BLADE'S Guide To
KNIVES
& Their VALUES

Edited by
Steve Shackleford

The Knives on the Cover

Front Cover:

The knives and knife boxes on the covers of *BLADE's Guide To Knives & Their Values* reflect a mix of the cutlery industry's past and present.

The knife at left on the front cover is the Kershaw Baby Boa, new for 2005. It features knifemaker Ken Onion's SpeedSafe® assisted-opening mechanism, 440A stainless blade steel, and a handle of 6061-T6 anodized aluminum with a smoked finish. Manufacturer's suggested retail price: **$74.95**.

Next to it is a Frary Boss barlow. From the collection of Pete Cohan, it was made in the 1880s. "The only other one I know of is in the Smithsonian," Pete noted. He values it at **$1,200**, though he said "there are people who would pay more."

Second from right is a Big Bear sub-hilt fighter by Blade Magazine Cutlery Hall-Of-Famer© Bob Loveless. The knife is courtesy of ABS master smith and purveyor Dave Ellis of Exquisite Knives, and he values it at **$20,000** plus on the secondary market.

At far right is a mint four-blade John Primble congress with a bone handle and fancy bolsters. It also is courtesy of Mr. Cohan and he values it at $150.

Back Cover:

Mr. Cohan also supplied all the knife boxes on the back cover. At left is a box for a John Primble pocketknife circa the early 1960s. Pete's value: **$30** (he said one in mint condition would bring **$40**). At upper right is a box for a John Russell Barlow circa the early 1900s. Pete's value: **$125**. Below it is a box for a Frary knife similar to the barlow on the cover, though different, from 1884. The box is very rare. Pete's value: **$200**.

The knife at left is a stag fixed-blade hunter with a leather pouch sheath by veteran knifemaker Bob Dozier of Springdale, Arkansas. The two-blade pocketknife is a Case/Tony Bose collaboration that was released in 2004. It is a modified muskrat pattern with a stag handle. What makes it "modified" is the wharncliffe blade. The Case pattern number is TB522004. Blade steel is ATS-34 stainless. Only 400 pieces were made. Manufacturer's suggested retail price: **$430**.

©2005 F+W Publications
Published by

kp books
An Imprint of F+W Publications

700 East State Street • Iola, WI 54990-0001
715-445-2214 • 888-457-2873
Our toll-free number to place an order or obtain
a free catalog is (800) 258-0929.

Library of Congress Catalog Number: 2005924772
ISBN: 0-87349-913-1

Designed by Patsy Howell
Edited by Steve Shackleford

Printed in United States of America

Table of Contents

Preface to
BLADE's Guide to Knives
& Their Values

You hold in your hands the sixth edition of what was formerly known as *Levine's Guide To Knives & Their Values*, originally written by Blade Magazine Cutlery Hall-Of-Famer© Bernard Levine in 1985. The new name of *BLADE's Guide To Knives & Their Values* was selected for a number of reasons, with two being foremost.

First, Mr. Levine is no longer associated with the book and has not been since the Fourth Edition. However, most of his past contributions to *BLADE's Guide* have been retained throughout this sixth edition. Simply put, without him, there would be no *BLADE's Guide*. As Pete Cohan noted, "Bernard Levine is the original author and creator of this comprehensive guide to knife collecting. We must recognize his remarkable knowledge of knives and knife lore and his very significant skills as a researcher and scholar in the matter of cutlery."

Second, Steve Shackleford, editor of the newly-named *BLADE's Guide*, is also editor of *BLADE®,* the world's No. 1 knife magazine. As a result, we decided to lend *BLADE's* name to *BLADE's Guide*, not only to differentiate it from past editions but to lend it *BLADE's* internationally known name for added credibility and marquee value.

If you own previous issues of this book, you will notice both similarities and changes. We have tried to preserve the best of Mr. Levine's vast knife knowledge while at the same time updating values and historical events. We also have reorganized the book, grouping some subjects differently and/or positioning them in new or different sections, to provide more structure and cohesiveness to individual themes and topics.

Whether a relatively new collector or a veteran, you will find this latest volume of immense interest and value. One point to remember throughout is this: Any product is only worth what the consumer is willing to pay for it. Period! Thus, in one particular marketplace a given knife may bring a specific value, but in another it may be less, or more. Values also fluctuate with the economy.

Another key to remember is that all values listed are for knives in new, mint and unsharpened condition—in other words, as close as possible to the condition in which they first arrived from the factory. Naturally, unused, mint condition knives are rarer than those that have been used once or more. The point here is that some people may own a well-used knife and feel it is worth a lot more than it actually is, just because the listed value for a similar model is fairly high.

Of great importance is the fact that this book is more than just a value guide, more than just a list of brands and patterns. It contains the greatest amount of reliable knife information in book form. It will guide you both in identifying and in understanding the type, the maker, the age, and the origin of any knife of any type that you might happen to be curious about. It includes old knives and newer knives, folding knives and fixed-blade knives, factory knives and handmade knives, valuable historical artifacts and common everyday tools. It includes all the varieties of knives used in peace and war, plus a broad selection of exotic knives from around the world.

Equally important, this book will show you how to estimate any knife's current value in the collector marketplace.

Unlike some value guides, which are often geared to experienced collectors, using this one does not oblige you to know anything about knives, about their numbering codes, or about knife terminology. Of course, if you are interested, such esoteric detail and much more is included, and practically every cutlery term used by knife collectors is defined and explained.

Those familiar with *BLADE* magazine know that it relies on no one person for its success but on the collective talents of a number of contributors—and such is the case with *BLADE's Guide To Knives & Their Values*. Though a number of individuals have contributed their knowledge, five stand out: Pete Cohan, Bill Claussen, Richard White, Dave Ellis and Larry Oden.

A board member of the National Knife Collectors Association and manager of the project to move the National Knife Museum to Smoky Mountain Knife Works in Sevierville, Tennessee, Cohan has totally overhauled *BLADE's Guide's* procedure for valuing standard American folding knife patterns (see Part 2, Section II). Instead of pinpointing exact values based on certain features of the knives, Pete's system describes how to determine a range of values that the knife is likely to bring according to a number of factors, including materials, special design features and others. Since the same knife will bring different value appraisals depending on the area of the country in which it is bought and sold and who is buying and/or selling it, we believe Pete's value-range system is much more realistic and thus much more reliable to you as a knife collector. He also supplied almost all new images for over 100 pages of the book—which in itself makes the ' a bargain for the cover price. Of everyone involved, Pete's contributions to *BLADE's Guide* are most significant.

Bill Claussen owns Northwest Knives & Collectibles, a retail knife shop in Salem, Oregon, and is co-author of *Sheffield Exhibition Knives*, a comprehensive historical and pictorial guide to the finest knives of nineteenth-century Sheffield, England, the legendary "City Of Steel." Bill has updated knife values in several areas of *BLADE's Guide*, including but not limited to Harley-Davidson knives, trappers, folders, folding dirks, fruit knives, American Indian knives, kitchen knives, knives and forks, and foreign, exotic, primitive and historical fixed blades.

A serious researcher and writer on the subject of all forms of antique knives—with an emphasis on antique pocketknives—Richard White is a field editor for *BLADE*, a staff writer for *Knife World*, author of the book, *Advertising Cutlery*, and has written for several other knife publications. His knowledge of antique advertising, military, stockman, Boy Scout and other knives and their values is reflected in his stories in *BLADE's Guide*.

Dave Ellis is a master smith in the American Bladesmith Society and a purveyor of handmade knives through his ExquisiteKnives.com, specializing in those of Cutlery Hall-Of-Famers Bob Loveless and Bill Moran. His stories on Loveless and Moran provide unprecedented information

in book form on the history and values of the knives of these two knifemaking legends.

Larry Oden is a long-time collector of Buck knives and a member of the Buck Collectors Club whose collector display of Buck knives has won many awards at such venues as the BLADE Show and others. Along with Joe Houser, he has totally revamped the sections on Buck folders, fixed blades and limited-edition knives in *BLADE's Guide*, making the *Guide* the most comprehensive and up-to-date source on Buck knife values extant.

Many others have contributed their knowledge of knife values, history, photographs and other information for *BLADE's Guide*. They include Cutlery Hall-Of-Famer Bill Adams; Roger Baker; Harold Bexfield; Cutlery Hall-Of-Famer Howard Cole; Eiler Cook; Jim Cooper; Anders L. Dahlman; Dennis Ellingsen; Terrill Hoffman; Bill Karsten; Joe Kertzman; Dr. James Lucie; Steve Morseth; Point Seven photo studios; Cutlery Hall-Of-Famer Houston Price; Siegfried Rosenkaimer; Rhett Stidham; Harlan Suedmeier; Jim Taylor; Vern Taylor; Larry Thomas; Geoffrey Tweedale; Cutlery Hall-Of-Famer Jim Weyer; Gordon White; and Mark Zalesky. We also thank the knife clubs who updated their club knife values for the book. If we have omitted anyone, please forgive us.

Others whose knowledge has played a crucial role in the information contained herein include the aforementioned Bernard Levine, Paul Davis, Jack Edmondson, and Cutlery Hall-Of-Famers B.R. Hughes, A.G. Russell and J. Bruce Voyles. We thank them all.

Introduction

Collecting Knife Lore

Knife collecting is a branch of treasure hunting. Similar to digging for pirate gold, searching for knives offers the challenge of the hunt, the thrill of discovery, and the concrete reward of the treasure itself.

The ongoing hunt for cutlery treasure applies as much to knife lore as it does to actual knives. When people ask us what we collect, the short answer is, "information." We get excited whenever we find a blade marking, catalog, billhead, letter, advertisement, brochure, label or directory listing that reveals a hitherto unknown facet of cutlery history—and also when collectors send us photocopies of such items, because it is the information that is most valuable to us. It lets us add to or correct our histories and brand lists, which in turn enable collectors to attach meaning, historical context, and value to knives that might otherwise have remained mere scraps of metal.

Why Bother with History?

History matters to knife collectors because knives do not just happen. People design knives, people make them and people sell them. People buy them, carry them, use them and lose them. Much of what makes knives interesting—and ultimately what makes them valuable—is people.

It is humbling to contemplate how little we actually know about the history of any knife, the real people who were really behind it. We are reminded of this every time we visit a place where knives are made, whether a big, modern cutlery factory or an individual knifemaker's workshop.

Each major knife factory employs hundreds of people, and its history could fill this book. Yet, today's big firms are only a handful of the hundreds of cutlery manufacturers that have flourished in just the past two centuries. Dozens of now-vanished cutlery firms were once at least as large as today's industry leaders, yet everything we know about most of the old companies is scarcely enough to fill out a single line of information in a brand list.

When that line of data includes a long span of years, such as 1818 to 1963, consider what this really means. It was five or six generations of people, thousands of men and women over the years whose life work has now vanished—save for the knives we preserve in our collections. It was a company that opened its doors before the first railroad track was laid, and that was still around well into the age of jet airplanes. It was a building to which hundreds of people walked ... later rode the streetcar ... perhaps later drove their cars ... every workday of their lives, often from childhood until advanced old age.

For many of them, the cutlery factory meant steady employment, a satisfying job, a comfortable family home. It meant friendships, romances and holiday picnics. However, for some it meant long, hungry layoffs in the bad years, and long, exhausting toil in the good ones. It might even have meant an early death from grinder's consumption, or from the flying fragments of a shattered grinding wheel.

To the larger world, cutlery factories meant knives—thousands of knives in hundreds of different styles. Yet, some person, somewhere, designed each one of those styles. Other people refined the materials that went into the knives. Forgers, grinders, cutlers and finishers actually made the knives, laboring in the hundreds of factories and workshops. Then, armies of jobbers and salesmen carried the finished knives around the world, and legions of retail merchants offered the knives for sale to the public.

Every one of the businesses had a story—the manufacturers, the wholesalers and the retailers. What's more, so did every one of the firms' owners and employees. Most of their life stories would have seemed ordinary at the time, but even the most ordinary aspects of distant times seem extraordinary to us now. The year 1818 was before electricity, before gaslight, before telegraph and telephone, before indoor plumbing.

Picture old Sheffield, England, with cobblestone streets. What was it like for an 11-year old English farm boy to be sent into Sheffield to be apprenticed to a cutler? What was it like for a Sheffield cutler, who had never before traveled even as far from home as London, to board a wooden ship and sail across the ocean to Connecticut? What were life and work and play like when he got there? And what about life in Solingen, in Thiers, in Nixdorf, in Maniago, in Seki City? What about life in Walden, New York, a century ago, or in Gladstone, Michigan, or Tidioute, Pennsylvania?

These are the sorts of questions that we like to ponder when we think about old knives. Whenever we look up a name in *BLADE's Guide to Knives and Their Values*, we are glad to find a little information about it, but always wish there could be more. Even when an entry is complete—and many are not—those few words and numbers are but the palest shadow of the real human stories that each listing so briefly summarizes.

Each Knife Has a Story, Too

And what of the knives themselves? It is astounding how much we take for granted about them, how little we really know. Look at a plain, old jack knife, such as a Russell. It appears so simple, but consider what it took to make it.

First, the blades and springs. Prior to 1907, when French metallurgist Paul Louis Toussaint Heroult introduced his electric furnace, knife blades and springs were forged from crucible cast steel, which was made by hand in fire-clay pots in Sheffield, 60 to 90 pounds at a time. Most of the iron to make the fine steel was mined in Sweden from a rich belt of meteorite impact that also supplied the cutlery industries of Eskilstuna, Sweden, and Solingen.

Next, the mounts. The copper to make nickel-silver bolsters and brass liners might have come from Michigan or Peru, the nickel from Canada or Russia, and the zinc from Mexico or Tennessee. Mild steel for rivets, bolsters and liners likely came from Pittsburgh, Pennsylvania.

Then, the handle material. Cocobolo wood was cut in the jungles of Central America, carried out on mule back, then loaded on ships bound for U.S. or European ports. Both ebony wood and elephant ivory were cut in equatorial Africa, carried to seaports by caravan, shipped from there to merchants in London, and then across the Atlantic to Boston or New York. Shells for pearl scales were brought up from the sea floor by divers in the Philippines. Antlers for stag scales might have come from the giant red deer of northern Europe, or from the sambar deer of southern Asia. Black buffalo horn came from the domestic water buffalo of the Far East. Ox horn and cattle shinbone might have come from the Chicago stockyards, but were more likely imported from the Argentine pampas.

All these materials were gathered together in J. Russell & Co.'s large, water-powered factory at Turners Falls, Massachusetts, built in 1870. Some of the people who actually made the knife might have been life-long Russell employees, perhaps even the sons or granddaughters of cutlers who had worked at the original Green River Works in Greenfield in the 1830s. Others would have been recent immigrants, recruited by the firm in England or Ireland.

The Knife's Journeys

The old knife's story did not end when it left the factory. Indeed, at that point its story had barely begun. It was part of an order that was shipped somewhere. How was it transported: by canal barge, railway, wagon or steamboat? Where was it sold and by what or whom: by mail-order catalog, Broadway department store, neighborhood cutlery shop, rural general merchant, pack peddler or military commissary?

Who bought the knife new: a schoolboy, a farmer or a sailor, perhaps? Who had it next and how did he acquire it? Did he find it on the side of the road, win it in a card game, pick it up on a battlefield, take it in a holdup, receive it as a gift or inherit it from a distant relative?

And then who had the knife, and then and then? And how did each of those people come to have it, and perhaps later come to lose it? And what, if anything, did each of them think about it?

Old knives in mint condition pose their own series of questions. Why was the knife never used? Where was it put away and why? Was it preserved for sentimental reasons (for example, "it belonged to Uncle Abner, who died in the Great War"), or was it merely forgotten at the back of a cupboard drawer?

Imaginary vs. History

Every period of time was different from every other in countless ways. With even a little study, we can begin to identify some of the more obvious changes from past to present (cars, television, stainless steel, plastic), and we can observe how these have affected our lives. With a little more study, we can free ourselves from today's more absurd misconceptions about the past.

For instance, "American Primitive" was a style of painting, not a style of life. Earlier times had simpler technology than we do now, but their language, manners, clothing and accouterments, even on the frontier, were a great deal more refined than ours are today—not better, kinder or wiser, but certainly more refined.

"All genuine records are at first tedious because, and insofar as, they are alien. They set forth the views and interests of their time for their time and come no step to meet us. However, the shams of today are addressed to us and are therefore made amusing and intelligible, as fake antiques generally are."—Jakob Burckhardt (1818-1897)

It would be impossible to recreate, or even to fully understand, a single moment of the past. No matter how much information we accumulate, our view could not help but be distorted—both by our knowledge of what came later, as well as by our present attitudes and values. And even when we try, the past recedes as we reach out to it. Light fades and focus softens. Facts are forgotten, meaning is lost.

To make matters worse, certain of the revisionists circle closer like vultures round a dying beast. They tear off fragments of the past, rending them beyond recognition to feed their frenzied imaginations.

Some of the revisionists seem to believe that nothing in the world had ever really changed until they appeared on the scene. To them, history is a branch of fiction. Historical figures are mythic heroes someone invented. To them, Davy Crockett and Donald Duck are drawn with the same pen.

As far as certain of the revisionists are concerned, it is a free country: they have just as much right to make up history as anyone else, and to create evidence to support their stories, too. What they appear to feel should have happened, what was significant, those are all the data that they seem to need or want. If the facts do not fit their imaginary histories, they change the facts.

Some of today's academic historians are misguided revisionists, too. They derive their modernist theories from argumentative or controversial writings, not from observation of the world—much the way romantically deluded collectors derive their misguided fantasies from movies and adventure novels, rather than from artifacts and firsthand accounts. Some of today's revisionist historians twist or invent evidence to support their imaginings. Then, to validate their inaccurate theories, they simply quote each other or else echo their mentors' unfounded pronouncements.

Cutlery and History

But real knives, or any real objects, can help to keep a historian honest. History tied to artifacts is brought down to earth by the solidity of its subject matter. We students of knives can theorize all we like, just like academic historians, but at the end of the day, if our theories do not fit our knives, then our theories have got to change.

And for those of you who asked, this is the reason why so much in this book has changed from each edition to the next.

Buying, Selling and Trading Knives

The true value of a knife, if such a thing exists, is the actual amount of money paid for it by a knowledgeable buyer to a knowledgeable seller in an unpressured transaction. In the real world, such conditions are not always met, so knives often sell for either less or more than they are "worth."

Uninformed sellers often undervalue their knives, furnishing real bargains to the lucky collector. Just as often, of course, an uninformed or misinformed seller will overvalue his knives, perhaps tempting some unlucky beginning collector into a costly and discouraging error.

Sometimes, a seller "needs the money" and must take less for a knife than he knows it to be worth. Other times a buyer "has to have" one knife in particular, and will grudgingly pay more for it than he believes it really to be worth. Then, too, all or part of many knife transactions is trade or barter, allowing both parties to greatly overvalue their knives.

If you have a knife to sell or if there is one that you are seeking to buy, how much it is "really" worth is up to you. The value estimates in this book will help you to form your opinions and become more knowledgeable as a buyer or seller. However, in the marketplace, as in the voting booth, the final decisions are yours and yours alone.

For example, if we estimate a knife to be worth $100 but it is worth only $50 to you, then don't pay more than $50 for it. On the other hand, if you are an advanced collector and would happily pay $200 for the knife, then by all means do so, and don't worry about what we say. Just don't be surprised if no one is willing to pay you $250 (or even $150) for it later on.

Supply and Demand

Blade Magazine Cutlery Hall-Of-Famer© Bernard Levine wrote in the October 1985 *Knife World* how fellow Hall-Of-Famer W.D. "Bo" Randall asked him why even a very ordinary knife by another Hall Of Famer, William Scagel, was worth so much more than some newer and much more finely finished handmade knives. (For more on Randall and Scagel, see the "Table of Contents" for the page number of Pioneers of Modern Handmade Knives and other related stories.) All Levine could do was shrug his shoulders and reply, "supply and demand," same as with any other antique or collectible object.

Scagel is viewed as the pioneer of 20th-century custom knifemaking. For this reason, many collectors want an example of his work. Others make a specialty of collecting his knives and other metal creations. This is the demand, and it seems to grow steadily.

The supply, by contrast, is very limited. Therefore, prices for Scagel knives continue to rise. This is the same reason that antique pocketknives and bowie knives continue to increase in value. The demand is growing while the supply is steady or shrinking (as knives are worn out or lost). In the short term, increasing demand and higher prices call forth increased supply, as it becomes worthwhile for more dealers to spend more time beating the bushes for more old knives to bring onto the collector market. The increased supply is a temporary effect, since the ultimate supply of old knives is, of course, limited.

The main point here is that collector value has little to do with "intrinsic" value in use, or even with replacement value. It also has very little to do with age or rarity. Many a rare old knife that is still useful is nonetheless nearly worthless on the collector market, simply because no one collects its type. Low demand or collector pleasure for a potential collector's item leads to low prices, whether the supply is low or high.

Evaluating Factory-Made Folding Knives

In *BLADE's Guide to Knives and Their Values*, most types of fixed-blade knives are evaluated individually. By contrast, the values of most factory-made folding knives are presented in charts. This is because the varieties of factory folding knives sold in the USA in the past century-and-a-half probably approach one million, so value tables are a practical way to cover the staggering variety in a single volume. The use of these tables is explained in the Introduction to Standard American Folding Knife Patterns (see the "Table of Contents" for the page number).

The factory folding knife value tables present a great deal of information in a compact and easy-to-use form. They are intended to cover the widest possible variety of knives. Even if you should find an old factory knife so odd that no one has seen one just like it, the tables will give you a general idea of what it is worth.

Evaluating Custom, Handmade Knives

The values of custom and handmade knives reflect, on the supply side, the time, skill and materials put into them by their makers. On the demand side, they reflect the fashions and tastes of the knife-buying public, both users and collectors.

The knife-buying public is truly diverse. Every day, sportsmen and budget-minded collectors buy hundreds of handmade knives in the $35 to $350 range. Just as surely, wealthy and sophisticated collectors pay $500, $1,000, $5,000 and sometimes much more for distinctive works of cutlery art. One such collector may entirely support half-a-dozen knifemakers.

However, this is not the whole picture. From time to time, ordinary men and women spend a month's pay on a special handmade knife that they had long been dreaming about. Rarely is this an impulse purchase. Perhaps it had taken six months or a year for the maker to fill the customer's order, while it may have taken the customer every day of that time to save up for the knife.

The market in handmade knives is volatile. New design fads come on suddenly, while old designs fade quietly away. Values on average trend upward, but the values of new basic handmade hunting knives have stabilized because of increased competition and improved techniques.

Meanwhile, the resale values of older handmade knives range all over the map. Today, there are a few early 1970s handmade knives that command 50 times their original price, but there are many others that will not bring what they cost new then.

What holds its value in handmade knives is quality. Quality means original, intelligent, consistent design; grace and elegance of line; flawless execution; appropriate use of extraordinary materials; and, finally, what one astute Japanese collector described as "knives that have a face." In other words, an aficionado of handmades does not need to see a great maker's mark to recognize the maker's work.

The handmade knife market is not just knives. More importantly, it is people. It includes makers with the integrity to continue to make quality knives, and buyers with the discernment to buy them.

The knife market also includes, like any other market, some people whose flair and showmanship entice customers into buying high-priced knives that are not really first class. Both extremes of knife quality are out there at every knife show, along with a lot of knives that fall somewhere in-between. The whole range of knifemakers is listed in *BLADE's Guide*.

Knives are popular right now, so almost all handmade knives have value. Quality knives will hold their value— or at least they will hold it as long as there are quality-conscious people who care about knives. Fad knives will remain popular, too, but this year's fad knives may not be worth much once next year's fads come along.

Buying a Handmade Knife

Some knifemakers do not accept orders but most do, and they therefore maintain waiting lists ranging from

weeks to years. Get on a maker's list and eventually you should receive exactly the knife you want.

Most makers also make knives to sell at shows. This may seem unfair to the customers on their waiting lists, but often it is a maker's only chance to craft knives that he himself wants to make, certainly a craftsman's prerogative. Also, a lot of customers won't bother with waiting lists, and would rather pay a premium to get immediate delivery. Why should only the knife purveyors profit from such impulse purchases?

Handmade knife purveyors offer immediate, or relatively immediate, delivery on new handmade knives, both at shows and by mail. Since purveyors often pay list price to makers for their knives, they must sell them for more to cover their overhead and make a profit.

In addition to stocking new handmade knives for immediate purchase, purveyors are the main source for handmade knives by retired or deceased knifemakers. Purveyors can also supply early knives or discontinued styles by active makers. They do this by buying knives or accepting consignments from collectors and estates. One thing purveyors cannot offer is personal contact between customer and knifemaker, an intangible benefit that is very important to many buyers and makers.

Fad knives will remain popular, too, but this year's fad knives may not be worth much once next year's fads come along.

Buying Wisely

To buy knives wisely, you need only to remember three principles:

First, select knives based on your own taste and judgment, buying only types or brands of knives that you really like. When you like a certain type of knife, you will develop a sense of its good features, as well as its potential problems. Unless you are willing to spend the time and take the financial risk of becoming a knife dealer or a purveyor, don't try to second-guess other collectors' tastes.

The second principle of buying wisely is to base the prices you pay on both condition and market. Don't pay high for knives in poor condition. On the other hand, occasionally stretch your budget to buy a fine handmade knife or a rare antique knife in pristine condition. Study ads, sale lists, knives for sale at shows, auction sale results and the estimated values in *BLADE's Guide* until you have a feel for current market values. Refuse to pay much more than going prices.

Third, be wary of a knife for sale at well below current market. Is it genuine or counterfeit? Is it original or reworked? What is the reputation of the seller? This last principle involves your interaction with a known seller/dealer/purveyor. Know whom you are dealing with before you make a serious purchase.

What Should You Collect?

There is a wonderful variety of interesting and potentially rewarding collecting specialties that knives offer. What's more, the whole field of knife collecting is still new enough that some of these specialties have barely been explored yet. In some specialties there is still relatively little competition. Thus, there is no better time than the present for a collector to start.

In this chapter we would like to give you a few suggestions about what sorts of knives you might consider collecting. Some people start out by collecting every knife that catches their fancy. This can be a costly and inefficient way to figure out what one really likes.

Try attending a knife show with the goal of buying just one knife that really pleases you. Once you have found that knife, do not stop looking but do look more objectively. Why do you like this knife, and not that one? Would you like to have other knives of this type, or would you rather that your next knife be something completely different?

Study knife collections on display. What impresses you about one display but not another? What might you have done differently? Would you like eventually to build a large collection, or would you prefer just to own a few choice items? Would you like to find a "keeper" every weekend, or would you rather wait for something really special to come along?

We strongly recommend specializing early, picking a specific theme for your collecting, or at least a general direction. This will focus your efforts and conserve your resources. Also, when and if your collecting tastes change, it is much easier to sell or trade out of a relatively organized collection (often all at once) than out of a random accumulation.

Old Factory Knives

In simpler times collectors of old knives chose their collecting specialties from among three basic areas: brands, handle materials and patterns. As knife collecting has developed, many more approaches have been explored, as set forth below. All of these areas offer potential for enjoyment, education, and perhaps even eventual profit. Which area and specialty you select is up to you.

No matter which specialty you choose, and we cannot repeat this too often, always seek out authenticity and excellent condition. If there is any chance at all that you (or your children) will want to display or sell your collection, then the extra trouble and expense that got you the best in your field can be amply rewarded.

Here are the broad categories of antique knife collecting, and some of the possible specialties within each. Let these ideas inspire you but do not be limited by them. Trust your own taste and interests.

Brands

The reasons why collectors choose to focus on particular brands are almost as varied as the brands themselves. The most common reason is that other collectors already collect the brands. Thus the popularity of Remington, Winchester, Case, Russell, Henckels, Keen Kutter and many others continues to grow. Collecting popular brands is fine and there are many knife guides that focus on such brands.

Another reason for picking a brand is personal association. This can be as simple as choosing a brand name that is the same as your own name. If your grandfather ran the knife company this would be an obvious choice, but even if the similarity is only a coincidence, it is still fun to find your own name (first or last) stamped on a blade.

Personal association can also mean picking a brand or brands made or marketed in your own hometown or home state. If there are no local brands or none that appeal to you, you might consider brands from another location that you enjoy visiting.

Personal association can just as well mean choosing knives of the same brand or the same pattern as your very first knife. It is remarkable how many major collections got started in such a manner.

Types of Brand

In the *Pocketknife Brand List* (see the "Table of Contents" for the page number), there is a column headed "Type of Firm." If you are considering collecting knives by brand, pay attention to this column. The type of brand often has an important influence upon the value and desirability of a knife. These are the basic possibilities.

Manufacturers' Brands

First, of course, is cutlery manufacturers' own brands. Manufacturers range from giant firms such as Henckels or W.R. Case & Sons, which have hundreds of employees, down to one-man operations such as Ostwald or Dooley. Knives from small, obscure shops are much rarer than knives from the big firms. In fact, they may be so rare that there is not much demand for most of them. Unless they are popular for some special reason, they may not attract the typical knife collector.

Some of the big cutlery manufacturers marketed knives under alternate or secondary brands. These knives were sometimes of lesser quality than the firms' first-line "name" brands. However, they were not manufacturing "seconds." They were just made plainer and simpler in order to sell at a lower price.

In the Old World many "manufacturers" were really *factors*, merchants who employed independent "contractors" or outworkers to make knives marked with the factor's name or trademark. A factor's warehouse was called a "factory," and that is the original meaning of the word. See *19th Century Sheffield Cutlery Firms and History of the Solingen Cutlery Industry* for more about factors and outworkers (see the "Table of Contents" for the page number).

Contract Brands

We have seen more than one collector disappointed after collecting a brand for a time, and then learning that the company in question never made a single knife. All of its knives were "contract knives" made by a variety of manufacturers.

There is absolutely nothing wrong with contract knives. However, if you are interested in knives actually made in a certain place, specializing in a contract brand may not be for you.

Here are the different types of contract brands.

Wholesalers' Brands

Wholesalers' contract brands break down naturally into two groups. First are the cutlery wholesale brands. Cutlery wholesalers and importers, many of them once based in New York City, distribute knives nationwide, sometimes even continent-wide or worldwide. They sell knives to retail stores, advertisers, and even to regional hardware wholesalers. Some of them, such as Wiebusch and Kastor, eventually bought the factories that made many of their knives.

The house brands of the regional hardware wholesalers constitute the second group of wholesale brands. Hardware brands may show a highly local flavor, both in trade names and in choices of patterns.

Most wholesale hardware firms served well-defined geographic areas, usually the trading area of one major city. Each wholesaler provided back-up inventory for dozens of small-town retail hardware and general merchandise stores. Competition between the wholesalers in most areas was intense. The larger wholesale hardware firms covered broader regions, and a few even distributed their house brands nationwide or internationally.

Just a small number of these wholesale hardware firms still remains. Some are once again selling private-brand knives.

Retailers' Brands

Not many retailers today are big enough to generate the minimum orders required for privately branded knives. Today, when several thousand is a typical minimum order, only the big catalog outfits can play the game. In the old days, when 10 dozen of a pattern was sufficient, many cutlery and sporting goods stores were able to carry their own private brands of knives.

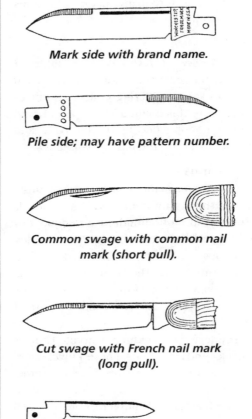

Mark side with brand name.

Pile side; may have pattern number.

Common swage with common nail mark (short pull).

Cut swage with French nail mark (long pull).

Pen blade with full tang bevel.

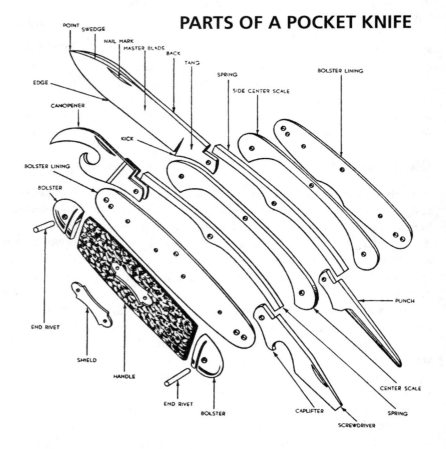

PARTS OF A POCKET KNIFE

From: Winchester Sales Manual, 1933. Bement, **The Cutlery Story,** *1950.*

The marks of some retailers, such as Sears Roebuck and L.L. Bean, can have just as much collector appeal as any maker's mark.

Advertisers' Brands

One additional type of knife branding has attracted a lot of collector interest. This area is privately branded advertising knives. Most advertising knives are tang-stamped with the name of the manufacturer, the wholesaler or the advertising specialty house from which they were ordered. By contrast, advertiser-branded knives, with such tang stampings as COCA-COLA or ANHEUSER-BUSCH, are rare, and many of them command high values. Some also have been counterfeited, and there are many current valid reproductions, so you must be careful in your collecting.

Handle Materials

There are collectors who specialize in any handle material you can think of, even the plainest ones. However, some of the favorites are pearl (shorthand for mother-of-pearl) and stag (shorthand for deer antler). Almost as popular are "bone stag" (bone jigged and dyed to resemble stag) and fancy colored celluloid. Ancient ivory and tortoise shell are also quite popular and add to the value of a quality knife.

An interesting area that is still under-appreciated is decorated metal handles. Both the Swedes and the Germans did remarkable things with selective etching, electroplating, gilding and enameling. Coin-like pressed metal handles are relatively more popular.

Knives with advertising on the handles are very popular, especially fancy ones designed for a major advertiser, such as Anheuser-Busch. Knives bearing advertising for local or regional firms may not command the highest prices, but they can form an interesting and attractive collection.

Knife Shapes and Patterns

The variety of knife patterns made over the years sometimes can seem endless, especially knives made

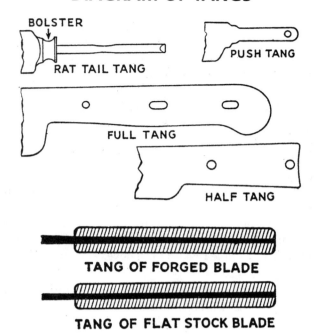

DIAGRAM OF TANGS

before circa 1850, which was when standardization began to be widespread. Every standard pattern can be a collecting specialty, and a large number of them already are. The value tables herein reflect the more popular patterns.

Of course, there is no rule that says you must collect just one pattern. It can make a lot of sense to collect functionally related patterns, such as cattle knives and premium stock knives, or boys' knives and barlows. It can also make sense to collect physically related patterns, such as the crown, the congress and the swayback.

There is another way to approach pattern collecting. Instead of specializing in one or a few patterns, it can be very interesting to collect one knife of every standard pattern. To be even more diverse, each of these knives might be of a different brand, and of course every handle material could be represented. Naturally, all of these knives should be in excellent to mint condition. A collection of this type would be a real challenge.

DIAGRAM OF PARTS OF A KNIFE

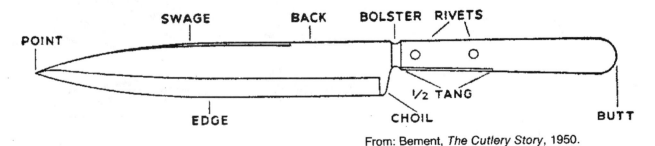

From: Bement, *The Cutlery Story*, 1950.

History

Collecting knives as history can be most interesting. There are two basic ways to go about this.

The most popular and the most costly, as well as the most risky, is to collect knives that reflect the "Big Picture," as it used to be called. These are the knives, including bowie knives, military knives, Indian trade knives and presentation knives, which were made and used in dramatic and dangerous times.

"Big Picture" historical knives are popular and costly, just as all fine historical artifacts are. They are risky because, being valuable and/or historically significant, they can be counterfeits or reputable reproductions that may have little collector value. If you want to get involved with such knives, you had better have deep pockets, as well as a lot of time to study and develop your expertise.

The other historical approach is to collect knives that reflect the history of knives. You can focus on company history, such as by collecting knives made by pioneer American knife manufacturers. You can focus on technical history by collecting "firsts": the first picture-handled knives, the first stainless steel knives, the first closed-back pocketknives. You can limit yourself to pocketknives, like the majority of collectors, or you can collect other types as well.

Instead of company or technical history, you can focus on cultural history. You could collect brands and styles known to have been used in particular places and times. Not just the dramatic places and times, either, and not just weapons. An 1830s American bowie knife might now cost as much as a house, but a carving set or a pen knife from that period may not cost much more than a new factory knife. Antique fixed-blade hunting knives have gained greatly in popularity in recent years, but they are still relative bargains, especially when compared to antique folding hunters.

Let us add that once you are willing to consider the "little picture," you need not limit yourself to the history just of knives. For example, you can collect knives that reflect the history of a trade or profession. You might focus on medical knives, veterinary knives, office knives, trappers' knives, miners' dynamite knives, farmers' or ranchers' knives, automobilists' knives, or anything else that interests you. Once you get into the spirit of the hobby, the hard part is not deciding what to collect, it is deciding what *not* to collect.

New Factory Knives

Don't let all this talk about history put you off if what really interests you is new knives. Many new factory knives are very nice indeed.

With new knives, just about the only limiting factor on your collection is your budget. Almost any new knife, except the most limited or exotic, can be had by anyone anytime he can afford the going price.

If you collect new knives, you have a budget and you have a collecting goal such as "all the current Buck knives," you can calculate just when your collection may be complete. If you like to go out every payday and buy a knife for your collection, old knives are probably not for you. New knives will be a lot more satisfying.

Another critical factor is time. Collecting old knives can require a lot of time spent visiting antique shops, flea markets and shows. With new knives, finding a cooperative local retailer who accepts special orders or else securing a handful of mail order catalogs (see the list of dealers/purveyors at the back of the book) can enable you to do a lot of collecting in just an hour or two per month.

TYPES OF WINCHESTER BOLSTERS

Threaded Bolster

Ribbed Bolster

Octagon Bolster

Square Bolster

Fluted Bolster

Rat Tail Bolster

Candle End Bolster

Threaded Rib Bolster

Spoon Threaded Bolster

Long Fluted Bolster

SHIELDS

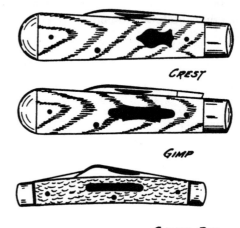

CREST

GIMP

CURVED BAR

A collection of new factory knives will take longer to appreciate in value. In fact, some may never be profitable. However, careful selection with emphasis on quality will help reduce your risk.

Of course, there is no guarantee of profit in any branch of knife collecting, nor in any other type of collecting, for that matter. However, we believe that both high-grade antique and new knives (factory and handmade) and high-grade modern handmade knives do offer a reasonable chance of eventual profit, if collected wisely and with a weather eye to the ever-changing market.

On the brighter side, collecting new factory knives is not nearly as unpromising financially as collecting, say, new postage stamps. With new stamps one is guaranteed to lose money every time that the postage rates go up.

Regardless of the financial prospects, people will continue to collect new postage stamps, and they will continue to collect new factory knives. And as long as they enjoy themselves, they are certainly getting their money's worth.

"Collectible" Knives

In the past 20 years or so, a lot of knives have come on the market which, though usually in unlimited quantities, have nonetheless been aimed mainly at the collector market. Such "collectible" knives most often have impressive "list" prices, but if you check mail order catalogs and ads you will find them offered regularly at a 50 percent or greater discount in "wholesale" quantities of three, or sometimes even one.

These collectible knives, especially the folders, are favored by some of the "courthouse" traders. Those are the fellows who entertain themselves by swapping old pocketknives, until collectors buy up all their good ones. Rather than trading old junkers, some courthouse traders now swap new knives.

Today, knife manufacturers and importers are highly conscious both of the popularity of knife collecting and also of their own history. They vie with each other to create new and different patterns. Many of these are aimed at the collector and trader markets. The manufacturers also provide frequent changes on the more popular traditional patterns.

The collector marketplace consigns most of these innovations to the low-end value group. This has ever been the fate of odd innovations in the cutlery field. Still, some of the innovations are genuine improvements and will be with us for a long time.

One sure way to keep up with the latest twists in factory knives is to obtain or look at each manufacturer's or importer's catalog as soon as it is available. If something

new appeals to you, buy it right away. Chances are that it will no longer be available six months or a year from now. In any case, current catalogs are the surest guide to the current prices of regular-issue current knives, so most of them are not included in this (or any other) value guide.

Commemorative Knives

Commemorative knives were inspired by the popularity of commemorative stamps and coins. They are knives with inscriptions on the handle or blade that commemorate an event. Most were made in the past 30 years, but there are a few older ones, such as a Henckels 200th anniversary knife from 1931.

Unlike souvenir knives (see the "Table of Contents" for the page number of Advertising, Figural, Character and Miniature Knives), commemorative knives are usually dated and made for a limited time in a limited quantity. Commemorative knives are usually standard patterns that have been dressed up with non-standard handle materials, shields or blade etchings. On rare occasions, they are specially designed patterns. (See Blade Magazine Cutlery Hall-Of-Famer© Bruce Voyles' *Commemorative Knives 1960-1990 IBCA*.)

Limited Edition Knives

A limited edition knife is a type of commemorative knife that does not commemorate anything in particular. Some limited edition knives are handmade or "benchmade" (benchmade means handmade by a small team, rather than by an individual maker, and is also the name of a factory knife company, Benchmade, in Oregon City, Oregon), and these types have been the most likely to appreciate in value. Most limited editions are factory made. Often they are serial numbered.

One class of limited edition knives is annual club knives issued by local and national knife collecting organizations (for more on them, see the "Table of Contents" for the page number of the section on club knives). Most local club knives are very limited in quantity. Often they are sold only to club members, though all clubs allow people to join and purchase knives by mail. An up-to-date list of knife clubs is published every month in *Knife World* magazine.

Why There Are Limited Edition and Commemorative Knives

Because of their special features and limited numbers, commemorative and limited edition knives, when new, sell for more money than similar plain knives. To be precise, commemorative and limited edition knives are given special features in order that they may be sold for a higher price.

> *A limited edition knife is a type of commemorative knife that does not commemorate anything in particular.*

While an element of sentiment may help to inspire issues of commemorative knives, the main reason that they and limited edition knives are made is for the seller's profit. (Of course, for those who sell knives, as for those who sell most anything, profit must be a key consideration or else they likely will be looking for other lines of work.) Even club knives are made to help augment the clubs' treasuries, while they also allow club members to purchase "something special."

Similarly, though some collectors buy limited edition knives simply because they like them, many who purchase them do so in hopes of future profit. With the supply of each issue fixed and the hobby of knife collecting growing, increased demand should lead to increasing values. In many knife club knives this has indeed proven true, though there are exceptions.

Limited Edition Knives Today

While retail sales of newly issued limited edition knives continue strong, the secondary or resale market for most limited edition factory knives is weak. Over the past five years, the resale prices of most good quality limited edition knives were around 50 percent of "retail list price." Today, some mail order distributors sell brand new limited edition knives at 50 percent off original "list price."

Limited edition knives made in the past 30 years number in the thousands. To build a representative collection of these now would take a substantial investment. Most collectors realize this and act accordingly. After all, it is their hard-earned money at stake. Most serious collectors, the ones who spend serious money, much prefer knives originally made to be used as knives to ones that were made specifically as collectibles.

As in other markets, low prices can attract the interest of speculators. Recall that in the 1950s good antique bowie knives sold for $5 each, and a collector who paid $10 for one was considered a fool. Not many years later those "fools" got to laugh all the way to the bank.

If 10,000 or 20,000 new people join the knife collecting fraternity in the next few years, they are going to want to buy something. Maybe the limited edition knives will seem pretty exciting to folks who missed out on the knives' original issue. An important rule for limited editions is to look at the knife, not just at the advertising for it. Is it made by a well-known firm? Is it at least as well finished as a comparably priced plain knife? Are the inscriptions and serial numbers neatly and permanently marked on the knife, not just printed on the box or on a slip of paper?

Is there a box for the knife, and is it of appropriate quality? A knife that was issued with a box is always worth much less if the box is missing or damaged.

Besides looking at the knife, look at the edition as a whole. Just how limited is it? You would be surprised at how many are "limited" to as many knives as the issuer can sell. Be more skeptical of any "limited" quantity much over 2,500. When you go to sell your knives, you want to be fairly confident that there will not be lots of others just like them on the market at the same time.

Serial Numbers

"Serial" numbers on limited edition factory knives are an artificial construct. Factory knives are generally made in large lots by mass production methods. Serial numbers, when used, are applied at random, either to parts before assembly or to finished knives after completion. In other words, the numbers have nothing to do with the sequence of manufacture.

Despite their limited significance, limited edition serial numbers do have some effect on the resale value of these knives. Serial number 1 of most knives commands a considerable premium. Numbers 2 through 10 also command a premium, though not as much as number 1.

When used on handmade knives, by contrast, serial numbers do often indicate real sequence of manufacture, either of a particular model or else of a maker's entire output. However, with low-numbered handmade knives one must usually perform a sort of mental balancing act.

On one side, a low number has more subjective appeal than a high number. On the other side, a low number usually means earlier work, which can mean lower quality or an obsolete style, and therefore a less desirable knife. On balance, a serial number on a handmade knife is less of monetary value than it is of informational value, often telling you when the knife was made, and sometimes even for whom it was originally made.

Handmade and Custom Knives

It is in the nature of handmade and custom knives that there be virtually endless variety among them. Indeed, this variety is largely the point of the existence of handmade knives. Even in the days when a factory knife line might have comprised two thousand patterns, there was still demand from customers for "something different." Today, when a good factory knife line includes only two or three dozen numbers, there is all the more reason for a discriminating knife user to consider a handmade knife.

It is not just discriminating knife users who buy handmade knives. To many collectors, modern handmade knives are the most exciting area of knife collecting. There are now thousands of knifemakers across the USA and around the world. Each of them tries each day to exact something new and special from his tools, his materials, his hands, and his mind.

In handmade knives, the advantages to the collector of specializing are nearly as great as they are in factory knives. Much as in the realm of factory knife collecting, many handmade knife collectors favor one or a select handful of makers. Others prefer to collect by pattern, style or handle material. A few collectors focus on knives made in one state or one region.

Custom Handmade Knives

Custom handmade knives can have a special appeal as well. In this area alone you can get exactly what you want in the way of a knife, made to order just for you.

Would you like a folding knife that is custom fitted to your hand, one with, say, a drop-point Stellite® blade, a concealed lock that works with one finger, rainbow-toned titanium handles, and a picture of your favorite dog engraved on the bolster? Some of the makers listed in this book will undertake to make a knife this special for you. It won't be cheap, but it will be as near to your wishes as a knife can be.

If you want a truly custom handmade knife, as opposed to a customized standard pattern, do bear in mind that its maker must recover all of his design and development costs for this new style of knife in the price that he charges you for it. If you are not willing to pay 50-500 percent extra for a one-of-a-kind design, it is unfair to ask a maker to create one for you.

The Winds of Change

For collectors concerned with the resale value of their handmade knives, keeping up with market trends is essential. Handmade knives are far more subject to the whims of fashion than are antique knives. This is most obvious in the steady decline of collector interest in handmade fixed blade hunting knives.

Until the mid-1980s, most collectors of handmade knives favored fixed blades. Today, a majority of handmade knife collectors mainly buy folders. This is why some top knifemakers no longer even make fixed blades.

In the past few years the U.S. market for fixed blade art knives has revived somewhat. However, for the most part, the market for handmade hunting knives has declined to the point where it has pretty much merged with the factory hunting knife market. This is great news for hunters, whose knife choices are now almost limitless, but it is very bad news for collectors who "invested" in handmade hunting knives at premium prices.

Handmade Folders vs. Handmade Fixed Blades

Twenty-five years ago, a good handmade hunting knife cost four to 10 times as much as the best factory hunting knife. Today, a substantially better handmade hunting knife can cost the same as or less than a good factory hunting knife.

Why has this happened? In part it is because factory hunting knives have gotten better over the years, and hence they have gotten more costly. Mainly, however, it is because the main market for handmade hunting knives today is hunters who want good knives.

Yes, there are still a few people who collect handmade hunting knives, but there are not enough of these collectors, as compared to the number of knifemakers, to inflate the prices of these knives beyond those of good factory knives. (There are a few exceptions that defy this rule, the most notable being the hunting knives of Blade Magazine Cutlery Hall-Of-Famer© Bob Loveless.)

Markets are shaped by supply and demand. Today, there are literally thousands of makers across the country (and around the world) supplying handmade hunting knives, many of very high quality (see "Table of Contents" for the page number of *20th Century Knifemakers*).

Because the competition in the hunting knife market is among makers—and not among buyers the way it is in the handmade folder market—most of today's handmade hunting knives must sell in the range of $35 to $350, if they are to sell at all. This is exactly the price range of good quality factory hunting knives.

Whatever cost advantages the factories might enjoy, because of mass-production and volume purchasing, these are counterbalanced by their added costs of management, of government regulation, and of wholesale and retail distribution. A skillful custom knifemaker with a well-organized shop is very nearly as efficient as a factory, but with a lot less overhead and capital outlay. Plus, he or she can offer customers the sort of personal contact, attention to detail, and array of custom features not possible from any factory, and at little or no additional cost to the purchaser.

Handmade folding knives are an entirely different story—at least for the time being. Today, handmade folders are in demand. Most sell for two-to-20 times the prices of the best quality factory folders.

The supply of fine handmade folders is severely limited. A majority of knifemakers is unwilling or unable to make folders, and some who do make folders are unable to match, let alone exceed, today's high factory standards. At the same time, the present demand for handmade folders is positively feverish. This is why the forces of supply and demand presently inflate their prices far above those of factory folders.

Yet, just as the market for handmade hunting knives has matured over the course of a generation, the handmade folder market, too, is eventually going to mature. The few very best and most original folder makers will still command a premium for their work, just as Bob Loveless still commands a premium for his hunting knives. However, the majority of makers who cannot or will not reach the most exalted peaks of craftsmanship—and marketing—will be obliged to compete on an ever-more-

> *If you are not willing to pay 50-500 percent extra for a one-of-a-kind design, it is unfair to ask a maker to create one for you.*

level playing field, both with the knife factories and also with dozens of new and constantly improving fellow custom knifemakers.

Misconceptions

Because the collector market for handmade knives is overwhelmingly a fashion market, some of its features are counterintuitive. People who observe this market from a distance often draw very wrong conclusions about it, which can lead them—and you—into costly errors. Let us try to set some of these misconceptions straight.

1) Extreme Rarity. A "unique" handmade knife is usually not a valuable knife. A maker's work must be available for collectors to take an interest in it. Therefore, the only knife ever sold by an obscure maker is usually next to worthless. The main exception is rare variants of common knives, such as special-order Randalls. These can be extremely valuable because a lot of people want them.

2) Deceased Makers. When a maker dies or retires, he ceases to innovate, attend shows, and influence or be influenced by fashion. The work he left behind begins to look old-fashioned. New and eager collectors never met him, perhaps have never even heard of him. Most of them want the newest and latest, but he is not providing it. They do not look twice at his knives, and they certainly do not buy them. Therefore, the values of his knives decline, often very substantially.

What about Blade Magazine Cutlery Hall-Of-Famer© William Wales Scagel? He died years ago but his knives are greatly in demand and rising in value.

This is true. However, Scagel's work is valuable not because he is dead but despite that fact. Scagel was a pioneer, innovator, artist and a historical phenomenon. Few makers are of his caliber but, for those who are, their work is already valuable while they are working, as Scagel's work was, and is likely to remain so long after they are gone. For most others, however, our experience thus far clearly indicates that the opposite will be true.

3) Early Knives by Prominent Makers. A few makers made great knives from day one. Most, however, learned on the job, and their early efforts are now very likely an embarrassment. To the historically minded collector those first attempts might have some value, but to the connoisseur of quality who buys only the best of today's new knives, those early works are of little or no interest.

4) Engraving and Decoration. The sad fact is that decoration of any sort usually diminishes the resale value of a high-grade modern knife to below the initial cost of knife plus decoration.

This is because the embellishment limits the potential market for the knife to only those few customers who happen to like that particular style or subject of decoration. Even sadder, unless the decoration on a knife was done by a really superior and well-known artist, embellishments will usually reduce the resale value of a knife below that of the exact same knife without decoration.

On the Cutting Edge: Fixed Blades

All is not bleak on the fixed blade front. There are three main areas of ongoing collector interest in the realm of handmade fixed blades. One is modern interpretations of traditional designs, such as famous American bowie knives, Renaissance left-hand daggers, and Japanese tantos. A few bladesmiths are making Indo-Persian- and Oriental-style knives and swords that rival the work of the greatest masters of the past. Some of the finest knifemaking being done today is in this area.

The second area is fantasy knives and swords—and even armor—both for wall display and for wear by re-enactors and the like. Fantasy knives are as fantastic as the maker or customer wants them to be. If you can imagine it, chances are that there is a wild-eyed maker who can build it for you.

The third area is combat and survival knives. Fine work continues to be done in this area.

On the Cutting Edge: Folders

Handmade folders are where most of the collector interest now lies, and where much of the collector money is now spent. At this writing, more and more custom knifemakers are finding inspiration in the traditional factory-made pocketknife patterns of the past. A few make straightforward replicas, while many others offer their own personal variants and interpretations to both collector and knife user alike.

Of course, the mainstream of handmade folding knives is still the modern locking folder, including the many Michael Walker-inspired locking liners (or "LinerLocks™," a name which Walker, Blade Magazine Cutlery Hall-Of-Famer©, trademarked). Tactical folders—folders with hi-tech materials and a "combat look," though most are largely used as utility pieces—were extremely hot in the '90s and continue to be sought today, especially by collectors in the 18- to 30-year-old range. A lot of collector attention also goes to small and elegant "gentlemen's knives," both plain (pioneered by Blade Magazine Cutlery Hall-Of-Famer© Ron Lake and Jess Horn) and fancy (pioneered by Henry Frank). The popularity of these small knives remains strong, in part because of their close kinship to fine jewelry.

Damascus folders have retained their popularity, and damascus knives of all types are especially sought after by European collectors. Increasingly, the high technical standards demanded of standard stainless and high-carbon-steel-blade handmade folders are coming to be expected of damascus folders, as well.

Titanium and niobium, and even aluminum, can be toned to a whole rainbow of colors by deft application of heat, electricity, and chemical reagents in a process called *anodization*. In the 1980s, Michael and Patricia Walker pioneered the application of this technique to folding knives. Today, toned bolsters and handles have moved from novelty to commonplace, and are even being offered on factory folders. They are still popular where aesthetically effective, but they no longer sell on novelty value alone.

Innovative blade locking mechanisms still excite some collector interest, but as with toned titanium, it takes more than mere novelty to catch the collector's eye today. There remains much untapped potential in this realm, both in innovation and also in improvements upon old locking principles. However, it takes a solid machine shop background for a maker to devise really practical and functional locks.

While growing numbers of custom knifemakers are finding inspiration in classic factory patterns, a few of today's knife factories have turned to prominent custom knifemakers for designs. These factory/custom collaboration knives were intended as upscale using

pieces, but some have become collector items in their own right.

Miniature Knives

Most miniature knives are too small to be functional, so they are really more jewelry than cutlery. They can be fixed blade or folding, though most handmade miniatures are still fixed blades.

Some custom knifemakers can be persuaded to make miniatures of their regular knives. A few makers specialize in miniature versions of other people's designs (such as Earl Witsaman's miniature Randalls). A growing number of makers do original work in miniatures, even branching out into tiny swords and axes.

Knifemaker Brochures

Most knifemakers offer printed brochures, though more and more are turning to providing those brochures in Web-page format on the Internet. Those who belong to The Knifemakers' Guild are required to offer brochures. Some collectors who do not have a whole lot of money to spend on knives also (or instead) collect these brochures. Considering the labor and expense of photography, layout and printing, we believe that makers are entirely justified in charging enough for their brochures to make a profit on them.

Brochures are an inexpensive way to look at a lot of fine knives. The better quality brochures might even increase in value as the years go by. Some old brochures by pioneer makers already command a premium ($5 to $25, occasionally more).

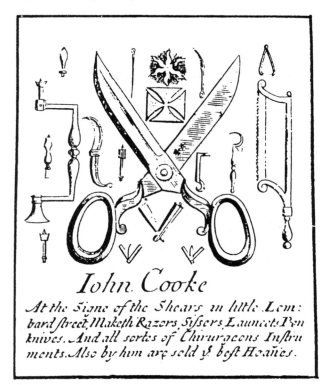

Two 18th Century London cutler's cards (courtesy Geoffrey Tweedale).

Knives as an Investment

There is no direct route to profit in buying and selling knives. However, there are a few rules that you can follow that should improve your chances of making money. Most of these rules apply equally well to buying any type of knife as an "investment," whether handmade, antique, commemorative or limited edition.

The first rule is so obvious that most people forget about it. This is that the profit, if any, comes in selling the knife. An "investment" knife is not a productive asset like a machine tool or a share in a business. It yields no return except capital gain, and that gain cannot be realized except by selling the knife.

Let's say that the "value" of your knife has doubled in three years. Where do you propose to sell the knife to realize the increase—at a show, through an ad? Have you anticipated how much shows and ads cost?

Perhaps you can sell it to a dealer. Of course, he will want his share of profit.

Obviously, it is possible to sell collectible knives at a profit, but you had better plan your method and figure in your overhead before you start spending money.

High-End Knives

In the years since knife collecting began its present rise in popularity, back in the early 1970s, the collector knife market has witnessed remarkable changes. Perhaps the most profound change in recent years has been the radical separation of "high-end" knives from all others.

What are high-end knives? These are extraordinary knives of interest to the collector or aficionado for whom cost is pretty much no object. Most of today's high-end knives fall into six categories.

1) Historical presentation knives of all types made for and given to prominent individuals. A splendid example is the five-blade pen knife made by James Ward & Co. of Bronxville, New York, and presented to President Abraham Lincoln in June 1863. The knife is in mint condition, is in its original box, and is accompanied by a hand-written note of thanks from Lincoln. The knife brought $99,825 at a Sotheby's auction in New York in January 1989.

2) Early bowie knives, including American bowies by prominent cutlers and surgical instrument makers, and Sheffield bowies of large size or of unusual design. Butterfield & Butterfield of San Francisco auctioned two important bowie collections in March 1992, and the best knives in that sale brought between $15,000 and $60,000 each. An I*XL exhibition bowie knife brought $132,000.

3) High-grade handmade sheath knives by well-documented American knifemakers of the first half of this century. The best known of these makers are discussed in Pioneers of Modern Handmade Knives (see the "Table of Contents" for the page number). In private sales, the better and rarer of these knives are bringing around $3,000-$4,000 each, with extraordinary examples selling for significantly more.

4) Select brands of American and English factory pocketknives made before 1942, in mint "as new" condition. Most favored are large, ornate folders, including the Very High rated folding hunters which have been popular for a quarter century now, as well as folding dirks and bowies, fancy figurals, and the larger and more elaborate whittlers and multi-blades. The price spread between the finest mint examples of these types and all other knives remains wide.

5) Superbly crafted antique traditional knives from such diverse locales as Lapland, Java, Argentina and India. This category is just beginning to emerge, as collector knowledge of and appreciation for these fine blades grow.

6) The finest of contemporary handmade folding knives, especially folders that have been magnificently gold inlaid and engraved.

High-End Prices

These high-end knives pose a perplexing dilemma for the compiler of a knife price guide. Everyone who follows the knife magazines is aware of the impressive prices that these fine knives can bring.

Yet, a close reading reveals that such prices are only realized by established specialty dealers or by international auction houses. Similar knives offered at knife shows or in antique shops will not bring a half, nor sometimes even a tenth, of the highly publicized high-end prices. As a rule, high-end knives, when sold in the ordinary course of business, are almost invariably purchased at wholesale by dealers.

The reason for this is simple. For the person who can afford to spend $50,000 on a modern pocketknife or $100,000 on an old one, his own time is far too valuable to spend days or weeks wandering through shows and shops looking for cutlery treasures. He would much prefer to retain a knowledgeable dealer to do that time-consuming legwork for him, and to pay for that time with the dealer's markup on the knives that he sells him. At least as important, the knife dealer insulates the wealthy collector from the aggravation and potential risk of trying to do business with strangers.

For the dealers and collectors who move in those exalted orbits, value guides have little meaning. When wealthy collectors want a knife, they will pay whatever it takes to obtain it. To them the cost is only money, money they have in abundance.

For the rest of us, however, the impressive prices often paid for high-end knives in those wealthy circles have little significance. This is why, in the body of this book, we do not list the prices that these knives bring at auction, or in private transactions between specialist dealer and wealthy collector.

Chances are that you are neither an auction house nor a prominent knife dealer. Those big numbers are dazzling but to mere mortals they are not useful. We cannot afford to pay those prices when we buy, and we cannot expect to realize them when we sell.

Let's suppose that you have found an extraordinary high-end knife, and that you want to sell it. Somewhere there are collectors who would like to buy your knife, but they do not want to give up their privacy. Yet neither knife nor money can change hands until the two sides are brought together. Enter the dealer. This is where dealers earn their cut. Wealthy collectors realize this. You should, too.

For many high-end knives, this book will help you to determine a fair price to expect a dealer to pay you for each one. If you are not in a hurry, you might eventually realize a larger sum by consigning the knife to a specialist dealer, rather than selling it outright.

The other side of the coin is that any knife dealer who needs to use this book (or any other book) to sell his or her own high-end knives is probably in the wrong business. A knife dealer's prices on rare and highly sought-after items must be set by his customers, by what the traffic will bear, not by any guidebook, no matter how conscientious it might be.

Similarly, a collector who fancies himself "advanced" and who spends thousands of dollars per knife, yet who asserts that dealer prices should match "book" prices, is either fooling himself or else trying to mislead a seller. The high-end knife market simply does not work that way, it never has, and we doubt that it ever will. Each high-end knife is a special event unto itself. Its real market price can only be determined in the real market.

The Handmade Market

The same sort of two-tiered market exists in high-end modern handmade knives as in high-end antique bowies. Ask almost any top-drawer knifemaker, and he will tell you that he sells the majority of his knives to dealers. These dealers must obviously be selling the maker's knives at a profit, or they would not continue to buy them.

Sooner or later most of these successful knifemakers will consider raising their prices, in order to try and capture the dealers' mark-up for themselves. However, the smart makers figure out that they have no way to reach most of the customers to whom the dealers have been selling their knives. The time that they will have wasted trying to reach those customers would have been more productively spent in the workshop, making more knives.

Knifemaking takes time, capital and skill, and so does knife selling. The types of skills required in these two complementary sides of the knife business are very different, but time and capital are largely interchangeable. Any time and capital that a knifemaker employs in selling knives diminish what he can use in making knives. Every maker must determine his own optimum mix of making and selling, but for an established maker, the established dealers provide a very cost-effective service.

Some dealers offer special advantages. Many handmade knife buyers live in foreign countries, and they do not like to bother with customs forms, currency exchange, shipping problems, and language barriers. Knife dealers in their own countries bring American handmade knives to them, managing all the delays and paperwork as part of the service that they offer.

Other well-to-do collectors are simply too busy or too impatient to wait for a knifemaker to fill an order, which can take weeks, months or years. When they want a knife they want it now, and they will happily pay extra to a dealer in order to get it promptly.

Collecting Knives to Use

How many people in the United States collect knives as a hobby? No one knows for sure but, based on the subscription and membership figures we have seen, we would say more than 50,000 but fewer than 150,000.

Let's try an easier question, at least one that sounds easy. Forgetting the "hobby" aspect, how many people in the United States simply collect knives?

We will bet you know the answer as well as we do. Think about it: Do you know any adult—not counting people in jail—who does not have a "collection" of knives? That's right, whether he or she believes it or not, almost every person in the USA collects knives—every man and woman, and even a lot more children than their parents may realize. After all, the knife is mankind's oldest and still most basic tool, and it would be passing strange if a person did not own at least a few knives.

Of course, most of these 200 million or so American adults collect knives only to use—or at least that is what they would probably say if asked. The fact is that most of them also have a few knives that they bought because they thought the knives looked neat, and thought that maybe some day they would use them.

See the section on Special Purpose Jack Knives.

MARBLE'S EXPERT KNIFE

These knives were particularly designed to meet the requirements of the professional hunter, trapper and guide who requires a thin keen edge for dressing skins and furs. The back of the blade is designed for scraping skins while on the forms. Has leather handle, aluminum tip. Length of blade 5 inches, weight 3½ ounces.

See the section on American Hunting Knives.

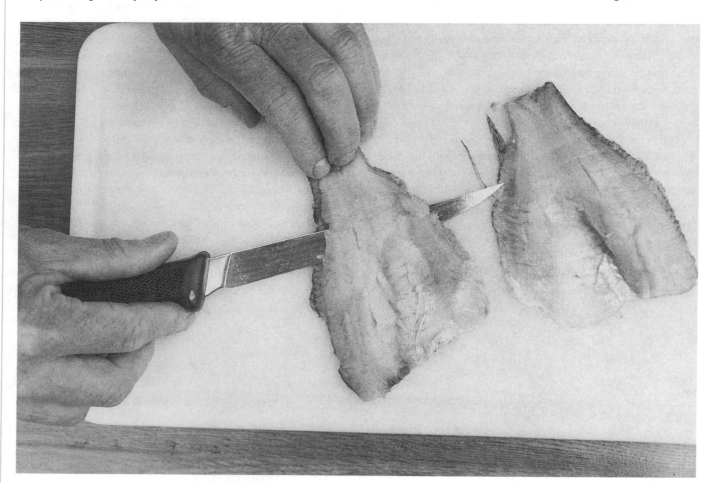

Some of the first real knife collectors were sportsmen such as fishermen, many of whom even today continue to use their knives to fillet their catch.

Blade Magazine Cutlery Hall-Of-Famer© Bernard Levine wrote that he used to travel a lot. When he sat next to someone on an airplane, he usually introduced himself. As soon as he told the passenger that he writes about knives, he indicated that he would brace himself. For the next five minutes, at least, the passenger was sure to tell him all about his or her knives.

The first serious knife collectors Levine met—people who spent a fair amount of their leisure time looking for knives to add to their collections—were those who collected knives to use. The majority of them were cooks, amateur and professional, men and women. Many were whittlers and wood carvers. Others were hunters, fishermen, butchers or gardeners.

People who collect knives to use are so diverse in background and interests that it is risky to generalize about them. Most are interested first and foremost in quality, though a few have picked up some truly odd notions of how to recognize it. We learned early on not to argue about this. Most knives work adequately, and people defend their beliefs about knives just as fervently as they do their ideas about guns, cars, love and religion.

Next to quality, these practical collectors are concerned with functional design. They have learned what types of knives work best for them, but they always have an eye out for something a little better.

Most of these collectors have one or a few favorite brands. Some are curious and try any brand that looks good. A hard-headed minority steadfastly ignores any writing on their blades.

Fifteen or 20 years ago, few of these collectors had any sense of the history of their knives. More recently, as more knife books, magazines, knife shows and cutlery Web sites have appeared, this has begun to change.

If you collect knives to use, you probably do not need much advice from us. However, since advice is our job, we will offer some anyway.

When you buy an old knife that appears unused, look up its value in this book before you sharpen it and use it. If it proves to be relatively valuable, you must decide if you want to destroy up to half of that value by sharpening the blade. Maybe having the knife to use will be worth the "cost" to you, but at least you will have a chance to choose before it is too late. See the section on Grading the Condition of a Knife and Blade Finishes (see the "Table of Contents" for the page number) for information on how to tell if an old knife is really unused.

If you are one of the noble fellowship of knife fanciers, you are in good company. People aware of the myriad possibilities in the world of knives are most often also aware of the countless other wonders the world has to offer. We agree with Socrates that "the unexamined life is not worth living." The knife is the most basic of our tools. If you do not know your knives, you cannot claim to know your world.

Building and Displaying Your Collection

Do you have tens of thousands of dollars to play with? Are you willing to go head to head with some very competitive and long-established collectors? If so, you can enter absolutely any area of knife collecting you choose.

However, no matter how deep your pockets and aggressive your fighting instincts, if you want to put together an outstanding collection of such popular items as American Bowie knives, Remington pocketknives, Loveless sheath knives, or Ron Lake folders, you would still need a lot of time and patience. Not only have the established big-league collectors scooped up the best examples on the market, they have earned the first shot at most of the new ones that are found or made.

If you do have the money and the drive, don't let our warning discourage you. Decide what you want and show the dealers or makers that you are serious (and appreciative). Courtesy, sincerity, and prompt payment without haggling will soon confirm your place in the big league, and your name will move up quickly on their lists.

At the other extreme, a collecting budget of as little as $10 or $20 a week can in a few years be parlayed into a pre-eminent collection of any of several hundred less popular types or brands of good quality or historically interesting knives. What it takes instead of a lot of money is a lot of time, patience, study, and effort. A little bit of advantageous trading and resale does not hurt, either, although this can involve extra time and risk.

Big league or little, as your collection grows, your knowledge of your chosen area or areas will grow, too. You might start to seek "go-withs" for your knives: ads, catalogs, original packaging and store displays, photos of knives being made or in use. Before long you will have enough knives and related material to put together a display that you can set up in your home, exhibit at knife shows, or loan to local banks or museums.

A good display is not cheap to build, but it can pay for itself in the satisfaction of enjoying your collection as a complete entity. There are also some nifty fringe benefits to displaying your collection at shows. One is the chance of winning awards, such as trophies, expense-paid trips, or one-of-a-kind handmade knives. Another is advertising value, such as when a visitor to your display says, "I've got a knife sort of like that one at home, only the handle is a different color. Would you like to have it?"

Planning Ahead

A well-planned and well-displayed collection offers immediate personal satisfaction and, if you ever decide to sell it, a good chance of eventual profit. Just as important to many individuals, a noteworthy collection can be a direct source of personal prestige.

If you have ever wanted to "make a name for yourself," building an interesting and informative knife collection can be a practical way to go about it. Knife journalists and

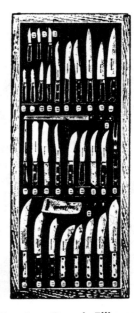

Courtesy Dennis Ellingsen

other collectors often mention outstanding collections in conversation and in print. Much of our own knife education has come from studying people's collections.

A collector who builds an organized and well documented collection may eventually find a permanent home for all or part of it in a museum. There the collection will bear his name for generations to come. Of course, museums rarely buy collections, so you may have to choose between prestige and profit.

Display

It is a fact much bemoaned, but a fact nonetheless, that the flashiest displays at knife shows are the displays that win the awards. Your collection may be the most interesting or the most valuable at the show, but if it does not attract attention by its presentation, and then hold attention by its organization, hardly anyone will ever know.

Think about the theme of your collection. That theme should be evident halfway across the room. One prize-winning collection of handmade knives made in California is displayed on a large wooden map of the state. Another collection of barber shop cutlery is displayed in a replica old-time barber shop. A large, magnificent wood carving would make a fine centerpiece for a collection of whittlers.

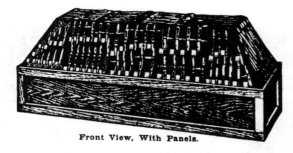

Front View, With Panels.

Think also about the organization of your collection. Your display should be arranged to make that organization clear to the viewer. A recent first-prize display of handmade knives relied on clearly labeled and dramatically lit thematic groupings to enchant visitors and judges alike. If you collect a single brand, try to show its evolution and diversity.

Just as there is no "right" kind of knife to collect, there is no "right" way to display your collection. Here are some good rules to follow, no matter what kind of display you are planning.

Make sure your knives are securely affixed to the display, but be careful not to damage them when mounting or removing them. Display valuable or fragile knives behind glass. Thieves are a problem, and so are fingerprints, which can leave permanent stains. Do not expose your display to direct sunlight. Do not store or display your knives in leather sheaths. Acid in the leather can corrode the blades and fittings.

CUTLERY DISPLAY BOXES.

For displaying and stocking cutlery in show cases. For use where dealers are not using the fixed Sampling Method. Boxes covered with black basket-weave paper and fitted with a removable tray at top. Tray lined with rich green plush. Top of tray has oval collar button knob, with letter "W" on top, also an attractively embossed label in red and gold attached to front of box.

Pen Knife Purse

Design your display in interchangeable modules. This has two benefits. First, it makes it easy to set up, take down, ship, and store your display, without having to take it completely apart. Second, as your collection grows and changes, you can add or modify one or several modules without having to redesign and rebuild the entire display. Be sure to leave room in your display for "go-withs" and for brief, legible labels.

Safety

If you plan to display your collection, take some elementary precautions ahead of time. In fact, every collector should take these precautions:

Do not leave your collection unattended in a parked vehicle, even in the trunk. Consider installing a safe and a burglar alarm in your home. Your safe or storage place should be in a climate-controlled part of the house to minimize the danger of rust.

Don't give out your home address. Do all your collecting business through a post office box. Also make sure your home address is not shown in the telephone directory. Most telephone companies will omit your address or substitute your post office box number at no charge.

Having a box number means that you cannot ship via United Parcel Service, unless dealing with people you know, or use an alternative address, such as a business. At this writing, U.P.S. will accept antique or handmade knives valued up to $50,000 for domestic air shipment, but will not transport "weapons" or "used goods" internationally. Registered Priority Mail is still a reliable choice, insuring up to $25,000.

When you handle knives at a show or at home, remember that, no matter how handsome, how ancient, or how valuable they might be, they are also usually very SHARP. Master knife photographer Blade Magazine Cutlery Hall-Of-Famer© Jim Weyer sticks mailing labels on to Band-Aid® brand bandages and hands them out as calling cards at knife shows. A lot of his "cards" get used.

If you accidentally drop a knife, get out of the way and let it fall. We don't care how valuable it is, hands and feet are still worth more.

Have at least as much respect for the point and edge of a knife blade as you do for the muzzle of a gun. Do not point or wave knives at other people (or at yourself). A knife might not have the range of a gun, but a knife is always loaded.

Knife Show Etiquette

Knife shows and combined knife and gun shows are held all over the country throughout the year. Some are sponsored by commercial show promotion companies. A growing number are sponsored by local, regional and national knife collecting organizations. For current listings, consult the show calendar sections in *BLADE, Knives Illustrated* and *Knife World* magazines, and on the Web at www. blademag.com.

Knife shows are a lot of fun. They are best, however, when visitors follow a few basic rules of courtesy. They are:

- Do not handle knives without permission;
- Never touch the blade or the edge of any knife offered or displayed as a collector's item;
- Never open more than one blade of a folding knife at a time;
- Do not block a sale table if you are only "window shopping";
- If you have brought knives to trade or sell, obtain permission before displaying them at or in front of someone's table, and;
- Do not interrupt or comment on any transaction.

Grading the Condition of a Knife

The National Knife Collectors Association (NKCA), with headquarters in Chattanooga, Tennessee, (POB 21070, Chattanooga, TN 37421 423.892.5007) has published a set of standards for grading old knives, especially pocketknives. Collectors and dealers have long used the NKCA standards. With the permission of the NKCA, we list the standards here.

As in the first edition of this book, we have followed the higher NKCA standards with our own modified terminology, which we believe is more accurate at reflecting the knife marketplace. However, any such standard grading terms are more suited to a guidebook than to a knife list. When listing an actual knife for sale, it is always better to describe its actual condition in detail rather than to just attach a grade label.

If you are building a serious collection, one that you one day hope to display or to sell, you should limit yourself to knives in Mint or Excellent Unsharpened (NKCA Near Mint) condition. Mint knives are more valuable than Near Mint, of course, but Mint knives are rare, expensive and fragile. A little abuse or neglect quickly turns them into Near Mint.

A Mint or Near Mint knife has the same shape it had when new. It looks exactly the way its maker intended it to look. That is why it is most suitable for a collection.

A Good (NKCA Excellent) or lesser-condition knife is still an example of its type and of its maker's work. However, it is not an entirely accurate example, since its shape has been modified by wear, use and sharpening.

Knives grading Fair or Poor are suitable for a serious collection only as examples of exceedingly rare or early patterns, brands or types of construction. To merit consideration, such a knife should be all original.

Some collectors and dealers insist on taking a Near Mint or even a Mint knife and buffing or polishing it up. This is a mistake. Over-eager polishing destroys any remaining original finish on a knife (see the "Table of Contents" for the page number of the section, Blade Finishes). It softens all contours and edges. It eliminates all traces of honest age, which may leave the very authenticity of the knife open to doubt. It substantially reduces the knife's value to a serious and knowledgeable collector.

N.K.C.A. GRADES

NKCA MINT: Absolutely new, exactly as shipped from the factory. A mint knife has no blemishes. It was never carried, never sharpened and never used. A mint knife may be lightly oiled and wiped with a soft rag. Any harsher cleaning will turn it into a Near Mint knife, with a 1/3 to 1/2 reduction in value.

NKCA NEAR MINT (also EXCELLENT UNSHARPENED): An unused knife with a few minor blemishes. It may show slight carry wear or age checking on the handles. The blades may have been lightly honed or may show slight discoloration, even a tiny rust spot or two. Any original blade etch must be present and clear. Most of the original finish (again, see Blade Finishes) must be present. The base prices in *BLADE's Guide To Knives And Their Values* are for knives in Near Mint or Excellent Unsharpened condition.

NKCA EXCELLENT (also GOOD): Up to 10 percent blade wear. All blades "walk and talk." (To "walk" is to operate smoothly under tension from the backspring. To "talk" is to snap crisply when opened or shut. A blade that does not walk and talk is said to be "lazy.") Blades or handles may be discolored or cleaned. Sophisticated collectors prefer discoloration to heavy cleaning. A heavily cleaned or buffed knife cannot grade higher than NKCA Excellent. A Good (NKCA Excellent) condition knife is worth about 25 percent less than an Excellent Unsharpened (NKCA Near Mint) knife.

NKCA VERY GOOD or **GOOD**: Up to 25 percent blade wear. Slight cracks or chips in the handles. May have one lazy blade. All stampings clear. No replaced parts. In *BLADE's Guide To Knives And Their Values*, NKCA Good or NKCA Very Good knives are described as "WORN." They are worth about 50 percent less than Excellent Unsharpened (NKCA Near Mint) knives.

NKCA FAIR: Up to 50 percent blade wear. Blades may be lazy. Large cracks or chips in the handles. Handles or blades may have been replaced with original parts (some dealers and repairmen have stocks of unused old parts; they and others also cannibalize broken knives for good parts). Stampings faint but legible.

NKCA POOR: Blades heavily worn. Handles broken or missing. Obviously replaced blade(s). Stampings faint or illegible.

Some Clues that Help
Date and Identify Knives

Materials

SHEAR STEEL: invented in the Middle Ages, but most knives marked SHEAR STEEL are 19th century.

CAST STEEL: also called crucible steel, *acier fondu, guss stahl* (G.S.): invented circa 1742 by Benjamin Huntsman of Sheffield for clock springs. First used for blades and pocketknife springs within about 30 years. In general use on better knives c1800-1920. Last made commercially about 1968. (For more about shear steel and cast steel, see the "Table of Contents" for the page number of Kitchen and Butcher Knives.)

HEROULT ELECTRIC STEEL: in 1907 French metallurgist Paul Louis Toussaint Heroult (1863-1914) designed the Heroult electric furnace for production of steel, which quickly became the standard method of making high-grade tool and cutlery steels, replacing crucible cast steel.

CHROME ALLOY STEEL (under 11 percent chromium): first experiments by Faraday and Stodardt in England, 1819; first blades by Berthier in France; first commercial application by Julius Baur in New York, 1865; occasional use for blades circa 1860s-1870s, but it rusts badly; not widely used in knives until the invention of ...

CHROMIUM PLATING: invented and first used 1924. Chrome-plated chrome-vanadium steel blades were commonly used on American fixed-blade knives circa 1935-65.

STAINLESS STEEL (over 11 percent chromium): invented in 1914 simultaneously by Elwood Haynes of Kokomo, Indiana, and Harry Brearley of Sheffield, England, who cooperated in its development and licensing. First commercial use in knives circa 1915. Widely used after 1919. Many 1920s stainless-steel-bladed pocketknives have carbon-steel springs. By 1930s, half of *total* cutlery sold in the U.S. was stainless steel, but while over 90 percent of table cutlery was stainless, over 90 percent of pocket cutlery was not. Today, nearly all new cutlery is stainless steel.

STELLITE: cobalt tungsten alloy, invented by Elwood Haynes in 1907, first used in knives 1910. Last commercial use in pocketknives, April 1920. Now used by some custom makers. It is a trademarked name of the Deloro Stellite Co.

SILVER: American change from COIN (90 percent) to STERLING (92.5 percent) standard: 1868 [see the "Table of Contents" for the page number of Silver Fruit Knives]. Central European silver usually marked in parts per 1,000 (e.g., "800" indicates 80 percent silver).

SILVER ELECTROPLATE: an improvement over ancient dip and c1742 close plating; first commercial use c1837 by Jean Christofle of Paris, France.

NICKEL SILVER or **GERMAN SILVER**: alloy of copper, zinc, nickel, invented c1810 by E.A. Geitner, Germany.

NICKEL PLATE: first used mid-1860s.

CAST IN PLACE TIN ALLOY ("PEWTER") BOLSTERS: first used on fixed-blade knives circa 1867, on pocketknives circa 1876. Still used on some scrapers.

ALUMINUM: first produced commercially by H. E. S. Deville in France 1854. First produced economically by Heroult in France and C.M. Hall in the U.S., 1886. Thereafter sometimes used for knife handles, bolsters and liners.

DURALUMIN ALLOY: invented 1910.

HARD RUBBER: patented 1844; first used for knife handles circa 1856.

CELLULOID: plastic material invented 1869 by John W. Hyatt; first commercial use 1872.

CLEAR CELLULOID HANDLES: invented and first used 1879 [see the "Table of Contents" for the page number of **Makers of Picture Handled Pocketknives**].

BAKELITE: plastic material invented 1909 by Leo H. Baekeland; made from formaldehyde and phenol, usually dyed and reinforced; used for knife handles c1920s-1950s.

Mechanisms

Integral iron bolsters and liners on pocketknives: Sheffield manufacture before circa 1860.

Long, narrow square kicks on pocketknife blades, to facilitate hand fitting: usually before circa 1860 (see the photo in and the "Table of Contents" for the page number of 19th Century Sheffield Cutlery Firms).

Wrought iron bolsters on steel-bladed table and kitchen knives: Sheffield manufacture before circa 1880 (see the photo in and the "Table of Contents" for the page number of Table Knives and Forks).

Fixed blades blanked on punch presses (tangs have uniform thickness, or else taper only toward the edge), first used circa late 1860s. Forged blades almost always have tangs that taper toward the end (however, many modern handmade knives have tangs tapered by grinding).

Linerlock™ (e.g., on electrician's knives): patented by Watson and Chadwick for Cattaraugus, 1906, in general use after about 1930. Name trademarked by Blade Magazine Cutlery Hall-Of-Famer© Michael Walker circa early 1990s.

Hollow-sheet steel handles secured by folded tabs, with thin celluloid covers: made after 1934, mainly by Elosi (Lohr & Stiehl), Imperial and Richards.

Pocketknife punches that identify contract manufacturers:

> Harrison patent punch blade dated June 10, 1902 (No. 701,878): made by New York Knife Co.
>
> Cooper patent punch blade dated April 25, 1905 (No. 788,022): made by Robeson Cutlery Co.
>
> Alvord patent punch blade dated October 16, 1906 (No. 833,146): made by Empire Knife Co.
>
> Carman patent punch blade dated April 7, 1908 (No. 884,350): made by Napanoch Knife Co.
>
> Mayer patent punch blade dated August 11, 1908 (No. 895,778): made by Camillus Cutlery Co.
>
> Fuller patent punch blades dated December 26, 1911 (No. 1,072,838) or February 15, 1916 (No. 1,171,422): made by New York Knife Co.

Blade Marking Technology

STAMPING: Deep-stamped brand markings were universal on all types of knives up until the 1880s. They are still universal on pocketknife tangs.

Up through about 1814, the stamping dies for these marks were hand cut and often appear relatively rough and simple. That year, the English law limiting blade stamping to the registered guild mark was repealed, while the introduction of mechanical reduction techniques (such as the reducing lathe) permitted the making of precise and complex stamping dies (see the photo in and the "Table of Contents" for the page number of 19th Century Sheffield Cutlery Firms).

ETCHING: Around 1880, deep etching was introduced as a lower-cost and potentially more elaborate alternative to stamping trademarks on fixed-blade knives. Under a glass, a deep-etched mark has slightly ragged edges and is clean inside. An older stamped mark is black inside, because it was applied prior to heat treating.

In the 1940s, the one-step electro-etch began to supplant the deep etch on fixed blades. It was also used on the blades of pocketknives, though not on their tangs. This etch has a fuzzy, frosty look. It has almost no depth, so it is readily worn away.

Decorative and trademark blade etching, in which the resist for a whole elaborate panel was first applied with a brass stencil, was used on razors and knives from around 1800 through the 1940s, and possibly later. Such an etch was done on a crocus polished surface (see the "Table of Contents" for the page number of Blade Finishes). Unlike electro-etch, it is sharp edged and bright. It has barely perceptible depth. The etching on current fakes is more deep and less crisp and bright than the real thing.

Helpful Markings

BRITISH MONARCHS: the inclusion of a Royal Cypher in an English blade stamp indicates that the firm had a Royal Warrant, usually meaning that a member of the Royal Household had purchased cutlery from the firm. A warrant did not expire with the death of the Monarch; we have some stainless steel knives made in the 1920s marked **V** (crown) **R**. ["Their Majesties" used circa 1892.]

> **G** (crown) **R** (hand cut stamp) [George II, III, and IV]: before 1830.
>
> **W** (crown) **R** [William IV]: 1830-1837.
>
> **V** (crown) **R** [Victoria]: 1837-1901.
>
> **E** (crown) **R** [Edward VII]: 1901-1910.
>
> **G** (crown) **R** (modern-style, multi-line stamp) [George V and VI]: 1910-1952.

COUNTRY NAME: The U. S. Tariff Act of 1890 requires manufactured goods imported to the United States in or after 1891 to be permanently marked with the name of the country of origin. Virtually every knife marked with the name of a country was made after 1890. Here are some country and related geographic and miscellaneous markings whose meanings may not be obvious.

PRUSSIA: dominant kingdom of the German Empire; name used on some Solingen export goods between 1891 and 1915.

RHINELAND or German **RHEINLAND**: part of Germany occupied by the Allies from 1919 to 1925; name sometimes used on German export goods.

AUSTRIA: before 1918 was shorthand for the Austro-Hungarian Empire. Knives so marked were made both in Austria and in Bohemia (now part of of the Czech Republic) between 1891 and about 1915.

CZECHOSLOVAKIA: created 1920. Knives so marked were made in Bohemia in the 1920s and 1930s.

MADE IN U.S.A.: first used by a few firms in the late 1910s or early 1920s. Uncommon until the mid-1960s when it was required on American-made knives exported to Canada. Nearly universal on American factory-made knives today.

OCCUPIED JAPAN: U.S. Occupation spanned 1945 to 1952.

SHEFFIELD (*NOT* used with "ENGLAND", i.e. pre-1891): seems to indicate goods made for export to the United States after about the 1830s. Sheffield steel goods were thought best by Americans, and half of Sheffield's mid-19th-century output was shipped to the USA. The English market then favored London cutlery, however, so a known post-1830s Sheffield mark lacking the word "SHEFFIELD" usually indicates that the piece was made for sale in Britain, or in one of the colonies.

In addition, a name above "SHEFFIELD" can be that of a merchant somewhere in Britain or the Commonwealth, rather than of a Sheffield maker or factory.

LONDON: made in London. London guild rules long forbade London cutlers from selling out-of-town cutlery stamped with their own touchmarks, but Sheffielders and Dutchmen often counterfeited London marks, such as the London guild's dagger mark, since those had the most prestige. After 1819, London cutlers could use the word "LONDON" on their own blades, but it became illegal for anyone to use the word "LONDON" on any cutlery made outside of the City.

A London street address *without* the word "LONDON" indicates that the item was made in Sheffield for a London cutlery merchant some time after 1819.

CELEBRATED, WARRANTED, CAST STEEL, ENGLISH STEEL, etc., without an English place name (such as "Sheffield"): often indicates a knife made in Germany or Austria-Hungary, mainly before 1891, for export to the United States.

STEEL (on shank of fork): Sheffield made, 19th century.

FOREIGN or **FOREIGN MADE**: made, usually in Germany, for export to England, after about 1926.

ZIP CODES: in U.S. addresses, after July 1, 1963.

Handle Materials

PEARL (mother-of-pearl): The inner lining of certain mollusk shells from off the coasts of the Orient and Australia.

ABALONE SHELL: The inner lining of a gastropod shell found off the coasts of California and Mexico. "Sea Glade" was Imperial's circa 1939 name for abalone shell bits in a clear matrix.

IVORY: Elephant tusks, usually from West Africa. Distinguished by extreme hardness and a delicate wood-like grain. White when fresh, ivories and bone age to a golden yellow color. Green-dyed ivory was popular in Europe from the 17th to the early 19th centuries.

MASTODON and **MAMMOTH**: Ancient mastodon and mammoth ivories found in the far northern climes (Alaska, parts of Canada and Russia, etc.) are often used on handmade knives. (As is walrus ivory [see following], mastodon and mammoth are often referred to as "fossil ivory," though the term "fossil" is a misnomer. A fossil, such as petrified wood, is replaced by the minerals in the surrounding soil, while ancient ivory is frozen in the ground.)

Tables full of ancient ivory slabs and other natural handle materials are common at knife shows.

WALRUS IVORY: Obtained from Alaska and the Russian Arctic. It has no grain but each tusk has an obvious crystalline-appearing core. Not used on factory-made pocketknives. Ancient walrus ivory is popular on handmade knives.

TORTOISE SHELL: Mottled brownish yellow shell of such sea turtles as the hawksbill, sometimes backed with gold leaf or orange paper to enhance its color. At one time, translucent cow horn was spotted to resemble tortoise shell.

BLACK BUFFALO HORN: Rich, glossy black horn obtained from the water buffaloes of Asia.

GRAY or **GREEN BUFFALO HORN**: Smooth horn often streaked with white, it is in fact usually cattle horn.

GENUINE STAG: Outside cut ("bark") of deer or similar antler, obtained originally from Hungary, Bohemia, Ceylon and China, with the best examples coming from India (Sambar stag), though India often bans the material's exportation (such a ban was in effect when *BLADE's Guide* was going to press). Its color is sometimes enhanced with dye, hence the distinctive orange tint of Case stag.

SMOOTH WHITE BONE: The shinbone of beef cattle, readily distinguished from ivory by its many tiny pores and lack of grain.

SCORED BONE: Smooth white bone cut with a grid or pattern of lines, used on inexpensive English knife handles in the late 18th and early 19th centuries.

JIGGED BONE or **BONE STAG** (called STAG in most knife catalogs): Mechanically gouged bone, or sometimes second-cut stag, that is usually dyed—often with potassium permanganate—to resemble genuine stag. With experience, one can often identify a knife's maker by the pattern and color of jigged bone. Distinctive patterns of jigged bone were sold to various knife companies by the Winterbottom Bone Co. of Egg Harbor, New Jersey, and by the Rogers Mfg. Co. of Rockfall, Connecticut.

EBONY: A hard, very fine-grained black wood from East Africa and Madagascar.

COCOBOLO: A hard, fine-grained, reddish-brown wood from Central America.

HARD RUBBER: Relatively soft material in black, reddish brown or white. When rubbed briskly, it smells like burning rubber. Rarely used on pocketknives.

CELLULOID: The first moldable synthetic plastic, made of cellulose nitrate treated with camphor and alcohol. It can be made in every color of the rainbow, or any combination of colors arranged in swirled or geometric patterns. It can be fabricated to simulate most natural materials, including ivory, horn, stag, pearl, amber, agate, tortoise shell and wood. It can also be made transparent and used to cover printed pictures (see the "Table of Contents" for the page number of the section, "Makers of Picture Handled Pocketknives").

"DELRIN": A modern moldable plastic material, not as versatile as celluloid, but much more durable.

"MICARTA®": A nearly indestructible laminated plastic material that can be machined and engraved.

BRONZE (copper and tin) and **BRASS** (copper and zinc): Sometimes employed as the handles of knives intended to be used around salt water.

NICKEL SILVER (originally called **GERMAN SILVER**): An alloy of copper, zinc and nickel used often for bolsters and sometimes for liners. Used for the handles of veterinary knives and of inexpensive knives with embossed advertisements and designs. For more on metal handles, see the "Table of Contents" for the page number of the sections, "Pen Knives" and also "Boy's Knives."

Learning to Recognize Fakes

The bane of the knife collector's existence is fakes. Every one of us has been taken in by fakes at one time or another, especially when we were just starting or branching out into a new specialty. Anyone who claims never to have been fooled by a fake probably just has not yet realized that he or she has been fooled.

There are countless ways to be fooled. Even if you could count the ways, clever rogues are out there right now dreaming up new ones. We strongly recommend the book *Counterfeiting Antique Cutlery* by Gerald Witcher.

Counterfeits

A counterfeit is a careful copy or imitation of a genuine item, one intentionally made to deceive the buyer. An authorized reproduction is not a counterfeit as long as it is clearly and permanently marked as a reproduction.

Knife collecting has some highly skilled counterfeiters. There are counterfeit antique knives so exact that even experts have difficulty spotting them. Old-style blade steels and finishing tools are more available than you might assume.

There have been some high-quality counterfeit knives in the market since 1970. You might think an individual with sufficient skill to replicate an 1830s American bowie knife or a 1920s American folding hunter accurately enough to fool an experienced collector would be able to get at least as much money for the same quality knife made of modern materials and marked with his own name—but such is not the case.

The recent sharp increases in prices for antique pocket cutlery and antique bowie knives, as well as growing interest in presentation antique knives with engraving and World War II vintage handmade combat knives, has made clever counterfeiting profitable. The potential for sophisticated fraud is now very real. Caution and skepticism are essential, not just for beginners but for all of us.

Indeed, collectors of recent and contemporary handmade knives must be increasingly cautious as well. Here, too, the potential for sophisticated fraud is growing every day. For example, Blade Magazine Cutlery Hall-Of-Famer© Bill Moran's knives have been faked and sold at outrageous prices.

Caution and skepticism should not diminish your enjoyment of knife collecting. They are essential attitudes in all types of collecting, from sports cards to fine arts to automobiles. By contrast, one thing that is certain to diminish your enjoyment of knife collecting is the belated discovery that you have spent $500 or $5,000 on a counterfeit knife.

Low-grade counterfeit knives abound. Some are such poor fakes that they are not even real knives. Their "blades" were never heat treated, their edges never sharpened. Nevertheless, even these awful, clunky objects fool some people.

The majority of counterfeits are real knives that are falsely marked. The markings, finish and handle materials on some counterfeits of popular brands are so poor and inappropriate that they are obvious to most collectors, yet even the worst of them sell briskly to inexperienced collectors, and greedy antiques dealers and flea-market merchants.

Remember, a low-quality knife with a high-quality name is almost always a fake.

James & Lowe, Sheffield

"JAMES & LOWE" was the legitimate mark of Fred James, the pre-eminent maker of bowie knives in Sheffield, England, in recent times. He died in 1985. Sandy Lowe, who also is deceased, was a cutler who worked with James.

Besides his James & Lowe knives, James made dozens of big, heavy, fake I*XL "California Knives." The fakes have bedeviled museums and collectors for the past two decades and more. The principal distributor of the fakes was the late Richard Washer of Sheffield. Many of these "Dickie Washer Specials" are shown in Washer's 1974 book on Sheffield markings and are captioned as authentic 19th-century pieces.

James once worked as a foreman for Wostenholm, but this does not make his "I*XL" knives genuine. They were not made for Wostenholm and they are certainly not antique. The oft-told story that they were old blades that James merely completed is false; they are made of modern steel.

Someone who has had the chance to examine genuine antique bowie knives made in Sheffield should have no trouble recognizing a James knife as modern. The color of the steel and the style of the finish are the most obvious clues. Also, his blade bevels, style of filework, and choices of guard materials and shapes are all distinctive and modern.

James knives that are marked "I*XL" are basically counterfeits. Many sold for hundreds of dollars in the early 1970s. However, James' James & Lowe-marked knives are genuine 1970s artifacts and worth more than the fake I*XLs.

Reworks

A rework or remanufactured knife is a knife that has been "improved." It can be a knife that was repaired with old or borrowed parts, or even one that was entirely assembled from old parts. It can be a knife that has had an undesirable brand removed and a desirable name put in its place. It can simply be a knife that has been so heavily cleaned and polished that it is no longer possible to tell what has or has not been done to it.

Unlike convincing counterfeits, which are rare, reworks are epidemic in knife collecting. A surprising number of people believe themselves to be competent at knife restoration. Most are not.

To start with, a competent and honest repairman uses correct, original parts. Incompetent, dishonest repairmen do not care if parts are correct and original, nor would they know where to get proper parts if they did care.

Strange as it may seem, however, a knife that is obviously made from mismatched parts may well be an authentic old knife. There are many documented instances of cutlery firms buying up the parts inventories of defunct competitors, using up the inventories of firms that they had taken over, and re-stamping blades made for contracts that had been canceled. Every hybrid knife must therefore be evaluated on its own merits.

There are a few competent repairmen who have the skill and the equipment to do a proper crocus or glaze finish. A not-so-smart repairman cannot resist the impulse to polish a knife inside before putting it back together. If the tang of a pocketknife has been buffed in places where a buffing wheel cannot reach, then you can be reasonably certain that the knife has been apart.

As far as fake markings go, a strong light and a good magnifier will show up just about all of them. Any mark struck a letter at a time on an "antique" manufactured knife is immediate bad news. So, too, is a ragged-edged or over-sized engraved mark, or any "cold-stamped" mark. (See *Counterfeiting Antique Cutlery*, by Gerald Witcher.)

When a mark is struck cold into steel, it remains clean inside the mark itself. (Note: Deep-etched marks on fixed-blade knives are also clean inside; this type of mark was not used on folding knives.) An authentic hot-stamped mark—or a mark stamped prior to heat treating—is black inside. Some fakers put black ink in their cold-stamped marks, though the ink is easily wiped away.

A cold-stamped mark has raised edges that you can feel. If the edges have been ground away, you can usually see where it was done. Sometimes, a fake mark shows through on the back of the blade. A real one never does.

When a blade's tang or ricasso has been ground down to remove an original mark, it can usually be seen by holding the knife with the edge away from you and sighting down along the side of the blade. If the area of the marking appears hollowed out or asymmetrical, it probably has been altered.

Of course, many fake or misleading markings on German-, Japanese- or Italian-made knives were applied at the factories. Just because a stamping is original to a knife does not necessarily mean that it is authentic.

If a pocketknife blade and its spring are not of the same thickness and color, then something is probably wrong. If a blade and its tang or ricasso are not of exactly the same color, then something is definitely wrong (see the "Table of Contents" for the page number of the section on "Table Knives and Forks" for the only exception to this rule). Fakers sometimes weld a replacement blade to a tang marked with a collectible stamping. Bubbles and gaps at the junction reveal sloppy welding, but the only clue to skillful welding may be a slight color difference.

Another certain giveaway on a reworked antique knife is glue. Glues were simply not used in knife assembly until quite recently. In particular, epoxy and cyanoacrylate (Super Glue®), both recent inventions, were not used in assembling antique factory-made knives. If a shield or handle is glued on—both should be pinned on— something is definitely amiss.

The only exception to the glue rule is that older, narrow-tang fixed blades had their handles attached with cutler's cement. Cutler's cement is made of rosin, beeswax and brick dust. It is dark brown and crumbly, smells bad and melts in boiling water.

German Fakes, Old and New

To guard against counterfeits and reworks, it is important to learn to distinguish German-made knives from the much more collectible American makes. This is especially true because the "conversion" of German pocketknives into counterfeit American ones is a practice that dates back more than a century.

As of 1891, imports to the United States must be permanently labeled to show country of origin. Early in the 20th century, small cutlery retailers often complained that shady importers were re-stamping German pocketknives to fool them and their customers, long before knife collecting was a popular hobby.

So how does one tell if an old pocketknife was made in Germany, especially when it is unmarked or when its mark suggests that it could be American? There are several useful clues. Here are the most common. Sometimes only one is present but often there are several:

- The combination of steel pivot pins with nickel-silver bolsters;
- Nickel-silver mounts with a dull, greenish-gray cast;
- Bolsters thinner than the bone or stag handle slabs;
- Golden or light-brown bone or stag slabs with shallow and uniform jigging;
- On small pen knives, the combination of short pearl handle slabs with very long nickel-silver bolsters; and;
- Tang stamping in a narrow sans serif typeface.

Do Your Homework

The best way to guard against counterfeits and reworks is to learn what correct knives look like. Study the colors of old steel and other metals. Examine the textures and finishes of old handle materials. Learn blade shapes and tapers, markings and finishes.

By first-hand observation, learn what was standard practice in these components for the makers in which you are interested, and also learn what was not. Study catalog illustrations and knives that you know to be authentic. Doing this also will help to protect you from the most obvious class of fakes: imaginary knives.

Imaginary Knives

For the purposes of this story, an imaginary knife is a fake that is made to look old and historically interesting, but that is in fact not based on any real prototype. The most remarkable thing about virtually all the imaginary knives that we have seen is that they are anachronistic. In other words, the technology to make them simply did not exist in the time from which they pretend to be.

If you know your cutlery, cultural and technological histories, you will recognize at first glance when a knife is imaginary.

The favorite marking on imaginary knives is WELLS FARGO & CO. Trust us: any knife that says WELLS FARGO on it is an imaginary one.

Any knife that has the maker's name misspelled on it is an imaginary one. We have seen a few contract knives that had the distributor's name spelled wrong, but these were tiny knives worth just a few dollars.

Any knife with the word "Gambler" or "Gambling" on it is an imaginary one. Professional gambling was and is a secretive profession. An awful lot of nice, old oyster knives are etched GAMBLER'S PUSH DAGGER or some such nonsense. They are in the same league as coins stamped 69 B.C.

In the realm of the technological, you should learn the difference between old celluloid and new plastic. You should learn the difference between a forged blade with its tapers in every direction, and a blanked blade with at most only one taper (toward the edge). Study the section, "Some Clues That Help Date and Identify Knives" (see the "Table of Contents" for the page number). It will help you identify most of the anachronisms that the makers and purveyors of imaginary knives cannot be bothered to avoid.

Celebrity Imaginaries

The usual subject of celebrity imaginary knives is James Bowie. The high priest of preposterous celebrity imaginary bowies was a writer named Raymond Thorp. His 1948 tome, *Bowie Knife*, was almost entirely a figment of his imagination, especially his drawings of how he thought bowie knives should have looked.

Brass-Handled Figural Knives

Modern reproduction, re-issue, imaginary and fake figural knives are usually made with die-stamped ("coined") solid brass handles. (For examples, see the knives labeled #8 and #16 in the group photo on the first page of the section on "Advertising, Figural, Character and Miniature Knives." See the "Table of Contents" for the page number). Modern makers and fakers employ brass handles because such handles are inexpensive to make today. Equally important, the supposedly "antique" look of brass, often combined with oak, also has been popular. All sorts of reproduction and imaginary items are made from or trimmed with polished brass, ranging from pocketknives to bathroom hardware to chandeliers.

This present popularity of "old-timey" brass is rooted in a popular misconception about the role of brass in "the old days." Although brass was indeed widely used generations ago, naked polished brass had only limited application in earlier times. It was used in some scientific and technical apparatus, such as microscopes, telescopes and measuring instruments. It was used in some rough outdoor and nautical hardware, such as padlocks, cleats and certain plain pocketknives. It was used in cannon barrels and later in metallic cartridge ammunition.

For most household applications, however, brass was protected either by plating or by toning. For example, brass was plated with silver for table use, nickel for plumbing fixtures or gold for eyeglass frames and watch-fob pen-knife handles. Brass was chemically toned or patined for lighting fixtures, builder's hardware and signs. Not only was plain, bare brass considered low class—"brassy" has never been a compliment—but bare brass is difficult to maintain.

Older figural knives most often have coined, nickel-silver handles. Some have aluminum handles (aluminum was favored by Peres of Solingen). A very few have pewter handles (favored by Frary of Connecticut). The brass-colored handles common on figural, six-blade utility knives produced in France are in fact usually made of plated white metal.

A figural knife with solid brass handles is almost always modern. If it bears old-style artwork or advertises a dated product, the knife is probably a fake.

Deane & Adams

Deane & Adams was the name of a respectable London gun merchant. However, in England—and, to a certain extent, in the United States—it is easy to buy up old names and trademarks and then do anything one pleases with them. Back in the 1960s and 1970s, Deane & Adams was used as the front name for a large and brazen purveyor of fake and imaginary collector items. The firm's two specialties were Old West and Nazi fakes. The latter-day

Deane & Adams was ostensibly a part of something called the Fairchild Organisation, though it was most likely a front name as well.

Besides selling fakes at retail in London, the owners of Deane & Adams published a thick and heavily illustrated mail-order catalog. Every single item sold through the catalog was either a counterfeit or an out-and-out imaginary knife.

To the practiced eye, D&A counterfeits look shoddy, while their dozens of imaginary items are outrageous. Despite the poor quality, Deane & Adams sold millions of dollars worth of their products to British and American dealers, who then offered the items to the public, often at a 1,000 percent or more mark-up.

Featured in the front half of the catalog are all the dozens of styles of "Wells Fargo" belt buckles, and other assorted imaginary brass buckles and belt plates, many marked "Tiffany & Co." on the back. Deane & Adams was the principal source for the ingenious but entirely fraudulent imaginary buckles. Dealer cost on them in the early 1970s ranged from $3 to $6 each.

Along with the buckles, the catalog includes all sorts of other fake and imaginary items, ranging from "bawdy house" tokens, to Nazi field telephones, to knives of all descriptions. The knives would be funny if so many beginning collectors had not fallen for them. Indeed, people still fall for them today, because the fake knives have now been around long enough to acquire a real patina of age.

One of the fakes is the "Barnum & Bailey Circus Guy Rope Knife." It is in fact just a cut-down chef's slicing knife.

Then there were the "Wells Fargo Express Mail Knives" and the nearly identical "Ku Klux Klan" knives. There were the "Tiffany" bowies and the "Civil War Liberty" bowies, the latter claimed to be generic, used by both North and South. There were the "Norwegian SS" bowies. There was even a variety of absurd "Gambler's" knives, including little "bowies" with bone dominoes for handle scales and ricassos stamped GAMBLER'S COMPANION/POKER & LIVE. Some of them are etched or stamped with collectible names, such as Keen Kutter.

We have seen many imaginary bowie knives, probably from the same English source, which have either a silver-plated or a stag or a hoof-shaped horn handle, and blades stamped "BEARDSHAW," a sad abuse of a good, old name. Often they have spurious blade etches, such as "FAMOUS" or "VICTORIAN." The latter is almost as phony as the "Original Bowie Knife" etched on modern German hunting knives.

Even wilder than those bowies was D&A's "Mattie Silks Sidewalk Girl Knife." It consisted of a slender dagger blade stamped M. PRICE/SAN FRANCISCO, a stubby pearl handle of the type made for disposable wedding-cake knives, and

an odd-shaped cast-brass latch lever stuck on as a guard, because it bears a vague resemblance to a knuckle bow. The knives could be purchased by the dozen, complete with an "antique" display case.

Another gem was the No. 247-A etched "New Bedford Whale Mincer" on the blade—and would a blade lie? Most likely it originally was a dough or griddle scraper, but "Whale Mincer" sounds so much more historical!

Moving from imaginaries to simple fakes, D&A offered unlimited quantities of "issue" military pieces: Fairbairn-Sykes commando knives, U.S. Mark 1 1918 LF&C knuckle-duster trench knives (made in England), and Nazi daggers in assorted models, all conveniently in mint condition.

Goose-Stepper Imaginaries

In addition to the counterfeit Nazi daggers, Deane & Adams offered a variety of imaginary Nazi knives of its own creation. One was the "Daimler-Benz Luftwaffe Survival Folding Knife." Another was the "World War Two Russian Front Disabled Veteran Knife Blade Buckle."

Best known of the fakes is the brass-handled "lazy-tongs" knife, ostensibly made by Eichorn. D&A called it the "NZ-418 SS Close Combat Push Knife." Being a "purely Aryan weapon," it was exclusively "used in the Scandinavian regions." The knife's design was based on a 1929 British patent; such knives were never made in wartime Germany.

Deane & Adams was not the only purveyor to concoct imaginary Nazi pocketknives. At almost any knife show, you will see nickel-silver-handled balloon whittlers and oval pen knives covered with Nazi-type regalia: swastikas, SS lightning flashes, a simulated Hitler autograph, and the words DRITTES REICH (Third Reich, misspelled). Perhaps such knives would have been big sellers in wartime Germany if someone had thought of making them then. However, they are strictly modern imaginary items.

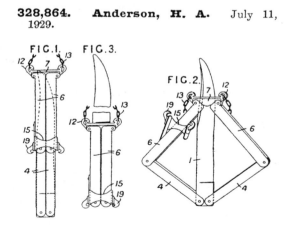

328,864. Anderson, H. A. July 11, 1929.

This 1929 design was "borrowed" by Deane & Adams to create an imaginary Nazi pocketknife widely sold in the 1960s.

Primitive Knives

There are a number of old, primitive-looking fixed blades circulating in the collector marketplace. Most are "mysterious" vintage knives cobbled together from a hodgepodge of old and not-so-old knife parts and other objects. Some have been crudely shaped and aged to look primitive. Some collectors equate crudeness with age or with frontier provenance. Such people are the prey of fakers who make crude, primitive-looking knives.

If you ever feel tempted to spend good money on such a knife, remember: Do your homework, for there are only a few really old "mountain-man knives." And even if some of today's weekend re-enactors favor knives made to look primitive, you can be sure that their frontier ancestors, whose lives often depended on their knives, would never have tolerated such poor cutlery.

Historical Fakes

Knife collecting has been around a long time. We have seen medieval inventories that list in detail a family's precious knives. Some had jeweled or inlaid and engraved hilts. Others had been presented by or to monarchs, ambassadors or distinguished clergymen. Some were wedding knives that commemorated important marital alliances. Even then there were famous knifemakers, and even then there were fakes.

We once saw a little Japanese dagger of inferior quality. It was signed Muramassa, the name of one of the most famous Japanese swordsmiths. Fake Muramassas are not unusual but this one was special because it appeared old enough to have been made in Muramassa's lifetime, which was about six centuries ago. Swordsmith Michael Bell informed us that Japanese sword collectors have a saying that for every 10 signed samurai swords, 11 of the signatures are fake.

A collector had a 16th-century European knife with a "matching" fork. The fork had been made in the late 19th century to enhance the value of the knife to collectors at the time, collectors who would not realize that eating forks had not been invented in the 16th century. Today, the 19th-century fake fork is an antique in its own right.

Self Defense

To sum up, if a knife seems too good to be true, chances are that it is. Put it down and walk away. Don't get into an argument with the seller. If the knife is a fake, he probably knows it and is not about to admit it.

If there is a knowledgeable dealer or collector available, ask him or her to take a look at the knife. He or she may not be able to give you a definite "yes" when the knife seems to be all right, but he/she can sure give you a definite "no" when it is not. All experts err occasionally because of ignorance or the exotic nature of a knife.

Most reputable dealers will, on request, guarantee to refund your money if a knife is shown to be a fake or otherwise not as represented. Such a refund guarantee is usually valid for from three to 10 days. Of course, if a knife is sold to you as a rework, do not ask for your money back when someone else confirms that it is a rework. There are a few dealers out there who are infamous for selling reworks. Keep your eyes and ears open; you will learn those dealers' identities soon enough.

What should you do if you make a mistake, if you get stuck with a fake and the seller either cannot be found or simply refuses to make good? You might be tempted to sell the fake to another collector and recover some of your money. Don't do it! Even if you sell the item as a fake, what will be remembered and passed on is that you sold it, not what you said about it at the time.

Your most valuable possession is your reputation. If you lose it, you will find that it is a very lonely world out there. Keep the fake as a reminder to be more careful in the future, destroy it, or donate it to the counterfeit study collection of the National Knife Collectors Association (for more information contact the NKCA, POB 21070, Chattanooga, TN 37421 423.892.5007).

Blade Finishes

To avoid being fooled by a reworked knife, it is essential to understand that no old-time commercial knife factory ever used rag buffing wheels. An old knife blade or handle that shows the softened edges and slightly wavy surface produced by rag wheel buffing has certainly been reworked. Even worse, a knife that shows signs of such buffing over the whole tang or on the inner surfaces of liners or springs has probably been taken apart, most likely for blade or handle replacement.

For polishing their knives, old-time cutlers used hard wheels. The wheels were either wood covered with leather—usually walrus hide—or hard felt. The surface of the wheel was coated with a mixture of glue and the proper abrasive, and the coating was painstakingly renewed at least once a day.

Even modern mass-produced knife blades, which are gang polished on special machines, are polished on hard wheels so that the edges and lines look clean. Inexpensive blades are polished by drum tumbling, which produces a very respectable looking finish that is almost impossible to fake.

Two different finishes were used on older knife blades: glaze and crocus. For a glaze finish, the abrasive glued onto the final polishing wheel was a very fine powdered emery. A true glaze finish (sometimes called "blue glaze") looks like a series of very fine, even parallel lines at right angles to the main cutting edge of the blade. There are collectors and dealers who fail to recognize this as an original finish and insist on buffing it out.

For a crocus finish, the abrasive on the final wheel was crocus of iron, an extremely fine-powdered iron oxide. A crocus polish is, in effect, a mirror finish. It is smooth and shiny. It shows undistorted reflections. By contrast, a rag wheel polish yields a wavy surface and distorted reflections.

The glaze finish was standard on all low-priced knives, including most plain jack knives. A crocus polish was sometimes used all around on the very finest pearl-handled dress knives.

Standard American practice on all but both the most inexpensive and costliest knives was to crocus polish the mark side of the master blade. Then, the polished mark side usually would receive a trademark etch. The back of the master blade and both sides of the other blade or blades would be glazed.

If you are or hope to be a serious collector willing to pay a premium for mint-condition knives, it is essential that you learn to recognize authentic crocus and glaze finishes. Get an experienced dealer or collector to show you what they look like.

Proper Cleaning

What is the proper way to clean an old knife? The most important rule is to work slowly and patiently. If you clean too little now, you can always clean more later. If you clean too much, however, you may hurt the knife, or at least reduce its value.

The first step is to remove any loose dirt, grease and lint. The tools to use are soft clean rags, wooden toothpicks and cotton swabs. Use the tools in conjunction with a light, non-drying, non-staining oil, such as Japanese sword oil. Japanese sword oil is made from Camellia flowers. It smells good and is good for your knives. It is sold by the Japan Woodworker and by Garrett Wade (see the "Table of Contents" for the page number of the section, "Some Specialist Dealers in Collectible Knives").

Put a drop of oil in each joint of the knife. Wipe down the handles and the blades with a soft rag. Use a drop or two of oil on the rag. Clean inside the knife with swabs and toothpicks. Use a toothpick to clean old grease out of jigged bone.

If there is a sticky residue on the handles as a result of old self-adhesive labels, try removing it with oily nail-polish remover applied to a rag. The active ingredient in the nail-polish remover is acetone, so work by an open window and do not breathe the fumes.

If there are spots of rust on the knife, oil them well and let the knife sit for several days. Then, carefully scrape away the actual rust with the tip of a sharp, stiff knife blade.

By scraping away only the actual rust, you leave intact any of the original finish that remains. Of course, if no original finish remains, then it can do no harm to carefully refinish the entire knife. For the best appearance of a pocketknife blade, and to keep from grinding into the tang, re-establish the choil—the notch in front of the tang—with a small triangular file.

Little, high-speed bench grinders are not meant for use on knives. If you plan to do much refinishing, invest in a small, high-quality belt sander from one of the dealers in knifemaking supplies listed in the *Knives Annual* edited by Joe Kertzman and published by F+W Publications, Inc.

Limits on Estimating the Age of a Knife

Automobile and firearms companies keep detailed serial-number records of production. On the other hand, cutlery companies make all their knives, except special limited editions, in large lots—a thousand of this pattern, ten thousand of that one, etc. When manufactured for inventory, knives from such a batch can remain in stock for several years. Therefore, it is usually not possible to tell exactly when a particular knife was made or sold. You would do very well to narrow it down to a five- or 10-year span. (It should be noted, however, that with the introduction of soft tooling—laser cutting, Computer Numerically Controlled [CNC] machining and other recent developments—more and more factory knives are being produced in smaller lots and a greater diversity of patterns. Knives made in such a manner do not tend to stay in stock as long as those made via the "large lot" method.)

Also, once a knife pattern has been discontinued, the usual practice in most firms has been to discard the production records. Until the recent upsurge in knife collecting, there was no practical reason to keep them. However, specifications, drawings and sometimes even leftover parts have generally been saved, at least until a major upheaval occurred, such as a three-shift war contract or a change of company ownership.

No old-time commercial knife factories ever used buffing wheels such as this modern model from the shop of ABS master smith Ed Fowler. (Fowler photo)

Rather than using a buffing wheel, clean the knife by hand as much as possible. Use soft, clean rags, wooden toothpicks and cotton swabs in conjunction with a light, non-drying, non-staining oil to remove any loose dirt. If it's a pocketknife, put a drop of oil in each joint. Clean inside the knife with swabs and toothpicks. Oil rusty spots, let the knife sit for a few days, and then carefully scrape away the rust with the tip of a sharp, stiff knife blade. Of course, if no original finish remains, then it can do no harm to carefully refinish the entire knife.

Introduction to Folding Knives

This section of the book, Folding Knives, is divided into three segments. They are:

1) **Factory Folding Knife Charts, Tables, and Histories.**

This segment includes the pocketknife blade charts; the pocketknife brand list of manufacturers' and distributors' brands; lists of old Sheffield, London and Salisbury cutlers; and several chapters on cutlery history of special interest to pocketknife collectors. The chapters include:

19th-Century Sheffield Cutlery Firms

The History of G. Wostenholm & Son

Swiss Multi-Blades

History of the Solingen Cutlery Industry

Bohemian Pocket Cutlery

Eskilstuna Pocket Cutlery

19th Century American Pocketknife Firms

Remington U.M.C. Pocketknives

Case, Western, Ka-Bar, Cattaraugus and Related American Brands

Winchester and Simmons

Imperial, Ulster, Schrade and Camillus

Gerber Folding Knives

Buck Folding Knives

Makers of Picture Handle Pocketknives

Embossed, Color Etched and Enameled Handles

Advertising, Figural, Character and Miniature Knives

Pocketknife Blade Openers

At the end of this segment are several chapters on recent limited-edition folding knives—and a few fixed blades—made primarily for sale to knife collectors.

2) **Standard American Folding Knife Patterns.**

This segment has an introduction and three parts. The three parts—Jack Knives, Pen Knives and Multi-Blades—comprise a series of detailed chapters on all the styles and patterns of pocketknives commercially made for the American market since about the middle of the 19th century. Each of the chapters on special-purpose patterns has its own value chart, while the standard shapes of jack knives and pen knives are included in combined value charts.

The introduction to this standard-pattern segment includes detailed instructions for using the value charts, and also a PICTORIAL KEY illustrating typical examples of the standard shapes and patterns. If you are not familiar with pocketknife pattern names, this pictorial key will help you to find the right chapter quickly.

3) **Foreign, Exotic, Primitive and Historical Folding Knives.**

This segment includes standard folding knife styles made before the middle of the 19th century, and also a selection of more recent pocketknife styles made in foreign countries for foreign markets. A special chapter describes "Contemporary French Cutlery." As there is a wide variation among all these knives, each type is described and valued individually.

Note: The names and markings of all makers of contemporary custom and handmade knives, both folding and fixed blade, have been combined into a new special segment in Part III, 20th Century Knifemakers (see "Table of Contents" for the page number).

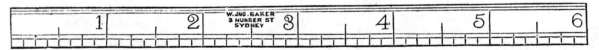

NOTE: THE SIZE OF A FOLDING KNIFE IS ITS LENGTH IN THE CLOSED POSITION.

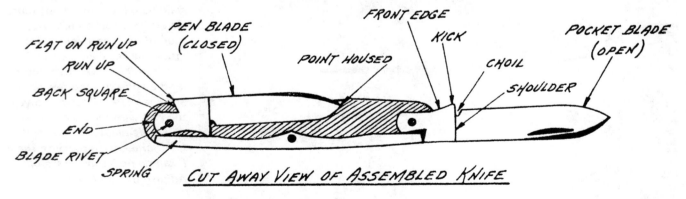

CUT AWAY VIEW OF ASSEMBLED KNIFE

Many pocketknives are not drawn full size, but the lengths of the handles are presented.
To get a good idea of the actual size, place your old knife on the sketch of the 6-inch rule shown.

Pocketknife Blade Charts

Schrade Cutlery Company Pocketknife Blades, 1926

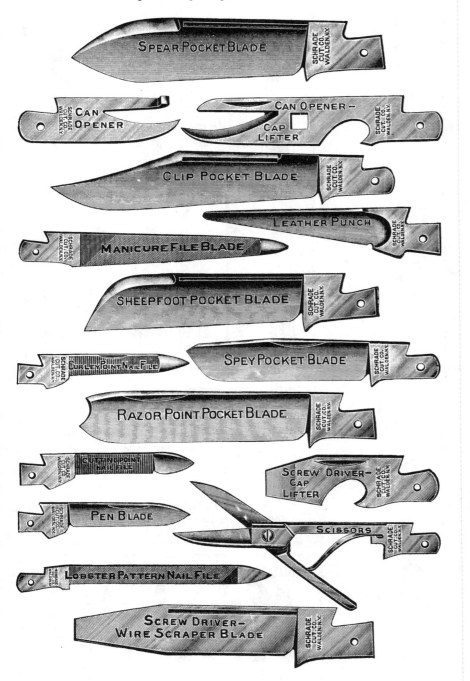

SPEAR POCKET BLADE

CAN OPENER

CAN OPENER — CAP LIFTER

CLIP POCKET BLADE

LEATHER PUNCH

MANICURE FILE BLADE

SHEEPFOOT POCKET BLADE

CURLEY POINT NAIL FILE

SPEY POCKET BLADE

RAZOR POINT POCKET BLADE

CUTTING POINT NAIL FILE

SCREW DRIVER — CAP LIFTER

PEN BLADE

SCISSORS

LOBSTER PATTERN NAIL FILE

SCREW DRIVER — WIRE SCRAPER BLADE

E.C. Simmons Blades, 1930

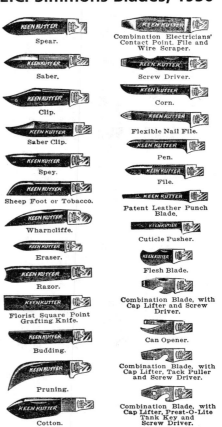

Spear.

Saber.

Clip.

Saber Clip.

Spey.

Sheep Foot or Tobacco.

Wharncliffe.

Eraser.

Razor.

Florist Square Point Grafting Knife.

Budding.

Pruning.

Cotton.

Combination Electricians' Contact Point, File and Wire Scraper.

Screw Driver.

Corn.

Flexible Nail File.

Pen.

File.

Patent Leather Punch Blade.

Cuticle Pusher.

Flesh Blade.

Combination Blade, with Cap Lifter and Screw Driver.

Can Opener.

Combination Blade, with Cap Lifter, Tack Puller and Screw Driver.

Combination Blade, with Cap Lifter, Prest-O-Lite Tank Key and Screw Driver.

NOTES:

Pocket blade means master blade, the principal blade in a pocketknife.

A **saber ground blade** is beveled for only part of its width, making it stouter than an ordinary blade.

The **cut-off pen blade** was also called a coping blade.

The **long curved spey blade** was later called the "Great Western spey blade."

The **Curley point** file was patented by J. Curley of New York in the 1880s.

The square hole in some opener blades is a Prest-O-Lite tank key, for the fuel tanks of a popular early brand of automobile headlight.

Remington replaced the one-piece can opener with the stronger Tillmanns two-piece can opener in 1924. It was patented in 1927.

In 1944, Imperial introduced the modern style of hooked "safety can opener" blade.

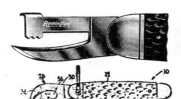

Remington two piece patented can opener

Imperial

Remington Blades, 1920

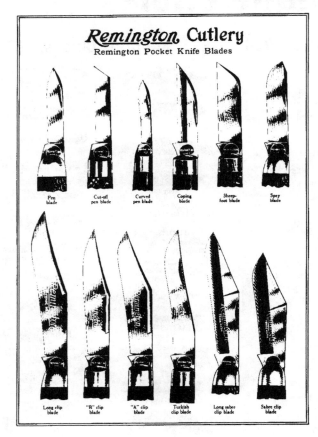

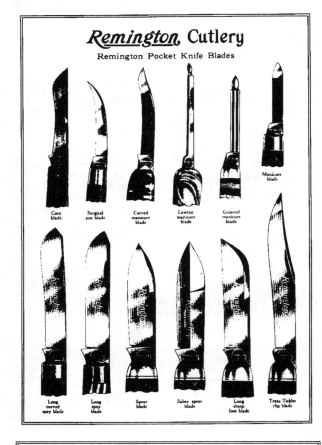

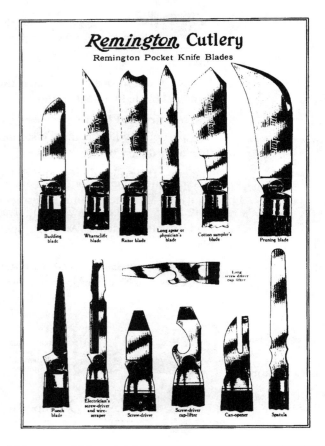

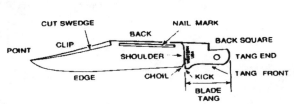

Parts of a regular clip master pocketknife blade. [From *The Knife Makers Who Went West*, copyright 1978 by Harvery Platts. Used by permission.]

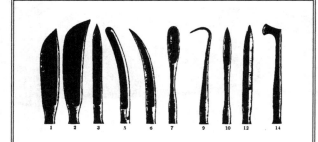

Surgical instrument knife blades, from a 1920s catalog (see *Folding Medical Instruments*).

1. Scalpel	7. Spoon
2. Bandage or operating knife	9. Tenotome
3. Straight sharp bistoury	10. Finger knife
5. Curved blunt bistoury	12. Minor Liston knife
6. Curved sharp bistoury	14. Gum lancet

Pocketknife Brand List

Introduction

The table starting on page 46 includes the brand markings on at least 99 percent of the factory pocketknives one encounters in the United States. The list has two purposes.

The first purpose is to provide you with a capsule history of each brand. This history includes:

- Who distributed the brand;
- Trademarks associated with the brand;
- What cutlery firm made the brand, when known;
- Where the distributor was located;
- What country or countries the brand was made in;

- What type of business the distributor was in; and
- What years it was in business.

NOTE: Partnership firms often changed names. If a knife's marking incorporates several names, you may find additional information by looking up each of these names separately in this list.

For brands and patterns not listed, consult either *Late 18th Century Sheffield Cutlers' Marks, London Pictorial Touchmarks, Salisbury Cutlers* (these immediately follow this brand list), *Foreign Exotic Primitive and Historical Folding Knives*, or else *20th Century Knifemakers*. Consult the Table of Contents for the page numbers.

Acknowledgements

In compiling and then revising this list, I received the help of many books, dealer sale lists, and individuals. The books we found most helpful were:

Goins' Encyclopedia of Cutlery Markings by John Goins

New England Cutlery by Philip R. Pankiewicz

Romance of Knife Collecting by Lavona and Dewey Ferguson

Collector Knives by Blade Magazine Cutlery Hall-Of-Famer© C. Houston Price (earlier editions by Cutlery Hall-Of-Famers James Parker and J. Bruce Voyles)

ABCA Price Guide to Antique Knives by J. Bruce Voyles

Register of Trademarks of the Cutlers' Company of Sheffield, 1919, 1953

Whyte's Sheffield Directory, 1893-94 [courtesy Frank Hudson]

The Sheffield Knife Book by Geoffrey Tweedale [courtesy Barry Swain]

Sheffield Bowie and Pocket-knife Makers by Richard Washer

Sword and Bayonet Makers of Imperial Germany by John Walter

Cutlery Made in Germany (1953 and 1983 Editions)

Wholesale Hardware Directory (1897 Edition)

1922 Merchandise Rating Register, Hardware Merchants of the World (incorporating the 28th Annual Historical Directory of the Wholesale Hardware Houses of the United States and Canada) [courtesy Ernie Modlin]

Kelly's Directories

Antique Medical Instruments by Elisabeth Bennion

The Old Knife Book by Tracy Tudor

The Encyclopedia of Old Pocketknives by Roy Ehrhardt

The Knife Collectors Handbook by Charles Frazier and Revis Ferguson

The Standard Knife Collector's Guide by Ron Stewart and Roy Ritchie

Knife Album by Robert Mayes

Dozens of collectors and dealers around the world helped us in our search for brands, and for information about them. Special contributions were made by Siegfried Rosenkaimer of Solingen; Geoffrey Tweedale; Frank Hudson and Barry Swain of England; Damien Lemaire of France; Capt. Anders L. Dahlman of Sweden; Aldo and Edda Lorenzi of Italy; Cutlery Hall-Of-Famer Albert M. Baer of Imperial Schrade; Elliott Kastor Bryer of New York; Nilo Miori of Camillus; Jim Taylor, formerly of Sheffield; Cindy Taylor; Ernie Modlin; Rhett Stidham; Tom Heitzman; Charlie Dorton; Adrian Van Dyk; Bill Lung; Oscar Hauenstein; Larry Angell; Charles Ochs; Don Lawrence of Ontario; Dick Fullerton; John Malaguerra; John J. Merrigan, Jr.; J. C. Hurt, Jr.; Marc Levine; Paul Dewey; Robert Suydam; and the readers of *Knife World* magazine, whose inquiries to Cutlery Hall-Of-Famer Bernard Levine's "Whut Izzit" column have been at least as educational to him as his replies have been to them.

If you have a knife marked with a brand not listed here, please send the publisher a copy of the marking, along with a description and a picture (tracing, photo, or photocopy) of the knife. If you have primary source documentary evidence that expands or corrects any of the information included here, please send a photocopy to: Managing Editor, KP Books, an imprint of F+W Publications, Inc., 700 E. State St., Iola, WI 54990.

Pocketknife Brand List

POCKETKNIFE BRAND	TRADEMARK (or reference)	LOCATION	MADE IN	TYPE OF FIRM	DATES
A.A.A. 1	see A.J. Jordan				
A.C.	in hallmark on silver fruit knives: see Albert Coles				
A. Co.	see Albertson Co.				
A.C.M. Co.	see Aerial Cutlery [Manufacturing] Company				
A.C.S.	see Alex. Coppel				
A. & F. Co.	see Abercrombie & Fitch				
A.K. & B.	The Kit (see Adolph Kastor & Brothers)				
A.M. & S.	see Arthur Marsh & Son				
A.W.W. & Sons	see A.W. Wadsworth & Sons				
Abbott, J(ames) M.		Oxford ME	USA	Mfr. (& Retail?)	c1860
Abercrombie & Fitch Co.	A. & F. Co.	New York NY	US/Ger./Eng	Retail	1892-c1978
Ablett, J.W.	sold in Canada	Sheffield	England	Mfr.?	recent
Ablett, Trevor		Sheffield	England	Hand mfr.	current
Acier Fondu	Cast Steel (French) (also on some old Sheffield blade)				
Adolphus Cutlery Co.	by A. J. Jordan	St. Louis MO	Ger./Eng.	Import brand	c1882-90s
Adwick, John		Sheffield	England	Mfr.	c1893
Aerial Cutlery Co.	Jaeger Bros.	Duluth MN	USA	Mfr.	1909-1912
Aerial Cutlery Co.	Jaeger Bros.	Marinette WI	USA	Mfr.	1912-1944
Afentakis	Greek military issue		Greece	Mfr.'s brand	c1967
Agate Wood	by Utica Cutlery Co.	Utica NY	USA	Mfr.'s brand	c1946
Ahrens, Ernst G.		Solingen	Germany	Mfr.?	c1910?
Ainslie-Martin Co.	Clark Ainslie & Co.-1900	Lynchburg	VA	Hdw. Whol. Ret.	1886-c1922
Aitor-Cuchilleria del Norte, S.A.	Aitor	Ermua, Vizcaya	Spain	Mfr.	current
Akron Cutlery Works		Akron OH	USA?		c1911-1928
Alamo			Japan	Import brand	recent
Albacete	(place name)	Spain			
Albert, Francis & Co.		Baltimore	MD	Hdw. Whol.	1887-19??
Albertson Co.	A. Co., was Hollingsworth	Kane PA	USA	Mfr.	c1930-1938
Alcas Cutlery Co.	Cutco; Wearever bought Kabar, Ka-Bar 1996. Also see Aurum (Etchings)	Olean NY	USA	Mfr.	1941-pres.
Alcoso	by Alex. Coppel	Solingen	Germany	Mfr.'s brand	c1933-pres.
Alexander		Sheffield	England	Mfr.?	c1860s
Alford, A.G.		Baltimore MD	England	Sporting goods	c1890
All Time Splendid Cutlery			England?	Export brand	
Alldis, J(ames)	probably by Excelsior	Torrington CT	USA?	Mfr.?	c1884
Allen Cutlery, Co.		Newburgh NY	USA	Mfr.	1917-1925
Allen, E.T.	The Club	San Francisco CA	England?	Whol. Import	1878-1899
Allen, Edgar; Imperial Steel Works	Stag (picture)	Sheffield	England	Steel Mfr. Ad	c1870-pres.
Allen, Joseph & Sons	NON-XLL (after 1838)	Sheffield	England	Mfr.	1810-1959
Allen, W.H. & G.W.		Philadelphia PA		Hdw. Whol.	1843-19??
Allen & Son	Square and Compass	Sheffield	England	Mfr.	c1818-1902
Alling, John, & Co.		Chicago IL		Hdw. Whol.	c1897
Alpha	see Harrison Brothers & Howson				
Altenbach, Peter, & Sohne	Swanwerk; also see Jowika	Solingen	Germany	Mfr.	1901-1996
Altman, B., & Co.		New York NY	Germany	Retail	c1900?
Ambacher, J.		Sandusky OH	USA	Mfr. & Retail	c1869-1891
Ambassador	by Colonial Knife Co.	Providence RI	USA	Mfr.'s brand	1951-pres.
Amefa	Dutch military issue		Holland?	Mfr.'s brand	c1960s-80s
America's Best	see Moore Handley Hardware Co.				
American Ace	see New Jersey Knife Co.				
American Blade Cutlery Co.	by Parker Cutlery Co.	Chattanooga TN	Japan	Whol. Import	1981-1990
American Cutlery Co.	pocketknives pre-1900	Chicago IL	USA	Mfr.	1879-c1923
American Hardware & Supply Co.	American Beauty	Pittsburgh	PA	Hdw. Whol.	1911-c1935
American Knife Co.		Thomaston CT (Thomaston CT called Plymouth Hollow CT to 1875)	USA	Mfr.	1849-1911
American Knife Co.	Kendal c1948; Bukar -1955	Winsted CT	USA	Mfr.	1919-1955
American Knife Co.	for Cole National Corp.	Cleveland OH	Japan/Ger.	Import brand	c1970
American Maid	see Utica Cutlery Co.			Mfr.'s brand	c1950

POCKETKNIFE BRAND	TRADEMARK (or reference)	LOCATION	MADE IN	TYPE OF FIRM	DATES
American Merchandise Co.			Ger./Japan	Import brand	
American Pocketknife Co.	Box 401	Massilon OH	USA?	Retail?	c1930s?
American Shear & Knife Co.	first pocketknives 1870	Hotchkissville CT	USA	Mfr.	1853-1914
Ames Manufacturing Co.	pocketknives marked Ames or Ames Cutlery Co. made in Germany, possibly for this firm, c1860-1890s	Chicopee Falls MA		Mfr. & Whol.	1829-c1935
Amicus	Rudolph Freund, now Degen	Solingen	Germany	Mfr., figurals	1899-pres.
Amory, Edward		Sheffield	England	Mfr.	c1893
Anderson, A(ndre) J.	marked knives pre-1915	Fort Worth TX	Germany	Retail gun shop	c1882-1963
Andrew, (William), & Tredway, A.	became A. Tredway & Co.	Dubuque IA	USA?	Hdw. Whol.	1853-1873
Andrew, J(ohn) H(enry), & Co.	Toledo, scimitar (picture)	Sheffield	England	Steel Mfr. ad	c1860-1960
Angel	(picture) see C.W. Engels				
Anglo-Pacific Cutlery Co.			Ger./Eng.	Import brand	19th cent.
Anheuser Busch	by Kastor, Wester, Konejung	St. Louis MO	Germany	Brewer Advt.	c1880-1914
Anheuser Busch	made by Camillus	St. Louis MO	USA	Brewer Advt.	c1932-1948
Ankeny, O.P.	made replacement blades	Elko NV	USA	Repairman	c1950s
Antelope	made for Griffon,	Keschner	Germany	Export brand	c1930
Anvil	see Colonial Knife Co.; (picture) see Meriden Cutlery Co.				
Aquila	= eagle (Italian)		Italy	Mfr.'s brand?	
Arbolito	= Little Tree (Spanish), see H. Boker (office in Mexico City 1865-pres.)				
Ardobo Cutlery Co.			Germany	Import brand	c1930
Argyle Cutlery Co.			Germany	Import brand	c1910
Aristocrat	see McCrory Stores				
Aristocrat Knives	Parkway Distributors	Panorama City CA	Ger./Japan	Import brand	1991-pres.
Ariston	sold in Canada		Germany	Import brand	c1960?
Arkansas Traveler	see Fones Bros.				
Arlington Cutlery Co.		New York	NY	Import brand	
Armax			USA		
Army & Navy Cooperative Stores Ltd.		London	England	Hdw. Retail	18??-pres.
Arnold (or Arnould)	(on a folding cutlass)	Namur	Belgium	Mfr. or Retail	c1900
Arrow Brand	see Adolph Blaich				
Arrow Co.			Germany	Import brand	c1920s?
Arrows (five) around circle	see Mueller & Schmidt				
Arrows (three) in fist	see Precise (International)				
Arrows (two) crossed, in circle	see China Light Ind.	Shanghai	China		
Art	see George Butler & Co.			Mfr.'s brand	1861-pres.
Art Knife Co.		Nicholson PA	USA		c1920?
Arundel & Mappin	see Joseph Mappin	Sheffield	England	Mfr.	1820s
Ashmore, John	Mary Ashmore after c1850	Philadelphia PA	USA	Mfr.	c1832-1858
Ashton, J.	see John Askham				
Askham & Mosforth	sales office in New York formerly Samuel Frost; then Frost, Askham & Mosforth; became John Askham	Sheffield/NYC NY	England	Mfr. & import	1853-c1856
Askham, John, (& Son)	Toboggan, J. Sharpe, J. Ashton, John Askham b1818-d1894; son Frank mfd. boxes after 1914	Sheffield/NYC NY	England	Mfr. & import	1856-1920s
Asprey	166 Bond Street	London	England	Retail jeweler	c1870-pres.
Asquith, Walter		Sheffield	England	Mfr.	c1893
Atco			Japan	Import brand	recent
Atkins, E.C., & Co.	saw escutcheon	Indianapolis IN	USA	Saw mfr. advt.	c1930s
Atkins, William	Turtle (picture)	Sheffield	England	Mfr.	c1848-1913
Atkinson Bros.	Bear (picture)/In Mind	Sheffield	England	Mfr.	c1845-pres.
Atlantic Cutlery Co.	imported by Wiebusch	New York NY	Germany	Import brand	pre-1915
Atlas Works	J. Russell & Co.	Turners Falls MA	USA	Mfr.'s brand	c1880
Attica Knife Co.		Attica NY	Germany?	Import	c1880s
Aurum (Etchings)	marked knives by Alcas	Garland TX	USA	Blade etcher	1974-c1991
Ausonia Nanutti Bettrame Spa.	Ausonia=Italy (Latin)	Maniago	Italy	Mfr.	current
Auto(matic) Knife Co.	Wilzin's patent probably absorbed by Hatch Cutlery Co. before 1898	Middletown CT	USA	Mfr.?	c1889-189?
Autopoint	makes advt. mechanical pencils; sold knives (incl. Remington) 1960's; in Janesville WI 1979-pres.	Chicago IL	USA	Advt. Specialty	1911-1979
Avery & Co.		Portland OR		Hdw. Whol. Ret.	1892-?
Ayer, Wells W.	agent for R. Bunting & Sons	Boston MA	England	Whol. importer	c1830s-80s
B4*ANY	see Frederick Ward, John Watts				

POCKETKNIFE BRAND	TRADEMARK (or reference)	LOCATION	MADE IN	TYPE OF FIRM	DATES
B. & B.	see Brown & Bigelow				
B.B. Knife Co.	see Beaver Brook				
B.P. Co. Ltd.	see Butterick Pattern Co.				
B.T. Co.	see Bridgeport Tool Co.				
Backhaus, F.W.	El Charro; baby riding crane	Solingen	Germany	Mfr.	1827-19??
Bagshaw, William		Sheffield	England	Mfr.	c1817-1852
Baker & Hamilton	B.H. & Pacific 1918-1945 Golden Gate Cutlery Co.: c1890s; Baker & Hamilton on tang: c1915-1918; DAMASCUS by New Haven or Eclipse: pre-1918; Stiletto Cutlery Co. New York: made by N.Y. Knife 1918-1931, by Union Cut. c1933-1942	San Francisco CA	USA/Ger.	Hdw. Whol.	1853-1981
Baker, John, & Co.	Wheeldon works	Sheffield	England	Mfr.	c1893
Baker, W. Jno.		Sydney, Australia	England	Retail Import	1888-pres.
Baldwin(, Harry D.,) Cutlery Co.		Tidioute PA, Jamestown NY		Mfr.	c1912-1932
Baldwin, A., & Co.	incorporated 1888	New Orleans LA	USA	Hdw. Whol.	1822-pres.
Balfour, Arthur, & Co.	Capital, Griffin	Sheffield	England	Steel Mfr. Advt.	c1870-1960
Balisong Inc.	became Pacific Cutlery Co.	Los Angeles CA	USA	Hand Mfr.	1979-1982
Balkanlux		Thiers?	France	Mfr.'s brand	
Balke & Schaaf	Lamb (picture)	Solingen	Germany	Mfr.?	1897-1970s
Banister & Pollard Co.		Newark NJ		Hdw. Whol. Ret.	c1922
Banner Cutlery Co.	Kastor brand?	New York NY	Germany	Import Brand	pre-1915?
Bannister, A.F., & Co.	Furness & Bannister 1867-85	Newark NJ	USA	Mfr. & Whol.	c1867-1915
Barber, Edward		Sheffield	England	Mfr.	c1893
Barber, James	Era	Sheffield	England	Mfr.	c1840s?
	acquired by Thomas Ellin & Co., then by Joseph Elliott			Mfr.'s brand	c1850-pres.
Barber, John		Sheffield	England	Mfr.	1810-1834
Barber, John, & Son		Sheffield	England	Mfr.	1834-c1852
Barber, William		Sheffield	England	Mfr.	c1893
Barclay Bros.		Sheffield	England	Mfr.	c1900
Barge, Henry	made congress knives 1859	Sheffield	England	Mfr.	1859-c1876
Barker	(Sheffield made)	Croydon (London)	England	Retail	20th c.?
Barker, C.B., & Co.	Howard Cut. Co., Owl Cut. Co., C.B. Barker and H. H. Howard. US knives by Napanoch. Brands sold to Wiebusch & Hilger	New York NY	US/Ger./Eng	Whol. & Import	c1880-1905
Barker, C.C.	(on handle)	Cumby TX	USA	Mfr. Blacksmith	c1920-1974
Barker-Jennings Hardware Corp.		Lynchburg VA	Germany	Hdw. Whol.	1887-19??
Barlow, Samuel	BARLOW, Z* Scimitar	Neepsend (Sheffield)	England	Mfr.	c1780-1840
Barlow Company	BARLOW/STAINLESS/JAPAN	Los Angeles CA	Japan	Advt. specialty	recent
Barnascone, Lewis, (& Son)	Grasshopper, Comb(ination) Lewis and Henry Bamascone were brothers from Switzerland, partners until 1868	Sheffield/Paris	England	Whol. & retail	1850s-1920s
Barnascone, Henry, (& Son)	Prolific, Hungry Wolf trademarks sold to Harrison Fisher & Co.	Sheffield	England	Whol. & retail	1868-1920s
Barnes, Edward, & Sons	U*S	Sheffield	England	Mfr.	c1833-c1888
Barnes, Frederic, & Co.		Sheffield	England	Mfr.	c1893
Barnes, Isaac		Sheffield	England	Mfr.	c1837-1870
Barnes & Miller Hardware Co.	Diamond (picture)	Memphis TN		Hdw. Whol.	c1910?
Barnett, G.W., Hardware Co.	incorporated 1903	Montgomery AL		Hdw. Whol.	c1900-1930
Barnett, O(scar), Tool Co.	J.C. Lewis Pat., H.H.H.	Newark NJ	USA	Mfr.	1900-c1915
Barnsley, T.C., Mfg. Co.		Oklahoma City OK	USA	Mfr.	c1898
Barnsley Brothers		Monett MO	USA	Mfr. & Whol.	1898-1906
Barnsley, George, & Sons	A Shoe (picture); Wide Awake	Sheffield	England	Indust. knife mfr.	1836-pres.
Barrel	(picture) see Daniel Peres or John Petty & Sons				
Barrett, C.	8 Strand	London	England	Retail	c1900?
Barrett Hicks Co.		Fresno CA	USA?	Whol. or Retail	c1920s?
Barron, G.C.W.	succeeded Robert Lingard	Sheffield	England		c1919
Barton, Samuel		Sheffield	England	Mfr.	c1893
Bartram, John		Sheffield	England	Mfr.	c1893
Basic Tools/Silver Falcon	made for Compass Industries	New York NY	Japan	Import brand	1986-pres.
Bassett (Jewelry Co.)	Rustless	Providence RI	USA	Jewelry Mfr.	c1922
Bastet, T.F.	Coutelier du Roi	Amsterdam Neth.	Fran/Ger.	Retail	c1860
Bateman, George		Sheffield	England	Mfr.	c1785

POCKETKNIFE BRAND	TRADEMARK (or reference)	LOCATION	MADE IN	TYPE OF FIRM	DATES
Bateman, Robert	Globe Works (tenant)	Sheffield	England	Mfr.	c1893
Batt, William, & Sons	Cricket bat (picture)	Sheffield	England	Mfr.	c1860-1910
Battle Axe Cutlery Co.	for A.R. Justice Co.	Philadelphia PA		Hdw. Whol. brand	1877-c1937
Battle Axe Knives	J.W. Hickey & T. Shouse	Winston-Salem NC	Germany	Retail Ltd. Ed.	c1980s
Bauer			Germany		c1930
Bauermann, Hugo	Huba, farmer (picture)	Solingen	Germany	Mfr.	current
Baum, Maurice	Albert works	Sheffield	England	Mfr.	c1893
Baus, Peter Daniel	Lerche (lark)	Solingen	Germany	Mfr.	1820-?
Baxter, Arthur, & Co.		Sheffield	England	Mfr.	c1893
Baxter, W. & J.A.	Congo Works	Sheffield	England	Mfr.	c1970
Bayes	made by Colonial		USA	Advt. specialty	
Bay State Mfg. Co.		Worcester MA	Germany?	Wholesale?	c1890?
Baylor, C.E., Co.		Morristown TN		Hdw. Whol.	1899-19??
Bayonne Knife Co.		Bayonne NJ	USA	Whol. (Mfr.?)	1888-c1910
Beach, W(illiam)	Catherine St.	Salisbury	England	Mfr.	1829-1880
Beacon Knife Co.			Ger./Aust.	Import brand	c1900
Beal, J. & J.	Josh. Beal (& Sons) Boar, Mule, Cauldron (picture) Endure; Whistle (picture) Sound; Church (picture) Conservative	Sheffield	England	Mfr.	c1870-1950s
Bean, L.L.	some by Union Cut. Co.	Freeport ME	USA	Retail	1912-pres.
Bear (picture)	see Atkinson Bros.; standing upright see Hessenbruch				
Bear MGC	was Parker-Edwards	Jacksonville AL	USA	Mfr.	1990-pres.
Beaver Brook Knife Co.	B. B. Knife Co.	Beaver Brook MA	USA	Mfr.?	c1880
Beaver Falls Cutlery Co.	Harmony Society	Rochester PA	USA	Mfr.	1866-1886
Bechon-Bechon or Bechon-Grassion	116 Bechon some probably made by Elsener of Switzerland c1915	St.-Remy-sur-Durolle	France	Mfr. (& Imp.?)	1871-1934
Beck & Gregg Hardware Co.	Dixie Knife	Atlanta GA		Hdw. Whol.	1883-1930s
Becker, J(ohann). H(einrich).	Hipp-Hopp, Stopp, Pascha	Solingen	Germany	Mfr.	c1901-1919
Beckett, Edward	U.S. agent for G. Wostenholm successor to Asline Ward	New York NY	England	Whol. Import	c1897-19??
Bedford, John, & Sons	owns Atkinson, Fullwood	Sheffield	England	Mfr.	c1865-pres.
Bednal, John, & Co.	Crispin works	Sheffield	England	Mfr.	c1893
Bee Hive	(picture) see Slater Bros.				
Beekman Cutlery Co., The			Germany	Import	c1900?
Belknap, Amos		St. Johnsbury VT	USA	Blacksmith	c1839-1883
Belknap, W.B., Hardware Co.		Louisville KY	USA/Ger.	Hdw. Whol.	c1840-1985
Belknap Hardware Co.	J. Primble India Steel Works	Louisville KY	USA/Ger.	Hdw. Whol.	c1890-1940
Belknap Hardware Co.	John Primble (see Primble) made by Boker, Camillus, Utica, Schrade	Louisville KY	USA/Ger.	Hdw. Whol.	c1947-1985
Belknap Hardware Co.	Bluegrass	Louisville KY	USA	Hdw. Whol.	c1898-1985
Belknap Hardware Co.	Pine Knot (see Pine Knot)	Louisville KY	USA	Hdw. Whol.	c1910-1934
Belvin	(in triangle)	Sheffield	England	Mfr's? brand	
Benchmade Knife Co.		Los Angeles CA	USA	Mfr.	1988-1989
Benchmade Knife Co.		Clackamas OR	USA	Mfr.	1989-circa 2000.
Benchmade Knife Co.		Oregon City OR	USA	Mfr.	circa 2000-pres.
Bench Mark Knives	Rolox	Gastonia NC	USA	Mfr.	1970s-1984
Bench Mark Knives	Rolox; sold by Gerber	Portland OR	USA	Distrib brand	1984-c1987
Bengall	see Luke Cadman, Thomas R. Cadman & Sons			Mfr.'s brand	1748-1965
Bennett, Sir John, Ltd.	factored by Viners		England	Retail	c1960?
Benoit	knives made in Laguiole	Aubin, Aveyron	France	Retail	c1900-1955
Beretta U.S.A. Corp.	subsidiary of Beretta/Italy	Accokeek MD	USA	Mfr. & Dist.	c1984-pres.
Berg, Erik Anton		Eskilstuna	Sweden	Mfr.	c1880-1920
Bering-Cortes Hardware Co.	BECO	Houston TX	USA?	Hdw. Whol.	1885-c1947
Berkshire Cutlery Co.	O-U-NO		Germany	Import Brand	c1890
Bernard et Chevalier	76 Bernard	Nogent	France	Mfr.	18??-pres.
Berns, Gebruder (Bros.)	Otter	Solingen	Germany	Mfr.	1867-1993
Bernstein, Samuel E.	Royal Brand Sharp Cutter (National Silver Company)	New York NY	US/Ger./Jap	Whol. & Import	c1890-1950s
Bert, H., & Co.		Sheffield	England	Mfr.?	c1890?
Bertram, C., Reihn. Sohn	Hen & Rooster (picture)	Solingen	Germany	Mfr.	1864-1983
Bertry-Pouzet	116	Thiers	France	Mfr.	1836-?
Besset-Laroche, Societe Nouvelle	31 Besset	Olliergues	France	Mfr.	
Best	Sailboat (picture)		Japan	Import brand?	c1950

POCKETKNIFE BRAND	TRADEMARK (or reference)	LOCATION	MADE IN	TYPE OF FIRM	DATES
Besteel Warranted			USA?	Discount brand	c1930s
Bhutta Bro.		Nizamabad	India	Mfr.	c1940
Biddle Hardware Co.	became Supplee-Biddle 1914	Philadelphia PA		Hdw. Whol.	1837-1914
Bierhof, Justus	sold in Holland	Ohligs	Germany	Mfr.?	c1920s-30s?
Biffar, Fred	Dixie Switch (by Camillus)	Chicago IL	USA	Retail?	1917-1922
Big Horn Mark	for H. Willis Co.	Louisville KY	Italy	Import brand	?-c1972
Bigelow & Dowse	was Horton & Cordis: 1839	Boston, Sprngf'ld MA		Whol. & Retail	1872-1954
Billings & Spencer Co., The	(knives c1890-1914)	Hartford CT	USA	Tool Mfr.	1872-1963
Billings, J.W.	X.X.L. Cutlery	Sheffield			c1880s
Billy Barlow	(on bolsters) see Lyon Cutlery Co.				
Bingham, C.T.	Late F. Fenney	Sheffield	England	Mfr.	1852-?
Bingham, W., Co.	XLCR, BBB. by Ulster Knife	Cleveland OH	USA	Hdw. Whol.	1841-c1930
Bingham & Ogden	Select, Arrow sold to Ford & Medley before 1919	Sheffield	England	Mfr.	1858-1938
Binghamton Cutlery Co.		Binghamton NY	USA	Mfr.	c 1900?
Birmingham Knife Factory	Birmingham was part of Derby	Derby CT	USA	Mfr.	c1849
Bisby, A.H., & Co.		Sheffield	England	Mfr.	c1945
Bishop & Co.		Sheffield	England	Mfr.	c1893
Blackjack Knives		Effingham IL	US/Japan	Mfr. & Import	1986-pres.
Blackwell, Alfred		Sheffield	England	Mfr.	c1893
Blaich, Adolph/J.S. Holler	Arrow Brand	San Francisco CA	Germany	Whol. Import	c1893-1915
Blaich, Adolph, Inc.	moved to Reno NV 1954 agent for J. S. Holler c1895-1906; later for Western States Cutlery Co.	San Francisco CA	Germany/US	Whol. Sport. Gds.	1885-c1988
Blake & Lamb	made by Utica Cutlery Co.	Utica NY	USA	Trap Mfr.	c1930
Bleckmann, J.E.	exported to England	Solingen	Germany	Mfr.	1808-c1980
Blish, Mize & Silliman Hardware Co.	Mohawk, some made by American Shear & Knife Co.	Atchison KS	USA	Hdw. Whol.	1871-pres.
Blitzknife	see W.F. Harwell				
Bluefield Hardware Co.		Bluefield WV		Hdw. Whol.	1898-19??
Blue Grass	see Belknap Hardware Co.				
Blue Grass Cutlery Co.	sells Winchester, Primble	Manchester OH	USA	Whol.	c1985-pres.
Blue Ribbon Cutlery Co.	see Belknap Hardware Co.				1910-ff.
Blyde, A.J.	Crutch (picture) Help J. Greenhough (1890s), Viena, Sure & Far The Golfer (picture)	Sheffield	England	Mfr.	1890s-1920s
Blyde, Edwin, Ltd.	Volunteer, Spur (picture)	Sheffield	England	Mfr.	1798-pres.
Blyde, John, Ltd.	Genius, Saturn (picture)	Sheffield	England	Mfr.	1841-1950s
Bob White Cutlery	Quail (picture)	Santa Fe TN	USA	Retail	c1979
Bocker, Karl	Ostrich (picture)	Solingen	Germany	Mfr.	1913-1920s
Bocking, William	True	Sheffield	England	Mfr.	1838-c1945
Bockla	Cut-Well		Japan?	Export brand	c1918
Boden, James		Sheffield	England	Mfr.	1841-c1876
Boentgen & Sabin, Bonsa-Werk	many trademarks	Solingen	Germany	Mfr.	1867-1983
Bofil		Vich, Catalonia	Spain	Mfr.	current
Boker, H(ermann), & Co.	H. Boker's Improved Cutlery Tree Brand. Merged into Boker U.S.A. 1917	NYC NY/Newark NJ	USA	Whol. & Import	1837-1917
Boker, Casa Roberto	Arbolito; H. Boker branch	Mexico City	Germany	Import agent	1865-pres.
Boker, U.S.A.	included Valley Forge	Newark NJ	USA	Mfr.	1899-1921
Boker, U.S.A.	sold to J. Wiss 1969	Maplewood NJ	USA	Mfr.	1921-c1978
Boker, U.S.A.	div. of Cooper Group	Apex NC	USA	Mfr.	c1978-1986
Boker, U.S.A.	owned by Heinrich Boker	Golden CO	Germany	Import agent	1986-pres.
Boker, Heinrich	Tree Brand. Arbolito	Solingen	Germany	Mfr.	1869-pres.
Boker, Henry	H.B. and 2 bird heads (pic) see Heinrich Boker (made for Australia?)				
Boker, R(obert) & H(ermann)	Cast Steel, see H(ermann) Boker				
Bolsover, Henry, & Co.		Sheffield	England	Mfr.	c1893
Bolsover, Thomas, & Sons	W.B I B	Sheffield	England	Mfr.	c1919
Bona-Fide	see John Wigfall & Co., Joseph Elliott				
Bonsa	see Boentgen & Sabin				
Bonsmann, E.		Solingen	Germany	Mfr.?	1861-c1920
Booker, Henry		Sheffield	England	Mfr.	c1893
Boom Fixer	see Union Cutlery Co.	Olean NY	USA	Mfr.'s brand	c1933
Boos, W(illiam) H. & W(illiam) M.	Mathias Boos & Son 1866-	Toledo OH		Whol. Import	c1895-1936
Booth Bros.	showed at 1867 Paris Expo	Newark NJ	USA	Mfr.	1864-1879
Booth Bros.		Boonton NJ	USA	Mfr.	1879-1889

POCKETKNIFE BRAND	TRADEMARK (or reference)	LOCATION	MADE IN	TYPE OF FIRM	DATES
Booth Bros.		Stockholm NJ	USA	Mfr.	1889-1903
Booth Bros.		Sussex NJ	USA	Mfr.	1903-1909
Bora	import by Ferhad Erdogan	Ashland OR	Turkey	Mfr.'s brand	current
Borgfeldt, George, & Co.	Twig, Nifty. Eagle agent	New York NY		Whol. & Import	c1895-1927
Borwick, (Roger)	Samuel Borwick after 1825	Sheffield	England	Mfr.	c1791-1860
Boss Barlow	(on bolsters) see Frary Cutlery Co.				
Bostwick Braun Co.	was Roff & Co. 1855-68	Toledo OH	USA	Hdw. Whol.	1868-pres.
Bowen Knife Co.	Bullet; was Collins Bros.	Atlanta, Waycross GA	USA	Mfr.	1973-pres.
Bower, F.A., Import Co.	Fabico; some by Buchel	Jacksonville FL	Ger./Japan	Importer	1950s
Bowie Knife	Boker brand?	Newark NJ	USA	Mfr.'s brand	c1950s?
Bowler, Thomas, J.	Bowler Cutlery Co.	Chicago IL	USA?	Hdw. retail	c1920s
Bowman's & Levan		Cleveland OH		Retail?	
Boy of America, The	(on handle) see J. Russell & Co.				
Boyle, Neil F., Hardware Co.Blackfoot &c		ID		Hdw. Whol. Ret.	c1922
Bracht, Fritz	Dovo (Hartkopf, Raucnerkopf)	Solingen	Germany	Mfr.	1930-pres.
Bradford, M(artin) L., (& Son)	became Bradford & Anthony	Boston MA		Retail	1845-1856
Bradford & Anthony	became Dame Stoddard.	Boston MA		Retail & Whol.	1856-1883
Bradford, R. & W.	9 Patricks Road	Cork	Ireland	Mfr.	c1850
Bradford, Samuel	Clonmel		Ireland	Mfr.	c1850
Bradlee, Samuel	sold to M.L. Bradford	Boston MA		Retail	1799-1845
Bradley, L(yman), & Co.	L. Bradley & George Beecher	Salem CT	USA	Mfr.	c1841-1844
Bradley, L(yman), & Co.	Salem became Naugatuck 1844	Naugatuck CT	USA	Mfr.	1844-c1851
Bradley, L(yman)	rep. American Knife Co. 1850s	Middlebury CT	USA	Wholesale	c1851-1896
Bradshaw, A.W., & Sons			Germany	Import brand	c1900
Bramah, J(ames)	worked for Joseph Rodgers	Sheffield	England	Cutler	c1940s
Bramhall, William		Sheffield	England	Mfr.	c1893
Brandford Cutlery Co.			Germany	Import?	c1870s
Branner, Gustav	Face, dagger in teeth (pic)		Germany	Wholesale	c1945-pres.
Brantford Cutlery Co.	Warranted Never Dull (see Butler Bros.?)			Whol. brand?	c1900?
Braunegger	W/J.S.		Germany?	Mfr.?	1880s
Breeds, K.	(Sheffield made)	Tunbridge Wells	England	Retail	c1900?
Brewster, C(harles) E., Co.		Dover NH		Retail Druggist	c1880s
Briat, Jean		Limoges	France	Retail?	
Bridge Cutlery Co.	Shapleigh Hdw. Co. brand	St. Louis MO	USA	Hdw. Whol. brand	c1902-1931
Bridgeport Hardware Mfg. Corp.		Bridgeport CT	USA	Mfr. & Whol.	c1897
Bridgeport Tool Co.	B.T. Co., Pequot Brand	New Haven CT	USA	Whol. (& Mfr.?)	c1910s-20s
Bright & Co.		Reading PA		Hdw. Whol.	c1909-?
Bright, John		Sheffield	England	Mfr.	c1893
Brighton Cutlery Works			Germany	Import brand	c1900?
Brintnall Terry & Belden	imported Wester & Butz	Chicago IL	Germany	Hdw. Whol.	?-1876
Bristoline			Germany	Advt. specialty	c1950s
Brit-Nife		St. Louis MO			
Broadbent, John		Sheffield	England	Mfr.	c1893
Broch (Charles) & Thiebes (Henry)	Climax; became Pape Thiebes	St. Louis MO	Germany	Whol. Import	c1890
Broch, W., & Co.		New York NY	Germany	Whol. Import	c1885
Brokhahne, William	Speed. To Wiebusch 1906	New York NY		Whol. Import	c1875-1906
Brookes & Crookes	Bell (picture)	Sheffield	England	Mfr.	1858-1957
Brookes, Thomas		Sheffield	England	Mfr.	c1893
Brooks, John		Sheffield	England	Mfr.?	
Brooksbank, Abram	Defiance, Cannon (picture) operated by Needham, Veall & Tyzack 1932-1965	Sheffield	England	Mfr.	c1849-1932
Brown & Bigelow	B. & B.; many made by Colonial 1931-c1977	St. Paul MN	US/Austr.	Advt. specialty	1896-pres.
Brown Brothers (Mfg. Co.)	Union Razor Co. bought Tidioute Cutlery Co., moved to Tidioute PA 1902, became Union Cutlery Co. 1909	Little Valley NY	Ger./USA	Whol. & Import	c1890-1902
Brown-Camp Hardware Co.	I.O.A.	Des Moines IA		Hdw. Whol.	1865-1959
Brown, Buster, Shoe Co.	by Camillus via Shapleigh	St. Louis MO	USA	Shoe Mfr. Ad.	c1930s
Brown, Edward, & Son		Sheffield	England	Mfr.	c1893
Brown, Hamilton, Shoe Co.	same as Buster Brown(?)		Germany	Shoe Mfr. Ad.	c1920s
Brown, John	Columbia Works	Sheffield	England	Mfr.	?-1839
Brown, The Ralph, Co.		San Francisco CA		Wholesale	c1910
Brown, W.S.	made by Peres	Pittsburgh PA	Germany	Retail?	c1905

POCKETKNIFE BRAND	TRADEMARK (or reference)	LOCATION	MADE IN	TYPE OF FIRM	DATES
Browne & Pharr	screws in bolsters	Atlanta, Waycross, GA	USA	Hand Mfr.	c1974
Browning	made knives c1969-1983	Morgan UT	US/Ger./Japan	Mfr. & Import	1875-pres.
Brueckmann, Ernst	Bridge (picture)	Solingen-Ohligs	Germany	Mfr.	1891-c1972
Brumby & Middleton	owned by E. Blyde 1930	Sheffield	England	Mfr.	c1893-19??
Brunswick Cutlery Co.	D.C. & H. economy brand	San Francisco CA	Germany	Hdw. imp. brand	c1897-1907
Brunton/Lakota	Hawk	Riverton WY	USA	Mfr.	current
Bte. SGDG	= Brevete sans garantie de gouvernement (French) = patent without government guarantee				
Buchel, Rolf Walter	Three Rams (picture)	Solingen	Germany	Mfr.	1946-pres.
Buck (Knives)	founded c1900 (see text) (smaller patterns made by Schrade 1966-68, Camillus 1968-84)	San Diego CA	USA	Mfr. & Whol.	1963-1980
Buck (Knives)		El Cajon CA	USA	Mfr.	1980-pres.
Buck Knives		Post Falls ID	USA	Mfr.	2005-pres.
Buck Creek	Austin Redman	London KY	Ger./Japan	Whol. Import	1970-1980s
Buck Creek	see Taylor Cutlery Co.	Kingsport TN	Japan	Import brand	current
Buck Cutlery Co.			Germany	Import brand	c1900
Buck, J.	Holborn Viaduct	London	England	Retail	c1910s
Buck & Hickman Ltd.		London	England	Tool Retail	c1920
Buck, Peter E., & Sons		Ashland PA	Germany	Hdw. Whol. Ret.	1863-19??
Bud Brand		Winsted CT	USA		
Buffalo Wholesale Hardware Co.	Buffalo Cutlery Co.(?)	Buffalo NY		Hdw. Whol.	1903-19??
Buhl Sons Co.	incorporated 1902	Detroit MI		Hdw. Whol.	1843-194?
Bull Head Cutlery Co.			USA?		c1930?
Bullard & Gormley Co.		Chicago IL		Hdw. Whol.	c1922
Bulldog Brand	for Charlie Dorton name sold to Parker's K.C.S. 1992	Kingsport TN	Germany	Whol. import	1980-1987
Bulldog Brand	by Olbertz for Parker KCS	Chattanooga TN	Germany	Whol. brand	1992-pres.
Bunny	see J. Curley & Brother				
Bunting Hardware Co.		Kansas City MO		Hdw. Whol.	c1922
Bunting, R(obert)	joined by son Richard		England	Mfr.	c1825-1841
Bunting, R(obert), & Sons	dist. by Wells Ayer, Boston	Sheffield	England	Mfr.	1841-1850
Bunting, R(ichard)	dist. by Wells Ayer, Boston	Sheffield	England	Mfr.	1850-c1883
Burger & Baumgard		New York NY		Whol. & Export	1876-19??
Burgin, J.S., & Son		Sheffield	England	Mfr.	c1893
Burgon, (Charles), & (James) Ball	Sound	Sheffield	England	Mfr.?	1866-c1917
Burkinshaw, Aaron	from Sheffield 1848, X-L	Buryville CT	USA	Mfr.	c1852-1853
Burkinshaw Knife Co.	Exile, Pain. Aaron d.1881	Pepperell MA	USA	Mfr.	1853-1881
Burkinshaw's, Aaron, Sons	Joseph (d. 1886), Fred (d. 1898) and Charles Burkinshaw; Alta Shattuck				1881-1920
Burkinshaw, William H.		Sheffield	England	Mfr.	c1893
Burnand, James, & Sons	Indian (pic), Self Defense	Sheffield	England	Trade knife mfr.	c1850-c1930
Burton, William		Sheffield	England	Mfr.	c1893
Busch, Adolphus	see Anheuser Busch				
Busch, Wilhelm, Soehne	part of Exporting Solingen	Solingen-Ohligs	Germany	Mfr.	1920-1960s
Buster, Frank, Cutlery Co.	Fight'n Rooster by Olbertz	Lebanon TN	Germany	Ltd. Edit. Import	1977-pres.
Butcher, W(illiam) & S(amuel)	Wade & Butcher, X.C.D. Sold to Sigmund Kastor 1913; sold to Durham-Duplex Razor Co., 1918	Sheffield	England	Mfr.	c1819-1959
Butler Brothers	Warranted Never Dull branches nationwide (may have used name Brantford Cutlery Co.)	Chicago IL	USA	Whol.	1877-c1940
Butler, George (& James), & Co.	Trinity Works, Cavendish Art (1861), Key (from Steer & Webster 1867); since 1952 Butler has been a retail brand	Sheffield	England	Mfr. & Retail	1768-1952
Butterick Pattern Co.	B.P. Co. Ltd.		Germany	Sewing Advt.	c1910
C.A.S. Iberia Inc.	Muela; Stephenson & Wilson	Hixson TN	Spain/Eng.	Import	1986-pres.
C.C.C.	may be Chipaway, Curtin & Clark, Camillus, Challenge, Continental, or Cattaraugus				
C.C. Knife Co.	see Central City Knife Co.				
C.E.B. Co.	see Charles E. Brewster Co.				
C.F. & R.	see Corbett, Failing & Robertson				
C.I.	see Compass Industries				
C.J.	(in flag) see Christopher Johnson				
C.K. Co.	see Colonial Knife Co.				
cMc	(on aluminum handle) see Cecil McCloud				
C.P. Wrench Co. Pat. 6/26/'08	Charles C. Fields	Bristol TN	USA	Mfr.	1908-?

POCKETKNIFE BRAND	TRADEMARK (or reference)	LOCATION	MADE IN	TYPE OF FIRM	DATES
C.W.F.	in hallmark on silver fruit knives: see Charles William Fletcher				
C.W.S. Unity	see Cooperative Wholesale Society Ltd. Whol. brand				
Cabau, Jean	J. Cab.	Paris	France	Mfr.	c1820-1870
Cadman, Luke	Bengall	Sheffield	England	Razor Mfr.	1748-c1870
Cadman, Thomas R., & Sons	pocketknives 1930s	Sheffield	England	Razor Mfr.	c1870-1965
Caire, J(ustinian), & Co.		San Francisco CA	France	Hdw. Retail	1851-1897
Caldwell, A(rthur) B., Cutlery Co.	sold by Van Camp Hdw. Co.	Indianapolis IN	Germany	Hdw. Whol. brand	c1910
California Notion & Toy Co.		San Francisco CA		Whol. Import	1894-c1930
Calmels, Pierre		Laguiole	France	Mfr.	current
Cam, James		Sheffield	England	Mfr.	c1893
CAM III Enterprises	Chuck A. Mahon III	Vacaville CA	Japan	Whol. Import	1977-pres.
Cambridge & Co.	(US Navy contractor)		England	Import?	c1900?
Camco	Camillus economy brand	Camillus NY	USA	Mfr.'s brand	1948-pres.
Cameron Knife Co.			USA?		c1920s?
Camillus/Cutlery Co./Camillus NY/USA	(mark used through WWII)	Camillus NY	USA	Mfr.	1902-pres.
Camillus/New York/USA	(mark used after WWII)	Camillus NY	USA	Mfr.	1902-pres.
Camp Buddy	by Thornton (see Federal Knife Co.)				
Canastota Knife Co.	dist. by Wm. Cornwall, NYC	Canastota NY	USA	Mfr.	1875-1895
Canton Cutlery Co.	W.S. Carnes, Car-Van	Canton OH	USA	Mfr.	1879-c1930
Canton Hardware Co.	Keen Edge	Canton OH	US/Ger.	Hdw. Whol.	1888-19??
Canton Knife Co.	see Novelty Cutlery Co.				
Canty H.T., & Co.		Sheffield	England	Mfr.	c1900?
Capewell, John F.		Sheffield	England	Mfr.	c1893
Capitol Cutlery Co.	owned by Van Camp Hdw. Co.	Indianapolis IN	USA	Mfr.	1904-1948
Capitol Knife Co.		Winsted CT	USA	Mfr. ?	c1940?
Cardinal Cutlery Co.		New York NY		Wholesale?	
Carhartt, Hamilton	knives c1910s?	Dearborn MI	USA?	Clothes Mfr.	1890-pres.
Carlin & Fulton Co.		Baltimore MD		Hdw. Whol.	1856-19??
Carlin, James F., Sons & Co.	became Carlin-Huffish Co.	Alexandria VA		Hdw. Whol.	1895-1906
Carlin-Hulfish Co.	Carhulco became Worth Hulfish & Sons; Worth Hulfish (1848-1930) joined English & Carlin 1863	Alexandria VA		Hdw. Whol.	1906-1919
Carlisle Hardware Co.		Springfield MA		Hdw. Whol. Ret.	1846-19??
Carlson-Lusk Co.	Tatro-Nif	Boise ID		Retail?	c1910
Carr Fast(ener) Co.	military knives		Australia	Mfr.?	1940s
Carr, Henry S., & Sons		Sheffield	England	Mfr.	c1893
Carrier Cutlery Co.	see Cronk & Carrier Mfg. Co.				
Cartailler-Deluc	92 Cartailler	Thiers	France	Mfr.	1898-pres.
Carter Skinning Knife	by Miller Bros.	Meriden CT	USA	Mfr.'s brand	c1880s
Carters/Hen & Rooster	made by Bertram	Scottsville KY	Germany	Retail	1969-1983
Cartier	made by Wostenholm	London	England	Retail jeweler	c1960s
Cartwright, Joseph		Sheffield	England	Mfr.	c1893
Car-Van S(teel) P(roducts)	see Canton Cutlery Co.				1911-c1930
Case Brothers & Co.	made by C. Platts & Sons	Gowanda NY	USA	Whol.	1896-1900
Case Brothers Cutlery Co.	Tested XX (by itself)	Little Valley NY	USA	Mfr.	1900-1912
Case Cutlery Co.	(branch of the above)	Kane PA	USA	Mfr.	1907-1911
Case Brothers Cutlery Co.	Tested XX (by itself)	Springville NY	USA	Mfr.	1912-1915
Case Mfg. Co.		Little Valley NY	USA	Whol.	c1898-1899
Case Mfg. Co.	for Case Bros.	Smethport, Warren PA		Mfr.	c1911
Case, J.D.	see Case Mfg. Co.	Little Valley NY	USA	Whol. brand	c1898-1899
Case, Jean	see Kinfolks Inc.				1928-1948
Case, W.R., & Son Cutlery Co.	(made by Napanoch)	Little Valley NY	USA	Whol.	1902-1905
Case, W.R., & Sons Cutlery Co.	(made by Platts)	Little Valley NY	USA	Whol.	1904-1905
Case, W.R., & Sons Cutlery Co.		Bradford PA	USA	Mfr.	1905-1920
Case, W.R., & Sons Cutlery Co.	W.R. Case & Sons	Bradford PA	Germany	Import	pre-1914
	mark used on current limited editions by Parker Knife Collectors Service				
Case W.R., & Sons Cutlery Co.	Case/Tested XX	Bradford PA	USA	Mfr.	1920-1940
Case, W.R., & Sons Cutlery Co.	CASE/XX	Bradford PA	USA	Mfr.	1940-1965
Case, W.R., & Sons Cutlery Co.	CASE XX/Made in U.S.A. owned by American Brands 1972-1988	Bradford PA	USA	Mfr.	1965-1990

POCKETKNIFE BRAND	TRADEMARK (or reference)	LOCATION	MADE IN	TYPE OF FIRM	DATES
Case, W.R., & Sons	Durango, made by Colonial	Bradford PA	USA	Whol. brand	c1975
Case, W.R., & Sons Cutlery Co.	CASE XX/Bradford PA/*USA* owned by James Parker 1988-1991; by River Associates 1991-93; by Zippo 1993-pres.	Bradford PA	USA	Mfr.	1988-pres.
Case Classics	see Golden Age Classics (Parker's Knife Collectors Services)				
Case Tested XX, W.R. Case & Sons	for Golden Age Classics	Chattanooga TN	Japan/USA	Ltd. editions	1990-pres.
Case XX Metal Stampings Ltd.	by Case for Canadian govt.	Pictou NS	Canada	Mfr.	1948-1950s
Casson, Jay, & Son		Sheffield	England	Mfr.	c1893
Catoctin Cutlery	Fox, Koncept	Smithsburg MD		Wholesale	current
Catskill Knife Co.	made by Camillus	Camillus NY	USA	Mfr's. brand	c1930s
Cattaraugus Cutlery Co.		Little Valley NY	USA	Whol.	1886-1891
Cattaraugus Cutlery Co.	Indian (picture)	Little Valley NY	USA	Mfr.	1891-1963
Cattaraugus Cutlery Company	Knife Collectors Club	Springdale AR	Ger./Japan	Retail brand	c1973-pres.
Cavendish	see George Butler & Co.			Mfr.'s brand	1860s-pres.
Caverhill, Learmont & Co.		Montreal, Quebec		Hdw. Whol.	1853-19??
Celebrate Cutlery Co.	see George Borgfeldt	New York NY	Germany	Import brand	c1920
Celebrated Cutlery			Ger./Aust.	Generic import	
Centazzo, Angelo, e Figli	M (as mountains)/C.A.F.	Maniago	Italy	Mfr.	?-1950
Centazzo, Angelo, Patin e Figli	Cavalier (Knight)	Maniago	Italy	Mfr.	1950-pres.
Central City Knife Co.	C.C. Knife Co.	Phoenix NY	USA	Mfr.	1880-1892
Central Cutlery Co.		Elizabeth NJ	USA	Mfr.?	c1926
Chaldecott		Sheffield	England	Mfr.	c1750
Challenge Cutlery Co.	owner: Wiebusch & Hilger	Sheffield or NYC	Engl./Ger.	Import	1867-1914
Challenge Cutlery Co.	owner: Wiebusch & Hilger	Bridgeport CT	USA	Mfr.	1891-1928
Chalmers, (Thos), & Murray, (Robt)	T.C. 1863-, R.M. 1764-	New York NY		Hdw. Whol.	c1900
Champion (Knife)	see Moore Handley Hardware Co.				
Champion & Co.	C in an oval agent for James Crawshaw pocketknives c1830; also manufactured scissors	Sheffield	England	Retail	1791-c1980
Champlin, J.B.F., & Son (Tint)	became Cattaraugus	Little Valley NY	Germany	Import	1882-1886
Chapman (E. Byron) Cut. (Mfg.) Co.	Chapman Hand Forged	Muncie IN	USA	Whol.	1915-1931
Charlesworth, Charles Henry		Sheffield	England	Mfr.	c1893
Charlottesville Hardware Co.		Charlottesville VA		Hdw. Whol. Ret.	1889-19??
Chason (or Chasson)		London	England	Surg. Instr.	c1790
Chatellerault	(place name)		France		
Chatillon, John, & Sons	pocketknives c1900-1937	New York NY	USA	Spring eq. mfr.	1835-pres.
owned Foster Bros.		Fulton NY	USA	Butcher k. mfr.	1883-1950s
Chester Brothers		Sheffield	England	Mfr.	c1893
Cheseterman, James, & Co.	made rulers for pen knives	Sheffield	England	Ruler Mfr.	
Chicago Small Fire Arms Co.	(small .22 cal. knife pistol) see U.S. Small Arms Co.				
China Light Ind. Prod. Imp. & Exp.	Fong Yuon/Whirling Square	Canton, Guangdong	P.R. China	Mfr.	current
China Light Ind. Prod. Imp. & Exp.	Crossed arrows	Shanghai	P.R. China	Mfr.	current
China Light Ind. Prod. Imp. & Exp.	Rose in circle	Tsingtao, Shantung	P.R. China	Mfr.	current
Chipaway Cutlery Co.	for E.C. Simmons Hdw.	St. Louis MO	US/Eng/Ger.	Hdw. Whol. brand	c1891-1907
Chipaway Cutlery Co.	for Frost Cutlery	Chattanooga TN	USA	Whol. brand	c1994-pres.
Christians, Gebruder (Bros.)	Fork (picture)	Solingen	Germany	Mfr.	1824-pres.
Christy (Russ J.) Knife Co.		Fremont OH	USA	Mfr.	1890-pres.
Claflin, H.B., & Co.	(US Navy contractor)				19th cent.
Clarenbach & Herder	became L. Herder & Son	Philadelphia PA	USA/Ger.	Mfr. & Retail	1847-1871
Clark Brothers	bought Northfield in 1919	Kansas City MO	US/Eng/Ger.	Mfr. & Import	1895-1929
Clarke, John, & Son	Wm. Rodgers, John Holmes trademarks now owned by Egginton Group Ltd.	Sheffield	England	Mfr.	1848-1980s
Clarke Shipping		Sheffield	England	Wholesale?	c1870
Clarke, Shirley & Co.	Boston Works. OIO was W. Shirley & Co., OIO mark sold to Harrison Fisher & Co.	Sheffield	England	Mfr.	1870s-?
Clauberg, F(rederick) A., & Co.	Mikado, Halberd	New York NY	Germany	Wholesale	1840-c1926
Clauberg, Wilhelm	Knight (sub. of A. Wingen)	Solingen	Germany	Mfr.	1810-1996
Clauss Cutlery Co.	S. & M. made some c1925	Fremont OH	USA	Whol. & Mfr.	1887-pres.
Clay Cutlery Co.	made by Robeson (?)	Andover NY	USA		
Clay, William		Sheffield	England	Mfr.	c1893
Clean Clipper	see Rector & Wilhelmy, Wright & Wilhelmy				
Clean Cut	Clover (picture) see Dunham Carrigan & Hayden. Made by N.Y. Knife Co. c1884-1912				

POCKETKNIFE BRAND	TRADEMARK (or reference)	LOCATION	MADE IN	TYPE OF FIRM	DATES
Clearcut	see The George Worthington Co.				
Clements	Hand Forged	Sheffield	England	Mfr.	20th cent.
Clim(Axe)	see Schmachtenberg				
Clipper Cutlery Co.	see Watkins Cottrell				
Clover Brand	for Kastor and Camillus	Camillus, NYC NY	Germany	Import brand	pre-1941
Clover Brand	made by Camillus	"Syracuse" NY	USA	Mfr.'s brand	c1941-2
Club, The	Dog's Head (picture) see E.T. Allen				
Clyde Cutlery Co.	sold pocketknives c1930s	Clyde OH	USA	Mfr. (& Whol.?)	1850-1960s
Coast Cutlery Co. by Western States Schrade, and Camillus.	by Western States, Schrade, and Camillus. Most marked knives made c1935-1942	Portland OR	USA	Wholesale	1919-pres.
Coca Cola	genuine, most by Camillus	Atlanta GA	USA	Bottler Advt.	1930s-40s
Coca Cola	counterfeit		Germany		1970s-80s
Coca Cola 5¢	(on handle) U.S.A. (on tang) fantasy made by Colonial Knife Co.				1980s
Cockhill, John C(reswick)		Sheffield	England	Mfr.	c1893
Coe, James, & Sons		Sheffield	England	Mfr.	c1893
Cogan, J.C., & Sons	son Charles Cogan	Wilmington IL	USA	Mfr.	1880-?
Cognet, Antoine & Gaspard	Douk-Douk (1930-), Tiki L'Ecureuil, El Baraka, Le Bundu (1956-), Le Boussadia (all sold in Africa)	Thiers	France	Mfr.	c1835-pres.
Cold Steel, Inc.	Lynn Thompson	Ventura CA	Japan	Import	1980-pres.
Cole National Corp.	Kabar (USA), Khyber (Japan), Sabre (Japan, Germany, Ireland, USA)	Cleveland OH	USA/Japan	Whol. & Imp.	c1960-1996
Cole, William H., & Sons	Baltimore MD			Hdw. Whol.	18??-19??
Colebrook Knife Co.				Import brand?	
Coleman-Western	was Western Cutlery Co. sold to Wilderness Forge 1990; sold to Camillus 1991	Longmont CO	USA	Mfr.	1984-1990
Coles	Hand Forged	New York NY	Germany	Whol. Import	c1960s
Coles, Albert	A.C. silver fruit knives	New York NY	USA	Mfr.	c1836-1880
Collings & Wallis		Sheffield	England	Mfr.	c1893
Collini, Ermenegildo	Italicus	Premana	Italy	Mfr.	1880-c1990
Collini, F.	makes for Klaas, Rifter	Melno	Italy	Mfr.	c1930-pres.
Collins Bros. (Walter, Michael)	made by Camillus sold to become Bowen Knife Co. 1973	Atlanta GA	USA	Ltd. Edition	c1970-1973
Colonel Coon	Racoon (picture), see Tennessee Knife Works				
Colonial Cutlery Co.	see Schwabacher Hardware Co.				
Colonial Knife Co.	many trademarks including Ambassador, Old Cutler, Ranger, Forestmaster, Shur-Snap, Topper	Providence RI	USA	Mfr.	1926-pres.
Colorado Cutlery Co.		Boulder CO		Import brand	
Colquhoun & Cadman	C & C, Go-ahead, Scroll	Sheffield	England	Mfr.	1890s-1920s
Colt	patent folder by Barry Wood, Venice CA, 1969-1973	Hartford CT	USA	Gun Mfr.	1837-pres.
Colt(ellerie) (Riun(ite)	see Coricama (Coltellerie Riunite di Caslino e di Maniago)				
Columbia Knife Co.			Austria?	Import?	c1900
Commander	(probably made for Metropolitan	Cutlery Co.)			
Commando	see George Schrade Knife Co.				
Compass Industries	C.I., Silver Falcon	New York NY	Japan/Ger./&c	Whol. importer	1936-pres.
Concord Cutlery Co.			Germany?	Import brand	c1880
Condor	Hoffman Design	Agoura Hills CA		Whol. importer	1984-pres.
Congreve, C(harles)	W(crown)R	Sheffield	England	Mfr.	1829-1843
Conn(ecticut) Cutlery Co.		Naugatuck CT	USA	Mfr.	1867-1883
Conn(ecticut) Cutlery Co.		Thomaston CT	USA	Mfr. ?	
Continental Cutlery Co.	see Clark Bros.	KC/NYC/Sheffield		Whol. brand	1915-1920
Continentale	sold in Britain		Germany	Import brand	c1920s
CoO Knife Co.	see Cooperative Knife Co. (but "CoO Knife Co./Walden N.Y." made by Walden Knife Co.)				
Cook Bros.		Sheffield	England	Mfr.?	c1890
Cooper & Co.	58 Picadilly	London	England	Retail	
Cooper Bros.			Germany	Import brand	c1900
Cooperative Knife Co.	became Ulster Knife Co.	Ellenville NY	USA	Mfr.	1871-1876
Cooperative Wholesale Society Ltd.	Unity; Vulcan Road	Sheffield	England	Wholesale	20th c.
Copley, J(ohn), & Sons	XX	Sheffield	England	Mfr.	c1824-1930s
Copley, William H.		Sheffield	England	Mfr.	c1893
Coppel, Alexander	Balance, Alcoso, A. C. S.	Solingen	Germany	Mfr.	1821-1985

POCKETKNIFE BRAND	TRADEMARK (or reference)	LOCATION	MADE IN	TYPE OF FIRM	DATES
Coquanoc Works	see Howard W. Shipley				
Corbett, Failing & Robertson	C.F. & R.; inc. 1893	Portland OR	USA	Hdw. Whol.	1851-19??
Coricama	COltellerie RIunite di CAslino e di MAniago Co-op 1887-1907; Albert Marx 1907-14; Gebr. Krusius 1918-75; Alexander SRL 1975-pres.		Italy	Mfr.'s brand	1887-pres.
Corliss Cutlery Co.			Germany	Import brand?	c1900
Corning Knife Co.	made by Camillus	Camillus NY	USA	Mfr.'s brand	c1930s
Cornwall Knife Co.	made by Camillus	"New York" NY	USA	Mfr.'s brand	c1930s
Cornwall Knife Works		Cornwall (?) CT	USA	Mfr.?	19th cent.
Cornwall, William M.	agent for Canastota	New York NY	USA	Whol.	c1880s
Corsan, Denton, Burdekin & Co.		Sheffield	England	Mfr.	1852-1859
Cosmo Mfg. Co.	some by Joseph Feist		Ger./Japan	Importer	c1920s-50s
Cousins, J., & Sons		Sheffield	England	Mfr.	c1893
Cowen, Samuel H.		Sheffield	England	Mfr.	c1893
Cowlishaw, John Yeomans	J.Y.C. Cowlishaw lived 1830-1895; firm made silver fruit knives 1854-c1920s	Sheffield	England	Mfr.	1854-1974
Cox & Son	Sheffield made	Southampton	England	Retail	c1920s
Craft	see Freeman, Delamater & Co.				
Craftsman (Sears Roebuck)	by Camillus, Schrade, Ulster tool brand used on pocketknives c1946-1991 (see Dunlap)	Chicago IL	USA	Retail brand	1926-pres.
Cranberry	see Luttrell Hardware Co., McClung Hardware Co.				
Crancer Hardware Co.		Leavenworth KS		Hdw. Whol.	1857-19??
Crandall Cutlery Co.	merged with W. R. Case	Bradford PA	USA	Mfr.	1905-1912
Crandall	for Parker KCS	Chattanooga TN	USA/Japan	Whol. brand	c1993-pres.
Crawshaw, James	sold by Champion & Co. invented lobster pen knife, quadrangular exposition and quill knife, before 1830	Sheffield	England	Mfr.	c1817-1850
Crescent Cutlery Co.	ex-Northfield employees	Northfield CT	USA	Mfr.	c1890s
Cresta		Sheffield	England		20th cent.
Creutzberg, George F.	Eagle/Phil'a, G.F.C.	Philadelphia PA	USA	Whol. & Seconds	c1875-1943
Cripple Creek	by Bob Cargill (see text)	Lockport IL	USA	Mfr. Ltd. Edit.	1981-1986
Cripple Creek	sold to Blackjack 1993	Old Fort TN	USA	Mfr. Ltd. Edit.	1986-1993
Cripple Creek Brand	Blackjack Knives	Effingham IL	USA	Mfr.'s brand	1993-1995
	mark returned to Cargill	Old Fort, Ocoee TN	USA	Mfr. Ltd. Edit.	1995-pres.
Critchfield		Sheffield	England	Mfr.	c1750
Criterion	see Alfred Field		Ger./Eng.?	Import Brand	
Croisdale		Leeds	England	Retail?	
Cromwell Criterion	probably Alfred Field				
Cronk & Carrier Mfg. Co.	Carrier Cutlery Co.	Elmira NY	USA	Mfr.	1900-1921
Cronk & Carrier Mfg. Co.	Carrier Cutlery Co.	Montour NY	USA	Mfr.	1921-c1928
Crookes Brothers		Sheffield	England	Mfr.	c1893
Crookes, G. or H., & Co.		Sheffield	England	Mfr.	c1836-1867
Crookes, John		Sheffield	England	Mfr.	c1893
Crookes, Jonathan	Heart and Pistol (picture)	Sheffield	England	Mfr.	c1780-1827
Crookes, Jonathan, & Son	Heart and Pistol (picture) sold to Joseph Allen c1910; sold to Herbert M. Slater 1947	Sheffield	England	Mfr.	1827-pres.
Crosman Blades	division of Coleman made by Alcas, Camillus, Utica	East Bloomfield NY	USA	Whol.	1982-1985
Crossland, John, & Son	+LAND; skull and bones	Sheffield	England	Mfr.	c1868-1924
Crouch, Jess	Schatt & Morgan foreman	Titusville PA	USA	Mfr.'s brand	c1920s
Crown Cutlery Co.		New York NY	Ger./Austr	Whol. importer	1910s-20s
Crown Cutlery Co.	made in US during WWI	New York NY	USA	Wholesale	c1916-1919
Crown with wings	see Olbertz				
Crownshaw	(Sheffield made)	Liverpool	England	Retail	c1870?
Crucible Knife Co.	sold by W. T. Grant, NYC	Lynn MA	USA	Mfr.?, Retail	1921-1932
Cruso	sold by H. S. & B.		Aust./Ger.	Import brand	c1913
Cunningham Hardware Co.		Mobile AL	USA/Ger.	Hdw. Whol.	1889-19??
Curley, J., & Brother (Terrence)	Bunny, Foxy Grandpa	New York NY		Whol/Imp/Invent	c1880-1925
Currey, Ltd.	all metal rigging knives	Chichester	England	Whol. export	present
Curtin & Clark Hardware Co.	C.C.C.	St. Jos., K.C. MO	USA	Hdw. Whol.	1890-c1920
Cussin & Fearn			USA	Retail (prize)	1930s

POCKETKNIFE BRAND	TRADEMARK (or reference)	LOCATION	MADE IN	TYPE OF FIRM	DATES
Cut Sure	see Kruse & Bahlmann				
CutAway	see Paxton & Gallagher Co.				
Cutco	see Alcas				
CutEasy	see Smith Brothers Hardware Co.				
Cutgud	see Washington Cutlery Co. (Milwaukee and Watertown Wisconsin)				
Cutino Cutlery Co.	some made by Challenge	Kansas City MO	USA	Retail?	c1914-1935
Cutlass	see Leppington (Cutlers) Ltd.				
Cutler Hardware Co.		Waterloo IA		Hdw. Whol.	1866-19??
Cut-Mor	see Moore(?)	Pomona CA		Retail brand	c1950?
Cutter	(picture of a boat) see Thomas Ellin & Co., Joseph Elliott				
Cutts, William H.		Southbury CT	USA	Mfr.	c1860s-70s
D.C.C.	see Davenport Cutlery Co.				
D.C. & H.	see Dunham Carrigan & Hayden				
D.E.	see Diamond Edge				
D.R.G.M.	= German Empire Utility Design (German) [Registered pattern] used 1871-1918, 1933-1945				
D.R.P. or D.R. Pat.	=Patented (German)				
D.S. & K	see Dame Stoddard & Kendall				
Dahmann, Herman	merged with A. Wingen	Solingen	German	Mfr.	1950s
Damascus	(for Baker & Hamilton) see Eclipse Cutlery Co. or New Haven Cutlery Co.				
Damascus Steel Products Corp.	DASCO. Knives 1930-42	Rockford IL	USA	Tool Mfr.	1922-pres.
Dame Stoddard & Kendall	D.S. & K., Hub was Bradford & Anthony; became Stoddard's, some made by Weyersberg	Boston MA	Ger./USA	Retail & Whol.	1883-c1932
Dana Hardware Co.	was Eaton Harrington & Dana	Boston MA		Hdw. Whol.	1820-c1915
DASCO	see Damascus Steel Products				
Davenport Cutlery Co.	D.C.C.	Sheffield	England	Mfr.?	c1939
David, G., Fils (Son)	L'Arbalete (crossbow)	St.-Remy-sur-Durolle	France	Mfr.	c1900-pres.
Davis, (David W.)	pat'd knife & corkscrew	Detroit MI	USA	Inventor	c1891
Davy, Abraham	(& Sons, after 1856)	Sheffield	England	Mfr.	c1836-1870
Dawes & Ball	pocketknives after c1935	Sheffield	England	Mfr.	1925-c1962
Dawson Hardened Copper Co.	probably the same as Hardened	Copper Cut. Co., New York NY			
Deakin, James, (& Sons)	Desk Bell (picture)	Sheffield	England	Mfr.	1867-c1960
Deakin, Reuss & Co.	Tiger; became Deakin, Sons	Sheffield	England	Mfr.	1872-1895
Deakin, Sons & Co.	Tiger, sold in S. America	Sheffield	England	Mfr.	1895-c1914
Deane (Dray) & Co.	Deane's/Monumen/A.D.1700	London	England	Whol. exporter	c1700-19??
DeBoer & Bach	D AND B	New York NY	US/Eng/Ger.	Whol. importer	c1915-1920
Decatur & Bull	Two Heads (picture)	Montreal, Quebec	Germany?	Hdw. retail	c1920s
Decatur & Hopkins Co.		Boston MA		Hdw. Whol.	1845-19??
Decora			Germany		c1930s?
Deerslayer	see Precise				
Defender (Pocketknife Co.)	.22 cal. knife pistols	Providence RI	USA	Mfr.	c1920
Defiance	Cannon (picture) see A. Brooksbank; after 1876 see J. Bedford				
Degen Knives	Stephan Hartkopf successor to Amicus, made by Gebr. Richartz	Los Angeles CA	Germany	Import	1987-pres.
Delmar Cutlery Co.			Germany?	Import brand?	c1910
Delta	see Hugo Linder				
DeLuxe	see Salm	Torrance CA	USA	Mfr.'s brand?	1918-1925
Demeritt, J(ohn)		Montpelier VT	USA	Cutler/gunsmith	c1850s
Denizet, H.		Langres	France	Mfr.	c1920s?
Depend	see W. Saynor				
Depend-on Me Cutlery Co.		New York NY		USA?	c1945
Depose	= Registered (design patent) (French)				
Derby Silver Co.	fruit knives c1880s	Derby CT	USA	Mfr. & Whol.	c1870-1933
Dewing Tyler & Co.		Worcester MA			c1820
Diamond Edge	(D-E). Shapleigh Hardware Co. until 1960, then an Imperial trademark				
Diamond Spear	frog (picture) see Brokhahne			Import brand	c1878-1906
Dickinson, E.M.	Screw (pic), Forward, Invicta sold to Needham, Veall & Tyzack	Sheffield	England	Mfr.	c1880-1940

POCKETKNIFE BRAND	TRADEMARK (or reference)	LOCATION	MADE IN	TYPE OF FIRM	DATES
Dictator	for S. H. Kress by Utica	New York NY	USA	Retailer brand	c1930s
Diefenthal, Josef Th.	Triskelion of 3 blades	Solingen	Germany	Mfr.	1908-pres.
Digby	by Graham Clayton	Sheffield	England	Hand mfr.	1974-pres.
Dinger, H.	(made in Solingen)	Kaiserslautern	Germany	Retail?	c1930s?
Dingo Cutlery					
Dirlam, J., & Sohne	Can't B Beat; Balmoral	Solingen	Germany	Mfr.	1856-pres.
Dispatch	see Peter L. Schmidt				
Disston Steel	commem. prob. by Camillus	Philadelphia PA	USA	Saw Mfr. ad	1940
Divine, Dwight, & Sons	Ulster Knife Co., Kingston, Ellenville Knife Co. Had been Cooperative Knife Co. Sold to Albert M. Baer	Ellenville NY	USA	Mfr.	1876-1941
Dixie Knife	see Beck & Gregg				
Dixie Switch, Dixie Guard	see Fred Biffar				
Dixon, James, & Sons	Trumpet (1879-)	Sheffield	England	Whol. & Mfr.	c1805-1990
Dixon Cutlery Co.	made in "Werwolf" Work		Ger./USA	Whol. Import	c1920s?
Dobson, George, & Sons		Sheffield	England	Mfr.	1864-1914
Dodge, J(oseph) & R(obert)	sold to F. Newton 1884	Sheffield	England	Mfr.	c1848-pres.
Dodson, A.		Sheffield	England	Mfr.?	c1941
Dodson Mfg. Co.		Chicago IL	USA	Ad. specialty?	c1937
Dollar Knife Co.	see Schatt & Morgan	Titusville PA	USA	Mfr.'s brand	c1927
Dolphin Cutlery Co.		New York NY	Germany	Whol. Import	1918-1920s
Domar Cutlery Co.	Theodore M. Green Co.	Oklahoma City OK	USA	Whol.	c1916-1920
Dooley	D with arrow	Cincinnati (?) OH	USA	Mfr.	c1950s ?
Dorken Brothers & Co.		Montreal, Quebec		Hdw. Whol.	1894-19??
Dorko	see Dorten				
Dorten	DORKO	Solingen	Germany	Mfr.	c1983
Double Sharp	# # see G. Ibberson				
Douk-Douk	Shaman (picture) see Cognet				
Dovo (Dorp & Voos)	sold to Fritz Bracht	Solingen	Germany	Mfr.	1900-1939
Drabble, Enoch		Sheffield	England	Mfr.	c1840
Drabble, James, & Co.	machine-made Bowies	Sheffield	England	Mfr.	1860-1888
Drabble & Sanderson Ltd.	Emperor (picture) SPQR	Sheffield	England	Mfr.	c1919
Drake Hardware Co.		Burlington IA		Hdw. Whol.	1864-19??
Draper, Edmund, & Co.		Sheffield	England		c1893
Dreisbach's Sons, C.		Lewisburg PA		Hdw. Whol.	1874-19??
Dreiturm	= Three Spires (German) see J. A. Schmidt				
Dreizack	= Trident (German) see Ed. Wusthof				
Drew & Sons	156 Leadenhall St. E.C.	London	England	Retail	c1910s
Droescher, Severin R.	S.R.D./Arrow	New York NY	Sweden & ?	Whol. Import	c1891-1924
Duane Cutlery Co.	(Kastor brand?)		Germany	Import brand	c1910
Dubost-St. Joanis	crescent (picture)	Thiers	France	Mfr.	c1900-19??
Due Buoi (Pietro Rosa)	Two oxen (picture)	Maniago	Italy	Mfr.	1887-pres.
Duke Peterson Hardware Co.		Baltimore MD		Hdw. Whol.	1904-?
Dumas-Aine, 32	= Dumas the elder (French) see Rousselon Freres et cie.				
Dumousset-Bechon	116 Bechon	St.-Remy-sur-Durolle	France	Mfr.	1931-1951
Dunham Carrigan & Hayden	Clean Cut, Springbrooke Comstock, Volka, Sequoia, Brunswick, Sunset	San Francisco CA	US/Ger.	Hdw. Whol.	1849-1964
Dunlap	by Camillus for Sears Tom Dunlap was the hardware buyer for Sears Roebuck; he created Craftsman tools in 1926	Chicago IL	USA	Retail brand	c1930s
Dunlap, J.	dist. by Schmachtenberg	New York NY	Germany	Import brand	1916-c1939
Dunn Bros.		Providence RI	USA	Jewelry Mfr.	1927-pres.
Dura-Edge	see Utica Cutlery Go.				
Durango	for W. R. Case by Colonial	Bradford PA	USA	Whol. brand	c1975
Durham-Enders Razor Co.	owned Wade & Butcher	Jersey City NJ	England	Mfr. and Importer	
Durham-Duplex Razor Co.	1918-1950s	NYC NY, Mystic CT	USA		c1908-1970
Dutwin, E., & Son		Port Jervis NY	USA?		
Duvert Freres (Bros.)		Thiers	France	Mfr.?	c1900
E.F. & S.	see Furness				
E.K.A.	see Eskilstuna Knivfabriks Aktiebolag				
E.P. Co.	see Eagle Pencil Co.				

POCKETKNIFE BRAND	TRADEMARK (or reference)	LOCATION	MADE IN	TYPE OF FIRM	DATES
E/crowned anchor	see Eskilstuna Jernmanufaktur	Aktiebolag			
Eadon, John		Sheffield	England	Mfr.	c1893
Eagle	has Frary patent bolster	Bridgeport CT	USA?		c1890
Eagle with Crown	(picture) see L. & C. Glauert or Ignaz Rosler's Sons Cutlery Works				
Eagle Brand	see Parker Cutlery	Japan			
Eagle Knife Co.	Hemming pat. 10/1/1918; sold to Winchester 1919	New Haven CT	USA	Mfr., Inventor	1916-1919
Eagle Pencil Co.	Eagle Cutlery Co., Magic	New York NY	USA	Mfr.	c1883-1945
Eagle/Phil'a	see Creutzberg				
Eagleton Knife Co.	made by Wester & Butz		Germany	Import brand	c1890
Early Bird	see Charles Ibbotson				
Eaton, T(homas) W.	Caledonian Knife	Sheffield	England	Mfr.	c1849-c1900
Ebel, Paul	two fish with crown	Solingen	Germany	Mfr.	1905-1960s
Ebro	see Adolph Kastor				
Echo	see Pauls Bros.				
Eclipse Cutlery Co.	Damascus (Baker & Hamilton)	San Francisco CA	US or Ger.?	Hdw. Whol. brand	c189?-1918
Edelmann			Germany?		c1860?
Edge Mark	for Gutmann Cutlery, Inc.	Mount Vernon NY	Ger./Japan	Import brand	c1950-pres.
Edgemaster	see Schrade Walden (Schrade Cut. Co. style)			Mfr.'s brand	
Edmunds, W.C., & Co.		Baltimore MD		Hdw. Whol.	1900-?
Edouard, Mure	716 Veritable Edouard	Le Roc (near Thiers)	France	Mfr.	19??
Edson Cutlery Co.			Germany	Import brand	c1900
Edwards & Sons	161 Regent St.	London	England	Retail	c1870s
Edwards & Walker Co.		Portland ME		Hdw. Whol.	1876-19??
Eigen, C.V.		Solingen	Germany	Mfr.?	
Ekco (Housewares Co.)	Pocketknives c1945-48 Edward Katzinger (1863-1939); first kitchen knives 1929; to Amer. Home Prod. Corp 1965	Chicago IL	USA/Canada	Mfr. & Whol.	1888-pres.
El Gallo	= Rooster (Spanish), see	Carl Schlieper			
Elberfield Cutlery Co.	made by Wester & Butz		Germany	Export brand	c1866-1891
Elberon Cutlery Works			Germany	Import brand?	
Electric Cutlery Co.	Friedmann & Lauterjung Made in Newark NJ c1890-1909, then sold to New York Knife Co., Walden NY	NYC NY, Newark NJ	USA	Whol. & Mfr.	1873-c1909
Electron	see J.A. Schmidt				
Elektronoris			Germany		c1920s
Elgin Cutlery Co.	Shure Cutter		USA	Whol.?	c1930
Elinox	see Karl Elsener				
Elk	see Premier Cutlery Co.				
Ellenville Knife Co.	see Dwight Divine, Ulster	Ellenville NY	USA	Mfr.'s brand	c1920s
Ellin, T(homas), & Co.	Sylvester Works acquired Cutler, Vulcan, ERA James Barber from other firms, sold to J. Elliott	Sheffield	England	Mfr.	1784-1944
Ellin, Thomas R(ichardson)	Footprint, Domino	Sheffield	England	Mfr.	c1860-1960
Ellingsen, O.	made by Gebruder Berns	Reykjavik, Iceland	Germany	Retail	c1960s
Elliot, William	owner Adolph Strauss 1907-18	New York NY		Whol.	c1880-1918
Elliott, George		Sheffield	England	Mfr.	c1893
Elliott, H., & Sons		Sheffield	England	Mfr.	c1893
Elliott, Henry		Sheffield	England	Mfr.	c1893
Elliott, John, & Sons		Sheffield	England	Mfr.	c1893
Elliott, Joseph	bought J. Wigfall 1870, bought Lockwood Bros. c1921; bought T. Ellin & Co., ERA James Barber, I. Wilson 1944; most of Lockwood's old I. & H. Sorby brands went to Turner, Naylor & Co.	Sheffield	England	Mfr.	1795-pres.
Ellis, I(saac), & Sons	Primus; sold to E. Blyde	Sheffield	England	Mfr.	c1839-1932
Eloi	see (Louis) Eloi Pernet				
Elosi	Ernst Lohr, Otto Stiehl pat.	Solingen	Germany	Mfr.	c1930s
Elsener, Karl	Elinox, Victoria, Victorinox	Ibach	Switzerland	Mfr.	1884-pres.
Ely, I.G., & Co.	Elyte (c1960-1980s)	Atlanta GA	Germany	Gift Wholesale	c1940s-80s
Elyria Cutlery Co.	became Clauss Cutlery Co.	Elyria OH	USA	Mfr. & Whol.	1878-1887
Elyte	see I.G. Ely Co.				
Emerson & Fisher, Ltd.		St. John NB		Hdw. Whol. Ret.	1870-19??
Emery-Waterhouse Co., The	Trustworthy	Portland ME	USA	Hdw. Whol. Ret.	1842-pres.
Emmons-Hawkins Hardware Co.	Emhawco (by Utica)	Huntington WV	US/Ger.	Hdw. Whol. Ret.	1875-1969
Empire Knife Co.	in West Winsted post-1880	Winsted CT	USA	Mfr.	1856-1930

POCKETKNIFE BRAND	TRADEMARK (or reference)	LOCATION	MADE IN	TYPE OF FIRM	DATES
Empire	for Parker KCS	Chattanooga TN	USA/Japan	Whol. brand	c1993-pres.
Empkie-Shugart(-Hill) Co.		Council Bluffs IA		Hdw. Whol.	1872-19??
Enderes, Original	some by Camillus	Guttenburg IA	USA	Tool Mfr. Whol.	1926-?
Enders, William	Oak Leaf, see E. C. Simmons	St. Louis MO	USA/Ger.	Hdw. Whol. brand	c1908-1929
Endure	see J. Beal				
Engels, C.W.	Angel (picture) S, Pilatus	Solingen	Germany	Mfr.	1884-1960s
Engels, F(riedrich) W., & Co.	Agent for C.W. Engels	New York NY	Germany	Import Agency	c1909-1943
English & Carlin	became J.F. Carlin & Sons	Alexandria VA		Hdw. Whol.	1844-1895
English Steel	(NOT marked Sheffield) see A. Feist & Co.				
Engstrom, John	JE/18/74; WieBusch import	Eskilstuna	Sweden	Mfr.	1874-1895
Enterprise Cutlery Co.	sold by Shapleigh	St. Louis MO	US/Ger.	Whol. brand?	c1918-1920s
Epstein, A.		Karlsruhe?	Germany	retail	c1907
Epworth, Thomas		Sheffield	England	Mfr.	c1893
Equip U.S.A.	Timberlite, Timberline	Mancos CO	USA	Mfr.	1991-1996
Erber			Ger./Austr.	Import?	c1890?
Erma			Germany	Import brand	c1950s?
Ern, C. Friedrich	Crown & Sword, Newton	Solingen-Wald	Germany	Mfr.	1873-1986
Eskilstuna	(place name)		Sweden		
Eskilstuna Jernmanufaktur AB	E on crowned anchor	Eskilstuna	Sweden	Mfr. & Whol.	1920-1970
Eskilstuna Kniffabriks AB	EKA. was H. Hallstroms	Eskilstuna	Sweden	Mfr.	1917-1925
Eskilstuna Knivfabriks AB	owned by John Elmquist 1917-46; son-in-law Torbjorn Evrell 1946-present				1925-pres.
Eureka Cutlery Co.	became Lackawanna	Nicholson PA	USA	Mfr.	1911-1915
Ever-Sharp	American Wholesale Co.	Baltimore MD	USA	Whol. & Retail	1920s
Everlastingly Sharp	see Schrade Cutlery Co.				
Everts, David	DES crossed flags	Solingen	Germany	Mfr.	1802-pres.
Everts, Ferd., Sohn & Co.	Schneidteufel; Okapi 1930s-	Solingen	Germany	Mfr.	1880-pres.
Excelsior Knife Co.	sold to Northfield c1884	Tortington CT	USA	Mfr.	1880-1884
Exclusive Cutlery Shop, The	T.E.C.S.	San Francisco CA	Ger./France	Retail	1911-1991
Executive	see Colonial Knife Co.				
Executive Edge	for B. & D. Trading Co.	Fair Oaks CA	Brazil	Import brand	current
Explorer	see Gutmann Cutlery Co.				
Explorer (Gutmann) Swing-Blade	Francis Boyd patent	Mount Vernon NY	Japan/USA	Import brand	1989-pres.
Eye Brand	see Carl Schlieper				
Eyewitness	Eye (picture) see Needham Veall & Tyzack				
Eyre, B(enjamin) J(ames), & Co.	bought W. Greaves 1850	Sheffield	England	Mfr.	18??-c1876
Eyre, Ward & Co.	B.J. Eyre & F. Ward	Sheffield	England	Mfr.	c1852-1869
Eyre, B.J., & Co.	(Wiebusch trademark)	New York NY	Engl./Ger.	Import brand	c1876-1915
F (anchor) F	see Franz Frenzel				
F.B. Trade Mark	see Forquignon				
F.K. Co.	see Fayetteville Knife Co.				
F. & L.	see Friedmann & Lauterjung				
F. & W. Mfg. Co.	see Foley & Williams Mfg. Co.				
Faber, Eberhard	A.W. Faber brand	New York NY	Germany	Pencil Mfr.	c1880
Fabico	see F.A. Bower Import Co.				
Fabyan Knife Co.	Q.E.D.	?NY	Germany	Import?	c1890?
Fairbanks Trading Co.		Fairbanks AK?	US/England	Retail?	c1900?
Fairfield Cutlery Co.		Bridgeport CT	USA	Mfr.?	c1884
Fairmount Cutlery Co.	Camillus brand	Camillus NY	USA	Mfr.'s brand	1930s
Fall River Knife Co.		Fall River(?) MA	Germany	Import brand	c1900
Fame	see W. Greaves or S. & J. Kitchin				
Famex or Famexi	see E. & F. Horster				
Fan Brand	see Carl Schlieper (not exported to U.S.)				
Farge	some made by Frenzel	Chatellerault	Fran./Aus.	Mfr. & Importer	?-c1914
Farr, Albert		Sheffield	England	Mfr.	c1893
Farr, John		Sheffield	England	Mfr.	c1821-1852
Farr, Joseph		Sheffield	England	Mfr.	c1893
Farr, William, H.	Portland works	Sheffield	England	Mfr.	c1893
Farragut Cutlery Co.	made by Camillus	"New York City" NY	USA	Mfrs. brand	c1920s
Farwell Ozmun Kirk & Co.	Henry Sears (1897-1959)	St. Paul MN	USA	Hdw. Whol.	1859-1959
Fawsitt, Humbert M., & Co.	Wentworth works	Sheffield	England	Mfr.	c1893

POCKETKNIFE BRAND	TRADEMARK (or reference)	LOCATION	MADE IN	TYPE OF FIRM	DATES
Fayetteville Knife Co.	F.K. Co.	Fayetteville NY	USA	Mfr.	?-1911
Featherweight	(aluminum frame) see Utica Cutlery Co.			Mfr.'s brand	1932-pres.
Federal Knife Co.	made by Camillus	"Syracuse" NY	USA	Mfrs.brand	c1920s
Federal Knife Company	Johnston, Thornton; sold to Colonial (Thornton is a district of Johnston)	Johnston RI	USA	Mfr.	c1945-1950
Fein Stahl	= Fine steel (German); usually not made for export				
Feist, A., & Co.	Lunawerk; English Steel	Solingen	Germany	Mfr.	1864-1939
Feist, Joseph	Omega; Solidus; Olifant	Solingen	Germany	Mfr.	1864-pres.
Felix, Gustav	Gloria-Werke	Solingen	Germany	Mfr.	1843-pres.
Felsenheld, E.		New York NY	US/Ger.	Mfr. & importer	c1900?
Fenny, Frederick Fox, Tally-Ho		Sheffield	England	Mfr.	1824-1852
Fenton, Joseph, (& Sons)	Gregory Fenton, Ltd. 1968-	Sheffield	England	Mfr.	1795-pres.
Field, Alfred, & Co.	Criterion, Cromwell? Progress, Bird Head (picture). Agent for Joseph Rodgers & Sons, George Korn	New York/ Sheffield	Eng/Ger./US	Mfr. & Whol.	1836-1942
Field, Marshall, & Co.	Marshall Field 1834-1906 Store formerly called Cooley, Wadsworth & Co.; Field hired 1856	Chicago IL	US/Eng/Ger.	Retail	1881-pres.
Fielding, John		Sheffield	England	Mfr.	c1848-1867
Fife Cutlery Co.	made by C. Bertram	Mount Sterling KY	Germany	Retail?	1968-1974
Fight'n Rooster	see Frank Buster Cutlery Co.				
Findlay, Roberts & Co.	IMA1	Baltimore MD	Germany?	Hdw. Whol.	c1897
Fine Steel	see Fein Stahl		Germany?	Export mark	c1890?
Finedge Cutlery Co.	Ostiso	New York NY	Germany	Whol.	1920s
Finnigan's	18 New Bond St. W	London/Man./ Liverp.	England	Retail	
Firth, Luke		Sheffield	England	Mfr.	c1849-1870
Fisher, A.	Man with fish (picture)	Solingen	Germany	Mfr.?	c1930s
Fisher, A.A., & Co.			New York NY	Whol.?	c1910?
Fisher, Harrison, & Co.	Trafalgar Works, Nelson crossed fish (picture); OIO brand from Clarke, Shirley & Co.; Harrison Fisher d. 1907; Hungry Wolf, Prolific (from Henry Bamascone); absorbed Needham, Veall & Tyzack 1975	Sheffield	England	Mfr.	1896-pres.
FishMaster	see Colonial Knife Co.	Providence RI	USA	Mfr.'s brand	c1950
Fiskars	now owns Gerber	Helsinki	Finland	Mfr.	1649-pres.
Fiske Kniv	= Fish Knife (Icelandic) (knives usually made in Germany)				
Fist (Faust) holding three arrows	(picture) see Precise (International)				
Fleron	Trenton NJ		USA?		c1910?
Fletcher, Charles William	C.W.F. silver fruit knives	Sheffield	England	Mfr.	1894-19??
Fletcher Hardware Co.	Fletcher Knife Co.	Detroit MI		Hdw. Whol.	1862-1913
Fletcher, John		Sheffield	England	Mfr.	c1893
Flint, A.W.	made in Sheffield		England	Import brand?	20th cent.
Flipnife	see Lectrolite Corp.				
Flockton Tompkin & Co.	Ye Cats; some by Nowill	Sheffield	England	Mfr. & Whol.	20th cent.
Florida Hardware Co.		Jacksonville FL	USA?	Hdw. Whol.	1875-19??
Flylock Knife Co.	by Challenge Cut. Co. George Schrade patent 3/5/1918	Bridgeport CT	USA	Mfr's. brand	1918-1928
Foley & Williams Mfg. Co.	F. & W. Mfg. Co.	Cincinnati OH	USA?	Retail	c1900
Folsom & Tillman	F & T (joined)	Helena GA		Hdw. Retail	c1908-?
Fones Brothers	Arkansas Traveler	Little Rock AR		Hdw. Whol.	1865-1920s
Fong Yuon	see China Light Ind.	Canton, Guangdong	China		
Ford & Medley	Emu	Sheffield	England	Mfr.	1872-c1930
Foreign (Made)	= made abroad, usually in Germany, for sale in Britain after c1926				
Forest King	by Schrade Cutlery Co.	Walden NY	USA	Mfr.'s brand	1934-c1942
ForestMaster	by Colonial	Providence RI	USA	Mfr.'s brand	1930s-pres.
Forged (Made in) USA	usu. by Camillus for Sears	Chicago IL	USA	Retail mark	c1930s
Fork	(picture) see Gebruder Christians				
Forquignon (Bros.)	F.B., LeRoi Corn Knife	Solingen?	Germany	Mfr.	c1900
Forschner (R.H.) Group	agent for Victorinox successor to Chas. Forschner & Sons, New York NY; also called Swiss Army Brands	Shelton CT	Switzerland	Whol. Import	1855-pres.
Fort Pitt Knife Co.		Tidioute PA	USA		
Foster Brothers Co.	bought by John Chatillon & Sons 1883, sold Foster Bros. & Chatillon contract pocketknives c1900-37	Fulton NY	USA	Butcher K. Mfr.	c1878-1950s
Foster, J.	made in Sheffield	Leeds	England	Retail	c1900?

POCKETKNIFE BRAND	TRADEMARK (or reference)	LOCATION	MADE IN	TYPE OF FIRM	DATES
Fox Cutlery Co.	(Koeller & Schmitz-1915)	Milwaukee WI		Whol.	c1884-1955
Fox Knives	imported by Catoctin	Maniago	Italy	Mfr.	current
Foxy Grandpa	see J. Curley & Brother				
Francis, Henry		Sheffield	England	Mfr.	c1893
Frankfurth, Wm., Hardware Co.	incorporated 1885	Milwaukee WI		Hdw. Whol.	1861-pres.
Frankonia Jagd	some made by Boker	Wurzburg, Franconia	Germany	Retail	current
Frary Cutlery Co.	A1, James Frary (-1881)	Bridgeport CT	USA	Mfr.	1876-1884
Frary, (James), & Son (Harry) Co.	became LaBelle Cutlery	Bridgeport CT	USA	Mfr.	c1881-1884
Fraser, Alexander, & Co.	Fraser & Co., Fraser Knife sold by Hudson's Bay Co. Winnipeg, Manitoba Retail c1870-1915	Sheffield	England	Mfr.	c1870-1914
Fraser, Walter S., & Co., Ltd.		Victoria, BC		Hdw. Whol. Ret.	1862-19??
Freeman, Delamater & Co.	Craft	Detroit MI		Hdw. Whol.	1890-c1908
Frenix	see Franz Frenzel	Nixdorf, Bohemia	Czecho.	Mfr.'s brand	c1920s
Frenzel, Franz	F (anchor) F imported by Wiebusch to the U.S., by Farge to France	Nixdorf, Bohemia	Aust-Hung.	Contract Mfr.	c1900
Fre(re)s Bro(ther)s (French)					
Freund, R(obert)		Solingen	Germany	Mfr.?	
Friedmann & Lauterjung	F & L (see also Electric)	New York NY	Ger./USA	Whol.	c1866-1909
Frontier	by Camillus for Imperial	Ellenville NY	USA	Mfr.'s brand	current
Frost, Samuel	joined Askham and Mosforth	Sheffield	England	Mfr.	c1820-1850
Frost, Askham & Mosforth	Samuel Frost died 1853 became Askham & Mosforth; Thomas Mosforth b. 1821	Sheffield	England	Mfr.	1850-1853
Frost Cutlery Co.	Surgical Steel, Falcon	Chattanooga TN	Japan	Whol/Ret/Import	1978-pres.
Frothingham & Workman, Ltd.		Montreal, Quebec		Hdw. Whol.	1809-19??
Frye, Phipps & Co.		Boston MA		Hdw. Whol.	1816-19??
Fuller Bros. (Ross & Fuller Assoc.)	Paragon Cutlery Co.	New York NY		Hdw. Whol. Exp.	c1868-19??
Fulton	see Montgomery & Co. or John Kenyon (also Fulltone)				
Fulton Cutlery Co.	sales office in NYC	Canal Fulton OH	USA	Mfr.	c1919
Funke, Leopold	(Bridge Cutlery ?)	St. Louis MO	USA	Mfr.?	c1876
Furness, Edward	Father of Barlows	Sheffield	England	Mfr.	c1900
Furness, Enoch, & Sons EF&S. Imported by Wiebusch		Sheffield	England	Mfrs.	c1870-1915
Furness, George		Sheffield	England	Mfr.	c1893
Furness, M., & Sons	1760. Imported by H.S.B.	Sheffield	England	Mfr.	1760-c1916
Furness, Matthew		Sheffield	England	Mfr.	c1893
G	= Guss Stahl (cast steel) (German)				
G.	in hallmark on silver fruit knives: see John Gorham				
G.B.D.	see A. Oppenheimer & Co.				
G.C. Co.	see Gutmann Cutlery Co.				
G.F.C. Phila.	see G.F. Creutzberg				
G. & J.B.	see George & James Butler				
gL*	see A. Feist & Co. Lunawerk				
G.M.L.	People's Cutlery Workshop	Leegebruch	E. Germany	Mfr.	?-pres.?
G.R.C. Co.	see Golden Rule Cutlery Co.				
G.R.W.	see J. Russell & Co. Green River Works		USA	Mfr.'s brand	
GS	= Guss Stahl (cast steel) (German)				
G. & S. Welkut	see Graef & Schmidt				
GT Knives	Greg Bark, Todd Jones	San Diego CA	USA	Hand Mfr.	1993-pres.
G.U.	in hallmark on silver fruitknives: see George Unite				
G.W. & H. Hdw. Co.	see Geller Ward & Hasner Hardware Co.				
G-96	see Jet-Aer				
Galahad	see Hadfields Ltd.				
Galliac	crowned Y	Paris?	France	Mfr.	c1810?
Galvanic 1882				Mfr.'s brand	c1880s
Gamble Stores	by Camillus (?)	Minneapolis MN	USA	Retail Hdw.	c1930s-50s
Garcia, Alvaro		Albacete	Spain	Mfr.	c1930s?
Gardner, Joseph	Gardner 1876 Joseph Gardner was the superintendent of Lamson & Goodnow	Shelburne Falls MA	USA	Mfr.	1876-1883
Gates, Albert		Sheffield	England	Mfr.?	c1850
Gebr(uder)	= Brothers (German)				
Geller Ward & Hasner Hardware Co.	G.W. & H. Hdw. Co.	St. Louis MO	USA	Hdw. Whol.	1902-c1937
Gellman Bros.	some by Lackawanna	Minneapolis MN	USA & ?	Retail?	c1920

POCKETKNIFE BRAND	TRADEMARK (or reference)	LOCATION	MADE IN	TYPE OF FIRM	DATES
Gem, Edward, & Co.	sold to Alfred Field	Sheffield	England	Mfr.	c1893
Genella, Charles	Spike, Little Buddy	Chattanooga TN	Japan	Import	c1978
Geneva Cutlery Co.	became Geneva Forge 1934	Geneva NY	USA	Mfr.?	1902-1934
Geneva Forge, Inc.	div. of E. Katzinger (EKCO)	Geneva NY	USA	Mfr.?	1934-1960
Gerber Legendary Blades	first pocketknives 1968 sold to Fiskars 1986, became Fiskars-Gerber	Portland OR	USA	Mfr.	1939-pres.
Gerber/Paul	design by Paul Poehlmann	Portland OR	USA	Mfr.'s brand	1978-1986
Gerber-Sakai	Silver Knight	Portland OR, Seki	Japan	Mfr.'s brand	1977-1995
Germania Cutlery Works	Nathan Kastor	Solingen-Ohligs	Germany	Mfr.	1892-1937
Gerson	melon testers	Boston MA and Middleboro MA	Fra/Ger./Italy	Food dist. ad	?-pres.
Ges. Gesch.	= Design patent ("legally registered") (German)				
Ghriskey's Sons, Charles M.		Philadelphia PA		Hdw. Whol.	1849-19??
Giant Grip			Japan?	Advt.?	c1930s
Gibbins, J., & Sons		Sheffield	England	Mfr.	c1893
Gilbert Collonge	Stag head (picture)		France	Mfr.'s brand	
Giesen & Forsthoff	G. (man) F.; Timor	Solingen	Germany	Mfr.	1920-pres.
Gilbert, Henry, & Son		Harrisburg PA	USA?	Hdw. Whol.	1840-19??
Gilbert/Saville Works	see Stauffer, Eshelmann & Co.				
Gilchrist, William	Celebrated Razor Steel	Sheffield?	England	Mfr.?	c1860s
Gill, George		Sheffield	England	Mfr.	c1893
Gill, George, & Sons		Sheffield	England	Mfr.	c1940
Gill, Henry	ex Northfield employee	Northfield CT	USA	Hand Mfr.	1931-c1960
Gillott, C.	Heart & Cross (pic)	Sheffield	England	Mfr.	c1848-1900
Gillott, George	Reliance works	Sheffield	England	Mfr.	c1893
Gits Razor Knife	(Gitsnife) by Gits Molding Co.	Chicago IL	USA	Plastics Mfr.	1938-c1950
Gladiator Cutlery	see Carl Wusthof, KG				
Glamorgan Works	see Joseph Haywood				
Glasner & Barzen			Germany	Advt. Specialty?	c1910
Glauert, L. & C.	Patriot, Crowned Eagle	Sheffield	England	Mfr.	c1893
Globe Cutlery Co.	Glico. Some by Robeson	NY, NY	Ger./USA	Wholesale?	c1900s-20s
Glossop		Sheffield	England	Mfr./now Retail	c1835-pres.
Gobernador	= Governor (Spanish) see Krusius, Gebruder Mfr.'s brand				
Golden Age Classics	old Case brands by Parker KCS	Chattanooga TN	USA	Ltd. editions	c1990-pres.
Golden Gate Cutlery Co.	see Baker & Hamilton	San Francisco CA	Ger./US?	Hdw. Whol. brand	c 1890s
Golden Rule Cutlery Co.	G.R.C. Co.	Chicago IL	USA	Mfr.	1911-c1924
Gomez/Albacete	see Martinez-Gomez S.A.E.Z.				
Gonon, Joseph	41 Gonon	Thiers	France	Mfr.	c1906
Gonon-Chassengue et Fils	41 Gonon	Thiers	France	Mfr.	1896-1931
	trademark owned by la Societe Generale de Coutellerie et d'Orfeverie, Paris				1931-1963
Gorham, John, Mfg. Co.	G. silver fruit knives	Providence RI	USA	Silver Mfr.	1831-pres.
Goshorn Hardware Co.	Goshorn Cutlery Co.	Charleston WV	Germany	Hdw. Whol. Ret.	1906-?
Gouverneur	= Governor (French and German) see Krusius, Gebruder			Mfr.'s brand	
Graef, A.	Made by Wester & Butz		Germany	Import brand	c1890
Graef (William) & Schmidt (Carl)	agency for J.A. Henckels	New York NY	USA/Ger.	Whol. Import	1883-c1948
Graef & Schmidt	G. & S., Welkut, Spider	NY, NY & Irvington NJ	USA	Mfr.	c1940-1952
Grafrath, Gebruder (Bros.)	Grawiso	Solingen	Germany	Mfr.	1869-pres.
Grammes, L.F., & Sons			Germany	Advt. Specialty?	c1930s
Grant, W.T.	Crucible Knife, Wearite	NY, NY (Lynn MA)	USA	Retail brand	c1920s
Graveley & Wreaks	some by William Sansom	New York NY	England	Retail Import	c1830-1837
Graves, J.G.	Enterprise	Sheffield	England	Mfr.	c1869 ff.
Grawiso	see Grafrath				
Gray & Dudley Hardware Co.	Washington Cut., Hermitage -was Gray, Fall & Co.-1895; knives by S & M?; brands assigned to Keith Simmons c1927	Nashville TN	US/Ger.	Hdw. Whol.	1862-c1927
Great American Tool Co.	Gatco, Timberline, Timberlite	Getzville NY	USA	Mfr.	1996-pres.
Greaves, Francis, & Sons	High Toned, Incise	Sheffield	England	Mfr.	c1850-1970s
Greaves, W(illiam)	Fame	Sheffield	England	Mfr.	1780-1816
Greaves, W(illiam), & Son	built Sheaf Works 1823-26 sold to B. J. Eyre 1850	Sheffield	England	Mfr.	1816-1850
Green Duck Co.		Chicago IL	USA?	Advt. Spec.?	c1910
Green, John		Sheffield	England	Mfr.	c1893

POCKETKNIFE BRAND	TRADEMARK (or reference)	LOCATION	MADE IN	TYPE OF FIRM	DATES
Green & Green		Sheffield	England	Mfr.	c1893
Green, Theo. M.	see Domar Cutlery Co.				
Greenbrier	see Lowenstein & Sons				
Greenhough, John	Viena Works made exposition knives; marks sold to A.J. Blyde, last used 1926	Sheffield	England	Mfr.	1867-1890s
Greenrice			England	Retail	
Gregory, G.	made fleams	Sheffield	England	Mfr.	c1820s?
Gregory, John E.	Smith's works	Sheffield	England	Mfr.	c1893
Greogry, William (& Sons)	W. (hammer) G., All Right sold to John Petty & Sons	Sheffield	England	Mfr.	1843-1907
Grieb, J. Matthew	father of Charles Grieb	New York NY	US/Ger.	Retail	c1860s-91
Grieb, Charles	lived 1868-1928	New Haven CT	USA	Mfr. & Retail	1893-1913
Greist Mfg. Co.	Buddy-Nife	New Haven CT	USA	Mfr.	c1926
Griffin's Waterproofer	made by E. B. Sears (see Dynamite Knives under Multi-blades, Plier and Wrench Knives)				
Griffon Cutlery Works	A.L. Silberstein & Co. Griffon XX; Carbomagnetic. Factory: Bridgeport CT; also Worcester MA c1918-1921	New York NY	USA/Ger.	Whol. & Mfr.	1893-pres
Guss Stahl	= Cast Steel (German)				
Gutmann Cutlery Co.	Explorer; Edge; G.C.CO.	Mount Vernon NY	USA/Ger./Jap.	Whol. Import	1947-pres.
Gutmann Cutlery Co.	Explorer; Edge; G.C.CO.; Walther knives	Bellingham WA	USA/Ger./Jap.	Whol. Import	circa 1995-pres.
H-B	(monogram on shield of Remington Scout knife) see Highlander Boys				
H. & B. Mfg. Co.	see Humason & Beckley				
H. & D. Co.		Chicago IL	USA	Mfr.?	c1910?
H.H.H.	see O. Barnett Tool Co.				
H.H.S.	see E. & F. Horster				
H.K. Co.	see Hollingsworth Knife Co.				
H.M.C. Cutlery Co.	Whale (picture)	New Bedford MA	Import brand?	M	
H.R.S. & Co.	see Henry Rodgers Sons & Co.				
H.S.B. & Co.	see Hibbard Spencer Bartlett				
H'Ville Knife Co.	see Hotchkissville Knife Co.				
H.W.G. Hdwe. Co.	see Hackett Walther Gates Hardware Co.				
Haag, F.G.	113 Canal Street, NY			Wholesale?	
Hackett, C.W., Hardware Co.	orig. Strong Hdw. Co. 1858	St. Paul MN		Hdw. Whol.	1889-1902
Hackett Walther Gates Hardware Co.	H.W.G. Hdw. Co.	St. Paul MN		Hdw. Whol.	1902-1912
Hackett-Gates-Hurty Co.		St. Paul MN		Hdw. Whol.	1912-pres.
Hackman Oy	nylon handle balisongs	Nurmi; Sorsakoski	Finland	Mfr.	1790-pres.
Hadfields Ltd.	Galahad, Hecla, Hadura	Sheffield	England	Steel Mfr.	c1861-19??
Hafters Cutlery Co.					c1920s?
Hagg & Co.		Eskilstuna	Sweden	Mfr.	c1920
Hague, George T.		Sheffield	England	Mfr.	c1893
Hague, Samuel		Sheffield	England	Mfr.	c1830s-50s
Hague, T.E.		Sheffield	England	Mfr.?	
Halberd	(picture) see Frederick A. Clauberg				
Hale Brothers	Horse head (picture)	Sheffield	England	Mfr.	c1871-1972
Hall, Charles	C. Hall	Sheffield	England	Mfr.	c1836-1872
Hall, Jonathan	I. Hall	Sheffield	England	Mfr.	1795-1830
Hall, J.		Bradford	England	Retail?	c1910?
Hall Hardware Co.		Minneapolis MN		Hdw. Whol.	1913-?
Hallstroms, Hadar, Knivfabriks	became E.K.A.	Eskilstuna	Sweden	Mfr.	1882-1917
Hamer & Sons		Sheffield	England	Mfr.?	
Hamilton Brown Shoe Co.	see Brown, Hamilton, Shoe Co.				
Hamilton Carhartt	see Carhartt, Hamilton				
Hammer Brand	(solid bolsters) see New York Knife Co.			Mfr.'s brand	c1880-1931
Hammer Brand	(shell handles) see Imperial Knife Co.			Mfr.'s brand	1938-pres.
Hammersfahr, Gottlieb	Nirosta, Pyramide	Solingen-Foche	Germany	Mfr.	1684-19??
Hancock, B(enjamin?)	U.S. Knife	Sheffield	England	Mfr.	1812-?
Hancock, Samuel, & Sons	Mazeppa, Zephyr	Sheffield	England	Mfr.	c1836-1924
Handarbeit	= hand made (German)				
Hanover Cutlery Co.			Germany	Import brand	
Happy Jack Cutlery	Chuck Garlits	Rosman NC	USA	Hand Mfr.	1987-1989
Harco	see Harwi Hardware Co.				

POCKETKNIFE BRAND	TRADEMARK (or reference)	LOCATION	MADE IN	TYPE OF FIRM	DATES
Hardened Copper Cutlery Co.	(copper blade)	New York (office)	USA?	Mfr.	c1920
Hardin (Wholesale)	by Olbertz for Geo. Smith	Kenova WV	Germany	Import	recent
Hardy Brothers Ltd.	Hardy's Anglers Knife Nos. 1-4 (marked on handle); knives made c1900 by G. Butler (Art), Sheffield	Alnwick	England	Tackle Mfr.	1880s-pres.
Hardy, Thomas, & Son	Freedom	Sheffield	England	Mfr.	c1868-1950s
Hargreaves Smith & Co.	Fryers, J. Smith & Co.	Sheffield	England	Mfr.	c1866-1920
Harper & McIntire Co.		Ottumwa, Cedar R. IA		Hdw. Whol. Ret.	c1867-19??
Harrington, Henry	Cutler to the People	Southbridge MA	USA	Mfr.	1818-1876
Harris Bros. & Co.		Chicago IL	USA?	Wholesale	c1915
Harrison Brothers & Howson	Crown (picture) Alpha succeeded William Sansom & Co. 1847; bought Charles Ibbotson & Co., 1902. Had offices in New York City and San Francisco c1890s. Sold to Viners, 1959	Sheffield	England	Mfr. & Whol.	1847-1959
Harrison Fisher	see Fisher, Harrison				
Harrison, W.W., & Co.		Sheffield	England	Mfr.	c1893
Harrod's	made by Ibberson	London	England	Retail	20th cent.
Harrop, Tom		Sheffield	England	Mfr.	c1893
Hart Cutlery Co.	some by Camillus	New York NY	Ger./USA		c1920s
Hart Hardware Co.		Louisville KY		Hdw. Whol.	c1897
Hartford Cutlery Co.		Tariffville CT	USA	Mfr.	c1880
Hartford Cutlery Co.	sold by Marshall Wells	Duluth MN	Ger./USA	Hdw. brand?	c1928
Hartkopf, Robert, & Co.	Winged lions some knives made for Utica Knife & Razor Company	Solingen	Germany	Mfr.	c1855-1957
Hartley, John		Sheffield	England	Mfr.	c1893
Harvard	see The George Worthington Co.				
Harwell, W.F.	Blitzknife	Charlotte NC	USA		c1947
Harwi, Alfred Jonathan, Hardware Co.	Harco (1910-)	Atchison KS		Hdw. Whol.	1875-19??
Hasons & Co.	Union Jack (pic)		England?		c1930s
Hassam (Brothers) (Frederick F. & Roswell H.)	was Kingman & Hassam c1853-1860 (successors to N. Hunt & Co.)	Boston MA	US/Ger./Eng	Retail (& Mfr.?)	1860-1872
					1886-c1888
Hatch Cutlery Co.	moved from Connecticut	Buchanan MI	USA	Mfr.	c1888-1899
Hatch Cutlery Co.	moved from Michigan	South Milwaukee WI	USA	Mfr.	c1899-19??
Haugh & Frisbie		New Haven CT	USA	Mfr.?	c1857
Haven, R.M.		Norwich CT	USA	Mfr.?	c1857
Haw (, George,) Hardware Co.		Ottumwa IA		Hdw. Whol.	1864-19??
Hawcroft, William, & Sons		Sheffield	England	Mfr.	c1893
Hayhurst, William		Sheffield	England	Mfr.	c1893
Haynes, Stellite		Kokomo IN	USA	Mfr. & Retail	1911, 1919
Hayward Key Knife	see Empire				
Haywood, Joseph	Teakettle (picture) Glamorgan Works, 1880; marks sold to Thomas Turner & Co. 1902	Sheffield	England	Mfr.	c1843-1902
Healy, Charles J.		New York NY		Whol. Import	1885-19??
Hearnshaw Bros.	John Bull (picture) associated with Thomas Ellin c1953	Sheffield	England	Mfr.?	c1953
Heathcote, Samuel		Sheffield	England	Mfr.	c1893
Heathcote, Thomas		Sheffield	England	Mfr.	c1893
Hecho en Mexico	= Made in Mexico (Spanish)				
Hedengram & Son		Eskilstuna	Sweden	Mfr.	c1900?
Heimerdinger, W.C.		Louisville KY		Retail	recent
Helena Hardware Co.		Helena MT		Hdw. Whol.	1870-19??
Heljestrand C.V.		Eskilstuna	Sweden	Mfr.	c1900
Hellberg, J.A.		Eskilstuna	Sweden	Mfr.?	1900-1978
Heller Bros.	Horse (picture) Nucut	Newark NJ	USA	Hoof knife mfr.	1870-1930s
Hello Boys	see J. Curley & Brother				
Hemming Brothers	Hemming Woodsman World's first successful automatic grinders 1903. Eagle Knife Co. 1916-1919	New Haven CT	USA	Mfr., Inventors	c1900-1924
Hen & Rooster	C. Bertram	Solingen	Germany	Mfr.'s brand	1864-1983
Hen & Rooster	by Klaas for Frost Cut	Chattanooga TN	Germany	Import brand	c1983-pres.
Henckels, J(ohann) A(braham)	Zwillingswerk (Twinworks)	Solingen	Germany	Mfr.	1731-pres.
Henckels, J.A.	pocketknives made by Henckels	exported to the USA			1883-1960

POCKETKNIFE BRAND	TRADEMARK (or reference)	LOCATION	MADE IN	TYPE OF FIRM	DATES
Henckels, J.A.	lower quality: made on contract for Henckels by Boker, Olbertz, etc.				c1952-pres.
Henckels, International	Half Twin with halberd		Brazil	Mfr.	c1970s
Henderson, Peter, & Co.	some by G. Butler	New York NY	Eng./Ger.	Retail?	c1880?
Henkels, Paul A. Solingen			Germany	Mfr.	1887-pres.
Henkle & Joyce Hardware Co.		Lincoln NE	USA	Hdw. Whol.	1900-c1934
Hennis	230 Coventry St., by Rodgers	London	England	Retail	c1900?
Henry, William, & Co.		Fort Worth TX		Hdw. Whol.	c1897
Herbertz, C. Jul.		Solingen	Germany	Mfr.	current
Herder, L.	was Clarenbach & Herder	Philadelphia PA	USA/Ger.	Mfr. & Retail	1871-1879
Herder, Charles	was L. Herder	Philadelphia PA	USA/Ger.	Mfr. & Retail	1879-?
Herder's	was Charles Herder	Philadelphia PA		Retail	?-pres.
Herder, Friedr., Abr. Sohn	Spade (after 1727), Pharus	Solingen	Germany	Mfr.	1623-1994
Herder, H(enriette)	Spade in frame	Solingen	Germany	Mfr.	1806-pres.
Herder, Richard Abr.	4-pointed star	Solingen	Germany	Mfr.	1885-pres.
Herder, Robert	4-leaf clover, Windmill	Solingen	Germany	Mfr.	1872-pres.
Hessenbruch, T.	became H. Hessenbruch Will Bear (picture of bear standing upright with staff) Inspection	Philadelphia PA	USA/Ger.	Hdw. Retail	c1873-1906
Hessenbruch, H(ermann), Co.		Philadelphia PA	USA/Ger.	Hdw. Retail	1906-c1926
Heyden, K.V.D.	Elephant head (picture)	Antwerpen	Belgium	Mfr.?	20th cent.
Hibbard Spencer Bartlett & Co.	O.V.B., True Value by New York Knife, Ulster, Camillus, Utica, etc. Became True Value Hardware Co.	Chicago IL	USA	Hdw. Whol.	1855-c1960
Hibbard Spencer & Bartlett	for Parker KCS	Chattanooga TN	USA/Japan	Whol. brand	c1993-pres.
Hickey, J(ohn) W., & Sons	see also Battle Axe Knives	Louisville KY	Germany	Retail Ltd. Ed.	1976-1980s
Hickok Mfg. Co.	KoiNife	Rochester NY	USA	Jewelry Mfr.	1937-1950s
Hickory	see Kelly How Thomson				
Hickory Hand Forged	see J.H. Sutcliffe Co.				
Hides, George, & Son	Excelsior	Sheffield	England	Mfr.	1790-19??
Higgins, J.C.	by Schrade Walden for Sears	Chicago IL	USA	Retail brand	c1960
High Carbon Steel	by Camillus usu. for Sears	Chicago IL	USA	Retail mark	c1930s
Highlander Boys	H-B on Remington shield	Denver CO	USA	Scouting org.	c1930
Hilger(, Hugo,) & Co. (& Sons)	merged with Wiebusch	New York NY	Germany	Hdw. Whol.	c1842-1864
Hilliard & Chapman		Glasgow	Scotland	Mfr.	c1850
Hilton, J(ohn)	some made for J. Curley	Woodbury CT	USA	Mfr.	c1896
Hinchcliffe, John	Bee Hive (picture) advertised "American Indian knives"; mark sold to Slater Bros.	Sheffield	England	Mfr.	c1841-1858
Hit	made by Colonial	Providence RI	USA	Mfr.'s brand?	
Hobbs Hardware Co., Ltd., The		London, Ontario		Hdw. Whol.	1876-19??
Hobson, Alfred, & Son	Current	Sheffield	England	Mfr.	c1837-1876
Hobson, Henry, & Sons	Express, Press (picture)	Sheffield	England	Mfr.	1860s-1920s
Hobson, John M.		Sheffield	England	Mfr.	19th cent.
Hobson, Thomas		Sheffield	England	Mfr.	c1893
Hoffman Hardware Co.		Los Angeles CA		Hdw. Whol.	1911-?
Hoffritz		New York NY	Ger./Fra.	Whol./Ret./Imp.	c1930-pres.
Holland, J.R.	British military issue		England	Mfr.	c1941-1945
Holler, J(ohn) S., & Co.	also see Adolph Blaich	New York NY	Ger./Engl	Whol. Import	c1867-1906
Holley, Alexander H.		Salisbury/ Lakeville, CT	USA	Mfr.	1844-c1850
Holley & Co./Holley & Merwin	Home (= HOlley & MErwin) partners Alexander H. Holley, Nathan W. Merwin, George B. Burrell	Lakeville CT	USA	Mfr.	c1850-1854
Holley Mfg. Co.	ceased distribution c1904	Lakeville CT	USA	Mfr.	1844-1930s
Holley	for Parker KCS	Chattanooga TN	USA/Japan	Whol. Brand	c1993-pres.
Hollinger Cutlery Co.		Fremont OH	USA	Mfr.?	c1919
Hollingsworth Knife Co.	formerly Kane Cutlery	Kane PA	USA	Mfr.	c1916-1930
Holly, Mason (Marks) & Co.	some by Western States Building sold to Marshall Wells, who used it 1931-1946	Spokane WA	USA	Hdw. Whol.	1885-1931
Holmberg, P.A.		Eskilstuna	Sweden	Mfr.	1900-1930s
Holmes, John, & Co.	sold to J. Clarke before 1900	Sheffield	England	Mfr.	1860-pres.
Holmes, Samuel, & Sons		Sheffield	England	Mfr.	c1893
Holtzapffel, John	invented ornamental lathe Holtzapffel & Deyerlain 1804-1827; Holtzapffel & Co. after 1828	London	England	Retail	1794-1938
Holtzapffel (& Co.)	64 Charing Cross Rd. SW	London	England	Tool retail	1821-1901
Holtzapffel & Co.	13 & 14 New Bond St.	London	England	Tool retail	1902-1907

POCKETKNIFE BRAND	TRADEMARK (or reference)	LOCATION	MADE IN	TYPE OF FIRM	DATES
Holtzapffel & Co.	53 Haymarket SW1	London	England	Tool retail	1907-1930
Holtzapffel & Co.	79 Wigmore St. W1 Sold to Sharpleshall Ltd., Regents Park Rd.	London	England	Tool retail	1931-1938
Holub (Opeartions)	made by Camillus	Sycamore IL	USA	Elec. Supply	c1970s
Home (Cutlery Co.)	see Holley & Co. / Holley & Merwin		USA	Mfr.'s brand	c1850
Honest Abe	Parker Cut. mail order	Chattanooga TN	Japan	Retail	c1987
Honeyman (De Hart) Hardware Co.		Portland OR		Hdw. Whol. Ret.	1878-19??
Honk Falls Knife Co.	in old Napanoch building	Napanoch NY	USA	Mfr.	1921-1929
Honk Falls Knife Co.	for Parker KCS	Chattanooga TN	USA/Japan	Whol. brand	c1993-pres.
Hopkinson, H.B.	ex-Northfield employee	Northfield CT	USA	Mfr.	c1885
Hoppe & Co.	Caelton	Sheffield	England	Mfr.	1890s-1920s
Hoppe's 9	Blackie Collins design	Coatesville PA	USA	Gun Care Mfr.	1995-pres.
Hoppe, Gebruder (Bros.)	owner Karl Joest	Solingen	Germany	Mfr.	1919-pres.
Horrabin, Vickers	sold to H.G. Long	Sheffield	England	Mfr.	c1893
Horridge, George		Sheffield	England		1890s-1910s
Horster, E. & F., Co.	HHS, Famex, Monika	Solingen-Wald	Germany	Mfr.	1850-pres.
Horton, Gilmore, McWilliams & Co.		Chicago IL		Hdw. Whol. Ret.	1843-19??
Horton, J(ames), & Co. Ltd.	Swordplay; Kaufmann agent	London, Hamburg	EngL./Ger.	Wholesale	c1930
Hotchkissville Knife Co.	made by Am. Shear & Knife	Hotchkissville CT	USA	Mfr's brand	c1870?
Hounam, J. & H.R.		Sheffield	England	Mfr.	c1893
House, Hasson Hardware Co.		Knoxville TN		Hdw. Whol.	1907-?
House, J.	119 King St. Hammersmith	London	England	Retail?	
Hovenden, R., & Sons		London	England	Retail	c1880s
Howard Cutlery Co.	for C.B. Barker Co.	New York NY	Germany	Import brand	c1880-1905
Howard Cutlery Co.	made for Barker by Canastota	New York NY	USA	Wholesale brand	c1881-1895
Howarth, J.	Meadow Works	Sheffield	England	Mfr.?	19??-pres.
Howden, D.H., & Co., Ltd.		London, Ontario		Hdw. Whol.	1900-?
Howe, John		Sheffield	England	Mfr.	c1893
Howes Cutlery Co.			Germany	Import brand	c1900
Hoyland		Hull	England	Retail?	
Huba	Farmer (picture) see Hugo Bauermann				
Hubertus Schneidwarenfabrik	Kuno Ritter, owner	Solingen	Germany	Mfr.	1932-pres.
Hudson Cutlery Co.		New York NY	US/Ger.?	Whol. Import	
Hudson Knife Co.			Germany	Import brand	c1920s
Hudson Valley Cutlery Co.		? NY	USA?		c1890?
Hudson's Bay Company	marked on tang: c1915	Winnipeg, Manitoba	US/Eng/Ger	Retail, Trading	1670-pres.
Huey & Philp Hardware Co.		Dallas TX		Hdw. Whol. Ret.	1872-19??
Hukill-Hunter Co.		Pittsburgh PA		Hdw. Whol.	1902-?
Hulfish, Worth, & Sons	was Carlin-Hulfish Co.	Alexandria VA		Hdw. Whol.	1919-1963
Hulley, George		Sheffield	England	Mfr.	c1893
Humason & Beckley Mfg. Co.	H. & B. sold to Landers, Frary, & Clark 1912	New Britain CT	USA	Mfr.	1852-1916
Humphreys, W.R., & Co.	Radiant, Lamp (picture)	Sheffield	England	Mfr.	c1880-1970
Hunold, Ernest	Hunoldine Steel	Providence RI	England	Importer	c1893-1909
Hunt, N(athaniel), & Co.	sold to Kingman & Hassam	Boston MA	US/Engl.	Mfr. & Retail	C1840-1853
Hunter, J.B., Co.	incorporated 1914	Boston MA	Germany	Hdw. Whol. Ret.	c1901-1960
Hunter, Michael, & Sons	Bugle, Buffalo, Llama bought Parkin & Marshall, Slack & Grinold; sold to Needham, Veall & Tyzack	Sheffield	England	Mfr.	1780-1910s
Hurt, Samuel		Sheffield	England	Mfr.	c1893
Hutton, Joseph	sold pocketknives c1860	Sheffield	England	Sickle mfr.	17??-19??
Hutton, William & Sons	W.H. & S. on handle	Sheffield	England	Mfr.	c1870
I. & J. Mfg. Co.	Shur-Lock, Irene & Joseph Hopta	Plainfield NJ	USA	Mfr.?	c1950
I.K. CO. or IKCO	see Imperial Knife Co.	Providence RI	USA	Mfr.'s brand	1917-1940s
I.N.(C.) Co.	see Iowan Novelty (Cutlery) Company				
IR	under Crowned Eagle (picture) see Ignaz Rosler, Sons Cutlery Works				
I*XL	see George Wostenholm (for owners of mark after 1971, see Rodgers Wostenhom Ltd.)	Sheffield	England	Mfr.'s brand	1787-1971
I*XL - Schrade	see Rodgers Wostenholm Ltd.		England	Mfr.'s brand	1977-1982
Ibberson, George, & Co.	Violin (after 1880), # #	Sheffield	England	Mfr.	1700-1988
Ibbotson, Charles, & Co.	Slash, Early Bird (1890-) sold to Harrison Bros. & Howson	Sheffield	England	Mfr.	c1868-1902
Ibbotson, Henry		Sheffield	England	Mfr.	c1893
Ibbotson & Horner	American Cutlery	New York? NY	USA	Mfr.	c1850

POCKETKNIFE BRAND	TRADEMARK (or reference)	LOCATION	MADE IN	TYPE OF FIRM	DATES
Ibbotson Peace & Co.	became W.K. Peace & Co.	Sheffield	England	Mfr.	c1847-1864
Ideal	I-D-L, for Belknap Hdw. Co.	Louisville KY		Hdw. Whol. brand	1890s
Ideal Knife Co.	IDEAL/U.S.A.	Providence RI	USA	Mfr.(?)	1924-c1986
Illinois Cutlery Co.		Chicago IL	USA		c1911
Imco	made by Richartz		Germany	Import brand	c1950s
Imperial Knife Associated Cos.	Ulster Schrade Imperial	New York NY	USA	Mfrs.	1947-pres.
Imperial Knife Co.	IKCO, Crown, Hammer	Providence RI	USA	Mfr.	1917-1987
Imperial Knife Co.	Jackmaster, Apex, etc.	Ellenville NY			1947-2004
Imperial Knife Co.	(multi-colored handles)	Providence RI	USA	Mfr.	c1925-1942
Imperial Knife Co.	Stag Cutlery Co.	Listowel	Ireland	Mfr. & Exporter	current
Imperial			Mexico		recent
Imperial R(azor) Co.	(Cutwell) Kastor's first brand	New York NY	Germany	Whol. Import	c1880s-90s
India Steel Works	(John Primble) see Belknap Hardware Co.				
Indian Ridge Traders		Royal Oak MI	England	Retail	recent
Indiana Cutlery Co.	see Wabash Cutlery Co.	Terre Haute IN	USA	Mfr's brand	c1932
Industry Novelty Co.		Chicago IL	USA?	Ad Specialty?	1908-1917
Inox(ydable)	= Stainless (French)				
International Cutlery Co.	Star. See Clauss	Fremont OH		Import brand?	c1890-19??
Interstate Hardware & Supply Co.		Bristol VA		Hdw. Whol.	1905-?
Invicta, The	see E.M. Dickinson				
Iowan Novelty (Cutlery) Co.	I.N.Co. or I.N.C.Co.	Cedar Rpds, Keota,IA	USA	prob. Whol.	c1910s
Iroquois	probably by Utica	Utica NY	USA	Mfr's brand?	c1930s-40s
Iroskeen	see I. Rosenbaum				
Isonit	see Needham Veall & Tyzack				
Ivanhoe	see Henry Rossell & Co.				
Iver Johnson S(porting) G(oods) Co.	by Russell, N.Y.K.Co., etc.	Boston MA	USA	Retail	c1912
Iversen & Albrecht	agent for J.A. Henckels	New York NY	Germany	Whol. Import	c1948-1960
Ives, W.A., Mfg. Co.		Meriden CT	USA	Mfr.	19th cent.
J.C.N. Co. (Pat. 11-9-37)	made by G. Schrade	Jersey City NJ (?)	USA	Ad. Spec.?	c1940
J.D. & S.	see James Dixon & Sons				
J.E./18/74	see John Engstrom				
J.M.	(Nogent-inox) see Jacques Mongin				
JR	in hallmark on silver fruit knives: see John Round & Son				
J.R & S	in hallmark on silver fruit knives: see Joseph Rodgers & Sons				
J.Y.C.	in hallmark on silver fruit knives: see John Y. Cowlishaw				
Jack Knife Ben	Benjamin W. Chon (b. 1863) Made by Napanoch (?-1919), Schrade Cut. Co. (?-1927), Utica Cut. Co., others	Chicago IL	USA	Retail	1887-1940s
Jack Knife Ben's Handy Dandy	by Schrade Cut. Co.	Chicago IL	USA	Retailer brand	c1904-1927
Jack Knife Ben	for Parker KCS	Chattanooga TN	USA/Japan	Whol. brand	c1993-pres.
Jack Knife Shop	Union Stockyards	Chicago IL	USA	Retail	
Jack-O-Matic	by Imperial Knife	Providence RI	USA	Mfr.'s brand	1943-1958
Jackmaster (Hammer Brand)	by Imperial Knife Co.	Providence RI	USA/Ireland	Mfr.'s brand	1938-pres.
Jackson, George		Sheffield	England	Mfr.	c1893
Jackson Knife & Shear Co.		Fremont OH	USA	Mfr.	c1899-1914
Jackson, William (& Co.)	Sheaf Island works	Sheffield	England	Mfr.	c1850s-90s
Jacobs & Co.	AdanaC (= CanadA)	? Canada	England	Retail?	c1910?
Jacoby & Wester	became Wester Bros.	New York NY	Germany	Whol. Import	1891-1902
Jaeger Bros.	see Aerial Cutlery Co.				
Jaeger, Joseph	Palm	Los Angeles CA		Whol. or Retail	c1891-1909
Janney, Semple & Co.	Janney, Semple, Hill c1920	Minneapolis MN		Hdw. Whol.	1857-c1950
Jarvis, James		Sheffield	England	Mfr.	c1893
Javorka			Austria?	Mfr.?	c1890?
Jeffrey	by Bertram		Germany	Retail	c1971
Jensen-King-Byrd Co.		Spokane WA		Hdw. Whol. Ret.	1883-19??
Jet-Aer Corp.	G-96	Paterson NJ		Whol. Import	1973-pres.
Jet Knife Corporation	Patent 2,416,277	New York NY	USA	Mfr.?	1947-?
Jim Bowie	see Carl Schlieper				
John Bull	see Hearnshaw Bros.				
John Jay	see Union Cutlery Co.				
Johnson, Christopher, (& Co.)	CJ in flag; to I*XL 1955	Sheffield	England	Mfr.	1836-c1956

POCKETKNIFE BRAND	TRADEMARK (or reference)	LOCATION	MADE IN	TYPE OF FIRM	DATES
Johnson Cutlery Co.	J.C./CO.	Des Moines IA	USA	Retail?	c1929-1931
Johnson, George, & Co.	Seven stars (picture)	Sheffield	England	Mfr.	1810-1855
Johnson, James		Sheffield	England	Mfr.	c1818-1853
Johnson Western Works	see Christopher Johnson & Co.				
Johnston	see Federal Knife Company				
Jonas & Colver	I C in spectacles	Sheffield	England	Steel Mfr.	c1892-1967
Jones, Thomas		Sheffield	England	Mfr.	c1893
Jordan, A(ndrew) J(ackson)	AAA1, Adolphus, Old Faithful A.J. Jordan b.1846; Twentieth Century Cutlery Co.; agent of Friedmann & Lauterjung	Saint Louis MO	Eng./Ger.	Whol. & Mfr.	1871-1929
Jordan, F.W.	probably by Krusius Bros.	New York?	Germany	Import brand	c1920s
Joseph, Nathan	Queen's Own Co.	San Francisco CA	England	Whol. Import	c1873-1894
Jowett, John	Royal Albion, Knowles	Sheffield	England	Mfr.	1870s-1920s
Jowika Stahlwarenfabrik	Weber & Altenbach Listowel, Ireland, factory now owned by Imperial Schrade, managed by Henry Weber	Solingen	Ger./Ireland	Mfr.	current
Judson Cutlery Co.		New York NY	Ger./US	Whol.	c1900-1940
Justice, A(lfred) R., Co.	Battle Axe Cutlery Co.	Philadelphia PA		Hdw. Whol.	1877-1937
K. & B. Cutlery Co.	see Kruse & Bahlmann Hardware Co.				
K.B. Extra	see Krusius Brothers				
K. & D.	see Kraut & Dohnal				
K.Z. & M.	see Krakauer, Zork & Moye				
K55K Black Cat	see Heinrich Kauffmann				
KA-BAR	(only mark) see Kabar Cutlery Co.				
KA-BAR/Union Cut. Co.	see Union Cutlery Co.	Olean NY	USA	Mfr.'s brand	1923-1951
KA-BAR/Olean N.Y.	see KA-BAR/UNION CUT. CO.				
KA-BAR/U.S.A.	see Kabar Cutlery Co.				
KA-BAR/(number) USA	see Kabar (Cole National)				
Kabar Cutlery Co.	KA-BAR, KA-BAR/U.S.A. successor to Union Cutlery Co.	Olean NY	USA	Mfr.	1951-c1966
Kabar	Cole National Corp. sold to Alcas Cutlery Co. 1996	Olean NY	USA	Mfr.'s brand	1996-pres.
Kai Cutlery Co.	makes some Kershaw, etc.	Seki City	Japan	Contract Mfr.	current
Kaleski's Settlers (Robert Kaleski)	made by Thomas Turner	? Australia	England	Writer	c1909
Kaliakin, John		Vyatka (or Kirov)	Russia	Mfr.	c1876
Kaminski Hardware Co., The		Georgetown SC		Hdw. Whol.	1865-19??
Kammerling, Carl, & Co.	owns P.L. Schmidt, Wintgen	Elberfeld	Germany	Mfr.	1904-pres.
Kamp Cutlery Co.			Germany		c1910
Kamp King see Imperial Knife Co.				Mfr.'s brand	1935-pres.
Kamphaus, P.	Granate (K.B. Dorndorf)	Solingen	Germany	Mfr.	c1797-pres.
Kamphausen & Pluemacher		Solingen-Ohligs	Germany	Mfr.	1860-19??
Kane Cutlery Co.	became Hollingsworth	Kane PA	USA	Mfr.	c1910-1916
Kane Cutlery Co.	for Parker KCS	Chattanooga TN	USA/Japan	Whol. brand	c1993-pres.
Karlsson		Eskilstuna	Sweden	Mfr.?	c1910
Kase (with soccer ball and foot)	by Boentgen & Sabin	Solingen	Germany	Mfr.'s brand	c1960s?
Kastor, Adolph, & Bros.	XLNT, EBRO, Clover Camillus, Koester's, Germania, Morley, Duane, Syracuse, Streamline, Stainless Cutlery Co., etc.	New York NY	Ger./USA	Whol./Imp./Mfr.	1876-c1947
Kastor, N(athan)	buyer for Adolph Kastor also see Germania Cutlery Works	Solingen-Ohligs	Germany	Factor, Export	c1885-1930s
Kaufmann, Heinrich, & Soehne	Mercator, K55K, Indiawerk imported to Great Britain by J. Horton & Co. Ltd. c1930	Solingen	Germany	Mfr.	1856-pres.
Kay, John		New Haven CT	USA	Mfr.?	c1857
Kaye	Sheffield made	Hull		England	Retail
Kaylan		Syracuse NY			
Keen Edge	see Canton Hardware Co. or Keith Simmons & Co.				
Keen Kutter	see Miller Brothers & Keep			Whol. brand	18??-c1873
Keen Kutter, Simmons	see E.C. Simmons Hdw.	St. Louis MO	USA	Hdw. Whol. brand	1868-1940
Keen Kutter	see Shapleigh Hdw.	St. Louis MO	USA	Hdw. Whol. brand	1940-1960
Keen Kutter	by Schrade for Val-Test	Chicago IL	USA	Whol. brand	1960-1965
Keen Kutter	for Frost Cutlery	Chattanooga TN	USA	Whol. brand	1991-pres.
Keen(e?) Cutlery Co.	made by Napanoch (1)	New York NY(?)	USA	Whol. brand?	19??
Keener Edge	see C.M. McClung Hardware Co.				
Kee-nife	see Imperial	Providence RI	USA	Mfr.'s brand	c1950
Keenwell Mfg. Co.	by Union Cutlery Co.	Olean NY	USA	Mfr.'s brand	c1910
Keidel, Henry, & Co.	Rangoon	Baltimore MD		Hdw. Whol.	1866-c1926
Keith Simmons & Co.	Keen Edge, Washington Cutlery (from Gray & Dudley c1927)	Nashville TN		Hdw. Whol.	1899-pres.
Kelley-How-Thomson Co.	Hickory (some by Napanoch)	Duluth MN	USA	Hdw. Whol.	1896-c1947
Kellogg Johnson & Bliss	made by Wester & Butz	Chicago IL	Germany	Advt. Spec.?	c1893

POCKETKNIFE BRAND	TRADEMARK (or reference)	LOCATION	MADE IN	TYPE OF FIRM	DATES
Kendal Mfg. Co.	see American Knife Co.	Winsted CT	USA	Mfr.	c1948
Kent/N.Y.C.	for Woolworths by Camillus	New York NY	USA	Retail brand	c1931-1955
Kentucky Cutlery Association·					
Kenyon, John, & Co.	Fulltone, Fulton, IK	Sheffield	England	Mfr.	c1870-1960
Kerau	see Sanderson Bros. (& Newbould)				
Kershaw Cutlery Co.	made by Kai and also in-house	Wilsonville OR	Japan	Whol. Import	1974-2004
Kershaw Cutlery Co.	made by Kai and also in-house	Tualatin OR	USA	Whol. Import & Mfr.	2004-pres.
Keschner, H.	Diamond, Antelope		Germany	Ad. Spec.?	c1920s?
Key	(picture) see Steer & Webster, George Butler & Co.				
Keys, Crossed	(picture) see Friedr. Herder. Abr. Sohn				
Keyes Cutlery Co.		Unionville CT	USA	Mfr.	pre-1893
Keyport Cutlery Co.		Keyport NJ	USA	Mfr.	c1911
Keystone Cutlery (& Hardware) Co.		Milwaukee WI		Hdw. Whol.	c1925-1938
Keystone Knife Co.	keystone shaped shield	Titusville PA	USA	Mfr.?	
Khyber	for Kabar (Cole National)	Cleveland OH	Japan	Import brand	recent
Kinfolks Inc.	Kinfolks, K.I., Jean Case	Little Valley NY	USA	Mfr.	1926-c1951
Kinfolks	mark bought by Robeson	Perry NY	USA	Mfr.'s brand	c1951-1965
Kinfolks	for Parker KCS	Chattanooga TN	USA	Whol. brand	c1993-pres.
King, H. & J.W.	Warranted 1869	New York NY		USA?	c1870
King Hardware Co.	The King Bee	Atlanta GA	USA?	Hdw. Whol.	1886-c1952
King's head in profile	see Weyersberg				
Kingman & Hassam	became Hassam Brothers (qv)				
Kingston	blade etch: see Ulster Knife Co.		USA	Mfr.'s brand	c1915-1958
Kingston (Knife Co.)	on bail of GI utility knife joint venture by Ulster & Imperial	Ellenville NY and Providence RI	USA	Mfr.	c1943-1945
Kinson Cutlery Co.		Richmond VA	USA?	Retail?	
Kippax, John	Kippax, Pearl	Sheffield	England	Mfr.	c1787
Kipsi Kut/Pokipsi N.Y.	see Poughkeepsie Cutlery Works				
Kirk, Henry		Sheffield	England	Mfr.	c1893
Kirk, James		Sheffield	England	Mfr.	c1893
Kitchin, S(amuel) & J.	XCD, Snake (picture), Fame	Sheffield	England	Mfr.	1855-1960s
Klaas, Robert	"Kissing" Cranes	Solingen	Germany	Mfr.	1834-1980s
Klaas, Robert	Cranes, for Smoky Mtn.	Sevierville TN	Italy	Retail brand	current
Klauberg, Carl. & Bros.	[or Clauberg] Damascene	New York NY	Germany	Whol. Import	c1819-1940
Klein, M(athias), & Sons	knives by Utica 1911-pres.	Chicago IL	USA	Electric Whol.	1857-pres.
Kleppish, Henry M.		New York NY		Whol. Import	1860-19??
KlicKer	see Shapleigh	St. Louis MO	USA	Hdw. Whol. brand	c1958
Klostermeir Bros. Hardware Co.		Atchison KS		Hdw. Whol.	c1900-?
Knapp & Spencer	Regent	Sioux City IA		Hdw. Whol.	1868-19??
Knauth, G(ustav) C.		Spring Valley, NYC NY	USA	Mfr.?	c1900-1941
Knecht, August		Solingen	Germany	Mfr.	c1910?
Knife Collector's Club	A.G. Russell III	Springdale AR	US/Ger.	Retail	c1974-pres
Knox-All	see Merrimac Cutlery Co.				
Koch, F.A., & Co.		New York NY	Ger./US	Whol.	1874-c1933
Koeller (Koller) F., & Co.	Elephant, Magna, WEXL	Solingen-Ohligs	Germany	Mfr.	1855-pres?
Koeller & Schmitz Cutlery Co.	see Fox Cutlery Co.				
Koester's, J(acob), Sons	see Adolph Kastor & Bros. (Koester was the German spelling of Kastor)				
KoiNife	see Hickok Mfg. Co.				
Koller, F.	variant of Koeller				
Koller, Hugo	Eagle	Solingen	Germany	Mfr.	1861-pres?
Komins Brothers		Philadelphia PA		Hdw. Whol.	1917-?
Kompak	see Napanoch (1)				
Koncept	Varitork. Catoctin distrib.	Smithsburg MD	USA	Mfr.	current
Kondratov, Demetrius	Imperial Eagle (picture)	Vyatka (or Kirov)	Russia	Mfr.	1870-1917?
Konejung, Hermann	Spectacles, Hammers	Solingen	Germany	Mfr.	1873-pres.
Korff & Honsberg	Cherub (picture)	Remscheid	Germany	Mfr.?	c1930s
Korn, George W(illiam)	1846-1919; Razor Co. 1900-25	NYC & Litt. Valley, NY	US/Ger.	Inventor & Imp.	c1880-1919
Korten & Scherf			Germany	Mfr.?	c1900?

POCKETKNIFE BRAND	TRADEMARK (or reference)	LOCATION	MADE IN	TYPE OF FIRM	DATES
Krakauer, Zork & Moye	K.Z. & M., Krack-A-Jack	San Antonio TX, El Paso TX, Chihuahua Mexico	USA?	Hdw. Whol.	1885-c1910
Krakauer, Zork Co.		El Paso TX, Phoenix AZ, Chihuahua	Mexico	Hdw. Whol.	c1910-?
Kraut(, Emil) & Dohnal(, Ignate)	K. & D., Topnotch	Chicago IL	USA?	Retail?	c1902-1937
Krebs, Peter Daniel	Lobster (picture)	Solingen	Germany	Mfr.	c1870-1954
Krespach, C.		Mainz	Germany	Retail	c1890s
Krieghoff, Heinrich, Waffenbrik	sold tool kit knives	Suhl	Germany	Arms mfr.	c1910?
Kroner, Fred, Hardware Co.		Lacrosse WI	Germany	Hdw. Whol. Ret.	1865-19??
Kruse & Bahlmann Hardware Co.	K. & B., Cut Sure	Cincinnati OH	USA	Hdw. Whol.	1858-1962
Krusius Brothers	K.B. Extra, Primrose	New York NY	Germany	Whol. Import	c1888-1927
Krusius, Gebruder (Brothers)		Solingen	Germany	Mfr.	1856-1983
Kunde & Co., Kuhn	budding & grafting knives	Dresden, Remscheid	Germany		?-pres.
Kutmaster	see Utica Cutlery Co.	Utica NY	USA	Mfr.'s brand	1937-pres.
Kutwell	made by Union Cutlery	Olean NY	USA	Mfr.'s brand	c1930s
Kwik Kut	Sears Roebuck's cheapest brand, made by Camillus	Chicago IL	USA	Retail brand	c1939
L.A. Co.			Germany	Import brand?	c1952
L.C.A. Hardware Co.	see Lee-(Clarke)-Coit-Andreesen Hardware Co.				
L.C. Co.	see Lackawanna Cutlery Co.				
L. Co., The	see Lockwood Luetkemeyer Henry Hardware Co.				
L.F. & C.	see Landers Frary & Clark				
L.K. Co.	see Liberty Knife Co.				
L.L.H. Co.	see Lockwood Luetkemeyer Henry				
L.V. Knife Association	see Little Valley Knife Association				
La Barge	= the godwit (bird)	Thiers?	France	Mfr.'s brand	c1900?
La Colombe	= the dove (French)	Laguiole?	France	Mfr.'s brand	current
LaBelle Cutlery Works	Smith Sutton & Co. formerly James D. Fray & Son Co.; managed by Harry L. Frary, son of J.D. Frary	Bridgeport CT	USA	Mfr.	c1884-1888
Lackawanna Cutlery Co.	L.C.Co.; was Eureka Cutlery	Nicholson PA	USA	Mfr.	1917-1930
Lackawanna Cutlery Co.	for Parker KCS	Chattanooga TN	USA/Japan	Whol. brand	c1993-pres.
Lacy's Deer Knife	by Joseph Rodgers	Sheffield	England	Mfr.'s brand?	c1830s
Lafayette Cutlery Co.	O.U.	110 Lafayette St, NYC	Germany	Whol. Import	c1910s-20s
Laguiole	(place and pattern name)		France		
Lakeside Cutlery Co.	sold by Montgomery Ward pocketknives made by Challenge Cutlery Co.	Chicago IL	USA	Retail brand?	c1922-1928
Lakota Corp.		Riverton WY	USA	Mfr.	current
Lamson & Goodnow	made folding knife & fork sets (slot knives) c1862-1880s	Shelburne Falls MA	USA	Mfr.	1844-pres.
Lamson & Goodnow	(pocketknives 1870s-80s made by Waterville, Gardner)	Shelburne Falls MA	USA	Whol.	1844-pres.
Lancaster	made by Schrade Walden		USA	Retail brand?	c1947-1954
Landers Frary & Clark (Universal)	(pocketknives 1914-1930s)	New Britain CT	USA	Mfr.	1862-1965
Landis Brothers (Henry, Reuben)	Pat. Nov. 11, 1879	Canton OH	USA	Inventors (Mfr)	c1879
Lane Bros.		"Sheffield"	Germany	Import brand	c1880s
Langbein, Charles		New York NY		Retail & Whol.	c1880s-90s
Langbein, William, & Bros.	L in swastika of 4 legs	New York NY		Whol. & Retail	c1900-60s
Langenberg, Jul.		Solingen	Germany	Mfr.	1879-?
Langley, Elliot W.		New York NY	USA?	Mfr.?	1892-?
Langres	(place name)		France		
Lark (Lerche)	see Peter Daniel Baus				
Larrabee & North		Chicago IL		Wholesale	?-1874
Laufbrunnen	= flowing well (German) see W. Weltersbach				
Lauterjung & Co.	Tiger, Cervo. (Eicker)	Solingen	Germany	Mfr.	1813-pres.
Lauterjung & Sohn	now called Puma-Werk (which see)				
Law Bros.	Celebrated Cutlery		Germany	Import Brand	c1890s
Law, Charles, & Sons		Sheffield	England	Mfr.	c1893
Law, Joseph	LIBERTY on bolster	Sheffield	England	Mfr.	c1820
Lawrence, G(eorge), H.	Laurel	Sheffield	England	Mfr.	c1919-1952
Lawton Cutlery Co.		Chicago IL	USA?	Retail?	c1895

POCKETKNIFE BRAND	TRADEMARK (or reference)	LOCATION	MADE IN	TYPE OF FIRM	DATES
Layman & Carey Co.	Dorsey & Layman-1873	Indianapolis IN		Hdw. Whol.	1865-c1920
Leas Hardware Co.		Delaware OH		Hdw. Whol.	1892-?
Leatherman Tool Group	plier knives	Portland OR	USA	Mfr.	c1984-pres.
LeBalkanique		Thiers?	France	Export brand	
Lectrolite Corp.	Flipnife	New York NY			c1947
Lee-(Clarke)-Coit-Andreesen Hdw. Co.	L.C.A. Coit (1914-)	Omaha NE		Hdw. Whol.	1881-19??
Lee Hardware Co.		Shreveport LA		Hdw. Whol.	1899-?
Lee Hardware Co.		Salina KS		Hdw. Whol.	1902-pres.
Lee, J.		Medway MA	USA	Mfr.?	c1830
Lehrkine & Daevel Co.		Milwaukee WI			
Lenox Cutlery Co.		New York NY	Germany	Import	c1909-1920
Leon, Abraham	Solly Street	Sheffield	England	Mfr.	c1850
Leonard, A.M., Inc.	(knives with this mark made for Leonard by Schrade before 1960)	Piqua OH	US/Ger./Eng	Horticultural Supply Retail	1885-pres.
Leppington (Cutlers) Ltd.	Cutlass	Sheffield	England	Mfr. or Whol.	c1950s-70s
LeRoi Corn Knife	see Forquignon				
Letang Hardware Co., Ltd.		Montreal, Quebec		Hdw. Whol.	1900-?
Levenson's Radio	sold knives in WWII	Sydney	Australia	Retail	1920s-1965
Lever Cutlery Co.		New York NY	USA?	Mfr.?	1898- ?
Levering A1 Knife Co.		New York NY		Whol.?	c1890?
Levigne	lizard (picture) see Pierre Tarry-Levigne				
Lewis & Bennett Hardware Co.	predecessor est. 1826	Wilkes-Barre PA		Hdw. Whol.	1912-?
Lewis Bros. (& Co.), Ltd.	Klean Kutter	Montreal, Quebec		Hdw. Whol.	1887-19??
Lewis, J.C.	Pat. 1900. see 0. Barnett Tool Co.				
Liberty Knife Co.	L.K. Co.	New Haven CT	USA	Mfr.	c1919-1925
Lincoln		Sheffield	England	Mfr.?	19th cent.
Lincoln Novelty Co.			USA	Wholesale	c1930s
Linden Knife Co.		Linden NJ			
Linder & Co.	Junkerwerk	Solingen	Germany	Mfr.	1887-pres.
Linder, C(arl) & R(obert)	crown/pruning knife absorbed by Carl Linder Nachf.	Solingen-Weyer	Germany	Mfr.	1842-1971
Linder, Carl, Nachf.	Rehwappen	Solingen	Germany	Mfr.	1908-pres.
Linder, Hugo	Deltawerk	Solingen	Germany	Mfr.	1878-1957
Lindsay, James C., Hardware Co.	Lindsay Mfg., True Blue	Pittsburgh PA		Hdw. Whol.	1867-c1926
Lindstrom, C.J.		Eskilstuna	Sweden	Mfr.	c1900
Lingard, Joseph	I-Fly, Shuttle (picture), XLNT marks owned by G. C. W. Barron 1919	Sheffield	England	Mfr.	c1842-1880s
Lingard, Robert	Pea croft	Sheffield	England	Mfr.	1862-1890s
Lion lying down	(picture) see C. Lutters				
Lion standing up	(picture) see Carl Spitzer				
Lipic, Joseph, Pen Co.		St. Louis MO	USA	Ad. Specialties	?-pres.
Lipscomb, H.G., & Co.	Watauga, Belle Meade	Nashville TN	USA	Hdw. Whol.	1891-19??
Little Valley Knife Association	forerunner of Crandall	Little Valley NY	USA	Whol.	1900-c1905
Little Valley Knife Association	for Parker KCS	Chattanooga TN	USA/Japan	Whol. brand	c1993-pres.
Lizrad	(picture) see Pierre Tarry-Levigne				
Llama	see Needham Veall & Tyzack				
Lloyd, Supplee & Walton	became Supplee Hdwe. Co.	Philadelphia PA		Hdw. Whol.	19th cent.
Lockwood E./Lockwood, Alfred L.	same as Lockwood Mfg.?	Springfield MA	USA?	Retail?	c1900
Lockwood Mfg. Co.		Boston, Chelsea MA	USA?	Retail?	c1900?
Lockwood Bros.	C+X, Pampa, Rhea (bird) merged with Joseph Elliott & Sons, 1919; Lockwood name last used c1933	Sheffield	England	Mfr.	1798-c1933
Lockwood Luetkemeyer Henry Hdw. Co. (The Luetkemeyer Co.)	Thelco, L.L.H.; formerly Lockwood-Taylor (1876-), H.W. Luetkemeyer (1848-), McIntosh Hdw. (1875-)	Cleveland OH	US/England	Hdw. Whol.	1848-19??
Logan, Gregg Hardware Co.		Pittsburgh PA		Hdw. Whol.	1831-19??
Logan/Smyth	Air Force contractor	Venice FL	USA?	Mfr.?	1986-1988
Long		Oxford	England	Retail?	c1880
Long, Hawksley & Co.	became H. G. Long	Sheffield	England	Mfr.	c1846-1911
Long, H(enry) G(odfrey), & Co.	was Long, Hawksley & Co. name and crossed swords mark (reg. 1833) last owned by H. M. Slater	Sheffield	England	Mfr.	1911-1991
Longden, John H., & Son		Sheffield	England	Mfr.	c1893
Lopez, F.		Albacete	Spain	Mfr.?	
Lord Bros.			Germany?	Import brand	c1880s

POCKETKNIFE BRAND	TRADEMARK (or reference)	LOCATION	MADE IN	TYPE OF FIRM	DATES
Lowe, F.G., & Sons		Sheffield	England	Mfr.	c1893
Lowenstein & Sons	Greenbrier	Charleston WV	USA?	Whol./Retail	c1900?
Lower, J.P., & Sons			Germany?	Export brand	c1880s
Lubin	perhaps Weinstock Lubin	San Francisco? CA	Austria?	Retail?	c1890s
Ludo Cutlery Co.		Solingen?	Germany	Mfr.'s brand	c1920s
Luetkemeyer, The, Co.	see Lockwood Luetkemeyer	Henry Hdw. Co.			
Luger Knife	see Track Knives (Luger shield: see Knife Collectors Club)				
Luna, Lunawerk	see A. Feist & Co.				
Lunt	Fleet Street	London	England		Retail
Luthe Hdw. Co. (Patrick & Luthe)	marked knives c1917 ff.	Des Moines IA	USA	Hdw. Whol.	1892-1955
Lutters, C., & Co.	Lion lying down (picture)	Solingen	Germany	Mfr.	1840-pres.
Luttrell, S(amuel) B(ell), & Co.	Cranberry; sold to McClung	Knoxville TN		Hdw. Whol.	1870-19??
Lux, Louis		New York NY	Germany	Whol. Import	c1920
Luxrite		Hollywood CA			
Lyon Cutlery Co.	resemble Frary knives	Bridgeport? CT	USA?	Import?	1880s
M.B. Co.	on silver plated fruit knives: see Meriden Britannia Co.				
M.B.C. Co.	probably Miller Brothers Cutlery Co.				
M/C.A.F.	(M as mountains) see Centazzo, Angelo e Figli			Mfr.'s brand	?-1950
M.C. Co.	Anvil (picture) see Meriden Cutlery Company				
M.C. Co.	(monogram) see Magnetic Cutlery Co.		USA	Whol. brand	c1910s
M.F. & S.	see M. Furness & Sons				
M. Fruit Knife Pat. Apr. 26,'81	see Miller Brothers Cutlery Co.				
M.K.L.	Finest Steel		Czecho.	Import brand?	c1920s
M.S.A. Co.	see Marble's Safety Axe Co.				
M.S. Ltd. XX	see Case XX Metal Stampings Ltd.				
M.W.H. Co.	see Marshall Wells Hardware Co.				
MacBrair Brothers & Co.		Sheffield	England	Mfr.	c1893
Machenbach, Karl Friedrich		Cologne	Germany	Adv. Spec.?	c1910?
Mack Hardware Co.	some made by F. Collini	Boston MA	Italy	Retail?	c1940
Macupa		Solingen	Germany	Mfr.'s brand?	
Magna	see F. Koeller & Co.				
Magnetic Cutlery Co.	O. & F. Maussner Blue Bird brand, made by Daniel Peres; M.C. Co. (monogram), made by Union Cutlery Co.	Philadelphia PA	Germany	Whol. (Ret?)	c1900-1932
Maher & Grosh	to Clyde OH 1963	Toledo OH	USA	Retail mail	1877-198?
Maine Cutlery Co.	for J.B.F. Champlin & Son	Little Valley NY	Germany	Import brand	c1883
Mairowttz & Buscher	M. & B.S., key and rope	Solingen	Germany	Mfr. ?	c1860s
Majestic Cutlery Co.			Germany	Import Brand	c1910
Maleham & Yeomans	(beware of fakes)	Sheffield	England	Mfr.	1876-1970
Malinda Works	see Abram Brooksbank				
Manby, George		Sheffield	England	Mfr.	c1893
Manchester			USA	Po'k. skeletons	c1920s?
Manhattan Cutlery Co.	see John Newton & Co.; imported by H. Boker & Co.			Mfr.'s brand	c1861-1916
Maniago	(place name)		Italy		c1300-pres
Maniago Knives Makers Association	MKM	Maniago	Italy	Mfr.'s assoc.	current
Manico, E.C., & Co.		Sheffield	England	Mfr.	c1893
Mann & Federlein		Solingen	Germany	Mfr.?	
Manson		Sheffield	England	Mfr.	19th cent.
Mantua Cutlery Co.			Germany	Import brand?	c1900
Manufacturer's Union Cutlery Co.		Chicago IL	England?	Whol.?	c1880s
Mappin, Joseph	Sun; Arundel & Mappin 1820s	Sheffield	England	Mfr.	1810-1841
Mappin Brothers	Frederick Thorpe Mappin absorbed William Sampson & Sons 1845; opened London shop 1845, London warehouse 1856; opened Queen's Cutlery Works 1851; sold to a jeweler 1889; sold to Mappin & Webb 1902	Sheffield	England	Mfr. & Retail	1841-1902
Mappin & Co.	became Mappin & Webb	Sheffield, London	England	Plater & Retail	1861-1868
Mappin & Webb	M Trustworthy, Tusca; Sun	Sheffield, London	England	Mfr. & Retail	1868-pres.
Mar, Al, Knives	Al Mar d. 1992	Lake Oswego OR	Japan	Whol. Importer	1979-circa 2000
Mar, Al, Knives	Al Mar d. 1992	Tigard OR	Japan	Whol. Importer	circa 2000-pres.
Marble's Safety Axe Co.	Marble's folding hunter made c1900-1942; see Fixed Blades, Amelican Hunting Knives	Gladstone MI	USA	Mfr.	1898-pres.

POCKETKNIFE BRAND	TRADEMARK (or reference)	LOCATION	MADE IN	TYPE OF FIRM	DATES
Marble's Safety Axe Co.	M.S.A. Co. pocketknives made by a contractor c1902-1908	Gladstone MI	USA	Whol.	1898-pres.
Marble's	by Olbertz for Parker KCS Marble's name restored to Marble Arms by court oeder August 1996	Chattanooga TN	Germany	Import brand	c1993-1996
Mark		Solingen?	Germany	Export brand?	c1850s
Marks, I.			England?	Retail?	19th cent.
Marples, Robert Henry	Well in (front) of all	Sheffield	England	Mfr.	18??-1950s
Marples, Thomas	T.M. silver fruit knives	Sheffield	England	Mfr.	1855-?
Marriott (Marriott & Atkinson)		Sheffield	England	Mfr.	c1840-1875
Marsden Brothers & Co.		Sheffield	England	Mfr.	c1893
Marsden, William W.		Sheffield	England	Mfr.	c1850-1870
Marsh, Arthur, & Son	A.M. & S. in ribbon	Sheffield	England	Mfr.	c1845-19??
Marsh Brothers (William & Thomas)	Pond Works, Roxo also called James Marsh & Co. (1815-1828), Marshes & Sheperd Pond Works (1828-1960s)	Sheffield, NYC NY	England	Mfr.	1631-1960s
Marshall Field & Co.	see Field, Marshall, & Co.				
Marshall, W. H.		Sheffield	England	Mfr.	c1893
Marshall Wells Hardware Co.	M.W.H. Co.; Zenith; Hartford branches at Portland OR, Spokane WA, Billings MT, Great Falls MT; Winnipeg, Edmonton, Vancouver	Duluth MN	USA	Hdw. Whol.	1888-1963
Marshes & Sheperd	Pond Works; see Marsh Brothers				
Martin Bros. & Naylor	became Martin & Hall	Shelffield, London	England	Plater & Retail	c1849-1854
Martin, Finlayson & Mather, Ltd.		Vancouver BC		Hdw. Whol. Ret.	1901-?
Martin Fre(re)s	= Martin Bro(ther)s	Perpignan	France	Retail?	c1930?
Martin, James	became W. H. Sample	Albany NY		Mfr. & Retail	1831-1871
Martinez-Gomez S.A.E.Z.	Martinez, Gomez	Albacete	Spain	Mfr.	current
Marx & Co.			Germany	Whol. Import?	c1880s
Marx Cutlery Co.		Boston MA	Ger./Brazil	Whol. Import	current
Masahiro Cutlery Co.	makes Al Mat Knives	Seki City	Japan	Contract Mfr.	current
Massillon Cutlery Co.	successor to Ohio Cutlery Co.	Massillon OH	USA	Mfr.	c1924-5
Mason, George		Sheffield	England	Mfr.	c1893
Mason, H.H.		Worcester MA	USA	Custom Mfr.	c1890
Mason & Sons		Canton OH			
Mason, William B.		Sheffield	England	Mfr.	c1893
Master Barlow, Master	made by Colonial	Providence RI	USA	Mfr.'s brand	1939-pres.
Master Mechanic	by Schrade for True Value			Whol. brand	current
Master Quality	see Montgomery Ward				
Maussner, Otto	in Solingen 1855-87, Riga 1887-90, Phila. 1900-10		Ger./Latvia	Whol. (Retail?)	c1855-1910
Maussner, Otto	(& Frank, after 1910) see Magnetic Cutlery Co.				
Maw, (J. &) S.		London	England	Mfr. & Retail	c1807-1901
May, F.P., Hardware Co.		Washington DC		Hdw. Whol.	1874-19??
Mayer, G.M.	Diamond (outline)	New York NY	Germany	Import	c1920
Mazeppa	see Samuel Hancock & Sons and B. Worth & Sons				
Mazer, G.	31 Royal Exchange	London	England	retail	c1910
McAvity, T., & Sons, Ltd.		St. John NB		Hdw. Whol. Ret.	1834-19??
McClory, John, & Sons	Scotia, Thistle (picture)	Sheffield	England	Mfr.	c1870-pres.
McClung, C(alvin) M(organ), & Co.	Cranberry, Keener Edge	Knoxville TN	USA/Ger.	Hdw. Whol.	1880-c1960
McCoy, Jos(eph) F., Co.	Monarch, Axiom was called McCoy & Sanders c1887	New York NY		Import	1805-19??
McCrory Stores	Aristocrat	New York NY		Retail	c1930s-50s
McGovern, Bernard	made knives for Frary, E.C. Simmons, Ephraim Turner (whip knife)	Bridgeport CT	USA	Contract Mfr. and Inventor	c1880s
McGregor-Noe Hardware Co.		Springfield MO		Hdw. Whol.	1866-19??
McIlwaine Linn & Hughes	Sterling Cutlery Co.	New York NY	Ger./Engl.	Whol. Import	1895-c19l4
McIntosh (-Huntington) Hdw. Co.	Heather; became L.L.H.	Cleveland OH		Hdw. Whol.	1875-1911
McKnight Wholesale Hardware Co.		Wichita KS		Hdw. Whol.	1891-19??
McLean, T.	Sheffield made		England	Retail?	c1890?
McL(endon) (Duncan) Hardware Co.	some by Schatt & Morgan	Waco TX	USA	Hdw. Whol.	1882-c1945
McLoud, Cecil	cMc on handle he was deaf and blind	New Orleans LA	USA	Shoemaker	died c1977
McPherson Bros.	some by Jos. Rodgers	Glasgow, Scotland	England	Retail?	c1910
Meeson, J.W., & Sons	J.W.M.	Sheffield	England	Mfr.?	c1840
Mehasco	see Merchants' Hardware Specialties, Ltd			Hdw. Whol. brand	
Melcher, Gust(av)		Solingen	Germany	Mfr.?	
Mella	Mella Brand	Solingen	Germany	Mfr.'s brand	c1950?
Mellowes & Co. Ltd.		Sheffield?	England	Mfr.?	c1900
Melrose Cutlery Co.			Germany	Import brand	c1920s

POCKETKNIFE BRAND	TRADEMARK (or reference)	LOCATION	MADE IN	TYPE OF FIRM	DATES
Melton Hardware Co., The		Meridian MS		Hdw. Whol.	1880-19??
Mercator	see Heinrich Kauffmann				
Merchants' Hdwe. Specialties, Ltd.	Mehasco	Calgary AB		Hdw. Whol.	1911-?
Meriden Britannia Co.	M.B. Co. on fruit knives	West Meriden CT	USA	Flatware Mfr.	1852-1893
Meriden Cutlery Co.	sold to L.F. & C. 1916 pocketknives made for Meriden by Southington and by Valley Forge	Meriden CT	USA	Mfr. & Whol.	1855-c1925
Meriden Knife Co.	made for Miller Bros.	Meriden CT	USA	Contract Mfr.	1917-c1932
Merit Import Co.	(Peter J. Michels Inc.)	New York NY	Germany	Whol. Import	c1922-1940
Merrimac Cutlery Co.	Knox-All		Germany	Import brand	
Metal Industries Ltd.		Shoranur, Madras	India	Mfr.	c1950s?
Meteor Industries	owned Rodgers Wostenholm	Sheffield	England	Mfr.	1982-1986
Met-Pro			Canada	Mfr.'s brand?	
Metropolitan Cutlery Co.	Commander(?), Metcutco	New York NY	Ger./US	Whol. & Import	c1918-1951
Michael, James R., Mf'g Co.	some by Miller Bros.	New York NY	USA	Military retail	c1889
Michigan Hardware Co.		Grand Rapids MI		Hdw. Whol.	1912-?
Middleton	Union Street	Sheffield	England	Mfr.?	
Mikov			Czecho.	Mfr.'s brand	c1948?
Miller Brothers	Wm. & Geo. Miller 1863-78; Wm. Rockwell 1878-.	Yalesville and Wallingford CT; moved to Meriden CT c1872, became...	USA	Mfr.	1863-1872
Miller Brothers Cutlery Co.	Trademark: screws in handles	Meriden CT	USA	Mfr.	1872-1926
Miller Brothers Hardware Co.	was Pogue, Miller & Co.	Richmond IN		Hdw. Whol.	1879-19??
Miller Brothers & Keep	M. & K.; Keen Kutter	Chicago IL	USA?	Wholesale	18??-c1873
Miller, David, & Son	Premier works, Broom	Sheffield	England	Mfr.	c1893
Miller Sloss & Scott	Stiletto sold to Pacific Hardware & Steel Co. 1901	San Francisco CA	USA	Hdw. Whol.	1891-1901
Miller, Thomas		Sheffield	England	Mfr.	c1893
Miller, Thomas T., Hardware Co.		Easton PA		Hdw. Whol.	c1856-19??
Miller, W.A.L.		San Francisco CA	USA	Ret. Jeweler	c1900
Miller-Morse Hardware Co., Ltd.		Winnipeg, Manitoba		Hdw. Whol.	1882-19??
Mills Cutlery Co.		Meriden CT	USA	Mfr.	
Mills, Frank (& Co.)	owned by J. Nowill 1950s	Shelffield	England	Mfr.	1860s-1970s
Mills, W(illis), & Son (Ernest)	began at Thomas Turner	Sheffield	England	Hand Mfr.	1921-1947
Mills, Ernest	made for Dunhill, Landell	Sheffield	England	Hand Mfr.	1947-1985
Milner, John	Intrinsic; Orient Works	Sheffield	England	Mfr.	1848-c1970
Milton, Joseph		Sheffield	England	Mfr.	c1893
Milward, James, & Co.			Engl./Ger.	Import brand?	
Missoula Mercantile Co.	Buffalo Brand (- c1917)	Missoula MT	USA	Whol. & Retail	1885-c1972
Mitchell & Co. Ltd.		Manchester	England	Mfr.?	c1910?
Mitchell-Powers Hardware Co.		Bristol VA		Hdw. Whol.	1882-19??
Mitsuboshi Cutlery Corp.		Seki City	Japan	Mfr.	current
Moede, Jurgen	Protea	Solingen	Germany	Mfr.	1963-pres.
Mogal, Mitchell, Inc.	Mogal/Made in U.S.A.	New York NY	USA	Whol.	c1924-1951
Mogal, Mitchell, Inc.	Romo	New York NY	Ger./It/Jap	Whol. Import	1924-pres.
Monarch	see Cole National or Jos. McCoy				
Monatte, A.	C*W		France	Mfr.?	c1900?
Mongin, Jacques	J.M. Nogent-Inox	Biesles, near Nogent	France	Mfr.	1946-pres.
Monika	see E. & F. Horster				
Monogram THCo.	see Turner Hardware Co.				
Monroe Hardware Co.	Monroe Cut. Feather Edge	Monroe LA	Germany	Hdw. Whol.	1889-19??
Montgomery & Co.	Fulton	New York NY	US/Ger.	Hdw. Whol.	1876-19??
Montgomery Ward	Lakeside, Wards, Power Kraft	Chicago IL		Retail	1872-pres.
Montgomery Ward	marked on tang	Chicago IL	USA	Retail brand	c1920s
Monumental Cutlery Co.	Wiebusch brand	New York NY	Ger./Engl.	Import brand	c1874-1893
Moore	some made by Imperial	Pomona CA	USA	Retail?	c1950
Moore Handley Hardware Co.	America's Best, Champion marked knives c1883-1962 made by New York Knife, Boker, Schrade, Camillus	Birmingham AL	USA	Hdw. Whol.	1883-1980s
Moreton, John, & Co.	Butterfly, Empress	Sheffield	England	Mfr.	1890s-1920s
Morgan's Sons, C.		Wilkes-Barre PA		Hdw. Whol.	1868-19??
Morgan Import Co.		New York NY	Germany	Import	c1910

POCKETKNIFE BRAND	TRADEMARK (or reference)	LOCATION	MADE IN	TYPE OF FIRM	DATES
Morley Bros. Hardware Co.	Wedgeway Cut. Co. 1887-1933	Saginaw, MI	USA?	Hdw. Whol.	1863-pres.
Morley-Murphy Hardware Co.		Green Bay WI		Hdw. Whol.	1904-?
Morley, W.H., & Sons	A. Kastor & Bros. brand	New York NY	Aust/Ger.	Whol. brand	c1913-1927
Morris Cutlery Co.		Morris IL	USA	Mfr.	1882-c.1930
Morse, B.H.	see Waterville Co.				
Morton, William, & Sons	175 Rockingham St.	Sheffield	England	Mfr.	c1868-1971
Morton's	West Street	Sheffield	England	Retail	pres.
Mosley, R.F., & Co. (Ltd.)	Rustnorstain 1914-	Sheffield	England	Mfr.	1860s-1968
Moulson Brothers	XLNT, Globe Works	Sheffield	England	Mfr.	19th cent.
Mount, J(ames) T., & Co.		Newark NJ	USA	Mfr.?	c1890
Mount Vernon Cutlery Co.			Germany?	Import brand	c1890
Muela	imported by C. A. S.	Iberia	Spain	Mfr.	current
Mueller & Schmidt Pfeilringwerk	Five arrows around circle	Solingen	Germany	Mfr.	1896-pres.
Mulberry Cutlery Co.	see Lewis Barnascone	Sheffield	England	Whol. brand	c1919
Muller, Aug.		Solingen	Germany	Mfr.	c1985
Mumbly Peg by Camillus		Camillus NY	USA	Mfr.'s brand	c1937-1960s
Myerson's Printing Co.	Myerson's Family Magazine	St. Louis MO	Germany	Advt. Premium	1906
N.B. Knife Co., The	see New Britain Knife Co.				
N.C. Co.	see Novelty Cutlery Co.				
N.L. Co.	see National Lead Co.				
N. & S.	see Naylor & Sanderson				
N. Shore Co.	see North Shore Co.				
Nachf(olger)	= Successor (German)				
Nagle Reblade Knife Co.	began in Newark NJ	Poughkeepsie NY	USA	Mfr.	1912-1916
Namur	(place name)		Belgium		c1600-pres.
Napanoch Knife Co. (1)	to Winchester & Honk Falls	Napanoch NY	USA	Mfr.	1900-1919
Napanoch Knife Co. (2)	J. Cushner, ex-Napanoch (1)	Napanoch NY	USA	Mfr.	1931-1939
Napanoch	for Parker KCS	Chattanooga TN	USA/Japan	Whol. brand	c1993-pres.
Nash Hardware Co.	Panther	Fort Worth TX	USA	Hdw. Whol.	1872-1975
Natenberg-Strauss Importing Co.	Reliance	Chicago IL	Ger./Czech.	Whol. importer	c1923
National Cutlery Co.	S&S	Detroit MI	Germany	Whol. importer	c1890-1907
National Lead Co.	N.L. Co.		Germany	Paint Mfr. Advt.	
Naugatuck Cutlery Co.		Naugatuck CT	USA	Mfr.	1872-1888
Naylor, Charles		Philadelphia PA	USA	Cutler	c1800?
Naylor, D.	Star/Arrow (picture)	Sheffield	England	Mfr.	c1800?
Naylor, George, & Son	Pret. 1741 (?) became Naylor & Sanderson	Sheffield	England	Mfr.	c1741-1795
Naylor & Sanderson	N. & S. was George Naylor & Son; became Sanderson Brothers (steel refiners and cutters)	Sheffield	England	Mfr.	c1795-1829
Needham, Robert A.		Sheffield	England	Mfr.	c1893
Needham, William	W.N. silver fruit knives	Sheffield	England	Mfr.	1891-c1920
Needham Bros.	Repeat (Wiebusch import)	Sheffield	England	Mfr.	1851-1940s
Needham, Thomas B.	Taylor's Eye Witness	Sheffield	England	Mfr.	1856-1879
Needham Veall & Tyzack (Ltd.)	Taylor's Eye Witness, Llama T.B. Needham, James Veall, Walter Tyzack; bought Nixon & Winterbottom c1897; bought Haywood's Glamorgan Works 1902; M. Hunter & Co. 1902; Southern & Richardson 1920s; Saynor, Cooke & Ridal 1948; sold to Harrison Fisher & Co. 1975	Sheffield	England	Mfr.	1879-1975
Neff Hardware Co.		Wheeling WV		Hdw. Whol., Ret.	1907-?
Neft Safety Nife	Pat. 11-9-1920 distributed by Valley Forge (Boker)	Newark NJ	USA		c1920-?
Neiman-Marcus		Dallas TX	Italy	Retail	current
Nelson Knife Co.	(possibly Nelson Hdw. Co. Roanoke VA)		USA?/Ger?		c1915
Neumeyer, (Gustav), & (A.J.) Dimond	Velox, Sphinx	New York NY		Whol. & Retail	c1905
Never Dull Cutlery Co.	see Butler Bros.				
New Britain Knife Co., The	The N.B. Knife Co.	New Britain CT	USA	Mfr.?	
New Century Cutlery Co.			Germany	Import brand	c1900
New England Cutlery Co.		Wallingford CT	USA	Mfr.?	c1860
New England Knife Co.				Whol.?	c1910?
New Haven Cutlery Co., "Damascus" by Boker for Baker & Hamilton		San Francisco CA	US/Ger.	Hdw. Whol.brand	c1890s
New Holland (Co.)	on Kutmaster bolster	New Holland PA	USA	Farm Eqpt. Ad.	c1960
New Jersey Knife Co.	American Ace	Newark NJ			c1919

POCKETKNIFE BRAND	TRADEMARK (or reference)	LOCATION	MADE IN	TYPE OF FIRM	DATES
New West R. & C.	made for Richards & Conover Hardware Co. (qv) by Boker c1910				
New York Cutlery Co.	Rowe & Post	New York		Import brand	c1875
New York Knife Co.	moved to Walden 1856	Matteawan NY	USA	Mfr.	1852-1856
New York Knife Co.	Hammer Brand (c1880-1931) Wallkill River Works (factory name, used as an economy brand c1928-1931)	Walden NY	USA	Mfr.	1856-1931
Newbould, John	532	NYC/Sheffield	England	Mfr. & Import	c1860s-90s
Newlin, Knight Hardware Co.		Philadelphia PA		Hdw. Whol.	1798-19??
Newton, Francis, & Sons	Premier, Swan (picture), Try, Juste Judicato (from J. & R. Dodge 1884)	Sheffield	England	Mfr.	1838-pres.
Newton, John (& Co.)	Manhattan Cutlery, Frog imported to U.S. by H. Boker & Co. Marks sold to John Watts 1916	Sheffield	England	Mfr.	1861-c1926
Nicholson, William		Sheffield	England	Mfr.	c1836-1864
Niesserons		Salem OR	France?	Retail?	c1890?
Nifty	see Borgfeldt				c1913
Nilsson, Axel	for J.M. Thompson Hdw. Co.	Minneapolis MN	USA/Ger.	Whol. brand?	c1900-1914
Nippel, F.A.	Solingen-Wald	Germany		Mfr.?	c1910?
Nirosta	= No Rust (German), see Gottlieb Hammesfahr				
Nixon & Winterbottom	N W; Pyramid (picture) sold to Needham, Veall & Tyzack 1897	Sheffield	England	Mfr.	1864-1950s
Nixon Hardware Co.		Rome GA		Hdw. Whol.	1894-1920s
No. 6 Sheffield Steel	Maltese crosses	Dehra Dun	India	Counterfeit	c1940s-70s
Nodder, John, & Sons		Sheffield	England	Mfr.	c1893
Noel, J.T.L.	45	Nogent	France	Mfr.?	
Nogent	(place name)	France			
NON-XLL	see Joseph Allen				
Norcliff		Sheffield?	England	Mfr.	18th cent.
Norman, James		Sheffield	England	Mfr.	c1893
Normark	Mfd. by E.K.A.	Minneapolis MN	Sweden	Whol. Import	1959-pres.
Norris, Samuel	*P Cast Steel	Sheffield	England	Mfr.	c1795-1815
North American Knife Co.		Wichita KS			c1920s
North Shore Co.		Chicago IL	USA	Ad. Specialty?	c1930s
North West Cutlery Co.			Germany	Import brand	c1890
Northfield Knife Co.	UN-X-LD run by Clark Bros. 1919-1929. Liquidated 1931, Name used by Henry Gill, d.1964	Northfield CT	USA	Mfr.	1858-1919
Northfield Knife Co.	for Parker KCS	Chattanooga TN	USA/Japan	Whol. brand	c1993-pres.
Norton, William	228 Solly Street	Sheffield	England	Mfr.	c1850s
Norvell Shapleigh Hardware Co.	see Shapleigh Hdw. Co. (some made by Empire Knife Co.)				1902-1920
Norvell, S(anders)	see Shapleigh Hardware Co.				1902-1920
Novco or Nov. Cut. Co.	see Novelty Cutlery Co.				
Novelty Cutlery Co.	Canton Knife Co., Novco August Vignos	Canton OH	USA	Mfr.	1879-c1949
Novelty Patent Nov. 11, 1884	made by Bernard McGovern				
Nowill & Kippax	Nowil/Kippax	Sheffield	England	Mfr.	c1787
Nowill, J(ohn), & Sons	Krosskeys, *D	Sheffield	England	Mfr.	1700-pres.
Nowill, John	J.N. silver fruit knives	Sheffield	England	Mfr.	c1840s
Nowill, Joseph	Geneva	Sheffield	England	Mfr.	c1787
Nowill, William	W.N. silver fruit knives	Sheffield	England	Mfr.	1825-?
Nunda Knief Works	see Woodworth Knife Works			Wholesale brand	
Nurten & Scherf			Germany	Mfr.?	c1900?
O. & L.H. Co.	see Orr & Lockett Hardware Co.				
O.C. Mfg. Co.	see Ohio Cutlery Co.				
OIO	see W. Shirley & Co., Clarke, Shirley & Co.; later to Harrison Fisher & Co.				
O.M.F.	(on W.W.I. Canadian sailor knives)				c1915
O.N.B., O.N.B. Barlow	probably A. Kastor & Bros.	New York NY	Germany	Import Brand	c1910
O.S.T. Cutlery Co.	by A.F. Bannister?	Newark NJ	USA		c1912
O.V.B.	(Our Very Best) see Hibbard	Spencer Bartlett			c1884-1960
O.V.B.	(Our Very Best) see Hibbard	Camillus NY	USA	Mfr.	circa 2002-pres.
Oak Leaf	see William Enders (Simmons Hardware Company brand)				
Oakley & Fox	made by Wostenholm	New York NY	England	Retail	c1870
Oakman Bros.		New York NY		Retail or Whol.	c1900
Oates, Albert	AOT, Current	Sheffield	England	Mfr.	1870s-1920s

POCKETKNIFE BRAND	TRADEMARK (or reference)	LOCATION	MADE IN	TYPE OF FIRM	DATES
Oates, Luke, & Co.		Sheffield	England	Mfr.	c1893
Oates, S.E., & Sons	S.E.O. & S. (by Furness?)	Sheffield	England	Mfr.?	pre-1915
Occident Cutlery Co.	sold by Seattle Hdw. Co.	Seattle WA		Hdw. Whol. brand	c1908
Odell Hardware Co.	Southern +(cross) Cutlery	Greensboro NC		Hdw. Whol.	c1873-19??
Oehm (& Co.)	some made by Miller Bros.	Baltimore MD	USA ?	Retail	c1860-1936
Ohio Cutlery Co.	O.C. Mfg. Co., Tru-Temper	Massillon OH	USA	Mfr.	1919-1923
Okapi	(picture) see Ferd. Everts	Sohn & Co.			
Oklahoma City Hardware Co.		Oklahoma City OK		Hdw. Whol.	1901-c1951
Olbertz, Friedrich	Olbos, Winged crown makes many current American private and limited edition brands	Solingen	Germany	Mfr.	1915-pres.
Olbos	see Friedrich Olbertz				
Olcut	see Olean Cutlery Co.	Olean NY	USA	Mfr.'s brand	1911-1920s
Old Cutler	by Colonial Knife Co.	Providence RI	USA	Mfr.'s brand	c1978-pres.
Old Faithful	see A.J. Jordan				
Old Hickory	see Ontario Knife Co.				
Old Timer	by Imperial Schrade on	Schrade and Ulster	U.S.A.	Mfr.'s brand	1959-2004
Olean Cutlery Co.	Olcut. Union Cut. Co.	Olean NY	USA	Mfr.'s brand	1911-1920s
Olsen Knife Co.	(Mfr. of sheath knives)	Howard City MI	Germany	Mfr. & Import	recent
Olsson, Emil		Eskilstuna	Sweden	Mfr.	1892-1968
Olympic Cutlery Co.		New York NY		Whol. brand?	c1910?
Omega	see Joseph Feist				
Ontario Knife Co.	Old Hickory pocketknives made by Queen Cutlery Co. after 1971	Franklinville NY	USA	Kitchen knives	1889-pres.
Opinel	Crowned Hand	Cognin, Savoie	France	Mfr.	c1890-pres.
Oppenheimer, A., & Co.	G.B.D.	Saddle Brook NJ	Japan/Italy	Pipe Mfr.	current
Orange Cutlery Co.	(ex Walden Knife employees)	Walden NY	USA	Mfr.	1923
Orgill Brothers & Co.		Memphis TN		Hdw. Whol.	1847-19??
Oriental Stainless	silver handle multiblades		Japan	Import brand	c1950s
Orr & Lockett Hardware Co.	O. & L.H. Co.	Chicago IL	Germany	Hdw. Whol. Retail	1872-c1927
Osbaldiston, Louis, & Co.	Hydra; pocketknives 1880-	Sheffield	England	Mfr.	1865-1940
Osborn Keene & Co.			Germany	Importer?	c1900?
Osborne, Edward	EO on Ibberson liner	Sheffield	England	Cutler	c1893
Osgood Bray & Co.	Three Stars some made by Burkinshaw		US/Ger.	Wholesale?	19th cent.
Ostdiek (Herman J.) Company, The	some by Case(?) c1915	Minneapolis MN	USA	Whol. & Import	1908-c1930s
Osterberg, Carl Victor		Eskilstuna	Sweden	Mfr.	c1920-1945
Ostiso	see Finedge Cutlery Co.				
Ostwald, P.W.	-O- (crude hand-made)	Baker OR	USA	Mfr. (Machinist)	c1930s-60s
Othello	Moor's head (picture) see Anton Wingen, Jr.				
Ott-Heiskell Hardware Co.	formerly Ott Bros. & Co.	Wheeling WV		Hdw. Whol.	1836-19??
Otter	see Berns Brothers (Gebruder Berns)				
Our Very Best	O.V.B., see Hibbard Spencer Bartlett	c1884-1960			
Overland Import Co.	Fred Mac Overland	Los Angeles CA	Germany	Import	c1952
Owl Cutlery Company	made for C.B. Barker c1880-1905; for Wiebusch & Hilger c1905-1910	New York	England	Import brand	c1880-1910
Oxley, J(ohn)	J.O.; knife & steel (picture)	Sheffield	England	Butcher k. mfr.	c1825-1980
*P	see Samuel Norris				
P.B.-A1	see Pauls Bros.				
P.K.	(on Barlow bolster) see Pine Knòt, James W. Price (Belknap Hardware Co.)				
P.N. Mfg. Co.	Novelty Pat. 11-11-84		USA		1880s
Pacific Cutlery	was Balisong Inc.	Los Angeles CA	USA	Mfr.	1982-1987
Pacific Cutlery Co.	D Cx	Sheffield	England	Export brand	c1890
Pacific Hardware & Steel	Stiletto Cutlery Co. made by Napanoch. P.H. & S. merged with Baker & Hamilton 1918	San Francisco CA	USA	Hdw. Whol.	1901-1918
Packard Hardware Co.		Greenville PA		Hdw. Whol.	1854-c1897
Pairpoint	plated fruit knives	New Bedford MA	USA	Glass Mfr.	c1890?
Pal Brand	imported by Utica K&R, Pal	Utica, Plattsburgh NY	Czech./Ger	Import brand	c1924-1939
Pal Blade Co./Pal Cutlery Co.	Mailman bros. of Utica K&R	Montreal/ Plattsburgh	Canada/USA	Mfr.	c1935-1953
Pal/Remington	both brands on same knife Pal bought Remington's cutlery division in 1940, used up all old parts.	Plattsburgh NY and Holyoke MA	USA	Mfr.	c1940-1942

POCKETKNIFE BRAND	TRADEMARK (or reference)	LOCATION	MADE IN	TYPE OF FIRM	DATES
Palfreyman, George		Sheffield	England	Mfr.	c1893
Palmer, William		Sheffield	England	Mfr.	c1893
Palo Alto Cutlery Co.			Germany	Import brand	c1880
Panther	see Nash Hardware Co.				
Paolantonio, J.		Frosolone?	Italy	Mfr.	
Pape Theibes Cutlery Co.	Unitas; was Broch & Thiebes	St. Louis MO	Germany	Whol. Import	c1903-1929
Paragon Cutlery (or Shear) Co.	see Fuller Bros.				
Paric, Robert	Ibr. Sophie Germain	Nogent?	France		
Paris Bead		Chicago IL			c1920s
Parisian Novelty Co.	wrapped celluloid handles	Chicago IL	USA	Advt. Specialty	1905-1985
Parker Brothers	76 Eyre St.	Sheffield	England	Mfr.	c1847-1860
Parker Cutlery Co.	James Parker Eagle, Parker Brothers, Parker-Edwards (Jacksonville AL), American Blade Cutlery; briefly owned W.R. Case & Sons, Cutlery World Stores. Bankrupt 1991.	Chattanooga TN	Japan/USA	Whol. & Mfr.	c1970-1990
Parker Frost Cutlery Co.	James Parker, James Frost	Chattanooga TN	Japan	Whol/Ret/Import	1976-1978
Parker's Knife Collectors Service	Buzz Parker new imports marked "W. R. Case & Sons," "Marbles," etc.	Chattanooga TN	Ger./Jap/US	Ltd. Editions	1990-pres.
Parker, Edward, & Sons	Perfect	New York?	Germany	Whol. importer	c1900
Parker, J.H.		Concord NH	USA?	Mfr.?	c1860s?
Parker & Field	made by Miller Bros.		USA	Retail?	c1900?
Parkin (William) & Marshall	Telegraph works; XL ALL sold to M. Hunter & Sons	Sheffield	England	Mfr.	1770-c1910s
Passaic Knife Co.		Newark NJ	USA	Mfr.?	c1920s?
Pastor Aleman	= German Shepherd (Spanish)	Mexico?	Jap./Ger.?	Import brand?	c1970s?
Pat. Ang.	= Patent angemeldet (patent pending) (German)				
Pathfinder/Big Chief	A. Kastor & Bros. brand	New York NY	Germany	Import brand	c1910
Patterson, Harral & Gray		New York NY		Hdw. Whol.	1874-19??
Pauls Bros.	Echo, P.B.-Al	N.Y.C. & Solingen	Germany	Mfr. & Import	c1880-1900
Pavian (-Adams) Cutlery Co.	Summit	St. Paul MN		Whol.	1906-c1920
Pavlovo, G(orod)	= City of Pavlovo (Russian) (place name)	Russia			
Paxton & Gallagher Co.	CutAway (-1906)	Omaha NE	USA	Hdw. Whol.	1864-c1959
Peace J.H., & Co.		Sheffield	England	Mfr.	c1893
Peace, W(illiam) K(irby), Co.	Eagle. Was Ibbotson Peace	Sheffield	England	Mfr.	c1867-pres.
Pearce, Edward, & Co.		Sheffield	England	Mfr.	c1893
Pearsall, Robert		New York NY		Hdw. Whol. Imp.	1895-?
Pearson, S., & Co.		Sheffield	England	Mfr.	c1893
Peavey, Andrew J.	knife pistol pat.3/27/	1866 S. Montville ME	USA	Inventor & Mfr.	1860s
Peeples Hardware Co.		Savannah GA		Hdw. Whol.	1899-?
Peerless Cutlery Co.	or Peerless Blade Corp.	New York NY	Germany	Whol. importer	c1930s
Pegasus	Winged horse (picture) see Henry Rogers Sons & Co.				
Pennsylvania Cutlery Co.		Tidioute PA	Germany?	Import?	c1914?
Pennsylvania Knife Co.	?	PA	USA	Mfr.?	c1914?
Peres, (Peter) Daniel, & Co.	Ale Barrel (pic)	Solingen	Germany	Mfr.	1792-pres.
Perigo Brothers	Dragon seated (picture)	Sheffield	England	Mfr.	1870s-1950s
Perkins, J. (or N.)		Newburyport MA			c1820s
Perlmann, Louis	Two fencers (picture)	Solingen, Leipzig	Germany	Retail?	1883-pres.
Pernet, (Louis) Eloi	Eloi; lived 1883-1963	Paris	France	Mfr.	1932?-1992
Pernet, Eloi	Eloi, Dominique Minel	Nogent	France	Mfr.	1992-pres.
Perret, Jean Jacques	Cup (picture) born 1730; wrote *The Art of the Cutler* (1771-72)	Paris	France	Mfr.	1753-1784
Personna		New York NY		Razor Mfr.	c1948
Peters, Gebruder (Bros.), Cutlery		Solingen-Merscheid	Germany	Mfr.	c1880
Peters, Walter	Laurus tool kit knives	Solingen	Germany	Mfr.	1936-pres.
Petty, John, & Sons	Perth works; barrel (picture, reg. 1791); bought William Gregory before 1919; bought Robert Hallam; Joseph Mills	Sheffield	England	Mfr. & Whol.	c1868-1986
Pfeifer			Germany	Mfr.?	19th cent.
Pfeilringwerk	= Arrow circle Works (German) see Mueller & Schmidt				
Pharus	see Friedr. Herder, Abr. Sohn				
Phelps, H.M.	see Waterville (?)				c1857
Phoenix Cutlery Co.	by Camillus?	Syracuse NY	USA		
Phoenix Knife Co.	was Central City Knife Co.	Phoenix NY	USA	Mfr.	1892-1916
Phoenix Knife Co.	for Parker KCS	Chattanooga TN	USA/Japan	Whol. brand	c1993-pres.

POCKETKNIFE BRAND	TRADEMARK (or reference)	LOCATION	MADE IN	TYPE OF FIRM	DATES
Pic	mountain peak (picture) see Precise (international)				
Pickering Hardware Co.		Cincinnati OH		Hdw. Whol. Ret.	1888-19??
Pickslay, Charles, & Co.	Royal York Works	Sheffield	England	Mfr.	c1840
Pictou Cutlery Co.	sold to W. R. Case 1948	Pictou NS	Canada	Mfr.	?-c1946
Pigott, James		Sheffield	England	Mfr.	c1893
Piggott, John	Cheapside, E.C.	London	England	Retail	c1890-1900
Pikaninny	see Hibbard Spencer Bartlett & Go.				
Pilatus	see Friedrich W. Engels		Germany	Mfr.'s brand	c1910?
Pilley, Edward		Sheffield	England	Mfr.	c1893
Pine Knot/James W. Price	made for Belknap Hdw. Co. Bird (picture). Some made by Union Knife Works, later by Robeson	Louisville KY	USA	Hdw. Whol.brand	c1910s-30s
Pitard (-Saxton) Hardware Co.	Gustave Pitard, John Saxton	New Orleans LA		Hdw. Whol.	1869-19??
Pitkin Cutlery Co.		Germany		Import brand	
Platt Sons	see Union Knife Works	Union NY			
Platts, C., & Sons	in old S. & M. plant	Gowanda NY	USA	Mfr.	1896-1897
Platts, C., & Sons	became C. Platts' Sons	Eldred PA	USA	Mfr.	1897-1900
Platts' C., Sons	merged with W.R.Case 1905	Eldred PA	USA	Mfr.	1900-1905
Platts Brothers		Union NY	USA?	Whol.	1905-1907?
Platts Brothers Cutlery Co.		Andover NY	USA	Mfr.	1907-c1909
Platts N'field	usually overstamped assembled from old Northfield Knife Co. parts by Ray Platts	Northfield CT	USA	Mfr.	post-1919
Platts	for Parker KCS	Chattanooga TN	USA/Japan	Whol. brand	c1993-pres.
Pli-R-Nif Co.		S.F., Berkeley CA	USA	Mfr.	1905-?
Plum, (Robert)	G. Plum after 1841	Bristol	England	Mfr.	c1822-1939
Pocket Pard	see Utica Cutlery Co.				
PocketEze	see Robeson				
Pocketknives crossed	(picture) see Carl Spitzer				
Pool, S.	51 Burlington Arcade W.	London	England	Retail	c1925?
Potter-Hoy Hardware Co., The		Bellefonte PA	USA?	Hdw. Whol. Ret.	1865-19??
Poughkeepsie Cutlery Works	Kipsi Kut, Pokipsi N.Y.	Poughkeepsie NY	USA	Mfr.	c1919
Powell, Thomas		Sheffield	England	Mfr.	c1893
Power Kraft	made for Montgomery Ward	Chicago IL	USA	Retail brand	c1939-pres.
Powder River, The	see Wyoming Knife Co.				
Practical Cutlery Co.	Walter Birch owner 1919	Sheffield	England	Mfr.	1890s-1920s
Pradel, A.	Extra Fine	Thiers?	France	Mfr.	
Pradel, C.	1er Choix (first choice)		France		
Pradel	= spear blade (French); also old Thiers trademark now owned by G. David Fils				
Pratt & Co.	probably made by Ulster	Buffalo NY	USA	Retail jeweler	c1830-19??
Precise (International)	Deerslayer; Pic (peak) Fist and 3 arrows (1954-1966) by Voos, Schlieper; agent for Wenger	Suffern NY	Ger./Japan	Whol. importer	1954-pres.
Premier Cutlery Co.	Lifetime, Elk	New York NY	Ger./Ital.	Whol. importer	1921-c1955
Premier Cutlery Co., Ltd.	Lifetime, Premcut	Toronto, Ontario	Ger./Japan	Whol. importer	1921-pres.
Prentiss Knife Co.		New York NY	USA?	Whol.?	c1910?
Pressner, M., & Co.	Sharpe, Non To Compare		Japan	Mfr.?	c1930s-40s
Press Button Knife Co.	licensed by George Schrade; division of Walden Knife Company	Walden NY	USA	Mfr.	c1892-1923
Presto	by George Schrade Knife Co.	Bridgeport CT	USA	Mfr.'s brand	c1925-1945
Pribyl, I(gnaz), & Son	Ignaz Sr. & Ignaz Jr.	Chicago IL	Germany?	Whol. & Retail	c1870s
Pribyl Brothers	Ignaz Jr. & Joseph	Chicago IL	Germany?	Whol.	c1880-1905
Price, James, W.	see Pine Knot				
Price, M(ichael)		San Francisco CA	USA	Mfr.	1856-1889
Primble, John, Indian Steel Works	for Belknap Hdwe. Co.	Louisville KY	USA/Ger.	Hdw. Whol.brand	c1890-1940
Primble, John	for Belknap Hdwe. Co. by Boker, Camillus, Utica, Schrade	Louisville KY	USA/Ger.	Hdw. Whol.brand	c1947-1985
Primble, John	made by Utica for Blue Grass Cutlery Company	Manchester OH	USA	Whol. brand	1985-pres.
Primrose	see Krusius Brothers				
Princeton Knife (Cutlery) Co.	see Wiebusch	New York NY		Whol. brand	c1905
Pritzlaff, J., Hardware Co.	Everkeen	Milwaukee WI		Hdw. Whol.	1850-1957
Proctor, B.J.			Germany		
Progress	see Alfred Field		Germany	Import Brand	
Prolific	see Henry Bamascone & Son	Harrison Fisher & Co.			
Pronto	by Colonial Knife. Co.	Providence RI	USA	Mfr.'s brand	c1926-1952

POCKETKNIFE BRAND	TRADEMARK (or reference)	LOCATION	MADE IN	TYPE OF FIRM	DATES
Protea	see Jurgen Moede				
Proto Tools		Fullerton CA	USA	Tool mfr. advt.	c1970s
Providence Cutlery Co.		Providence RI	USA	Mfr.	c1917-pres.
Providence Cutlery Co.			Germany	Import Brand	c1880-1915
Puma, Puma-Werk	was Lauterjung & Sohn	Solingen	Germany	Mfr.	1769-pres.
Pyramid	(picture) see Gottlieb Hammesfahr				
Q/Crown	see Queen Cutlery Co.				
Quail	(picture) see Bob White Cutlery				
Queen City Cutlery Co.	now Queen Cutlery Co. acquired Schatt & Morgan 1928	Titusville PA	USA	Mfr.	c1920-1945
Queen Cutlery Co.	Q/Crown, Queen Steel	Titusville PA	USA	Mfr.	1945-pres.
Queen's Cutlery Works	see Mappin Brothers				
Queen's Own Co.	see Nathan Joseph	San Francisco CA			
Quick Point	made/sold knives 1930s-40s some made by Remington, Winchester (and so marked)	St. Louis, Fenton MO	USA	Advt. Specialty	1928-pres.
R. & C.	see Richards & Conover Hardware Co. (made by Ulster c1910)				
Rabone Bros. & Co.	(US Navy contractor)		England	Export brand	c1865
Race Brothers	Certified Cutlery		Germany?	Import brand	c1880s?
Ragg, John & William	Napoleon, Paragon, Plantagenet, Pawn (picture); founder Richard Ragg 1601; now Granton Ragg Ltd.	Sheffield	England	Mfr.	1831-pres.
Rainbow	made for Boker USA	Providence RI	USA	Whol. brand?	c1933-1954
Rampur State	(place name)		India		pre-1949
Rampur U(ttar) P(radesh)	(place name)		India		post-1949
Ramsay Brothers	(Sheffield made)	Whitehaven	England	Retail	
Ramsbottom, Walter, J.	Luz, Spinning Wheel	Sheffield	England	Mfr.	1870s-1920s
Ramsden, B.W., & Co.		Sheffield	England	Mfr.	c1893
Randall, Hall & Co.		Chicago IL		Wholesale	c1875
Ranger	see Colonial Knife Co.	Providence RI	USA	Mfr.'s brand	1938-pres.
Ran-tan-Ka-rus	see Smith & Hemenway				
Raola Hardware & Iron Co.	Raola			Hdw. Retail(?)	
Rattler Knife Co.	Austria			Import brand	c1910
Raucherkopf	= smoking head (German) see Voelker Foerst & Merten or Fritz Bracht				
Rawson & Nourse	Eagle (picture)	Grafton MA	USA?	Mfr.?	c1840s?
Rawson, James	to Westville (New Haven) 1853	Birmingham CT	USA	Mfr.	c1846-1853
Rawson, James	& Son (James F.) after 1875	New Haven CT	USA	Mfr.	c1853-1890
Rawson Brothers	Rooster/S; winged cross	Sheffield	England	Mfr.	1870-1980
Ray, Tom, Cutlery Co.		Kansas City MO		Whol.	c1910
Raynes, Thomas	Permanent Scissor Works	Sheffield	England	Mfr.	1874-1960
Razor	(picture) see R. J. Roberts				
Rector & Wilhelmy	Clean Clipper (arrow) was Larson & Wilhelmy. To Omaha NE 1883. Became Wright & Wilhelmy 1902.	Nebraska City NE	USA	Hdw. Whol.	1871-1902
Red Devil S. & H. Co.	see Smith & Hemenway				
Red Diamond		? NY	USA		
Red Stag	for Goodwin Enterprises	Chattanooga TN	Germany	Ltd. Edit. Imp.	c 1983-pres.
Redfern, Edwin		Sheffield	England	Mfr.	c1893
Regal Cutlery Co.	see H. Boker	New York NY	Germany	Import brand	c1906
Regan, Marvel, & Co.	Columbia Works	Sheffield	England	Mfr.?	c1880?
Reico			Germany		
Reilly & Guy		New York NY		Ship Hdw. Whol.	1878-19??
Reliance	see Natenberg-Strauss Importing Co.				
Remington Arms Company/U.M.C. (Union Metallic Cartridge Co.)	made knives 1919-1940	Bridgeport CT	USA	Mfr.	c1828-pres.
	REMINGTON (in circle), usually have pattern number on reverse tang				1919-1940
	REMINGTON (in circle) S: stainless steel blades				c1939-1940
	Remington "straight line" assortment knives, some by Camillus, G. Schrade				c1933-1940
Remington	reissue made by Camillus	Bridgeport CT	USA	Whol.	1982-pres.
Remington	(on handle) U.S.A. (on tang) fantasy made by Colonial Knife Co.				1980s
Renshaw, T(homas), & Son	Stand	Sheffield	England	Mfr.	c1840-1900
Retru-Gros, A.	Marteau (hammer)	Thiers	France	Mfr.	c1900
Rev-O-Noc	(Conover backwards) see Hibbard Spencer Bartlett				

POCKETKNIFE BRAND	TRADEMARK (or reference)	LOCATION	MADE IN	TYPE OF FIRM	DATES
Revitt, Frank		Sheffield	England	Mfr.	c1893
Reynolds, Frederick	mainly razors until 1922	Sheffield	England	Mfr.	1845-1945
Rice Lathrop & Clary		Winsted CT	USA	Table Cutlery	1856-1861
Rice & Lathrop	became Lathrop & Barton	Winsted CT	USA	Table Cutlery	c1862
Richard, S(tephon), Co.	Richard's (made kitchen knives)	Southbridge MA	US/Ger./Eng	Whol.	c1862-1908
Richards & Conover Hardware Co. (George Ricahrds & John Conover)	New West by Boker; Rich-Con, R. & C. by Ulster Knife Co. Branch at Oklahoma City OK c1910	Kansas City MO	USA	Hdw. Whol.	1875-1956
Richards Bros. (& Sons) Ltd.	Street lamp, tent (pics) Owned by Gebr. Richartz (Wm. Muller, mgr.) 1934-1977; owned by Imperial Knife Co. 1977-1982; by Western Knives 1982. Owned Rodgers Wostenholm 1975-1982	Sheffield	England	Mfr.	1934-1982
Richardson, E.C.	101 Duke Street	Sheffield	England	Mfr.?	
Richardson, W.		Sheffield	England	Mfr.	c1893
Richartz, Gebruder, & Soehne	Whale	Solingen-Ohligs	Germany	Mfr.	1900-pres.
Richmond Cutlery Co.			Germany?		19th cent.
Richmond Hardware Co.		Richmond VA	USA/Ger.	Hdw. Whol. Ret.	1903-?
Richter, R.J.	fantasy Nazi pen knives	?	Ger./Swed.	Importer?	c1963
Rigid Knives	owner Z. Dean Parks	Santee CA	USA	Mfr.	c1970-1980
	name sold to Smoky Mtn.	Lake Hamilton AR	USA	Mfr.	c1980-1987
Rigid	Smoky Mountain Knife Works	Sevierville TN		Retail brand	current
Ritter, Kuno	see Hubertus				
Riverside Cutlery Co. N.Y.	made for Dunham, Carrigan & Hayden, probably by Boker		USA		c1918
Rivington Works	see Alfred Williams				
Robbins Clark & Biddle	became Biddle Hdw. (?)	Philadelphia PA		Hdw. Whol.	1837-?
Roberts, R(obert) J., Razor Co.	Razor. Sold to Boker 1905	New York NY	Germany	Whol. Import	c1870-1940
Roberts, William H.	54 Holly St.	Sheffield	England	Mfr.	c1890s
Roberts, Hardwicke & Taylor	became Roberts, Sanford...	Sherman TX	Eng/Ger.	Hdw. Whol.	c1881-?
Roberts, Sanford & Taylor	Texoma knives 1909-50	Sherman TX		Hdw. Whol.	1881-pres.
Robertson, Foster & Smith, Ltd.		St. John NB		Hdw. Whol.	1892-19??
Robeson Cutlery Co.	ShurEdge, PocketEze, Premier	Rochester & Perry NY	USA	Mfr. & Whol.	c1894-1948
Robeson Cutlery Co.	Robeson Shuredge USA	Rochester NY	US/Ger.	Mfr. & Whol.	1945-1965
Robeson Cutlery Co.	Robeson USA, made by Camillus Robeson pocketknife brand owned by Ontario Knife Co., Franklinville NY 1971-1977 and circa 1990s	Rochester NY	USA	Wholesale	1965-1971
Robinson Bros. & Co.		Louisville KY		Hdw. Whol.	1878-c1925
Robinson, Herbert	Grinder (picture)	Sheffield	England	Mfr.	c1873
Robinson, Samuel		Sheffield	England	Mfr.	c1860-1876
Robinson, W.H.		Sheffield	England	Mfr.	c1893
Rochester P'a	see Beaver Falls				
Rockford Cutlery Co.		Rockford IL	USA		c1915?
Rodgers, James		Sheffield	England	Mfr.	1825-1850s
Rodgers, Joseph, & Go.		Sheffield	England	Mfr.	c1893
Rodgers, Joseph, & Sons	(1764), No.6 Norfolk St.	Sheffield	England	Mfr.	1682-1971
Rodgers, R., & Son	Pick and Shovel	Sheffield	England	Mfr.	c1893
Rodgers Wostenholm Ltd.	bought by Richards Bros. 1975; Richards bought by Imperial Knife Co. 1977 (see Schrade-I*XL); bought by Meteor Industries 1982; names used by Egginton Group 1986-pres.	Sheffield	England	Mfr.	1971-1986
Rodgers, William	I Cut (Blade) My Way trademarks sold to John Clarke & Son c1855; to Egginton Group mid 1980s	Sheffield	England	Mfr.	1830-c1855
Roeger, Gebruder (Brothers)		Solingen	Germany	Mfr.?	
Rogers & Baldwin Hardware Co.		Springfield MO		Hdw. Whol.	1885-19??
Rogers, Henry, Sons & Co.	Pegasus, H.R.S. & Co.	Sheffield	England	Mfr.	c1880-1950s
Rogers Cutlery	Meriden Britannia Co. silver plated fruit knives circa 1890	Meriden, Hartford CT	USA	Silver plate	c1847-pres.
Romo	Rosenbaum & Mogal 1917-1924, Mitchell Mogal, Inc., 1924-present	New York NY	Ger./It/Jap	Whol.	1917-pres.
Rose in circle	(picture) see China Light Industrial...	Tsingtao, Shantung, China			
Rosenbaum (I.) & MOgal (M.)	Romo	New York NY	Ger./It/Jap	Whol.	1917-1924
Rosenbaum & Mogal	Romo	New York NY	USA	Wholesale	c1917-1918
Rosenbaum, I(saac)	Iroskeen	New York NY		Whol.	1924-1950s
Rosler's, Ignaz, Sons Cutlery Works	crowned eagle (picture) IR	Nixdorf, Bohemia	Aust-Hung.	Mfr.	1794-c 1918
Ross & Fuller Association	see Fuller Bros.				
Rossell, Henry, & Co.	Ivanhoe, Victory	Sheffield	England	Steel Mfr.	c1877-19??

POCKETKNIFE BRAND	TRADEMARK (or reference)	LOCATION	MADE IN	TYPE OF FIRM	DATES
Rostfrei	= Stainless (German)				
Roth, John		New York NY	Germany	Import	c1920s?
Round, John, & Son	J R silver fruit knives 1874-	Sheffield	England	Mfr.	1847-1932
Rousselon Freres et Cie.	32 Dumas-Aine	Thiers	France	Mfr.	1921-pres.
Rowbotham, H., & Co.		Sheffield	England	Mfr.?	c1954
Rowbotham, T.E., & Son		Sheffield	England	Mfr.	c1820
Rowbotham & Wingfield	see (Wade) Wingfield & Rowbotham				
Rowe & Post	New York Cutlery Co.	New York NY		Import	c1875
Roxo	see Marsh Bros.				
Royal Brand Sharp Cutter	see Samuel E. Bernstein				
Rudolph & West Co.		Washington DC		Hdw. Whol.	1885-?
Runkel Bros.	made by Wester & Butz		Germany	Chocolate Advt.	c1920s
Ruppertz, R.	Scissors (picture)	Solingen	Germany	Mfr.?	c1900?
Russell Locknife	Rudolph Grohmann's	Pictou NS	Canada	Hunting K. Mfr.	c1970s?
Russell, A.G.	see Knife Collectors Club				
Russell, J., & Co.		Holyoke MA		Hdw. Whol.	1848-19??
Russell, J(ohn), & Co.	Green River Works, R/arrow Made pocketknives 1875-1917,1920-1941	Turners Falls MA	USA	Mfr.	1834-pres.
Russell	"reproduction" Barlows		Germany	Counterfeits	1971
Russell	100th Anniversary reissue Barlow: made by Schrade				c1975
Ryalls & Heathcote		Sheffield	England	Mfr.	c1836-1870
Ryalls, John, & Sons		Sheffield	England	Mfr.	c1893
S. & A.	see Sperry & Alexander				
S. & M.	see Schatt & Morgan				
S.C.C.	see Schrade, Ellenville NY				
S.C. Co.	see Schrade Cutlery Co., Walden NY				
S.E.O. & S.	(on bolster) see S. E. Oates				
S.M.F.	(under picture of king) see Stocker & Co.				
SPA	Best Steel	Seki City?	Japan	Mfr.?	c1950s?
S.R. & Co.	see Sears Roebuck & Co.				
S.R.D./Arrow	see Severin R. Droescher				
S.W.C.	see Schrade Walden Cutlery Co.				
Sabre	for Cole National	Cleveland OH	Jap/Ger./US	Import brand	c1960-1980
Saint Lawrence Cutlery Co.	see Schmachtenberg Brothers				
Salm, John	marked DeLuxe (1918-1925)	Torrance CA	USA	Mfr.?	1918-1935
Sakai, Susumo	Gerber-Sakai	Seki City	Japan	Mfr.	1977-pres.
Salt Lake Hardware Co., The	branch at Pocatello ID	Salt Lake City UT		Hdw. Whol.	1888-19??
Samco	see Sanders Mfg. Co.				
Sample, W.H. (& Sons)	succeeded James Martin	Albany NY	USA	Mfr/Whol/Ret.	1871-1937
Sanders Manufacturing Co.	Samco	Nashville TN	USA	Advt. Specialty	current
Sanderson Bros. (& Newbould)	was Naylor & Sanderson	Sheffield	England	Steel Mfr.	1829-pres.
Sanderson, James		Sheffield	England	Mfr.	c1893
Sanderson, Thomas		Sheffield	England	Mfr.	c1893
Sansom, William, & Co.	Crown (picture) Alpha made knives for Gravely & Wreaks, NYC (-1837). Became Harrison Bros. & Howson	Sheffield	England	Mfr.	1796-1847
Santa Fe Stone Works	handles inlaid in USA	Santa Fe NM	Japan	Handle Mfr.	c1986-pres.
Sargent, (Jim), Co.	Sarco; Sargent USA by Queen	Florence AL	US/Jap/Ger	Retail	current
Sarry, A.		Thiers	France	Mfr.	c1930s
Sarubi, J.		Providence RI	USA?	Retail?	c1930?
Sauvagnat-Aine	59 Sauvagnat	Thiers	France	Mfr.	?-pres.
Savage Cutlery Co.			Germany?	Import brand	c1890
Savage, George, & Son (John)		Sheffield	England	Mfr.	c1840-1864
Savery		Thiers	France	Mfr.	
Savigny		London	England	Mfr. & Retail	c1720-1850
Saville (Works)	see Stauffer, Eshelmann & Co.				
Saville Cutlery Co.		Sheffield	England	Mfr.?	c1920s
Savoy Cutlery Co.			Germany	Import brand	c1910
Saxonia Cutlery Co.			Germany	Import brand?	c1936?
Saynor, Samuel & John		Sheffield	England	Mfr.	c1810
Saynor, Samuel, & Son	Rainbow	Sheffield	England	Mfr.	c1820s
Saynor, Samuel	became Saynor & Cooke	Sheffield	England	Mfr.	c1833-1852
Saynor & Cooke	horticulture knives	Sheffield	England	Mfr.	1852-1876
Saynor Cooke & Ridal	Saynor, Obtain, Rainbow sold to Needham, Veall & Tyzack; Saynor marks now used by Harrison Fisher & Co.	Sheffield	England	Mfr.	1876-1948

POCKETKNIFE BRAND	TRADEMARK (or reference)	LOCATION	MADE IN	TYPE OF FIRM	DATES
Saynor, W(illiam), & Co.	Depend, Pioneer, Lineal	Sheffield	England	Mfr.	1865-1958
Scagel, William Wales	kris (picture)				1903-1961
Scagel	for Parker KCS	Chattanooga TN		Whol. brand	c1993-pres.
Schatt & Morgan		Gowanda NY	USA	Mfr.	1890-1895
Schatt & Morgan	S. & M.; sold to Queen City	Titusville PA	USA	Mfr.	1895-1931
Schatt & Morgan	reissues by Queen	Titusville PA	USA	Mfr.'s brand	1991-pres.
Schaw-(Ingram-)Batcher Co., The		Sacramento CA		Hdw. Whol.	1890-?
Schlechter, E., & Sohn		Solingen	Germany	Mfr.?	c1930?
Schlieper, Carl	Eye Brand, Fan, El Gallo	Solingen	Germany	Mfr.	1769-pres.
Schmachtenberg Bros.	J. Dunlap, Clim(Axe) Anchor and Swords (picture), Saint Lawrence Cutlery Co.	NY & Solingen	Germany	Mfr. & Whol. Imp.	1887-c1939
Schmid, J(ohn) M., & Son		Providence RI		Retail	1857-1964
Schmdit, Carl, Sohn	Church (or house?), Ram	Solingen	Germany	Mfr.	1829-pres.
Schmidt, J.A., & Sohne	Dreiturm (Three Spires)	Solingen	Germany	Mfr.	1829-pres.
Schmidt, Peter Ludwig	now part of Kammerling	Elberfeld	Germany	Mfr.	c1895-pres.
Schmidt & Ziegler	Bull (picture), El Toro. Imported by the H. Willis Co. (Harlan Willis Burbank), Louisville KY	Solingen	Germany	Mfr.	?-c1972
Schmidtberg, P.		Solingen	Germany	Mfr.	c1930
Schneider, Wenzel		Prague, Bohemia	Aust-Hung.	Contract Mfr.	19th cent.
Schnetzler, Wild & Co.	Solly Steel works	Sheffield	England	Mfr.	c1893
Schoverling, Daly & Gales		New York NY		Sporting Goods	1865-19??
Schrade Cutlery Co.	sold to "Kingston" 1946	Walden NY	USA	Mfr.	1904-1946
Schrade Walden	Schrade Cut. Co. style division of "Kingston;" Imperial Knife Associated Companies after 1947	Walden NY	USA	Mfr.'s brand	1946-1950s
Schrade Walden	Ulster style division of Imperial Knife Assoc1ated Companies. Became "Schrade" 1973.	Ellenville NY	USA	Mfr.'s brand	1950s-1973
Schrade	Uncle Henry, Old Timer division of Imperial Schrade	Ellenville NY	USA	Mfr.	1973-2004.
Schrade	(see Taylor Cutlery)				2004-pres.
Schrade-I*XL	see Rodgers Wostenholm Ltd.		England	Mfr.'s brand	1977-1982
Schrade, George, Knife Co.	Presto (H), Commando George Schrade died 1940. Firm owned by Boker 1956-1958	Bridgeport CT	USA	Mfr.	c1929-1958
Schrade/NY USA/Warren	see Warren Tool Co.				
Schumachner, E.		Solingen	Germany	Mfr.?	
Schwabacher Hardware Co.	Colonial Cutlery Co.	Seattle WA	US/Ger.	Hdw. Whol.	1864-pres.
Schwartz, M.	Briener Strasse		Germany	Retail?	
Scotia	Thistle (picture) see John McClory & Sons				
Sears, E(dward) B.	joined father Henry Sears in 1878				
Sears, Henry, & Co.	in Rockford IL c1870	Chicago IL	USA	Mfr.	1865-1878
Sears, Henry, & Son 1865	for Farwell Ozmun Kirk	Chicago IL	USA	Hdw. Whol.brand	1878-c1959
Sears Roebuck & Co.	see Wilbert, T.T.C., Sta-Sharp, Dunlap, Kwik Kut, Craftsman Retail 1886-pres.				
Sears Roebuck & Co. Chicago/ Napanoch Knife Co. N.Y.		Chicago IL	USA	Retail brand	c1900-1902
Sears Roebuck & Co.	marked on tang	Chicago IL	USA	Retail brand	1886-c1902
Sears	marked on tang	Chicago IL	USA	Retail brand	1991-pres.
Seattle Hardware Co.	Occident Cutlery Co.	Seattle WA		Hdw. Whol.	1885-19??
Seit	= since (German)				
Sellers, John, & Sons	S and Dagger (1838)	Sheffield/NY, NY	England	Mfr. & Import	1820-1950s
Seltzer-Klahr Hardware Co.		Philadelphia PA		Hdw. Whol.	1857-19??
Semmes Hardware Co.		Savannah GA		Hdw. Whol.	1898-?
Seneca Cutlery Co.	by Utica Cutlery Co.	Utica NY	USA	Mfr.'s brand	c1932-1942
Shamrock, Charles	OK		Germany?	Import brand?	c1880s?
Shapleigh, A.F., Hardware Co.	Diamond Edge (after 1888)	St. Louis MO	USA/Ger.	Hdw. Whol.	1843-1960
Shapleigh, A.F., Hardware Co.	Keen Kutter (after 1940)	St. Louis MO	USA	Hdw. Whol.	1843-1960
Sharp Cutter, Royal Brand	see Samuel E. Bernstein				
Sharpe, J.	see John Askham				
Sharpe & Smith		Chicago IL		Surg. Inst.	
Shaw, George		Sheffield	England	Mfr.	c1893
Shaw, S(tan)	began at Ibberson's 1941	Sheffield	England	Mfr.	c1972-pres.
Shaw, William	W.S.	Sheffield	England	Mfr.	c1847-1871
Sheard, W.F.		Tacoma WA		Retail?	
Sheffield	(place name)		England		
Sheffield Cutlery Co-operative Society Limited		Sheffield	England	Mfr.	c1893

POCKETKNIFE BRAND	TRADEMARK (or reference)	LOCATION	MADE IN	TYPE OF FIRM	DATES
Shelburne Falls Cutlery Co.	made for Lamson & Goodnow by Waterville	Shelburne Falls MA	USA	Whol. brand	c1870s-80s
Sheldon & Hammond	Shelham, Excalibur, Ventura	? Australia	Japan	Import	current
Sheldon, John		Sheffield	England	Mfr.	c1893
Sheldon, Thomas		Sheffield	England	Mfr.	c1893
Shelham	see Sheldon & Hammond				
Shelton, Clark R.		Birmingham and Westville (Derby) CT	USA	Mfr.	c1849-51
Sherwood, (Charles E.)	became Camillus 1901	Camillus NY	USA	Mfr.	1894-1896
	sold to Adolph Kastor & Bros.				1898-1901
Shipley, Howard W.	Coquanoc Works	Philadelphia PA	USA	Mfr.	c1876
Shirley, W., & Co.	OIO. Boston Works became Clarke Shirley & Co. before 1879	Sheffield	England	Mfr.	1860s-70s
Shumate Cutlery Corp.	also Shumate Razor Co.	St. Louis MO	USA	Whol.	1884-c1928
Shur Kut				Mfr.'s brand	
ShurEdge	see Robeson				
Shur-Lock	see I. & J. Mfg. Co.				
Shur-Snap	by Colonial Knife Co.	Providence RI	USA	Mfr.'s brand	c1948
Sickles & Preston (& Nutting) Co.		Davenport IA		Hdw. Whol.	c1852-19??
Siegel		Schorndorf?	Germany	Retail?	c1890
Silberstein, A.L., & Co.	see Griffon Cutlery Works				
Silver Falcon	see Compass Industries				
Silver Eagle	renamed Silver Knight	Portland OR	Japan	Mfr.'s brand	1977-1978
Silver Knight	made by Sakai for Gerber	Portland OR	Japan	Mfr.'s brand	1978-1995
Silver Sword	by Camillus	Camillus NY	USA	Mfr.s brand	c1982-pres.
Silver, S.W., & Co.	Cornhill	London	England	Retail	c1910?
Simav	Italian Navy issue	Naples	Italy	Mfr.'s brand	c1940
	Keen Kutter, Chipaway inc. 1874; merged with Winchester 1922; sold to Shapleigh Hdw. Co. 1940. 1922 branches at Philadelphia PA, Sioux City IA, Minneapolis MN, Wichita KS, Toledo OH	St. Louis MO	USA	Hdw. Whol.	1868-1960
Simmons Hardware Co.	economy brand tang stamp	St. Louis MO	Germany	Hdw. Whol. Import	c1890-1940
Simmons Hardware Co.	Hornet (picture)	St. Louis MO	Germany	Hdw. brand	c1890s
Simmons Worden White Co.	SWWCo. made by Camillus	Dayton OH	USA	Tool Mfr. Advt.	c1937 ff.
Simonds Mfg. Co.	Simonds Saw Co. with saw shaped shield. Probably by Camillus	Fitchburg MA	USA	Saw Mfr. advt.	c1940
Singleton, W., & Priestman, E.	W. Singleton & Co.	Sheffield	England	Mfr.	c1861-1936
Slack & Grinold	Bon Accord, Onward	Sheffield	England	Mfr.	c1893
Slater Brothers	Bee Hive (picture) reorganized as Herbert M. Slater, Venture Works	Sheffield	England	Mfr.	1858-1901
Slater, Herbert M(arriatt)	Venture, Bee Hive bought J. Crookes, H.G. Long. Some recent knives made in Japan. W. D. Slater d. 1994	Sheffield	England	Mfr.	1901-1991
Sloss & Britain		San Francisco CA		Hdw. Whol.	1915-?
Smethport Cutlery Co.	sold to W.R. Case	Smethport PA	USA	Mfr.	1907-1909
Smith, C.		Lowell MA			c1860s
Smith, G.F., & Son		Scarborough	England	Retail	c1900?
Smith, James	patent lock	Sheffield	England	Mfr.?	c1835
Smith, John		Sheffield	England	Mfr.	c1893
Smith, Robert G.	Reliance works	Sheffield	England	Mfr.	c1893
Smith & Clark	ivory fruit knives	Bronxville NY	USA	Mfr.?	c1850
Smith & Hemenway	Red Devil S. & H. Co. made by Utica Cutlery Company; Ran-tan-Ka-rus. Also in Irvington NJ (1956)	Utica & New York NY	USA	Hdw. Whol.	c1890-1936
Smith & Hopkins		Naugatuck CT	USA	Mfr./Buttons	1848 ff.
Smith & Patterson		New York NY	Sweden	Whol. Import	1893-c1910
Smith & Wesson	S. & W. Made knives 1974-86	Springfield MA	USA	Gun Mfr.	c1852-pres.
Smith & Wesson	by Vermont Cutlery Co.	West Rutland VT	USA	Whol. brand	1986-1993
Smith & Wesson	for Taylor Cutlery Co.	Kingsport TN	?	Whol. brand	1993-pres.
Smith Brothers Hardware Co.	CutEasy (knives c1903-)	Columbus OH	USA	Hdw. Whol.	1893-c1959
Smith, Sutton & Co.	see LaBelle Cutlery Works				
Smoky Mountain Knife Works	now owns Klaas, Rigid	Sevierville TN		Retail	current
Snappy, Shur-Snap	see Colonial	Providence RI	USA	Mfr.'s brand	1948-c1958
SOG Specialty Knives	Tomcat, Stingray, Air-Sog	Edmonds WA	Japan	Import	1985-circa 1995
SOG Specialty Knives	Topo Meridian, SOG Bowie, SEAL Pup	Lynnwood WA	Japan	Import	circa 1995-pres.

POCKETKNIFE BRAND	TRADEMARK (or reference)	LOCATION	MADE IN	TYPE OF FIRM	DATES
Solingen (place name)	Germany				
Sommers, G., & Co.		St. Paul MN		Whol.	1882-19??
Son Bros. & Co.	Son & Briggs 1869-72 owned Yale Cutlery Company, Connecticut	San Francisco CA	US & ?	Whol. & Import	1869-c1919
Sorby, I. (John)		Sheffield	England	Mfr.	1780-1827
Sorby, I. & H. (John & Henry)	I.H.S., Punch, Sheep sold to Lockwood c1850; trademarks to Elliott, and to Turner, Naylor & Co. c1921	Sheffield	England	Mfr.	1827-c1850
Sorby, I.	Punch (picture) see Turner, Naylor & Co.				
Southern & Richardson	Nest (1880), Cigar, Squatter formerly Wilson & Southern; merged with Needham, Veall & Tyzack 1920s	Sheffield	England	Mfr.	1847-1975
Southington Cutlery Co.	dist. by Meriden Cut. Co.	Southington CT	USA	Mfr.	1867-c1914
Spade, Three Spades	(picture) see Friedr. Herder, Abr. Sohn				
Spear Cutlery Co.			Ger./Aus.		pre-1915
Speer Hardware Co.		Fort Smith AR		Hdw. Whol.	1886-19??
Sperry & Alexander	S. & A., Centaur	New York NY	USA?	Whol.	1893-1920s
Spider in web	(picture) see Graef & Schmidt				
Spitzer, Carl Gustav	Standing Lion (picture) pocketknife (picture), etc.	Solingen	Germany	Mfr.	1863-197?
Spitzhoff		Nogent?	France?	Mfr.	
Spoutnik	Rocket (picture)		France	Mfr.'s brand	c1962
Sprague & Miller	also Sprague & Root; Sprague & Boyden; Sprague, Boyden, & Welch: see Waterville Co.				
Spratt's	(dog stripper)	Nwrk/Berlin/London	England	Dog Food Mfr.	c1912
Spring Cutlery Co.			England		c1890
Springbrooke Knife Co.	made for Dunham, Carrigan & Hayden; pocketknives by New York Knife; fixed blades by L.F. & C.	San Francisco CA	USA	Hdw. Whol. brand	c1895-1920
Springer	(on handle of switchblade) see Carl Wusthof KG or W. Weltersbach				
Spyderco	Clipit	Golden CO	Japan	Whol. Import	current
Sta-Sharp	made for Sears by Camillus	Chicago IL	USA	Retail brand	c1924-1941
Stacey Bros. & Co.	Ark. (to Thos. Ward?)	Sheffield	England	Mfr.	1847-1941
Stacey, Henry V.		Sheffield	England	Mfr.	c1893
Stacey, James E., & Co.		Sheffield	England	Mfr.	c1893
Stag Cutlery Co.	owned by Imperial Schrade formerly owned by JOWIKA	Listowel	Ireland	Mfr.	?-pres.
Stainless Cutlery Co./N.Y. City	Camillus/Kastor brand	Camillus NY	USA	Mfr.'s brand	1924-1930s
Stamm, Gebruder (Bros.)	Original Tidax	Dusseldorf	Germany	Retail?	c1930s
Standard Cutlery Co.	Meriden CT (?)		Eng./Ger./US	Whol.?	c1900
Standard Knife Co.	owned by two Case Brothers	Little Valley NY	USA	Whol.	1901-1903
Standard Knife Co.	made by W.R. Case & Sons	Bradford PA	USA	Mfr.	1920-1923
Standard Knife Co.	for Parker KCS	Chattanooga TN	USA/Japan	Whol. brand	c1993-pres.
Standart Bros. Hardware Co.	incorporated 1902	Detroit MI		Hdw. Whol.	1863-19??
Stanifroth, William Thomas	Wings (picture, 1852); Ascend	Sheffield	England	Mfr.	1849-1920s
Stanley Knife, The (Henry M.)	Brookes & Crookes	Sheffield	England	Mfr.'s brand	1872-1920s
Star Sales Co.		Knoxville TN		Whol. & Import	current
Stauffer, Eshelman & Co.	Saville (Works), Seco	New Orleans LA	Germany	Hdw. Whol.	1825-c1914
Staysharp Cutlery Co.			USA?	Wholesale?	c1930?
Stead, J., & Co.	Steadfast	Sheffield	England	Mfr.	c1930s-60s
Steer & Webster	Key (picture) Castle Hill Works, sold to Geo. Butler & Co. 1867	Sheffield	England	Mfr.	c1833-1867
Steinfeld, Albert, & Co.		Tucson AZ		Hdw. Whol.	1854-19??
Stellite	see Haynes Stellite				
Stephenson & Wilson	British military knives	Sheffield	England	Mfr.	1937-pres.
Sterling	stamped on steel handle		Australia	Mfr.'s brand	c1940s
Sterling (Cutlery Co.)	see McIlwaine Linn & Hughes				
Sterling Service	see J.M. Thompson Hardware Co.				
Stevens, J., & Son	(surgical instruments)	London	England	Mfr. & Retail	1830-19??
Stevenson	(on bail of GI utility knife)		USA	Mfr.'s brand?	c1945
Stiletto	made for Miller Sloss & Scott; Pacific Hardware & Steel; Baker Hamilton & Pacific				
Stiletto Cutlery Co., New York	made for the above firms by Napanoch c1901-1917; by New York Knife c1920-1931; by Union Cutlery c1933-1942	San Francisco CA	USA	Hdw. Whol. brand	c1900-1942
Stocker & Co.	Solingen Metallwarenfabrik S.M.F. (after 1933)	Solingen	Germany	Mfr.	1897-197?
Stoddard's	was Dame Stoddard & Kendall	Boston MA		Retail	c1932-pres.
Stollberg (& Clapp) Hdw. Co., The		Toledo OH		Hdw. Whol. Ret.	1878-19??
Stones		Derby	England	Retail	

POCKETKNIFE BRAND	TRADEMARK (or reference)	LOCATION	MADE IN	TYPE OF FIRM	DATES
Stratton & Terstegge Co.	Stratco	Louisville KY		Hdw. Whol.	1862-19??
Strauss, A(dolph), Company	bought William Elliot	New York NY		Whol. Import	c1907-1918
Straw, William	38 Essex St.	NY, NY	USA	Mfr.	c1844
Streamline	see Camillus Cutlery Co.	Camillus NY	USA	Mfr.'s brand	1936 ff.
Strevell-Paterson Hardware Co.		Salt Lake City UT		Hdw. Whol.	1888-19??
Stringer, John		Sheffield	England	Mfr.	c1893
Suffolk Cutlery Co.			Germany	Import brand	c1880s
Summit Cutlery Co.	see Pavian Cutlery Co.				
Sunshin	Rising Sun (picture)		China?	Mfr.'s brand?	
Superior Cutlery			Ger./Aust.	Generic Import	
Superota, Le			France	Mfr.'s brand?	current
Supplee Hardware Co.	Crown & arrow (picture)	Philadelphia PA		Hdw. Whol.	18??-1914
Supplee-Biddle Hardware Co.	Supplee and Biddle merged	Philadelphia PA		Hdw. Whol.	1914-?
Sutcliffe, J(ohn) H., & Co.	Hickory Hand Forged	Louisville KY	USA	Ret. Mail Order	c1900
Svoboda, B.	for Liberty Organization	Montrose CA	Ger./Japan	Whol. brand	c1950-pres.
Swain, (James P.), Cutlery	knives 1858-	Bronxville NY	USA	Mfr.	c1840-1898
Swan Works	see Altenbach				
Swanner, (Stan) Cutlery Co.	Swans (picture)	Fairfield OH	US/Ger	Retail, Whol.	1979-pres.
Swift, Joseph, & Co.		Sheffield	England	Mfr.	c1893
Swiss Army Brands	see R.H. Forschner				
(Swiss Army Knife)	see Elsener or Wenger				
Sword & Shield			Germany	Import brand	recent
Sword	Sword Brand after 1942, by Kastor and Camillus			Mfr.'s brand	c1906-pres
Swordplay	see J. Horton & Co. Ltd.	London, Hamburg	England	Wholesale brand	c1930
Syraucse Knife Co.	Camillus brand	Camillus NY	USA	Mfr.'s brand	1930s
Syracuse Knife Co.	Imported by Camillus		Poland	Import brand	1975-1976
T.B. & M.	see Turton Bros. & Matthews				
T.C./1972/U.S.A.	see Thompson Center Arms				
T.E.C.S.	see Exclusive Cutlery				
T.M.	in hallmark on silver fruit knives: see Thomas Marples				
T.T.C. Diamond Brand, N.Y.	sold by Sears Roebuck	Chicago IL	USA	Retail	c1909
Talbot, Brooks & Ayer		Portland ME		Hdw. Whol.	1902-?
Tampa Hardware Co.	W.C.T.	Tampa FL		Hdw. Whol.	1900-c1930
Tarry-Levigne, Pierre	Lizard (picture)	Thiers	France	Mfr.	c1864-19??
Tatro-Nif	see Carlson-Lusk Co. (Tatro Winfield buyer)				
Taylor, John	(eye) Witness 1838-	Sheffield	England	Mfr.	c1820-1856
Taylor's (eye) Witness	Thomas B. Needham	Sheffield	England	Mfr.'s brand	1856-1879
Taylor's (eye) Witness	Needham, Veall & Tyzack	Sheffield	England	Mfr.'s brand	1879-1975
Taylor Cutlery Co.	Stewart Taylor	Kingsport TN	Japan	Whol. Import	current
Taylor, Arthur W.		Sheffield	England	Mfr.	c1893
Taylor, George H., & Brother	Times works	Sheffield	England	Mfr.	1850s-1920s
Taylor, H.H.	HTH	Sheffield	England	Mfr.	c1919
Taylor, H.H., & Bro.	(US Navy contractor)	Sheffield	England	Mfr.	c1855 ff.
Taylor, Henry	Acorn	Sheffield	England	Mfr.	c1858-1927
Teague Hardware Co.		Mobile AL		Hdw. Whol.	1892-19??
Tekna (Design Group)		Belmont CA	USA	Mfr.	recent
Tenk Hardware Co.		Quincy IL		Hdw. Whol.	1865-19??
Tennessee Knife Works	Colonel Coon brand by Adrian Harris; sold to W.R. Case & Sons	Columbia TN	USA	Mfr.	1978-1988
Terrier Cutlery Co.	made by Robeson	Rochester NY	USA	Mfr.'s brand?	c1910-1916
Thalson Paratrooper	see YAX				
The W. & H. Co.	see Whitehead & Hoag				
Theile & Quack	Wade B(ros.), Tyler, A*1 made by Wester & Butz, Gebruder Weyersberg	Elberfeld	Germany	Whol. Export	c1866-1890
Thelco	(= The L. Co.) see Lockwood Luetkemeyer Henry Hardware Co.				
Thiers	(place name)		France		
Thistle Cutlery	see Clauss Cutlery Co.	Fremont OH	Germany	Import brand	
Thomas Mfg. Co.	sold HHH, American Shear	Dayton OH	USA	Retail by mail	1907-1911
Thomas-Ogilvie Hardware Co.		Shreveport LA		Hdw. Whol.	1907-?
Thomaston Knife Co.		Thomaston CT	USA	Mfr.	1884-c1930
Thompson & Gascoigne	became Empire Knife Co.	Winsted CT	USA	Mfr.	1852-1856
Thompson, Edward Lauders, & Co.		Sheffield	England	Mfr.	c1893
Thompson, J.H., (Cutlery) Ltd.		Sheffield	England	Mfr.	c1955

POCKETKNIFE BRAND	TRADEMARK (or reference)	LOCATION	MADE IN	TYPE OF FIRM	DATES
Thompson, J.M., Hardware Co.	Sterling Service	Minneapolis MN	Ger./Eng.	Hdw. Whol.	1900-c1922
	Axel Nilsson		USA/Sweden		
Thompson S., (& Son) (& O'Neill)	6 Henry Street	Dublin	England?	Retail?	c1833 ff.
Thompson Center Arms	T.C./1972/U.S.A. made by Camillus, supplied by Blackie Collins, sold by Trend Products, Dublin OH	Rochester NH	USA	Whol. prototypes	1972
Thomson-Diggs Co., The	Century (- 1935)	Sacramento CA		Hdw. Whol.	1884-?
Thornhill, W.	Tree (picture)	London	England	Mfr. & Retail	19th cent.
Thornton	see Federal Knife Company				
Thorpe, George		Sheffield	England	Mfr.	c1893
Thorpe, Joseph		Sheffield	England	Mfr.	c1853-1873
Thorpe, T.		Sheffield	England	Mfr.	
Tidioute Cutlery Co. (1)	to Union Razor Co. 1902	Tidioute PA	USA	Mfr.	1897-1906
Tidioute Cutlery Co. (2)	to Baldwin Cutlery Go.	Tidioute PA	USA	Mfr.	1909-1916
Tiemann, (George) & Co.	surgical instruments	New York NY	USA	Mfr.	1826-pres.
Tiger Brand	see Lauterjung & Co.				
Tillotson, Thomas & Co.	Columbia Place 1852-	Sheffield	England	Mfr.	1760s-1863
Tilquin		Brussels	Belgium	Mfr. or Retail	
Timberline	Vaughan Neely, Bill Sanders	Mancos CO	USA	Hand Mfr.	1982-1988
Timberline, Timberlite	by Equip U.S.A. 1991-1996, by Great American Tool Co. 1996-present	Mancos CO	USA	Mfr.'s brands	1991-pres.
Timms, James		Sheffield	England	Mfr.	
Timpson, C., & (Jos. A.) Tucker	167 South St.	NYC	USA?	Hdw.Whol. & Mfr.	1863-1872
Tina	budding & grafting knives		Germany	Mfr.'s brand?	c1890-pres.
Tingle, William H.		Sheffield	England	Mfr.	c1893
Tips, Walter, Co.	some by Colonial 1930s	Austin TX	USA	Hdw. Whol.	1862-pres.
Tisane de la G[ran]de Chartreuse	on clasp knife blade = infusion of Chartreuse (French) = light or Golden Chartreuse	Grande Chartreuse	France	Liqueur Advt.	pre 1903
Tischer & Reisinger		Dayton OH		Hdw. Whol.	1884-19??
Tisdale, Benjamin H.	lived 1791-1881;	Providence RI	USA	Silversmith and Jeweler	c1824
	made silver fruit knives	Newport RI	USA	Silversmith and Jeweler	c1840-1881
Toboggan	(picture) see John Askham				
Toledo	(place name)	Spain			
Toledo Cutlery Co.			Germany	Import brand	c1890s
Tompkin	see Flockton Tompkin & Co.				
Tonerini		Scarperia	Italy	Mfr.	c1945
Topper, Junior Topper, Sport Topper	see Colonial				
Torner's Celebrated Cutlery	probably Thiele & Quack				
Torrey, J. R., Razor Co.	Mfr. after c1880 factory organized by Joseph Turner and William Cowlishaw	Worcester MA	USA	Mfr. & Import	c1858-1963
Tower Brand, The	see J.S. Holler				
Towika	actually Jowika (Stahlwarenfabrik)				
Towle (Silversmiths)	silver fruit knives	Newburyport MA	USA	Mfr.	c1970s?
Towle Stainless	for Towle Mfg. Co.	Newburyport MA	Germany	Whol. import	c1978
Townley Metal & Hardware Co.		Kansas City MO		Hdw. Whol.?	1884-pres.
Townsend, Francis J.	Life	Sheffield	England	Mfr.	c1893
Track Knives - Luger Knife	1/100, Ray Schmidt et al	Whitefish MT	USA	Custom Ltd. Ed.	1976
Tracy & Robinson (& Williams)		Hartford CT		Hdw. Whol.	1835-19??
Tracy-Wells Co., The Columbus OH				Hdw. Whol.	1885-19??
Trail Blazer	see The George Worthington Co.				
Travelers Premium Company	tool kit knives		Germany	Retail?	c1900?
Treat Hardware Co.		Lawrence MA		Hdw. Whol. Ret.	1859-19??
Tredway, A., & Co.	was Andrew & Tredway	Dubuque IA	USA?	Hdw. Whol.	1873-c1929
Treliving & Smith	made by Thomas Turner	?	England	Retail?	c1840?
Treman, King & Co.		Ithaca NY		Hdw. Whol. Ret.	1844-19??
Trenton Cutlery Co.	sold to Boker c1906	Trenton NJ?	England	Import	c1880-1906
Trickett, Albert		Sheffield	England	Mfr.	18??-c1939
Trickett, James		Sheffield	England	Mfr.	c1879
Trident	(Dreizack) see Ed. Wusthof				
Tritch, The George, Hardware Co.	made by Ulster	Denver CO	USA	Hdw. Whol.	1859-19??
Troll			Germany	Export brand?	c1920s
Trout Hardware Co.	Square Deal	Chicago IL		Hdw. Whol.	c1896-1907
Tru-Temper	see Ohio Cutlery Co.				

POCKETKNIFE BRAND	TRADEMARK (or reference)	LOCATION	MADE IN	TYPE OF FIRM	DATES
True Value	see Hibbard Spencer Bartlett & Co.				
Trumpet or Cornet	(picture) see Gebruder Weyersberg				
Trustworthy	see Mappin & Webb				
Tryon, Edward K.	3/T. Some by Utica	Philadelphia PA	US/Engl.	Retail & Whol.	1811-c1952
Tuna Valley Cutlery Co.	possibly a Case brand	Bradford PA	Germany?	Import brand?	c1890s
Tunnel City		Tunnel City WI		Mfr.?	
Turner, (C.W.) Hardware Co.	Monogram THCo	Muskogee I.T./OK		Hdw. Whol.	1887-c1901
Turner, Edward		Sheffield	England	Mfr.	c1893
Turner, Ephraim	whip knife by B. McGovern	Fort Worth TX	USA	Inventor	c1884
Turner, Thomas, & Co.	Encore 1805-, Teakettle 1902-, Norfolk St. c1820s; Suffolk Works built c1834; see also: Warranted Really Good; bought Wingfield & Rowbotham, 1898; Haywood, 1902. Turner's sold to Viners 1932	Sheffield	England	Mfr.	1802-1932
Turner, Naylor & Co.	I. Sorby, Punch (picture)	Sheffield	England	Tool Mfr. Whol.	c1930s
Turton Brothers & Matthews	T.B. & M., Locomotive	Sheffield	England	Mfr.	c1860-1950s
Tuska Moto			Japan?		
Twentieth Century Cutlery Co.	made for A.J. Jordan	Saint Louis MO	USA?	Whol. brand	c1890-1906
Twig Brand	see Borgfeldt			Whol. brand	c1911
Twigg, S., & Sons		Sheffield	England	Mfr.	c1893
Twigg, W., & Sons		Sheffield	England	Mfr.	c1893
Twinworks, Twins	(picture) see J.A. Henckels				
Twitchell Bros.		Naugatuck CT	USA	Mfr.	
Twitchell, Homer	became pres. of Conn. Cut Co.	Naugatuck CT	USA	Mfr.	c1850-70s
Tyas, William, & Sons		Sheffield	England	Mfr.	c1893
Tye, Edwin, & Son	Ellis's wheel	Sheffield	England	Mfr.	c1893
Tyler Celebrated Cutlery	see Theile & Quack				
Tyzack, W.A., & Co. Ltd.	Stella, Horseman (1909-)	Sheffield	England	Mfr.	c1850-1953
U.K. & R.	see Utica Knife & Razor Co.				
U.M.C.	(Union Metallic Cartridge) see Remington (circle)				
U.N. Co.	see United Novelty Co.				
U.R. Co.	see Union Razor Company				
U*S	see Edward Barnes & Sons				
U.S.A.	(bone handles and steel mounts) made by Kingston for U.S. Army				
U.S.A.	(plastic handles and upset tip bolsters) usually Colonial				
U.S.A. Q.M.C./J.P.N.Z. 10158	U.S. Army Quartermaster Corps		Austria?	Military contr.	c1900
U.S. Cutlery (or Knife) Co.		Terre Haute IN	USA?		
U.S. Cutlery Co.	Vulcan	St. Louis MO		Wholesale	c1900?
U.S. Small Arms Co.	small knife pistol	Rochester NY, Chicago	USA	Mfr.	c1914-1923
Udahl	see Julius Uellendahl				
Uellendahl, Julius	Udahl. Sold in Ireland	Solingen-Wald	Germany	Mfr.	1904-c1970
Ulery, U(lysses) J., Co.	metal handles, by Napanoch	New York NY	USA	Whol.	c1902-1919
Ulmer, A(dolph)	C.F. Ulmer after 1890	Portland ME	Germany	Retail	1869-1928
Ulster Knife Co.	Dwight Divine & Son had been Cooperative Knife Co.; foreclosed by Dwight Divine 1876; sold to Albert M. Baer 1941	Ellenville NY	USA	Mfr.	1876-1941
Ulster USA	Albert M. Baer	Ellenville NY	USA	Mfr.	1941-1943
	became Kingston 1943, Imperial Knife Assoc. Cos. 1947			Mfr.'s brand	1945-pres.
UN-X-LD	see Northfield Knife Co.				
Uncle Henry	by Imperial Schrade (after Henry Baer)			Mfr.'s brand	1967-2004
Underwood, H.	56 Haymarket	London	England	Mfr. & Retailer	c1820-19??
Unger Bros.		Newark NJ	USA	Mfr.	c1919
Union Hardware & Metal Co.		Los Angeles CA		Hdw. Whol.	1882-?
Union Knife Co.	(beware of counterfeits)	Naugatuck CT	USA	Mfr.	1851-1885
Union Knife Works		Union NY	USA	Mfr.	c1911-1913
Union Razor Co.	became Union Cutlery	Tidioute PA	USA	Mfr.	c1902-1909
Union Cutlery Co.	moved to Olean NY	Tidioute PA	USA	Mfr.	1909-1911
Union Cutlery Co.	KA-BAR (first used 1923)	Olean NY	USA	Mfr.	1911-1951
Union Cutlery Co.	Ka-Bar	Cleveland OH	USA	Reissue	1979-1996
Union	(in map of N. America) see Union Cutlery Co.				
Unitas	see Pape Thiebes Cutlery Go.				
Unite, George	G.U. silver fruit knives	Birmingham	England	Mfr.	
United Cutlery Co.	170 E. Houston/230 Canal	New York NY	Aust./Ger.	Import	c1901-1920

POCKETKNIFE BRAND	TRADEMARK (or reference)	LOCATION	MADE IN	TYPE OF FIRM	DATES
United Cutlery Co.	made picture knives	Canton OH	USA	Mfr.	c1919
United Cutlery Co.	Smoky Mountain Knife Works	Sevierville TN	Japan/Ger.	Wholesale brand	current
United Knife Co.		Litchfield CT	USA	Mfr.?	c1860
United Knife Co.	ex-Northfield employees	Northfield CT	USA	Mfr.	c1885
United Machine Tool Co.	United (Navy pilot knife)	Grand Rapids MI	USA	Mfr.	c1943
United Metal Co., The		Shoranur, Madras	India	Mfr.	c1950?
United Novelty Co.	U.N. CO.	New York NY	USA	Advt. Specialty?	c1918
Unity	see Cooperative Wholesale Society Ltd. Whol. brand				
Universal	see Landers Frary & Clark (trademark adopted c1890s; sold to General Electric 1965)				
Unwin & Rodgers	NON-XLL-1865, Superlative Rockingham Works 1849; Globe Works from J. Walters 1865; made knife pistols 1839-	Sheffield	England	Mfr.	1833-c1910
Utica K(nife) & R(azor) Co.	Pal; owned by Joseph Abraham, Utica NY; and Samuel Mailman, who opened Pal Cutlery Co. (which see) c1935	Montreal	USA/Ger.	Whol. Import	c1924-1935
Utica Cutlery Co.	Kutmaster, Seneca, Agate	Utica NY	USA	Mfr.	1910-pres.
V.C. & Co.	see Vom Cleff & Co.				
V.F.	(in circle) see Valley Forge / Boker				
Val-Test Extruding	Keen Kutter (by Schrade)	Chicago IL	USA	Wholesale	1960-1965
Valley Falls Cutlery Co.		Valley Falls NY? RI?	USA?	Mfr.?	c1915?
Valley Forge Cutlery Co.		Newark NJ	USA	Mfr.	c1892-1899
Valley Forge/VF (in circle)	owned by Boker USA	Newark NJ	USA	Mfr.'s brand	1899-c1950
Valor Corporation	also Valco	Miami FL	Ger./Jap/Pak.	Import	1970-pres.
Value Received	pen knife (picture) see William Thomas Staniforth			Mfr.'s brand	1884-1920s
Van Camp Hardware & Iron Co.	sold knives-c1960 owned Capitol Cut Co. c1904-1948	Indianapolis IN	US/Germany	Hdw. Whol.	1876-pres.
Vance, J(ames) M., & Co.		Philadelphia PA	USA?	Hdw. Whol.	1776-19??
Veall, J.	joined T.B. Needham 1876, died 1906: see Needham, Veall & Tyzack				
Velox	see Neumeyer & Dimond				
Venture	see Slater				
Verinder	St. Pauls (Sheffield made)	London	England	Retail	c1900?
Veritable	= Genuine (French)				
Veritable Laguiole	see G. David Fils				
Vermont Cutlery Co.	Vermont Hardware Co.(?) probably made by Wester & Butz	Burlington? VT	Germany	Hdw.? Whol. brand	1871-19??
Vermont Knives	made Smith & Wesson	West Rutland VT	USA	Mfr.	1986-1993
Vernon, R., & Sons	sold to Beckett Steel Co.	Sheffield	England	Mfr.	1893-1904
Verry		Paris	France	Mfr.	c1870s?
Victor	tool kit knives		USA?		c1910?
Victoria	see Karl Elsener	Ibach, near Zurich	Switz.	Mfr.'s brand	1909-pres.
Victorinox	see Karl Elsener	Ibach	Switz.	Mfr.'s brand	1921-pres.
Victory Cutlery Co.		New Haven CT	USA	Mfr.?	c1925
Vignos, August	see Novelty Cutlery Co.				
Viking	see Eric Wedemeyer				
Village Blacksmith	see Washington Cutlery Co.				
Vincenzo & Piscitelli	look like Imperial	Frosolone	Italy	Mfr.?	c1950s
Viners, Ltd.	A. & E. Viener 1900-1925 bought Thomas Turner, 1932; Harrison Bros. & Howson, 1959. Largest in Sheffield 1965	Sheffield	England	Mfr.	1925-1982
Visconti, A.	Biscia, Serpe (Snake)	Canzo, Como	Italy	Mfr.	1882-pres.
Vittur, B.D.		New Orleans LA		Retail?	
Voelker Forst & Merten	Raucherkopf (smoking head)	Solingen-Hoehscheid	Germany	Mfr.	1920-19??
Voight, Starr & Co.		New York NY		Hdw. Whol.	1889-19??
Volka	for Dunham Carrigan	San Francisco CA	Germany	Hdw. Imp. brand	c1903
Vom Cleff & Co.	V. C. & Co.	New York NY	Ger./Eng.	Whol. Importer	1887-c1930
Vonnegut,(Clemens) Hardware Co.		Indianapolis IN		Hdw. Whol.	1852-1965
Voos, (Ernest) (Cutlery Co.)	Voos/Arrow; some by Empire	New Haven CT and Cheshire CT	USA/Ger.	Mfr. & Whol.	1923-pres.
Voos, Emil		Solingen	Germany	Mfr.	current
Voos, August & Co.	Voss Cutlery Co.	New York NY	Germany	Whol. Import	c1900-1939
Vulcan	see Thomas Ellin & Co., Joseph Elliott				
Vulcan Knife Co.	(may be U.S. Cutlery Co. St. Louis MO)		Germany	Import brand?	c1895
Vulcanite Knife Co.	Goodyears Pat. 5/6/1851	New York NY	USA	Mfr.?	1850s
W. & A. Co.		Providence RI	USA	Whol. Jeweler?	c1911
W. & H.	(in a flag) see Walker & Hall				

POCKETKNIFE BRAND	TRADEMARK (or reference)	LOCATION	MADE IN	TYPE OF FIRM	DATES
W. & H. Co., The	see The Whitehead & Hoag Co.				
W.H. & S.	see William Hutton & Sons				
W.B./Speed	see Brokhahne or Wiebusch				
WB (joined)	see White Brothers				
W.B. & P.	see Wood, Bicknall & Potter				
W.C.T.	see Tampa Hardware Co.				
W.N.	in hallmark on silver fruit knives: see William Needham or William Nowill				
W.R.B. Co.	see Will Roll Bearing Co.				
W'vill Co.	see Waterville Co.				
Wabash Cutlery Co.	(Indiana Cut. Co. c1932)	Terre Haute IN	USA	Mfr.	1921-1935
Wade,(Robert)	joined W. & S. Butcher as their American agent, 1819; eventually changed their US brand to Wade & Butcher	Sheffield, NYC	England	Mfr.	c1810-1819
Wade & Butcher	see W. & S. Butcher	Sheffield	England	Mfr.'s brand	c1819-1918
Wade & Butcher	Durham-Duplex Razor Co.	Jersey City NJ	US/Engl.	Mfr.'s brand	1918-1959
(Wade) Wingfield & Rowbotham	sold to Thomas Turner	Sheffield	England	Mfr.	c1825-1898
Wade B(ros.) Celebrated Cutlery	see Theile & Quack				
Wadsworth, A.W., & Sons	part of A. Kastor & Bros.	New York NY	Aust./Ger.	Import brand	c1905-1922
Wagner, Wilhelm	W/W	Solingen	Germany	Mfr.	1876-197?
Wahkonsa Cutlery Co.					
Wain, John		Sheffield	England	Mfr.	1890s-1920s
Walden Knife Co.	sold to E.C. Simmons 1902 moved to New Haven CT and merged with Winchester 1923	Walden NY	USA	Mfr.	c1870-1923
Walker & Co.		Sheffield	England		
Walker & Hall	W. & H. (in a flag)	Sheffield	England	Flatware Mfr.	1845-1960s
Wallace Bros.	a few pocketknives c1900	Wallingford CT	USA	Flatware Mfr.	c1895-1955
Wallkill River Works	N.Y. Knife Co. brand	Walden NY	USA	Mfr.'s brand	1928-1931
Waltco Saf-T-Sheath			USA	Mfr.	1950s-60s
Walter Brothers'	imported by Wiebusch	New York NY	Germany	Import brand	pre-1915
Walters, John, & Co.	Globe Works	Sheffield	England	Mfr.	c1841-1865
Waltham Cutlery Co.		Waltham MA (?)	US/Ger.	Wholesale?	c1910s
Walton's Thumb	Olson Industries	Denver CO		Mfr.'s brand	?-c1989
Wandy		Milan	Italy	Mfr.'s brand	1950s?
Ward, Asline	U.S. agent for G. Wostenholm (b.1821-d.1905); succeeded by Edward Beckett before 1897	New York NY	England	Import	c1850-189?
Ward, Charles, F.		Sheffield	England	Mfr.	c1893
Ward, F(rederick) & Co.	B4*ANY owned Eyre Ward & Co. with B. J. Eyre & Co. c1852-1869; Mark sold to John Watts	Sheffield	England	Mfr.	c18??-1890s
Ward, J(ames), & Co.	ivory fruit knives, etc.	Bronxville NY	USA	Mfr.	c1860s
Ward, J.	Atlas Works (J. Russell)	Turners Falls MA	USA	Mfr.'s brand	c1880s ff
Ward, Merriam & Co.		Boston MA		Retail	c1870
Ward, Thomas & Sons	see Stacey Bros.	Sheffield	England	Mfr.	c1850-pres.
Ward & Morton		Sheffield	England	Mfr.	c1893
Wardle, Henry		Sheffield	England	Mfr.	c1893
Wardlows, S. & C.		Sheffield	England	Steel Mfr.	c1850s-pres.
Wards	made for Montgomery Ward & Co. by Utica (and some possibly by Winchester)	Chicago IL	USA	Retail brand	c1935-50s
Wards	blade etched Western Pride made for Montgomery Ward by Western States	Chicago IL	USA	Retail brand	1930s-40s?
Wards Master Quality	made for Montgomery Ward	Chicago IL	USA	Retail brand	recent
Warenzeichen	= trademark (German)				
Warman & Ely		Philadelphia PA	USA	Retail?	c1860s
Warner, E., & Co.		Sheffield	England	Mfr.	c1893
Warner Hardware Co.		Minneapolis MN		Hdw. Whol. Ret.	1901-?
Warranted Really Good	by Thomas Turner & Co. used on knives made for the U.S., also usually marked "Made Expressly For America"	Sheffield	England	Mfr.'s brand	c1810s-50s
Warren	re-bladed Remington frames	Baker OR	USA	Customizer	c1930s
Warren Brothers			Germany?	Import brand?	c1890?
Warren, J.M. & Co.	incorporated 1887	Troy NY		Hdw. Whol. Ret.	1809-19??
Warren Pearl Works		Philadelphia PA	USA?	Pearl Mfr.?	c1890?
Warren Tool Co.	made by Imperial Schrade	Rhinebeck NY	USA	Tool Mfr. Ltd. Ed.	1982
Warwick Knife Co.		Warwick NY	USA	Mfr.	c1907-1928
Washington Cutlery Co.	Anchor (picture), see Gray & Dudley Hardware Co. and Keith Simmons & Co.				

POCKETKNIFE BRAND	TRADEMARK (or reference)	LOCATION	MADE IN	TYPE OF FIRM	DATES
Washington Cutlery Co.	made Village Blacksmith butcher knives; sold Washington Cutlery Co. and Cutgud (c1898-1909) pocketknives	Watertown, Milw. WI	USA	Whol. (& Mfr.?)	1898-1940
Watauga	see H.G. Lipscomb & Co.				
Waterbury Cutlery Co.		Waterbury CT			
Waterville (Cutlery or Mfg.) Co.		Waterbury CT	USA	Mfr.	1843-c1913
Watkins Cottrell Co.	Clipper (after 1901)	Richmond VA		Hdw. Whol.	1867-pres.?
Watkinson, Jonathan	Watkinson	Sheffield	England	Mfr.	c1787
Watson, John, Inc.		Houlton ME		Hdw. Whol.	1870-19??
Watts, John	first cutlery 1888 B4*ANY mark from F. Ward 1890s; Frog (picture) from J. Newton 1916	Sheffield	England	Mfr.	1765-pres.
Wearever	see Alcas				
Webb, H.W. & Sons		Baltimore MD		Hdw. Whol. Ret.	1850-19??
Webster, William, & Son		Sheffield	England	Mfr.	c1893
Weck, Edward, & Sons	c1940 made by Schrade	New York NY	Ger./USA	Wholesale	c1893-1943
Wedemeyer, Eric	Viking E.W. (by Union Cut.)	New York NY	USA	Retail?	c1930s
Wedgeway Cutlery Co.	for Morley Bros. Hdw. Co.	Saginaw MI	USA?	Hdw. Whol.brand	1887-1933
Weed & Co.	branch at Rochester 1911	Buffalo NY		Hdw. Whol. Ret.	1818-19??
Weeks Hardware Co.		Scranton PA		Hdw. Whol. Ret.	1907-?
Weidmannsheil	= "Good hunting!" (German) and stag (picture), see W. Weltersbach				
Weiland, Charles, Inc.		New York NY		Hdw. Whol.	1882-19??
Weis, John		Nashville TN	Germany	Retail?	
Weise, F.		New York NY	USA?		c1860?
Weiss, John & Son 1830-83; & Sons 1883-		London	England	Mfr. & Retailer	1787-pres.
Welkut	see Graef & Schmidt				
Welliver, W.W., Hardware Co.		Danville PA	Germany	Hdw. Whol. Ret.	1880-19??
Weitersbach, William	Springer, other marks	Solingen	Germany	Mfr.	1882-pres.
Wenger	(Swiss Army) Wengerinox; bought by Victorinox in 2005	Delemont	Switz.	Mfr.	c1908-pres.
Werwolfwerk	imp. by Dixon Cut. Co.		Germany	Mfr.?	c1920s
Weske Cutlery Co.	mainly made fixed blades	Sandusky OH	USA	Mfr. & Retail	c1946-1952
WEST-CUT	by Western Cutlery	Boulder CO	USA	Mfr.'s brand	c1958
West Virginia Cutlery Co.				Whol.?	
Westaco	see Western States Cutlery				
Westby, Joseph	Westby b. 1854 d. 1929	Sheffield	England	Mfr.?	1876-1965
Westby, John		Sheffield	England	Mfr.	c1893
Wester & Butz	many brands; Wester Bros.	Merscheid	Germany	Mfr.	1832-1966
Wester Bros.	Anchor-Star-Arrow was Jacoby & Wester; US agent of Wester & Butz; pre-1915 jack knives made in USA	New York NY	US/Germany	Whol. & Import	1902-c1967
Wester Bros.	(no Anchor Logo)	New York NY	USA	Whol.	c1906
Wester Stone Co.	see Wester Bros.	New York NY	Germany	Import brand	c1915
Western Cutlery Co.	for Wiebusch & Hilger	New York NY	Ger./Aust.	Import brand	c1874-1914
Western Knives	owned Richards Bros.	Sheffield	England	Holding Co.	c1982
Western States Cutlery Co.	became Western Cutlery 1956	Boulder CO	USA	Mfr.	1911-1956
Western States Cutlery Co.	Tested Sharp Temper (tic-tac-toe) blade etch			Mfr.'s brand	c1911-1941
Western Cutlery Co.	moved to Longmont 1978	Boulder CO	USA	Mfr.	1956-1978
Western Cutlery Co.	became Coleman-Western 1984	Longmont CO	USA	Mfr.	1978-1984
Western Cutlery Co.	made by Camillus formerly Coleman-Western	Camillus NY	USA	Mfr.'s brand	1991-pres.
Westersson, A.J.		Eskilstuna	Sweden	Mfr.	c1900
Westmark	see Western Cutlery Co.				
Westpfal, (August), Cutlery Co.	Standpoint	New York NY		Retail	c1920-1951
Westpfal, Frederick (& Bro.)	Acme	New York NY	Germany/US	Whol. & Retail	c1884-1940
WEXL	see American Shear & Knife Co. or F. Koeller & Co.				
Weyde, Max		Solingen	Germany	Mfr.	c1980s
Weyersberg, Gebruder (Bros.)	Comet, King, A* 1, etc.	Solingen	Germany	Mfr.	1787-pres.
Whale	(picture) see Richartz				
Wharton, H.	Crown (picture) Cast Steel		Germany?		
Wheatley Bros.	Wheat Sheaf marks sold to Needham, Veall & Tyzack	Sheffield	England	Mfr.	1878-1936
Wheaton & Bennett	104 Oxford Street	London	England	Retail	
Wheelhouse, Thomas		Sheffield	England	Mfr.	c1893
Whirling square in circle	(picture) see China Light Industrial Products ... Candon, Guangdong				
White, Matthew	OVO	Sheffield	England	Mfr.	c1847-1869
White Brothers	WB (joined)	New Orleans LA	Germany	Retail	c1900-1950

POCKETKNIFE BRAND	TRADEMARK (or reference)	LOCATION	MADE IN	TYPE OF FIRM	DATES
Whitehead & Hoag, The, Co.	made by Boker USA	Newark NJ	USA	Advt. Specialty	c1870-1959
Whitfield Hardware Co.	Wire Grass	Hawkinsville GA		Hdw. Retail	c1910
Whiton Hardware Co.	Alki, Olympic	Seattle WA		Hdw. Whol.	1888-c1925
Whitt-L-Kraft	see Cattaraugus Cut. Co.	Little Valley NY	USA	Mfr.'s brand	c1931-1954
Whittingslowe	marked on metal handles	Adelaide	Australia	Mfr.	c1940s-?
Whittles & Froggatt		Sheffield	England	Mfr.	c1850s
Wibbeltrath, Hermann	Steeple (picture)	Solingen-Ohligs	Germany	Mfr.	c1860
Wichard	W (in pentagon)		France	Mfr.?	current
Wichita Cutlery Co.		Wichita KS		Whol.?	
Wick, Albert or William		New York NY	Germany	Whol.	19th cent.
Wiebusch & Hilger	Western Cutlery Co. Monumental Cutlery Co., Walter Bros., &c; agent for many scissor and tool firms. Bought B.J. Eyre 1876; built Challenge Cutlery Co. 1891; bought C.B. Barker 1905. Frederick Wiebusch (d. 1893), Wm. S. Hilger, Charles F. Wiebusch, Walter M. Taussig	New York NY	US/Ger./Eng.	Whol/Imp/Mfr.	1864-1928
Wigfall, John, & Co.	Bona-Fide; sold to Elliott	Sheffield	England	Mfr.	1843-1911
Wilbert Cutlery Co.	made for Sears Roebuck by Napanoch and Empire	Chicago IL	USA	Retail brand	c1909
Wilcox/45 Edgeware Road	made in Sheffield	London	England	Retail	c1900
Wilcox, Louis N., & Son		Baltimore MD		Hdw. Whol.	c1922
Wild, Arthur E.		Sheffield	England	Mfr.	c1893
Wild, John, Jr., & Ebenezer & W.	Celebrated American Cutlery	New York NY	USA	Mfr.?	c1850
Wild, Joseph		Sheffield	England	Mfr.	c1893
Wilford Cutlery Co.	Great Western Works	Sheffield	England	Mfr.	c1840s-80s
Wilkinson Sword Ltd.		London & Sheffield	England	Whol. & Mfr.	c1905-pres.
Wilkinson, H.Y., Cutlery Co.		Sheffield	England	Mfr.?	c1900
Wilkinson, W(illiam), (& Son)		Sheffield	England	Mfr.	c1760-1892
Will,(Frederick) & (Julius) Finck	factory (1863-1905) made fixed blade knives; pocketknives marked Will & Finck were imported	San Francisco CA	Ger./Eng.	Mfr. & Retail	1863-1932
Will & Finck	for United Cutlery	Sevierville TN	Japan	Whol. brand	current
Will Roll Bearing Co.	W.R.B. Co. (by Baldwin?)	Terre Haute IN	USA	Whol.?	c1920s
Williams (Brothers) Cutlery Co.		San Francisco CA		Retail	c1900-pres.
Williams, Alfred	Rivington Works, EBRO took over W. & S. Butcher. Imported by Kastor.	Sheffield	England	Mfr.	c1900-1946
Willis Co., The H.	Harlan Willis Burbank imported Schmidt & Ziegler, Big Horn brand	Louisville KY	Ger./Italy	Whol. import	?-c1972
Wilmington	see J.C. Cogan & Son's	Wilmington IL			
Wilson & Hawksworth		Sheffield	England	Mfr.	1825-1832
Wilson, Hawksworth & Moss	Joshua Moss was US Rep.	Sheffield	England	Mfr.	1832-1846
Wilson, Hawksworth & Ellison	became steel-maker, 1850s	Sheffield	England	Mfr.	1846-1850s
Wilson, Joseph F.		Sheffield	England	Mfr.	c1893
Wilson & Southern	became Southern & Richardson	Sheffield	England	Mfr.	1828-1847
Wilson, W., & Sons		Sheffield	England	Mfr.	c1893
Wilson Cutlery			Germany	Import brand	c1900
Wilton, Henry		New York NY	Germany	Import	c1900
Wilzin's patent	see Auto(matic) Knife Co.				
Wimberly & Thomas Hardware Co.	marked knives c1903-1920s predecessor established 1887	Birmingham AL	USA/Ger.	Hdw. Whol.	1903-1982
Winchester (Repeating Arms Co.)	made knives 1919-1942 bought Napanoch and Eagle 1919, Simmons Hdw. and Walden Knife Co. 1922	New Haven CT	USA	Mfr. & Whol.	c1865-pres.
Winchester/New Haven, CT	premiums made by Schrade	New Haven CT	USA	Gun Mfr. ad	c1978
Winchester	contract-made knives sold in Germany by Winchester-Germany. Knives MARKED Winchester/Germany are fakes.	Ratingen, Germany	Ger./Japan/It.	Whol. & Retail	1960s-pres.
Winchester	authorized new issues made by Utica, Queen, and Camillus for Blue Grass Cutlery Corp.	Manchester OH	USA	Whol. brand	c1985-pres.
Winchester	Z.I. Molina contract-made knives sold in France, licensed by Winchester-France	St-Jean-Bonnefonds	Japan/Italy	Whol. & Retail	1980s-pres.
Winchester	(on handle) U.S.A. (on tang) fantasy made by Colonial Knife Co.				1980s
Winchester Cutlery Co.			Germany	Import brand	
Wing, E(benezer), & Co.		West Goshen CT	USA	Mfr.	c1860s
Wingen, Anton, Jr.	Othello	Solingen	Germany	Mfr.	1888-1996
Wingfield & Rowbotham	see (Wade) Wingfield & Rowbotham				
Winkler, Victor	Wiso, made by J. Moede	Solingen	Germany	Whol. brand	c1980s
Winter, J.	17 St. Philips Terrace	Sheffield	England	Mfr.?	c1850

POCKETKNIFE BRAND	TRADEMARK (or reference)	LOCATION	MADE IN	TYPE OF FIRM	DATES
Wintgen, Ewald, & Co.	now part of Kammerling	Elberfeld	Germany	Mfr.	
Wire Grass	see Whitfield Hardware Co.				
Wire Jack	see George Schrade Knife Co.	Bridgeport CT	USA	Mfr.'s brand	c1926-1956
Wismar Cutlery Co.	Germany			Import brand	c1900
Wiso	see Victor Winkler				
Wiss, J(acob) & Sons		Newark NJ	USA	Scissor Mfr.	c1848-pres.
Witness	Eye (picture) see Needham Veall & Tyzack				
Witte, Alexis	Solace	New York NY		Wholesale	1878-c1930
Witte, (Ernest) Hardware Co.	F. Wiebusch a partner c1865	St. Louis MO		Hdw. Whol.	1849-pres.
Witte, Francis T., Hardware Co.		New York NY		Hdw. Whol. Ret.	1880-19??
Witte, John G., & Brother		New York NY		Import	1868-?
Wolf, Chris	Schatt & Morgan foreman	Titusville PA	USA	Mfr.'s brand	c1920s
Wolf & Co.	made by D. Peres		Germany	Advt. Specialty	c1910?
Wolfertz, C.F., & Co.	(Mfr.1862-c1920)	Allentown PA		Mfr. then Whol.	1862-c1944
Wolstenholme, George	became Wostenholm	Sheffield	England	Mfr.	1745-c1775
Wood Knives	Barry B. Wood Engineering, Design, & Services. Also made Colt knives 1969-1973	Venice CA	USA	Mfr.	1969-1977
Wood, Barry B.	B.B.W. Now Wood, Irie & Co.	Venice CA	USA	Hand Mfr.	1972-1991
Wood, Irie & Co.	Barry Wood, Michael Irie	Colorado Springs CO	USA	Hand Mfr.	1991-pres.
Wood, Alexander & James	also Wood, Vallance & Co. affiliates at Winnipeg, Regina, Vancouver, Calgary, Nelson BC, and Toronto	Hamilton, Ontario		Hdw. Whol.	1849-19??
Wood, B., & Sons		Sheffield	England	Mfr.	c1893
Wood, Bicknall & Potter	W.B. & P.	Providence RI	Germany?	Retail	c1890?
Wood, Frank	Rudder, I Guide	Sheffield	England	Mfr.	c1893
Wood, Joseph	Jos. Wood & Co. after 1871	York	England	Retail & Mfr?	c1799-1935
Woodbury Cutlery Co.		Woodbury CT	USA	Mfr.?	19th cent.
Woodhead, George (& Son)	G.W.*I.	Sheffield	England	Mfr.	c1845-1870s
Woodward Hardware Co.	Gordon Roswell Woodward	Cairo IL		Hdw. Whol.	1861-1960s
Woodward Wright & Co.		New Orleans LA		Hdw. Whol.	1867-19??
Woodworth Knife Works	pocketknives by Case c1912	Nunda NY	USA	Butcher Knife Mfr.	1876-c1917
Worth, B., & Sons	Mazeppa (ex-Hancock), Nunic	Sheffield	England	Mfr.	c1874-1960
Worth Hulfish & Sons	see Hulfish, Worth, & Sons; also Carlin-Hulfish Co.				
Worthington, The George, Co.	Trail Blazer, Harvard, Clearcut	Cleveland OH		Hdw. Whol.	1829-c1949
Wostenholm, George	Rockingham Works First U.S. sale (by Naylor & Sanderson) 1830; moved to Washington Works 1848	Sheffield	England	Mfr.	1815-1848
Wostenholm, George	I*XL Washington Works	Sheffield	England	Mfr.	1848-c1870s
Wostenholm, George	I*XL Celebrated	Sheffield	England	Mfr.	c1860s-90s
Wostenholm, George	I*XL, ENGLAND on blade	Sheffield	England	Mfr.	c1891-1971
Wostenholm, George	I*XL: (for owners of name after 1971, see Rodgers Wostenhom Ltd.)				
Wostenholm, J(oseph), & Co.	- & Sons after 1854	Sheffield	England	Mfr.	c1848-1867
Wragg Brothers		Sheffield	England	Mfr.	c1893
Wragg, David D.		Sheffield	England	Mfr.	c1893
Wragg, John, & Son	Crossed blades (picture) Joseph Wragg; bought mark and Advance Works from E. Blaydes; sold to W. R. Humphreys	Sheffield	England	Mfr.	1880-1900
Wragg, Samuel C. (& Sons)	Sheaf Island Works	Sheffield	England	Mfr.	c1830s-60s
Wragg, Samuel C.	for United Cutlery	Sevierville TN	Japan	Whol. brand	current
Wragg, William H(enry)	contract multiblades	Sheffield	England	Hand Mfr.	1871-1955
Wragg, Eric, M.	son of Wm. H. Wragg	Sheffield	England	Hand Mfr.	1946-1994
Wragg, William, & Sons		Sheffield	England	Mfr.	c1893
Wright, A.W.	sold in Canada	Sheffield	England	Mfr.?	recent
Wright, S., & Co., Ltd.		Sheffield	England	Mfr.	c1970
Wright & Wilhemy	Clean Clipper (arrow) knives by Boker, Ulster. Called Rector & Wilhelmy to 1902; in Nebraska City to 1883	Omaha NE	USA	Hdw. Whol.	1871-pres.
Wusthof, Carl, KG	Gladiator, Hejo, James	Solingen	Germany	Mfr.	1895-pres.
Wusthof, Eduard	Dreizack (Trident) factory built 1832; pocketknives discontinued c1955	Solingen	Germany	Mfr.	1814-pres.
Wyeth Hardware & Mfg. Co.	Wyeth's Warranted Cutlery	St. Joseph MO	USA/Ger.	Hdw. Whol.	1860-pres.
Wyoming Knife Co.	moved to Colorado	Casper WY	USA	Mfr.	c1974-1984
Wyoming Knife Co.	The Powder River folder	Fort Collins CO	USA	Mfr.	1984-pres.
XCD	see W. & S. Butcher				
XLCR	see W. Bingham				

POCKETKNIFE BRAND	TRADEMARK (or reference)	LOCATION	MADE IN	TYPE OF FIRM	DATES
XLNT	see Adolph Kastor & Bros., or Joseph Lingard				
XL N.Y.	see Ulster Knife Co.				
XX	see W.R. Case, or J. Copley (also used by Osborne on fixed blades)				
Xcelite	now part of Cooper Group	Orchard Park NY	USA	Elec. Tool Mfr.	1921-1973
Y-B Cigars			USA?	Cigar Mfr. Ad	c1920s?
Yale Cutlery Co.	owned by Son Bros. S.F. CA	Meriden CT	USA	Mfr.?	c1883- ?
Yankee	see Colonial Knife Co.				
Yankee Cutlery Co.	J. Reichard & Co.	New York NY	Germany	Import Brand	1903-1950s
Yax	Thalson Paratrooper		Germany?		c1950?
York Cutlery Co.		York PA	Germany	Import	c1955
Young, M.S., & Co.		Allentown PA		Hdw. Whol.	1843-19??
Young, W.	32 Arcade (Sheffield made)	London	England	Retail	c1890?
Yudelman, Israel Sjambok		Sheffield	England	Plater & Mfr.	c1900-1925
Zak		?	Germany	Import brand	c1910?
Zavialoff, Alexis	Imperial eagle (picture)	Vyatka (or Kirov)	Russia	Mfr.	c1870s
		Pavlov	Russia	Mfr.	c1900
Zenith	see Marshall Wells Hdw. most made by New York Knife Co.; some made later by Camillus	Duluth MN	USA	Hdw. Whol. brand	c1893-1917
Zenith			Germany	Mfr.'s brand	recent
Zest International	Zest		Minneapolis MN	Import	current
Zion's Co-op Mercantile Institution		Salt Lake City UT		Whol. Retail	1868-?
Zinn, Edward	Open Easy	New York NY	Germany?	Import	c1920
Zippo Mfg. Co.	pocketknives 1964-pres. bought W.R. Case & Sons Cutlery Co. 1993	Bradford PA		Mfr.	1932-pres.
Zwillingswerk	= Twinworks (German) see J.A. Henckels				

NUMBERS AS TRADEMARKS

3C	see Cattaraugus Cutlery Co.					
3/T	see Edward K. Tryon					
No. 6 (Norfolk Street)	see Joseph Rodgers & Sons (this mark was often counterfeited in India)					
No. 6 Sheffield Steel	Maltese crosses	Dehra Dun	India	Counterfeit	c1940s-70s	L
20th Century Cutlery Co.	see Twentieth Century Cutler Co., A.J. Jordan					
31 Bessett	see Besset-Laroche, Societe Nouvelle					
32 Dumas-Aine	see Rousselon Freres et Cie					
41	see Gonon					
59	see Sauvagnat-Aine					
76	see Bernard et Chevalier					
92	see Cartailler-Deluc					
116	see Bertry; Bechon; Dumousset					
716	see Edouard					
1700	see Nowill					
1741	see Naylor					
1760 M. F. & S.	see Furness					
1765	see John Watts					
1776	see Krusius Brothers or Sanderson Brothers					
1834	see J. Russell & Company					
1855	see Meriden Cutlery Company					
1865	see Henry Sears & Sons					
1874	see John Engstrom					
1876	see Joseph Gardner or Frary Cutlery Co.					
2284833, P2689400, 2479855 (U.S. patent numbers)	see Imperial Knife Co. (made after 1954)					
For PUNCH BLADE patent numbers, see page 31						

Pattern Year						
1976	1977	1978	1979	1980	1981	1982
507 Lockback						
X	X	X	X	X	Bear	Bighorn
					$36	$36
508 Folding Hunter						
Eagle/ Whales	Eagle/ Banner	Bear/Fish	Bear/ Hunter	Turkeys	Raccoons	Bison
$75 [#260]	$63 [#261]	$50 [#261]	$40	$40	$45	$38
500 Large Lockblade						
X	X	X	Bison	Rams	Bucks	Deer
			$37	$24	$24	$25
503 Small Lockblade						
X	X	X	Trout	Bass	Gar	Trout
			$24	$25	$19	$20
505 Stockman						
X	X	Canada Geese	Gulls	Raccoons	Dog/ Pheasant	Mallards
		$34	$28	$25	$25	$20
506 Barlow						
X	X	Raccoons	Raccoon	Ducks	Fox	Squirrel
		$23	$21	$16	$16	$15
502 Sharp Finger						
Whales/ Ship	Eagle/ Banner	Bear/Fish	X	Pronghorn	Ram	Cougar
$60 [#152]	$40 [#155]	$30 [#155]		$24	$20	$20
501 Drop Point						
X	X	X	Buck			
X	X	X	$24			
509 Little Finger						
X	X	X	X	X	Canada Geese	Raccoon
					$20	$20

Pattern Year						
1983	1984	1985	1986	1987	1988	1989
507 Lockback						
Mustang	Raccoons	Bears	Turkeys	Wolves	Cougar	Bear & Cub
$37	$37	$30	$30	$29	$29	$29
508 Folding Hunter						
Rams	X	X	X	X	X	X
$35						
500 Large Lockblade						
Raccoons	Moose	Beavers	Mallards	X	X	X
$23	$23	$21	$20			
515 4" Lockback						
X	X	X	X	X	X	Dog/Rabbit
						$21
524 Tradesman						
X	X	X	X	Badger	Grizzlies	X
				$16	$16	
511 Cub Lockback						
X	Chipmunk	Raccoon	Opossum	Frog	Weasel	X
	$18	$20	$16	$16	$16	

505 Stockman						
Rabbit	Duck Decoy	Weasel	Coyotes	Retriever	Skunks	Wood Ducks
$20	$18	$18	$18	$18	$16	$16
506 Barlow						
Owl	Boar/Dogs	Pheasant	Pup/Decoy	X	X	X
$14	$12	$12	$12			
503 Small Lockblade						
Catfish	Trout	Alligator	Steelhead	Otters	Sunfish/ Perch	Two Bass
$18	$18	$17	$16	$15	$16	$16
513 Bearhead						
X	X	X	X	Mallards	Beaver	Eagle
				$16	$16	$16
502 Sharp Finger						
Bear/Dog	Elk Bugling	Fawn	Raccoon	Polar Bear	Pheasant	Coon Hunt
$18	$16	$16	$17	$16	$16	$17
509 Little Finger						
Eagle	X	X	X	X	X	X
$20						
518 Gut-hook Hunter						
X	X	X	X	X	X	Ram
						$18

Pattern Year						
1990	1991	1992	1993	1994	1995	1996
507 Lockback						
Foxes	Elk	Bear	Bobcat	Wolves	Cougar	Bison
$28	$28	$29	$30	$30	$31	$32
503 Small Lockblade						
Trout	Fisherman	Geese	Pike	Bass	Crappies	Salmon
$14	$15	$15	$15	$15	$16	$16
505 Stockman						
Bird Dog	Geese	Quail	Loons	Geese	Pheasant	Snow Geese
$16	$17	$17	$17	$17	$18	$18
511 Cub Lockback						
X	X	Squirrel	Woodcock	Scorpion	X	X
		$17	$17	$17		
513 3" Bearhead						
Raccoons	Eagle	Fox	Rattler	Armadillo	Raccoon	Woodpecker
$16	$17	$17	$17	$17	$17	$18.
515 4" Lockback						
Turkeys	Raccoons	Mtn. Goats	Owl	Blue Heron	Osprey	Bighorn Ram
$21	$22	$23	$24	$24	$24	$25
502 Sharp Finger						
Horses	Hunter	Bighorn	Buck	Two Elk	Antelope	Moose
$16	$17	$17	$18	$18	$19	$19
518 Gut-hook Hunter						
Buck	Bear	X	X	X	X	X
$19	$20					
296 Trapper						
X	X	X	X	X	Beaver	Wolverine
					$18	$20

Cutlery Centers Past and Present

ARGENTINA: Buenos Aires and Salta.

AUSTRIA: Steyr and Vienna.

BELGIUM: Namur, Gembloux and Oliergues.

BOHEMIA (part of Austria-Hungary until 1921, then part of Czechoslovakia): Nixdorf and Prague.

CANADA: Pictou, Nova Scotia, and St. John, New Brunswick.

CHINA: Canton, Dalain, Shanghai and Tsingtao.

ENGLAND: London, Birmingham and Sheffield (including Rotherham, Barnsley and Penistone; also Stannington; Wadsley; Heely; Attercliff; Dungworth; Darnall; Worrall; Bradfield; Bridgehouses; Storrs; Bents Green; Owlerton; Little Common; Hill-Top; Pitsmoor; Milnhouses; Cherry Tree Hill; Hirst; Brightside; Sandy-Gate; Sowden; Neepsend; and other nearby villages).

FINLAND: Helsinki, Kauhava and Rovaniemi.

FRANCE: Paris, Langres, Thiers (including Saint-Remy-sur-Durolle, Le Roc and Olliergues), Chatellerault, Nogent, Biesles, Nontron, Laguiole, Cognin, Moulins and St. Etienne.

GERMANY: Nuremberg, Munich, Augsburg, Steinbach, Passau, Solingen (including Ohligs, Remscheid, Merscheid, Wald, Foche, Weyer and Hoehscheid), Elberfeld and Esslingen.

INDIA: Shoranur, Rampur, Dehra Dun, Gujarat and Salem.

IRAN: Zenjan and Isphahan.

IRELAND: Listowel and Cork.

ITALY: Maniago, Caslino, Frosolone, Canzo, Premana, Forno-Canvese, Asso, Brescia and Mondolfo.

JAPAN: Seki City, Sakai, Kurume, Osaka and Nara.

LEBANON: Jezzine.

MEXICO: Oaxaca, Leon and Jalisco.

NETHERLANDS: Amsterdam.

NORWAY: Christiania (now Oslo) and Bergen.

RUSSIA: Pavlovo, Vyatka (or Kirov), Slatoust and Moscow.

SPAIN: Toledo, Ermua (Vizcaya), Albacete and Vich.

SWEDEN: Boden, Eskilstuna and Mora.

SWITZERLAND: Ibach, Delemont, Aarau, Geneva and Le Sentier.

UNITED STATES

ALABAMA: Jacksonville.

ARKANSAS: Springdale and Lowell.

CALIFORNIA: San Francisco, San Marcos, Torrance and Ventura.

COLORADO: Boulder, Golden, Lakewood and Longmont.

CONNECTICUT: Meriden, Bridgeport, New Britain, New Haven, Waterbury (Waterville section), Naugatuck, Hotchkissville, Lakeville, Winsted, Northfield, Thomaston (Reynolds Bridge section), Shelton, Southington and Putnam.

FLORIDA: Vero Beach.

IDAHO: Boise, Idaho Falls and Post Falls.

ILLINOIS: Chicago, Havana and Morris.

MARYLAND: Baltimore and Crisfield.

MASSACHUSETTS: Boston, Southbridge, Shelburne Falls, Greenfield, Turners Falls, Worcester, Chicopee, Ayer, Pepperell, Northampton and Canton.

MICHIGAN: Gladstone and Grand Ledge.

NEW HAMPSHIRE: Antrim.

NEW JERSEY: Newark, Irvington and Maplewood.

NEW YORK: New York, Bronxville, Walden, Ellenville, Olean, Utica, Camillus, Napanoch, Little Valley, Elmira, Perry, Rochester, Franklinville and Poughkeepsie.

NORTH CAROLINA: Asheville and Waynesville.

OHIO: Canton, Clyde, Fremont and Wauseon.

OREGON: Portland, Eugene, McMinnville, Oregon City, Tigard, Tualatin and Wilsonville.

PENNSYLVANIA: Philadelphia, Beaver Falls-Rochester, Bradford, Titusville, Tidioute, Kane and Chester.

RHODE ISLAND: Providence.

TENNESSEE: Chattanooga, Kingsport and Sevierville.

TEXAS: Dallas and Denison.

UTAH: Morgan.

VIRGINIA: Marion.

ALABAMA: Jacksonville.

WASHINGTON: Bellingham and Lynnwood.

WISCONSIN: South Milwaukee, Watertown and Marinette.

Late 18th Century Sheffield Cutlers' Marks

The first Sheffield city directory was published in 1740, but the most comprehensive Sheffield directory of the 18th century was the one of 1787. The 1787 directory includes an extensive classified section. For all the makers and factors of finished cutlery, the classified listings show name, address and touch-mark.

A *factor* was a person or firm who sold cutlery made for him/it and marked with his/its brand by independent workmen called "little mesters." In Sheffield, the factoring system was called "liver and draw." The workmen (forgers, grinders, handle and fitting makers, and "cutlers" or final assemblers) delivered the week's finished goods to the factor, and then drew their pay, as well as their parts and material for the following week.

Most of the knives made in Sheffield at that time were marked only with a maker's or factor's touch-mark. Therefore, to identify the mark on an 18th-century Sheffield knife, you need to have an illustrated listing like the one included in the 1787 directory.

Around 1814, legal and guild rules changed, permitting the use of the maker's or factor's full name on finished cutlery. If he chose, he could add his address, and he could include his word or pictorial mark as well. Advances in die-sinking technology made such elaborate stamping dies affordable.

Although the 1787 Sheffield directory was reproduced in 1969 (by Da Capo Press), the reproductions are now almost as difficult to find as original copies. Therefore, we have reproduced all parts of that directory that identify cutlers' touch-marks. We would like to thank Tom Heitzman for permission to reproduce from his copy of the directory.

Knives with any of these touch-marks are very rare. Their values range from high to very high.

The high values are due in part simply to age and rarity. More important, however, is that the large majority of cutlery sold in the United States in the decades around 1800 was made in Sheffield by or for people listed in the 1787 Sheffield city directory. To the contemporary American collector or historian, these knives are therefore of particular interest.

PEN and POCKET KNIVES
in general.

Manufacturers in SHEFFIELD.

Name	Mark
BARNES Isaac, Campo-lane	BARNS
Barnes Thomas, Smithfield	LOVE
Barlow John, Campo-lane	BARLOW
Bateman George, Smithfield	BATEMAN
Beardshaw William, Silver-street	PASTO
Beardshaw John, Holles Croft	BEARDSHAW
Beet and Senyers, Pea Croft	BRET OBTAIN RAINBOW
Bradshaw Wm. Holles Croft; *Pockets only*	BRADSHAW
Briddock Martin, Lambert Croft	BRID-DOCK
Brightmore William, Broad-lane	LONDON CITY
Broadhead William, Holles Croft	B O→W
Broomhead, Hinchliffe, and Co. Brinsworth's Orchard	BROOMHEAD
Broomhead Joseph, Lambert Croft; *Jacks*	⚓PYL
Brown George, Coalpit-lane	BROWN
Burch George, Spring-street	SMEG
Butler William, Trinity-street	BUTLER
Cadman George, Back-lane	CUPID
Cawton Joshua, and Sons, Snighill	☉ CAW-TON
Clark Jonathan, Norfolk-street	LARK
Crabtree Thomas, Pea Croft	CRABTREE
Creswick Joseph, Queen-street	LAVORO
Crookes James, and Son, New-street	W D DAY
Davison Lemuel and Co.	IMPERIAL
Fowler Isaiah, Coalpit-lane	CROS P ROOM METAS
Fox and Norris, Westbar	
Fox William, do.	FOX
Green James, Norfolk-street	J. GREEN
Green Jonathan, Bailey Field	ZA
Hague and Nowil, Garden-street	D EHONG FUEL
Hall Thomas, Meadow-street	
Hall Henry, Union-street; *spotted and Wood Pockets*	
Harrison John, and Son, Holles Croft	I H
Hawksworth Christopher, Silver-street	O CH
Higginson Samuel, Burgess-street	STAR
Ibberson John and George, Gibralter	K
Jervis William, White Croft	
Jervis John, Meadow-street	C
Justice Paris, Spring-street	PARIS WAR
Kay Samuel, Pinston-lane	
Kelk Charles, Westbar-green	KEMP
Kemp Isaiah N. Norfolk-street	PIT
Kennington James, Blind-lane	PEARL
Kippax John, China-square	ESAU SULTAN
Kirkby and Borwick, Longstone-lane	EDEN
Kirkby Mary, Brinsworth's Orchard	S L
Knowles Francis, White Croft	LEVIK
Levick John, and Son, Pond-lane	MERIT
Loy William, Far-gate	⛧O+
Ludlam Widow, and Sons, Burgess-street	ETNA
Marriot Luke, Coalpit-lane	
Martin Charles, Pond-lane	ORMUS
Matthews John, Smithfield	TOURS
Mickelthwaite, and Co.	ZACA +
Mycock John and Joseph, Burgess-street	PENG
Mycock Joseph, Church-lane; *Pockets*	M
Naylor and Son, Coalpit-lane	PRET
Nowil and Kippax, High-street	NOWIL KIPPAX
Nowil Joseph, Copper-street; *also Jacks*	GENEVA
Newton Edmund, Back-lane	ACUTE
Owen Robert, Westbar-green	GOLD
Patten Hannah, and Son, Silver-street	NANTZ
Patten George, Coalpit-lane; *also Jacks*	PATEN
Priest Francis, Pea Croft	PRIEST
Proctor Charles, and Luke, Milk-street; *Hunters Knives and Butchers Steels only*	L.P PROSPER
Ratcliff Widow, Paradise Square	CROIX
Roberts John, Pinston-lane	HOTEL
Rodgers Joseph, and Maurice, Norfolk-str	* ✠
Roebuck, and Co. Lambert Croft	ROEBUCK
Rose William, Coalpit-lane	
Shepherd Robert, Norfolk-street	<✠
Shipman Æneas, Silver-street	ANON
Smith William, and Co. Coalpit-lane	IFS
Smith John, Grindle-gate	SPARLIN
Spurr Peter, Church-lane	SPUR
Staniforth, Parkin, and Co. Sycamore-str.	HAGUE SHEMEL
Stead Richard, Silver-street	STEAD
Sutton Jonathan, Meadow-street	BAM
Sykes Samuel, Holles Croft	BUDA
Tarbotton Thomas, Scotland-street	QUEEN
Taylor Samuel, Pea Croft	BEET

Name	Mark
Travis Nathaniel, White Croft -	IN BILBO
Urton William, and George, Colston Croft	URTON TAGLIO
Water Godfrey, and Son, Pond-lane -	WATER REMUS
Wigfall William, Pea Croft -	J. WATKIN- SON
Watkinson Jonathan, Silver-street	
Wild Jonathan, Sims Croft -	SIAM
Wild William, Trinity-street -	GLOBE
Wilkinson John, Lambert Croft -	AN & C
Withers Benjamin, and Co. Far-gate -	ESPANGE
Wright William, John, and Robert, Smithfield -	◇ ♡ ☿ ⚘ CV ⚹ 8

Manufacturers the NEIGHBOURHOOD.

Name	Mark
BARLOW Samuel, Neepsend -	N ° ↝
Baxter John, Bridgehouses; *Hunters only*	24 N
Carr John, Neepsend - -	CARR
Hawksworth Thomas and Jonathan, Attercliff -	+ + SX CASAN +
Warburton Samuel, Bridgehouses -	LIFE
Yates George, Bridgehouses - -	⚘ R 3

Common POCKET and PENKNIVES.

Manufacturers in SHEFFIELD.

Name	Mark
ALSOP Luke, Coalpit-lane -	HA +
Bishop Thomas, China Square -	STATE
Butler Stephen, Townhead Well -	BAKU
Crookes Jonathan, Scotland-street -	↝ ◁ +
Dixon James, Campo-lane -	DIXON
Duke Henry, Trinity-street -	READ
Dungworth Jonathan, Meadow-street -	1772
Drabble Enoch, Green-lane -	USE +
Fox John, Park -	FOX
Hancock Charles, Scotland-street -	QUEBEC
Hibbert Samuel, Bailey Field -	SOL
Hutton Henry, Coalpit-lane -	HUTTON
Lindley William and Son, Ponds -	SAILOR BOLD
Littlewood and Hatfield, Park -	⚲ IL
Marsh Hannah, Park -	UPHONY ⚘
Oates John, Little Sheffield -	Y ⚘ OATES
Osborne George, Porto Bello -	DRAFT

Name	Mark
Parkin Thomas, Scotland-street -	LOUIS
Priest Joseph, Young-street -	DUNBAR +
Revel Joseph, do. -	PINK
Revel Benjamin, Pea Croft -	JOLLY SAILOR
Spencer Widow, Westbar-green -	↝ ↯ ◁
Smith Widow, Broad-lane End -	+ ↯ + ✳
Swinden Matthew, Holles Croft -	⚘ M S
Taylor Paul, Pond-lane -	⚘ P T
Turner Samuel, China-square -	◇ IVORY
Twigg Jonathan, Broadlane End -	TWIGG
Ward James, Spring-street -	W D S
Waterhouse Jeremiah, Scotland-street -	➤ ◇ +
Wild John, Holles Croft -	⚜ WILD

Manufacturers in the NEIGHBOURHOOD.

NOTE. Those who make Penknives, have the Word *Pen* put against their Names; the others make only *Couteaux.*

Name	Mark
ALMON John, Cherry-tree Hill -	ALMON ⚜
Ashell George, Attercliff, *Pen* -	CRUZ
Abel John, Bents Green -	ABEL
Abel William, Little Common -	+ ↯ ↯ +
Barker William, Wadsley -	◁ N ⚹
Bateman Ralph, Wadsley -	ROD
Beatson George, Gleadles -	⊣ MYR
Beatson Luke, do. -	◁ ⊢ ⚹
Beighton, William, Edge -	⊙ N ⚹
Boulsover Timothy, Park -	JOVIL
Bowden Joseph, Worral -	⚘
Bradshaw William, Crooks -	E N E
Bradshaw James, do. -	✿ ⊢
Briggs William, Toadhole -	BRIGS
Bruck John, Hill-top -	BRUCK
Brookshaw Sampson, Little Common -	SAMP
Brown George, Heely -	FIR
Brown John, do. -	Γ ◁
Burdekin John, Stannington -	23 B
Burley Nicholas, Onesacre -	Z ⚹ ✿
Burley George, do. -	ASTRON
Close Godfrey, Heely -	⚘ + ⚘
Close Francis, Newfield Green -	CLOSE
Coldwell Joseph, Dungworth -	GES
Denton William, Bents Green -	SOU
Dewsnap Thomas, Tom-lane -	DUSNAP
Drabble Enoch, Dungworth -	➤ ⚘ ◁

Name	Mark
Drabble William, do.	GOSLAR
Drabble Joshua, do.	SADU
Dungworth Joseph, Hirst	◁ϝⱶ→
Dyson William, jun. Shotnell	AJAX
Garret Joseph, Birley Edge	1765
Gill Samuel, Heely	ASHDOD
Gill Thomas, do.	⊀⊢◁
Gill Jonathan, do.	VENLO
Gill Joshua, do.	SEALED
Gillat Samuel, do.	⊟Ⓞ✠✝
Gillat William, do.	SYNO
Gillat Henry, do.	⊟Ⓒ✷
Gillat Thomas, do.	ℵ⊢ϙϝ
Goddard John, Attercliff; *Pen*	⊕✳✝
Green Moses, Wadsley	⫶⫶⫶ ⫶⫶⫶
Green Widow, Worral	⊢Ⓞ◡
Hague William, Dungworth	DRIVE
Hallam Francis, Darnall; *Pen*	F H ✝
Hallam Thomas, sen. Heely; *Pen*	HALM
Hallam Thomas, jun. do.	HALM
Hallam Jonathan, Heely	CEYX
Hallam Joseph, Little Common	SPELL SPELL
Hartley Joshua, Mill Lee	HARTLY
Hawksworth George, Dungworth	G³H
Hill James, Piper House	⊢⊟⌐
Hobson John, Bell Hague	N I P
Hobson Amos, Malin Bridge	▷✕⊢⫣
Hobson Joseph, Owlerton	◁✣Ⓞ
Hobson Jacob, do.	Ⓞↄ✷
Hoole William, Crooksmoor	⬚⫧
Howard Joseph, Storrs	✳⊟ϝ
Hoyle Ralph, Dungworth	ANCONA
Ibbotson Widow, Coldwell	PASO
Innocent John, Darnall; *Pen*	LUTON
Jones Widow, and Sons, Greenhill	JONES
Kinder John, Attercliff; *Pen*	BOSTON
Kinder John, Hirst	X❤ UBIA
Kirkby and Himsworth, Cros Pool	TOR✝
Leadbeater George, Stannington	▷⊢✝Ⓞ
Lingard Joseph, Milnhouses	ᛉC✝
Lingard John, do.	ᛉC✝◁
Lingard Thomas, do.	⌐⊢ON
Lowe Richard, Stannington	◡⫴✝C
Marshall William, Bents Green	✝⫴⧫✝
Memmot George, Heely	ᛉⓄ✝
Memmot Amos, Heely	⋊Ⓞⴰ
Memmot Samuel, do.	RUSO
Middleton John, Wadsley	ARM
Newton John, Sharrowmoor; *Pen*	⟶✓Ⓞ
Nicholson John, Darnall; *Pen*	SAX
Nichols Abraham, Stannington	JAN. 20
Nichols John, Storrs	⟶✦⤙
Nixon Thomas, Dungworth	◁ 20
Oates Matthew, Bents Green	ELT
Owen George, Bridgehouses	STEADY
Platt William, Cowms	W. PLAT
Priest John, Bents Green	NINE
Priest William, do.	PRIEST
Ransley Henry, Stannington	◁⊟✳ϝ
Revel Abraham, Little Common	EPHOD
Rose John, Wadsley	✳⋈C
Rose John, jun. do.	MOPED
Senior Joseph, Slaylee	I C
Shaw Samuel, Heely	◡ ✝ϝ
Slack Isaac, and Co. Crooksmoor	ϙ ♣
Slack Jonathan, Steel Bank	ↄ⫴◀
Staniforth George, Bridgehouses	✝ SENT
Stones Joseph, sen. Park	STONES
Stones Joseph, jun. Heely	93✝
Stones Thomas, do.	◡ϝ✝
Stringer Joseph, Slaylee	⩊Ⓞ✳
Taylor Philip, Birley Car; *Pen*	ℵⓄ⌐ BON
Thompson John, and Son, Heely	COUTEAU
Turner Stephen, Hirst	S T
Turner Joseph, Hilltop	P Y
Turner John, do.	Ⓞ✝P
Tricket William, Morwood	AEUN
Tricket William, Storrs; *Pen*	ℵ⫴ϝ
Tricket John, Wadefield House	EMER
Tricket John, Dungworth	ℵⴰ
Tricket James, Bierly Car	EDG
Twigg John, Attercliff	LUCK
Watson John, Sandygate	6 ∀
Watson Thomas, do.	∀ V
West John, Storrs	WEST
Wigley Joshua, Bradfield	EWTO
Wright John, Dungworth	WRIGHT

Names omitted in their proper Places.

ABDY John, Howard-ſtreet ; *Couteau and Graver Maker* -	✱ A
Cooper Sheldon, Gibralter, *Pen and Pocket Knives in general* - -	COOPER
Drabble Samuel, Broad-lane, do. -	ORRERY
Greaves Thomas, Church-lane, do. -	◄♈⊶

RAZORS.

Manufacturers in SHEFFIELD.

ASH Richard, Young-ſtreet -	RAY ♔
Birks William and John, Norfolk-ſtreet - -	⊥⊥ & ⊥ &
Brammall Nicholas, White Croft -	CALVIN
Brightmore John, Croſs Field -	CITY
Brittain, Wilkinſon, and Brownell, Arundel-ſtreet - -	EXCELLENT FRANCE VRAI
Broomhead, Hinchſliffe, and Co. Brinſworth's Orchard - -	BROOMHEAD
Broomhead Joſeph, Lambert Croft -	⚥ PYL
Cadman Luke, Surrey-ſtreet -	BENGALL
Cadman David, Longſton-lane -	SENEGAL
Dewſnap George, and William, Lambert Croft - -	SORBON
Dewſnap Francis, Wicker -	♀ MECCA
	FARA
Fox and Norris Weſtbar -	⚐ P ROOM MΞΞΛS
Fox William, do. - -	FOX ⚔
Greaves William, Burgeſs-ſtreet -	GREAVES
Hall Jonathan, China-ſquare -	GRATIAN
Hallam James, Norfolk-ſtreet -	⇥ PARIS
Harriſon John, Campo-lane -	HARRISON
Hudſon John, Weſtbar-green -	CUSCO
Juſtice Paris, Spring-ſtreet -	+ PARIS
Kirkby Samuel, Lambert Croft -	⚓ · R M
Green James, Norfolk-ſtreet -	J. GREEN
Leadbeater John, Copper-ſtreet -	ITALY
Lindley John, Spring-ſtreet -	⟋+
Marriot Luke, Coalpit-lane -	⤢ ◄✱✠
Parkin Joſephus, Campo-lane ; *alſo Jacks*	HOLLAND +
Parker Widow, Pea Croft -	PARKER +
Patten Hannah, and Son, Silver-ſtreet	NANTZ

Pryor Michael, Burgeſs-ſtreet -	N⌐8❍
Revel George, Ratten Row ; *alſo Jacks*	↕ ✠ GR BELVOIR AMSTERDAM
Roberts Joſeph, and Co. Garden-ſtreet	
Rodgers Joſeph, and Maurice, Norfolk-ſtreet - -	✱ ✠ RODGERS
Roebuck, and Co. Lambert Croft -	ROEBUCK
Rowland Widow, Back-lane -	♈ R
Shepherd John, Holles Croft -	♛ WOLF
Smith Thomas, Scotland-ſtreet -	LEIPZIG ✠ SMITH
Staniforth, Parkin, and Co. Sycamore-ſtreet - -	SHEMEL PARKIN
Staniland Richard, Burgeſs-ſtreet -	♁ RICH ◆
Warburton Thomas, Burgeſs-ſtreet .	+ LISBON
Withers Benjamin, and Co. Far-gate .	ESPANGE
Wright William, John, and Robert, Smithfield ; *alſo Jacks*	◄Ɛ⌐C 8♂◄ ✕ ✠

Manufacturers in the NEIGHBOURHOOD.

BRAMMALL John, Storrs .	JOPPA
Hall John, Sharrowmoor .	LIMRICK
Lindley Samuel, Attercliff .	LONDON N 3
Palfreyman George, Stannington .	CC
Pitchford Jonathan, Stumperly .	P⸺FORD ♀
Revet John, Stannington .	VIRGIL
Revet Richard, do. ·	✱∽ HOMER
Shaw John, do. .	CLAYTON
Worrall John, do. ·	♅ HORACE
Warburton Samuel, Bridgehouſes .	LIFE

LANCETS and PHLEMES.

ASH Richard, Young-ſtreet ; *Lancets*	RAY ♔
Brightmore John, Croſs Field	CITY
Butler William, Trinity-ſtreet ; *Phlemes*	BUTLER
Creſwick Joſeph, Queen-ſtreet ; *Phlemes*	LAVORO
Fox William, Weſtbar	FOX ⚔
Hallam Mary, Norfolk-ſtreet ; *Lancets*	⇉ PARIS
Hallam James, do. do.	⇥ PARIS
Proctor Jonathan, Coalpit-lane ; *Phlemes*	PROCTOR
Pryor Michael, Burgeſs-ſtreet ; do.	N⌐8❍
Roebuck, and Co. Lambert Croft -	ROEBUCK
Watkinſon Jonathan, Silver-ſtreet -	J. WATKINSON

SPOTTED KNIVES.

Manufacturers in SHEFFIELD.

BEELY Thomas, Ponds	MARS
Beet Edward, Lambert Croft	↩ BEET
Hall Henry, Union-ſtreet	7 H →
Marples Samuel, Holles Croft	Z ↩ +
Race Richard, Cleekham Bowling-green	R R ∽
Shipman Æneas, Silver-ſtreet	VERNON
Swallow Joſeph, Smithfield	↩ H
Swann Joſeph, Gibralter	9 L ⚜
Townſend James, Holles Croft	66 T

Manufacturers in the NEIGHBOURHOOD.

ASHALL John, Darnall	1756
Atkinſon Richard, Grayſtones	R·A
Bancroft Robert, Stannington	I C ⚜
Barnes Joſeph, Owlerton	I B
Bateman Ralph, Wadſley	ROD
Beldon Joſeph, Darnall	9 ⚜ +
Brammall Thomas, Wiſewood	M
Briddock Martin, do.	GHUR
Burch Joſeph, Stannington	IB Z +
Burley John, Stannington	* ♡
Carr Thomas, do.	⚜
Carr James, do.	D 2 *
Creſwick John, Sandy-gate	CAVE
Crownſhaw Ralph, Wadſley	ICUNE
Dyſon William, ſen. Shotnell	DYSON
Dyſon Charles, Stannington	ROPA
Ellis John, Wadſley	ſ o *
Eyre William, Darnall	Q KING
Fearn Thomas, Roebuck Houſe	TABLE
Fenton Hugh, Malin Bridge	DISH
Furnace Luke, Stannington	1760
Graſon Joſeph, Darnall	FIRMUM
Green Jeremiah, Worrall	M S G ω +
Hague William, Dungworth	DRIVE
Hague John, Wadſley	♡ 8 +
Hallam John, Walkley	ASAY
Hallam Robert, Dungworth	ISAY
Hallam George, Owlerton	G+C
Hawley John, Stannington	IH 70
Hobſon Benjamin, Hilltop	MINE
Hobſon Jonathan, Wadſley	NORCOPPIN
Hobſon Thomas, Bradfield	HOBSON
Hobſon George, ſen. Worrall	LASS
Hobſon George, jun. Bradfield	◊ LASS
Hoyle Jeremiah, Wadſley	6 ✠ ⚜
Howard John, do.	R ✠ *
Howard Jonathan, Toadhole	S 6
Ibbotſon John, Stannington	IBBOTSON
Ibbotſon Henry, Sowden	G G o
Jebſon Joſeph, do	GLAD
Jenkin James, Attercliff	⚷ 8
Johnſon Samuel, Wadſley	GLUTIA
Kay Thomas, do.	* ONE
Lingard Joſeph, Worrall	Z 6 *
Marſh Thomas, Darnall	9 ✠ +
Marſh William, do.	IRISH
Matthewman William, Wadſley	✠ ✠ ✠
Milnes Benjamin, Worrall	MILNS
Nichols Sarah, Stannington	S 3 +
Nichols Abraham, do.	JAN. 20
Nut Joſeph, Wadſley	Z 3
Oates Matthew, Stannington	9 ♡ →
Oates William, do.	* W
Oxley Thomas, Stannington	4 6 C
Parkin William, Tom-lane	✠ P ✠
Roſe Benjamin, Wadſley	9 ſ
Roſe John, jun. Wadſley	ROSE
Roſe Joſeph, do.	DONIA
Saunderſon Jeremiah, Holdworth	MERE
Staniforth Aaron, Worrall	A S +
Stringer Joſeph, Wadſley	W S *
Stringer Charles, do.	C SER
Skelton Jonathan, Stumperley	VINE
Tricket John, Stannington	EMIR
Tricket John, Dungworth	Z S
Turner Samuel, Fullwood	TURNER
Walker Samuel, Sowden	SALAD
Webſter William, Whiteley Wood	
Whiteley Joſeph, Edgefield	OGNIL
Wilkinſon and Twigg, Attercliff	LA ✠ ⚜ ⚷ ✠ O
Wilſon, Robert, Wadſley	WILSON
Wilſon Joſeph, Damflaſk	RAPAN
Wood George, Darnall	3 G ⚜
Wood John, do.	EPIC
Woolhouſe Michael, Worrall	TREE
Youle Robert, Darnall	ALO*

Stamped Brafs, White Metal, and Metal Framed KNIVES.

BEELY Thomas, Ponds ; *Brafs ftamped*	MARS
Baxter John, Bridgehoufes ; *White Metal, and Metal framed, only*	24 N
Binney Jofeph, Broad-lane End ; *White Metal, Metal framed & Japanned* .	THAT
Greaves Thomas, Church-lane ; *Brafs framed, only* . . .	◀ ☉ ⊣
Harrifon John, and Son, Holles Croft ; *White Metal, and Metal framed, only*	H ⊰⊹
Harwar Charles, High-ftreet ; *Japanned only*	DECEM
Jervis William, White Croft .	✝⊕⊹
Jervis John, Meadow-ftreet ; *White Metal, and Metal framed*	♉ C
Ludlam Widow, and Sons, Burgefs-ftr. do.	ETNA
Naylor and Son, Coalpit-lane ; do. .	PRET
Patten Hannah, and Son, Silver-ftreet .	✝ NANTZ
Patten George, Coalpit-lane . . .	✠ PATEN
Ratcliff Robert, Lambert Croft ; *Brafs ftamped only*	✝ R R
Rodgers Jofeph, and Maurice, Norfolk-ftreet ; *White Metal, and Metal framed*	✳ ✠ RODGERS
Smith William, and Co. Coalpit-lane .	⊹✠⊹ IEf
Turner Samuel, China-fquare ; *White Metal Metal fnamed, and Japnnned* -	◈ IVORY
Water Godfrey, and Son, Pond-lane ; do	WATER
Webfter Jofeph, Hartfhead ; *Brafs ftamped*	⊠⊠◇ O T W
Wilfon Samuel, Eyre-ftreet ; do. .	
Wilfon John, Brinfworth's Orchard ; *Wh. Metal and Metal framed only* .	BILBOA
Wilfon Jofeph, Carver-ftreet ; *White Metal, and Metal framed only* .	IDEA
Withers Benjamin, and Co. Far-gate .	ESPANGE

TABLE KNIVES, Silver and Plated.

BELDON, Hoyland, and Co. Burgefs-ftreet	PLUTUS
	⚔ ⚔
Birks William, and John, Norfolk-ftreet	FABRE
Dewfnap John, Queen-ftreet .	SOUND
Dewfnap Joshua, Trinity-ftreet .	W. GREEN & Co
Green William, and Co. Eyre-ftreet	SUPER Z C
Hoyland, Clarbour, and Barnard, Hill-Foot . . .	CLARBOUR ✠ SURIOUS
Hunter and Twigg, Back-lane .	WATCH HUMBLE
Law Thomas, and Co. Norfolk-ftreet .	✠ ✠ LAW L&Co.
Littlewood John, Silver-ftreet . .	ARGENT ♀
Roberts Jacob, and Samuel, Union-ftreet	✠ ✠ PAPA ABBA
Settle Thomas, and Co. Brinfworth's Orchard . . .	✠ S E T
Smith Nathaniel, and Co. Wain-gate .	Z+✠ S
Staniforth, Parkin, and Co. Sycamore-ftreet . . .	⚔ ⚔ PARKIN
Sutcliff, Sporle, and Co. King-ftreet .	SHEMEL S. S. & Co.
Sykes, and Co. Pinfton-lane .	SYKES ♘
Tricket, Haflehurft, Whiteley, and Pryor, Hill Foot . . .	✠ OVA OPUS

TABLE KNIVES, in general.

BARNES Thomas, Smithfield -	LOVE
Beet John, Norfolk-ftreet .	CIRCLE
Beet Widow, and Sons, Broad-lane .	BEET
Birkinfhaw Francis, Silver-ftreet .	MIZZEN
Bramhall James, Porto Bello .	BEST STEEL
Brightmore John, Crofs Field .	CITY
Bright Lydia, Holles Croft . .	CHEAPSIDE ✠
Brittain, Wilkinfon, and Brownell, Arundel-ftreet .	GB VRAI FRANCE
Brittain Benjamin, Hawley Croft .	EXCELLENT PRIVATEER
Broomhead, Hinchfliffe, and Co. Brinfworth's Orchard . .	BROOMHEAD
Broomhead and Ward, Eyre-ftreet .	↜ ⚔
Butler Stephen, Townhead Well .	⚜ BAKU
Carlton John, Far-gate . .	P
Carnell Jofeph, Weftbar-green .	PLANT ARMIS

Name	Mark
Cawton Joſhua, and Sons, Snig-hill	⊙ CAWTON
Colley and Brady, Burgeſs-ſtreet	WALDO
Crooks John, Smithfield	OCOLOS
Dickinſon Thomas, Furnace-hill	OPHIR
	✠ RIR
Dunn William, and Co. Grindle-gate	w DUNN
Emerſon Robert, Burgeſs-ſtreet	JACHIN
Eyre John, and Co. China-ſquare	EXTRA
Green John, Sims Croft	W. LOY
Green Thomas, Spring-ſtreet	✠ SOLYMA
Hawkſworth and Sharrow, Grindle-gate	HAWKS-WORTH
Holmes and Nicholſon, Pond-lane	♔ PHARPAR
Hoyland, Clarbour, and Barnard, Hill-Foot	♔ SUPER z c CLARBOUR
	✠ SURIOUS
Hudſon Joſeph, and Co. Coalpit-lane	EMB✠
Hunter and Twigg, Back-lane	WATCH HUMBLE
Jebſon Matthew, Weſtbar-green	GOZO
Loy William, and Co. Pond-lane	≤ 0 ✤
Loy Jonathan, Coalpit-lane	LOY
Naylor George, and Son, do.	PRET
Oates Chriſtopher, Holles Croft	C. OATES
Owen Robert, Weſtbar-green	✠ GOLD
Parker Ebenezer, Eyre-ſtreet	WITSIUS
Parker Ann, Pea Croft	✠ PARKER
Roberts Jacob, and Samuel, Union-ſtreet	+ + PAPA ABBA
Salt John, Holles Croft	〓 ⊣ ◇ ✤
Shepherd Edward, Far-gate	◁ ✠
Shepherd Robert, Norfolk-ſtreet	◁ ⌐ ✤
Smith Samuel, Scoltand-ſtreet	♔ S S
Smith Widow, Broad-lane End	✳ + ∽ +
Staniland John, do.	GRACE
Stanley Samuel, Scotland-ſtreet	℥ STANLEY
Staniforth, Parkin, and Co. Sycamore-ſtreet	⚔ PARKIN
Teal William, Shudehill	SHEMEL TEAL
Tillotſon Thomas, Coalpit-lane	ALBION
Trickitt William, and Thomas, Arundel-ſtreet; alſo Deſk Penknives	KOLA TURIN
Walton Richard, White Croft	▭ WALTON
Warburton Samuel, Holles Croft	WARBURTON
Wilkinſon Thomas, Blind lane	+ PLANT
Windle Edmund, Lambert Croft	𝄢 E W
Woolhouſe Joſeph, do.	SWAIN
Wright William, John, and Robert, Smithfield	⊙ ⇵ – C ∞ ◁◇ ✕ ✤

TABLE KNIVES, common.

Manufacturers in SHEFFIELD.

Name	Mark
ASHFORTH Samuel, Park	IE ⇵ + ✠
Broomhead Benjamin, and Joſeph,	⇵ ✤ + H H 5
Cadman Peter, and Co. Norfolk-ſtreet	𝆔
Kent Richard, and Son, do.	W. KENT
Midgley Thomas, Dixon-lane	NIZZA
North William, Little Sheffield	NORTH
Parker Samuel, Scotland	YTHEL
Paſs John, Sheffield Moor	PASS
Ryals Joſhua, and Son, Brinſworth's Orchard	TEEN ◇ IS
Timm John, Back-lane	+ UGGU
Waterhouſe Jeremiah, Scotland-ſtreet	⊳ 0 +

Manufacturers in the NEIGHBOURHOOD.

Name	Mark
ASHFORTH John, Shire Green	⚚ W A
Green George, Storrs	XERXES
Holland Robert, Grimeſtorpe	⊃ S ✤
Hydes Thomas, Pitſmoor	⤳ ✤ x ✤
Kent Richard, Brightſide	𐤄 ◁ ✤
Milner George, do.	U ⋀ ◇ ✤

Masters of the Sheffield Cutlers Guild, 1624-1905

The mastership in the Sheffield Guild was largely a ceremonial office, the term of service being one year, beginning in September. The man elected was generally a prominent and prosperous member of the guild, so the list on this and the facing page is in effect a list of the leading cutlers of Sheffield down through the years. Since service as master required both time and expenditure, some prominent cutlers declined election, obliging them instead to pay a fine. While most masters were working cutlers, some were cutlery factors, edge tool makers or file cutters.

From the early 19th century on, more and more of the masters were steelworks proprietors, cutlery manufacturers and factory owners rather than working cutlers, although most of the owners and managers had grown up in the cutlery trades and knew how to make knives—had they been so required. Many of the men were the directors of large, old firms that bore the names of others.

The list was copied from Robert Leader's *History of the Company of Cutlers in Hallamshire in the County of York* (Sheffield, Pawlson & Brailsford, 1905, two volumes). There were cutlers in Sheffield long before 1624, but the records of the Guild only go back that far. Names marked with a bullet (•) were included in the 1787 Sheffield Directory, and the man's listed trade is included here.

The spelling of family names was subject to whimsy until well into the 19th century. Sorsby, Sorsbie and Sorby were probably related, as were Barlowe and Barlow, Brelsforth, Breilsforth and Brailsford, etc.

1624 Robert Sorsby	1655 Thomas Pearson	1685 Thomas Tucker	1715 William Moor
1625 John Rawson	1656 John Webster	1686 Benjamin Kerkbie	1716 Thomas Broadhead
1626 William Warter	1657 Malin Sorsbie	1687 John Webster junr.	1717 John Guest
1627 Wm. Web[s]ter	1658 John Rawson	1688 Robert Breilsforth	1718 Tobias Ellis
1628 Robert Sorsby	1659 William Creswicke	1689 James Webster	1719 Peter Symon
1629 John Webster	1660 Stephen Carr	1690 Joseph Downes	1720 James Longsden
1630 William Creswicke	1661 Robert Allin	1691 Jno. Webster, Church lane	1721 James Crawshaw
1631 Robert Stacie	1662 James Staniforth		1722 John Smith
1632 James Creswicke	1663 James Newton	1692 Thomas Johnson	1723 Jonathan Moor
1633 George Valliance	1664 John Pearson	1693 John King	1724 Jeremy Beet
1634 William Walker	1665 Thomas Jeninges	1694 John Trippett	1725 Thomas Redforth
1635 Thomas Creswicke	1666 Nathaniel Robbinson	1695 Robert Spooner	1726 John Tooker
1636 Richard Wilkinson	1667 George Creswicke	1696 Christ'r Brumhead	1727 Andrew Wade
1637 John Crooke	1668 John Webstarr	1697 Richard Downes	1728 Andrew Wade
1638 James Creswicke	1669 Robert Soresbie	1698 Andrew Wade	1729 Thomas Cotton
1639 Robert Carr	1670 Edward Barlow	1699 Benjamin Pearson	1730 Sam. Wainwright
1640 Robert Skargell	1671 Richard Parramour	1700 Robert Savage	1731 Thomas Wilson
1641 Thomas Milward	1672 Mathew Arnold	1701 Richard Marsh	1732 John Ward
1642 Richard Slack	1673 John Sutton	1702 Ephraim Nicholls	1733 Cotton Watkin
1643 Richard Base	1674 Castle Shemield	1703 John Pearson	1734 John Osborne
1644 William Pell	1675 William Crawshaw	1704 Edward Sanderson	1735 Joseph Turner
1645 William Warter	1676 James Newton	1705 Joseph Nutt	1736 Joshua Cawton
1646 Thomas Ludlam	1677 John Pearson	1706 Ezra Cawton	1737 Joseph Shepherd
1647 Malin Sorsby	1678 Thos. Jenings the elder	1707 George Cartwright	1738 Joseph Kenyon
1648 Robert Brelsforth		1708 John Downes	1739 Jonathan Dixon the younger
1649 Richard Jackson	1679 Joshua Baies	1709 James Hoole	
1650 George Barnesley	1680 Jonathan Webster	1710 John Morton	1740 Jonathan Dixon the elder
1651 William Birley	1681 Robert Nicholls	1711 Samuel Smith	
1652 Thomas Bate	1682 John Winter	1712 Samuel Twible	1741 Richard Kent
1653 Edward Barlowe	1683 Edward Badger	1713 Thomas Tooker	1742 Thomas Rose
1654 William Crawshawe	1684 William Ellis	1714 Jonathan Birks	1743 George Marriott

1744 John Spooner
1745 Joseph Leathly
1746 Robert Dent
1747 Edward Windle
1748 Leonard Webster
1749 George Smith
1750 William Hides
1751 Thomas Newbold
1752 Joseph Parkin
1753 Thomas Law
1754 Joseph Owen
1755 William Webster
1756 Benjamin Withers
1757 John Wilson
1758 Jonathan Moore
1759 Joseph Ibberson
1760 William Webster
1761 Willliam Parker
1762 George Greaves
1763 Joseph Hancock
1764 •Samuel Bates [files]
1765 Joseph Bower
1766 William Birks
1767 John Turner
1768 •Thomas Beely [cutler]
1769 Jeremiah Ward
1770 •Joshua Cawton [cutler]
1771 •William Trickett [cutler]
1772 •Robert Owen [cutler]
1773 •George Brittain [factor]
1774 Joseph Kenyon
1775 John Winter
1776 •John Green [cutler]
1777 Samuel Norris
1778 William Linley
1779 •Josephus Parkin [cutler]
1780 John Rowbotham
1781 •Peter Spurr [cutler]
1782 •Joseph Hawksley [files]
1783 •William Fowler [scissor-smith]
1784 •Benjamin Broomhead [factor]

1785 •Thomas Settle [silver cutler]
1786 •Samuel Wilson [cutler]
1787 •Jonathan Watkinson [cutler]
1788 •Thomas Nowill [cutler]
1789 •Thomas Tillotson [cutler]
1790 Joseph Ward
1791 •George Wood [scissorsmith]
1792 •John Henfrey [scissorsmith]
1793 Thomas Warris
1794 •Benjamin Withers [factor]
1795 •William Birks [cutler]
1796 Joseph Fletcher Smith
1797 John Linley
1798 Samuel Broomhead Ward
1799 •Benjamin Vickers [scissor-smith]
1800 •Samuel Newbould [edge tools]
1801 Joseph Bailey
1802 Joseph Withers
1803 •James Makin [forks]
1804 William Nicholson
1805 •John Eyre [cutler]
1806 John Sorby
1807 Peter Brownell
1808 Ebenezer Rhodes
1809 Robert Brightmore
1810 John Tillotson
1811 John Eadon
1812 James Smith
1813 John Holt
1814 Joseph Parkin
1815 James Makin
1816 Thomas Asline Ward
1817 George Tillotson
1818 John Fox
1819 John Hounsfield
1820 Joseph Dixon Skelton
1821 William Colley
1822 Thomas Champion

1823 Thomas Dewsnap
1824 Peter Spurr
1825 Henry Moorhouse
1826 William Sansom
1827 Samuel Hadfield
1828 James Crawshaw
1829 Philip Law
1830 Enoch Barber
1831 John Blake
1832 Thomas Dunn
1833 Thomas Ellin, sen.
1834 John Sansom
1835 John Spencer
1836 Thomas Blake
1837 John Greaves
1838 Samuel Hadfield
1839 Samuel Smith
1840 James Moorhouse
1841 Thomas Ellin, jun.
1842 William Broadhurst
1843 Thomas Wilkinson
1844 Francis Newton
1845 William Butcher
1846 Thos. Burdett Turton
1847 Henry Mort
1848 Frederick Fenny
1849 Henry Atkin
1850 Samuel Scott Deakin
1851 William Webster
1852 Michael Hunter
1853 Wm. Anthony Matthews
1854 Thomas Moulson
1855 Frederick Thorpe Mappin received Baronetcy 1886
1856 George Wostenholm
1857 William Hutchinson
1858 Robert Jackson
1859 Robert Jackson
1860 Michael Hunter, junior.
1861 George Wilkinson
1862 Henry Harrison
1863 Thomas Jessop
1864 Charles Atkinson
1865 John Brown
1866 John Brown knighted August 1867
1867 Mark Firth
1868 Mark Firth

1869 Mark Firth
1870 William Bragge
1871 Thomas Turner [jr.]
1872 Thomas Edward Vickers
1873 Samuel Osborn
1874 George Wilson
1875 Edward Tozer
1876 Edward Tozer
1877 David Ward
1878 Wm. Henry Brittain
1879 Jos. Burdekin Jackson
1880 William Chesterman
1881 John Edward Bingham received Baronetcy 1903
1882 Albert Alsop Jowitt
1883 George Barnsley
1884 John Edward Bingham
1885 Charles Belk
1886 Geo. Francis Lockwood
1887 James Dixon
1888 Saml Earnshaw Howell
1889 Saml Gray Richardson
1890 Robert Colver
1891 Robert Belfitt
1892 John Furniss Atkinson
1893 George Howson
1894 Charles Henry Bingham
1895 Henry Herbert Andrew
1896 Sir Alexander Wilson, Bart. received Baronetcy 1897
1897 Maurice George Rodgers
1898 Frederick Charles Wild
1899 Robert Abbott Hadfield
1900 Richard Groves Holland
1901 Arthur Robert Ellin
1902 Albert John Hobson
1903 Michael John Hunter
1904 George Hall
1905 Sydney Jessop Robinson

Cutlers' Company of London Recorded Pictorial Touchmarks, Principally of the 17th Century

Notes:
1. *The dagger was the mark of the Cutlers' Company of London.*
2. *(F) after a name indicates "foreigner," not a native of London.*
3. *Dates thus [1650-] are dates of earliest noted recording. In many cases (especially 1606-) first use was earlier. Dates thus [-1650] are dates of last use, due either to death, to abandonment, or to transfer.*

MARK	CUTLER	DATES
A (letter)	William Lloyd	1609-
A (letter)	William Eaton	1618-
A and crown	Joseph Arnold	1703-
A with dagger	Sebright Orrenge	1606-
A with dagger	Jacob Ashe	1634-
Acorn	John Whatford	1606-
Acorn	Thomas Eament	1609-
Acorn	Thomas Camell	
Acorn	John Bird	
Acorn	Thomas Isaack (infringed by William Perkins, John Arnold)	1648-
Acorn	John Barford	1668-
Anchor	James Marson	1606-
Anchor	Thomas Murston	-1611
Anchor	William Maddox	1611-
Anchor	Peter Bell	1640-
Anchor	William Justice	1664-
Arrows (see Cross arrows)		
Artichoke with dagger	Thomas Busshell	1629-
Artichoke	Thomas Busshell	1664-1673
Artichoke	Ephraim Howes [How]	1673-
B (letter)	John Branckston	1606-1610
B	Thomas Browne	1610-
B	William Blick	1681
B and crown	Isabel Robinson	1645-
B and crown	Elizabeth Robinson	-1650
B and crown	Clement Bell	1650-
B	Clement Bell	1664
Beads (see Bunch of beads)		
Bell	Simon Rug	1607-
Bell	Thomas Scrag	1609-
Bell	Clement Bell	1664-
Bell	Glenham Wheatcroft	1681-

MARK	CUTLER	DATES
Bended bow and arrow	Robert Wilkenson	1625
Black heart and dagger	Nathaniel Swayne (infringed by Henry Stanehurst)	1628-1647
Black heart	Paul Young	1647-
Blackamoor's head	Lawrence Bret (F)	1631-
Blackamoor's head	Abraham Smith	1650-
Blackberry (see Artichoke)		
Blazing star	Peter Brylman	1606-
Blazing star	Walter Hughes	1638-
Blazing star	John Hathaway	1689-
Bolt and tun	Thomas Williams	1626-
Broad arrowhead	William Barrett	1639-
Broad arrowhead	Edmund Kitchins	1664-
Buck's head	William Pettie	1626-
Bunch of beads	Richard Steeds	1613
Bunch of beads	William Eaton	1616
Bunch of beads	John Miles	1619-
Bunch of beads	Philip Bowen	1635-
String of beads	Joseph Davis	1646-
Bunch of grapes	Lambert Williams	1606-1622
Bunch of grapes	William Ball	1627-1664
Bunch of grapes	William Rush	1664-1683
Bunch of grapes	William Foote	1683-
Bunch of grapes and spur rowell	Gabriel Briggs	1661-
Bunch of grapes and spur rowell	John Mumford	-1669
Bunch of grapes and spur rowell	Daniel Tredwell	1669-1677
Bunch of grapes [and spur rowell]	Peter Perkins	1677-
Bunch of grapes and spur rowell	William Laughton	1693-
C (letter)	Christopher Butler (F)	1606-
C and crown	William Justice	1656-
C and crown	George Cooke	1686-
Cardinal's staff	George Lomeley	1606-
Case of knives and coronet	Richard Ward	1718-
Charing Cross	Thomas Almond	-1648
Charing Cross	George Walker	1648
Charing Cross	James Edmonson	1648-
Close Helmet	William Stevens	1621-
Coney	Daniel Coney	1691-
Crescent (see half moon)		

MARK	CUTLER	DATES
Cross (see also Charing Cross, Spanish Cross, Standing Cross)		
Cross (plain)	Awsten Johnson	1606-1612
Cross (plain)	George Skuyt	1615
Cross and crescent	William Marlar	1519-
Cross and half moon	Joseph Smith	1687-
Cross and crown	Philip Brown	1671-
Cross and fleur de lis	Jervis Boswell	1714-
Cross and star	John Cooke	1671-
Cross arrows	John Counyne (F)	1627-
Cross daggers	John Butler	1659-
Cross keys	John Bushell (infringed by George Lomely, Thomas Lumley)	1606-
Cross keys	William Gardiner	1676-
Crosse sceptres	Thomas Bradford	1664-
Crosse sceptres	Anne Gardner	-1664
Crosse sceptres	Job Worrall	1684-
Crossbow	William Crane	1606-
Crosslets	Samuel Gilbert	-1650
Crosslets	Henry Callis	1650-
Crown and dagger	John Gillet (crown infringed by William Sherebrook)	1606-
Crown	Thomas Justice	1664-
Crown	Paul Browne	1677-
Cup	Thomas Mardell	1645-
Cup	Nicholas Pace	-1655
Crown and P	Nicholas Pace	1655-
Cup	Matthew Peck	1655-
D (letter)	James Dod	1620-
Daffadoundilley (daffodil)	Leonard Vdall	1636-
Dagger	company mrk	
Daggers (see Cross daggers)		
Dart and half moon	Jeremiah Holcrofte	1676-
Dart and star	Edward Dorning	1687-
Diamond and crown	Arnold Smyth	1619-1621
Diamond and crown	Morrice Bowen	1621-
Diamond and coronet	Richard Brown	1723-
Diamond and dagger	Tho. Sharford	1606-
Diamond and dagger	Henry Smartwhite	1704-
Diamond and star	Thomas Panton	1664-
Dolphin	Henry Dyke	1610-
Dolphin	Jonas Melcher	1622-
Dolphin	John Melcher	-1651
Dolphin	John Hyegate	1651-1657
Dolphin	Adam Ball	1657-
Dolphin	Adam Piggott	1664-
Double crescent	Robert Hynkeley	-1452
Double crescent	John Leylond	1452-
Double crescent	Thomas Jackson	1519-
Double Heart	Bartholomew King	1664-
E (letter)	Richard Ellarie	1606-
E (letter)	Thomas Walker	1619-
Eight (figure)	Richard Barnes	1607-
Ermine and coronet	Thomas Huett	1703-

MARK	CUTLER	DATES
F (letter)	William Lloyd	1609-
Falchion [short sword]	William Sherebrook	1617-
Falchion	Zachariah Sellers	-1686
Falchion	Christopher Morgan	1686-
Faulchion and heart	Samuel Stanton	1679-
Filbert (see acorn)		
Filbert with the dagger	John Arnold	1633-1664
Five (figure) and dagger	John Phillips	1606-
Five (figure) and crown	John Bathoe	1664-
Flaming sword with R.B.	Richard Birch	1621-
Flaming sword, G, three half moons	John Milborne (F)	1644-
Flaming sword	John Garner	c1660-
Flaming sword and ball	Richard Piggott	1679
Flaming sword and star	Thomas Walsingham	1675-1679
Flaming sword and heart	Timothy Tindall	1676-1679
Flaming sword and half moon	Glenham Wheatcroft	-1679
Flaming sword and half moon	William Stevens	1699-
Flaming sword and crown	William Wood	1704-
Fleur de lis	John Mercer	1519-
Fleur de lis	John Wessell	1606-1645
Fleur de lis	Walter Powell	1645-
Fleur de lis, crown, and dagger	Jeremy Knowles (F)	1637-1642
Fleur de lis and crown	George Spencer	1642-1650
Fleur de lis and crown	Walter Powell	1650
Fleur de lis and crown	George Parker	1679-
Fleur de lis and dagger	John Wessell	1606-
Fleur de lis and dagger	John Gaudy	1702-
Fleur de lis and half moon	Samuel Miller	1686-
Flying serpent	James Tusley	1673-
G (letter)	Gregorie Evers (F)	1606-
G (letter)	George Lomeley (mark abandoned 1613 due to counterfeiting)	-1613
Gilleflower	William Eaton	1632-
Globe	Melser Gisbert	1608-
Goat's Head	Robert Lister (F)	1633-
Grapes (see Bunch of grapes)		
H (letter)	Robert Hobs	1606-1621
H (letter)	Thomas Horsey	1621-
H	Henry Sergeant	1654-1664
H	Bridget Sergeant	1664-
Halberd	Robert Barnes	1616-
Halberd	Thomas Bickerstaffe	1678-

MARK	CUTLER	DATES
Halberd and crown	George Drew	1681-
Halberd and diamond	Peter Hathaway	1698-
Halberd and heart	Peter Tax	1698-
Two half moons	Thomas Jackson	1519-
Three half moons	Thomas Lamyan	1519-
Half moon	Nathaniel Mathewe (infringed by Charles Fynch)	-1610
Half moon	-Moorebread	1610-
Half moon	John Tinne	1675-
Half moon and crown	Simon Weaver	1664-
Half moon and dagger	Richard HIll	1694-
Half moon and heart	Richard Kettlebuter	1636-
Half moon and heart	Elizabeth Kettlebuter	1664-
Half moon and O	John Cornelius	1655-
Half moon and P	John Cornelius	1664-
Half moon and P	John Kettlebuter	1688-
Half moon and heart	John Kettlebuter	1693-
Half moon and star	John Taylor	1647-
Hammer	Thomas Hedden [Heddinge]	1612-1619
Hammer	Andrew Rosse [Rose]	1619-
Hammer	Edward Sadler	1620-1625
Hammer	Henry Willoughby	1695-
Hammer and heart	John Whitten	1710-
Hand	John Brannes (F)	1606-
Hand	Edward Thomas	1609-
Hand	Thomas Lambert	1614-
Hand	Thomas Hunt	1644-1658
Hand	Henry Parker	1658-1663
Hand	John George	1663-
Hart's horn	Reynold Collyns	1610-
Heart	Frederick Cheretree	1606-1608
Heart	John Cuny	1608-
Heart	Timothy Cockrell	1674-1676
Heart	Stephen Price	1676-
Heart and cross	Francis Hibbert	1662-1665
Heart and cross	Henry Letherland	1665-
Heart and crown	John Bell	1650-
Heart and crown	Thomas Justice	1653-
Heart and crown	John Bell (infringed 1686 by Ephraim How)	1673-
Heart and crown	Ephraim How	c1703
Heart and dagger	John Almond	1620-
Heart and dart	John Wharrey	1667-
Heart, fleur de lis, and dagger	Peter Spitser	1698-
Heart and spade	Thomas Spicer	1703-
Heart and weeping tear	John Harrington	1674-
Heart (also see black heart double heart)		
Helmet (see Close helmet, Morion)		
Herring	Richard Herring	1606-
Horseshoe	Tho. Barrat	1606-
Horseshoe	William Rush	-1664
Horseshoe	Robert Ashwood	1664-
Horseshoe and crown	William Rush	1643
Hunter's horn	Haunce Smyth	1606-

MARK	CUTLER	DATES
I.M.	Johnathan Miner	1688-
K and dagger	William Knowles	1661-
Key and crown	Jarvis Allison	1640-
Keys (see Cross keys)		
King's head	Haunce Smyth	1613-1626
King's head	Abraham Smyth	1626-
L (letter)	Zachariah Lowen	1657-
L and crown	Enoch Taylor	1640-
L and crown	William Laughton	1676-
Leopard's head	William Balls	1622-
Leopard's head	Robert Wilkenson	1625-
Leopard's Head	Jeremy Draper	1647-
Lion	Henry Neve	1612-
M (letter)	Robert Dobson	1606-
M	Thomas Moakeson (Moulson) (infringed by Marmaduke Redditt)	1642-1670
M	Marmaduke Redditt (Reader)	1664-
Mace	John Best	1689-
Maidenhead	John Bell (F)	1632-1648
Maidenhead and N	Nicholas Waterson	1648-1664
Maidenhead	John Bell	1664-1668
Maidenhead	Philip Penn	1668-
Moon (see Half moon, Crescent)		
Morion [helmeted] head	Melcher Thomas (Domas)	1608-
Morion head	Oliver Plucket	1611-
Morion head	Litle Haunce Smyth	1613-
Morion head (on sword blades)	Robert South (King's Cutler)	1632-
N (letter)	Samuel Nicholson	1606-
N and coronet	William Norwood	1695-
N and maidenhead	Nicholas Waterson	1648-1664
NOW (imitating Ephraim How)	(counterfeit)	c1703
O and heart	John King	1664-
O and half moon	John Cornelius	1655-
P (letter)	William Hanwick	1606-
P and Crown	Nicholas Pace	1655-
P (letter)	Nicholas Pace	1664-
P with dagger	Robert Preston	1637-
Pincers (open)	John Melser	1622-
Pincers and crown	William Wolfe	1645
Pineapple	Matthew Smith	1686-
Pistol	Edward Badcock	1655-
Pistol	Robert Worth	1710-
Poleaxe (hatchet fashion)	John Woodley	1664-
Pomengranate	Edmond Chapman	1612-
Pomengranate	John Knolls	1624-
Pomengranate	William Rush	1637-
Portcullis	William Bates?	c1607
Punchinello	Robert Telby	1668-
R (letter)	Ralph Leachworth	1621-
R with dagger	John Browne	1606-
R and crown	Samuel Swallow (infringed earlier by Thomas Swalloe)	1631-

MARK	CUTLER	DATES
Ragged staff and dagger	William Preston (F)	1634-
Ragged staff	Jasper Greene	1680-
Rose	William Browne	1606-
Rose	John Martin	1619-
Rose	Henry Parker	1664-
Rose	Daniel Tredwell	1664-1669
Rose and crown	William Hoy	1686-
Rose and crown	Jarvis West	1710-
Rose bud	Thomas Mardell	1640-
S (letter)	Thomas Okys	1519-
S (Romayne letter)	John Whitfield	1607-
Scallop shell and dagger	Paul Mathewe	1608-
Sceptre	Albord Johnson	1606-
Sceptre	Aaron Freeman	1695-
Sceptre and club	Henry Fowle	1692-
Sceptre and cross	Moses Carr	1686-
Sceptre and crown	Benjamin Beard	1685-
Sceptre and diamond	Thoams Butterfield	1684-
Sceptre and diamond	William Page	1699-
Sceptre and globe	Thomas Thompson	1694-
Sceptre and half moon	William Deane (infringed by Henry Grew, Moses Carr)	1677-
Sceptre and half moon	Robert Browne	-1694
Sceptre and half moon	- Harman	1694-
Sceptre and spade	Thomas Butterfield	1702-
Sceptre and star	Samuel Grover	1677-
Sceptre and star	Thomas Stanton	1685-
Sceptres (see Crosse sceptres)		
Serpent and cross	Robert Littlewood	1664-
Serpent, dagger, standing cross	Henry King (F)	1637-
Serpent (see Flying serpent)		
Shepherd's hook	Widow Harblet	1606-
Sickle	Bellam Careles	1609-
Six (figure) and half moon	Edward Grange	1664-
Snuffers	George Lomely	1613-
Spade and crown	John How	1709-
Spanish cross	Henry Callis	1664-
Spectacles	Charles Fynch	1606-
Spectacles	John Seymer	1647-
Spread eagle	Abraham Brock	1619-1623
Spread eagle	John Skegg	1707-
Spur rowell with dagger	Peter Browgh	1606-
Spur	Abraham Brock	1623-
Spur rowell and bunch of grapes	Gabriel Briggs	1661-
Standing Cross	John Almon[d]	1606-
Standing Cross, serpent, dagger	Henry King (F)	1637-
Standing Cross	Thomas Mason	1664-
Standing Cross	Thomas Deanne	1668-
Star	Thomas Dowling	1603-
Star	John Virgyn	1622-

MARK	CUTLER	DATES
Star	Job Hunt	1664-
Star (see also Blazing star)		
Star and crown	William Holland	1703-
Star and half moon	John Taylor	1647-
Star and half moon	Thomas Squire	1677-
Star, pierced	Marian Garret	1519-
Star with dagger	Tho. Dowlinge	1606-
Sun	John Langford	1609-
Sword	Leonard Leadman	1693-
Sword and cross	Jeffery Gunn	1681-
Sword and crown	John Perry	1693-
T (letter)	Henry Stanus	1606-
T (letter)	Joseph Stanhowse	1664-
T and dagger	Giles Lyndesey	1677-
T B and Crown	Rejoyce ffox	1677-
Thistle	John Jencks	1606-
Thistle	Joseph Jencks (infringed by William Rush)	c1638
Thistle	John Arnold	1656-
Thistle	George Arnold	1664-
Three (figure) with dagger	Peter Cornelius	1606-
Three (figure)	Arnold Cornelius (see V)	1620-1629
Three (figure)	Lawrence Shepard	1629-
Three (figure)	William Boswell	1664-1666
Three (figure)	Robert Tallby	1668-
Three and crown	Robert Lister	1640-
Three leaved grass	Wicker Bunt	c1600
Three leaved grass	Robert South	-1606
Three leaved grass	Andrew Rose (see Trefoil)	1606-
Tobacco pipe	Richard Piggott	1682-
Tongs, fire	John Arnold	1606-
Tongs, fire	William Savage	1636-1666
Tongs, fire	Wm. Boswell for Thos. Elliot	1666-1668
Tongs, fire	William Boswell	1668-1673
Tongs, fire	Jarvis Boswell	1675-
Trefoil	John Pascall	1519-
Trefoil	Andrew Rosse [Rose]	-1619
Trefoil	Thomas Heddinge [Hedden]	1619-
Triangle	Benjamin Stennet	1688-
True-love knot	Christopher Butler	1614-
Unicorn head with dagger	Peter Spitser	1621-
Unicorn head	Peter Spitzer	1664-
V (letter)	Arnold Cornelius	1629-1664
V (letter)	Widow Cornelius	1664-
V (letter)	Thomas Elliott	1673-
V and heart	Miles Tillyard	1645-
V and star	Zachariah Seller	1673-
W (letter)	William Hethe	1519-
W (letter)	William Bate[s]	1607-
Weeping tear (on razors)	George Stocton	1664-
X (letter)	Gregorie Edwards	1615-
Y (letter)	William Boswell	1668-
Y with dagger	Joseph Surbut [Serbert] (F)	1631

Masters of the London Cutlers Guild, 1584-1922

Lists of London cutlers go back two centuries prior to 1584, but the list of masters and wardens is complete only from that date forward. Up until the early 19th century, the London Guild was both more powerful and more prestigious than its rival in Sheffield. A principal activity of the London Guild throughout most of its history was endeavoring to suppress the counterfeiting of its marks by the "foreigners" in Sheffield.

Each year saw the election of a master and two wardens in the London Guild, each of them prominent in the trade.

Until 1626, masters and wardens usually served two terms. Most of the wardens went on to become masters. A few cutlers declined election to masterships, choosing instead to pay fines. Where applicable, they are included here in parentheses.

This list is derived from Charles Welch's *History of the Cutlers' Company of London* (by the company, 1923, two volumes).

1584 Roger Knowlls
1585 Richard Mathew
1586-87 Richard Vale
1588-89 Richard Mathew
1590-91 Richard Hawes
1592-93 Thomas Porter
1594-95 Thomas Greene
1596-97 John Gardiner
1598-99 Thomas Asshott
1600-01 Henry Siddon
1602-03 Oliver Pluckett
1604-05 George Ellis
1606-07 Thomas Porter
1608 Oliver Plucket
1609-10 Christopher Hatfield
1611-12 Reynold Greene
1613-14 Henry Adams
1615-16 Thomas Chessheire
1617-18 Miles Bancks
1619-21 John Porter (James Tackley, fined)
1622-24 George Harberd
1625-26 William Davis
1627 Thomas Tuck
1628 Henry Withers
1629 Robert South
1630 Edmund Hutchenson
1631 John Berrey
1632 Adam Ward
1633 Francis Fullwell
1634 Francis Cob
1635 Thomas Taylor
1636 Joseph Rogers
1637 George Moore
1638 Edward Hynson

1639 Thomas Byewater
1640 William Cave
1641 Thomas Hart
1642 Gabriel Partridge
1643 Thomas Beedham
1644 Robert Fowlzer
1645 William Tooley (Richard Bates, fined)
1646 Isaac Ash
1647 Thomas Cheshire
1648 Percival Moore
1649 Edmund King
1650 Thomas Parsons (Col. Lawrence Bromfeild, fined)
1651 Thomas Freeman (Edmund Warnett, fined) (Richard Evans, fined)
1652 George Sanders
1653 Henry Beale
1654 Richard Batson
1655 Thomas Hopkins
1656 Jacob Ash
1657 Walter Gibbons
1658 Ald. John Maniford
1659 Robert Carrington (John Partridge, fined)
1660 Tobie Berrey
1661 William Fulwell
1662 William Carter
1663 Thomas Bywater
1664 Richard Tredwell
1665 Thomas Smyth
1666 Jeremiah Greene
1667 John Flampstead
1668 Capt. Edward Ball

1669 Robert Saywell
1670 Robert Raystrick
1671 Richard Hopkins
1672 Thomas Birtwhistell
1673 Henry Whittaker
1674 Thomas Dermer (Capt. Thomas Powell, fined)
1675 William Paxton
1676 Thomas Bradford
1677 Thomas Hooker
1678 Simon Weaver
1679 Capt. Richard Blaney
1680 Robert Grymes
1681 John Howes
1682 Adam Ball
1683 Edward Faulkingham
1684 Thomas Pennington
1685 William Chiffinch
1686 Francis Browne
1687 John Hawgood
1688 Daniel Wilson
1689 Anthony Clapham
1690 Thomas Tunn
1691 Samuel James
1692 John Kettlebuter
1693 John Godman
1694 Abraham Smith
1695 John Wilcox
1696 William Mereden
1697 Richard Wise
1698 Henry Benson
1699 Richard Geast
1700 Clement Tookie
1701 Richard Hopkins
1702 John Woodcraft
1703 Capt. John Frith
1704 Humphrey Bellamy

1705 Nicholas Levett
1705-06 Ephraim How
1707 Anthony Ball
1708 John Merreden
1709 Thomas Powell
1710 Philip Mist
1711 Joseph Shepheard
1712 Edward Patterson
1713 Richard Piggott
1714 Richard Kay
1715 Job Worrall
1716 Edward Williams
1717 William Powell
1718 Edward Tompkins
1719 Guy Stone
1720 Anthony Russell
1721 Charles Thompson
1722 William Smith
1723 Sir Richard Hopkins
1724 John Bully
1725 Peter Spitzer
1726 Thomas Barugh
1727 Richard Chapman
1728 Thomas Cox
1729 John Bully
1730-31 John Fisher
1732 Thomas Horne
1733 Amos White
1734 Francis Hyde
1735 Thomas Allcroft
1736 Charles Cotton
1737 Jarvis Boswell
1738 Thomas Bibb
1739 William Falkener
1740 Thomas Yelloley Edward Holden
1741 William Chambers
1742 William Loxham

1743 Samuel Smyth
1744 Benjamin Cox
1745 Henry Collett
1746 Thomas Geary
1747 George Fisher
1748 Charles Cotton
1749 Wm. John Andrews
1750 John Bennett
1751 William Collins
1752 William Hardy
1753 Joseph Hatton
1754 Thomas Crouch
1755 James Cullum
1756 Thomas Cross
1757 Robert Perry
1758 John Baldwin
    Edward Loxham
1759 John Chambers
1760 George Gibson
1761 John Carman
1762 Joseph Miller
1763 James Richardson
1764 Thomas Dunnage
1765 Thomas Reid
1766 Francis Thurkle
    (George Watson,
    fined)
1767 Joseph Bayzand
1768 John Beaumont
1769-70 Joseph Hatton
1771 Thomas Dealtry
1772 Joseph Fisher
1773 Peter Cargill
1774 Thomas Squire
1775 William Ayres
1776 Joseph Miller
1777 John Beaumont
1778 Thomas Copous
1779 John Bennett
1780 Henry Allen
1781 John Bell
1782 James Scott
1783 James Looker
1784 Robert Lepper
1785 James Beavan
1786 John Copous
1787 Yeeling Charlwood
1788-89 Thomas Patrick
1790 John Phipps
1791 John Dunnage
1792 William Pepys
1793 John Bennett
1794 Edward Dowling
1795 Francis Thurkle
1796 George Jeffreys
1797 Robert Loxham
1798 James Looker

1799 Robert Huddy
1800 Charles Biggs
1801 John Foulds
1802 Edward Parry
1803 John Gent
1804 Thomas Squire, Jun.
1805 George Skelton
1806 John Dowling
1807 Joseph Thos. Rolph
    Charles Biggs
1808 Robert Taber
1809 James Dunnage
1810 George Skelton
1811 Robert Loxham
1812 John Greer
1813 William Ayres
    John Beaumont
1814 Geo. Moses Thurkle
1815 Henry Wm. Looker
1816 William Pryor
1817 James Carden
1818 James Priest
1819 Yeeling Underwood
1820 Stephen Boyce
1821 Richard Johnstone
1822 Wm. Hasledyne Pepys
1823 William Ayres
1824 Abraham Skynner
    Geo. Moses Thurkle
1825 William Squire
1826 Richard Rees
1827 Walter Allen Meriton
1828 Wm. Hasledyne Pepys
    (Henry Verinder,
    fined)
1829 Ald. Henry
    Winchester
1830 William Pryor
1831 James Johnston
    (Zechariah Uwins,
    fined)
1832 William Johnston
1833 Henry William
    Looker
1834-35 John Wort
    (Thomas Johnston,
    fined)
1836 Henry Verinder
1837 Henry Thos.
    Underwood
1838 Zachariah Uwins
1839 William Squire
1840 Thomas Higgs
1841 James Copous
1842 Joseph Hoppe
1843 Walter Allen Meriton
1844 Henry Verinder

1845 John Evans
    (Sir John Hall, fined)
1846 Edward Stammers
1847 Thomas Boot
1848 Peter Paterson
1849 Wm. Hallett Hughes
1850 Thomas Pocock
    (James Lee, fined)
1851 Thomas Barnjum
    Thomas Pocock
1852 Charles Greer
1853 Ald. Sir Robert Walter
    Carden
1854 Robert Burra
1855 Geo. Frederick Davis
1856 Richard Lloyd
1857 William Squire Pryor
1858 Thomas Hammant
1859 Thomas Boot
    (John Pryor, fined)
1860 Joseph Fisher
1861 Capt. Wm. Liveing
1862 Geo. Frederick
    Carden
1863 Thomas Dunnage
1864 James Rhodes
1865 Ald. Sir Robert Walter
    Carden
    (Richard James Rees,
    fined)
1866-67 William Anderson
1868 Henry Graves
1869 Frederick Smith
    James Rhodes
1870 Thomas Gotch
    Pocock
1871 Wm. Grenville
    Johnston
1872 Wm. Adam Oldaker
1873 Richard Tress
1874 John Llewellyn Evans
    Henry Graves
1875 James Nairne Scott
1876 Ald. Sir Robert Walter
    Carden
    (James Beaumont,
    fined)
    (Henry Carnegie
    Carden, fined)
1877 Henry Graves
1878 Thomas Gotch
    Pocock
1879 Wm. Adam Oldaker
1880 Alfred Pockock
1881 John Parry Edkins
    (George Tyler, fined)
1882 Joseph Thorne

1883 Richard Gore Lloyd
1884 Samuel Poynton Boot
1885 Robert Balls Hughes
1886 Ebeneezer Pocock
1887 Robert Greer
    (Dr. Charles Welch,
    fined)
1888 James Greer
1889 Horace Charles Lloyd
1890-91 Richard Jas.
    Cheeswright
1892 Joseph Morton
1893 Ebeneezer Wm.
    Williams
    Joseph Morton
1894 Francis George Boot
1895 Robert Perkins
1896 Jos. Underwood
    Morton
1897 Henry Wm. Ashmole
1898 William Cumin Scott
1899 James Alfred Rhodes
1900 Edward Beaumont
1901 Henry Ross Boot
1902 Algernon Graves
1903 Thos. Alfred Dunnage
1904 Benjamin Pratt
1905 James Beaumont
    Waller
1906 Charles James Scott
1907 Charles Welch
1908 Edm. Walter
    Rushworth
1909 Alfred Pocock
1910 Francis Wm. Williams
1911 Ald. Sir Walter
    Vaughan Morgan,
    Baronet
1912 William Alfred
    Herbert
1913 George Pocock
1914 William Price Pepys
1915 Alfred James Thomas
1916 Wm. Coppard
    Beaumont
1917 Dr. Chas. Geo.
    Beaumont
1918 Dr. Samuel Welch
1919 Percy Rogers Pocock
1920 Frederick Richard
    Cheeswright
1921 Macdonald
    Beaumont
1922 Edwin Hedley
    Williams

Salisbury Cutlers

Before 1800 the city of Salisbury, Wiltshire, was even better known than Sheffield for high-grade knives and scissors. Salisbury, or New Sarum, was founded in 1220; a "Cutiller" named Sebode was recorded there in 1270.

In the 1720s, at least a dozen Salisbury master cutlers employed apprentices. The most prominent was William Strugnell, who became mayor in 1721. Joseph Blackhead, who had been apprenticed to Francis Barber in 1719, was taking on apprentices of his own by 1728. Later in the 18th century, the leading Salisbury cutlers were the Goddards. James Goddard was mayor in 1793, while Thomas Goddard became mayor in 1797. Both supplied cutlery to King George III and to the Prince Regent, the latter who would become George IV.

Until the 1780s, Salisbury cutlers stamped their blades with pictorial or initial touch-marks. From the 1780s onward, they marked their blades with their full names, usually followed by the old town name, SARUM.

According to The Victoria County History of Wiltshire, "The trade continued throughout the 19th century; 7 cutlers are listed in a directory of 1822 and 10 in one of 1830. George III patronized members of the Botly family ... It was the custom to meet the London and Exeter coach and display cutlery to the passengers, and ... it was 'no uncommon thing' to take 70 pounds from a single coach.

"William Beach received an honourable mention for his cutlery at the Great Exhibition [of 1851], and in 1862 exhibited a case containing knives, scissors, razors, and daggers at the International Exhibition in London."

C.N. Moore adds, in *Wiltshire Industrial Archaeology*, "There was some connection between Salisbury and Sheffield, as shown by Thomas Neesham, who came from Sheffield to be an 'improver' or assistant to Mr. Shorto of Queen Street, and who in 1817 set up his own business in New Canal.

" ... An advertisement of about that time mentions that [the Neeshams] were making sportsmen's knives and puzzle knives, and ... miniature knives ... One, in the shape of ... Lady Ilchester's leg, is in the [Salisbury] Museum. There is also in the Museum a giant pen knife that was used by the Shortos as a trade sign, and in the window of Neesham's shop there used to be a giant pen knife with a hundred blades. [William] Beach ... in 1874 made a bowie knife for William Blackmore ... before he set out for New Mexico."

In 1895, Salisbury still offered high-grade cutlery. The leading firm at the time was James Macklin and Son. However, "by the end of the 19th century[,] the Salisbury cutlery industry was in a sad state of decline. Many of the cutlers were importing Sheffield pieces. Robert Macklin, who was first apprenticed [to] and then took over the Botlys' business in Catherine Street in 1880, had two cutlers still working for him in 1896. Macklin became Mayor during the Great War [1914-1918], and was knighted ... The last working cutler, however, was Henry Neesham, who continued to work until his death in March 1914, aged 88."

NAME	ADDRESS	ACTIVE DATES
William Baker		1710-1725
Thomas Baker	('knife blade maker')	1720
Francis Barber		1718-1719
William Beach	Catherine Street	1829-1880
James Bennett	Market Place	1826-1844
William Best	Bedwyn Street	1838-1839
Joseph Blackhead		1728-1730
Botly & Son	Market Place	1791-1844
Jane Botly	Ox Row	1838
Henry Botly	7 Catherine Street	1838-1880
Thomas Brathatt		1620
William Brathatt		1620
Richard Bryant		1720-1725
W.H. Brown	33 High Street	1903-1915
James Crabb	Market Place	circa 1790
Bennet Eastman	Fish Row	1649-1650
Fox		circa 1780
Francis Gilbert	Silver Street	1844
James Goddard	Queen Street	1753-1793
Thomas Goddard	Queen Street	1797-1798
Francis Gregory		1716
Thomas Long		1744
James Macklin	7 Catherine Street	1880-1915

NAME	ADDRESS	ACTIVE DATES
William Mullens	High Street	1720-1732
Thomas Neesham	New Canal & Oatmeal Row	1817-1855
Henry Neesham	Oatmeal Row	1855-1914
Thomas Obourne		1712-1726
John Page	Queen Street	1755-1757
Charles Power		1713-1725
Jane Price	Oatmeal Row	1838-1839
Francis Thomas Price	Oatmeal Row	1844
John Pring		1741-1758
Read		1780?
Henry Shorto	Queen Street	1791-1832
John Skilton		1711-1716
William Snook		1741-1753
William Snook	Catherine Street	1791-1843
Richard Speering	('sword cutler')	1712-1713
William Speering		1719-1721
William Strugnell		c1720
John Troke	(also watchmaker)	1791-1798
Webb	(also gunsmith) Queen Street	1790-1830
John Whately		1718-1721
John & Thomas Wilkes		1791-1798

19th Century Sheffield Cutlery Firms

By Geoffrey Tweedale

(Editor's note: Geoffrey Tweedale of Manchester, England, is the author of The Sheffield Knife Book: A History and Collector's Guide *[1996; available from Knife World Publications, POB 3395, Knoxville TN 37927] and* Steel City: Entrepreneurship, Strategy and Technology in Sheffield, 1743-1993 *[Oxford University Press, 1995].)*

The 19th century was the golden age of Sheffield cutlery. The town's cutlery industry was firmly based on its citizens' centuries-old skills in knifemaking, and it had been given further impetus in the 18th century by Benjamin Huntsman's invention of crucible cast steel (1742) and by the growth of colonial and export markets. In 1824, there were over 8000 workers in Sheffield's cutlery and tool trades; by 1850, the number had doubled.

Most of the men were independent or semi-independent craftsmen, the "little mesters." However, so strong was the demand for Sheffield cutlery after 1800 that large-scale firms began to appear, some of whose near-legendary names were to greatly enhance Sheffield's growing world reputation.

Sheffield's larger firms of the 19th century offered a full range of steel products, and some even made their own steel. However, even the largest spread their risks by buying specialty patterns from outworkers, and by renting out space within their "works" to individual craftsmen. Thus, Sheffield's traditional hand skills in forging, grinding, and "cutlering" (assembly and finishing) reigned supreme, even in the big factories. Power forging of table knife blades did not come to Sheffield until the 1870s, four decades after its first use in the United States. Power forging of pocketknife blades was unknown in Sheffield until the 20th century.

Sheffield and the United States

The stimulus for the growth of large cutlery firms in Sheffield in the early 19th century was the burgeoning American market. Indeed, Sheffield was already so dependent on the American trade in the 18th century that the interruption of the trade due to the American Revolution (1776-1783) caused considerable distress in the town.

Further hardship followed for Sheffield craftsmen during the embargoes of the Napoleonic Wars, especially during the War of 1812 (1812-1815), when all trade between Britain and the United States was halted. By 1812, some major Sheffield firms had been devoting nearly all of their energies to the American market.

Chief among them was the firm of NAYLOR & SANDERSON, which traced its history back to the 16th century. The Naylors were cutlers in Coalpit Lane who, by 1800, had joined the Sanderson family in Carver Street Lane.

The leading light of the joint firm was George Naylor. In 1812, he told a Parliamentary Committee that his firm had been engaged in the U.S. trade for six years and sent five-sixths of its goods to the USA. George Naylor retired in 1829, at which point the firm was re-formed as Sanderson Brothers, thereafter concentrating on tool steel.

After 1815, Sheffield's trade with America expanded enormously. The edge-tool firm of JOHN SORBY & SONS was typical of the old established Sheffield firms that exploited the new opportunities. The Sorby family had resided in Sheffield for at least 300 years, and, in 1620, a Robert Sorsby was the first Master Cutler of the town's Cutlers' Guild. By the early 19th century, I. Sorby & Sons had built up a network of close family relationships and business interests in the town, chief of which was led by John's son, Henry Sorby. (See the section, "American Indian Trade Knives.")

The year 1816 saw publication of the first-ever-illustrated catalog of Sheffield tools and cutlery. Compiled by Joseph Smith, the *Explanation or Key to the Various Manufactories of Sheffield* showed all the various patterns made in Sheffield specifically for the American market. At the time, Smith's *Key* was a financial failure for its publisher, but today provides a priceless glimpse of early 19-century Sheffield export cutlery. (See the section, "Foreign, Exotic, Primitive, and Historical Folding Knives.")

The steel, tool and cutlery firm of MARSH BROTHERS paid particular attention to the U.S. market early in the 19th century. Founded in 1631, it traded as JAMES MARSH & CO. from 1815-1828, and also as MARSHES & SHEPHERD. James Marsh opened an office and warehouse in Philadelphia in 1817. In 1828, Marsh Bros. began manufacturing at the Pond Works in Sheffield. In the 1830s and 1840s, the firm opened additional offices and warehouses in Boston and New York for the sale of its table cutlery and spring knives.

In 1823, the profits of the American trade enabled WILLIAM GREAVES & SONS to begin building its famous Sheaf Works. When completed in 1826, at a total cost of 50,000 pounds, it was the first factory in Sheffield to bring together all the stages of cutlery manufacture, from the converting of Swedish iron into steel right up to packing the finished knives. In an 1849 directory, the firm described itself as "American Merchants," offering a wide variety of steel and cutlery products. In 1850, the Greaves firm was taken over by BENJAMIN JAMES EYRE & CO., which, by 1852, had combined with FREDERICK WARD & CO. (B4-ANY) to form EYRE, WARD & CO.

Wade & Butcher

Another firm that established its reputation in the United States during this early phase of expansion was WILLIAM & SAMUEL BUTCHER, a partnership formed by two brothers in 1819. For a time, it occupied the "Philadelphia Works." The brothers were a highly successful team, though William Butcher (c1791-1870) became the more prominent of the two in Sheffield town affairs (he was Master Cutler in 1845).

The Butcher firm had a New York office headed by another Sheffield man, Robert Wade. This led to the famous mark WADE & BUTCHER being stamped on most of its export products. A shrewd businessman, William Butcher sent large quantities of barlows, bowie knives and razors to the USA, alongside heavy consignments of steel and files. Butcher's works were sold after his death but the new owners continued the cutlery side of the business, using the Wade & Butcher mark well into the 20th century.

Similarly, THOMAS TURNER & COMPANY found the American trade lucrative. Turner established his business in 1802, and by the 1820s was located in Norfolk Street. In about 1834, the firm opened its Suffolk Works to produce a wide range of cutlery, tools and steel. T. Turner & Co. catered to American tastes by stamping its pocketknives with quaint Americanisms and catchy slogans, such as "Warranted Really Good," "Made Expressly For America," "Warranted To Strike Fire," and "Alabama Hunting Knife."

Thomas Turner, Jr. (1829-1916) led the firm until his retirement in 1893, helped by his brothers, Benjamin and William. By 1905, T. Turner & Co., under new management, absorbed two other old cutlery firms, WINGFIELD, ROWBOTHAM & CO. and JOSEPH HAYWOOD, and employed about a thousand men.

Also prominent was WILSON & HAWKSWORTH, established in 1825 to manufacture cutlery. The firm's American traveler, Joshua Moss, was particularly successful, and was admitted to the partnership in 1832, when the business became WILSON, HAWKSWORTH, & MOSS. By 1846, when another partner, Joseph Ellison, joined the firm, it relinquished most of its interests in cutlery to concentrate on crucible steel making.

MAPPIN BROTHERS also grew rapidly before 1850, having developed from the engraving business of Joseph Mappin, founded in 1810. The firm began manufacturing cutlery by the 1820s, a business that was cultivated by Joseph's eldest son, Sir Frederick Thorpe Mappin (1821-1910). In 1851, Mappin Bros. moved into the Queen's Cutlery Works, Baker's Hill, which in the 1860s employed over 200 men. By then, the works enjoyed a great reputation for its sportsman's knives, some of which contained 19 blades and/or tools, while its spring knives were produced in several thousand different patterns and variations. Frederick's younger brother, John N. Mappin, managed a separate concern in the 1860s, MAPPIN & WEBB, which absorbed Mappin Bros. in 1902. Thereafter, the firm increasingly specialized in silver-plated wares and, more recently, jewelry.

In the "glorious year of prosperity 1835," as one newspaper described it, when over half the town's exports went stateside, Sheffield's U.S. cutlery trade reached a peak. Thereafter there was a decline, but the USA still took a quarter of English hardware exports until 1860.

Sheffield directories show that many Sheffield cutlers cleverly exploited new fashions across the Atlantic in the 1850s and 1860s. HENRY BARGE specialized in three- and four-blade congress knives. JOHN HINCHCLIFFE produced "fancy spring, lock, sneck, dagger, and American Indian Knives." UNWIN & RODGERS manufactured its "patented pistol-knife." The "Boston Works" of RICHARD BUNTING supplied fancy folding knives to its American agent, Wells W. Ayer of Boston. JONATHAN CROOKES & SON (founded 1780) made private-brand cutlery for American retailers such as Martin Bradford of Boston. Both SLEIGH ROWLAND (active c1830-1850) and LUKE BOOTH (died 1855) made table cutlery for American homes, while HENRY C. BOOTH's Norfolk Works made bowie knives, as did SAMUEL WRAGG & SONS (active 1830s-1860s) and GEORGE WOODHEAD (active 1845-1870s). Other makers, such as JOHN ASKHAM (1818-1894), advertised knives made especially for the American market. However, of all the cutlery firms that catered to America at the time, none were as successful as Rodgers and Wostenholm, which together dominated the U.S. cutlery market.

J. Rodgers and G. Wostenholm

Joseph Rodgers & Sons had an unequaled reputation in the 19th century for the quality of its products. Its famous and much imitated mark—the Star and Maltese Cross—was granted in 1682. By the early 19th century, Rodgers was prospering in Norfolk Street, owed most to the direction of John Rodgers (1779-1859). He widened its product range, won a Royal Warrant by providing cutlery for the Prince Regent, and established the company's famous showroom in the 1820s. There, visitors might stand in admiration before Rodgers' remarkable display knives, such as the Year Knife and the famous Norfolk Knife (see the section, "Showpiece and Exposition Knives") made for the Great Exhibition of 1851.

A member of the Rodgers firm resided permanently in New York to foster the U.S. trade. The trade was a decisive factor in the firm's expansion into the world's largest cutlery factory by 1850. Rodgers was incorporated as a limited company in 1871 with a capital of 130,000 pounds, and remained among the largest Sheffield firms for the remainder of the 19th century.

REGISTERED TRADE MARK.

GRANTED 1682.

JOSEPH RODGERS & SONS
had an unequaled reputation in the 19th century
for the quality of its knives. Its famous and
much imitated mark was the Star and Maltese Cross.

By the mid-19th century, Rodgers had been joined at the front rank by GEORGE WOSTENHOLM & SON. Founded in 1745, Wostenholm operated at the Rockingham Works in Sheffield until the third-generation head of the enterprise, George Wostenholm (1800-1876), decided to relocate to a larger facility in 1848. The facility was the Washington Works on Wellington Street, where he brought together 300-400 workers to supply the American market with all types of cutlery.

The firm catered to the U.S. trade almost exclusively, with Wostenholm himself crossing the Atlantic 30 times in search of orders. Wostenholm had a New York office, headed by Asline Ward (1821-1905), which distributed its prestigious I*XL brand name throughout the USA. The firm became the most prolific maker of bowie knives, which, under Wostenholm, reached a high level of artistry and craftsmanship. Wostenholm's became a limited company in 1875, with a capital of £100,000.

Later Firms

After the American Civil War (1861-1865), Sheffield firms continued to cater to the demand for "American novelties." Among the most successful was the Atlantic Works of BROOKES & CROOKES, which was founded in 1858 by Thomas Crookes (1825-1912) and John Brookes. Crookes, soon aided by the second and third generations of his family, was the guiding hand in the business, which won a first-class prize at the Philadelphia Centennial in 1876. The firm, which by the 1890s employed over 150 men, specialized in elaborate sportsman's and lady's knives, and in ornate bowie and hunting knives.

HARRISON BROTHERS & HOWSON also pursued the U.S. trade vigorously after 1865, with its high-quality table, pocket and silver-plated articles. Founded in 1796 by WILLIAM SANSOM, a Master Cutler who had secured a Royal Warrant for his products, the business was acquired in 1847 by James W. Harrison, William Howson and Henry Harrison (c1825-1893). The latter built up the firm's American trade, which, by the 1890s, had agencies in New York on West Broadway, and in San Francisco on Sutter Street. By 1896, the company employed over 700 men. It opened new premises in Carver Street in about 1900, and shortly afterward absorbed the pocketknife business of CHARLES IBBOTSON.

Sheffield's traditional expertise also attracted American entrepreneurs. In 1885, ANDREW J. JORDAN (c1846-1929), a St. Louis merchant, opened a factory in Sheffield. It was first at Baker's Hill and then at the India Works in Furnival Street. He sent only the highest quality goods to the United States, especially kitchen knives, since it was said that he would not deal in machine-made articles (see the section, "Kitchen and Butcher Knives").

The Decline

By the 1890s, Sheffield's American trade was in serious decline. The town was increasingly unable to compete against the less expensive, machine-produced and attractively advertised knives of its U.S. competitors, who were also insulated by an ever-rising wall of protective tariffs. The American frontiersman no longer carried a Sheffield bowie, and Sheffield cutlers, when not emigrating themselves, were looking elsewhere toward developing colonial markets.

Nonetheless, several Sheffield firms achieved a measure of success in the period, including GEORGE HIDES & SON

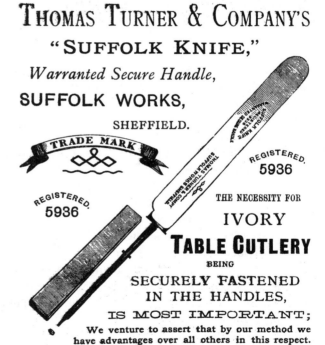

GOLD MEDAL awarded to THOMAS TURNER & Co., at South African International Exhibition, Cape Town, 1877.

THOMAS TURNER & COMPANY'S "SUFFOLK KNIFE,"

Warranted Secure Handle,

SUFFOLK WORKS,

SHEFFIELD.

TRADE MARK

REGISTERED. 5936

REGISTERED. 5936

THE NECESSITY FOR

IVORY

TABLE CUTLERY

BEING

SECURELY FASTENED IN THE HANDLES,

IS MOST IMPORTANT;

We venture to assert that by our method we have advantages over all others in this respect.

The TANG being made strong the *whole-length* of the Handle, and A CROSS PIN, (*as shown in the sketch*) being inserted into a small Groove, and turned into a Cavity Inside the Handle, (made for its reception) forms an INTERNAL LOCK: an OVAL RIVET, fastened upon the *Square Tang* of the *Head* PREVENTS the possibility of the Blade TURNING ROUND in the Handle, or becoming Loose in any way.

THOMAS TURNER & COMPANY found the American trade lucrative. Turner established his business in Sheffield in 1802, and by the 1820s was located in Norfolk Street. In about 1834, the firm opened its Suffolk Works to produce a wide range of cutlery, tools and steel.

(est. 1609), CHAMPION & CO. (est. 1791), and MICHAEL HUNTER & SON (est. 1780).

Another firm, GEORGE IBBERSON & CO., not only produced high-quality pocketknives but also assisted in a major breakthrough in cutlery technology. The Ibberson family had been involved in cutlery manufacture in Sheffield since 1666, and had been granted 28 freedoms of the Cutlers' Company since 1700. In 1914, Joseph Ibberson, in collaboration with Thomas Firth & Sons, steelmakers, and Harry Brearley, inventor, hardened and ground the first knife blades made of stainless steel.

By the First World War (1914-1918), American tariffs had effectively ended Sheffield's U.S. trade. Only premier pocketknife firms such as Wostenholm's could maintain a token presence in the USA. Even that trade was ended in the 1920s, when additional U.S. tariffs, the terrible losses Sheffield men had suffered on the fields of Flanders in World War I, new health and safety rules that closed most of the smaller Sheffield firms, and aggressive new competition from American pocketknife firms such as Remington, Case, Schrade and Western States, combined to send Sheffield's cutlery trade into a decline that has continued unabated to this day.

None of Sheffield's great American trading firms are now in existence. Their factories have all been demolished. Their only memorial is the thousands of handmade knives that they sent out, which are now scattered all around the world.

The History of G. Wostenholm & Son

(Editor's note: The following information was obtained from Harold Bexfield, James Taylor, Geoffrey Tweedale, and the collection of Wostenholm manuscripts Blade Magazine Cutlery Hall-Of-Famer© Bill Adams obtained from the Sheffield City Libraries.)

In 1745, George Wolstenholme began the manufacture of knives and razors in the village of Stannington, near Sheffield. He was then 28 years old, and, from the age of 13 in 1730, had been an apprentice to master cutler John Darwent of Stannington.

That "first George Wolstenholme" came of a formerly landed Saxon family of Lancashire. In the 15th century his ancestor, John Wolstenholme, had moved about five miles from Sheffield. Under Cromwell in the 1650s, the family had lost its estates. Several of the family's members became farmers near Stannington. George Wolstenholme was the first of the family to become a cutler.

George trained his son, Henry, in the cutler's trade. In 1757, Henry was granted the trademark SPRING and joined his father in business. Henry named his second son George, and apprenticed him in about 1788 to a Sheffield cutler named John Mickelthwaite.

The second George gained the Freedom of the Cutler's Company in 1799, and eventually succeeded to his father's business. He relocated the firm to Sheffield proper, and by 1815 was occupying part of the steam-powered Rockingham Works. That was the year that he shortened his surname to Wostenholm.

His son, the third George Wolstenholme, had been born in 1800, and by 1824 was working for his father. He was entered a master cutler in 1826, and was granted the trademark I*XL (I Excel). This mark originally had been granted to another cutler in 1787.

In 1830, the Wostenholms arranged with William Stenton of Naylor & Sanderson, then the leading supplier of Sheffield cutlery to the U.S. market, to bring some of their I*XL cutlery to America. The venture proved so successful that the Wostenholms determined to devote all their efforts thenceforth to catering to the burgeoning American demand.

In 1832, father and son entered into partnership as "George Wostenholm & Son." The second George died in 1833, leaving the third George in sole charge. In 1848, he relocated to the large and modern Washington Works. The Washington Works reflected Wostenholm's dedication to making knives for Americans, as did his crossing the Atlantic 30 times to promote his wares. By the 1850s, I*XL was the most popular brand of cutlery in the United States.

The third George Wostenholm died in 1876. The firm continued to prosper until the 1890s. In 1891, 1897, 1901 and 1909, ever-steeper "protective" tariffs imposed by the United States virtually closed the American market to English cutlery, save at vastly inflated prices. The I*XL directors tried to shift their sales to other markets, such as Canada and Australia, but the markets were smaller and less prosperous than America's. Besides, other competitors were already established in those markets.

In the First World War, the British War Ministry stockpiled a large supply of military knives, then drafted all the younger English cutlers. Hundreds of them, ill trained and poorly led, died at Ypres and in other battles (36 died from Wostenholm alone), and no one took their place in Sheffield.

Strict labor and social welfare regulations, enacted as war measures but continued afterward, further crippled the cutlery industry, and largely destroyed the ancient system of cottage outworkers on whom all the Sheffield

Two Blades
No. 2—Brown Bone Handle, 3⅝ Inches long. Steel
Linings. One Large and One Small Spear Blade;
Highly Glazed........................Per Dozen, $7.00

This I*XL barlow is from a 1914 American hardware catalog. Comparable U.S.-made knives sold for $4 a dozen.

firms depended for specialty and limited-production patterns. The Depression and then World War II, with the accompanying round of social regulations, further hurt the cutlery industry.

Sheffield's cutlery firms did not share in the post-war prosperity, and their decline continued unchecked. The paltry assets of failed firms were often acquired by the survivors. Between 1955 and 1968, Wostenholm acquired Christopher Johnson, Champion Ltd., and several others. In 1971, Wostenholm was taken over by its old rival, Joseph Rodgers & Sons. The Washington Works were torn down, and Rodgers-Wostenholm moved to Guernsey

Road. In 1975, the joint firm was acquired by Richards Bros., which had been founded in 1934 as an offshoot of the Richartz firm of Solingen. Its Morse Street plant, built by manager Wilhelm Muller in 1946, was the largest pocketknife factory in Europe. Its specialty was sheet-metal, shell-handled knives made under Lohr and Stiehl's patents (as were Richartz and Imperial Jackmasters). At its peak it employed 800 people, and made 70 percent of the pocketknives in Sheffield, and 40 percent of the scissors.

In 1977, Richards Bros. was sold to Blade Magazine Cutlery Hall-Of-Famer© Albert M. Baer of Imperial Knife Associated Cos. He consolidated operations at the Morse Street plant, where about 100 of the cutlers worked on Schrade-I*XL knives. After five years without showing a profit, Baer sold Rodgers-Wostenholm to Meteor Industries, a government contractor. He sold the balance of Richards Bros. to a firm called Western Knives, which went bankrupt within four months.

The Morse street factory was demolished in 1984. Today, the Rodgers and Wostenholm trademarks are owned by the Egginton Group of Allen Street, Sheffield.

Swiss Multi-Blades

Is there a person anywhere in America, or the whole world, for that matter, who would fail to recognize a bright red Swiss Army Knife? The sleek little multi-blades now turn up everywhere, from the Space Shuttle in orbit, to TV adventure shows, to ads for all sorts of products that claim to be the metaphorical "Swiss Army Knife" of their particular industries. Conversely, some advertisers have turned the marketing ploy around, equating a little red multi-blade to their competitors' diminutive products, while portraying their own products as "real, full-sized tools."

After litigation in New York City—during which one federal judge (later reversed) decreed that bright-red-handled pocketknives made in China could be sold as "Swiss Army" knives—the exclusive right to use the term "Swiss Army Knife" now belongs equally and exclusively to the two Swiss firms that actually make knives for the Swiss Army. Of course, the actual Swiss Army-issue knives never had bright red handles.

The Swiss have been making multi-blades for a little over a century, and have ruled this segment of the market for a generation. Yet, the multi-blade folder has been around for more than 250 years (see the section, "Foreign, Exotic, Primitive, and Historical Folding Knives"), so the Swiss in fact were latecomers to this specialty.

The two makers of modern Swiss Army knives, Victorinox and Wenger, were not even multi-blade

pioneers in their homeland. In 1876, a Geneva cutler named C.F. Schneider showed complex multi-blade folders at the U.S. Centennial Exposition in Philadelphia, alongside Jacques Le Coultre of Sentier, Switzerland, who showed his patented frame-back razors. Another Geneva cutler named Forestier produced high-grade horticultural cutlery. One of old San Francisco's pioneer knifemakers, Jacob Hermann Schintz (1827-1908), emigrated from Switzerland in the 1850s.

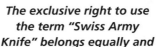

The exclusive right to use the term "Swiss Army Knife" belongs equally and exclusively to Victorinox—maker of the "official" Swiss Army knives—and Wenger—maker of the "genuine" Swiss Army knives. Each has a similar though different shield of a white cross on a red background that it puts on the handles of its knives. Wenger's shield is the more rounded of the two.

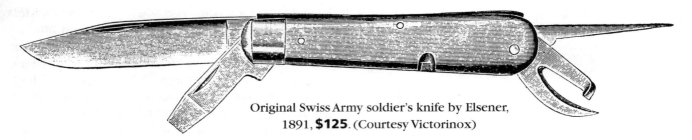

Original Swiss Army soldier's knife by Elsener,
1891, **$125**. (Courtesy Victorinox)

Elsener-Victorinox

In 1884, a 24-year-old cutler named Karl Elsener returned to his native Switzerland after having served knifemaking apprenticeships in Paris, France, and in Tuttlingen, Germany, where he had become a journeyman.

Elsener aspired to be a large-scale manufacturer, not merely a local craftsman. The opening of the St. Gotthard Pass railroad in 1880 made industrial development feasible in Switzerland's remote mountain canton states. Elsener selected for his cutlery factory the former Koller mill on the Tobelbach River in the village of Ibach in the canton of Schwyz. The building became the nucleus of a factory complex that was to serve the Elsener family firm until 1943.

From the beginning, Elsener brought in master cutlers from abroad, as well as local farm boys from Schwyz, to train as apprentices. In 1890, he organized the Association of Swiss Master Cutlers. The primary goal of the organization was to produce soldiers' pocketknives for the Swiss Army, knives that would take the place of ones then being imported from Solingen.

The first Swiss-made pocketknives for the Swiss Army were delivered in October 1891. The Swiss soldier's knife of 1891 was a multi-blade built on a tapered regular jack frame. It had wooden handles and heavy bolsters at the narrow end similar to the later electrician's knife.

The soldier's knife had four blades: a clip blade, a screwdriver, a can opener and a punch—much like the Boy Scout and Girl Scout knives introduced in the United States 20 years later. Except for the substitution of dark-red fiber handles in 1908, and of stainless steel blades in 1951, the design remained virtually unchanged until 1961. Since then, the Swiss soldier's knife has been a four-blade equal-end with checkered, aluminum-alloy handles.

The Officer's Knife

Elsener soon added a variety of commercial multi-blade patterns to the output of his growing enterprise. He named each pattern after its intended customer: the schoolboy's knife, the cadet knife and the farmer's knife. In 1897, he introduced the pattern that would eventually win his firm worldwide success: the officer's knife.

The Swiss Army issues a soldier's knife to every enlisted man, but not to commissioned officers. In 1897, Elsener conceived of the officer's knife as a practical private purchase item. Since every male Swiss citizen serves in the Swiss Army, either as a soldier or as an officer, the market for the knives seemed assured.

The new knife was an equal-end with six blades: spear master, screwdriver, can opener and pen-clip on the front, and a punch and corkscrew on the back. Each spring acted on three blades, so the six-blade officer's knife was no bulkier than the four-blade soldier's pattern. The Swiss government granted Elsener a design patent for the knife on June 12, 1897. It was similar to knives made for generations in England, France, Germany and Bohemia, but in Switzerland it was regarded as a novelty.

The Schweizer Offiziersmesser found immediate success, and not just with Swiss officers. By 1903, Elsener was offering more than a dozen variations on the basic 9cm (3-5/8-inch) red-handled multi-blade. Available implements, besides the six in the original No. 205, included hoof picks, scissors, champagne wire cutters, saws, shot-shell extractors, gimlets and cigar punches.

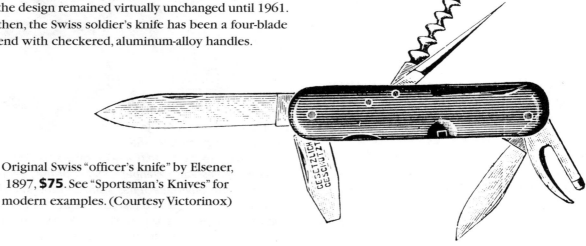

Original Swiss "officer's knife" by Elsener,
1897, **$75**. See "Sportsman's Knives" for
modern examples. (Courtesy Victorinox)

Each full-sized model could be had with a bail or an inlaid Swiss cross escutcheon for a few cents extra. In 1909, the Swiss escutcheon became standard.

Other pocketknife styles that Elsener then offered included a two-blade, red-handled, modestly priced student knife; a half-dozen variants on the wood-handled soldier's knife; and another half-dozen variants on the curved, wood-handled, Prussian-style farmer's knife, with from one to four utilitarian blades/tools (clip, hooked pruning blade, saw and harness mending needle).

In 1909, Elsener's mother, Victoria Elsener-Ott, passed away. In her memory, he adopted her Christian name VICTORIA as the trademark on all his wares. Elsener died in 1918, leaving the firm to two of his sons, Carl and Alois. Alois would leave the firm in 1929. Today, the company is owned and managed by direct descendants of Karl and Carl Elsener.

After World War I, business for the Victoria firm was slow. Then, in 1921, stainless steel became available in Switzerland. On their new stainless knives, the Elsener brothers adopted the trade name VICTORINOX— VICTORIA plus INOX, which is short for inoxydable, French for stainless.

The Swiss defensive build-up during World War II led to increased business for Victorinox. The firm erected a completely new factory complex in 1943, followed by much larger additions in 1946, 1969 and 1976.

Beginning in the late 1940s, Victorinox knives were sold at American military post exchanges throughout Europe. This, more than any other factor, made red-handled "Swiss Army" knives familiar to American consumers. Today, Victorinox Swiss Army knives are sold in the United States by Swiss Army Brands.

Wenger

Victorinox has never had a monopoly on the manufacture of Swiss Army soldiers' knives. Recall that, back in 1891, it was not Karl Elsener personally but the Association of Swiss Master Cutlers that was contracted to supply knives.

The "Avis" to Elsener's "Hertz" in Swiss pocketknife manufacture is Wenger of Delemont, a town in Bern canton that specializes in precision manufacturing. Delemont is in the French-speaking region of Switzerland, while Ibach is in the German-speaking region.

In the vicinity of Delemont in the 1890s were several rival small-scale cutlers. One of them was Monsieur P. Boechat, who began in the cutlery business in the nearby village of Courtelle in 1893. Soon afterward, the Councilor of Delemont granted Boechat a subsidy of 20,000 francs to relocate his cutlery works to the town. Boechat's move further intensified local competition.

At the time, a Protestant minister named Theodore Wenger traveled a local circuit preaching the gospel to the cutlers in the Delemont area. A second-generation master cutler, Wenger had earned a reputation for fairness in resolving disputes among his colleagues around Delemont.

Wenger encouraged cooperation among local cutlers. They formed a consortium, with Boechat's firm as the nucleus, so they could pool raw material purchases, skilled labor and marketing. In the early 1900s, The Rev. Wenger was chosen to direct the consortium. In 1908, their firm was incorporated as WENGER S.A.

Ever since 1908, the Swiss Army has divided its soldier's knife purchases 50-50 between Elsener and Wenger. Today, both Victorinox and Wenger are world leaders in cutlery design and manufacturing technology, as well—of course—as in sales.

(Editor's note: In 2005, Vicorinox bought Wenger. According th reports, Wenger's production facilities would remain in Delemont, with no reduction in jobs there.)

History of the Solingen Cutlery Industry

By Siegfried Rosenkaimer

(Editor's note: Siegfried Rosenkaimer is the proprietor of Carl Linder, Nachf., of Solingen, manufacturer of sheath knives. He is an avid collector of artifacts and documents pertaining to the history of German cutlery.)

Solingen can now look back on more than 630 years since it was first chartered as a town in 1374. About 1,400 years before that, the Romans had founded the city of Cologne on the Rhine, 20 miles away from Solingen. For the Roman inhabitants of Cologne, Solingen was deep inside the dangerous country of the German tribes, up on high ground and hidden in the thick forests. After the Romans had left, the Solingen area served for almost 1,500 years as a retreat and refuge for the German rulers of Cologne. They built a strong castle in Solingen in 1118.

Several natural advantages led to the development of what was to be the cutlery industry of Solingen. The forests offered virtually an unlimited supply of wood for making charcoal. The creeks revealed deposits of iron ore by leaving reddish-brown sediments on their way to the Rhine. Most of all, nearby Cologne, the wealthiest trading center in Germany, was prepared to pay a fair price for "cold steel."

For hundreds of years, Solingen was to supply the blades for swords and other edged weapons to Cologne. In those days, Solingen was not allowed to sell its blades anywhere else. Skilled Cologne craftsmen would add handles and sheaths, and then ship the finished swords worldwide. Even though the blades usually bore the names of now famous Solingen swordsmiths, and sometimes even the word SOLINGEN, the weapons were known to all as "Cologne Swords."

The Thirty Years War (1618-1648) brought misery to Germany. Some of her fine craftsmen emigrated to France, Russia, England and the British colonies—including America among the latter. Before the end of the 17th century, sword makers from Solingen had founded the "Hollow Swordblade Company" in Newcastle-upon-Tyne, England.

Whereas Solingen had been exporting cutlery to England in the mid-16th century, by the mid-18th century the tables had turned. England then led the world in technology, and Sheffield, with its crucible cast steel, led the world in cutlery. Cast steel's fine grain allowed Sheffield cutlers to perfect the "black" or mirror finish on their blades, and to forge delicate little pen blades for their pocketknives.

Peres

Since 1600, Solingen had been ruled by the Duke of Bavaria. Solingen cutlers were organized in guilds. Only the privileged were allowed admission to the guilds to work as smiths, grinders, hardeners, blade traders, or even manufacturers.

Peter Daniel Peres, born in Solingen in 1776, did not belong to the "privileged" of any guild. He was a merchant and had started his own cutlery trading business in 1792, at the age of 16. When first he encountered the competition of fine English cutlery, he realized that nothing supplied by the Solingen guilds could compare.

In 1805, Peres applied to Duke Maximilian for permission to be the first to manufacture "Fine Pen Knives" in Solingen, arguing that no such thing was being made there yet, and therefore the guild rules banning competition did not apply. The Duke was persuaded, and soon Peres was operating Solingen's first water-powered pocket and pen knife factory.

Not long afterward, Duke Maximilian traded Solingen to Napoleon Bonaparte, Emperor of France, as part of the arrangement by which France recognized the promotion of Maximilian to the status of King of Bavaria. Napoleon abolished all the privileges and monopolies of the Solingen guilds, and by so doing fostered competition and rapid development among the many capable craftsmen and merchants who long had been suppressed by the guilds' rules. After Napoleon's fall in 1815, Solingen became part of the Kingdom of Prussia.

In the first half of the 19th century, several important companies were established in Solingen to produce and sell pocket cutlery. At the time, most of the manufacturers were factors rather than actual factory owners in today's sense.

The factors ordered blades from the smiths and had them ground and finished by the grinders. They got bolsters from the casters, scales from the grip makers, and springs from the springmakers. Etchers might then decorate the blades and chiselers might engrave the mounts. Two more craftsmen would assemble and finish the knives.

All the craftsmen were outworkers who labored at home. Almost every home in or near Solingen then had its little workshop in the back. The craftsmen of the former guilds could now share their knowledge with assistants and apprentices. The rising volume of trade allowed increasing specialization, which in turn helped foster finer workmanship. Only the final inspection and packing were done at the factor's warehouse. In a limited way, this system is still in operation today.

Some of the important Solingen firms dating from before 1850:

Founded	Name	Trademark
1684	Gottlieb Hammesfahr	Pyramide
1727	Friedr. Herder Abr. Sohn	Ace of Spades
1731	J.A. Henckels	Twins
1787	Gebruder Weyersberg	Corneta
1792	P. Daniel Peres	Barrel
1806	David Everts	DES/Eiffel-Tower
1820	Pet. Dan. Baus	Lerche (Lark)
1821	Alexander Coppel	ACS/Scale
1824	Gebruder Christians	Fork
1832	Ed. Wusthof	Trident
1840	C. Lutters & Cie.	Lion lying down
1842	Carl & Robert Linder	Pruner/Crown

After 1850

Around mid-century, Solingen was making a fresh start. Crucible steel was readily available in Germany, in particular from the Krupp works in Essen, 25 miles from Solingen. Henckels pioneered the use of steam power for knifemaking, and other firms soon followed

suit. The steel mills and coal mines of the nearby Ruhr district drew immigrants from eastern Europe, while railroads and steamships opened up the world's markets to Solingen cutlery, and helped bring an incredible rise in demand, especially from the United States. The 1870-71 war between France and Germany found Solingen as supplier of thousands of bayonets and swords to the new and growing German Imperial Army.

In the following years of reckless financial speculation, hundreds of companies were founded in Solingen, most of them having only a very short existence. Nonetheless, Solingen grew rapidly, the population doubling between 1870 and 1900. The rapid growth of a few larger cutlery firms was equaled in importance by the proliferation of hundreds of small units, most of them making cutlery components. By 1900, Solingen's cutlery exports topped those of England, France and the United States combined. The figures for 1913: Solingen $10 million, Sheffield $4 million and the United States $1 million.

After 1918

World War I interrupted this development. Germany was cut off from its export markets. By the end of the war, other countries, especially the United States, had developed their own cutlery industries. Germany's hyperinflation and desperation for hard currency in the early 1920s prompted the United States and Britain to enact anti-dumping laws

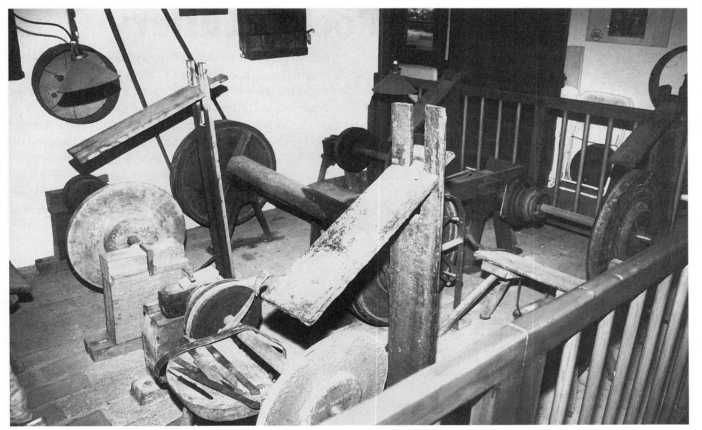

Water-powered grinding shops ground blades for the Solingen cutlery industry. This is a grinding room in the Balkauser Kotten on the Wupper River outside Solingen. The Balkauser Kotten was in operation at least as early as 1715.

and punitive tariffs (up to 420 percent). Other former markets, such as Russia, were closed completely. Solingen exports fell by 80 percent compared to pre-war levels. Many Solingen firms went bankrupt.

The advent of the Third Reich in Germany led to a brief revival in Solingen, especially in the production of daggers and bayonets. Yet, the Second World War brought physical destruction in Solingen far worse than the economic hardship that had followed World War I. Many factories were completely destroyed. Molds, records, machinery and tools were lost. After the war, Allied trade and manufacturing restrictions delayed Solingen's revival for more than a decade.

Recent Years

By the mid-1950s, older workers in Solingen had made a new start. German labor was still comparatively cheap. Germany's "Economic Wonder" was not limited to the Volkswagen "Beetle." During the 1950s and 1960s, some of the old pocketknife makers still offered fine handmade knives. Unfortunately, the younger generation was not to step in. Gradually, the small firms went out of existence as the old craftsmen retired. Machinery began to replace handwork as the cost of labor climbed and unemployment fell below 1 percent.

The 1970s brought another change. Social legislation pushed the real cost of labor to soaring heights. New laws and regulations of the social-liberal government elevated costs even more. This raised the price of German exports in foreign markets, while opening Germany's home market to cheaper imports. Another wave of bankruptcies and cutlery plant closings followed, to the point where hardly any low-priced knives are now made in Solingen.

Solingen's splendid infrastructure has nonetheless managed to survive the turmoil of the 20th century. Today, cutlery casters also supply the car industry. Umbrella frame makers who once rolled sheet metal for ferrule makers now supply components to the electronics industry. Yet, all these specialty firms still also supply components to the Solingen cutlery industry.

Science now is as much a part of cutlery making as skill and experience. Solingen firms have pioneered the development of fully automatic stamping, grinding and polishing equipment. Cutlery production machinery made in Solingen is today in operation in knife factories around the world, especially in the USA.

Bohemian Pocket Cutlery

Before World War I, much of the least expensive cutlery sold in the United States came from Solingen. However, a large number of low- to middle-priced pocketknives sold in the USA at that time, especially fancy multi-blades, came instead from Austria-Hungary. Specifically, they came from Bohemia, which in 1921 became part of Czechoslovakia.

We have identified two large firms in Nixdorf, Bohemia, that made a wide variety of fancy folding knives in that period. One was the firm founded by Ignaz Rosler in 1794. In 1817, he and his nephew, Josef Emanuel Fischer, built the Nixdorf Fine Steelware Factory. His sons later built the nearby Ignaz Rosler's Sons' Cutlery Works. Its specialty was multi-blades for export. Both factories were active exporters at the end of the 19th century.

The other Nixdorf firm was that of Franz Frenzel. Wiebusch & Hilger of New York marketed his knives in the United States in the late 19th and early 20th centuries.

In addition, the firm of Wenzel Schneider in Prague, the capital of Bohemia, made pocketknives for export. Schneider exhibited his wares at the 1876 Centennial Exposition in Philadelphia.

Eskilstuna Cutlery

(Editor's note: The following information is from Capt. Anders L. Dahlman of Lund, Sweden, author of Kniven—en Personlig Betraktelse, *1993.)*

The two traditional knifemaking centers in Sweden are Eskilstuna and Mora. In the 20th century through to today, Eskilstuna has specialized in folding knives, Mora in sheath knives.

Retreating Ice Age glaciers in southeast Sweden left behind a chain of large lakes, the lowest being Lake Malaren, which discharges into the Baltic Sea at Stockholm. Eskilstuna is at the opposite end of the lake, 50 miles west of Stockholm, where the quick-flowing Torshalla River drains Lake Hjalmaren into Lake Malaren.

The town was first called Tuna, and dates to the Bronze Age. By the 11th century, it was an active center of Viking raiders. In the 1070s, an English monk named Eskil undertook missionary work in Sweden, and was consecrated a bishop at Strangas, near Tuna. Swedish King Inge supported Eskil's work but was murdered and succeeded by King Sweyn the Bloody. In 1080, Bishop Eskil protested the Vikings' return to their traditional religion, so Sweyn ordered him stoned to death. Eskil was canonized, and when Sweden was Christianized once again, the town was renamed Eskilstuna in his honor.

The falls of the Torshalla were a barrier to commerce, but they are a steady source of waterpower. Moreover, Sweden was rich in timber for charcoal, and in high-grade meteoric iron ore for steel making. (Swedish iron supplied the steel and cutlery industries of both Sheffield and Solingen.)

In 1600, Prince Regent Charles, who had established Lutheranism in Sweden in 1593—he later reigned as King Charles IX, 1604-1611—began a war against his exiled Catholic cousin, King Sigismund III of Poland. To assure his supply of arms, Charles ordered each of his provinces to supply specified quantities. These proved insufficient, so he sent out troops to destroy village smithies, and to round up the smiths and bring them in chains to Eskilstuna. There they were put to work in new centralized establishments. This marked both the birth of the steel industry in Eskilstuna and the birth of Swedish socialism.

Charles IX's son, Gustavus II, conquered Livonia from the Poles, but died in battle. Under his heir, Queen Christina, a German or Dutch ironmaster named Reinhold Rademacher set up a large center of forges and foundries in the Livonian port of Riga—now the capital of Latvia—in 1649. In 1654, King Charles X saw that Riga was vulnerable to Russian conquest—it fell to Russia in 1710—so he relocated the new enterprise to Eskilstuna.

His court architect, Jean de la Valee, then laid out a new forge town in Eskilstuna. It was planned to consist of 120 smithies, each occupied by two independent smiths. In fact, only 19 of the smithies were ever built, but they continued in use for generations, the last one operating until 1925. The five that remain have been made into a museum of iron working.

Eskilstuna Firms

Dozens of firms have made cutlery in Eskilstuna. We have seen examples by the following: Erik Anton Berg (c1880-1920); John Engstrom (1874-1895, imported to the USA by Wiebusch); Eskilstuna Jernmanufaktur AB (1920-1970); Hagg & Co. (c1920); Hadar Hallstroms (became EKA, see below); Hedengram & Son (c1900); C.V. Heljestrand (c1900); J.A. Hellberg (c1900-1978); P.A. Holmberg (1900-1930s); Karlsson (c1910); C.J. Lindstrom (c1900); Emil Olsson (1892-1968); Carl Victor Osterberg (c1920-1945); and A.J. Westersson (c1900). Several 19th-century Swedish cutlery firms are listed in the appendix, "Cutlery Exhibitors at the 1876 Centennial Exhibition." From 1814 to 1905, Norway was a dominion of Sweden, so many Norwegian-style knives were—and are—made in Eskilstuna. See the section, "Foreign, Exotic, Primitive, and Historical Fixed Blade Knives."

EKA

The only pocket cutlery firm remaining in Eskilstuna is EKA. It traces its roots to Hadar Hallstroms Knivfabriks, founded in 1882. Hadar Hallstrom's knife factory exported many knives to the United States. Some circa-1900 catalogs of northern and western U.S. hardware firms offered Swedish knives; knives exported after 1891 are marked SWEDEN.

In 1917, the Hallstrom factory was acquired by John Elmquist, who changed the factory's name to Eskilstuna Kniffabriks, and adopted the trademarks E.K.A. and KNIFBOLAGET ESKILSTUNA. In 1925, the spelling was changed to Eskilstuna Knivfabriks and KNIVBOLAGET (the latter mark was last used c1944). The firm's EKA marking also has varied. EKA in a circle was used circa 1927-1943. E.K.A. was used circa 1950-1965. The current EKA mark, with "falling" letters, was adopted in 1967.

John Elmquist died in 1946 and was succeeded by his son-in-law, Torbjorn Evrell. In 1952, Evrell modernized the plant, replacing the old water-powered belt system with electric motors. After that, he continued to update the plant's equipment and methods, as well as its lines of knives.

EKA's best-known knives are fancy lobster pen knives with metal handles. Originally, the knives had "Swedish-

Advertising knives are an EKA specialty.

etched" gun-metal handles—90 percent copper, 10 percent tin—embellished with gold, silver and enamel. EKA's most recent handles are painted brass, though some are done in 18k gold or gold plate. EKA also makes distinctive styles of lightweight folding hunters.

EKA knives are distributed in the United States by the Nichols Company, P.O. Box 473, Woodstock, VT 05091.

19th Century American Pocketknife Firms

The first knifemakers to work in the United States usually called themselves "cutlers and surgical instrument makers." They had learned their trade in the Old World, mainly in England, but also in Germany, France and the Low Countries.

In her book, *History of the Cutlery Industry in the Connecticut Valley* (1955), Martha Taber reports having found a reference to such a cutler working in Pennsylvania in 1698. The earliest such listing we have seen is from the 1780s (see the section, "Bowie Knives").

Any such skilled artisan would have been able to make a first-class pocketknife, but if he actually had done so, it would have been on special order only. Even with shipping added in, the commercially made Sheffield product would have been less expensive than his, and of at least equal quality. We have yet to see an 18th-century pocketknife that is demonstrably of American make.

The 19th century is altogether a different story. Beginning after the War of 1812—perhaps even before—a number of Yankee artisans and entrepreneurs, most with Sheffield backgrounds, began to manufacture pocketknives in America.

To drive their wheels, hammers and bellows, these first American pocket cutlers used small waterpowers in the hilly regions of southern New England. To sell their goods, they employed the fabled "Yankee peddlers," and they also contracted with created wholesale firms in New York City, New Haven and Boston.

The first pocketknife firms in New England apparently were one-man operations and their names have not come down to us. The first American manufacturing cutler whose name we know—as opposed to a surgical instrument maker who made knives to order—was Henry Harrington of Southbridge, Massachusetts. He opened his first shop in 1818 and was active until his death in 1876. The firm he founded is still flourishing as Russell-Harrington. We have seen razors and bowie knives by Harrington, but not a pocketknife. To find the first American manufacturers

who specialized in pocket cutlery, we must turn to Connecticut.

Connecticut Firms

Taber reports that the pocket cutlery industry of Connecticut began before 1800 as a part of the workshop production of "Yankee notions" to be sold by itinerant peddlers throughout the new nation. The notions included "buttons, spoons, forks, thimbles, tin pans, small brass castings, pocket books, and pocketknives." She found that the production had expanded to factory form by the late 1820s.

The 1840s

The first reasonably firm date we have for pocketknife manufacture in Connecticut is 1841, the approximate date of the founding of LYMAN BRADLEY & CO. of Naugatuck. We do not know how long the early factory lasted, but Bradley himself was active both as a distributor and as a manager of other cutlery firms until the 1890s.

Two years later, in 1843, the WATERVILLE MANUFACTURING CO. of nearby Waterbury was

The Waterville Manufacturing Co. of Waterbury, Connecticut, was established in 1843. The firm grew to be one of the largest U.S. pocketknife producers of the 19th century.

The American Knife Co. of the Reynolds Bridge section of Plymouth Hollow, Connecticut, was founded in 1849 and survived until about 1911.

established by G. Kendrick. Lyman Bradley was one of its managers in its formative years. By 1850, it had 200 workmen. The firm grew to be one of the largest U.S. pocketknife producers of the 19th century. The Waterville name survived for seven decades, to 1913, under at least three different groups of owners.

The HOLLEY CO. was founded in 1844 in Lakeville, up in the northwest corner of Connecticut. It, too, grew to be an important firm.

About 1904, the owners of Holley decided not to adopt the machine methods then coming to dominate the industry. (The first practical automatic grinding machine, the Hemming, made in New Haven, was introduced in 1903. Virtually every Hemming machine ever made is still in use.) Instead, they gave up their national distribution and continued to make knives by hand for local sale up into the 1930s.

The remainder of the 1840s saw the establishment of several small pocketknife firms in Connecticut, and one large one. The small firms included SMITH & HOPKINS of Naugatuck (circa 1848), and also CLARK R. SHELTON and the BIRMINGHAM KNIFE WORKS, both of Derby (circa 1849). Some of the shears makers in Cornwall Bridge at the time also seem to have made pocketknives.

The large firm was the AMERICAN KNIFE CO. of the Reynolds Bridge section of Plymouth Hollow (renamed Thomaston in 1875). The American Knife Co. was founded in 1849 and survived until about 1911.

Do not confuse this firm's knives with those of the AMERICAN KNIFE CO. of Winsted, Connecticut, in business from 1919-1955. (Two other Winsted firms of the 1910s and 1920s were BUD BRAND CUTLERY CO. and the CAPITOL KNIFE CO.)

The 1850s

The UNION KNIFE CO. was established in Naugatuck in 1851. The small firm lasted until 1885. It was not related to the later Union Cutlery Co. of Olean, New York.

The following year, 1852, THOMPSON & GASCOIGNE opened a knife factory in Winsted. In 1856, it changed hands and was renamed the EMPIRE KNIFE CO. In 1880, the factory was moved to the old Lathrop and Barton table cutlery plant in West Winsted. Empire grew to be a large

firm that did a lot of private-brand contracting. Charles L. Alvord, Empire's president from about 1890 to 1923, was a leader in the fight for tariff protection for the American cutlery industry. Empire went out of business in 1930.

HUMASON & BECKLEY of New Britain was founded in 1853. It did a moderate business until 1912, when it was sold to LANDERS FRARY & CLARK. L.F. & C. (founded 1865) was the largest cutlery firm in the world at the turn of the 20th century, but it did not make pocketknives. L.F. & C. turned H. & B. into its pocket cutlery division about 1914, and continued making pocketknives into the 1930s.

In an 1857 Connecticut business directory, we found listings for three pocketknife firms whose knives we have never seen. Perhaps they subcontracted to one of the larger firms, or perhaps they were distributors. Their names were JOHN KAY of New Haven, HAUGH & FRISBIE, also of New Haven, and R.M. HAVEN of Norwich.

In 1858, the NORTHFIELD KNIFE CO. was established in Northfield. The first cast-iron-handled jack knives were made there in 1862. Its UN-X-LD knives were made until 1919, at which time the factory was bought by Clark Brothers of Kansas City, which ran it for 10 years. Next, a former employee named Gill moved some of the equipment to a nearby site and resumed making "Northfield" knives by hand until about 1960.

The 1860s

In 1863, MILLER BROTHERS (George and William) commenced operations in Yalesville and Wallingford. It moved to Meriden in 1872. Miller Brothers was an important firm that did a lot of private brand contracting. Its knives are of exceptional quality. Many have the handle scales secured by tiny brass screws, a Miller Brothers trademark registered in 1870. Any older American knife with such screws is a contract knife made by Miller Brothers.

In 1878, Miller Brothers was reorganized under William Rockwell, who soon took the lead in the American cutlery industry's fight for tariff protection. The effort bore fruit in the Tariff Acts of 1890, 1897 and 1901. Consequently, Sheffield and Solingen, finding the U.S. market nearly closed to their knives, instead began exporting unemployed cutlers to work in what had become a flourishing American cutlery industry.

U.S. consumers paid dearly for the tariffs in inflated prices and lost markets, but Rockwell and a few other factory owners profited handsomely from them. Miller Brothers even managed to win U.S. Navy contracts for sailor knives away from Sheffield suppliers, who had enjoyed a lock on the business since the American Navy had first set sail.

Miller Brothers got out of the knife business—in favor of steel pens—in 1926. The firm went out of business in 1943.

Both the SOUTHINGTON CUTLERY CO. of Southington—whose pocketknives were distributed by the Connecticut table cutlery giant, Meriden—and the CONNECTICUT CUTLERY CO. of Naugatuck were established in 1867. Connecticut Cutlery lasted until 1883, Southington until about 1914.

The 1870s

In 1870, the American Shear Co. of Hotchkissville (founded 1853) changed its name to the AMERICAN SHEAR & KNIFE CO. and began making pocketknives. Some of its blades were marked H'VILLE (Hotchkissville) KNIFE CO. The concern lasted until 1914.

The NAUGATUCK CUTLERY CO. of Naugatuck began in 1872 and lasted until 1888. About the same time, TWITCHELL BROTHERS had a pocketknife plant in Naugatuck. We do not know its dates.

In 1876, James D. Frary of Bridgeport, one of the founders of Landers, Frary & Clark, established the FRARY CUTLERY CO. It was the most "hi-tech" pocketknife operation of its time. Frary had about a dozen patents and employed more than 750 people, mass-producing inexpensive yet serviceable knives that are now quite rare (the Smithsonian Institution has a fine collection of them).

In 1881, Frary sold the firm and its two plants to Messrs. Trunk, Bliss and Healy, who seem to have run it for only about three years. Meanwhile, James Frary and his son, Harry, had started JAMES D. FRARY & SON CO., also in Bridgeport. In 1884, they sold the new firm to Smith, Sutton & Co., who renamed it the LABELLE CUTLERY WORKS. LaBelle was still active at the end of the decade, with Harry L. Frary as superintendent.

The 1880s and 1890s

The EXCELSIOR KNIFE CO. of Torrington was founded in 1880. It lasted only until 1884, when it was bought out by Northfield.

Another small firm, the THOMASTON KNIFE CO. of Thomaston, began about 1887. It lasted until 1923.

CHALLENGE CUTLERY CO. of Bridgeport was started by the important New York wholesale firm of Wiebusch & Hilger in 1891. It was liquidated upon the death of Mr. Wiebusch in 1928.

HATCH CUTLERY CO. began in Bridgeport in 1886, and its knives were distributed by Wiebusch. It moved to Michigan before 1890, and then to Wisconsin by 1899.

Finally, around the turn of the 20th century, the BILLINGS & SPENCER tool company of Hartford began to manufacture a few novel and expensive styles of knives. One was an early type of "butterfly knife" (see the section, "Foreign, Exotic, Primitive, and Historical Folding Knives").

Until 1940, Connecticut, as the home of both Remington and Winchester, continued to dominate pocketknife manufacture in the United States. Today, oddly enough, not a single factory pocketknife is made anywhere in the state.

Massachusetts Firms

Throughout the latter part of the 19th century, Massachusetts at least equaled Connecticut in the production of fixed-blade knives. However, it never offered serious competition in pocketknives.

A few Massachusetts men might have made pocketknives before 1850, but no such knives of provable age and origin have been found. We earlier met HENRY HARRINGTON of Southbridge (active 1818-1876). We found a reference in a 1922 magazine to a razor supposedly made by a J. LEE of Medway, circa 1830. The Ames Manufacturing Co. of Chicopee (1829-1900) seems to have sold the pocketknives with AMES on the tangs, but we suspect that they were made on contract for Ames later in the century.

The Bay State's first documented pocket cutler was AARON BURKINSHAW. He left Sheffield for Connecticut in 1846. In 1853, he moved to Pepperell, Massachusetts, and built a large factory. He pioneered brand name advertising of cutlery to consumers. His 1876 illustrated catalog, another innovation, featured horticultural knives, New England whalers, and Sheffield-style pen and jack knives. His trademarks "Exile" and "Pain" may have reflected his view of life in New England. Burkinshaw died in the early 1880s, leaving the firm to four of his 15 children. Fred, a younger of Burkinshaw's sons, was the last owner, closing the factory in 1920.

Shelburne Falls

During the Civil War, LAMSON & GOODNOW of Shelburne Falls (founded 1844), one of the "big three" of American table cutlery production—Russell and Meriden were the other two—began to make folding knife/fork and knife/fork/spoon combinations. Some of the Connecticut pocketknife firms made the combos as well, and all are prized by military knife collectors, though they were never a government-issue item. According to research by Cindy Taylor, the "slot knives" were the only folders made by Lamson & Goodnow. Later pocketknives with the Lamson & Goodnow name or marked SHELBURNE FALLS CUTLERY CO. were made on contract by others, including Waterville and, possibly, Joseph Gardner.

Gardner was the superintendent of the Lamson & Goodnow plant. In about 1876, he is reported to have opened a small pocketknife factory nearby. Knives marked GARDNER 1876 probably came from the shop.

Russell

In 1875, the famous John RUSSELL Green River Works, originally founded in Greenfield in 1834, but since 1870 located at Turners Falls, began to make pocketknives. Russell made a full line but one specialty was its American version of the traditional barlow knife. Within a generation, "Russell" and "barlow" were almost synonymous in many parts of the country.

Russell pocketknife production was suspended during World War I. Manufacture, mainly of the barlows, was resumed in 1920, and continued even after Russell's merger with Harrington in 1933 and the move to Southbridge in 1936. In 1941, Russell barlows were discontinued.

The J.R. TORREY RAZOR CO. of Worcester, established in 1858, apparently made some pocketknives late in the 19th century. At least, knives with their stamping are known, and Torrey was certainly equipped to make them.

A small pocketknife firm was active in Massachusetts around 1880. It was the BEAVER BROOK KNIFE CO. It was in the town of Beaver Brook, but both the company and the town disappeared before the turn of the 20th century. Its knives were usually marked B.B. KNIFE CO.

Like Connecticut, Massachusetts is out of the running as far as pocket cutlery goes. A good number of fixed-blade knives are still made there, however.

New York Firms

From the opening of the Erie Canal in 1825 until about a generation ago, New York City was the center of cutlery distribution for the entire United States. Virtually every American knife manufacturer who aspired to a national or world market had either an office or an agent in New York. Despite its centrality, New York City itself was never a significant manufacturer of pocket cutlery, largely due to its lack of water power. However, surgical instrument making was an important endeavor in the city, and a few firms did try pocketknife production there on a small scale, most notably the firm of John, Ebenezer and W. WILD in the 1850s.

Rural Bronxville, 17 miles north of downtown, was a different story. In the 1860s, it boasted at least three pocketknife firms: JAMES WARD & CO. (makers of a knife presented to Abraham Lincoln in 1864; see the section, "Knives as an Investment"); SMITH & CLARK; and JAMES P. SWAIN. A local specialty was ivory-bladed folding fruit knives.

Industry developed in upstate New York a little more slowly than it did in New England. The first recorded

In 1880, over 70 men worked the exhaust-hooded grinders situated at the far right beneath the windows of the John Russell Manufacturing Co. (Russell Harrington Cutlery photo)

upstate knife company grew to be one of the most important—NEW YORK KNIFE CO. It was founded in 1852 in Matteawan, since renamed Beacon, by 16 Sheffield cutlers who had quit Waterville in a pay dispute. In 1856, the young firm was moved across the Hudson to Walden. Almost all of its considerable output was pocketknives, which were among the finest ever produced.

One of the original 16 Sheffield cutlers was Thomas Bradley. His son, Tom Bradley Jr., became president of New York Knife in 1870. He was elected to Congress in 1902, and sold the firm to C.B. and James E. Fuller in 1903.

About 1880, New York Knife had adopted its familiar "Hammer Brand" and arm-and-hammer trademark. In 1928, it began using its Wallkill River Works name on a low-cost line of knives. James Fuller ruined the firm by trying to auction a full year's output on one day, Sept. 15, 1930. Within months, New York Knife was out of business. In 1936, Imperial bought the Hammer Brand trademark.

The 1870s

The next important New York state pocketknife firm was the WALDEN KNIFE CO. in Walden. Walden Knife was founded by some disgruntled New York Knife Co. employees in 1869 or 1870. Like New York Knife, it did a large business in private-branded contract knives.

In 1902, Walden Knife was purchased by one of its important customers, the E.C. Simmons Hardware Co. of St. Louis. In 1923, after Simmons had merged with Winchester, the Walden plant was liquidated and the equipment moved to the Winchester plant in New Haven.

The CO-OPERATIVE KNIFE CO. was established in Ellenville in 1871. (Knives marked "Co-O. Knife Company, Walden N.Y." were made by Walden Knife Co.) It really was a cooperative endeavor, managed jointly by the Sheffield cutlers who started and staffed it.

Co-Operative failed in 1876 and was taken over by its principal creditor, Dwight Divine Sr., who renamed

In 1891, J.B.F. Champlin hired Harvey Nixon Platts away from Northfield to launch the Cattaraugus Cutlery Co. This is how the buildings of the old manufacturer appeared circa 1980 in Little Valley, New York.

it ULSTER KNIFE CO. Dwight Divine Jr. ran it for many decades. Ulster later became part of Imperial Schrade.

The CANASTOTA KNIFE CO. was organized in the village of Canastota in 1875. It survived there until 1895.

The 1880s to 1900

Two small upstate New York knife companies began late in the 19th century. The CENTRAL CITY KNIFE CO. started in Phoenix in 1880. It was renamed PHOENIX KNIFE CO. in 1892, and failed in 1916. FAYETTEVILLE KNIFE CO., whose starting date is not known, burned down in 1911.

In 1886, J.B.F. Champlin, formerly a salesman for the New York City importer FRIEDMANN & LAUTERJUNG, started his own jobbing firm in Cattaraugus. In 1891, Champlin hired Harvey Nixon Platts away from Northfield to launch the CATTARAUGUS CUTLERY CO. in the pocketknife manufacturing business. (Platts was later a co-founder of W.R. Case & Sons and the founder of Western States.) Champlin and Platts purchased the equipment of the defunct Beaver Falls Cutlery Co. of Pennsylvania. Cattaraugus was a major firm in the pocketknife industry until 1963. It was also strong in fixed blades. After World War II, its main product was plastic-handled kitchen knives.

In 1892, Charles SHERWOOD started a small pocketknife plant in Camillus. For a few years after 1894, he leased it to Robeson. In 1902, he sold it to the major New York importer, Adolph Kastor & Bros., who renamed it CAMILLUS CUTLERY CO., as it is still called today.

Millard Robeson, a jobber in Elmira since 1879, first produced knives in Sherwood's plant in 1894. In 1898, he opened his own plants in Rochester and Perry.

Robeson died in 1903, but the ROBESON CUTLERY CO. continued until 1940. It was reorganized then by Emerson Case and continued manufacturing until 1965. From then until 1977, Robeson was a brand name used on contract knives made for ONTARIO KNIFE CO. In the early 1990s, ONTARIO reintroduced the Robeson name on a line of pocketknives.

The NAPANOCH KNIFE CO. of Napanoch started in 1900. Napanoch made extremely high-quality knives.

The Winchester Arms Co. bought Napanoch in 1919 and moved its equipment to New Haven, Connecticut, to become the heart of its new pocketknife operation. Most of Napanoch's employees went along to New Haven.

A few of the Napanoch people stayed behind to start HONK FALLS KNIFE CO. in the old Napanoch building. It lasted until 1929. In 1931, a man named Cushner bought the Napanoch name from Winchester and revived the old firm in a small way at the old location, where it lasted until 1939.

CARRIER CUTLERY CO. (Cronk & Carrier Mfg. Co.) also started in 1900. Located in Elmira, it continued in business until 1921.

New Jersey Firms

Booth Brothers

The oldest recorded pocketknife firm in New Jersey was BOOTH BROTHERS. Thomas Booth of Sheffield established it in Newark in 1864. In 1867, Booth Brothers exhibited pocketknives at the world exposition in Paris. In 1879, the firm was moved to Boonton, New Jersey, on the Morris Canal.

In dry years, water flow in the canal was not sufficient to power the knife factory's trip hammers and grinding wheels. As a result, in 1889 Booth Brothers moved again, this time to Stockholm, New Jersey, on the Pequannock River. The site had been used for iron working since the 18th century.

In 1903, the City of Newark bought the Booth Brothers property to add to municipal watershed holdings. The pocketknife firm then moved to Sussex, New Jersey. It went out of business in 1909. (See Edward Lenik, *Booth Brothers Knife Factory* 1969, North Jersey Highlands Historical Society.)

Boker/Valley Forge

New Jersey's principal claim to cutlery fame was for the production of scissors and shears. Newark was the home of Rochus HEINISCH, a Swiss emigre who had come to the United States in 1825. Heinisch invented the modern style of bent tailor's and dressmaker's shears, as well as the technique of inlaying steel cutting edges into iron shear frames.

In 1847, another Swiss emigre named Jacob Wiss came to Newark and went to work for Heinisch. The following year he started his own scissors firm, also in Newark. In 1914, JACOB WISS & SONS, by then under the direction of the sons, bought out Heinisch's firm. Wiss was already recognized as the world's pre-eminent scissors firm. In 1969, Wiss acquired H. Boker & Co.

HERMANN BOKER & CO. is one of the oldest names in American cutlery. The firm was founded in New York City in 1837 by Hermann Boeker, a recent arrival from Germany. H. Boker & Co. was mainly a cutlery importing firm, but it also imported tools and steel.

Hermann Boeker, and his brother Robert, scions of a long line of German tool makers, had started a plant to make sabers in Remschied in 1829, across the river from Solingen. Seeing their future in opening up the North American market, the two brothers crossed the Atlantic in 1837, Hermann to New York, Robert to Canada. Hermann soon moved his headquarters and warehouse to Newark, New Jersey, although he retained a sales office in New York City. Later, in 1865, Robert established a branch of H. Boker & Co. in Mexico City, called Casa Roberto Boker, which is still active today.

In 1869, Hermann and Robert's cousin, Heinrich Boeker, joined forces with cutler Hermann Heuser to open a factory in Solingen to manufacture "Tree Brand" (trademark of the family's Remschied works) pocketknives, razors and scissors for both H. Boker and Casa R. Boker to sell in North America. The plant, HEINRICH BOKER & CO., is still one of Germany's leading producers of pocket cutlery. Besides Heinrich's Tree Brand cutlery, H. Boker & Co. also imported Sheffield cutlery under trademarks that Heinrich had purchased, including Manhattan Cutlery Co., John Newton & Co., Regal and, later, Trenton Cutlery Co.

In 1899, in response to increasing tariffs on imported cutlery, H. Boker & Co., which was still controlled by Hermann Boeker's descendants, began to manufacture pocketknives in Newark. The factory was called the VALLEY FORGE CUTLERY CO. John Goins reported that Valley Forge was an already existing firm, founded in 1892, which Boker purchased.

In the Valley Forge factory, Boker produced both Boker and Valley Forge knives and hand tools. The firm also did a great deal of private brand contracting. One of its biggest customers was the Newark advertising specialty firm of WHITEHEAD & HOAG. Its knives were tang-stamped THE W. & H. CO.

In 1921, Boker sold the Valley Forge plant and moved its U.S. operations to a new complex of buildings in Maplewood, New Jersey. Boker continued to use the Valley Forge trademark on some knives until about 1950. Afterward, all knives made in the Maplewood plant were marked BOKER/U.S.A. Boker bought the George Schrade Knife Co. in 1956, but closed it down in 1958 when switchblade knives were banned in U.S. interstate commerce.

Founded in New York City in 1837, Hermann Boker & Co. is one of the oldest names in American cutlery. After a series of sales and buyouts that began in 1899 and spanned almost 90 years, the Boker U.S.A. name, trademarks and distribution rights were sold in 1986 to Heinrich Boker of Solingen, Germany, where Boker knives are still made. This is a picture of the Boker plant as it appeared in Solingen in 1999. Boker's U.S. sales office is in Golden, Colorado.

When Wiss bought Boker U.S.A. in 1969, the only change it made was to stop importing German Boker scissors. Then, about 1978, Wiss sold Boker to the Cooper Tool Group of North Carolina. Cooper ran Boker as a subsidiary until 1984, when the Maplewood plant was closed and the domestic manufacturing of Boker knives was halted. In 1986, Cooper sold the Boker U.S.A. name, trademarks and distribution rights to Heinrich Boker of Solingen. Boker's American sales office is now in Golden, Colorado. (See Ernst Felix, "The Boker Story," unpublished m/s, 1986.)

Pennsylvania Firms

Philadelphia

Cutlery has been made in Pennsylvania since the 17th century, and Philadelphia was America's distribution hub until the 1820s. Several cutlers made knives and surgical instruments there to order, but the earliest identified thus far who advertised pocketknife production was John ASHMORE. He also made table cutlery and bowie knives from about 1832 until his death in 1850. His widow, Mary, then took over and ran the firm until 1858.

CLARENBACH & HERDER, later called L. HERDER & SON, was founded in Philadelphia in 1847. Herder's was a cutlery retailer that in its early days also manufactured scissors and bowie knives. Pocketknives with the Herder's brand are also known, but it is not clear if Herder's made or just distributed them.

C.F. Wolfertz

An old Pennsylvania firm that definitely made pocketknives was the C.F. WOLFERTZ Co. of Allentown. The firm was organized in 1862. Like many 19th-century cutlers working in cities, Wolfertz at first used dog-powered treadmills to drive his wheels. The firm made cutlery until the early 1920s, when it became a distributor only. In 1944, the firm dropped its cutlery lines in favor of home furnishings.

COQUANOC/WORKS/PHILAD. regular jack with "Oroide" handles. (Photo courtesy Bernard Schreiber and R.J. Cundiff)

Beaver Falls

The BEAVER FALLS CUTLERY CO. was located in Beaver Falls in the extreme western part of Pennsylvania, and also in the adjoining borough of Rochester. The firm made all types of cutlery. We believe the pocketknife department was in Rochester, because some of the smaller knives are marked ROCHESTER PA only.

The Beaver Falls firm, indeed the whole town, was founded in 1866 by the Harmony Society, a religious sect that began in 1805. The Harmonists had created the town of Economy in 1825, just south of Beaver Falls.

Beaver Falls Cutlery Co. rapidly outgrew the ability of the Harmonists to staff it, so, rather than being Harmonists, most of the 300 employees were hired. In 1872, after a wage cut, the employees went out on the first strike in the history of the American cutlery industry. The firm brought in 200 Chinese strikebreakers from New Orleans in order to keep running, and the strike was eventually settled.

Beaver Falls went out of business in 1886. In 1891, Cattaraugus bought the company's remaining tools and equipment.

Howard W. Shipley

At the 1876 Centennial Exhibition in Philadelphia, one of the many cutlery exhibits was a display of pocket cutlery made at the COQUANOC WORKS of HOWARD W. SHIPLEY. The Coquanoc works were located at the northwest corner of Ninth Street and Columbia Avenue, right in Philadelphia.

The Smithsonian Institution has a copy of Shipley's price list circa 1876, evidently given out at the fair. The list includes 192 distinct patterns with from one-to-five blades. Handle materials included "Oroide" (a bronze-like alloy), cocoa (cocobolo), ebony, bone, buffalo horn, stag, pearl, ivory and tortoise shell. We have seen only one Coquanoc Works pocketknife.

Schatt & Morgan/Queen City

In the early 1890s, J.W. Schatt and C.B. Morgan founded the NEW YORK CUTLERY CO., an import house in New York City. Schatt previously had worked for the Torrey Razor Co. Morgan had worked first for C.B. Barker, whose HOWARD CUTLERY CO. knives were made by Canastota, and then for his brother, Frank Morgan, owner of the BAYONNE KNIFE CO., a New Jersey cutlery importer, in business 1888-1898.

Soon after, Schatt and Morgan decided to open a factory in Gowanda, New York. They called it the SCHATT & MORGAN CUTLERY CO. In 1896, they sold the plant to Charles Platts and relocated their operations to Titusville, Pennsylvania, the "Queen City" and birthplace of the American petroleum industry. Schatt preferred Gowanda, where he continued to live, and Morgan bought him out in 1911.

In 1922, several Schatt & Morgan supervisory personnel started QUEEN CITY CUTLERY CO. on the side. They reportedly used S. & M.'s facilities to make some of their components, and were finally fired as a result around 1928. Shortly afterward, S. & M. went out of business, and the owners of Queen City bought the plant and equipment. In 1945, Queen City changed its name to QUEEN CUTLERY CO., under which name it still operates today. As of this writing, Queen was offering a line of pocketknives sporting the Schatt & Morgan brand.

Tidioute

The TIDIOUTE CUTLERY CO. was founded in Tidioute, Pennsylvania, in 1897. The firm's claim to fame is that it was bought in 1902 by the Brown Brothers' UNION RAZOR CO., also of Tidioute. Union Razor was renamed UNION CUTLERY CO. in 1909. When Booth Brothers of Sussex, New Jersey, went out of business in 1909, its tools and equipment were sold to "a firm in Tidioute, Pennsylvania," which no doubt was Union.

Union Cutlery Co. moved to Olean, New York, in 1911. It adopted the trademark KA-BAR in 1923. (See the section, "Case, Western, Ka-Bar, Cattaraugus, and Related American Brands" for more on KA-BAR, and also for information on C. PLATTS & SONS of Gowanda, New York, and Eldred, Pennsylvania.)

For more information on American cutlery manufacturers, see the sections, "American Knifemakers and Cutlery Merchants of the Bowie Knife Period" and "Kitchen and Butcher Knives."

Remington U.M.C.

Remington is one of the most popular brands of knives to collect. Among the reasons why are:

- Remington knives have a close association with firearms, as do the equally popular Winchester knives;
- Remington knives are of the highest quality, handsome and well made (though with certain intentional exceptions);
- Remington made pocketknives in an incredible variety, more than a thousand patterns all told, and;

- Though hardly common, Remington knives are still relatively abundant, much more so than earlier brands. Of course, old Remingtons in mint condition are very scarce, but even they are available—at a price.

Note: The last digit in a Remington pattern number indicates the handle material and can warn you of an incorrectly re-handled knife. The code: 1-Redwood; 2-Black; 3-Bone Stag; 4-Pearl; 5-PyREMite; 6-Genuine Stag; 7-Ivory or White Bone; 8-Cocobolo; and 9-Metal.

Remington Cutlery Chronology

Based on original research by Dennis Ellingsen.

Nov. 11, 1918	World War I ends. U.S. government cancels almost all outstanding war contracts.
April 1919	Remington plans a cutlery operation in nearly new but now idle Bridgeport, Connecticut, military ammunition plant; hires C.W. Tillmanns and his team of Solingen cutlers away from Valley Forge (Boker). Tillmanns and crew had worked for Camillus until 1915, left for Utica when ordered to work on an Allied navy knife contract, thence to Boker. Like Boker, Remington makes Tillmanns cutlery production manager, also hires A.H. Willey, 21-year Boker veteran. Remington already employs many cutlers who had been idled by wartime steel restrictions.
September 1919	Remington begins plant conversion. It will use new machine methods and interchangeable parts. Publication of Remington Cutlery Catalog No. 1, with 150 pages of pocketknives, starts. Company introduces its "acorn" shield to indicate punch-blade knives (copied from Boker, as were most of Remington's standard pocketknife patterns).
Feb. 9, 1920	Remington knife production begins with the R-103 regular jack. The company frames the first R-103s for presentation. All Remington cutlery is to be sold through hardware wholesalers. All knives are to be marked REMINGTON, no private brands. Company begins an aggressive consumer and trade advertising program.
June 1920	Remington ships more than 500 dozen pocketknives.
May 15, 1921	Remington salesmen blanket the country, taking orders to be filled through hardware jobbers.
July 1921	More than 2000 retailers in 47 states (Nevada the only one not included) carry Remington pocketknives.
Oct. 1921	Pages 151-182 of Catalog No. 1 are published; total number of patterns is over 600. Remington offers pre-packaged mixed "assortments."
March 1922	Remington doubles its knife production capacity.
July 1922	Pages 183-214 of Catalog No. 1, containing 100 more patterns, are published. U.S. Trademark 151,481 is registered for PyREMite, Remington's brand of patterned celluloid, in use since 1919.

September 1922	Remington announces the first "Bullets," the R-1123 (bone stag) and R-1128 (cocobolo) large trappers (then called "hunting knives"). By 1930, there are to be 12 standard styles of "Bullets": large, highly finished, outdoorsmen's pocketknives with distinctive Bullet shields.
1923	Remington is authorized to make Official Boy Scout Knives and introduces the RS-3333 utility knife with the Official Boy Scout shield (formerly, it had the acorn SCOUT KNIFE shield).
1924	Remington introduces Tillmans' two-piece, patent-pending can opener for scout and utility knives (patent issued July 12, 1927).
1925	The Remington Catalog C-5, illustrating 927 patterns of pocketknives, is published. The company introduces its first six patterns of fixed-blade hunting knives with sheaths.
April 1926	Remington introduces six more sheath knife patterns, retailing for $2-$6 each. Remington sells knives in 48 states and more than 60 foreign countries.
February 1927	Remington introduces kitchen knives.
August 1930	The second edition of Catalog C-5 is published.
February 1931	Remington announces that pocketknife production exceeds 10,000 knives per day (more than 2,860,000 per year). A Remington survey reveals that a pocketknife's "half-life" averages about two years.
Aug. 3, 1933	In financial difficulty—probably due to numerous hardware wholesaler failures—Remington is rescued from bankruptcy and acquired by DuPont.
1936	Remington DuPont issues a new catalog. The pocketknife line is reduced to 307 patterns.
Late 1930s	Remington DuPont introduces the Remington straight-line-marked assortment knives, most or all of them contract made.
1939	Remington introduces its first stainless pocketknives. They have an "S" in the tang stamping.
Nov. 12, 1940	Remington announces re-conversion to military small arms production and the end of cutlery production. Industry rumors say the Remington cutlery division lost $2 million in 1940. Remington sells its cutlery parts and equipment to Pal Blade Co.
1982	Remington offers the first of an annual series of reissue "Bullet" knives, contract made by Camillus, that were still in production when this book was published in 2005.

Case, Western, Ka-Bar, Cattaraugus and Related American Brands

Case Bros. & Co.
Gowanda, NY
1896-1900
Jean and Andrew Case
John D. Case 1896-1898
Jobber (for C. Platts & Sons)

Case Bros. Cutlery Co.
Little Valley, NY
1900-1912
Jean, John D. & Andrew Case
Elliot J. & Dean J. Case, J.Russell Case
Manufacturer

Case Bros. Cutlery Co.
Springville, NY
1912-1915
Jean & John D. Case
Manufacturer

W.R. Case & Son Cutlery Co.
Little Valley, NY
1902-1905
J. Russell Case
Jobber (for Napanoch)

W.R. Case & Sons Cutlery Co.
Little Valley, NY
1904-1905
J. Russell Case, H.N. Platts
Jobber (for C. Platts' Sons)

W.R. Case & Sons Cutlery Co.
Bradford, PA
1905-present
H.N. Platts left 1911
J. Russell Case d.1953
John O'Kain retired 1971
Russell B. Osborne d.1975
1972-1988: division of American Brands
1988-1991: owned by James Parker
1991-1993: reorganized by River
Associates
1993-present: owned by Zippo
Manufacturer

American Knife Co.
Reynolds Bridge, Plymouth Hollow, CT
1849-1911
C.W. Platts, cutler 1864-1872
Manufacturer

Northfield Knife Co.
Northfield, CT
1858-1919
C.W. Platts, Superintendent 1872-1896
H.N., Charlie, Ray, Joe and Frank Platts
(apprentices)
Manufacturer

C. Platts & Sons Cutlery Co.
Gowanda, NY
1896-1897
C.W. Platts H.N., Charlie, Ray, Joe and
Frank Platts (cutlers)
Manufacturer

C. Platts & Sons Cutlery Co.
Eldred, PA
1897-1900
C.W. Platts (d.1900)

C. Platts' Sons Cutlery Co.
1900-1905
H.N., Charlie, Ray, Joe and Frank Platts
Manufacturer

Case Mfg. Co. (also J.D. Case)
Little Valley, NY
1898?-1899?
John D. Case
Jobber

Standard Knife Co.
Little Valley, NY
1901-1903
Elliot J., & Dean J. Case
Jobber

Case Cutlery Co.
(Case Bros. Cut. Co. 2nd plant)
Kane, PA
1907-1911
Jean Case
Manufacturer

Robinson Cutlery Co.
Springville, NY
1921-present
1921: founded by J. Russell Case
and George Robinson
c1925-present: owned by the Robinson
and Skerker families
Manufacturer of kitchen knives

Alcas Cutlery Co. (CUTCO)
Olean, NY
1941-present
W.R. Case and ALCOA 1941-1972
ALCOA 1972-1984
Independent 1984-present
Acquired Ka-Bar brand from Cole
National 1996
Manufacturer

Union Knife Works
Union-Endicott, NY
c1911-1913
Charlie Platts, Superintendent, Joe Platts,
Foreman
Manufacturer

Eureka Cutlery Co.
Nicholson, PA
1911-1915
Charlie Platts, Superintendent c1913
Manufacturer

Thomaston Knife Co.
Thomaston, CT
1887-c1930
Charlie Platts, Manager
1916-c1930
Manufacturer

Remington Arms Co.
Cutlery Division
Bridgeport, CT
1919-1940
Charlie Platts, Cutler c1930
Manufacturer

Platts Bros. Cutlery Co.
Andover, NY
1907-1909
Charlie, Ray, Joe & Frank Platts
Manufacturer

Western States Cutlery Co.
Western Cutlery Co.
Boulder & Longmont, CO
1911-1991
Harvey Nixon Platts d.1947
Harlow & Reginald Platts
Harvey Platts retired 1984, d.1996
1911-1920 jobber [for American Shear,
Valley Forge, Thomaston, W.R.
Case, Utica, Eureka, Challenge, Clyde]
1920-1991 manufacturer
1984 sold to Coleman
(called Coleman/Western)
1990 sold to Wilderness Forge
(Wyoming) 1991 brands, machinery,
tooling sold to Camillus 1991-present
brand made and sold by Camillus

Friedmann & Lauterjung
(Electric)
New York, NY
c1866-c1909
J.B.F. Champlin, salesman 1866-1882
Importers and jobbers

J.B.F. Champlin & Son
Little Valley, NY
1882-1886
J.B.F. & Tint Champlin
Importing jobber

Cattaraugus Cutlery Co.
Little Valley, NY
1886-1963
J.B.F. Champlin d.1903
Tint Champlin (retired 1928, d.1938)
J.B.F. (Jack) and Phillip Champlin, H.N.
Platts 1891-96
C.W., Charlie, Ray, Joe & Frank Platts
1894-96
W.R., Jean, John D. & Andrew Case
1886-87
Jobber 1886-1891
Manufacturer 1891-1963

Little Valley Knife Association
Little Valley, NY
1900-1905
Herbert E. Crandall
Jobber

Crandall Cutlery Co.
Bradford, PA
1905-1912
(sold to W.R. Case & Sons)
Herbert E. Crandall
Manufacturer

Kinfolks
also made Jean Case 1928-1948
Little Valley, NY
1925-c1951
Dean J. Case d.1951

J. Russell Case and Tint Champlin 1925-28
Jean Case 1928-1935, J. Elliot Case
Manufacturer

Robeson Cutlery Co.
Rochester and Perry, NY
c1879-1977
Emerson E. Case president 1940-1965
Jobber c1879-1894
Manufacturer 1895-c1965
Jobber c1965-1977
Brand sold briefly under Ontario in
1990s

Burrell Cutlery Co.
Ellicottville, NY
1940-present
Harold W. Burrell 1940-1950
Dean Burrell, Addie Case Burrell
and John Kerns
Manufacturer (kitchen knives, razors)

Brown Brothers Mfg. Co.
Brown Brothers Knife Co.
Little Valley, NY
c1890-1902
Tidioute, PA
c1902-1909
Wallace R. & Emerson Brown
Manufacturer and importer

Tidioute Cutlery Co.
Tidioute, PA
1897-1906 (sold to Brown Bros. 1902)
Manufacturer

Union Razor Co.
Tidioute, PA
1902-1909
Wallace R. Brown
Manufacturer

Union Cutlery Co.
Tidioute, PA
1909-1911
Wallace R. Brown
Manufacturer

Union Cutlery Co.
Olean, NY
1911-1951
KA-BAR brand 1923-1951
Wallace R. & Emerson Brown
Danforth Brown
Manufacturer

Ka-Bar Cutlery Co.
Olean, NY
1951-c1966
Ka-Bar brand since 1951
Danforth Brown d.1956
Manufacturer

Cole National Corp.
Cleveland & Solon, OH
1966-present
Ka-Bar and Khyber brands
Manufacturer at Olean, NY 1966-1977
Jobber and importer 1977-present
Sold Ka-Bar brand to Alcas 1996

Case Pocketknife Patterns

Among collectors of factory pocketknives, W.R. Case & Sons has been the most popular brand for more than 40 years. Interest in Case is so widespread that it is the only pocketknife brand in which minor differences in marking, and even minor variations within a pattern, can sometimes have major effects on value. In fact, it would take entire books to cover the field of Case pocketknives to the satisfaction of advanced collectors.

Luckily for Case fans, such books exist. The most detailed is *The American Premium Guide to Knives and Razors, Fourth Edition*, by Jim Sargent. Also very thorough are *The Official Price Guide, Collector Knives, Eleventh Edition*, by Blade Magazine Cutlery Hall-Of-Famer© C. Houston Price, and *The IBCA Price Guide to Antique Knives, Second Edition*, by Cutlery Hall-Of-Famer J. Bruce Voyles. *The Case Knife Story* by Allen Swayne shows 76 Case tang stampings. For Case specials and limited editions, see the *1985 Case Pocket Price Guide, Third Edition*, by Jim Sargent and Jim Schleyer, as well as *Counterfeiting Antique Cutlery, 1997 1st Edition*, by Gerald Witcher.

For full-time knife dealers and advanced Case collectors, the specialized books are essential. However, most people will find all the information they need about Case knives in *BLADE's Guide To Knives and Their Values*.

In the section, "Pocketknife Brand List", there are more than 17 Case listings. These are all the important Case brand variations. When you use these listings in combination with the pocketknife pattern chapters, you will be able to establish the age and current market value of almost every Case knife.

Case Pattern Numbers

A real advantage of using *BLADE's Guide* for estimating the value of Case knives and other collectible brands is that you do not have to know a thing about pattern numbers to look up a knife. Though recent Case knives have the number stamped on the back of the master blade tang, older Case knives generally do not. This often confuses the beginning collector when he tries to use other books.

Even though you do not need pattern numbers to use *BLADE's Guide*, you will need to know them if you want to get further into Case, or if you want to understand the private language used by Case collectors.

The W.R. Case & Sons pattern numbering system is probably the most rational of any pocketknife brand. However, like the English language, the code has its share of contradictions, ambiguities and exceptions.

The first digit (disregarding 0) in each pattern number is the handle material code. Knowing this code can help you spot a knife that has been incorrectly re-handled. A letter prefix in place of the first digit can indicate handles of metal, fancy celluloid or recent limited-edition materials.

The handle codes are:

Numbers:

1 = Walnut
2 = Smooth black composition
3 = Smooth yellow composition
4 = Smooth white composition (rare)
5 = Genuine stag (most Case genuine stag is dyed an orange color). Also, second-cut stag
6 = Bone stag (jigged bone). Also, synthetic bone stag, including "rough black" from the 1940s, and "Delrin" used more recently
7 = Imitation tortoise shell (rare); maple (current)
8 = Genuine pearl; and **9** = Imitation pearl ("cracked ice")

Letters:

Metal:

M = Base metal
S = Silver or gold plate
T = Toledo scale
W = Wire

Fancy Celluloid:

B = Onyx, agate or Christmas tree; **BM** or **H** = Brown mottled (butter and molasses); **G** or **P** or **Y** = Assorted colors; **GS** = Gold stone; **HA** = High art (picture handle); **R** = Candy stripe, and **RM** = Red mottled

Recent Materials:

A = Appaloosa; **E** = Engraved brass; **W** = White bone; **SR** or **SG** = Smooth red or green bone; **G** = Green Delrin or bone; **P** = Pakkawood®; **I** or **IS** = Imitation ivory; and (**S** = Scrimshaw)

The second digit in a Case pattern number indicates simply the number of blades in the knife.

The remaining two digits (sometimes three digits, rarely four) refer to a particular "handle die," or shape. A pocketknife shape is called a "handle die" because the liners, which determine the shape, are stamped with a set of steel dies.

Following are the Case handle-die codes. An incorrect code on a blade usually indicates that the blade was taken from another knife for repair or replacement. However, in the old days, some of the codes were used on two or three different specialty (or even contract) patterns.

W.R. CASE & SONS HANDLE DIE CODES

00 = 4 5/8-inch swell-center clasp jack OR 5 1/2-inch melon tester;
01 = 2 5/8-inch equal end pen;
02 = 3 3/8-inch barehead slim jack;
03 = 4-inch budding and grafting OR 3 5/8-inch curved jack;
04 = 3 3/8-inch regular jack;
05 = 3 3/4-inch barlow;
06 = 2 3/8-inch regular jack;
07 = 3 1/2-inch serpentine jack;
08 = 3 1/4-inch swell-center serpentine pen;
09 = 3 3/8-inch barlow OR 3 1/4-inch gunstock budding;
10 = 3 1/8-inch sleeveboard jack;
11 = 4 3/8-inch swell-center regular jack;
011 = 4-inch pruner;
14 = 3 3/8-inch slim jack, cap bolsters;
15 = 3 5/8-inch gunstock jack;
16 = 3 3/8-inch regular jack;
17 = 4-inch curved jack;
18 = 3 1/2-inch junior premium stock;
19 = 4 1/8-inch slim regular jack;
20 = 2 3/4-inch serpentine jack (Peanut);
21 = 3 1/4-inch wharncliffe pen;
23 = 3 5/8-inch slim swell-center jack;
24 = 3-inch regular jack;
25 = 3-inch swell-center jack;
26 = 3-inch dog-leg jack;
27 = 3-inch swayback pen (old);
27 = 2 3/4-inch baby premium stock and jack (new);
027 = 2 3/4-inch sleeveboard pen;
28 = 3 1/2-inch easy open sleeveboard jack;
028 = 3 1/2-inch serpentine jack;
29 = 2 1/2-inch curved regular jack;
30 = 3 1/4-inch equal-end pen;
31 = 3 3/4-inch (approx.) regular jack;
031 = 3 3/4-inch (approx.) barehead regular jack;
32 = 3 5/8-inch gunstock premium stock and jack;
33 = 2 5/8-inch square-end baby prem. stock, pen, jack;
34 = 3 3/4-inch crown jack;
35 = 3 1/4-inch regular jack;
36 = 4 1/8-inch equal-end jack;
37 = 3 1/2-inch swell-center jack (old);
37 = 3 5/8-inch clasp jack (modern, Sod Buster Jr.);
38 = 4 5/8-inch clasp jack (Sod Buster);
39 = 4 3/4-inch pruner;
40 = 4 7/16-inch serpentine jack;
42 = 2 7/8-inch crown pen;
43 = 5-inch daddy barlow;
44 = 3 1/4-inch square-end junior premium stock and jack;
45 = 3 5/8-inch equal-end jack, cattle and utility;
045 = 3 5/8-inch utility with English can opener;
46 = 4 3/8-inch rigging knife OR 3 5/8-inch equal-end pen;
046 = 3 3/4-inch eureka cattle knife;
47 = 3 7/8-inch premium stock and jack;
48 = 4-inch (approx.) slim serpentine jack;
49 = 4-inch (approx.) serpentine jack;
50 = 4 3/8-inch sunfish (Elephant Toenail);
050 = 5 3/8-5 1/2-inch swell-center hunting knife;
0050 = 5 1/8-inch swell-center hunting knife;
51 = 5 1/4-inch curved regular hunting knife;
051 = 3 7/8-inch fishtail with guard (old);
051 = 3 3/4-inch curved regular jack (new);
52 = 3 3/4-inch curved regular jack take-apart;
052 = 3 1/2-inch congress;

053 = 2 3/4-inch equal-end pen;
54 = 4 1/8-inch standard trapper;
055 = 3 1/2-inch equal-end jack and cattle;
056-057 = 2 1/2-inch curved regular jack;
57 = 3 3/4-inch equal-end office knife;
58 = 4 1/4-inch folding hunter;
058 = 3 1/4-inch shadow equal-end pen;
59 = 5-inch modern folding hunter;
059 = 3 1/4-inch equal-end pen;
60 = 3 7/16-inch (approx.) equal-end pen;
61 = 2 7/8-inch slim equal-end pen OR 4 3/8-inch switchblade;
62 = 3 1/8-inch wide equal-end pen;
062 = 3 5/16-inch utility knife;
63 = 3 1/8-inch equal-end pen;
063 = 3 1/16-inch sleeveboard pen;
64 = 3 1/8-inch equal-end pen;
65 = 5 1/4-inch clasp folding hunter;
66 = 3 1/8-inch junior premium stock;
67 = 3 1/4-inch swell-center balloon pen;
68 = 3 1/4-inch congress;
69 = 3-inch congress;
70 = 3 1/8-inch swell-center congress;
71 = 3 1/4-inch equal-end pen OR 5 3/8-inch switchblade;
72 = 5 1/2-inch extra-wide clasp (Bulldog, Buffalo);
75 = 4 1/4-inch square-end premium stock and jack;
76 = 3 5/8-inch sleeveboard pen;
77 = 3 1/8-inch sleeveboard pen;
78 = 3 1/16-inch crown pen;
79 = 3 1/8-inch (approx.) equal-end pen OR 3 1/4-inch leg knife;
079 = 3 1/4-inch sleeveboard pen;
80 = 3 7/8-inch serpentine pen;
81 = 3-inch candle-end lobster pen;
82 = 2 3/4-inch square-end regular jack;
83 = 3 1/2-inch swell-center balloon pen;
083 = 3 3/16-inch sleeveboard lobster pen;
85 = 3 5/8-inch square-end regular jack;
086 = 3 1/4-inch square-end regular jack;
87 = 3 1/2-inch gunstock pen;
087 = 3 1/4-inch junior premium stock and jack;
88 = 4 1/8-inch congress;
088 = 3 1/8-inch sleeveboard lobster pen;
089 = 3 1/16-inch equal-end lobster pen
90-0090 = 3 3/8-inch equal-end utility;
090 = 2 1/4-inch lobster pen;
91 = 4 1/2-inch oval pen;
92 = 4-inch square-end premium stock and jack;
93 = 3 15/16-inch square-end premium stock;
093 = 5-inch tickler and fish knife;
94 = 4 1/4-inch equal-end jack and cattle OR 4 1/4-inch canoe cattle (Gunboat);
094 = 4 1/2-inch tickler;
095 = 5-inch tickler and fish knife;
96 = 4 1/4-inch slim square-end equal-end pen;
096 = 3 1/8-inch tickler;
97 = 5-inch folding hunter (Shark Tooth);
097 = 5-inch leg knife;
098 = 5 1/2-inch tickler and fish knife;
99 = 4 1/8-inch regular jack;
099 = 2 7/8-inch equal-end lobster pen;
102 = 2 3/4-inch sleeveboard lobster pen;
105 = 3 1/8-inch lobster pen;
109 = 3 3/8-inch swell-center serpentine cattle knife;
131 = 3 5/8-inch canoe cattle and jack, and;
145 = 4-inch equal-end utility.

Winchester and Simmons

The Winchester Repeating Arms Co. of New Haven, Connecticut, and the E.C. Simmons Hardware Co. of St. Louis, Missouri, shared a common history for less than a decade, but it is the period in the 1920s that is of the greatest interest to knife collectors.

At the end of the First World War, Winchester, like rival Remington, had found itself with extra production capacity and investment capital. Management sought new uses for these resources and the first choice was cutlery. Rather than developing cutlery capacity from scratch, as Remington was doing, Winchester bought two very different existing firms to form the basis of its cutlery operation.

In New Haven, Winchester bought the Eagle Knife Co. from the Hemming Brothers. The Hemmings had invented and patented the world's first successful automatic blade-grinding machines. They also had developed automatic punch presses for blanking blades. Winchester wanted the machines, and the know-how to apply them, for its own operation.

In upstate New York, Winchester bought the Napanoch Knife Co., a traditional pocketknife firm founded in 1900. Winchester moved most of Napanoch's equipment and all of its employees who were willing to relocate to New Haven, and then sold the land and buildings to a group of the remaining employees, who turned it into the Honk Falls Knife Co.

Winchester began to manufacture pocketknives sporting blades blanked from chrome-vanadium tool steel. Though great at edge holding, the material made ugly knives that no one would buy. What Winchester really needed was more hardware marketing savvy. To acquire it, Winchester merged with the Simmons Hardware Co. in 1922.

Simmons Hardware had begun as a regional hardware wholesaler in St. Louis after the Civil War, much like hundreds of other similar firms all over the United States. Unlike most hardware wholesalers, however, Simmons had grown and expanded aggressively in pursuit of a national market. The Simmons "Keen Kutter" brand had become known all over the country.

In pocket cutlery, "Keen Kutter" was Simmons' premium brand, used mainly on American-made knives. The company's lower-priced knives, most of which were made in Germany, were tang stamped "Simmons" or "Simmons Hardware Co." Some of the latter have a picture of a hornet stamped on the reverse tang, and the older "Simmons Hornet" knives are popular with collectors.

Simmons did not just contract with manufacturers for its private-brand Keen Kutter merchandise; whenever it could, it bought them out. By so doing, it could give priority to its own production and then use excess capacity to make a profit supplying some of its competitors.

For pocketknife production, Simmons bought the Walden Knife Co. of Walden, New York, in 1902. Thus, in 1922, when Winchester bought Simmons, it also got the Walden Knife Co. Walden's equipment was moved to New Haven in 1923. Thenceforth, former Walden and Napanoch staff made Winchester and Keen Kutter pocketknives on Walden equipment in Winchester's New Haven plants.

Eschewing fancy alloys and much of the Hemmings' automatic machinery, the company's cutlers forged pocketknife blades from plain old carbon steel.

Winchester-Simmons was a large, integrated firm. It manufactured firearms, ammunition, cutlery, tools, flashlights, batteries and a variety of other hardware. In addition, it bought a wide range of private-branded hardware items. It did most of its own wholesale distribution through offices in Atlanta, Boston, Chicago, Minneapolis, "Pacific," Philadelphia, St. Louis, Sioux City, Toledo and Wichita. It actively encouraged independent hardware retailers to become franchised "Winchester Stores," carrying Winchester-brand merchandise exclusively. Stores that did not join the Winchester retail network were still encouraged to carry Winchester or Keen Kutter cutlery, as well as Winchester firearms and ammunition, which were also distributed through other wholesalers.

Winchester-Simmons grew and prospered through the 1920s, but after 1929 the two firms went their separate ways. Thereafter, Winchester concentrated on manufacturing and distribution, while Simmons once again became strictly a hardware wholesaler. In 1940, Simmons was acquired by its long time St. Louis rival, the Shapleigh Hardware Co. Keen Kutter became Shapleigh's second brand, after its own Diamond-Edge. Following the Shapleigh firm's demise in 1960, Imperial acquired the Diamond-Edge mark, while "Keen Kutter" vanished from the marketplace.

> *Rather than developing cutlery capacity from scratch, as Remington was doing, Winchester bought two very different existing firms to form the basis of its cutlery operation.*

In the 1930s, Winchester strove to maintain its reputation for quality cutlery, but in the face of mechanized cost-cutting rivals such as Imperial, Colonial, Utica and Camillus, it had to adapt. In 1933, the firm introduced, tentatively at first, light-gauge, machine-made assortment knives. The original plan was that the knives would be the "entering wedge" to help Winchester salesmen get their better knives onto retailers' shelves, but assortments soon became a major part of Winchester's business (see Blade Magazine Cutlery Hall-Of-Famer© Bernard Levine's related story in *Knife World*, January 1988). The combination of Winchester markings only on one blade, no pattern number and rough black handles indicates an inexpensive "assortment" knife from the 1930s. In some instances, the assortment knives had multi-colored celluloid handles instead.

With America's entry into World War II in December 1941, Winchester began a rapid phasing out of most of its consumer-oriented manufacturing. The firm's cutlery manufacturing ceased in early 1942.

Winchester has not made any knives since, but in recent years the firm's German and French distribution agencies have had Winchester-brand knives contract made for sale in their European markets. Winchester USA has licensed Blue Grass Cutlery of Manchester, Ohio, to distribute new Winchester-brand knives in the United States.

Imperial, Ulster, Schrade and Camillus

The following chronologies are based on information from Blade Magazine Cutlery Hall-Of-Famers© Albert M. and Henry Baer, Dick Fullerton, Julian Raper, Elliott Kastor Bryer, George M. Schrade, Nilo Miori, Cutlery Hall-Of-Famer Houston Price, John Goins, Alfred Lief, Dennis Ellingsen and Siegfried Rosenkaimer.

Imperial Knife Co.

1916. Brothers Michael and Felix Mirando, cutlers from Frosolone, Italy, leave Empire Knife Co., Winsted, Connecticut, to go to Providence, Rhode Island. They start Imperial Knife Co. in a blacksmith shop rented from a cousin.

1917. The company delivers its first knives to the Hayward Jewelry Co., Attleboro, Massachusetts. They are 2 5/8-inch cigar-cutter "skeletons" (see the section, "Pen Knives") to which jewelry firms attached precious metal handles and bails. Imperial introduces the IKCO tang stamping.

1918. A small space is rented in what would become the main Imperial plant, on what is now Imperial Place. At first, all of Imperial's output is skeleton knives for the large jewelry industry in Providence. It also makes IKCO two-blade sailor knives for the U.S. Navy.

1919. Dominic Fazzano joins Imperial as a partner.

1921. Imperial has 100 employees and an entire floor in the factory, begins direct marketing of "shadow knives"— skeletons to which celluloid handles are affixed.

By 1940, Imperial's daily production exceeded 100,000 knives.

1922. Imperial begins the distribution of bolstered jack and pen knife patterns, using bone stag handles, as well as various patterns of multi-colored celluloid.

1936. Imperial introduces Jackmaster pocketknives with pressed sheet metal handles, licensed from Ernst Lohr and Otto Stiehl (Elosi) of Germany. The processes for making the knives are steadily improved, and receive many patents. Imperial buys the Hammer Brand trademark of the defunct New York Knife Co. for use on the Jackmaster knives.

1939. Imperial owns and uses the entire five-story factory.

1940. Imperial's daily production exceeds 100,000 knives.

1943-1945. Blade Magazine Cutlery Hall-Of-Famer© Albert M. Baer, owner of Ulster Knife Co., involves Imperial in a joint venture to produce millions of knives for the government under the name Kingston Cutlery Co., an old Ulster trademark.

Ulster Knife Co.

1871. Cooperative Knife Co. of Ellenville, New York, founded by emigrant Sheffield cutlers.

1876. Cooperative Knife Co. fails. It is taken over by Col. Dwight Divine, a banker, and renamed Ulster Knife Co.

1919-1941. Divine's son declines to modernize Ulster, retains Sheffield hand methods, loses money every year.

1941-1942. Albert M. Baer (see Camillus, below) buys Ulster from C. Dwight Divine Jr. With Edward Wallace and Frank Kethcart, he thoroughly modernizes the plant for mass production. Baer is joined by his brother, Blade Magazine Cutlery Hall-Of-Famer Henry ("Uncle Henry") Baer.

1941-1945. Albert M. Baer serves on the Army Advisory Board of the Office of the Quartermaster General.

1943. Baer organizes Kingston Cutlery Co., a joint venture with Imperial, to make government-contract knives.

1945-46. Kingston forms the Vulcan Safety Razor Co., and it begins to make kitchen knives. It acquires Schrade Cutlery Co. of Walden, New York, renaming it Schrade-Walden.

1947. Kingston Cutlery Co. dissolved. Ulster and Imperial merge to form Imperial Knife Associated Cos. owned by the Baers, the Mirandos and Fazzano.

George Schrade

1892-93. George Schrade (1860-1940) of New York City patents an improved switchblade with its release button in the bolster (see the section, "Switchblade Jack Knives"). He forms Press Button Knife Co., but, unable to find enough cutlers, sells an interest in Press Button to

Walden Knife Co. and moves it to the facilities in Walden, New York.

1903. Schrade sells all of Press Button to Walden Knife Co. (by then a subsidiary of E.C. Simmons Hardware Co.).

1904. George Schrade and two of his brothers, Louis and William, form Schrade Cutlery Co. in Walden to apply the latest machine methods and interchangeable parts to pocketknife production. Like Walden Knife Co., Schrade Cutlery Co. does much private-brand contract work.

1906-07. George Schrade patents an improved switchblade with the button on the side, and with a safety slider. The "Safety Push Button Knives" are made by Schrade Cut. Co.

1910. George Schrade patents an automatic knife-shield-inletting machine, then sells his share of Schrade Cut. Co. to Louis so he can travel to Europe with his son, George M. Schrade, to market the machines.

1911-1916. George Schrade resides in Solingen, where he develops the Springer switchblade. In 1916, the German government confiscates his assets, so he returns to the United States. He patents a spring-loaded weaver's scissors.

1917. George Schrade licenses Flylock (patented 1918) to Challenge Cutlery Co., Bridgeport, Connecticut, which he then joins. Schrade Cutlery Co. opens a branch factory at Middletown, New York, managed by George's brother, Joseph Schrade.

1925. George Schrade patents a bone-jigging machine.

1926. George Schrade patents the Wire Jack.

1928. George Schrade patents an automatic knife handle routing machine.

1928-29. Challenge Cutlery Co. closes after the death of owner Charles F. Wiebusch. George Schrade forms the Geo. Schrade Knife Co. in Bridgeport with some Challenge machinery and makes Presto switchblades, Wire Jacks and other plain knives.

1932. Schrade Cut. Co.'s Middletown branch is closed.

1937. George Schrade patents the flying jack and the pull-ball knife, simplified types of switchblades.

1940. George Schrade passes away. George M. Schrade and his son, Theodore, continue Geo. Schrade Knife Co.

1946. Kingston Cutlery Co. buys Schrade Cutlery Co., renames it Schrade-Walden Cutlery Co.

1956. Boker of Newark, New Jersey, buys Geo. Schrade Knife Co., but closes it in 1958 when Congress bans switchblades.

Imperial Knife Associated Cos.

1952. Henry Baer made president of Schrade.

1957-58. Schrade factory is relocated from Walden to be consolidated with the Ulster factory in Ellenville.

1959. Schrade's Old Timer brand is introduced.

1960. Imperial acquires Diamond-Edge trademark from the defunct Shapleigh Hardware Co. of St. Louis.

1965. Imperial becomes a partner in Durol (est. 1634) of Thiers, France; makes blades for electric carving knives.

1967. Schrade's Uncle Henry brand is introduced.

1977-1982. Imperial owns Richards Bros., Ltd., of Sheffield, the British licensee of the Lohr and Stiehl patents, and since 1975 the owner of Rodgers-Wostenholm. Schrade I*XL knives made at the Morse Street factory.

1983-86. Martin F. Zorn becomes president of Imperial.

1984. Albert M. Baer buys out his partners, renames the firm Imperial Schrade Corp. All pocketknife and hunting knife operations consolidated in a large modern factory in Ellenville, except the Jackmaster knives, which were made in the Stag Cutlery, Ltd., factory in Listowel, Ireland.

1986-2004. Walter Gardiner is president of Imperial Schrade.

June 1987. Henry Baer passes away.

1992. Albert M. Baer, chairman of Imperial Schrade, celebrates his 70th year in the cutlery industry.

1993. Imperial Schrade sales and administrative offices are relocated from New York City to the factory at Ellenville.

1997. Albert M. Baer passes away.

2004. On its hundredth anniversary, Schrade ceases knife production. Stewart Taylor of Taylor Cutlery buys all of Schrade's intellectual property—the Schrade trademarks and patents, tooling, etc.—and United Cutlery, Smoky Mountain Knife Works and Blue Ridge buys all of the existing Schrade knife parts that the "old" Schrade had not assembled into completed knives.

The Kastor Family

1841. Aaron Koester (1822-1885) leaves Wattenheim, Germany, for Natchez, Mississippi, where he prospers as a merchant.

1847. Aaron becomes a naturalized U.S. citizen in Vicksburg, anglicizes Koester to Kastor.

1864. Six months after Union forces take Vicksburg, Aaron Kastor goes to New York City, exchanges $250,000 in greenbacks for $100,000 in gold, and then goes to England, France and Germany to buy hardware.

1865. Aaron joins the firm Bodenheim, Meyer & Co. of New York City, wholesale importers of guns, cutlery and hardware from England, Belgium and Germany, whose primary market had been the American South. Henry Bodenheim (1823-1873) had lived in Vicksburg until 1865.

1867. Aaron becomes a partner in Bodenheim, Meyer & Kastor.

1870. Aaron's nephew, Adolph Kastor (1856-1946), emigrates from Wattenheim and works for Bodenheim, Meyer & Kastor. Adolph's father was Jacob Koester (1824-1911).

1873. Henry Bodenheim dies; firm becomes Meyer & Kastor. Adolph Kastor's older brother Nathan (1854-1932) immigrates to New York City and joins the firm as a stock clerk.

Oct. 1, 1876. Aaron Kastor parts from Abraham Meyer, does business as A. Kastor, hardware importer, in New York.

1879. Adolph Kastor takes his first annual hardware-buying trip to Europe for his uncle's firm.

1883. Adolph Kastor, returning from a sales trip to Cuba, meets a German pocketknife manufacturer. Kastor buys the man's samples and the line sells so well he decides to import cutlery exclusively for sale to jobbers.

1885-1886. Nathan Kastor lands Montgomery Ward and Marshall Field accounts, then goes to Solingen, Germany, on a cutlery buying trip, where he stays to open a permanent buying office.

c1888. Adolph, Nathan and Sigmund (1866-1947) Kastor form A. Kastor & Bros. at 109 Duane St. with backing from Jacob; are later joined by August Kastor (1870-1950). A. Kastor & Bros. adopts four-leaf "Clover Brand" symbolizing the brothers (registered 1906). Other brands include EBRO, XLNT (English), Koester's, Imperial Razor, Morley, Wadsworth, Duane, Parker, Majestic, Argyle, Corliss, etc. (German).

1892-94. Nathan Kastor opens the Germania Cutlery Works factory in Ohligs, Germany, to manufacture Kastor brands.

c1904. Nathan Kastor leaves Kastor Bros. firm, though he continues to supply cutlery to it.

1912. Kastor Bros. imports German pocketknives for U.S. Army Medical Department. Sigmund Kastor leaves Kastor Bros.

1913. Sigmund buys controlling interest in Wade & Butcher of Sheffield, exports its straight razors to America.

1918. Sigmund sells Wade & Butcher to the Durham Duplex Razor Co. of Jersey City, New Jersey.

1932. Nathan Kastor dies, succeeded at Germania by his nephew William Hartley [Hertz]. August Kastor retires, sells his shares in Kastor Bros. to Albert M. Baer.

1937-38. Nazis close and liquidate Germania Cutlery Works; it becomes an umbrella firm. Hartley immigrates to America.

Camillus

1894. Charles Sherwood builds a small pocketknife factory in Camillus, New York, west of Syracuse.

1896-98. Sherwood leases his plant to Robeson.

1897. U.S. Tariff Act (Dingley Tariff) nearly doubles prices of imported knives.

1902. Adolph Kastor buys Sherwood's pocketknife plant, renames it Camillus Cutlery Co. He and Nathan reorganize it on a division of labor basis rather than handicraft.

c1904. Adolph's son, Alfred B. Kastor (1889-1963), joins Kastor Bros., replacing Nathan, who remains in Ohligs.

1906. Camillus introduces Crossed Swords trademark.

1914-1918. Camillus makes military knives for Canadian, British and U.S. navies, the Red Cross, and the Dutch. German foreman Carl Tillmans and crew quit in protest in 1915 (see the section, "Remington U.M.C.").

1922. Albert Baer, grandson of Henry Bodenheim, becomes a salesman for Kastor Bros.

1923. Baer lands the Sears Roebuck account. Camillus uses Sta-Sharp, Dunlap and Kwik-Kut brands on Sears knives.

1924. Camillus begins to make Stainless Cutlery Co. brand pocketknives with stainless steel blades.

1927. Adolph Kastor retires and is succeeded by his son, Alfred.

1930. Albert Baer signs Babe Ruth to endorse autographed baseball-bat figural knife, first of many endorsements.

1934. Camillus registers Kent trademark, used exclusively on knives for F.W. Woolworth.

1936. Stream Line trademark registered. Other Camillus brands include Camco, Syracuse Knife Co., Mumbly Peg, and High Carbon Steel, U.S.A. Hundreds of private contract wholesale and retail brands also made. Camillus becomes the leading American supplier of private-brand knives.

1938. Albert Baer leaves Kastor Bros. but retains a major stake in the firm, acquired from August Kastor.

1942-45. Camillus makes millions of knives for the government, creates many important military designs.

1947. Kastor Bros. name dropped in favor of Camillus.

1963. Death of Alfred Kastor. Ownership of Camillus passes to Albert M. Baer's two daughters.

1990. Camillus buys stake in Smoky Mountain Knife Works, Sevierville, Tennessee, where part of its factory collection is now on display.

1991. Camillus buys rights to Western name, begins producing Western knives shortly thereafter.

Imperial, Ulster, Schrade and Camillus

Makers of Picture-Handle Pocketknives

Celluloid

In 1872, inventor John Wesley Hyatt introduced celluloid to the manufacturing world. Made of cellulose nitrate treated with camphor and alcohol, celluloid was the first practical, moldable synthetic plastic.

Other moldable materials based on rubber, gutta-percha or shellac had been known for several decades; they all had severe limitations. For instance, the materials were naturally opaque, and all but hard rubber could be made only in black or dark brown. White or red "hard" rubbers were fairly soft and nearly impossible to keep clean. Also, early hard rubber could not be precisely molded and, worse, it smelled bad.

Shellac-based compounds, such as the ones used for daguerreotype cases, were hard but brittle. They could be molded precisely for ornamental use but were not suitable for rough use, such as on a knife handle.

By contrast, celluloid proved to be a nearly ideal synthetic material for decorative practical applications such as handles, buttons and combs. Its liabilities are that it is flammable, shrinks as it ages and, under certain circumstances, breaks down chemically, releasing acid vapors that damage the steel blades and springs of the knife it is on and of any nearby knife. Manufacturers learned to minimize shrinkage of finished products by curing or pre-shrinking the celluloid in moderate-temperature ovens for long periods of time before final shaping. Changing the basic chemical formulation of the celluloid was required to solve the acid-vapor problem.

On the plus side, celluloid could be precisely molded. It is hard and shiny, making it easy to keep clean, yet it is not brittle. It can be made in every color of the rainbow, or any combination of colors arranged in any swirled or geometric pattern one desires.

As a result, celluloid can be fabricated to simulate most natural materials. Imitation ivory, horn, stag, pearl, amber, agate, tortoise shell, and even wood were purchased by cutlery firms for knife handles. Most intriguing of all, at least to people a century ago, celluloid can be made perfectly clear.

Picture Handles

It was celluloid's "magical transparency" that in 1879 caught the attention of Reuben and Henry Landis of Canton, Ohio. They realized that a knife handle made of clear celluloid could cover a picture or inscription on paper, and the whole "sandwich" would be at least as durable as most other handle materials. The paper could be written or drawn on, printed or lithographed. It even could be a tiny unmounted photographic print.

The Landises applied for a patent on the idea in July 1879 and received the patent (number 221,467) on Nov. 11. While they were waiting for the patent, they licensed two local entrepreneurs who started up rival firms to manufacture knives with the new-style picture handles.

Canton Cutlery equal-end whittler, knife co. ad, **$150**.

Canton Cutlery and Novelty Cutlery

One of the entrepreneurs was Dr. W. Stuart Carnes, who founded the Canton Cutlery Co. on West Tenth St. in Canton. The other was the postmaster of Canton, a one-armed Civil War veteran named Major August Vignos.

Like Carnes, Vignos apparently believed that picture handles were a nifty innovation, sure to become popular. However, Vignos did not stop there. Paper is so cheap and easy to work with, there was no real reason for any two picture-handled knives to be alike. Vignos's new enterprise, the Novelty Cutlery Co. at 515 McGregor Ave.—which he later ran as a branch of his Canton Knife Co.—would offer its customers any images they liked under the clear handles of their knives.

Customers could, of course, choose from a book of standard designs. However, Vignos encouraged them to submit their own art work or, even better, their own photograph, to be reproduced in miniature under the handle of a knife. In addition, such printed copy as a name and address, a greeting, an ad or a political slogan could be included under the handle as well.

Marketing

Thus, Vignos' Novelty Cutlery Co. was entirely a custom- or special-order concern, one that specialized in nationwide and even international business. Nothing like it had been seen in the cutlery industry before.

In one move, Vignos bypassed the whole elaborate network of national cutlery distributors (most located in New York City), regional hardware wholesalers, and local cutlery and hardware retailers. Just the Novelty factory needed to maintain an inventory and, except for samples, the inventory was only of parts and unassembled knives.

In assembling a pocketknife, the bolsters and handle scales are first affixed to the liners. Then the handles, springs and blades are pinned together.

Vignos's unit cost per knife was much higher than usual because of the required photo reduction, typesetting and custom assembly. However, by cutting out most of the middlemen and eliminating finished inventory, he kept the cost per knife to the consumer competitive with other brands.

Vignos had to market his knives virtually direct from the factory to the retail customer. He realized that the volume of correspondence marketing virtually direct would require could very well bankrupt him. Therefore, he adopted the idea of local agents, the sales method used by most book publishers at the time.

Any ambitious man or boy with a couple of dollars in capital could become a Novelty Knife agent. Each agent bought an illustrated catalog and, when he could afford it, he supplemented the catalog with samples.

The agent showed the catalog and samples everywhere he went and solicited orders. He answered the customer's questions. He wrote up individual orders to the factory in a standard format, with no instructions left out or garbled. He made sure that the correct pictures and copy were enclosed. In return, he took a commission out of the printed list price he charged the customer.

Because they paid the cost of their own catalogs and samples, the agents, in effect, cost Vignos nothing. As a result, he lined up as many of them as he could. Most of his ads were to recruit agents, not to sell knives.

Hence, there were thousands of Novelty agents. They could do as much or as little business as they wanted, as long as they paid in advance for every knife that they ordered.

With his novel product and his bold marketing plan, August Vignos was a great success. One mark of his success is that he was chosen to be the American juror for the cutlery exhibits at the 1900 World's Fair in Paris (the fact that he was of French descent and spoke the language did not hurt, of course). Judging from the account of Camille Page, the French juror at the fair and the first cutlery historian, the fair's display of knives was very likely the finest ever exhibited.

Competitors

Another mark of Vignos's success was that his business was emulated, more or less exactly, by several competitors. His first rival was his Canton neighbor, Dr. Carnes, with his Canton Cutlery Co.

Aerial Cutlery balloon double-end jack, knife co. ad, **$225**.

Like Vignos, Carnes began in 1879. Though never as well known as Vignos, Carnes also was successful. His firm made picture-handled knives until about 1930. Then it changed direction and name—to Car-Van Steel Products—and carried on until 1949.

Potential rivals to the two Canton, Ohio, picture-knife firms had to wait until the Landis patent expired before they could jump into the competition. Meanwhile, the evidence suggests that, in addition to his army of individual agents, Vignos sold knives through several agencies that did enough business, perhaps as advertising specialty dealers, to demand their own tang stamps. We believe that this accounts for knives with such stampings as INCO (Iowa Novelty Co.) of Keota, Iowa, and Novelty Cutlery Co., Brooklyn, New York.

Aerial

The first serious competition to the Ohio firms came from the Jaeger brothers of Duluth, Minnesota. In 1909, they started the Aerial Cutlery Co., whose main stock in trade was picture-handled knives. In 1912, the Jaegers moved their operations to Marinette, Wisconsin.

A 1925 Aerial agent's catalog, reproduced in Tracy Tudor's *Old Knife Book* (1978), shows a wide variety of patterns and an even wider variety of pictures. They include bathing beauties and fashionable ladies, lodge emblems, occupational symbols and scenes, patriotic and political motifs, college banners, cartoon figures, animals, vehicles, ships, buildings and sample advertisements. Near the end is a blank form for ordering personalized knives.

About 1925, the Jaeger brothers began to transfer their interest from knife manufacturing to the wholesaling of barber and beauty supplies. The transition was gradual and was not complete until about 1944, when the last picture-handled Aerial knives were put into storage.

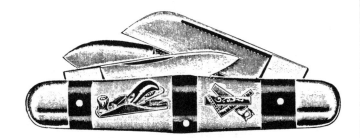

Aerial Cutlery balloon cattle knife, union symbols, **$130**.

Aerial Cutlery equal-end whittler, lodge symbol, **$95**.

Thirty years later, several thousand of the stored knives found their way into the collector marketplace. This accounts for the high proportion of Aerials that are now seen in mint condition.

Golden Rule

The next picture-knife competitor on the scene was the Golden Rule Cutlery Co. of Chicago. It began making picture knives in 1911, and its catalogs and business methods were very similar to those of Novelty and Aerial. (Golden Rule and Novelty catalogs of 1918 are reproduced in the fourth edition of Blade Magazine Cutlery Hall-Of-Famer© Dewey Ferguson's *Romance of Knife Collecting*, 1976.) Golden Rule went out of business in about 1924.

Lackawanna and Wabash

At least two other pocketknife firms made picture-handled knives. One was the Lackawanna Cutlery Co. of Nicholson, Pennsylvania. The firm began as the Eureka Cutlery Co. in 1911, changing its name in 1915. We believe

Golden Rule Cutlery slim equal-end jacks, military symbols, **$150**.

Novelty Cutlery senator pen, military picture, **$65**.

that picture knives marked NICHOLSON were also made by the firm. Most Lackawanna picture knives have a diamond-shaped, gold-flake "tinseloid" border around the picture or inscription. Lackawanna went out of business in 1930.

The other firm was the Wabash Cutlery Co. of Terre Haute, Indiana, in business from 1921 to 1935. As with Lackawanna, picture knives were not the firm's main business.

Novelty (Epilogue)

August Vignos died in 1925. His son, Alfred, succeeded him as president of Novelty Cutlery Co. By that time, popular interest in custom picture-handled knives was beginning to decline, though competition among the makers was at its height.

Unlike the others, Novelty proved strong enough to weather the Depression without any change in direction. It even hung on through the war years, though U.S. celluloid production ceased in about 1940 (other less flammable and more stable plastics replaced celluloid). However, Novelty Cutlery Co. found no place in the post-war world. It went out of business in 1948.

Evaluating Picture-Handle Knives

To estimate the value of a picture-handle knife, first figure the value of an identical shape, brand and condition of knife with a patterned celluloid handle. Then, add the value of the image.

PICTURE (and text)	ADD
Local business advertisement	$20-50
Lodge, fraternal, union or local politics	$40-80
Animals	$40
Fashion or bathing beauty	$50
Nude or nudes	$75
Early transportation: car, train, wagon	$50-100
Early transportation: ship, airplane, dirigible	$60-90
Famous person; military or historical scene	$50-100
Nationally advertised product	$50-100
Knife company advertising	$75-125
National political campaign or issue	$60-200
Aerial Cutlery balloon cattle knife, union symbols	$130
Novelty Cutlery senator pen, military picture	$65
Canton Cutlery equal-end whittler, knife co. ad	$150
Aerial Cutlery balloon double-end jack, knife co. ad	$225

Introduction to the Standard American Folding Knife Patterns

By Pete Cohan

The folding knives covered in "Standard American Folding Knife Patterns" are the types and patterns that have been made for commercial sale in the United States from about the mid-20th century up to today. Included are knives made in America and those made abroad for export to the USA as well.

Most knives made for American customers in this period fit into a definite range of shapes and patterns. In the segments that follow, all of the standard shapes and patterns are described, illustrated and valued in great detail, along with all of their variations. The history of each type, as far as it is known, is included in its segment.

"Standard American Folding Knife Patterns" is divided into three chapters: Jack Knives, Pen Knives and Multi-Blades.

Jack Knives are relatively plain, sturdy knives. Standard jack knives are single-ended and have their blade or blades hinged at one end. There are also a few styles of stout double-ended jack knives.

Pen Knives are small, lightweight, double-ended knives. They have two, three or more lightweight blades hinged in both ends. However, some of the smallest pen knives, now called quill knives, are single ended, like tiny jack knives.

Multi-Blades, as the name implies, have a multitude of blades, from two or three up to a hundred or more. At least one of the blades is either a special-purpose pattern, such as a spey blade, or a special implement (other than a cutting blade, a nail file or a leather punch). It can be a can opener, a champagne wire cutter, a hoof pick, a wrench or even a dinner fork. Multi-blades are usually large and sturdy, like standard jack knives. They are almost always double ended.

Some folding-knife forms, due to their construction, blade type or arrangement or special application, resist being placed in the foregoing categories. Such knives are covered in Part 2 of Section II, "Multi-Blade Knives," and/or Part 3 of Section II, "Foreign, Exotic, Primitive and Historical Folding Knives."

Since the beginning of organized pocketknife collecting, certain knife patterns have become very popular and probably will continue to be a dominant factor in the collector market.

Valuing Pocketknives: The Basics

The valuing of a pocketknife using the value tables provided in this part of *BLADE's Guide* is based on two major collecting factors, namely, knife pattern and the tang mark identification of the maker's name or mark, and/or the distributor/retailer brand mark.

The values you may get based on pattern and mark are not precise even if the condition of your knife meets all other criteria set forth in this guide. The values are estimates and provide you with a range in which your knife falls. It is very useful information but is no assurance that you can then sell your knife for your estimated value. Collector marketplace conditions will ultimately determine the value of your knife.

A very large number of collectors focus collecting on a specific knife pattern. Since the beginning of organized pocketknife collecting, certain knife patterns have become very popular and probably will continue to be a dominant factor in the collector market. The value tables found in the following chapters reflect this high level of collector interest in certain patterns by the higher value ranges indicated for the patterns.

While there are well over 3,000 cutlery names or marks, fewer than 200 of the marks, be they manufacturer or distributor/retailer brands, have become widely collected in the pocketknife market. The names and brands most sought after by the collector will tend to be in the higher value ranges of the tables provided. To be sure, there are exceptions. For instance, certain very collectible patterns, such as any good-quality four-blade congress or large folding hunter, may have higher values irrespective of the tang mark. The opposite is also true. A tang mark may be so sought after that the pattern has little effect on the higher value it has in the collector marketplace.

The following lists are provided as "shorthand" references to some of these manufacturers' marks and names, as well as distributor/retailer marks and brands that are typically on the higher end of the value range. This listing of brands/marks is for knives in the period 1960 and before. While there are some post-1960 exceptions, such as Buck, W.R. Case & Sons, Case Classics, Belknap Hdw. (John Primble & Blue Grass), new production Winchester, Remington marks, Schatt & Morgan, Robeson and a few others, the brand marks of interest and of higher value are those used by the original manufacturer or distributor, not by recent authorized use of the mark or name.

List A:

American Shear and Knife Co.
Beaver Falls Cut. Co./Mason & Sons
Belknap Hdw./Blue Grass/John Primble
Boker
Camillus Cutlery Co. (early)
Case (all 1960 and earlier marks)
Cattaraugus
Challenge Cut. Co.
Crandall Cut. Co.
Empire Knife Co.
J.A. Henckels
Hibbard, Spencer & Bartlett
Holley Cut. Co.
Humason and Beckley (H&B)
I*XL-George Wostenholm
Jack Knife Ben
Landers, Frary and Clark (LF&C)
Maher and Grosh
Miller Bros.
MSA/Marble's
Napanoch
Needham, Veall & Tyzack (Taylor Eye Witness)
New York Knife Co.
Northfield Knife Co.
Novelty Cut. Co./Canton Cutlery Co.
C. Platts & Sons
Queen Cut. Co.
Remington
Joseph Rodgers
J. Russell
Schatt & Morgan/Queen City Cut. Co.
Schrade, Walden
Schrade Cut. Co.
George Schrade Knife Co.
Shapleigh Hdw. Diamond Edge
Simmons Hdw. Co./Keen Kutter
Ulster
Union Cut. Co./Kabar
Wade and Butcher
Walden Knife Co.
Waterville Manufacturing Co.
Western States/Western, Boulder
Wilbert Cut. Co.
Will & Finck
Winchester
W.H. and/or Samuel C. Wragg

In addition to the foregoing list, there are several early New England cutlery marks that have a considerable collector following. As a result, the values of the knives of these early American cutlery firms all fall in the higher ranges on the appropriate value table. Some specific examples are:

Buck Bros.
Burkinshaw
Excelsior and Naugatuck Cut. Co.
James Frary & Sons
Gardner
Hatch
Hatch Cutlery Co.
LaBelle Cutlery Works
Southington Cut. Co.
Union Knife Co.

For a comprehensive review of these important early U.S. firms, see *New England Cutlery* by Philip Pankiewicz, Hollytree Publications, Gilman, CT 06336. If your knife has an early New England mark, it will be a higher-value piece.

There are also a large number of collectors who specialize in any pattern of pocketknife that has a particular local or regional brand mark on the tang. Many such knives have somewhat higher values, particularly in regions where the knives were distributed. Some specific examples:

Bigelow & Dowse (Wismar)
W. Bingham & Co. (BBB and XLCR)
Coast Cutlery
Gray and Dudley
Marshall Wells Hdw. Co.
Moore-Handley Hdw.
Pacific Hardware & Steel/Baker & Hamilton
Utica Cutlery (UTK, PocketPard, etc.)
Van Camp Hdw. & Iron
Witte Hdw. Co.
Wyeths Warranted Cutlery

In the late 19th and early 20th centuries, a novel form of pocket cutlery was developed and made by two firms as advertising, promotional, marketing and novelty knives. The history of this specialty is very interesting. Picture-handle and advertising knives have a fairly large collector following that has made some of the knives quite valuable. Handle condition is a critical factor. With clear celluloid handles that can decompose and pictures that fade, the handle becomes the most important consideration in valuing the knives. The knives are addressed in Part 1 of Section II, "Makers of Picture Handle Pocketknives"; "Advertising, Figural, Character and Miniature Knives"; and "Advertising Cutlery's Rich Potential."

There are separate value listings in Section IV of *BLADE's Guide* that address several brands and marks that have been produced since 1960. If your knife is a post-1960 piece, then these lists could be very helpful.

There is also a developing collector interest in pocketknives and fixed blades that have tang marks capitalizing on non-cutlery brand names which have a considerable and often very enthusiastic following. Examples are the Harley-Davidson knives, Smith & Wesson-marked knives, and the large number of private, limited-issue knives made by Camillus or Imperial Schrade and others with such names as Adolphus Busch, Mac Tool, Ace Hardware, L.L. Bean, Ducks Unlimited, National Rifle Association, Skoal and John Deere.

A great many pocketknives circulating today are only good for their intended purpose as a cutting tool. Thousands of low-cost pocketknives were imported from Europe, primarily Germany. There were also many inexpensive English-made knives that were exported to the USA. In recent years, a very sizable number of pocketknives have been imported from Japan, India, Pakistan, China and Taiwan. Some of the Japanese imports are of excellent quality and design. Many others are low-cost knock-offs of popular American patterns. The lower-quality part of this tide of imports is currently of little collector value.

While both imported and American-made economy pocketknives will be found in excellent-to-mint condition, they tend to have minimal collector value. Perhaps some of these brands will become collectible. Only time will tell. Most of the knives are on the lower end of the range in the value tables.

Pocketknives in the past 10 years have gained much new collector interest with the "reincarnation" of many old-style patterns, handle materials, and historic cutlery brands in the collector-oriented issues. Some notable examples include the CASE CLASSICS, a modern WINCHESTER and REMINGTON line of pocketknives, SCHATT & MORGAN and ROBESON, BULLDOG BRAND, FIGHT'N ROOSTER, the SCHRADE HERITAGE series, BLUEGRASS BRAND, and the QUEEN and KA-BAR collector series. There are many more that entered this market with varying degrees of success.

Section I of *BLADE's Guide* provides useful information regarding what to collect, but what you collect is your decision and the pleasure you get from whatever knives you collect is of real importance.

Valuing Pocketknives: The Procedure

Estimating the approximate value of a collectible pocketknife is not a science, it is more an art. As previously stated, two very important elements can be identified most of the time, namely, pattern and maker/distributor mark. The condition of the knife must be excellent to mint and

> *In recent years, a very sizable number of pocketknives have been imported from Japan, India, Pakistan, China and Taiwan.*

unsharpened. Other factors directly impacting value are identified in Section I under "Some Clues That Help Date and Identify Knives." What is nearly as important and far more subjective is just how "collectible" the knife really is to the pocketknife-collecting public. *BLADE's Guide* helps you by merging what are, at present, very collectible marks with the pattern tables, which are designed to reflect current pattern popularity (see "Pictorial Key to Standard American Folding Knives," Part 2, Section II). With some practice, you can arrive at an estimated value that will be quite useful even if not absolute.

Anyone using the system provided in *BLADE's Guide* must be very candid in evaluating his knife's condition, and likewise very willing to adjust the dollar value provided in the value tables when the knife in question does not meet the criteria for the higher estimated values.

There are many thousands of "collectible" pocketknives but that does not mean each of the knives has a "high value" expressed in terms of dollars and cents. Other books and guides available to the knife-collecting public address several very popular brands in great detail. Current, up-to-date editions of such books can provide more specific value information for those particular brands. *BLADE's Guide* will provide you with useful values for almost any pre-1960 pocketknife listed in "Standard American Folding Knife Patterns" when you observe the following steps:

Steps to Follow

Carefully inspect the knife to determine its condition. See Section I, "Grading the Condition of a Knife," including the NKCA standards, and the pocketknife terminology in "What Should You Collect?/ Parts of a Knife."

Determine the knife pattern by using the pattern charts in Part 2 of Section II, "Pictorial Key to Standard American Folding Knives." You should also look carefully at the knives pictured in each pattern group of *BLADE's Guide*.

Check all blades for a mark that is most often found on the tang of the largest blade. There may be marks on other blades of the knife. See Section I under "Some Clues That Help Date and Identify Knives."

Review the "shorthand" reference lists of highly collectible brands and marks, etc., outlined earlier in this story under "Valuing Pocketknives: The Basics." If the knife you are trying to value is on the lists, check the "Pocketknife Brand List" in Part 1 of Section II for more information. If the mark is not on the shorthand reference lists, carefully review the "Pocketknife Brand List" to identify the mark to determine the time period used, country of origin, etc. (Also, see Section I, "Some Clues That Help Date and Identify Knives.")

Consider the additional traits found in the "Other Factors Check List" in the following segment of this story and make adjustments in your overall description of your knife. (Also see "Grading the Condition of a Knife," "Some Clues That Help Date and Identify Knives," and "Handle Materials" in Section I.)

If your knife has a brand name or mark that is on any of the "shorthand" lists outlined earlier in this story, place your estimate at the mid-point on the value range for the appropriate pattern. Each trait in the "Other Factors Check List" (see following) that has a positive sign in brackets [+] will move your estimated value up one step. Each factor that has a negative sign in brackets [-] reduces the estimated value by one step. If the knife has a desirable handle material, move your estimate up one step toward the high end of the range; if not, move it down one step. When you have completed this process, should your estimate fall between listed values, take the mid-point between the two values. For example, for $125 and $75, the mid-point would be $100.

If your knife does not have a brand name or mark on any of the aforementioned "shorthand" lists, check the "Pocketknife Brand List" in Part 1 of Section II to determine its approximate date of use or manufacture. Begin your knife estimate at the point marked "LM" (Low/Medium) on the value range charts in Standard American Folding Knife Patterns. As outlined in the preceding step "F," for each positive factor, handle material, etc., move your estimate one step toward the high end of the range. For each less desirable feature, move your estimate toward the lower end of the range. Keep in mind that your knife may well have some considerable value if it meets most of the more collectible factors. On the other hand, it can be of much less value if it is a current or recent production, or a knife for which there is little or no collector demand. Again, if your estimate falls between two listed values, calculate the mid-point between the two.

MOST IMPORTANTLY, if the knife you are trying to value is not excellent to mint and unsharpened, then its value is reduced well below the values provided in the tables and on the knives illustrated herein. To arrive at a realistic estimate of value, you must be objective about the condition of your knife. Improperly cleaned, restored, re-pinned and re-bladed knives or handle cracks can all reduce the value and, in some cases, make the knife of no collector value.

Other Factors Check List

In the following, a positive sign in brackets [+] indicates that the factor or trait typically adds value to the knife, and a negative sign in brackets [-] typically reduces value:

1. Is the knife an "old" brand name but in current or recent production? (See Sections I and IV.) [-]
2. Are there special-purpose blades or tools in the knife? [+]
3. Is there a special grind on the main or other blades? For instance, is it or are they saber ground? [+] Is there a blade etch? [+}
4. Do any of the blades lock and is there anything unusual about the lock mechanism? [+]
5. Are the bolsters stamped or "fancy" in form or style? [+] Is the knife shell handled or does it have crimped-on bolsters? [-]
6. Overall size: The price of a knife generally increases with size—4 inches or more in the closed position—with certain exceptions. [+]
7. Handle materials that add value are generally the following (also, see Section I under "Handle Materials"): a) Mother-of-pearl, elephant ivory, tortoise shell, deer horn, stag, horn, bone, abalone, certain gemstone inlays [+], and; b) The presence and type of shield. [+]
8. Handle materials that generally do not add to the value of a knife (with some known exceptions) are: a) Old celluloid patterned or solid, Delrin, aluminum, plain brass, iron, stamped metal, hard rubber, "Bakelite," and wood (pressed or laminated). [-]
9. Handle materials that, contrary to items in the preceding #8, generally add to the value of the knife: Fancy celluloid such as waterfall, Christmas tree, candy stripe, goldstone, red-and-white/blue flag, and clear plastic with pictures/advertising. [+]
10. Overall condition of the knife, if not mint/excellent unsharpened: a) Very good condition, little wear, reduces value by half and more on lower-quality knives [-], and; b) Extensive use and cleaning, re-handling and re-blading can put a knife in the low-value category and, in many instances, reduce its worth to "parts" value only. [—]

To become really informed on knife values and collector trends, you need to attend knife shows and sales where there are many collectors/dealers. Do not go to

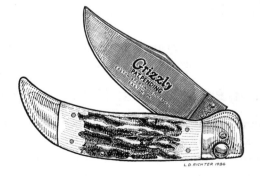

Ka-Bar Grizzly. (drawing by Larry Richter)

buy the first time, but rather to look and take note of the prices asked for knives that interest you. You will find that the range of prices from dealer to dealer on the better-known brands will not vary greatly. On the other hand, you will find that the prices on many other brands will vary considerably. The variation is largely dependent on collector interest. Prices will vary on knives by pattern and brand according to geographic region. What is "hot" in the U.S. Northeast may be very different from what is "hot" in Texas, California or Tennessee. You should keep notes on prices asked; this will be an important reference (base line) as you become more involved in knife collecting.

Other sources of current knife values are the many legitimate knife auctions held by knowledgeable auction houses. Attend an auction as an observer and keep a written record of the prices paid. If you cannot attend the auction, you can get a copy of the prices realized from the auctions for a small fee. The provision of the auction catalog with the prices paid of each lot is a very useful tool in valuing knives in the present time.

In recent years, Internet auction sales of all types of cutlery have become popular. In most Internet auction sales, there are severe limitations imposed on the buyer since all that they are able to see of the knife is a scanned photograph. While there are many good value opportunities to buy recent production knives through such e-business auctions, the buying of antique cutlery, and, in particular, high-dollar antique cutlery, can carry a real risk. Suffice it to say that most knowledgeable collectors will exercise great caution in their purchases and, as always, "buyer beware."

The most important thing to remember is that knife collecting should not be based on the premise that the value of each knife you collect will increase with time. There will always be knives that will make great gains in popularity and value, but there will be a great many more that will not. Collect for your personal enjoyment and the pleasure you get from owning cutlery which pleases you, as well as the fellowship provided by those you meet with the same interest.

Pictorial Key to American Folding Knives

Standard Jack Knife Shapes

EQUAL-END JACK

REGULAR JACK

SLIM JACK

CURVED REGULAR JACK

SLEEVEBOARD JACK

JUMBO JACK

CURVED JACK

SWAY-BACK JACK

CONGRESS JACK

CROWN JACK

SWELL-END JACK

JACK with EASY OPEN NOTCH

SWELL-CENTER JACK

BALLOON JACK

SWELL-CENTER REGULAR JACK

GUNSTOCK JACK

PREMIUM JACK

SERPENTINE JACK

WHARNCLIFFE JACK

SLIM SERPENTINE JACK

EUREKA JACK

CANOE JACK

SURVEYOR JACK

FISHTAIL JACK

FISH JACK

Double-End Jack Knives

FARMER'S JACK

MOOSE (TEXAS JACK)

BALLOON

JUMBO

SUNFISH

Named Jack Knife Patterns

HARNESS KNIFE

ELECTRICIAN'S KNIFE

PRUNING KNIFE

MAIZE KNIFE

COTTON SAMPLER

Named Jack Knife Patterns *(continued)*

BUDDING & GRAFTING KNIFE

BUDDING KNIFE

FLORIST'S KNIFE

MELON TESTER

SAILOR'S (ROPE) KNIFE

SAILOR'S (RIGGING) KNIFE

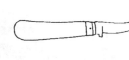

RASE KNIFE (TIMBER SCRIBER)

PHYSICIAN'S KNIFE

SPATULA KNIFE

CORN KNIFE

SPEY KNIFE

SPEY KNIFE

FLEAM

BOY'S KNIFE

BARLOW KNIFE

ENGLISH JACK

TICKLER

FISH KNIFE

MUSKRAT

DOUBLE-END TRAPPER

LIGHT TRAPPER

STANDARD TRAPPER

LARGE TRAPPER

FOLDING HUNTERS

FOLDING BOWIE

SWITCHBLADE JACK

SILVER FRUIT KNIFE

Advertising, Figural, Character, and Miniature Knives

ADVERTISING PEN KNIFE

FIGURAL JACK KNIFE

CHARACTER KNIFE

Standard Pen-Knife Shapes

SENATOR or EQUAL-END PEN KNIFE

SLEEVEBOARD PEN

OVAL PEN

CONGRESS KNIFE

GUNSTOCK PEN

CROWN PEN

MODERN CROWN PEN

SWELL-CENTER PEN

PREMIUM PEN

PREMIUM PEN

WHARNCLIFFE KNIFE

DOG-LEG PEN

SWELL-CENTER SERPENTINE

SWELL-CENTER CONGRESS

MECHANICAL PEN

WHITTLERS (large blade on two springs; each small blade on one spring)

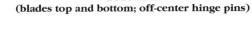

**LOBSTERS
(blades top and bottom; off-center hinge pins)**

SWITCHBLADE PEN

QUILL KNIFE

LETTER-OPENER KNIFE

OFFICE KNIFE

Multi-Blades

HORSEMAN'S KNIFE

SPORTSMAN'S KNIFE

CHAMPAGNE PATTERN

OPENER KNIFE

KNIFE-FORK-SPOON COMBO

SCOUT-UTILITY KNIFE

UTILITY KNIFE

CATTLE KNIFE

CATTLE KNIFE

CATTLE KNIFE

PREMIUM STOCK KNIFE

PREMIUM STOCK KNIFE

PLIERS KNIFE

TOOL KIT KNIFE

Jack Knives

"Jack knife" is a general term for the simplest form of folding knife. The standard jack knife is single-ended. Its blade is (or blades are) hinged at one end of the handle. There are also a few large, heavy-duty, double-ended jack-knife patterns. Double-ended jack knives have a large blade in each end and are covered in a separate chapter.

Small knives with blades pivoted at both ends are called "pen knives." Tiny, single-ended knives with just a short pen blade are called "quill knives." Though they are constructed like jack knives, quill knives were the original pen-sharpening knives, so they too are classed as pen knives. See the "Introduction to Standard American Folding Knife Patterns," Part 2, Section II, for more detailed definitions of jack knives and pen knives.

In this chapter, we describe the standard jack-knife handle shapes made or sold in the United States during approximately the last century-and-a-half. Each has a descriptive name; some have several names. In addition, a number of specific combinations of shape, size, blades, bolsters, handle material or fittings have distinctive "pattern" names.

Within each description of a shape, we mention the named patterns that are made in that shape. For full details and prices on these named patterns, you should refer to the appropriate segments in this section under "Jack Knives."

Jack knives made for other markets than the United States, and those made before the middle of the 19th century, are included in Part 3 of this section, "Foreign, Exotic, Primitive, and Historical Folding Knives." Figural jack knives shaped like shoes or other objects are included in Part 1 of Section II, "Advertising, Character, Figural, and Miniature Knives."

Decorated jack knives with silver blades and bolsters are called "fruit knives." They were intended to aid in the nibbling of fresh fruit, and were a popular keepsake gift through about the 1920s. All silver fruit knives, regardless of shape, are covered in "Silver Fruit Knives."

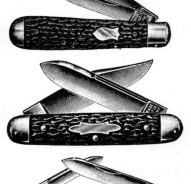

(From top) A regular jack, a double-ended jack and a pen knife.

Origins

The origin of the term "jack knife" has been lost in time. It may come from "jack" the sailor, "jack" the common workman, "jack" meaning *roughly made*, "jack" meaning *smaller*, or even from "jack" meaning *jacket*.

In Scotland, a large clasp knife was long called a "jacktoleg," but no one knows where that term originated either. Folklore has it that the word was a corruption of "Jacques de Liege," supposedly a Flemish cutler named Jacques in or from Liege. We suspect that this explanation has no more substance than do the modern legends about bowie knives.

Jack knives have been made in the widest variety of sizes of any pocketknives. American production jack knives are mainly between 2 1/2 - 5 1/2 inches long closed. This is the size range that concerns us here. Big folding bowie knives and dirks have their own segment in this section ("Folding Dirks and Folding Bowie Knives"). Large European clasp knives are included in Part 3 of this section, "Foreign, Exotic, Primitive, and Historical Folding Knives." Giant Showpiece and Exposition Knives are included under "Multi-Blade Knives" in this section. Tiny quill knives and watch fob knives are included under "Pen Knives" in this section.

Springs

At its simplest, a folding knife needs only a handle, a blade, and a pivot pin. It does not even need a backspring. Jack knives without backsprings are sometimes called "penny knives." Penny knives are included in Part 3 of this section under "Foreign, Exotic, Primitive, and Historical Folding Knives."

Bolsters

Because they have blades only at one end, jack knives do not require two sets of bolsters. Jacks with bolsters at the blade end only are called "barehead" or "single-bolster" jacks. Bolsters on the "head" end of a jack knife (the non-blade end) are called "cap bolsters." When referring to patterns that never have cap bolsters, such as the barlow, the adjective "barehead" is omitted.

Some knives without solid bolsters instead have wide, round, reinforcing washers at the ends of the hinge pins. Collectors call pins with such washers "bird's-eye rivets."

On double-ended knives, the bolsters at the master-blade end are the front bolsters. Those at the opposite end are the rear bolsters. Small knives with no bolsters at all are called "shadow knives."

A barehead jack knife.

Standard Jack Knife Shape Value Table

Base prices for JACK KNIVES of indicated shape with: handles 3 1/4 to 3 3/4 inches long; bolsters and cap bolsters; bone stag (jigged bone) or scored-bone handle scales; two blades: master blade plus pen. Excellent unsharpened condition.

NOTE: DOUBLE-END JACK KNIVES (including SUNFISH), and also the following named jack knife patterns all have separate segments in *BLADE's Guide*.

Most of these segments have their own value tables: Special Purpose Jack Knives, including HARNESS, ELECTRICIAN'S, PRUNING, MAIZE, COTTON SAMPLING, BUDDING, FLORIST'S, MELON TESTING, SAILOR'S, RASE, PHYSICIAN'S, SPATULA, CORN, SMOKER'S, BOX, and VETERINARY KNIVES; BOY'S KNIVES; BARLOW KNIVES; ENGLISH JACKS; TICKLERS (POWDER-HORNS) and FISH KNIVES; TRAPPERS and MUSKRATS; LARGE TRAPPERS; FOLDING HUNTERS (four types); FOLDING DIRKS and BOWIES; and SILVER FRUIT KNIVES.

VALUE RANGE

SHAPE	VERY HIGH (VH)	HIGH (H)	MEDIUM (M)	LOW / MEDIUM (LM)	LOW (L)
EQUAL-END	$360	$225	$125	$80	$40
SLIM EQUAL-END	200	100	60	50	40
REGULAR	250	175	90	45	15
SLIM (REGULAR)	275	175	75	45	15
CURVED REGULAR	275	175	100	50	25
SLEEVEBOARD	175	125	60	40	15
JUMBO	450	275	175	120	65
CURVED	250	150	100	50	20
SWAYBACK	225	150	80	55	30
CONGRESS	250	165	75	55	35
CROWN	225	150	85	60	40
SWELL-END (Tear Drop and E-O)	300	200	100	50	25
SWELL-CENTER (Small "Coke" Bottle)	375	250	125	85	45
BALLOON	185	125	75	50	25
SWELL-CENTER REGULAR	500	275	150	70	40
GUNSTOCK	500	375	225	150	90
PREMIUM	350	225	150	75	50
GUNSTOCK PREMIUM	275	195	90	60	35
HUMPBACK PREMIUM (Sowbelly)	450	300	190	150	125
SERPENTINE (also Peanut)	275	150	90	45	25
WHARNCLIFFE	275	200	125	90	60
SLIM SERPENTINE	250	175	100	50	30
EUREKA	350	250	160	115	75
CANOE or SURVEYOR	500	350	200	150	100
FISHTAIL	325	225	100	70	45
FISH	325	225	125	80	40

Many Pocket Knives are not drawn full size, but length of Haft (or Handle) is stated. To get a good idea of the actual size, place your old knife on the sketch of six-inch rule shown below.

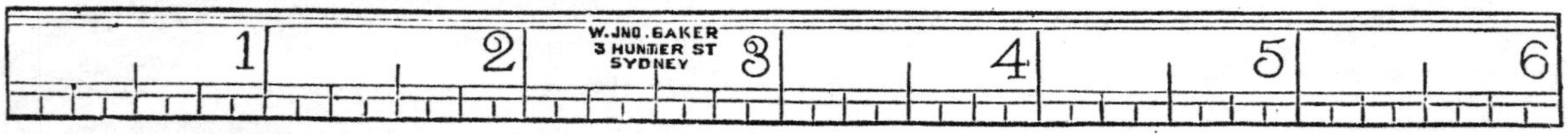

```
      1        2   W.JNO.BAKER  3      4      5      6
                   3 HUNTER ST
                   SYDNEY
```

NOTE: THE SIZE OF A FOLDING KNIFE IS ITS LENGTH CLOSED.

Examples of Typical Jack Patterns

(Napanoch and Cattaraugus)

"NAPANOCH" Wharncliffe Jack Knife

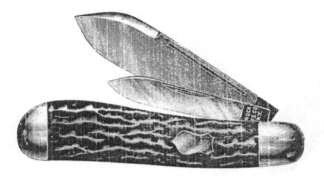

Actual Size　　　　　　　*3 1/2 inches long*

No. 2570—Patent Stag Handle. 1 Spear Blade. 1 strong Pen Blade. Nickel Silver Shield, Cap and Bolster. **$125**.

"NAPANOCH" Light Jack Knife

Actual Size　　　　　　　*3 1/4 inches long*

No. 28—Patent Stag Handle. Brass lined. 1 large Spear Blade. 1 strong Pen Blade. Nickel Silver Shield. Steel Bolster and Cap. **$150**.

Boker Tree Brand, 3", gunstock jack, bone, **$275**.

Cattaraugus, 3 3/4", two blades, brass lined, nickel-silver bolsters, full polish, fancy Fiberloid handle, **$90**.

"NAPANOCH" Mechanic's and Farmer's Knife

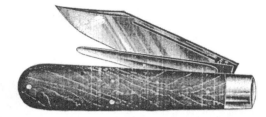

Actual Size　　　　　　　*3 1/2 inches long*

No. 206—Cocobolo handle, brass lined, 1 strong clip blade, 1 patent leather punch, steel bolster, **$100**.

The strongest leather punch on the market. Punch closes into the handle as perfectly as a blade. Very easy to sharpen. The punch will hold an edge a long time, and can be ground until worn out.

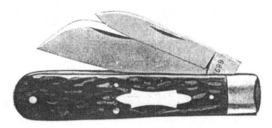

No. 21839—3 3/8", large sheepfoot and pen blade, brass lined, nickel-silver bolster, full polish, stag, shielded.

Cattaraugus, 3 3/8", two blades, brass lined, nickel-silver bolsters, full polish, ebony handle, shielded, **$100**.

Boker Tree Brand, 3 1/4", double-end jack (equal end), bone, **$250**.

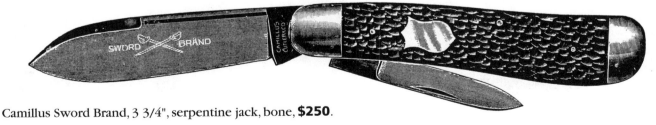

Camillus Sword Brand, 3 3/4", serpentine jack, bone, **$250**.

Equal-End Jacks

Boker Tree Brand, 3 5/8", bone handle, **$175**.

New York Knife Co., two large blades, bone stag, **$300**.

No. 6294 Case, 4 1/8", bone stag:
Tested XX, **$375**; XX, **$300**.

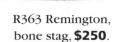

R363 Remington,
bone stag, **$250**.

Camillus Sword Brand, 4 1/8", ebony wood handle, **$200**.

Slim Equal-End Jacks

New York Knife Co., engraved aluminum, **$100**.

R1855 Remington,
3 3/8", plain celluloid,
$100.

326011 Robeson, barehead,
3", plain celluloid, **$75**.

Boker Tree Brand, bone handle, **$175**.

Regular Jacks

Boy's Knife

Barlow

No. K1108 Keen Kutter,
one blade, barehead,
3 3/8", bone stag, **$100**.

Electrician's Knife

Stabber Pattern

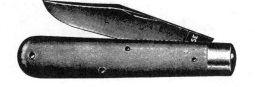

No. 3124 1/2 Case, one blade,
barehead, 3", plain celluloid: Tested XX,
$120; XX, **$75**.

English Jack

Remington, bone stag, **$200**.

Ulster Knife Co., saber ground blade, genuine stag, **$150**.

J. Russell, two large blades, barehead, 3 5/8", wood, **$175**.

No. 2203 3/4 Schrade Cut. Co.,
fancy bolsters 3 1/2", bone stag,
$145.

Marshall Wells, 3 1/2", bone handle, **$175**.

Slim Jacks

4 5/8" Melon Tester

3 1/2" Physician's Knife

Challenge (USA), 3 1/4", wood.

Hibbard Spencer & Bartlett, 3 1/2", coffin bolster cap, bone stag, **$275**.

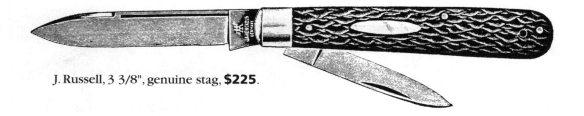

J. Russell, 3 3/8", genuine stag, **$225**.

Curved Regular or Clasp Jacks

Henry Sears & Son, saber-ground blade, 3 1/2", patterned celluloid, **$125**.

Case Tested 6207, 3 1/2", bone handle, **$250**.

Curved Regular Barlow. **$325**.

Ulster Knife Co. (for Bingham), wood, **$150**.

Sleeveboard and Jumbo Jacks

Keen Kutter, 3 3/8", patterned celluloid (green and black), **$125**.

Case Tested 6214 1/2, 3 3/8", bone, **$200**.

Winchester, 3 1/4", bone stag, **$160**.

Ulster Knife Co., bone stag.

Stiletto (P. H. & S.), 3 1/2", bone stag, **$175**.

Blades at Wide End

H. Boker (USA), 3", patterned celluloid, **$75**.

Jumbo Jacks

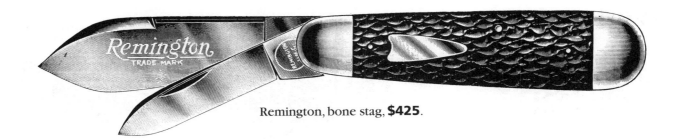

Remington, bone stag, **$425**.

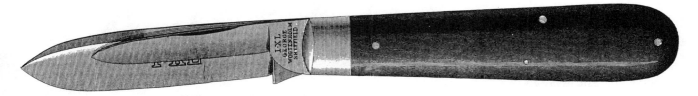

I*XL George Wostenholm, 4", ebony, barehead, **$250**.

Curved Jacks and Congress Jacks

Joseph Rodgers, 3 3/8", 2-blade curved jack, stag, **$275**.

Pruning Knife

Ulster Knife Co., two large blades, barehead, wood, **$150**.

Keen Kutter, one saber-ground blade, barehead, 3 1/4", wood, **$75**.

J. Russell, barehead, 3 5/8", buffalo horn, **$300**.

No. 2394 1/2B Schrade Cut. Co., barehead, 3 9/16", plain celluloid, **$75**.

Sway-Back Jacks

Joseph Rodgers, one blade,
barehead, 3 1/2", wood, **$200**.

Keen Kutter, 3 1/2", wood, **$175**.

Congress Jacks

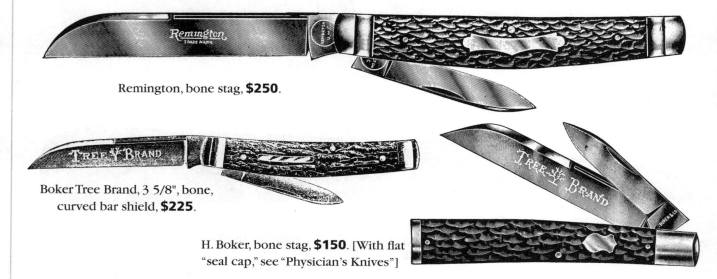

Remington, bone stag, **$250**.

Boker Tree Brand, 3 5/8", bone,
curved bar shield, **$225**.

H. Boker, bone stag, **$150**. [With flat
"seal cap," see "Physician's Knives"]

Crown Jacks

L.F.&C., fancy bolsters, 3 7/8",
bone stag, **$200**.

Crown Pen Knife

H. Boker, bone stag, **$200**.

Schrade Cut. Co.,
3 1/2", bone, **$200**.

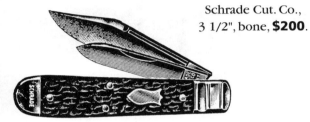

Keen Kutter, fancy bolsters, smooth white bone,
$225.

Swell-End Jacks

Winchester, patterned
celluloid, **$175**.

TWO BLADES, 1 Large Clip and
1 Pen; Large Blade Full Polished;
Nickel Silver Bolster, Cap, Shield
and Lining.

Per Dozen
No. 2098—3⅜ IN.; GREEN CELLU-
LOID HANDLE $18.70

OUR NEW ''PROD-KNIFE''
WITH STIFF HOLLOW SPOON-BIT BLADE
A PERFECT TOOL FOR BORING HOLES IN WOOD, LEATHER, ETC.

Ulster harness or teamster's knife, punch blade, barehead, wood, **$125**.

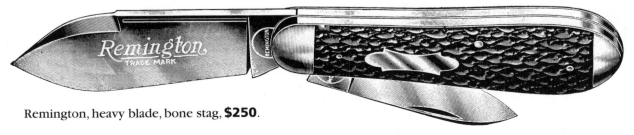

Remington, heavy blade, bone stag, **$250**.

Easy-Openers

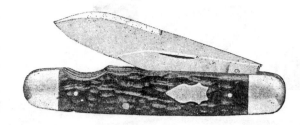

Cattaraugus, 3 3/8", E.O. worm-groove bone, **$200**.

H. Boker, gunstock E-O, 2 7/8", bone stag, **$175-$200**.

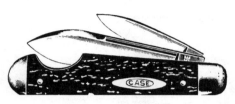

No. 6228EO Case Tested XX, swell-end E-O, 3 1/2", bone stag, **$250**.

No. 2423EO Schrade Cut. Co., slim equal-end E-O, 3 1/8", bone stag, **$90**.

KA-BAR 6228 EO, 3 7/8", bone, **$225**.

Swell-Center Jacks

Ulster (for Bingham), stabber jack (saber ground), barehead, wood, **$175**.

3-1/2" Stabber Pattern

Case Tested 32025 1/2, 3", composition, **$300**.

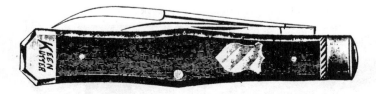

Gun Stock Jack. Keen Kutter "gunstock," fancy bolsters, ebony, **$275**.

Schrade Cut. Co., fancy bolsters and seal cap, 4", bone stag, **$350**.

Balloon Jacks

Keen Kutter, wood, **$100**.

H. Boker, 2 7/8", bone stag, **$125**.

Marshall Wells (NYK), 3 1/2", bone, **$200**.

Swell-Center Regular Jacks

Maher & Grosh, 4", w/etch, bone, **$275**.

No. 6211 Case Tested XX.
4 3/8", bone stag, **$695**.

Joseph Rodgers, saber-ground blade, barehead, 4 1/2", genuine stag, **$475**.

Gunstock Jacks

Budding Knife

I*XL-G. Wostenholm, 3 5/8", bone, **$400**.

Premium Jacks

(Pre-1910 equal-end) Ulster Knife Co., bone stag, **$175**.

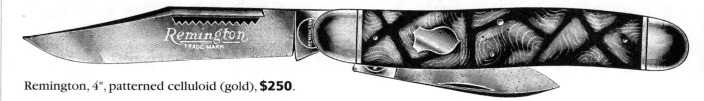

Remington, 4", patterned celluloid (gold), **$250**.

Case Tested 6244,
3 1/4", bone,
$275.

Case Tested 62087,
3 3/8", bone,
$275-$300.

Serpentine Jacks

J. Russell, 3 1/2", wood, **$250**.

"PEANUTS"

Ulster Knife Co., fancy
bolsters, 3 1/8", smooth
white bone, **$200**.

No. 62028 Case, 3 1/2", bone stag:
Tested XX, **$250**; XX, **$175**.

No. 8220 Case
Tested XX, 2 7/8",
pearl, **$350**.

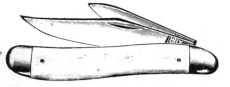

I*XL G. Wostenholm,
3 1/2", stag, **$275**.

Remington, 3", bone stag, **$225**.

J. Primble India Steel Works (Belknap
Hdw.), 2 13/16", fancy celluloid
(candy stripe), **$200**.

Wharncliffe Jacks

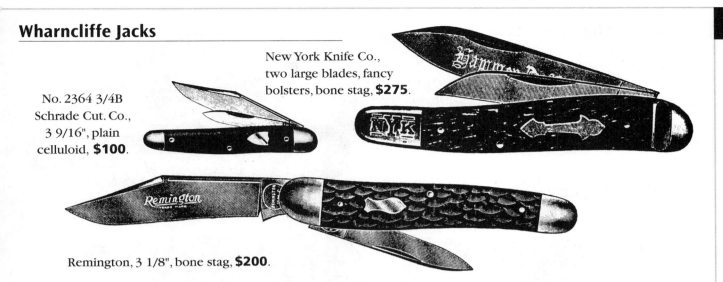

No. 2364 3/4B
Schrade Cut. Co.,
3 9/16", plain
celluloid, **$100**.

New York Knife Co.,
two large blades, fancy
bolsters, bone stag, **$275**.

Remington, 3 1/8", bone stag, **$200**.

Slim Serpentine or Crooked Jacks

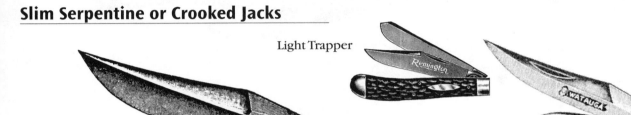

Light Trapper

WATAUGA (H.G. Lipscomb Co.),
4", 2 blades, bone, **$225**.

Napanoch, saber-ground blade, barehead, 3 13/16", bone stag, **$275**.

Ulster Knife Co., saber-ground blade, barehead, 3 7/8", bone stag, **$200**.

Eureka Jacks

Hibbard Spencer & Bartlett
(NYK), 3 5/8", 2 blades,
bone, fancy bolsters, **$300**.

New York Knife Co., fancy bolsters, bone stag, **$350**.

Canoes and Surveyor Jacks

H. Boker, canoe,
fancy bolsters, bone
stag, **$300**.

Surveyor Jack

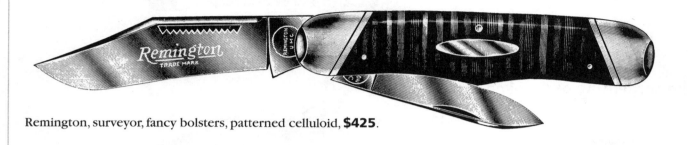

Remington, surveyor, fancy bolsters, patterned celluloid, **$425**.

Fishtail and Fish Jacks

No. 61051, Case Tested XX,
one blade, fancy bolsters, 3 7/8",
bone stag, **$400**.

John Primble (Belknap Hdw.),
3 7/8", bone, **$275**.

Fish Jacks

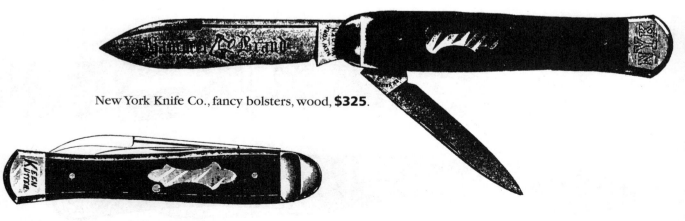

New York Knife Co., fancy bolsters, wood, **$325**.

Keen Kutter, fancy bolsters, wood, **$275**.

Double-End Jack Knives

Ordinarily, jack knives have all their blades in one end, while knives with blades in both ends are either pen knives or multi-blades. However, certain patterns of folders with blades in both ends are too large and robust to be called pen knives, while they are too simple, with only two blades, to be called multi-blades. These are the double-end jack knives.

One unusual type is the double-end "melon tester." The long, thin knife with a slim spear blade and a pen blade is covered under "Special Purpose Jack Knives." So is the smaller double-end "florist's knife."

VALUE RANGE

SHAPE	VERY HIGH (VH)	HIGH (H)	MEDIUM (M)	LOW / MEDIUM (LM)	LOW (L)
SUNFISH (see table under *Sunfish*)					
FARMER'S JACK	$325	$250	$125	$100	$75
TEXAS JACK (Moose)	350	275	150	125	100
DOUBLE-END PREMIUM	250	175	100	70	45
EQUAL-END BULL-HEAD	300	225	120	85	50
JUMBO and BALLOON	475	350	200	175	150
EUREKA and SURVEYOR	400	325	175	140	100
CANOE	375	275	175	130	90

Farmer's Jacks

An even more unusual type of double-end jack is the Wharncliffe-shaped "farmer's jack." Its two blades are a pruning blade in the wide end and a spey or budding blade in the narrow end.

Base values for DOUBLE-END JACK KNIVES of the indicated shapes, from 3 9/16 to 4 3/8 inches long, two large blades, full bolsters and bone-stag handles. Excellent, unsharpened condition.

NOTE: For MELON TESTERS and FLORIST'S KNIVES see the segment on "Special Purpose Jack Knives"; for MUSKRATS and DOUBLE-END TRAPPERS see the segment on "Trappers, Muskrats and Large Trappers."

Schrade Cutlery Co., **$150**.

Schrade Cut. Co., farmer's, 4 1/8", bone stag, **$200**.

H. Boker, farmer's, 3 3/4", bone stag, **$125**.

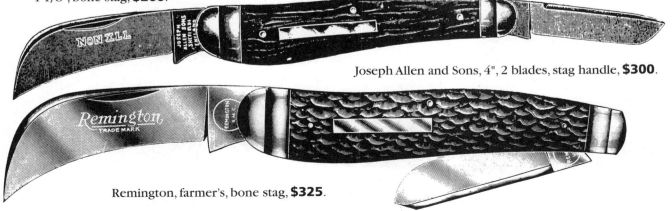

Joseph Allen and Sons, 4", 2 blades, stag handle, **$300**.

Remington, farmer's, bone stag, **$325**.

Stock-Knife-Type Double-End Jacks

With the exception of the sunfish, the farmer's jack and the double-end melon tester, all double-end jack knives are built on either cattle-knife- or premium-stock-knife-handle frames (see "Multi-Blade Knives"). In the early years of the 20th century, the names "cattle knife" and "stock knife" were sometimes used for two-bladed knives. Since the 1920s, however, the names have been used only for knives with three or more blades. Larger two-bladed versions are considered jack knives, no matter if they are single-ended or double-ended. Smaller, two-bladed, double-ended versions that are 3 1/2 inches long or less and come with a pen second blade are pen knives.

The single-ended jack that is based on the premium stock knife is called the "premium jack." The premium jack has several double-ended counterparts. The most impressive of these is the TEXAS JACK or MOOSE.

Texas jacks are big, usually at least 3 7/8 inches long. Their size may account for their "Texas" name, while the large blade out each end may have reminded someone of a bull moose's giant antlers.

The master blade of a Texas Jack is always a wide clip. The second blade is a spear or a long, wide spey.

Slender, double-end premium jacks with either a slender clip and a long spey or else two clip blades are considered double-end trappers (see "Trappers, Muskrats and Large Trappers").

DOUBLE-END PREMIUM JACKS are serpentine or, rarely, sleeveboard knives with a clip blade in one end and a small spey or a pen in the other. Small versions with a pen blade are pen knives.

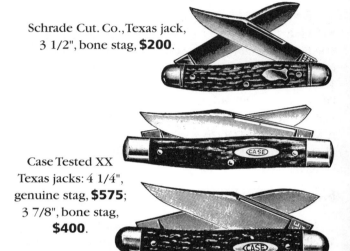

Schrade Cut. Co., Texas jack, 3 1/2", bone stag, **$200**.

Case Tested XX Texas jacks: 4 1/4", genuine stag, **$575**; 3 7/8", bone stag, **$400**.

Winchester double-end premium jacks, bone stag, 4", **$350**; 3 1/4", **$225**.

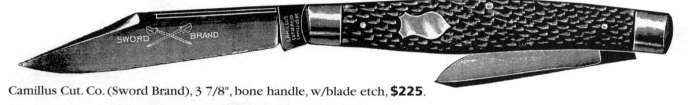

Camillus Cut. Co. (Sword Brand), 3 7/8", bone handle, w/blade etch, **$225**.

Remington double-end premium jack, patterned celluloid: 4" (brown agate), **$300**.

H. Boker, double-end premium jack, bone stag, **$165**.

J. Primble India Steel Works (Belknap Hardware), sowbelly Texas jack, 3 7/8", bone stag, **$450**.

Cattle-Knife-Type Double-End Jacks

The BULL-HEAD or equal-end double-end jack knife is a two-blade version of the standard cattle knife. It has spear or clip master blades. The second blade may be a spey, a sheepfoot, a clip, a punch or a pen. In 1919, Remington used the term GENERAL SERVICE KNIVES for its 3 5/8-inch double-end, equal-end jack knives that had pen second blades.

The rarest double-end jack knives are the ones built on fancy cattle-knife-handle dies. They are the large sleeveboard or JUMBO; the swell-center or BALLOON; the swell-center serpentine or EUREKA; the CANOE; and the SURVEYOR or swell-center canoe. The last of most of them were made in the 1920s and 1930s. Western States apparently had made double-end jacks in the surveyor pattern by special order only. The pattern actually may have been a Utica contract knife.

Camillus Cut. Co. (Sword Brand), 3 5/8", jumbo jack (double end), ebony handle, **$375**.

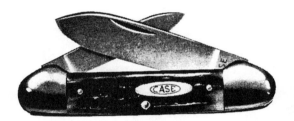

Case XX 52131, stag handle, **$425**.

Winchester balloons, bone stag; 3 1/2", **$295**; 3 7/8", **$400**.

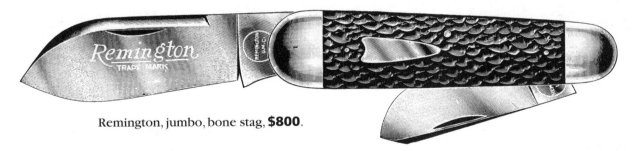

Remington, jumbo, bone stag, **$800**.

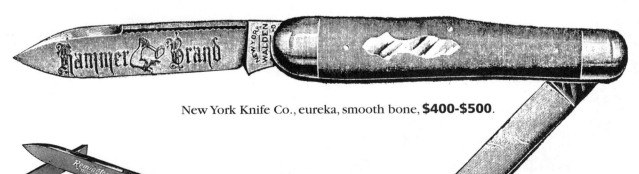

New York Knife Co., eureka, smooth bone, **$400-$500**.

Remington, bull-head (oval), 4 1/2", bone stag, **$650**.

Sunfish

Odd as they may seem, the farmer's jack and the eureka look ordinary compared to the "sunfish" (also called "elephant's toe-nail," "Old English rope knife," and "vest-pocket axe"). Sunfish are massive equal-ends (or rarely swell-centers) at least 3 3/4 inches long, and usually longer. They are much wider than Remington's "general service knives."

The master blade of a sunfish is a spear point nearly the size of a tea plate. The second blade is a "pen" blade that is bigger than many spear blades.

It seems to be a mid-to-late-19th-century American pattern, perhaps with a Scandinavian influence. Sunfish were popular in the northern Midwest and the South. They were favored by framing carpenters and by men who strung trolley and telegraph lines. Sunfish are still made, and quite a few pre-1930 pieces are available.

Most sunfish have bone-stag handles. Mother-of-pearl, genuine stag, tortoise shell, wood and celluloid are not common. Horn, ivory and smooth-bone handle scales were used on sunfish many years ago. Case's recent elephant toenails have laminated wood handles, though there are several modern sunfish with bone handles, both in sets and as commemorative pieces.

Base values for SUNFISH up to 4 1/2 inches long, with bone-stag, smooth-bone or horn handle scales. Excellent, unsharpened condition.

Sunfish are very popular among collectors. Any early example in good condition commands a high price. Mother-of-pearl-handled examples, such as by Case Bros. (made also on contract for Marble's; see "American Hunting Knives"), are particularly valuable. *Beware of counterfeits!*

VALUE RANGE

VH	H	M	LM	L
$2,000	$1,500	$750	$550	$350

Napanoch, bone stag, **$1,200**.

OLD ENGLISH ROPE KNIFE USED
ON SAILING VESSELS
No. 6250—Length closed 4 3/8".
Case Tested XX, bone stag, **$1,500**.

Marble Safety Axe Co.,
3 7/8", pearl, **$2,200**.

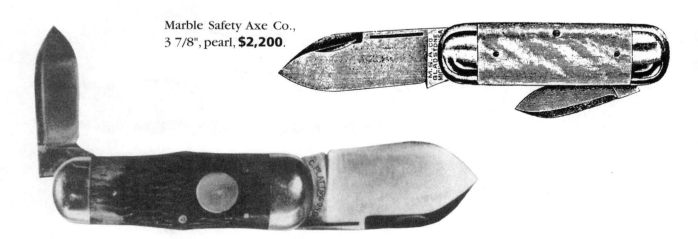

C. Platts' Sons, swell-center, 4 3/8", bone stag, **$1,500**. (courtesy Harvey Platts)

Named Jack Knife Patterns

Special Purpose Jack Knives

The preceding chapters describe the various shapes or "handle dies" of standard American jack knives. The chapters in this section describe special jack-knife *patterns* that are built on some of these handle dies. Most of the patterns have special styles of blades designed for specific tasks. The patterns are:

HARNESS KNIVES
ELECTRICIAN'S and **JANITOR'S KNIVES**
PRUNING KNIVES
MAIZE KNIVES
COTTON SAMPLERS
BUDDING and **GRAFTING KNIVES**
FLORIST'S KNIVES
MELON TESTERS
SAILOR'S ROPE KNIVES
RASE KNIVES or **TIMBER SCRIBERS**
PHYSICIAN'S KNIVES
SPATULA or **PALETTE KNIVES**

CORN KNIVES
BOX KNIVES and **SMOKER'S JACK KNIVES**
SPECIAL SPEY and **VETERINARY KNIVES,** including **FLEAMS**

The chapters on special-purpose jack knives are followed by the rest of the standard American-named jack-knife patterns. They are:

BOY'S KNIVES
BARLOW KNIVES
ENGLISH JACKS
TICKLERS and **FISH KNIVES**
TRAPPERS, MUSKRATS and **LARGE TRAPPERS**
FOLDING HUNTERS and **AMERICAN CLASP KNIVES**
FOLDING DIRKS and FOLDING BOWIE KNIVES
SWITCHBLADE JACK KNIVES

Following them is the chapter **SILVER FRUIT KNIVES**, which bridges the gap between jack knives and pen knives.

Harness Knives

In the 19th century, a jack knife with a punch blade was often called a "harness knife" or a "teamster's knife."

In the days when a leather harness connected your wheels to your horsepower, a broken strap could be anything from an inconvenience to a disaster. For quick field repairs, a leather punch was essential. The harness knife is the simplest and least expensive pocketknife that includes a punch.

- The value of a harness knife is 25 percent greater than the value of an identical jack knife with an ordinary pen blade as the second blade. Estimate the value from the "Value Table for Standard Jack Knife Shapes" in the chapter on "Jack Knives," moving up one "step" for the punch blade.

Schrade Cutlery Co., 3 1/2", ebony handle, **$195**.

H. Boker, slim equal-end, 3 1/8", bone stag, **$125**.

Press Button (G. Schrade), bone handle, 3 5/8", **$225**.

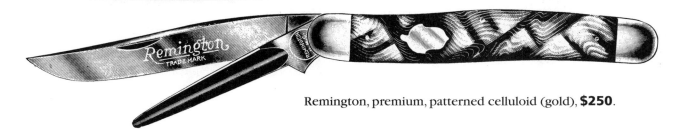

Remington, premium, patterned celluloid (gold), **$250**.

Electrician's Knives

The electrician's knife is identified by the combination of a spear master blade with a locking screwdriver-wirestripper blade. The design is based on the military specification of "TL-29." The knives are often called TL-29s, and government-issue examples usually have "TL-29" marked on them. "TL" means "Tool for Linemen."

The original TL-29 specification of World War I called for a 3 5/8-inch sleeveboard handle with wooden scales. The screwdriver on the first version has oval cutouts on both sides. Its lock is internal and is released by depressing the folded main blade. This version is usually called the Signal Corps knife. According to Blade Magazine Cutlery Hall-Of-Famer© M.H. Cole, over a quarter million of them were made for the government in 1917-1918. They usually have military markings on the shield. Many more were made for commercial sale.

The revised TL-29 specification of the 1930s called for a 3 3/4-inch regular jack, usually with a bail. Its screwdriver has a single cutout on the back. Its lock was patented by Watson and Chadwick for Cattaraugus on July 3, 1906, and is the forerunner of today's Michael Walker LinerLock™. The scales are wood, black plastic or, rarely, jigged bone.

Electrician's knives have long been made for civilian as well as military use. A major supplier was Mathias Klein & Sons electrical supply in Chicago. Knives marked M. KLEIN were made for it.

A few variations on the two TL-29 patterns have been offered for sale. Signal-Corps-size knives with just a screwdriver-wirestripper blade were made in the 1920s. These "Radio Knives" have a back lock.

Another Signal-Corps-size knife has a blade in each end. Its master blade is sometimes a sheepfoot.

Some firms offered full-sized electrician's knives with a pruner master blade. The hooked blade is used for stripping insulation from heavy cable.

Base values of ELECTRICIAN'S KNIVES with wood handles. Excellent, unsharpened condition.

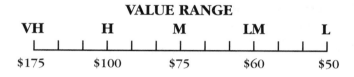

VALUE RANGE

VH	H	M	LM	L
$175	$100	$75	$60	$50

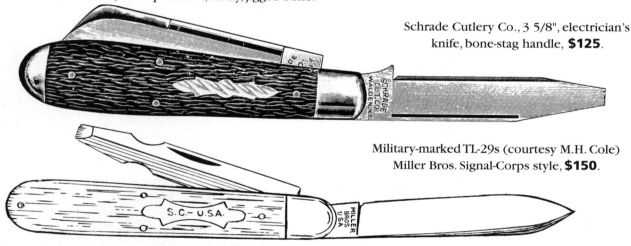

Schrade Cutlery Co., 3 5/8", electrician's knife, bone-stag handle, **$125**.

Military-marked TL-29s (courtesy M.H. Cole) Miller Bros. Signal-Corps style, **$150**.

Janitor's Knives

The belt-and-suspenders man can have both the spear-point *and* the hawkbill in his electrician's knife, along with the screwdriver blade. W.R. Case & Sons called such three-blade models "janitor's knives."

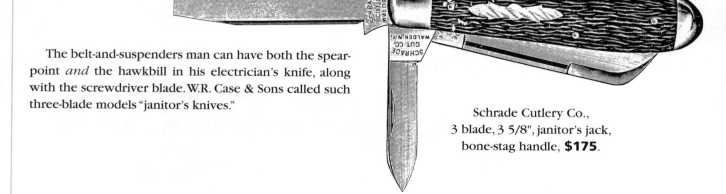

Schrade Cutlery Co., 3 blade, 3 5/8", janitor's jack, bone-stag handle, **$175**.

Pruning Knives

Ordinarily, the presence of a hawkbill blade indicates that a knife is a pruning model. Besides being used to strip electrical insulation, pruning knives are used for cutting such materials as sheet rock, carpet, linoleum, roofing paper and string.

In earlier times, pruning knives actually were used for pruning shrubs and fruit trees. Some still use them for pruning today.

Pruning knives are relatively large curved jacks. There is some variation of shape and size among them. The most obvious variation is that some have rounded head ends—the non-blade ends—while others have flat heads, usually protected by metal "seal caps."

Most pruning knives are single bladed. A few have a second blade, usually a pruning saw. The farmer's jack (see "Double-End Jack Knives" in the chapter on "Jack Knives") has a pruning blade in one end and a spey or budding blade in the other.

Circa 1900, Wostenholm made a changeable blade pruner that came with a hawkbill blade and a saw, and also sheepfoot and spey blades for grafting. When latched into place, any of the three knife blades—though not the saw—folded, just as in an ordinary jack knife. The end cap was the latch lever.

Hardwoods were the most common handle materials for pruners. Stag also was favored because its natural curves and rough texture make for a firm grip. Cow horn and bone stag also were used, all of which help make pruning knives an attractive and interesting collectible.

Base values of PRUNING KNIVES with one hawkbill blade, rounded head end, bone-stag-handle scales and front bolsters. Excellent, unsharpened condition.

VALUE RANGE

VH	H	M	LM	L
$200	$150	$100	$75	$50

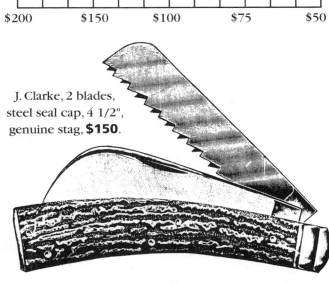

J. Clarke, 2 blades, steel seal cap, 4 1/2", genuine stag, **$150**.

Geo. Wostenholm (1899 Edmonds patent) changeable blade, genuine stag, **$675**.
(Photo courtesy Allen Dellenbaugh)

G. Wostenholm, 3 3/4", 2 blade, Wharncliffe pruner, **$225**.

J. Russell, 4 1/4", genuine stag, **$275-$300**.

Joseph Rodgers, 4", single-blade pruner, stag handle, **$200**.

Maize Knives

A close cousin of the pruning knife is the maize or corn-topping knife, originally used for harvesting grain sorghum. Its curved jack handle is similar to some pruner handles, but its short, rounded blade is distinctive. Do not mistake a worn-out or broken pruner for a maize knife.

Values for MAIZE KNIVES in excellent, unsharpened condition.

VALUE RANGE

VH	H	M	LM	L
$275	$240	$180	$120	$60

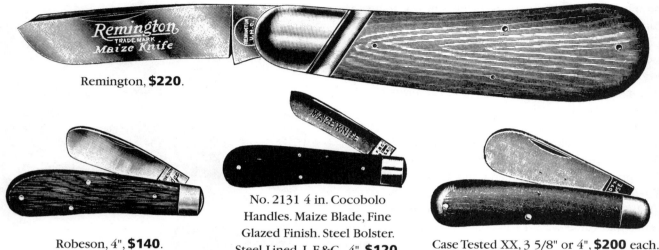

Remington, **$220**.

Robeson, 4", **$140**.

No. 2131 4 in. Cocobolo Handles. Maize Blade, Fine Glazed Finish. Steel Bolster. Steel Lined. L.F.&C., 4", **$120**.

Case Tested XX, 3 5/8" or 4", **$200** each.

Cotton Samplers

Another cousin of the pruning knife is the cotton-sampling knife. Cotton buyers used cotton samplers to cut samples out of bales. Maher & Grosh of Ohio advertised cotton samplers a century ago as folding skinning knives.

Like maize knives, cotton samplers have curved jack handles, usually with wooden handle scales. Their blades, however, are distinctive. The straight section next to the tang is blunt.

A few cotton samplers, instead of having the rounded blade, have a broad square-point blade. It is heavy and even wider than a rope-knife blade, and also may be etched COTTON SAMPLER or COTTON KNIFE.

There is more collector interest in cotton samplers than pruners or maize knives. They are attractive knives and rare in excellent condition.

Values for COTTON SAMPLERS in excellent, unsharpened condition.

VALUE RANGE

VH	H	M	LM	L
$500	$350	$275	$200	$125

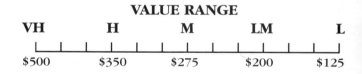

Joseph Rodgers, 4 5/8", cotton sampler w/bail, stag handle, **$400**.

J. Russell, 4 1/4", **$475**.

Remington, **$550**.

Budding and Grafting Knives

While pruning knives moved to the city and found new jobs, budding and grafting knives stayed down on the farm. Perhaps this is why budding and grafting knives seldom get recognition from collectors.

Grafting, the more general term, is the attachment of living *scions*, or cuttings, from one species or variety of tree, shrub or vine to the limbs or stump of another species or variety. The stock or host variety may have sturdy branches or hardy and disease-resistant roots, while the grafted variety produces the best fruit or blossoms. Often, the grafted variety is a sterile hybrid that produces no seed and can be propagated only by grafting. Sometimes, branches are added to a tree simply to increase its production.

Budding is a specialized type of grafting used on roses and young fruit trees. Individual buds of the desired variety are inserted under the bark of the stock plant.

Patch budding is a technique used on pecan trees. A precise square of bark with a bud in the center is cut from one tree and placed in an identical square hole in the bark of the stock tree. To cut the precise squares, a two-bladed *pecan budding knife* is used. It has a thick spacer separating the blades.

The blade of a budding and grafting knife, which is often beveled just on one side, cuts off the scions and cuts the incisions in the stock. The spud—or opener or shaft—is used to open the incisions.

On some knives, the spud, which can be fixed or folding, projects from the head ends. Such a spud is made of ivory, bone or a non-tarnishing metal. It even can be an extension of the handle. On other knives, the spud is a projection on the back of the blade.

Several handle dies were used on budding and grafting knives. The most common is an equal-end or sleeveboard that has a single blade with a spud on its back. Small swell-end and regular jacks were made both with just a single "budding" or spey-type blade, and also with a folding spud in the opposite end. Small gunstock budding knives have a little clip blade at the narrow end and a fixed spud at the wide end. Budding knives that have the spud integral with the handle have two or three distinctive shapes.

There is some collector interest in budding and grafting knives. Since they are uncommon, their values are increasing.

Base values for BUDDING and GRAFTING KNIVES with smooth bone or horn handle scales. Excellent, unsharpened condition.

VALUE RANGE

SHAPE	(VH)	(H)	(M)	(LM)	(L)
EQUAL-END or SLEEVEBOARD	$200	$100	$80	$60	$40
SWELL-END or REGULAR	150	90	60	35	25
Ditto with spud	175	125	75	45	30
GUNSTOCK	200	150	80	50	40
INTEGRAL SPUD	175	125	75	45	30
PECAN (2 blades)	450	300	175	125	100

Case Tested XX, pecan budder, 3 3/8", walnut, **$375-$400**.

H. Boker, gunstock, plain composition, **$125**.

G. Wostenholm, 4", ivory spud budding knife, **$175**.

Schrade Cut. Co., sleeveboard, blade with spud, 4", plain celluloid, **$75**.

Remingtons, plain celluloid, integral spud, 3 3/4", **$125**; swell-end with spud, **$150**.

Joseph Rodgers, 4 7/8", 2-blade budding knife, horn handle w/ivory spud, **$225**.

Florist's Knives

The inscription "Say it with Flowers" on the white-composition handles most readily identifies a florist's knife. There are two types. Most are slim serpentine jacks with a single, short sheepfoot or "budding" (spey-type) blade. Usually they have bird's-eye rivets and a bail.

Double-end florist's knives are equal-ends, usually with a sheepfoot in one end and a "budding" blade in the other. Replacing one of the blades with a V-shaped weed digger turns the knife into a "greenskeeper's knife."

Base prices of FLORIST'S KNIVES with one or two blades, white composition handles, and bird's-eye rivets. Excellent, unsharpened condition.

VALUE RANGE

VH	H	M	LM	L
$175	$125	$90	$75	$60

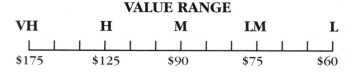

Remington, 2 blades, bolsters, **$175**.

Schrade Cut. Co., double-end, weeding blade, bolsters, 4", **$165**.

G. Wostenholm, 4 1/4", florist's knife, ivory handle, **$175**.

Melon Testers

A melon tester is a long, slim regular jack with a spear master blade. Other names for the pattern include *citrus knife* and *sausage knife*. The melon tester is a relatively modern pattern, first offered in the 1930s, though long, lightweight jack knives were popular in Europe in the 18th century.

Most melon testers have just the one spear blade. Some also have a long pen blade. A few recent melon testers have a serrated master blade, which are even more collectible.

Double-end melon testers also have been made. The unusual knives may come in an odd shape, such as an elongated swell-center serpentine.

Melon testers are much less valuable than other long folding knives, though a number of collectors like them. Those with a blade etch are particularly desirable.

Base values of MELON TESTERS with composition handles and one or two blades. Excellent, unsharpened condition.

VALUE RANGE

VH	H	M	LM	L
$225	$175	$100	$75	$50

Shapleigh Hdw., 5 3/4", ivory celluloid, **$90**; 4 1/2", double-end, pearl celluloid, **$125**.

ESPECIALLY MADE
FOR CUTTING FRUIT
Stainless Steel Spring and Blades
Suitable for Citrus Fruits; also Many
Other Uses; Brass Lining;
Nickel Silver Bolsters; Length
Closed 4 1/2 inches; Length of
Large Blade 3 11/16 inches;
Large Spear and Small Pen Blades;
Full Polished and Etched.

Case Tested XX, double-end, 4 1/4", bone stag, **$200**.

(Contemporary) Schrade, 4 11/16", white composition, **$40** list.

SAUSAGE SAMPLING KNIFE
Suitable for the Packing House Trade; used as Sausage Sampling Knife. Also Many Other Uses. Brass Lining, Length Closed 5 3/4 inches; Length of Blade 4 7/8 inches; Large Spear Blade; Glazed and Etched.

Case U.S.A., 5 1/2", serrated melon tester, white composition handle, **$175**.

Sailor's Rope Knives
(including U.S. and Foreign Military)

The ordinary sailor's knife is a curved jack or a curved regular jack with a single sheepfoot or flaring "rope" blade. The special straight-edged blades are used to cut rope cleanly by laying the rope on a wooden surface and hammering the blade through it with a belaying pin. Between this rough use and the hazards of salt water, it is not surprising that old sailor's knives in good condition are rare.

Ordinary sailor's knives are fairly large, at least 4 inches long closed. They usually have a bail so they can be secured from falling overboard.

Smaller curved jacks with a stout sheepfoot blade are called *New England Whalers*. They may have gotten their name from being a handy size for working with light harpoon line. New England Whalers may be drilled for a lanyard, but they have no bail.

There are also regular, curved regular and swell-end jacks, usually with a single clip blade, that were sold and used as rope knives. Values of these and of New England Whalers should be estimated from the "Value Chart for Standard Jack Knife Shapes" in the "Jack Knives" chapter.

Since the late 19th century, some sailor's knives have been made with an auxiliary folding marlinespike. The marlinespike is used in splicing and fancy knot work.

Some English knives have the marlinespike beside the blade. However, the more usual place is on the back. If the marlinespike locks open—often the bail is the lock release—the knife is a "rigger's knife." If it does not lock, the knife is a "yachtsman's knife." Some recent yachtsman's knives also have a shackle key.

Base values for SAILOR'S KNIVES. Excellent, unsharpened condition

*All knives with military markings have added value.

ORDINARY with Wood or Composition Handles

VALUE RANGE

VH	H	M	LM	L
$375	$250	$125	$100	$75

RIGGING or YACHTSMAN'S with Composition Handles

VALUE RANGE

VH	H	M	LM	L
$250	$175	$100	$80	$65

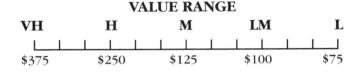

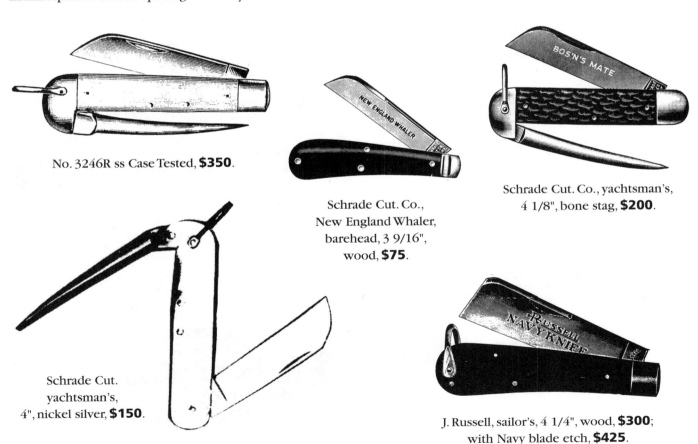

No. 3246R ss Case Tested, **$350**.

Schrade Cut. Co., New England Whaler, barehead, 3 9/16", wood, **$75**.

Schrade Cut. Co., yachtsman's, 4 1/8", bone stag, **$200**.

Schrade Cut. yachtsman's, 4", nickel silver, **$150**.

J. Russell, sailor's, 4 1/4", wood, **$300**; with Navy blade etch, **$425**.

Sailor's Knives *(continued)*

Below are brands or marks on various forms of sailor's knives:

New York Knife Co. 6027 (see image at bottom of page): **$175**.

Schrade Cut. Co. 2353 Navy (second from bottom, right): **$150**.

W.R. Case & Sons 6202EO: **$200**.

Napanoch Knife Co.: **$250**.

IKCO (Imperial), rough black handles: **$75**.

Cattaraugus Cutlery Co.: **$175**.

Union Cutlery Co.: **$150**.

Empire Knife Co.: **$175**.

Challenge Cutlery Co.: **$100**.

Miller Bros. Cut. Co.: **$150**.

Camillus Cutlery Co.: **$100**.

Valley Forge Cutlery Co.: **$125**.

Schatt & Morgan Cutlery Co.: **$175**.

Robeson Cutlery Co.: **$175**.

Ministry of Defence Approved List Supplier. Approval No. 05/29

Recent British military knives: 1P Army: **$20**; 2P Army: **$30**; 3P Army: **$50**; 2P Navy: **$40**; 35090 (life raft): **$40**; Yacht: **$45**. (Illustration courtesy Ron Braehler) For World War II Australian versions, see the part on *"Foreign, Exotic, Primitive and Historical Folding Knives."*

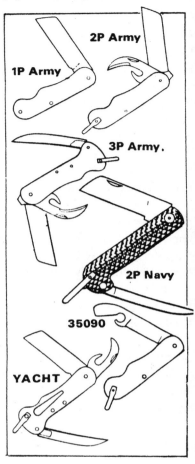

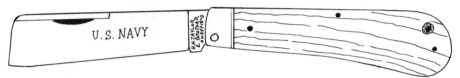

U.S. Navy knife by H.H. Taylor & Bro. of Sheffield, recovered from stores of the *U.S.S. Cairo*, sunk in the Yazoo River in 1862. 4 3/4" closed, genuine stag, **$825**. (Illustration courtesy *Knife World*)

Sailor's knife from Smith's Key, 1816, integral bolster-liners, scored bone, **$375-$500**.

Keen Kutter contract knife, made by Camillus c1915 for an Allied navy (French or Canadian), 4 7/8" closed, checkered black fiber handles, **$250** (**$175** as is). (Dennis Ellingsen photo)

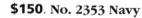

$150. No. 2353 Navy Navy Knife, Easy Opener, 3 1/4 inches long; 2 blades (regulation navy pocket blade and nail pen); brass lined; nickel silver bolsters and shackle; cleaned inside; pocket blade crocus polished on one side; Bone Stag handle.

U.S. Navy World War I issue seaman's jack knives, 3" closed, rope blade, manicure blade, shackle, most with bone-stag handles. The pattern is similar to the "No. 2 Boy Scout" (see "Utility and Scout Knives" in the chapter on "Multi-Blade Knives").

Rase Knives or Timber Scribers

Though gouge-type blades were almost never used in multi-blade knives, they were routinely used in jack knives that were specially designed for them. Jack knives with gouge-type blades are called *timber scribes* or *timber scribers*. Another name for them is *rase knives* or *race knives*, with "race" used in the sense of a groove. *Rase* is pronounced *raze*.

Rase knives were designed for cutting lines and markings into wood. They are used with a pull stroke, which accounts for the distinctive "L" or "7" shape of the blade. The bent shape also ensures that the U-shaped cutting edge is safely housed when the blade is folded.

Historically, the principal use of the rase knife was to scribe ownership and destination markings on wooden barrels and crates. Almost every commodity in the 19th century was shipped in wooden containers, so you can see how important rase knives were.

On occasion, rase knives also were used for whittling markings off, or "e-RASE-ing" them. More often, though, a larger tool called a *scorp* or *inshave* was used to remove markings so containers could be recycled.

Rase knives were used by carpenters and boat builders to put a permanent mark on wood. On wooden boats, the waterline is sometimes scribed so that it is easy to find when it comes time for another coat of paint.

Among the several variations of rase knives, there is even a double-edged version, which seems to defeat the purpose of having the blade fold. Most rase knives have just the scriber blade, though some have an ordinary spear or clip blade as well.

An often-seen rase knife is the version made by New York Knife Co. in a choice of wood or "Goldine" (bronze) handles. Old bronze- or brass-handled knives were made for use around salt water.

There are also fixed-blade rase knives, some of them quite elaborate. They were sometimes called cellarman's knives, as they were used in wine cellars.

Base prices of RASE KNIVES with one rase blade and wood handles. Excellent, unsharpened condition.

VALUE RANGE

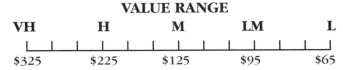

VH	H	M	LM	L
$325	$225	$125	$95	$65

New York Knife Co., wood, **$175**.
Wester Bros., double-ended, wood, **$250**.

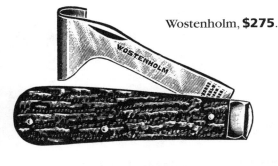

Wostenholm, **$275**.

C.B. Timpson & Tucker,
brass, **$300**.

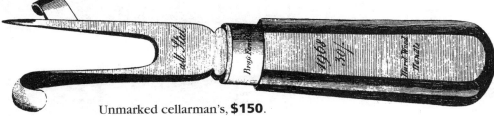

Unmarked cellarman's, **$150**.

J. Clarke, two blades, genuine stag, **$275**.

Physician's Knives

The "physician's knife" is the most refined variety of slim regular jack. The standard version is a slender, straight-sided knife, usually about 3 1/2 inches long. It has a flat "seal" cap. A rare variant is the serpentine or gunstock version.

Not all physician's knives are jack knives. Another style is a long, slim equal-end or sleeveboard "whittler" (see the "Whittlers" segment in the chapter on "Pen Knives").

Years ago, the distinction between the physician, who treated illness with medicines, and the surgeon, who treated by operating, was much more pronounced than it is now. The *physician's knife* is so called because it is primarily designed for preparing medicines.

The narrow spear master blade was intended for scooping powders from vials, and for loosening powders if they got caked. The flat seal cap, often of coin silver, was used for crushing powders and pills—hence the collector's name for the pattern, the "pill-buster." The second blade of a pill-buster is sometimes a flexible spatula, used for mixing powders or salves. More often it is a slim pen blade.

Though a physician's knife could be used for emergency surgery, this was *not* its intended function. The one example seen had a scalpel blade but was advertised as a *veterinary* knife.

For surgeons' emergency use, specialty surgical instrument makers made folding pocket instruments. The little knives have simple, two-piece handles, usually of tortoise shell or horn. They usually have open backs without liners or backsprings (see the chapter on "Multi-Blade Knives").

The physician's knife is a premium pattern. It was made with good handle materials—bone stag, mother-of-pearl, horn and ivory—and even celluloid. The knives are still made today but are intended for collectors rather than for physicians.

Base values of PHYSICIAN'S KNIVES with bone-stag handles, spear master blade and pen or coping second blade. Excellent, unsharpened condition.

VALUE RANGE

VH	H	M	LM	L
$375	$275	$175	$100	$70

Miller Bros., 3 3/4", physician's knife, 2 blades, bone handle, **$250**.

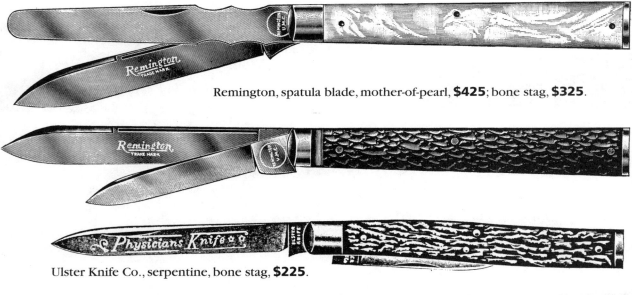

Remington, spatula blade, mother-of-pearl, **$425**; bone stag, **$325**.

Ulster Knife Co., serpentine, bone stag, **$225**.

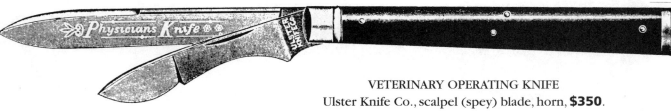

VETERINARY OPERATING KNIFE
Ulster Knife Co., scalpel (spey) blade, horn, **$350**.

Physician's Knives *(continued)*

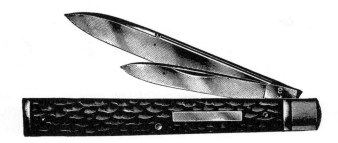

H. Boker, bone stag, **$200**.

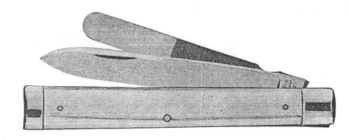

No. 22753 Spat.—2 15/16" Large Spear and Spatula blade. Brass lined. Nickel silver bolsters. Cap. Full polish. Mother of Pearl handle. CATTARAUGUS, **$250**.

Spatula Knives

Some physician's knives have a flexible folding spatula as a second blade and are called *spatula knives*. A few cutlery firms used the blade by itself in a smaller folding knife, usually sleeveboard shaped. It, too, was used by physicians, but also by artists as a folding palette knife. Most have wooden handles but a few have fancier handle materials. They seem to have gone out of production by the time of the Second World War.

Base values of SPATULA KNIVES with wooden handles. Excellent condition.

VALUE RANGE

VH	H	M	LM	L
$225	$150	$120	$90	$75

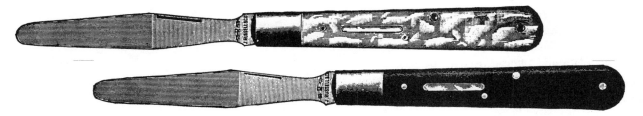

J. Russell, mother-of-pearl, **$250**; wood, **$150**.

Corn Knives

Corn knives are made for cutting corns off a person's toes, and that is about all. To cut corns easily, the blades are tempered very hard and ground extra thin, which makes them too delicate for most other tasks. Corn knives have a characteristic blade shape and many say CORN KNIFE on the handle or the blade.

If you wear fashionably tight shoes, you will eventually need to use a corn remover. Since the 1930s, less-risky rasps, abrasive materials and chemical preparations have supplanted corn knives.

Base vales of CORN KNIVES with smooth bone or celluloid handles marked "Corn Knife," one blade and no bolsters. Excellent, unsharpened condition.

VALUE RANGE

VH	H	M	LM	L
$140	$100	$75	$55	$35

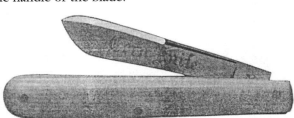

No. 10851—3 1/8" Corn Knife. Brass lined. Glaze finish. French ivory handle. CATTARAUGUS: **$75**.

Joseph Rodgers, corn razor, 3 3/8", white bone handle, **$150**.

Corn Knives *(continued)*

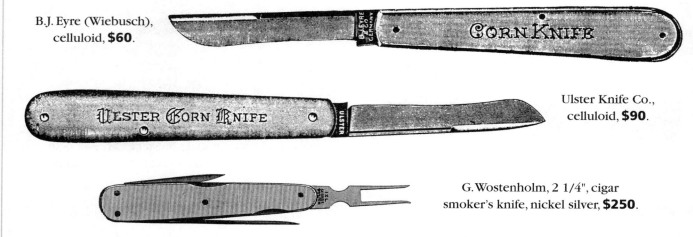

B.J. Eyre (Wiebusch),
celluloid, **$60**.

Ulster Knife Co.,
celluloid, **$90**.

G. Wostenholm, 2 1/4", cigar
smoker's knife, nickel silver, **$250**.

Box Knives and Smoker's Knives

There are two jack-knife patterns that are often confused with the pill-buster. Like the physician's knife, the *box knife* and the *smoker's knife* both have special-purpose metal caps.

The box knife has a little steel hammerhead for a cap. Its main blade is a spear. Its second blade is a combination pry bar and nail puller. Box knives were used for opening and closing the small wooden boxes in which cigars, sugar, chocolate and cheese used to be sold. Most box knives advertise one of the aforementioned products.

Folding box knives are rare. They were used in homes and in fine shops. Most box knives were fixed blades, and most of the blades were very plain. Production of folding box knives seems to have ceased in the 1920s.

The *smoker's jack knife* has the cap modified as a pipe tamper. Like the box and physician's knives, its main blade is a long spear. Its second blade can be a pen, a pipe reamer or a cigar punch. Some versions of the pattern are still made, usually with metal handles.

Base values of BOX and SMOKER'S (jack) KNIVES with metal handles, two blades. Excellent, unsharpened condition.

Box Knives

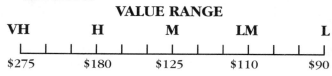

	VALUE RANGE			
VH	**H**	**M**	**LM**	**L**
$275	$180	$125	$110	$90

Smoker's Knives

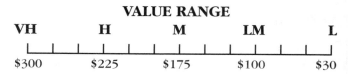

	VALUE RANGE			
VH	**H**	**M**	**LM**	**L**
$300	$225	$175	$100	$30

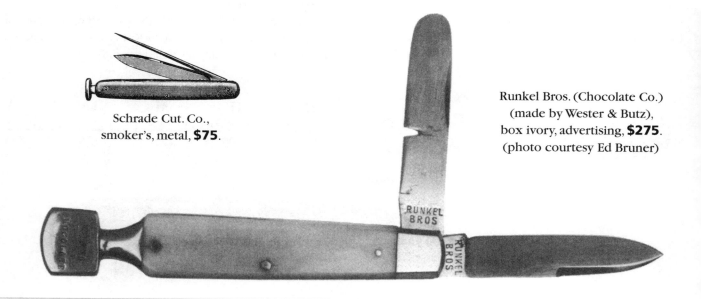

Schrade Cut. Co.,
smoker's, metal, **$75**.

Runkel Bros. (Chocolate Co.)
(made by Wester & Butz),
box ivory, advertising, **$275**.
(photo courtesy Ed Bruner)

Special Spey and Veterinary Knives

Several special patterns of jack knife were made for use by amateur and professional veterinarians. The most common sort were spey knives for speying or altering young animals.

Special spey knives are regular jacks, curved regular jacks, serpentine jacks or sometimes another shape, all with a spey master blade. Most are single bladed, though rarely they have a second blade, a pen or, on some English spey knives, a hawkbill or a sheepfoot.

One American style of the 1930s-'50s is called a "rooster nutter." The little metal-handled curved regular jack has a spey blade and a castrating hook. Though supposedly designed for castrating chicks, the hook is also used on cattle and hogs.

Rooster-nutter values as illustrated here: **$90-$225**. For others, use the "Value Table for Standard Jack Knife Shapes" in the chapter on "Jack Knives."

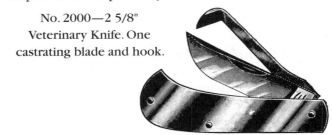

No. 2000—2 5/8"
Veterinary Knife. One
castrating blade and hook.

Fleams

The fleam is an old style of veterinary knife used for bleeding livestock. Cattle often were bled on the nose. The point of a fleam blade was placed on the nose, and the back of the blade was struck with a "bloodstick." Automatic spring-powered fleams that need no bloodstick were made in the 18th and 19th centuries.

Fleams look like the one in the accompanying picture, though sometimes fancier. Handles are brass, usually with cow-horn handle scales. Sometimes the whole handle is horn. Most fleams have three blades but some have only two. They never have backsprings. Horseman's knives (see the chapter on "Multi-Blade Knives") often have a fleam blade hidden in one handle.

Values: Three blades, plain: **$125**; fancy, **$195-300**.

Automatic (in fitted
case): **$300-$675**.

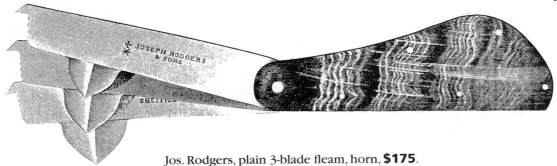

Jos. Rodgers, plain 3-blade fleam, horn, **$175**.

Other Veterinary Knives

One odd veterinary knife is not really a knife at all. It is a little folding saw in a regular jack handle. The *cockspur saw* is used for sawing the spurs off the legs of fighting cocks to make room for razor-sharp steel spurs, or "gaffs."

Values: NOVCO picture handled: **$575**.

Another odd one is an equal-end double-end jack with two comb-like blades. Some have a round shield with a terrier's head. The "dog-stripping" knife is used for grooming kinky-haired breeds.

Values: Remington: **$300**. Case Tested: **$375**. Spratts (a dog food producer): **$200**.

R4733
DOG STRIPPING KNIFE.
Stag Handle; Brass Lined;
Mirror Finished Blades;
Nickel Silver Trim. Length,
closed, 3 3/4 inches.

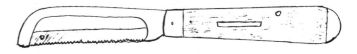

Unmarked: **$275**.

Boy's Knives

A boy's knife is a small (3 1/2 inch or under) regular jack or curved regular jack, ordinarily with a single spear blade. Some have a pen blade as well.

Into the 1930s, most boy's knives sold for 10 cents or less, so their construction is the most economical possible. Some have "DIME" or "5¢ KNIFE" on the handle.

Metal Handles

Integral metal handles make an inexpensive but sturdy boy's knife. The earliest mass-produced type was the flat "coined"-brass handles made in New England and New York in the 1850s and 1860s. The knives have an elaborate design that usually includes the manufacturer's name.

In 1862, Samuel Mason of Northfield Knife Co. patented the use of low-cost "malleable cast iron with a rough or corrugated exterior, in imitation of buckhorn" for jack-knife handles. Many iron-handled boy's knives have trademarks, such as Northfield's "UN-X-LD" or Russell's "Boy of America," incorporated into the casting.

Frary Cutlery Co. introduced cast-tin-alloy- or pewter-handled boy's knives around 1880. One style with a blunt-ended blade, called the "Our Boy," was for younger boys. Others were souvenirs of new hit operettas by Gilbert and Sullivan. Cut-rate German cutlery firms copied Frary's methods and continued to use them after James Frary left the business in the late 1880s.

Both the iron- and pewter-cast-handled types were eclipsed in the early 20th century by boy's knives with still-lower-cost handles of pressed mild steel. Less expensive yet were knives with one-piece, folded-sheet-steel handles, such as the Allen, patented in 1917, and the Eagle of 1918. Joining them on the market in about 1926 was the "wire jack" invented by George Schrade (see "Easy Openers" in the "Names, Illustrations and Descriptions" segment of the chapter on "Jack Knives").

Circa 1934, Ernst Lohr and Otto Stiehl (ELOSI) of Solingen, Germany, introduced thin plastic covers for low-cost (5-25 cents) pocketknives with sheet-steel shell handles, licensing the technique to Imperial (USA) and Richards (UK). The handle, made by Imperial Stag in Listowel, Ireland, and a flat plastic handle made by Colonial, were the standards on modern low-priced boy's knives.

Besides metal and plastic, boy's knives were handled in wood, horn and low-grade smooth bone. Some boy's knives came with a shackle and chain for attachment to a belt or suspender button.

Unmarked (Germany), chain, 2 7/8", stamped steel, advertisement, **$45**.

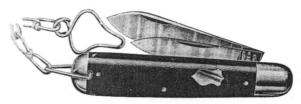

Actual Size   *3 1/4 inches long*

No. 26—1/2X Ebony Handle. Brass lined. 1 large Spear Blade. 1 strong Pen Blade. Chain. Nickel Silver Shield. Steel Cap and Bolster. Per Dozen $22.35 NAPANOCH, **$150**.

H. Boker, stamped steel, trademark, **$75**.

J. Russell, 3" or 3 3/8", wood, **$175**.

Winchester chain, 3 1/2", wood, **$150**.

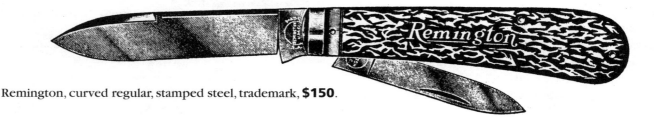

Remington, curved regular, stamped steel, trademark, **$150**.

Boy's Knives *(continued)*

Most boy's knives are still inexpensive on the collector market. A variety of the little knives, together with old photos, advertising and boy's toys, make a very interesting display.

Base values for BOY'S KNIVES with cast or stamped iron or steel handles, or with smooth bone, horn or wood handle covers, one or two blades. Excellent, unsharpened condition.

VALUE RANGE

VH	H	M	LM	L
$175	$125	$90	$60	$30

Lenox Cut., Germany, 2 3/4", embossed metal, 2 blades, **$75**.

Eagle patent, easy open, 3", sheet steel, **$45**.

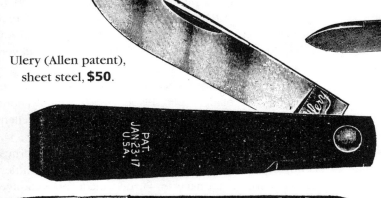

Ulery (Allen patent), sheet steel, **$50**.

Western Cut Co. (Germany), curved regular, 3 1/2", stamped steel, trademark, **$45**.

J. Russell, 2 3/4", Boy of America, cast metal, **$250**.

Armstrong, Germany, 2 3/4", embossed metal, **$65**.

Schrade Cut. Co., 3 1/4", "Boy Scout," official, **$160**.

Armstrong, Germany, 2 3/4", embossed metal, 5¢, **$65**.

Walter Bros. (Germany), curved regular, chain, 3 1/4", adv't, **$75**.

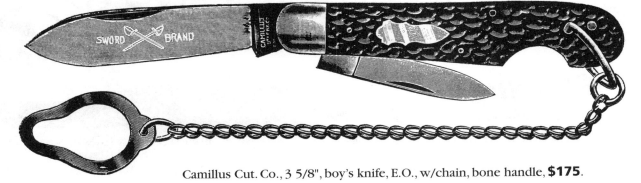

Camillus Cut. Co., 3 5/8", boy's knife, E.O., w/chain, bone handle, **$175**.

Barlow Knives

A modern Barlow knife is a regular jack or, rarely, a sleeveboard jack, with extra-long bolsters and no cap bolsters. Many pre-1840s barlows were curved regular jacks, as were a small number of more recent ones.

The barlow is a sturdy pattern intended for the working man. The long bolsters are usually iron and most often are stamped with a trademark.

Traditional barlow-handle scales are smooth, flat bone. Some are left natural but most are dyed brown or red. Recent barlows have plastic handles. Older deluxe barlows have jigged bone, stag or even mother-of-pearl handles. Some, the "Southern pattern," have fancy stamped bolsters.

There are two basic classes of barlow. One class is standard barlows, which are around 3 3/8 inches long closed. The other class is "daddy" or "grand-daddy barlows," usually 5 inches long. The unusual "baby Barlow" is a lower-quality knife under 3 inches long.

Both standard and daddy barlows can have clip or spear master blades. Both can be single-bladed or have a pen second blade.

Standard barlows also can have a sheepfoot, spey or "razor" master blade. Daddy barlows can have a fish-scaler back on the master blade, or, on those with one blade, a lock. A few are easy-openers.

The Barlows

The Barlows were a family of cutlers in Sheffield, England, prominent in the 17th and 18th centuries. The first well-known Barlow in Sheffield was Edward Barlow*e* (note the "e"), who was elected master of the Cutlers' Guild in 1653.

According to John Goins, the original Barlow of barlow knife fame was Obadiah Barlow, who started in business in 1667. His grandson, John, succeeded him in 1710 and John Junior of Campo Lane succeeded John in 1745. In their time, the family seems to have had exclusive use of the word BARLOW *by itself* as a trademark on pocketknives. John Junior, the last in the family line, died in 1798.

While not directly related to Obadiah Barlow, another cutler of the same period was Samuel Barlow of Neepsend, near Sheffield. His trademark in 1787 was a sideways "Z," a small circle and a picture of a scimitar. After 1798, he added the word BARLOW to his mark. He worked until the 1830s. A fairly good number of Samuel Barlow's knives found their way to America. They are rare and very collectible.

Base values for BARLOW KNIVES with clip or spear master blade, pen blade, and smooth-bone, horn, patterned-celluloid or wood handles. Excellent, unsharpened condition.

An important supplier of barlow knives was the Furness family of Liberty Hill, Stannington, near Sheffield. Cutlers named Furness, Furnace or Furniss made pocketknives there since at least 1760. Furness barlows were widely sold in America from well before 1870 to about 1915. Markings include Enos Furness & Sons (EF&S), M. Furness (MF&S), Martha Furness (S.E. OATES), Edward Furness (ED F&S), and George Furness (GF&S).

VALUE RANGE

SHAPE	(VH)	(H)	(M)	(LM)	(L)
DADDY BARLOW	$650	$375	$225	$150	$90
STANDARD BARLOW	1,200	600	300	150	75
BABY BARLOW	200	125	75	50	35

BARLOW, 3" curved regular, from *Smith's Key* (1816), integral bolster-liners, single blades, spotted horn: top has fancy bolsters, **$1,200**; bottom has plain bolsters, **$900-$1,000**.

No. 42. WHITE BONE HANDLES. 3 3/8 inches.

No. 52. BUFFALO HORN HANDLES. 3 3/8 inches.

Russell Barlows with shields: **$750-$800** each.

Standard Barlows

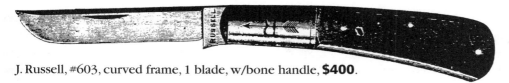

J. Russell, #603, curved frame, 1 blade, w/bone handle, **$400**.

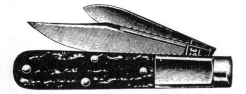

Case Tested XX, fancy bolsters, 3 3/4", genuine stag, **$350**.

S.E. Oates (by Martha Furness), one blade, 3 3/8", bone, **$150**.

Ulster Knife Co. (for W. Bingham), mother-of-pearl, **$500**.

E.C. Simmons, Keen Kutter, 3 5/8", 2 blades, bone handle, **$150**.

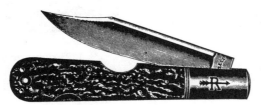

Hibbard Spencer Bartlett, razor blade, 3 1/2", bone, **$150**.

Daddy Barlows

Robeson, 1 blade, 5", bone, **$250**.

J. Russell, 1 blade, 5", bone, **$475**; easy-open, 1 locking blade, genuine stag, **$750-$800**.

Western States, "Tested Sharp Temper," 1 blade, 5", bone, **$395**.

Remingtons, 5", bone: 2 blades, **$425**; 1 locking blade, **$650**.

English Jacks

"English Jack" is a term that was commonly applied to deluxe, large-sized (over 4 inches), slim, regular and sleeveboard jack knives. Premium handle materials, fancy bolsters and locking master blades are often seen on them.

English jacks most often have a single clip blade. Others have a spear blade instead. Some have a pen second blade.

Most of the large-size jack knives exported from England to the United States from the mid-19th to the early 20th centuries fit the definition. However, "English jack" is an American term and was used equally on large, high-grade, straight jack knives made in the USA.

English jacks are similar in proportion to large "daddy" barlows. They may have appealed to the prosperous Southern or Western customer who had grown up with and liked barlow knives, but who wanted something a little dressier. For a man who was used to a straight one- or two-blade jack knife, a curved four-blade tobacco knife or three-blade premium stock knife just did not fit the bill.

The English jack is less bulky and thus easier to carry in a pocket than clasp knives or folding hunters, though its master blade is almost as long as theirs. In a pinch, a lockback English jack can serve adequately as a defensive weapon. Very large and ornate English jacks are often classed with folding bowie knives. They are very collectible and have a large following.

Base values for ENGLISH JACKS 4 to 4 1/2 inches long, plain bolsters, bone-stag or fancy celluloid handles, non-locking master blade. Excellent, unsharpened condition.

VALUE RANGE

VH	H	M	LM	L
$575	$475	$325	$225	$150

R1343 Nickel Silver Trim Stag Handle; Brass Lining Length, closed 4 1/4 inches.

R1153 Nickel Silver Trim Stag Handle; Brass Lining Length, closed, 4 3/8 inches.

Remingtons, 2 blades, bone stag: fancy bolsters, **$450-$500**; plain, **$375-$400**.

William Rodgers (John Clarke), 4 1/2", genuine stag, **$325**.

G. Wostenholm I*XL, 4", 2 blades, w/stag handle, **$475**.

No. 1863
3/4 Schrade Cut. Co., 4 1/2", bone stag or candy stripe, **$200**.

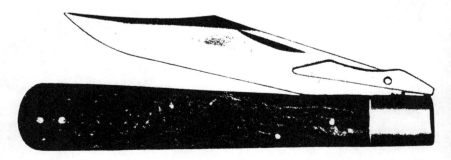

No. 6165 Lg. Union Cut. Co., lockback, folding guard, bone stag, **$525**.

Winchester 2907, 2 blades,
4 1/4", bone stag, **$575**.

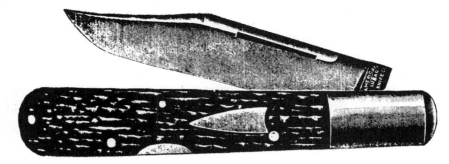

American Shear & Knife Co., lockback, bone stag, **$450**.

ONE BLADE. Large Spear.
Full Polished; Nickel Silver Bolster,
Cap and Shield; Brass Lining.
Per Dozen
No. K1683—4 1/2 IN. STAG
HANDLE $19.80
Keen Kutter, bone stag, **$400**.

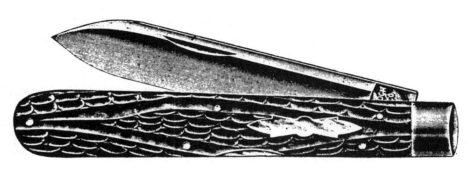

Napanoch, lockback, 4 5/8", bone stag, **$525**.

J. Primble (Belknap Hdw.)
2 blades, 4 1/2", bone stag, **$400**
(an ancestor of the melon tester).

Challenge, lockback, 4 1/2",
bone stag, **$300**.

Lock back hunting. One blade, half crocus polished.
German silver bolster. Brass lined. Length 4 1/2 inches.
Stiletto, lockback, bone stag, **$425**.

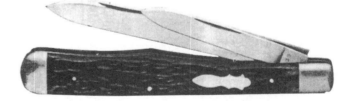

No. 2239—4 1/2" Long spear point and long pen blades.
Brass lined. Nickel silver bolsters. Glaze finish. Stag
handle. Shielded. CATTARAUGUS: **$400**.

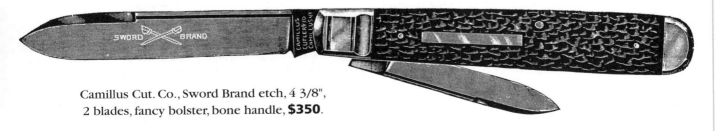

Camillus Cut. Co., Sword Brand etch, 4 3/8",
2 blades, fancy bolster, bone handle, **$350**.

Ticklers and Fish Knives

The "tickler" is the American clasp-knife pattern that looks most like the southern European clasp knife, or *navaja*. It is a slender serpentine jack knife with a pointed "head" or non-blade end. Most are 5 inches long closed or longer.

Ticklers have several picturesque names. Many collectors, especially Case collectors, call them "Texas toothpicks." Others call them "powder-horns."

A pearl-celluloid-handled tickler was described in 1933 as "a beautiful Saturday Evening special, society, or switch knife" by the Chicago hardware wholesaler, Hibbard Spencer Bartlett & Co. Other distributors called ticklers "tango" or "dance" knives, or "Dixie razors."

The master blade of a tickler is always a clip point, either flat or saber ground. Many ticklers are single bladed. Others have two blades, a clip and a pen.

A special type of tickler, called a "fish knife," has either a fish-scaler-blade back or a second blade that combines a fish-scaler and a hook disgorger. For convenience, a few other specialized fishing patterns are included in this chapter.

The American-made tickler seems to have been introduced in the 1890s. The high cutlery duties imposed by the Tariff Acts of 1890 and 1897 raised the prices of foreign knives, including clasp models, and made it possible for American firms to compete with the imports. The fish-knife version of the tickler seems to date from the 1920s.

Among collectors, ticklers are not as popular as other big American clasp knives. Collectors of specialty knives and antique fishing tackle seek specialized fishing knives, such as the Case "Fly Fisherman." Some of this popularity has begun to spill over into tickler-pattern fish knives.

Base values for TICKLERS over 4 1/2 inches long with bolsters and cap bolsters, bone-stag or horn handle scales, flat-ground master blade plus pen. Excellent, unsharpened condition.

VALUE RANGE

VH	H	M	LM	L
$425	$375	$200	$150	$100

Winchester, 1 blade, 4 1/4", bone stag, **$375**.

Maher and Grosh, 5", picked bone handle (Dixie Razor), **$275**.

Western States, "Dox Fish Gaff," 5", aluminum, **$175**.

Makes a crackerjack carpenter's, mechanic's, teamster's, fisherman's sportsman's, hunter's or trapper's knife. Ideally suited for sticking, skinning and cleaning game or fish. Substantial enough for heavy work. Has a large comfortable handle affording a firm grip. A real knife for the in or out doors man. Also makes a beautiful Saturday Evening special society or switch knife.
Hibbard, one long substantial clip point blade, Full Mirror Polished on both sides. Super Pearl Indestructible handle, brass lined, fancy nickel silver cap and bolster. Length when closed 5 in., w't per doz. 2 lbs.
C9711Y4 . . . . each $0.50

Hibbard Spencer Bartlett, one blade, patterned celluloid: saber ground, fancy bolsters, 5", **$125**.

Fly Fisherman
Length closed 3 7/8"
Fly Fisherman – Nickel silver handle with cutting and scissors on one side and pick and file on other. Screwdriver on one end and ball on other end.

Case Fly Fisherman:
Tested XX, **$375-$425**, XX, **$300**.

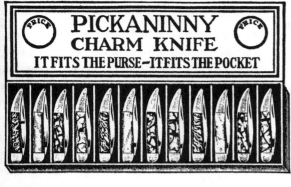

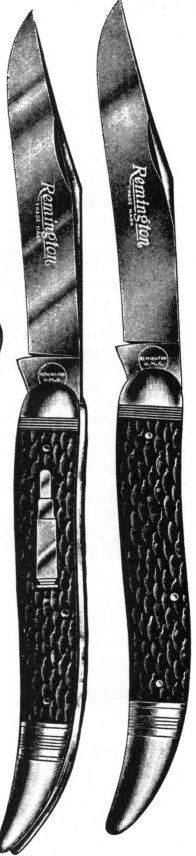

Hibbard Spencer Bartlett, one blade, patterned celluloid, 2 1/2" charm knife **$35**.

Remingtons, bone stag: 1 blade, bullet shield (R-1613), **$2,000**; 1 blade, **$525**.

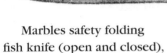

Marbles safety folding fish knife (open and closed), nickel plated, **$350**.

Case, 5", 1 blade, bone stag: Tested XX, **$425**; XX, **$300**.

Case Tested XX, fishing, 5 1/2", plain celluloid, **$275**.

Western, fishing, 4 3/8", plain celluloid, **$150**.

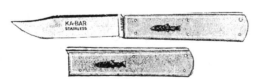

KA-BAR T-61 fish knife, Ivoroid handle, **$125**.

Robeson, 1 blade, 5" candy stripe celluloid, **$150**.

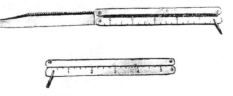

KA-BAR S.S. folding fish knife w/rule, 5 1/2", **$85**.

Trappers, Muskrat, and Large Trappers

A "trapper" is a jack knife with two specific full-length blades. The master blade is a clip point with a very long clip. The second blade is a long spey. The standard trapper (or heavy trapper) is around 4-4 1/4 inches long closed. It is built on the swell-center-regular-jack handle die.

Light trappers are built on 3 3/4-inch or larger slim-serpentine handle dies. The light trapper was most likely introduced before the First World War, the standard trapper not until the mid-1920s.

Mini-trappers are compact, trapper-style knives, both standard and lightweight, around 3 1/4 to 3 1/2 inches long closed. They were introduced in the 1970s.

Premium trappers are built on serpentine-premium-stock handles, both round-end and square-end. They range from 3 5/8-4 3/8 inches long.

Double-end trappers are similar to premium trappers, only with one blade in each end. A variant of the double-end trapper is the muskrat. It has two identical "muskrat-clip" blades, one in each end.

Large trappers remain extremely popular, but the once-intense interest in collecting standard trappers has cooled some. This is because of the number of counterfeit antique trappers, especially Case trappers, in the collector market. (For more on possible counterfeit Case trappers, see the book, *Counterfeiting Antique Cutlery*, by Gerald Witcher.) The standard trapper is a simple pattern to make, and the high prices fetched by old trappers proved an irresistible lure to shady operators in all parts of the country. Advanced collectors will still pay a hefty premium for authentic old trappers, but many trappers with "old" markings are not authentic. For detailed information on Case trappers, consult the references listed in "Case Pocketknife Patterns" in the "Pocketknife History" chapter of the section on "Folding Knives."

Base values for TRAPPERS of the indicated style, over 3 5/8 inches long, with bone-stag handles. Excellent unsharpened condition.

SHAPE	(VH)	(H)	(M)	(L)
STANDARD TRAPPER	$400	$325	$125	$75
Case Tested XX	500-1,200	n/a	n/a	n/a
LIGHT TRAPPER	300	200	100	60
PREMIUM TRAPPER	325	225	150	90
DOUBLE-END TRAPPER	275	200	100	60
Remington equal-end "Bullets" R4353	1,200	n/a	n/a	n/a
Remington equal-end "Bullets" R4466	1,800	n/a	n/a	n/a
MUSKRAT (two clip blades)	525	350	200	100

Premium trapper: Western States "Mountain Man," 4 3/8", genuine stag, **$600**.

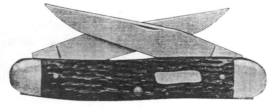

No. 22199—3 1/2" Two Sabatur blades. Brass lined, nickel silver bolsters. Full polish, stag handle, shielded. Cattaraugus: **$200**.

R4353 OUTDOORMAN'S KNIFE. Convenient to carry in pocket – has round Nickel Silver Bolsters and full sunk joints. Correct shaped blades for sticking and skinning. Stag Handle, Brass Lined. Length, closed, 4 1/4 inches.

Double-End: Remington Bullet, bone stag, **$2,000**. 1985 reissue, plastic, **$150** (mint).

R-4593 MUSKRAT KNIFE. Designed from suggestions of Muskrat Trappers. The long, keen, slender lance allows the perfect removal of pelts without perforation, increasing their value. Ideal for skinning all small fur bearing animals. Both blades alike, Mirror Finished, Stag Handle; Brass Lining; Nickel Silver Bolsters. Length, closed, 3 7/8 inches.

Muskrat: Remington, bone stag, **$250**.

Double-end trapper: Western States, 3 7/8" bone stag, **$600**.

Standard trapper: Case Tested XX, 4 1/8", genuine stag, **$995**; Case XX, **$295**.

Light trapper: Schrade Cut. Co., 3 7/8", bone stag, **$200**.

Large Trappers

The large trapper, like the standard trapper, is built on the swell-center-regular-jack handle die. At 4 1/2 inches, it is not much longer than the standard trapper, but it is nearly twice as wide and heavy.

One of the first and best-known large trappers was the 6 1/2-ounce Remington R1123 "Old Reliable" with a bullet shield, introduced in September 1922. Similar knives were also introduced by Utica and by Union. In 1928, Western States introduced the 5230, a large trapper with self-guard bolsters and over-size caps.

Remington later introduced a three-quarter-scale "large" trapper. The R1173 "Baby Bullet" is 3 1/2 inches long but has the same proportions as the R1123. The Baby Bullet is much rarer than the larger one.

Values for LARGE TRAPPERS in excellent, unsharpened condition, with appropriate etch. Only a few firms made large trappers.

Remington R1123, bone stag, **$2,000**.
Remington R1128, cocobolo, **$1,600**.
Remington R1173, baby, bone stag, **$2,500**.
Remington re-issues, plastic handles, stainless blades, made by Camillus: R1123, **$300** (mint) and R1173 "baby," **$150** (mint).
Utica "Nessmuk" pattern with buffalo head shield, bone stag, **$950**; celluloid, **$650**. (Utica made Hibbard Spencer Bartlett, Maher & Grosh, Royal Brand)
Western States, genuine stag, **$850**; celluloid, **$450**.
Case Tested XX 62100 "saddlehorn," bone stag: **$975**.
Union/Ka-Bar, genuine stag, **$800**; bone stag, **$750**.
Bowen, **$175** (mint).
L.L. Bean, **$300** (mint).
Camillus wildlife, **$60** (mint).

Western States No. 5230

R1123
R1123 "OLD RELIABLE." Very popular with Hunters and Trappers throughout the world. One strong heavy gauged blade for sticking and general use, another strong blade for skinning, both blue glazed. Stag Handle, Brass Lined, Nickel Silver bolster, flush square joints, hole in butt end for thong. Length, closed, 4 1/2 inches.

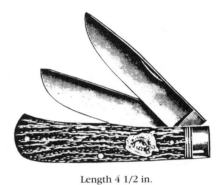

Length 4 1/2 in.
Nubuck Stag Handle
Sportsman's, Camping or Hunting Knife
Two blades, large clip
and special hunters blade.
C229Y3..........................each $1.00
Hibbard Spencer Bartlett & Co.,
made by Utica.

R1173

Folding Hunters, American Clasp Knives

"Folding hunter" is a broad term that includes large swell-center jack knives; various medium-to-large folding lock knives; and most modern American-style clasp knives. These types of knives are included in this chapter. The only exceptions are the Marble's Safety Hunting Knives, which are included with the other Marble's knives in the "American Hunting Knives" segment of "Section III, Fixed Blade Knives."

Some collectors use the term "folding hunter" to describe just about all types of large jack knives, including daddy barlows, English jacks, ticklers, large trappers, folding dirks and folding bowie knives. These knives are all covered in other chapters of this book.

Swell-Center Hunting Knives

Five-inch and larger swell-center jack knives are called "swell-center hunting knives." The big Coke-bottle shaped knives were the standard American folding hunting knives of the late-19th and early-20th centuries.

In the 19th century, swell-center hunting knives most often were handled in ebony, but also in cocobolo, smooth white bone, horn or genuine stag. Later ones were offered with bone stag, celluloid, or laminated wood. Some 20th-century examples have enlarged front bolsters.

Most swell-center hunting knives are single-bladed, the blade usually being a clip or a saber-ground clip. A few firms offered narrow versions of the pattern, which sometimes have a slim spear master blade. Some swell-center hunters were made with a locking blade, usually with the release forward of the center swell. A few had a folding guard.

On two-bladed swell-center hunting knives, both blades are normally full length, usually a saber clip and a heavy spear. Some have a saw as a second blade.

Swell-center hunting knives remained popular through the 1940s, though they steadily lost ground to fixed-blade hunting knives and clasp-type folding hunters. Case had discontinued all but one of its many versions by 1940, and dropped that one, the C61050 SAB, in 1976. Remington never made the pattern, but Winchester made the popular model 1920, identical to the earlier Napanoch X100X.

Base values for SWELL-CENTER HUNTING KNIVES with bone-stag handles, one non-locking blade or one blade and saw, bolsters and caps. Excellent, unsharpened condition.

VALUE RANGE

VH	H	M	L
$1,200	$650	$375	$200

Winchester Model 1920: $1,000.
Napanoch Model X100X: $1,150.

No. 12829—5 3/8" "King of the Woods." This knife is made especially for Big Game Hunters. Blade has Clip point and 3 3/4" cutting surface. Built exceptionally strong. Brass lined. Nickel silver bolsters. Hole drilled for ring or thong. Full polish. Stag handle. Spring lock, which holds blade in position when open. **$850.**

No. 12839—Same as above but has additional back lock and a nickel silver guard which comes into place at end of handle when blade is open and also shielded. **$950.**

No. 12819—Same as 12829 with the exception of no spring lock. **$650.**

CATTARAUGUS

Union Cutlery Co., Dog-Head shield, back lock, 5 1/4", bone stag, **$900**.

Western States, barehead, 5", patterned celluloid, **$425**.

Miller Bros., back lock, 5 3/8", bone stag, **$650**.

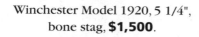

Winchester Model 1920, 5 1/4", bone stag, **$1,500**.

Napanoch Model X100X (predecessor of the Winchester Model 1920), bone stag, **$1,500**.

Ulster Knife Co., wood, **$650**.

Swell-Center Hunting Knives *(continued)*

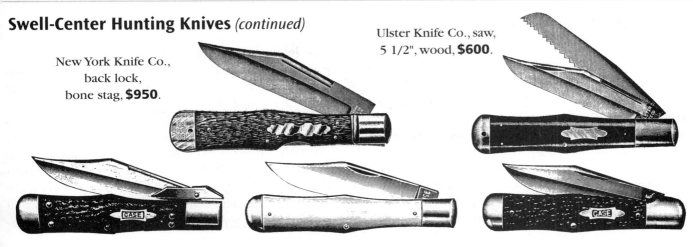

New York Knife Co.,
back lock,
bone stag, **$950**.

Ulster Knife Co., saw,
5 1/2", wood, **$600**.

Case Tested XX, back lock, folding
guard, 5 1/2", bone stag, **$1,500**.

Case Tested XX, 5 1/8",
plain yellow celluloid, **$495**.

Case Tested XX, 5 3/8",
bone stag, **$650**.

Swell-Center, Hunting and Lock Knives

Since the mid-19th century, the swell-center-regular-jack handle die has been used for lockback folding hunters. The attractive knives usually have a single clip blade. The only old names we have seen for the knives are "lock knife" and "hunting knife," which both referred to other patterns as well.

In the 1920s and 1930s, Remington and Utica made single-bladed folding hunters on their swell-center-regular-large-trapper handles (see "Trappers, Muskrats, and Large Trappers" in this chapter). More recently, versions of the single-blade style were introduced by Western, and by other firms and individual knifemakers,

particularly Jess Horn. As with its other "bullet" patterns, Remington has issued plastic-handled replicas of the original, which were made for Remington by Camillus.

Base values for SWELL-CENTER REGULAR HUNTING and LOCK KNIVES, standard (narrow) width, with bone-stag handles, one *locking* blade. Excellent, unsharpened condition, with appropriate etch.

VALUE RANGE

VH	H	M	L
$700	$650	$375	$175

Remington R1303 bone stag: $1,500-1,750.
Remington R1306 genuine stag: $1,750-1,950.

B1531, DH, SH, Lock Knives. 4 1/2
ins. handles, lock blades, iron
bolsters, nickel silver
name plates, shackled.
Wostenholm: **$400**.

Case, narrow, folding guard,
bone stag, Tested
XX, **$850**; XX,
$300; XX
U.S.A., **$250**.

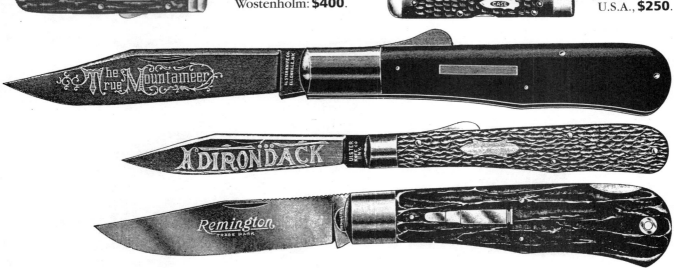

Third from bottom: Ulster Knife Co., wide, wood, **$700**. Second from bottom: Ulster Knife Co., narrow, bone stag, **$600**.
Bottom: Remington R1306, wide, genuine stag, **$2,000**; 1984 reissues (mint), full size, **$175**; baby size, **$200**.

Clasp-Type Folding Hunters

The first clasp knives were made from the ends of cow, goat, or sheep horns that were slotted to contain a blade. The blade was shaped to fit the natural curve of the horn so that the tip of the horn covered the point of the blade. Early styles of clasp knife that were used in the United States are shown in Part 3, "Foreign, Exotic, Primitive, and Historical Folding Knives, of this section."

Since the turn of the century, American cutlery firms have made several styles of folding hunter inspired by traditional clasp knives. The plainest and rarest of the clasp-type folding hunters has a simple curve like a curved regular jack. Some collectors call the knives "bananas." In Sheffield, some were called the "church-window" pattern after the Gothic-window-like decoration on their bolsters.

In the 1920s, Case pioneered clasp-type folding hunters with a center swell on top. Case's standard -65 pattern is still offered, but the extra-wide -72 pattern was discontinued circa 1980. A few other firms still offer clasp-type folding hunters, but the knives' popularity is long past.

Long, slender American clasp knives with pointed heads are called "ticklers." A tickler with a fish scaler added is called a "fish knife." Ticklers and fish knives are not classed as folding hunters. For more on them, see the "Ticklers and Fish Knives" segment in this chapter.

Base values for CLASP-TYPE FOLDING HUNTERS with one or two blades, bolsters and caps, bone-stag and plain- or patterned-celluloid handles. Excellent, unsharpened condition, with appropriate etch.

	VALUE RANGE			
SHAPE	(VH)	(H)	(M)	(L)
CURVED REGULAR	$1,500	$850	$400	$225
SWELL CENTERS:				
EXTRA-WIDE	1,400	900	450	250
STANDARD	650	450	300	175
EXTRA-SLIM	500	400	250	150

Imperial, curved regular, hatchet blade, patterned celluloid, 5 1/8", **$250**.

Schrade, 227UH standard, recent (1972-1986 last list **$42**), 5 1/4", Delrin plastic, **$50** with sheath, **$40** without.

No. 62100 Case Tested XX, **$1,250**.

Case Tested XX, curved regular, 5 1/4", bone stag, **$950**.

Western States, extra-wide, 5 1/2", plain celluloid, **$750**.

R1253
HUNTER'S KNIFE, with heavy double sabre clip blade, crocus polished and etched. Stag Handle; Nickel Silver Cap and Bolster. Brass Lined. LOCK BACK. Length, closed, 5 1/4 inches.

Remington, curved regular, bullet shield, **$2,000**.

Case Tested XX, standard, 5 1/4", genuine stag, **$500**.

Western, extra-slim, 5 1/4", patterned celluloid, **$175**.

Modern Folding Hunters

The majority of modern American folding hunters are streamlined versions of the clasp knife. They have lost their upswept, pointed handle ends and retain only enough curve for a comfortable grip. The original version of this modern classic was the Buck 110 Folding Hunter, introduced in 1963 and inspired by the World War II lifeboat knife (see "Buck Folding Knives" and "Sailor's Knives").

Since the late 1960s, almost every pocketknife company doing business in the United States has offered numerous variations on this immensely popular design.

| SHAPE | VALUE RANGE | | | |
	(VH)	(H)	(M)	(L)
MODERN FOLDING	n/a	n/a	$25	$5
FARMER'S CLASP	$150	n/a	17	4

Base values for MODERN FOLDING HUNTERS and FARMER'S CLASP KNIVES, with one blade, wood or·horn handle scales. Excellent, unsharpened condition.

Farmer's Clasp Knife

Before World War I, German firms such as Henckels and Herder introduced a light, simple, clasp-type folder with wood handles and no bolsters called a *Schlactmesser Zum Zulegen* (folding butcher knife). Though Union Cutlery soon copied the German style of farmer's clasp knife, the pattern had negligible sales in the United States until 1967, when Case introduced its 4 5/8-inch "Sod Buster" with black composition handles and bird's-eye rivets. A locking-liner version and a smaller 3 5/8-inch "Sod Buster Jr." came out in 1970. Today, German and Swedish firms make plastic-handled versions in a variety of sizes and colors.

Spyderco Custom Collaborations: C37 Michael Walker lightweight (bottom left), Zytel® handle, **$75** list; Michael Walker C22 Swiss made, **$435**; Bob Terzuola C15, **$150**; C19 Jr. **$125**; Wayne Goddard C16, **$155**; C18 Jr. **$140**; C20 Baby **$53**; Frank Centofante C25, **$125**; Jess Horn C27 jigged bone, **$450**; C34 Micarta, **$120**; C38 Lightweight, **$70**; Jot Singh Khalsa C40 black Micarta, **$133**; Howard Viele C42 Micarta, **$150**.

1990s Benchmade Panther; **$50** list.

Folding Sportsman III #6406 Single,
4" trailing point blade. Length open: 9 1/4".
Leather sheath included. Gerber Folding Sportsman III (discontinued 1995), 4 1/2", wood, **$108.20** list.

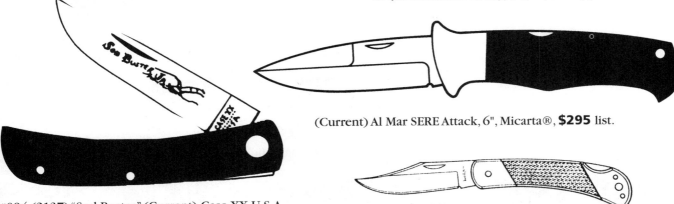

(Current) Al Mar SERE Attack, 6", Micarta®, **$295** list.

#094 (2137) "Sod Buster" (Current) Case XX U.S.A.
Sod Buster, Jr., 3 5/8", plastic, **$27** list.

(Current) Kershaw Wildcat Ridge II, 4 7/8",
plastic **$59.95** list.

#250 (P197L SSP) "Shark Tooth"
Contoured black laminated hardwood
handle, etched blade, 5" closed; weighs 10 oz.
(Current) Case XX U.S.A. Shark Tooth, 5", laminated wood, **$65** list.

C37 Michael Walker lightweight,
Zytel® handle, **$75** list.

SIZE CLOSED - 5 inches
UNCLE HENRY BEAR PAW

SIZE CLOSED - 5 inches
UNCLE HENRY PAPA BEAR

(Contemporary) Schrade folding hunting knives,
list prices: **$53.95**, **$59.95**.

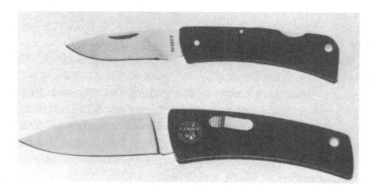

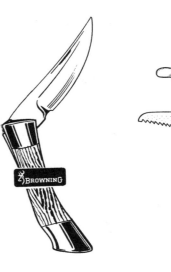

Blackie Collins designed Gerber L-S-T (**$28.60** list)
and Bolt Action (**$56** list, discontinued 1997).

Left: Browning Stalker (**$60** ebony, **$85**
stag), designed circa 1967 by Gil Hibben,
discontinued 1994. Right: Big Game,
ebony, **$78** list; stag, **$104** list.

Left: Spyderco C35
"Q" Clipit,
cut-out blade and
nylon handle, **$39** list.

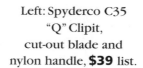

(Current) A.G. Russell General Purpose One Hand Knife, **$79.97** list.

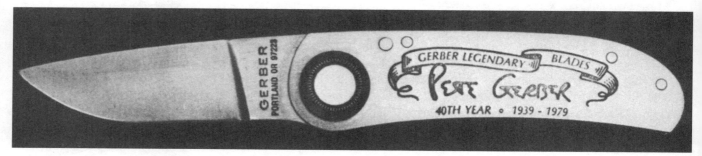

Gerber Paul (discontinued 1986): standard **$200-250**; limited edition, **$300-400**.

Folding Dirks and Folding Bowie Knives

By Roger Baker and Bernard Levine

(Editor's note: Roger Baker has collected folding dirks and folding bowies for more than 25 years. Bernard Levine is a Blade Magazine Cutlery Hall Of Famer©, former editor of this book and a widely recognized authority on the values and history of most all antique knives.)

The terms "folding dirk" and "folding bowie knife" are used, often interchangeably, to refer to large, well-made, usually ornate jack knives of the mid-19th century that were designed primarily as weapons. Strictly speaking, "folding dirk" refers only to such knives that have double-edged "dirk" or dagger blades. "Folding bowie," the more general term, encompasses larger folding dirks, as well as big folding combat knives with clip-point or spear-point blades.

Folding dirks and bowies were the pocket-carry counterparts of the better-known fixed-blade bowie knives. Bowie knives leapt to national attention in 1827 with the notorious Sandbar Fight involving James Bowie and remained in vogue for about half a century. The bowie knife and the Colt revolver, introduced in 1835, were the characteristic sidearms of the American frontier. Pundits labeled them America's outstanding contributions to 19th-century civilization.

Judging by the relative numbers of surviving examples, the folding bowie may have been just as popular as the less costly fixed blade in the 1830s, the enthusiastic early years of the bowie trend. By the 1850s, the big folders were in eclipse. After the Civil War, only small folding dirks were still available.

Almost all folding dirks and bowie knives are over 4 1/2 inches long closed. They are generally slender, and most have a cross-guard integral with the front bolsters.

Almost every older folding dirk and bowie we have seen was made in Sheffield. Most of them were made for sale in the United States. However, those marked with the name of another English city, such as London or Bristol, and most of those with lions in the decorations were made for sale in England. A German style of folding bowie is described later in this chapter.

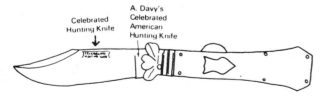

A. Davy's
Celebrated
Celebrated   American
Hunting Knife   Hunting Knife

Sheffield folding bowie, 6 1/4 inches long closed, marked A. DAVY'S/ CELEBRATED/AMERICAN/ HUNTING KNIFE on tang and CELEBRATED HUNTING KNIFE on blade. Cow horn ("English buffalo") handles. 1836-1856. Value **$5,000**. (illustration courtesy Michael Stephen and *Knife World*.)

Ornamental appearance was an important consideration in the design of folding dirks and bowies. Consequently, they were made in a wide variety of shapes. Another factor in their diversity of shape is that most were made from circa 1830 to 1860, before mass production and pattern standardization had taken hold in the cutlery industry.

Not only are the shapes of the big knives varied; so too are their decorations. Their bolsters are almost always ornately embossed.

Though the knives were handmade, their fancy nickel-silver bolsters were mass-produced. Standard designs were stamped out by specialist firms and sold to all the makers. Some of the original dies used to stamp these fancy mounts still exist, which helps account for a certain amount of counterfeiting—most of which is inept—and questionable repair work.

The design motifs of the mounts are an important factor in estimating the value of a folding dirk or bowie. Bolsters with political or patriotic symbols are worth about 50-150 percent more than similar knives without.

Perhaps the most desirable motif is the "half horse half alligator." This imaginary beast symbolized the "Hunters of Kentucky" in a song of the same name dating from the War of 1812. An equally valuable and even rarer motif is the bust of Mexican War hero Gen. Zachary Taylor.

Bolsters with the American eagle are also popular. So, too, are cross guards with an artillery horse, a cannon, and a liberty pole and cap. (1850s German copies of the design look more like a duck, a drainpipe and a crutch.) Cross guards with the motto "Liberty and Union" in a banner reflect the sentiments of Daniel Webster's famous "Constitution and Union" speech of 1850. The knives bearing the imperial lion—the lion being a British symbol—are also popular among American collectors, though less so than the knives with American symbols.

Handle materials on folding dirks and bowies are generally of high quality. Genuine stag, ivory and mother-of-pearl are the most often encountered. Horn and tortoise shell are more unusual. We have not observed bone or wood handles on them, but some may exist.

Makers

In contrast to standard production folding knives, the maker of a folding dirk or bowie is not a major factor in estimating its value, except insofar as the name and blade markings help to date the knife. The earlier circa 1830s knives, which also tend to be larger and more elaborate, are the most valuable. See "Some Clues that Help Date and Identify Knives" in Section I and also the "Pocketknife Brand List" segment in the "Factory Folding Knife Charts, Tables and Histories" chapter of Section II for specific information.

From the knives we have seen, the principal firms that made folding dirks and bowies seem to have been Samuel C. Wragg, William and Samuel Butcher, George Wostenholm & Sons, and Robert and Joseph Lingard. Many other Sheffield names are found on the knives as well.

Folding dirks and small folding bowies, top to bottom. Values approximate. (Roger Baker collection)

A   Unmarked, 4 3/4", ivory handles, **$2,000**.

B   W(crown)R/THOMAS/BARNES/PATENT/DIRK, 6 1/8", ivory handles, **$3,000**.

C   I*XL/GEORGE/WOSTENHOLM/SHEFFIELD, 5 1/2", LIBERTY & UNION guard, ivory handles, **$2,500**.

D   SAMUEL C. WRAGG/FURNACE HILL/SHEFFIELD/ IMPROVED PATENT CUTLERY, 5 1/4", carved mother-of-pearl handles, worked nickel-silver spring cover, **$3,500**.

E   REGISTERED BY GOVERNMENT/FEBRUARY 9, 1850, No. 2180/LINGARD/PEACROFT/SHEFFIELD, 5 3/4", two-blade switchblade (press small blade to operate), stag handles. [Switchblades are illegal to own in many states.] **$5,000**.

F   ARTHUR/LINLEY & CO./SHEFFIELD, 5 1/8", two blades, mother-of-pearl handles, **$3,000**.

Collecting Folding Dirks and Bowies

The Sheffield folding bowie is fascinating in its historical lore, mechanical workmanship, and elegant beauty. It is frustrating to search for these rare pieces of Americana. It can be devastating to the wallet to acquire one. However, even a single fine example can be considered a respectable collection.

Folding dirks and bowies will never grow to be a popular collecting field simply because there are too few good specimens available to supply a large market. Likewise, there cannot really be a "market value" for a particular type, since almost every one of the knives is different, as is every transaction among the few collectors in the field.

The knives in the accompanying photographs illustrate the range of sizes, makers and decorations that exist. The values given are estimates only. However, they can serve as a guide to evaluating similar knives. The value of a particular knife is substantially influenced both by its condition and by the condition of the market. The

Folding bowie knife and large folding dirks. Values approximate. (Roger Baker collection)

Third from bottom: SAMUEL C. WRAGG/No. 2-/FURNACE HILL SHEFFIELD, 6 1/4", heavy saber-clip blade, wide stag handles, eagle pommel, **$14,500**.

Second from bottom: Unmarked, 9", ivory handles with etched panel, **$4,500**.

Bottom: NON-XLL/UNWIN & RODGERS/SHEFFIELD, 8 1/8", mother-of-pearl handles, **$8,000**.

knives in the accompanying illustrations are in as good a condition as any that are known.

Be extremely wary of folding dirks or bowies that have been heavily cleaned or buffed. Their mechanisms are delicate, and many broken ones have been incorrectly restored. Fresh buffing can conceal sloppy repair work. It can also indicate a counterfeit.

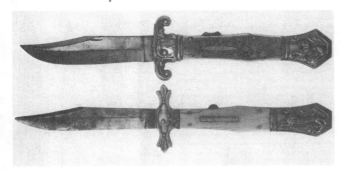

Folding bowies. Values approximate.
(Roger Baker collection)

Top: MILLS/120 HOLBORN/LONDON, 7", lion pommel, etched ivory handles, **$15,000**.

Bottom: W(crown)R/GEORGE WOSTENHOLM & SONS/CELEBRATED IMPROVED CUTLERY/ ROCKINGHAM WORKS/SHEFFIELD/WARRANTED OF THE BEST QUALITY, 7", half-horse-half-alligator pommel, ivory handles, **$14,500**.

German-Style Folding Bowies

German folding "bowies" are well made but not nearly as valuable—or as old—as their English counterparts. The standard style has a blade several inches longer than its handle. Folded, it can be used as a handy utility knife; open, it can be a formidable weapon. A knife of this type usually has two locks. A standard back lock keeps the blade open. A button-type lock in the front of the handle keeps it closed.

Case made a knife of the type, as did some of the English firms. The Marble's safety hunting knife was an American improvement on the design (see the "American Hunting Knives" segment in Section III). More recent versions, usually with brass mounts, have been made in India and Pakistan. International copying of knife patterns is as much a part of cutlery history as it is of the cutlery industry today.

See Part 3 of Section II, "Foreign, Exotic, Primitive, and Historical Folding Knives," for information on other large European jack knives.

German-style folding bowie knives, values in excellent, unsharpened condition, with sheath.

Sheath missing: subtract 20 percent.
German brand (rated Very High or High): **$300**.
German brand (rated Medium to Low): **$120**.
English brand (rated Very High or High): **$375**.
English brand (rated Medium to Low): **$200**.
Case 551 stag or 661 bone stag: **$625**.
Indian or Pakistani: **$25**.
Indian or Pakistani with metal blade guard: **$50**.

Folding bowies. Values approximate.
(Roger Baker collection)

Top: W(crown)R/W. BUTCHER/SHEFFIELD, 7 1/8", horsehead pommel, heavy spear blade, ivory handles, **$10,500**.

Bottom: SNOW/PORTSEA/OF THE BEST QUALITY, 5 7/8", horsehead pommel, saber-clip blade, ivory handles, **$14,500**. ("Portsea" is part of Portsmouth, England.)

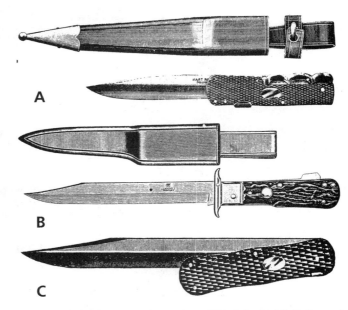

Expanding Bowie Knife. Can be used as a 4" Blade Locked, Fully Opened as an 8" Blade Locked. In Leather Sheath.

German-Style Folding Bowies, all sold with sheath.

A Hart German export circa 1905. 4" handle, 7" blade. Ebony handles, folding guard, **$120**.

B German export by J.A. Henckels circa 1935. 4 5/8" handle, 8 3/8" blade. Stag handle scales, folding guard, **$300**.

C. Sheffield export by John Clarke & Son, circa 1924. 4" handle, 8" blade. Ebony handle scales, no guard, **$200**.

Switchblade Double-End Jack Knives

The switchblade double-end jack knife was made before World War I. In the 1920s, Schrade Cutlery Co. made both shadow and bolstered 3 3/4-inch equal-ends with a spear master blade and either a large clip or a punch second blade.

"Outing Knife," Imitation Buckhorn Handle.
"Coaching Knife," Imitation Buckhorn Handle.

Switchblade Jack Knives

Switchblade knives have been illegal to sell in interstate commerce since 1958, as well as illegal to possess in most states. Despite—or because of—this, there is a lot of collector interest in them. We do not recommend buying or keeping switchblades, except where they are legal, and you definitely should never mail them.

"Patent Press Button" Lock Back.

$150.

$2,500.

Flylock Pattern $550.

$350.

$1,000.

$700. $600. $550.

Springer Pattern $250.

Silver Fruit Knives

By Bill Karsten

Bill Karsten is the author of Silver Folding Fruit Knives. *Bill Claussen upgraded the values of the knives in October 2004.*

Decorated Jack Knives

Knives with silver blades—sometimes silver plated or gold—are called *fruit knives.* They were intended to aid in the nibbling of fresh fruit and were a popular keepsake gift up through about 1930.

The earliest-known folding fruit knives were made in France in the 17th century. They were double-ended with one silver or gold blade, which resisted staining from fruit acids, and one steel blade. Examples in excellent condition are worth **$2,000** and up.

Another early style of French fruit knife has no backspring. In this style, two blades pivot on a common hinge pin, one blade on each side of the knife. Examples have been called *Berge knives* at least since the 19th century. Before that, they were called *crutch knives* or *balance knives.* Fine French Berge knives with tortoise-shell handles and gold trim, in excellent original condition, will bring **$3,000** to **$3,500**, and like other "high-end" knives, some have brought considerably more at recent auctions. Examples in good condition, as usually found, are worth about **$500** to **$900**.

English Fruit Knives

Silver fruit knives were made in England, mainly Sheffield and Birmingham, beginning in the 18th century. The English also made folding-silver-fruit-knife-and-fork sets for traveling.

Early French couteau sans clou pin-less fruit knife.

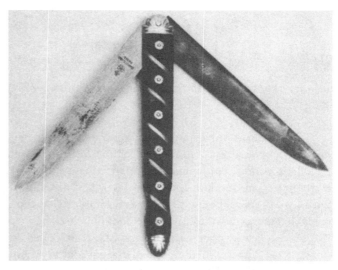

French Berge knife. (Smithsonian Institution)

Most English silver work is *hallmarked.* England has had a hallmark system since the 14th century. Official silver assay offices were opened in Sheffield and Birmingham in 1773. Fruit knives made in either place after that date are marked accordingly. A full hallmark includes the following stamps: city code (a crown for Sheffield, an anchor for Birmingham); sterling mark (a lion passant); year code (a letter); maker's or "sponsor's" (seller's) initials; and duty stamp (the monarch's profile). Before 1830, sometimes only the sterling mark and the duty stamp were used. The duty stamp was dropped in 1890.

Fruit knives of the Georgian period, prior to 1830, are simple in design yet tasteful and elegant. Often, the blade is engraved along the back edge. Handle scales are generally thin-beveled mother-of-pearl or tortoise shell. Many have a silver shield engraved with the recipient's name or initials. Backsprings are chased with a diagonal or, later, a cross-hatch pattern. Some have long, ringed bolsters or silver end caps.

Typical Sheffield hallmark (John Nowill).

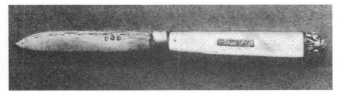

Typical Georgian fruit knife.

Fancy shaped Victorian fruit knife in mother-of-pearl.

Exceptional English fruit knife hallmarked 1924.

795—CARVED PEARL HANDLE FRUIT KNIFE; 3 1/2 in. Haft: Sterling
Silver Blade . . . . .17/6 each, post free.

Sheffield fruit knife from the 1920s.

Georgian fruit knives are the aristocrats of silver fruit knives. Individual knives or forks sell for **$200-$300** in excellent condition, depending on the quality of work. Matching knife-and-fork pairs are worth **$400-$600**, with cased pairs being the most desirable. The most valuable Georgian fruit knives have gold blades. Sheffield had no gold assay office until 1904, so the gold blades are unmarked. However, their Georgian designs identify them. They are worth **$550** and up.

Beginning with the reign of William IV (1830-37) and continuing through the Victorian era (1837-1901), English design and decoration changed greatly. Fruit knives were made in more exotic shapes, their mother-of-pearl, tortoise-shell, silver or ivory handles engraved in various floral or geometric themes. Some of the finest mother-of-pearl or shell handles featured *pique*—pin-work patterns of tiny silver pins painstakingly hand inletted into the scales. Presentation pieces were engraved, usually on the blade, with dates, initials, names or even brief inscriptions.

Georgian and most Victorian fruit knives are single bladed. Some later editions have a second blade—a slim, curved, unsharpened seed or nut pick. Also, some knife-and-fork pairs were made as a single unit, the two parts held together by small lugs that fit into slots (hence the name "slot knives").

Many English silversmiths made fruit knives. Two whose work was outstanding were George Unite (G.U.) of Birmingham and John Yeomans Cowlishaw (J.Y.C.) of Sheffield. One of the most prolific, whose work is often encountered in the United States, was Thomas Marples (T.M.) of Sheffield.

A number of factors affect the value of Victorian fruit knives, including the color of the mother-of-pearl (the more colorful, the better); the quality and extent of the engraving or pin work; the age (a good silver hallmark book is essential to determine age); the shape and size; the number of blades; and the maker. Most important, a knife that is well proportioned and pleasing to the eye is worth more than a heavy, ostentatious piece.

Good-quality Victorian single-bladed knives or forks in excellent condition range in value from **$125-150**. Knives with seed picks can bring a slight premium. Take-apart or matching silver knife-and-fork sets are worth **$300-$350** in excellent condition. Worn or damaged fruit knives bring less than a third of the listed values, often much less.

Most 20th-century English fruit knives were mass-produced. Decoration was often pressed or etched rather than cut by hand. The design and quality of the later knives are usually inferior to the older ones. The decline foreshadowed the end of the age of fruit knives. Later pieces of ordinary quality are worth **$90-$120**.

American Fruit Knives

Except for the brief period of 1814-1830, the United States had no standardized hallmark system like England's. American silversmiths used all sorts of marks, such as initials, full names, pictorial symbols, simulated hallmarks, fineness designations such as COIN (90 percent silver) or STERLING (92.5 percent), or no mark at all.

American fruit knife marked STERLING.

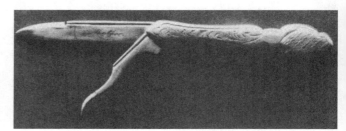

American fruit knife marked COIN.

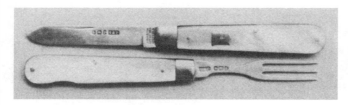

Victorian take-apart fruit knife and fork.

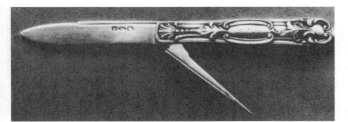

Coles fruit knife.

Gorham fruit knife.

There are perhaps 20,000 American silver marks listed in various reference works. However, just two firms, Cole and Gorham, made a large proportion of American silver fruit knives.

Albert Coles of New York was active from about 1836-1880. He produced a large volume of work, much of it for other makers. His mark is in three parts: an eagle, his initials (A.C.) and a man's profile.

Coles' fruit knives are well above average in quality. They feature heavy, ornate silver handles. Most have a nut pick. His backsprings are nicely chased in a ladder and cross-hatch design.

John Gorham of Providence, Rhode Island, founded one of America's largest silver companies in 1831. Gorham's early mark was also in three parts: a letter (G), an anchor, and a lion passant facing left. In 1868, when America substituted the sterling for the coin standard, Gorham turned the lion around to face right. The change can help date his knives.

Gorham's best fruit knives are perhaps even finer than Coles'. Examples in top condition by either firm are valued at **$100-$150**. American pieces marked simply COIN or STERLING are less desirable and are valued at **$80-$120**.

Embossed plated fruit knife with figure of a girl.

Empire plated flop-over fruit knife.

Plated Fruit Knives

Silver-plated fruit knives are generally unmarked. They range from unattractive to beautiful. If you are not sure whether a knife is silver or plated, *gently* flex the blade a *little bit*. If it feels soft and stays bent, it is silver. (Afterward, carefully straighten it back out.) If it feels springy, it is plated. *Do not file a knife to do an acid test, or you will destroy much of its value.* Plated fruit knives are worth **$40-$70** in excellent condition.

The Empire Knife Co. of Connecticut made an odd silver-plated fruit knife. Its blade and seed pick project from opposite ends of a common tang. The tang is secured in the end of a springy steel handle. The blade unit can be pivoted so that one end or the other is exposed. The knife is worth about **$60**. Other base-metal novelty fruit knives are worth **$30-$55**.

Fruit knives frequently can be found at antique shops and shows, though some antique dealers ask excessive prices. English knife dealers bring many fine early examples into the USA. A large collection can include 300 or more pieces, all different.

William Needham Fruit Knives

William Needham manufactured silver fruit knives with mother-of-pearl handles in Sheffield from about 1891-1920. He offered scores of patterns, ranging from the plainest to the most elaborate engraved, carved and pique models. Most were of exceptionally high quality, especially for the last years of the fruit-knife era.

Needham published a handsome catalog, from which came the accompanying illustrations (courtesy William Adams). Needham's name appears nowhere in the booklet, allowing it to be used by cutlery or jewelry retailers to solicit special orders from customers. However, all of the knives included have his initials—WN—as part of their hallmarks. The date letters on the fruit knives cover the years 1902-1907, but the dates on the silver-handled, steel-bladed knives on the last two pages of the accompanying illustrations span from 1910-1916.

One knife from the last page has stainless steel blades. Stainless was invented in 1914 and used briefly for knives in 1915. Its production was then suspended until 1919, as chromium was required to make tool steel for the war effort. Thereafter, stainless steel blades soon made silver-bladed fruit knives obsolete.

All That Glitters

English silver fruit knives are beautiful, glittering, delicate and gem-like, in stark contrast to the conditions under which they were made. Silver finishers, many of them women, were among the lowest paid of Sheffield craftspeople. Their starting wage early in the 20th century was six shillings per week. The hours were long, the work was filthy, and the workshops were cold, damp and ill lighted. All but the strongest died young of tuberculosis.

Even more unhealthful was the working of mother-of-pearl, because pearl dust is highly toxic. A single exposure can induce fever and tremors. Repeated exposure is inevitably fatal.

The chief reward enjoyed by the people who made the beautiful fruit knives in Sheffield was the satisfaction of a job well done. Most were paid so little that they could never hope to own a single example of their own handiwork.

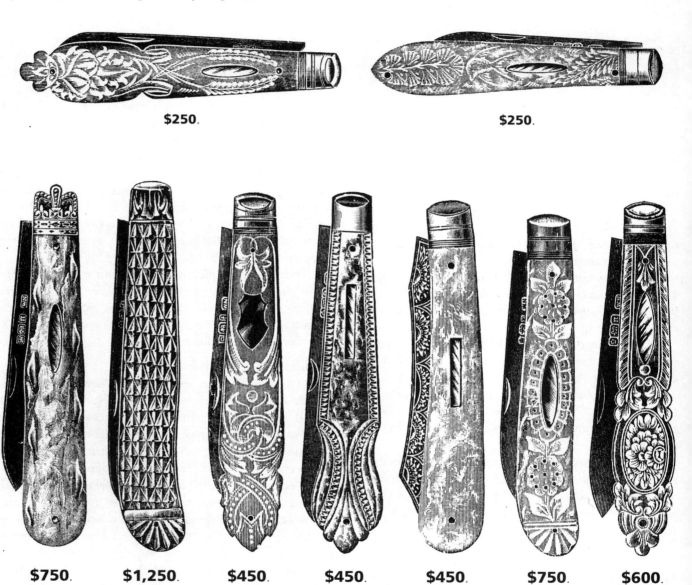

$250. $250.

$750. $1,250. $450. $450. $450. $750. $600.

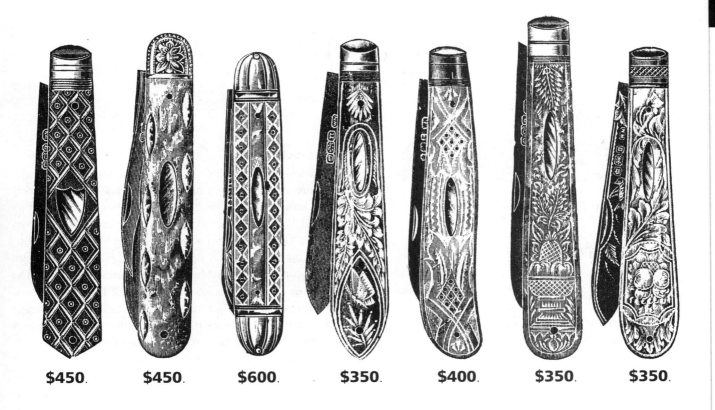

$450. $450. $600. $350. $400. $350. $350.

$250. $150.

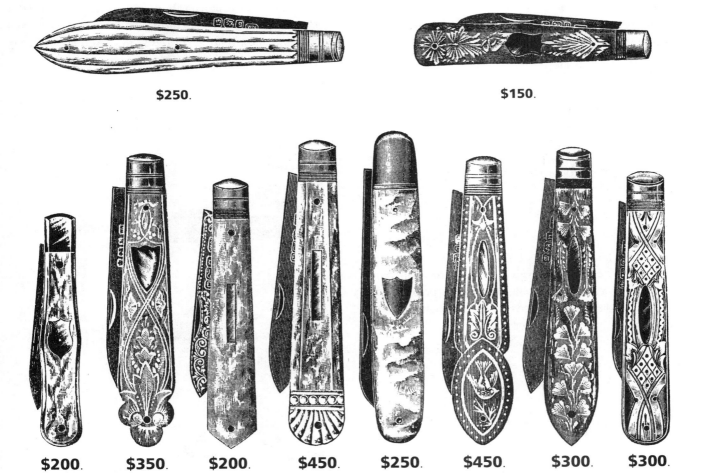

$200. $350. $200. $450. $250. $450. $300. $300.

Pen Knives

Pen Knife

Crinking

Pen Knives and Quill Knives

Pen knife refers to a small folding knife with blades in both ends. Almost invariably, one or more of the blades is a pen pattern.

The pen blade and the pen knife originally were designed for sharpening quill pens. Quill pens were first employed in the early Middle Ages and their use was standard in the Western world until the 19th century. Though steel pens had been made before then, they did not become common until after 1828, when Josiah Mason began mass-producing them in Birmingham, England.

It is remarkable that quill pens have been gone for generations now, but pen blades and pen knives are still very much with us. A sharp little blade still has plenty of uses.

The earliest folding pen knives usually seen are from the 18th century, when their main use still was for sharpening quill pens. Folding pen knives may have been used before that time to cut book papers or trim candle wicks.

Unlike modern "pen knives," which by definition have at least two blades, many of the pen knives from the 18th and 19th centuries have only one blade. Collectors now call little single-bladed folding pen sharpeners "quill knives." The diminutive pieces have their own segment ("Quill Knives") in this chapter.

Construction

Double-ended knives, including pen knives, historically require more labor to make than standard single-ended jack knives. At least one spring in almost every double-ended knife must be adjusted to bear smoothly on two blades. The blades themselves must be "crinked" or bent sideways so that each opposing pair can close into the same slot without one blade banging against the other. (On some modern knives, such as those made by Victorinox, asymmetrical grinding has taken the place of crinking.) In addition, most pen knives are premium-quality knives requiring a higher degree of finish than jack knives.

As a result, pen knives—when new—have usually cost more than jack knives of comparable size and quality. In fact, most manufacturers a generation and more ago used to charge more for their top-of-the-line pen knives than they did for any of their jack knives, no matter how large.

These relative original values do *not* carry over into the collector market, however. Most collectors find big knives more appealing than small ones, and naturally will pay more for what they like better.

Bolsters and Backs

Pen knives can have full bolsters, tip bolsters or no bolsters at all. They can have plain liners or liners milled like the edge of a dime. They can have engraved bolsters with plain or engraved handles. They can even have "closed backs."

Full Bolsters

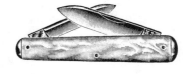

Tip Bolsters

Quill Knife

No Bolsters (Shadow)

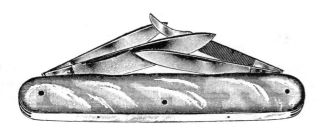

Solid Mother-of-Pearl Closed Back

On a knife with a closed back, both handle liners are made from a single piece of metal that is wrapped around the backsprings. On a jack knife or a stock knife, a closed back is often a mark of inexpensive construction. On a pen knife, it most often is; however, some of the finest pen knives were made with closed backs.

Joints

A pen knife can have one of three types of joint: *common, half-sunk* or *sunk*. The type of joint is defined by how much the "run ups" or back ends of the blades protrude from the handles when the blades are closed.

The most elegant type of joint is the *sunk joint*. With sunk joints, the back corners of the blades are completely "sunk" within the handles so as not to catch on clothing or break up the lines of the handle.

Many pen knives with sunk joints must have little beveled notches cut into the handles beside the nail nicks of the blades, or else the blades cannot be opened. Though similar, the notches are not the same as the easy-open notches on some jack knives, since they do not permit the blades to be grasped with the fingertips.

Some large jack knives have over-sized bolsters that cover the run ups of the blades. Though similar in function, this type of reinforced construction is not called a sunk joint. Some fancy slim jacks and English jacks do have true sunk joints.

Half-sunk joints are only half as elegant as sunk joints. The back corners of the blades stick out a little bit but so do the nail nicks, so notches do not need to be cut in the handles. Half-sunk joints are sturdier than sunk joints.

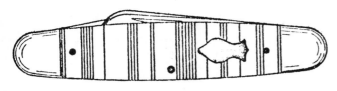

Sunk Joints

Half-Sunk Joints

Common Joint

Common joints are the least costly of the three types to make, but they are also the sturdiest when the knife is open and in use. In a common joint, the back corners of the blades stick out quite prominently when the blades are closed.

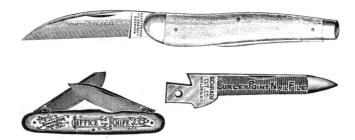

Blades

The spear master blade is standard in most pen-knife patterns of the past century and a half. Important exceptions include congress knives with a sheepfoot master blade and serpentine pens that often have a clip master blade; some are Wharncliffe knives with Wharncliffe master blades. (See "Pocketknife Blade Charts" under "Factory Folding Knife Charts, Tables and Histories" in Section II.)

Pen knives do not have spey blades except for some "office knives" that have a spey-like blade intended to serve as an ink eraser. An office knife is a large equal-end pen knife with white ivory, bone or celluloid handles. OFFICE KNIFE in fancy letters is usually etched or stamped on the front handle. Office knives are covered in the "Mechanical Pen Knives/Office and Letter Opener Knives" segment of this chapter..

Many pen knives have a manicure blade, something not ordinarily found in jack knives. Manicure blades have been made in at least half-a-dozen varieties. Some pen knives with manicure blades also have a little folding scissors.

Pen knives, mainly equal-ends, have been fitted with a variety of mechanisms to assist in the opening of the blades.

Ring Opener

Pen Knife Handle Materials and Skeleton Knives

Mother-of-pearl seems to be the most common handle material on older pen knives. However, it is unusual to find an older pen knife in mother-of-pearl with its handles still intact. Ivory also was used on many pen knives.

Metal handles of one sort or another are also common on pen knives. The least-expensive metal handles are plain nickel silver, aluminum, pewter and "gun metal" (an alloy of copper and tin).

The next step up in cost is decorated metal handles: the nickel-silver handles decorated with stamping, the aluminum with stamping or engraving, and the gun metal with color etching, selective plating or enameling. For more on decorated handles, see "Advertising, Figural, Character, and Miniature Knives."

The fanciest metal handles are covered with silver or gold. Ordinary ones are thin sheets of the precious metal secured to the brass liners of "skeleton knives." The thin sheets often are engine-turned or have some simple engraving. Low-cost versions of the flat handles are merely sheet brass that is silver or gold—or even chromium—plated.

The best metal handles are elaborate stampings or investment castings of gold or silver applied by jewelers to "skeleton knives." Such handles may have jewels or panels of semi-precious stones, such as gold-bearing quartz, set into them.

A "skeleton knife" is a completely assembled and finished pen knife lacking bolsters and handle covers. Jewelers buy them and dress them up any way they like. Many early American pen knives of the sort were sold exclusively by jewelry stores.

A few firms have specialized in the manufacture of skeleton knives. Wostenholm of Sheffield, England, seems to have made a lot of them for the American market up until around 1910. Miller Bros. and Empire, both of Connecticut, made large numbers in the early 20th century. The Imperial Knife Co. got its start in 1916 making skeleton knives for the wholesale jewelry trade in Providence, Rhode Island.

Besides mother-of-pearl—occasionally abalone as well—and the various metals, almost any other handle material that you can name has been used on pen knives. Jigged bone and celluloid were common in the first half of the 20th century. Smooth bone, tortoise shell and horn

Skeleton with Gold-Plated Covers

were popular in the 19th century. However, genuine stag and wood are very unusual on pen knives, having been considered more appropriate on larger or coarser knives.

Sometimes, you may find a pen knife with two different factory-original handles, either mother-of-pearl and brown bone or black plastic and white plastic. Some of the knives are salesman's samples. Most are "magician" knives that, with careful manipulation, can be made to appear to "change color."

Lobsters

The main structural division in pen knives is between ordinary spring-back knives and "lobster-spring" knives. A "lobster" knife has its spring or springs—often a single "split" or branched spring—inside the middle of the handle. This allows it to have blades on both top and bottom, as well as at one or both ends. A lobster pen always has its pivot pins set off to the sides of the long axis of the knife.

We do not know for certain why the knives are called "lobsters." It may be because the action of two blades, pivoting at the corners of one end of a knife, is reminiscent of the action of lobster claws.

Lobster-spring pen knives were made in a number of standard shapes. Most of the shapes have exotic-sounding names, and some have more than one name. Their names, descriptions and values are covered in the "Lobster Pen Knives" segment of this chapter.

Lobster pen knives are flat and lightly constructed. A wide variety of thicker multi-blade folders resemble lobsters in that they have blades both top and bottom. The more-robust knives are covered in the chapter, "Multi-Blade Knives."

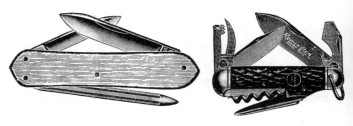

Lobster   *Multi-Blade*

Whittlers

The main structural division in spring-back pen knives is between ordinary pen knives and "whittlers." Most three-blade pen knives of all shapes are constructed as whittlers.

Most whittlers have two springs. The large, thick master blade, at one end of the knife, bears on *both* of the springs. The two thin small blades at the other end of the knife each bear on one of the springs. Some whittlers have three backsprings and are a special class of whittler.

Whittler

Years ago, knife manufacturers did not usually distinguish their whittlers from their other pen knives. Today, however, whittlers are a separate and important collecting specialty. Therefore, in *BLADE's Guide*, all whittlers—regardless of shape—are described and valued together in one chapter.

Value Table for Standard Pen Knife Shapes

Base values for PEN KNIVES of the indicated shape, over 2 15/16 and up to 3 3/4 inches long closed; pen or manicure second blade; brass or nickel-silver liners, nickel-silver trim; full bolsters; bone stag (jigged bone) handles. Excellent, unsharpened condition, with appropriate etch.

NOTE: The following special types of pen knife have their own separate chapters and value tables: WHITTLERS, LOBSTERS, QUILL KNIVES, and OFFICE and LETTER OPENER KNIVES. MECHANICAL PEN KNIVES, EMBOSSED, COLOR-ETCHED and ENAMELED HANDLES, and ADVERTISING, FIGURAL, CHARACTER and MINIATURE KNIVES have their own segments elsewhere in *BLADE's Guide,* but they use this value table.

VALUE RANGE

SHAPE	VERY HIGH (VH)	HIGH (H)	MEDIUM (M)	LOW / MEDIUM (LM)	LOW (L)
TWO-BLADE SENATOR	$150	$125	$60	$45	$30
THREE-BLADE SENATOR (not a whittler)	150	125	75	50	35
FOUR-BLADE SENATOR	200	150	75	50	35
SLEEVEBOARD	165	135	75	50	35
OVAL or CIGAR	175	150	75	50	35
TWO-BLADE CONGRESS	250	175	100	70	45
FOUR-BLADE CONGRESS	650	350	225	160	100
"GUNSTOCK"	600	375	250	180	125
CROWN or COFFIN (barrel-shaped)	300	200	100	70	40
MODERN CROWN (rectangular)	125	75	50	35	25
SWELL-CENTER and BALLOON	375	250	150	100	45
PREMIUM (SERPENTINE)	225	150	90	60	35
WHARNCLIFFE	300	225	125	100	80
"DOG-LEG" SERPENTINE	275	150	100	70	45
SWELL-CENTER SERPENTINE	250	175	100	75	50
SWELL-CENTER CONGRESS or SWAY-BACK	450	350	175	130	90

Skeleton Knives with Gold-Filled or Plated Covers

There is limited collector interest in the metal-handled watch-fob knives known as *skeleton knives*, which had gold-filled or plated covers. However, if the fobs are true miniatures—for example, less than 1 inch long—there is a good market for them.

Value of any style in excellent, unsharpened condition:

VALUE RANGE

VH	H	M	LM	L
$125	$100	$60	$45	$30

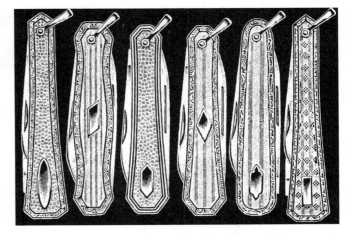

An illustration from 1925 of skeleton knives.

Some Typical Examples

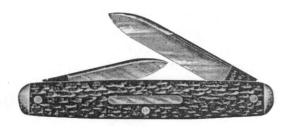

Actual Size　　　**No. 2361**　　　*3 1/8 inches long*
Patent Stag Handle.　　　　　　Nickel Silver lined, **$85**.
Nickel Silver Shield and Tipped.　　　Half-sunk Joints.
CATTARAUGUS, **$100**.

No. 5260
Length closed 3 7/16"
Case XX, **$90**.

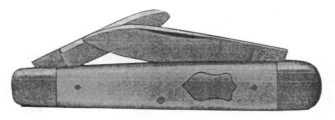

No. 22223—3 5/16" Two blades. Brass lined.
Nickel silver bolsters. Crocus finish. Mother-of-pearl handle. Shielded.
CATTARAUGUS, **$125**.

No. 22153—3 1/8" Two blades. Brass lined. Nickel silver bolsters.
Crocus finish. Mother-of-pearl handle.
CATTARAUGUS, **$165**.

Boker Tree Brand, 3 1/4", 4 blades, swell center
serpentine, mother-of-pearl handle, **$165**.

G. Wostenholm, multi-blade pen with button
hook, tortoise-shell handle, **$175**.

Hibbard Spencer Bartlett, 2 5/8",
sleeveboard, easy opener,
mother-of-pearl handle, **$125**.

No. 22639—3" Two Blades. Brass lined.
Nickel silver bolsters. Full polish. Stag handle. Shielded.
CATTARAUGUS, **$100**.

NOTE: THE SIZE OF A FOLDING KNIFE IS ITS LENGTH IN THE CLOSED POSITION.

Senator or Equal-End Pens

Pen knives have been made in a good variety of shapes over the years, though not in as many shapes as jack knives. Some pen-knife shapes are similar to those of jack knives, but the majority are different.

By far the most common pen-knife pattern, the "senator" is similar in shape to the equal-end jack knife. The senator pen is round-ended and symmetrical like the equal-end jack, but is proportionally narrower.

Some manufacturers called all of their equal-end pen knives "senators," while others limited the name to knives of intermediate proportions. The latter firms called very narrow equal-end pen knives "regular pens." The same firms called very wide or large pen knives "oval" or simply "equal-end."

Senator pens can have two, three or four blades. On rare occasions they have even more. Most three-blade senators are "whittlers."

The master blade of a senator pen is a small spear point. The second blade in a two-blade senator is either a pen blade or a nail file. Three-bladed senators that are not whittlers are the same as the two-bladed ones, except for the addition of a full-length blade. The latter can be a special manicure, a scissors, a corn blade or, rarely, a sheepfoot. Most four-bladed senators have a spear, two pens and a file.

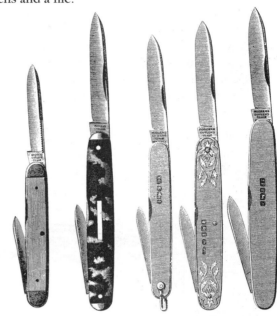

Joseph Rodgers (from left): 2 1/4", ivory, **$100**; tip bolsters, 2 3/4", tortoise shell, **$125**; 2 7/16", sterling, **$100**; 2 11/16", embossed sterling, **$125;** 2 3/4", sterling **$100**.

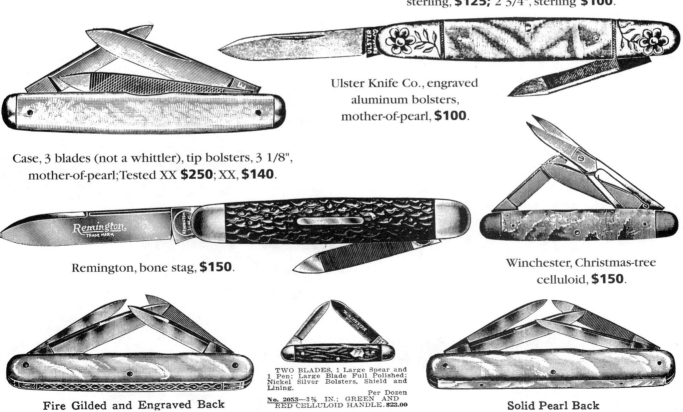

Ulster Knife Co., engraved aluminum bolsters, mother-of-pearl, **$100**.

Case, 3 blades (not a whittler), tip bolsters, 3 1/8", mother-of-pearl; Tested XX **$250**; XX, **$140**.

Remington, bone stag, **$150**.

Winchester, Christmas-tree celluloid, **$150**.

Fire Gilded and Engraved Back

H. Boker, 4 blades, shadow bolsters, milled liners, worked back, 2 11/16", mother-of-pearl, **$200**.

TWO BLADES, 1 Large Spear and 1 Pen; Large Blade Full Polished; Nickel Silver Bolsters, Shield and Lining.
Per Dozen
No. 2053—3⅜ IN.; GREEN AND RED CELLULOID HANDLE. **$23.00**

I*XL G. Wostenholm, 3", 2 blades w/scissors, **$150**.

Solid Pearl Back

H. Boker, 4 blades, shadow bolsters, milled liners, fancy (mother-of-pearl) closed back, 2 11/16", mother-of-pearl, **$200**.

Sleeveboard Pens

A "sleeveboard pen" has round ends like a senator, but its handle tapers. It is shaped like the old sleeveboards once used for ironing shirt sleeves. Sleeveboard pen knives ordinarily have the master blade in the wider end. Fat, heavy-duty sleeveboards are called "jumbo knives." Two-bladed jumbos are covered in the "Double-End Jack Knives" segment of the "Jack Knives" chapter. Three-bladed jumbos are detailed in the "Whittlers" segment of the chapter on "Pen Knives" and the "Cattle Knives" segment of the chapter on "Multi-Blade Knives."

No. 62079 1/2
Case, 3 1/4", bone stag:
Tested XX, **$175**;
XX, **$125**.

Remington,
mother-of-pearl,
$200.

Ulster Knife Co.,
tip bolsters,
plain celluloid,
$75.

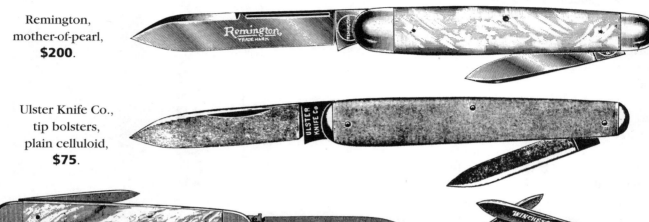

I*XL G. Wostenholm, 3", 2 blades w/file/manicure, mother-of-pearl, **$160**.

Winchester, 3 3/8", bone stag, **$150**.

Anglo-Saxon, Milton, Oval or Cigar Pens

The Anglo-Saxon pattern is a large—sometimes over 4 inches long closed—equal-end or slightly tapering pen knife with curved sides. Both the senator and the sleeveboard, which are closely related to the oval pattern, have straight sides.

Oval pen knives usually are of premium quality and have sunk joints. Large oval pen knives are very rare. Most of the few 20th-century examples are whittlers.

H. Boker, tip
bolsters, 2 5/8",
bone stag, **$75**.

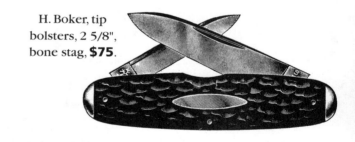

Joseph Rodgers, 4 blades, 3 1/4", mother-of-pearl, **$175**.

Winchester, 2 5/8",
mother-of-pearl,
$150.

Joseph Rodgers, 2 1/4",
tortoise shell, **$150**.

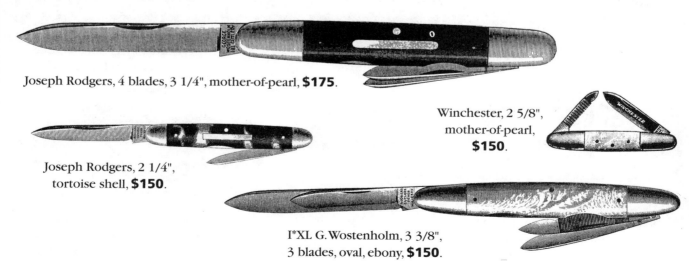

I*XL G. Wostenholm, 3 3/8",
3 blades, oval, ebony, **$150**.

Congress and Tobacco Knives

The "congress" knife is curved in the shape of a crescent. It usually has squared corners, though a few have rounded corners. Congress knives can have two, three, four, five, six or eight blades. They always have a sheepfoot master blade.

The largest congress knives are 3 1/2 to over 4 inches long. The large congress patterns often were called "tobacco knives" because they were favored for carving bite-sized chews from plugs of chewing tobacco. Larger whittlers of various shapes were also sometimes called tobacco knives. True tobacco knives never have a manicure blade.

It seems that the congress knife appeared on the scene some time in the first third of the 19th century. It is one of the earliest patterns created specifically for the American market. In the late 1800s, Joseph Rodgers offered the U.S. market over 20 different variations of the congress knife. Knife fanciers have long speculated on the origins of the names "senator" and "congress" as pocketknife designations, but no solid evidence has yet surfaced.

Not only is the congress a classical American pattern, for most of its history it was a Southern one. English firms and the big Northeastern cutlery manufacturers, such as Remington and New York Knife Co., made congress knives in large numbers, but they mainly distributed them through wholesalers in the Southeast.

An appealing feature to look for on congress knives, one also found on barlows and other patterns made for the Southern market, is fancy bolsters. Fancy bolsters are often accompanied by fancy handle materials, such as mother-of-pearl.

On the night he was shot, April 14, 1865, President Abraham Lincoln was carrying a six-bladed, ivory-handled congress knife. The knife is now on display in the Library of Congress. It is marked WILLIAM GILCHRIST'S CELEBRATED RAZOR STEEL.

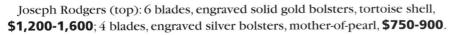

Joseph Rodgers (top): 6 blades, engraved solid gold bolsters, tortoise shell, **$1,200-1,600**; 4 blades, engraved silver bolsters, mother-of-pearl, **$750-900**.

No. 7763
Schrade Cut. Co., 3 7/8",
bone stag, **$225**.

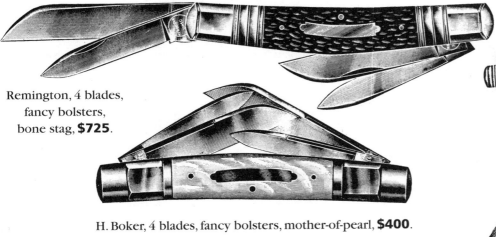

Remington, 4 blades,
fancy bolsters,
bone stag, **$725**.

H. Boker, 4 blades, fancy bolsters, mother-of-pearl, **$400**.

W.H. Morley, 4 blades, fancy
bolsters, 3 3/4", genuine stag,
$250.

I*XL G. Wostenholm, 3 1/4", 4 blades, ivory handle, congress, **$525**.

Winchester, 3 1/4",
mother-of-pearl, **$225**.

Congress and Tobacco Knives *(continued)*

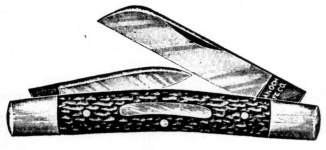

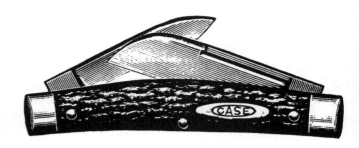

"NAPANOCH" Congress Knife

Actual Size   **No. 2280**   *3 1/4 inches long*

Napanoch Knife Co., bone stag, **$400**.

Case Tested XX, 4 1/8", bone stag, **$300**.

I*XL G. Wostenholm, 3 1/4", 4 blades, congress pen, stag, **$400**.

"Gunstock" Pens

There is almost no such thing as a *gunstock pen knife*. One exception was made by Case, the 3 1/2-inch round-ended -87 pattern. It is sort of a sleeveboard with a step instead of a ramp. It was offered with mother-of-pearl or stag handles.

Another exception is the *gunstock lobster* or *orange blossom*, covered in the "Lobster Pen Knives" segment of this chapter. Yet another exception is a sort of double gunstock pen knife made in Sheffield in the 19th century.

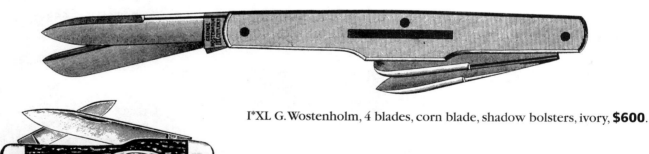

I*XL G. Wostenholm, 4 blades, corn blade, shadow bolsters, ivory, **$600**.

Case Tested XX, 3 1/2", genuine stag, **$550**.

Crown or Coffin

The scarce 19th-century crown or coffin pattern looks more like a slender barrel or cask than a crown or coffin. More than anything, it looks like a congress knife with a straight handle. Indeed, the coffin may be the direct antecedent of the congress pattern. Another possible ancestor of the congress is the English sort of "double gunstock" pen knife mentioned in the preceding "'Gunstock' Pens."

Coffin pen knives are slender and have squared corners and convex sides. They can have two, three or four blades, and horn, ivory or tortoise-shell handles.

A few 20th-century firms made pen knives that are nearly rectangular. We call them *modern crowns*. The Case -78s and the Wallkill River Works "closed backs" by New York Knife Co. are examples.

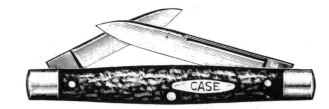

Case, 3", bone stag: Tested XX, **$175**; XX, **$150**.

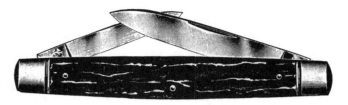

H. Boker, genuine stag, **$125**.

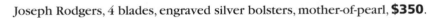

Joseph Rodgers, 4 blades, engraved silver bolsters, mother-of-pearl, **$350**.

Winchester, tip bolsters, 3", bone stag, **$125**.

Ulster Knife Co.; 4 blades, mother-of-pearl, **$225**; 2 blades, ivory, **$200**.

I*XL G. Wostenholm, 3 3/8", coffin, 3 blades w/file, ivory, **$300**.

Modern Crown Pens

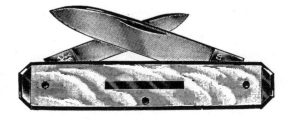

H. Boker, tip bolsters, 2 5/8", mother-of-pearl, **$75**.

Wilbert, 2 3/4", crown pen, celluloid, **$100**.

Swell-Center and Balloon Pens

Swell-center pens have a center swelling with slightly pointed bulges top and bottom. The two basic types of swell-center pen knives are the equal-ended, which are simply called "swell-center," and the tapered, which are called "balloon" or "swell-center balloon." Balloon knives have bulbous, rounded ends shaped like hot-air balloons. Some symmetrical swell-centers have the round type of end as well. Others have pointed ends.

Western States called a small swell-center pen with pointed ends the *Northfield pattern*—no doubt a tribute to the founder of Western States, Harvey N. Platts, who worked for the Northfield Knife Co. in Connecticut early in his career.

In the 1870s, several American pocketknife firms, including Shipley of Philadelphia and Holley of Lakeville, Connecticut, called their small, round-ended swell-center pens "Jenny Lind" knives. They were honoring the immensely popular concert singer who was known to her American fans as the "Swedish Nightingale." Some firms called the style the "buttercup."

LADIES' OR GENTLEMEN'S KNIFE
No. 2180

2 7/8 inches long, pearl handle, German silver lined, two blades, German silver bolster. This is of the very highest quality. There are none better made.

American Shear & Knife Co.,
2 7/8" buttercup, mother-of-pearl, **$175**.

Joseph Rodgers: 4 blades, engraved silver bolster, 3 1/4",
mother-of-pearl, **$300**; 5 blades, fancy bolsters, 3 3/4", ivory, **$475**.

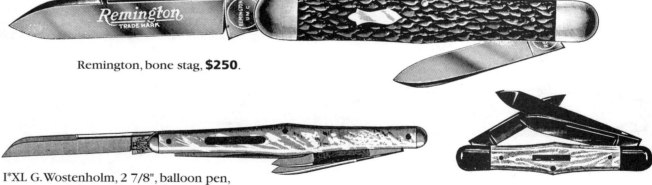

Remington, bone stag, **$250**.

I*XL G. Wostenholm, 2 7/8", balloon pen,
4 blades w/file, mother-of-pearl, **$275**.

Western States, 3 blades,
not a whittler, 3",
patterned celluloid, **$165**.

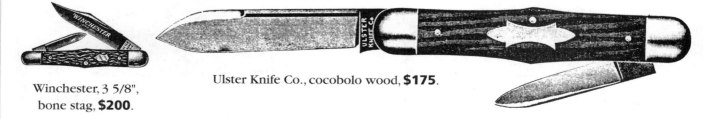

Winchester, 3 5/8",
bone stag, **$200**.

Ulster Knife Co., cocobolo wood, **$175**.

Serpentine Pen Knives

As with serpentine jacks, serpentine pen knives include all more or less S-curved pen knives, whether tapered or equal-ended. Equal-end—or nearly so—serpentine pen knives are two-blade versions of the junior premium stock knife, so they are often called *premium pen knives.* Like stock knives, most premium pen knives have clip master blades and come in both round-end and square-end versions.

Markedly tapered serpentine pen knives are often called "dog-legs." However, if they have Wharncliffe master blades, they are called Wharncliffe knives.

A Wharncliffe blade has a straight edge like a sheepfoot. However, its back is gently curved and its point is more acute. Lord Wharncliffe, for whom the pattern was named, and who in fact designed it, was a noble patron of Joseph Rodgers & Sons of Sheffield around 1820.

If the second blade of a double-ended serpentine knife is anything other than a pen blade or a nail file—for example, a spey, a spear or a punch—then the knife is considered a double-end jack knife rather than a pen knife.

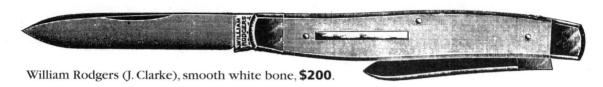

William Rodgers (J. Clarke), smooth white bone, **$200**.

Premium Pen Knives

Hibbard, Spencer & Bartlett (NYK), 3", serpentine pen, mother-of-pearl, **$150**.

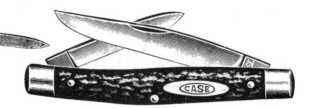

Case, 3 1/4", bone stag:
Tested XX, **$200**; XX, **$150**.

Wharncliffe Knives

I*XL G. Wostenholm, 3 1/8", Wharncliffe, 3 blades, mother-of-pearl, **$350**.

Joseph Rodgers, 4", genuine stag, **$400**.

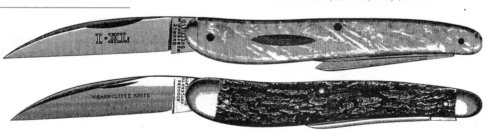

"Dog-Leg" Serpentive Knives

Schrade Cut. Co., 3 9/16", black celluloid, **$100**.

Winchester, tip bolsters, 3 3/8", bone stag, **$125**.

Case Tested XX, bone stag, **$275**.

Camillus Sword Brand, 3 3/8", 2 blades, "dog-leg" serpentine, bone, **$200**.

Schrade Cut. Co., tip bolsters, 3 1/4", bone stag, **$125**.

Swell-Center Serpentine

The *swell-center serpentine* looks similar to the *sway-back* (see following "Swell-Center Congress or Sway-Back"), the main difference being that its handle is tapered rather than being equal-ended. It advertises that it is *not* a congress-derived pattern by almost always having a clip or a spear master blade, rather than a sheepfoot.

The swell-center serpentine pen knife is similar in shape to the "Eureka" jack knives and cattle knives. However, it is both slimmer in proportion and smaller.

Like most other pen-knife shapes, the swell-center serpentine often was used for whittlers. Collectors sometimes use the term *half-whittler* for other pen knives with clip master blades.

H. Boker, 4 blades, glove-buttoner blade,
tip bolsters, 2 3/4", mother-of-pearl, **$150**.

New York Knife Co., 5 blades, tip bolsters, bone stag, **$425**.

I*XL G. Wostenholm,
2 7/8", swell-center serpentine,
barehead, mother-of-pearl, **$150**.

Swell-Center Congress or Sway-Back

The great majority of congress knives have squared corners, while only a few have rounded ones. There exists a curved pattern with rounded corners similar to a round-ended congress, only with a swell in the middle of the back. It is called the "sway-back" or "swell-center congress."

Swell-center congress pen knives are small knives of premium quality. They usually have sunk joints, milled liners and fancy handles, such as mother-of-pearl or tortoise shell. Older sway-backs are often *shadow knives*

(made without bolsters). Most sway-backs display their kinship to congress knives by having sheepfoot master blades. However, they also were made with clip-point and Wharncliffe master blades.

J. Primble India Steel Works (Belknap
Hdw. Co.) 3", patterned celluloid, **$250**.

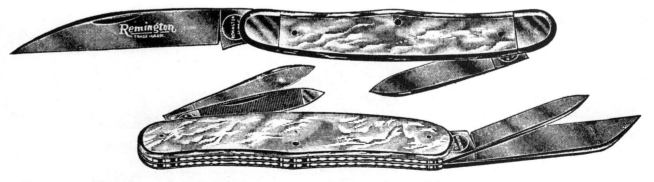

Remingtons: 4 blades, shadow bolsters, milled liners, worked back, mother-of-pearl, **$750**; 2 blades, mother-of-pearl, **$450**.

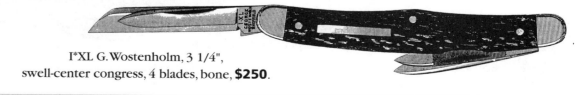

I*XL G. Wostenholm, 3 1/4",
swell-center congress, 4 blades, bone, **$250**.

Whittlers

"Whittler" is a modern collector's term that refers to a particular type of construction and blade arrangement. Any pen knife with such a blade arrangement and design is considered a whittler, regardless of shape or handle die. Many whittler-pattern knives are found in large frames that could be classified with the multi-blades.

A whittler is a three-blade knife with a large blade in one end and two small cutting blades of equal length in the other end. Some whittlers have two springs. Each small blade bears on one of the springs. The large blade is extra thick and bears on both springs. The thick master blade bearing on two springs is the most distinctive feature of this type of whittler.

The majority of whittlers have a center divider that separates the tangs of the two small blades, and that also separates the two springs for part of their length. This divider can be seen along the back of the knife, where it tapers to nothing just past the center pin.

Other whittlers show no divider at the back. Often, the two springs of this type are tapered and not separated at all. A very small divider separates the tangs of the two small blades at the end of the knife. An early ancestor of this type of whittler construction is shown in Part 3 of this Section, "Foreign, Exotic, Primitive, and Historical Folding Knives."

Whittlers range in size from ladies' pen knives under 2 inches long closed, on up to heavy cutting tools over 4 inches long. Sometimes, larger whittlers were called *carpenter's knives*.

Many small pen knives with the whittler's construction and blade arrangement have a manicure blade in place of one of the small cutting blades. The knives are not considered "true" whittlers by some collectors, but they are not out of place in any whittler collection.

The whittler has always been a premium-priced knife. A lot of fit and finish work is required in its manufacture. Firms that manufactured low-cost knives did not make whittlers, except in Germany around the turn of the 20th century. Even the lower-priced German ones have high-grade mounts and handle materials. Most whittlers have brass liners and nickel-silver bolsters. Some have nickel-silver liners.

Another type of whittler has three backsprings. Some are pen knives, others small cattle knives and jumbos. Today, collectors everywhere call the knives "three-spring whittlers," and they will pay a premium for them. The knives are rare and very collectible.

Handle Materials

Handle material on whittlers runs the gamut. Wood, often ebony, seems to have been very common on American-made whittlers in the 19th century, but it is almost unknown after World War I. (A rare exception is the golden-laminated "Propwood" used by Schrade Walden circa 1948.) Ivory and smooth white bone also are common on 19th-century whittlers, but are rarely found on whittlers made in the 20th century. Green cow horn was a popular early material that continued in use through the 1930s. Aluminum was used by a few firms, such as Holley.

Mother-of-pearl was the top-of-the-line handle material for whittlers in the 20th century. Even less-expensive German whittlers made at the turn of the 20th century usually have mother-of-pearl handles. In the 19th century, mother-of-pearl shared the spotlight with tortoise shell. A few mother-of-pearl whittlers are still being made, usually in limited editions. Genuine stag also was used on whittlers, though much less often than mother-of-pearl.

In the first half of the 20th century, the standard handle materials for whittlers were bone stag and celluloid. Celluloid used on whittlers was mainly in its imitative forms: imitation ivory, horn and wood, plus all the different colors of imitation mother-of-pearl.

Since whittlers were premium-priced knives, multi-colored celluloids were rarely used on them. However, clear-celluloid "picture handles" were fairly common. "Slick" black composition has been used widely since the 1920s. Rough black was used in the 1940s, while various synthetics and laminated woods have been used in addition to bone and stag in recent times.

Collecting Whittlers

With all the variety of whittlers, a collection of them can be as narrow or as diverse as you wish. Some big

No. 32139—3 1/2" Large caribou and two pen blades. Brass lined. Nickel silver bolsters. Crocus finish. Stag handle. Shielded.
CATTARAUGUS, **$450**.

No. 32866—3 5/8" Carpenter's Knife. Large spear point blade. Small scribing blade. Pen blade. Brass lined. Nickel silver bolsters. Crocus finish. Ebony handle. Shielded.
CATTARAUGUS, **$300**.

W. JNO. BAKER 3 HUNTER ST SYDNEY

1   2   3   4   5   6

Many Pocket Knives are not drawn full size, but length of handle is stated.
To get a good idea of the actual size, place your old knife on the sketch of the 6-inch rule shown above.

NOTE: THE SIZE OF A FOLDING KNIFE IS ITS LENGTH CLOSED.

firms, such as Remington and Ulster, made nearly a hundred varieties of whittlers. English-made whittlers are particularly collectible because they are of very high quality and the English firms that made them no longer exist. You can collect all types, or just one brand, one shape, one handle material, or whatever you find appealing. Many knife collectors want whittlers, and demand for the knives is strong among brand and handle-material collectors as well.

Value Table For Whittlers

Base values for WHITTLERS 3 1/4 to 4 5/8 inches long with three cutting blades, full bolsters and bone-stag handles. Excellent, unsharpened condition.

VALUE RANGE

SHAPE	VERY HIGH (VH)	HIGH (H)	MEDIUM (M)	LOW / MEDIUM (LM)	LOW (L)
EQUAL-END	$325	$250	$150	$120	$90
SLEEVEBOARD	450	300	175	135	100
LOCKBACK SLEEVEBOARD	500	350	175	150	125
JUMBO	700	400	250	200	150
PHYSICIAN'S	475	300	250	175	100
OVAL or CIGAR	1,000	600	300	225	125
CONGRESS	400	325	175	125	90
SWELL-CENTER CONGRESS	375	250	150	120	90
SERPENTINE	325	175	125	100	75
WHARNCLIFFE	675	400	250	200	150
SWELL-CENTER SERPENTINE	400	325	225	150	90
NORFOLK	800	525	350	275	200
LOCKBACK NORFOLK	1,200	600	475	375	275
SWELL-CENTER and BALLOON	575	300	200	135	75
SWELL-CENTER (non-standard)	500	250	175	125	100
CROWN	200	100	75	60	45

Novelty Cut. Co., 2 7/8", swell-center whittler, transparent celluloid, **$275**.

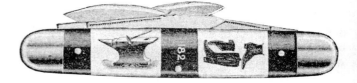

Novelty Cut. Co., 3 7/8", equal-end whittler, transparent celluloid, **$250**.

I*XL G. Wostenholm, 2 1/2", congress whittler w/file, mother-of-pearl, **$175**.

Equal-End Whittlers

Whittlers have been made in almost every variety of handle shape and size used for standard two- and four-blade pen knives. Ordinary *equal-end* or *senator whittlers* are the most common. However, most of them, especially the smaller ones, have a nail-file blade. The master blade in an equal-end whittler is almost always a spear point.

H. Boker, file blade, fancy bolsters, bone stag, **$200**.

American Shear & Knife Co., file blade, 3 1/8", mother-of-pearl, **$275-325**.

Remington, mother-of-pearl, **$395**.

Winchester, punch blade, 3 3/8", patterned celluloid (gray), **$175**.

I*XL G. Wostenholm, 3", whittler, stag, **$250**.

Sleeveboard Whittlers

Sleeveboard whittlers are also relatively common. The larger of them are true whittling knives, often with a stout clip or saber-clip master blade. The two small blades on the heavier sleeveboards are usually a pen blade and a sharp-pointed coping blade. A few sleeveboard whittlers, mainly from before the First World War, have locking main blades.

H. Boker, lockback, bone stag, **$275**.

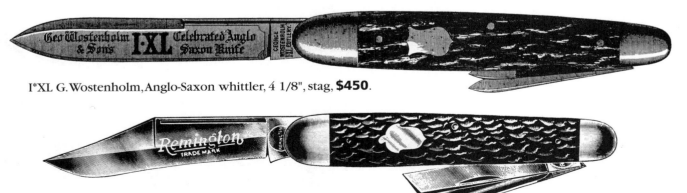

I*XL G. Wostenholm, Anglo-Saxon whittler, 4 1/8", stag, **$450**.

Remington, saber-ground blade, punch blade, bone stag, **$425**.

Jumbo Whittlers

Big sleeveboard whittlers are called "jumbos." *Jumbo whittlers* have been given all sorts of special names. Among them are "engineer's knife" (Western States) and "Swedish pattern electrician's knife" (Boker). All jumbo knives are relatively rare and valuable.

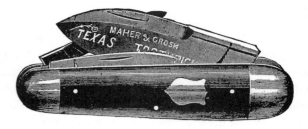

Maher & Grosh, 3 3/4", jumbo whittler (Ulster?), ebony, **$400**.

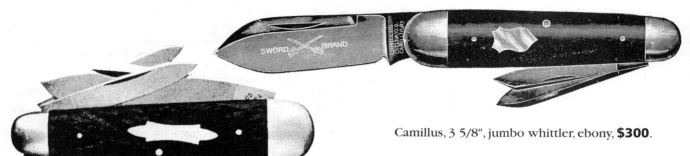

Camillus, 3 5/8", jumbo whittler, ebony, **$300**.

Cattaraugus, 3 1/2", jumbo whittler, stag, **$375**.

Three-Blade Physician's Knives

Long, slim whittlers were made in a variety of shapes, including equal-end, sleeveboard and swell-center serpentine. The knives always have long, slim spear master blades. They were often listed in old catalogs as *physician's knives*. In collections they are usually included with physician's-pattern jack knives, also called "pill-busters." They are a rare pattern and demand high prices in excellent-to-mint condition.

Winchester, bone stag, **$350**.

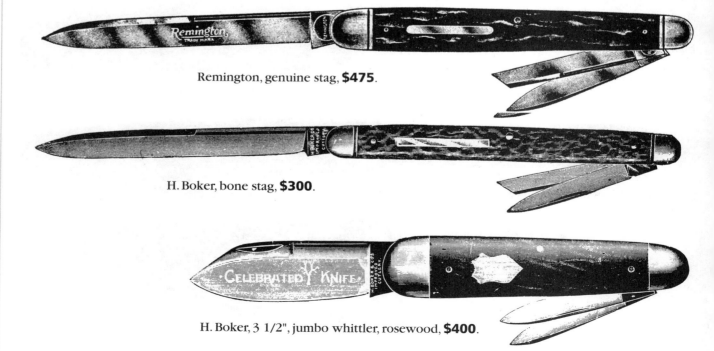

Remington, genuine stag, **$475**.

H. Boker, bone stag, **$300**.

H. Boker, 3 1/2", jumbo whittler, rosewood, **$400**.

Oval or Cigar Whittlers

Oval "cigar" whittlers are quite rare. They are generally premium-quality knives with sunk joints and spear master blades.

Perhaps the most valuable Case pen knives are the __91 pattern 4 1/2-inch cigar whittlers. A Tested XX 3391, 5391 or 6391 can bring **$2,000** in mint condition, considerably more than the Remington R7756 of the pattern.

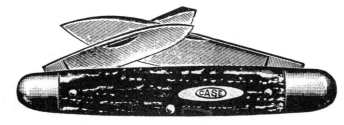

Case Tested XX and Case XX 5391, genuine stag, **$1,200** and **$2,000,** respectively.

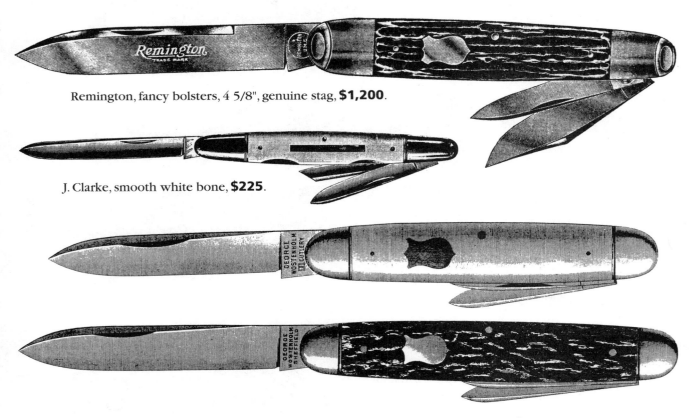

Remington, fancy bolsters, 4 5/8", genuine stag, **$1,200**.

J. Clarke, smooth white bone, **$225**.

(Top) I*XL G. Wostenholm, 3 3/4", "cigar"-pattern whittler, ivory, **$600**.
(Bottom) I*XL G. Wostenholm, 4 1/4", "cigar" (oval)-pattern whittler, stag, **$800**.

Gunstock Whittlers

The only gunstock whittler we are aware of is the "orange blossom." (See the "Lobster Pen Knives" segment in this chapter.) We have seen old catalog pictures of small gunstock premium knives that appear to be whittlers, and they probably have three backsprings.

Winchester, 3 1/8", gunstock whittler, bone, **$150**.

Congress Whittlers and Three-Blade Tobacco Knives

Congress whittlers are relatively rare. They exhibit all the variations in size, handles and bolsters that other congress knives do. Most smaller congress "whittlers" have manicure blades, while larger "tobacco knives" with whittler construction do not. Just about all congress and swell-center congress knives have sheepfoot master blades.

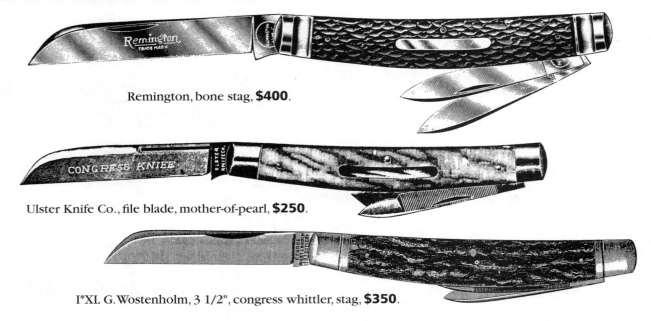

Remington, bone stag, **$400**.

Ulster Knife Co., file blade, mother-of-pearl, **$250**.

I*XL G. Wostenholm, 3 1/2", congress whittler, stag, **$350**.

Swell-Center Congress Whittlers

Swell-center congress or *sway-back "whittlers"* probably should not be counted as whittlers at all. They are lightweight, premium-quality knives and most have a manicure blade. However, since they are constructed like whittlers, they are included here for consistency.

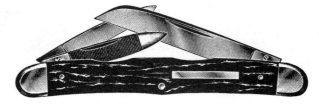

H. Boker, file blade, 3 1/16", genuine stag, **$200**.

Keen Kutter, 2 7/8", whittler (no bolsters), mother-of-pearl, **$150**.

Case Tested XX, file blade, 3 1/8", bone stag, **$350**.

Remington, file blade, patterned celluloid (gold bronze), **$375**.

Serpentine and Wharncliffe Whittlers

Serpentine whittlers are almost as common as sleeveboards. Heavier serpentines or "dog-legs" usually have clip master blades. Slimmer serpentines more often have spear master blades.

Some firms made *Wharncliffe whittlers*—serpentines with a Wharncliffe master blade. All Wharncliffe knives, especially Wharncliffe whittlers, are a very popular knife pattern.

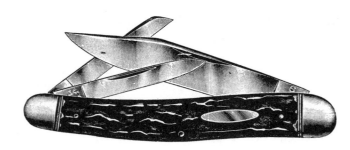

H. Boker, genuine stag, **$250**.

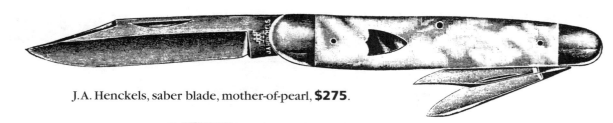

J.A. Henckels, saber blade, mother-of-pearl, **$275**.

Ulster Knife Co., 3 3/16", mother-of-pearl, **$300**.

Winchester, 3 3/8", serpentine whittler w/file, slick black, **$200**.

Winchester, punch blade, 3 1/4", bone stag, **$275**.

Schrade Cut. Co. No. 81004 3/4 STG: saber-ground blade, 3 7/8", bone stag, **$225**.

Schrade Cut. Co., 3 1/4", bone stag, **$250**.

Joseph Rodgers, 3 3/16", genuine stag, **$675**.

Ulster Knife Co., file blade, mother-of-pearl, **$325**.

I*XL G. Wostenholm, 4", Wharncliffe whittler, ivory, **$600**.

Swell-Center Serpentine and Norfolk Whittlers

Swell-center serpentine or serpentine balloon whittlers were made with both clip-point and spear-point master blades. Case's -08 handle die is a popular small version of the pattern.

A specific ornate version of the swell-center serpentine whittler is called the *Norfolk whittler*. It has a distinctive saber-clip blade used in no other knife. We have seen examples by Rodgers and by Remington. Some have locking main blades. The special lockback patterns are "top of the line" with whittler collectors.

No. 6308
Case Tested XX,
3 1/4", bone stag,
$375.

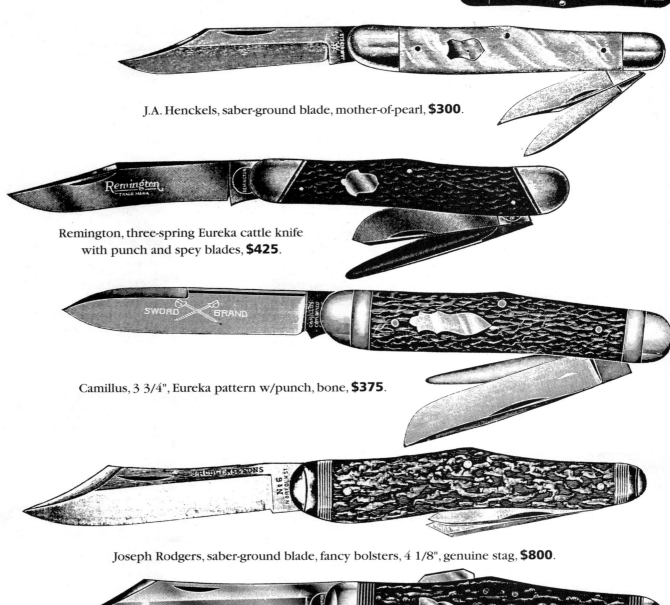

J.A. Henckels, saber-ground blade, mother-of-pearl, **$300**.

Remington, three-spring Eureka cattle knife
with punch and spey blades, **$425**.

Camillus, 3 3/4", Eureka pattern w/punch, bone, **$375**.

Joseph Rodgers, saber-ground blade, fancy bolsters, 4 1/8", genuine stag, **$800**.

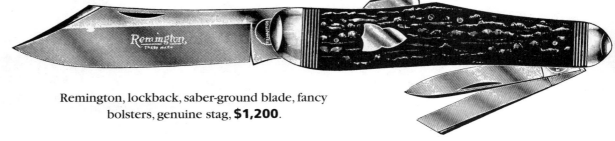

Remington, lockback, saber-ground blade, fancy
bolsters, genuine stag, **$1,200**.

Swell-Center Whittlers

Swell-center whittlers almost always have balloon ends. Knives with ends of other shapes command a premium. The master blade can be either a spear or a clip. Many collectors consider the swell-center balloon whittler to be one of the most attractive pocketknife patterns.

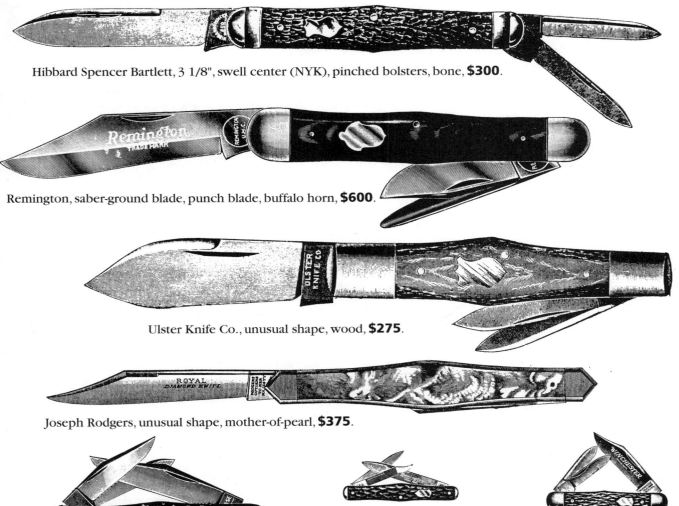

Hibbard Spencer Bartlett, 3 1/8", swell center (NYK), pinched bolsters, bone, **$300**.

Remington, saber-ground blade, punch blade, buffalo horn, **$600**.

Ulster Knife Co., unusual shape, wood, **$275**.

Joseph Rodgers, unusual shape, mother-of-pearl, **$375**.

Case, 3 1/2", bone stag:
Tested XX, **$185**; XX, **$125**.

Remington, file blade, tip bolsters, 3", bone stag, **$250**.

Winchester, 3 1/2", bone stag, **$225**.

Crown Whittlers

Nineteenth-century American pocketknife price lists include various sizes of three-blade crown pen knives, and many of them were whittlers. The pattern is very rare now.

Humason & Beckley, file blade, tip bolsters, 3 1/4", mother-of-pearl, **$150**.

Ulster Knife Co., 3 1/8", ivory, **$200**.

Lobster Pen Knives

James Crawshaw, a cutler and merchant who worked in Sheffield from about 1817 to 1850, invented a new style pen knife in the 1820s. An 1831 history described it as "the lobster-knife, by which four blades open upon one spring ... [which] instead of forming the back, as in the old method, is placed along the middle of the handle, and between the scales or sides of the handle, so that it works on each side, and hence admits of blades at each end, and even any number of them. The mode of slitting the spring gave rise to many-bladed knives in all their varieties. Mr. Crawshaw took out no patent, but is a wholesale manufacturer." (The historical quoted material is courtesy of Geoffrey Tweedale.)

Traditional lobsters use Crawshaw's fragile, single slit spring, but modern machine-made versions use a pair of more durable, simple springs tabbed together back to back. Because the spring or springs are in the middle, a lobster pen knife always has its pivot pins set off to the sides of its long axis—hence, the resemblance of the pivoting blades to the waving claws of a lobster.

Lobster pen knives are flat and lightly built. Heavy-duty knives with blades both top and bottom are covered in the chapter on "Multi-Blade Knives" in this section. Except for a few in the "Sheffield" pattern, lobsters never have full bolsters.

Lobster-spring pen knives were made in a number of standard shapes. Most have exotic sounding names, and some have more than one name. Most lobster shapes have rounded ends, but some have pointed ends. The pointed ones have "candle-end" as part of their names.

No. 4003—5 3/4" Spear and pen blades. Scissors. Manicure blade in the back. Silver lining. Full polish. Genuine Pearl handle. CATTARAUGUS, **$125**.

No. 300-Ori.—3" One large blade, pen blade and manicure blade in back. Brass lined. Full crocus finish. Oriental mother-of-pearl handle. CATTARAUGUS, **$75**.

Lobsters often have bails so that they can be hung from a watch chain, a feature that may or may not affect the knives' values.

VALUE TABLE FOR LOBSTER PEN KNIVES

Base values for LOBSTER PEN KNIVES of any size, with three blades (except where indicated), bone-stag (jigged-bone) handles, and with or without bail. Excellent, unsharpened condition, with etch where appropriate.

VALUE RANGE

SHAPE	VERY HIGH (VH)	HIGH (H)	MEDIUM (M)	LOW / MEDIUM (LM)	LOW (L)
TWO-BLADE OVAL or CHARM	$100	$75	$50	$35	$15
THREE-BLADE OVAL	125	90	75	50	30
EQUAL-END	150	100	75	60	40
SUNFISH LOBSTER	150	100	60	45	30
DOLPHIN (FISH CANDLE-END)	175	125	75	60	50
SLEEVEBOARD	90	70	50	30	20
"SHEFFIELD"	125	80	50	40	30
SERPENTINE SLEEVEBOARD	150	100	60	45	30
FANCY SLEEVEBOARD	165	125	75	60	50
SERPENTINE CANDLE-END (2 blades)	90	60	45	30	20
GUNSTOCK (3 blades)	225	175	125	100	75
ORANGE BLOSSOM (4-blade GUNSTOCK)	375	275	150	125	100

| 1 | 2 | W. JNO. BAKER 3 HUNTER ST SYDNEY 3 | 4 | 5 | 6 |

Many Pocket Knives are not drawn full size, but length of handle is stated.
To get a good idea of the actual size, place your old knife on the sketch of the 6-inch rule shown above.

NOTE: THE SIZE OF A FOLDING KNIFE IS ITS LENGTH CLOSED.

Oval Lobsters and Charm Knives

The simplest lobster is the two-blade oval. It has a small spear blade on top and a manicure blade on the bottom. A candle-end or pointed two-blade oval lobster is called a "charm knife."

Three-blade oval lobsters have a pen blade facing the spear blade. The style is tapered but has curved sides, unlike a sleeveboard, which has straight sides. Another name for the style is the "frog" pattern.

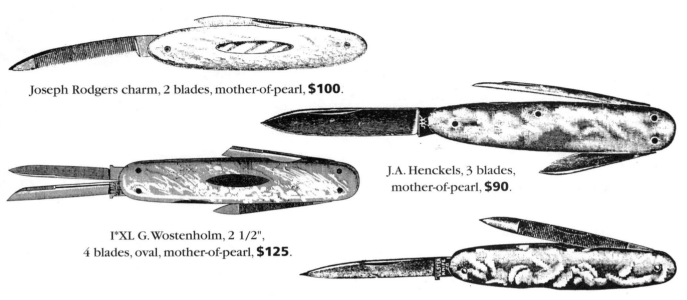

Joseph Rodgers charm, 2 blades, mother-of-pearl, **$100**.

J.A. Henckels, 3 blades, mother-of-pearl, **$90**.

I*XL G. Wostenholm, 2 1/2", 4 blades, oval, mother-of-pearl, **$125**.

Ulster Knife Co., 2 blades, mother-of-pearl, **$75**.

Equal-End Lobsters

The most common lobster pen is the equal-end. Some are rounded at the ends, like other equal-end knives. Others are oblong, sort of a round-cornered rectangle. A few are quite rectangular, complete with sharp corners. Oblong lobsters are often pinched in slightly top and bottom.

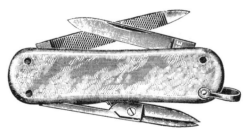

Case Tested XX, scissors, mother-of-pearl, **$175**.

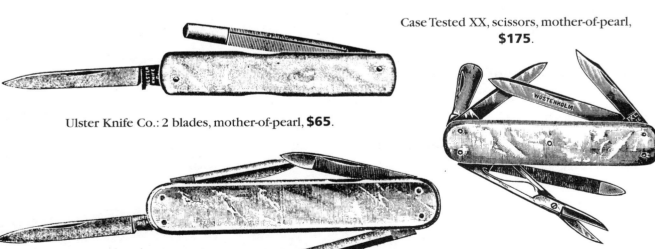

Ulster Knife Co.: 2 blades, mother-of-pearl, **$65**.

American Shear & Knife Co., 4 blades, mother-of-pearl, **$150**.

I*XL G. Wostenholm, 3", 6 blades w/manicure blade, mother-of-pearl, **$150**.

Sunfish Lobsters and Dolphins

Equal-end lobsters with pointed "candle" ends and pinched sides are usually given fish names. Those pinched near one end so that they look like a *planarian*—the flatworm beloved of biology teachers—are called "fish candle-end lobsters," or "dolphins." Those pinched in the middle are called "sunfish lobsters." ("Sunfish" alone is the name of a large double-end jack knife, also called "elephant toenail.")

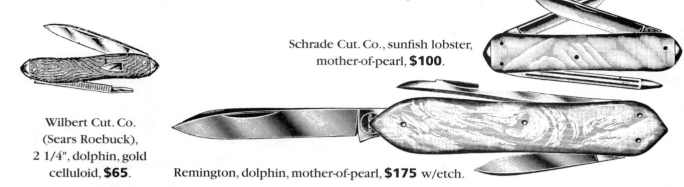

Schrade Cut. Co., sunfish lobster, mother-of-pearl, **$100**.

Wilbert Cut. Co. (Sears Roebuck), 2 1/4", dolphin, gold celluloid, **$65**.

Remington, dolphin, mother-of-pearl, **$175** w/etch.

Sleeveboard Lobsters

Sleeveboard lobsters, like other sleeveboard knives, are tapered and have straight sides and round ends. Most sleeveboard lobsters have three blades, as on the oval frog pattern, but they also are seen with two and as many as six blades. The sleeveboard is one of the most common lobster patterns.

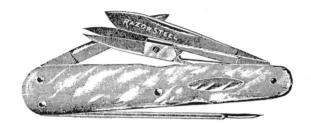

Maher & Grosh, 3 1/8", 4 blades w/scissors, mother-of-pearl, **$90**.

Sheffield Pattern Lobsters

One type of sleeveboard lobster has a cutout most of the length of its back in order to accommodate a large manicure blade as thick as the entire knife. Western States called the style the "Sheffield pattern." The knives sometimes have full bolsters.

Joseph Rodgers, 2 5/8", 3 blades, Sheffield pattern w/corkscrew, ivory, **$125**.

Joseph Rodgers, mother-of-pearl, **$100** (also for ivory).

Serpentine Sleeveboard Lobsters

Unlike the standard sleeveboard lobster and the Sheffield pattern, both of which are common, the serpentine sleeveboard lobster is very rare. The pattern is one of the most elegant "lobsters." Winchester called the style the "curved balloon lobster."

Joseph Rodgers, 3 1/4", serpentine, mother-of-pearl, **$150**.

American Shear & Knife Co., fancy patterned celluloid (waterfall), **$135**.

Fancy Sleeveboard Lobsters

Perhaps more elegant and rarer than the serpentine sleeveboard lobster is the straight sleeveboard, which is pinched in three or four times along the sides. The *fancy sleeveboard* may once have had a special name; if so, it has been lost.

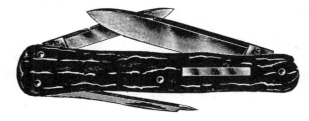

H. Boker, genuine stag, **$135**.

Joseph Rodgers,
3", "ripple" sleeveboard,
4 blades, ivory, **$165**.

Serpentine Candle-End Lobsters

The S-shaped pattern known as the *serpentine candle-end lobster* is relatively common. Examples always seem to have only two blades. Round-ended, two-blade serpentine lobsters are very unusual, though their value is the same as the candle-ends.

Hibbard Spencer
Bartlett, 2 7/8",
serpentine candle-
end, embossed
Ivoroid, **$75**.

Gunstock Lobsters and Orange Blossoms

One of the most appealing styles of lobster is the gunstock, sort of a swell-center sleeveboard. It can have three or four blades. One of the blades is a long manicure blade on the back.

Four-blade gunstock lobsters have a top deck like a whittler. The double-thick spear master blade rides on the full width of the spring at the narrow end. Two small blades ride on the split ends of the spring at the wide end.

The four-blade gunstock lobster whittler is called the "orange blossom," named by Tom Bradley, Jr., of the New York Knife Co. in honor of his Civil War regiment, the 124th New York Volunteer Infantry (the Orange Blossom Regiment). In the 1920s and 1930s, a mother-of-pearl-handled orange blossom was one of the most expensive pocketknives a person could buy. Remington's R6454 mother-of-pearl orange blossom cost nearly 2 1/2 times more than the company's R1123 large trapper with bullet shield ($8 versus $3.35 in 1925). The relative values, of course, do not hold in today's collector market.

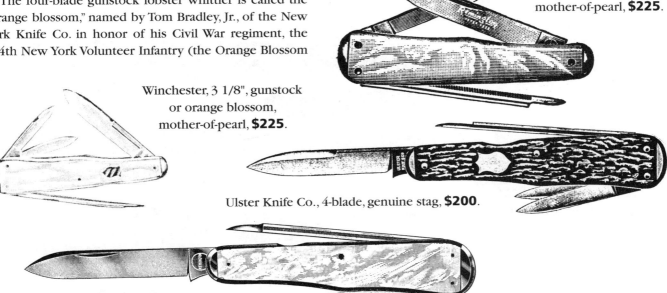

Remington, 3 blades,
mother-of-pearl, **$225**.

Winchester, 3 1/8", gunstock
or orange blossom,
mother-of-pearl, **$225**.

Ulster Knife Co., 4-blade, genuine stag, **$200**.

Remington R6454, 4-blade, mother-of-pearl, **$300**.

Quill Knives

Quill knives are the tiny "pen" knives used up into the early part of the 20th century for sharpening quill pens. The Rodgers examples shown on this page and also the pen machine shown in the "Industrial Knives" segment of the Special Section of Section III, "Fixed Blade Knives," are from a 1912 catalog. Folding quill knives were sometimes included in fancy manicure, sewing and travel kits.

Quill knife blades usually are a pen or coping style, but sometimes are a clip or a curved bistoury-like shape. The blades are always tiny, rarely more than half the length of the small handles, which are typically about 2 1/2 inches long. On single-bladed quill knives, the "head" of the spring ordinarily fills the extra space in the handle.

By the latter part of the 19th century, almost all new quill knives were single-bladed. However, a few double-ended ones with two blades were still made.

At the time of their greatest popularity, before about 1830, many quill knives were made with two or more blades. Most of them were double-ended but some were single-ended, like miniature jack knives. However, all the blades are the same tiny size; none is a larger "master blade."

In the 1820s, Sheffield's James Crawshaw, the inventor of lobster pen knives, also invented "quadrangular" (four-cornered) quill knives. They are shaped like a needle case or a miniature cigar. In its simplest form, the knife has eight tiny blades, four in each end, one every 90 degrees. The pattern also was made with two, three, four, up to 12 blades in each position, yielding a knife with 16, 24, 32, up to 96 tiny blades. They usually have ivory handles, but there are a few with checkered and pique (pin-worked) mother-of-pearl. In excellent condition they are worth from **$500** up to more than **$3,500**. With some blades broken, as the knives usually are found, figure about **$150-300**. Crawshaw also pioneered use of this construction for big exposition multi-blades (see the Bradford knife in the 'Showpiece and Exposition Knives' segment of the following chapter, "Multi-Blade Knives").

The "quadrangular" pen knives and other multi-bladed quill knives were not standard American patterns, though some were no doubt used in the USA. Various other styles of multi-blade quill knives were made throughout Western Europe in the eighteenth and nineteenth centuries (see Part 3 of this section, "Foreign Exotic Primitive and Historical Folding Knives").

Values for single-bladed QUILL KNIVES of any shape, wood, bone or horn handles, in excellent condition.

VALUE RANGE

VH	H	M	LM	L
$150	$100	$90	$75	$60

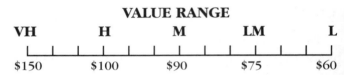

I*XL G. Wostenholm, 2 7/8", swell center quill knife, ivory, **$150**.

Quill knives by Joseph Rodgers and Ulster Knife Co.: horn, **$125** each; ivory and stag, **$150**; mother-of-pearl, **$150**.

Mechanical Pen Knives

Some pen knives, mostly equal-ends, have mechanical devices to open the blades. The simplest are blade attachments such as Joseph Rodgers' "Pellett" lifts. Next simplest are turn-rings or ring openers. A German firm made flush-mounted, cam-locking ring openers in single- and double-ended versions that are very rare and of high value.

Spring-open knives date back to the 18th century. Some rare 19th-century ones have spring-assists to open the blades about 30 degrees when a lever is pressed. The Wilzin mechanism was used on two- and four-blade senators, with one lever for each blade, and on medium-sized double-end jacks, making the patterns of higher value.

There have been dozens of other "trick" opening mechanisms used on pen knives and small jack knives. They generally increase the value of a knife.

All push-button and switchblade knives are illegal in interstate commerce.

Press Button, 3 5/8", early 1900s, w/punch, bone, **$200**.

Slide button: Case Tested XX, 3 1/4", metal handle, **$90**.

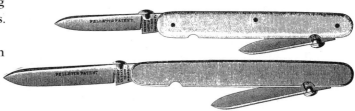

Joseph Rodgers senators, (W.W. Pellett 1893 patent) blade lifts: shadow, 2 1/2", ivory, **$125**; 2 3/4", plain nickel silver, **$75**.

H. Boker senator, ring opener, fancy celluloid (waterfall), **$45**.

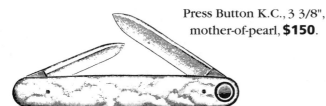

Press Button K.C., 3 3/8", mother-of-pearl, **$150**.

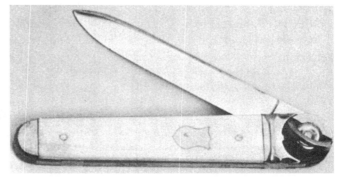

Unmarked (C. Hollweg 1886 patent) cam-lock ring opener, ivory, **$300** (courtesy Wiebusch Collection, Smithsonian).

Wilzin ad from October 1891 Harper's. Stag (bone stag), **$150**; "Silverine' (fancy n/s) **$120**; fancy aluminum, **$125**; ivory, **$200**; mother-of-pearl, **$200**; decorated Sterling, **$200**.

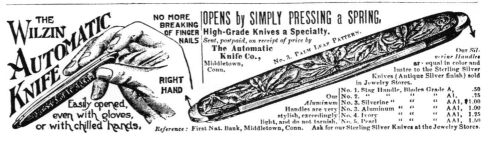

Office and Letter-Opener Knives

Office Knives

An "office knife" is a relatively large equal-end pen knife that has a spear master blade for opening letters and a spey-type blade intended to serve as an ink eraser. Most office knives have white handles. Many 20th-century ones have celluloid handles. Older ones have bone or even ivory. OFFICE KNIFE in fancy letters is usually etched or stamped on the front handle.

An office knife is a working knife for a clerical worker. The comparable fixed-blade version is the ink eraser shown in the "Tradesmen, Craftsmen and Special Purpose Knives" segment in the Special Section of Section III, "Fixed Blade Knives."

VALUE RANGE

SHAPE/HANDLE VARIATIONS	VERY HIGH (VH)	HIGH (H)	MEDIUM (M)	LOW / MEDIUM (LM)	LOW (L)
OFFICE HANDLE	$150	$75	$45	$30	$15
w/ivory handles	185	100	80	60	40
w/bone handles	160	90	65	50	30
w/o 'OFFICE KNIFE' on handle	—	—	—	35	10

Letter-Opener Knives

A letter-opener knife is a pocketknife handle with a folding blade in one end, usually a small spear or a spey-type eraser blade. The other end is a fixed letter opener. Most of the letter openers are slender, but some are as wide as their handles. Letter-opener knives often have advertising or presentation inscriptions on the handle or on the letter-opener blade.

There is some interest in letter-opener knives. On occasion, owners cut off the letter opener and offer the

handle as an ordinary knife. Close inspection will always reveal the unwise modification.

Base values for OFFICE KNIVES and LETTER-OPENER KNIVES with celluloid handles. Excellent, unsharpened condition.

VALUE RANGE / LETTER-OPENER KNIFE

VH	H	M	LM	L
$100	$75	$50	$30	$15

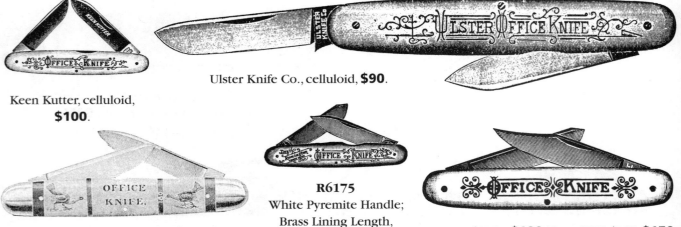

Keen Kutter, celluloid, **$100**.

Ulster Knife Co., celluloid, **$90**.

Novelty Cut. Co., 3 3/4", equal-end, clear celluloid, **$100**.

R6175
White Pyremite Handle; Brass Lining Length, closed, 3 3/4 inches. Remington, celluloid, **$150**.

Case XX 42057, **$100**; Tested XX 4257, **$150**.

RLO 44
Remington letter-opener knife, mother-of-pearl, **$150**.

No. L1824M
Schrade Cut. Co. letter-opener knife, celluloid, **$75**.

Embossed, Color Etched and Enameled Handles

Boker embossed, **$35**.

New York Knife Co., 1915 World's Fair, **$300**.

Boker embossed dogs, **$90**.

Remington R7319 embossed art deco, **$250**.

Gold, green, red and white, designed enameled handle, brass lined, **$50-$75**.

Henckels Toledo scales hunting scene, **$150**. (Black iron with design in gold and silver wire.)

Boker etched bird scene, **$90**.

Henckels embossed champagne pattern, **$125-250**.

Boker color-etched gun-metal train, **$100**.

Gun-metal handle, fire-gilded design, **$60**.

Swedish etching on gun-metal handle, **$60**.

Advertising Knives

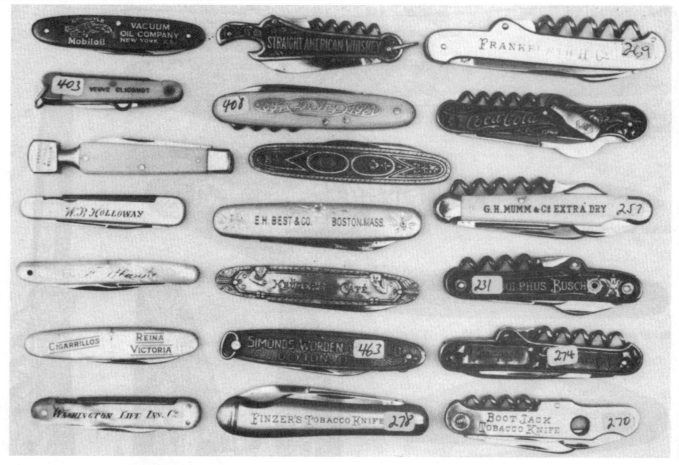

Advertising knives circa 1910-1930, by Wester & Butz of Solingen, except as noted. Courtesy Ed Bruner.

First column, *top to bottom:*

1. Senator pen, grey gun metal with red and silver, for Mobil. **$75-100**.
2. Lobster pen, ivory, Stanhope viewer, for C.F. Schmidt & Peters Veuve Clicquot champagne. **$300**.
3. Box knife, stamped iron hammer and etched ivory, for Runkel Bros. Vienna Sweet Chocolate. **$225**.
4. Lobster, etched pearl, for W.B. Holloway, Harvard Brewery. **$150-175**.
5. Serpentine pen, etched pearl, for C.F. Blanke. **$100**.
6. Senator pen, etched pearl, for Reina Victoria Cigarillos. **$150-175**.
7. Lobster, etched pearl, for Washington Life Insurance. **$125**.

Second column, *top to bottom:*

8. Fred Herbertz & Co., Solingen, opener knife, embossed brass for "Juarez Straight American Whiskey." Probably an "imaginary knife," c1970. **$35**.
9. Opener knife, inlaid celluloid, for De Vry 1897-1927. **$75**.
10. Equal-end pen, toledo scales, for Neckarsulmer Fahrzeugwerke (NSU Automotive Works). **$65-85**.
11. Schrade Cutlery Co. equal-end pen, stamped and engraved aluminum, for Best & Co. Knoxall Textiles. **$75**.
12. Equal-end pen, embossed nickel silver with Katzenjammer-type kids, for Kruger's Cafe. **$185-200**.
13. SWWCO/Made in USA (by Camillus) turn-ring pen, embossed brass, for Simonds Worden White Co. **$90**.
14. Easy-open jack, nickel silver, FINZER's TOBACCO KNIFE. **$100-125**.

Third column, *top to bottom:*

15. Champagne pattern, nickel silver for Frankfurth & Co. **$75**.
16. Pseudo-champagne pattern, brass "COCA-COLA." "Imaginary knife" c1970. **$40**.
17. Champagne pattern, etched ivory, for G.H. Mumm & Co. Extra Dry Veuve Clicquot Champagne. **$225-250**.
18. N. Kastor, Ohligs, Germany, champagne pattern, enameled and gift brass, Stanhope viewer, for Adolphus Busch. **$425-500**.
19. Champagne pattern, embossed nickel silver, winery scene on reverse for Mercier & Co., Epernay, Champagne. **$200-225**.
20. Champagne pattern with cigar cutter, stamped nickel silver, BOOT JACK TOBACCO KNIFE. **$150-175**.

Souvenir whittler made by Wester & Butz for the 1893 World's Columbian Exposition, Chicago. **$225-250**. (Courtesy Ed Bruner, David Minor photo.)

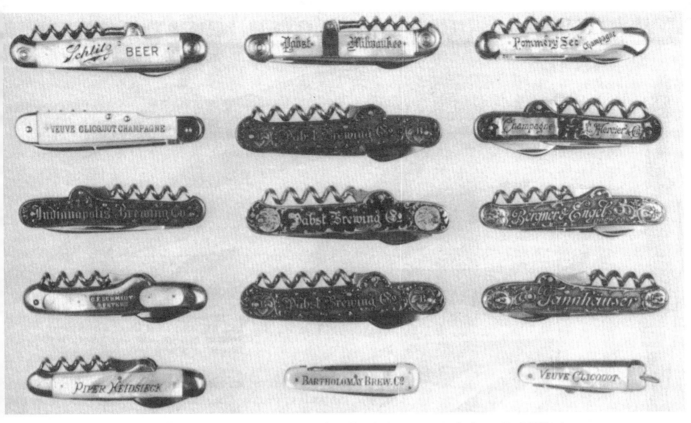

*Beer and champagne advertising knives made in Germany before World War I,
most from the Wester Bros. and Wester & Butz showrooms. Courtesy Ed Bruner, David Minor photo.*

First column, top to bottom:

1. Wester Bros. 3 1/2" pearl, Schlitz Beer, "The Beer That Made Milwaukee Famous." **$350.**
2. No brand, 3 3/8" ivory, C.F. Schmidt & Peters Veuve Clicquot Champagne. **$185.**
3. Indianapolis Brewing Co. 3 3/8" brass, Progress brand beer. **$200.**
4. No brand, 3 1/4" nickel silver with pearl inlays, C.F. Schmidt & Peters (champagne). **$250.**
5. Anheuser-Busch/Wester Bros. 3 1/4" pearl, Piper Heidsieck (champagne). **$400-425.**

Second column, top to bottom:

6. No brand, 3 1/2" pearl, Pabst (beer), Milwaukee. **$325-350.**
7. Wester Bros. 3 5/8" brass, Pabst Brewing Co., Milwaukee. **$125-150.**
8. A. Graef 3 5/8" gilt brass with red enamel, Pabst Brewing Co. **$325-350.**
9. Wester Bros. 3 5/8" brass, Pabst Brewing Co., Milwaukee. **$150-175.**
10. Bartholomay Brew. Co. 2 3/8" pearl Sheffield lobster pattern. **$175-200.**

Third column, top to bottom:

11. A. Graef 3 1/8" pearl, Pommery "Sec" and Pommery "Brut" Champagnes. **$250-275.**
12. Fritz Reuter, Washington D.C., A. Graef, 3 3/8" brass, H. Mercier & Co. Champagne, Epernay. **$175-200.**
13. Wester Bros. 3 3/8" nickel silver, Bergner & Engel Brewing Co., Tannhauser (beer). **$150-175.**
14. Bergner & Engel 3 1/4" nickel silver, Bergner & Engel Brewing Co., Tannhauser (beer). **$150-175.**
15. Eagleton Knife Co. 2 1/4" pearl modified Sheffield lobster pattern, Veuve Clicquot (C.F. Schmidt & Peters Champagne). **$160-175.**

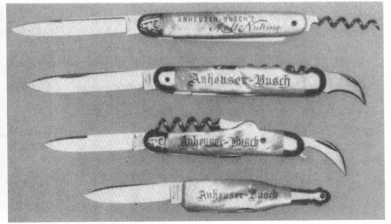

Pearl Anheuser-Busch advertising knives with Stanhope viewers, from the Wester Bros. and Wester & Butz showrooms. Opener and champagne patterns **$450-500** each; bottle figural **$450-475**.
Courtesy Ed Bruner, David Minor photo.

Advertising, Figural, Character, Miniature Knives

Figural knives are knives shaped like other objects, or like animals or people. The oldest style, dating back at least 1,800 years, is the leg knife. Eighteenth-century examples were called "Princess Legs," and are worth at least **$200-250**. Little 19th-century ones (top left) are worth **$150-200**. Twentieth-century American "ballet knives" have a shoe that serves as a cap lifter. They are worth from **$125** (Boker, H. Sears 1865) to **$250** (Remington). Other figurals, such as guns or shoes, are worth **$50-250**, depending on quality. Figurals shaped like vehicles or nudes can be worth up to **$300**. Modern reproductions (most have brass handles) are worth **$20**.

Character knives (Popeye, Hopalong Cassidy, Buck Rogers, etc.) by Camco (plastic handles) or Imperial (sheet metal handles) are worth up to **$200** in mint condition. New lithographed plastic-handled ones by Colonial (marked MADE IN U.S.A.) are worth **$5-10** each.

Some miniature knives are functional (bottom left) while others are strictly charms. Value range is from **$15** (below) to **$150**, also depending on quality.

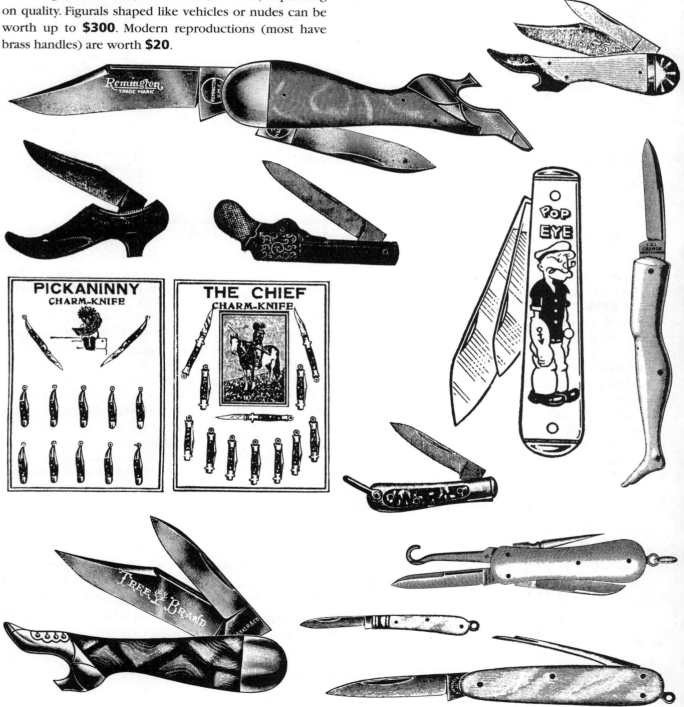

Character Knives

Dick Tracy (Camco), **$150-175**.
Red Ryder (Camco), **$175-200**.
Buck Rogers (Camillus), **$275-300**.
(Dennis Ellingsen photo)

Others:

H.M.S. Pinafore (Frary), **$350**.
Roosevelt Bears
    (Teddy B and Teddy G), **$200**.
Jimmie Allen (Robeson), **$225**.
Popeye (Imperial), **$250**.
Buster Brown (Imperial, etc.), **$250**.

Lone Ranger (Camco), **$100**.
Silver Bullet (Camco), **$75**.
Hopalong Cassidy (Imperial), **$75**.
Roy Rogers (Colonial), **$75**.
Roy Rogers 3-blade (Ulster), **$175**;
    2-blade, **$150**.
Davy Crockett (Imperial, Colonial),
    $75.
Rin-Tin-Tin (Colonial), **$75**.
New "Riders of the Silver Screen"
(Camillus), **$35** each.
New "Riders of the Silver Screen"
(Colonial), **$10-15** each.

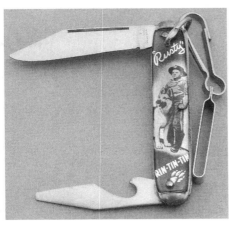

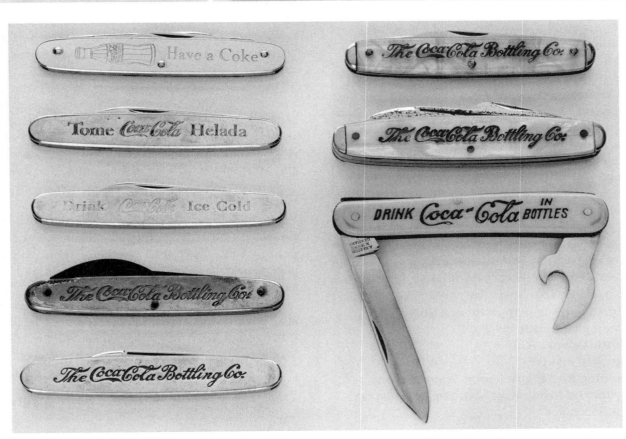

Coca-Cola advertising knives, courtesy Tom Williams and Camillus Cutlery Company.

First Column, metal handles (values **$125-200**):
"Have a Coke": CAMILLUS/STAINLESS (**$50-225**).
"Tome Coca-Cola Helada": CAMILLUS.
"Drink Coca-Cola Ice Cold": CAMILLUS.
"The Coca Cola Bottling Co." The first is a brass-handled sample with unmarked blades. The reverse handle is marked "1899 - 50th Anniv. - 1949." The second is STAINLESS CUTLERY COMPANY (made c1925-1940). Its reverse handle is marked "Delicious and Refreshing."

Second column:
"The Coca-Cola Bottling Co." The first is marked CAMCO/U.S.A. The second is an unmarked sample from 1945, probably a CAMCO also. Both have cracked ice celluloid handles. Values: **$125-200**. The third is "Drink Coca-Cola in Bottles": A. KASTOR & BROS./GERMANY (c1920s). Value: **$250**.

Multi-Blade Knives

Multi-blades are folding knives that have a multitude of blades. The multitude can be as small as three—rarely, two—and as great as 100 or more.

At least one of the blades in a multi-blade is either a special-purpose blade, such as a spey blade, or a special implement, other than a nail file or a leather punch, which are sometimes used in three-bladed pen knives. The special implement may be a can or bottle opener, a champagne wire cutter, a hoof pick, a wrench or even a dinner fork. There are 100-bladed showpiece knives in which all 100 blades are different.

Like standard jack knives, multi-blades are usually large and sturdy. Like standard pen knives, multi-blades are almost always double-ended.

There are many standard patterns of multi-blades, most with their own special names. However, there are no standard-named shapes for multi-blades as there are among jack knives and pen knives. Multi-blades are classified by structure and function.

If someone refers to an equal-end jack or an equal-end pen, his meaning is clear. However, if he refers to an "equal-end multi-blade," his meaning is not clear. He could mean a utility knife or a cattle knife, or a sportsman's knife or a bottle-opener knife.

As a result, there is no segment on "standard" multi-blade shapes in the BLADE Guide. Instead, each type of multi-blade is treated separately. The types are listed below. In the types marked with an asterisk (*), there is either so much or so little diversity that the examples shown for the types are valued individually in order to serve as a guide. The other types have value tables.

* **Horseman's and Sportsman's Knives**
* **Champagne Patterns**
* **Bottle Opener Knives**
* **Smoker's Knives**
* **Folding Knife-Fork-Spoon Combinations**
  Scout and Utility Knives (includes Military)
  Cattle Knives
  Premium Stock Knives
  Junior Premium Stock Knives
* **Plier and Wrench Knives**
* **Special-Purpose Multi-Blades**
  Tool Kit Knives
* **Showpiece and Exposition Knives**
* **Folding Medical Instruments**

Horseman's and Sportsman's Knives

Horseman's and sportsman's knives are the original multi-blades. Sometimes they are all called "combination knives." They have been made in an incredible variety of shapes and blade combinations over at least the past 300 years. A selection of older versions is shown under Part 3 of this section, "Foreign, Exotic, Primitive, and Historical Folding Knives."

Horseman's Knives

A horseman's knife can have anywhere from three to over 40 blades. What distinguishes it from other multi-blades, and especially from sportsman's knives, is that it has a hoof pick—sometimes called a stone hook—for cleaning horses' hooves. Also, horseman's knives often have a fleam blade for bleeding foundered horses (see "Special Spey and Veterinary Knives" for more about fleams).

Most horseman's knives are made in a standard shape. The shape is pinched at the end where the larger blades are hinged, giving a sort of bottleneck appearance. The shape allows the hoof pick to open 180 degrees. However, as the accompanying illustrations show, horseman's knives also were made in other shapes, while the "standard" horseman's shape also was used on some sportsman's knives that have no hoof pick.

An interesting feature of larger, standard-shaped horseman's knives is that they often have a curved cutout in the handle, under the stone hook. The inside of the hook usually has teeth opposite the cutout. The cutout lets the arm of the hook double as a nutcracker.

Most horseman's knives sold in America were made in Sheffield. Some were made in Germany, sometimes of lesser quality. A very few were made in the United States. See the following pages for information on values.

Horseman's Knives: Values

Any American-made horseman's knife is worth at least **$400**. Standard-shape Sheffield examples with genuine stag handles—the usual material—are worth from **$500** for small ones up to about **$1,200** for large ones.

No. 1047
St w/r•Sportsman's Knife, Pearl Scales, German silver bolsters, shield and shackle, brass lining, two blades, mirror finish, leather punch, corkscrew, hoof cleaner, steel tweezer, steel pin, screwdriver.
J.A. Henckels, small size, mother-of-pearl, **$450-500**.

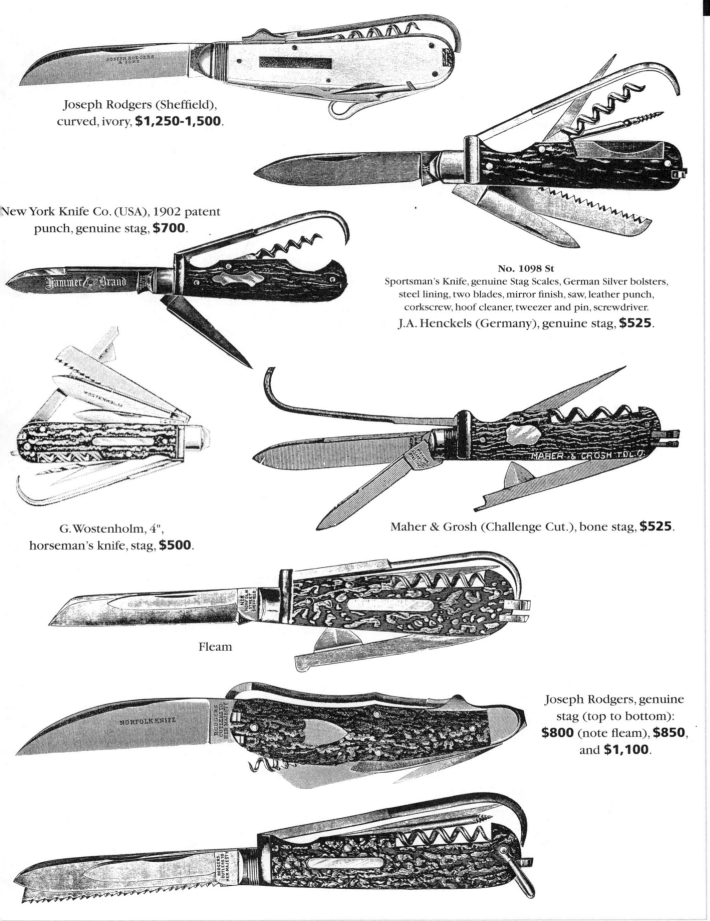

Joseph Rodgers (Sheffield), curved, ivory, **$1,250-1,500**.

New York Knife Co. (USA), 1902 patent punch, genuine stag, **$700**.

No. 1098 St
Sportsman's Knife, genuine Stag Scales, German Silver bolsters, steel lining, two blades, mirror finish, saw, leather punch, corkscrew, hoof cleaner, tweezer and pin, screwdriver.
J.A. Henckels (Germany), genuine stag, **$525**.

G. Wostenholm, 4", horseman's knife, stag, **$500**.

Maher & Grosh (Challenge Cut.), bone stag, **$525**.

Fleam

Joseph Rodgers, genuine stag (top to bottom): **$800** (note fleam), **$850**, and **$1,100**.

Horseman's and Sportsman's Knives

The three pieces shown here have nickel-silver handles for use near salt water. top: Rodgers (horseman's), 4 1/2", with shotshell extractor, buttoner, harness mending bolts, British oval-style tin opener, etc., **$650**; middle: J.A. Henckels, 7 blades, "compass-joint" w/marlinespike, **$450**; and bottom: J.A. Henckels, 4 blades, including marlinespike, **$375**.

I*XL G. Wostenholm, sportsman's knife,
4", nickel-silver handles, **$275-300**.

Sportsman's Knives

"Sportsman's knife" is really a catchall term for the larger and more elaborate multi-blades that do not have a specific application, such as horseman's knives. There is probably more variety in sportsman's knives than in any other type. Though loaded with many blades, some sportsman's knives are no bigger than pen knives. Others are big enough for two-handed use. The modern "Swiss Army" knife is a type of sportsman's knife.

Sportsman's knives are so diverse that their values must be estimated on a knife-by-knife basis. Brand name has some effect but is not as significant as on some other knives. The main factors are quality, condition, size, number of blades, unusual features and handle material. The sportsman's knife is very collectible and can demand premium prices if it is in very fine condition. Moreover, the ones made by English makers are most desirable. The examples herein show the range.

Camillus Cut. Co., 3 3/4", bone stag,
Prest-O-Lite, nickel-silver bolsters, **$400**.

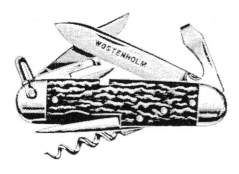

G. Wostenholm, 3 7/8", 6-blade utility,
bone stag, **$325-350**.

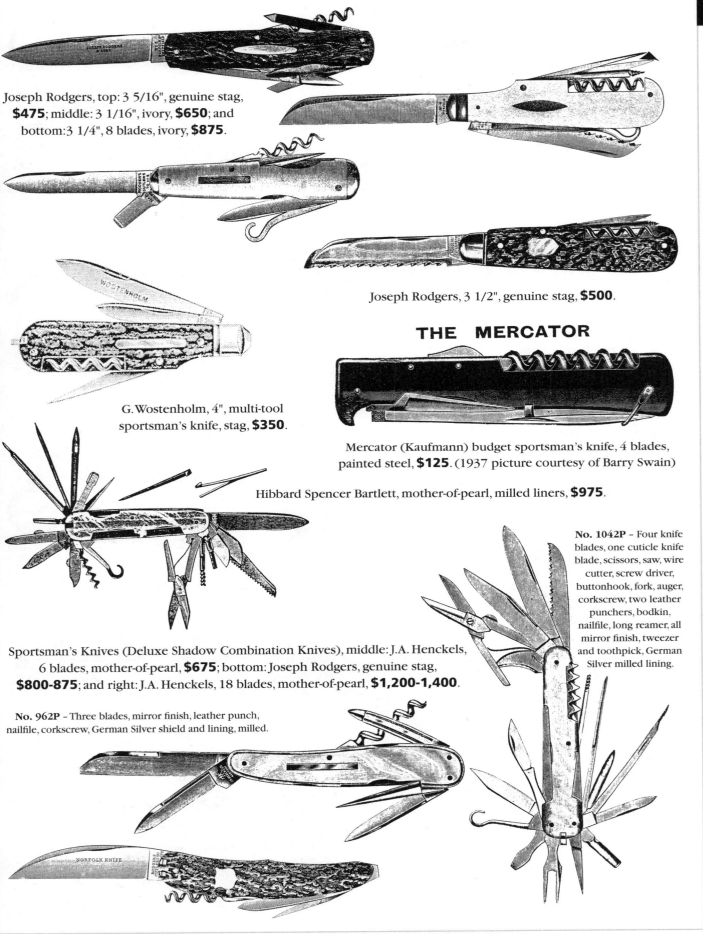

Joseph Rodgers, top: 3 5/16", genuine stag, **$475**; middle: 3 1/16", ivory, **$650**; and bottom: 3 1/4", 8 blades, ivory, **$875**.

Joseph Rodgers, 3 1/2", genuine stag, **$500**.

THE MERCATOR

G. Wostenholm, 4", multi-tool sportsman's knife, stag, **$350**.

Mercator (Kaufmann) budget sportsman's knife, 4 blades, painted steel, **$125**. (1937 picture courtesy of Barry Swain)

Hibbard Spencer Bartlett, mother-of-pearl, milled liners, **$975**.

No. 1042P – Four knife blades, one cuticle knife blade, scissors, saw, wire cutter, screw driver, buttonhook, fork, auger, corkscrew, two leather punchers, bodkin, nailfile, long reamer, all mirror finish, tweezer and toothpick, German Silver milled lining.

Sportsman's Knives (Deluxe Shadow Combination Knives), middle: J.A. Henckels, 6 blades, mother-of-pearl, **$675**; bottom: Joseph Rodgers, genuine stag, **$800-875**; and right: J.A. Henckels, 18 blades, mother-of-pearl, **$1,200-1,400**.

No. 962P – Three blades, mirror finish, leather punch, nailfile, corkscrew, German Silver shield and lining, milled.

Champagne Patterns

CHAMPAGNE patterns always have a corkscrew, usually on the back. Older ones—from before about 1925—also have a champagne-wire-cutter blade. Later versions have a crown cap lifter instead but are nonetheless called champagne patterns. Note that a "champagne knife" is a fixed blade with a champagne-wire-cutter blade only. Champagne patterns are very popular and make an impressive exhibit when properly displayed. Values have a wide range, with the type of handle material exerting a significant influence.

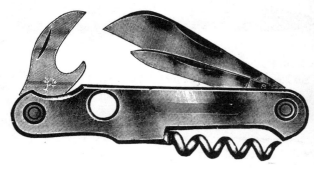

H. Boker, nickel silver, cigar clipper, **$175**.

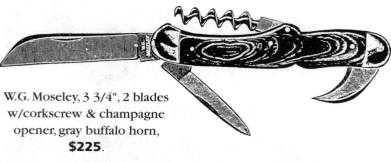

W.G. Moseley, 3 3/4", 2 blades w/corkscrew & champagne opener, gray buffalo horn, **$225**.

A. Kastor (Germany), 3 1/2", 2 blades w/corkscrew & champagne opener, stag, brass lined, crocus polished, **$200** (mother-of-pearl: **$250**).

Henry Sears & Son, 3 1/4", bone stag, **$275**.

Keen Kutter, 3 1/4", mother-of-pearl, **$300**.

Schrade Cut. Co., patterned celluloid, **$150**.

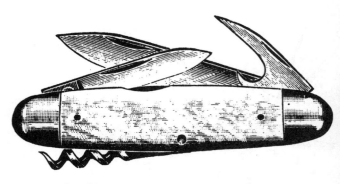

Case Tested XX, mother-of-pearl, **$675**.

Remingtons: genuine stag (left), **$600**; mother-of-pearl (right), **$950**.

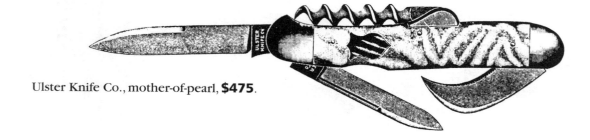

Ulster Knife Co., mother-of-pearl, **$475**.

Bottle Opener Knives

A BOTTLE OPENER knife is a pen knife or small jack knife with either a corkscrew in the back, or a cap lifter built into the handle or one of the blades.

"NAPANOCH" Gentleman's Knife

H. Boker, 3 1/4", black-and-white celluloid, **$125**.

Napanoch, bone stag, **$275-300**.

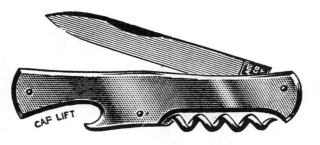

Schrade Cut. Co., nickel silver, **$60**.

Stiletto (P.H.&S.), bone stag, **$225**.

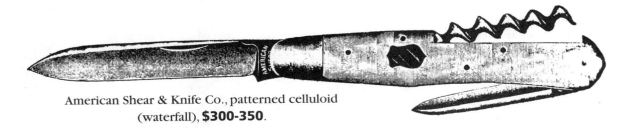

American Shear & Knife Co., patterned celluloid
(waterfall), **$300-350**.

Smoker's Knives

SMOKER'S KNIVES are multi-blades, some or all of whose blades are designed for use on pipes or cigars.

The blades or fixtures can include cigar cutters for clipping off the ends of cigars; long, thin cigar punches for opening an airway down the center of a cigar; cigar forks for holding short cigar stubs without burning one's fingers; pipe tampers; and pipe-bowl reamers. A simpler style of smoker's knife is included under the "Special Purpose Jack Knives" segment of the chapter, "Named Jack Knife Patterns."

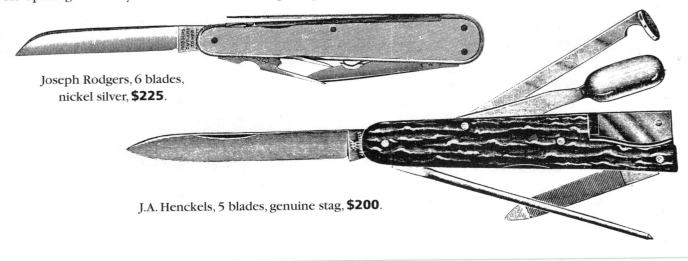

Joseph Rodgers, 6 blades,
nickel silver, **$225**.

J.A. Henckels, 5 blades, genuine stag, **$200**.

Folding Knife-Fork-Spoon Combinations

Most folding knife-fork-spoon combinations take apart into two or three pieces. In the early 19th century, take-apart versions were called "slot knives" because of the tab and slot mechanism that joins the pieces.

Slot knives with forks seem to have been made for as long as people have eaten with forks, which has been since the late 17th century. Some older French examples consist of a pair of knives slotted together. Today, they are called "friend knives," though, in fact, well-mannered people ate with pairs of knives before use of the eating fork became popular. For older or silver-bladed "slot knives," see Part 3 of this section, "Foreign, Exotic, Primitive, and Historical Folding Knives," or the "Silver Fruit Knives" segment of the chapter, "Named Jack Knife Patterns."

The first American slot knives seem to have been made in the 1860s. Ames Cutlery Co. patented one type in 1861. American Knife Co. patented another in 1862. Lamson & Goodnow made many in the period, as did other American pocketknife companies then in business.

American slot knives were popular with Federal troops in the Civil War, though they were never an issue item. Older American examples had wooden handles, and many had tin-plated blades.

In World War I the American Red Cross purchased millions of non-take-apart folding knives with wooden handles, steel mounts, a single spear blade and a folding spoon. One hundred eighty thousand such "Red Cross knives" were ordered in October 1917 alone. They were included in soldiers' gift boxes, paid for out of private donations. Camillus was a leading supplier. Today, the knives are often misidentified as Civil War artifacts. Value **$90-150**.

A European style of fold-up eating set has full, separate handles for each implement, and was sold with a fitted case. Values: bone, horn, or wood set **$150**; single item **$35**. Ivory set **$250**; single item **$65**.

Ulster Knife Co., two parts, wood, **$275**.

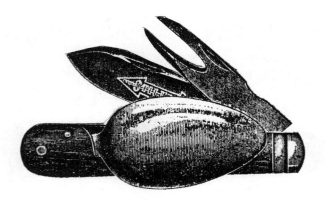

Stiletto slot knife (made by Ulster for Pacific Hardware & Steel); its fork functions as a can-opener and it has a cap-lifter on its side, 4 3/8", wood, **$375**.

W.R. Case & Sons, 4 1/2", "Hobo" knife-fork-spoon combo, bone, **$375-475**.

VALUE RANGE

VH	H	M	LM	L
$600	$500	$400	$250	$175

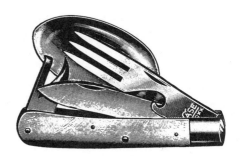

No. 3452
Case Tested XX, 3 3/4",
yellow celluloid, **$700**.

No. Y249K&F _Handles slip apart forming general utility knife and fork combination. Amber composition handles. Size over all 3⅞".

No. Y349KFS Handles slip apart forming three piece utility set. Amber composition handles. Size over-all 3⅞".

Western States, **$475**.

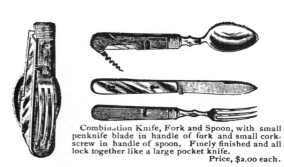

Combination Knife, Fork and Spoon, with small penknife blade in handle of fork and small corkscrew in handle of spoon. Finely finished and all lock together like a large pocket knife.
Price, $2.00 each.

COMBINATION CAMP KNIFE, FORK AND SPOON.

European style, cased set of three:
wood or horn, **$275**; ivory, **$450**.

Knife

Fork and Cap Lifter

Spoon and Can Opener

Camillus Cutlery Co., 3", English-style
blade, bone stag, **$275-300**.

Vest Pocket Knife and Fork
WITH IMITATION LEATHER CASE ½ x 1¼ x 4 INCHES.

PARTLY OPENED

The most convenient and lightest two-piece set ever devised. It is strong, carefully fitted and beautifully finished in nickel—a pleasing addition to any outfit.
A fork is a necessity on any trip and this knife will save you from dulling your hunting knife when cutting meat on a plate.
No. 60.   3½ ounces; nickel plated; with case; prepaid...................$1.50

Marble's (German made), **$300-350**.

Utility and Scout Knives

By Dennis Ellingsen, with value adjustments by Pete Cohan.

Dennis Ellingsen collects scout and utility knives.

Utility Knives

The utility knife is an equal-end multi-blade pattern. The standard utility knife is 3 5/8 inches long closed and has two backsprings and a bail. Ordinarily, it has four blades: a spear master blade, a punch, a can opener and a screwdriver-caplifter.

There are several uncommon variations on the basic design. There are both smaller and larger sizes. There are a few three-blade versions, lacking one of the tool blades. There are five-blade versions, with the fifth blade a stubby Phillips screwdriver.

There is also a six-blade version. It has a pen blade in place of the punch on top, and a corkscrew and punch on the bottom. In the 1920s, the version was called the *picnic knife* or, by some firms, the *army and navy pattern*.

The standard four-blade utility knife seems to have been a cross between the American equal-end cattle knife and German and Swiss multi-bladed hunter's and soldier's knives, a hybrid that was conceived some time around 1900. However, four-blade utilitarian multi-blades date back at least to the 18th century (see Part 3 of this section, "Foreign, Exotic, Primitive and Historical Folding Knives").

The American utility pattern was offered as an inexpensive, homegrown substitute for the costly horseman's and sportsman's knives long imported from Europe. The foreign multi-blade patterns had been popular in the United States for some time, but had never been produced in quantity in America because of higher labor costs. The Tariff Acts of 1890, 1897 and 1901 made even the imported horseman's and sportsman's knives much more expensive, so U.S. firms began to offer the utility knife as a less costly substitute.

The six-blade utility knife, with punch and corkscrew on the back, began as a European (German, Bohemian, French and Swiss) effort to make more inexpensive versions of a traditional multi-blade, while retaining the most important blade, the corkscrew, for Europeans. Some U.S. firms made a six-blade pattern. It has become a very collectible multi-blade, bringing top dollar when found in excellent condition.

Base values for UTILITY KNIVES (other than Official Scout) with four blades, bone-stag, smooth-bone or genuine stag handles, and full bolsters. Excellent, unsharpened condition, with etch as appropriate.

VALUE RANGE

VH	H	M	LM	L
$850	$500	$300	$200	$125

Camillus Cut. Co., 3 5/8", utility, bone, **$250**.

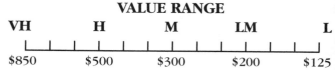

No. 42209-B—3 5/8" The American Scout knife. An all around good knife for outdoors. It has a large spear point cutting blade, can opener, combination cork-screw and cap lifter and punch blade. CATTARAUGUS, **$325**.

Schrade, #9593, 3 3/8", 4-blade utility, bone stag, **$225**.

Schrade, #S9463 Prest-O-Lite key, 3 5/8", bone stag, **$250**.

Schrade, #9466, 3 5/8", mother-of-pearl, **$375-400**.

Schrade, #9464, 3 5/8", R-W-B celluloid, **$300-350**.

Six-Blade Utility Knives

HERE'S the Bird for K.P.— the Remington Camp Knife

A *Man's Knife* — Remington Steel, made to the exacting Remington standards of quality and accuracy — with clean cutting edges that stay keen a long time.

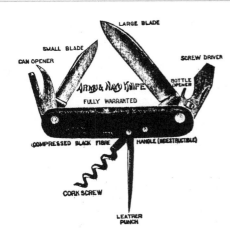

Remington, one-piece can opener, 3 5/8", bone stag, **$500**.
(Remingtons with a 2-piece can opener were first made in 1924.)

Daniel Peres, sold by Von Lengerke & Antoine, Chicago (1925), no bolsters, 3 5/8", plain celluloid, **$125-175**.

J.A. Henckels, genuine stag, **$250**.
(Note European-style leather punch with eye.)

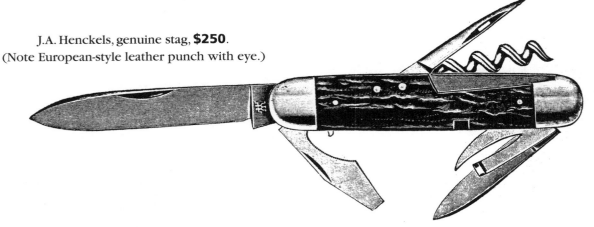

Four-Blade Utility Knives

Remington, 3 3/8", R-W-B celluloid, **$525**.

Keen Kutter, 3 1/2", bone stag, **$350**.

Schrade Cut. Co., 3 5/8", utility, **$250**.

Camillus Cut. Co., Sword Brand etch, 3 5/8", mother-of-pearl, nickel-silver bolsters, **$375-400**.

Napanoch, Prest-O-Lite key, bone stag, **$375**.

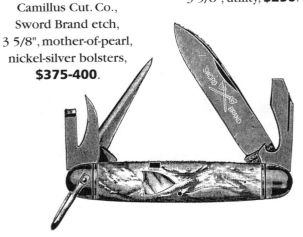

Large Size Utility Knives

Western States "Kit Carson," 4 3/4", bone stag, **$900-1,100**. Similar knife by Utica, **$650-800**.

Case Tested 6465SAB, 5 1/4", green bone, saber-ground blade, **$2,000-2,400**.

Case Tested 6465, flat ground, bone, **$2,400**.

New York Knife Co. "Buffalo Bill," 5", bone stag, **$850-950**.

Remington R4243 "Bullet," 4 13/16", bone stag, **$2,000**.

Boy Scout Knives

What brought the four-blade utility knife widespread popularity in the United States was its designation in 1910 or 1911 as an official style of pocketknife for the Boy Scouts of America (B.S.A.). The scouting organization was founded in 1910, modeled after the British organization established in 1908. British scout knives look like British military rigging knives. Before World War II, Ulster made rope knives for the B.S.A Sea Scouts (see "Sailor's Rope Knives" in the chapter, "Named Jack Knife Patterns").

Until 1922, New York Knife Co. was the only firm authorized by the B.S.A. to make Official Boy Scout knives. All Official Boy Scout folding knives have a special shield (see following page and/or pages). Until late 1922, New York Knife's Official shield was a banner with the words BE PREPARED. Also, the master blade etch on the knives indicate that they were Official, though today the etch is often worn away.

In the early days of scouting, New York Knife Co. offered two styles of Official Boy Scout knives. The utility pattern was the No. 1 Boy Scout. The No. 2 Boy Scout was an easy-open regular jack with a sheepfoot blade, a pen blade and a bail. The World War I U.S. Navy sailor's knife looks similar. The utility pattern ultimately eclipsed the smaller jack knife.

New York Knife's monopoly extended only to Official scout knives. Most all of its rival pocketknife firms made unofficial scout knives. They gave the knives such unauthorized markings as SCOUT KNIFE, CAMP KNIFE, MADE FOR SCOUTS, or even BOY SCOUT. In 1923, Remington and Ulster (Dwight Divine) obtained permission to make Official Scout utility knives.

Many firms also made easy-open scout-type jack knives similar to the New York "No. 2 Boy Scout"—some with unauthorized BOY SCOUT shields. However, only Landers Frary & Clark, in the 1930s, made any that were "Official." Even the Remington R963 with a Boy Scout hat shield was not Official.

Scouting catalogs in the late 1920s offered folding knife-fork-spoon sets by George Schrade Knife Co. using George Schrade's patented "wire-jack" construction. However, it was not until the late 1940s that the sets began to bear the Official Boy Scout designation.

New York Knife Co. went out of business in 1931. It was replaced on the Official Boy Scout Knife roster by Cattaraugus and Landers Frary & Clark. In the early 1930s, Cattaraugus offered a modified utility pattern called the "Whitt-L-Kraft." L.F.&C. ceased pocketknife production in 1938 or 1939, while Cattaraugus stopped making pocketknives in the 1950s.

Remington sold its cutlery division to Pal in 1940. Pal made Official Boy Scout Knives until 1948. Pal was the first firm to use plastic handles on Official Boy Scout Knives. In 1947 and 1948, Camillus briefly made Official Boy Scout knives.

Also after the war, Ulster, Schrade and Imperial merged to form Imperial Knife Associated Cos. Both the Imperial and Ulster brands have since appeared on Official Boy Scout utility knives. Buck offered Official Boy Scout lockback folding hunters. Today, Camillus, Victorinox and Wenger make Official knives, or reasonable facsimiles.

Girl Scout and Camp Fire Girls Knives

Though the Girl Scouts of America were established in 1912, the earliest Official Girl Scout knives we have seen date from the 1920s. The first were by Ulster (Dwight Divine), followed some time after 1927 by Remington. Both firms made only junior-sized—3 3/8-inch—Girl Scout utility knives with bone-stag handles. In the mid-1930s, Remington also made an equal-end-pen Girl Scout knife with two blades and a bail.

Later in the 1930s, Utica/Kutmaster began making Official Girl Scout Knives. The company made both junior and full-sized versions with clear-celluloid-over-green handles. In addition, Utica/Kutmaster made Featherweight (aluminum-framed) one- and two-blade Girl Scout knives with black or green handles. The company also made small knives for the Brownie Scouts. The little knives have clear-over-red-celluloid handles.

The Camp Fire Girls was established in 1911. By 1915, if not earlier, it had an official knife made by New York Knife Co. The knife has the motto WOHELO (Work Health Love) on the shield. In the 1920s, Remington and Ulster also made Official Camp Fire Girls knives. Some of the official knives have a manicure blade.

Utica/Kutmaster began to make Camp Fire knives in the 1930s. They did not have a special WOHELO shield, the only official designation being in the blade etch.

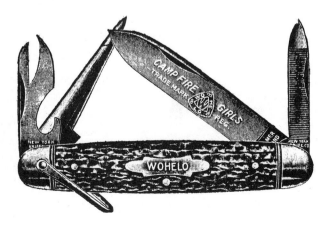

New York Knife Co. Camp Fire circa 1915, **$600**.

No. 1004. SCOUT KNIFE. Usually the first acquisition of a Scout. Stag handle, large polished cutting blade etched with official emblem, screw driver, can opener and boring tool for leather articles. Equipped so as to be hung on the Scout belt. Prepaid.....**$1.00** Given for 2 subscriptions to BOYS' LIFE.

No. 1005. SCOUT KNIFE. This also is official and is designed for those Scouts who prefer a two-bladed knife. Ebony handle. One small blade and one large, opening without use of finger nail. Has shackle for hanging on Scout's belt. Prepaid...............50c Given for 1 subscription to BOYS' LIFE.

New York Knife Co. pre-1923 Official knives: **$375** each.

Approved and licensed by the Boy Scouts of America.

Official Scout, length when closed 3¹¹⁄₁₆ in. large clip point cutting blade highly mirror or crocused polished on front side and etched with official Boy Scout Emblem, combination screw driver and wire scraper blade, combination can opener and crown cap bottle opener and Patent Knurled Genuine Harrison Leather Punch or Gouge Blade. Stag handle, brass lining, nickel silver bolsters, toggle and shield. The shield is stamped with the official Boy Scout Fleur-de-lis Insignia and the words "Be Prepared," w't per doz. 2¾ lbs.

C9744Y4 ....each **$1.50**

New York Knife Co. post-1923 Official knife, **$375**.

Official Boy Scout Knives

ULSTER   HAMMER   REMINGTON

Above: After 1921 and until 1948, each authorized official manufacturer adopted its own distinctive version of the Official Boy Scout shield. The shields alone enable you to identify the makers of older Official Scout knives.

(Shield chart from 1929)

No. 64900. Size 3⅝". Ulster Official knife. Also in less expensive knife No. X350ST with bone stag handle. With pearl composition handle, X350 Comp.

Ulster Official knife sold by Western States circa 1941, **$300**.

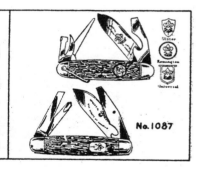

OFFICIAL BOY SCOUT KNIFE
Stag handle; heavy cutting blade; screw driver; bottle and can opener; punch blade.
No. 1496 "REMINGTON" $1.50
No. 1502 "ULSTER"   1.50
No. 1585 "UNIVERSAL"   1.50

WHITT-L-KRAFT KNIFE
Excellent for whittling, carving, cutting and all other handicraft work. Has four blades.
No. 1087 $1.50

No. 1087

Official knives circa 1932.

RS 4783

OFFICIAL KNIFE BOY SCOUTS OF AMERICA
STAG HANDLE; THREE BLADES, 1 Large Spear, Crocus Polished and Etched with Scout Insignia; 1 Combination Bottle-Opener and Screw Driver, 1 Can Opener, Both Blue Glazed. Nickel Silver Lining, Bolsters and Emblem Shield, Snap-on Nickel Plated Shackle.
Length, closed, 3½ ins.

Remington, small 3-blade (1936), **$425**.

No. D2589—Whitt-L-Kraft Knife. 3½"   4 Blades consisting of one large spear point for coarse work, one small blade, with 45 degree offset point for fine work; hollow chisel blade for extra-fine close-in work; and a scraper blade for finishing, which is also a combination can opener, bottle opener and screw driver. Full polish, brass lined, Nickel silver bolsters. Stag handle with shield bearing Scout Insignia. With or without bale.

Cattaraugus, **$475**.

Remington Boy Scout Knives

$500.

$500.

$1,000.
(Rare!)

$450.

RS 3333
Official Knife
Boy Scouts of America

RC 4523
Official Knife
Boy Scouts (Spanish)

RS 4233
Official Knife
Boy Scouts of America

RS3333
OFFICIAL KNIFE

1936 Official. **$225-275**.

Top left: pre-1923 non-official. Above three: c1925 Official.

Non-Official circa 1921: bone stag, **$400**.

R 963

R 963 Stag
R 965 Flag Pyremite

OFFICIAL KNIVES

Compiled by Dennis Ellingsen (Values revised September 2004; for knives in mint condition, unsharpened)

OFFICIAL BOY SCOUT KNIVES

Brand	Blades	Description	Mfrs Model #	BSA #	Value
New York Knife	4	3 5/8" "Be Prepared" banner shield		1004	$375.
New York Knife	2	wood "Be Prepared" banner shield		1005	375.
New York Knife	2	bone "Be Prepared" banner shield		1450	450.
New York Knife	4	3 5/8" oval shield, spear blade	BS1	1566	300.
New York Knife	4	3 5/8" oval shield, clip blade	BS1	1566	300.
New York Knife	2	punch oval shield	BS2	1568	375.
New York Knife	4	3 3/8" oval shield	BS4	1567	300.
New York Knife	4	pearlized handles	BS3	????	775.
Remington	3	3 3/8" junior size	RS4773	????	450.
Remington	3	3 1/2" mid size	RS4783	1494	300.
Remington	4	3 5/8" standard size	RS3333	1496	300.
Remington	4	3 5/8" std. size, Spanish	RC4523	????	1,000.
Remington	4	3 3/8" junior size	RS4233	1497	400.
Remington	1	4 1/2" blade (fixed)	RH50	1559	250.
Remington	1	4" blade (fixed)	RH51	1561	250.
Ulster Dwight Divine	4	3 5/8" bone	47553L5	1502	125-200.
Ulster Dwight Divine	4	3 3/8" junior size	47488L5	1503	125-200.
Ulster Dwight Divine	2	two cutting blades	243L5	1504	250.
Ulster Dwight Divine	3	3 3/8" junior size	1513		125-200.
Ulster Dwight Divine	2	Sea Scout w/marlinespike (see Sailor's Knives)		1128	750.
Ulster Knife	4	3 5/8" genuine mother-of-pearl	4063L	????	850.
Ulster U.S.A.	5	3 5/8" white plastic w/Phillips screwdriver		1046	45.
Ulster U.S.A.	4	3 5/8" standard		1996	45.
L.F.&C.	4	3 3/8" junior size	04667	1586	250.
L.F.&C.	4	3 5/8" standard size	04666	1585	200.
L.F.&C.	3	3 3/8" junior size		1564	300.
L.F.&C.	2	3 1/2" mid size	02668	????	300.
Cattaraugus	4	Whitt-L-Kraft	D2589	1087	475.
Cattaraugus	3	Whitt-L-Kraft	C2589	1122	475.
Marble's	1	Woodcraft (fixed)	1560	1560	300-500.
Marble's	1	Sport (fixed)	1562	1562	300-525.
George Schrade	3	Chow kit knife/fork/spoon (red)		1384	100.
Pal Blade	4	bone or plastic		1495	75.
Pal Blade	3	bone utility		1493	100.
Pal Blade	1	4 1/2" blade (fixed)	RH50	????	100-150.
Pal Blade	1	4" blade (fixed)	RH51	????	100-150.

Brand	Blades	Description	Mfrs Model #	BSA #	Value
Ka-Bar	1	3 1/2" blade (fixed) (1941)		1554	250.
Ka-Bar	1	5" blade (fixed) (1941)		1553	200.
Ka-Bar	1	4" blade (fixed) w/spike (Voyageur)		1555	350.
Ka-Bar	3	knife/fork/spoon, take-apart, yellow		1382	550.
Kingston	4	MIL-K metal handles, blade etch (c1946)			125.
Imperial	4	3 5/8" hot-stamped shield (1949-52)		1045	45.
Imperial	4	3 5/8" standard		1996	35.
Imperial	4	white cracked-ice handles		1052	80.
Imperial	5	w/Phillips screwdriver		1046	75.
Imperial	3	"whittler"		1047	65.
Imperial/Frontier	2	Leader's		1066	50.
Camillus	4	plastic handles		1996	40.
Camillus	4	cracked-ice (Nu-pearl) handles		1052	45.
Camillus	3	"whittler" – white, black or brown		1047	30.
Camillus	5	w/Phillips screwdriver		1046	35.
Camillus	1	mini lockback		1065	35.
Camillus	1	large lockback		1371	60.
Camillus	1	3 1/2" blade (fixed) white		1373	45.
Camillus	1	3 1/2" slide-lock		1372	40.
Camillus	1	"Adventure"		1375	40.
Camillus	1	lockback		1370	45.
Camillus	3	2 1/4" Eagle Scout, red/white/blue		1995	65.
Camillus	3	2 1/4" Explorer, green		1998	45.
Western	1	4 1/2" blade (fixed)		1378	45-60.
Western	1	5" blade (fixed)		1379	50-75.
Western	1	4" blade (fixed)		1381	65-80.
Western	1	4 1/2" blade (fixed) Delrin handle		1367	50.
Western	1	3 1/2" blade (fixed) Delrin handle		1364	45.
Schrade Walden	2	clip & pen, Delrin handle	708	1043	30.
Schrade Walden	2	with file, stainless handle	778	1060	30.
Schrade USA	3	whittler - Delrin handles	863	1047	45.
Buck	1	Scoutlite red handles	412	1381	90.
Victorinox	3	Boy Scout Classic		1394	35.
Victorinox	6	Boy Scout Tinker		1395	35.
Victorinox	8	Boy Scout Huntsman		1396	60.
Victorinox	7	Boy Scout Adventurer		1397	40.
Victorinox	1	Boy Scout Century		1383	20.
Victorinox	7	Boy Scout Mechanic		1882	65.
Wenger	7	Scout Special		1391	40.
Wenger	9	Young Hunter		1382	45.
Wenger	5	Viceroy		1393	30.

OFFICIAL GIRL SCOUT KNIVES

Brand	Blades	Description	Mfrs Model #	BSA #	Value
Remington	4	3 3/8" bone handles		R4373	$575.
Remington	2	Pen knife w/bail		R4723	500.
Remington	2	Easy-opener		R963-X	675.
Remington	1	4" blade (fixed)		RH251	300.
Ulster	2	3 3/8" bone		Y503	150.
Ulster	2	3 3/8" bone, easy-opener			450.
Ulster Knife	4	3 3/8" bone, many variants	Y501		150.
Ulster Dwight Divine	4	3 3/8"	M301		200.
Ulster	4	3 3/8" genuine mother-of-pearl		4066	550.
Marble's	1	4" blade Sport (fixed) leather handle			500.
George Schrade	3	Chow kit - knife/fork/spoon (green)			50.
Kutmaster (Utica)	4	3 3/8" mottled green celluloid handles			75.
Kutmaster	4	3 3/8" clear plastic over green handles			45.
Kutmaster	4	3 5/8" clear plastic over green handles		11-310	45.
Kutmaster	4	3 3/8" green plastic w/hot stamp shield			30.
Utica	2	3 3/8" bone handles, aluminum liners		11-312	100.
Utica	2	3 3/8" plastic handles, aluminum liners		11-312	45.
Utica	4	3 3/8" mottled green celluloid handles			75.
Utica	4	3 3/8" green plastic handles			30.
Utica	4	3 3/8" bone handles			45.
Pal Blade	4	3 3/8" bone, etch only, no shield (c1946)			150.
USA (Pal)					90.

OFFICIAL CAMP FIRE KNIVES

Brand	Blades	Description	CF #	Value
New York Knife	4	3 3/8" bone handles		$600.
Ulster	4	3 3/8" bone handles	4533	375.
Remington	4	3 3/8" bone handles		600.
Ka-Bar	3	3 7/8" knife/fork/spoon, take-apart, yellow		700.
Kutmaster	4	3 5/8" black plastic handles		45.
Kutmaster	4	3 3/8" black plastic handles		45.
Utica	1	sheath knife		125.

OFFICIAL CUB SCOUT KNIVES

Brand	Blades	Description	Mfrs Model #	BSA #	Value
Camillus	3	white handles		1885	$20.
Camillus	3	blue or black handles		1885	20.
Imperial	3	blue or black handles		1885	30.
Buck	1	Cublite blue handles	414	1884	65.
Victorinox	2	Feather Weight		1865	20.

OFFICIAL BROWNIE KNIVES

Brand	Blades	Description	Value
Kutmaster (Utica)	1	clear plastic over red handles	$45.
Kutmaster	1	clear plastic over red, locking blade	45.
Utica	1	brown plastic handles	30.

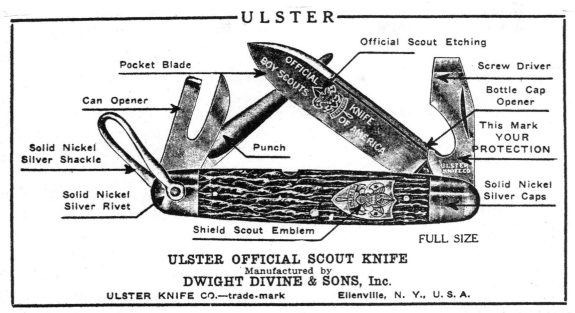

ULSTER

Official Scout Etching

Pocket Blade

Screw Driver

Can Opener

Bottle Cap Opener

Solid Nickel Silver Shackle

Punch

This Mark YOUR PROTECTION

Solid Nickel Silver Rivet

Shield Scout Emblem

Solid Nickel Silver Caps

FULL SIZE

ULSTER OFFICIAL SCOUT KNIFE
Manufactured by
DWIGHT DIVINE & SONS, Inc.
ULSTER KNIFE CO.—trade-mark   Ellenville, N. Y., U. S. A.

ULSTER

SPECIFICATIONS

POCKET BLADE—A special feature of the pocket blade is the special high temper, which insures a durable blade and a keen cutting edge. Due to the careful grinding, the blade can be easily re-sharpened with a few strokes on an oil stone, holding the flat side of the blade at an angle of 20 degrees on the stone.

SCREW DRIVER—Carefully designed for the radio amateur, finished to a narrow edge for fine instrument work, yet strong and durable enough for the heavier work on bicycle, gun or car.

BOTTLE OPENER—An indispensable article at home or in camp for removing caps from bottles and other receptacles with metal caps.

CAN OPENER—One of the most useful tools in the knife. Much careful study has been devoted to the Ulster design and manufacture. A special feature is the groove which guides the opener exactly on the lip of the can and prevents the tool from slipping. This added convenience prevents many an ugly scratch on sharp tin edges.

SPRINGS—Vital parts of every knife are the springs. The Springs of the Ulster Official Scout Knives are scientifically and accurately hardened and tempered and highly polished, the tension carefully adjusted.

PUNCH—A convenient tool for camp and hike. Rigidly tested before leaving the factory, can be depended upon to withstand hard usage.

LOOP—Made of heavy guage nickel silver wire, riveted to a solid pin through the bolster. The loop turns easily and is closely adjusted.

SPECIFICATIONS

STEEL LINER—In the frame between the punch blade and can opener there is a small plate of steel or spacer. This makes a light, compact knife frame of strong, rugged construction.

HANDLES—The stag handles are of selected American bone stag, carefully treated to wear well. The stag handles are closely fitted to the metal scales and securely riveted.

SCOUT INSIGNIA—The Boy Scouts of America have licensed the Ulster Knife Company to manufacture the Official Boy Scout Knife, bearing the official Scout insignia upon the shield and blade, together with the Boy Scout motto, "Be Prepared." This shield and etching is an assurance to you that the knife is able to meet the same tests as our samples tested and approved by the United States Bureau of Standards. Each Ulster Knife bears the Ulster Knife Co. trademark upon blade tangs guaranteeing to you a thoroughly high quality product carefully designed to fill all the needs of the Boy Scout.

Ulster Official Boy Scout Knives are suplied in three sizes—the regular large 3⅝-inch pattern, No. 47553 L 5; the Junior size, four-blade 3⅜-inch pattern, No. 47488 L 5, and the standard two-blade pattern, 243 L 5.

Each Scout and patrol wishes to excel in scouting activities. Start right. Secure an official Ulster Scout Knife and "Be Prepared" for all emergencies.

Ulster 47553L5 Official Boy Scout knife, **$200-300**.

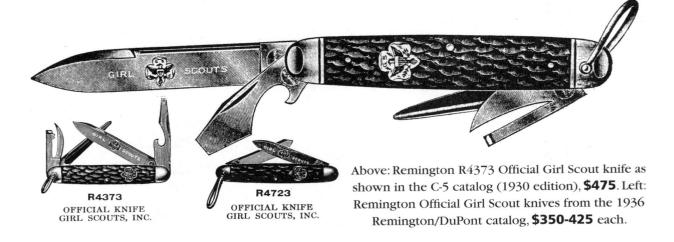

R4373
OFFICIAL KNIFE
GIRL SCOUTS, INC.

R4723
OFFICIAL KNIFE
GIRL SCOUTS, INC.

Above: Remington R4373 Official Girl Scout knife as shown in the C-5 catalog (1930 edition), **$475**. Left: Remington Official Girl Scout knives from the 1936 Remington/DuPont catalog, **$350-425** each.

U.S. Military Utility Knives

From the introduction of the utility pattern early in the 20th century, cutlery manufacturers advertised one or another version of the four- or six-blade utility knife as an "army and navy" or "military" pattern. Individual servicemen undoubtedly bought lots of the knives. However, with only one exception, the U.S. government seems not to have issued any multi-blades until just before World War II.

The one documented exception was purchased by the Army Medical Department prior to World War I. It was a 3 1/2-inch barehead swell-center regular pattern with bone-stag handles. It had a corkscrew on the back, a spear master blade marked MED.DEPT./U.S.A. and A.KASTOR & BROS./GERMANY, and a saw blade marked KASTOR over a contract date (the dates are usually 11-8-12 and 10-22-14). Value **$350**.

During World War II, the U.S. government purchased millions of utility knives for issue to soldiers, marines and Navy hospital corpsmen. Most had the standard four blades—on rare occasions, three—bone-stag handles and steel mounts. Some had shields marked with such branch initials as U.S.A., M.D.-U.S.N., U.S.N. and U.S.M.C., marks that significantly increase the value of the knives. Most had no shield or military markings and, as such, do not command a higher price.

About 1944, the Army and Marine Corps switched to checkered stainless steel for utility knife handles, though

(drawings by Blade Magazine Cutlery Hall-Of-Famer© M.H. Cole)

the blades were still carbon steel. In 1958, the branches switched to stainless steel blades.

For Army commandos and mountain troops, beginning in 1942, Ulster made junior-sized utility knives. The knives had an added Phillips screwdriver, either as a fifth blade or welded to the extra-wide bail, and a sheepfoot or spey blade in place of the cap-lifter. Handles were bone stag, mounts were steel, and the bail or shield usually was stamped "U.S." Value **$300-350**.

The oddest G.I. folder of the war was the Navy pilot's survival knife. It was 6 inches long, with blackened steel mounts and checkered, black-plastic handles secured by screws. It had a stout, saber-ground clip blade with a liner-type lock in one end, and a flexible, fine-toothed saw in the other. Some had a bail at the saw end. The sheath was canvas. The knives were made by Colonial Knife Co. and United Machine Tool Co. of Grand Rapids, Michigan.

Other military folding knives are found under the "Special Purpose Jack Knives (Electrician's Knives and Sailor's Knives)" segment of the "Named Jack Knife Patterns" chapter, and the "Cattle Knives" segment of this chapter. G.I. folding machetes are included with "U.S. Military Fixed Blade Knives" in the Special Section of Section III, "Fixed Blade Knives."

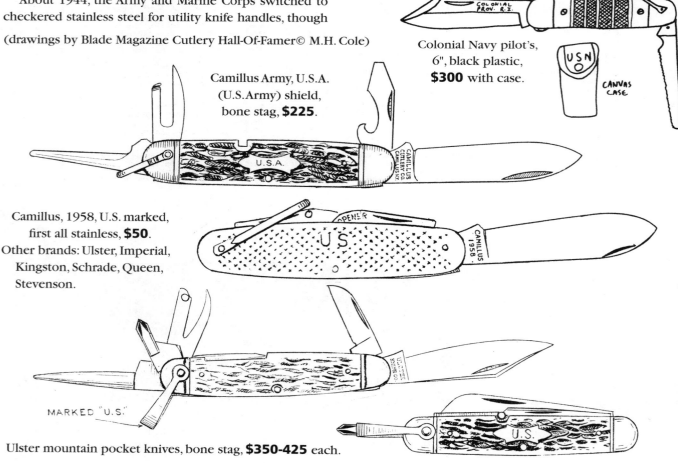

Colonial Navy pilot's, 6", black plastic, **$300** with case.

Camillus Army, U.S.A. (U.S. Army) shield, bone stag, **$225**.

Camillus, 1958, U.S. marked, first all stainless, **$50**. Other brands: Ulster, Imperial, Kingston, Schrade, Queen, Stevenson.

MARKED "U.S."

Ulster mountain pocket knives, bone stag, **$350-425** each.

Cattle Knives

The cattle knife is a heavy-duty three-bladed pocketknife, ordinarily 3 5/8 or 3 3/4 inches long. Some are junior sized, as small as 3 1/4 inches. Others, such as the Case 94s, are as large as 4 1/2 inches. A very few cattle knives have four blades and are the most popular with collectors.

As the name suggests, the cattle knife was designed for work on and around livestock. The type seems to have been introduced in about the 1870s.

The standard cattle knife has the same round-ended equal-end shape as the equal-end jack, and was probably derived from it. At least 90 percent of cattle knives are standard equal-ends, though a few have been made in other shapes. They include:

the "Premier" or serpentine;

the "Eureka," or swell-center serpentine;

the "Balloon" or straight swell-center.

the "Jumbo" or heavy sleeveboard;

the "Canoe," which looks like its namesake, and;

the "Surveyor," sort of a swell-center canoe.

Two-bladed versions of the knives are found in the "Jack Knives" chapter, including the chapter's "Double-End Jack Knive"s segment.

The master blade of a cattle knife is most often a spear blade, though many, including most Case cattle knives, have clip master blades. A few have sheepfoot master blades. The second blade is usually a spey, while the third can be a sheepfoot, pen or a punch.

An unusual type of cattle knife has three backsprings. The type, unlike three-backspring whittlers, must have a punch or spey blade as the second blade and a sheepfoot or pen blade as the third.

The "premier" or equal-end serpentine cattle knife was the ancestor of the more slender premium stock knife, introduced in the 1890s. Premier cattle knives have spear master blades. Stock knives have clip master blades. Some transitional cattle knives are slender like stock knives but have spear master blades.

During the First World War, both Camillus and Simmons Hardware sold 4 1/4-inch equal-end cattle knives handled in wood to the U.S. Army Signal Corps. In World War II, Camillus made a bone-handled equal-end cattle knife as a "utility knife" for the U.S. Army Air Corps.

Plain celluloid and bone stag are the most common handle materials on cattle knives. Fancy ones were made with patterned celluloid or, sometimes, mother-of-pearl. Wood and genuine stag handles seem to have had very limited use on cattle knives after about 1930.

Army Air Corps Utility Knife

Camillus, bone stag, military issue, **$175**.

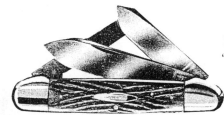

KA-BAR, 4 3/8", "Gunboat," bone stag, **$600**.

KA-BAR, 3 1/2", canoe w/punch, bone stag, **$375**.

Base values for CATTLE KNIVES over 3 7/16 through 3 15/16 inches long, with bone-stag or patterned-celluloid handle covers, and three blades.

Excellent, unsharpened condition, with etch as appropriate.

VALUE RANGE

SHAPE	VERY HIGH (VH)	HIGH (H)	MEDIUM (M)	LOW / MEDIUM (LM)	LOW (L)
STANDARD EQUAL-END	$500	$425	$300	$235	$175
PREMIER (serpentine)	500	400	275	200	150
EUREKA (swell-center serpentine)	650	475	300	235	175
BALLOON (straight swell-center)	600	425	275	200	125
JUMBO (heavy sleeveboard)	850	500	375	300	250
CANOE (or "GUNBOAT")	1,200	875	450	350	300
SURVEYOR (swell-center canoe)	950	450	275	200	150

Standard Cattle Knives

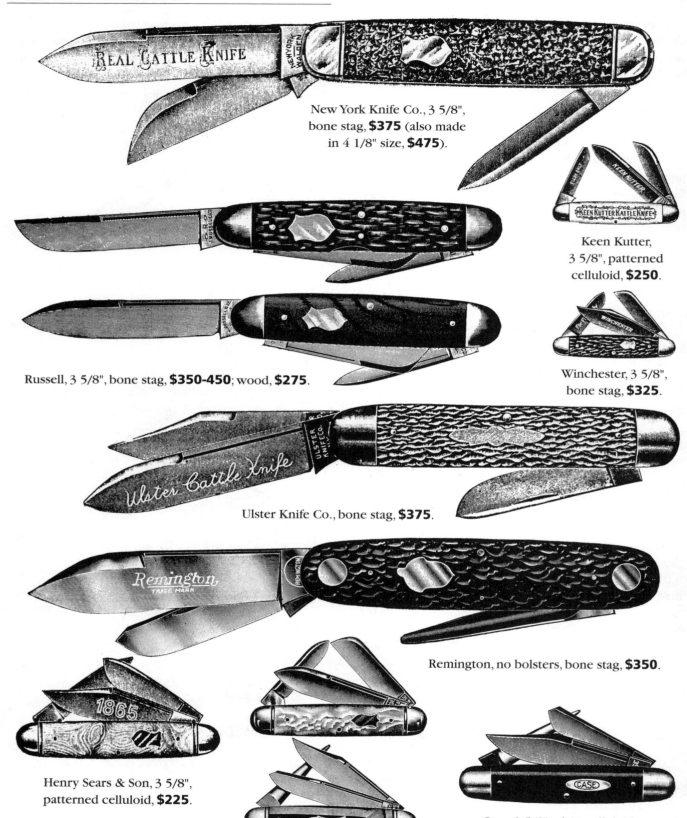

New York Knife Co., 3 5/8", bone stag, **$375** (also made in 4 1/8" size, **$475**).

Keen Kutter, 3 5/8", patterned celluloid, **$250**.

Russell, 3 5/8", bone stag, **$350-450**; wood, **$275**.

Winchester, 3 5/8", bone stag, **$325**.

Ulster Knife Co., bone stag, **$375**.

Remington, no bolsters, bone stag, **$350**.

Henry Sears & Son, 3 5/8", patterned celluloid, **$225**.

Schrade Cut. Cos., 3 5/8": mother-of-pearl, **$350**; patterned celluloid, **$195-225**.

Case, 3 5/8", plain celluloid: Tested XX, **$250**; XX, **$210**.

Cattle Knives (Four Blades)

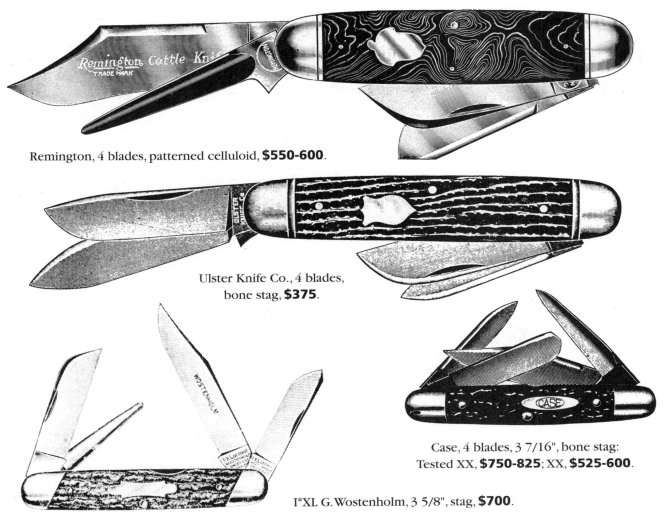

Remington, 4 blades, patterned celluloid, **$550-600**.

Ulster Knife Co., 4 blades,
bone stag, **$375**.

Case, 4 blades, 3 7/16", bone stag:
Tested XX, **$750-825**; XX, **$525-600**.

I*XL G. Wostenholm, 3 5/8", stag, **$700**.

No. B160 The Celebrated Wostenholm I*XL Farmer's
Knife.

Cattle Knives (Junior Size)

H. Boker, 3 3/16" fancy bolsters, bone stag, **$225**.

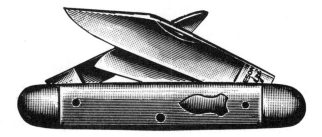

Robeson ShurEdge, 3 3/8", plain celluloid, **$175**.

Remington, 3 3/8", mother-of-pearl, **$425-500**.

Cattle Knives (Fancy, Three Backspring)

Winchester junior premiers: 3 1/4" patterned celluloid, 3 blades, bone stag, **$200** (left) and **$275** (right).

Keen Kutter, Eureka, bone stag, **$475**.

No. K738¾—3¾ INCH STAG HANDLE; THREE BLADES.

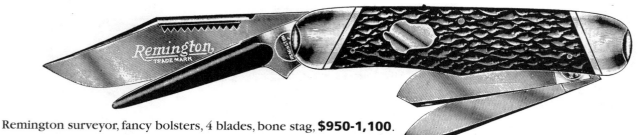

Remington surveyor, fancy bolsters, 4 blades, bone stag, **$950-1,100**.

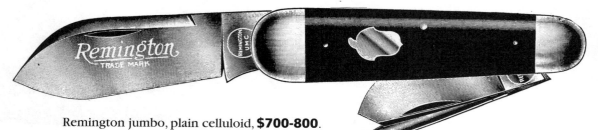

Remington jumbo, plain celluloid, **$700-800**.

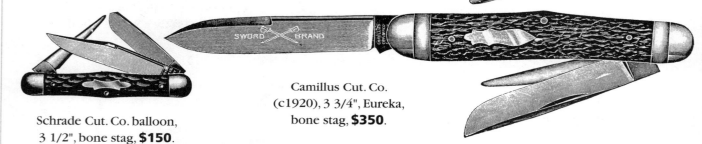

Schrade Cut. Co. balloon, 3 1/2", bone stag, **$150**.

Camillus Cut. Co. (c1920), 3 3/4", Eureka, bone stag, **$350**.

Remington, equal-end, three backsprings, patterned celluloid (gold pearl), **$600**.

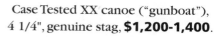

Case Tested XX canoe ("gunboat"), 4 1/4", genuine stag, **$1,200-1,400**.

Each blade on separate spring.

Each blade on separate spring.

Henry Sears & Son three-springs: surveyor, 3 7/16", patterned celluloid, **$450**; Eureka, 3 5/8", bone stag, **$400**. Note punch and spey secondary blades.

Premium Stock Knives

The PREMIUM STOCK KNIFE is a serpentine-shaped double-end pocketknife that ordinarily has two springs and three blades. Some stock knives have four blades, and a few have five or as many as six. Five- and six-bladed stock knives have three springs. Any stock knife under 3 1/2 inches long closed is called a "Junior Premium Stock Knife."

The premium stock pattern was introduced about 1890 as a less bulky and dressier version of the cattle knife. The stock knife was designed as a rancher's pattern, so it was at first marketed mainly in the West.

The master blade of a stock knife is always some type of clip point. The second blade is usually a spey for castrating young animals or for skinning. The remaining blade or blades can be a pen, sheepfoot or harness punch.

Stock knives are made in two basic shapes, square end and round end. Simmons Hardware Co. called round-ended stock knives the "Vaquero" pattern. Schrade Cutlery Co. called square-ended ones the "Texas" pattern. A heavily curved, round-ended premium stock knife is called a "hump-back" or a "sowbelly." Square-ended stock knives with a center "swell" on top are called "gunstock premium stocks."

On older stock knives, the most common handle material is jigged bone. Next is celluloid. Genuine stag is much less common, though a few firms, such as Case and Henckels, used it extensively. Stock knives with mother-of-pearl handles, called "stockman's Sunday dress knives," are rare and much sought after by collectors.

Wood handles occasionally were used on premium stock knives before 1940. Ivory and horn appear rarely on the pattern. Metal handles were used by a few firms but were not popular. Most modern stock knives have plastic handles, though Case continued to use bone on several of the patterns.

Up until the late 1940s, even the plainest stock knives were considered "premium" or high-priced knives. Around that time, however, cost-conscious manufacturers began to compare the stock knife to other three-bladed patterns. They recognized that the stockman requires much-less-skilled hand fitting than any whittler. In the past half century, as a consequence, the stock knife and junior stock knife have become the standard—and often the only—three-blade patterns made by many pocketknife firms.

Up until the 1920s, all sorts of jack and pen knives, especially serpentines, were sometimes called "premium stock knives." Since then, however, two-blade knives with stock-knife-like handles have been called premium jacks if they are single-ended (see the chapter, "Jack Knives"); Texas jacks if they are large and double-ended (see the "Double-End Jacks" segment of "Jack Knives"); or premium pen knives if they are small and double-ended (see the chapter, "Pen Knives").

Older and larger premium stock knives are of particular interest to brand collectors, especially the hump-back-shaped, mother-of-pearl-handled, and four-, five- and six-blade versions. Some collectors specialize in stock knives.

If you want to collect recent factory folding knives, rather than antiques, premium stock knives are a good choice. Many brands and variants have been made in recent years.

Base values for PREMIUM STOCK KNIVES with 3 1/2-4 inch handles, bone-stag (jigged-bone) handle covers, and three blades.

Excellent, unsharpened condition, with etch as appropriate.

VALUE RANGE

VH	H	M	LM	L
$1,000	$700	$300	$200	$150

Cattaraugus—3 7/8" Large clip, long spey, sheepfoot and punch blades. Brass lined. Nickel silver bolsters. Full polish. Stag handle. Shielded. **$450**.

No. K4429.
FOUR BLADES, 1 Large Clip, 1 Large Sheep Foot, 1 Large Spey Point and 1 Pen, Full Polished; German Silver Shield and Lining.

Keen Kutter Vaquero, 4-blade premium stockman, mother-of-pearl, **$375**.

No. 341 STOCK AND CASTRATING OR SPAYING KNIFE

Stock Knife, 3 Blades—$1.50
Weight, 3½ ounces

Cut shows exact size and style of knife. 60,000 sold in three years   Retails in far west at $2 00.

Has long bowie point blade, small blade, and the sheep foot "tobacco" or scribing blade—all are very thin and as carefully made and tempered as a $2 razor.   Don't hone them still thinner and expect them to cut wood.

This knife is our best seller and it ought to be, for it is the best knife for the money ever made.

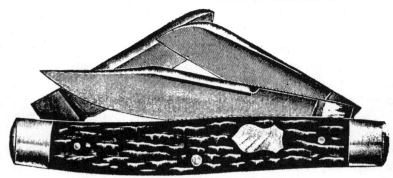

American Shear & Knife Co., bone stag, **$525**.

Remington, lock punch, genuine stag, **$1,150**. (Rare!)

533750
Solid nickle silver handle
Length closed 4 in.

Robeson, solid metal, **$150**.

No. X6374. Over-all size 3⅞". Bone stag handles. Also made with punch blade in place of sheep-foot, No. X6374P.

Western States, bone stag, **$500**.

Winchester Gunstock (stockman),
3 3/4", bone stag, **$375**.

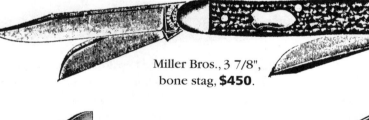

Miller Bros., 3 7/8",
bone stag, **$450**.

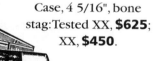

Case, 4 5/16", bone
stag: Tested XX, **$625**;
XX, **$450**.

H. Boker, long spey, bone stag, **$600**.

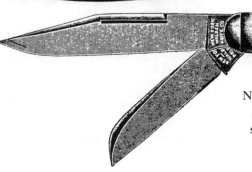

New York Knife Co.,
3-blade premium
stock knife, bone,
$400-450.

Keen Kutter, gunstock,
3 3/4", bone stag, **$350**.

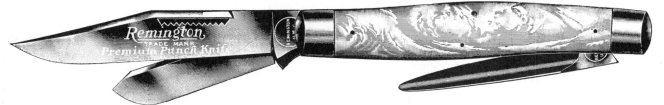

Cutlered by Master Cutlers—All Blades Full Crocus Polished, Punch Blade Blued and Crocus Polished, Back Springs Crocus Polished, Full Milled Nickel Silver Linings, Linings Full Burnished and Polished, Clip Blade Etched

Remington, milled liners, mother-of-pearl, **$1,200**. (Rare!)

3 Blade, Crocus Polish, Etched, Full German Silver Mounted, Ranch Knife, Pearl Handle.

Ulster Knife Co., mother-of-pearl, **$450**.

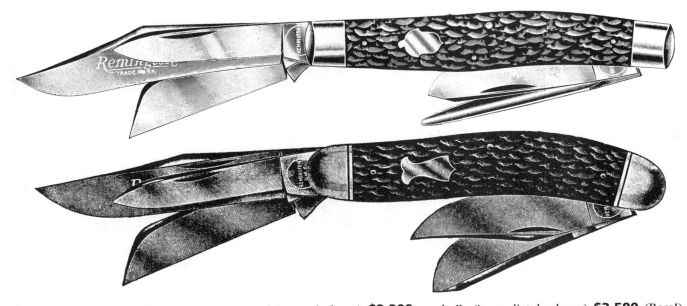

Remingtons, 5 blades, bone stag: square end (second, above): **$2,200**; sowbelly (immediately above): **$2,500**. (Rare!)

PREMIUM STOCK

Schrade Cut Co., #M9806, 4 blades, 4", mother-of-pearl, **$525**.

Case Tested XX, 5 blades, 3 7/8", bone stag, **$2,200-2,400**.

HANDLE—Bone stag.
BLADES—Four: saber clip, pen, spey and sheepfoot.
BOLSTER—Nickel silver.
LINING—Brass.

John Primble, 4", 4 blades, bone, **$325**.

Case Tested XX, 4 blades, bone stag, **$850-900**.

Junior Premium Stock Knives

JUNIOR *premium stock knives* are small versions of premium stock knives. They are not really big enough for frequent work on animals, but how many current owners of junior or full-size stock knives continue to use them on livestock?

The first junior stock knives, in the 1910s, were 3 3/8 inches long. Most are still around that size. However, many have been made in smaller sizes more recently, some as little as 2 1/2 inches.

The traditional, small three-bladed knife is the whittler, but a junior stock knife of the same size and comparable quality takes so much less labor to make that it can be sold for two-thirds—or even half—the price. As a result, junior stock knives largely have replaced whittlers in modern pocketknife lines.

There is less variation in junior stockmen than in full-size stock knives. One odd junior stock variant is the Remington R100 series of "Dollar Knives." They have one-piece, closed-back frames with integral bolsters.

Junior stock knives are not as popular as full-size stock knives among pattern collectors, probably because of their small size. Older ones are of considerable interest to brand collectors.

Base values for JUNIOR PREMIUM STOCK KNIVES with 3-3 1/2-inch handles, full bolsters, bone-stag or horn handle covers, and three cutting blades. Excellent, unsharpened condition, with etch where appropriate.

VALUE RANGE

VH	H	M	LM	L
$400	$325	$250	$175	$125

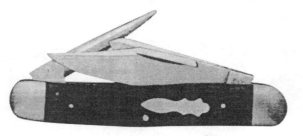

No. 32189-G—3 7/16" Clip, spey and punch blades. Brass lined. Nickel silver bolsters. Crocus finish. Stag handle. Shielded. Cattaraugus: **$325**.

No. 32249—3" Small stock pattern. Large clip, small sheepfoot and spey blades. Brass lined. Nickel silver bolsters. Crocus finish. Stag handle. Shielded. Cattaraugus: **$225**.

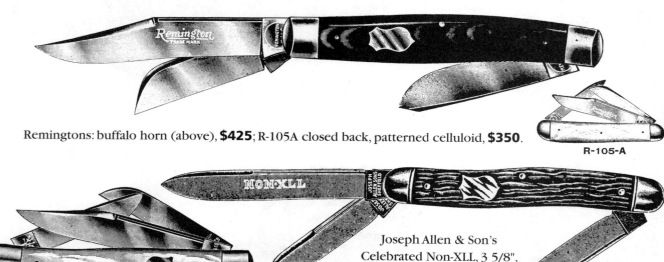

Remingtons: buffalo horn (above), **$425**; R-105A closed back, patterned celluloid, **$350**.

R-105-A

H. Boker, mother-of-pearl, **$400**.

Joseph Allen & Son's Celebrated Non-XLL, 3 5/8", 3-blade junior premium stock, bone, **$295**.

Ulster Knife Co., punch, bone stag, **$300**.

LIGHT "OUTING KNIFE" WITH BELT-PUNCH BLADE.

Plier and Wrench Knives

American Plier Knives

By Blade Magazine Cutlery Hall-Of-Famer© Houston Price, Publisher, *Knife World*

PLIER KNIVES are multi-blades about the size and shape of an equal-end cattle knife (3 1/2-4 1/4 inches long). They incorporate a small but functional pliers either as a separate blade or as a part of the handle.

Lewis Patent

The American plier knife most often found is the "HHH" made by the Oscar Barnett Tool Co. of Newark, New Jersey. The knives are based on U.S. Patent No. 662,005 issued to James C. Lewis of Tracy, California, on Nov. 20, 1900. Most have "Trade HHH Mark" etched on the blade or stamped on the plier handle.

Barnett went out of business in about 1915. In the 15 years that HHH knives were produced, many hardware wholesale houses distributed them, as did such national retail mail-order firms as Sears Roebuck and the Thomas Manufacturing Co. of Ohio. Consequently, the knives can be found all over the country, though rarely in good condition.

HHH knives have brown, jigged-bone handles. They have a spear master blade and a punch. One end of the center liner projects for use as a screwdriver. The pliers incorporates a wire cutter and the end of its handle doubles as a hoof pick.

HHH knives were made with a variety of markings. Some have an O. BARNETT TOOL CO. tang stamping, while others have J.C. LEWIS PAT. NOV. 20, 1900. Some have two patent numbers stamped on the side of the plier handle (in addition to the aforementioned one, the other is 606,547 from June 28, 1898).

The original retail price for the HHH knife ranged from 92 cents in the Sears "big book" up to $2.75 in the 1910 Thomas catalog. Current value is about **$150** for a knife in used condition with no blades broken, and about **$400-475** for an excellent, unsharpened example.

Undy Patent

Less common than the HHH is the Valley Forge plier knife patented by Charles Undy of Newark, New Jersey, on Sept. 11, 1923. A 1925 Von Lengerke & Antoine retail catalog offered it as a "'Radio Knife."

The Valley Forge plier knife has brown, jigged-bone handles, a spear master blade, and a screwdriver/wire-stripper blade. The spring-loaded pliers folds into the handle.

Most of the knives are tang stamped VALLEY FORGE CUTLERY CO., NEWARK N.J. U.S.A. Some are stamped H. BOKER & CO'S IMPROVED CUTLERY, U.S.A. Boker had owned Valley Forge since 1899. Boker/Valley Forge also made the knife on contract for Case, and examples exist

H.H.H. ad from 1910 Thomas Mfg. Co. catalog.

with three different Case stampings. All the knives have PAT APPL'D FOR stamped into one handle.

When new, the knife sold at retail for about $2.00. Current values range from **$275-500**, though unusual CASE stampings may go to **$1,000**.

Morley

The imported Morley plier knife was made for and sold by an American firm. Marked W.H. MORLEY & SONS/GERMANY, it was imported by Adolph Kastor & Bros. of New York, owners since 1902 of Camillus Cutlery Co.

The Morley knife has brown, jigged-bone handles. The blades are a spear and a pen. The plier handle has a screwdriver tip and is held shut by the bail.

The knife probably dates from the mid-1920s. Its value is **$275-325** in excellent condition.

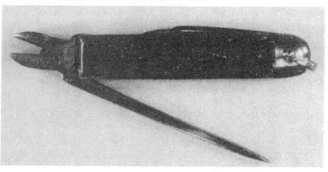

Morley plier knife.

Heilrath Patent

One of the rarest of plier knives also has the simplest mechanism. It was patented May 23, 1905 (No. 790,432) by Christian Heilrath of Sacramento, California. He transferred his patent to G.M. Parkinson, who manufactured the knives under the name PLI-R-NIF.

The PLI-R-NIF measures 4 1/4 inches closed. Its appearance is that of two single-blade knives, each with a spring whose end is shaped into one jaw of the pliers. The two parts are joined by the pivot of the pliers. Friction between the two nickel-silver inner liners keeps the pliers shut when not in use.

The few known PLI-R-NIFs have a spear master blade. The second blade is either a screwdriver or a punch. The

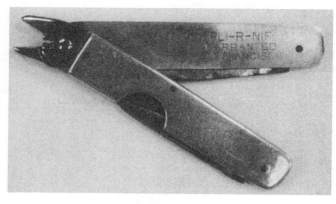

Heilrath PLI-R-NIF.

In 1982, Tim Leatherman of Leatherman Tool Group in Portland, Oregon, sparked a renaissance of plier knives that continues to expand.
Above: Leatherman Mini-Tool (current) about **$50**; original model, about **$65**; and Super model, about **$75**. Others include: Gerber Multi-Plier, about **$60**; SOG Power Plier, about **$60**; BuckTool, about **$65**; A.G. Russell Pocket Tool Box, **$50**; and Victorinox Mechanic, **$45**.

punch's handle has an easy-open notch. Handle scales are aluminum and some have stamped advertising.

The usual marking is PLI-R-NIF/WARRANTED/SAN FRANCISCO in large letters on one liner. PAT'D MAY 23, '05 may be stamped on the master blade tang or on one of the handles.

The offices of Parkinson's PLI-R-NIF Co. were in San Francisco until the 1906 earthquake and fire. Afterward, they were across the bay in Berkeley at 2700 Dana St. Distribution was limited, probably just to the West Coast. Current value is **$350-450**.

There are U.S. patent drawings of other plier knives, such as a bicyclist's version by John Watts of Sheffield from 1897, and a changeable-blade model by Frederik Nielsen of California from 1925. Value **$225-275**.

Wrench Knives

Toward the close of World War I, Cattaraugus introduced a multi-blade with a built-in wrench. It has brown, jigged-bone handles. Its mechanism was patented March 5, 1918 (No. 1,258,396) by Tint Champlin, son of the firm's founder, J.B.F. Champlin.

The wrench is a sliding alligator or bulldog type. The master blade is a screwdriver/wire-stripper; the other blade is a punch. Most are marked PATENT APPLIED FOR. Value: **$475-700**.

The first Cattaraugus wrench knife, it was made for a short time only. In about 1920, the firm replaced it with two knives that have a standard crescent wrench at one end. The 1-W has a spear blade and punch. The 3-W has a spear blade and a screwdriver/cap-lifter, of which two variations are known. They are worth about **$575** each in excellent condition.

Also in the 1920s, Aerial Cutlery Co. offered a picture-handled knife—the D399 "Alligator Special"—with an alligator wrench built into one end. It has mother-of-pearl

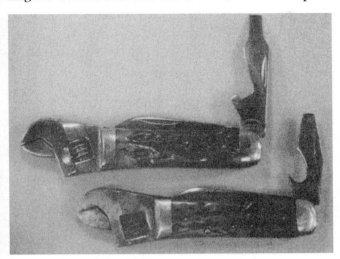

1920s (top) and 1930s Cattaraugus 3-Ws.

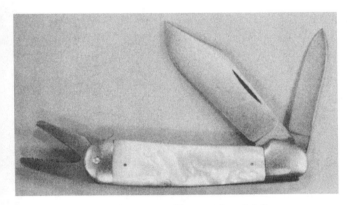

Aerial D399 "Alligator Special."

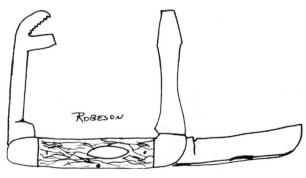

Robeson radio electrician's knife.

handles, which are probably not original. A picture-handled example is worth about **$175** in excellent condition.

In the same time period, Robeson offered a radio electrician's knife with a hawkbill master blade, a large screwdriver, and a small, folding alligator wrench. The knife is worth about **$400**.

An all-steel C.P. Wrench Co. knife circa 1908 from Bristol, Tennessee, is worth about **$350**. It is a rare and unusual piece.

Imports

More recently, both plier and wrench knives have been made in France, Germany, Italy and Japan for export to the United States. The French knives are of the highest quality and are worth **$75-100**. Depending on quality, German and Italian ones are worth **$35-75**. Japanese ones are worth about the same.

Dynamite Knives

Closely related to plier and wrench knives is the large variety of crimping knives made especially for miners, road builders and others who work with explosives. One rare type is Charles Griffin's "Griffin's Waterproofer" of 1892, manufactured for Griffin by Edward B. Sears of Chicago. It is a 4 1/2-inch barehead regular jack. Its single, modified spear blade, combined with a hole in the bolsters, allow it to be used for crimping blasting caps. A special cap tool is seated inside the back wooden handle scale.

The dynamite knife in the accompanying photograph, made in Germany for the Koehler Mfg. Co. of Marlborough, Massachusetts, is more typical. Values of older examples in excellent condition range from **$300-550**.

Koehler Mfg. Co. dynamite knife.

Special-Purpose Multi-Blades

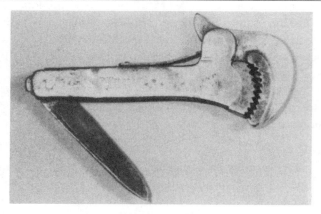

C.P. Wrench Knife, Bristol, Tennessee,
all steel, circa 1908. **$350** (in unused condition).
(courtesy Howard Melnick)

Wrench/screwdriver knife made by Tiger (Lauterjung
& Co.), Solingen, for Barnette, Newark, New Jersey.
May have been used to install door latches. **$225**.
(courtesy Howard Melnick)

Monkey wrench knife made in Italy circa 1950s,
stainless steel. **$125**. (courtesy Howard Melnick)

Robeson automobilist's jack knife with spear blade,
punch blade, and combination screwdriver, wire stripper,
cap lifter, Prest-O-Lite key; advertising Moore Oil Co.
$375. (courtesy Howard Melnick)

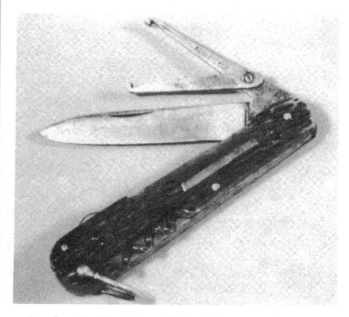

Stag-handled English multi-blade by H.G. Long & Co.
with a patented, adjustable shot-shell extractor. **$400**.
(courtesy Howard Melnick)

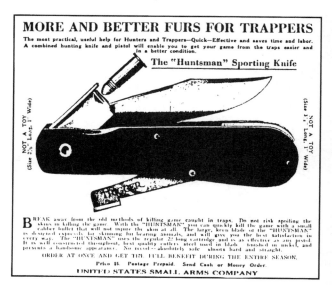

United States Small Arms Co. .22 caliber knife pistol.
(courtesy Jim Booker).
Note: This knife is illegal. **$800-950**.

Special-Purpose Multi-Blades *(continued)*

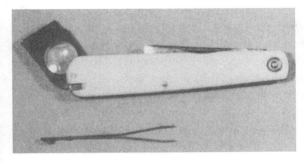

Ivory-handled budding-style knife with magnifier and tweezers, possibly used by stamp collectors. **$375**. (courtesy Howard Melnick)

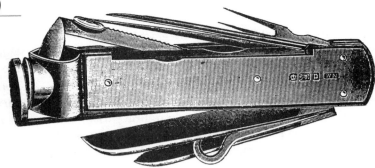

Cigar-cutter knife with silver handles hallmarked 1907, sold by William Needham of Sheffield. **$375-400**. (courtesy Blade Magazine Cutlery Hall-Of-Famer© William Adams

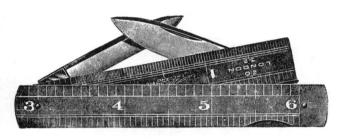

All-steel Sheffield pen knife with James Chesterman folding rule, 20th century. **$175**. Some of these are still made. (courtesy Howard Melnick)

William Langbein, New York, swell-center balloon whittler with typographer's punch blade, master-blade etch advertising R. Hoe & Co. printing presses. **$375**. (courtesy Howard Melnick)

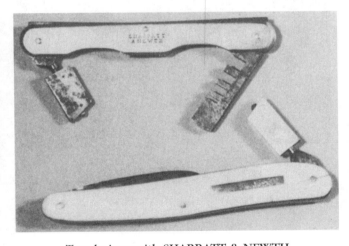

Two knives with SHARRATT & NEWTH diamond-glass-cutter blades. Top: all steel by Sharrat & Newth, **$275**. Bottom: ivory handles by J. Nowill, **$525**. (courtesy Howard Melnick)

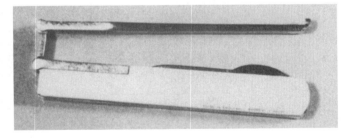

Ivory-handled nutcracker knife sold by Asprey, London; has a champagne-cutter blade and a silver fruit blade hallmarked in the 1920s. **$700-850**. (courtesy Howard Melnick)

Above: Ruler comb-i-nation (note the comb in the "handle") knife made in Sheffield, England, from *Smith's Key*, 1816. **$650-700**. (courtesy EAIA) Left: Folding rule with pen-knife blade made in Sheffield, from *Smith's Key*, 1816. **$500**. (courtesy EAIA)

Tool Kit Knives

Since the 18th century, if not earlier, specialty cutlers have contrived to include more and more tools in handy-sized multi-blade knives. Of course, the more tools that are included, the more delicate each one has to be. This is why so many older, complex multi-blades have broken blades or tools; they did not stand up to heavy use.

As an alternate way to get a lot of tools into a small knife handle, some cutlers made tool kit knives. A *tool kit knife* is a standard-sized jack-knife handle that resides in a fold-up kit with an assortment of sturdy blades and tools—or at least they are sturdier than the tools in one-piece multi-blades.

The tools with a tool kit knife include, at a minimum, a knife blade, file, saw and screwdriver. Often there are several types and sizes of each of the foregoing, and also a gimlet, punch, chisel, ruler, can and bottle openers, cook pullers, and a small hammer.

The tool kit handle has an opening in one end for attaching the tools. Sometimes there is a second opening in one side of the handle for attaching the gimlet or cork puller. The highest-quality tool kit handles have a separate detached spear blade. The kits with a permanent fixed blade in the handle are usually of lesser quality.

In the best tool kits, each tool pushes straight into the handle opening and locks rigidly in place, thus preventing the tools from shutting on your fingers. Modern knife-axe hunting-knife sets and 18th-century changeable-blade carving knives use the same mechanism.

Less costly kits do not have the mechanism. They have a fixed pivot pin in the open end of the handle, while each tool has a hooked tang. The tang is hooked on to the pin, and the tool is pivoted into place. Tools in this type of knife usually do not lock. (See "Pruning Knives" for another type of changeable-blade mechanism.)

Base values for TOOL KIT KNIVES with original leather or plastic cases, bone-stag or picture handles, all original tools, and in excellent condition.

VALUE RANGE

VH	H	M	LM	L
$800	$600	$400	$275	$150

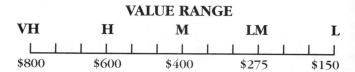

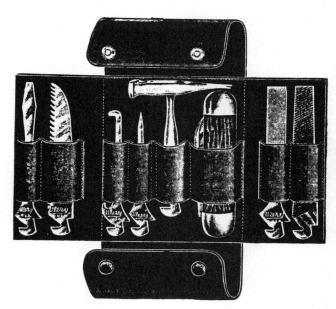

Ulery, wood handles, **$225**.

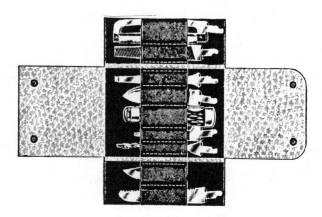

Napanoch, bone-stag handles, **$675-725**.

Handles may be purchased separately
Price 75c each

No 1300

Any tool or blade may be purchased separately
Price 25c each

New York Knife, large set with 2 bone-stag handles, **$800**. (courtesy Alan Weinstein)

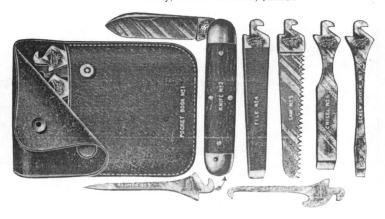

Ulery, 7-piece kit, **$275**.

Showpiece and Exposition Knives

Showpiece and exposition knives are one-of-a-kind or, rarely, limited-production knives. They were made to serve as the centerpiece of a store or exposition display case. Most are either very large, very ornate or both.

Every showpiece knife should be evaluated on its individual merits. Big, elaborate ones with 20 or more blades can be worth from **$5,000** to over **$150,000**; giant jack knives and pen knives are worth from **$1,000** to **$6,000**.

Showpiece jack knives (not shown): New York Knife Co. "Giant Exhibition Knife," 11", double-end jack, wood, two blades, two bails, c1929, **$2,800**. Case display knife, 11 1/2", swell-center jack, black plastic, **$1,100**.

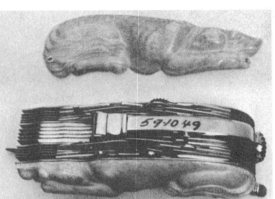

Bohemian showpiece knife c1900, 5 1/2", carved ivory handles. Value, **$5,500**. (Wiebusch Collection, Smithsonian Institution)

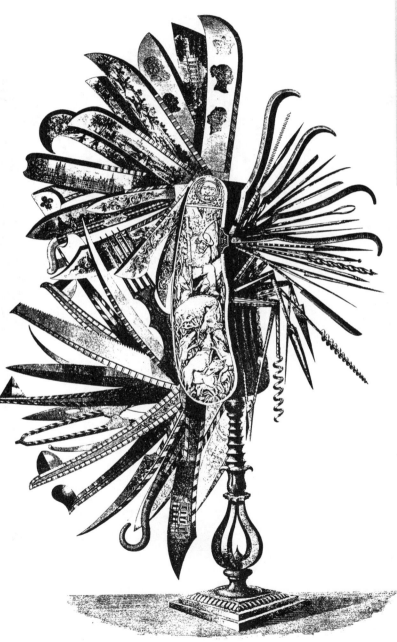

The Joseph Rodgers Norfolk Sportsman's Knife, mid-19th century. Handle length: 14 1/2". Total height open on stand: 38". Approximate value, **$350,000**.

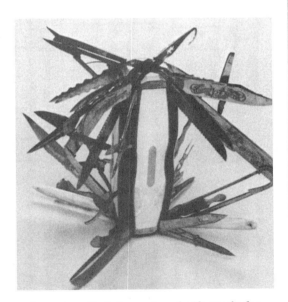

Ivory-handled showpiece knife made for Martin L. Bradford of Boston c1850. Courtesy the National Knife Museum collection. Approximate value, **$35,000**. (Phil Pankiewicz photo)

Folding Medical Instruments

In the 19th century, folding pocket instruments were made for surgeon's emergency use. They are distinguished by small size, unlined, flat handles—usually tortoiseshell or horn—open backs, and extremely fine finish. Many are double-ended, almost all have blade stops at 180 degrees, and many lock open. A very few have spring backs with locks.

The accompanying illustrations are from a c1874 catalog of Tiemann & Co., New York (courtesy of George Sarris). Values indicated are for examples in excellent condition with any legible maker's mark.

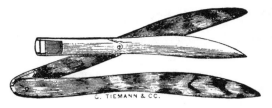

Seton Needle. Used for the procedure called *setaceum*—introducing a silk string under the skin to induce the formation of pus. Value, **$150**. Larger versions included in pocketknives were used to inoculate cattle against blackleg disease and have values ranging from **$150-300**.

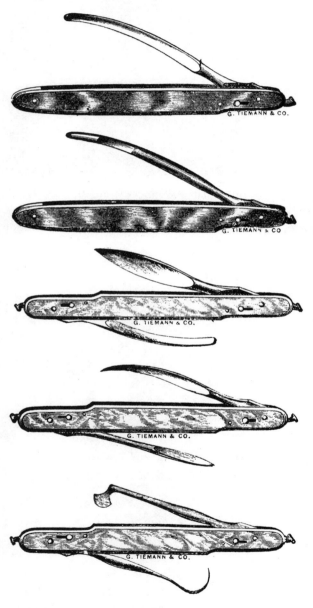

Thumb Lancet. Used for phlebotomy or bloodletting. Bleeding was a popular "cure-all" up until about 1870. This style of folding thumb lancet was introduced in the 17th century and was in common use throughout America during much of the country's early history. Value, **$90-150**.

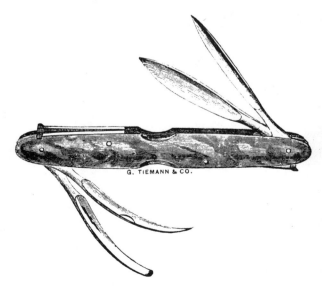

Slide Catch Pocket Instruments. 1 blade, **$125**; 2 blades, **$165-200**. Examples shown, top to bottom: curved probe-pointed bistoury; Cooper's hernia knife; scalpel and probe-pointed bistoury; sharp-pointed bistoury and tenotome; and gum lancet and tenaculum (hook).

Spring Catch Pocket Instruments. 2 blades (not shown), **$150**; 4 blades, **$350**; and 6 blades, **$475**.

Foreign, Exotic, Primitive and Historical Folding Knives

In this section are the basic types of folding knives used in Europe and Asia in the past several hundred years. Until the 20th century, folding knives were far more common in Europe than in Asia, while they were virtually unknown in Africa and Oceania (the islands of the central and South Pacific Ocean). Older Asian folders differ in detail from European ones, but they are similar to them in basic design. Therefore, the knives examined in this part of the *BLADE Guide* are divided primarily by type, not by geographic region.

From the earliest colonial days into the 19th century, North American settlers used many of the older types of European folding knives. However, none of the types, so far as we can determine, was regularly offered for sale in the USA after about 1860.

Of course, in the past few years, cutlery traditions throughout the world have changed drastically. Modern versions of some foreign-style knives, such as the Opinel penny knife, have carved a small niche for themselves in the American market.

Though the older foreign styles lost favor in 19th-century America, most of the standard American patterns that replaced them trace their ancestry to the older types, particularly to the penny knife, the quill knife, and the *Navaja*, or Spanish clasp knife. Information on this evolution is included in the various pocketknife-pattern chapters of the *BLADE Guide*.

Some of the old patterns are still made and sold in the Old World. However, just as in America, most foreign countries and cutlery-producing districts have developed their own modern patterns. Since the modern "exotic" patterns occasionally turn up on the collector market in the United States, a sampling of them is included herein as well.

Penny Knives

"Penny knife" is a modern adaptation of an old term for the simplest sort of jack knife. A penny knife consists of a more-or-less cylindrical, one-piece handle, a blade and a pivot pin. Often, the hinged end of the handle is reinforced by a sheet-metal ferrule that functions like the bolsters on a spring-back knife. Most penny knives are very plain, but some exhibit fancy turning or ornate figural carving.

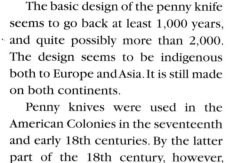

Roman folding knife with metal handle. (courtesy Pagé)

The basic design of the penny knife seems to go back at least 1,000 years, and quite possibly more than 2,000. The design seems to be indigenous both to Europe and Asia. It is still made on both continents.

Penny knives were used in the American Colonies in the seventeenth and early 18th centuries. By the latter part of the 18th century, however, American demand for folders was almost entirely for spring-back knives.

Many of the older penny knives that turn up in the United States today were brought there by tourists or immigrants in the 20th century, or else late in the 19th century. Even the oldest ones found in the USA only rarely can be proven to have been used in America in Colonial times. This is because antique dealers were importing the knives for collectors even a century and more ago, much as they do now. Dated archaeological sites and period paintings are the only sure sources of information on "authentic" Colonial knives.

Other Spring-less Folding Knives

Not all knives made without springs are "penny knives." Many early pruners and clasp knives have no springs. More important, most 19th-century-and-earlier folding medical instruments have no backsprings, either.

The distinguishing marks of old folding medical instruments are: small size, flat profile, two-piece handles—usually tortoise shell—with the back completely open, bird's-eye rivets instead of bolsters, and extremely fine finish. As with knives, but unlike straight razors, most have some sort of blade stop at 180 degrees. 19th-century folding medical instruments are sometimes double-ended and often have a locking mechanism. (See the "Folding Medical Instruments" segment of the chapter, "Multi-Blade Knives.")

English medical bistoury, circa 1815. Value, **$50**.

Italy. Boot (*Stivale*) Figural Penny Knife.

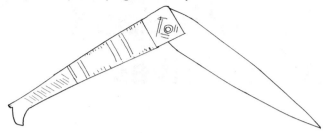

About 2-6 inches long closed. Horn handle. Brass or steel ferrule. Leaf-shaped blade. 18th-20th centuries, possibly older. Example shown 4 1/2 inches, 19th century. Value, **$35**. Larger or finer examples higher. Courtesy Bill Karsten.

France. 1771 Factory Penny Knives.

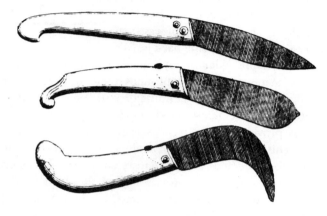

Three-to-6 inches long closed. One-piece handle of horn or wood. Thumb tab on tang. Mass-produced in St. Etienne using waterpower. From Fougeroux de Bondaroy, *L'Art du Coutelier en Ouvrages Communs*, 1771. Value, **$75**.

Similar knives handmade elsewhere in Europe. Blades stamped with picture, letter or word trademarks until c1815. Paris marks (all records lost) usually small, with logo and initial letter. See Sheffield, London and Salisbury lists for English marks. Marks on back of blade often Spanish. Italy and Austria still used pictorial marks after 1900.

France. Modern Penny Knife.

This style made from 1 3/4 to 11 inches closed. Wooden handle. Iron ferrule. On larger sizes, ferrule rotates to lock the blade. Made by Opinel of Cognin, Savoie, since about 1890. Value, **$8-18** in standard sizes, **$90** for 11-inch giant. Courtesy Gutmann Cutlery Co.

China. Large Penny Knife.

Four-to-5 inches long closed. Forged blade, wood handle, iron ferrule. Value, **$20-40**. Drawing from Pagé, c1900.

Italy (Scarperia). Figural Penny Knives.

About 3 1/2 inches long closed. Carved boxwood handles representing mythic(?) figures. Glass bead eyes. Steel ferrules. Pictorial maker's marks. In Italy this pattern is called *Temperino di Scarperia* (pen knife of Scarperia). Circa 1900? Value, **$50-100**; with plain wood handle, **$10**.

Italy (Scarperia?). Figural Penny Knife.

About 3 1/2 inches long closed. One-piece bone handle carved as bust of woman. Example above has bird's-eye rivet, gilt design on blade; typical *temperino* has ferrule, plain blade. 18th to 19th centuries. Value about **$150**. Courtesy Smithsonian Institution, Wiebusch Collection.

Japan. Higonokami Penny Knife.

About 3 1/2 inches long closed. Handle of wood or steel (steel handle with name and maker's marks). Blade of thin steel plate laminated to iron, ground on one side

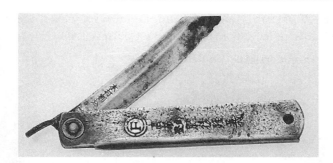

only. Blade stop on tang. 18th to 20th centuries. Value, **$10-20**.

China. Razor and Small Penny Knife.

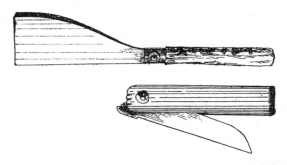

About 3 1/2 inches long closed. One-piece handle of wood or horn. Wedge blade (razor, above, top) or thin blade (knife). Bird's-eye rivet. Some have sheet-metal ferrule. 19th to 20th centuries. Value, **$5-20**. Drawings from Page, c1900.

France and England. Straight Jack Knives.

Three-and-a-half to about 8 inches long closed. Distinctive features may include: prominent rosette-type

(Above) France, 18th-century Deluxe Jack Knife. Drawing from Pagé. Value about **$450**.

(Right) 18th-century French Folding Couteaux (Knives) from Perret, *The Art of the Cutler*, 1771.

A. (Fig. 29), "*Couteau a la Charoloise*" or "*Couteau a crosse*" (la crosse=gunstock), so-called because of the roundness at the end of the handle. Value about **$130** for a plain example.

B. (Fig. 30), "*Couteau a poincon*" (punch knife), a double-ended spring knife with stag handles. Note that the French punch blade has an eye so that it can be used for stitching harness and as a seton for inoculating cattle. Value about **$125**. (A more recent clasp version is called a *Laguiole*.)

C. (Fig. 31), Gunstock knife with a cork-pulling hook, rosewood handles cut obliquely to reveal the grain. Value about **$250**, because of the cork-puller.

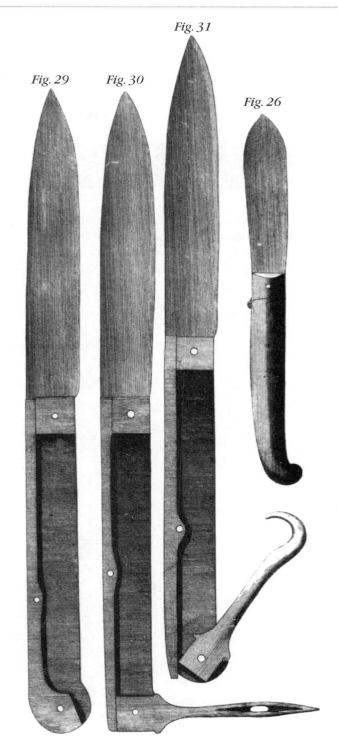

D. (Fig. 26), "*Couteau Eustache Dubois*", the most common pattern at the time, consists of a blade with stop, a wooden handle, and a single pin. Value about **$75**.

This penny knife pattern was mass-produced in factories. The others, with springs, were handmade.

Note the square tangs that exactly fill the joints in all three positions. These "square-and-clean joints" were common practice on 18th-century French and English spring-back knives.

rivets on French knives; fancy-worked bolsters integral with liners on English knives; tang shaped to fill the "square and clean" joint; thin, flat handles; wood and horn, when used, sawed "on the bias" to display their grain; tiny nail mark; superb workmanship. 17th to early 19th centuries.

England. Straight Jack Knife.

Six inches long closed. Cut steel gadroon bolsters integral with liners, horn handles, square and clean joint. Tang stamped WATKINSON (Jonathan Watkinson, Silver Street, Sheffield, was the Master of the Sheffield cutler's guild in 1787). Value, **$500**.

Straight Jack Knives

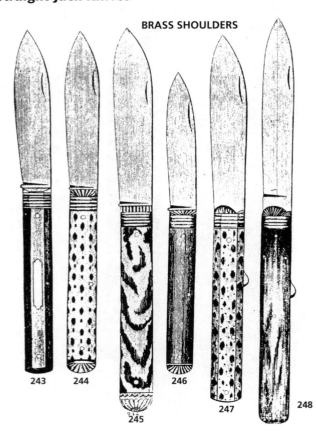

BRASS SHOULDERS

243   244   245   246   247   248

Illustrations from an 1816 Sheffield catalog of cutlery and tools available for export to the United States (*Smith's Key*; see "19th Century Sheffield Cutlery Firms"). Handles of carved ivory, bone, horn, wood and tortoise shell (see knife above labeled "245"). The ones labeled 244 and 247 are "spotted knives," with clear horn handles spotted to resemble tortoise. "Brass shoulders" may mean "white" brass or nickel silver, invented in 1810. Those labeled 247 and 248 are lockbacks. Similar knives also offered with corkscrew on back. Values range from **$150** (plain) to

$1,000 (fancy). See "Late 18th Century Sheffield Cutlers' Marks" to identify makers' marks. Courtesy EAIA.

France. Corsican "Vendetta" Knife.

A folding version of the Mediterranean dagger. Five to 10 inches long closed. Iron mounts, including long, self-guard bolsters. Bone handles often etched with traditional decorations. Semi-lock blade (has no lock release), usually with Thiers maker's mark, often etched in Italian, "Corsican Vendetta," on the front and either "Death to Enemies" or "May My Wound be Fatal" on the back. 19th to 20th centuries.

Example shown above is 8 inches long closed, marked VERITABLE FARGE (Thiers). 20th century. Value, **$150**. Courtesy Bill Spivey.

Austria or Germany. Dice Knife.

Four inches long closed. Spear and manicure blades. Removable plated dice cup containing bone dice, bone handles etched in German "Lots of Luck." Circa 1900. Some were exported to the USA. Value, **$350**. Courtesy Smithsonian Institution, Wiebusch Collection.

Japan and Germany. Japanese Airplane Knives.

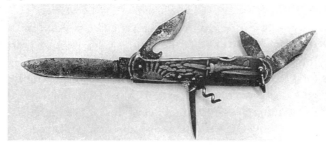

Various styles of jack knives and multi-blades with stamped metal handles showing Japanese World War II aircraft and marked SHARPE, NON TO COMPARE. c1940. Value, **$75**. Courtesy Garvis Keasler and *Knife World*.

Contemporary French Cutlery

By Damien Lemaire

The centers of cutlery manufacture in France today are Thiers, Nogent, Cognin, Laguiole, Langres, Nontron and Biesles. Paris and Chatellerault used to be important centers but are no longer.

Biesles is the home of master cutler Jacques MONGIN, who was designated a *Meilleur Ouvrier de France* for his superb craftsmanship. Some of his fine knives are sold in the United States.

Nontron, according to an article in the *Gazette des Couteaux*, a knife magazine published in Paris, is the oldest center of cutlery craftsmanship in France that still produces the traditional styles. Indeed, Nontron may well be the birthplace of the French folding knife. Records from the 15th century show that cutlers from all over France, even Paris, worked for a time in Nontron to improve their skills.

Traditional Nontron knives have special, reinforced ferrules and boxwood handles. Since about 1900, the boxwood has been decorated with burned-in designs. A local specialty is miniature knives. Prominent names in Nontron's past were BERNARD and PETIT. The best-known traditional cutler there now is Mr. CHAPERON.

OPINEL pocketknives from the town of Cognin in Savoie can be found in every general merchandise store in France. Prices range from **$8** for the smallest size to **$90** for the giant (11 inches closed) No.13. Most popular are the No. 8 and No. 9. Ordinarily, they have carbon steel blades and plain beech-wood handles, but the No. 8 is available with stainless steel and *pallisandre* (rosewood) for **$14**. Opinels are carried by hunters, fishermen, students and scouts all over France. In the South (Languedoc, Roussillon), winegrowers use Opinels as "table cutlery."

The 1992 Winter Olympics were held in Savoie, and Opinel issued a knife to commemorate the occasion. It has white handles imprinted with the Olympic symbol.

Courty et Fils in Paris offer CUSTOM OPINELS. They are No. 8s and No. 9s that have either straight or Yatagan-style handles made of ivory, buffalo horn or "blonde" cow horn. Cost ranges from **$40** to **$170**.

The LAGUIOLE is a style of pocketknife that originated in the town of Laguiole. Laguioles are not as popular as Opinels, in part because they cost more (**$15** to **$120**). They are handled in horn, ivory or rosewood, and can have a punch blade and a corkscrew. Their blades are always carbon steel. Unlike Opinels, Laguioles have a backspring. Traditionally, the free end of the spring is decorated with an engraved bee.

Laguioles are carried by many knife users, and also by farmers in the South. In France, a Laguiole is regarded as a good present for a friend. Laguioles are often used as props in TV and magazine ads for traditional French products such as cheese and wine.

The master maker of Laguiole knives is Pierre CALMELS of Laguiole, the great grandson of the inventor of the Laguiole style. However, if you want a Calmels knife, you have to go to Laguiole and buy it directly from him. Other brands of Laguioles include G. DAVID's *"a L'arbalete"* (Crossbow brand), La Lucrece, Rossignol, and "MC" (the *Maison des Couteliers* in Thiers). G. David even makes an automatic, or switchblade, Laguiole.

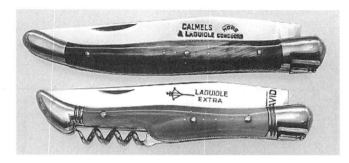

The *VENDETTA CORSE* or Corsican "vendetta" knife is sold primarily in Corsica. Some of the knives, such as the "Veritable Farge," are made in Thiers, decorated in Corsica and sold mainly to tourists. Others are made in Corsica and are sold largely to Corsicans. The best-known maker there is Mr. ANTONNINI in Bastia. Another maker is Mr. CECCALDI. His knives are shaped like Laguioles and are handled with local Corsican woods. Some Ceccaldi knives are sold by a retailer in Lyon.

Handmade sheath knives in France came mainly from the ARDENNLAME shop. The shop closed in 1986. Similar knives are now made at the *Maison des Couteliers* in Thiers, a museum established in 1982.

Automatic knives can be found in every gun shop in France. Inferior-quality ones are imported from Italy, while better ones come from Solingen, Germany. Prices range from **$10** to **$45**. Automatics are illegal to carry in France.

In fact, in France it is illegal to carry any knife, even a Laguiole, an Opinel or a pen knife. Enforcement usually depends on the knife, the person carrying it, the situation, the time of day, and the attitude of the policeman.

VICTORINOX, ELINOX, and WENGER Swiss Army knives are very popular in France. Many students carry either a Victorinox or a copy. The copies come from France (made in Nogent, Biesles and Langres); Spain (made by Aitor and ICA); and Germany (made by Wingen and Puma). Prices range from **$10** up to **$70** for the "survival Victorinox," which comes with a survival kit in a belt sheath.

AMERICAN knives, mainly sheath knives and big lockback folders such as those by Buck, Gerber and others, are popular in France, but very expensive. Buck sheath knives cost between **$70** and **$200**. Buck 110 and 112 folding hunters cost from **$100** to **$200**. The Buck Statue of Liberty commemorative sold for **$500**. In France, a Randall knife is considered a bargain at **$400**.

A Selection of French Pocketknife Styles, after the catalog of the *Etablissements Therais.*

1. Gouttiere (gutter)
2. Langres
3. Tonneau (barrel)
4. Tiredroit (straight pull)
5. Fenerol
6. London (English style)
7. Donjon (castle keep)
8. D'electricien (electrician's)
9. Yssingeaux
10. & 11. Pradels (the blade shape is called *Pradel*)
12. Queue de Poisson (fishtail)

13. Aurillac(ois)
14. De mineur (miner's)
15. De berger (shepherd's)
16. Allemand (German style)
17. Belge (Belgian style)
18. Pradel Yatagan
19. Alpin (Alpine)
20. Aveyronnais
21. Prussien (Prussian style)
22. Pietain

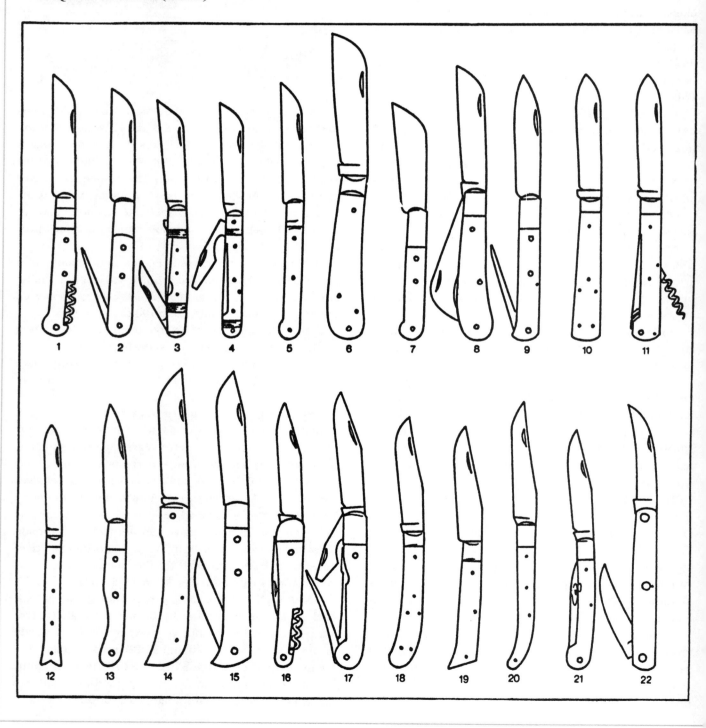

Italian Pocket Cutlery

Italy has an ancient pocket-cutlery tradition, perhaps the most ancient in the world. The oldest surviving folding knives date from the latter period of the Roman Empire.

The tradition of fine pocketknife making is still alive in Italy, and much of it is indeed very traditional. Many of the patterns made there today date back at least to the Middle Ages; some may be older.

Around 1900, Camille Page listed the principal cities in Italy that ever had a cutlery industry. Those marked (*) in his list were still producing cutlery in 1900. Today, the leading center of Italian cutlery made for export is Maniago, in the foothills of the Alps north of Venice. Knives for domestic consumption in Italy are still made in Scarperia, Canzo, Caslino and Frosolone. Two of America's leading pocketknife firms, Imperial and Colonial, were both founded by cutlers who had emigrated from Frosolone. As of 2004, such American cutlery companies as Lone Wolf Knives, Xikar and others were having some of their knives made in Italy.

Italian Pocketknife Patterns

The accompanying sketches and descriptions are from an illustrated chart provided by Aldo and Edda Lorenzi, the leading retail cutlers in Milan. They also provided copies of *Coltelli d'Italia* by Giancarlo Baronti (1986) and *I Coltelli di Scarperia* by Luciano Salvatici (1992).

Note that the fishtail pattern—often mistakenly called the "stiletto"—is absent from the chart. That is because it is French rather than Italian in origin. The fishtail is made in Italy mainly for export.

Values of the knives depend more on age, workmanship and condition than on pattern; range from **$10** (modern mass-produced) to **$150** or more (older hand-crafted).

ARBURESE: Old Sardinian shepherd's pattern first made in Arbus (near Cagliari). Skinning blade. Cow-horn handles riveted to false spring; no backspring. Modern ones have nickel-silver fittings, stainless blades.

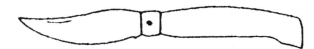

BERGAMASCO: Traditional pattern from Lombardy, common until the mid-19th century. Used by herdsmen of the Bergamo Valley. Solid horn-tip handle, no backspring.

CACCIA MUGELLANO (Mugellan hunting knife): A Tuscan hunter's pattern made in Scarperia, widely used. Usually has horn handles, iron mounts. Modern ones stainless. Derived from older sportsman's multi-blades.

Italian Cutlery Centers
(*still active in 1900*)

REGION	CITY	REGION	CITY
Piedmont:	Biella	**Lombardy:**	Asso*
	Forno-Canavese*		Brescia*
	Masserano		Canzo*
	Netro		Caslino d'Erba*
	Saglano-Micca		Cortenuovo
	Turin		Maccagno
	Vernante		Nerso
Venice:	Maniago *	**Naples:**	Campo-Basso
Tuscany:	Mondolfo*		
	Scarperia*		

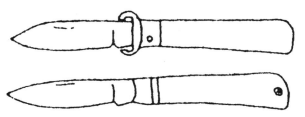

Only tool now sometimes included is the shot-shell extractor.

FIORENTINO: This "Florentine" pattern has been made in Scarperia at least since 1800 and is popular all over Italy. One-piece handle of horn or yew wood has a brass circle at end. Carbon-steel blade, backspring.

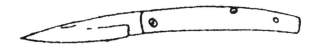

GOBBO ABRUZZESE (Abruzzi hunchback): Popular in Abruzzo, Molise and the lower Lazio, it resembles knives described in ancient Roman chronicles. The handle is a solid horn tip, bent forward in "hunchback" shape.

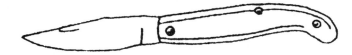

MAREMMANO: Popular since the mid-19th century in the Tuscan and Latian Maremma (marsh districts). Solid horn handle with longitudinal grooves. Backspring. Blade either scimitar-shaped (clip) or leaf-shaped (spear).

PATTADA O RESOLZA SARDA: Originally from Sardinia, now popular all over Italy. Flat, cow-horn handles. Traditional type has false spring, or no spring. Modern

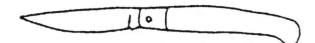

type has spring, brass liners, brass bolsters (sometimes), stainless blade. Made in a range of sizes.

RASOLINO (Little Razor): Popular in central and southern Italy. The keen, razor-shaped, carbon-steel blade was used for grafting various plants, and also for castrating small animals. Handle of hollowed horn, with a backspring.

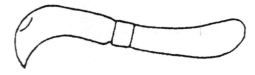

RONCHETTO VALTELLINESE: An ancient pattern used in Valtellina, mainly for grapevine growing. Sickle-shaped, carbon-steel blade, solid handle, no spring.

TRE PIANELLE: A traditional knife from Scarperia. The name (which translates as *three flats*) derives from its saber-ground, double-edged blade, now illegal in Italy. One-piece handle of solid horn with brass disk, carbon-steel blade and spring.

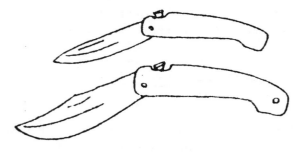

VERNANTIN: A Piedmontese pattern, it came from Vernante, Cuneo. Popular in Liguria since the early 1800s. Horn or yew handle. Scimitar-shaped or straight-edged carbon-steel blade. It has no spring, so the tang end is flattened to form a thumb stud, which rests in a notch in the back of the handle when the blade is open.

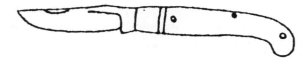

ZUAVA: An all-purpose pattern made in Scarperia. Popular in Tuscany. Horn handles, iron liners, backspring, carbon or stainless blade, made in a range of sizes.

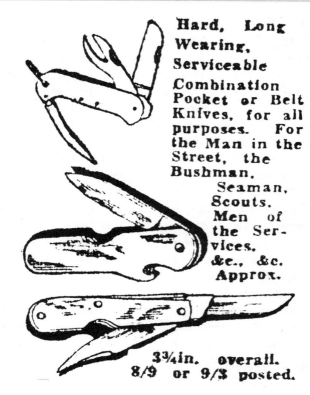

Hard, Long Wearing, Serviceable Combination Pocket or Belt Knives, for all purposes. For the Man in the Street, the Bushman, Seaman, Scouts, Men of the Services, &c., &c. Approx. 3¾ in. overall. 8/9 or 9/3 posted.

Australia. Wartime Pocketknives.

About 3 3/4 inches long closed. All steel, usually plated. Often marked on front handle. Australia made no pocketknives in peacetime, but during World War II could not obtain sufficient supply from Britain or America, so local metal-products firms (e.g., Carr Fastener) made basic patterns, mainly for the military. Examples from a May 1945 ad for Levenson's Radio, a Sydney retailer. Value, **$25**. Courtesy George Nisselle.

Lebanon. Bird figural knife.

Three-to-5 inches long closed. Horn handles, brass fittings, and turquoise, coral and ivory inlays. Made in Jezzine. 20th century. Also made as fixed blades. Value, **$40-60**. Inexpensive versions with plastic inlays, **$10**. Courtesy Betty Pittman and *Knife World*.

Germany. Folding Hunting Knives.

Folding versions of the *Jagdmesser*, and similar styles. Three-and-a-half-to-6 inches long closed. Stag handles,

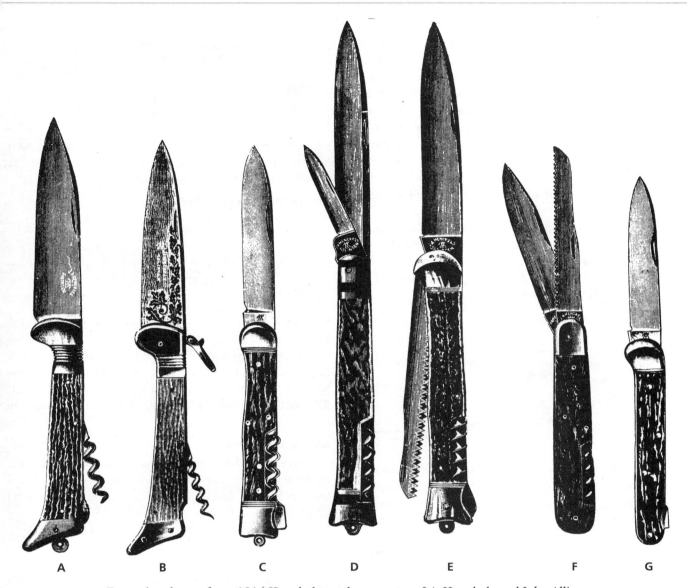

Examples shown from 1914 Henckels catalog, courtesy J.A. Henckels and John Allison.

nickel-silver mounts. Those labeled "A" and "B" (above) have heavy blades with front locks. The plain blade version, "A," value, **$600**. The damascus blade with gilt oak leaves, "B," **$1,500**. Those labeled "C," "D" and "E," fishtails, have respective values of **$150**, **$250** and **$300**. Those labeled "F" and "G," **$175** each. Some were exported to the United States.

Example shown 4 1/4 inches long closed. One-piece, black-lacquered steel handle, center lock. Marked K55K and MERCATOR. Black Cat Knife made by Kauffmann. 20th century. Value about **$22**. Courtesy Gutmann Cutlery.

Germany. Jewish Sabbath Knife.

Five-and-one-half inches long closed. Silver handles with engraved, mother-of-pearl panels. Inscribed in Hebrew, "Honor the Sabbath; The Way of Hillel." Some have corkscrew. For preparing bread and wine on Friday evening. Example shown has unmarked blade. Some are

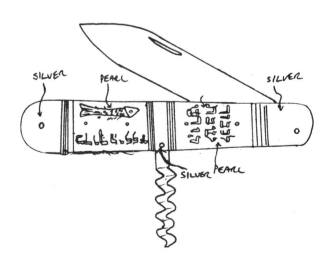

marked SOLINGEN. Circa 1900. Value, **$275**. Courtesy Harvey Reisberg and *Knife World*.

Clasp Knives

A traditional clasp knife is a large, single-bladed jack knife with an upwardly curved handle that tapers to a point. Clasp-knife handles are curved and pointed because they originally were made from the solid ends of goat, sheep or cow horns that were split or slotted to contain the blade. The tip of the horn covers the point of the blade, the blade having been shaped to fit the natural curve of the horn.

Traditional-style clasp knives are still made in southern Europe and Mexico. They are often called by their Spanish name, *navaja*.

The leaf-shaped clasp-knife blade may be the earliest pocketknife blade type, as it is the easiest to forge. Horn-handled clasp knives with leaf-shaped blades are still made today in Spain, for example, by an old outfit called BOFIL in Vich, Catalonia. The value of one is about **$8**.

Spain. NAVAJA (Clasp Knife).

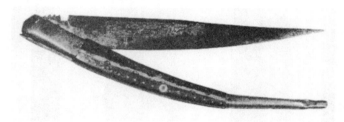

Four to 12 or more inches long closed. Handles usually horn. Brass or iron bolsters. Often decorated with pin-work, inlays or engraving. Long, slender navajas worn tucked behind belt. Ratcheted blade lock. 18th to 20th centuries.

The example shown is a mid-18th-century navaja bandolera; floral design on blade indicates it was made in Andalucia. Value, **$225-250**. Courtesy Eiler R. Cook.

Larger and finer examples, value up to **$400**. Recent small examples made in Albacete, Spain, value, **$20-30**. Plain examples made in Mexico, value about **$15**.

France. Chatellerault Clasp Knives.

Five to 12 inches long closed. Handles horn, wood or bone (sometimes etched). Clip blade. Iron mounts. Cap-bolster finial is a row of three balls. 18th to 19th centuries. The knives were made in Chatellerault, mainly for export to Spain, Latin America and the USA.

Example shown 8 1/4 inches long closed. Standard pattern. Early-to-mid 19th century, collected in North Carolina. Value, **$450**. Courtesy Smithsonian Institution.

Example shown 10 1/2 inches long closed, probably sold in Spain, 19th century. Brass back on blade. Value, **$250**. Courtesy Smithsonian Institution.

France. Hunter's Clasp Knife.

From about 4 inches long closed up to two-hand size. One-piece-stag (shown) or horn-tip handle. External backspring. *Cran d'arret* (stopping-notch) lock with pull-ring release. Yatagan blade. Late 19th and 20th centuries. Some are handmade, high quality. Value, **$20-50** small; **$35-200** medium; **$100-500** large, depending on quality.

Austria. Clasp Knife.

Four-to-5 inches long closed. Standard pocketknife construction, but decoration indicates it was made for Eastern Europe. Example shown, 4 inches long. Nickel silver and horn. 19th century. Value **$75-100**. Courtesy Smithsonian Institution, Wiebusch Collection.

Hungary. Modern Clasp Knife.

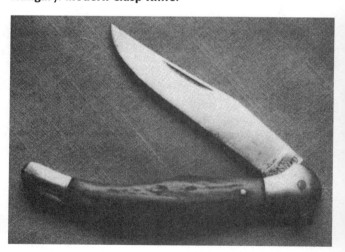

Four-and-a-half inches long closed. Stag handles. Stainless blade marked NEH/ROSTFREI. Made in Hungary circa 1980s. Value about **$35**. Courtesy Michael Bell.

England. Clasp Knives.

Three to 12 inches long closed. Long, iron bolsters, usually integral with liners. Late 17th to early 19th

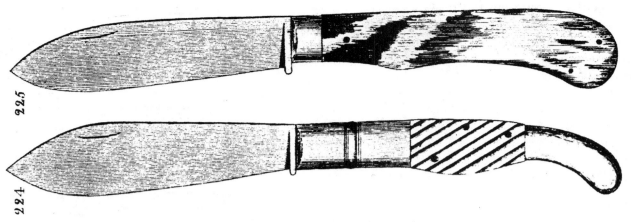

centuries. A popular style in the American Colonies, often found in archaeological sites. Value, **$250** and up. (See "Late 18th Century Sheffield Cutlers' Marks" for more information.)

Illustrations from *Smith's Key*, 1816. These two patterns (above) then offered in 1/4-inch increments from 3-5 1/2 inches long closed. Handles of cow horn or diagonally grooved bone. Value, **$200** and up. Courtesy EAIA.

Western Europe. Fancy Clasp Knives.

Very large, ornate folders. Possibly made as weapons or tools, but probably made for collectors.

Example shown above from France, 9 1/2 inches long closed. Iron mounts. Two-handed grip of tortoise shell, stag and ivory. Lock-release lever. Two rings. 19th century. Value, **$3,500**. Courtesy Robert Soares and Hugh Hayes.

Example shown below, Western Europe. We have seen examples marked ARNOLD/NAMUR (Belgium). Nine inches long closed. Switchblade, with external thumb-release trigger that hooks over back of blade. Stag or ivory handle. Steel mounts, trigger and guard. 19th century. Example shown has etched blade and bolsters. Courtesy Smithsonian Institution, Wiebusch Collection. (Switchblades are illegal to own or sell in most U.S. states. Check local and state laws for more information.)

Germany and Austria. Deerfoot Clasp Knife.

Four-and-a-half to 6 inches long closed. Lockback with folding or fixed guard, nickel-silver mounts, deerfoot handle. Late 19th and 20th centuries. Example shown from a 1910 catalog. Value, **$75**. Some were exported to the USA.

Germany and Austria. Clasp Knife.

LOCK-BACK

Four-and-a-half to 6 inches long closed. Lockback, usually with two blades, corkscrew. Steel bolsters, stag or bone-stag handles. Late 19th and early 20th centuries. Example shown from a 1914 catalog. Value in excellent condition, **$100**. Some were exported to the USA.

China. Clasp Knife.

About 3 1/2 inches long closed. Brass handle shaped like seed pod. Brass spring. Brass blade inlaid with steel cutting edge. Circa 1900. Value, **$75**. Courtesy Blade Magazine Cutlery Hall-Of-Famer© James B. Lile.

China. Squirrel Figural Knife.

About 3 inches long closed. Brass or nickel silver Asian-pet-squirrel-figural handle with engraved "fur." Copper rivet "eye." Some, such as example shown, have openwork copper inlay in blade. 20th century. Value about **$30**.

Quill Knives

(See the "Quill Knives" segment in the chapter, "Pen Knives," for more information on quill knives.)

English Quill Knives from *Smith's Key*, 1816. Two-and-a-half-to-3 inches long closed. Made in a variety of shapes, handle materials and decoration. Value, **$35** (plain) to **$175** (very fancy). Courtesy EAIA.

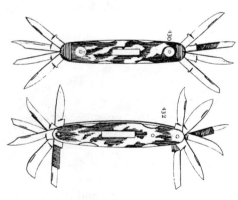

Double-ended, double-sided quill knives made in England from *Smith's Key*, 1816. Note that they are not lobster patterns. Blades in multiples of four. Value, **$250-750**, depending on decoration and number of blades. Courtesy EAIA.

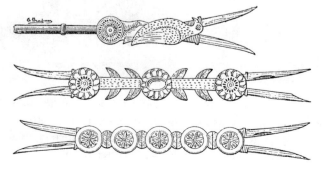

French multi-bladed quill knives. About 3 inches long closed. Carved ivory or mother-of-pearl handles. Early 19th century. Value **$500** each.

England. Double-ended Quill Knives.

From *Smith's Key*, 1816, courtesy EAIA.

Double-ended quill knife. About 4 inches long closed. One of many popular shapes. Value about **$250**.

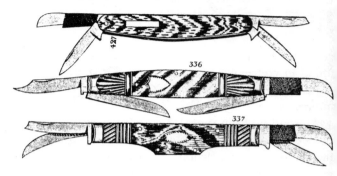

Four-bladed quill knives, 2 1/2 to 3 inches long closed. Three of many varieties. The one labeled "427" is an early congress pattern. Value, **$150** (plain) to **$750** (fancy).

Balance Knives

A "balance knife" or "crutch knife"—both names were used in 18th-century France—is a double-sided knife with usually two and sometimes four blades. The tang of each blade appears to be "split," though it was formed by folding around a mandrel. The blades are pivoted on a single pin with their tangs interleaved. Thus, the "run-up" of one blade serves to stop the opposite blade in the open position.

India or Sri Lanka (Ceylon). Two-bladed Coir Knife.

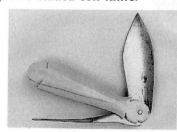

About 3 1/4 inches long closed. Deeply hollow-ground steel blade, steel pick. Pick is blunt on recent examples. Both blades usually have an engraved silver panel inlaid along the back. Ivory or wood one-piece handle. Most shaped as shown, but we have seen one shaped like a regular jack. Reportedly a rug weaver's knife. *Coir* is a material used for rug warp. 18th to 20th centuries. Value, ivory **$130**, wood **$50**.

France. Balance Knife (or Berge Knife).

About 4 inches long closed. Tortoise-shell or mother-of-pearl handles with gold or silver trim. One gold and one silver blade, or one silver and one damascus steel. 18th to 19th centuries ("Berge knife" is a 19th-century term

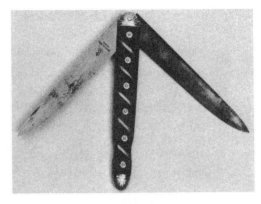

for model). Example shown nineteenth century by Cardeilhac of Paris, silver and damascus blades, gold trim. Value, **$2,400** to **$2,800** in excellent condition, **$400** to **$900** in good condition. Courtesy Smithsonian Institution, Wiebusch Collection. (See the "Silver Fruit Knives" segment in the chapter, "Named Jack Knife Patterns," for more information.)

Multi-Blades

Multi-blades have been around at least since the 18th century. This is a sampling of older styles.

England. Multi-Blade.

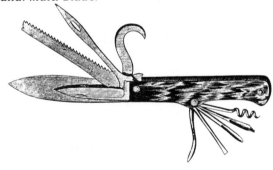

About 4 inches long closed. Multi-blade with tortoise, horn (as shown) or stag handles. Ten blades, as shown, value, **$750**. Six blades, similar shape, value, **$350**. Four blades, value, **$200**. From *Smith's Key*, 1816, courtesy EAIA.

England. Horseman's Knife.

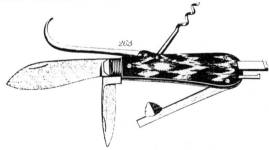

About 3 1/4 inches long closed. Note fleam blade and hoof pick. Value, **$375**. From *Smith's Key*, 1816, courtesy EAIA. Similar knife with two or three small blades hinged inside the hoof pick, value, **$1,500**. We have seen a *functional* 42-bladed knife of the type and size, its silver fruit blade hallmarked for the year 1790. It was in near-mint condition. Value, **$3,800**.

England. Snuff Box Knife.

About 3 inches long closed. Two to four blades. Hinged or rotating snuff-box lid. Tortoise, mother-of-pearl or ivory handles. Value, **$250-350**. From *Smith's Key*, 1816, courtesy EAIA.

Australia. Station and Farmers Knives.

184—BAKER'S SIX. Specially designed for use among stock. Six Blades, Finest Quality and Finish, in Stag Haft. Size 3½in. (as illustration), **21/-**; larger size, 4in. Haft, **24/-** each, post free.

Three-and-a-half-to-4 inches long closed. Equal-end handle die. Four, five or six blades. Fancy bolsters. Bone-stag handles. Made in Sheffield. Value, 3 1/2-inch: four blade, **$90**; five blade, **$165**; 6 blade, **$210**. Special speying knife: four-blade with four identical hawkbill blades, value **$110**. From a 1924 W. Jno. Baker, Sydney, catalog.

China. Doctor's Knife.

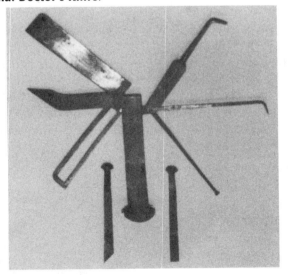

Brass handle. Includes cutting blades, saw, forceps, probes. Used by Chinese army surgeons. 20th century. Value about **$150**. Courtesy Frank Phelps and *Knife World*.

France. 18th-Century Multi-Blades.

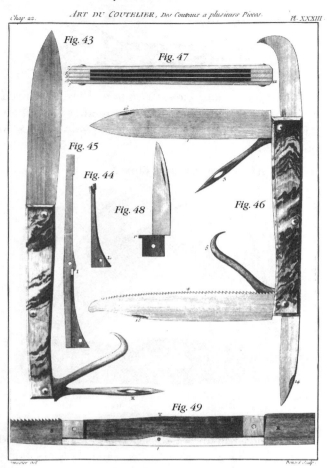

Images above are from Perret, *The Art of the Cutler*, 1771 and include:

A. (Fig. 43) Three-bladed, single-spring "traveler's knife," structurally a predecessor of the whittler. The spacer (Fig. 44) affixed to the spring (Fig. 45) separates the two small blades, a harness punch and a cork-puller hook. Value, **$600**. With pen blade (*canif*) in place of hook, value, **$300**.

B. (Fig. 46) Six-bladed, three-spring "amateur gardener's knife." It has two handle scales and two interior liners (Fig. 47). "Crinking, blade adjustment, and position of nail marks are critical for smooth working." The ancestor of most sportsman's and utility knives. Value, **$600**.

France. 20th-Century Multi-Blade.

About 4 inches long closed. From a 1936 catalog: "Country knife, flat handle, mottled horn, with reinforced end and ring, strong knife blade, saw, pruning blade, punch." Made in Thiers by Rousselon Freres & Cie. DUMAS/AINE 32 brand. Value, **$65**. Courtesy Damien Lemaire.

Austria-Hungary. Strikefire Multi-Blades.

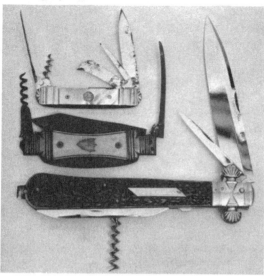

Two-and-three-fourths-to-6 inches long closed. Various patterns with a heavy steel bar covering the backsprings. The bar was used with a flint for striking fire for lighting pipes and cigars. Value, **$125-750**. Courtesy Smithsonian Institution.

Bavaria. Take-apart Knife-and-Fork Kits.

Courtesy Smithsonian Institution, Wiebusch Collection.

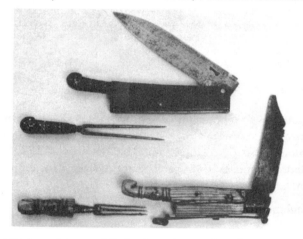

Examples shown 4-5 inches long closed. Decorated bone, ivory, horn or wood handles. Locking knife blades. Removable forks. 18th to 19th centuries. Value, **$250**.

Example shown 7 inches overall. Springless folding knife, horn or wood handles. Removable fork and two skewers. Tin-alloy decorations. Eighteenth to nineteenth centuries. Value, **$450**.

England and France. Slot Knife.

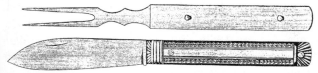

Four-to-5 inches long closed. Take-apart knife-and-fork combination. Fork part may have spoon in opposite end. Handles of plain horn or wood, or fancy carved ivory or mother-of-pearl. 18th to 19th centuries. Example shown from *Smith's Key*, 1816, courtesy EAIA. Value, **$250** (plain) to **$750** (fancy). (See also the "Silver Fruit Knives" segment of the chapter, "Named Jack Knife Patterns.")

France. Friend Knife.

About 4 inches long closed. Slot knife with identical halves. 18th to 19th centuries. Value, **$85** (plain) to **$300**.

Secret Knives

The term "secret knife" (translation of the 18th-century French *couteau a secret*), does not refer to any particular shape or style. Rather, it refers to any knife that contains a hidden mechanical contrivance, such as a locking or unlocking mechanism, or hidden extra blades.

We consider secret knives to be one of the most fascinating areas of knife collecting. Quite a variety of them was made from the 17th through the early 19th centuries. Some simpler designs were made more recently. All types of early secret knives are rare.

Spain (?). Concealed-Blade Secret Knife.

About 4 inches long closed. Penny-knife type with one-piece horn handle. Blade stop is in fact part of the small blade, which is nested into the back of the hollow large blade. Circa 19th century. Value, **$350**. Courtesy Lawrence Bireline and *Knife World*.

Germany. Pivot-liner Secret Knife.

About 4 inches long closed. Inner wrap-around-back liner pivots inside outer wrap-around-end liner. Button in handle releases inner liner. Jigged-bone handles. "WERWOLF No. 100" trademark. Circa 1900. Value, **$175**. Some made for export to the United States.

France. Ruler Secret Knife.

About 6 3/4 inches long closed. Steel mounts, ivory scales with engraved markings. Looks and works like a folding rule. Open length of rule is one French royal foot (13 English inches), divided into 12 *pouces*, which are divided into twelfths (*lignes*). To open blade without opening ruler, flip up the L-shaped steel cover (at right in above picture), which exposes the nail nick. 18th century. Value, **$550**.

France. Multi-Blade Pivot-Handle Secret Knife.

Five-and-a-half inches long closed; nearly 1 inch wide and 1 inch thick. Wood handles; iron mounts. Made in two sections, each with four blades, two on top and two on bottom. Blades cannot be opened until tapered, square-cross-sectioned rods that block the springs are pushed out with one of the picks hidden in the handle scales. Nest of six saw blades pivoted between the two sections. To open the saw blades, use a pick to press a serrated spot on one of the center liners. This releases a latch at one end of the handle and allows the two sections to pivot at the other end. Some French single-bladed secret knives use a similar pivot mechanism. 18th century. Value about **$2,000**. Courtesy Smithsonian Institution, Wiebusch Collection.

France (also other countries). Pivot-Handle Secret Knives.

Three to 8 inches long closed. Three stout pins set in blade tang. Center is pivot pin that joins blade to handles. Other two pins are stop pins, one protruding on each side, to stop handles in open and closed positions. Most older types have separate mechanism to lock handles together.

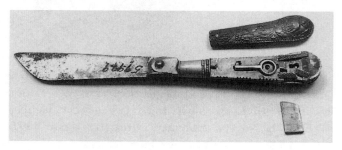

Earliest types from 17th and 18th century France, also possibly Germany and the Low Countries, have actual locks that keep handles from pivoting, and to prevent use by anyone who does not know the "secret." Usual type has two or three combination dials in front handle or cap (see below). Example above has pressed-horn-handle cover clipped to checkered-steel bands on liner by a concealed brass latch-piece (bottom right). Push out latch-piece; remove handle; take out key; unlock knife; close or open blade; lock knife; reassemble. Value, **$750** up. Courtesy Smithsonian Institution, Wiebusch Collection.

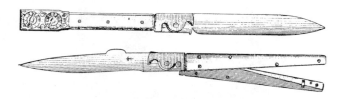

Some later types, from 18th to early 20th centuries, have sliding bolster with long pin inside one handle that engages eye in other handle to lock knife either open or closed. Circa 1770 example, above, has handles tapered to allow knife to be used as a plug bayonet. Value, **$350** and up.

Axel Hasselstrom received U.S. Patent 426,445 for the exact same mechanism on April 29, 1890. W. Bradley and A.B. Ball received a British patent for a simpler version with a single stop pin on May 14, 1898. Values of factory versions, often without secret locks, **$75-150**.

Custom maker Barry Wood patented this version without separate latch in 1972 (No. 3,702,501). Value about **$500**. Dark-red-handle version made for Colt, 1969-1973, **$250-350**.

France, Germany, U.S.A., Philippines. Butterfly Knife.

Two to 8 inches long closed. A pivot-handle knife similar to the previous ones, except that the half handles are side by side rather than back to back. The latch mechanism is at the end, not internal. Evidently a French invention, 18th or early 19th century. Several styles were made in Germany in the 1880s and exported to the USA. Miller Bros. of Connecticut patented a sheet-metal-handled version in June 1887. Butterfly fruit knives were made in England under H.H. Field's British patent of May 3, 1898. A stout version was patented in the USA by Charles Billings of Connecticut in 1908; the knives were made by Billings and Spencer with nickel-plated, knurled-steel handles.

Because it has no backspring, the butterfly knife can be made using simple technology. It is the national folding knife of the Philippines. Usual materials there are brass frames, horn handles.

Values: French with champagne blade **$200**; German with stag handles **$150**; Philippine **$15-75**, depending on size and quality; Japanese or Italian **$5-35**. Finnish by Hackman, nylon handles, **$30**; American versions: Miller Bros. **$175**; Billings & Spencer **$550**; Waltco, circa 1950s, **$95**; California made by Bali Song, Inc., **$125-275**. (Bali Song, Inc., was the predecessor of Pacific Cutlery, Corp., both of which were under the direction of Les de Asis. Both are now defunct. Today, the butterfly knife tradition of each company lives on through Benchmade Knife Co. in Oregon City, Oregon, which continues to make its own butterfly knives with De Asis as CEO.)

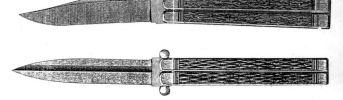

1885 German "Springless Marvels" with stag handles by Bontgen & Sabin. Courtesy Siegfried Rosenkaimer.

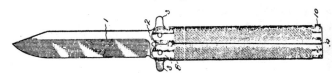

Circa 1908 Billings & Spencer butterfly knife courtesy William Lipes and *Knife World*.

Germany or Austria. "Reverse Butterfly" Secret Knife.

Split-handle knife with handles pivoted at opposite end from blade. Example shown 4 1/8 inches long closed. Stag handles. Circa 1890s. Value about **$250**. Courtesy Smithsonian Institution, Wiebusch Collection.

Fixed Blade Knives

The section "Fixed Blade Knives" begins with the history of the most celebrated of all American knives, the bowie. The "Bowie Knives" segment explains the origin, development and variety of this classic piece in the period of its common use, circa 1827-1872. The text is followed by an expanded list of "American Knifemakers and Selected American Cutlery Merchants of the Bowie Knife Period."

The segment following it is "American Indian Trade Knives." The third segment traces the evolution of "American Hunting Knives," factory-made fixed blades designed primarily for sport.

Then we turn to handmade knives. First comes a series of short segments about some of the "Pioneers of Modern Handmade Knives," men whose influence can be seen in almost every fixed-blade knife sold in the United States today.

Following it is an updated listing of "Today's Knifemakers." The segment has been revised with complete contact information, including addresses and phone numbers, where available. Next comes a detailed history of "United States Military Fixed Blade Knives," illustrated with the superb drawings of Blade Magazine Cutlery Hall-Of-Famer© M.H. Cole. It is followed by a brief segment on "Foreign Military Fixed Blade Knives," including basic information on "German Third Reich Knives" and a segment on "Commercial Daggers and Survival Knives."

After these comes a wide-ranging look at ancient and modern fixed-blade knives from around the world. Much of it was written by Eiler R. Cook, with contributions by other prominent specialists.

Finally, there are segments on "Kitchen and Butcher Knives," "Table Knives," "Carving Sets," and "Industrial Knives."

Note: Throughout the "Fixed Blade Knives" section, each knife or type of knife is valued individually.

Bowie Knives

The Sandbar Fight

The story of the bowie knife began Sept. 19, 1827, on a Mississippi River sandbar just above Natchez. At that place was held what the participants called an "interview" to settle an "affair of honor"—in other words, a duel. Duels were a common enough occurrence in the Old South, but this particular "interview" turned into a melee. Even though the initial encounter proved harmless to the two principals involved, the meeting swiftly degenerated into a "rough fight" among the dozen men present, leaving two of them dead and two others wounded.

One of the wounded men was Blade Magazine Cutlery Hall-Of-Famer© James Bowie (1796-1836), a young planter and land speculator then residing in Avoyelles Parish, Louisiana. Bowie was a friend of Samuel Wells, one of the principals in the duel.

In the rough fight, Bowie had been shot in the thigh and knocked down. He was then, according to the published account of Mr. Wells, set upon by a member of the opposing party, Major Norris Wright, who attempted to stab Bowie with a sword cane.

By then Bowie had already emptied both of his single-shot pistols. To defend himself, he drew from under his coat a large hunting knife that his brother, Rezin Bowie, later indicated he had given James for his protection. James struggled up to a sitting position and, with one blow of the knife, killed Major Wright. Wright's friends later told a story much less flattering to Bowie—that he had first shot Wright, *then* stabbed him—but it was Wells' version that was most widely circulated at the time.

The incident, which came to be called the "Sandbar Fight," attracted intense popular and journalistic interest. The image of a wounded man lying on the ground and struggling just to sit up, his guns empty and useless, yet who managed by one blow of a knife to slay an opponent who was attacking him with a sword, caught the fancy of the nation.

In the popular mind, Bowie's feat was attributed not so much to the pluck and desperation of the man as to some special, undefined virtue of his knife. " Bowie knives" quickly became a fad, then a fashion, then a fundamental fixture of the American scene. Young men of Bowie's planter class in the South came to be called the "bowie-knife-and-pistol gentry." And then, in 1836, Bowie's dramatic martyrdom in defense of the Alamo in Texas guaranteed that his name would forever be linked to the knife that bore his name.

Personal Defense

In 1807, the introduction of percussion pistols had revolutionized personal defense. Both more reliable and more compact than their flintlock predecessors, "cap-and-ball" pistols could be carried concealed discreetly. This was a timely invention, since civilian wear of the small sword had by then gone out of fashion in America.

However, the usual "brace" or pair of single-shot pistols meant that a man had only two shots to deal with any opponents, assuming that both pistols happened to work. (For improved reliability, men often paid professional gunsmiths to load their pistols for them.) After discharge, a pistol was useful only as a bludgeon. For backup, therefore, men often carried a dirk, dagger, clasp knife or sword cane. Hence, when the bowie knife came along, it was perceived as a substantial improvement over the more familiar edged weapons of the time.

For the next half-century the bowie knife was among America's most popular sidearms, joined in the spotlight in the late 1840s by the "Colt's" cap-and-ball revolver. A pair of Colt revolvers might hold 10 or 12 rounds, but the percussion system never was reliable enough for a prudent man to stake his life solely on his pistols. Come rain, snow, sleet or gloom of night, a bowie knife was always loaded and never failed to fire.

Edwin Forrest's Claim

What exactly is a bowie knife? At the beginning, in 1827, it was simply "a knife like Bowie's." There have been a number of contenders for the title of "original bowie knife," one of the more recent being the Edwin Forrest knife.

According to Edwin Forrest, he received a knife from James Bowie soon after the Sandbar Fight. Forrest (1806-1872) was America's first genuinely popular entertainment celebrity. He had gone on the New York stage in 1820, and by 1826 was the idol of the city. Then he had made a national tour, and everywhere he performed he inspired near riot and mass hysteria, much the way later generations would be driven wild by Valentino, Elvis and the Beatles. According to the story Forrest told his biographers, he had met James Bowie in 1824 while performing in New Orleans. (See "In Search of the Sandbar Knife, Part III," by J.R. Edmondson, April 2003 *BLADE®*.)

Much more so than Bowie, Forrest was a flamboyant and extravagant man, famous for his violent public quarrels. He was also a master of self-promotion. As William C. Davis wrote in *Three Roads to the Alamo*: "A lot of nonsense has been written about Bowie and Forrest, most of it generated by Forrest himself … It was pure fiction from an actor who also invented much of his life history."

Nonetheless, by several reports, Forrest's arms collection was world renowned. It included custom weapons made for his own use, over-sized stage weapons made for his performances, and weapons that reportedly had belonged to emperors, kings and generals.

According to Forrest, in a letter accompanying the knife, Bowie told Forrest that the knife he had given the actor was *the* famous knife that all the newspapers were so excited about, and he thought that Forrest might want to add it to his collection. In later years, Forrest displayed the knife in his cabinet of arms in his mansion in Philadelphia. However, according to Edmondson, the letter that Forrest claimed Bowie wrote to accompany the knife "is unknown to virtually all" Bowie historians. "To my knowledge," Edmondson noted, "such a letter, or even a photocopy of it, has never been displayed for public consumption."

Actor Edwin Forrest claimed that this was the knife used by James Bowie in the Sandbar Fight. (formerly from the collection of Blade Magazine Cutlery Hall-Of-Famer© William R. Williamson, courtesy Hall-Of-Famer William Adams; Hall-Of-Famer Bruce Voyles photo)

Forrest's cabinet of arms remained sealed after the actor's death. In the 1960s, the late William R. Williamson, eminent bowie collector and Blade Magazine Cutlery Hall Of Famer©, had learned of its existence but concluded that it had been destroyed in a fire that damaged Forrest's mansion in 1873. Then, in 1988, he found that the cabinet was still intact and that Forrest's heirs intended to liquidate it. Museums obtained most of the famous arms, but Williamson bought the bowie knife, the cabinet and several of Forrest's personal weapons.

The knife is large and plain, similar in shape to an Indian trade scalper (see the following segment, "American Indian Trade Knives"), though longer and more stout. The handle slabs are checkered and secured by three large rivets with silver burrs. Though its sheath is silver mounted, the knife does not look professionally made. As Edmondson wrote, though it qualifies as a "large butcher knife" thanks to its 12-inch blade, it far exceeds the dimensions reported by Rezin Bowie and others. Nor do the checkered scales resemble the "handle corrugated with braids of steel" mentioned in William Rounseville Alger's biography of Forrest.

Is the Forrest knife the original bowie? Some think it is, others do not. Without Bowie here to tell us himself, it appears no one will ever know for sure.

Early Bowie Knives

The Sandbar Fight took place before the invention of photography, and even before the common use of engraved drawings in newspapers and magazines. The fame of the bowie was spread at the time through written accounts of the Sandbar Fight, along with descriptions by journalists who had not actually seen the knife.

Nonetheless, men all over the country wanted to have a "Bowie's knife." They could only guess what one should look like, but they did their best to match the descriptions. Bowie knives were made long and short; light and heavy; single edged and double edged; straight backed and curved backed; clip point and spear point; plain and decorated; fixed blade and folding (see the "Folding Dirks" and "Folding Bowie Knives" segment in the chapter, "Named Jack Knife Patterns"); and with a cross guard—or two—and without. Few of them probably looked much like Bowie's knife, but hardly anyone knew it, and apparently no one cared. To their makers and to their owners, all the knives were bowies.

Though shape, size and decoration varied widely in the first two decades of the bowie knife era, all bowie knives had one thing in common: They were designed primarily as weapons. The coffin-shaped hilt on many early bowie knives might well have been symbolic. A sense of propriety prompted most people then—including Rezin Bowie—to call them "hunting knives." In fact, many of the knives were similar to the stout knives and short swords then used by European sportsmen to kill stag and boar. (See Part III of Section II, "Foreign Exotic, Primitive, and Historical Fixed Blade Knives.")

Like the European hunting knives and hangers of that period, fixed-blade bowies were sold with sheaths fitted to be thrust through or suspended from a belt. That way one's bowie knife would always be handy for attack or defense. But unlike a European gentleman, who only wore his hunting knife when on the chase, many Americans wore their bowie knives all the time.

Original Makers?

Who made the bowie knives to meet the burgeoning demand? In particular, who made the very first, the *original,* bowie knife?

Rezin Bowie later wrote that he had made the knife that he had given to his brother James prior to the Sandbar Fight. According to Rezin:

"The first Bowie knife was made by myself in the parish of Avoyelles, in this state, as a hunting knife, for which purpose, exclusively, it was used for many years. The length of the blade was nine and one quarter inches, its width one and a half inches, single edged and blade not curved. Colonel James Bowie had been shot by an individual with whom he was at variance and as I presumed a second attempt would be made by the same person to take his life, I gave him the knife to use as occasion might require, as a defensive weapon. Some time afterwards, and the only time the knife was ever used for any purpose other than that for which it was intended, or originally designed, it was resorted to by Col. James Bowie in a chance medley, or rough fight, between himself and certain other individuals with whom he was inimical, and the knife was then used only as a defensive weapon and not till he had been shot down; it was then the means of saving his life. The improvement in its fabrication and the state of perfection which it has since acquired from experienced cutlers, was not brought about through my agency. I would here also assert that neither Col. Bowie nor myself, at any period of our lives ever had a duel with any person whatsoever."

Rezin's granddaughter and grandson claimed that Rezin's use of the word "made" should not be taken literally, that Rezin had in fact commissioned the knife from a neighbor and sometime employee of the Bowie brothers named Jesse Clifft (whose name also appears as *Clift* on some documents). If true, then Clifft would most likely have forged the blade at his own blacksmith shop, located in nearby Marksville, the seat of Avoyelles Parish. A sheriff's inventory of Clifft's blacksmith shop still survives from 1830, when Clifft migrated to Texas.

Also, according to *James Bowie and the Sandbar Fight* by James L. Batson, another Bowie brother, John J. Bowie, said, "'James Bowie had a knife made to meet his fancy by a common blacksmith named Snowden.' C.K. Ham and Annie M. Bowie, John Bowie's granddaughter, allowed that Love or Lovell H. Snowden made the knife."

James Black

On Dec. 8, 1841, James P. Jett, editor of the weekly Washington, Arkansas, *Telegraph*, wrote an editorial page critical of violence. Washington, 250 miles north

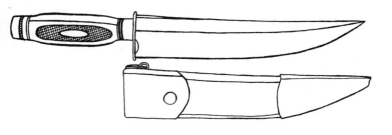

Style of bowie knife made by Daniel Searles for Rezin Bowie, circa 1830. Checkered ebony handle typical of surgical instrument maker's work, silver mounts. 14" overall. Value, **$45,000** and up. (drawing by Joanna Spivey)

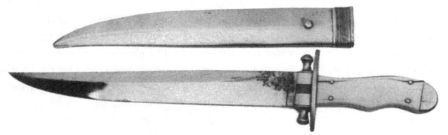

Straight-backed bowie with long false edge, marked SIRHENRY/A PARIS. Ivory handles, two nickel-silver guards, sheath. 14 3/4" overall. 1830s-1840s. Value, **$7,500** and up. (courtesy Smithsonian Institution) [Knives are valued with their sheaths.]

of Marksville, Louisiana, was then the seat of Hempstead County. The essay begins thus (it is reprinted in full from a story in *Knives '88* written by Blade Magazine Cutlery Hall-Of-Famer B.R. Hughes): "*The Bowie Knife. This far-famed deadly instrument had its origin we believe in Hempstead County. The first knife of this kind was made in this place by Mr. James W. Black for a man named James Bowie who was killed at the Alamo, in Texas, and hence is sometimes called the Black knife, sometimes the Bowie knife ... Whilst on this subject we cannot forbear mentioning the sad dispensation with which Mr. James W. Black has been visited. Several years since [in 1839] he lost his eyesight ...*"

Jett was not the only person in Washington, Arkansas, to whom James Black (1800-1872) had confided his story. After 1842, blind and near penniless, Black was cared for by the family of Dr. Isaac N. Jones, whose young son Daniel Webster Jones (born in 1839) would grow up to become governor of the state (1897-1901). As a boy, Daniel Jones had heard Black's tales of knifemaking. Nearly half-a-century later, in 1903, Jones recounted Black's story in print. He placed the claimed first meeting of Black and Bowie "about 1833 or 1834," six years *after* the Sandbar Fight. Moreover, Jones' knowledge of damascus was sketchy at best, though it is arguable whether that failing necessarily discounts his memories of Black.

At the time, Jones' story was little noticed outside of Arkansas. But earlier published claims of Black's primacy—echoing Jett's 1841 editorial—reportedly had been denied by several members of the Bowie family. They knew the real story, they insisted, and it had nothing to do with Arkansas or James Black.

Though there were inaccuracies in Jones' story, there was also the following. According to Jones, James Black also claimed to have been apprenticed to a silver worker in Philadelphia as a youth. As Jones wrote, "*James Black was born in a village in the state of New Jersey on May 1, 1800. At the early age of eight he ran away from home and went to Philadelphia, where he was apprenticed to a manufacturer of silver-plated ware named Henderson ... His apprenticeship expired in 1818. He had become quite expert in the silver-plating business and intended to make it his occupation for life.*"

If this were true and Black really had been a silver worker, then he would have known how to make a silver-mounted knife to the high standards of the time. Any knives he made would not have been plain or crude.

Unfortunately, Black did not mark his knives with his name, so it is virtually impossible to trace any one knife to him. Some bowie authorities do not give much credence to Black as a maker of bowie knives. However, according to Edmondson ("In Search of the Sandbar Knife, Part II," March 2003 *BLADE®*), researchers such as Bill Worthen, executive director of the Arkansas Historical Museum, Black descendant Lu Waters and B.R. Hughes "have uncovered a vast amount of circumstantial evidence that support Black as the maker of a number of unmarked, silver-mounted, coffin-pommeled bowies." (For a picture of an example of such a knife, Bowie No. 1, see page 35 of *The Antique Bowie Knife Book* by Terry Moss and Blade Magazine Cutlery Hall-Of-Famers© William Adams and J. Bruce Voyles.)

Black might well have made bowie knives for customers in Arkansas in the 1830s, perhaps even one for James

Unmarked 15 1/2" bowie, virtually identical to a marked knife made by Henry Schively. Checkered horn handle, nickel-silver mounts, leather of sheath inscribed "Crocket." Family tradition has it that the knife was given to Henry Clay by his fellow Whig, David "Davy" Crockett (1786-1836), before Crockett left for Texas in 1835. It may be the "large butcher knife" presented to Crockett in Philadelphia during his 1835 speaking tour of the Northeast. Value, **$45,000** and up. (Jim Taylor photo, courtesy town of Bedford, Massachusetts)

Unsigned bowie in the Spanish style, almost certainly made by Samuel Bell. 13" overall, engraved silver handle inlaid with mother-of-pearl panels, engraved and fitted silver sheath marked with owner's name: Geo. W. Kelley. Value, **$50,000** and up. (courtesy J.E. Stafford; Blade Magazine Cutlery Hall-Of-Famer© Jim Weyer photo)

Bowie. Nonetheless, without Bowie around to testify to that fact, it seems no one will ever know for sure.

Raymond Thorp

In 1925, Raymond Thorp published the first of a series of articles on the history of the bowie knife. At first he stuck closely to Jones' account, but later appears to have added his own embellishments, all of which culminated in his 1948 book, *Bowie-Knife*. In this widely read volume, he claimed that there had been a relationship between James Black and James Bowie.

Expanding upon Jones' tale, Thorp portrayed Black as a fearsome backwoods alchemist who created the bowie knife, a radical improvement on "Bowie's design." Bowie took the knife and proceeded to use it in various encounters.

Without benefit of evidence, Thorp reconstructed in detail the lost "true" bowie knife that Black had forged by processes now forgotten. Thorp's drawings of "true" bowie knives accompanied his tale, and plenty of Thorp-style bowies have been made since that time.

Also since that time, novelists, movie producers, and even museum curators and historians seem to have drawn upon Thorp, treating his interpretations as fact, most notable being Paul Wellman and his best-selling novel, *The Iron Mistress*. As a result, Thorp's version of the bowie knife story is the one that entered popular awareness.

A particularly persistent error of Thorp's was to draw a distinction between "Arkansas Toothpick" and "Bowie-Knife." The term "Arkansas toothpick" was a circa 1840s synonym for "bowie knife." The term was sometimes etched or stamped on the blades of Sheffield bowies of various sizes and shapes. The term did not refer to any specific style of knife, such as a double-edged dagger, as Thorp asserted.

Cutlers

The "true story" of the bowie knife, as far as it can be determined, is different from Jones or Thorp's versions. Neither man realized that several of what are believed to be Rezin Bowie's knives survive to this day. One was made by Daniel Searles and has the inscription "presented by Rezin Bowie to Lt. H.W. Fowler of the U.S. Dragoons." The knife is on display in the Alamo. Another, known as the Jesse Perkins bowie, was made by Henry Schively and is housed in the Mississippi State Historical Museum in Jackson, Mississippi. Both are fancier than Rezin's

description of the original knife but are believed to have been made to the same basic design. Their provenance is documented in Bowie family correspondence.

One or more highly skilled merchant craftsmen—custom knifemakers, "experienced cutlers" and surgical instrument makers—could be found in nearly every American city of the day (see the list at the end of this segment). Most of them advertised "cutlery of all descriptions on hand and made to order." Two such cutlers—Searles and Schively—were the ones who made the aforementioned knives in the 1830s that have been attributed to Rezin Bowie. Searles was of Baton Rouge, Louisiana, just down river from Avoyelles Parish. Schively was of Philadelphia, his shop a block or two from the office of a doctor who reportedly treated Rezin Bowie in Philadelphia in 1832.

Cutlers and surgical instrument makers throughout the United States were the first beneficiaries of the bowie knife. In some towns, gunsmiths, silversmiths or even blacksmiths such as Clifft were called upon to make bowie knives. In fact, in 19th-century American cities, cutlers, gunsmiths and silversmiths were respected middle-class professional men with glass-fronted, downtown shops.

Though sometimes very plain, American cutler-made bowie knives are the most highly prized by today's collectors. Any large or fancy bowie knife made by one of the U.S. cutlers active in the 1820s or '30s is now worth at least **$20,000** in excellent condition. Later or plainer cutler-made bowie knives are worth at least **$2,500**. Exceptional design, workmanship, size, condition or historical association can add substantially to the values.

European cutlers also joined in the bowie movement, some by sending knives, others by coming to America. Fancy handmade bowies from Paris, some with damascus steel blades, found favor in the old South (value, at least **$2,500**). We have seen examples by Cabau (circa 1825-1835), by Picault (circa 1840-1880), and by "Sirhenry" (dates unknown). Some London-made hunting knives might possibly have been brought to the United States, though virtually all the English bowie knives sold in America came from Sheffield.

Early Sheffield Bowie Knives

News of the Sandbar Fight and the growing American demand for "Bowie's knives" would have reached England before the end of 1827. Sheffield knives had long been sold in the United States, but it was only after the War of 1812, which had hurt their business badly, that the city's cutlery manufacturers had begun to cater to American tastes. (See the "19th Century Sheffield Cutlery Firms" segment in the "Pocketknife History" chapter of Section II.)

By coincidence, the first full-fledged cutlery *factory* in Sheffield had just been completed in 1826 after four years of construction—the Sheaf Works of William Greaves & Son. Besides Greaves, some of the other important Sheffield manufacturers involved very early in the bowie knife trade were William & Samuel Butcher; Samuel C. Wragg; James Rodgers; Enoch Drabble; Charles Congreve; and George Wostenholm's Rockingham Works.

Wostenholm first sent his I*XL cutlery to the United States in 1830, and thereafter devoted nearly all of his considerable energies to American sales. In 1848 he occupied Sheffield's largest factory yet, named the Washington Works in honor of the American trade. Until the 1890s, Wostenholm's cutlery dominated the American market.

The earliest Sheffield bowies were characterized by an astonishing variety of blade and handle shapes, and decoration. The big, fancy, odd-shaped Sheffield bowies of the early period (circa 1827-1845) are nearly as rare and valuable as their plainer American counterparts, with values ranging from **$7,500** on up. Plainer early examples are worth at least **$2,000** in excellent condition.

By the late 1840s, scores of Sheffield firms were making bowie knives and other cutlery for America. Most of the Sheffield firms listed as active in the mid-19th century made, or at least sold, bowie knives. (See the "Pocketknife Brand List" under Part 1 of Section II, "Factory Folding Knife Charts, Tables and Histories".) Other firms, such as Woodhead & Hartley, Broomhead & Thomas, James Westa, James Burnand, Thomas Tillotson and John Coe, seem to have specialized in bowies. However, some common but undocumented "Sheffield" names on bowies, such as Manson and Alexander, may have been import brands, not makers. Values, **$500** and up.

Even in the factories, Sheffield cutlery was almost entirely handmade. However, one element of "mass-

Large clip-point bowie marked JAMES RODGERS/ROYAL CUTLERY/SHEFFIELD and CAST STEEL BOWIE KNIFE; rosewood handle trimmed with nickel silver, circa 1840. Value, **$14,000** and up. (courtesy Blade Magazine Cutlery Hall-Of-Famer© M.H. Cole)

production" then prevalent in Sheffield contributed to the great popularity and relatively low cost of Sheffield bowies in the United States. This element was the production of fancy but inexpensive nickel-silver handle fittings, and eventually of entire hollow handles (mistakenly called "cutlery handles" by bowie collectors today).

Nickel silver—or German silver or "white brass"— an alloy of copper, zinc and nickel, had been invented around 1810. Soon it was being rolled like silver into thin sheets, which were then pressed into three-dimensional decorative shapes using steel dies. The hollow shapes were then filled with "rozzil"—cutler's cement, made of rosin, beeswax and brick dust—or sometimes with lead.

Myriad designs of furniture and handles were formed of sheet nickel silver by specialist firms in Sheffield. They sold their wares to all the cutlery makers there. Many designs were created just for the American market. (See the "Folding Dirks and Folding Bowie Knives" segment of the chapter, "Named Jack Knife Patterns," for examples.)

Collectors should note that some original forming dies—such as the big horse head—have survived and now are used to make both reproduction and counterfeit knife fittings. Also be aware that neither brass fittings of any type, nor ornate nickel-silver castings, were ever used on 19th-century Sheffield bowie knives, though both were used on English counterfeits of the 1960s and '70s.

Note, too, that Sheffield-style, embossed nickel- and sterling-silver mounts were not used on American-made bowie knives, but only on American carving sets (whose handles are now often used on counterfeit bowies). American cutler-made bowies usually have plain coin-

Clip-point bowie marked WOODHEAD & HARTLEY, made c1850 by George Woodhead, 36 Howard Street, Sheffield; ivory scales, half-horse, half-alligator pommel, Gold Rush etch. Value, **$20,000** and up. (courtesy Hugh Hayes)

Coffin-hilt bowie with long false edge, marked on butt MARKS/& REES/CIN Al. Rosewood handle wrapped with silver-copper alloy, silver rivets. 13 1/2" overall. 1840s. Value, **$20,000** and up if excellent, **$3,500** as is. (courtesy Donald Euing)

Bowie-period dagger by John Walters, Sheffield. Etched CALIFORNIA TOOTHPICK/GOLD SEEKER'S PROTECTOR. Value, **$2,500** ($650 as is). (courtesy Bob Macon)

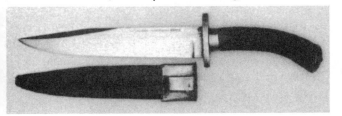

Clip-point bowie marked CHEVALIER'S CALIFORNIA KNIFE, by John D. Chevalier of New York. Stag handle. Value, **$6,500** as is. (courtesy Hugh Hayes)

silver or steel mounts; sometimes, silver-plated brass or nickel silver (Chevalier, Will & Finck); rarely, patinated bronze (Roby); or a silver-copper alloy (Marks & Rees). American factory bowies were mounted in steel, in plain nickel silver, or, rarely, in plain brass (Ames, Ashmore, H. Huber).

Two other forms of bowie decoration popular in 19th-century Sheffield had the aspect of mass-production. One was *decorative blade etching*. The resist for these complex etched designs was applied with reusable brass stencils, some of which survive today in collections. The other was the deep stamping of blades with trademarks, mottoes, decorative devices, complex hunting scenes, and political symbols or slogans. Deep-stamped decoration went out of fashion in the 1850s, but poor-quality counterfeits were made a century later, using old stamps and old horn handle scales on newly made blades with solid brass mounts.

1840s and 1850s Bowie Knives

Aside from their decoration, Sheffield bowie knives were forged, ground and finished by hand, as were the American bowies made by cutlers and surgical instrument makers. Beginning in the 1830s, America began to develop a mechanized, factory-based cutlery industry. Mass-production methods were applied to components of table, butcher and industrial knives, and pocketknives.

However, it was not until the Mexican War (1846-1848) and the California Gold Rush (1849-1852) had begun to spur new demand for bowie knives far exceeding any in the past that the young American firms first made any factory bowie knives—or at least any that we know of now. Best known are the 1,000 Ames rifleman's knives made for the Army in 1849. (See "United States Military Fixed Blade Knives" in the "Special Section" of this section.)

A byproduct—and therefore an indicator—of factory mass-production was uniformity. By the late 1840s, the wild variety of the early bowie era was largely past. Shapes had become standardized, options more limited. Some

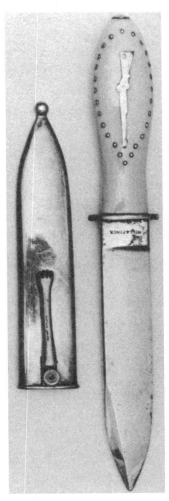

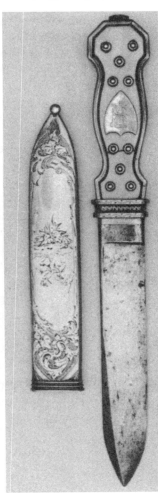

San Francisco Bowie Knives

Left: Will & Finck, walrus-ivory handle, silver studs, gold-rifle handle inlay, nickel-silver sheath. Circa 1871. Value, **$30,000** and up. Plain walrus-ivory handle, value, **$25,000** and up.

Right: Michael Price, hollow, cast-coin-silver handle, ivory panels, gold rivets and shield, engraved silver sheath. Value, **$55,000** and up if excellent, **$20,000** and up as is. (both courtesy Hugh Hayes)

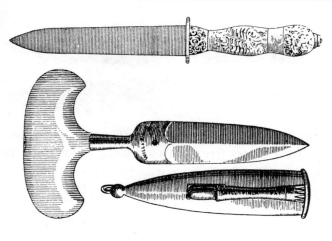

San Francisco Bowie Knives

Top: Will & Finck, nickel-silver handle inlaid with abalone shell. Value, **$25,000** and up with nickel-silver sheath. Bottom: Will & Finck dirk or push dagger, walrus-ivory handle, nickel-silver sheath. Value, **$30,000** and up. (both of the above Will & Fincks are circa 1896; line drawings courtesy California Historical Society)

new bowies were still fancy, a few elegant, but more and more were uniform.

In California, however, demand for fine bowies was so great that a local cutlery industry sprang up in San Francisco to fill it, a tiny workshop industry that, from 1852-1915, created its own rich and distinctive styles. (See Blade Magazine Cutlery Hall-Of-Famer© Bernard Levine's *Knifemakers of Old San Francisco*, 1978; also *Knives '82*.) Fancy San Francisco bowies are now among the most sought after by collectors, commanding prices upward of **$20,000** in excellent condition.

By contrast, the least-appreciated bowie knives today are the smaller American factory-made types, products of Northeastern table cutlery, kitchen knife and edge tool firms from the 1840s-1870s. Values are **$400-3,500**. (See the "American Hunting Knives" segment in this section for additional information about brands and markings.)

Sheffield cutlery firms responded to the California Gold Rush by unleashing a flood of inexpensive bowie knives etched with motifs such as *CALIFORNIA KNIFE, GOOD AS GOLD, GOLD SEEKER'S DEFENDER*, etc. Similar knives

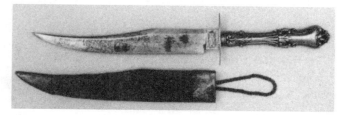

Clip-point bowie marked TILLOTSON/COLUMBIA PLACE/SHEFFIELD. Etched eagle. Nickel-silver "cutlery" handle filled with cutler's cement. Value, **$950** (**$450** as is). (courtesy Bob Macon)

Typical small Sheffield dirk. Value, **$250** (plain) to **$600** (decorated and etched), with sheath.

went along on Australia's 1852-1853 Gold Rush. Despite their low quality, the knives have a value of **$350-1,500** in excellent condition with the etching clear and sharp. (Beware of deeply etched fakes.) Some larger, fine-quality bowie knives also bear Gold Rush legends.

Civil War Bowie Knives

A decade after the Gold Rush, with the start of the Civil War, demand surged again for bowie knives. Bowies had long been popular in the South, and this inspired some Southern politicians, particularly Gov. Joseph E. Brown of Georgia, to order large numbers of massive, locally made bowie knives, many with D-guards, for issue to Confederate troops and home guards. However, it took two hands to maneuver a 10-pound rifled musket, so a big, heavy knife was an encumbrance on the march. Troops in the field usually discarded them.

Most Confederate bowies were blacksmith made and are plain and unmarked—and, therefore, readily counterfeited. Today they are of relatively modest value, usually **$500-1,500**. Nonetheless, high-grade, cutler-made bowies of similar styles can command upward of **$7,500**, substantially more if marked or otherwise attributable.

In Massachusetts, the two leading makers of Federal swords also made small quantities of bowie knives during and after the war. The Ames Mfg. Co. of Chicopee had been in the sword business since 1829. C. Roby & Co. of West Chelmsford had made farm tools for sale in the South until the war broke out, and then had switched to swords. The bowie knives from both firms are distinctly sword like, with brass or bronze mounts and often with fancy, etched blades. They are the only authentic American-made bowies with etched blades, and their freehand etching looks very different from the stencil etching done then in Sheffield.

Note that every knife we have seen with a purported Confederate or Yankee *presentation etching* on the blade has been a modern fake. Authentic 19th-century presentation inscriptions on knives were neatly *engraved* on escutcheons or mounts. For a blade—such as that of a sword—to be presentation etched, it had to be made to order. The oldest, authentic, presentation-etched bowie knife we have seen, with the exception of a fancy dagger by the Ames Mfg. Co., was made for an English customer in Sheffield in June 1923.

Unmarked Georgia-type D-guard bowie, wood handle, steel guard. Value **$450** and up.
(courtesy Blade Magazine Cutlery Hall-Of-Famer© William Adams)

Large clip-point Wostenholm bowie presented
by a Civil War colonel to an Army surgeon.
Mother-of-pearl handles. Value, **$4,500** and up.
(courtesy Bob Macon)

Officers and men on both sides of the Civil War sometimes carried small, lightweight bowie knives or dirks. Most were low-cost Sheffield or American factory knives, as only a man of means could afford to spend anywhere from **$10-$300** for a made-to-order bowie knife from a cutler. In daguerreotype portraits, Civil War soldiers are often portrayed holding bowie knives and pistols, but we suspect that many of the knives and guns were props that belonged to the photographers rather than their subjects.

Decline and Revivals

Soon after the Civil War, bowie knives, along with the percussion pistols that they accompanied, were rendered obsolete as back-up weapons by the center-fire metallic pistol cartridge. The reliable, quick-loading, waterproof ammunition was first made about 1866, but the Colt Single Action Army revolver, introduced in 1873, made the brass cartridge universally accepted. Since an edged weapon was no longer essential to back up one's personal firearms, the bowie knife faded quietly away.

Yet, the bowie's soul has survived. In the 1880s, the knife's soul transmigrated into the mass-produced bowie-style hunting knife beloved of greenhorn outdoorsmen. (See the "American Hunting Knives" segment in this section.) Then, in the 1940s, after two generations in limbo, the bowie's soul was reincarnated in the combat utility knives of World War II. (See the "United States Military Fixed Blade Knives" segment in the "Special Section" of this section.) And now that knives are so popular to collect, the once fearsome bowie has become an art form. (For more about antique bowie knife values, see "Knives as an Investment" in Section I.)

Because of today's astronomical values, the bowie market is awash in counterfeits, some of them now 30 or 40 years old. Most fake bowie knives are of atrocious quality, but even the worst ones can fool experienced collectors who do not pay close attention. An occasional fake is very well done but usually it will have at least one damning clue, so study every knife carefully. The best insurance is to buy only from reputable dealers who stand behind their merchandise. Even then, it pays to have your knife authenticated.

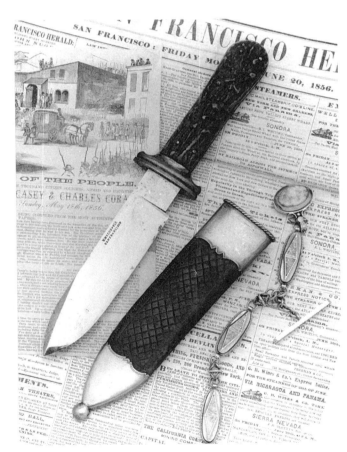

The only known bowie by San Francisco's pioneer cutler, Hugh McConnell, it sold at auction in 1992 for **$60,500**. It is now valued at **$100,000** and up.
(courtesy Butterfield & Butterfield)

This sketch of a J. English & H. & F.A. Huber "Sheffield Works" bowie is from the logo of the Antique Bowie Knife Association (ABKA) and is courtesy of the ABKA. In 1834, English & Huber advertised tools for nearly every trade, along with: "Indian Tomahawks with Pipe and Spear; Indian Knives; Beaver Traps; Bowie Knives; Hunting Knives, Buck handle, $9/doz.; Hunting Knives, Leather Scabbard, Brass mounted, $36/doz.; Hunting Knives, Leather Scabbard, Ebony handle, Silver mounted, $72/doz.; Hunting Knives, Silver Scabbard, $96/doz.; Dirk Knives, Buck, Ivory, and Pearl Handles; Pocket, Pen, and Desk Knives ..." A detailed description of the firm's "Sheffield Works" in the Germantown section of Philadelphia survives from 1840. Value with ebony handle, sheath, **$25,000** and up.

Large "Hunting Knife, round stag handle, Leather Scabbard, Brass mounted," marked H.HUBER/C.STEEL/ PHILAD, made by Henry Huber. Similar blade style to earlier English & Huber knives. Value, **$50,000** and up. Only two are known to exist. (courtesy Bill Claussen)

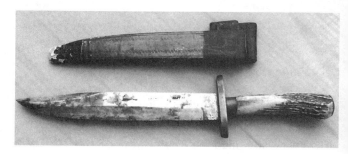

Large, plain, factory-made bowie marked ASHMORE/WARRANTED/CAST STEEL, made in Philadelphia. Stag handle, brass mounts, leather sheath. Value, **$6,000** and up.

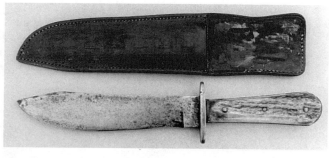

John Todt San Francisco bowie or hunting knife, 8" blade, brass guard, stag; probably from the time of the Alaska Gold Rush, circa 1898. Leather sheath with leather lining. Value, **$4,000** and up. (courtesy Bill Claussen)

Bowie by Roby Mfg. Co., West Chelmsford, Mass. (1867-1875). Ebony grip, patinated bronze mounts, steel guard, fully etched blade (both sides) with engraved details. Value, **$6,000** and up. (courtesy Peter McMickle)

American Knifemakers and Selected American Cutlery Merchants of the Bowie Knife Period

NOTES:

1. Those firms or individuals marked with a "?" are not known to have made or sold bowie knives, or no knives with their marks have been found. For the others, we have seen authentic, marked knives, in some cases accompanied by credible contemporary documentation.
2. Dates are years worked, unless otherwise noted.
3. S.I.M. = Surgical (or dental) instrument maker. A cutler or surgical instrument maker made knives to order or for direct sale. A cutlery manufacturer made knives for wholesale distribution.
4. The larger Sheffield firms had sales offices or agents in the United States, mainly in New York. They are not listed here. (See "19th Century Sheffield Cutlery Firms" in the "Pocketknife History" chapter of Section II; also, the "Pocketknife Brand List" under "Factory Folding Knife Charts, Tables and Histories" in the same section.)
5. Listings are arranged by location, then roughly in chronological order. This is because most American bowie makers worked in distinctive local styles that evolved over time. Any knife inconsistent with the location and time period of the name marked on it should be considered with extreme caution.

Please help to improve this list. If you have a bowie knife, medical instrument, or other cutlery item marked with any name in this list that is preceded by a "?," or if you have an authentic, marked American bowie knife and the name is not on this list, please send a photo of the piece, along with a close-up or careful copy of the mark, to *BLADE's Guide*, 700 E. State St., Iola, WI 54990.

THE SOUTH (Information from James L. Batson, Cecil Anderson, Jim Blackburn, and Blade Magazine Cutlery Hall-Of-Famer© William Adams.)

ALABAMA

James Conning, Mobile, 1840-1871; Importer (Dealer) and Sword Mfr.

Calvin Key, Lauderdale County, 1848-1866 (came from Tennessee, went to Hood County, Texas); Gunsmith and cutler, worked with Asa Richardson

Asa Richardson, Tuscumbia, c1840-1880; Gunsmith and cutler

Louis Crenshaw, Hope Hull (Montgomery), c1861; Blacksmith and cutler

T.L. Pruett, Prattville, c1861

Alexander McKinstry, Mobile, c1861; Dealer

ARKANSAS

? James Black, Washington, c1826-1839; blacksmith (born New Jersey 1800, may have been a silver-plater's apprentice in Philadelphia 1808-1818, claimed to have made a knife for James Bowie c1833, died Washington, Arkansas 1872).

GEORGIA

William J. McElroy, Macon, c1846-1888; Tinsmith

Charles Heinz, Atlanta (from Columbia, South Carolina), 1855-1905; Gunsmith, Cutler

Daniel C. Hodgkins & Son(s), Macon, c1860s; Cutlers & S.I.M.s

Etowah Iron Works (Mark A. Cooper), Etowah, c1860s

Bell & Davis, Atlanta, c1861

LOUISIANA

? Jesse Clifft, Marksville, Avoyelles Parish, Louisiana, c1823-1830 (then to Texas); Blacksmith (born Pittsylvania County, Virginia 1800). A neighbor of the Bowies, reportedly made at least one knife for Rezin Bowie.

Daniel Searles, Baton Rouge, c1828-1860; Gunsmith, Cutler, Engraver (born 1782 Anne Arundel County, Maryland; to Ohio 1804; to Cincinnati and first offered "swords, dirks" 1806; to Indiana 1809; to Louisiana 1817; to Baton Rouge 1828; suicide there 1860). Appears to have made at least one knife for Rezin Bowie.

Rees Fitzpatrick, Baton Rouge, c1833-1839 (then to Natchez, Mississippi); Gunsmith & cutler (born Ohio 1808; died Natchez 1868)

? Thomas A. Potts, New Orleans, c1838; Cutler?

F.C. Goergen, New Orleans, died 1849; Importer (dealer)

Alfred H. Dufilho, Sr., New Orleans, 1853-c1878; Cutler & S.I.M. (Born Paris, France, 1833; died 1907)

(J.P.) Lasserre, New Orleans, c1860; Cutler?

Cook & Bros., New Orleans, c1860

MISSISSIPPI

Rees Fitzpatrick, Natchez, 1838-1867 (from Baton Rouge, Louisiana); Gunsmith & cutler

G.W. Stalans, Jonesboro, c1861

SOUTH CAROLINA

Charles Heinz, Columbia, 1841-c1855 (then to Atlanta); Gunsmith (born Germany 1824; died Georgia 1906)

Henry Reinhardt, Charleston, c1852; S.I.M.

Courtney, Tennent & Co., Charleston, c1856-1864; Importer (dealer)

John Holmes, Charleston, c1840; Gunsmith (dealer?)

TENNESSEE

Samuel Bell, Knoxville, 1819-1852 (then to San Antonio, Texas); Silversmith, cutler, importer, mayor (born 1798; died Texas 1882). Knives stamped BELL/ KNOXVILLE, probably made for him in Sheffield.

R. Alldeon, Memphis, c1860; Cutler

Leech & Rigdon, Memphis Novelty Works, Memphis, 1860s (during the Civil War moved to Columbus, Mississippi, Greensboro and Augusta, Georgia); Mfr.?

Gitter & Moss, Memphis, 1860s

Schneider & Glossich, Memphis, 1860s

VIRGINIA

? Hiram Peabody, Richmond, c1850s-1860s; Dealer

Burger & Bros., Richmond, c1860s; Sawmakers, cutlers

Lan & Sherman, Richmond, c1861; Cutlers

? Boyle, Gamble & MacFee, c1861; Sword mfrs.

? Clarkson & Co., Richmond, c1861; Dealers?

THE MIDDLE ATLANTIC STATES

DISTRICT OF COLUMBIA

Thomas Lamb, Washington City, c1840; Cutler & S.I.M.

MARYLAND

Baltimore makers and dealers

? Samuel Ball, c1796-c1830; Cutler

Samuel Jackson, c1833-c1870; Cutler & S.I.M.

? Benjamin Daffin, c1835-?; Cutler (dealer?)

Charles C. Reinhardt, c1837-1869; Cutler & S.I.M.

Frederick Kesmodel, c1850s; to San Francisco c1856; returned to Baltimore c1872; Cutler & S.I.M. (firm called M. Kesmodel in the 1940s)

NEW JERSEY [Information from *Early Tools of New Jersey and the Men Who Made Them* by Alexander Farnham, 1984.]

Newark makers and dealers

Rochus Heinisch, 1825-1914; Scissors Mfr. (bowies 1860s)

? Alfred B. Seymour, ????-1838; Cutler and tool mfr.

Alfred Hunter, c1835-1865 (from New York City); Cutlery mfr.

H. Boker & Co.; Importer (see New York City makers and dealers)

? Aaron Crawford, c1838-1880; Cutler & Tool Mfr.

? Joseph English, (from Philadelphia), c1842-1856; Cutler & Tool Mfr., succeeded by:

? William Dodd, 1856-c1861 (to New York City); Cutler & Tool Mfr., succeeded by:

? Charles S. Osborne & Co., c1861-1905 (since 1905 has been in Harrison); Cutler & Tool Mfr. (Osborne lived 1818-1896)

? Henry Sauerbier, c1848-1887; Cutler & Swordsmith

? John Garside, c1850; Table Cutlery Mfr.

? Furness & Bannister, c1860?; Table Cutlery Mfr.

? Charles Ranke, c1860?; S.I.M.

Outside Newark

? Henry Seymour, Elizabeth, c1860-??.; Scissors Mfr.

? Thomas Johnson, Little Falls, c1860?; Cutler

? J. Nicol, Orange, c1860?; Cutler

? Beverly Cutlery Works, Beverly, c1860?; Cutlery Mfr.

NEW YORK

New York City makers and dealers

(Note: This list excludes most of the cutlery importers, wholesalers, manufacturers' agents and retailers in mid-nineteenth-century New York City, some of whom likely sold bowie knives marked with their own names. (Many of the firms are included in the "Pocketknife Brand List" segment of Part I, and "Factory Folding Knife Charts, Tables and Histories" in Section II.) In addition to the cutlers and S.I.M.s who were active for a span of years prior to about 1870, many others worked briefly in New York City and elsewhere in the state. (Information from Mark Indursky.)]

? William Fosbrook, c1787-1819; Cutler & S.I.M. (Wm. Fosbrook & George B. Smith, c1794; Hdw. Retail)

? George B. Smith, c1801-1805; S.I.M.

? James Anderson, c1796-1801; Cutler & S.I.M.

? William Pintard, c1810-1850; Cutler & S.I.M. (from Philadelphia)

? Carl Klauberg, c1819-1940; Cutlery Mfr. & Importer

? Rose & Sellers, c1823-1828; Cutlers, became:

Peter Rose, 1828-1845; Cutler & S.I.M.

George Tiemann & Co., 1826-pres.; Cutler & S.I.M. (George Tiemann born USA 1795; died 1868)

? Frederick S. Liese, c1829-1862; Turner & S.I.M.

Graveley & Wreaks, c1830-1837; Cutlery importer (dealer)

Alfred Hunter, c1830-1835; Cutler, then to Newark, New Jersey

Wolfe & Clarke, c1830s; Cutlers?

John C. Nixon & Son, c1830s-1864; Cutlers, became:

George W. Nixon, 1864-c1870s; Cutler

? William O. Starr, c1834-1858; S.I.M., became:

? W.O. & W.S. Starr, 1858-??; Guns

John D. Chevalier, c1835-1859; Cutler & Dental I.M.; became:

John D. Chevalier & Sons, 1859-1866

William R. Goulding, c1837-1853; S.I.M., became:

? W.R. Goulding & Thaddeus H. Walsh, 1854, became:

? W.R. Goulding Jr. & William F. Ford, 1855-1857, became:

? George Wade & W.F. Ford, 1857-1866, became:

? William F. Ford & Co., 1866-19??; S.I.M. represented by Shepard & Dudley c1870-1894

Hermann Boker & Co., 1837-pres. (see "19th Century American Pocketknife Firms" segment of the chapter, "Pocketknife History," in Section II for details) (to Newark, New Jersey, c1840, but retained New York City office); Cutlery Importers

? A.R. Moen, c1842-1851; Cutler

? William E. Rose, c1842-1852; Cutler & S.I.M.

? Christian F. Oberlander, c1842-1860s; Cutlery Mfr.

? Herman Hernstein, c1843-1867; S.I.M., became:

? Albert L. Hernstein, c1867-1896

? George Saphar, c1844-1857; Cutler

? Joseph Henley, c1847-1851; Cutler and

? James Dempster, c1849-1851, 1855; S.I.M. became:

? Dempster & Henley, c1851-1855; Cutler & S.I.M.

August Eickhoff, c1848-c1900; Cutler

Ibbotson & Horner, c1848; Cutlery Mfrs. (New York office?)

? Charles E. Morson, 1848-55; S.I.M.

? Amedee Alviset c1848-1860s; Cutler (retail?)

? Frederick Moeller & A. Kammerer, c1850; Cutlers & S.I.M.

? George Clark, c1850-1857; Cutler

? Louis Kroeber, c1850-1860s; Cutler

? John Vincent, c1850-1857; Cutler

? A.& J. Saunders, c1850-1857; Cutlers

? Augustus Voillard, c1850-1860s; Cutler

? Frederick G. Wheeler, c1850-1859; Cutlery Mfr.

? Henry Zindel, c1850-1860s; Cutler

John Waite, c1851; Cutler

? Louis Drescher, c1851-1853; S.I.M.

? Peter W. Bain & V.W. Brinckerhoff, c1851-1855, S.I.M., became:

? V.W. Brinckerhoff, 1855-1862, S.I.M; 1862-1868, Retail

? Thomas Heokler, c1853; S.I.M.

? S.C. Herschfeld, c1853; S.I.M.

? C. Kruger & Co., c1853; S.I.M.

? Ferdinand Wiese, c1853-1885; Cutler

? Otto Corsepius, c1853-1857; S.I.M.

Ferdinand G. Otto & Augustus Koehler, c1853-1860; Cutlers & S.I.M., became:

? F.G. Otto & John Reynders, 1860-1875; S.I.M.

? John D. Erbig, c1855-1857; Cutler

? Louis Glanz, c1855-1860s; Cutler & S.I.M.

? Huntley & Fargis, c1855-1858; Cutlers

? John Herdfelder, c1855-1859; Cutler

? Frederick Jetter, c1855-1858; Cutler [may have become

? Jetter & Scheerer, active c1890s]

? Samuel Ruchty, c1855-1858; Cutlery Mfr.

? Claude F. Vuargnoz, c1855-57; Cutler

Baldwin, Hill & Co., c1857-??; Wholesale (dealers)

? Edward Bajot (& John T. Knapp), c1858-1869; Dental I.M.

? Eschmann, Beckett & Co., c1859-1868; S.I. Import

? Philip Schmidt, 1862-1878; S.I.M., became:

? P.H. Schmidt & Son, 1878-??

? William Dodd, c1863-1876 (from Newark, New Jersey); Cutler

Tiffany & Co.; Fancy Goods retail, 1837-present (& Silver Mfr. after 1868).

(Note: Tiffany sold a few ornate, silver-mounted presentation swords and knives. Every plain knife we have seen marked "Tiffany" was a fake.)

Outside New York City

? R.P. Lathrop, Albany; 1832-??, S.I.M., succeeded by:

? James Martin, Albany; ????-c1880, S.I.M.

? Herman Spangenberg & Elias Y. Hawley, Albany, c1860; S.I.M.s

? R.D. Buffham, Rochester, c1851; Cutler

? Henry Clifton, Rochester, c1840s-1860s; Cutler

? John Crane, Rochester, c1851; Cutler

? J. Kedzie & Co, Rochester, c1851; Cutlers

? Sanborn & Stratton, Rochester, c1851; Cutlers

? John Denman, Rochester, c1859; Cutler

? Bushnell, Rochester, c1860s; S.I.M. [made custom pocket axe for "Nessmuk" (George W. Sears) author of *Woodcraft*]

? George Shepard, Utica, c1851; Cutler

? J. Pearson, Syracuse, c1851; Cutler

? Jacob Mantl, Syracuse, c1859; Cutler

? N. Moershfelder, Buffalo, c1859; Cutler

? John C. Sieffert, Buffalo, c1859; S.I.M.

? J. Sigwald, Buffalo, c1859; Cutler

? F.&C. Gram, Buffalo, c1859; Cutlers

? James Howgate, Poughkeepsie, c1859; Cutler

? C. Clifton, Troy, c1859; Cutler

PENNSYLVANIA

Philadelphia makers and dealers

Schively family, 17??-c1875; Cutlers & S.I.M.s

(John Schively died c1790)

(Henry Schively, Sr., active 17??-c1813)

Henry Schively, Jr., active c1810-1849. Appears to have made at least one knife for Rezin Bowie.

? George and Charles Schively, active c1847-c1875

? William Pintard, c1801; Cutler & S.I.M., then to New York

Stevens, circa 1820s; Cutler.

? Charles Naylor, c17??; Cutler

? William Rose, 1798-1880s; Saddler Knife, Sword, and Tool Mfr. (since 1880s has been in Sharon Hill)

? Henry (Jr.) & Frederick A. Huber, ????-1826; Saddlery Hardware Mfr. and Importer, became:

Joseph English & H.&F.A. Huber "Sheffield Works," 1826-c1837; Cutlery and Hardware Mfr. & Importer, became (after J. English left for Newark, New Jersey):

? H.&F.A. Huber, c1837-c1842; Mfr. and Importer, became (after death of Frederick A. Huber):

H. Huber, c1842-??; Cutlery Mfr.

John Ashmore, c1832-c1850; Cutler & Mfr., became:

? Mary (Mrs. John) Ashmore, c1850-1858; Cutler & Mfr.

Clarenbach & Herder, 1847-1871; Cutlery Mfr., became:

? L. Herder & Son, 1871-1879; Mfr. & Retail, became:

? Charles Herder, 1879-??; Mfr. & Retail (later became Herder's)

J. J. Teufel & Bro., c1860s?; Cutlers & S.I.M.s

? Snowden, c1860s?; S.I.M.

Outside Philadelphia

James Bown & John Tetley, Enterprise Gun Works, Pittsburgh, c1848-1862; Gunsmiths, Cutlers, became:

James Bown (1862-1871), became:

James Bown & Son (1871-?)

NEW ENGLAND

CONNECTICUT

Collins & Co., Hartford (Collinsville), 1826-1966; Axe and Machete Mfr.

? Thomas Rawling & William Jepson, New Haven, c1831-1864; Cutlers and File Makers

Leverett Belknap, Hartford, c1840-1852; Gunsmith and cutler

? Lyman Bradley (& Co.), Salem/Naugatuck, 1841-c1851; Cutlery Mfr., became:

? Lyman Bradley & Co., Middlebury, c1851-1896; Wholesale [Note: We saw a counterfeit Bradley with a stainless guard.]

? Pratt Ropes (Webb) & Co., Meriden, 1845-1855; Table Cutlery Mfr. became:

? Meriden Cutlery Co., 1855

New England Cutlery Co., Wallingford, c1850s-1860s; Cutlery Mfr.

George Stewart, Norwich, c1850s-1860s; Gunsmith & Cutler

? Alexander Haugh, New Haven, c1856-1864; Cutler [also Haugh & (John) Kay; Haugh & Frisbie; Haugh & Riggs]

? Ebenezer Dewitt Riggs, New Haven, c1864-1874; Cutler

H. Wilkinson, Hartford, c1860s; Cutler (Dealer?)

? Rice Lathrop & Clary, later Lathrop & Barton, West Winsted, 1850s-1880; Cutlery Mfr.

Charles E. Billings, Hartford, c1868; patent bowie pistol.

MAINE

James M. Abbott, Oxford, c1860; Cutler?

MASSACHUSETTS

? Samuel Bradlee, Boston, 1799-1845; Cutler (Dealer); became:

Martin L. Bradford (& Son), Boston, 1845-1856; Retail; became:

? Bradford & Anthony, Boston, 1856-1883; Retail; became:

? Dame Stoddard & Kendall, Boston, 1883-c1932 (now Stoddard's); Retail

Henry Harrington, Southbridge, 1818-1876; Cutler, became:

? Dexter Harrington & Son, 1876-1933; Mfr., became:

? Russell-Harrington Cutlery Co., now part of Hyde Tool

Ames Mfg. Co., Chicopee and Cabotville, c1829-1900; Sword & Cutlery Mfr. (see "United States Military Knives" in the "Special Section" of this section)

Ward M. Cotton, Leominster, c1829-1875; Machinery Mfr. (knives c1860s)

John Russell & Co., Greenfield, 1834-1870; Turners Falls, 1870-1933; Table and Kitchen Cutlery Mfr. (merged 1933 with D. Harrington in Southbridge.)

Zeitz & Co., Boston, c1830s-1850s; Cutler & S.I.M.(?)

? John Ames, Sharon, 1835-1857; Butcher Knife Mfr.; became:

? H. Augustus Lothrop, Massapoag Works, Sharon, 1857-1900; Butcher Knife Mfr.

? Codman & Shurtleff, Boston, (1838) 1855-pres., S.I.M.

Nathaniel Hunt, Boston, c1840-1853; Cutler, succeeded by:

Frederick F. Hassam, Boston, c1853-1856; Cutler (Dealer?); became:

Kingman & Hassam, Boston, 1856-1860; Cutlers (Dealers?); became:

Hassam Brothers (Frederick F. & Roswell H.), 1860-1866; Cutlers; succeeded by:

? D.C. Bates & Co.

Lamson & Co., S. Falls Works, Shelburne Falls, 1842-1844; Cutlery Mfr.; became:

Lamson & Goodnow, S. Falls Works, Shelburne Falls, 1844-present; Table and Kitchen Cutlery Mfr.

? South River Cutlery Co., Conway, c1851-1856; Table Cutlery Mfr.

Buck Brothers, Worcester, 1853-1864; Millbury, 1864-19??; Edge Tool Mfrs.

? Christopher Roby & George Stark, West Chelmsford, 1853-1858, Agricultural Implements, became:

? C. Roby & Co., 1858-1861, Agric. Implements, became:

C. Roby & Co., 1861-1867, Sword Mfr., became:

Roby Mfg. Co., 1867-1875, Sword Mfr. (Note: Fake Roby bowies have cast brass mounts, while the genuine examples have steel guards and patinated bronze fittings.)

Steven Taft, Millbury, c1860s; Edge Tool Maker

George M. Thompson, R.P. (Rockport?), Essex County, c1860s; Blacksmith and cutler

? John and Robert Murphy, Boston, Mansfield, Ayer, 1850-pres.; Industrial Knife Mfr.

? Stephen Richard Co., Southbridge, c1862-1908; Cutlery Mfr.

Fritz Franz, Boston, ????-1901; Cutlery Mfr., became:

? Fritz Franz & Co., Boston, 1901-1905, became:

? Fritz Franz & Son, Boston, 1905-1915

RHODE ISLAND

John M. Schmid, Providence, 1857-1871; Cutler & S.I.M.

? J.M. Schmid & Son (Albert), Providence, 1871-1964; Cutlery Dealers

? Charles A. Ruff, Providence, c1860s; S.I.M.

VERMONT

Amos Belknap, St. Johnsbury, 1839-1883; Blacksmith, cutler

John Belknap, St. Johnsbury, c1860; Cutler

Silas Walker, Bennington, c1862; Cutler?

THE MIDWEST

MISSOURI

St. Louis makers and dealers

? August Kern, c1850s, Cutler

? Jacob Blattner, c1840s-1860s; S.I.M.

? Peter Huffschmitt, c1859; Cutler

? A.M. Leslie, c1859; S.I.M.

? George Leyser, c1859; Cutler

? Frederick Mack, c1859; Cutler

? August Trumper, c1859; Cutler & S.I.M.

? Ph. Werber, c1860; S.I.M.

Outside St. Louis

? Sam. Dresser, Pleasant Mt., c1840s-1870; Gunmaker and Cutler, succeeded by:

? Sam. Dresser Jr., c1860-1910

OHIO

Cincinnati cutlers and surgical instrument makers

(Daniel Searles, 1806-1809; Gunsmith and cutler, advertised swords and dirks; thence to Indiana & Louisiana)

Marks & Rees, c1833-1839; Cutlers & S.I.M.s, became:

? William Z. Rees, 1839-c1860s; S.I.M.

Rudolph Hug, c1853-1882; S.I.M.

? Joseph Billet, c1859; Cutler

? M. Dolph, c1859; S.I.M.

? John Luther, c1859; Cutler

? L. Schreiber, c1859; Cutler

? H.R. Sherwood, c1859; S.I.M.

? Sprenger & Emrich, c1859; Cutlers, became:

Phil. Emrich, c1860s; Cutler

? Louis & Max Wocher, c1859; S.I.M.s

? F.A. Zimmer, c1859; Cutler

Outside Cincinnati

Andrew G. Hicks, Cleveland, c1846; Cutler (see "United States Military Knives" in the "Special Section" of this section)

THE WEST

CALIFORNIA

San Francisco makers and dealers

? Justinian Caire, 1851-1897; Importer (Dealer)

Hugh McConnell, 1852-1863; Cutler & S.I.M., became:

Frederick Will & Julius Finck, 1863-1905 (-1932); Cutlers, Locksmiths, & S.I.M.s (Dealers after 1905) (F. Will, S.I.M., from Albany, New York; retired 1883)

? Henry Bayley, 1852-1858; S.I.M. (from England)

John W. Tucker, c1854; Jeweler (Dealer)

Frederick Kesmodel, c1856-1867; Cutler & S.I.M. (also worked in Baltimore); sold out to Will & Finck

Michael Price, c1856-1889; Cutler & S.I.M. (from Limerick, Ireland)

Jacob H. Schintz, c1860-1906; Cutler & S.I.M.; foreman for M. Price 1869-1874 (from Switzerland)

Michael J. Hayes (& Son), 1887-1901; Cutlers; foreman for M. Price 1874-1887 (from Limerick, Ireland)

Frederick O. Hartenstein & Co., 1869-1876; Cutlers

Adolph Rau & John Kohnke, 1871-1875; Cutlers, became:

Adolph Rau & John Todt, 1875-1880; Cutlers, became:

John Todt, 1880-1915; Cutler, succeeded by:

? George J. Zett, Cutler

? Bauer Brothers (John and Louis), 1872-1887; Cutlers & Tool Makers

Nathan Joseph & Co., 1875-1894; Importer (Dealer)

Outside San Francisco

? "Uncle Billy" Allison, Yolo County, c1850s; Cutler

Horace Hall Rowell, Sawmill Flat, c1857-1875 (then to Sonora); blacksmith, gunsmith

? Frank Schilling (& Son), San Jose, 1862-1980s; Gunsmith, Cutler & S.I.M.

Fred Watson, Colusa, c1890; Cutler?

TEXAS

Samuel Bell, San Antonio, c1852-1882; Silversmith, Cutler (came from Knoxville, Tennessee)

UTAH TERRITORY

? William Walker, Salt Lake City, c1851; Cutler

American Indian Trade Knives

Contemporary collectors have a passion for everything to do with American Indians. They seek Indian-made knives of all types, both old and new, as well as manufactured knives that were traded to Indians in the past.

Prior to European contact, Indians shaped knife blades and projectile points from bones or sharp stones, such as flint or obsidian. The stones were found only in certain areas, so both finished blades and the raw material for making them had been items of trade among Indian tribes centuries before Europeans arrived. Stone knives are a specialized field unto themselves. This chapter is limited to steel-bladed trade knives.

Steel Knives Used by Indians

From the time of their first contact with European explorers, traders and settlers, American Indians were eager to acquire knives with steel blades. Steel blades are not any sharper than stone, but they are much more durable. Indians received knives as gifts during trade or treaty negotiations. They exchanged pelts for knives from fur traders. When the opportunity arose, most Indians saw nothing wrong in stealing knives and other goods from the settlers who were expropriating their lands and resources.

Indians used any steel knives they could obtain. From Indian sites archaeologists have excavated all sorts of cutlery items, most of them imported from Europe. Some of the items had been adapted to other than their original uses, such as dinner knives and broken swords made into sheath knives, razors and pen knives converted to woodcarving knives, and ink erasers used as arrow points.

Though Indians used all types of blades, distinctive styles of knives were made especially for trade to them. Trade knife designs were based in part on the Indians' practical needs, their aesthetic preferences, and on minimizing the cost of the knives to the trading companies.

Sheffield-made Cartouche Knives
About 5" to 7" blade. Applied bolsters, probably wrought iron. Handles bone (top), wood (bottom) or silverplated. From *Joseph Smith's Explanation or Key, to the Various Manufactories of Sheffield, 1816.*
Value, **$50**. (courtesy EAIA)

Over the years, favored shapes, styles and brands evolved gradually, reflecting both the changes in European cutlery technology and the steady move westward of the fur trade. A few particular styles were favored in particular regions. Until recent times, some of the same or similar knife styles also were traded to aboriginal people in other parts of the world.

Cartouche Knives

A common sort of knife found in excavated Indian sites, especially from the first half of the nineteenth century, is essentially a pointed dinner knife. In circa-1820s Hudson's Bay Co. records, examples of the type are called "cartouche knives." They were traded to the Indians in large numbers but not merely for dining. We do not know the source of the name.

Most cartouche knives had pointed blades, but dubbed (round-end) and sheepfoot (straight-edged) types have been excavated from Indian sites, too. Examples in the Hudson Bay Co. collection have either forged or applied bolsters. They have pinned, two-piece handles, narrower than scalper or butcher knife handles (see following), though some excavated cartouche knives have one-piece handles affixed to rat-tail tangs.

Scalper, Dag, and Butcher Knife

Artists who traveled through the wilds of North America in the nineteenth century made hundreds of drawings and paintings of Indians in every part of the continent. Their artwork shows how Indians carried knives, most often in a deep sheath worn at the side or at the small of the back. However, the pictures show few details of the knives themselves, the artists being more interested in the faces of their subjects or their elaborate attire. For example, the many knives in George Catlin's drawings, done in the 1830s and 1860s, all look just about the same.

A few of the artists, most notably Rudolph F. Kurz in the 1850s, paid close attention to every detail, including the knives. Kurz collected Indian artifacts and studied them before drawing them. He traded knives to Indians for their art and handiwork. Kurz noted that women wore their knives at the back all the time, while men only did so when traveling. The few violent men who carried dags ordinarily wore them tied to the wrist, concealed under the blanket, with the blade lying flat along the forearm.

Most of the knives that Catlin and Kurz depicted were a type that archaeologists commonly find in Western Indian sites. The pattern was called the "scalper." The scalper is a medium-sized knife, usually about 12 inches long overall, with a 7-inch blade about 1/16-inch thick. The lightweight blade has a curved cutting edge, a straight or slightly up-

Indian artist's depiction of scalping.

curved back, and a keen point—similar to the blade of a 1950s household slicing knife. The tang is short and the dark-red wooden handle, in a diamond cross section, is secured by three rivets, the latter usually made of steel wire.

Unlike the double-edged dag, which was rarely carried and was strictly a weapon, the scalper was common. It was used for every type of cutting chore by both men and women. Around 1850 the trade price of a scalper in the Missouri basin was about $1.50, or two knives for one finished buffalo robe. The price fell to $1 around 1855.

The ledger of a Montana fur-trading fort from the 1850s includes many references to "knife," "scalper" and "butcher knife." There are a few references to "pocket knife," "knives & forks" and "scissors."

The stouter clip-point "butcher knife" cost up to twice as much as the scalper, and lacks the keen point so useful for delicate work. We assume that this explains why butcher knives were much less commonly traded.

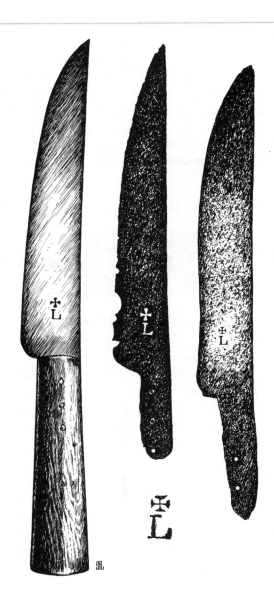

Rablia[?], meat hunter at Fort Union and one of 300 half-breed children of the fort's founder, Kenneth McKenzie, is depicted holding a dag. (painted circa 1858 by William Cary)

Sheffield Trade Scalpers

About 7" (not including tang) flat-ground, lightweight, single-edged steel blades. Examples shown marked with the Maltese cross over the letter "L," the mark used on trade blades that apparently belonged to Lockwood Bros. of Sheffield. (drawings by Steve Allely) Mint example (left) is unsold stock of the Hudson's Bay Co. Plain, dark-red wooden handle of diamond cross section affixed by three steel rivets. We have not seen an authentic unused example like this for sale, though its value would exceed **$3,000**.

(courtesy Hudson's Bay Co. and Lower Fort Garry National Historic Site, Selkirk, Manitoba)

Relic blade (center) is one of several excavated at the site of a North West Co. trading post near Pine City, Minnesota. The post was active circa 1804-1810.

Relic blade (right) was found atop a butte above the Quinn River in Humboldt County, Nevada. The area was visited by traders as early as 1828. However, it is likely that both sites subsequently were used by Indians.

Value as is, **$250** each.

The predecessor of the dag was called the "bayonet." Lighter and more acutely pointed than the dag, the bayonet blade was widely traded c1750s-1820s, possibly later. Since Indians used the bayonet as a lance or war-club blade, it was usually traded unhandled. Also traded without handles were most crooked knife blades used in woodworking. The Indians carved their own handles for the blades. Iron arrow points were also traded unmounted.

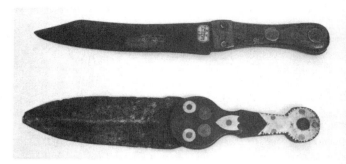

Sheffield Trade Chopping(?) Knife

(Top) About 13" overall. Heavy clip blade. Horn or wood handles. Brass or iron rivets and pinned-on bolsters. Example shown marked JUKES COULSON STOKES & CO./SHEFFIELD (a firm of factors that specialized in trade goods). Mid-19th century. Blade heavily worn. Value as is, **$2,500**. (courtesy Smithsonian Institution) This style knife, except without bolsters, was made into the 1960s by S. & J. Kitchin, Ltd. Value, **$300**.

Sheffield Trade Dag with Factory Grip.

(Bottom) *Dague* (pronounced "dag") is French for "short, wide dagger." About 13" overall. Wide, lightweight, double-edged steel blade. Flat horn handles with inlaid brass decorations. Example shown stamped in relief inside a dentate (toothed) border: I. SORBY (John Sorby, who was Master of the Sheffield Cutlers' Guild in 1806; marking used circa 1780-1827). Value, **$5,000**. (courtesy Smithsonian Institution)

Sheffield Trade Dag Blade (or "Bayonet")

About 6" (not including tang), flat-ground, double-edged steel blade. Two notches allow it to be inlaid into handle scales or lashed to a pole, as in lances or Confederate guard spontoons. Example shown marked JUKES COULSON/STOKES & CO. Early nineteenth century. Value, **$3,000**. (courtesy Donald Euing)

1851 Drawing by Rudolph F. Kurz showing a Plains Indian warrior's mode of wearing a trade scalper in the small of his back while traveling.

Imported Trade Dag Blade with Custom Grip

Trade knives were not used by Indians only. The blade of this example, similar to the one above, is marked BAL.../NEW Y... Carved maple grip with one copper rivet, four brass rivets, and two screws securing brass mounts. Mounts stamped E. RICKETTS (possibly the Evan Ricketts who was listed in St. Louis in 1858). Confiscated as evidence by Frank Beller, deputy sheriff (1887-1891 and 1895-1900) of Park County, Montana. Value, **$1,000**. (courtesy George Stahl)

Sheffield Trade Dag with Factory Grip.
This outstanding example of a Sheffield trade dag is marked in relief inside a dentate border:
I. & H. SORBY (John Sorby and his son Henry. Marking used after 1827; Sorby and its trademarks sold to Lockwood Bros., 1850). It has horn handles with brass inlays in the form of stylized pelts. Value, **$6,500**.
(courtesy Museum of the Fur Trade, Chadron, Nebraska)

Imported Trade Dag with Factory Grip.
8 1/2", convex-ground, double-edged steel blade marked BALDWIN HILL & CO./NEW YORK CAST STEEL. Factory handles are flat, reddish-brown wood panels secured by six brass rivets and decorated with a burned-in picture of an Indian firing a trade gun over a stump. Note that the disc-shaped pommel is smaller than on English factory dags. Imported by Baldwin, Hill & Co., a New York City wholesaler listed in 1857 only. Probably made in Germany. Value, **$3,500**. (Blade Magazine Cutlery Hall-Of-Famer® J. Bruce Voyles photo, courtesy Donald Euing and Hall-Of-Famer William Adams)

Brands and Makers

A blade stamping on many scalpers found in Western Indian sites is a Maltese cross over the letter "L." The mark has baffled and misled archaeologists for years, because a single fancy table knife with plated brass mounts found in an eighteenth-century Eastern site bears a similar mark. Recent research in Sheffield trademarks should clear up the confusion. The one table knife is unrelated to the later scalpers. It was made by Thomas Law of Norfolk Street, Sheffield, a mid-to-late eighteenth-century "Plate Worker" and maker of "Silver and Plated Table Knives."

However, by the early nineteenth century, the Maltese-cross-over-L mark belonged to Lockwood Bros. (founded in 1767, moved to Sheffield from Ecclesfield in 1798). Lockwood made tools and also sold cutlery. In 1850, Lockwood took over John & Henry Sorby of Spital Hill (founded 1780), makers of tools and Indian trade knives. About 1919, Lockwood became part of Joseph Elliot & Sons, who still listed the Maltese cross/L mark in 1952. The Maltese cross/L-marked scalpers were made for the trade by Lockwood Bros.

A similar-looking mark belonged to a Hiram Cutler in the 1850s, and then to Joseph Rodgers & Sons after that. We do not know who—if anyone—used the mark earlier. We have seen relic scalper blades marked **G** (crown) **R** or **W** (crown) **R/FURNISS & Co**. Apparently, they were made by a member of the Furniss family (also spelled Furness) in Sheffield, or in nearby Stannington, prior to about 1840.

In 1803, on their transcontinental trek, Lewis and Clark had brought along dozens of John Wilson knives made in Sheffield, handing them out as presents and in trade, as well as using some themselves. We do not know what patterns the knives were. Evidently, both Indians and settlers considered **I. WILSON** to be a premium brand. Wilson butcher knives were made until about 1970, when thousands of unused examples were dumped on the collector market. The mark "HUDSON BAY Co." on some of the later knives is spurious.

American-made butcher knives, such as by J. Russell & Co. and Lamson & Goodnow, were first mass-produced in the 1840s, but were even more expensive than the Wilsons. We suspect that their high cost explains why it appears that they were not used in the fur trade in the 1840s or 1850s. However, American knives did supplant, or at least supplement, the trade knives imported from England and Germany into the Missouri basin during the latter part of the Civil War. See the following segment, "American Hunting Knives," for more about them.

Recognizing Fakes

Practically all areas of knife collecting are subject to fakery, but none more so than Indian knives. A majority of purported Indian knives, whether stone or steel bladed, are fakes of one sort or another.

As a collector of Indian trade knives, you have no sure way to protect yourself from the artful faker. However, the more you know about the history of knife design and manufacturing technology, the less likely you are to be fooled. You may never be certain if a particular knife was ever traded to or used by an Indian, but you can learn to judge when and where just about any knife was made.

You must learn to distinguish the tapered tang of a forged blade from the parallel-sided tang of a blade blanked from sheet steel, a technique first used on low-cost knives about 1870 (though roll-forging of blade blanks dates back to 1805, and some blades are still forged today). You must learn to distinguish the color and texture of old shear steel and crucible cast steel from those of more modern steels (though cast steel was made until 1968).

Portrait Sketches by George Catlin
(Top right) Clermont, head chief of the Osage. His war club is fitted with a trade "bayonet" or dag blade (1834).
(Above) Mahtahptaha—roughly translated, "he who rushes through the middle"—a young Mandan warrior. He wears his scalper in a sheath thrust under his belt (1832).
(Bottom right) Stanaupat—roughly translated, "the bloody hand"—head chief of the Riccarree (Arikara), holds his scalper. His robe is fringed with scalp locks (1832).

You must learn where and how various types of blades were marked so you can recognize phony markings and blades that have been reshaped. The common form of fakery is often revealed by a mark being too close to the point or edge, or by the edge being steeply beveled. You must learn to distinguish deep-etched marks, first used in the 1880s, from stamped marks, especially dentate-border-relief stamps that were last used in the 1830s (though simple stamped marks are still used on some knives today).

You must learn which handle and mount materials were used in particular times and places, and which were not. You must learn how handles and mounts were fabricated and attached. You must learn that even the most inexpensive trade knife was neatly ground and finished, not crude and "primitive." Indians invested days of labor—mainly the women—in new trade knives, and they expected them to look good.

Closely examine as many old knives of all types as you can. Once you have become familiar with old butcher knives and cleavers, you will be able to spot the ones that have been "converted" to look like scalpers and trade choppers. Read and re-read "Bowie Knives and Kitchen and Butcher Knives" in this section, and "Some Clues That Help Date and Identify Knives" in Section I. The information may seem trivial compared to the romance and "feel" of a knife, but romance and emotion are the con man's stock in trade. If you pay a real price, we think you should get a real knife—but to get a real knife in the world of Indian pieces, you had better do your homework, and do it well.

Attribution

Fanciers of Indian knives are subject to the usual perils of overzealous "restoration," calculated counterfeiting and outright imaginary pieces. However, the most common form of Indian knife fakery, and usually the most difficult to detect, is *false attribution*.

Many "fake" Indian trade knives are in fact genuine old knives. What makes them fakes is that the decoration, sheath or context in which they are alleged to have been found—in other words, the factors that reputedly make them Indian—are fake.

A beaded or tack-work sheath might be genuine, though not necessarily old. Large numbers of the sheaths were made on reservations in the 20th century for sale to tourists. However, odds are high that the knife in such a sheath will not be the knife that the sheath originally was made to hold. In many instances, the aforementioned "tourist sheaths" were made oversized to fit almost any knife. A plain, old butcher knife worn down to shapelessness might be Indian or "primitive" frontier, but it is far more likely that it is neither. A worn-out knife is just a worn-out knife, and any story with it is just a story.

Remember: Buy the knife, not the story. A worn-out knife, even if authentic, has little monetary value.

Most serious collectors are not much interested in whether or not their knives have an Indian association, mainly because the documentation of purported Indian trade objects is both difficult to verify and easy to fake. Genuine museum artifacts are rarely sold, but fake Indian items—and even some real ones—are often accompanied by fake museum documentation.

Weapons of the Assiniboine

July 6th, we were visited by a band of 14 Assiniboines, part of a war party of fifty ... They had only three guns, a few carried common lances, and all had a knife; the leader was armed with a stick in which were inserted three blades of butcher's knives.

John James Audubon 1843
(artist and naturalist)

Firearms are certainly much valued by [Assiniboine and other Plains] warriors. Indeed, they are the principal arms, but bows and arrows are used fully as much by mounted men. The difficulty appears to be the loading of the gun on horseback. If possible they carry both on their war expeditions, also some are armed with lances, war clubs, and battle axes ... used only in melees at close quarters ... The metal arrow point is superior to the flint one formerly used, and more easily procured. The arrows for battle are barbed and tied on loosely, so that an attempt to withdraw the arrow invariably leaves the iron in the wound...

The stone war club is the most efficient weapon in battle ... The weight of the stone is about 5 pounds. The handle is made of elastic sinew and cannot be broken ... Tomahawk[s] and battle axes are not thrown at their enemies, as generally represented, but are secured to the wrist by a strong cord, and only used at close quarters; as also the lance and knife. The scalping knife is of English manufacture, a logwood or brazilwood handle [both of these tropical South American dyestuff woods are deep red in color], and soft steel blade about 8 inches long and 1 1/2 inches wide, sharp on one edge [i.e., single-edged, not double-edged], and with the point turned like a butcher knife [i.e., not centered like a dagger]. These are the kinds of knives mostly used by all Indians for hunting and all purposes, though Wilson's butcher, Cartouche, eye dagues [dags, sometimes pronounced "daggies"], and other knives can be had. Most Indians at all times carry knives of some kind and scalps are taken off with whatever knife they happen to be in possession of at the time.

Edwin Thompson Denig 1858
(resident trader to the Assiniboine since 1835)

PRUSSIAN CROWN

Fancy Hardwood Handle, Fastened with Brass Rivets. Full Scale Tang. White Metal Bolster. Extra High Grade Prussian Steel Blade with wide Swage; Carefully Tempered, Ground and Sharpened. Highly Finished.

No. 5692—Length of Blade, Inches	6	7	8
Per Dozen	$5.50	6.50	8.00

½ Dozen in a Box.

German Export Butcher or Sheath Knife

10-12" overall. Blanked blade, sheet-metal bolsters, wood handles, fancy rivets and "Prussian Crown" escutcheon, often with unidentified man-and-tree logo, sometimes marked with importer's brand. An old man from a Northwest reservation told us that the low-quality knives sometimes were used as trade goods in the early twentieth century. Example shown from a 1914 West Virginia wholesale hardware catalog. Value, **$15-30**; American-made version, **$50-75**.

What collectors seek instead are the *types* of knives known to have been traded. The cautious collector closely studies the knife itself rather than relying on affidavits, attribution, accessories or aura. (On the other hand, with knives in most other categories, documentation *is* important as far as authentication is concerned.) Advanced collectors pay a hefty premium for "mint" or unused trade-type knives. However, Indians used their trade knives, and used them hard. If a trade-type knife has survived in excellent or mint condition, it very likely was never traded.

Trade Type Knives

What types of knives were actually used in the trade? Much of the interpretive material written in recent years about Indian trade knives has been based on false assumptions and romantic beliefs, notions that have little or no basis either in trade documents or in genuine artifacts. In previous editions of this book, some of those errors have been repeated, and a few new ones have been added. For example, Sidney R. Baxter & Co. of Boston made industrial knives in the 1940s, and the Baxter "trade dagger" shown in an earlier edition of this book was in fact made from the blade of the firm's World War II combat knife. As a philosopher once said, "*If you don't learn something useful from your mistakes, you shouldn't make any.*"

For the present edition of *BLADE's Guide*, this segment of the book is based on three types of primary sources.

First is relic knives found in archaeological sites. Second is knives collected directly from North American Indians by nineteenth-century anthropologists. Third is artwork and firsthand accounts set down by individuals who traveled or lived among the Indians in the eighteenth and nineteenth centuries. There is one account written by a seventeenth-century French fur trader, but it included no pictures or descriptions of his knives.

On these pages are shown the better-known styles of knives that were made for trade to Indians. Knives of these types are valuable to collectors whether or not the knives have any Indian association.

BUTCHERS' KNIVES.— HAND FORGED. DIAMOND SHAPED HANDLES.

No. 4576

HALF TANG.

				6	7	8	9	10	11	12	inches.
No. 4576	Beechwood Handles,	Iron Pins	... ...	19/3	26/3	32/6	38/6	46/6	57/0	65/9	per doz.
No. 4608	Boxwood	do.	do.	... ...	22/6	30/6	36/6	43/9	51/9	61/9	72/3	,, ,,
No. 4609	Rosewood	do.	do.	... ...	22/6	30/6	36/6	43/9	51/9	61/9	72/3	,, ,,

THROUGH TANG.

				21/3	28/6	34/6	41/6	49/9	59/6	69/0	,, ,,
No. 4610	Beechwood Handles,	Iron Pins	... ...	21/3	28/6	34/6	41/6	49/9	59/6	69/0	,, ,,
No. 4611	Boxwood	do.	do.	... ...	24/3	32/6	38/6	46/6	55/0	65/0	73/9	,, ,,
No. 4612	Rosewood	do.	do.	... ...	24/3	32/6	38/6	46/6	55/0	65/0	73/9	,, ,,

I. Wilson Trade-Type Butcher or Sheath Knives

6-12" forged blades. Beech, box or rosewood/diamond-cross-section handles. Full or half tang. Marked SHEFFIELD, ENGLAND. From Wilson's circa 1933 catalog. Value, **$50-100**.

Crooked Knives

About 9" overall. Curved blade with relatively straight cutting edge, often with blunt-end, bent tip. Handle of wood, bone or antler. String, sinew, or metal ferrule. Handles and mounts usually made by owner. Indian or Eskimo man's knife for the carving of canoes and other wood. Held blade down with thumb in rest. Primarily traded and used in Canada and Northwestern USA, 18th to 19th centuries.

Do not confuse with similar carver's hook made in Italy that has a round-end handle with no thumb rest. Value, **$10**.

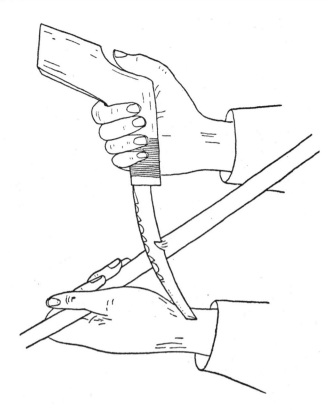

Eskimo crooked knife from "The Man's Knife Among the North American Indians," by Otis Tufton Mason, 1899. Value, **$450**. (courtesy Smithsonian Institution)

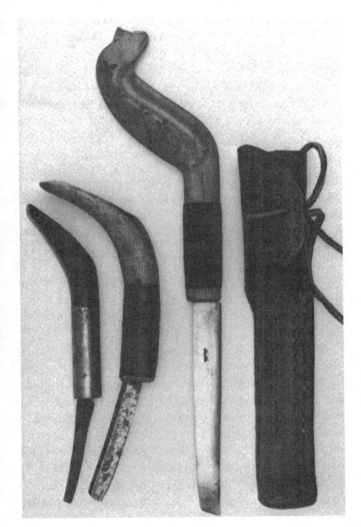

Left: two c1900 crooked knives with worn blades, one probably a "recycled" straight razor. Stag handle, wood handle, metal ferrules. Value, **$75-175** each. Right: twentieth-century factory example. Blade marked SHEFFIELD/ENGLAND. Boxwood handle carved as animal. Green cord ferrule. Leather side-open sheath. Value, **$300**.

Ooloo (with trade blade)

Blade up to 6" across. Handle usually bone or walrus ivory. Eskimo woman's knife for scraping seal skins. Similar knives used throughout Eskimo regions of the Arctic. 18th to 20th centuries.

Older ooloos often lack a distinct tang.

Example shown above circa 1960s. Value, **$50**.

Older examples can be much more valuable. Do not confuse with similar-shaped chopping knives or saddler's knives (see "Kitchen and Butcher Knives" and "Industrial Knives" later in this section). (courtesy Eiler R. Cook

American Hunting Knives

The hunting knife, in one form or another, has been with the human race since before the dawn of history. However, the *American sport hunting knife* is a recent creation, one that first appeared a little over a century ago.

In earlier times, "hunting knife" usually meant a large, stout knife, even a short sword, used as a hunting weapon for killing big game. (See "London hunting knife" and "Hanger or hunting sword" in Part 3 of Section II, "Foreign, Exotic, Primitive, and Historical Fixed Blade Knives".) The very first "bowie" was such a hunting knife (see "Bowie Knives" in this section). The term "hunting knife" could also refer to a butcher or skinning knife carried by a hunter for the field dressing of game.

The invention of high-powered rifles and ammunition in the latter part of the nineteenth century meant that even the desk-bound merchant or clerk could safely go hunting on weekends or vacations. Yet, the leisure-time hunters still needed knives to skin and dress their game.

Thus it was from the butcher knife, primarily, that the modern American sport hunting knife evolved. In its modern form, an American hunting knife is smaller, stouter and fancier than most butcher knives (see "Kitchen and Butcher Knives" in the "Special Section" of this section). Usually it is equipped with a finger guard and a fitted sheath (though also see "Folding Hunters and American Clasp Knives" in the "Named Jack Knife Patterns" chapter of Section II).

Gutting, skinning, disjointing and boning are butcher's tasks, well performed with butcher's tools. For meat hunters and sportsmen alike, a butchering kit was as essential as their weapons, clothing and shoes. Standard butcher tools served well but, by the 1870s, cutlery makers and merchants were calling certain small-sized butcher knives "sheath knives" or "hunting knives." A 4 to 8-inch-bladed knife was convenient to carry in a hunting bag, or Indian-style in a deep, drop-in sheath.

Butcher-Style Hunting Knives

By the 1880s, American cutlery firms were offering refined versions of their butcher patterns explicitly as hunting knives. The knives might have stouter blades or fancier handles than standard types, and sometimes even guards and sheaths. Yet, they still looked like butcher knives.

However, a new breed of sport hunters and recreational outdoorsmen wanted something more. Though they needed the practical utility of the humble butcher knife, they longed for the elegance of what had become the obsolete bowie. They were willing to pay a premium for knives they would wear only while hunting and fishing, knives intended for peaceful camp use—skinning and butchering game, slicing bacon, chopping kindling, etc.—deluxe sportsman's knives designed exclusively for their leisure-time pursuits.

Colclesser Bros.

In 1926, William Monypeny Newsom wrote at length about bowie and hunting knives in his book, *The Whitetail Deer*. Newsom lamented the closing of the butcher knife manufacturer that had made his favorite outdoor knives, Colclesser Bros. Cutlery Co. of Eldorado, Blair County, Pennsylvania. Colclesser also had made small double-bitted camp-axe heads designed by "Nessmuk"—a.k.a. writer George Washington Sears. Nessmuk's original axe had been custom made to his design in the 1860s by a surgical instrument maker named Bushnell in Rochester, New York.

In the 1890s, another noted sporting writer, Horace Kephart, sent a sketch (see accompanying line drawing, courtesy Willis Hobart) of his 5-inch-bladed, dream hunting knife to Colclesser Bros., and Colclesser obliged by making up a prototype. Kephart's sketch was reproduced in *Hunting & Fishing* magazine, July 22, 1897. Colclesser responded to the publicity with a campaign of small ads in the magazine, such as the following:

HUNTER'S AXES.-"Nessmuk" and others, weight 8 to 20 ozs.; the Kephart knife; knives made to order, hand made, excellently tempered; belts, sheaths, etc., furnished.

To this day, we have never seen a Colclesser-marked knife or axe. An excellent example might be worth **$300.**

Hunting Knives, Apache Style

The Apache Indians taught me to use a common butcher knife in camp, and for any knife larger than a pocket size, one will not go far wrong in selecting a first-class butcher knife, with a common, straight wood handle, and a broad, thin blade, slightly pointed. Five inches should be the limit in length of blade, and four inches will be better. Like the Apaches ... have the sheath deep enough to cover half the handle, leaving a portion exposed, which may be grasped by the thumb and finger only in drawing. I like the Apache method of carrying a thin whetstone in a separate pocket in the same sheath with the knife.

[Perry D. Frazer, "Canoeing," *Shooting & Fishing* magazine, May 27, 1897 (courtesy Willis Hobart)]

A

Butcher-Style Hunting Knives

Lightweight American Butcher-style "Hunting Knives"

Lightweight blade 4-10" long, usually forged. Acute clip point. Cocobolo handles secured with steel or brass pins. The principal mid-19th-century American makers were J. Russell & Co. and Lamson & Goodnow, but many other American brands were made (see "Kitchen and Butcher Knives" in the "Special Section" of this section), as well as imported English and German versions.

The earliest Russell stamping (c1835-1875) has neat, tiny letters and no diamond trademark. Value of a plain example with the mark, **$175**; with later-stamped or deep-etched marks (as shown) **$65**; with recent-etched mark, **$12**.

Similar plain examples stamped LAMSON GOODNOW & CO./S. FALLS WORKS (earliest mark, c1844-1855), **$160**. Stamped LAMSON & GOODNOW MFG. CO./S. FALLS WORKS (1855-c1870), **$125**. Lamson & Goodnow knife with stamped anchor or USA map trademark, $35; with surface etched mark, **$10**. A consignment of butcher knives with pinned, flat-steel bolsters, blades stamped LAMSON & GOODNOW MFG. CO./PATENTED MARCH 6, 1860, was recovered from the steamboat *Bertrand* that sank in the Missouri River on its way to Fort Benton, Montana Territory, in 1865. Value, **$145**.

Many variations of this basic style were offered:
Ebony or rosewood handles: add **$10**.
Stag or ivory handles: add **$100**.
Handles checkered: add **$20**.
Pinned, flat-steel bolsters: add **$20**.
Fancy cast-pewter bolster(s): add **$35**.
Integral forged bolster and cap: add **$100**.
Cross-guard: add **$100**.

Examples shown (above and right) are marked J. RUSSELL & CO./GREEN RIVER WORKS. They date circa 1890s and have either later-stamped or deep-etched marks. Values:
A: plain **$65**.
B: fancy cast-pewter bolsters **$95**.
C: stag handles, integral bolster and cap **$260**.
D: checkered ebony handles, cross-guard **$190**.

Heavyweight American Butcher-style "Hunting Knife"

(Right) Heavy, tapering forged blade 5-10" long. Usually with checkered ebony handles. Examples with early-stamped marks, **$300**. Later marks, **$100**. Stag handles, add **$50**. Blade Magazine Cutlery Hall-Of-Famer© Bob Loveless said that the pattern inspired his dropped hunter with tapered tang.

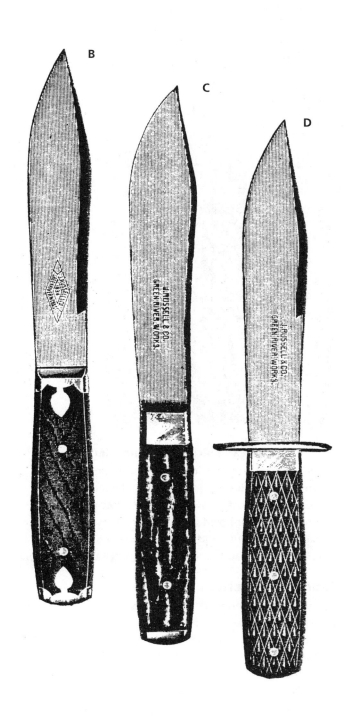

B

C

D

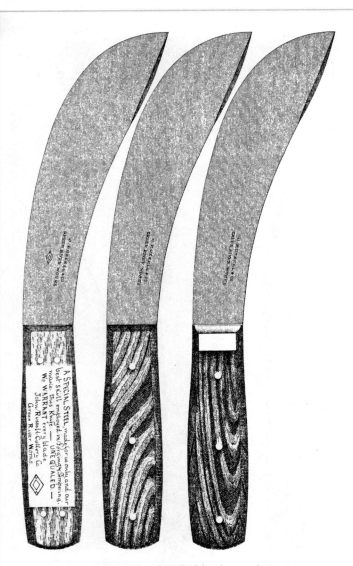

American Butchers' Skinning Knives

5-7" forged steel blade with tapered tang. Pinned wooden handles. Sometimes have flat steel bolsters (after 1860) or cast-pewter bolsters(after c1867). Later examples have uniform tangs, larger rivets. See previous page for markings and values (see also *Kitchen and Butcher Knives* in the *Special Section* of this section).

Hunting in America

The American hunting knife is the sporting knife of the middle-class American. It reflects a social revolution in the United States that is so profound yet so familiar that most Americans are not aware of it.

In much of the Old World, the only people legally permitted to hunt were aristocrats who owned large estates. Anyone else who hunted was a poacher, a criminal. Aristocrats hunted for pleasure. Poachers hunted for food, either for themselves or to sell, often at the risk of their lives.

In America in the early days, and even up into the twentieth century, so much of the country was wild and game was so abundant that anyone who wanted to hunt

could hunt. Wealthy rural landowners had brought with them from Europe the sport of hunting for pleasure. Poor people had brought with them—or had learned from the Indians—the skills of hunting to fill the larder. In the new, free country, there were few restrictions on what and where the poor could hunt.

To the middle-class American of the mid-nineteenth century, the upwardly mobile craftsman, clerk, merchant or professional man, hunting had two bad associations. On one hand, hunting was a sport of self-styled aristocrats. The middle-class American did not like aristocrats or anything about them, though his wife, daughters and even he might have wished that he would become one.

On the other hand, hunting was one of the harsh necessities of survival in the rural world he recently had left. If he had grown up on a farm, as most Americans did in the nineteenth century, he might have enjoyed hunting on the lucky occasions when the weather was mild and game was plentiful. However, poor farm boys had to hunt often, in good weather and bad. When game was scarce, they had no choice but to spend longer hours hunting, no matter how cold, wet and miserable the conditions were.

Of course, after the middle-class American had lived in town for a few years, or maybe a generation or two, then country life began to acquire a romantic aura. He forgot the cold and the wet, and that most of the time he had hunted barefoot, wearing the only shirt and britches that he owned. What he remembered was the clean air, the sense of freedom, and the majestic buck that had been out of range.

The Outdoors Revolution

Here, then, is the germ of the social revolution, of ordinary citizens redefining the great outdoors from a place of toil and hardship to a place of sport and leisure. This is the beginning of hunting as a middle-class sport, at the time a uniquely American phenomenon.

The townsmen and city men returned to the country to hunt, not because they had to, as their parents had, or as they themselves had often been compelled to as boys. They went strictly for sport, to recapture the best feelings of their youth, or of their fathers' and grandfathers' fireside tales.

The men did not go out to hunt as Old World aristocrats, with jumping horses, packs of dogs or an army of beaters. Instead, they hunted like country boys, usually on foot, alone or with a few friends, with a dog or two and maybe a packhorse. They went as country boys who had "made good," with all the fine gear that they ever had dreamed about: waterproof boots, a warm coat, a Winchester rifle or Remington shotgun, and, of course, a hunting knife.

The new popularity of hunting as a sport was just one facet of the outdoors revolution of the late nineteenth and early twentieth centuries. The Boy Scouts, Girl Scouts and

Camp Fire Girls were all established around 1910. (See the "Utility and Scout Knives" segment of the chapter, "Multi-Blade Knives," in Part 2, Section II.) The National Park Service was established in 1916 to manage the nation's nine public recreation wilderness areas, eight of which had been created since 1890.

Bowie-Style Hunting Knives

The bowie knife as a sidearm was a great fad beginning in 1827, and an established trend for the next half-century. By the mid-1870s, however, the bowie largely had been supplanted for self-defense by the cartridge revolver, though a few big-city cutlers still made true bowies up into the 1910s.

Despite the transformation, when the novice American sportsman ventured out to challenge the fields and streams, after having lived all his life in a city or town, the knife he imagined he should be carrying was still the bowie knife. Consequently, most of the commercial hunting knives sold in the United States in the last decades of the nineteenth century look a lot like bowies, with a stout, wide blade, usually a clip point and saber ground, and fitted with a big, double cross-guard. The bowie-style hunting knife remained popular through the 1920s, and it is still made today. We doubt that it will ever disappear entirely.

It is not very difficult to learn to distinguish post-circa-1880 bowie-style hunting knives from real 1820s-1870s bowies. One telling characteristic is the shape of the handle. Most of the later hunting knives have straight-sided handles that taper toward the end. We have yet to see the handle shape on an early bowie knife (see the accompanying sidebar for the possible origin of the shape). Another indication of a later hunting knife is a cross-guard with ball-shaped ends, which usually signifies early-to-mid-twentieth-century manufacture—though we have seen some earlier exceptions.

Yet another useful clue is the construction of the original sheath, when it is present. All the bowie-style hunting-knife sheaths that we have seen were made of solid leather. As a rule, they are flat, two-piece, stitched leather sheaths, similar to inexpensive, modern sheaths. Some are one-piece leather sheaths stitched up the back.

J. Russell bowie-style hunting knives circa 1900, made with 5-, 6-, 7-, 8- and 9-inch blades; standard sheath. Value, **$750-1,250**.

Contemporary Views of the Bowie-Style Hunter

In his 1926 book *The Whitetail Deer*, William Monypeny Newsom wrote of the bowie-style hunter, "several foreign cutlery companies make this 'American pattern' knife. A representative of one of these houses told me that this English knife is a copy, in shape, of the one Colonel [Buffalo Bill] Cody had with him when he took his [Wild West] show to England [in 1887 or 1892], when this cutlery house purchased it, putting it on the market as the True American Hunting Knife."

If Newsom was correct, it could mean that the bowie-style hunter had the same origin as today's yoked "Western" shirt designed by Cody as a prop for his show. Newsom then added, "Be that as it may, it is this general pattern built on Bowie lines that we see in the sporting-goods stores today, and at the belt of many modern deer hunters," a fact the writer deplored. "One look at this knife will make it obvious that it has no place in the woods these days." (*The Whitetail Deer* book quoted herein is courtesy of Jim Rohl.)

"Nessmuk"—a.k.a. George Washington Sears—had even stronger words. In the 1920 edition of his 1884 book, *Woodcraft*, he wrote, "The 'bowies' and 'hunting knives' usually kept on sale are thick clumsy affairs with a sort of ridge along the middle of the blade, murderous-looking but of little use; rather fitted to adorn a dime novel or the belt of 'Billy the Kid,' than the outfit of the hunter."

In the same vein, in 1897, Horace Kephart of St. Louis, Missouri, wrote, "The conventional bowies are poorly tempered, too thick to be whetted, and shaped so that they are good for nothing but stabbing, which is about the last thing a sensible man ever has occasion to do. Every green hand, when he buys his first hunting knife, thinks of bears—bears that charge at sight, and engage the hunter in a rough-and-tumble of the good old dime novel kind. This disease is as inevitable as measles. Every fall I hunt bears, and every fall the bears run away." (The preceding quoted material is from *Shooting & Fishing* magazine, May 13, 1897, courtesy Willis Hobart.)

Two weeks later, Perry D. Frazer, editor of the "Canoeing" column in *Shooting & Fishing*, added, "By all means the novice should avoid buying the misnamed hunting knives, which have thick clipped-point blades and imitation stag horn hafts. I have heard but one person say a good word for these store knives, and he said that when driven into a tree the haft made an elegant peg to hang rifle or hat on."

By contrast, the original sheaths of just about all real bowie knives were not made simply of leather. The standard Sheffield bowie sheath had a pasteboard body covered with a thin, morocco-like-leather veneer, usually dyed and gold stamped, and reinforced with a nickel-silver throat and tip. The original sheaths rapidly wore out and sometimes were replaced later with all-leather ones.

American and better-quality Sheffield bowies might have had solid leather in place of the pasteboard and veneer for the body of the sheath, but the metal ends were still present. The best American sheaths, and an occasional English one, were solid metal, sometimes with a leather frog (belt hanger) or even a leather over-sheath.

HUNTING KNIVES

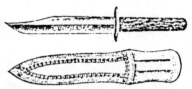

High carbon steel saber clip swaged blade, highly tempered and polished, glazed finish. Scale tang stag handle. Three nickeled pins. Nickel silver guard. Complete with russet embossed leather sheath.

Winchester

The only fixed-blade hunting knives sold by Winchester in the USA were of a bowie style in the early 1920s. The only marking on the No. 1981 (5-inch blade) and No. 1982 (6-inch blade) is the *Winchester* trademark etched on the bevel of the blade. The rare knives are worth at least **$650** in excellent condition. Identical knives marked Walden Knife Co. or E.C. Simmons Keen Kutter are worth about **$450**.

Bowie-Style Brands and Markings

Usually, the best evidence for recognizing a bowie-style hunting knife is the markings. For example, any bowie-style knife by Landers Frary & Clark (often marked L.F. & C. or UNIVERSAL) was made after about 1890.

J. Russell & Co. bowie-style knives with either an etched marking or a diamond trademark were made after about 1880. Even though Russell advertised them as "bowie knives" up into the 1910s, they were made after the bowie-knife era had ended, and are in fact bowie-style hunting knives.

Knives sold by Bridgeport Gun Implement Co. date from the 1880s and after. Many of the knives' blades were imported.

American Bowie-Style Hunting Knives

Values in excellent condition, without sheath:

Russell with stag handles:**$750-1,250** depending on size.

Landers Frary & Clark (L.F. & C.), heavy blade, stag handle, solid cast guard: **$320**.

Landers Frary & Clark (Universal), light blade, rough black celluloid handle, flat guard: **$125**.

Lamson & Goodnow "Hercules," heavy blade, stag: **$300**. Winchester: **$650+**. Keen Kutter: **$450**.

Walden: **$400**.

Bridgeport Gun Implement Co. (B.G.I. Co.; sold by Hartley & Graham c1889): **$425**.

Gelston Mfg. Co. (sold by Orvis circa 1892): **$200**.

Most other American brands: **$100-350**.

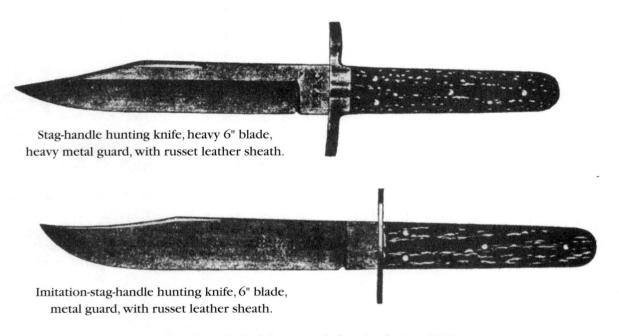

Stag-handle hunting knife, heavy 6" blade, heavy metal guard, with russet leather sheath.

Imitation-stag-handle hunting knife, 6" blade, metal guard, with russet leather sheath.

Landers Frary & Clark bowie-style hunting knives, 1910s.
Top: heavy version, stag: **$320**. Bottom: lightweight version, celluloid: **$125**.

Bowie-Style Imports

Any Sheffield knife marked ENGLAND was made after 1891 and is not a true bowie. Several Sheffield brands of bowie-style knives were made only in the later period. The knives are still common and are increasing in popularity.

The most common later Sheffield brand is NON-XLL by Joseph Allen & Sons, in business c1886-1947. Another common brand is Alfred Williams, sold from the late 1890s to at least 1918 by Kastor, usually with Kastor's EBRO trademark.

English knives marked CHALLENGE, a trademark of the New York import firm Wiebusch & Hilger, are also from the latter period. However, many important English firms, including Wostenholm, Rodgers, W. & S. Butcher, Slater Brothers, and Joseph Elliott, made both real bowie knives and also later-bowie-style hunting knives.

Any German-made or German-marked knife in the "bowie" style is a hunting knife from after the mid-1880s. Most are from after the First World War.

Sheffield Bowie-Style Hunting Knives

(straight, tapered handle and/or ENGLAND in marking). Jigged-bone handles. Blade up to 7 inches long. Value in excellent condition, without sheath:
Joseph Allen (NON-XLL): **$125**.
Alfred Williams (EBRO): **$125**.
I. Wilson: **$125**.
Challenge: **$125**.
Joseph Elliott: **$125**.
Joseph Rodgers or George Wostenholm I*XL: **$275**.
Wade & Butcher "Hunter:" **$175**.
Slater Brothers (Venture): **$175**.

German Bowie-Style Hunting Knives:

Very High (e.g., Henckels): **$100**.
High (e.g., Wingen): **$45**.
Medium (e.g., Richartz): **$20**.
Low/Medium: **$10**.

The First American Sport Hunting Knives

True American hunting knives—practical camp or skinning sheath knives designed for the prosperous sportsman and man of leisure—seem first to have been made in San Francisco in about the late 1860s or early 1870s. They were expensive handmade knives, some custom made, or as the term was then, "made to order."

In his book, *Knifemakers of Old San Francisco*, Blade Magazine Cutlery Hall-Of-Famer® Bernard Levine wrote that, "[the knifemakers] of Old San Francisco made

the most exotic, the most costly, and perhaps the most beautiful knives ever produced in the United States." More recently, their knives have been equaled by the best of today's custom knifemakers, and perhaps even surpassed, but their place in history as design pioneers remains secure.

Circa-1870 San Francisco was a natural place for the hunting knife to appear. The city was energetic and wealthy. Many of the residents had braved the hardships

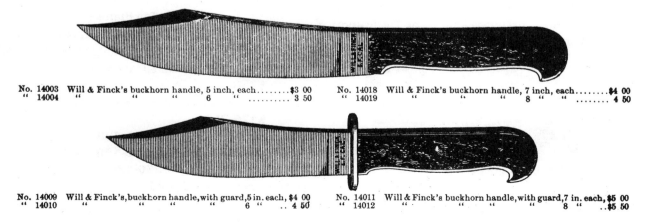

No. 14003 Will & Finck's buckhorn handle, 5 inch, each........$3 00
"   14004   "   "   "   "   6   " 3 50

No. 14018 Will & Finck's buckhorn handle, 7 inch, each........$4 00
"   14019   "   "   "   "   8   "   " 4 50

No. 14009 Will & Finck's, buckhorn handle, with guard, 5 in. each, $4 00
"   14010   "   "   "   "   6   "   .. 4 50

No. 14011 Will & Finck's buckhorn handle, with guard, 7 in. each, $5 00
"   14012   "   "   "   "   8   "   ..$5 50

Will & Finck, San Francisco, California hunting knives with elk-antler handles, from the Will & Finck 1896 mail-order catalog. Value range: **$1,200** (small, without guard) to **$4,500** (large, with guard). (courtesy California Historical Society)

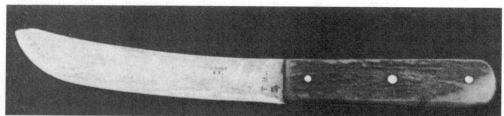

Top: Michael Price, San Francisco, classic California hunting knife. Circa 1870s-1880s. Elk-antler handles. Value, **$1,500**. (courtesy Donald Euing) Similar knife with walrus-ivory handles, **$1,800**.

Bottom: John Todt, San Francisco, hunter's skinning knife with elk handles. Value, **$750**. (courtesy Doug Royal.)

of the round-the-Horn passage, the overland trek from Missouri, the gold mines of central California, or the silver mines of Nevada. Now free of the necessity, many San Franciscans and other California townsmen remained outdoorsmen by choice.

The climate and situation of northern California were ideal for hunting, fishing and camping. For seven months of the year, sportsmen could be sure of mild weather and no rain. An hour by boat north or east of San Francisco or an hour south on horseback brought one to the edge of unbroken miles of wild forest and field. A leisurely half-day train ride would bring one to the heart of the Sierra Nevada Mountains.

Successful Californians wanted the best of everything, at home and in the field. It was for them that Michael Price, Will & Finck, John Todt, and others made California hunting knives (see "American Knifemakers and Cutlery Merchants of the Bowie Knife Period" in this section).

California hunting and camp knives clearly show their mixed parentage. In profile they look like butcher knives. In heft and handle material, they resemble fine bowies. An innovative feature on most of their blades is a sharp false edge, which is designed for chopping wood and bone. Because it is not meant for stabbing, it is not as sharp or as acute as the false edge on a bowie-knife blade. The feature has been used on many later hunting knives.

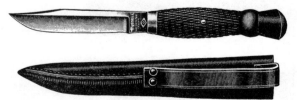

No. 32 – Hunt Knife, Sole Leather Sheath.
Forged. Scored Solid Ebonwood Handle. Nickel Ferrule.
Blade length, 4½ in.   Per dozen, **$30.00**
No. 33 — Same as above. Blade length, 6 in.
                                              Per dozen, **$31.00**

Thistle Top

Toward the end of the nineteenth century, a novel style of factory-made hunting knife appeared. In its catalogs, the famous New York City sportsman's outfitter, Abercrombie & Fitch (established 1892), took credit for the knife's design. The "Abercrombie & Fitch Specials" were made by J. Russell & Co. in two blade sizes: 4 1/2 and 6 inches. Cutlery firms other than Russell made similar knives, and other retailers than A. & F. sold them.

The knives have one-piece, checkered ebony handles with integral, thistle-shaped pommels. The shape suggests that the design might be a "modern" utilitarian interpretation of the Scottish dirk (see Part 3 of Section II, "Foreign, Exotic, Primitive, and Historical Fixed Blade Knives"). The fact that many of the knives were made in Sheffield suggests that the design might have originated in Britain.

Whatever its origin, the thistle-top hunter must stand as one of the first mass-produced sheath knives designed specifically for hunting as a sport. Its popularity seems to have lasted only until about the middle 1910s, by which time it had been supplanted by the more practical Marble's knives and their many eventual imitators.

Thistle Top Hunters

Values in excellent condition, without sheath:
Russell 6-inch marked "Abercrombie & Fitch": **$300**.
Russell 4 1/2-inch marked "Abercrombie & Fitch":
   $250.
Russell not marked "Abercrombie & Fitch":
   $125-250.
Other American makers: **$90-180**.
Rodgers or Wostenholm: **$90-180**.
Other English makers: **$50-120**.
German makers: **$35-75**.

Webster L. Marble
Marble's Knives and Axes

The knifemakers of old San Francisco sold their camp and hunting knives mainly to California sportsmen. Abercrombie & Fitch, in its early years, sold mainly to the East Coast market. It took a Michigan sportsman with an inventive turn of mind to bring the sportsman's hunting knife to the rest of the United States. His name was Webster L. Marble.

Marble was born into a prosperous manufacturing family in Wisconsin in 1854. The family soon moved to Vassar, Michigan, and then to Traverse City, on an arm of Lake Michigan. Marble's father taught him outdoor skills, hunting, fishing and trapping. As a young man, he worked as a timber cruiser and surveyor.

Never satisfied with existing methods and equipment, Marble experimented with new and practical designs. In 1898, he built a small factory in Gladstone, Michigan, to manufacture the waterproof match safe and the safety pocket axe that he had invented.

The following year, Marble took in a partner named Frank H. Van Cleve, and they began to advertise their products in national outdoors magazines. In 1901, they introduced their first hunting knife, the Ideal. In 1902, they added a folding hunter, invented by Milton H. Rowland, which combined the virtues of the Ideal with those of the company's folding safety axe.

More knife designs and phenomenal success followed rapidly. Most of the cutlery illustrated herein is from Marble's 1908 catalog. The Special (No. 57) may have been Marble's version of the Michael Price California hunting knife.

Webster Marble (left) and Frank Van Cleve display their wares at a sporting goods show in New York's Madison Square Garden c1905. (Union View Co. photo, courtesy Bill Lung.)

The pocketknives shown in this catalog, with the exception of the Safety Hunting Knife, were contract knives. By design and pattern numbering, several were made by Case Bros. of Little Valley, New York. A few patterns were also imported from Germany. The pocketknives were offered from about 1902 to 1908. Others, made by Union Cutlery, were offered until circa 1915.

Marble's was the first knife company to bring the stacked-leather-washer handle into widespread use and

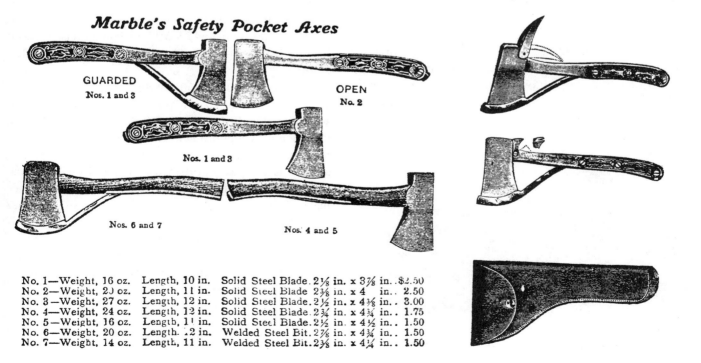

Marble's Safety Pocket Axes

GUARDED
Nos. 1 and 3

OPEN
No. 2

Nos. 1 and 3

Nos. 6 and 7

Nos. 4 and 5

No. 1—Weight, 16 oz.	Length, 10 in.	Solid Steel Blade.	2⅛ in. x 3⅞ in.	$2.50
No. 2—Weight, 20 oz.	Length, 11 in.	Solid Steel Blade	2⅜ in. x 4 in.	2.50
No. 3—Weight, 27 oz.	Length, 12 in.	Solid Steel Blade.	2½ in. x 4⅜ in.	3.00
No. 4—Weight, 24 oz.	Length, 12 in.	Solid Steel Blade.	2¾ in. x 4¾ in.	1.75
No. 5—Weight, 16 oz.	Length, 11 in.	Solid Steel Blade.	2½ in. x 4½ in.	1.50
No. 6—Weight, 20 oz.	Length, 12 in.	Welded Steel Bit.	2⅞ in. x 4¾ in.	1.50
No. 7—Weight, 14 oz.	Length, 11 in.	Welded Steel Bit.	2⅜ in. x 4¼ in.	1.50

oon to anyone who must carry a large axe.

Marble's Camp and Chopping Axes

We have been requested so frequently by our sportsmen friends to furnish them with large axes of the same temper and quality as our popular line of Safety Pocket Axes that we now offer a very superior line of chopping and camp axes.

The reason for this demand was that it is almost impossible for one to buy a large axe that is guaranteed and that is fit to use without considerable grinding.

We guarantee these axes to be absolutely perfect in quality and temper, and the handle to be strong and true. Each axe is finely polished, ground to a keen cutting edge ready for immediate use and is furnished with an edge protector.

No. 10   Weight 2   lbs. Handle 26 in. with protector..... $1.50 prepaid
No. 11   Weight 2½ lbs. Handle 28 in. with protector...... 1.50 prepaid
No. 12   Weight 3   lbs. Handle 30 or 32 in. with protector 2.00 prepaid
No. 13   Weight 3½ lbs. Handle 30 or 32 in. with protector 2.00 prepaid
No. 14   Weight 3½ lbs. Handle 30 or 32 in. double bitted,
with two protectors.................................... 2.50 prepaid

Marble's Axe Edge Protector

This edge protector will be very much appreciated on account of the safety and convenience with which this style of axe may be carried in wagon, canoe or pack. The protector may be attached or detached in an instant and may be carried in the vest or coat pocket without inconvenience.

Marble's Axe Edge Protector is made in sizes to fit axe blades from 4 inches to 5½ inches in width. Price . . . . 25 cents, prepaid

Marble's Camp Axe and Edge Protector

If Edge Protector attached, **$450**;
Edge Protector alone, **$75**.

acceptance in the United States. We do not know the origin of this handle construction. However, the oldest examples we have seen were knives and machetes made by Collins & Co. of Connecticut as early as the 1850s. Italians and South Americans have long made knife handles from stacked horn, bone and metal washers.

In 1911, the Marble Safety Axe Co. (M.S.A. Co.) became the Marble Arms & Mfg. Co. In 1953, it became Marble Arms Corp. Today, the company is known as Marble's Outdoors and remains in Gladstone, Michigan.

Not shown in the 1908 catalog are several important Marble's knives that came later. One was the Woodcraft, whose design was patented in 1916. Another was the Sport knife, a smaller version of the Expert, introduced about 1930. Ideals with 4 1/4-inch blades were introduced after World War I, in place of the Canoe, which was discontinued.

In 1930, Marble died at the age of 76. The company he had founded continued to thrive, but it had faced increasingly stiff competition since the early 1920s. None of the competitors ever quite matched Marble's in quality, though most offered lower prices.

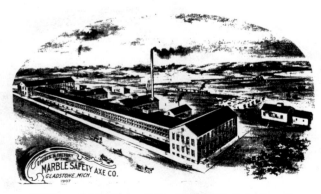

Offices and factory of the Marble Safety Axe Co.

MARBLE'S WOODCRAFT KNIVES

Marble's Woodcraft w/original leather sheath.

In the 1930s, some Woodcraft and Sport knives were made as Official Boy Scout and Girl Scout knives. Also in the 1930s, Marble's introduced the Outer's Knife and the Outdoor knife. Both were lightweight, inexpensive knives with integral hilts. The Outer's had jigged-bone-slab handles, while the Outdoor had a one-piece wooden handle.

During World War II, virtually every American cutlery firm made large numbers of government-model sheath knives—that is, every cutlery firm except Marble's. We do not know the reason for this but it could have been Marble's higher costs. Military buyers did buy most of Marble's 1941-45 commercial inventory and output, including large numbers of 5-inch Ideals used as aircrew survival knives. Many wartime Ideals have black Bakelite pommels.

After the war, the market for sheath knives was glutted with surplus military models. Since sheath knives were Marble's main line, the company's business suffered.

In 1957, Marble's cooperated with the Navy to develop the new jet pilot's survival knife. (See "United States Military Fixed Blade Knives" in the "Special Section of this section.") Marble's made some of the early production, but Camillus underbid it. Marble's issue knives have plain, blued mounts, value, **$475-500**. Its commercial versions have polished mounts and colored fiber spacers, value, **$300.**

Starting in the mid-1960s, Marble's offered most models with an optional "Tiger-Wood" handle. New models were long-handled versions of old standbys: Maverick (Woodcraft), Longhorn (Ideal), and Hunter (Expert). The Sport knife was renamed the Campcraft. Its 1970s version, as well as the little Sportsman and Skin-Dress-Filet, look much like knives by Western. Most later Marble's knives have a distinctive lower case marking: Marbles/Gladstone/Mich.

In the years since the 1950s, Marble's knife output declined steadily. The firm suspended knife production around 1977. Today, the new owners are producing a quality line of hunting knives and related cutlery.

Original Marble's knife sheaths have their own considerable value.
When a Marble's knife is found in an original sheath, it has significant impact on value.

Sheath Values:

a. Embossed or "carved," standard-size sheaths, **$60-150**.

b*. Coquina outfit with knives (Ideal) and others, stag pommel steel, **$5,000-6500**.

c. Tube sheath, **$100-125**; also pouch sheath w/stone, **$200-300**.

d. Plain sheaths, various, **$40-75**.

Gift Sets:

Match safe and compass in original box, five variations, **$150-175**.

Ideal knife and sheath, pin on compass and match safe in original box, eight variations, **$250-400**.

g. B.S.A. sheath, **$50-75**.

h. G.S. sheath, **$75-125**.

Aluminum sheath protector w/sheath, **$90-100**.

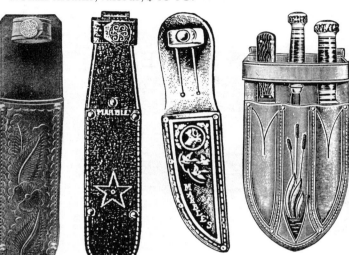

a   b*

b   a

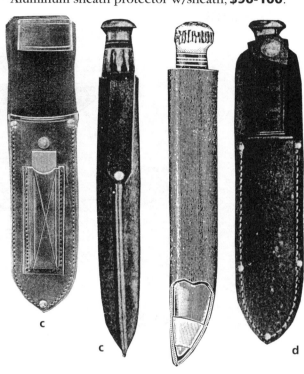

c

c   d

g

h   GIRL SCOUTS

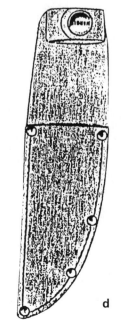

d   d

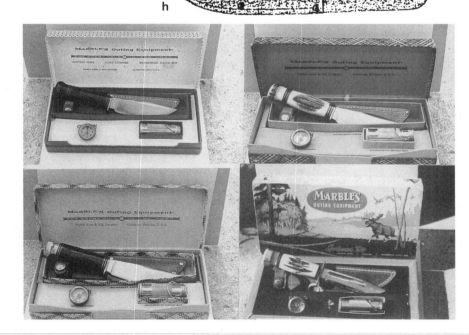

Fish Knife Folded

LOOK FOR THE NAME, MARBLES BEFORE YOU BUY.

MARBLE'S OUTER'S KNIVES

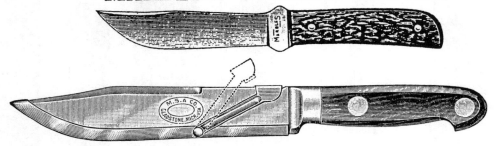

Camp Knife w/protector.

Compass No. 1

Prepaid.

No. 1.—Jewel Capped Needle, Revolving Celluloid Dial . . . $1.50
No. 2.—Jewel Capped Needle, Stationary Card Dial 1.25
No. 3.—Plain Needle, without Jewel, Stationary Card Dial . 1.00
Plain Compasses, Waterproof Screw Cases.
No. 4.—Plain Needle, Stationary Dial, without Bracket 75
No. 5.—Jewel Needle, Stationary Dial, without Bracket . . . 1.00
No. 6.—Jewel Capped Needle, Revolving Dial, without Bracket, 1.25

Any of these compasses will be fitted with magnifying lens at an additional cost of $1.00 each. These lenses give a particularly rich appearance.

Compass No. 2

Marble's Waterproof Match Box

A knurled and nickeled cylinder of drawn brass, which closes with an air and water-tight joint. It is about the size of a 10-gauge shot-gun shell and holds as many matches. A waterproof match box is cheap life insurance to the man who is "caught out" in wet weather. It means warmth, dry clothes, comfort and something hot to eat and drink. No experienced woodsman or sportsman thinks of going into the forest or camp without one of those little life-savers.
Price by mail, postpaid, 50 cents.

Match box parts:—
Rubber gasket, 5c.   Brass washer, 5c.   Screw, 5c.

The cut shows new style. It has solid top with no screw or brass washer. The knurled flange holds gasket securely in place.

Waterproof Match Box
(OPEN)

Instantaneous Rubber Boot Repairer

If you should stub a hole in your boot when miles from camp on a wet day you could quickly repair it with this device. No cement used. It cannot come off. You should always have both sizes in your sporting coat pocket, thus insuring yourself against wet feet. The two plates are concave and circular. The lower plate has a threaded pivot which projects through hole in upper plate and the two are held tightly together by a flush nut. Cannot hurt the foot.

Diameter ¾ inch, with key, postpaid, 15c.
Diameter 1 inch, with key, postpaid, 15c.   Two sizes, with key, postpaid, 25c.

Cut represents cross section of patch applied to a piece of rubber. Key is for turning up nut, only.

Current values of Marble's knives and axes in excellent, unsharpened condition:

AXES: Examples marked "M.S.A.":

First Type (head secured by screw): **$1,000-$1,500.**
Second Type (as illustrated in the 1908 catalog):

1. **$1,000.**	2 1/2. **$1,000.**	5. **$350.**
2. **$800.**	3. **$800.**	6. **$400.**
2-P. **$1,500.**	4. **$500.**	7. **$600.**

Third Type (squarer butt, 2 screws per handle):
$450.   3. **$450.**
Non-Folding: **$225-450.**

W.L. Marble's, M.S.A., Marble's Sheath Knives

Knife values are with sheath.
(Sheaths shown later in this segment)
Examples marked W.L. Marble's: add **$200-300.**
Examples marked M.S.A. Co.: add **$100-350.**
M.S.A. Co. with thicker blades, made 1901-1905 (very rare): add **$300-400.**
Marble's Safety Axe Co., marked Ideal: add **$300.**

Ideal:

	Blade length:	
	5"-6" (4 1/4")	7"-8"
Rubber-handle Ideal:	**$2,000** up	—
Stag-handle Ideal:	**$450** up	**$800-1,500.**
Leather with stag butt:	**$350** up	**$500-900.**
Leather with lignum vitae:	**$400** up	**$1,200-1,800.**
Leather with aluminum butt:	**$200** up	**$400-700.**
Leather with Bakelite butt:	**$250** up	—

Note: After 1942, all Ideals had double guards; guard does not affect value. Later 4 1/4" Ideal valued same as 5".

Yacht Knife: (a lightweight, drop-point Ideal): 5 1/2" blade. Very rare.

Stag-handle Yacht Knife:	**$2,500-3,500.**
Leather with stag butt:	**$1,800-2,800.**

Canoe: 4 1/2" blade. Very rare.

Stag-handle Canoe:	**$1,200-1,800.**
Leather with stag butt:	**$700-1,100.**

Expert: 5" or 6" blade.

Cocobolo-handle Expert:	**$1,200-2,000.**
Leather-handle Expert:	**$250.**
Stag-handle Expert (post-WWII):	**$175-250.**

Trailmaker: 10" blade.

Stag-handle Trailmaker:	**$1,500** up
Leather with stag butt:	**$900** up
Leather with aluminum butt:	**$700** up

Haines: 6" blade. Very rare.

Stag-handle Haines:	**$2,500** up
Rubber-handle Haines:	**$4,000** up
Special: 5" blade. Stag:	**$2,500** up

Dall DeWeese: 4" blade.

Stag:	**$1,200-1,600.**

Skinning: 5" blade.

Stag:	**$1,500** up

Coquina Outfit:

Iincludes 1 Ideal, 1 Skinning, 1 leather or stag-handled Sharpening Steel, in a 3-pocket sheath. Named for "Coquina" (pen name of G.O. Shields, editor of *Shields' Magazine*). Value, **$6,000** up.

Sharpening Steel only:

Stag:	**$500.**
Leather:	**$400.**

Camp Carver: 8" blade.

Stag:	**$3,000** up

Camp or Kitchen Knife: 6", 7", 8"

Wood handle, with guard:	**$1,000** up

No. 79—2½-inch blade.

No. 80—2½-inch blade.

No. 81—3½-inch blade.

Handy Fish Knife: Several styles.

Wood handle, nickel-silver fish:	**$1,200-1,800.**
Trout Knife: 5 5/8" all steel:	**$250-400.**

MARBLE'S NEW TROUT KNIFE

Woodcraft: 4 1/2" blade.

Stag-handle Woodcraft:	**$350** up
Leather with stag butt:	**$275** up
Leather with aluminum butt:	**$175** up
ditto, Official Boy Scout:	**$400** up
ditto, Buster Brown:	**$400** up
Sport Knife: 4" blade.	
Stag-handled Sport Knife:	**$400** up
Leather with aluminum butt:	**$150** up
ditto, Official Boy Scout:	**$400** up
ditto, Official Girl Scout:	**$400** up

Outer's: 4" blade.

    Bone-stag handles: **$200** up

Outdoor: 4 1/2" blade.

    Wood handle: **$150** up

Post World War II (lower case mark)

	Stag	Wood	Leather
Maverick/Woodcraft	$250	$175	$150
Longhorn/Ideal	$250	$200	$150
Hunter/Expert/Stag	$175	$150	$150
Campcraft, Sportsman, S-D-F	—	$75	$50

Marble's Safety Folding Knives

Safety Hunting Knife

Pre-World War I: Swell-center; thong hole in extension guard; lobed folding hilt. M.S.A. CO.

	Blade length		
	4 1/4"	5"	6"
Rubber handles, name in ribbon	$1,200 up	$2000	
Rubber handles, name in panel	$1,100 up	$1,800 up	$3,000 up
ditto, plain bolsters:	$1,000	$1,500	
Stag handles:	$1,800 up	$1,900 up	$4,000 up
ditto, plain bolsters:		$1,600 up	$1,700 up
Pearl or ivory handles:	$3,500 up	$4,500 up	$8,000 up

"Safety Hunting"—
Stag Horn Handle

Post-World War I: Regular jack; nail nick in extension guard; straight folding hilt. MARBLE'S.

    Stag handles: **$700** up   **$900** up

All Metal Safety Knives; Gadgets:

Safety Carver:	**$500** up
Safety Fish Knife:	**$300** up
Safety Saw:	**$700** up
Screwdriver:	**$250** up
Match Safe:	**$40** up

Butcher-Style Sport Hunting Knives

Between the 1910s and the 1930s, some butcher knife firms made sporty hunting knives that still showed a butcher-knife heritage. The knives are rare today, suggesting that they were not widely popular when new. By contrast, the firms' low-cost fishing knives were big sellers.

The Ellery Hunter

The Ellery hunter was a modified butcher's skinning knife sporting a black, self-guard wooden handle and was sold with a fitted sheath. It was designed by William Ellery, owner of Ellery Arms Co., a San Francisco outfitter and sporting goods retailer in business from 1909-1933. Ellery secured a design patent in 1916, though the knife was featured in the June 1913 *Outing* magazine.

Henckels made the first Ellery hunters in Solingen. Even after 1933, Henckels showed the knife in its American catalogs. From 1915 into the 1930s, the pattern also was made in the United States, some on contract.

    Values:

J.A. Henckels:	**$60**.
L.F. & C.:	**$50**.
Union Cutlery:	**$70**.
Keen Kutter:	**$75**.
Maher & Grosh:	**$50**.

Landers and Lamson

Landers Frary & Clark's hybrid Pathfinder, Kodiak, Pioneer and Ranger of 1931 combined the blade shapes and rivets of butcher knives, the Yankee bolsters of carving knives—extended into integral guards—and the checkered wood handles of fish knives. Value, **$150** each. (Courtesy of Dennis Ellingsen and Bill Claussen.)

Lamson & Goodnow put a turned stag handle with a metal spacer on a light 5-inch blade. We have seen one Lamson & Goodnow-marked example, its blade etched NATIONAL SPORTSMAN HUNTING KNIFE (a magazine premium). Example shown sold by retailer Maher & Grosh in 1929. Value, **$250.**

Fishermen's Knives

Some firms made little butcher-style fish knives with a clip blade, scaler back and a checkered handle. Older types have a deep clip for gutting, steel bolster and a sheath. Value, **$50**. 1920s-30s deluxe versions have pewter bolsters and tropical hardwood handles. Premium brands

(Russell, Case, Remington, Ka-Bar, etc.) value, **$20-30**. Other types, value, **$2-5**.

A few also made odd-shaped pan-fish knives. Of them, only the Marble's have caught on with collectors.

Case/Kinfolks: **$35**. Henckels: **$75**. Wadsworth: **$30**.

20th Century Sheffield-Made American-Style Hunting Knives

For nearly two decades after Webster Marble introduced his Ideal pattern, in 1901, none of the old-line American cutlery firms challenged his dominance of the sport-hunting-knife market, but not so Sheffield's cutlery manufacturers. They were desperate. They had been badly hurt by U.S. tariffs (see "19th Century Sheffield Cutlery Firms in the Pocketknife History" chapter of Section II), and could only still compete in high-markup items, such as bowie-style hunting knives. Could there be room for them in the new sport-hunting-knife market, too? By about 1907, both Rodgers and Wostenholm were offering Marble's lookalikes. Later, Wostenholm sold I*XL versions of American hunting knives through Canada's Hudson's Bay Co. stores.

Wade & Butcher

The most successful Sheffield firm to compete with Marble's was W. & S. Butcher. The Wade & Butcher-brand hunting knives are shown in a circa-1919 U.S. catalog, and may have been sold before then. The 4-inch-bladed "Boone" was clearly inspired by the 4 1/2-inch-bladed Marble's Woodcraft of 1916, but the Boone cost nearly twice as much.

The 4 3/4-inch "Teddy" looks like the Boone but cost a third more because it was the first stainless steel hunting knife on the market. Stainless steel had been invented in 1914 by Harry Brearley of Sheffield and Elwood Haynes of Kokomo, Indiana, working independently. The two

"TEDDY"

Made of the famous patented "Firth Sterling Stainless Steel" that resists corrosion by salt air or rain. Blade, 4¾ in. Handle of variegated segments of richly colored leather, brass and bakelite, nickel silver hilt and polished aluminum head.

C6752 Price, each ....$4.35 net

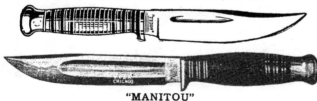

"MANITOU"

Wade & Butcher hunting knives from a 1925 Von Lengerke & Antoine catalog. Values: Manitou/Pioneer **$150**; Teddy (or Boone, not shown) **$125**. (courtesy Frank Gamble)

inventors pooled their patents and collected royalties from every steel firm in the world. The first firm to make stainless blade steel was Thomas Firth & Sons of Sheffield, whose "Firth Sterling" brand was used in the Teddy.

A 1925 U.S. catalog offered, in addition, Wade & Butcher copies of the Marble's Ideal in 4-, 5-, 6-, 7- and 8-inch-blade versions. We have seen them advertised both as the "Pioneer" and the "Manitou."

Strangely, though Wade & Butcher hunting knives are marked Sheffield, England, they likely were made, or perhaps just assembled, in America. W. & S. Butcher had been American owned since 1913, when Sigmund Kastor bought it. In 1918, he sold it to the Durham Duplex Razor Co. of Jersey City, New Jersey. We have heard of, but have not seen, evidence that the hunting knives were made in Durham's Jersey City factory.

The Marble's-inspired knives marked E.M. Dickinson, Sheffield, cost 10 percent more in a 1918 U.S. catalog than the real thing. A knife like No. 355 (see accompanying illustration), but with a single guard, is a Royal Air Force Servicing Commandos knife, sold by W. & S. Butcher to the British Ministry of War in 1943.

1912 "Hunting Knife" Distributors

The following 16 American firms were listed as suppliers of "hunting knives" in the 1912 *Sporting Goods Trade Directory*:

Billings & Spencer (made "butterfly" folding knives);

H. Boker & Co. (made folding hunters; imported Manhattan Cutlery bowie-style from Sheffield);

Colclesser Bros., Eldorado, Pa. (butcher style);

Alfred Field & Co. (imported Joseph Rodgers);

A. Kastor & Bros. (imported Alfred Williams bowie-style);

R.C. Kruschke, Duluth, Minn. (no information);

Landers Frary & Clark (made butcher and bowie-style);

Marble's (sport-style);

William Mills & Son, New York (no information);

Northfield Knife Co. (made folding hunters; may have made bowie-style);

Jno. Russell Cutler Co. (made butcher and bowie-style);

Smith & Hemenway Co. (wholesale);

Edw. K. Tryon Co. (wholesale and retail);

U.J. Ulery Co. (wholesale);

Wiebusch & Hilger (imported Challenge bowie-style), and;

Wilkinson Shear & Cut. Co., Reading Pa. (no information).

Eight of the firms were also listed under "sportsmen's knives," which included Abbey & Imbrie (fishing tackle wholesale and retail) and Goodell Co. (made butcher-style).

MARBLE PATTERN

No. 350

Marble pattern blade, forged from best quality razor steel, brass guard, laminated leather handle, stag tip, with leather sheath.

No. 355

Regular clip blade, forged from best quality razor steel, brass guard, laminated leather handle, stag tip, with leather sheath.

Values:

Ideal style, stag butt: **$150**.   Plain butt: **$75**.

Bowie style: **$125**.   R.A.F. by Butcher: **$135**.

Wm. Rodgers and Bell Bowie

The most prolific Sheffield maker of U.S.-style hunting knives sold in Britain was John Clarke & Son (William Rodgers brand). Similar knives marked BELL BOWIE were made for a peddler named Jack Bell (c1900-1980). He had premises in Mappin Street, Sheffield, above a 'little mester,' Sam Hancock, who made bowie knives and throwing knives, along with the hunting knives stamped BELL BOWIE. Jack Bell traveled across the North of England by bus and train, selling knives from big suitcases. (Information courtesy Frank Hudson.)

Values:

Wm. Rodgers, **$10-30**.   Bell Bowie, **$20-50**.

1919 American "Hunting Knife" Makers

The Cutlery Makers of America published by *American Cutler* magazine in 1919 listed the following 11 American makers of fixed-blade hunting knives:

J. Chatillon & Sons, New York (Foster Bros. butcher-style);

Clyde Cutlery Co., Clyde, Ohio (probably butcher-style);

Goodell Co., Antrim, New Hampshire (butcher-style);

Harrington Cutlery Co., Southbridge, Mass. (butcher-style);

Marble Arms & Mfg. Co., Gladstone, Mich. (butcher-style);

Lamson & Goodnow Mfg. Co., Shelburne Falls, Mass. (bowie and butcher-style);

Landers Frary & Clark, New Britain, Conn. (bowie and butcher-style);

Old File Cutlery Co., Havana, Ill. (butcher-style);

Ontario Knife Co., Franklinville, New York (butcher-style);

J. Russell Cutlery Co., Turners Falls, Mass. (bowie and butcher-style), and;

Stephen Richard Co., Southbridge, Mass. (butcher-style).

After World War I

Jaeger Brothers

One of the first American entrants into the sport-hunting-knife market after World War I was Jaeger Bros. of Marinette, Wisconsin, owners of the Aerial Manufacturing Co. (See the "Makers of Picture Handle Pocketknives segment in the chapter, Pocketknife History," in Section II.) In a catalog from around 1920, Jaeger Bros. offered three new hunting knife models:

K17B "Trailer": 5-inch straight blade, single guard;

K16B "Ranger": 5-inch straight blade, double guard; and;

K18B "Trapper": 5-inch skinning blade, single guard.

All three have stacked washer handles, not leather, but fiber, hardwoods and brass. The knives were marked "Jaeger Bros." The original price, $3.50 each, included a sheath. Current value, **$90**.

The firm also offered a small bowie-style "Belt Hunting Knife" marked AERIAL with picture handles for **$3**.. Current value, **$75-175** (depending on the picture).

Union Cutlery Co. (Ka-Bar)

An upstate New York pocketknife firm, Union Cutlery Co. offered three styles of fixed-blade hunter's skinning knives in an undated catalog that was issued sometime before 1923, when the firm adopted the Ka-Bar trademark, and after 1919, when stainless steel became available for commercial use. All three models, as well as 5-, 6- and 7-inch bowie-style hunting knives, were offered in a choice of stainless or carbon steel. The first models are worth **$175-275** now. Contract brands (e.g., Henry Sears & Son) are worth less. (Also see "The Ellery Hunter" earlier in this segment.)

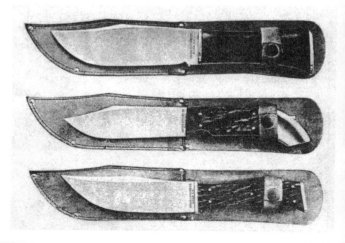

Ka-Bar

In the next few years, Union/Ka-Bar added dozens of other hunting knives to its product line. Their values, with Union Cutlery markings, are **$50-275**. Larger sizes and fancy handle materials command the higher values. The 2000 and 3000 series knives, which have hollow "match-safe" handles, are worth **$150-250** (see "Hollow Handle History" in *Knives '88*).

LITTLE HUNTER A   **$150.**

A great little knife designed for the use of the boy who wants a knife with the style and quality of a big knife. Length over all—6½". Two color unbreakable handle, genuine stag butt, nickel silver guard—grooved blade.
Little Hunter A—3½" blade with sheath $2.00

LITTLE HUNTER S   **$175.**

Same size as Little Hunter A except sabre blade. genuine stag handle and butt, nickel silver guard.
Little Hunter S—3½" blade with sheath $2.00

No. 3000   **$150-250.**

Threaded knob at end of handle, has reliable compass set into the under side of it. Knob opens water-proof match compartment in composition rubber handle. Thumb notch in blade is finely corrugated.
No. 3000—4½" blade with sheath $3.00

No. 2000

Same as No. 3000 except handle is aluminum.
No. 2000—4½" blade with sheath $3.00

No. 2071   **$150-250.**

Aluminum handle with match case and compass same as No. 2000—same blade as No. 571.
No. 2071—5" blade with sheath $3.25
No. 2071—6" blade with sheath 3.50

No. 3071

Same handle as No. 3000 with No. 571 blade.
No. 3071—5" $3.25

No. 386SS   **$50.**

A knife designed especially for nautical purposes. Heavy stainless steel blade and marlin spike. Both fit into a special sheath with separate compartments for knife and spike. Nickel silver bolsters and cocobola handle. Handle is shaped to fit in the hand.
No. 386SS knife, spike and special sheath $4.50

Remington and Pal

As recounted in *Remington U.M.C. Pocketknives*, the Remington Arms Co. entered the pocketknife business in 1919. After just a few years of applying sophisticated technology and aggressive advertising, Remington came to dominate the pocket cutlery industry.

In 1925, Remington management decided that the American hunting knife was more than a passing fad and entered that market as well. The company started out with six patterns but soon dropped one (the RH-35). In 1926, it added six more patterns. In typical Remington style, the company emulated its competitors' most successful patterns, plus a few novel designs of its own. Then, as Remington gained market experience, it dropped some patterns and added others. Kitchen, butcher and industrial knives were added to the company line in February 1927. Most Remington hunting knives are worth **$75** to **$325** in excellent condition, depending on size and handle material. Official Boy Scout sheath knives are worth **$100**, while the rarer Official Girl Scout sheath knives are worth **$200**.

Late in 1940, Remington sold off its entire cutlery division to the Pal Cutlery Co. of Plattsburgh, New York. We do not believe that Pal made hunting knives before 1940, but made plenty afterward. Most were made with Remington tooling and have Remington Hunting (RH) pattern numbers. Many were made for the government during the Second World War. (See the "United States

Complete display as shown, **$3,500.**
The knives are valued at **$200** each.

OFFICIAL GIRL SCOUT.

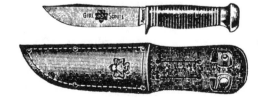

$450.

Military Fixed Blade Knives segment in the "Special Section" of this section). Most Pal hunting knives are worth **$50-75**.

REMINGTON

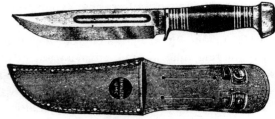

No. RH-36

Blades are solid forged from the highest grade of blade steel, specially tempered and hardened. Full sabre shape with stiff, keen, durable edges. Solid aluminum head. Solid sole leather sheath with loop belt attachment.

No.	Length blade	Wt. each	Each
RH-36	6 ¼ in.	11 ½ ozs.	$4.00

No. RH-35

Highest grade blade steel, tempered and hardened. Full sabre shape, keen edges. Solid aluminum head, handle of solid brass, fibre and sole leather washers. Sheath with loop belt attachment as furnished with RH-36 knife.

No.	Length blade	Wt. each	Each
RH-35	5 ¼ in.	11 ozs.	$3.75

No. RH-34

Highest grade of blade steel, forged and tempered. Full sabre shape, stiff, durable edges. Swelled grip handles, aluminum head, half hilt. Sheath with loop belt attachment as furnished with RH-36 knife.

No.	Length blade	Wt. each	Each
RH-34	5 in.	9 ½ ozs.	$3.50

No. RH-33

Highest grade of blade steel. An ideal camper's and outdoor knife. Solid aluminum top, sabre blade, durable keen edges. Half hilt. Sheath with loop belt attachment as furnished with RH-36 knife.

No.	Length blade	Wt. each	Each
RH-33	4 ½ in.	9 ½ ozs.	$3.00

No. RH-32

Highest grade of blade steel. A knife similar to the RH-33, but lighter weight. Complete with sheath with loop belt attachment as furnished with RH-36 knife.

No.	Length blade	Wt. each	Each
RH-32	4 ½ in.	8 ozs..	$2.50

All above, one in a box.

RH-36	Today's value:	**$350**.
RH-35	Today's value:	**$350**.
RH-34	Today's value:	**$300**.
RH-33	Today's value:	**$325**.
RH-32	Today's value:	**$350**.

Case, Cattaraugus, and Kinfolks

W.R. Case & Sons first got involved in sport hunting knives in November 1925. That year, Case and Cattaraugus jointly founded Kinfolks, Inc., in Little Valley, New York, primarily to manufacture hunting knives for the two pocketknife firms to sell. It is thus no accident that early Case and Cattaraugus hunting knives look similar. Case's first model was the No. 63-6, which resembles the No. 62-5 (see accompanying illustration) but has pinned-on bolsters and caps, and a 6-inch blade.

Later, the three firms went their own ways in the design and manufacture of hunting knives. Kinfolks marketed many under its own name, as well as under the name of Jean Case. Kinfolks also made contract knives. The most interesting Kinfolks hunting knives have imitation-amber-celluloid handles.

Case is still a force in the hunting knife market. As with Remington, however, Case hunting knives are not nearly as highly regarded by collectors as Case pocketknives. The value range for most of them in excellent condition, with sheath, is **$75-350**. Larger and more handsome ones are worth the most. As with Ka-Bar, Case's hollow-handle match safe model (No. 309) is worth much more, about **$375**. Some military knife collectors will pay up to **$375** for bone-handled "pig sticker" models, such as the 62-5 and the 63-6, though we have seen examples for sale at well under **$100**.

Case also made a changeable-blade hunting knife with three blades. It is called the "Sportsman's Set." A complete Sportsman's Set with sheath is worth about **$2,500**. A similar unbranded set marked HOBO only is worth about $800.

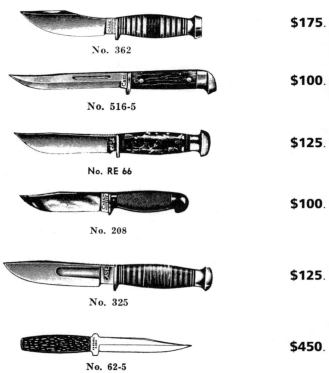

No. 362 — $175.

No. 516-5 — $100.

No. RE 66 — $125.

No. 208 — $100.

No. 325 — $125.

No. 62-5 — $450.

Kinfolks knives with amber-celluloid handles, made on contract for Shapleigh Hardware Co. Value, **$100** each. Similar Kinfolks knives with leather handles, **$75**.

Cattaraugus and Kinfolks went out of business in the 1960s. Their hunting knives are generally worth about 75 percent of the value of similar styles of Case knives.

Knife-Axes

Case, Ka-Bar, and Kinfolks, and also Western States (see next page), offered an odd gadget called a "Knife-Axe" that has a little more collector appeal than their regular hunting knives. A Knife-Axe is a hunting knife handle with two interchangeable snap-in blades, a knife and a hatchet (see "Tool Kit Knives" for a similar mechanism). All three pieces fit into a special sheath.

Case

Knife-axes, values of complete sets:
Case Tested XX, Case XX, or **Case:**
    Stag: **$475**.   Wood: **$325**.   Celluloid: **$400**.
Case XX/Made in U.S.A.
    Stag: **$450**.   Wood: **$200**.
Ka-Bar or Stiletto knife-axe set: **$300**.
Kinfolks knife-axe set, celluloid: **$175**.
Western States knife-axe set, celluloid: **$225** up.

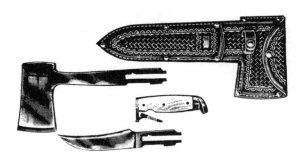

The example shown is Western States' second model, made 1947-1957. The first model, c1934-1942, uses a thumbscrew in place of the lever.

Western States

A contemporary name brand in American hunting knives is Western. Made today by Camillus and from 1984 to 1991 by Coleman, Western knives originally were manufactured by Western States Cutlery Co. of Boulder, Colorado. Western States offered its first fixed-blade hunting knife in 1928. The first pattern was the little number 63, an inexpensive, scale-tang, self-guard knife. The design was emulated a few years later by Marble's as the "Outer's."

The second pattern was, of all things, a bowie-style hunter, the number 45. However, it was followed in short by many more modern and practical styles. Most older Western States sheath knives are worth **$50** to **$275**.

In 1934, Western States patented a new type of hunting knife construction (Patent No. 1,967,479). It used a full-width tang open along the center. The construction was used on both leather- and celluloid-handled knives. Most knives with the construction also have a streamlined pommel. Western States made knives of the type on contract for a number of other firms, including Boker, Coast Cutlery, and Montgomery Ward (Ward's Western Pride).

$85.

No. 238   Blade 4½". Over-all size 8⅜". Composition pearl handles.

$100-125.

No. BX43   Blade 4¾". Over-all size 8½". Varigated colored bakelite handle. Also made in black bakelite handle with decorated red ring next to front guard. **No. BX43R.**

$150.

No. L36KG   Blade 5½". Size over all 9⅝". Decorated leather handle. Heavy brass guard.

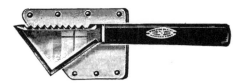

Fish knife
$100 up.

No. 990   Blade 3⅛". Over-all size 7¾". Highest quality stainless steel blade.

$50.

$60.

$85-100.

$75-85.

$125.

"39" SERIES

A
B
C
D

A. **$55**. Leather handle
B. **$65**. Celluloid handle
C. **$70**. Jigged-bone handle
D. **$75**. Stag handle

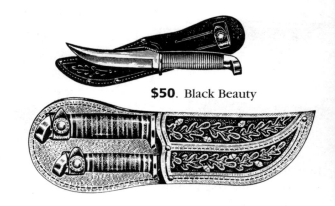

$50. Black Beauty

$125. Double set

Other Brands

In the 1930s, Imperial, Utica, Camillus and Colonial each offered at least a few patterns of hunting knives. In the 1940s, the same firms made sheath knives for the government, and were joined in the endeavor by Queen, Boker and Robeson. (They also were joined by most of the previously mentioned firms that were already in the sheath knife business. See the "United States Military Fixed Blade Knives" segment in the "Special Section" of this section.) Schrade-Walden—which went on to become Imperial-Schrade—first made sheath knives after the war. None of these firms' commercial hunting knives have yet attracted much collector interest. Their value is using value, in the range of **$5-75**.

153UH
9 ¼" **Golden Spike**
w/Sheath
$59.95
Schrade+ Steel®

Modern Schrade
(made at the old plant in Ellenville, New York)

Gerber Fixed Blade Sport Knives

*Editor's note: The information for the following is from Gerber's archives, supplemented by interviews with Ham Gerber, **Blade Magazine** Cutlery Hall-Of-Famer© Pete Gerber, Dave Murphy, Arden Manning, Doug Hutchens, and Ron Robley. There is some disagreement about details of the early years, 1938-1966.*

GERBER LEGENDARY BLADES began with the chance meeting of a civil servant who had a streak of entrepreneurship, and an entrepreneur with an unusual idea.

In the fall of 1938, David Zephaniah Murphy (1895-1972) was a blacksmith employed by the city of Portland, Oregon. In his spare time, he made carving knives with sharp tool-steel blades and neatly molded aluminum handles. He would make a batch of knives, then carry them around town to sell. Soon they were selling so well that he quit his day job.

Murphy would call on the larger firms around Portland, where his prospects were good for making multiple sales. One of the large firms was the commercial printing shop and advertising agency of Joseph Roman Gerber (1891-1966). Gerber had attained success by understanding that any product's style and pizzazz were just as important to its market success as its quality and design.

Gerber liked Murphy's knives but not Murphy's sales approach. Murphy sold his knives door to door for inexpensive prices, but Gerber envisioned selling the knives—under the Gerber name—through fancy retailers across the country at big prices, for example, a set of three in a wooden box for $25. All it would take was a little hype, publicity and marketing savvy, and Gerber specialized in all three.

The men made a deal. Murphy would make knives marked GERBER. Gerber, meanwhile, would secure walnut boxes from Ace Woodworking, and handle the promotion, marketing and finances. He agreed to pay Murphy $1 per knife, plus a half share of the profits at the end of each year. Gerber had little interest in knives. He left the marketing to his eldest son, Francis "Ham" Gerber—who spent his honeymoon trip in 1940 setting up Gerber dealerships across the United States—and the bookkeeping to his wife. Joe only stepped in at the end of each year to make sure that there were no profits left to divide up with David Murphy.

In 1940 Murphy got suspicious, and raised the up-front price to $1.25 per knife. In 1941 he got fed up, and refused to deliver 300 finished GERBER-MURPHY knives. He resumed making his own MURPHY designs, and began selling them direct to Gerber's first and biggest retailer, Abercrombie & Fitch of New York City, for $2.50 apiece.

The day after the Japanese bombed Pearl Harbor, Murphy discontinued making carving knives and began producing combat knives, boasting that his small shop was the first U.S. cutlery factory to convert to war production. He reluctantly sold the last 300 Gerber knives to Joe Gerber, who promptly delivered them to A. & F.—who then had custom sheaths made for some of the 6-inch-blade Joyeuse carvers, the "first" Gerber sheath knives (value, **$750**). The knives bear all three names: Gerber, Murphy and Abercrombie & Fitch (the sheaths are labeled "Abercrombie & Fitch").

Soon after, Gerber dropped out of the knife business for the duration of the war. Ham Gerber served two years in Burma as a pipeline construction engineer, carrying a presentation-etched Murphy Combat knife. His younger half-brother, Joseph Jr.—"Pete"—was still in school.

Gerber's Knives

After the war ended in 1945, the Gerbers got back into the knife business. They rented a loft above Oregon Wood Products Co. in Portland, who made the cases for the postwar Gerber steak and carving knives. Ham was named president. He had chosen the "Legendary" names for Gerber blades: Excalibur, Balmung and Joyeuse, plus Miming the steak knife (later joined by Durendal, Ron, Snickersnee, Flamborge, Curtana, Morglay, Trident and Siegfried). Pete, then a senior in high school, drove around to auto repair shops in his Model A Ford to buy old aluminum heads and pistons, which were melted in a crucible, right above the woodshop, and cast into knife handles. Gerber's postwar blades, through 1948, were recycled power hacksaw blades, ground to shape while still hard (at a Rockwell hardness of 62 Rc).

As before the war, Gerber focused on its Legendary Blades, the carvers and steak knives. Most Gerber retailers were small-town jewelry stores, though outfitter Abercrombie & Fitch was again foremost among them.

Meanwhile, A. & F. was pressing to have a Gerber sheath knife to offer its sportsmen customers, so Ham reluctantly came up with a design that he called the A. & F. Hunter. The blade of the first purpose-built Gerber hunting knife (value, at least **$500**) was merely a modified small carver pattern, but the handle was special. Its finger-grip shape and streamlined contour had been created during the war by an industrial designer named Thomas Lamb. Lamb had been granted a design patent for it in December 1945.

Gerber's knife production in 1945 and 1946 had been hit or miss. The staff was new and designs and methods were still in flux. However, in 1947, Gerber Legendary Blades hit its stride. The A. & F. Hunter was first made that September (109 total for the year). The stamping on all the Gerber knives produced that key year included the date, 1947.

Shorty and Fisherman

In spring 1948, an outdoorsman named Hale Woolf of Kalispell, Montana, asked Gerber if it would make a small hunting knife for him to its standards but to his design, which he provided in a sketch. Gerber obliged with two prototypes, made and shipped in April. Woolf liked them and so did others. Regular production of the "Shorty" began in July.

However, fancy jewelry stores were not the ideal venue to sell hunting knives. Ham began to set up a second network of "Shorty Dealers"—gun shops and sporting goods stores. A few stores carried the full Gerber line, but only A. & F. had its exclusive "Hunter." One small hunting knife does not make a line, so in June 1950 Gerber introduced its second sheath knife for general distribution, the Fisherman—a Miming steak knife blade with a shortened handle, offered with an optional fitted sheath.

1951

In 1951, Pete Gerber graduated from college and became company president. This freed Ham to travel for most of the year, setting up Gerber dealerships around the USA. The year was also marked by a machinists' union strike, and by relocation to another rented factory.

For collectors, 1951 left other legacies. Late in the year, the Gerber handle's truncated look was changed to a more streamlined shape that terminated in a rounded point. The older design was David Murphy's, and he had won back its exclusive use in court. Ham had created a new look, which remained in production for four decades, until 1990.

Also in 1951, Gerber experimented with its first non-metallic handle material. Aluminum was in short supply, as new jet aircraft were rushed to completion for the Korean War. Gerber did not have enough aluminum to fill orders, so the balance of knives that year were made with handles of "jet," not the real, polished hard coal, but jet-black, polished Bakelite. However, upscale Gerber buyers wanted metal, not plastic, and jet was quickly discontinued. We have seen exactly one Jet Shorty and one full set of Jet Carvers (at least $500 for either). There were also Jet Pixies—the new name for the redesigned little Fisherman.

1950s and 1960s

Between 1952 and 1959—though exactly when is not certain—Gerber added three more sporting knives for its "Shorty Dealers." Most likely the first of them was a slightly modified 1947 A. & F. Hunter, renamed for wider circulation. A Gerber booklet dated March 1959 calls it the Big Hunter, but two or three years later the name was assigned to a newer knife, while the former A. & F. Hunter began to be called the Lamb Handled Hunter, after its designer, Thomas Lamb. In 1965 the knife was again renamed (the Magnum); in 1970 it became the Magnum Hunter.

Also shown in 1959 was the Flayer, a skinning blade with a carver handle (the same as "Big Snick"). The same handle was used a few years later on the new Big Hunter which was not quite as big as the Magnum. Around the same time, Gerber introduced its 5-inch sportsman's steel.

Technology did not stand still, either. In 1950, Gerber began to chrome plate its blades. In 1953, molding of handles was supplanted by more precise die casting, and thereafter the handles were chrome plated, as well.

In the late 1950s, Jerry Beason, Gerber's rep in Alaska persuaded the factory to start making double sheaths each of which held a large knife, along with either a Pixie or a sportsman's steel.

Mark II

By 1966, America was deeply involved in the Vietnam War. Gerber decided that the firm could contribute to the war effort by offering a high-quality, practical combat knife for sale directly to American troops in Southeast Asia. The dagger it produced in its newly built factory in Southwest Portland—first occupied that February—was designated the Mark II. (The smaller Mark I dagger was not introduced until 1976, after the Vietnam War had ended.)

The Mark II was based on a sketch provided by Army Capt. C.A. "Bud" Holzman. The knife's drop-forged, double-edged blade was stout and sharp, and the cast-in-place textured aluminum grip was nearly indestructible. The knife was sold with an equally stout leather sheath, and had a Sportsman's Steel in a sheath pocket available as an extra-cost option.

The aluminum handles of the first Mark IIs had a surface texture called Steel Grip, a sprayed-on, molten-stainless-steel finish. Some collectors call it "Cat's Tongue." Starting in 1966, the Steel Grip handle also was offered on all Gerber hunting knives as an extra-cost option.

In 1968, Steel Grip was supplanted by Armorhide, an electrostatically applied, tinted-epoxy-powder coat baked on to the aluminum handle. Armorhide was standard on the Mark II and optional at first on the hunting knives, but within a year all the chrome-plated hunting knives had been discontinued. Armorhide fishing and diving knives—the Coho, Muskie, Trout and Neptune—were introduced.

The first Armorhide handles were gray and later were changed to black. In the early 1970s, Gerber's dive knives were made in safety orange and lemon yellow, and the Coho fish knives in tangerine. In 1970, the company's kitchen knives were offered in avocado, tangerine, pineapple and eggshell Armorhide.

The early evolution of the Mark II is summarized in the accompanying chart prepared by Doug Hutchens, former production manager at Gerber (Hutchens now is with Lone Wolf Knives). The Mark II is still made today, and Gerber has since added many other survival knives (see "Modern Commercial Daggers and Survival Knives" in the "Special Section" of this section).

Presentation

Gerber carving knives, with their handsome wooden boxes, were a popular presentation item on all sorts of occasions, from weddings to retirements. Mark II knives were sometimes factory etched for presentation to outstanding servicemen. In 1971, Gerber began to offer presentation-grade sporting knives as well. The Presentation Series began with five robust hunting-blade styles in two metals (stainless and tool steel) and two handles (wood and stag). Brown DuPont Hypalon "CushionGrip" handles were an option for a few years. In 1985, the series was reduced to two, the 400S and the 525S. From 1977 until the mid-1980s, Presentation Mark IIs and Mark Is also were offered. In 1987, Fiskars bought Gerber.

Al Mar

In 1971, Al Mar joined Gerber as a package designer. It turned out that Mar also had some very definite ideas about knife design. Many of his designs were a bit too radical for the Gerber of the 1970s, which was the main reason Mar left to found his own knife company, Al Mar Knives, in 1979 (the original Al Mar knives were made by Masahiro Cutlery Co. of Seki, Japan). However, before Mar's departure, Gerber did put several of his knife designs into production.

One of Mar's first knife efforts for Gerber, the Custom Series of six hunting knives introduced in 1975, proved to be a failure. The knives were sound, combining the classic pre-1951 Shorty with the latest design look of Blade Magazine Cutlery Hall-Of-Famer Bob Loveless, but the smooth, green nylon handles apparently were not. Substituting ebony the next year, then stag, did not help much.

In 1976, Gerber discontinued most of its original hunting knife designs, which by then were nearly 30 years old. In their place came a new Armorhide-handled series designed by Mar, using similar blades to the Custom Series. Mar's series was successful and remained a Gerber mainstay until 1989.

Mar passed away in 1992. Al Mar Knives continues today under the direction of Gary Fadden in Tualatin, Oregon.

Pete Kershaw

In 1966, when Gerber opened its big new factory, the staff was expanded as well. One new employee was a salesman named Pete Kershaw. By 1974, Kershaw had become Gerber's national sales manager and saw a rosy future in the sport knife market. However, Gerber's emphasis then was still on its Legendary line, so Kershaw decided to start his own firm, like Gerber, also in Oregon. He arranged an alliance with Kai Cutlery of Seki, Japan, which would manufacture Kershaw-designed sporting knives to be sold in the United States by the new Kershaw Cutlery Co.

Kai bought the company from Pete Kershaw in 1980 and, in 1996, built a manufacturing facility in Wilsonville, Oregon. Kershaw revolutionized the factory knife industry in the late 1990s by introducing custom knifemaker Ken Onion's assisted-opening folding-knife designs. Pete Kershaw retired as company president in 1998. In 2004, the company moved to a state-of-the-art factory in Tualatin, Oregon.

Columbia River Knife & Tool

Formerly of Kershaw, Paul Gillespie and Rod Bremer founded Columbia River Knife & Tool (CRKT) in 1994. Headquartered in Wilsonville, Oregon, the company bases most of its folding and fixed-blade designs on those of some of the world's leading custom knifemakers, including though not limited to Blade Magazine Cutlery Hall-Of-Famers© Ron Lake and Michael Walker, as well as Harold "Kit" Carson, Jim Hammond, Pat and Wes Crawford, Greg Lightfoot, Allen Elishewitz, Barry Gallagher and others. For the most part, CRKT's "factory/custom collaboration" and other knives are made in Taiwan and are a low-to-medium cost alternative to similar yet higher-end knives. Gillespie retired from the company in 2004 and CRKT continues today under Bremer's direction.

For more about Gerber and Murphy, see "Pioneers of Modern Handmade Knives" in this section, and "Modern Commercial Daggers and Survival Knives" in the "Special Section" of this section.

Chronology of Gerber Sheath Knives

Fixed Blade Sport Knives/Outdoor Knives
  Unplated molded aluminum blunt-end handles
      Abercrombie & Fitch Gerber/Murphy Hunter:
        late 1941
      [Gerber/Murphy 6" Joyeuse carving knife,
        also marked ABERCROMBIE & FITCH;
        some were equipped with sheaths by A. & F.,
        which were also marked]
  Unplated molded aluminum handles,
    with sheath
      Gerber Abercrombie & Fitch Hunter:
        9/1947-4/1953
      [Thomas Lamb handle patent, 12/1945]
      [Production. 1947: 109; 1948: 221]
      Shorty [blunt end handle]: 7/1948-late 1951
      [2 prototypes made 4/1948]
      [Production. 1948: 895; 1949 (est.): 1,400]
      Shorty [pointed end handle]: late 1951-early 1954
      Fisherman [blunt end handle]: 6/1950-late 1951]
      Pixie [pointed end handle]: late 1951-early 1954
  Jet handles (smooth molded black Bakelite),
    with sheath
      Shorty [pointed end] Jet handle: late 1951
      Pixie [pointed end] Jet handle: late 1951
  Chrome-plated die-cast pointed-end aluminum
    handles, with sheath
      Lamb Handled Hunter: late 1950s-1969
      [similar to A. & F. Hunter, called Big Hunter in 1959,
        called Magnum after 1965]
      Big Hunter: early 1960s-1969
      Flayer: late 1950s-1969
      Shorty: 1954-1969
      Pixie: 1954-1969 (available through 1972)
      Big Snick carver, optional sheath: late 1960s
      Durendal carver, optional sheath: late 1960s
  Steel Grip handles, with sheath: mid 1965-late
    1967
      [sprayed molten stainless steel coating,
        "Cat's Tongue"]
      Lamb Handled Hunter/Magnum; Big Hunter; Flayer;
      Shorty; Pixie; Durendal [also see Mark II, below]
  Sportsman's Steels for sharpening
      5" Sportsman's Steel: early 1960s-1993
      8" Sportsman's Steel: 1971-1989
  Two-piece sets in double sheath
  Chrome plated handles
      Pixie plus ...
      Lamb Handled/Magnum; Big Hunter;
      Flayer; Shorty: early 1960s-1969
      Sportsman's Steel plus ...
      Magnum; Big Hunter;
      Flayer; Shorty: mid-1966-1969

Steel Grip handles
  (same combinations as above): 1967-1968
  Armorhide handles (sprayed resin coating),
    with sheath
      [remaining patterns called Pro-Guide series after
        1/1986]
      Magnum/Magnum Hunter: 1968-1976
      [called Magnum Hunter after 1970]
      Mini-Magnum: 1969-1976, 1981-1989
      Big Hunter: 1968-1976
      Flayer: 1968-1976
      Shorty: 1968-1976, 1981-1989
      Pixie: 1968-1990
      Coho: 1968-1990
      Coho, tangerine Armorhide: 1971-1974
      Muskie: 1968-1990
      Trout & Bird: 1969-1990
      Neptune Dive Knife, orange Armorhide:
        mid-1968-1972
      Neptune Dive Knife, yellow Armorhide:
        1972-late 1974
      (tallow impregnated leather sheath)
  Two-piece sets in double sheath, Armorhide
    handles
      Pixie plus...
      Magnum; Big Hunter;
      Flayer; Shorty: 1968-1976
      Pixie plus Mini-Magnum: 1969-1976
  Sportsman's Steel plus...
      Magnum; Big Hunter;
      Flayer; Shorty: 1968-1976
      Steel plus Mini-Magnum: 1969-1976
      Steel plus Neptune Dive: 1969-1971
  Armorhide handles, new series
    (design by Al Mar), with sheath
      A-325 Game & Fish: 1976-1986
      A-400 Drop Point All Purpose: 1976-1989
      A-400 Camouflage handle: 1984-1989
      optional camouflage sheath
      A-425 Utility Skinning: 1976-1989
      A-450 General Utility: 1976-1985
      A-475 Drop Point Large Game: 1976-1989
  Pro-Hunter series hunting knives, slab handles,
    with sheath
      renamed Pro-Guide II series 1990. (1989-??)
      Pro-Hunter/Pro-Guide: Skinner; Drop Point; Clip
        Point; Caper
  Special-purpose cutting tools
      Moose Hook, Aluminum handle: 1968-1970
      Sport Axe, Black: late 1989-present
      Camp Axe, Black: 1993-present
  Professional fillet knives, various handles,
    sheath optional
      Fisher 5, orange ABS plastic: 1976-1980
      Fisher 8, orange ABS plastic: 1976-1980

Fisher 12, orange ABS plastic: c1976?
Balance Plus 7 1/2" Fillet: 1985-1987
Classic Walnut 7 1/2" Fillet: 1985-1987

GERBER INTERNATIONAL imported fixed blade
knives,
made by Sakai Cutlery, Seki City, Japan (1983-1985)
Skeleton Utility (2 models); Skeleton Hunting
(2 models);
Skeleton Survival (3 models); Exchange Blade
(2 models).

Presentation Series hunting knives, with sheath
400 - 4" skinning blade
400S wood: 1971-??
400HS stag, high speed steel: 1971-1973
400HS wood, high speed steel: 1974
400CG CushionGrip (DuPont Hypalon): 1979-1991
425 - 4 1/4" hunting and camping blade
425S wood: 1971-1985
425HS stag, high speed steel: 1971-1973
425HS wood, high speed steel: 1974
425CG CushionGrip: 1979-1985
450 - 4 1/2" fish and game blade
450S wood: 1971-1985
450HS stag, high speed steel: 1971-1973
450HS wood, high speed steel: 1974
450CG CushionGrip: 1979-1985
475 - 4 3/4" big game blade
475S wood: 1971-1985
475HS stag, high speed steel: 1971-1973
475HS wood, high speed steel: 1974
475CG CushionGrip: 1979-1985
525 - 5 1/4" heavy duty hunting blade
525S wood: 1971-??
525HS stag, high speed steel: 1971-1973
525HS wood, high speed steel: 1974
525CG CushionGrip: 1979-1991

Custom Series hunting knives, with sheath
(design by Al Mar)
Green Nylon handles (1975-76)
300A, 300B, 325, 375, 425, 475
Ebony Handles (1976-78)
C300A, C300B, C325, C375, C425, C475
Stag Handles (1979-1982/83)
C300A, C300B, C325, C375, C425, C475

MARK II
Mark II, Steel Grip handle: 1967-1968
Mark II, gray Armorhide handle: 1968-1978
Mark II, black Armorhide handle: 1978-??
Mark II-D Dive Knife, yellow Armorhide: 1970-1974
(tallow impregnated leather sheath)
Mark II gold plated 6224: 1973
Mark II Presentation Grade: 1977-1985
Mark II Presentation Grade, stag: 1982-1985
Mark II, blackened blade: 1982-1986, 1991-??
optional camouflage sheath: 1984-1986

MARK I
Mark I: 1976-??
Mark I Presentation Grade: 1977-1984
Mark I Presentation Grade, stag: 1982-1984
Mark I, blackened blade: 1982-1986, 1991-??
Mark I Tactical 5610: 1988-1994
Mark I Tactical, blackened blade: 1991-1994

PRESIDENT'S COLLECTION in Walnut Chest
(1979-1983)
MK-I & II, Presentation, wood handles
MK-I & II, Engraved Presentation, wood handles
MK-I & II, Stag handles
MK-I & II, Stag handles, engraved

BOARD MEMBERS' PRESENTATION SETS
(25 sets made, never sold)
MK-I & II, Presentation, carved ivory eagle head,
boxed: c1986

COMMAND
Command I: 1980-1994
Command I, blackened blade: 1982-1986,
1991-1993
Command II (with or without Steel): 1980-1985
Command II, blackened blade: 1982-1985
optional harness, fits Command I & Mark I
(two sizes): 1981-1985

GUARDIAN (design by Blade Magazine Cutlery
Hall-Of-Famer© Bob Loveless)
Guardian: 1981-1991
Guardian Back-Up, blackened blade: 1991-present
Guardian, blackened blade: 1982-1985
Guardian, camouflage: 1983-1991
Guardian I: 1981-1985
Guardian I, blackened blade: 1982-1985
Guardian I, camouflage: 1983-1985
Guardian II (with or without Steel): 1981-1985
Guardian II, blackened blade: 1982-1985
Guardian II, camouflage: 1983-1990
Guardian Presentation: 1981-1985
Guardian Set in wood box: 1982-1985
Guardian Deluxe Set in wood box: 1982-1985
Guardian Camouflage Set in wood box: 1983-1985
Optional harness: 1981-1986

FRISCO SHIV (design by Blade Magazine Cutlery
Hall-Of-Famer© Blackie Collins)
Frisco Shiv M-11, M-12, M21: 1982-1985
Frisco Shiv M-13, M-22: 1982-1988
Frisco Shiv M-13/M-22 combo set: 1982-1984

TAC-II: 1986-1991

SOS 20153 all metal with folding blade cover:
1986-1988

BMF - Basic Multi Function / LMF - Light Multi
Function
BMF 8" blade, sawteeth: 1986-1988
BMF 8" blade, no sawteeth: 1987-1988

BMF 9" blade, no sawteeth: 1988-??
BMF 9" blade, sawteeth: 1989-??
LMF with sawteeth: 1987-1988
LMF no sawteeth: 1987-1988
LMF Tactical 6" blade, no sawteeth: 1988-??
LMF Tactical 6" blade, sawteeth: 1989-??
BOWIE
Bowie Utility: 1989-??
Bowie Utility, Cordia Wood Ltd. Ed.: 1991
Bowie Utility, Stag Ltd. Ed.: 1991
Patriot, Black Blade: 1992-??
Clip-Lock (River Knives)
(Design by Blackie Collins)
Single Edge, Black: 1986-??

Single Edge, Orange: 1986-1988
Double Edge, Black: 1986-1990
Double Edge, Orange: 1986-1990
Survivor, Black: 1988-1994
Survivor, Orange: 1988
Survivor, Yellow Sheath: 1991-1992
Survivor, Pink Sheath: 1991
RiverMaster, Black: 1992-??
Dive/Whitewater Auxiliary Sheath: 1986-present
Moray Dive Knife: 1992-??
Buddy System II Black or Blue: 1992-1993
River Shorty Whitewater/Dive Knife (Italy):
1993-present

MARK II SERIAL NUMBER CHART (1967-1981)

(also see Modern Commercial Daggers and Survival Knives in the Special Section of this section).

YEAR SOLD	QUANTITY	SERIAL # RANGE of KNIVES MADE	DISTINCTIVE FEATURES ADDED OR CHANGED DURING YEAR
Called "Mark II Combat Knife"			
1967	(3,631)	1,001-3,750	5-degree offset narrow forged wasp-body blade, brown sheath with right strap
		3,751-5,000	changed to straight narrow forged wasp-body blade
1968	(4,022)	5,001-9,900	
1969	(4,070)	9,901-14,350	change from Steel Grip handle to gray Armorhide handle
1970	(4,765)	14,351-19,300	change sheath to left strap, Dive Knife version first offered
Called "Mark II Survival Knife"			
1971	(3,817)	19,301-23,750	
1972	(4,049)	23,751-28,000	offer fine serrations as option
1973	(4,769)	28,001-32,900	change to wide hand-ground wasp-body blade, Gold Plated blade offered
1974	(6,024)	32,901-39,000	yellow Dive Knife version discontinued
1975	(5,014)	39,001-44,015	
1976	(7,628)	44,016-54,434	coarse serrations standard, change to green painted sheath
1977	(8,191)	54,435-63,648	change to black sheath, Presentation Grade introduced
1978	(9,411)	63,649-76,001	change to black Armorhide handle
1979	(10,720)	76,002-85,000	change to straight-edge blade; President's Collection introduced
1980	(10,493)	85,001-100,810	
1981	(13,946)	100,811-112,000	

Note: *the option of a Sportsman's Steel in a pocket on the Mark II sheath was offered from the beginning of production.*

Pioneers of Modern Handmade Knives

Scagel Knives

By Dr. James Lucie

Editor's note: Dr. James Lucie not only was a friend of the late William Scagel, but his physician in later years. A journeyman smith in the American Bladesmith Society, Dr. Lucie also makes handforged Scagel-style knives and is a collector of original Scagel knives. All values shown are for original Scagel knives in excellent to mint condition and were furnished by Mr. Gordon White, a noted collector of Scagel, Remington and Marble's knives.

No story on Blade Magazine Cutlery Hall-Of-Famer© William "Bill" Scagel could ever convey the profoundly artistic and rare nature of his work. You must know a few things about this truly great artist, who was ahead of his time, to even begin to appreciate and understand the astronomical rise in the value of his knives.

The sixth and last child of John and Annie Lee Scagel, William Wales Scagel was born on Abraham Lincoln's birthday, Feb. 12, 1875, in Brooke Township of Sarawak, County Grey, Ontario, Canada. When he was 6, his family moved to Sarnia, Ontario, where his father established a boat-building business. Annie Lee was the sister of James Paris Lee, the inventor of the Lee-Enfield rifle. Genealogical records reveal that Bill's great-grandfather was Jacob Scagel, who came to America in 1715. Jacob later joined the Continental Army and fought with Gen. George Washington at Valley Forge, the Battle of Saratoga and at Yorktown.

By the turn of the twentieth century, Bill had served in the British Maritime Service and had traveled the world. Following his tour of duty, he came to the United States in 1900 and worked at a lumber camp in Wisconsin for several years. The lumber camp had a barracks that housed 80 people, but Bill would not live among them. He went down the trail a way, pitched a tent and lived there, working as a lumberjack during the day and making knives at night.

In 1910 he moved to Durand, Michigan, and worked as a troubleshooter for the Grand Trunk Railroad. He was listed in the Durand City Directory in 1907 with his spouse, Alice. It is believed he had been married, divorced and then remarried in Durand. There are no known children from the marriage. He later moved across the Michigan peninsula to Muskegon, where the 1920 census indicates that he was naturalized in 1910 and was "divorced." The City of Muskegon's 1920 Directory lists him as "cutlerer, maker of surgical instruments and metal fabricator."

He set up his blacksmith shop in the Jackson Hill area of Muskegon in 1920, where he began making his famous knives and axes. He actually began making fine cutlery in 1910, as is noted on his letterhead. During this period of his life, he resided in the lumber camp in Wisconsin and then Durand, Michigan, doing cutlery work without the benefit of a well-equipped shop.

Scagel made miniature knives over a period of at least 20 years. The model at right with a bone sheath was made for a man's watch chain in 1934. The tiny knife at left, made in 1936, was for the lady grocer where Bill shopped. The knife at center was made in 1950. Very rare, the Scagel miniatures that have been offered in recent years have been in the **$5,000-10,000** value range.

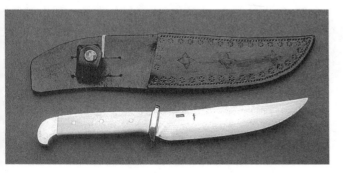

The ivory-handled hunter was made by William Scagel between 1940-1942. With a decorated sheath and in excellent to mint condition, it is valued at **$15,000-22,000**.

In 1936, a fire burned his blacksmith shop on Jackson Hill. He immediately built a shed of corrugated sheet metal and started again. It is interesting that old timers who knew Bill said he believed the fire was a result of arson.

In 1937, he moved eight miles southeast of Muskegon to the village of Fruitport, on Spring Lake. There he procured an odd-shaped acre of ground and built what was to be his final home and shop. He called the new place "Dogwood Nub." There he erected a large windmill, dug a well, and constructed living quarters over his shop.

He had had a rather bitter feud with the local power company and, as a result, refused its power. He used surplus World War I submarine batteries hooked up to his windmill for his power supply. He outfitted his shop with a rather elaborate system of large leather belts and pulleys. They connected a line shaft running off a Montgomery Ward hit-and-miss gas engine. Besides being a master metal worker, he also was an accomplished carpenter and spent many years improving and adding to his new place.

He built a beautiful log cabin on the front of his property, replete with artistic stained glass windows. The second floor, with its counterbalanced staircase, was where he spent many hours doing his oil paintings. Bill was a prolific reader and spent many an evening devouring books under flickering kerosene lanterns. He was an accomplished horticulturist, planting many rare varieties of dogwoods, fruit trees and other strange, exotic plants, many of which are still there today. At one time he did a detailed study of common weeds and classified them as an "order," doing elaborate pencil drawings of them, which in and of themselves are works of art.

A stroll through the Scagel property reveals a multiplicity of elaborately handforged, whimsical garden figures of immense beauty and imagination. Iron cattails and leaves, frogs, snakes climbing vines, and forged camp and bowie knife blades embedded in cement harps and lyres dominated the area. A beautifully made weathervane depicting a hunter and his dog greeted any visitor who drove up to the gate.

He was an accomplished boat builder, having fabricated an all-metal boat and sailed across Lake Michigan with his dog. Besides making cutlery, one of his greatest talents was his ability as an artist in sheet metal. He made magnificent copperware, Dutch ovens, steins, coffee and tea pots, and fry pans with long rosewood handles, all tinned for food and beverage use. You can only look with amazement at the perfect crimping and geometrical lines and proportions of his handiwork—which becomes all the more astonishing when you consider the lack of adequate power to his shop.

As the writer, I feel it incumbent upon me to clear up—finally, I hope—much misinformation as to Scagel's mystique and personality. You have all heard descriptive terms such as "loner," "recluse," "hermit," "mean spirited" and "woman hater" to describe Scagel. None, absolutely none, of these are even close to the truth.

It is true he was not the most gregarious of people and he preferred a rather solitary lifestyle. However, he was committed to doing "his thing," that is, the working of metal and making magnificent pieces of art, whether they were knives, frying pans or anything else. It is true he had two failed marriages, and I have heard from a number of old timers who knew Bill well the various reasons for the failures, and never heard any two reasons alike. Bill simply refused to talk to anyone about his past.

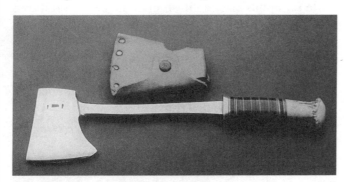

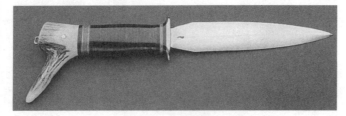

The classy Scagel hatchet (top) was created in 1935 and sports a brass guard and a handle of leather-and-fiber washers and a stag pommel. In excellent to mint condition, the hatchet will go for **$12,000-22,000**. Scagel made the combat knife (immediately above) for a U.S. Marine serving in the Korean War in 1950. The guard is polished brass, the handle is of leather washers, and the pommel is stag. Few were made, and values for examples in mint condition start at around **$18,000-25,000**.

Typical of the hunting knives William Scagel created is this model with a brass guard and ancient ivory scales. The sheath is leather. For examples in mint condition, values begin at around **$15,000-22,000**.

I did not come into his life as his physician and friend until 1956, when he was 81, and sustained a wrist injury that I attended. I do know that if you essentially kept your mouth shut, Bill would take a liking to you. A more helpful or friendly soul simply did not exist. You could engage in opposite dialogue if you did not become dogmatic or controlling about it. His political beliefs were to the far, far right. He had the great, old, early American idea that if you did not work, you did not eat.

As to religion, he insisted he was an atheist. Yet, I have often wondered what went through his mind each springtime when all the strange and exotic rare seeds he planted in his garden would burst forth in full bloom.

During the polio epidemic of 1939, physicians would bring measurements of afflicted children for him to make beautiful, ornate and perfectly functional braces so the children could walk and get around. For this he never rendered a charge. I have seen several of the braces and they go beyond one's imagination. Each was stamped with his kris mark and "handmade WW Scagel."

I do not mean to portray him as a saint. Like all of us, he had his faults. He was more introverted than need

be. If you hurt his feelings or did or said something he considered a slight, he took it very personal and was most loath to ever forgive and forget. He would not go on about it—it just stopped right there, never again to be noised about. I recall asking him once why he did not like "so-and-so," and his reply was generally along the line of, "You do not need to know that."

Sporting Goods Houses

Concerning aspects of his business, he made knives and axes for resale. They were sold through Abercrombie & Fitch of New York; Von Lengerke and Antoine of Chicago; Von Lengerke and Detmold of New York (the latter two sporting goods houses were owned by Abercrombie & Fitch); Pacific Arms Co. of San Francisco, California; and Alcook, Late & Wetwood of Toronto, Ontario, Canada, and its branch office in London, England. This is an area on which I have spent much time, study and research.

With the help of taped interviews of some of Bill's old-time friends who were very close to him, I have formed an opinion and arrived at a sort of timetable chronology of the interaction he had with the sporting goods houses. After examining several hundred Scagel knives and axes over a 30-year span, I have never seen a knife or ax with a Pacific Arms Co. logo or an Alcook, Late & Wetwood of Toronto or London logo. I simply believe they do not exist. I believe they were sold through these houses but

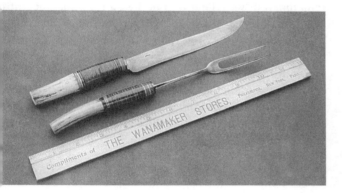

Over the years, Scagel made a wide variety of carving sets. Fashioned in the late '40s, this one features handles similar to his hunting knives—leather washers and horn. Depending on their condition and whether the sets are two or three piece, values begin at around **$6,000-15,000**.

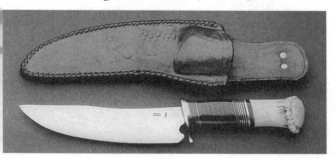

In prime condition, the rare bowie-style campknife measures 13 inches overall. The obverse side of the blade and the tooled leather sheath are stamped "Abercrombie & Fitch." In mint condition, the model would fetch a value of about **$25,000-35,000**.

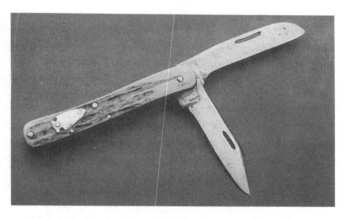

The twin-bladed Scagel folder has seen lots of use. It is also fairly rare. Values for mint models start at around **$8,000-20,000**.

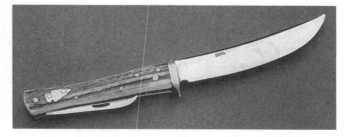

In mint condition, the Scagel hunter with folding blade in the handle is quite rare (only 12 were made). Values start at **$25,000-30,000**.

Bill never had a stamp with their logo in his possession. He did have in his workshop stamps of VL&D, VL&A and A&F.

The taped interviews were very revealing, especially since three of the interviewees who did not know each other said essentially the same thing concerning these houses. They tell of how during the Great Depression of 1929 Bill was notified by VL&A that, because of the Depression, it could not sell the knives for the prevailing prices of the time, and wanted to lower them. This inflamed Bill so much that he asked for the return of all of his merchandise, and he in turn went about the area selling it.

I have several such knives in my collection. From 1929 on, Bill never again made any knives or axes to be sold though these houses. This prompted me to assemble a collection of VL&A catalogs, which I was able to do spanning the years 1921-1933. Interestingly enough, the last catalog to feature his work was dated 1929. So, can we take the position that any knife stamped VL&A, VL&D or A&F was made before and up to 1929? I believe it to be true.

However, I have seen one exception. About five years ago, I acquired a knife marked VL&A that the owner says he bought from Bill in 1943. I cannot explain it but am taking the position that it was an old blade Bill had lying around in his shop. Years earlier it had been stamped VL&A and since it was during the World War II years, with a scarcity of good steel and Bill's penchant for being frugal, he simply finished it up for the customer. There may be other exceptions, though I have not seen them.

Stamps & Steels

Being a creature of habit, Scagel had a system of stamping that must be explained. The explanation should prove helpful to the dealer and collector alike.

If a blade is stamped with a company logo, then it will have no kris, and the "WW Scagel handmade" stamp will be in smaller-case letters than a knife or ax that was purchased at his shop. There also usually will be a "USA" on the commercial variety and not on the ones purchased at his shop. I fully realize that rarely is there an "always" or "never" to most rules. However, I have yet to see an exception. Further, I should be most grateful if some reader can provide me with adequate proof that one exists.

Bill made many butcher knives for the local butchers in our area. Almost all the knives have the smaller-case-letter stamp and no kris, though plainly are stamped with a "USA." This is not so for the typical household cutlery made for the general populace; most of the kitchen knives have the kris and no "USA."

It has been said that Bill made knives from OCS (old Chevrolet springs). This is not true. He used old car springs but not for cutlery. He was very critical about his steels.

His main suppliers were Ryerson Steel of Chicago and SKF Steels of New York. During World War II he used Timken bearing races—but not the bearings themselves— which he was able to obtain from a friend. Probably his biggest supplier was Jessops Steel, whose steel came from a rolling mill in Washington, Pennsylvania, and was called "Swedish Silver Steel" in those days.

I have a letter in my possession dated 1933 from SKF Steels of the Detroit, Michigan, branch. In the letter, SKF wishes to know why it had not received an order from Bill for a long time. Years later, an old friend of his remembered Bill telling him he had a big squabble with SKF over something and he never order from it again.

The Brunswick Pool Table and Bowling Ball Co. was located in Muskegon. Bill had some close friends who worked there, and they supplied him with all the ivory, rosewood and Michigan hardrock maple that he needed. Indeed, I was most fortunate to acquire nearly a lifetime supply of the materials from Bill's shop after his passing.

Categories

I think it important to the collector to categorize Scagel's knives and axes. Trends in any collectibles tend to swing in and out of favor depending on the current vagaries of the time. Except for one knife style, no attempt

The author's camp knives are replicas of Scagel models. The blades are forged 5160 steel, while original Scagel spacers and crown-stag handles finish the pieces in style. The author's list price: **$1,500-1,850** each, depending on handle style.

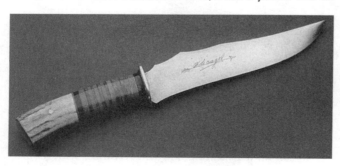

This is Scagel's personal hunter, which probably served him for many other needs, too. Value? Don't ask.

is made here to get into which are the rarest. The exception is the hunting knife with the folder blade in the handle. Bill made only 12 of them, and 12 only. I consider them the rarest and most valuable, though his bowies have to follow as a close second. My listing is not an attempt at establishing rarity; rather, it is for placement in a certain category. The list should comprise the following:

Folders;
Hunters with folder(s) in the handle;
Bird-and-trout knives;
Hunters;
Camp knives;
Fighters, both double and single edge;
Bowies;
Utility knives;
Carving sets;
Matching steak knife & fork sets;
Miniatures;
Butcher knives—commercial;
General kitchen knives, large and small;
Fish and filleting knives; and
Axes—two varieties.

Scagel's axes are very interesting. I consider them rare and very desirable. There are two kinds: (1) General camp ax, rather medium to large size and quite hefty, and (2) the hiking or military backpack axe—which is smaller and more petite—and generally was made with a knife that had a closely matching handle. The latter classification I find to be very rare. Examples are absolute works of art.

Epilogue

Lastly, this article would not be complete without dissemination to the world of knives regarding Scagel's passing. It was on a cold day, March 25, 1963, that I was called to Bill's place and found him lying on the floor in

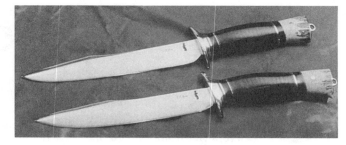

The author patterned these two pieces after Scagel knives, forging the blades from 5160 or 1084 steel. Overall length: 14 inches each. Brass fittings and Scagel leather washers and stag pommels complete the packages. The author's list prices: **$1,800-2,000** each, depending on handle style.

a dazed condition. He had been trying to fix the grate on his wood-burning stove, which long had been cold. The water in a tin cup sitting on a table was frozen. He was in the final stages of irreversible, full-blown, congestive heart failure and renal shutdown.

With great difficulty and much hassle, I got him into my car and took him to the hospital, where he died the following day. I have always regretted this final act on my part, as all I accomplished was to make his last and final day on Earth completely miserable. I should have just sat there, cradling his head in my lap, and let him quietly go to a more peaceful world. His final act of giving was to will his remains to the University of Michigan Medical School for anatomical dissection purposes.

Author's note: The genealogical portions of this article must be credited to Ms. LaRie Jensen of North Salt Lake City, Utah. She has done a most thorough and admirable task of digging out the facts of the Scagel family tree, going back to Jacob Scagel in the year 1715. I owe her more gratitude than I can possibly put into words. Thank you, LaRie.

The author was not only Scagel's physician and friend but, since Scagel's passing, has striven to emulate the master by creating Scagel-style knives, such as this large hunter with a leather handle and brass pommel. The author's list prices: **$950-1,250**, depending on handle style.

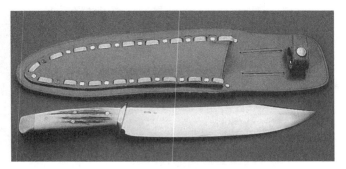

While a majority of the knives Scagel created were standard sizes, he did make bowies on occasion. The big model, with brass fittings and stag handle is in excellent condition and quite rare. The fancy leather sheath is in mint condition, too. The model will go for around **$30,000-40,000**.

Knife-Crafters

Giles Wetherill

Giles Price Wetherill (1903-1974) of Philadelphia literally was a custom knifemaker. In 1937 he told a reporter from *Popular Science* what he meant by "Custom-Built:"

"In making special designs for customers, Wetherill, whenever possible, 'tailors' the knives to the physical 'build' of the men who will use them. He takes seven measurements, including the length of the arm and the forearm, before he begins work on the design of the knife. Usually, he submits three or four patterns, out of which the purchaser chooses one. When an exclusive pattern is desired—that is, one which is not to be sold to anyone else—an additional 'design charge' of $25 is added."

For the time, Wetherill's prices were very high. He charged as much as $1,200 for some of his fancier knives.

As Phillip Krumholz learned from Wetherill's family ("The Forgotten Knifemaker," *Knife World*, January-March

The Knifecrafters Sheath Knives are strictly hand made, very unique in design as will be seen from the above cuts, and differ radically from all machine made knives. Each one is ground by hand from a piece of excellent forged bar steel, and the temper is exactly right. Handles are of the best walnut. They are ordinarily provided with wooden sheaths which grip the knife so tightly that it cannot fall out, and there is no danger of the knife cutting the person in such a sheath. The cuts above show some of the designs, which are priced as follows:

	Knife and Sheath
Fishing Knife, length of blade 6¹⁄₁₆″	$24.00
Scimitar Skinning Knife, length of blade 4½″ to 7½″	24.00
Shark Knife, length of blade 7″	16.00
Viking Curved Draw Knife, blade 5⁵⁄₁₆″, no sheath	14.00
Gilmore Hunting Knife, blade 7⁵⁄₁₆″	32.50
Whelen Wilderness Hunters Knife, 5½″ blade	20.00

We can also have Knifecrafter Sheath Knives built to order to your own specifications, carrying out all your pet ideas, and will be glad to submit an estimate on receipt of sketch and specifications.

1989), Wetherill made knives from 1931 to about 1940. He used the name "Knife-Crafters," but most of his knives, made in 115 styles, were unmarked.

On page 117 of an undated mail-order catalog, probably from the spring of 1937, a Washington, D.C., outfitter called The National Target & Supply Co. showed half-a-dozen "Knifecrafters Sheath Knives." They are identical to some of the knives shown in the *Popular Science* magazine article (catalog courtesy Mark Newcomer).

The "Viking Curved Draw Knife" was in fact Wetherill's interpretation of an American Indian crooked knife. (Collector John L. Malaguerra has a Scagel crooked knife that he bought new in 1928 for use on a Canadian wilderness adventure.) Wetherill's "Whelen Wilderness" butcher-style hunting knife was named for, and perhaps designed by, Col. Townsend Whelen (1877-1961), famous writer and marksman.

Another famous customer was Western author and dedicated angler Zane Grey (1872-1939). He bought several Wetherill knives about 1938, now in the collection of Dan Brock.

We have never seen any Wetherill knives for sale on the open market. An excellent example should bring at least **$2,500**. However, we have seen low-quality, factory-made versions of the "Fishing Knife," value about **$10**.

Howard James

Knives we have seen that were actually marked "Knife-Crafters" were not made by Wetherill. They were made during the 1940s by another man in Philadelphia, Howard James.

In the aforementioned *Knife World* article, Mr. Krumholz wrote that James' Knife-Crafters "business lasted for only a short time, but while in operation, a large quantity of throwing knives were produced which relied heavily on a design Wetherill developed nearly ten years before: the Phantom... [They] carried the distinctive Knife-Crafters

Set of three small Howard James "Knife-Crafters" throwing knives in leather roll-up sheath, value **$600-$1,000**.

trademark where the letters F in the name were tiny knives."

We have seen at least three different styles of Knife-Crafters-marked throwing knives. The largest, the Phantom, has a wide slot cut into the handle designed to put the center of balance closer to the point. Value, **$75-150** each.

Donald Moore; Kennedy Arms; Eske/Nevis

Based on information from Douglas Moore and M. W. Silvey.

Donald W. Moore c1900-1965. (courtesy Douglas Moore)

Donald W. Moore of Minneapolis, Minnesota, was the quintessential part-time knifemaker. Born around 1900, he grew up on a farm and joined the Army just after the Great War, hoping to learn to fly. However, the Army put him in the cavalry, in charge of a string of horses just like back on the farm, so he requested a discharge. Then he went to work for a railroad.

In the 1930s, having acquired some experience in woodworking, Moore and four cousins looked for a business unaffected by the Depression. They tried house building but few people then could afford new houses. Then they turned to casket building. Depression or not, people still died, so the cousins founded the Minneapolis

Casket Co., of which Donald Moore was to become president.

After returning home from the casket company each evening, Moore would nap briefly, then go down to the basement to make knives. In the 1930s, he made kitchen knives from saw steel and with cast-aluminum handles, both singly and in sets. Each set of six came in a wooden knife block, made from casket-factory scraps. He sold the knives around town, his only advertising being word of mouth.

When war came, Moore expanded his knife production. He poured a concrete slab in the basement, on which he set up a grinding shop under the porch, and a casting shop under the house. His brother Ralph came to live in the house and, after his shift at a local defense plant, would help out casting handles.

The Moores made combat knives with aluminum handles, some marked MOORE on the handle, others marked with the name of Moore's only retailer, Kennedy Brothers Arms Co. of St. Paul, across the Mississippi River. Some of the Moore combat knives have brass guards. Moore's son, Doug, then in his early teens, riveted the sheaths for all the combat knives, and when an order was ready for Kennedy Arms, Doug brought the knives there by streetcar. (Kennedy Arms also sold stout daggers with blued blades, wooden handles and brass guards backed with fiber, though they were made by someone else.)

Ordinarily, Donald Moore sold the knives that he made, but if a serviceman came to his house in uniform, Moore would give him a knife for free. After the war, some of these men expressed their appreciation by presenting war souvenirs to Doug, such as swords, pistols and bayonets.

Donald Moore returned to making kitchen knives in the evenings after the war, though he also would make sheath knives to order. He had made enough profit from the knife business during the war to pay off his mortgage, and to buy a new 1946 Plymouth for cash.

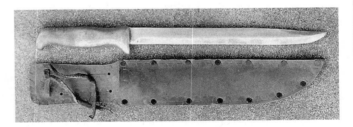

Douglas Moore's own custom MOORE knife, riveted sheath.

KENNEDY/ ARMS/ ST. PAUL dagger, value about **$400**.

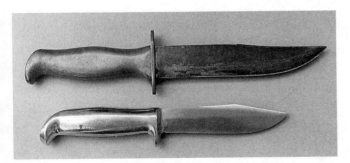

Above: (Top) MOORE/MPLS combat knife with brass guard, value about **$300**. (courtesy Douglas Moore) (Bottom) MOORE hunting knife, value about **$150**.

Moore retired from the casket company in 1965. His plan was to move north, to rural Nevis, Minnesota, and make knives in partnership with his brother-in-law, Albin Eskelson. However, Moore died a few weeks after retiring. Eskelson made knives similar in style to Moore's. They are stamped ESKE/NEVIS in a small circle on the handle.

Moore-marked knives are scarce today. Aluminum-handled MOORE or MOORE/MPLS combat knives bring at least **$250**, the wooden-handled Kennedy Arms daggers at least **$400**.

Randall Made, Orlando, Florida

All values courtesy of Rhett Stidham

W.D. "Bo" Randall was—and still is—the most influential knifemaker of the past half century. The influence of Randall design and construction on other knifemakers and on manufacturers, too, is easy to see, but just as important has been the example of his well-publicized career. A charter member of the Blade Magazine Cutlery Hall-Of-Fame©, Randall showed hundreds of would-be knifemakers that it is possible for one craftsman to "re-invent" mankind's oldest tool, and to create a globe-spanning business and reputation in the process.

The Beginning

The story of how W.D. Randall the orange grower became W.D. Randall the knifemaker has been told so many times that it has acquired something of the flavor of legend.

One day in the summer of 1937, near the shore of Walloon Lake in Michigan, Randall saw a man scraping paint from a boat with a remarkable-looking knife—a knife that proved to be one made by Blade Magazine Cutlery Hall-Of-Famer William Scagel (see "Scagel Knives" earlier in this segment). The fellow would not desist from abusing the knife, nor could he be persuaded to part with it. Randall therefore determined to try his hand at making one like it for himself.

Within five years this personal challenge had turned into a hobby, and the hobby into a booming business. Half-a-century and 200,000 handmade knives later, Randall had become the best-known knifemaker of the century.

Not long after having seen that first Scagel knife, Randall sought out its maker, and the two men became friends. Randall began to collect Scagel knives and eventually accumulated about 30, which are now on display in the Randall knife museum, which adjoins the Randall knife shop in Orlando. The centerpiece of the collection is that first paint-scraping Scagel, a gift many years later from its original owner.

Here is how Randall described what happened after that lakeshore encounter with a Scagel (copyright 1996 *Randall Made Knives,* used by permission):

"I challenged myself to make a knife that was just as good, or at least make the best knife I could make ... Before long I had a shop with a small forge and I put a lot of time into crafting knives that I could be proud to make and use myself. And [then] I began selling them at my father-in-law's clothing store in Orlando.

"As an outdoorsman, I took a lot of personal satisfaction in creating knives that were simple in design but very functional. And a growing business evolved among friends, fellow sportsmen, and sales to a few large sporting goods stores [most notably, Abercrombie & Fitch of New York]. Through it all, I managed our family's citrus groves and I continued to think of my hand-made knives as an avocation.

"Then World War II began. A young sailor asked me to make him a knife for use in man-to-man combat. When his friends saw it, they placed orders, and their friends placed orders, and my knives were used in combat, and a reporter wrote a story and ... [a]ll hell broke loose. Suddenly, unexpectedly, we were in the knife business, as envelopes addressed simply to 'Knife Man, Orlando, Florida' arrived on the doorstep.

"I built a full-scale shop and for the first time began using apprentices. With demand so strong, it was tempting to develop mass production methods. But now, more than ever, I wanted Randall Made to stand for quality and dependability, because servicemen were telling how much they relied on my knives.

"One wrote, 'It was a terrible thing at close range. (Your knife) would cut a man's head nearly off with a quick swing ... I also used that knife to open cans, cut wood, dress water buffalo ... and it stayed sharp. I was offered all kinds of trades, but I wouldn't part with it.'

Blade Magazine Cutlery Hall-Of-Famer©
Walter Doane "Bo" Randall 1909-1989

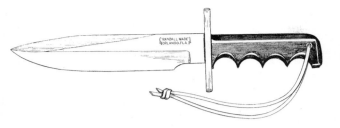

Randall Model 14, about **$290**. (drawing by Blade Magazine Cutlery Hall-Of-Famer© M.H. Cole)

"Since that time, Randall Made knives have been used extensively by soldiers and Marines, flyers and sailors, generals and infantrymen. Our customers have also included astronauts, government agents, celebrities, statesmen and royalty ...

"The first seven Gemini astronauts carried specially designed (Model 17) Randall Made knives ... General William Westmoreland wore his Randall while commanding forces in Vietnam ... there's a Randall Made in the Museum of Modern Art and the Smithsonian Institution.

"During World War II, one Army Air Force Captain was so enthusiastic about his first Randall that he ordered two more, saying, 'I have become your personal representative.' His name is Ronald Reagan ...

"Most importantly to me, there are thousands upon thousands of individuals who choose Randall Made knives because they need a superbly crafted knife they can count on in the home and in the field. Or, as is often the case today, they've wanted to have a Randall Made knife in their collection.

"For some years now, my son, Gary, has been instrumental in the business. He is honored, as I am, that

RANDALL VALUES AND MORE
BY RHETT STIDHAM

To receive the latest Randall catalog, including color pictures, prices, options and delivery times, send $2.00 ($5 for international customers) to: Randall Made Knives, P.O. Box 1988, Orlando, FL 32802, or view the Randall catalog online at http://www.randallknives.com.

For many years the Randall customer was able to order a customer-designed knife, but that is no longer the case. Only Randall-authorized designs, as shown in the Randall catalog, with allowed options, may be ordered. At this writing, September 2004, the Randall delivery time is 47 months. (Since the delivery time changes often, please contact the Randall shop for updates.) A $20 deposit is required for each knife ordered.

Also, in the past, the Randall shop and many authorized dealers stocked Randall knives for immediate delivery. Today, that is not the case. Most authorized Randall dealers are sold out on delivery knives for one to two years. Therefore, many models sell on the after market for **$100-200** over the Randall list price. In fact, Randalls are among the most-sought-after collectible straight knives.

Many Randall collectors, novice and veteran, are members of the Randall Knife Society, with the current membership at over 1900. The organization offers four collector-type newsletters quarterly that keep members up to date on Randall shop news and what is happening in collecting old and new Randalls. Also, periodically, a club knife is offered to the membership. (For Randall club knife values, see the "Knife Club Limited Edition Knives" segment

in the chapter, "Commemorative, Knife Club, and Limited Edition Knives" in Part 1 of Section II.) For information on the Randall Knife Society, write P.O. Box 158, Meadows of Dan, VA 24120 or visit the RKS Web site at http://www.randallknifesociety.com.

The collecting of older Randall knives can involve lucrative values. Many 1940s-era Randalls command values of **$2,000-5,000**, with an ultra-rare knife bringing as much as **$10,000**. Vietnam-War-era Randalls are the most-sought-after Randalls by collectors. Combat models with green tenite or brown Micarta® handles are relatively common but still bring values in the thousands.

The sheath for the Randall is almost as important as the knife. Most serious collectors do not consider the package complete unless a Randall knife has the proper sheath. In the 1940s, Randall sheaths were made mostly by H.H. Heiser (Denver, Colorado) and Clarence Moore (Orlando, Florida), with Heiser making Randall sheaths until about 1962/63. Moore made Randall sheaths into the early-to-mid 1950s. In 1963, Maurice Johnson, a retired state policeman from Indiana, became the only Randall sheath maker until the early 1980s. Maurice sold out to his son, Johnny Johnson, who made sheaths for Randall until Johnson's death in December 1991.

Greg Gutcher, Sullivan's Holster Shop, Tampa, Florida, today is the only maker of Randall knife sheaths. Sullivan's started making sheaths for Randall in January 1987 on some models and, since December 1991, has been the only Randall sheath maker.

Randall Made knives are on display in museums, as well as in many private collections ... But frankly, our favorite models are those specifically designed to be carried and used day in and day out, year after year. The reason is because, like many of you, Gary and I are both sportsmen, so we make knives we want to use ..."

W.D. "Bo" Randall passed away Dec. 25, 1989, at his home after visiting with his family earlier in the day. Bo and his son Gary had managed the business side by side for over 25 years. Gary Randall continues the tradition of hand crafting knives that bear the Randall Made trademark, along with his sons of the next Randall generation, Jason and Michael Randall.

To learn more, see the 1993 book *Randall Made Knives, the History of the Man and his Blades*, by Robert L. Gaddis; *The Randall Saga* (1992), by Dominique Beaucant; *Randall Fighting Knives in Wartime* (2002), by Robert E. Hunt; and *The Randall Chronicles* (2003), by former Randall shop foreman and *BLADE®* field editor, Pete Hamilton.

The Knife Museum

The Randall knife museum adjoins the shop in Orlando. Back in the 1960s, W.D. Randall bought a large collection of knives that a physician had been assembling since 1900. They and Randall's Scagels became the core of the museum.

The museum also displays all sorts of Randall memorabilia, including many testimonial letters from famous customers. Perhaps most interesting are the showcases containing one of virtually every Randall knife ever made, both regular models and special-order designs.

Special Designs

Bo Randall kept a file of some of the original sketches submitted for special-order knives. A sketch for a diver's

About 1200 Model 1's marked RANDALL MADE/SPFLD. MASS. were made in 1943-1945 under license by William F. Larsen of Springfield at the Northampton (Massachusetts) Cutlery Co. Sheaths by Southern Saddlery Co., Chattanooga. Excellent to mint value, **$3,000-5,000**. (drawing by Blade Magazine Cutlery Hall-Of-Famer© M.H. Cole)

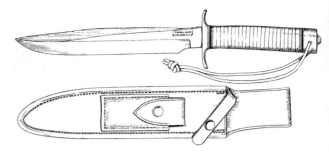

The Randall Model 1, 1940s era, excellent to mint value, **$3,500-5,000**, with the very first 1943 Model 1's commanding **$7,000-10,000**. A 1963 brown-button, Johnson-sheathed Model 1 is valued at up to **$3,000**. Later 1960s Model 1's with Johnson rough-back sheaths are valued at **$800-1,500**. (drawing by Blade Magazine Cutlery Hall-Of-Famer© M.H. Cole)

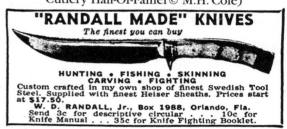

A 1947 ad from Field & Stream *shows an early Randall Model 3. (courtesy Greg Plass)*

This Model 12-6" Sportsman's Bowie, with walnut handle, was made for Robert Abels, pioneer bowie collector and author. Value, **$5,000**. (Rhett Stidham collection)

1991 Randall Knife Society club knives. Value, **$550** (Micarta® handle), **$595** (stag). (photo by Blade Magazine Cutlery Hall-Of-Famer© Jim Weyer)

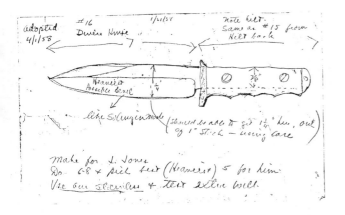

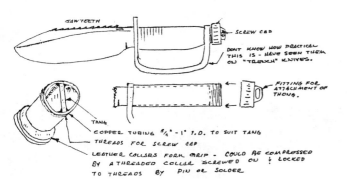

knife was sent to Randall in January 1958 by novelist James Jones, long a devotee of Randall knives. He wanted five made just like it. The design was adopted as the Model 16 in April 1958.

Capt. George W. Ingraham, 94th Medical Detachment, U.S. Army, sent Randall a sketch from Vietnam in January 1963. It was of his design for a rescue-and-survival knife for helicopter pilots and crew members, based on the Randall Model 14 "Attack."

The sawteeth were for cutting through aluminum and plexiglas on wrecked aircraft. The hollow handle would hold matches, water purification tablets, Dexedrine (stimulant), and Demerol (pain killer).

The hollow handle was not a new idea. Compare the match-safe knives made in the 1930s and 1940s by Ka-Bar (see the "American Hunting Knives" segment earlier in this section) and Case (see the segment on "United States Military Fixed Blade Knives" in the following "Special Section"). Ingraham's reason for having minimal survival needs stored in the knife handle was very simple. In his words, "no one is foolish enough to waste time hunting through wreckage for his survival gear when the gas tank may explode at any minute."

The Randalls experimented with the design and made several changes to keep costs reasonable. They eliminated the knuckle bow and shortened the tang. They replaced the threaded end with a rubber crutch tip. They used stainless steel for the handle instead of copper and they left the metal bare. This way, the user could wrap the handle with fishing line, tape, cord, boot laces, or whatever

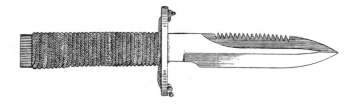

Randall Model 18. Value, **$1,500** for model shown. Value with rubber crutch-tip butt, **$2,000-3,000**. (drawing by Blade Magazine Cutlery Hall-Of-Famer© M.H. Cole)

he might find useful. The knife then became the Model 18 in the Randall line. Later, a threaded buttcap was offered as an option. The original cost was **$28.50** with sheath.

Morseth Knives

By Steve Morseth and Blade Magazine Cutlery Hall-Of-Famer© Bernard Levine

Steve Morseth was Harry Morseth's grandson.

Harry Morseth

In 1906, a 17-year-old Norwegian youth named Harry Morseth left his parents' homeland to settle in the United States. He traveled across the country, to the vicinity of Everett, Washington. On the map, that part of Washington looks as if it had been transplanted from the coast of Norway. There, in 1910, Morseth found work in the Walton lumber mill. Forty years later he retired from Walton Lumber Co. as mill foreman, but along the way had decided to embark upon a second career in the knife business.

In the 1950s, Morseth wrote:

"Frankly, I'm a crank about knives. I've been going hunting since I was a boy in Norway … and from first hand experience I've learned what hunters want and need from an all-purpose hunting and skinning knife. The precise details of knife design and construction have been of life-long interest to me, including blade steel, temper, shape, width, length, thickness, taper, bevel, tang, [guard], handle and sheath. For my own pleasure, and as a hobby, I have made an endless number of knives and sheaths to develop the most nearly perfect combination of features."

In 1934, Morseth made his first knife for commercial sale. It was a hunting knife similar in design to the Marble's knives then in vogue. Like many of the Marble's models, Morseth's first knife had a stag handle and a crown-stag butt. Unlike the Marble's knives, which have pinned, two-piece, stag handles, his knife had a one-piece handle.

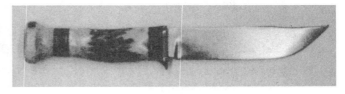

Original 1934 Morseth knife.

Original Morseth marking, 1949-1973.

For the blades of his first commercial knives, Morseth used a material familiar to him from the sawmill: planer-blade steel. The steel worked well but not as well as the laminated steel in knives from his old home in Norway.

Laminated Steel

One of the strengths of the samurai swords of old Japan is that their blades are laminated. A thin cutting edge of extremely hard steel is laminated between layers of tough, resilient iron or mild steel. The hard steel edge provides keen cutting ability, while the blade's mild sides support the edge and keep the blade from breaking.

Independently of the Japanese, the Norwegians discovered the virtues of laminated steel for blades. Unlike Japanese laminated blades, which are forged painstakingly by hand, Norwegian laminated blades are mass produced in a rolling mill. The outer layer of mild Norway iron is wrapped around and welded to the core of high carbon steel in one continuous operation. Many an inexpensive Norwegian *Tollekniv* (see Part 3 of Section II, "Foreign, Exotic, Primitive, and Historical Fixed Blade Knives") has a composite blade made in such a manner.

In 1939, Morseth went to Norway and visited the factory where strips of laminated blade steel were rolled. He ordered a batch of the steel and returned home. However, before his order could be shipped, World War II began, Norway was conquered, and all of its steel output was given over to Nazi war production.

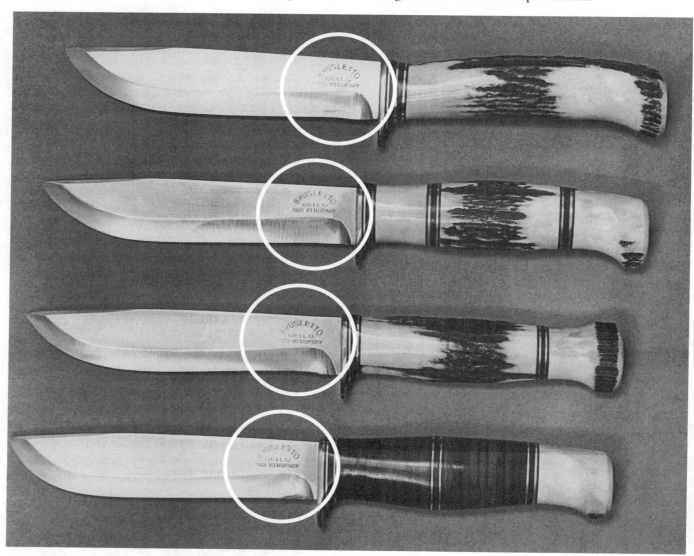

In 1949, Morseth received his first shipment of laminated steel in blade-blank form from Norway. Because the shipment consisted of blade blanks and was not simply raw steel stock, U.S. Customs required that the blanks be marked to show their origin. Consequently, the first laminated Morseth blades are stamped BRUSLETTO/GEILO/MADE IN NORWAY.

In the 1940s, Morseth continued to make knives out of planer-blade and other tool steels. Finally, in 1949, he received his first shipment of laminated steel.

Actually, what he received was not steel bars. Instead, he received blade blanks that had been stamped out to his own design in the factory. Because the shipment consisted of blade blanks and was not simply raw steel stock, U.S. Customs required that the blanks be marked to show their origin. Consequently, the first laminated Morseth blades are stamped BRUSLETTO/GEILO/MADE IN NORWAY.

Morseth Laminated Knives

By 1949, Morseth had refined his techniques and blade design considerably. At the time, all Morseth hunting knives had the same 5-inch blade style, the one he had settled upon as ideal. He hardened his blades to a Rockwell of 63 Rc, significantly harder than the 57 Rc Brusletto used on its blades.

Morseth offered four handle options with his basic blade: Model 1 had a one-piece stag handle; Model 2 had his distinctive three-piece stag handle; Model 2A had his original two-piece stag handle; and Model 3 had a leather-washer handle with a stag butt. Until 1951, all Morseth knives had brass guards. After that time, the guards were nickel silver.

Morseth knives were expensive for their day. A Model 1 cost $18, 2 and 2A cost $16, and 3 cost $14. The price of each knife included an ingenious Morseth Safe-Lok sheath

2,650,008
SCABBARD
Harry Morseth, Everett, Wash.
Application June 18, 1951, Serial No. 232,177
1 Claim.   (Cl. 224—2)

A scabbard for a hunting knife or the like comprising a relatively flexible outer case providing an elongated pocket open at its upper end, a liner for the pocket secured to the outer casing and comprising a flattened, relatively rigid, fiber tube that is substantially coextensive with said pocket and is closed at its lower end, the front and back walls of the liner tube at the upper end portion of the same being flared outwardly to receive therebetween the hilt end portion of a knife, and said liner tube being provided in the upper end portion thereof with recesses extending longitudinally along the side edge portions thereof inwardly from the upper end of the same between said outwardly flared portions of the front and back walls, said recesses being adapted to receive the ends of the hilt of a knife positioned in the liner tube, and said recesses being similarly formed and each having an enlarged lower part and a restricted upper portion leading outwardly therefrom and having outwardly converging walls adapted to yieldingly embrace the hilt of a knife positioned in the liner tube and to retain the same therein against accidental displacement.

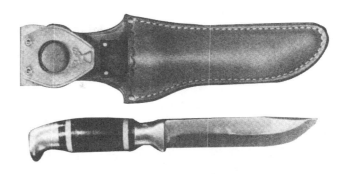

1953 Morseth $8.95 utility knife.

(U.S. Patent 2,650,008 granted 1953). The leather sheath is lined with vulcanized fiber (the same material used for handle spacers). The fiber protects the leather—and the wearer—from the point and cutting edge of the knife, and its springiness helps retain the guard of the knife in place. The leather hold-down collar slips over the handle for further protection. Of the Safe-Lok, Blade Magazine Cutlery Hall-Of-Famer Bob Loveless said in "A Pirate Looks At 70," January 2001 *BLADE®:* "The best sheath in the world was the Morseth [Safe-Lok] sheath ... There's no knife sheath better for safety."

New Models

The prices of Morseth knives put them out of reach of most sportsmen. In 1953, demand for high-priced handmade knives was the slackest it had been since before World War II. In consequence, Morseth began to offer a relatively inexpensive, plain utility knife.

The knife had a 5-inch blade and a leather-washer handle with aluminum-alloy mounts. The first ones had white fiber spacers, though most of the later ones did not. With a plain Safe-Lok sheath, the knife cost $8.95. It was produced until about 1960.

In 1954, responding to revived customer demand, Morseth added another model to his practical but limited line. The new knife was called the Morseth Bowie. It differed from the older models in that it had a 6-inch blade with a sharp false edge.

The new knife was offered in a choice of one-piece stag, three-piece stag, or leather-washer-and-stag handles. In addition, the bowie and the original hunting knife were

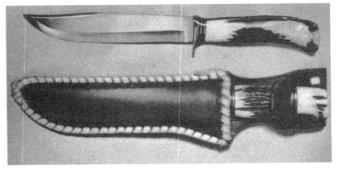

1954 Morseth 6" modified bowies.

offered with a one-piece, Scandinavian-style wooden handle. Wood options were ebony, teak and purple heart. In addition, the Safe-Lok sheath could be had in a plain stitched version, as well as the original fancy laced style.

Later Years

In 1956, Morseth moved across the strait from Everett to the village of Clinton, Washington, on Whidbey Island. A few minor design changes can help to distinguish later Morseth hunting knives from earlier ones. In 1958, the nickel-silver handle spacers were replaced with white fiber ones. In 1961, the guard was made slightly curved instead of straight as it had been.

In 1961, Morseth's grandson, Steve, began to make knives. As Steve described it,

"By early 1965 it was pretty much decided I had the necessary ability (or stupidity), and a corporation would be formed and I would take over the manufacture of the 'Morseth' knife … In January 1966 Harry Morseth retired from knifemaking and the corporation was formed. Immediately I ordered laminated bar stock and blade blanks in 5mm stock (3/16-inch) for my five new models."

Steve Morseth began his manufacturing with a total of seven models. They were:

1) Original Morseth 5-inch-blade hunting knife;
2) 6-inch-blade modified bowie, introduced 1954;
3) 5-inch-blade modified bowie;
4) Morseth Michigan with a 3 3/4-inch blade;
5) Morseth Cascade Skinner with a 4 1/4-inch blade;
6) Military Survival with a 6-inch blade; and
7) Military Survival with a 7-inch blade.

Harry Morseth in the 1950s.

Models 6 and 7 included a special quick-draw military sheath with a stone pocket, and as an option could be fitted with a lugged, double-brass guard. All models were offered with a choice of wood, leather, one-piece-stag or three-piece-stag handles. Besides making the standard Morseth models, Steve also made many custom knives.

Division

After a rich life and an eventful knifemaking career, Harry Morseth passed away on Oct. 9, 1967. On Dec. 14, 1971, Gordon Morseth, Harry's son and Steve's father, and owner of a controlling interest in the corporation, Morseth Sports Equipment Co., Inc., sold the corporation to Blade Magazine Cutlery Hall-Of-Famer© A.G. Russell.

After 1971, Russell manufactured MORSETH knives in Springdale, Arkansas, while Steve Morseth made S. MORSETH knives in Washington until his death in 1995. Russell has continued to use imported laminated steel for his MORSETH knives, while Steve Morseth had switched to 154CM, a modern stainless alloy. Steve had continued to make the Safe-Lok sheath, while A.G. makes standard leather sheaths for his MORSETH knives.

PRICE GUIDE TO OLDER MORSETH KNIVES

Original Morseth from planer blade: **$700**; with copper-lined sheath used prior to fiber lining: **$2,500**.

Morseths marked BRUSLETTO/GEILO/MADE IN NORWAY with Safe-Lok sheath. No sheath, subtract 30 percent.

5-inch-blade original design:
   Stag **$700**   Leather **$400**   Wood **$300**.

5-inch-blade utility, leather and aluminum: **$110**.

6-inch-blade modified bowie:
   Stag **$700**   Leather **$400**   Wood **$300**.

1966-1972 Models

5-inch-blade modified bowie:
   Stag **$600**;   Leather **$300**   Wood **$250**.

Morseth Michigan with 3 3/4-inch blade:
   Stag **$600**;   Leather **$300**   Wood **$250**.

Morseth Cascade Skinner with 4 1/4-inch blade:
   Stag **$600**;   Leather **$300**   Wood **$250**.

Military Survival with 6-inch blade:
   Stag **$600**;   Leather **$300**   Wood **$250**.

Military Survival with 7-inch blade:
   Stag **$600**;   Leather **$300**   Wood **$250**.

Lugged hilt on military survival: add **$40**.

F. J. Richtig

By Harlan Suedmeier

Harlan Suedmeier, RFD #2, Box 299-D, Nebraska City, NE 68410, collects Richtig and Floyd Nichols knives.

Believe it or not, the only knifemaker ever featured in Ripley's "Believe It or Not" was Frank Joseph Richtig of Clarkson, Nebraska. In the Nov. 18, 1936, installment of Ripley's syndicated newspaper feature, Richtig was sketched cutting a steel buggy axle into slices by hammering one of his butcher knives into the axle. In the 1930s, with his wife Mary, Richtig traveled to fairs and carnivals around the Midwest, performing the dramatic axle-slicing demonstration with his handmade knives.

Richtig was born to Czech immigrant parents on a Colfax County, Nebraska, farm on Dec. 28, 1887. In 1906, at age 19, he went to work as an apprentice in a blacksmith shop. Two years later, he and a partner set up their own shop in Clarkson. They operated the blacksmith business and sold Dodge and Dort automobiles until 1923, when Richtig sold his share to pursue another interest.

In 1916, Richtig had begun experiments in the heat treating of knife steels, culminating in his purchase of a Paragon electric heat-treat oven. In July 1925, he leased a shop and began to produce knives. He built much of his own machinery, including grinders, double-wheel buffers and casting equipment. He used the casting equipment to pour and mold aluminum-alloy handles onto the tangs of his blades. The cast handles were both durable and sanitary.

Richtig's main production was 11 styles of aluminum-handled kitchen and butcher knives, most made in several choices of blade length and thickness. Current values range from **$75** for a paring or steak knife to **$400** for a cleaver or big butcher knife.

Frank Richtig, with combat knives and miniatures.

Richtig also made aluminum-handled hunting knives in half-a-dozen standard models, plus at least a dozen custom or special-order styles. They are now worth from $150-650 each.

Before and during World War II, Richtig made daggers, hunting knives and fighters that had brass guards and butts, and handles made of thin, stacked-leather washers with brass and fiber spacers. The tangs were extended and drilled to make a lanyard loop. His few postwar sheath knives lack the loop, and the handles are made of thick washers with few spacers. The knives are now worth from **$800** for postwar examples, up to around **$4,500** for really fine older ones. The sheaths for Richtig's combat knives were made by saddler Alfred Cornish of Omaha, Nebraska.

Besides his functional knives, Richtig made a wide variety of miniature knives and hand tools that could be worn as jewelry. They are worth **$100** and up.

Richtig died in 1977 after a knifemaking career spanning more than half-a-century. He took his "secret" heat-treating method with him to the grave. [See *Knives '84*, page 40, and *Knives '88*, page 30.]

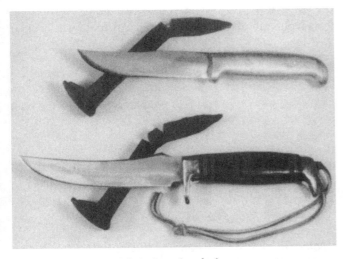

Richtig hunting knives.

Floyd Nichols

By Harlan Suedmeier

Floyd F. Nichols of David City, Nebraska, was a welder turned artist. He began to make small bronze, silver and copper Western scenes about 1927. Instead of the casting process, he used an acetylene torch to build them. He also made silver bits and spurs, custom jewelry, and elaborately carved-and-painted wooden figures.

A World War I veteran, Nichols turned his hand to making combat knives in World War II. He forged and ground the blades from manganese steel, and then tempered them to be somewhat soft on the theory that, in battle, a bent knife is more useful than a broken one. He formed the handles by wrapping 1/8-inch brazing or welding rod around the tang, sometimes using filler under the wrapping to make the handle easier to hold. The butt was a small knob attached to the tang, often inlaid with either a buffalo nickel or an Indian-head penny. He usually stamped the owner's name, serial number, and home town in the edge of the brass guard. Like Richtig, Nichols had his leather sheaths made by Alfred Cornish. Altogether, Nichols made about 1,200 knives.

Nichols died Nov. 17, 1958, after a long bout with cancer. Today, his knives are worth from **$1,500** to **$4,000** or more for a really fine example.

A Nichols combat knife.

Floyd Nichols with his torch sculpture.

A.C. Cornelison

By Larry Newell

Larry Newell is A.C. Cornelison's grand nephew.

*A.C. Cornelison
in the early 1950s.*

Asa Calvin Cornelison was born Aug. 10, 1908, in Texas. As a boy he moved to Scottsboro, Alabama. He forged knives there beginning in 1938 until 1950, when he moved to Detroit to work for Champion Sparkplug. During World War II, he served in the Army Air Corps repairing aircraft machine guns, also making knives on the side. He retired to Alabama in 1970.

In the late 1930s, he advertised his "World Famous Hunting Knives" in half-a-dozen outdoor magazines, including the *American Rifleman*, which reported in the December 1938 issue's "Trade Dope" section: "Custom Jackknife for outdoorsman is made entirely of Chrome-Vanadium tool steel, by A.C. Cornelison … at $6.50. There are sticking and skinning blades … Length closed 4 1/2 inches. Weight 8 ounces; number of parts, four … Purpose of design, great strength, durability, and reliability for explorers and other outdoorsmen who must depend on their pocket knife miles from shipping points."

Besides his tough, all-steel folders, Cornelison made fixed-blade hunting knives with stag handles, as well as plain, unhandled knives, which he gave to friends and relatives. He also made a few switchblades.

In the 1940s, Cornelison made his "Soldier's Knives," 6-inch-bladed daggers with cast-aluminum handles. According to Cornelison, "The mold was hot and filled with melted aluminum. The [stainless steel] blade was taken from the high temperature furnace and the end of the blade was pushed down into the mold, overflowing the surplus aluminum. The calcined clay mold was broken

Folder marked on the handle CHROMIUM VANADIUM STEEL/A.C. CORNELISON/SCOTTSBORO, ALA. U.S.A.

off after cooling." He also made big 19-inch brush knives with riveted aluminum handles.

Cornelison knives are rare, and are worth **$500** and up. The folders we have seen were marked on the handle, while the straight knives were marked on the blade.

R.H. Ruana

Based on information from Mel Fassio, Gregory Daschle, Ken Warner, and Bill Lung.

Blade Magazine Cutlery Hall-Of-Famer® Rudolph H. Ruana was born April 11, 1903, in Alexandria, Minnesota. When he was small, his family moved to North Dakota. In the early 1920s, Ruana served as a blacksmith in the Third Field Artillery, Sixth Division, United States Army. It was here that he reportedly made his first two knives, out of an old Ford leaf spring.

In March 1932, Ruana married Helmi Hellman in New Leipzig, North Dakota. In 1937, they headed west and joined other families of Finnish descent in the little towns just east of Missoula, Montana—Milltown, Bonner and West Riverside—the area then called *Finntown*. Ruana found work as a welder and mechanic at a garage in Bonne and, in 1938, began to make hunting knives on a regular, part-time basis.

Ruana continued to make knives throughout the 1940s, but demand for them was never steady enough for him to go full time. Finally, in 1953, he decided the time was right, so he bought the garage in Bonner, moved his knifemaking equipment there and became a full-time maker.

Ruana knives are unmistakable in style. As Ruana described them in his January 1966 catalog: "These knives are made by a combination of handcraft processes and the use of modern power tools. The blades are made of finest Hi-Carbon spring steel, forged with a modern power hammer, freehand hollow ground, individually oil quenched and heat treated. The handles are made of aluminum, cast directly on the tang, with native Montana elk horn inserts beveled and riveted."

In 1966 his line consisted of 12 standard hunting knife models, two big deluxe models, and the deluxe hatchet. All told, over the years, Ruana offered almost 40 models, including some big bowie knives, and he also made some special-order knives.

In 1964, when Ruana's three sons were grown, he realized that none of them wanted to join him in the knife business. He announced to the family that he was planning to shut down the business and retire in four years, when he turned 65. His son-in-law, Victor Hangas, did not approve of Ruana's plan to shut down the business, and he also did not like his job with the telephone company. Hangas soon quit his job and went to work for Ruana, gradually taking on more and more of the knifemaking tasks.

With the future of the business assured, Ruana stayed on. Indeed, he did not retire until 1983, when he was 81.

He died on April 29, 1986, but Ruana knives are still made the old way in Bonner by Victor Hangas. For information write: Ruana Knife Works, Box 520, Bonner, MT 59823. Current prices for Ruana knives made by Hangas range from **$75** to **$400**, higher for special orders. (For more on Rudy Ruana, see *Hear The Hammer: The Story of Montana's Ruana Knives*, by Smith, Towsley and Mandell. For your copy of the book, contact Ruana Book, Box 8141, Missoula, MT 59802.)

John Ek

Based on information from Robert Buerlein.

John Ek, like W.D. Randall, came to prominence in the world of knives during World War II. However, Ek was the head of a hand knifemaking operation rather than being a knifemaker himself.

A machine shop owner in Hamden, Connecticut, Ek began to manufacture commando knives of his own design in 1941. His first two models were plain, straight-bladed knives with shaped maple handles, no guards, and cast-in-place lead rivets. The Model 1 is single-edged with a sharp false edge, while the Model 2 is double-edged. Eventually there were to be 10 models during the war, all of them distinctive, no-frills Ek designs.

Ek sold his knives to active-duty military personnel only, and, beginning in late 1943, registered each knife's serial number to its original owner. At the peak of wartime production, Ek employed three shifts working seven days a week making knives, and he is reported to have sold over 100,000 knives by war's end.

In 1949, Ek moved to Miami, Florida. There his shop continued to make knives for private sale to military men, and thousands of Ek/Miami knives saw service in Korea and Vietnam.

Ek died in October 1976 and his son Gary took over the business. In 1982, Gary moved it to Richmond, Virginia. Subsequently he sold the Ek Commando Knife Company to the old Blackjack Knives of Effington, Illinois. At last report, Gary Ek had returned to Miami to hand craft knives under the "Ekknives" trademark.

World War II Ek knives are scarce now, especially those in excellent condition. Most were carried overseas by combat troops, and many were lost or broken in the field.

John Ek, Hamden, Connecticut, Model 4. (drawing by Blade Magazine Cutlery Hall-Of-Famer© M.H. Cole). Values of Hamden-marked knives: Models 1, 2, 5, 6, 7, 9, 10: about **$400**. Models 3, 4: about **$450**. Model 8: about **$600**. Ek Miami-marked knives, all models, about **$450**.

John Nelson Cooper

Based on information from Blade Magazine Cutlery Hall-Of-Famer© B.R. Hughes, Jack Lewis, Roger Combs, Don Nagel and Alex Collins.

John Cooper is remembered as the "Knifemaker to the Stars" of Hollywood in the 1960s and 1970s, but he first made knives in Tremont, Pennsylvania, in 1924, where he was born in 1906. He began with kitchen knives, graduating to field knives in 1927. He worked as a welder, making knives in his spare time. In the Army in World War II, he was stationed in the Panama Canal Zone, where he continued to make knives in his spare time, for fellow GIs.

Discharged in 1945, Cooper settled in Virginia Beach, Virginia. There he set up a shop to make hunting knives, and continued to work as a welder. In 1950, he started to make combat knives for soldiers going to Korea.

In 1964, Cooper moved to Burbank, California. He became a full-time knifemaker in partnership with part-time maker/part-time actor, Don Nagel, and with his own nephew, George Cooper. George handled sales at gun shows. In 1967 and '68, Cooper secured patents on his method of brazing the guard to the blade, thereby forming a smoothly curving, dirt-proof and nearly indestructible junction.

Besides Nagel, Cooper took on as assistants Jody Samson and Alex Collins, both of whom would go on to become established knifemakers in their own right. About 1978, John Cooper and another assistant, Clifton Lenderman, set up shop in Lufkin, Texas. Cooper retired in November 1981 but authorized Lenderman to keep making "Cooper" knives. John Cooper died in 1987. In his six-decade career, he is believed to have hand made anywhere from 15,000-24,000 knives. (For more information see *John Nelson Cooper* by William A. Martin and Paul Charles Basch, ISBN 0-944194-25-7.)

David Zephaniah Murphy

Based on information from Dave Murphy and Blade Magazine Cutlery Hall-Of-Famer© Pete Gerber.

In the late 1930s, David Z. Murphy, a blacksmith for the city of Portland, Oregon, began to make knives in his spare time. He ground the blades out of scrap tool steel and melted down old Ford automobile pistons to cast the aluminum from them into handles. He sold his carving knives door-to-door, which was how he met advertising man Joseph R. Gerber. Gerber conceived the idea for Gerber Legendary Blades (see "American Hunting Knives" earlier in this section) and contracted with Murphy to make sets of GERBER carving knives for him.

On Dec. 8, 1941, Murphy shifted all of his production to combat knives. His first effort was the MURPHY COMBAT JR., made with a carving knife handle. After 200 "Juniors" (current value, at least **$1,200**), he ordered dies for a full-size combat model marked MURPHY COMBAT KNIFE on the handle (value, **$750**). Murphy's son, David M., who started working in the knife shop at age 12, said that they made over 90,000 combat knives during the war.

After the war, David Z. Murphy resumed making civilian knives, spending much of his income on litigation against Gerber. Most of the MURPHY steak and carving knives in circulation date from this period (value, **$10-75**). (MURPHY industrial knives came from J. & R. Murphy of Massachusetts.) Murphy went bankrupt in 1954. Frank Barteaux then acquired the Murphy workshop, where he established the Barteaux Machete business. David Z. Murphy died Aug. 23, 1972. The younger Dave got back into knifemaking in 1981, even making reissue MURPHY COMBAT knives (about **$150**), but retired in 1994.

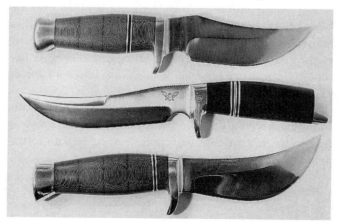

John Nelson Cooper's Alaskan, Aleutian and Siskiyou skinners with Micarta® handles sold for **$45-60** new in 1972. They and other utilitarian Cooper knives are now worth about **$1,400** each, with sheath. Larger and fancier Cooper bowies and daggers bring **$2,500-4,500**. (Joseph Rychetnik photo)

Joseph R. Gerber (left) and David Z. Murphy from a circa-1940 Gerber brochure. Gerber is testing the edge of a knife.

Buck Fixed Blade Knives

By Vern Taylor with updates by Joe Houser and Larry Oden

Editor's note: Vern Taylor founded the Buck Collectors Club in 1988. After more than a quarter century as a sales representative for Buck Knives, he retired to his ranch in northern California in the early 1990s. Vern passed away in June 2003. Joe Houser and Larry Oden of the Buck Collectors Club have expanded and updated Vern's following original article. For additional values and history of Buck Knives, see "Buck Folding Knives". Values are for knives in excellent, unsharpened condition.

You can find new Buck knives today in most good sporting goods, hardware and cutlery stores. For the dedicated collector, however, there is a treasure trove of old Buck knives out there also, just waiting to be discovered. Finding the knives is, of course, a lot more of a challenge.

Many of the older Buck knives are distinctively different from the ones made now. Others look similar to new knives, but they can be distinguished from the new ones by differences in markings and construction details.

In this segment you will find descriptions of the basic types of Buck fixed-blade knives made over the years. You will see how to identify and date the major variations in each type. You also will find an estimate of the current value for each variation in excellent, unsharpened condition. The detailed history of the Buck family of knives and all their variations would take a whole book in itself.

The basic categories of Buck knives are easy to distinguish. Any of the categories might make an interesting collecting specialty. In most of the categories it should be relatively easy to assemble a complete collection. Even the earliest Buck knives were sold by mail all over the country, so no matter where you live, you have a good chance of adding such knives to your collection.

Buck Principles

Millions of knives have been made bearing the Buck name, a name recognized and respected around the world. One reason for the company's good reputation is that it has never sold seconds. Blade Magazine Cutlery Hall-Of-Famer© Al Buck, the founder of the modern company, established as his policy, "If it's not the best we can do, it's not good enough to put our name on."

For many years, Buck destroyed any knives that were not up to the standards Al Buck had set. Today, knives rejected for cosmetic flaws—not structural flaws—are shipped to Christian missionaries in third-world countries, who barter the knives to local people for goods and services. Since the missionaries are usually short of cash, the arrangement benefits both them and the people they try to convert to Christianity.

The History of Buck

It was near the turn of the century that Hoyt Heath Buck, Al Buck's father, made his first knife. He was a blacksmith's apprentice and had discovered a new and effective method of tempering. He used his method in rebuilding worn-out grub hoes that he fitted with new cutting edges by forge-welding used-up horseshoer's files to them. H.H. Buck's rebuilt grub hoes lasted many times longer than new ones.

One day, one of Hoyt Buck's satisfied customers asked the young blacksmith to make a knife for him. The knife was more than satisfactory and, before long, Buck was making knives regularly. He used the same type of files and the same tempering method that he used in rebuilding hoes.

H.H. Buck and his wife, the former Daisy Green, lived in the Tacoma, Washington, area from about 1908 to 1930. Buck worked in the state's logging industry but also made knives in his spare time.

Hoyt and Daisy's first child, Al Buck, was born in 1910. They named him Alfred Charles after the traveling evangelist who had inspired Hoyt to become a born-again Christian. The event was to play a major part in the future of the family and the destiny of the company called Buck Knives.

In 1932, Al Buck left home to join the Coast Guard. He served for eight years, until 1940. Upon his discharge he settled in San Diego, California.

Early Buck Knives

By the beginning of World War II, Hoyt Buck had been ordained as a minister and was pastor of a small church in Mountain Home, Idaho. His small forge was set up next to the church. He made knives there for the local people. He also worked as millwright supervisor at the Anderson Ranch Dam.

When hometown boys left for military duty in the war, many of them wanted good knives. Hoyt responded to the need by making more knives than he ever had made before. The war brought the kids from rural Idaho together with young men from all over the country. In barracks and foxholes thousands of miles from home, the Idaho country boys spread the fame and reputation of Buck knives.

In 1945, Hoyt and Daisy Buck moved to San Diego to join their son, Al. The brutal Idaho winters had proven damaging to Daisy's health. Hoyt persuaded Al to join him in making knives to be sold by mail through outdoor magazines. Hoyt guessed that many of the readers of *Field and Stream, Outdoor Life,* and *Sports Afield* were the same young men who already had heard about the Buck knife from an Army buddy or Navy shipmate. If the Bucks could find just a few hundred customers from among those readers, it would be enough to launch them in the knifemaking business.

From 1945-49, Hoyt and Al Buck made knives for sale by mail. Nearly all the Buck knives thus far and for the next decade-and-a-half were fixed blades. In this period, Al Buck worked as a bus driver. When he drove days, he made knives at night.

Most of the blades for the Buck knives of the late 1940s and early '50's were made either from old files or power-hack-saw blades. The usual handle material was Lucite™, a trademarked name for an acrylic plastic, in a variety of bright colors. Later, the favored handle material was lignum vitae, a heavy, durable wood from the trees of tropical America. Some knives at the time were handled in elk horn, others in ironwood cut in the deserts east of San Diego.

In 1949, H.H. Buck passed away. For the next 10 years, Al Buck continued to make knives alone in his shop at 1272 Morena Ave. in San Diego. The war in Korea brought a severe downturn in his business. Unlike the situation at the start of World War II, the U.S. military had a large inventory of issue knives, so it discouraged the troops from buying their own. After the truce was signed in July 1953, the fortunes of Buck Knives turned upward even more markedly than they had after World War II.

Though they are getting increasingly difficult to locate, knives from Buck's early years can still be found today. Major variations have been identified and are outlined in the following text. The knives are categorized by group, with their differences noted. From 1942-45, Hoyt made over 2,000 knives. It is hard to say how the knives were made or if they were stamped, though it is likely that they were stamped BUCK. Hoyt did all the blade grinding and shaping until his death in 1949. Thenceforth, Al took over those duties. The values listed in the following paragraphs are for knives in excellent condition with the sheath.

Group One

Group one knives were stamped on the right side with a large (3/32-inch), four-strike stamp. *Four strike* means that each letter of the word BUCK was individually stamped onto the blade. Handles were of slab or stacked Lucite, or Masonite™, a trademarked name for a type of fiberboard. The handles in this group tended to be more distinctive than later groups. Many unusual color combinations were used. There was usually a pin through the pommel. The sheath was unmarked and made of leather. The snap on the keeper strap was usually flat and painted. Circa 1930s-'46. Value, **$600**.

Group Two

Group two knives were stamped on the right side with a smaller four-strike stamp. The handles were of stacked Lucite in many unusual color combinations. Black was offered as an option in this group. There was usually a pin through the pommel. The sheaths were the same as those in group one, though you may find a group two knife in a sheath with the word BUCK stamped on the pouch. The keeper snap had a convex, nickel-silver snap. Circa 1946-47. Value, **$600**.

Group Three

Group three knives were stamped on the right side with a single strike stamp. Handles were of various colors of stacked Lucite and often had one or more solid white spacers in the middle. There was usually a pin through the pommel. The sheaths were like those in the other groups discussed thus far. Circa 1947. Value, **$600**.

Group One knives include, from left:
with clear Lucite spacers (value: **$700**);
with rare slab Lucite handle, orange (value: **$500**)
and with Masonite handle (value: **$600**).

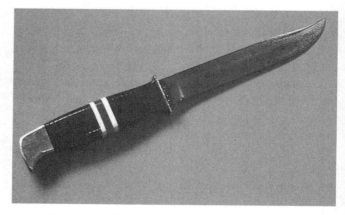

This red, white and blue Lucite-handle knife
from Group Two has a value of **$500**.

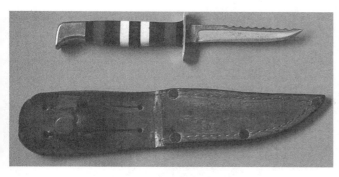

A multi-colored Lucite-handle knife from Group Three has a value of **$600**.

Group Four

Group four knives were stamped •BUCK• on the right side. The word BUCK was a single strike and the dots were individually stamped. There was a pin through the pommel. Sheaths were like those on group two knives. Circa 1947-48. Value, **$550**.

Group Five

Group five knives were stamped •BUCK• on the right side as were the knives in group four, and there was a three-strike model number stamped on the other side. Buck added the model numbers sometime around 1948. It was the last group with knives made by Hoyt Buck, who passed away in 1949. Circa 1948-51. Value, **$500**.

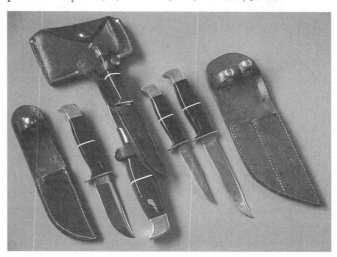

From left, all from Group Five: A blue-and-white Lucite-handle knife (value: **$500**); a green-and-white Lucite "Woodsman set" with axe (value: **$1,400**); and a black-and-white Lucite "Ranger set" (value: **$1,300**).

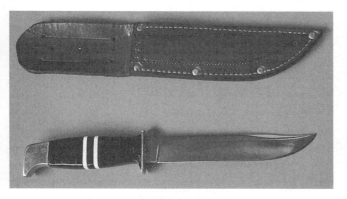

The green-and-white Lucite-handle knife from Group Four carries a value of **$600**.

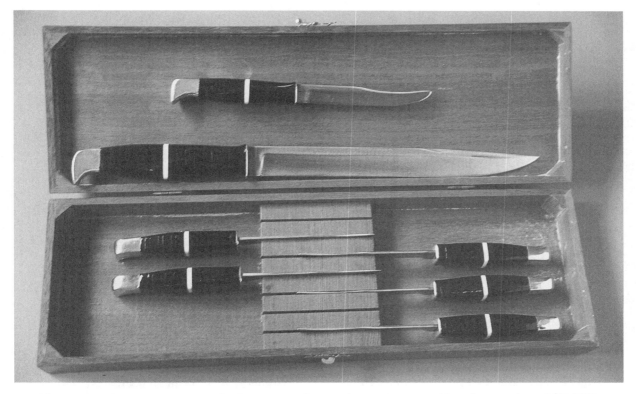

The extremely rare Group Four barbecue set of seven knives in a wood box has a value of **$3,000**.

Group Six

Group six knives were similar to group five knives except they were stamped •BUCK• on the left side and the model number was stamped on the right side. Most group six knives had a pommel rivet and handle spacers made of thin brass, paper or leather. Lignum-vitae handles were used for the first time by Buck on group six knives, as was the Buck name signed with an electric pencil. Circa 1951-54. Value, **$400**.

The value for this red-and-white Lucite-handle knife from Group Six is **$300**.

Group Seven

Group seven knives were stamped •BUCK• on the left side with no model number and no pommel rivet. It was the last blade stamping used on full-Lucite-handled knives. Handles of lignum vitae were common in this group as well. Circa 1954-55. Value, **$400**.

Group Eight

Group eight knives seem to be the rarest, as only two have ever been identified. They were described in a *Field and Stream* ad from 1955 as having handles of lignum vitae with dural (or duraluminum, a strong, lightweight, rust-resistant aluminum alloy) and Lucite trim. Elk handles

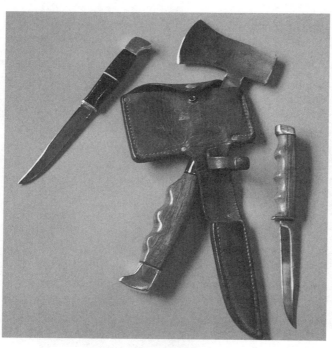

These Group Seven pieces include a black-and-white Lucite-handle piece (value: **$300**) and a lignum vitae "Woodsman set" with axe (value: **$1,200**).

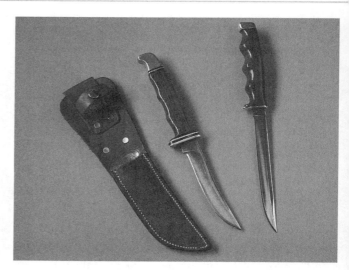

Group Nine knives and their values: A lignum-vitae-handle piece (left) with aluminum and leather spacers (**$350**) and one with a lignum-vitae handle and "BUCK" inscribed on the blade with an electric pencil (**$300**).

also were used. The blade was usually stamped •BUCK•, BUCK or signed with an electric pencil. Circa 1955. Value, **$500**.

Group Nine

Group nine knives were stamped BUCK on the left side or signed on the right. Group nine marks the end of Buck's lignum-vitae handles. Multiple spacers of aluminum, leather and sometimes brass were added to each end of the handle. Circa 1955-56. Value, **$300**.

Group Ten

Group ten knives were stamped BUCK on the left side of the blade. The handles were made of ebony or elk horn. Multiple handle spacers of dural, leather and, occasionally, brass were used. Circa 1956-61. Value, **$200**.

From left: These Group Ten knives consist of, from left: an elk handle with aluminum and leather spacers (value: **$300**) and an ebony handle with aluminum and leather spacers (value: **$300**).

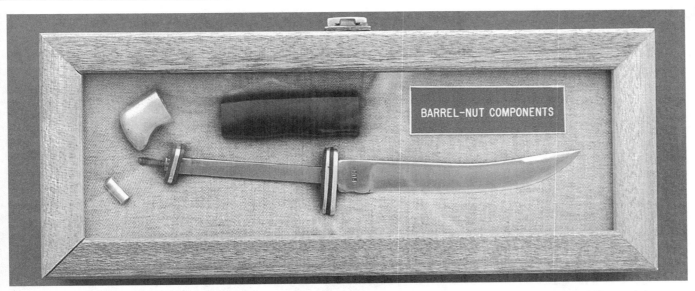

In the early "barrel-nut models," a barrel nut was inserted in a blind hole in the butt and screwed down tight. If the hole proved too deep, a plug of aluminum that matched the butt was inserted into the hole.

Factory Production Knives

In 1959, Al's son, Blade Magazine Cutlery Hall-Of-Famer© Charles T. "Chuck" Buck, completed his tour of duty in the U.S. Navy and joined his father in the business. Most of their daily living money at the time was earned by selling and sharpening the old reel-type lawnmowers. Buck Knives was incorporated in 1961 and stock was sold. The workshop was moved from Morena Ave. to a corrugated metal building at 3220 Congress St. near Old Town in San Diego. Production began there with three employees.

Until that time, the Bucks had cut out individual hunting knife blades on a band saw or fashioned them from files. The time-consuming job gave way to having them forged by a commercial forging company in Los Angeles.

Al Buck took to the road in his Volkswagen bus. He set out to persuade sporting goods dealers that his $13-$20

knives were a bargain, even though competitive hunting knives then sold for $8. Often, when he returned from a sales trip, Al would help make knives to fill the orders he had sold.

Buck knives had long been tested and demonstrated by driving the blade straight and true through a bolt or a heavy nail. It was around the early '60s that Buck adopted a picture of the test/demo as a trademark. We have talked to several of Buck's first dealers who still remember Al demonstrating his knives on 10-penny nails.

Identifying Early Factory Production Buck Knives

In the early 1960s, the Buck line consisted of seven fixed-blade hunting knives and one fillet knife. The designs were very similar to the ones cut from steel blanks and old files a few years earlier. The models were:

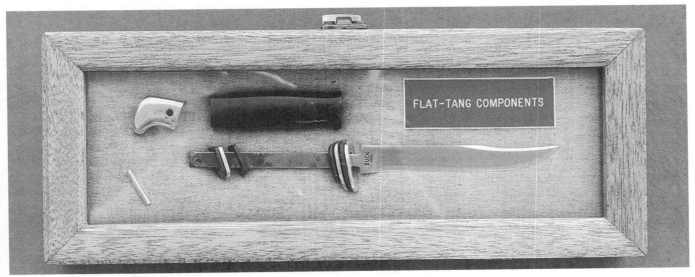

In 1962, Buck switched knife construction over to a flat tang. The butts were pressed on and pinned in place through a hole drilled from the side through the butt and tang. These are called "flat-tang models."

120 General
105 Pathfinder
103 Skinner
116 Caper (added late '62)

119 Special
118 Personal
102 Woodsman
121 Fisherman
(flat tang only, added '64)

The knives were stamped on the blade with just the one word, BUCK. Only the 121 Fisherman was never made in a barrel-nut configuration. The Model 116s were made both with and without guards.

The earliest production Buck knives were assembled in the same manner as the handmade knives of the '40s and

Knives with the three-line stamp of BUCK/MODEL#/U.S.A., circa 1972-85, with model numbers, names, handle materials and values, are, from top: 107 Scout (Micarta®), **$100**; 105 Pathfinder (phenolic), **$65**; 116 Caper (phenolic), **$75**; 121 Fisherman (phenolic), **$65**; 102 Woodsman (phenolic), **$65**; 119 Special (phenolic), **$75**; 118 Personal (phenolic), **$65**; 120 General (phenolic), **$100**; 103 Skinner (phenolic), **$65**; and 124 Frontiersman (Micarta), **$125**.

'50s. The tangs were threaded. A barrel nut was inserted in a blind hole in the butt and screwed down tight. If the hole proved too deep, a plug of aluminum that matched the butt was inserted into the hole. The knives are called the "barrel-nut models."

In 1962, Buck switched knife construction over to a flat tang. The butts were pressed on and pinned in place through a hole drilled from the side through the butt and tang. These are called "flat-tang models." The standard-production Buck knives of the early '60s had handles of black phenolic resin, a thermosetting resin similar to the material used for the handles of some of today's Buck fixed blades. At the time, however, white handles were also available on special order. The white handles were discontinued when it was learned that the white melamine resin material cracked in cold climates. In addition, custom handles, mainly of desert ironwood and elk-horn tips, were also available.

The original standard sheath was black leather with a keeper strap. When the 121 Fisherman was introduced, two keeper straps were sometimes used on the sheath. The familiar flap-over style sheath came into use about 1965.

In about 1967, Buck began to market knives in Canada. Consequently, the blade stamping was changed to BUCK/U.S.A. The stamping remained in use until about 1971, when Buck began to stamp a model number on the knives in a three-line arrangement: BUCK/MODEL#/U.S.A. Initially, the stamp was read with the knife pointed down (inverted) but, sometime around 1972, the stamping orientation was changed to be read with the knife pointed up.

The three-line stamping remained in use until 1986, when Buck started using year marks. (See "Buck Folding Knives" for a chart of the year symbols.) Also during this period, Buck reduced the combined number of Micarta® spacers used at the pommel and guard from four to three and, later, to two.

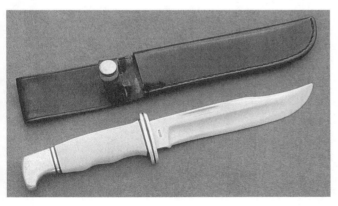

The Model 119 Special was very popular when it was first introduced in 1961. Its manufacturer's suggested retail price was $20. A barrel-nut model, it has a white melamine resin handle with aluminum fittings and a 440C stainless blade stamped BUCK. Value, **$400**.

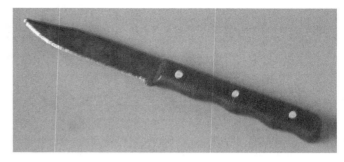

This utility knife with a linen Micarta® handle has a value of **$250**.

In about 1982, Buck switched from 440C stainless steel to 425 modified stainless steel across the product line. (Metallurgical testing is necessary to ascertain the steel.) The 425 modified remained the standard production steel until about 1992, when Buck switched to 420HC stainless.

Since 1964, Buck has added many new models, both fixed blade and folding. However, the 116, 118, 120 and 121 models have been discontinued. As an aside, it is fairly common to find flat-tang models of the era stamped BUCK•. The significance of the dot is unknown. Other than the dot, there seems to be nothing different about knives stamped BUCK or BUCK•. For more information on Buck, see the chapters "Buck Folding Knives," "Buck Custom and Limited Edition Knives," and "Modern Commercial Daggers and Survival Knives."

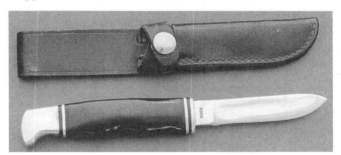

The Model 116 Caper was added to the Buck line in 1962 and was made both with and without a guard. The blade is stamped BUCK. Its original manufacturer's suggested retail price was $16. Its value today: **$250**.

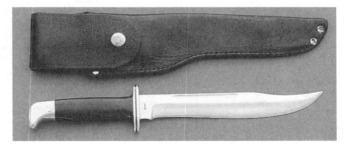

The Model 120 General was introduced in 1961 with a manufacturer's suggested retail price of $22. This one was made between 1962-64. The handle is ironwood, very rare in production knives. Value, **$300**.

Blade Designs of the Buck Knife are the result of a vast compilation of sketches and descriptions suggested by professional sportsmen. Each knife is designed to fulfill a specific purpose . . . years of research and field testing went into each design.

GENERAL — Model #120 — Heavy Bowie-styled knife similar in shape to the #119 but with 7¼" blade. This knife is used by many as a survival knife. Good for all-around camp use, chopping, game and as a fighting knife. **$22.00**

SPECIAL — Model #119 — A practical Bowie-styled knife with a 6" blade and blood groove. Beautifully balanced and shaped. Designed for heavy all-around knife work. **$20.00**

CAPER — Model #116 — A short 3¼" blade designed for saving the trophy. Best suited for working around the horns and ears. It is also a splendid knife for pan fish, small game and birds. **$14.00**

SKINNER — Model #103 — Wide 4" blade, heavy, fine edge. Weight, size and design of this knife makes the toughest skinning jobs simple. **$18.00**

PATHFINDER — Model #105 — This heavy duty, 5" blade is a wonderful all-purpose knife for general outdoor use. Much heavier blade than Model #118. For those who need a rugged knife. **$16.00**

WOODSMAN — Model #102 — A 4" straight blade with a fine point for fish and small game. **$13.00**

#104 TWINSET
#104 Twinset (shown) combines the #102 Woodsman and the #103 Skinner in a combination sheath. **$28.50**

#115 SPORTSMAN'S SET
Combines #118 Personal with the #103 Skinner in a combination sheath. **$29.50**

#117 TROPHY SET
Combines #116 Caper with the #103 Skinner in a combination sheath. **$29.50**

HUNTER'S AXE — Model #106 — 4" head 2½" cutting edge, 10½" over-all. Triple plated high impact tool steel. Ideal for dressing big game and for all-around camp and trail use. **$20.00**

PERSONAL — Model #118 — This famous Buck knife combines the skinning sweep of the wide skinner with a 4½" slender blade of a small game knife. **$14.00**

FOLDING — Model #110 — 4" blade pivots on ¼" bearing and has positive lock in open position. Handle of golden-grain Macassar ebony wood with solid brass bolsters and liner cast in one piece. May be carried in pocket or sheath. An ideal heavy duty outdoor knife for those preferring a folding blade. Over-all length 5". **$16.00**

FISHERMAN — Model #121 — This "fisherman's dream" is 10 inches over-all with a gentle curving flexible blade for perfect filleting, it also has a scaler added for extra convenience. This is the perfect knife for all kinds of fishing from ultra light to deep sea sport fishing. **$14.00**

Left and above: These images from a circa 1964 Buck catalog show some of the company's production models and manufacturer's suggested retail prices.

Post-1968 knives marked BUCK/U.S.A
Values: **$75** (smallest) to **$125** (largest).

United States Military Fixed Blade Knives

NOTE: The line drawings in this segment are reproduced from *U.S. Military Knives Bayonets and Machetes, Books III & IV,* copyright 1979 and 1990, by permission of the author and publisher, Blade Magazine Cutlery Hall-Of-Famer© M.H. Cole. The superb volumes are available from IDSA Books, 1324 Stratford Dr., Piqua, OH 45356.

The value estimates in this segment were prepared with the assistance of several collectors and dealers who specialize in U.S. military knives. Most important was the work of Larry Thomas, co-founder in 1987 of the American Military Edged Weaponry Museum, 3562 Old Philadelphia Pike, P.O. Box 6, Intercourse PA 17534, and Bill Claussen of Northwest Knives & Collectibles, 355 Court St. NE, Salem, OR 97301.

WARNING: We have seen fakes of the following U.S. military knives: Hicks knife, Ames 1849, Model 1887 hospital bolo, Model 1917-1918 trench knife, Mark 1 trench knife, Mark 2 (1219C2), M3 trench knife, Case V-42, smatchet, pig sticker, Camillus Marine Raider stiletto, and Vietnam-era S.O.G. knife. Also, the so-called "1st Ranger Battalion knife" has proven to be an Australian commercial knife not connected to the 1st Ranger Battalion. Time and rising values are sure to bring forth additional fakes, imaginary knives and replicas.

A legitimate reproduction is one that is clearly and permanently marked as a reproduction. Some presentation-grade reproductions cost as much as the original knives they replicate.

For information on U.S. military folding knives, see the segment on "Special Purpose Jack Knives" (electrician's knives and sailor's knives) in the chapter, "Named Jack Knife Patterns," and the "Multi-Blade Knives" chapter (scout utility knives and cattle knives), both in Part 2, Section II. For folding machetes, see below.

Introduction

From the earliest days of the Republic, the U.S. military has furnished its enlisted soldiers and sailors with weapons. Depending on period and branch of service, the weapons have included muskets or rifles (with bayonets), pistols and swords. Commissioned officers purchase their swords, but enlisted men in branches that used swords were issued them.

However, with the exception of a few rifleman's knives in the 1840s-60s, no U.S. branch of service issued sheath knives to its men until after 1880. The first standard-issue, U.S. military sheath knife was the Army Model 1880 Hunting Knife. The Navy did not get around to issuing sheath knives until World War II, though American sailors have been supplied with folding knives since well before the Civil War.

Of course, this does not mean that soldiers before 1880 did not use sheath knives. At least on active duty, many of them did. It simply means that there were no standard patterns of sheath knives that were made or purchased by the government for issue to the troops.

Rifleman's Knives

In the decades before the Civil War, companies of trained riflemen were the elite combat troops, both of the U.S. Army and the state militias. Soldiers in regular line outfits used smoothbore muskets.

Unlike the regular troops who furnished their own knives, riflemen were sometimes issued belt knives for use as tools and weapons. Two types of rifleman's knives from the 1840s have been identified, as has another rare type made in 1861.

Hicks Knife

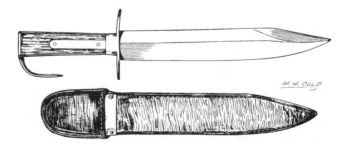

The earliest is the Hicks knife made by Andrew Hicks of Cleveland, Ohio, circa 1840. It has a 10-inch blade, a brass guard, and a brass-bound, wooden handle. Some examples have a brass half-knuckle bow, while others have an iron buttcap. The sheath is black leather. No surviving examples have any government markings, and evidence for their having been issued is circumstantial. Documents indicate that some knives made by Hicks were purchased by an arsenal, but the knives were not described.

1849 Ames Rifleman's Knife

In 1849, the Army let its first contract for a specific pattern of knife. It ordered 1,000 knives from the Ames

Manufacturing Co. of Cabotville, Massachusetts, for the Regiment of Mounted Riflemen. (Most of the knives were never issued.)

The Ames rifleman's knife is a spear-point bowie with a 12-inch blade, brass mounts and walnut handles secured by iron rivets. It has a black leather sheath with a brass throat, tip and frog stud.

The front ricasso is lightly marked AMES MFG. CO./CABOTVILLE/1849. The rear is marked US/WD. The guard is stamped WD and JWR. The frog stud is stamped D.

The Ames sheath is much sturdier than the Hicks sheath. Perhaps for this reason Ames knives are usually found with their original sheaths, while Hicks knives usually are not.

A well-made counterfeit of the Ames knife has been on the market for several years. Its ricasso stampings are much deeper than those on the original, and one of the inspector's initials on the guard is incorrect.

1861 Ames Rifleman's Knife

Nothing is yet known of the history and production of the 1861 Ames rifleman's knife, save the date and the manufacturer. The knife has a 12-inch spear-point blade, a brass guard, and a brass handle shaped like a tapered sword grip. The sheath is black leather with a brass throat and tip.

- -

RIFLEMAN'S KNIVES, current values for knives in excellent condition.

Hicks knife, any variant: **$8,000-12,000**.
   with original sheath: add **$1,500**.
1849 Ames knife with sheath: **$6,000-8,000**.
   sheath missing: subtract **$2,000**.
Counterfeit 1849 Ames knife: **$300**.
1861 Ames knife with sheath: **$5,000-6,000**.
   sheath missing: subtract **$1,000-1,500**.

- -

Ames Civil War Militia Knife

Several variants of the ornate Ames Civil War militia knife with wood or horn handle and cast-brass mounts were made, apparently for members of the Massachusetts militia companies that employees of the Ames Sword Co. joined during the Civil War. While not a government-issue pattern, it was nonetheless a U.S. military knife. Value with sheath: **$1,500-1,800**.

Model 1880 Hunting Knife

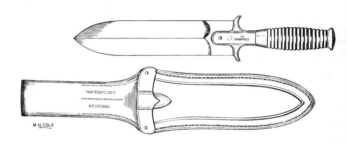

The Model 1880 was the first general-issue Army sheath knife. As such, it has been the subject of much study. The full story of its development, production and use was told in the book *Light But Efficient* (1973) by Albert Hardin and Robert Hedden.

The Model 1880 Hunting Knife has an 8 1/2-inch-long and 2-inch-wide steel blade, a stout metal guard—some are iron, most are brass—and a turned hardwood handle. All were issued in a stout, black leather sheath with a brass throat, though there is a variety of sheath attachments.

The Model 1880 was designed to serve three functions in the Indian campaigns on the plains: as a butcher knife for cattle and wild game, an entrenching tool and a last-ditch weapon.

In the field, the Model 1880's main function proved to be digging firing positions ("rifle pits"), so in 1890 its designation was changed to "Model 1890 Intrenching Knife." In fact, the Model 1880/1890 knives are similar in shape to the flat-bladed, short-lived Model 1873 Intrenching Tool.

Approximately 11,000 Model 1880s and 500 Model 1890s were made, all at Springfield Armory. The sheaths were made at Watervliet Arsenal and, later, at Rock Island Arsenal. The Model 1880s are serial numbered in two series.

MODELS 1880 and 1890, current values for knives in excellent, unsharpened condition. For mint condition, add 150 percent. For worn condition, subtract 50 percent.

Model 1880, iron guard, no sheath: **$800**.

Model 1880, brass guard, no sheath: **$250**.

Model 1890, brass guard, no sheath: **$700**.

(all Model 1890s are dated 1892)

Unmodified sheath, leather belt loop: **$175**.

Varney sheath with hinged brass catch: **$400**.

Sheath with brass hook: **$125**.

Model 1873 Intrenching Tool: **$175** w/sheath.

(like M1880 but has sheet steel blade)

Sheath only for M1873, with ring: **$50**.

Bolos and Hospital Corps Knives

Model 1887 Bolo

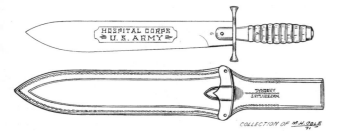

The U.S. Army's next issue knife looks like a longer, slimmer version of the Model 1880. It is the Model 1887 Hospital Corps Knife. It has a 12-inch bright blade with an etched panel. Its wood handle and leather sheath look similar to those of the Model 1880.

About 1,000 of the knives were made, also at Springfield Armory. They were intended for the use of field hospital personnel in clearing brush and cutting saplings for making emergency litters and shelters. There are two variations in blade shape.

MODEL 1887 BOLO, current values for knives in excellent, unsharpened condition. For mint condition, add 150 percent. For worn condition, subtract 50 percent.

Knife only, straight cutting edge: **$1,100**.

Knife only, bellied cutting edge: **$1,200**.

Sheath, unmodified leather belt loop: **$150**.

Sheath with brass hook: **$150**.

Similar knife by COLLINS & CO.: **$950**.

Model 1904 and Model 1909 Bolos

The Army's experience in the Philippine Islands during and after the Spanish American War demonstrated the value of a heavy-bladed, bolo-type knife for campaigning in the jungle. Consequently, the Ordnance Department came up with a variety of bolo designs in the next two decades.

The first and most handsome—and most expensive—of them was the Model 1904 Hospital Corps Knife. It has a 12-inch blade, walnut handles and a brown leather sheath. The first 7,000 or so had a leather belt loop on the sheath. The remainder of the nearly 40,000 made at Springfield Armory between 1904 and 1915 had a steel belt loop. All but a few first-year Model 1904s were serial numbered.

The Army's second bolo, the Model 1909 with a 14-inch blade, is larger than the Model 1904. It is also plainer in construction. More than 17,000 were made at Springfield Armory between 1909 and 1915. Another 58,000 were made on contract in 1917 by the Philadelphia toolmaker, Fayette R. Plumb.

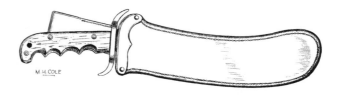

MODEL 1904 and MODEL 1909 BOLOS, current values for knives in excellent, unsharpened condition. For mint condition, add 100 percent. For worn condition, subtract 50 percent.

Model 1904 knife only: **$200-250**.

Sheath with leather loop: **$75**.

Sheath with steel loop: **$60**.

Similar bolo by COLLINS & CO.: **$650**.

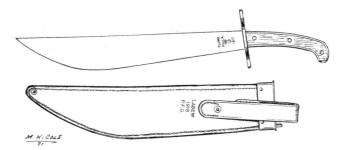

Model 1909 S.A. (Springfield) knife only: **$300**.

Rock Island sheath for S.A.: **$75**.

Model 1909 PLUMB knife only (dated 1917): **$135-175**.

LADEW sheath for PLUMB: **$75**.

Similar bolo by COLLINS & CO.: **$950**.

Model 1910 and Model 1917 Bolos

The Army's third bolo, the Model 1910, seemed to be the Army's acknowledgement that, outside of the jungle, a really big knife is more an impediment than a useful tool. The stout, simple bolo with a 10 3/8-inch blade was

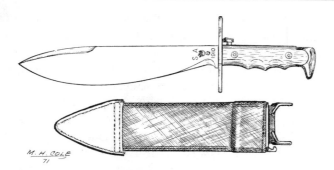

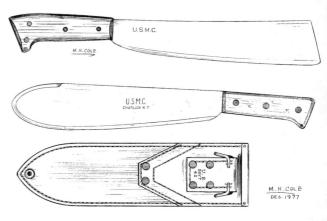

intended as a general-purpose chopping and digging tool. In World War I, its principal use was in clearing fields of fire for machine gun emplacements.

The Model 1910 has wooden handle scales and a steel pommel and guard. It has a button latch to engage a hook on the sheath. Nearly 60,000 Model 1910s were made at Springfield Armory up through 1918.

The standard sheath is wood with a metal throat. It is covered with cloth and has a leather tip. It is the first Army knife sheath to have wire hooks for hanging from a cartridge belt. Experimental all-metal sheaths were made on contract by Landers Frary & Clark in 1918.

The Model 1917 Bolo is identical to the Model 1910, except that the button latch was eliminated. The Model 1917 C.T. is further modified in having the pommel integral with the tang. The 1917 models were made on contract by two firms: Plumb and the American Cutlery Co. of Chicago. The latter was a manufacturer of low-priced kitchen knives. A.C. Co. went out of business shortly after World War I.

So many bolos were made, particularly the Model 1917s, that even World War II did not exhaust the supply. Model 1917s are still very common.

- -

MODEL 1910 and MODEL 1917 BOLOS, current values for knives in excellent, unsharpened condition. For mint condition, add 100 percent. For worn condition, subtract 75 percent.

Model 1910, knife only: **$125-150**.
Model 1917 PLUMB, knife only: **$65-75**.
Model 1917 C.T. PLUMB, knife only: **$65-75**.
Model 1917 C.T. A.C. Co., knife only: **$65-75**.
Cloth-covered sheath: **$20**.
Metal L.F. & C. sheath: **$25**.

- -

U.S.M.C. Bolos

With World War II on the horizon, the Army found that it had all the bolos it could use left over from 1918. Since 1898, the Marine Corps had used a square-point "intrenching machete" with wood handles and a stiff sheath covered with canvas and leather. Very few were in inventory in 1941.

In 1942, for war production, this bolo design was modified to have a round sharpened end, and was furnished with a sturdy leather sheath. The bolo-type

knives were issued mainly to Navy hospital corpsmen serving with the Marines.

- -

U.S.M.C. BOLOS, current values for knives in excellent, unsharpened condition. For mint condition, add 75 percent. For worn condition, subtract 75 percent.

Square point, knife only:
COLLINS & CO. No. 1001: **$300-350**.
DISSTON: **$225-275**.
YANKEE TOOL CO.: **$400**.
Sheath for square point: **$50**.
Round point, knife only:
PLUMB or CLYDE: **$150-175**.
VILLAGE BLACKSMITH: **$100-125**.
CHATILLON, BRIDDELL or unmarked: **$60-70**.
BOYT sheath for round point: **$20**. Dated '42, add 50 percent.

- -

Machetes

In addition to issuing bolos to the troops, the U.S. military also issued machetes for use in jungle terrain. Though the first machetes issued were not recorded, they were probably commercial patterns.

The Collins Model 1005 "U.S. [Army] Engineers Machete (Bolo Type)" was introduced in 1913. It has a heavy curved blade about 15 1/4 inches long, handle scales of wood or horn, and a leather sheath, often with brass trim. The 1005 machete was in regular use through the 1940s.

A rare World War I-era machete is the Collins No. 37 U.S. Signal Corps "Brush Cutting Machete," with its straight 17 3/4-inch blade, brass-mounted, leather-washer handle, and leather sheath stamped U.S./SIGNAL CORPS.

Bannerman's

Collins U.S. Engineers (Bolo Type): **$50-70**.

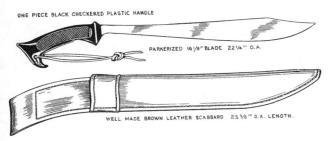

ONE PIECE BLACK CHECKERED PLASTIC HANDLE

PARKERIZED 16⅛" BLADE 22¼" O.A.

WELL MADE BROWN LEATHER SCABBARD 23⅜" O.A. LENGTH.

Unmarked Cruver U.S.A.A.F. survival: **$200-250**.

In World War II, large numbers of standard straight-bladed machetes were purchased by the military. Most had 18-inch blades, but the Navy also used some with 22- and 26-inch blades. Eighteen-inch machetes are still standard issue.

In 1934, the military adopted the Collins No. 18 bowie-knife-style machete as a survival knife for inclusion in the bail-out kit of pilots flying over tropical areas.

The No. 18s are 14 inches long overall and have either a green-horn or a black-composition handle. The sheath is brown leather. Black-handled versions were made during World War II by Case, Western, Kinfolks and several Australian firms. In the Pacific Theater, No. 18s were issued to several Marine units, particularly Carlson's Second Marine Raiders. The knives do not have Marine Corps markings (the USMC markings on some are spurious).

From 1940 to 1945, an elegant 16-inch-blade survival machete with a molded, checkered, black-plastic handle was made for the U.S. Army Air Force by Cruver Mfg. Co. of Chicago, using unmarked Collins No. 1253 blades. The machetes have been misidentified both as O.S.S. and as paratrooper issue.

In 1942, the Army Air Force adopted a survival machete with a 10-inch blade for inclusion in the bail-out kit in place of the Collins No. 18. Case, Camillus, Cattaraugus and Imperial all made plastic-handled folding models, while Case made a wood-handled fixed blade with a sheet-steel edge cover (in *Knives '85*, Daniel Edward "D.E." Henry gives evidence that the fixed-blade Case was designated the V-44). (For more on Collins machetes, see *Collins Machetes and Bowies 1845-1965* by Daniel Edward "D.E." Henry. For your copy, contact KP Publications, 700 E. State St., Iola, WI 54990-0001.)

MILITARY MACHETES, current values for knives in excellent, unsharpened condition. Mint condition add 75 percent, worn condition subtract 50 percent.

Collins U.S. Signal Corps (Brush Cutting) with military marked sheath: **$100-125**.

18-inch military marked, U.S. made: **$25-45**.

18-inch military marked, foreign made: **$15-20**.

Canvas sheath for 18-inch: **$15**.

Leather sheath for 18-inch: **$25**.

Hard plastic and metal sheath for 18-inch: **$12**.

22-inch Navy marked: **$40-50**.

26-inch Navy marked: **$50-85**.

Sheath for 22-inch or 26-inch: **$15**.

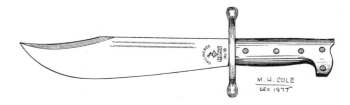

M. H. COLE
DEC 1977

Pilot's survival bowie/machetes, with sheaths:

Collins No. 18 horn handle: **$500-600**.

Black handle: **$300-350**.

Case XX: **$300-350**.

Western: **$500-600**.

Kinfolks: **$300-350**.

Australian:

Wood handle: **$350-400**.

Black handle: **$300-350**.

Brass D-guard, 3-point knuckle bow: **$500-600**.

Aluminum D-guard: **$500-600**.

[USMC markings on some bowie/machetes are fake]

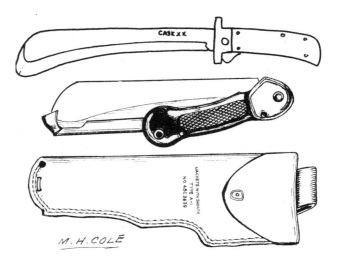

CASE XX

MACHETE WITH SHEATH TYPE A-1 NO. 45C3639

M. H. COLE

Post-1942 pilot's survival machetes:

Case V-44 fixed blade, with edge cover: **$125-150**.

Case folding: **$100-125**.

Camillus folding: **$75-125**.

Cattaraugus folding: **$75-125**.

Imperial folding: **$125-135**.

Holster sheath for Imperial: **$50**.

Trench Knives

First World War

Almost all the military-issue knives considered so far in this segment primarily were tools. Except in dire emergencies, they were too heavy and unwieldy to serve as weapons.

When the United States entered the First World War in Europe in 1917, the troops clamored for an issue-combat knife suitable for trench warfare. Both sides equipped their line outfits with good-quality trench knives (see the following segment, "Foreign Military Fixed Blade Knives"). The Army responded but in a manner that was less than satisfactory.

The first effort, designed by the Philadelphia saw-making firm of Henry Disston & Sons, seems to have been inspired by nineteenth-century bayonet design, spiced up with a little dime-novel fantasy: the Model 1917-1918 trench knife. It has a slim—and brittle—triangular blade, a wooden handle, and an imposing but impractical iron "brass-knuckles" hand guard. There are several variations, all listed below.

The first American trench knife, the Model 1917-1918 had several problems. It could be used only for stabbing or punching, not cutting. The blade was delicate and easily broken. The "knucks" were poorly designed. Therefore, an improved model was developed, the Mark 1.

The Mark 1 trench knife has a cast-brass handle with separate finger holes, and a skullcrusher spike on the butt. The blade is copied almost exactly from the very effective French-issue trench knife. Indeed, the first Mark 1s were made for the U.S. Army by a French firm. Later ones were made by three of the contractors that made the Model 1917-1918.

Second World War

After 1918, no more "knuckle knives" were made for the Army, though existing stocks were issued to soldiers and marines in 1941-43. Also, during World War II, several aluminum- or brass-handled types were offered for private sale. Some were made and sold in Australia and New Zealand. [Note: In California and several other states, it is illegal to own or sell "brass knuckles," with or without knife blades attached.]

- -

"KNUCKLE-DUSTER" TRENCH KNIVES, current values for knives in excellent, unsharpened condition. For mint condition, add 100 percent. For worn condition, subtract 50 percent.

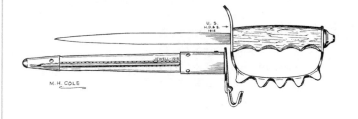

MODEL 1917-1918 TRENCH KNIFE

H. D. & S. flanged guard, knife only: **$550-600**.
A. C. Co. flanged guard, knife only: **$150-200**.
O.C.L. flanged guard, knife only: **$325-400**.
(Oneida Community Ltd.)
L. F. & C. 6-knobbed guard, knife only: **$250-300**.
L. F. & C. 7-knobbed guard, knife only: **$450-500**.
Leather sheath: **$50**.
Leather sheath with iron throat and tip: **$100**.

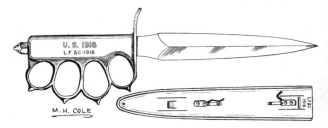

MARK 1 TRENCH KNIFE

AU LION (on blade), knife only: **$200**.
L. F. & C., knife only: **$200**.
H. D. & S., knife only: **$550-600**.
O.C.L., knife only: **$800**.
Steel sheath: **$75**.

WORLD WAR II KNUCKLE KNIVES

Crude, brass-handled Australian
(misidentified as 1st Ranger Battalion);
unmarked or stamped US.
Large size: **$800-900**.
Small size: **$900-1,100**.
Leather sheath: **$150**.
Examples marked CASE XX are fakes.
New Zealand, checkered aluminum, flimsy bow:
$100-150.
EVERITT, well made, aluminum: **$600-800**.

M3 Trench Knife

When the United States entered World War II late in 1941, existing stocks of Mark 1 Trench Knives were issued and used. By that time, however, the Army had realized that the Mark 1 was too much hardware for the job.

In 1943, a new and much superior trench knife was introduced—the M3. It has a straight, sturdy blade suitable for utilitarian cutting and chopping chores, as well as for stabbing in combat. It has a leather-washer handle and steel fittings.

In 1944, the M3 was superseded by the M4 bayonet for use with the M1 carbine. The M4 has the same handle and blade as the M3, but has bayonet-style fittings.

Over 2.5 million M3s were made on contract in 1943 and 1944. There are many variations of blade and guard markings, and also of handle shapes. Some are very rare. Few M3s entered the surplus market after World War II, and none of the variations can be considered common, particularly in good condition.

The M3 was still in use during the Korean War. Some M3s were then rehandled in Asia with scored hardwood handles.

M3 TRENCH KNIVES, current values for knives in excellent, unsharpened condition. Mint condition add 100 percent. Worn condition or re-worked or parts replaced, subtract 50 percent.

M3s marked on blade: "U.S. M3" plus ...

AERIAL/MARINETTE, WIS.: **$400**.

H. BOKER & CO./U.S.A.: **$350**.

CAMILLUS: **$225**.

CAMILLUS 1943: **$400-450**.

CASE: **$225**.

CASE 1943: **$500**.

IMPERIAL: **$150**.

IMPERIAL 1943: **$350**.

KINFOLKS INC.: **$300**.

KINFOLKS INC. 1943: **$450**.

PAL: **$200**.

PAL 1943: **$325-350**.

R.C. CO. (Robeson): **$500**.

• UTICA: **$150**.

• U.C.-1943 (Utica): **$300**.

M3s marked on crossguard ...

U.S./M3/A.C.C. (probably Aerial): **$250-300**.

US/M3/BOKER: **$250-300**.

US M3/CAMILLUS: **$150-200**.

USM3/CASE: **$375**. CASE: **$325**.

USM3/IMPERIAL: **$250**.

US/M-3/UTICA: **$125-150**.

U.S.M3/K.I.(Kinfolks): **$200-225**.

U.S./M3/PAL: **$125-150**.

Commercially sold M3s

Camillus #MK3 Trench knife 1996 issue price **$49.95**.

Camillus #M4 Bayonet 1996 issue price **$53.95**.

Unmarked: **$75**.

"Kutmaster/MADE IN U.S.A.": **$75**.

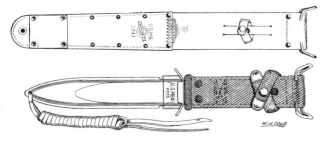

PAL BLADE CO./MADE IN U.S.A. (on ricasso): **$300-400**.

Sheaths for M3s:

M6 leather sheath, metal reinforced: **$200**.

M8 plastic sheath, canvas belt loop: **$30**.

M8A1 plastic sheath, wire belt hook: **$15**.

Plain leather commercial sheath: **$15**.

Special Combat Knives

Fairbairn Variants

Early in World War II, the U.S. military issued several types of slender daggers suitable mainly for silent assassination. The "stickers" closely resemble a well-known prototype, the British Fairbairn-Sykes commando stiletto, first made in 1940. Apparently, one of the U.S. military-issued daggers is a British Fairbairn. It is the unmarked O.S.S. (Office of Strategic Services, forerunner of the C.I.A.) stiletto with the distinctive "pancake-flapper" metal and leather sheath. Value with sheath: **$1,000**.

An American-made version of the Fairbairn is the Camillus Marine Raider Stiletto. It has a lightweight, checkered-zinc handle and a slim, double-edged blade etched with the Camillus trademark and "U.S.M.C." in a fancy scroll. The leather sheath usually was reinforced with a square metal plate near the tip. Fewer than 15,000 were made. Value: **$1,000-2,000**. Parkerized variant: **$1,500-2,500**.

A 1990 Camillus reproduction, #MRSI—with a 7-inch blued blade, USMC gold etching and pewter handle—was introduced at a manufacturer's suggested retail price of **$240**.

The basic Fairbairn is a fragile knife that is awkward to hold and use. In 1942 and '43, Case unveiled an improved version called the V-42 for the use of the First Special Service Force.

The V-42 has an oval leather handle, rather than a round metal one. In order to protect the fingers, it has a wide guard and a ricasso. Production models are distinguished by a pointed steel "skullcrusher" pommel, grooves in the leather handle, and a "thumbprint" pressed into the ricasso. Prototypes have a round butt, smooth handle and no "thumbprint." The sheath is leather with reinforcing staples at the throat. Three thousand six hundred V-42s were made. (For more on the knives of World War II, see *Knives of the United States Military World War II* [ISBN 0-9655544-1-4] by Michael W. Silvey, and *Commando Dagger* [ISBN 0-87364-311-9] by Leroy Thompson.)

Values: Issue, **$3,000**; Prototype, **$3,000-4,000**.

Smatchet

Besides promoting his dagger design, W.E. Fairbairn urged the U.S. military to adopt the "smatchet" as a combat knife. The smatchet is a large—16 inches overall—but lightweight bolo-type knife with a leaf-shaped blade. Fairbairn managed to convince only the O.S.S., which ordered a number of smatchets, all unmarked, from W.R. Case & Sons. The blade is parkerized, the handle is brown wood and the pommel is white metal. The sheath is black leather over plywood. (Beware of fakes.)

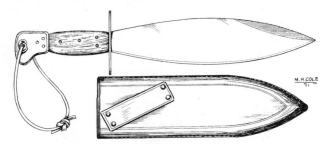

Value with sheath: **$900-1,000**.

There are also second and third model smatchets. Handles are black plastic, pommels are bird's-head shaped, and sheaths are brown leather. The second model's blade is polished bright, while the blade and pommel of the third are parkerized.

Values with sheath: Second, **$650-750**; Third, **$800-900**.

In 1944, Ulster Knife Co. made 10,000 unmarked smatchets for the O.S.S., based on samples supplied by Case. They had black parkerized blades, wood handles and zinc pommels. The entire lot reportedly was lost at sea.

Ulster also made a variety of other unmarked (sterile), special-order knives for the O.S.S. Ulster's president, Blade Magazine Cutlery Hall-Of-Famer© Albert M. Baer, was the cutlery industry representative on the Army Advisory Board (QMG) from 1941-45.

Australian-Made Commando Knives

Simple and well designed, Australian-made commando knives have a 5 1/2-inch spear-point blade and wooden-slab handles. The blade is marked with an Australian name— Gregsteel, East or Barker—and on many, either the blade or the guard is marked "U.S. 1944." The sheath is leather. Many were issued both to American and Commonwealth troops fighting in the Pacific.

Value in excellent condition, with sheath:
With U.S. markings: **$300**.
Without U.S. markings: **$200**.

Combat Utility Knives

U.S. Navy Mark 1

In World War II, the Navy broke with tradition and decided to issue a survival-type sheath knife to its sailors. The knife's main function was to cut the lashings that secured the release mechanism on all Navy life rafts. The first design, the Mark 1, was a very practical, 5 1/8-inch-blade utility knife. The Navy needed a lot of them right away, so they were made in more than three dozen handle, fitting and marking variants by most of the large American cutlery firms then in business.

In addition, individual procurement officers were allowed to buy sheath knives for their men on the open market. The official issue of some of the commercial knives is well documented, and a determined interviewer could probably prove that just about every pattern of 5- to 7-inch-blade commercial hunting knife available in the early 1940s found its way onto a Navy ship.

Mark 1s were made in such vast quantities that unissued lots of them still turn up on the surplus market, usually for between **$50** and **$75** each. The Mark 1 is the most common U.S. military knife on the collector market, but it would be a real challenge to acquire one of each variation in excellent-to-mint condition.

In his *U.S. Military Knives Bayonets and Machetes, Books III & IV*, Blade Magazine Cutlery Hall-Of-Famer© M.H. Cole illustrates 42 Mark 1 variations. The value range of many of them is as indicated in the previous paragraph, but the rarer variants have begun to increase in value. Following are the basic types. Within them are many variations of fittings and blade finishes. It seems likely that additional variants will be identified in the future.

- -

U.S.N. MARK 1 UTILITY KNIFE, current values for knives in excellent, unsharpened condition. Mint condition add 40 percent. Good, used condition subtract 75 percent.

Flat-steel-butt versions:
KA-BAR/OLEAN N.Y.: **$80-100**.

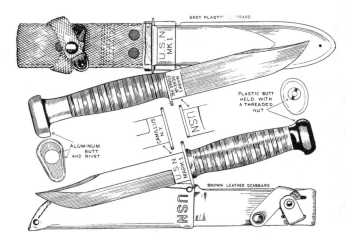

WESTERN/BOULDER COLO.: **$90-100**.
CAMILLUS/N.Y.: **$60**.
IMPERIAL/PROV. R.I.: **$60-70**.
SCHRADE-WALDEN/N.Y. U.S.A. (postwar):
   $40-50.
Black-plastic-butt versions:
CAMILLUS/N.Y.: **$45-55**.
BOKER & CO./U.S.A.: **$150-175**.
Black-rubber-handled version:
COLONIAL: **$60-70**.
Wooden-butt versions:
PAL, GENEVA FORGE or ROBESON:
   $75-85 each.
Aluminum-butt versions:
PAL or RH(PAL)35: **$30-50**.
ROBESON SHUREDGE/NO. 20: **$55-65**.
GENEVA/FORGE INC.: **$65-75**.

U.S. Marine Corps 1219C2 and Navy Mark 2

Until the spring of 1943, Marines in the Pacific Theater generally purchased their own sheath knives prior to going overseas. The most popular knife then, because it was supplied through Marine Corps post exchanges on the West Coast, was the Western States L-77. (For more on it, see the following "Commercial Combat Utility Knives.") Large numbers of L-77s were sold to marines throughout the war, and during the Korean conflict as well. Also widely used in 1942 and early 1943 were commercial hunting knives, World War I Army trench knives, and two issue knives: the Marine Raider stiletto and the "Gung Ho knife" (the Collins No. 18 machete), both mentioned earlier in this segment.

Eventually, the experiences of the first island jungle campaigns were distilled into a superior new U.S.M.C. combat utility knife designated the 1219C2. Its design, with a stout, 7-inch clip-point blade, was developed by Col. John M. Davis and Maj. Howard E. America, working with Camillus Cutlery Co., and was adopted Nov. 23, 1942. The first production run of 2,100 knives was shipped Jan. 27, 1943.

Meanwhile, the Navy had found that the Mark 1 was not stout enough for the hard use sometimes afforded it. Therefore, the Navy also adopted the 1219C2, designating it the Mark 2. Marines often used knives with U.S.N. markings when the Navy knives were all that was available.

The 1219C2 was popularly called the "kabar" because about a million of the wartime U.S.M.C.-issue knives were made by Union Cutlery Co. of Olean, New York, and were boldly marked with Union's KA-BAR trademark. However, Camillus made even more of the 1219C2s, while Pal and Robeson made large quantities, too. As with the Mark 1 and the Army M3, the Mark 2 was issued either with a leather sheath or with a hard-fiber-and-metal sheath.

1219C2/MARK 2 COMBAT KNIFE, current values for knives in excellent, unsharpened condition. Mint condition add 50 percent. Good, used condition subtract 50 percent.

   U.S.N. marked knife, or with no branch marking.
   First version with threaded tang. Marked on ricasso.
CAMILLUS, N.Y.: **$75**.
KA-BAR/OLEAN, N.Y.: **$175**.
Pinned or riveted butt. Marked on ricasso.
CAMILLUS, N.Y.: **$75**.
KA-BAR or KA-BAR/OLEAN, N.Y.: **$175**.
ROBESON SHUREDGE: **$150**.
PAL or RH(PAL)37: **$75**.
PAL w/aluminum MK 1 butt: **$350**.
Marked on guard.
KA-BAR: **$100**. CAMILLUS, N.Y.: **$75**.
R.C.C. (Robeson): **$150**.
U.D.T.(?) version: no handle grooves, bright blade.
   Guard marked KA-BAR USN MK2.
Blade fullers (grooves): **$400**.
No blade fullers: **$500**.
Post-World War II two-line markings on ricasso.
U.S./CONETTA (Stamford, CT c1961): **$45**.
U.S./UTICA CUT. CO.: **$45**.
U.S./CAMILLUS N.Y.: **$35**.
U.S./M.S.I.: **$60**.
U.S./ONTARIO: **$25**. (current issue)
U.S.N. sheaths.
One-piece leather: **$30**.
Two-piece leather: **$25**.
Gray plastic with canvas belt loop: **$15**.
U.S.M.C.-marked knife, marked on ricasso.
CAMILLUS, N.Y.: **$150**.
KA-BAR: **$250**.
PAL: **$150**.
ROBESON SHUREDGE: **$450**.
Marked on guard.
CAMILLUS: **$100**.
Leather sheath for U.S.M.C.: **$50**.
Leather sheath for U.S.M.C. marked "PAL": **$85**.

Cattaraugus and Case made utility knives with heavy, 6-inch blades and steel butts for the Army Quartermaster Department. Their main use was for opening and closing wooden crates, though as surplus they were later advertised as "Commando Knives." The Cattaraugus is still very common.

CASE 337-6" Q: **$175**. CASE XX 337-6": **$150**.
CATTARAUGUS/225Q: **$150**.

Commercial Combat Utility Knives

The Navy and Marine Corps standard-issue Mark 1 and Mark 2 were not the only U.S. combat-utility sheath knives of World War II. Many others were made for commercial sale and purchased by procurement officers and by individual GIs. Some resemble the standard patterns or the M3, while others are quite distinctive. Most have leather-washer handles, while virtually all have leather sheaths and a military appearance.

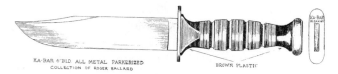

Union/Ka-Bar made about 500,000 6-inch-bladed, guard-marked combat knives that look like scaled-down Mark 2s. Value: **$85**. Case, Camillus, Kinfolks, Queen City, Pal and Robeson each made similar blade-marked knives. All had 6-inch blades, except for the Camillus and one of the three Case variants, which had 5-inch blades. Values: **$125-175**.

Case also offered a 7-inch-bladed, double-edged dagger or stiletto with a Mark 1-like handle and a black-plastic butt. Value: **$800** with standard sheath; add 50 percent for special 20-inch leather sheath.

In addition, Case continued to make its prewar No. 309 hollow-handle hunting knife with a match-safe in the butt. Value: **$700**, with sheath.

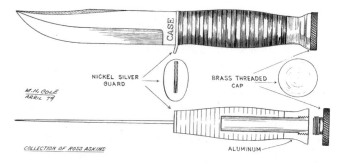

Some GIs bought Case Model 562-6" "pig-stickers," plain, self-guard butcher's sticking knives with wood handle slabs and leather sheaths.

Values with sheath: Case: **$400**. Case XX: **$400**. Some have jigged-bone handles. Value: to **$500**.

Besides several standard-issue patterns, Western States Cutlery Co. offered three distinctive commercial military knives. The W31 Parachutist was a small—8 5/8 inches overall—utility knife with a cocobolo handle. It was the only commercial version of the prototypes developed by Camillus for the Marine parachute regiments. Value: **$3,500**.

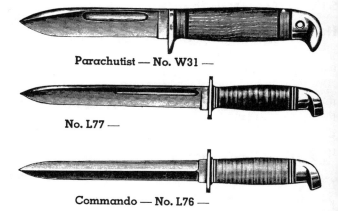

Western's 11-inch-overall Commando came with either a fullered, single-edged blade (L-77: **$700**), or a plain, double-edged blade (L-76: **$2,500**.). The L-76 was offered as an improved version of the Marine Raider stiletto, though it was never formally adopted.

The 10 1/8-inch-overall Shark was Western's version of the 6-inch-blade combat utility knife. It has a blued, fullered blade, a cross guard, and an aluminum bird's-head pommel. Value: **$200**.

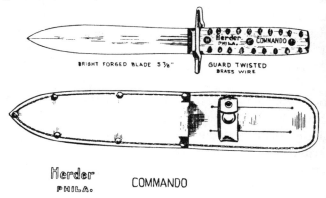

Several prominent cutlery retailers, such as Herder's of Philadelphia, M. Kesmodel of Baltimore, Kennedy Bros. of St. Paul, and Williams Bros. of San Francisco, commissioned the manufacture of distinctive, private-brand, combat utility knives for sale to GIs during the war. Value: **$250-500**.

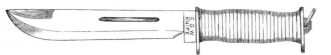

E.G. Waterman of New York City sold two models of World War II commercial combat knives by mail. Their leather or grooved-wood handles were secured to the tangs by a bent wire ring. Values: **$60** with scaler on the blade spine, **$40** plain, with sheath. No sheath, subtract **$15**.

Home-Front Combat Utility Knives

During World War II, a handful of custom knifemakers, most notably Blade Magazine Cutlery Hall-Of-Famer© W.D. "Bo" Randall and John Ek, gained national attention for making high-quality sheath knives of novel design. Indeed, for a time, Randall found demand for his Model 1 so great that he allowed a contractor in Springfield, Massachusetts, to make knives to his specifications.

Two custom makers who specialized in cast-aluminum-handled knives found a national market for their combat knives during World War II. They were David Z. Murphy of Gresham, Oregon (marked MURPHY COMBAT on the handle), and F.J. Richtig of Clarkson, Nebraska. Richtig also made knives with more ordinary handles. For more information Murphy, Richtig and other 1940s knifemakers, see "Pioneers of Modern Handmade Knives" earlier in this section.

Besides the full-time custom makers, thousands of home craftsmen, defense plant machinists, Army Air Force mechanics, and Navy Sea-Bees made hundreds of thousands of knives or parts knives during the war, either for themselves or to be sold or given to servicemen bound overseas. Indeed, Blade Magazine Cutlery Hall-Of-Famer© M.H. Cole, the military knife historian and artist, made many such knives himself.

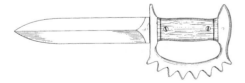

Knuckle knife by Blade Magazine Cutlery Hall-Of-Famer© M.H. Cole.

Almost all of the home-front knives are unmarked, though a combination of luck and detective work may allow you to identify some. Most look similar to commercial and issue knives of the 1940s. Many include typical materials of the time, such as purplish aircraft canopy Plexiglas™ fabricated into a stacked-washer handle. (Some call knives with such handles "theater knives.") The value of most such unmarked knives is between **$15** and **$75**, depending mainly on workmanship and condition.

L.F. Baker 1944 patent combat knife.

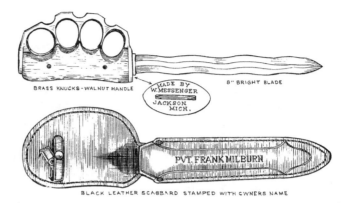

W.H. Messenger knuckle knife.

Marked knives by documented makers are another story. For them, the values start at **$1,000** and can climb well past **$3,000**. Besides makers discussed in detail in *Pioneers of Modern Handmade Knives,* documented makers include A.G. Bimson of Berthoud, Colorado; Taylor E. Huff of Fort Knox, Kentucky; Leo F. Baker of Chicago; Ernest Warther of Dover, Ohio; Herman Grieshaber of Chicago; William H. Messenger of Jackson, Michigan; Ben Rocklin of Chicago; and Merrill E. Brown of New Albany, Indiana. Research continues to document others.

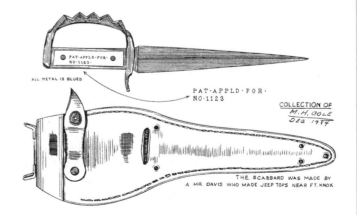

Taylor Huff 1944 patent knuckle knife.

A few categories of World War II knives fall in between standard made and expedient. One is the trench knives made early in the war from blades and parts of the Garand bayonet. The knives look like cut-down and sharpened bayonets, except that they have no slots or other fittings for attachment to a rifle. Value: **$40-50**.

Another example is the ANDERSON/GLENDALE/CALIFORNIA knives with molded-plastic handles, and blades made from one-third of a Patton Model 1913 cavalry saber blade. Other knives made from old sword blades have stitched leather handles. The knives were sold by sporting goods dealers in Philadelphia and Chicago, and possibly elsewhere. All are worth about **$300-400**.

Jet Pilot's Knife

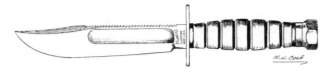

The World War II U.S. Navy pilot's bail-out knife was a big, 6-inch folder with a clip blade and a saw. (See the "Utility and Scout Knives" segment of the "Multi-Blade Knives" chapter in Section II.) The knife was costly and the saw was fragile. Many Navy pilots carried Mark 1s instead. Army Air Force planes often carried 5-inch Marble's Ideal hunting knives in their survival kits. (See "American Hunting Knives" earlier in this section.)

In the mid-1950s, the Navy ordered a new style of pilot's knife that combined the features of the Mark 1, the Mark 2 and the folder. The *jet pilot's knife* is as stout as the Mark 2; as small and handy as the Mark 1 (the first models had 6-inch blades but, since 1962, all have had 5-inch blades); and has sawteeth on the blade spine. The first ones were made by Marble's.

JET PILOT'S KNIFE, value in excellent condition.
6-inch blade, with sheath:
Marble's: **$800**; Commercial version: **$300**.
Camillus with screw pommel: **$175**.
Camillus with pinned pommel: **$125**.
5-inch blade, with sheath:
Camillus: **$50**.
Ontario: **$20**.
Utica: **$200**.
Milpar, leather handle, blade marked: **$150**.
Milpar, aluminum handle and guard: **$450**.

Diver's Knives

Most military diver's knives are very rare. One you may encounter is the Navy hard-hat diver's knife. It was used in the Navy yards and was also stowed in the escape hatches of submarines. Most do not have Navy markings. (See "The Diving Knife" by Eric Brooker, April 1989 *BLADE®.)*

There are two basic styles. The oldest is about 12 1/2 inches long and has a flat, spring-loaded, cast-brass sheath. Most U.S. models were made by Morse Diving Equipment of Massachusetts (established 1837). Value: **$225-275**.

European models were an inch longer and were made by Siebe Gorman & Co. London (established 1819). (See "Foreign Military Fixed Blade Knives" later in this section.) Value: **$300-350**.

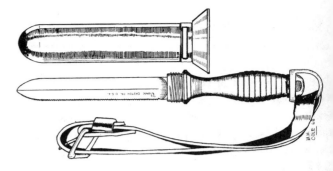

The more common version, the Mark V, was first used by the Navy in 1915. It has a 6 1/2-inch spear-point blade with sawteeth on one edge, a turned wooden handle and brass mounts. The knife screws into a massive, cylindrical brass sheath, allowing it to be used as a mallet. Value in excellent condition, with sheath:
Blade marked KA-BAR: **$500**.
Morse, Schrader, DESCO, Vince or unmarked: **$200-250**.
Other Navy diver's knives:
Imperial Non-Magnetic, with sheath: **$1,500**.
SeaFloat Team (SEAL support), molded plastic handle: **$45**.
See also U.S.N. Mark 2, U.D.T. versions.

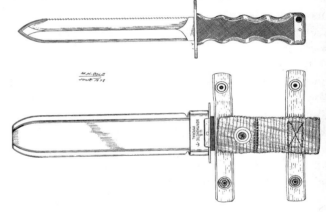

Imperial non-magnetic diver's knife, 1962.

Vietnam-Era S.O.G. Knives

During the Vietnam conflict, the U.S. Army's Special Forces commissioned a combat knife for members of its S.O.G. ("Studies and Observation Group") teams. The S.O.G. knives were made in Okinawa and bear no maker's markings. Value: **$1,200-2,000**.

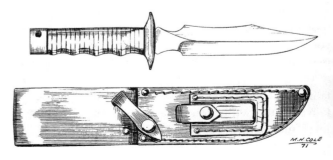

Some later knives are lightly etched with the Special Forces badge and the inscription "5th SPECIAL FORCES GROUP (Abn)/ VIETNAM." Value: **$2,000**. A variant by "Japan Sword" with a longer, slimmer blade may have been used by the C.I.A. Value: **$2,000** and up. Be aware that the knives have been extensively reproduced, copied and counterfeited.

U.S. Military Mess Cutlery

During and after the Civil War, the U.S. Army Medical Department bought plain table knives and forks for the use of men in hospitals. Field-mess utensils were still the responsibility of the troops.

Beginning in the mid-1870s, the Army began to issue mess knives and forks stamped out of sheet steel and that featured integral, cast-iron handles japanned black. Though usually marked "U.S." only, they were probably made by J. Russell & Co. Value: **$50**/pair.

A less expensive version was introduced circa 1892. Examples are stamped-sheet-steel knives and forks with a soft-metal bead cast around the perimeter of the full tangs to make a rudimentary handle. The 5 1/2-inch pointed knife blades are stamped "U.S.", while the forks are stamped "U.S." on the back of the shank. Both are stamped in the handle J. WARD & Co. PAT. DEC. 19, 1892. J. Ward was J. Russell's economy brand. Value: **$45**/pair.

In about 1903, a cast-in-place aluminum handle was substituted for the bead cast. Blades were made slightly wider and shorter (5 inches), and were sometimes tin-plated. The mess-kit knives were made in the Rock Island Arsenal in Illinois, and so are marked "R.I.A. U.S." and with the date on the handle. Value: **$15**. Circa 1913, the mess-kit knife blade was shortened to 3 5/8 inches. Value: **$12**.

Thenceforth, mess forks were no longer made to match the knives. The forks and matching tablespoons were stamped from sheet steel and then plated, first with tin and, in later years, nickel. Value: **$4**. Eventually, they were to be made of stainless steel.

After the United States entered World War I in April 1917, mess-kit cutlery was again supplied by contractors. Aluminum-handled knives were made in 1917 by L.F. & C. and by American Cutlery Co. (A.C. Co.). A 1918 contract was filled by the International Silver Co. (I.S.C.) of Meriden, Connecticut. Value: **$8**. Forks and spoons were made by Wallace Bros. Works (WB/W). In the 1930s, surplus mess utensils, especially I.S.C. 1918 knives, were used by the Civilian Conservation Corps (CCC) of President Roosevelt's "New Deal."

Circa 1941, large, oval holes were added at the ends of the utensil handles to allow them to be hung from the handles of mess-kit plates, and then dipped in a hot sterilizing solution after use. From 1941-43, to conserve aluminum, many mess-kit knives were made with black-plastic handles, some by L.F. & C., some by Goodell, and some in Australia. Value: **$6**. Later, most were made with a smooth alloy handle and have no maker's mark. Value: **$2**.

In recent years, the Army has used simple mess knives stamped from sheet stainless steel. Most were made by Utica Cutlery Co. (U.C. Co.). Value: **$2**. In addition, the Army and Navy have bought tons of knives, forks and spoons for mess hall and hospital use. Most were plain but the Navy favored a fancy anchor-and-shell pattern for officers' messes. Look for such handle stampings as: U.S.Q.M.D. or Q.M.C. (Quartermaster's Department or Corps), U.S.A. M.D. (Army Medical Department), or U.S.N. Value **$2-5**.

Military mess cutlery and flatware.
Top group: two plated mess-kit spoons and two plated mess-kit forks; silver-plated teaspoon, U.S.Q.M.D.

Main row, from left: Russell knife and fork, c1860s, wood handles stamped "US," probably from an Army hospital contract; J. Ward 1892 patent knife and fork, both marked "U.S."; Navy officers' mess silver-plated knife and fork; five aluminum-handled mess-kit knives: two R.I.A long blade; R.I.A. 1913 short blade; A.C. Co. 1917; L.F & C. 1917; three silver-plated forks: Q.M.D., U.S.A.-M.D., U.S.N.; silver-plated steel knife, MED. DEPT. U.S.A.; two plastic-handle mess-kit knives: L.F. & C., Australia.

Foreign Military Fixed Blade Knives

Introduction to German Third Reich Knives

Historical information and photos courtesy LTC Thomas M. Johnson (retired)

Germany's National Socialist Third Reich (1933-1945) employed an array of elaborate uniforms, decorations and accouterments to foster popular involvement in the Nazi party and regime. Dress daggers in more than 60 patterns and variants, made by dozens of cutlery firms in Solingen, were an important part of the regalia.

To the Allied soldiers who overthrew the Third Reich, the fancy Nazi regalia made ideal war souvenirs, especially the distinctive dress daggers. Indeed, the daggers proved

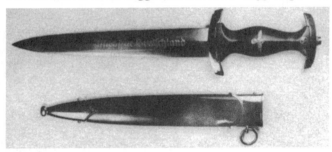

1. SA (*Sturmabteilung* or Storm Trooper's) dagger. The paramilitary SA was established in 1921. By 1934, it had over 4 million members. The SA dagger, adopted in 1933, was the first official Nazi dress weapon, and is by far the most common. All SA members could wear the daggers, which were sold through retail stores. Brown wood grip. Blade etch "*Alles fur Deutschland*" (All for Germany). Early versions, **$550**. Later (RZM marked), **$400**. The scarcer SS (*Schutzstaffel* or Elite Guard) dagger is similar, but has a black wood grip, blade etch "*Meine Ehre heisst Treue*" (My honor is loyalty). Early versions, **$1,800**. Later (RZM marked), **$1,400**. (Thomas Johnson photo)

2. HJ (*Hitler Jugend* or Hitler Youth) knife. Formally organized in 1935, and made mandatory for children 10 to 18 in 1939, the HJ imposed political indoctrination and military training. The HJ knife was an award for passing proficiency tests, and was sold by retail stores for 4 marks. Black, molded grip. Blade etch "*Blut und Ehre*" (Blood and honor) was omitted after August 1938. Value, **$275**. (Thomas Johnson photo)

For more information on Third Reich knives, consult the series *Collecting the Edged Weapons of the Third Reich* by LTC Thomas M. Johnson (retired). Contact Johnson Reference Books, 312 Butler Rd. #403, Fredericksburg VA 22405.

so popular that unofficial production of the more common patterns continued after World War II, to the point that parts knives, replicas and counterfeits may now outnumber the millions of authentic knives produced in the Nazi period.

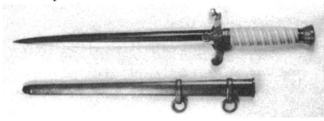

3. Army (*Heer*) officer's dagger. Throughout the Nazi period, the German army maintained its separate identity, as reflected by the token swastika on this dagger, adopted in 1935. White, yellow or orange grip. Value, **$425**. (David Delich photo)

4. 1937 Pattern Air Force (*Luftwaffe*) officer's dagger. The German air force, under Hermann Goring, was more closely tied to the Nazi party than the army. White, yellow or orange wire-wrapped grip. Value, **$475**. (David Delich photo)

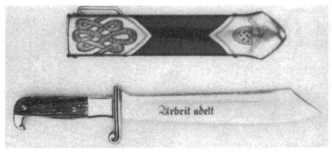

5. RAD (*Reichsarbeitsdienst* or Reichs Labor Service) hewer. The RAD was organized circa 1930. The hewer was designed as a chopping and digging tool. Stag grips. Blade etch "*Arbeit adelt*" (Labor ennobles). Value, **$700**. (David Delich photo)

Notwithstanding the large variety produced, most of the Third Reich daggers ordinarily encountered are of the five most common types. They are the storm trooper's dagger, Hitler youth knife, army officer's dagger, *luftwaffe* officer's dagger and Reich's labor service hewer.

Plug bayonet. Western Europe, 17th-18th centuries. About 20-24" overall. Triangular, single-edged blade. Turned wooden handle with pronounced swell near guard. Brass ferrule, pommel and cross-guard. Used jammed into the muzzle of the musket, or as a knife. Value, **$450.** (courtesy California Academy of Sciences, Rietz collection)

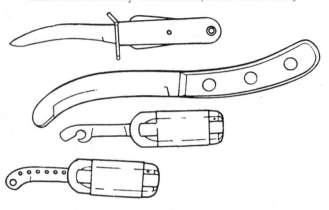

Above, from top: AEK—Aircrew Emergency Knife; 4" blade. Grippers in handle lock it into the steel sheath, which is stitched to a life vest. Value, **$75.**
F2—Firefighter's Quick Release knife; 6" blade. Safety-point rescue knife to cut seat belts. Value, **$30** w/sheath.
A90—Sailor's Floating knife; 2 3/4" blade. Safety-point knife with tin-opener end, lightweight handle, and stitch-down sheath for use in rubber dinghies. Value, **$25.**
A1—Dinghy Sailor's Floating Knife; 2 1/2" blade. Simple safety-point knife. Value, **$25** with stitch-down sheath.

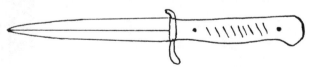

German World War I trench knife. About 10 1/2" overall. Single-edged blade with sharp false edge, some fully double edged. Wood or steel handle. Iron guard. Black, sheet-steel sheath. Value, **$75-100.**

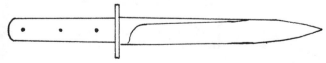

Austro-Hungarian World War I trench knife. About 13" overall. Single-edged blade with sharp false edge. Wood handles. Steel guard and sheath. Value, **$75-125.**

Values listed are for examples with knives and sheaths in excellent condition. Add 30-50 percent for mint condition; subtract 20-30 percent for very good condition.

British World War II Sykes-Fairbairn commando knife. About 11 1/2" overall. Metal handle secured by nut. Leather sheath. Values with broad arrow issue mark: checkered, **$175**; beads and ribs, **$275**; ribbed, **$100.** Turned wood handle, **$195.**
Example shown, current commercial, ribbed, **$35.** (courtesy of the old Gutmann Cutlery Co.)

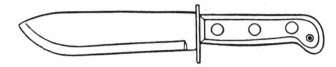

Knives approved for purchase by the British Ministry of Defence, from a 1981 Joseph Rodgers catalog. (Above) JS—Jungle Survival Knife; 7" blade. Value, **$50** with sheath. (courtesy Ron Braehler and *Knife World*)

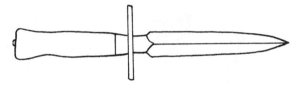

French World War I trench knife. About 11" overall. Double-edged blade with maker's mark or Thiers trademark registry number on ricasso (31-Besset; 41-Conon; 76-Bernard; etc.). Turned wooden handle. Steel mounts. Steel sheath with wire belt loops. Value, **$165.**

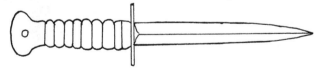

Dutch combat knife. About 13" overall. Blued, double-edged blade. Wooden handle. Oval steel guard. Leather sheath. Value, **$190.**

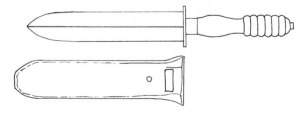

Hard-Hat Diver's Knife. About 13 1/2" long, has flat, spring-loaded, cast-brass sheath. Made by Siebe Gorman & Co. of London (established 1819) and used by most European navies. Value, **$200-250.**

Modern Commercial Daggers and Survival Knives

Early 20th Century Commercial Dirks and Daggers

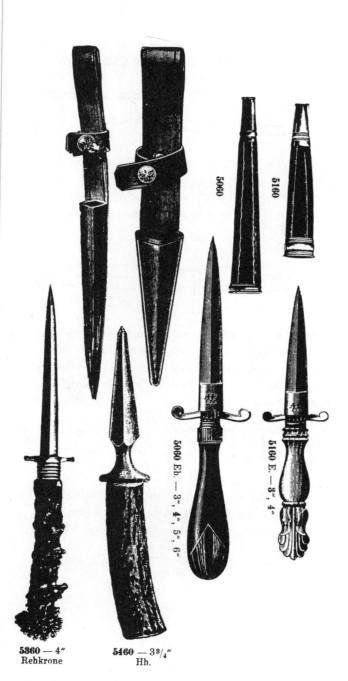

5060

5160

5060 Eb. — 3″, 4″, 5″, 6″

5160 E. — 3″, 4″

5360 — 4″
Rehkrone

5460 — 3⅜″
Hh.

Henckels daggers shown half actual size. Handles of roebuck crown antler, stag antler, ebony and ivory. Value, **$120-200** with sheath. (courtesy John Allison)

DIRKS

JOSEPH ALLEN & SONS, SHEFFIELD, ENGLAND

Best Quality English Steel Blades; Double Edge; Full Polished; Complete with Black Leather Sheaths

Per Dozen

No. 1168—Solid Twisted Pearl Handle; German Silver Hilt and Fancy Knurled Bolster; Length of Blade 4½ inches; Weight per Dozen 1⅝ lbs............................$32.00

Per Dozen

No. 1183—Solid Genuine Stag Handle; German Silver Hilt; Scored Bolster and Plain Seal Cap; Length of Blade 4½ inches; Weight per Dozen 2½ lbs.....................$20.00

Dirks imported by Shapleigh Hdw. Co.. Value, **$175** and **$125**. (courtesy John H. Murphy)

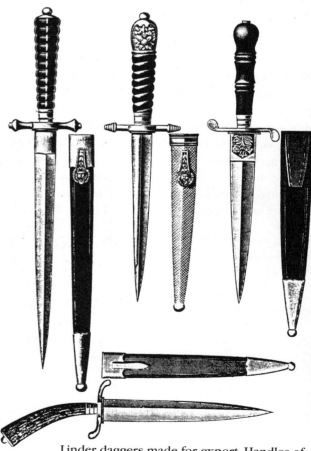

Linder daggers made for export. Handles of horn, celluloid, ebony and stag, **$135-200**.
(courtesy Siegfried Rosenkaimer)

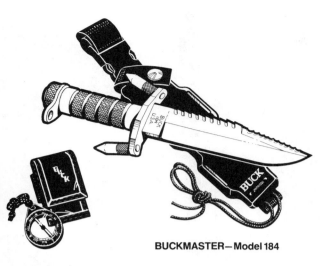

BUCKMASTER—Model 184

The Buck Buckmaster had a manufacturer's suggested retail price (MSRP) of **$227**.

Schrade Extreme Survival, 12 1/4" overall, had a manufacturer's suggested retail price (MSRP) of **$150**.

The Buck/Phrobis III M9 bayonet system was complex enough to impress the Department of Defense to make it the Army's bayonet circa 1990. It had an MSRP of **$211**.

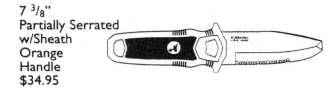

7 ³/₈"
Partially Serrated
w/Sheath
Orange
Handle
$34.95

Each knife comes equipped with a two sheath system. Delrin® sheath can be strapped to arm, vest or ankle.
Attach the webbed nylon sheath for comfortable belt wear.

Schrade Multi Purpose/Adventure; 7 3/8" overall, black, blue or orange, had an MSRP of **$34.95**.

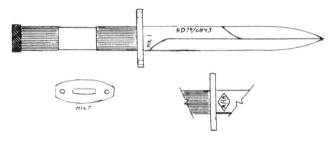

Angus Arbuckle, 1979 South African Defense Force (S.A.D.F.) combat survival knife, all steel, **$250** (courtesy John Rullman and *Knife World*)

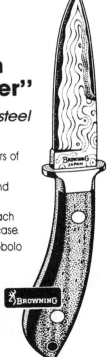

Limited Edition "Classic Fighter"

A classic, Damascus steel collector's knife.

- Blade forged from over 200 layers of steel.
- Styled with a "fighting" blade and handle.
- Edition limited to 1,000 knives. Each comes in a velvet-lined walnut case.
- Stainless steel bolsters and cocobolo hardwood handles.

For the 1988 "Classic Fighter," Browning's suggested retail price was **$350**.

SOG Specialty Knives recreated the Vietnam War-era S.O.G. (Studies and Observation Group) knife. Unmarked originals were made in the Far East in the 1960s. This higher-grade replica "SOG Bowie" has a leather-washer handle and blued blade and fittings. In 2004, the manufacturer's suggested retail price (MSRP) was **$284.95**. The MSRP for the SOG Trident, a stainless steel and Micarta® version, was also **$284.95**. The SOG Tigershark, with Kraton rubber handle, had a 2004 MSRP of **$154.95**.

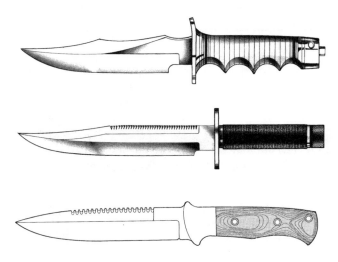

(Above, from top) Al Mar Knives' Micarta®-handled version of the Special Forces S.O.G. knife had a manufacturer's suggested retail price (MSRP) of **$282**; the SF-10 survival knife with a cord-wrapped hollow handle had an MSRP of **$230**; and the S.E.R.E. (Survival, Evasion, Resistance, Escape) serrated Model V with Micarta® handles had an MSRP of **$298**. As of 2004, all had been discontinued.

Lynn Thompson's Cold Steel Trailmaster Bowie has a Kraton® rubber handle. In 2004, the Carbon V steel version of the knife had a manufacturer's suggested retail price of **$184.99**.

Blade Magazine Cutlery Hall-Of-Famer© Rex Applegate, author of *Kill or Get Killed*, together with British Capt. W.E. Fairbairn, designed the Applegate-Fairbairn combat knife and combat smatchet. Handmade models by William Harsey had maker's list prices of **$285** and **$675**, and three boot-size versions had list prices of **$350-375**. (Those list prices probably are more now.) New production A-F combat knife by Boker, manufacturer's suggested retail price (MSRP) about **$135**; production smatchet by Boker, MSRP about **$235**. Applegate-Fairbairn combat folder by Gerber, **$135** MSRP.

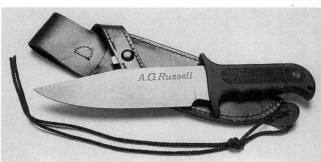

Blade Magazine Cutlery Hall-Of-Famer© A.G. Russell's forged, integral Sting of 1977, now discontinued, last had a manufacturer's suggested retail price (MSRP) of **$65**. Russell's camp knife, with a glass-reinforced Zytel® handle and a secret compartment, had an MSRP of **$60**.

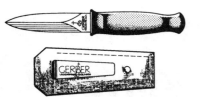

The Guardian® #5800: 3⅜" blade. Overall length, 7¼". Black Cordura sheath/belt clip.

Guardian® Camouflage #5816: 3⅜" blade. Overall length, 7¼". Weight 3.5 oz. Camouflage Cordura sheath included.

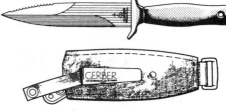

Command I™ Survival Knife #5900: 4¾" blade. Overall length, 9". Included: Black Cordura belt/boot sheath with quick-release thumb snap.

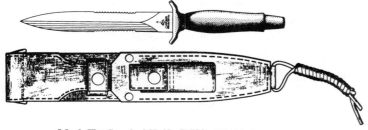

Mark II™ Survival Knife #5700: 6¾" blade. Overall length, 12". Included: Black Cordura sheath with accessory pocket.

Mark I™ 5600 Survival Knife: 4¾" blade. Overall length, 9". Included: a Black Cordura belt/boot sheath with quick-release thumb snap.

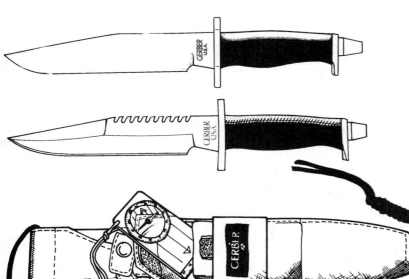

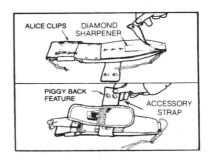

Basic Multi-Function Survival System™ (BMF™) 8" Bowie style blade with chisel tooth saw #5910, without saw teeth #5920. Overall length, 13". Blade thickness, .250". Weight, 15 oz.-28.6 oz. w/sheath. Black Cordura Sheath, diamond hone, and compass included. Unique strap allows attachment of survival pouch or folding knife sheath.

Above: Beginning in 1966, Gerber made combat-survival knives, with the Mark II (see Gerber Fixed Blade Knives) leading the way. The little Guardians had manufacturer's suggested retail prices (MSRPs) of **$76** each. The Command I (**$82** MSRP) was discontinued in 1994. The classic Mark II had an MSRP of **$106**, the smaller Mark I, **$89**. The newer BMFs, with 9-inch blades, had MSRPs of **$252** and **$276**. The similar 6-inch bladed LMFs had MSRPs of **$182** and **$204**.

Right: Aitor's Jungle King from Spain has enough accessories to outfit the whole family. It had a manufacturer's suggested retail price of **$320**.

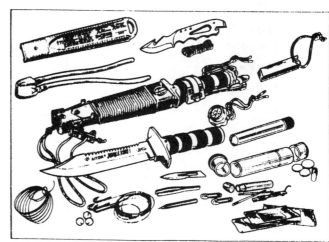

Modern Commercial Daggers and Survival Knives

Foreign, Exotic, Primitive and Historical Fixed Blade Knives

By Eiler R. Cook and Blade Magazine Cutlery Hall-Of-Famer© Bernard Levine

Mr. Eiler R. Cook is a collector of exotic knives and owner of Historic Edged Weaponry in Hendersonville, North Carolina. He provided illustrations and descriptions for nearly two-thirds of the knives and swords shown in this section. Mr. Bernard Levine is the former editor of this book, has authored several other knife books and is a regular columnist for Knife World. *Additional information has been provided by Lester Ristinen (Scandinavian knives) and Dave Schmiedt (Indonesian and Philippine knives). All values have been updated by Bill Claussen of Northwest Knives & Collectibles in Salem, Oregon.*

In this section we describe the basic types of fixed-blade knives used in the four corners of the world. We illustrate at least one example of each type and provide an estimate of that example's current value on the American collector market.

The knives are arranged geographically by region:

- A: Latin America
- B: Scandinavia
- C: Europe
- D: Africa
- E: Middle East and Indian Sub-Continent
- F: East and Southeast Asia
- G: Malaysia, Indonesia, and the Philippines
- H: Australia

At the end of the section is a brief summary of some modern, high-grade reproductions of some foreign and exotic knives and swords.

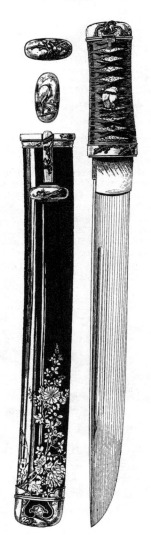

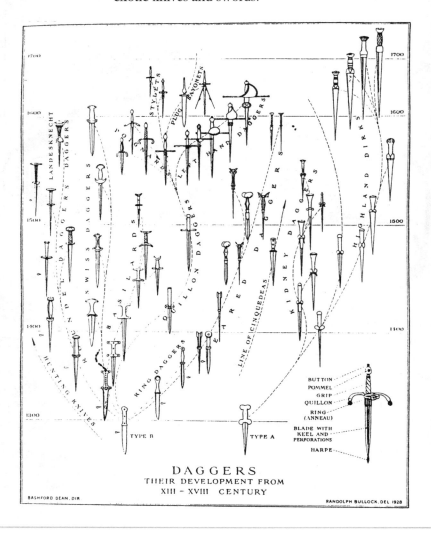

DAGGERS
THEIR DEVELOPMENT FROM
XIII – XVIII CENTURY

BASHFORD DEAN, DIR.

RANDOLPH BULLOCK, DEL. 1928

Area A: Latin America.

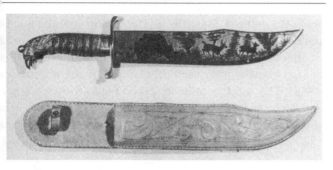

A.1. Mexico. Hunting knife.

About 14 inches overall. Both sides of blade usually etched with scenes or "dichos" (slogans). Handle is stag, sometimes snakeskin. White metal fittings. Hand-tooled leather sheath. 19th to 20th centuries. Example shown made in 1966 by Casa Aragon of Oaxaca, for six generations among Mexico's finest bladesmiths. Value, **$350**. Silver mounts, add 50 percent. Lower-quality examples with horn handles, aluminum or brass mounts, subtract 75 percent.

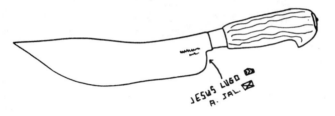

A.2. Mexico. Utility knife.

About 12 inches overall. Horn or wood handle with brass mounts. Crude workmanship. 20th century. Example shown made in Jalisco circa 1970. Value, **$8**. (image courtesy *Knife World*)

A.3. Guatemala. Highland Indian knife.

About 10 inches overall. Carved horn handle. Leather sheath. 19th to 20th centuries. Examples shown circa 1960. Value, **$10-40**.

Crude handcrafted knives sold in highland markets.

A.4. Argentina (also Uruguay). PUNAL or gaucho knife.

About 10 inches overall. Sheath usually metal, rarely wood handle and leather sheath. 17th to 20th centuries.

The gauchos are the cowboys of the pampas or prairies of southern South America. The CUCHILLO, or knife, in its various forms (PUNAL, FACON, DAGA, etc.) is a central part of their life and lore.

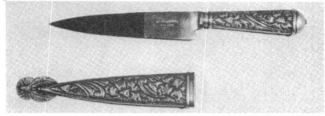

A.4.1. Most modern PUNALES have crude decoration and are poorly fitted, though some nice ones are still made. Example shown: PUNAL with tooled-silver mounts and gold trim made in Argentina circa 1940. Value, **$190**. Plated or base metal mounts, subtract 25 percent.

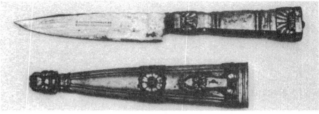

A.4.2. 19th-century PUNALES have finer engraving, often have gold rosettes on silver mounts. Blades—frequently whole knives—made in England, Germany or France. Old, fine-silver handles sometimes fitted with recent, poor-quality, Argentine-made replacement blades (subtract 75 percent). Example shown: 19th-century PUNAL with silver mounts and original blade. Blade made by Joseph Rodgers & Sons of Sheffield. Mounts marked L.COSTA. Value, **$450**. (photo courtesy California Academy of Sciences, Rietz Collection)

A.4.3. Seventeenth to eighteenth century PUNALES were made in Spain, look similar to Mediterranean daggers but with all silver mounts. Usually have ornate steel bolster, silver-overlaid ricasso, and chasing on blade. Pictorial touchmarks on back side of blade. Example shown: 18th-century PUNAL made in Spain. Value, **$375**.

A.5. Brazil (also Argentina). FACON.

About 10 inches overall. Metal mounts. Nineteenth to twentieth centuries. Spear-point gaucho knife, a more modern design than the PUNAL. Doubled-edged version called DAGA in Argentina. Example shown has aluminum mounts, from Rio Grande do Sul, Brazil, circa 1970. Value, **$45**.

A.6. Northern Argentina (Salta). PUNAL SALTENO.

About 18 inches long overall. Double-edged or fullered, single-edged blade. Silver mounts, including ornate, tapering handle and wide guard. 16th to 20th centuries. Example shown *galloneado* style, presented to President Juan Carlos Ongania in 1967. Value, **$950**. (photo and description courtesy Dr. Armando J. Frezze, Juez de Corte, Salta, Argentina)

A.7. Venezuela. LANZA.

About 15 inches overall. Steel lance head with long socket that serves as a handle when LANZA is used as a dagger. Unmounted LANZA carried in belt sheath, while its pole is carried by a servant. 17th to 19th centuries. Example shown, 19th century. Value, **$250**.

A.8. Central America. Spanish Colonial dirk.

About 16 inches overall. Hardwood handle, sometimes of wood discs separated by brass spacers. 18th to 19th centuries. Value, **$100-350**, depending on age and quality. Example shown, early nineteenth century.

A.9. Central America. MACHETE.

About 25 inches overall. Hilts of horn, wood or plastic. Leather scabbard. 19th-20th centuries. Stainless-bladed example shown made in West Germany, 1967, scabbard made for it in El Salvador. Value, **$125**. Plain local blade and scabbard, value, **$15-35**.

Hundreds of different shapes of MACHETES have been made, each for a specific region, crop or type of vegetation.

Until the mid-1960s, the best known in Latin America were made by the Collins Co. of Connecticut, who also made U.S. military MACHETES. The Collins brand name is still used in Central America. MACHETES made in England (such as Martindale's Crocodile brand from Birmingham) and in Germany were used in Asia and Africa. For more on MACHETES, see U.S. "Military Fixed Blade Knives" earlier in this section.

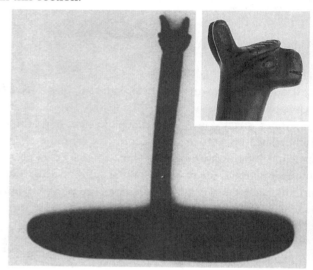

A.10. Peru. TUMI.

About 6 inches wide. Solid wrought copper. Llama-head finial. Pre-Columbian Inca sacrificial knife. All known authentic examples in museums. Example shown, 20th-century reproduction. Value, **$125**.

A.11. Chile. CORVO.

About 11 inches overall. Forged, hooked blade. Segmented handle of horn or bone with metal spacers. 18th to 20th centuries. Example shown from Pag, c1900. Value, **$150**. Current Chilean-Army-issue corvo has black-plastic grips; value with military sheath, **$60**. (image courtesy Atlanta Cutlery)

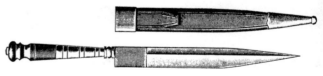

A.12. Brazil. FACA DE PONTA.

About 11 inches overall. Narrow, triangular blade, often with multiple fullers. Local-made FACA blades plated, unsharpened. Fancy horn handle and leather sheath. 19th to 20th centuries. Brazilian Indian trade dagger. Value, **$95** local made, **$125** German made. Example shown by Linder c1900.

Area B: Scandinavia.

B.1. Lapland. Handmade Lapp STUORRANNIIBI or LEUKU.

About 10 inches overall. Wood handle. Carved reindeer-horn sheath with reindeer-hide throat. Example shown, late 19th century. Value, **$400**.

B.2. Finland. Modern LEUKU or Finnish sheath knife.

About 8 inches overall. Wood handle—usually birch—with white-metal mounts. Ornamented leather sheath. 19th to 20th centuries. Example shown circa 1950s, value, **$75-150**.

Larger-size LEUKU, about 12 inches overall, used by Lapp trappers, add 25 percent. Russo-Finnish War commemorative inscription, add 25 percent. Leukus are sold worldwide. Leukus by J. Marttini and Lauri Tuotet, both of Rovaniemi, are sold in the United States.

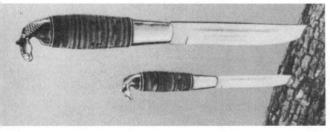

B.3. Finland. Horsehead PUUKKO.

About 6-8 inches overall. Plastic or pressed birch-bark handle, brass or nickel-silver mounts. Horsehead-shaped pommel. Leather sheath. 20th century. Value, **$75**. Made in Kauhava, exported to the United States since the 1910s. (photo courtesy Gutmann Cutlery)

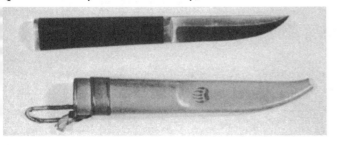

B.4. Finland. Modern-style PUUKKO.

About 8 inches overall. Dark-nylon handle with brass or silver mounts. Leather sheath. 20th century. Example shown circa 1970, value, **$90**. This knife designed by Tapio Wirkkala.

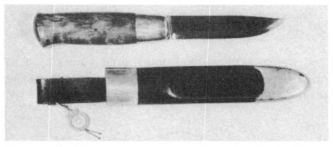

B.5. Norway. TOLLEKNIV or Norwegian whittling knife.

About 8 inches overall. Standard types have hardwood handles with white-metal, pewter or silver mounts. Leather sheath with matching fittings. 19th to 20th centuries. Value, **$75-150**. Example shown is David-Andersen's "Peer Gynt" knife with silver mounts, circa 1963. Value, **$150-200**.

B.6. Norway. STASKNIV (deluxe Sunday or fancy knife).

Examples have carved wood, bone or ivory (walrus) handles with metal mounts and matching sheaths of the same material. A few have crossguards. Mainly 19th century. Value, **$150** (wood or bone), **$275** (ivory). Example shown has curly birch handle and sheath, engraved, nickel-silver mounts. Made by Jean Mette of Kristiania (now Oslo). Depending on age and handle material, up to **$1,500**. (photo courtesy Bill Spivey)

B.7. Sweden. Hunting knife.

About 9 inches overall. Had laminated blades until c1990 (now special order only). Birch handle. Now have plastic sheaths. 20th century. Made in Mora, value, **$10-50**. (photo courtesy Gutmann Cutlery)

B.8. Sweden. SLOYD (manual training) knife.

About 5 inches overall. Wooden handle with iron or brass mounts. Fiber sheath or no sheath. 19th and 20th centuries. Value, **$10-20** (small and plain) to **$35-75** (large and decorated).

SPECIAL SECTION

SLOYD KNIVES

No. 2 Sloyd Knives. Oval Cocobolo Handles. 2⅝ in. Sabre Through Tang Blades.

No. 52 Sloyd Knives. Same as No. 2 except Handles are Varnished Beech.

Weight per dozen 1¼ lbs.

A simple whittling and utility knife. Identical knives made in USA. Example shown, American, c1930. (image courtesy Jim Emerson)

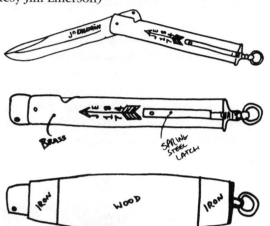

B.9. Sweden. Barrel knife (folding SLOYD).

Several sizes, average 6 inches long overall. Narrow, straight blade. Barrel-shaped birch handle, steel fittings, brass liners. Mid-19th century to circa 1952. Example shown circa 1900. Value, **$100-400**.

This is a fixed blade that takes apart to fold up. Made in Eskilstuna by several firms, including John Engstrom (marked JE/1874 on liners) and Erik A. Berg.

Area C: Europe.

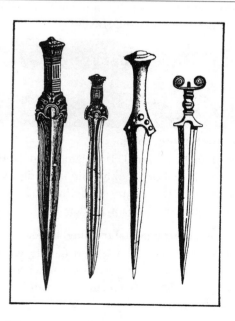

C.1. Western Europe. Bronze Age daggers.

About 8-15 inches overall. Bronze blades. Riveted or integral bronze handles. Circa 500 B.C. and earlier European bronze daggers are rare and valued in the **$1000s**. Virtually all known examples were found in excavations. Most are in museums.

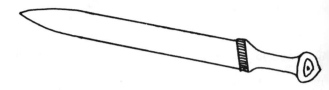

C.2. Northwestern Europe. SAX (SCRAMASAX).

About 10 inches overall, up to short sword length. Straight, single-edged blade. Flat, rounded pommel. Flat wood or horn grips. No guard. Leather or wood sheath or scabbard. Migration period to circa 15th century.

The Sax was the belt knife and short sword of the Germanic tribes in the Dark Ages, and later of the Vikings. All known authentic Saxes are from excavations and are in relic condition. Most are in museums. A few have sold in the **$1000s**.

C.3. Western and Central Europe. Rondel dagger.

About 12 inches overall. Narrow, straight blade. Disc-shaped guard and pommel. An aristocratic dagger of the 14th to 16th centuries. Authentic examples valued at **$1,500** and up, depending on quality and condition.

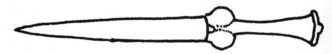

C.4. Western Europe. Ballock or kidney dagger.

About 12 inches overall. Straight blade. Carved, one-piece phalliform hilt with integral, ballock-shaped guard. 14th to 17th centuries. Predecessor of the Scottish DIRK. Value, **$1,000** and up.

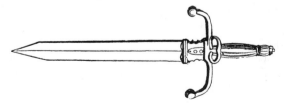

C.5. Western Europe. Parrying daggers.

C.5.1. Quillon dagger. About 12 inches overall. A simple dagger with forward projecting crossguard. 13th to 16th centuries. Value of original examples, **$1,000** and up.

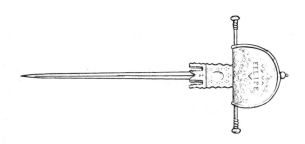

C.5.2. MAIN GAUCHE ("left hand") parrying dagger. About 20 inches long. A long, slender dagger with guard and handle like a sword. A "modern" refinement of the medieval Quillon Dagger. Used in combination with a sword. 16th to 18th centuries. Value, **$1,000** and up.

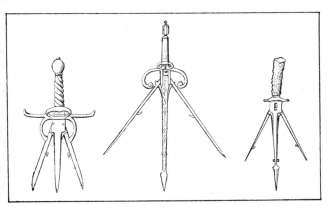

C.5.3. Three-bladed parrying dagger. About 20 inches long. A combined dagger and sword "catcher." 17th to 18th centuries. Value, **$1,000** and up.

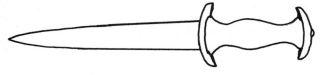

C.6. Western Europe. BASELARD.

About 15 inches overall. Sharp, pointed double-edged blade. Handle shaped like capital "I." Fourteenth to sixteenth centuries, revived by German Nazi party in 1930s. Early baselards are very rare outside of museums. Value in the **$1000s**. For Third Reich SA and SS versions, see "Foreign Military Fixed Blade Knives" earlier in this section.

A popular dagger in the late Middle Ages, the Baselard originated in Basel, Switzerland.

C.7. Scotland. DIRK.

Usually about 19 inches overall. A nineteenth- to twentieth-century dress dirk has a wood or horn handle, often with Celtic weave carving and a thistle-shaped butt. Earlier examples may have bone or metal grips. Often silver mounted. Leather sheath with metal mounts, sometimes holding an eating knife and fork. Middle Ages to 20th century. Value, **$200-1,500**, depending on age and quality of workmanship.

C.7.1. Early dirk. Example shown circa seventeenth to eighteenth centuries (excavated). The handle was probably bone, with wrought-iron mounts. Value, **$1,500**. (photo courtesy California Academy of Sciences, Rietz collection)

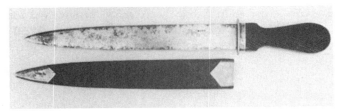

C.7.2. DIRK. Example shown, early 19th-century flat dirk for concealment. Made by Boog of Edinburgh. Checkered-boxwood handle, silver mounts. Value, **$500-1,500**.

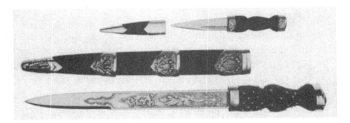

C.7.3. Dress DIRK. Example shown, current replica, made in India. Value: dirk, **$150**; *sgian dubh* (smaller knife in photo), **$40**; both with sheath. Knife courtesy A-C Enterprises. (photo by Blade Magazine Cutlery Hall-Of-Famer© Jim Weyer)

C.8. Scotland. SGIAN DUBH ("black knife").

Up to 8 inches overall. Blackwood or horn handle with carved weave design, silver or plated mounts, pommel usually set with large *cairngorm* (smoky yellow quartz). Black leather sheath with matching mounts. Mid-18th to 20th centuries. Example shown circa 1930. Value, **$140**. Older or with regimental crest, add 50-100 percent; modern, subtract 50 percent.

Pronounced *SKEEN-du*. Worn in top of right stocking as part of Highland dress. Each Highland regiment had its own model with distinctive crest.

C.9. England. London hunting knife.

At least 12 inches overall. Stout spear-point blade. Stag, boxwood, ebony or ivory handle with steel, nickel-silver or sterling mounts. Brown or black leather sheath, usually with matching mounts. Late 18th to early 20th centuries. Stouter than most bowie knives, these hunting weapons were used by English gentle-man adventurers to kill large game, mainly deer and boar. Examples marked LONDON were made in London, usually by surgical instrument makers, and of the highest quality. Those marked with a London street address only were made in Sheffield for a London retailer (subtract 40 percent). Value, **$750-2,500**.

Example shown made circa 1815-1830 by the London surgical instrument firm of John Weiss (1787-present). Ebony and nickel silver handle. The knife is from the Walter Moreau collection.

The ROSENKAIMER FAMILY and THEIR LINDER WORKSHOP

By Siegfried Rosenkaimer

About Linder

Centuries ago, the Solingen cutler's guild boasted quite a few members named Linder. Most of them were grinders. When Napoleon Bonaparte abolished the guilds circa 1805, he made everyone free to run his own business. Several of the Linders took the opportunity to found workshops, and they began selling their own products to the trade.

The Linder family was divided into several branches. One branch opened the Carl & Robert Linder firm in 1842. Its 239-page catalog for the year 1880 shows a complete line of cutlery.

Also circa 1880, a Wilhelm Linder had established his own specialized workshop for the production of hunting knives. His son, Carl Linder, carried on the trade and registered his name with the local trade authority on Oct. 10, 1908.

Carl Linder died in 1937. His widow sold the firm and its trademarks to my father, Paul Rosenkaimer (1899-1985), who renamed the firm Carl Linder Nachf. (successors). I became proprietor when my father passed away. My wife, Doris, and my two sons help run the company: Stephan Rosenkaimer is the office manager and Peter P. Rosenkaimer is a tool-and-die maker and an artist. Since he was 5, in 1965, Peter has been using the machinery in the workshop to make his own knives (P.P.R. brand). On one special project, he worked more than a year to complete a 7 1/2-foot-long showpiece sword for display in the office of a major Solingen export house.

The Rosenkaimers

The Rosenkaimers can be traced back at least seven generations in the Solingen municipal archives. Most of them were farmers who worked part time making knives and umbrella frames. They settled in small towns and villages that today are suburbs of Solingen.

My mother's family, the Seilheimers, were in sidearm—bayonets and hunting swords—production for generations. They were swordsmiths and brass workers. Paul Seilheimer, my maternal grandfather, started his own firm in 1917. It was merged into Carl Linder Nachf. in the mid-1960s.

From my grandfather's firm we inherited a great number and variety of old molds, samples, production tools and books. To this legacy was added, in 1971, the knifemaking department of the old Carl & Robert Linder firm, which was then closed down.

Both of the old firms long had engaged in the production of traditional Bavarian sheath knives. Today, Carl Linder Nachf., using many of the old tools and methods, ranks as the leading producer of this line. We also offer both collector knives, such as the giant "Alamo Bowie" that is 25 inches long and weighs 4 1/2 pounds, and also contemporary American-style hunting knives.

I have always taken an interest in history. Whenever an old Solingen company has closed down, I have tried to buy and save its old literature, catalogs, samples, and production parts and pieces. I donated some of the material to the Museum of Industry, which opened in Solingen in 1986. In addition, I have used some of the old tooling to make limited editions of historical knives and edged weapons.

Siegfried Rosenkaimer
Carl Linder Nachf.
Erholungstrasse 10
D-5650 Solingen 11
Germany

C.10. Northern Europe. HAUSWEHRE ("home defense").

Up to 15 inches overall. Wood, stag, bone or horn handle. Drop-in leather or cloth-over-wood sheath worn hung from belt. Middle Ages to 18th century.

Common person's all-purpose belt knife. May appear similar to Mediterranean daggers, but usually wider. Known mainly from artwork. Example shown in a 16th-century painting. Value, perhaps **$500** and up.

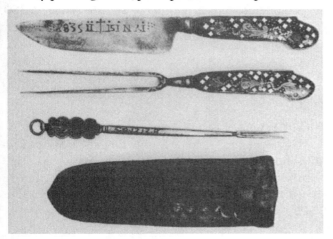

C.11. Bavaria (southern Germany). TROUSSE (hunting set).

Up to 8 inches overall. Pewter brass or silver handles with inlaid horn (usually) or stag panels and decorative rivets. Leather sheath holds matching knife and fork and, often, a sharpening steel. The steel, often hollow, unscrews to reveal skewer, marrow fork or corkscrew. Late 18th to early 20th centuries. Value, **$100-350**, depending on quality. Silver mounts, add 50 percent. Corkscrew inside sharpening steel, add 300 percent. Factory-made, subtract 50 percent. Example shown dated on blade 1835. Value, **$250**. (photo courtesy Smithsonian Institution, Wiebusch Collection)

This type of trousse was derived from the larger trousses of the 15th to 16th-century nobility. There is often a date on the handle, blade or sheath. Earliest we have seen is 1799. Most trousses are handmade and look much older than they are. Late ones are factory made and highly finished, but of lesser quality.

C.12. Germany and Austria. JAGDNICKER or WEIDMESSER ("hunting knife"). Also called TRACHTENMESSER ("dress knife").

About 8 inches overall. Handle usually stag—one piece with ferrule and cap, or two-piece riveted—or else chamois horn or deerfoot. Leather sheath with metal throat and tip but no belt attachment. Worn in Lederhosen pocket. 18th to 20th centuries. Value, **$30** for little-known brands, up

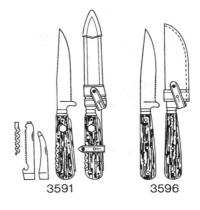

3591　　3596

to **$120** for well-known makes such as Puma, Henckels, Boker and Linder. Examples shown, current Puma. Silver mounts, add 50 percent. Folding blades in handle, add 50 percent.

C.13. Germany, Austria, Czechoslovakia. Deerfoot knife.

About 9 inches overall. Handle made from a deer's foot with the fur still on it. Leather sheath with nickel-silver fittings. 19th to 20th centuries. Example shown, current, courtesy Gutmann Cutlery. Value, **$45**.

Many of the knives were and are made for export to the United States (on them, the markings are in English). Folding versions also are made.

C.14. Germany. Hanger or hunting sword.

12 inches long up to short sword size. Usually stag handled. Often has crossguard (with hoof-shaped quillons) and counter-guard like a sword. Leather sheath/scabbard with metal fittings. 18th to 20th centuries. Value, **$300-1,500**, depending on quality and embellishment. Example shown from 1914 catalog, has side knife. Value, **$1,750**. (image courtesy J.A. Henckels and John Allison)

Used for killing and disjointing large game animals, and for personal defense. Also serves as a badge of rank among professional German foresters. Stag and boar are still hunted with spear and short sword.

C.15. Germany. Export Daggers and Knives.

A few examples of the many standard styles distributed around the world. Late 19th century to present. Value range, **$15-175**, depending on finish, condition and handle material.

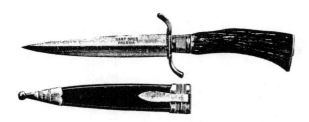

C.15.1. Export Dagger. 10 inches overall. Stag handle, black leather sheath. Nickel-silver mounts. Example shown from a 1903 American hardware catalog. Value, **$125**.

C.15.2. Export Dagger. 11 inches overall. Ebony handle, black leather sheath. Nickel-silver mounts. Example shown from a 1903 American hardware catalog. Value, **$175**.

C.15.3. Export Knife. About 11 inches overall. Leather and aluminum handle. Current example. Value, **$30**. (photo courtesy Gutmann Cutlery)

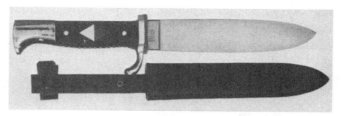

C.15.4. Youth Knife. About 10 inches overall. Plastic handles. Plated mounts. Metal and leather sheath. Current example by Wingen. Value, **$50**. (photo courtesy Gutmann Cutlery)

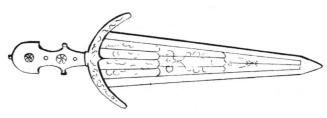

C.16. Southern Europe, mainly Italy. CINQUEDEA.

Up to 18 inches overall. Wide, heavy triangular blade, often fullered and pierced. Ornate handle. 15th and 16th centuries. Value, **$1,000** and up.

C.17. Southwestern Europe. Mediterranean dagger.

8-18 inches overall. Every possible handle and sheath material, from plain bone or horn, to mother-of-pearl or agate, to gold and jewels. Middle Ages to 19th century. Value range, **$100-1,000s**.

For centuries, the Mediterranean dagger was the standard belt knife of southern Europe and of Spanish areas of the New World. The earliest bowie knives of the 1830s looked similar. The South American gaucho's PUNAL is still made in this shape, though with all-metal mounts.

Small, fancy example, probably eighteenth century, from Sardinia. Double-edged, triangular blade. Mother-of-pearl and tortoise-shell handle mounted in silver. Silver-mounted, green morocco sheath. Value, **$350**. (photo courtesy California Academy of Sciences, Rietz Collection)

C.17.1. Canary Islands knife.

About 9 inches overall. Flexible forged blade. Stacked-horn-and-brass handle. Leather tab sheath worn inside waistband. 18th to 20th century. Value, **$100-350**. Example shown handmade in 1992 by Woodson Gannaway. Value, **$325**.

C.18. France. D'Estaing Knife.

About 13 inches overall. Ebony or ivory handle, silver or steel mounts. Designed as a combination dinner knife, carving knife and sidearm by Admiral Count d'Estaing, circa 1780, upon his return to France from service in the American Revolution. Made in Paris and later in Thiers. Value, **$150-350**.

C.19. Italy. STILETTO.

About 12 inches overall. Slender blade with two, three or four edges. Often all steel. 17th to 20th centuries. 19th-century engraving of a group of fine, old, all-steel STILETTOS. Value, **$500** each and up.

C.20. Austro-Hungarian Empire. Fancy dagger.

About 16 inches overall. Ornate metal guard. Wood sheath with matching metal fittings. 19th century. Example shown, circa 1825. Value, **$450.**

C.21. Russia (Caucasus). KAMA or KINDJAL.

About 20 inches overall. Semi-circular pommel with narrow grip, usually of wood, horn, ivory or silver embellished with *niello* (designs incised on metal filled with a black metallic alloy). Wood sheath covered with velvet, leather or matching silver. 18th to early 20th centuries.

The word "Kindjal" is the Russian version of the Arabic word "Khanjar." Both simply mean "knife." The KAMA is the traditional knife of the Cossacks. A similar knife may have been used in Persia.

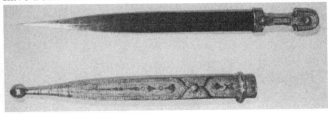

C.21.1. Example shown silver mounted, circa 1900. Value, **$650.** Plain horn handle, subtract 50 percent. Fine ivory mounts, add 30-50 percent.

C.21.2. KAMA reportedly collected in Persia in the nineteenth century. Value, **$450.**

C.22. Greece. KOPIS.

Ancient Greek bronze combat knife with curved blade and concave cutting edge. Known mainly from artwork and literature.

C.23. Greece. MACHAIRA.

Ancient Greek bronze combat knife with curved blade and convex cutting edge. Known mainly from artwork and literature.

The KOPIS and the MACHAIRA seem to be the ancestors of many more modern knives, including the KAMA, KHANJAR, KUKRI and JAMBIYA.

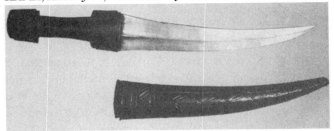

C.24. Balkans (Albania). Eastern European JAMBIYA.

About 15 inches overall. Handle of horn, wood or metal. Leather, wood or metal sheath. 18th century or earlier through early 20th century. Example shown late 19th century. Value, **$150.** Full silver mounts, add at least 200 percent.

The JAMBIYA is of Arab origin. It spread throughout Moslem-ruled lands from Eastern Europe through the Middle East to India in the period of the Ottoman Empire. Shape and decoration vary from region to region.

C.25. France. Satanic dagger.

About 10-15 inches overall. Curved or straight, double-edged blade. Cast-bronze handle depicting devils, satyrs, skeletons, snakes, goats, owls or other satanic devices. Metal sheath. Very high quality. Usually unmarked. Late 18th and early 19th centuries. Used by members of the satanic cults that arose in western Europe in the aftermath of the French Revolution and the Napoleonic Wars. Value, **$600** and up.

The example shown has a bronze skeletal figure of death as a grip. Its tombstone-shaped guard is marked CI GIT, French for "Here lies ..." and is entwined by a snake. Its damascus steel blade and bronze sheath are similar in shape to those of the daggers worn by the Mamelukes of Napoleon's Imperial Guard, made in Klingenthal Arsenal in 1813. Value, at least **$3,000.** Knife courtesy R.G. Fillmore. (T. Bruce photo)

Area D: Africa.

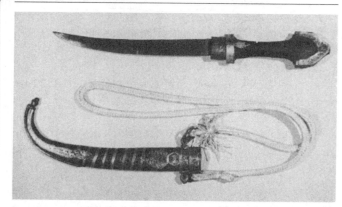

D.1. Morocco (Mokhazni tribe). KOUMMYA.

About 15 inches overall. Curved, single-edged blade, usually European made. Wood handle with flared pommel trimmed with brass or silver. Wood sheath with two suspension rings, matching trim. 18th to 20th centuries. Example shown, brass and silver trimmed, circa 1950. Value, **$150**. Fine silver mounts, add 200 percent.

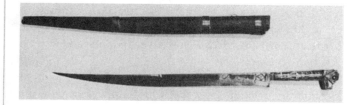

D.2. Morocco. FLYSSA.

Around 18 inches overall. Brass-inlaid, iron handle integral with blade. Blade may be brass inlaid as well. Mythic-animal-head pommel. Wooden sheath with brass bands. 18th to 20th centuries. Example shown, late nineteenth century. Value, **$190**.

This is the national dagger of the Kabyle people, a fiercely independent branch of the Berbers.

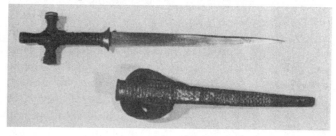

D.3. North Africa. TELEK (Tuareg arm dagger).

About 18 inches overall. Cross-shaped handle with leather and brass binding. Worked leather sheath with typical arm loop. 18th to 19th centuries. Example shown, mid-19th century. Value, **$275**.

Used by the nomadic Tuareg warriors of the Sahara desert region. Worn upside down on the left arm for quick draw with the right hand. (For more information, see "The Knives of the Blue Men of the Desert" in the March/April 1989 *BLADE®*.)

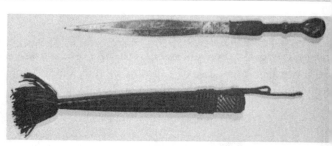

D.4. North Africa (Tunisia, possibly Senegal). Dagger.

About 14 inches overall. Leather-covered wood handle with rounded-knob pommel. Tooled-morocco sheath with tassel. 19th to 20th centuries. Example shown, early 20th century. Value, **$110**.

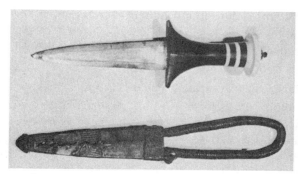

D.5. Sudan. Arm dagger.

About 9 inches overall. Wood and ivory handle with circular pommel and flaring self-guard. Leather sheath with arm band for wear on upper arm. 19th century. Example shown, late 19th century. Value, **$150-2,500**. A primitive African knife of very good quality.

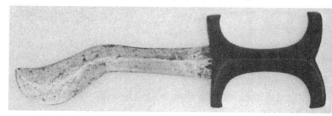

D.6. Sudan. Arm Knife.

About 12 inches overall. Similar to Sudan arm dagger except for pommel and blade shape. Ebony handle. Lightweight, well-tempered, double-edged blade. 19th century. Value, **$125**.

D.7. Central Africa. Dagger.

About 15 inches overall. Leaf-shaped blade with median ridge. Carved wood handle, leather sheath. Example shown probably early 20th century. Value, **$150-500**. (photo courtesy California Academy of Sciences, Rietz Collection)

D.8. Southwest Africa (Ovamboland, Namibia). Dagger.

About 10 inches overall. Carved wood handle and sheath, often bound with brass wire. 18th to 19th centuries. Example shown, nineteenth century. Value, **$100-150**.

Spear-shaped blade tapers to almost a needle point, as on certain bronze-age swords.

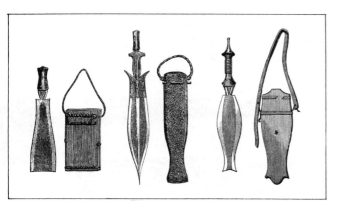

D.9. Central Africa (Zaire). War knife (center) and two parade knives.

Illustrations from a 19th-century book. Forged blades with complex fullers. Carved wood handles, sometimes with brass or copper trim. Wood sheaths bound with leather or wicker. Value, **$200-1,000**, depending on quality.

D.10. South Africa. German-style Hunting knife.

11 inches overall. Nickel-silver handle with horn scales. Blade etched BUSHMAN'S FRIEND. Other styles of hunting knives with this blade etch were sold in Africa, also in Australia. Made by John Clarke of Sheffield, England, circa 1950s. Copied from a German design. Value, **$60**.

"Bushman" is a British colonial term common both in Africa and Australia. It is roughly equivalent to such American terms as "woodsman" and "frontiersman."

D.11. Morocco. KHODMI.

About 11 inches overall. North African version of Mediterranean dagger. Thick blade usually has chasing and

inlaid copper mark. Horn or wood handle partly wrapped with wire. 19th to 20th centuries. Value, **$55**.

Area E: Middle East and Indian Sub-Continent.

E.1. Western Persia (ancient Luristan). Bronze dagger.

About 14 inches overall. Solid cast bronze with edges of blade hammered to work-harden them. Originally had inlaid bone, wood or hardstone handle scales. Example shown, before 700 B.C. Value, **$300** and up. With original handles, add 100 percent.

These daggers were grave goods and have survived in relatively large numbers. There are several variants, particularly with larger pommels.

E.2. Arabian Peninsula. JAMBIYA.

About 14 inches overall. Curved, double-edged blade with median ridge or groove. Wood, horn, ivory or metal self-guard handle. Curved or L-shaped sheath of leather or wood covered with leather, cloth or metal. Middle Ages to present. Example shown, silver mounted, probably 19th century. Value, **$450**. (photo courtesy California Academy of Sciences)

The JAMBIYA or Arab dagger was the free-man's belt knife wherever Moslems ruled. Eastern Europe, North Africa, Turkey, Persia and India all had variations of the JAMBIYA. Contemporary handmade examples in Yemen and Oman cost from **$300** for plain ones, to **$800** for a nice silver-mounted one, to **$3,000** or more for one with a black-market rhinoceros-horn handle and silver trim.

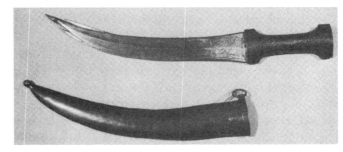

E.3. Persia (Iran). JAMBIYA.

About 16 inches overall. Metal handle with gold-inlay designs and flat-topped, Indo-Persian-style pommel. Metal sheath. 18th to 19th centuries. Value, **$100**. Example shown, mid-19th century, has unusual blade tip that divides into five points for added shock power for stabbing. Value, **$450**. More ornate examples with jeweled handles, add 100 percent and more.

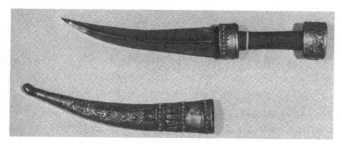

E.4. Iraq. JAMBIYA.

About 15 inches overall. Wood grip with embossed, silver-covered guard and pommel. Silver-covered wood sheath. Silver sometimes inset with turquoise or coral. 18th to 20th centuries. Example shown, 20th century. Value, **$230**. More ornate examples are more valuable.

E.5. Turkey. Dagger.

About 15 inches overall. Curved blade with Arabic inscription. Ivory grips. Hook-like pommel and guard of ebony. Brass sheath. 19th to 20th centuries. Example shown, early 20th century. Value, **$125**.

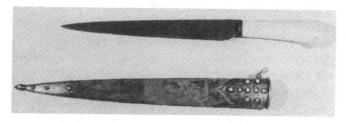

E.6. Afghanistan (also Persia, Northern India, Central Asia, Armenia, Turkey). KARD.

About 14 inches overall. Forged bolster. Thick blade, usually straight, sometimes curved. Ivory, jade or metal handle. Sheath of velvet-covered wood with ornate metal throat and tip. Middle Ages to nineteenth century. Example shown, circa 1800, damascus steel blade, ivory handle, sheath fittings embellished with turquoise. Value, **$700**.

Jade handle, add 50 percent. Non-damascus-steel blade, subtract 50 percent. Blade damascened in gold or silver, add 25 percent. Metal handle, subtract 75 percent.

The KARD was Persian in origin, brought to Afghanistan and northern India by the Mughals in the 16th century. A larger version was used in Central Asia. KARDS sometimes were concealed in canes or riding crops.

E.7. Afghanistan. SALWAR YATAGHAN (Khyber knife).

14 inches up to sword size. Triangular blade with T-shaped cross section. Leather sheath covers entire knife. Horn, bone or ivory (usually walrus) handle. 17th to 20th centuries. Example shown probably 19th century, ivory handle. Value, **$375**. (photo courtesy California Academy of Sciences, Rietz Collection)

We once saw a superb 19th-century Khyber knife made by Joseph Rodgers & Sons of Sheffield. Value, **$1,500**.

E.8. Northern India (also Persia). PESH-KABZ.

Up to 18 inches overall. Narrow, straight, bolstered blade, usually T-backed like a Khyber knife, but narrow and stiff for piercing chain mail. Handle often walrus ivory. Sheath of metal or leather over wood. 17th to 19th centuries. Example shown probably 18th century. Value, **$300**. (photo courtesy California Academy of Sciences, Rietz Collection)

E.9. India. KATAR.

About 15 inches overall. All steel. Handles may be damascened in gold. Some have two additional blades that spring out to the sides when the two handle sections are squeezed together. 16th to 19th centuries. Example shown probably 19th century. Value, **$270**. Ornate damascening, add 100 percent. Triple-bladed, add 100 percent.

Like the Moslem PESH-KABZ, the Hindu KATAR was designed for piercing chain mail. It was used with a punching blow. The side rails were used for parrying.

E.10. Southern India (Madras). Bowie-type knife. (Not illustrated.)

About 14 inches overall. Heavy, single-edged clip- or spear-point blade. Crossguard. Handle often of ivory. Looks similar to American or English bowie knives, but marked ARNACHELLUM/SALEM or AUSTIN/TRICHINOPOLY. 19th century. Value, **$750**.

E.11. S.W. Asia, from Arabia through Northern India. KHANJAR.

About 14 inches overall. Slightly recurved, double-edged blade. Indian examples often have blade decorations. Pistol-grip-, horse-head- and lotus-blossom-shaped handles range from plain metal to finest jade. Sheath of velvet-covered wood. 17th to 20th centuries. Example shown, 20th century. Value, **$75**. Ornate examples with jewelled or jade handles valued at **$1,000** and up.

Smaller knives of the shape with multi-piece, hardstone handles are made in Assam and Burma. Value, **$50** and up. An Indian version with a fan-shaped pommel is called a KHANJARLI.

E.11.1. KHANJAR by Joseph Rodgers & Sons from a 1912 catalog. Value, **$5,000**.

E.12. Southern India. PICHANGATTI ("hand knife").

About 13 inches overall. Heavy, straight clip-point blade. Round-end, pistol-grip handle with horn or silver scales. Wood sheath with silver or brass mounts. 18th to 20th centuries. Value, **$100**. Silver mounts, add 100 percent. A similar-shaped blade was also used on a polearm.

E.13. Nepal. Gurkha KUKRI (also KHUKURI).

About 16 inches overall. Heavy, forward-curved blade. Plain wood or ivory handle with ridge around middle. Wood sheath covered with leather or velvet, often holds

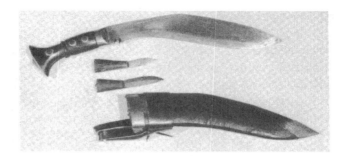

two miniature KUKRIS. Ancient times to present. Example shown, 1950s. Value, **$95**. Chrome-plated blade with black handle, marked INDIA, subtract 75 percent. Ivory handle, add 200 percent.

In addition to being the national knife of Nepal, used as both a jungle brush knife and weapon, the KUKRI was an issue arm of the Nepalese Gurkha troops serving in the British Army.

E.14. Sri Lanka (Ceylon). PIHA-KAETTA.

About 12 inches overall. Narrow, heavy blade inlaid and overlaid with engraved silver or brass panels. Ornate handle of wood, horn or ivory, often trimmed with metal. Equally ornate wood sheath with metal mounts. Seventeenth to twentieth centuries.

E.14.1. Example shown mounted in ivory and brass, 19th century. Sheath missing. Value, **$375**. Plainer example, subtract 50 percent. Fine ivory and silver mounts, add 50 percent. (photo courtesy California Academy of Sciences, Rietz Collection)

E.14.2. PIHA-KAETTA. Example shown mounted in horn, silver and brass. Wood sheath mounted in silver and brass also contains an ornate skewer. Probably 19th century. Value, **$450**. (photo courtesy California Academy of Sciences, Rietz Collection)

Area F: East and Southeast Asia.

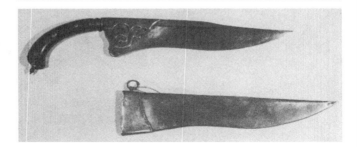

F.1. Southeast Asia (Burma south to Malaya). Knife.

About 16 inches overall. Kopis-shaped blade with carved-metal side plates. Pistol-shaped horn or wood grips. 19th century. Example shown, value, **$230**.

F.2. Tibet. PHURBU.

Six to 20 inches overall. Short, triangular, pyramidal blade. Heavy, elaborate handle. All-brass or iron blade with brass or wood handle. Tibetan Buddhist ritual knife. Example shown, all brass, 18th to 19th century. Value, **$600**. (photo courtesy Museum of Historical Arms, Miami Beach, Florida)

F.3. Bhutan, Tibet. Bhutan Dagger.

About 15 inches overall. Straight blade. Wood grip wrapped with silver wire. Wrought silver pommel. Silver-mounted leather sheath. 18th to 19th century. Example shown, circa 1880. Value, **$250**. For mounts of low-silver-content alloy, subtract 30 percent.

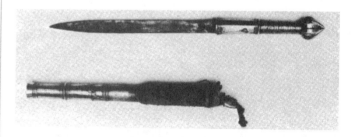

F.4. Burma and Thailand (Mountain regions). DHA.

About 15 inches overall, up to sword length. Plain, slender blade. Handle/hilt of silver over wood (usually) or of ivory, with onion-shaped pommel. Sheath/scabbard of silver over wood with flat bottom. Red carrying cord. 18th to 19th centuries. Example shown, late 19th century. Value, **$200**. Exceptional silver work, add 100 percent.

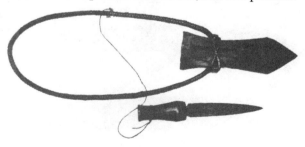

F.5. Taiwan. Formosan aboriginal dagger.

About 14 inches overall. Wooden handle and sheath with braided shoulder loop. 17th to 18th centuries. Example shown, 20th-century replica. Value, **$75**.

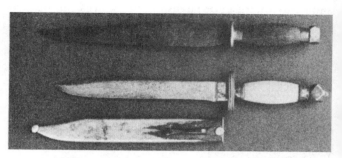

F.6. China. Combat knife (Chinese "bowie").

About 13 inches overall. Sharp, pointed, diamond-shaped, single-edged blade. Fluted handle of red wood or ivory with brass ferrules, heavy oval guard, and faceted pommel. Flat wooden sheath. 19th century. Unmarked examples made both in China and California. Example above (top), value, **$500-1,000**. Example above (bottom) made by Will & Finck of San Francisco, mounted in ivory and silver with silver-plated sheath, value, **$7,000**.

F.7. China. Double dagger.

Up to about 24 inches overall. A pair of matching knives with handles and mounts flat on one side so they nest together in one sheath. Blades may be sword style as in example shown, may be combat-knife style, or have broad, triangular blades with knuckle bows (called "butterfly knives" [not to be confused with the folding *butterfly knife* many associate with the Philippine Islands]). Wooden handles. Brass or iron mounts. Wooden sheath with metal fittings. 19th to 20th centuries.

Example shown has engraved brass fittings and tortoise-shell veneer on sheath, circa 1900. Value, **$500-1,500**. (photo courtesy John Crain)

A fine-quality, undecorated pair of iron-mounted butterfly knives would be worth about **$750-1,500**.

F.8. China, Mongolia and Tibet. Trousse.

Up to about 12 inches overall. Stiff, slender food-preparation knife with forged bolster. Handle scales of

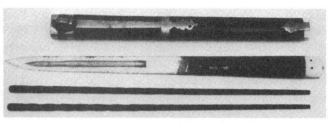

wood or horn with ivory or bone ends. Wooden sheath with metal and ivory mounts, usually wrapped in ray skin or metal. Holds pair of chopsticks of ivory, bone or wood. 18th to early 20th centuries. Example shown has sheath wrapped in black, lacquered ray skin, ebony chopsticks. Value, **$500**. (photo courtesy California Academy of Sciences, Rietz Collection)

Miniature trousse, handle and sheath covered in tortoise shell, silver chopsticks. Value, **$225**.

F.8.1. Some larger trousses are accompanied by a trousse-shaped dagger. Example shown, Chinese trousse with iron mounts, wood handles and bone ends on dagger and knife, bone chopsticks. Dagger blade marked "59" in Chinese. Value, **$350**.

A fine example of this type with laminated blades and matching mounts would be worth up to about **$2,000**.

F.8.2. Some Tibetan and Mongol trousses have metal-covered sheaths, often inset with large, colorful, uncut stones. Example shown has plated mounts, early 20th century. Value, **$250**.

Best-quality Tibetan and Mongol trousses have heavy silver mounts with flat, flaring bottoms, inset orange and blue stones, fine-quality blades. Value, **$500** up.

F.9. China. Western-style dagger.

Lightweight, straight double-edged blade. Brass mounts. Steel sheath with brass mounts. Late 19th and 20th

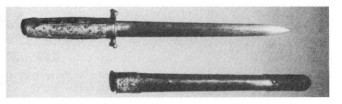

centuries. Example shown has designs of crossed U.S. and Nationalist China flags, U.S. Marine Corps emblem, dragons. Value, **$275**. Strictly Chinese decoration, subtract 50 percent.

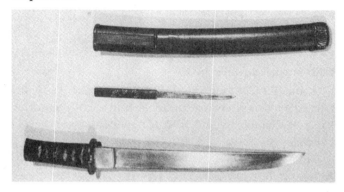

F.10. Japan. TANTO.

Up to 18 inches overall. Stout, laminated single-edged blade, polished to reveal grain. Tang may be signed. Copper or silver blade collar (*habaki*). Small iron or copper alloy guard (*tsuba*). Wood handle (*tsuka*) covered with ray skin (*sa-me*) and usually wrapped with braid, secured by single peg (*mekugi*). Matching decorated buttcap (*fuchi*), ferrule (*kashira*) and grip ornaments (*menuki*). Lacquered wood sheath may also have metal mounts. As in example shown, sheath may hold auxiliary knife (*kogatana*; handle called *kodzuka*). Fourteenth century to present. Example shown dated Feb. 2, 1855. Value, **$1,700**.

The TANTO originally was meant to be worn with armor, its main function being to cut the wearer out of his armor if he fell in the water. A similar dagger without a guard is sometimes called an AIKUCHI. Value of a Japanese tanto depends on quality of blade, fame of maker, quality of mounts and condition. *Do not* polish or oil a tanto. Consult an expert. Depending on quality and condition, *kodzuka* alone may be worth **$50-350**.

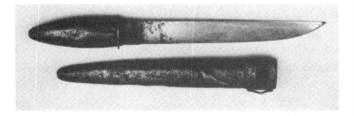

F.11. Japan. KAIKEN or KWAIKEN.

About 12 inches overall. Slender, single-edged blade, usually laminated. Blade collar (*habaki*). One-piece handle of wood or metal over wood. Matching sheath. Mounts may look like fan or other culturally related object. 15th to 19th centuries. Example shown, 19th century. Value, **$350**. (photo courtesy California Academy of Sciences, Rietz Collection)

This is the traditional woman's dagger, worn concealed in the *kimono* (dress). The knife's primary function was self-defense.

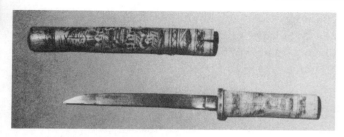

F.12. Japan. Souvenir knife.

About 1-2 feet long. Inferior blade and collar (*habaki*). Carved bone or, rarely, ivory mounts, 19th to 20th centuries. Value of example shown, **$90**. Exceptionally fine carving will increase the value **$100-200**.

Area G: Malaysia, Indonesia and the Philippines.

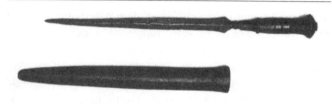

G.1. Malaya. LADING TERUS.

About 18 inches long overall. Narrow, stout double-edged blade resembling a lance head. Turned wood handle and rounded wooden sheath. 18th to 19th centuries. Example shown 19th century. Value, **$200-300**.

G.2. Malayan Archipelago. BADE BADE (RENTJONG).

About 11 inches long overall. Slightly curved, single-edged blade. Hardwood handle with right angle bend to facilitate quick draw. Wooden sheath. 19th century to present. Example shown has blade etched with Arabic writing, 1970s. Value, **$125**.

G.3. North Borneo. BARONG.

About 20 inches overall. Broad, leaf-shaped single-edge blade. Wood handle, rarely ivory. Wooden sheath. 19th

century or earlier to present. Example shown, late 19th century, well made with ornamental carving. Value, **$250-300**. Plainer modern example, subtract 50 percent. Ivory handle, add 50 percent.

The Moro jungle and combat knife was the inspiration for the various U.S. Army bolos.

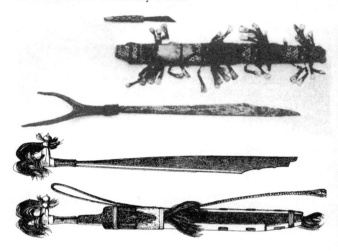

G.4. Sarawak, Malaysian Borneo. MANDAU (PARANG-ILANG).

About 25 inches overall. Stag-tine handle decorated with paint and cord. Wooden sheath decorated with paint, cord, fur, teeth and beads, also holds small 6-inch knife. The traditional knife of the Dyak headhunters of central Borneo. 18th to 20th centuries. Value of authentic examples, **$300-1500**, depending on quality of decoration.

Example, top, 20th-century tourist version. Value, **$100-150**. Example, bottom, from a 19th-century book illustration. Value, **$450**.

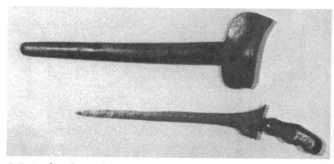

G.5. Malaysia and Indonesia. KRIS.

About 18 inches overall. Slim, delicate double-edged blade with elaborately wrought, pointed self-guard. Blade, usually "pamur" (welded damascus), may be straight or wavy. Carved wood or, rarely, ivory handle with worked metal ferrule or ring. Streamlined wooden sheath with boat-shaped throat. Throat may be ivory to match hilt. 14th to 20th centuries.

Krisses vary widely in quality and value. Many small and badly worn old krisses were sold in the USA in the 1970s at under **$10** each. They are not worth over **$25** now. However, a very fine kris in superb condition is worth perhaps **$450-1,000**.

G.5.1. KRIS. Example shown (previous page) from Java, circa 1800. Wooden mounts. Value, **$210**.

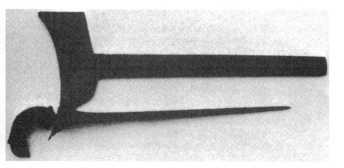

G.5.2. KRIS. Example shown from Malaya, 19th century. Note rectangular sheath throat. Value, **$250**.

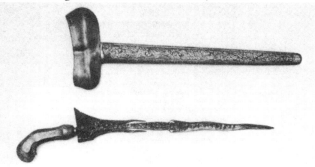

G.5.3. KRIS. Example shown from Malaya or southern Thailand. Note unusual "barbs" on blade and decorated sheath. Probably 19th century. Value, **$310**.

G.5.4. KRIS (KERIS MAJAPAHIT). Example shown from Java. Sheath and figural handle wrapped with metal and set with stones. Believed to be the earliest style of kris. 18th-century blade in 20th-century mounts. Value, **$550**.

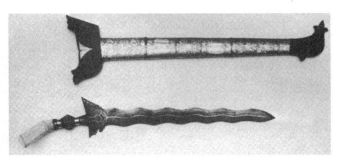

G.6. Philippines (Mindanao or Jolo). Moro KRIS.

About 24 inches overall. Shaped like Malay kris but larger and sturdier. Wood or ivory hilt. Wood scabbard usually wrapped with metal. Fifteenth to twentieth centuries. Example shown has ivory hilt and silver-wrapped scabbard. Early 20th century. Value, **$475**. Plain example, subtract 60 percent.

This is the short sword of the Muslim Moros of the southern Philippines. The example shown is one of a pair given by a *hadji*, a Moslem who has been to Mecca, to his favorite son.

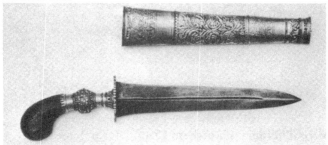

G.7. Philippines (Jolo). PUNAL.

About 13 inches overall. Double-edged blade. Curved wood handle with metal mounts. Metal-covered wooden sheath. 15th to 20th centuries. Example shown has silver mounts, 20th-century. Value, **$1,000**. Plain example, subtract 75 percent or more.

"Punal" is Spanish for "dagger"; the same word is used for the gaucho knife. This type of "punal" is a dagger of the Moros. The example shown is one of a pair that belonged to a chieftain ("datu") on Jolo Island.

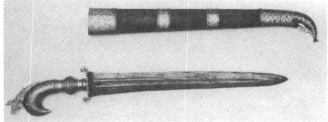

G.8. Philippines (Northern Mindanao). Moro dagger.

About 23 inches long overall. Double-edged blade with fuller. Elaborate bird's-head ("sarimanuk") handle of a silver-copper alloy. 18th to 20th centuries. Example shown, 19th-century blade in 20th-century mounts. Value, **$300**. A Maranao Muslim weapon.

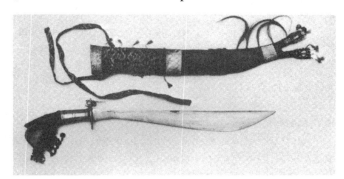

G.9. Philippines (Davao del Sur, Mindanao). BOLO.

About 14 inches long overall. Wood handle and sheath with metal trim and woven decorations. From the non-

SPECIAL SECTION

Muslim Bagobo tribe. 18th to 20th centuries. Example shown, early 20th century. Value, **$100-150**.

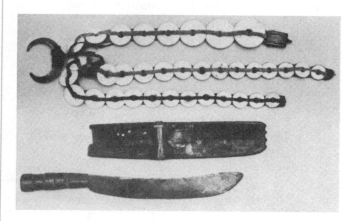

G.10. Philippines (Northern Luzon). Ifugao knife.

About 16 inches overall. Crude wooden handle and sheath. 18th to 20th centuries. Example shown circa 1900, with belt of fish-bone discs and boar's teeth attached to circa-1898 U.S. Army web belt. Value, **$175**.

The Ifugao were headhunters in the mountains of northern Luzon.

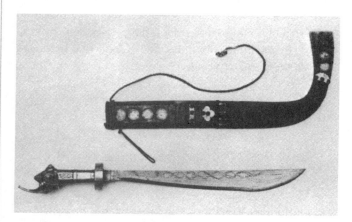

G.11. Philippines (Panay). SANDUKO BOLO.

About 30 inches long overall. Elaborate hilt wrapped in silver and gold. Wood scabbard decorated with old Spanish coins (earliest on example shown: 1777). 18th to 19th centuries. Example shown, late 19th century. Value, **$525**.

A rare weapon used by the Mondo tribe of Panay Island.

AREA H: Australia.

H.1. Australia. Sheath knives and sets.

About 10 inches overall. Wood handles. Knives made in England. Fancy leather sheaths made in Australia. Early 20th century. Examples shown from W. Jno. Baker, Sydney, 1924 catalog. Value range: plain knife, **$25**; with sheath, **$65**; "Oriental Design" knife, **$150**; with sheath, **$200**; complete sets, **$250-450**.

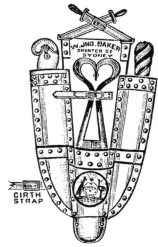

W. JNO BAKER NEW DESIGN DAGGING AND SKINNING OUTFIT.

Outfit consists of Red Tang Double Hollow-ground Dagging Shears, Boundary Rider's Skinning Knife, and Steel for sharpening same. The Sheath is of the Very Best Leather. The whole riveted throughout for lasting wear, with Loops to attach to saddle, and double-hand girth strap.

No. 24—Outfit, with Plain Beech Handle Knife and Steel, complete, **27/6.**

No. 26—With Strong Rosewood Handle, Knife and Steel, complete, **30/-.**

No. 27—With Oriental Design Knife (No. 1) and Horn Steel, as illustrated, complete, **35/-.**

Any of the above posted, 1/3 extra. Flaps fitted over Knife and Steel, as in No. 17, 2/- extra per outfit.

The Sign of Good Cutlery AT THE HOUSE OF STEEL FOUNDED A·D·1888

430—W. JNO. BAKER BUSH KNIFE, specially designed by W. Jno. Baker for Australian Use; Extra Strong Good Steel Blade, Good Grip Rosewood Handle, **6/9** each. W. Jno. Baker Registered Collar Cap Sheath, No. 436, **2/-** extra. Plain Sheaths, without Cap and Collar, **1/6** extra.

111—W. JNO. BAKER CAMP KNIFE, Good Grip Rosewood Handle, Extra Fine Steel 5in. Blade, **5/-**; 5½in. Blade, **5/6** each. W. Jno. Baker Patent Collar Cap Sheath, No. 436, **2/-** extra. Plain Sheath, without Cap and Collar, **1/6** extra.

109—W. JNO. BAKER SPEAR KNIFE, Rosewood Handle, Extra Good Steel, 5in. Blade, **4/3**; 5½in. Blade, **4/9** each. W. Jno. Baker Patent Collar Cap Sheath, No. 436, **2/-** extra. Plain Sheath, without Cap and Collar, **1/6** extra.

114—W. JNO. BAKER BOAT KNIFE, Good Grip Rosewood Handle, Extra Fine Steel, 5in. Blade, **5/6** each. W. Jno. Baker Registered Collar Cap Sheath, No. 436, **2/-** extra. Plain Sheath, without Cap and Collar, **1/6** extra.

The Sign of Good Cutlery

436 — COLLAR CAP LEATHER SHEATH, designed by W. Jno. Baker for the Australian Bush. The Sheath is rivetted right round, a collar on the top protects and strengthens the top, a cap of double leather prevents the point from piercing the bottom. An ideal Sheath for rough wear.

W. JNO. BAKER BOUNDARY RIDER'S SHEATH KNIVES—
No. **1** Oriental Design (as illustration), knife only .. **9/6** eac
No. **3** Quite Plain, Rosewood Handle, knife only .. .. **4/6** eac
No. **4** Quite Plain Beech Handle .. .. **4/-** eac

Post free.

W. Jno. Baker Registered Collar Cap Sheath, No. 436, fitted t above for **2/-** each extra.

4—W. JNO. BAKER BOUNDARY RIDER'S SHEATH KNIFE specially designed by W. Jno. Baker for Australian use; Good Steel Blades, Good Grip, Plain Rosewood Handle, **4/6** each Plain Beech Handle, **4/-** each. Plain Sheath, **1/6** extra; Collar Cap Sheath, **2/-** extra.

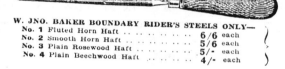

W. JNO. BAKER BOUNDARY RIDER'S STEELS ONLY—
No. **1** Fluted Horn Haft .. .. **6/6** each
No. **2** Smooth Horn Haft .. .. **5/6** each
No. **3** Plain Rosewood Haft .. .. **5/-** each
No. **4** Plain Beechwood Haft .. .. **4/-** each

In Australia, a "boundary rider" is a skilled hand on a "sheep station" (a sheep ranch). W. Jno. Baker, a retailer, was established in 1888. The firm is now on Pitt Street in Sydney.

H.2. Australia. Bowie Knife.

Argonauts in the Australian Gold Rush (1852-53) bought Sheffield bowie knives much like those sold in California (see "Bowie Knives" earlier in this section). Some of the knives bear such slogans as FOR AUSTRALIA or AUSTRALIAN CAMP KNIFE. Others have retailer's marks such as G.B. MODINI/SYDNEY.

Example shown by Thomas Short, Jun., Sheffield, circa 1850s. Blade etched FOR AUSTRALIA. Value (with blade etch), **$1,000**. (illustration from the A.A. Wood Collection, courtesy Kenneth Burton, *A Sure Defence; the Bowie Knife Book* [K.J. Burton, 7 Vincent St., Balmain, N.S.W. 2041, Australia])

Foreign, Exotic, Primitive and Historical Knives

Kitchen and Butcher Knives

Kitchen knives are so much a part of daily life for most of us that it may be hard to picture them as collector's items. However, when you include people who collect knives as tools to use, we believe that there are more people who collect kitchen knives than all other types of knives combined.

Just about all people who collect kitchen knives collect them to use. Therefore, unlike in other areas of knife collecting, mint or unused examples do not command much of a premium in price over knives in excellent condition, at least not at the present time.

Knives in excellent original condition are of course worth more than worn or restored pieces, though an artistically re-handled kitchen knife can be worth almost as much as an all-original one. People who collect kitchen knives to use generally take good care of them, so that even years of use do not significantly reduce their value.

Historically Interesting Brands

There is one class of kitchen and butcher knives that is worth more to collectors who will not use them than to those who will: knives by prominent early-to-mid nineteenth-century American cutlery factories and individual cutlers (see "American Knifemakers and Cutlery Merchants of the Bowie Knife Period" and "American Hunting Knives"). Early kitchen and butcher knives with the old names are worth two to five times as much as the very best using knives of the genre.

European and American kitchen knives made before 1800 are even rarer than early nineteenth-century ones. In the United States, they are so rare that they are less valuable than many later knives. However, they are still worth a good deal more as keepers than as users, especially since their blade quality is not very high.

Blade Steel

We have found that good-quality, modern stainless steel knives, when *properly sharpened,* are superior in use to *most* older knives, even the very best. Stainless steel knives can be made at least as sharp as carbon steel ones, and they do not stain. Also, most modern synthetic handles will not rot, split or fall off.

The president of a major knife company has said that preferring carbon steel kitchen knives over stainless steel ones is like preferring vacuum-tube radios over transistor ones. Tube radios and carbon steel kitchen knives were fine in their day, and now they can be fun to collect and use.

Carbon steel kitchen knives do win out over stainless steel ones in one major respect—they are a lot more interesting to collect.

Stainless steel knives have been made for almost 85 years, and the best ones have been of superior quality for over 45. In most of this recent period, design and workmanship have not been paramount concerns, and decoration has been almost nonexistent.

Carbon steel knives have been around for many years. The variety of their designs is almost endless. The workmanship on the better-quality older knives is astounding. Some of them even have exquisite decoration.

Premium Brands

People who collect kitchen knives are concerned primarily with quality. They look at brand names, not so much for their historical significance the way other collectors do, but as indications of quality. Several old brands have a dedicated following based, in most cases, on the consistent high quality of the products of those manufacturers.

We have found that older professional-style knives by any of the reputable makers are almost always of excellent quality. The differences *in use* between the best and the ordinary are, in our experience, relatively slight. However, differences in use *are* there, and the differences in fit, finish and choice of materials are often obvious. If you want to own the best, here are some names for you to consider.

A.J. JORDAN

There are several older kitchen knife brands that are consistently superb. One of the best is A.J. Jordan.

A.J. Jordan kitchen and butcher knives are something of an anomaly. Andrew Jackson Jordan was an American from Saint Louis. His kitchen knives were made in Sheffield, in a plant called the East India Works on Furnival Street, that he owned and controlled. No other knives look anything like them. The only other Sheffield kitchen knives that compare to Jordan in quality are older knives by Joseph Rodgers & Sons.

In addition to kitchen and butcher knives, Jordan also distributed other types of cutlery. However, his carving sets, table knives, pocketknives and razors all appear to be contract made, and, though good, are not of the exceptional quality of his kitchen knives.

In his catalogs, Jordan claimed that his kitchen and butcher knives were THE BEST ON EARTH. Though his was an era of exaggerated advertising claims—as many such claims often are—Jordan's claim, as far as we can tell, was close to being true.

All Jordan kitchen and butcher knives have "seasoned Persian boxwood handles." The costly wood is a light golden color, takes a high polish, and wears almost like iron. Many of Jordan's handle and blade shapes are original

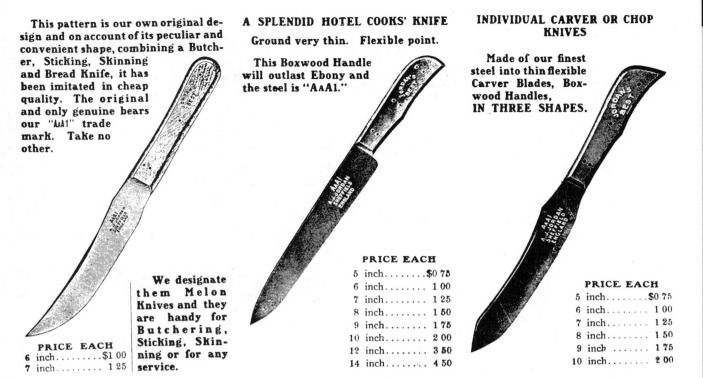

This pattern is our own original design and on account of its peculiar and convenient shape, combining a Butcher, Sticking, Skinning and Bread Knife, it has been imitated in cheap quality. The original and only genuine bears our "AA1" trade mark. Take no other.

PRICE EACH

6 inch........$1 00
7 inch........ 1 25

We designate them Melon Knives and they are handy for Butchering, Sticking, Skinning or for any service.

A SPLENDID HOTEL COOKS' KNIFE

Ground very thin.   Flexible point.

This Boxwood Handle will outlast Ebony and the steel is "AaA1."

PRICE EACH

5 inch	$0 75
6 inch	1 00
7 inch	1 25
8 inch	1 50
9 inch	1 75
10 inch	2 00
12 inch	3 50
14 inch	4 50

INDIVIDUAL CARVER OR CHOP KNIVES

Made of our finest steel into thin flexible Carver Blades, Boxwood Handles, IN THREE SHAPES.

PRICE EACH

5 inch	$0 75
6 inch	1 00
7 inch	1 25
8 inch	1 50
9 inch	1 75
10 inch	2 00

A.J. Jordan knives, values in excellent condition:
chef knives: **$90-125**;
small slicing or boning knives: **$60-95**;
skinning knives: **$125-150**;
large carving or butcher knives: **$75-90**.
(from a 1912 catalog, courtesy David Jordan).

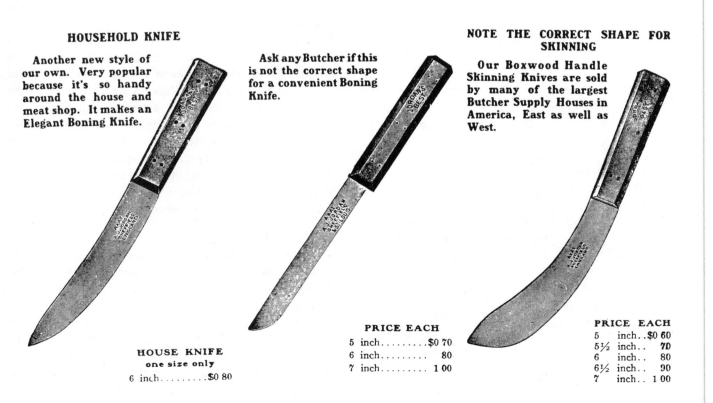

HOUSEHOLD KNIFE

Another new style of our own. Very popular because it's so handy around the house and meat shop. It makes an Elegant Boning Knife.

HOUSE KNIFE
one size only

6 inch........$0 80

Ask any Butcher if this is not the correct shape for a convenient Boning Knife.

PRICE EACH

5 inch	$0 70
6 inch	80
7 inch	1 00

NOTE THE CORRECT SHAPE FOR SKINNING

Our Boxwood Handle Skinning Knives are sold by many of the largest Butcher Supply Houses in America, East as well as West.

PRICE EACH

5 inch	$0 60
5½ inch	70
6 inch	80
6½ inch	90
7 inch	1 00

and distinctive. Jordan kitchen knives are lightweight and do not have bolsters.

For blades, Jordan used a special formula of *double shear steel*. Jordan acknowledged that cast steel was usually superior to shear steel, but he asserted that his shear steel was better than any other steel.

Shear steel was made by case hardening thin, wrought-iron bars in charcoal, breaking them up and forge welding them into a solid mass. If shear steel is hardened, broken up and re-welded, it becomes double shear steel. Cast steel was made by melting wrought iron in a sealed crucible with charcoal and flux. Cast steel for general knife use was last made in 1968.

Jordan was in business from about 1870 to about 1926. He distributed his knives all over the United States. However, based on a selection of testimonial letters that he published in 1912, 95 percent of his business was done from Virginia south and from Indiana west. Of the 71 letters: 12 were from California; six each were from Illinois and Minnesota; five were from Tennessee; four each were from Alabama, Georgia and Colorado; three were from Louisiana; two each were from Arizona, Kentucky, Mississippi, Oregon, Pennsylvania, Texas, Virginia and Washington; and one each was from Florida, Iowa, Indiana, Kansas, Massachusetts, Missouri, Montana, North Dakota, New Mexico, Ohio and South Carolina.

Sheffield Brands

To repeat, from the viewpoint of quality in use, most older professional-style knives are a good deal more than adequate. Even the majority of older household-style knives work very well, assuming, of course, that they are properly heat treated, ground thin enough at the edge, and correctly honed and steeled regularly.

FACTORY

SHEFFIELD, ENGLAND.

Joseph Rodgers c1900 butcher knife. Value **$150**. Not shown: chef's knife: **$100**; slicer: **$65**.

For those who want the very best and who are willing to spend time and money to find it, Jordan is not the only brand that will satisfy. We already mentioned that knives by Joseph Rodgers & Sons of Sheffield are superb. This applies mainly to Rodgers' nineteenth-century knives, which can be identified by the V (crown) R royal cypher in the blade stamping. All of Rodgers' many types of cutlery made in the Victorian era are of the same high standard.

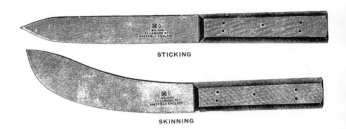

I. Wilson c1914 sticking knife (**$150-175**) and skinning knife (**$125-175**). Butcher knives (not shown): **$60-90**.

Another English brand that was very good, at least in the nineteenth century, was John Wilson (I. Wilson, 1750-c1970). The firm made butcher and industrial knives only. Though Wilson blades were good, their handles and tangs were inferior to Jordan's and usually need repair.

As for other Sheffield brands of kitchen knives, their quality varies widely and few, if any, are consistently good. Sheffield cutlers using traditional hand methods tried to compete with the far more efficient cutlery industries of America and Germany. Many cut corners and most let their standards fall to try to stay competitive rather than adopt improved methods. In consequence, one knife with a certain name may be of fine quality, while another with the same name may be flawed. When the English finally got around to standardizing their knife quality after World War I, they set the standard very low. Old Sheffield kitchen and butcher knives are historically interesting but, as utility knives, most are of uncertain using quality at best.

German Brands

In the United States in the nineteenth century, "Made in Germany" was nearly synonymous with "inferior quality." Most German cutlery manufacturers had decided that there were only two ways for them to compete in the American market: inexpensive prices and misrepresentation. Either they sold low-quality, mass-produced knives at prices so cheap that no one in the world could compete with them, or they sold barely adequate goods marked with American- or British-sounding brand names.

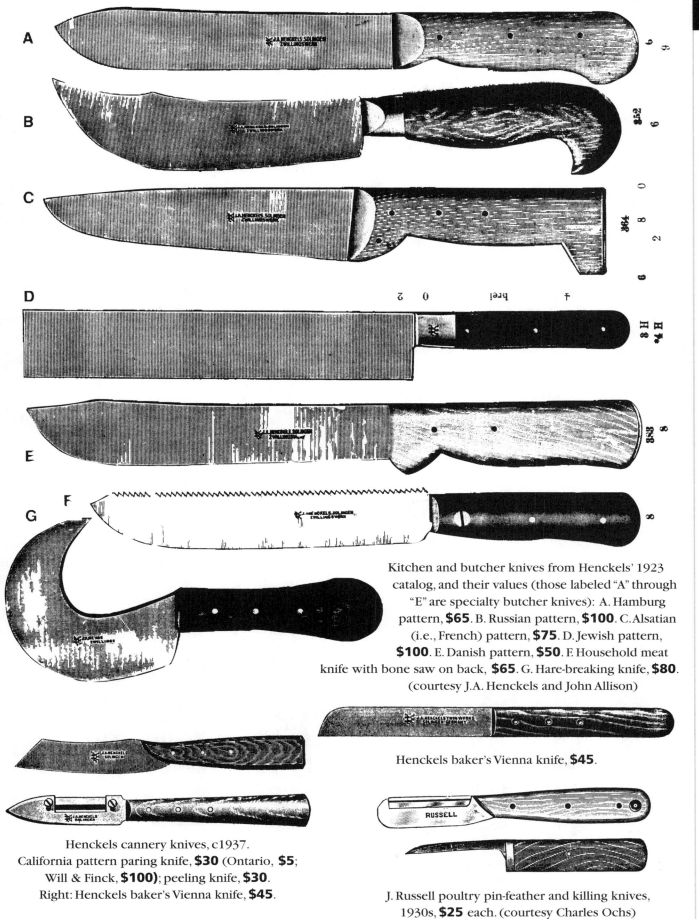

Kitchen and butcher knives from Henckels' 1923 catalog, and their values (those labeled "A" through "E" are specialty butcher knives): A. Hamburg pattern, **$65**. B. Russian pattern, **$100**. C. Alsatian (i.e., French) pattern, **$75**. D. Jewish pattern, **$100**. E. Danish pattern, **$50**. F. Household meat knife with bone saw on back, **$65**. G. Hare-breaking knife, **$80**. (courtesy J.A. Henckels and John Allison)

Henckels baker's Vienna knife, **$45**.

Henckels cannery knives, c1937. California pattern paring knife, **$30** (Ontario, **$5**; Will & Finck, **$100)**; peeling knife, **$30**. Right: Henckels baker's Vienna knife, **$45**.

J. Russell poultry pin-feather and killing knives, 1930s, **$25** each. (courtesy Charles Ochs)

J.A. HENCKELS

A few German pocketknife firms bucked the aforementioned trend by selling good knives in America under their own names. The first German kitchen and butcher knife firm to try the positive approach was J.A. Henckels, Twinworks, of Solingen. It is thanks largely to the promotional efforts of Henckels and the superb quality of its merchandise, especially between the two World Wars, that "Made in Solingen" now has such a positive meaning for American consumers.

Henckels entered the American market in 1883, when the firm was already 152 years old. It opened a retail store in New York City and arranged for wholesale distribution by a firm called Graef & Schmidt, succeeded 65 years later by Iversen & Albrecht. Since 1960, Henckels has managed its own distribution.

Like Rodgers of Sheffield, Henckels made almost every type of cutlery, most of it first rate. It made thousands upon thousands of patterns. It also published very nice catalogs, and many of the illustrations in this chapter are from Henckels' 1930s American-line catalog.

Mincing knife by Gershom Wakeman Bradley, Weston, Connecticut, 1876. Value, **$65-90**. (courtesy Arthur Sainsbury)

Henckels 1930s carving and butcher knives: ham slicer (square point), beef slicer (round point), scimitar steak knife (curved blade), butcher knife (clip point). Values: Large sizes: **$40-60**; Small sizes: **$30-40**.

Henckels 1930s bread knife (**$45**), German-style butcher knife (**$50**; same style by Village Blacksmith **$65**), French pattern slicer (**$25**), and forged-bolster slicer (**$45**).

J. A. HENCKELS TWIN BRAND CUTLERY

COOK'S KNIVES

No. 108 — Cook's Knife, 9″, 10″, 11″, 12″, 13″ and 14″. Sabatier shape, glazed blade with heavy heel, polished black wood handle, German silver tubular rivets, scale tang.

No. 102 — Cook's Knife, 8″, 9″, 10″, 11″, 12″ and 13″. Sabatier shape, glazed blade, polished black wood handle, two German silver rivets, one German silver tubular rivet, scale tang.

No. 225 — Cook's Knife, 9″, 10″, 11″ and 12″. Sabatier shape, glazed blade, polished black wood handle, two German silver rivets, one German silver tubular rivet, scale tang.

No. 100 — Cook's Knife, 7″, 8″, 9″, 10″, 11″ and 12″. Sabatier shape, glazed blade, polished black wood handle, polished steel ferrule, through tang.

No. 101 — Cook's Knife, 3″, 3⅞″, 5″, 6″, 7″, 8″ 9″, 10″ and 12″ narrow glazed flexible blade, polished black wood handle, German silver ferrule, through tang.

Much-sought-after Henckels chef's knives from the 1930s. Note GRAND PRIZE markings. Most also are stamped with model number and length. Values: Model No. 108 (heavy, with flexible point): **$150-250**; 102 (standard): **$90-125**; 225 (no bolster): **$40-60**; 100 (one-piece handle): **$60-90**; 101 (narrow): 3″-5″: **$40**; 6″-8″: **$50**; 9″-12″: **$60**.

Thanks both to its earlier promotional efforts and its more recent advertising campaigns, Henckels is the best-known name and most sought after among collectors and users of older kitchen knives. Today, Henckels limits its production almost entirely to kitchen and butcher knives, and is still one of the most popular brands in the United States.

Henckels 1930s paring knives. Values: **$20-35**.
Decorating knife: **$40**.

Henckels 1930s household cleaver (**$40**),
lobster splitter (**$100**), and boning knife (**$35-50**).

F. DICK

Though Henckels has been a leader in butcher and kitchen knives in the American market for over a century, it has never been a serious contender in the specialized area of sharpening steels. Henckels makes them and sells them, but few professionals buy its brand.

In the nineteenth century, the leading sharpening steels sold in the USA were the I. Wilson brand from Sheffield. Beginning almost a century ago, however, F. Dick steels were made available in America. They were so good and so attractive that, despite their relatively high cost, no other maker could offer serious competition.

The firm of Friedrich Dick in Esslingen, Germany, was established in 1788. Unlike Henckels, Dick's cutlery production has always been limited to "professional cutlery": cook's knives, butcher knives and steels. It also has manufactured machine tools.

F. Dick knives are first class, as good as any made in Solingen. However, its sharpening steels are what the firm is best known for in the United States.

In its earlier days, F. Dick offered a bewildering variety of steels. The plainest have turned wooden handles. Those next up the ladder have stag or fancy metal grips. The top of the line have elaborately turned and machined cow-horn handles, often inlaid with panels of nickel silver or even mother-of-pearl. A nice-looking one of these fancy steels in excellent condition is worth **$150** to **$200**. Stag- or metal-handled Dick steels are worth **$50** to **$75**, wood-handled steels **$25** to **$30**. I. Wilson steels are worth about two-thirds of these values, while other good brands in excellent condition are worth about a half.

The business end of a Dick steel can be round, oval, square or flat in cross section. The very best, called *slicks*, are as smooth and nearly as hard as glass. Slicks are used by packing-house butchers and anyone who requires a *really* sharp edge. They cost more than fine-cuts, which are made for ordinary use. Dick has never sold coarse steels.

We have met several people who collect fancy old Dick steels, and many who use them. To determine if an old steel is still usable, examine it for crosswise nicks. Even one nick is liable to chip your knife blades and is enough reason to reject a steel for use.

Then, try the steel out with a sharp but expendable knife. Old steels sometimes were used as fire pokers, which drew their temper and ruined them. If the knife bites into the steel, the steel's temper has been drawn and the steel is useless. However, if the handle looks nice, even a ruined steel has some value as a wall decoration.

JOHN WILSON'S

TRIDENT

A first-class brand of German kitchen and butcher knives widely sold in the United States today is Trident, made by Eduard Wusthof of Solingen. Though Wusthof is an old firm, founded in 1814, it did not enter the American market until 1959. Therefore, there are hardly any older Trident knives in the USA to attract collectors.

French Sabatiers

Both to the trained chef and to the knowledgeable amateur cook, the most basic kitchen knife is the "French chef's knife." The modern form of the knife dates to the latter part of the nineteenth century and is attributed to a Frenchman named Sabatier. John Goins, on page 214 of his *Encyclopedia of Cutlery Markings*, reports that the Frenchman was a Thiers cutler named Jean Augustin Sabatier, who went into business in 1846. We also have seen it claimed that Sabatier was a master chef.

COOKS' KNIVES

GENUINE FRENCH SABATIER

Original La Trompette by Sabatier, c1914. Value in excellent condition: 6"-8": **$65**; 10"-12": **$75**.

To this day, most French-made chef's knives are called *sabatiers*. The sabatier design is a refinement of the traditional French butcher knife.

In the United States up through World War I, the standard, French-made sabatier chef knife was the Trumpet Brand, *La Trompette*. Goins states that it was J.A. Sabatier's own brand, and remained in his family until 1920. From 1920 to 1941, it belonged to a Louis S.M. Pouzet. Trumpet sabatiers have high-quality, lightweight blades, but their one-piece ebony handles are weak and brittle. American and German firms copied the original Sabatier design, defects and all. They also made improved versions with full tangs and riveted slab handles. Several French firms make both types today.

American Kitchen and Butcher Knives

As mentioned, most early-to-mid-19th-century American brands of butcher and kitchen knives are more valuable as historical artifacts than tools. Several more recent American brands are equal in quality to the better imports, but, since they are less well known, they are often less expensive.

HARRINGTON

Henry Harrington was one of the first American manufacturing cutlers. He worked from 1818 to 1876. Any knife with his mark is a valuable artifact. Knives by his son, Dexter Harrington, and by their successors are of excellent quality for use, and some are now collected.

Pre-war Dexter skinning knife with guard: **$35**.

Pre-Second-World-War professional knives by the Harrington firm are very neatly stamped HARRINGTON CUTLERY CO. (curved)/DEXTER/SOUTHBRIDGE, MASS. They usually have rosewood handles that are often marked DEXTER as well. More recent Dexter professional knives still have the handle stamping, but the blade markings are electro-etched.

Older Dexter Harrington industrial knives and some kitchen knives are marked D. HARRINGTON & SON/ SOUTHBRIDGE, MASS. The most interesting ones are marked D. HARRINGTON & SON/CUTLERS TO THE PEOPLE/SOUTHBRIDGE, MASS., probably as a foil to Joseph Rodgers' CUTLERS TO HER MAJESTY.

RUSSELL

John Russell opened his Green River Works in Greenfield, Massachusetts, in 1834. In 1870 his successors moved the firm to Turners Falls, to what was at the time the largest single cutlery factory in the world.

Since 1933, Russell knives and Dexter knives have been made in the same factory in Southbridge, Massachusetts. Dexter is the premium brand. Older Russell butcher and kitchen knives have a historical value to collectors.

LANDERS FRARY & CLARK

Landers Frary & Clark (L.F. & C.) of New Britain, Connecticut, was founded in 1862 or 1863, and incorporated in 1865. George Landers was a hardware manufacturer, James Frary was an inventor and maker of scales and cutlery, and Clark was an attorney.

The firm first made hardware and scales. In 1866, L.F. & C. constructed a new building and began to make table cutlery. Within a few years, it had added butcher and kitchen knives to its line. By 1903, Landers Frary & Clark was the biggest cutlery firm in the world, and was also a pioneer in small electric appliances. Pocket cutlery was not added until 1914, and was dropped in the 1930s. L.F. & C. was acquired and liquidated by General Electric in 1965.

L.F. & C. sold butcher and kitchen knives under a multitude of brand names over the years. In addition to its full name, L.F. & C. used LANDERS, AETNA WORKS and UNIVERSAL. It used the names SAMUEL LEE on cleavers and LEE'S on sharpening steels. It acquired the names PUTNAM and OLD PUT when it bought the Putnam Cutlery Co. in 1909. L.F. & C. acquired the name MERIDEN and the anvil trademark when it bought the old Meriden Cutlery Co. in 1916. It used BLUE in a diamond on the handles of professional knives in the 1930s and after.

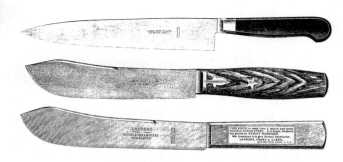

L.F. & C. butcher knives (**$45** plain, **$75** fancy) and cast-bolstered chef knife (**$45**).

Landers Frary & Clark made some absolutely first-rate knives. L. F. & C. professional knives marked DOUBLE SHEAR STEEL or GRAND PRIZE/ ST. LOUIS 1904 are usually top drawer. The company also made some low-cost lines of adequate but not extraordinary quality.

Other American Brands

Several high-quality American makers of kitchen and butcher knives have almost been forgotten today. Any of their knives would be a valuable find to a collector who likes to use fine old cutlery.

NICHOLS BROS.

Nichols Bros. of Massachusetts—also known as American Tap & Die Co.—made professional knives, cleavers and steels from about 1878 to the 1920s. Some of the knives are marked W.R. NICHOLS, and the company also made private brands, such as GLOEKLER of Pittsburgh. Eager to compete with Wilson and Jordan, Nichols advertised that its knives also were made from English double shear steel.

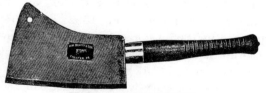

BEATTY BUTCHERS' CLEAVERS
Polished Cast Steel Blades. Varnished Hickory Turned Handles.

Beatty Cleaver, c1914: **$30-60**.

BEATTY

William Beatty & Son of Chester, Pennsylvania, made meat cleavers in about the same period. Its cleavers have turned, one-piece wooden handles and a distinctive blade profile.

REGULAR BUTCHER KNIFE
Anthracite Blue

Village Blacksmith, c1914 butcher knife: **$50**.

VILLAGE BLACKSMITH

From 1898-1940, the Washington Cutlery Co. of Watertown, Wisconsin, made butcher and household knives of crucible steel under the Village Blacksmith brand. Its forged-bolster household butcher knife was copied from a German pattern.

OLD FILE

The Old File Cutlery Co. of Havana, Illinois, made butcher and kitchen knives under the Old File brand from 1906 to 1966. The knives were not really made from files, as some might assume from the company's name.

FOSTER BROS.

In 1883, John Chatillon & Sons Co. of New York City, a half-century-old maker of scales, acquired the Foster Bros. Cutlery Co. of Fulton, New York, founded in 1878 by Frank and Allie Foster. Chatillon expanded the Foster Bros. line to over 500 items. During World War II, Foster made 250,000 cleavers for the military, plus thousands of bolos and other knives. Chatillon closed Foster Bros. in the 1950s and sold the name to the Columbia Cutlery Co.

EKCO, GENEVA FORGE

In 1881, a tinsmith named Edward Katzinger (1863-1939) came to Chicago from Budapest. In 1888, he founded the E. Katzinger Co. to make commercial baking pans. Ekco grew rapidly through acquisition and expansion, and the Ekco trademark appeared on housewares of all types. In 1929, Ekco bought its first cutlery firm, A. & J. Mfg. Co. of Binghamton, New York, maker of low-cost household knives. Ekco moved A. & J. to Chicago in 1931. In 1934, Ekco bought Geneva Cutlery Co. of Geneva, New York, renaming it Geneva Forge, which was moved to Canton, Ohio, in 1958. Ekco's premium Flint line of household knives compares favorably with any of the time. Since 1965, Ekco has been part of American Home Products Corp.

Collectible Brands

Many of the firms best known today for pocketknives, such as Case, Remington and Winchester, also made kitchen and butcher knives. (Case still offers steak knives today.) Values usually range from **$15** to **$75**. Perhaps the most amusing are the c1920s Robeson "Red Pig" knives. The knives have an oval brass shield in the front handle embossed with a pig, though the Robeson blade etch is usually worn away. A set of 10 comical postcards promoting the knives is worth **$200-300**, while an unsharpened Red Pig knife might be worth **$75-125**.

Beginning in the 1930s, many consumer-oriented knife firms—including Case, Remington, Ontario, Clyde, L.F. & C., Goodell, Shapleigh, etc.—offered low-cost household butcher knives with blanked, "dimpled" blades, inaccurately promoted as being hammer-forged. Value: **$10** to **$45**.

Small and Local Firms

The American firms named so far were relatively sizable commercial undertakings. A multitude of smaller firms, sometimes consisting of only one or two men, also made butcher and kitchen knives, often for local sale only. Despite—or because of—the fact that they were usually handmade, knives by the little firms vary widely in quality.

Knives by small manufacturers are rare and documentation of the firms' existence is even rarer. We found documentation of a two-man firm called J.E. Harris & Son of Warrensburg, Missouri, that made butcher knives in 1917. Collector Dennis Ellingsen tracked down the story of the Barr brothers, who opened a small cutlery factory in Eugene, Oregon, in 1891, specializing in butcher knives and sack needles. Hugh and William Barr left town in 1911 and established a larger factory in Oakland, California. Ed Goodchild bought the factory in Eugene and made R. & G. brand knives there until 1920.

No. 2583 – Lamb Splitter
Blade length, 12 in.   Approximate weight, 1 lb. 12 oz.
                              Per dozen, **$46.00**

J. Russell lamb-splitting cleaver, 1930s, **$90**. (courtesy Charles Ochs) Larger butcher's cleavers, **$50-100**.

Research is usually required to distinguish butcher knives made locally from contract knives made by large national firms, and stamped with the name of a local merchant. Bill Joliff tracked down a long-forgotten firm that made a specialty of this sort of contract work. It was the Woodworth Knife Works of Nunda, New York.

NUNDA KNIFE WORKS

Charles R. Woodworth (1831-1903) first made knives and sold them door to door in the 1850s. In 1878 he founded Woodworth Knife Works. His son, Fred, took over the firm in 1886. It apparently had closed by 1919, though that closing date cannot be confirmed.

According to Woodworth's 1912 catalog, the firm's specialty was making low-cost, primitive-looking, private-brand butcher knives for small-town blacksmiths. This allowed the village blacksmiths to sell the Woodworth knives as their own product. These excerpts from the catalog tell the story:

"Butcher Knives Made For Blacksmiths * Stamped with Your own name ... Buy $5.00 worth of our finished knives and we will stamp Your Name on each knife free ...We Sell to Only One Smith in Each Town. $5.00 Trial Assortment No. 1. Consisting of 42 Assorted Knives that you can easily sell for $15.00 to $18.00 ... Free - One knife blade just as forged [and] One in the rough partly finished ... ready for blacksmiths to finish as their own ... In all parts of the country we have satisfied customers who have built up a paying business selling our knives ..."The Woodworths had testimonial letters to prove the latter claim, including one from Smith & Sons and New Pine Creek, Oregon, a brand we actually have seen.

1919 list of American kitchen, butcher, and industrial knifemakers, compiled by *American Cutler* Magazine.

American Cutlery Co., Chicago, Ill.
Arcade Mfg. Co., Freeport, Ill.
E.C. Atkins & Co., Indianapolis, Ind.
Geo. H. Bishop Co., Lawrenceburg, Ind.
John B. Black Co., Chester, Pa. (Beatty cleavers).
W.G. Brown Mfg. Co., Kingston N.Y.
Buffalo Knife Co., Buffalo, N.Y.
Camillus Cutlery Co., New York.
W.R. Case & Sons, Bradford, Pa.
J. Chatillon & Sons, New York (Foster Bros.,   Fulton, N.Y.).
Christy Knife Co., Fremont, Ohio (bread knives)
H. Clauss Mfg. Co., Tipton, Ind.
Clyde Cutlery Co., Clyde, Ohio
W.H. Compton Shear Co., Newark, N.J.
Cuba Knife Co., Cuba, N.Y.
C.D. Dickinson & Son, North Hadley, Mass.
Henry Disston & Sons, Philadelphia, Pa.
W.H. Dollar Mfg. Co., Camden, N.J.
Empire Knife Co., Winsted, Conn.
Goodell Co., Antrim N.H. (now the Chicago Cutlery factory).
Harrington Cutlery Co., Southbridge, Mass.
Theo. Harrington, Southbridge, Mass.
H.C. Hart Mfg. Co., Unionville, Conn.
E. Hendricks, Inc., New York
C.& A. Hoffman, Philadelphia, Pa. (butcher's steels)
Hollinger Cutlery Co., Fremont, Ohio
Hyde Mfg. Co., Southbridge, Mass.
William Johnson, Newark, N.J.
Knickerbocker Mfg. Co., Belleville, N.J.
Lamson & Goodnow Mfg. Co., Shelburne Falls, Mass.
Landers Frary & Clark, New Britain, Conn.
Meriden Cutlery Co., Meriden, Conn.
J. Miller, New York.
R. Murphy & Bro., Ayer, Mass.
Robert Murphy's Sons, Ayer, Mass.
North Wayne Tool Co., Hallowell, Me.
Northampton Cutlery Co., Northampton, Mass.
Old File Cutlery Co., Havana, Ill.
Oldham Saw Works, Brooklyn, N.Y.
Ontario Knife Co., Franklinville, N.Y.
C.S. Osborne & Co., Newark, N.J.
L.D. Parkhurst, Danielson, Conn.
A.C. Penn, Inc., New York.
Poughkeepsie Cutlery Works, Poughkeepsie, N.Y.
Reading Saddle & Mfg. Co., Reading, Pa.
Stephen Richard Co., Southbridge, Mass.
Robeson Cutlery Co., Rochester, N.Y.
Rose & Bros., Sharon Hill, Pa.
J. Russell Cutlery Co., Turners Falls, Mass.
Simonds Saw Co., Fitchburg, Mass.
Smith & Hemenway, Irvington, N.J. [Red Devil]
Tuck Mfg. Co., Brockton, Mass.
Union Cutlery Co., Canton, Ohio
United Cutlery Co., Canton, Ohio
Vanator Cutlery Co., Grand Ledge, Mich.
Walden Knife Co., Walden, N.Y.
Washington Cutlery Co., Watertown, Wis.
Western States Cutlery & Mfg. Co., Boulder, Col.
L. & I.J. White, Buffalo, N.Y.
Wiebusch & Hilger, New York; agents for: American
    Tap & Die Co. (Nichols Bros.) Dunn Edge Tool Co.

(See "American Knifemakers and Cutlery Merchants
of the Bowie Knife Period" for more
fixed-blade knife manufacturers.)

Table Knives and Forks

Most people own a couple of dozen table knives and forks and never give them a second thought. Yet, table cutlery has an interesting history. Because they are so universal and have been around for so long, table knives and forks provide a medium by which the technological, cultural and artistic evolution of cutlery can be traced most readily.

In the Middle Ages, a person would likely own just one knife, which he carried with him and used for eating and every other cutting chore. A wealthy woman might carry a matched pair of knives so she could eat without soiling her fingers.

In the sixteenth century, the Italians began to use scaled-down carving forks for eating. The fashion of eating with forks spread to Germany and France, and then, after the Restoration (1660), to England and her American colonies.

English eating knives from medieval times had riveted bolsters. About 1555, Richard Matthews of Sheffield introduced the forged wrought-iron bolster welded to a steel blade. It became standard construction in Sheffield until the late 19th century. American inventors re-introduced both cast and riveted bolsters on inexpensive knives in the late 1860s.

The American table cutlery industry began in 1834. See "American Knifemakers and Cutlery Merchants of the Bowie Knife Period" for the names and dates of the important 19th-century U.S. table cutlery manufacturers.

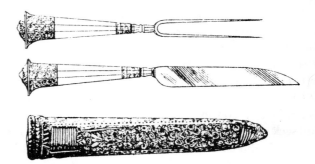

17th century set, **$400**.
(L. Bement, *The Cutlery Story*)

18th-century English table knife, scored bone, **$60**.

Small dessert pairs by the American "big three":
Pratt Ropes & Webb, Lamson & Goodnow,
and J. Russell. Marks and bolsters indicate c1850.
$60 per pair in mint condition.

Left: 16th-century English pair of knives
(wedding set), ivory, **$500**. (courtesy Smithsonian).
Center: 19th-century child's set, English, **$75**.
16th-century English knife, **$450**.

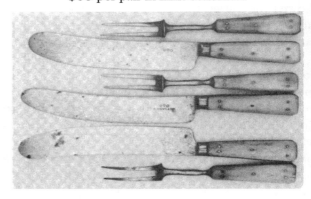

Early 19th-century knives and forks by Sleigh Rowland
or Sheffield, bone. Back of knife blade exhibits typical
"puddled" weld between iron bolster and steel blade.
$45-60 per pair in excellent condition.

Carving Sets

A carving set, consisting of a knife, fork and sharpening steel, was a fixture of every well-dressed dinner table until a generation or two ago. Deluxe sets might include two to five different knives, each with a fork, steel, corkscrew, bone holder, skewer puller, marrow scoop, cheese scoop, and poultry shears. From the 16th to the mid-19th centuries, the carving set usually matched the table knives and forks.

The most celebrated American carving sets were made by San Francisco cutlers Will & Finck, Michael Price and others (see "American Knifemakers and Cutlery Merchants of the Bowie Knife Period").

A carving knife alone is worth 50 percent of the value of a set. Forks and steels alone are worth about 10 percent of that value. An original fitted case adds about 20 percent to the value.

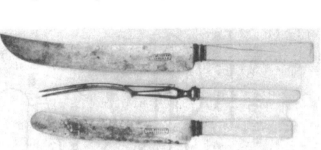

W. & S. Butcher matched carving.

Bread knife, carved boxwood, **$90**.

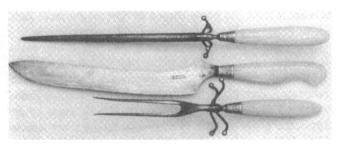

Michael Price, San Francisco set, walrus ivory, **$525**.

Lamson & Goodnow classic
New England pair, c1860: **$150**.

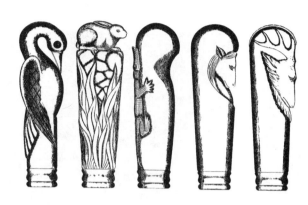

Russell sets with carved walrus ivory: **$475**.

No. 329—Genuine Stag Handles, Especially Selected. Solid Forged Octagon Steel Bolsters. German Silver End Plates. 8 inch Swaged Spanish Slicer Blade. Full Crocus Polished..................................Per Set,

No. 298—Genuine Stag Handles, Especially Selected. Fancy German Silver Ferrules and End Plates. 8 inch Fancy Swaged Turkish Cimeter Blade. Full Crocus Polished...Per Set,

No. 300—Genuine Stag Handles, Carefully Selected and Finely Finished. Fancy German Silver Ferrules and End Plates. 8 inch Swaged French Slicer Blade. Full Crocus Polished.................................Per Dozen,

Carving knife styles, values for 3-piece sets: two 19th-century English styles (note iron caps), **$75**; four c1910 American styles (some German made), **$60**.

Trade, Craft, and Artisan Knives

Tradesmen's, craftsmen's and artisans' knives are made for a specific cutting or shaping purpose by individual workers. Some of the knives have multiple functions, such as "shoe knives," but the most interesting ones are highly specialized.

Collecting these specialized knives is becoming very popular. There is considerable interest in ink-eraser knives, which are both attractive and provide many variations in shape and handle material. In recent years, several remarkable collections of eraser knives have been developed and beautifully displayed.

Some examples of these specialized knives and their values: pen machine: **$150**; ink eraser: plain **$15-50**, bone or advertising **$75**, ivory, mother-of-pearl, or picture

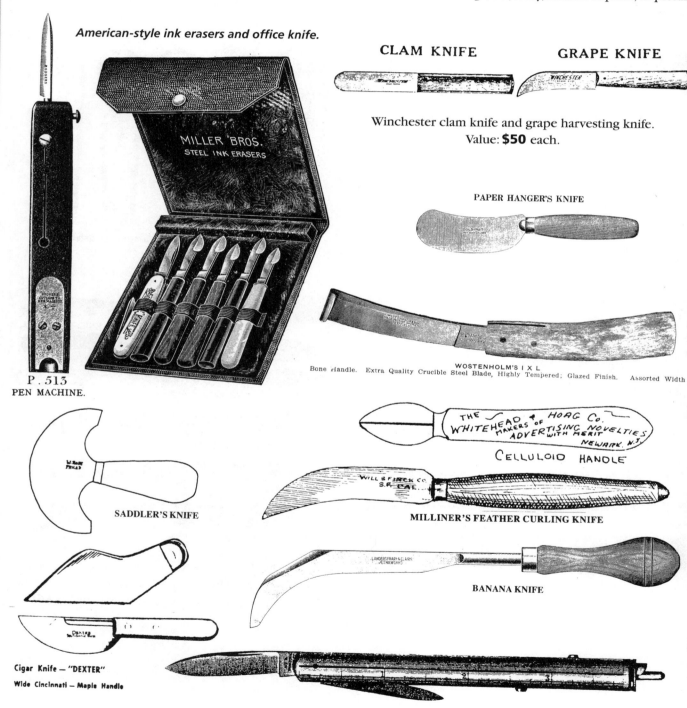

American-style ink erasers and office knife.

MILLER BROS. STEEL INK ERASERS

P . 513
PEN MACHINE.

CLAM KNIFE   **GRAPE KNIFE**

Winchester clam knife and grape harvesting knife.
Value: **$50** each.

PAPER HANGER'S KNIFE

WOSTENHOLM'S I X L
Bone Handle. Extra Quality Crucible Steel Blade, Highly Tempered; Glazed Finish. Assorted Width

SADDLER'S KNIFE

THE WHITEHEAD & HOAG Co.
MAKERS OF ADVERTISING NOVELTIES WITH MERIT
NEWARK. N.J.
CELLULOID HANDLE

MILLINER'S FEATHER CURLING KNIFE

BANANA KNIFE

Cigar Knife — "DEXTER"
Wide Cincinnati — Maple Handle

Joseph Rodgers 4" pencil knife w/rule on frame, metal handle. Value, **$200**.

handle **$50-125**; oilcloth knife: light push-tang **$15**, heavy forged **$50** (San Francisco maker **$375**); saddler's knife: **$35-50** (San Francisco **$125**); furrier's knife (all metal): **$20-50**; cigar knife: **$15**; oyster knife: **$10** (San Francisco **$75**; with ivory handle **$150**); feather curling knife: **$35** (San Francisco **$125**); plain "push-tang" knives: **$10-25**; and farrier's (horseshoeing) knife: plain **$35-50**, changeable blade **$40-65**.

OILCLOTH KNIVES.

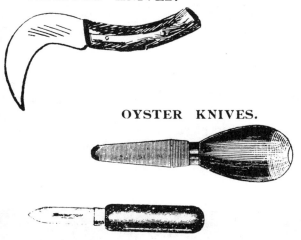

OYSTER KNIVES.

Winchester oyster knife. Value, **$45**.

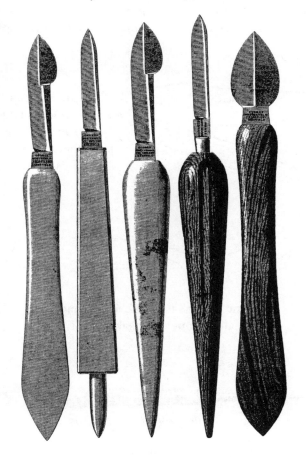

I*XL G. Wostenholm eraser knives. Value, **$65-125** each.

SHOE KNIVES.

Any size of either of these shapes, or any other shape, made to order, of superior quality, stamped "A J. WILKINSON."
EXACT SIZES AND STYLES.

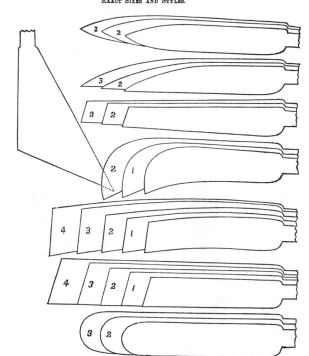

Various shoe knife blades (made to order) w/wood handles. Value, **$30-45**.

Glazier's (glass worker's) stopping knife, w/rosewood handle. Value, **$45**.

Woodwind-reed maker's knife. Value, **$125**.

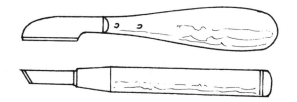

Wood-engraving knives (signmaker). Value, **$50-75** each.

As you might expect, almost every trade and craft developed specialized hand cutlery. While most of the cutting and shaping actions the specialized hand implements were used for are now done by machine, many of these implements can still be found. They represent the zenith of the use of special-purpose knives and are becoming a collectible in their own right.

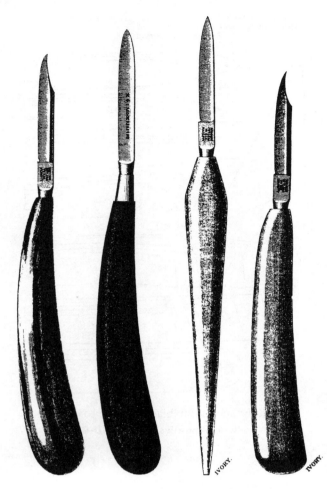

Joseph Rodgers desk knives (various examples). Value, **$45-100** each.

Basket makers picking knife (top) and shop knife (bottom). Value, **$25-50** each.

All shoe-knife blade styles are mounted in a hardwood handle w/brass ferrule. This 7 1/4" piece is a typical example.

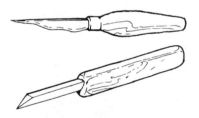

Organ builder's knives: voicer's knife (top) and nicking knife (bottom). Value, **$75-100** each.

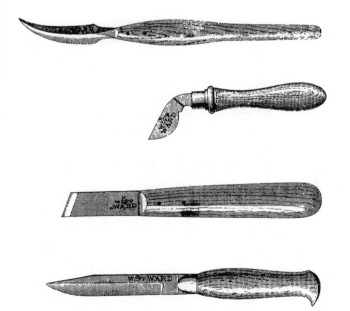

W. Ward chip-carving knives. Value, **$60-75** each.

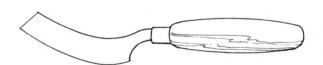

Piano maker's felt knife for hammers and damper felts. Value, **$65**.

Scale Tang Striking Knife.

Pattern maker's striking (line) knife, w/rosewood handle. Value, **$60**.

The Holy Grail of Handmades?

Bob Loveless is a living legend and his knives are among the most coveted anywhere

By Dave Ellis

When the name of Blade Magazine Cutlery Hall-Of-Famer© Robert W. "Bob" Loveless is mentioned, the first thing that comes to my mind is the Father of Modern Handmade Knives.

Bob has been making knives since 1954 and is credited with many of the features found on the knives of today. He supplied knives to Abercrombie & Fitch and firmly established himself as a force to be reckoned with in the small but growing knifemaking community.

Some of Bob's contributions to the modern handmade knife include the full-tapered tang, dropped hunter—or "drop-point hunter," as many call it—sub-hilt fighter and many more. Bob also pioneered the use of such modern stainless steels as 154CM in 1970, ATS-34 in 1980 and BG-42 in 1990. He played a pivotal role in the formation and success of the first knifemaker organization of the modern handmade movement, The Knifemakers' Guild, as well as the Japanese knifemakers' guild. Not one to rest on his laurels, Mr. Loveless is continually looking for new ways to improve his time-tested designs.

The Designs Work!

In my humble opinion, no other knifemaker's knives are as collectible and readily saleable as those made in the Loveless Shop. Over the years I have owned over 300 Loveless knives and one thing remains constant—the designs work!

Bob's knives are sound and the workmanship is top notch. Not only is it attractive but a Loveless knife will skin with the best of them. Loveless fighters almost float in your hand, and all of Bob's knives become an extension of your grip, creating fluid movement and cuts. An absence of sharp corners, palm swells where they belong, clean grind lines and perfect mirror polishes, all are staples of Loveless knives.

R.W. "Bob" Loveless—the master of his knife shop domain. (photo by Blade Magazine Cutlery Hall-Of-Famer© Jim Weyer, from Logos of the Loveless Legend)

The Loveless Shop also creates some of the nicest and most well-thought-out sheaths that I have seen. With weep holes for fluids and great stitching, they ride well on the belt and each Loveless knife fits into the wet-formed leather like a glove.

Bob has had many outstanding makers work in his shop. Probably the most famous is Steve Johnson. Steve has made quite a name for himself since leaving the Loveless Shop. Japan's Yoshihito Aida, Germany's Dietmar Kressler and many other famous knifemakers also have graced the Loveless Shop over the years. As these pages were being written, Jim Merritt was working alongside Bob and had been doing so for many years.

Loveless knives have gotten so popular that one of Bob's entry-level hunters will run you close to **$3,000**. A 6-inch fighter or Big Bear Fighter will really put a dent in your pocketbook! The fighter will start at about **$6,000**, and the Big Bear—well, how does **$20,000** plus sound? These are secondary market prices as the Loveless Shop has essentially stopped taking orders per Bob. Many folks are still waiting for their 4-year-old orders to be filled.

Here is a really handsome utility knife with the double nude logo, and engraved nickel-silver guard and Loveless bolts. On top of the tang is a nickel-silver insert engraved "R.W. Loveless," which indicates that this was a personal knife of Bob's. Approximate value: $9,000. (photo by Blade Magazine Cutlery Hall-Of-Famer© Jim Weyer, from Logos of the Loveless Legend)

Here's a very nice example of Bob's dropped hunter—probably his most recognizable design—with the rare signature logo. The handle is lignum vitae and the guard is nickel silver. Approximate value: $4,000. (photo by Blade Magazine Cutlery Hall-Of-Famer© Jim Weyer, from Logos of the Loveless Legend)

As Bob gets on in years—he was in his mid-70s as of this writing—you can expect to see fewer knives coming from his shop. He produces his knives using the stock-removal method. Paul Bos, one of the best, heat treats Bob's blades and has done so for many years.

Loveless Logos

Loveless knives have had many different maker's marks over the years. The Delaware Maid logo graced his knives until about 1969. Bob continued to make knives under the Delaware Maid mark and, as today, many of his knives featured a reclining nude woman—aka "the naked lady"—etched in the blade.

Bob moved to Modesto, California, in 1959. Around the mid-'60s, he used the Loveless-Parke logo, which graced a grand total of just 36 Loveless knives. Around 1969, he started using the Lawndale mark.

Bob' first full-time helper was Steve Johnson. Steve joined the Loveless Shop in 1971. Knives bearing the Loveless/Johnson logos are some of the most valuable. Steve worked in the shop for about three years. "Loveless & Johnson makers Riverside, California" is an extremely rare logo used on only three knives. I am fortunate to own one of the three and have turned down **$20,000** for it. Another somewhat rare logo is the signature logo, which Bob does not use very often. The modern Riverside logo and Riverside double nude logo were first used in the early 1980s and are still used today.

As of this writing, I am collecting a good number of knives with the Loveless/Merritt logo. I believe that it is one of the rarest of Loveless logos. I am receiving more and more requests for Loveless/Merritt knives, especially from Italy, where some of the top Loveless collections are found. Also as of this writing, the Japanese market for Loveless knives is starting to heat up again, and, of course, the United States is a hotbed of Loveless knife collectors.

This is a very collectible "New York Special," one of the Holy Grails of Loveless knives. Only seven were made in this configuration. It has the Riverside logo and green Micarta® scales—a Loveless favorite—with a snap inset in the handle and a corresponding snap on the sheath. The author said he has never owned one. Approximate value: $25,000. (photo by Blade Magazine Cutlery Hall-Of-Famer© Jim Weyer, from Logos of the Loveless Legend)

A shortened Wilderness model, the Mini Wilderness with a rare signature logo has a cocobolo handle and a nickel-silver guard. There are very few of these knives around. In fact, many Loveless fans have not even heard of the hard-to-find model. Approximate value: $9,000. (photo by Blade Magazine Cutlery Hall-Of-Famer© Jim Weyer, from Logos of the Loveless Legend)

There were three knives from the Loveless Shop with this ultra-rare "Loveless & Johnson makers Riverside, California" logo. This fine example has an ebony handle and nickel-silver guard. There is a brass initial plate on the spine, a very unusual addition to a Loveless knife. Approximate value: $20,000. (photo by Blade Magazine Cutlery Hall-Of-Famer© Jim Weyer, from Logos of the Loveless Legend)

Loveless made very few gut hooks. This one, a skinner with a wood Micarta® "improved" handle, sports a Lawndale logo Approximate value: $6,000. (photo by Blade Magazine Cutlery Hall-Of-Famer© Jim Weyer, from Logos of the Loveless Legend)

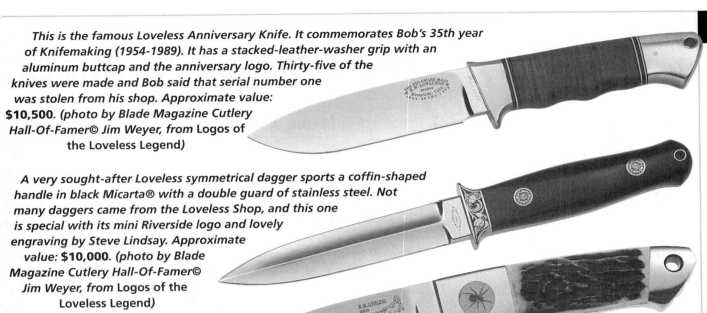

This is the famous Loveless Anniversary Knife. It commemorates Bob's 35th year of Knifemaking (1954-1989). It has a stacked-leather-washer grip with an aluminum buttcap and the anniversary logo. Thirty-five of the knives were made and Bob said that serial number one was stolen from his shop. Approximate value: $10,500. (photo by Blade Magazine Cutlery Hall-Of-Famer© Jim Weyer, from Logos of the Loveless Legend)

A very sought-after Loveless symmetrical dagger sports a coffin-shaped handle in black Micarta® with a double guard of stainless steel. Not many daggers came from the Loveless Shop, and this one is special with its mini Riverside logo and lovely engraving by Steve Lindsay. Approximate value: $10,000. (photo by Blade Magazine Cutlery Hall-Of-Famer© Jim Weyer, from Logos of the Loveless Legend)

This is an integral dropped hunter in stag with a double nude logo. Most Loveless integrals went to Japan. This one has an ivory disc inset in the bolster with color scrimshaw by the late Rick Fields. It is among the author's favorite Loveless knives. Approximate value: $14,000. (photo by Blade Magazine Cutlery Hall-Of-Famer© Jim Weyer, from Logos of the Loveless Legend)

Keys To Loveless Knife Values

By Dave Ellis

There are a number of factors to consider when buying a knife made by Blade Magazine Cutlery Hall-Of-Famer© Bob Loveless.

One important aspect to keep in mind is condition. If the knife is mint or near mint, it will bring the highest dollar.

If you come across a Loveless knife with age patina, even a bit of pitting, I would recommend using nothing stronger than, say, Simichrome polish to clean the blade. Reworking any knife is not usually a good idea, and a keen eye will tell you if a knife has been re-buffed, ground or otherwise altered. Older knives can be expected to show some age. In such cases, the effects of age really do not affect the value of the knives drastically.

The book, *Logos of the Loveless Legend*, by the late Al Williams, with photographs by Cutlery Hall-Of-Famer Jim Weyer, is a really good guide to the various logos that the Loveless Shop has used over the years. The book consists of many fine pieces that Al collected, some extremely rare and desirable. (Several of the book's pictures accompany this story.)

Any knife pictured in the book increases in value if only for the providence of being part of Al's collection—and also for being "immortalized" in such a fine book. Al always looked for the rarest and most desirable knives, and his collection reflected his approach. You can expect to pay approximately **$500-$1,000** more than usual for a knife that is in the book. In fact, some are considered much more valuable than the same model not in the book. Once the bulk of the Williams collection was sold to J.W. Denton and some of the knives reached the general public, the Loveless craze was fueled beyond what it ever had been—and it has been a hot market for many, many years.

Since he was instrumental in the formation and success of The Knifemakers' Guild, Loveless and his knives had quite an impact on the Guild—not only in the knives made by Guild members, but the many new users and collectors he brought into the fold. When Bob exhibited at a Guild Show, his many followers would flock to his table and, of course, also spend their hard-earned dollars at other makers' tables. Makers who have worked in the Loveless Shop are currently in the upper echelon of the craft, in particular Steve Johnson and Dietmar Kressler, two of knifemaking's top names.

Following are most of the Loveless logos used over the years. Each logo is valued using a star system, with five stars being the most valuable, four stars the next most valuable, etc.

- Delaware Maid: 5 Stars;
- Loveless/Johnson: 5 Stars;
- Loveless/Merritt Logo: 5 Stars;
- Loveless & Parke: 4-5 Stars;
- Signature Logo: 4-5 Stars;
- Double Nude: 4 Stars;
- Lawndale: 3-4 Stars;
- Wood/Loveless: 3 Stars, and;
- Riverside: 3 Stars.

There are many variations of the logos, such as single nude, "Loveless & Johnson makers Riverside, California," large print, small print, etc. Each variation, depending on rarity, can affect value.

The No. 1 Name in Bladesmithing

Bill Moran's knives are some of the most valuable pieces of cutlery art known to man

By Dave Ellis

Blade Magazine Cutlery Hall-Of-Famer© Bill Moran is the "Father of American Bladesmithing," "The Father of Modern Damascus," "The Father of the American Bladesmith Society," and has inspired more people to take up hammer and tongs to make knives than anyone ever. He forged his first blade around 1941! From Bill's Lime Kiln Maryland Shop come some of the most valuable pieces of cutlery art known to man.

Mr. Moran forges to shape, grinds, heat treats and finishes each and every knife the old fashioned way— by hand. (Editor's note: Due to the physical wear and tear that often affects a person of his advancing years—at this writing, Mr. Moran had just turned 80—he forges few, if any, knives today.) He has been credited with the reintroduction to America of damascus steel, an accomplishment that dates back to the early 1970s.

A Moran creation will run you anywhere from **$2,000** up to and over **$30,000**. Do not get too excited, as Bill's current backlog is running approximately 25 years. Very few people will get to see a new Moran knife in their lifetime, let alone be able to afford one.

I have owned and still own many of Bill's wonderful knives, from some of the older Lime-Kiln-stamped variety, to some of the more modern M.S.—or American Bladesmith Society "master smith"—stamped pieces. Each has

This WFM-marked bowie was made circa 1946. The handle is rosewood with brass fittings. Overall length: 15 3/8 inches. The sheath is leather. Value: $6,000. (Blade Magazine Cutlery Hall-Of-Famer© Houston Price photo from the book, The Master of the Forge, by Price and Hall-Of-Famer B.R. Hughes)

One of Bill's ultra-rare 50-year knives, this Southwestern bowie boasts a stag and curly maple handle with wire inlay and a wood-lined leather sheath. Overall length: 15 1/4 inches. Value: $18,000. (Blade Magazine Cutlery Hall-Of-Famer© Jim Weyer photo from the book, The Master of the Forge, by Hall-Of-Famers B.R. Hughes and Houston Price)

A Moran bowie with the Lime Kiln stamp sports a curly maple handle and brass guard and pommel, both of the latter fileworked. Overall length: 15 1/4 inches. The sheath is plain leather. Value: $5,000. (Blade Magazine Cutlery Hall-Of-Famer© Jim Weyer photo from the book, The Master of the Forge, by Hall-Of-Famers B.R. Hughes and Houston Price)

This Moran clip-point utility knife boasts a Lime Kiln stamp. The early 1960s hunter has a nice rosewood handle and brass fittings. Overall length: 9 1/2 inches. Value: $3,000. (Blade Magazine Cutlery Hall-Of-Famer© Jim Weyer photo from the book, The Master of the Forge, *by Hall-Of-Famers B.R. Hughes and Houston Price)*

ts own magic surrounding it and t is interesting to see the different variations as his knives have evolved over the years.

A knife made by Bill Moran is guaranteed to be razor sharp. Bill uses a convex grind—also called *cannel* or *appleseed* grind—and he gets a wicked cutting edge. Most of his blades are buffed to a mirror finish.

Bill likes natural handle materials and uses a lot of curly maple, rosewood and, on occasion, stag and ivory. He favors embellishments such as silver wire inlay and fileworked guards and buttcaps. Silver half moons adorn the handles and sheaths of his fancier pieces. On older Lime Kiln knives he used handles of rosewood, curly maple and ebony. Most of his older knives have brass fittings, while the fittings of his more recent pieces are nickel silver, steel or damascus.

The Knives and Their Values

Early Lime-Kiln-stamped Moran hunters start at around **$2,500** and go as high as **$5,000** or more for rare examples. A nice Lime-Kiln-stamped bowie or camp knife can easily set you back **$4,500** or more. Bill's Rio Grande camp knife was an immediate hit with his customers and can be purchased—if you are lucky enough to find one for sale—for around **$5,000**.

Mr. Moran's Vietnam fighter—the M-7—is a rarity and can easily cost **$5,500** plus. An ST-23 combat knife, which followed the M-7, is an unquestionable treasure and you can expect to empty your wallet of at least **$7,000** for one; a really nice example with a special sheath can climb to **$10,000** plus. Following the ST-23 is Bill's famous—and almost impossible to find—ST-24 fighter. A longer and leaner version of the ST-23, the last I heard it ran for almost **$15,000**.

Bill's quillon dagger has a W.F. Moran stamp, fluted ivory handle with twisted wire, and a steel guard and pommel. Overall length: 12 1/4 inches. The sheath is curly maple with wire inlay and ivory throat and tip. Value: $21,000. (Blade Magazine Cutlery Hall-Of-Famer© Jim Weyer photo from the book, The Master of the Forge, *by Hall-Of-Famers B.R. Hughes and Houston Price)*

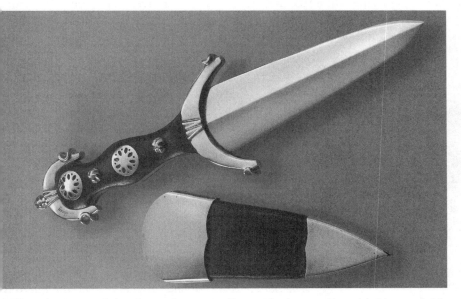

Bill made seven of the cinquedea, an Italian-style dagger. He said this one is his most detailed knife. The handle is rosewood and the fittings are brass, and the leather sheath has brass mounts. Overall length: 14 5/8 inches. Value: $20,000. (Blade Magazine Cutlery Hall-Of-Famer© Jim Weyer photo from the book, The Master of the Forge, *by Hall-Of-Famers B.R. Hughes and Houston Price)*

Bill made the blade shorter than usual on this ST-24 combat knife. The handle is curly maple with wire inlay. Overall length: 14 1/2 inches. He decorated the wood-lined sheath with a raised design. Value: $18,000. (Blade Magazine Cutlery Hall-Of-Famer© Jim Weyer photo from the book, The Master of the Forge, by Hall-Of-Famers B.R. Hughes and Houston Price)

Carbon Steel vs. Damascus

The aforementioned values are all based on the knives having carbon steel blades. In the case of damascus steel, you can expect to pay **$10,000** for a smaller hunter and upward of **$30,000** for an all-out bowie or ST-24 with all the bells and whistles—damascus blade, damascus fittings, special sheath, wire inlay, etc. (All values are based on the secondary market.)

Contemporary Moran carbon steel knives are not exactly inexpensive. A nice Maryland camp knife or bowie easily can cost **$12,000** plus. Then there are the rarer Moran knives, such as the cinquedea, of which Bill made so few. Finding one of them is almost impossible. If you are able to locate one, expect to *start* at **$20,000**.

Blade Stamps

The Moran Shop has had many blade stamps over the years. Bill's first stamp, used in the late 1940s, was his initials—WFM—in block letters. In the mid-1950s, he started using his now famous Lime Kiln stamp—"By W.F. Moran Lime Kiln MD." Bill used the stamp until 1973, even though he had moved his shop to Middletown, Maryland, by then.

Beginning in '73, Bill started using the Moran stamp—simply "MORAN." Occasionally you will see it used in conjunction with another stamp, such as "M.S." Bill still uses this stamp.

Also in 1973, he began the use of damascus and employed the "DAMASCUS" mark with his name stamp until the end of the decade. He earned his ABS "M.S." stamp in 1981. He uses a smaller "MORAN" stamp for his miniature knives. His most recent stamp is "50 yrs." He employed it on 50 knives celebrating his 50th year of knifemaking, first using the stamp in 1989.

Sheaths as Art

Bill's sheaths are works of art in themselves. His early sheaths typically were plain leather with a keeper strap. If you were lucky, he may have affixed a silver half moon on the front of the sheath. Eventually, Bill went with a basswood-lined-leather or a full

A Moran ST-23 fighter features a W.F. Moran stamp and a curly maple handle with filed brass guard and butt. Overall length: 13 inches. Value: $9,000. (Blade Magazine Cutlery Hall-Of-Famer© Jim Weyer photo from the book, The Master of the Forge, by Hall-Of-Famers B.R. Hughes and Houston Price)

For a knife by Bill Moran, it does not get much better than an ST-24 in damascus with the MORAN stamp. The handle is wire-inlaid curly maple and the guard is pierced. Overall length: 15 1/8 inches. A raised design embellishes the wood-lined leather sheath. Value: $28,000. (Blade Magazine Cutlery Hall-Of-Famer© Jim Weyer photo from the book, The Master of the Forge, by Hall-Of-Famers B.R. Hughes and Houston Price)

wooden sheath (the latter typically had silver wire inlay).

Most of his modern sheaths are wood-lined leather with a raised pattern on the front. On rare occasions, his fancy sheaths can have steel, nickel silver or even damascus throats and tips. Bill also used ivory. I have seen a few Moran sheaths made of shark skin, typically in a pouch-style design.

Maintaining a Moran

All of Mr. Moran's knives are forged of non-stainless steels, so a bit of upkeep is necessary. Do not store the knives in their sheaths. Keep the blades clean and covered with a top-quality gun oil. (I use Breakfree with nice results.) A bit of Renaissance Wax on the handles and sheaths should be sufficient to keep them looking their best.

I try to buy Moran knives that were well maintained. Expect to find light patina and/or spotting on Lime Kiln blades and fittings. I have found that, in general, the light patina and/or spotting does not affect the knife's value. If the blade has deep pitting, I recommend that you pass on the knife. On newer-marked Moran blades, try to buy those in near mint condition with original sheaths.

Moran Sheath Value Guide

Bill Moran's sheaths are a story in their own right. Depending on materials used and how they are made, the sheaths can add significant value to a Moran knife. Each sheath is valued using a star system, with five stars being the most valuable, four stars the next most valuable, etc.

- Wooden sheath with silver wire inlay: 5 Stars;
- New style wood-lined leather sheath with raised leather design: 4-5 Stars;
- Wood-lined leather sheath with throat and tip (steel or ivory is better than brass for fittings): 4 Stars;
- Wood-lined leather sheath: 3-4 Stars (rating varies depending on the quality of the half moon and other accouterments);
- Leather sheath with a silver half moon: 3 Stars;
- Wooden sheath: 3 Stars, and;
- Plain leather sheath: 1-2 Stars.

Moran Stamp Value Guide

Most of Bill Moran's knives can be valued based on their tang stamps. The rule of thumb is that newer Moran knives bring higher values. As for Moran sheaths, they also have different values.

Below is a value guide for Moran knives based solely on their tang stamps. Each stamp is valued using a star system, with five stars being the most valuable, four stars the next most valuable, etc.

- Damascus—Bill started using this stamp in 1973 and discontinued it around 1979. It was always used along with the MORAN stamp: 4-5 Stars;
- 50 yrs.—Starting in 1989, Bill began his 50-years knife project. The stamp appears only on 50 knives celebrating his 50th anniversary of knifemaking: 4-5 Stars;
- WFM—Bill's first stamp used in the late 1940s: 4 Stars;
- MORAN—He started using this stamp in 1973 and still uses it today: 3-4 Stars;
- M.S.—Denotes a master smith with the American Bladesmith Society, first used by Bill in 1981: 3-4 Stars;
- W.F. Moran—Bill used this stamp starting in 1980, typically on larger knives. It is not seen much anymore: 3-4 Stars;
- Moran (small print)—Bill used it on his miniature knives: 3 Stars, and;
- By W.F. Moran, Lime Kiln MD—This is a very common stamping first used in the mid-1950s and continued until 1973: 2-3 Stars.

Today's Knifemakers

Introduction

"Today's Knifemakers" is a list of knifemakers' names and contact information. The goal was to list as many as we could of the world's individual knifemakers who make and sell knives. The main purpose of the list is to allow collectors, purveyors, makers and anyone else interested in handmade knives to contact the maker of their choice. Each listing includes the maker's name, business name (if any), address, phone and fax number, where applicable.

Some History

Knives have been handmade since the beginning of time, or at least since the beginning of knives. Even in factories, many knives have been—and still are, to a certain extent—handmade, though more and more are going to CNC (Computer Numerically Controlled) knifemaking operations. Indeed, prior to 1903, when the first successful automatic grinding machine came into general use, all factory knives were essentially handmade.

To the modern collector, the term "handmade knife" refers to a knife that is essentially the work of a single craftsman, though a growing number of makers are farming out certain of their knifemaking operations. Before 1900, single-author knifemaking was an ancient and long-recognized craft or profession. Its practitioners were called "cutlers." The most skilled were also called "surgical instrument makers."

To be accessible to their customers, many cutlers worked downtown in larger cities. Most cutlers were retail merchants, as well as being craftsmen. Most knife manufacturers, by contrast, built their factories in small towns, where land, labor and water power were cheap and readily available.

We included every 19th-century American cutler whom we can identify in the list of "American Knifemakers and Selected American Cutlery Merchants of the Bowie Knife Period" (see "Bowie Knives"). A few knife manufacturers are included in the list as well, the rest being recorded in the pocketknife, hunting knife and kitchen knife lists.

The Way Knives Changed

As mechanization took over in the knife factories (after 1903, thanks to the Hemming grinder) and in the mills that made tool and blade steel (after 1907, thanks to the Heroult electric furnace), knife prices were forced down worldwide. Soon, the traditional urban cutlers largely vanished from American cities, no longer able to compete with the mass producers. The few cutlers who remained in business were reduced to retailing and re-grinding.

At the same time, the sharply lowered cost of high-grade tool steel, both new and scrap, suitable for blades and the ready availability of metal-working tools—especially the low-cost surplus tools abundant after World War I—opened up the possibility of hobby knifemaking to anyone who was so inclined. The newly popular home-mechanic-type magazines encouraged the pursuit.

For the first four decades of the twentieth century, very few of the new breed of largely rural home and hobby knifemakers actually made a living at their craft. There were about a hundred knife factories in America during the 1920s and '30s, and each one offered hundreds or even thousands of patterns in a range of price and quality, from bare-bones basic to elegantly deluxe.

Manufacturers of premium-quality knives, such as Marble's, Ulster, New York Knife and Remington, had the high end of the market well covered. A $3 Remington or $5 Marble's was equal in quality to most $20 or $30 handmade hunting knives. Consequently, very few knifemakers of the period, certainly fewer than a dozen, even bothered trying to improve on the most expensive factory knives.

Most makers then, if they sold their knives at all, tried to undercut the lowest factory knife prices. Usually they did so by bypassing distributors and retailers, and selling their knives for pennies.

The 1940s, '50s and '60s saw a steep decline in the number of knife factories in the USA, and in the quality and diversity of knives that the remaining manufacturers offered. During World War II, with factory knives in short supply and production limited to government models, hundreds of men handcrafted combat and utility knives for themselves, for gifts and for sale (see "U.S. Military Fixed Blade Knives" in this section). In the 1960s, American knife manufacturers very nearly abandoned the high end of the market to German imports, and to the handful of quality knifemakers around the country then struggling to make ends meet.

By the late 1960s, more and more knifemakers were refining their work and raising their prices to meet the neglected demand for quality. Initially, most of the buyers for their upscale handmades were sophisticated knife users, such as sportsmen, soldiers and explorers. Then, with a little help from the federal Gun Control Act of 1968—which limited collectors' access to collectible guns—many of the same collectors "discovered" handmade knives. Today, the craft of knifemaking has once again become a respected and sometimes well-compensated profession, much as it had been for several centuries prior to 1900.

International Knifemakers

The past two decades have seen a revival of quality knifemaking in most parts of the world, a renaissance that has paralleled, and often imitated, developments in the USA. For many international knifemakers, a test of success has been to offer their knives in the American market, which means that increasing numbers of fine international handmades have found their way into American collections.

Most, if not all, of the makers included in this list are working now. The names, addresses and phone numbers, where available, were gleaned from the *Knives* annual, the directories of the American Bladesmith Society and The Knifemakers' Guild, and other sources. We would certainly welcome the contact information of other working knifemakers for inclusion in future editions.

Values?

These listings do not include values. Due to the copious number of makers worldwide and the many models they offer, to do so would take a book at least the size of *BLADE's Guide*. For the price ranges most of the makers listed here ask for their knives, see KP Publishing's *Knives* annual. Anyone serious about handmade knives should have that book, too. (It is available from KP Publishing, 700 E. State St., Iola, WI 54990 800.272.5233.)

Instead of trying to include the values of knives by each maker in this list, we will tell you how to evaluate almost any handmade knife, the same way that we do when we write a formal appraisal.

Anyway, price ranges do not help you to evaluate a particular handmade knife in hand. Their main use is in helping you choose a maker's knife/knives based on your budget. (In addition to price ranges, the *Knives* annual also lists active knifemakers' addresses and phone numbers, and summarizes their offerings. [The *Knives'* contact list is drawn on heavily for *BLADE's Guide's* list.] Plus, each volume includes lots of great knife photos, feature articles, and a directory of manufacturers, embellishers, suppliers and more.)

There are two things to consider about the values of handmade knives. The first is that we have observed that virtually all signed or attributable handmades, even many lesser-quality ones, either are collected by somebody or at least are useful to somebody, and therefore have some value. In other words, the mere fact that a signed knife's maker is known and listed here or somewhere else means that someone will likely pay at least $50 for the knife; this is certainly not true of factory knives.

Second, there are always a few makers at any given time whose work commands a substantial premium, above even their own "list" prices. However, this sort of knifemaking stardom is subject to rapid change. Moreover, the popularity of certain aspects of a particular maker's work may not extend to all of his work (such as straight-carbon-steel blades by a maker best known for damascus steel, or fixed-blade knives by a maker best known for folders). Therefore, value ratings for the knives of presently popular makers are subject to change much more frequently than those of antique knives.

Evaluating a Handmade Knife

But what *about* values?

Some past editions of this book allowed the reader to evaluate less than 5 percent of handmade knives, so not much has really been sacrificed here in return for a substantial gain in contact information—which is crucial for you to determine a handmade knife's value. So instead of trying to include the values of knives by each maker in this list, we will tell you how to evaluate almost any handmade knife, the same way that we do when we write a formal appraisal.

First, telephone the maker. Describe the knife that you have, and ask what he would charge to make a similar knife today.

A few makers will terminate the conversation, which is understandable because they may suspect you are "feeling them out" in order to compete with them. Some will tell you to buy one of their brochures, which is fair. Most, however, will simply answer the question.

If they currently have a "list price" for a knife like yours, figure that you will be able to realize between 50-100 percent of the list price for your knife, depending on its condition and on how big and diverse the market is in which you offer it. There are exceptions to this rule of thumb; read on for some ways to identify the main ones.

Next, ask the maker if there is presently active demand for this particular type of knife. If the answer is *yes* and the maker adds that the pattern is back ordered, you can conclude that your knife is very likely worth a premium over the maker's "list price." It is on this premium that professional handmade knife purveyors make a profit.

If the maker says *no* and adds that he has not sold a knife like it in a while, you should conclude that the market value of your knife is substantially *less* than its replacement cost.

Novice collectors often think that a discontinued knife must necessarily be worth a premium. The fact is, usually, that a maker—handmade or factory—discontinues a pattern because no one wants it, or at least no one who is willing to pay what the maker considers a fair return on his time and effort. If it were worth a premium over this "cost," the maker would probably resume making it.

If the maker is no longer around or is no longer making the type of knife that you are evaluating—for example, it might have a mark or a type of construction that the maker no longer uses—you then need to contact a purveyor. Most purveyors, of course, do not give their services away for free and will charge an appraisal fee. However, if you do business regularly with a purveyor, either buy from or sell to him or do favors for him—such as customer referrals—then he will likely be willing to share information with you free of charge. And if a purveyor is kind enough to give you this valuable information, do not insult him by arguing. Disregard his opinion if you must, but keep your opinion of your knife's value to yourself.

So where do knife purveyors get *their* prices? Beginners and non-collectors often assume that they get them from value guides, such as this book. That is not true.

Knife value guides are a lot like the stock tables in the *Wall Street Journal*. The charts tell you at what prices shares sold for at the close of business yesterday. *They do not tell you what they should sell for today, let alone what they will sell for tomorrow.* Knife purveyors determine knife values the same way that stockbrokers determine stock values—through discovering day by day what their customers are actually willing to pay.

Whither Now?

Like the *Pocketknife Brand List*, this *Knifemaker List* is a work in progress. It is as complete as we could make it up to press time, but we fully expect it to keep growing larger and more detailed as time passes. If you have contact information about any knifemakers not listed, or if you have additional or more accurate contact information about makers who are listed, please share it with us.

Today's Knifemakers

A

BBOTT, WILLIAM M.
ox 102A, RR #2, Chandlerville, IL
627, Phone: 217-458-2325

BEGG, ARNIE
92 Kenwick Cr., Huntington
each, CA 92648, Phone: 714-848-
97

BERNATHY, PAUL J.
33 Park St., Eureka, CA 95501,
hone: 707-442-3593

CKERSON, ROBIN E.
9 W Smith St., Buchanan, MI
9107, Phone: 616-695-2911

DAMS, LES
413 NW 200 St., Hialeah, FL
3015, Phone: 305-625-1699

ADAMS, WILLIAM D.
O Box 439, Burton, TX 77835,
hone: 713-855-5643, Fax: 713-855-
638

ADDISON, KYLE A.
09 N. 20th St, Murray, KY 42071,
hone: 270-759-1564

ADKINS, RICHARD L.
38 California Ct., Mission Viejo,
CA 92692-4079

AIDA, YOSHIHITO
6-7 Narimasu 2-chome, Itabashi-
u, Tokyo 175-0094, JAPAN, Phone:
1-3-3939-0052, Fax: 81-3- 3939-
058

AKAHORI, YOICHIRO
-5-4 Fujieda, Fujieda City,
hizuoka, JAPAN 426-0006 54-641-
830

ALBERICCI, EMILIO
9 Via Masone, 24100, Bergamo,
ITALY, Phone: 01139-35-215120

ALCORN, DOUGLAS
14687 Fordney Rd., Chesaning, MI
48616 Phone/Fax 989-845-6712

ALDERMAN, ROBERT
2655 Jewel Lake Rd., Sagle, ID
83860, Phone: 208-263-5996

ALDRETE, BOB
PO Box 1471, Lomita, CA 90717,
Phone: 310-326-3041

ALEXANDER, DAVID
4801 West Lattin, West Richland,
WA 99353 509-627-6237

ALEXANDER, DARREL
Box 381, Ten Sleep, WY 82442,
Phone: 307-366-2699

ALEXANDER, EUGENE
Box 540, Ganado, TX 77962-0540,
Phone: 512-771-3727

ALEXANDER, JERED
213 Hogg Hill Rd., Dierks, AR
71833, Phone: 870-286-2981

ALLEN, MIKE "WHISKERS"
12745 Fontenot Acres Rd.,
Malakoff, TX 75148, Phone: 903-
489-1026

ALLISON, DANIEL
4820 Wyoming, Kansas City, MO
64112 816-931-4279

ALLRED, BRUCE F.
1764 N. Alder, Layton, UT 84041,
Phone: 801-825-4612

ALVERSON, TIM (R.V.)
4874 Bobbits Bench Rd., Peck, ID
83545, Phone: 208-476-3999

AMERI, MAURO
Via Riaello No. 20, Trensasco St.
Olcese, 16010 Genova, ITALY,
Phone: 010-8357077

AMES, MICKEY L.
1521 N. Central Ave., Monett, MO
65708-1104, Phone: 417-235-5941

AMMONS, DAVID C.
6225 N. Tucson Mtn. Dr., Tucson,
AZ 85743, Phone: 520-307-3585

AMOR JR., MIGUEL
485-H Judie Lane, Lancaster, PA
17603, Phone: 717-468-5738

AMOS, CHRIS
550 S Longfellow, Tucson, AZ
85711, Phone: 520-271-9752

AMOUREUX, A.W.
PO Box 776, Northport, WA 99157,
Phone: 509-732-6292

ANDERS, DAVID
157 Barnes Dr., Center Ridge, AR
72027, Phone: 501-893-2294

ANDERS, JEROME
155 Barnes Dr., Center Ridge, AR
72027, Phone: 501-893-9981

**ANDERSEN, HENRIK
LEFOLII**
Jagtvej 8, Groenholt, 3480,
Fredensborg, DENMARK, Phone:
0011-45-48483026

ANDERSON, MEL
17158 Lee Lane, Cedaredge, CO
81413-8247, Phone: 970-856-6465,
Fax: 970-856-6463

ANDERSON, GARY D.
2816 Reservoir Rd., Spring Grove,
PA 17362-9802, Phone: 717-229-
2665

ANDERSON, TOM
955 Canal Rd. Extd., Manchester,
PA 17345, Phone: 717-266-6475

ANDRESS, RONNIE
415 Audubon Dr. N, Satsuma, AL
36572, Phone: 251-675-7604

ANDREWS, DON
N. 5155 Ezy St., Coeur D'Alene, ID
83814, Phone: 208-765-8844

ANDREWS, ERIC
132 Halbert Street, Grand Ledge,
MI 48837, Phone: 517-627-7304

ANDREWS II, E.R. (RUSS)
131 S. Sterling Av., Sugar Creek,
MO 64054, Phone: 816-252-3344

ANGELL, JON
22516 East C .R .1474, Hawthorne,
FL 32640, Phone: 352-475-5380

ANKROM, W.E.
14 Marquette Dr., Cody, WY 82414,
Phone: 307-587-3017, Fax: 307-587-
3017

ANSO, JENS
GL. Skanderborgvej, 116, 8472
Sporup, DENMARK, Phone: 45
86968826

ANTONIO JR., WILLIAM J.
6 Michigan State Dr., Newark, DE
19713-1161, Phone: 302-368-8211

AOUN, CHARLES
69 Nahant St., Wakefield, MA
01880, Phone: 781-224-3353

APELT, STACY E.
8076 Moose Ave., Norfolk, VA
23518, Phone: 757-583-5872

APPLEBY, ROBERT
43 N. Canal St., Shickshinny, PA
18655, Phone: 570-542-4335

APPLETON, RAY
244 S. Fetzer St., Byers, CO 80103-
9748

ARBUCKLE, JAMES M.
114 Jonathan Jct., Yorktown, VA
23693, Phone: 757-867-9578

ARCHER, RAY and TERRI
PO Box 129, Medicine Bow, WY
82329, Phone: 307-379-2567

ARDWIN, COREY
4700 North Cedar, North Little
Rock, AR 72116, Phone: 501-791-
0301, Fax: 501-791-2974

ARNOLD, JOE
47 Patience Cres., London, Ont.,
CANADA N6E 2K7, Phone: 519-
686-2623

ARROWOOD, DALE
556 Lassetter Rd., Sharpsburg, GA
30277, Phone: 404-253-9672

ASAY, DOUG
424 N 3rd St., Jefferson, OR 97352
503-266-9050

ASHBY, DOUGLAS
10123 Deermont, Dallas, TX 75243,
Phone: 214-238-7531

ASHWORTH, BOYD
1510 Bullard Place, Powder Springs,
GA 30127, Phone: 770-422-9826

ATKINSON, DICK
General Delivery, Wausau, FL
32463, Phone: 850-638-8524

**AYARRAGARAY, CRISTIAN
L.**
Buenos Aires 250, (3100) Parana-
Entre Rios, ARGENTINA, Phone:
043-231753

AYEN, DOUGLAS
1273 Crums Church Rd., Berryville,
VA 22611-2415 540-955-6389

AYERS, WILLIAM
320 Linder Ave., Kuna, ID 83634
208-922-9295

B

BAARTMAN, GEORGE
PO Box 1116, Bela-Bela 0480,
Limpopo, SOUTH AFRICA,
Phone: 27 14 736 4036, Fax: 27 14
736 4036

BABCOCK, RAYMOND G.
179 Lane Rd., Vincent, OH 45784,
Phone: 614-678-2688

BACHE-WIIG, TOM
N-5966, Eivindvik, NORWAY,
Phone: 4757784290, Fax:
4757784122

BACA, EDDIE
POB 5611, Santa Fe, NM 87502
505-438-8161

BACON, DAVID R.
906 136th St. E., Bradenton, FL
34202-9694, Phone: 813-996-4289

BAGLEY, R. KEITH
Old Pine Forge, 4415 Hope Acres
Dr., White Plains, MD 20695,
Phone: 301-932-0990

BAGWELL, MARION
POB 1200, Reidsville, NC 27323

BAILEY, RYAN
4185 S. St. Rt. 605, Galena, OH
43021, Phone: 740-965-9970

BAILEY, JOSEPH D.
3213 Jonesboro Dr., Nashville, TN
37214, Phone: 615-889-3172

BAILEY, KIRBY C.
2055 F.M. 2790 W., Lytle, TX
78052, Phone: 830-772-3376

BAKER, VANCE
574 Co. Rd. 675, Riceville, TN
37370, Phone: 423-745-9157

BAKER, RAY
PO Box 303, Sapulpa, OK 74067,
Phone: 918-224-8013

BAKER, WILD BILL
Box 361, Boiceville, NY 12412,
Phone: 914-657-8646

BAKER, HERB
14104 NC 87 N., Eden, NC 27288,
Phone: 336-627-0338

BAKER, STEPHEN
718 E. Kasson Rd., Maple City, MI
49664

BALBACH, MARKUS
Heinrich - Worner - Str. 3, 35789
Weilmunster-Laubuseschbach/Ts.,
GERMANY 06475-8911, Fax:
912986

BALDWIN, PHILLIP
PO Box 563, Snohomish, WA 98290, Phone: 425-334-5569

BALL, KEN
127 Sundown Manor, Mooresville, IN 46158, Phone: 317-834-4803

BALLESTRA, SANTINO
via D. Tempesta 11/17, 18039 Ventimiglia (IM), ITALY 0184-215228

BALLEW, DALE
PO Box 1277, Bowling Green, VA 22427, Phone: 804-633-5701

BANFIELD, MARK D.
POB 143, Bay L'Argent, Newfoundland CANADA A0E 1B0 709-461-2259

BANKS, DAVID L.
99 Blackfoot Ave., Riverton, WY 82501, Phone: 307-856-3154/ Cell:307-851-5599

BARDSLEY, NORMAN P.
197 Cottage St., Pawtucket, RI 02860, Phone: 401-725-9132

BAREFOOT, JOE W.
117 Oakbrook Dr., Liberty, SC 29657

BARKER, REGGIE
603 S. Park Dr., Springhill, LA 71075, Phone: 318-539-2958

BARKER, ROBERT G.
2311 Branch Rd., Bishop, GA 30621, Phone: 706-769-7827

BARLOW, JANA POIRIER
3820 Borland Cir., Anchorage, AK 99517, Phone: 907-243-4581

BARNES, MARLEN R.
904 Crestview Dr.S., Atlanta, TX 75551-1854, Phone: 903-796-3668

BARNES, AUBREY G.
11341 Rock Hill Rd., Hagerstown, MD 21740, Phone: 301-223-4587

BARNES, JACK
PO Box 1315, Whitefish, MT 59937-1315, Phone: 406-862-6078

BARNES, ERIC
H C 74 Box 41, Mountain View, AR 72560, Phone: 501-269-3358

BARNES, WILLIAM
591 Barnes Rd., Wallingford, CT 06492-1805, Phone: 860-349-0443

BARNES, GREGORY
266 W. Calaveras St., Altadena, CA 91001, Phone: 626-398-0053

BARNES, GARY L.
Box 138, New Windsor, MD 21776-0138, Phone: 410-635-6243, Fax: 410-635-6243

BARNES, MARLEN R.
904 Crestview Dr. S, Atlanta, TX 75551-1854 903-796-3668

BARNES, WENDELL
2160 Oriole Dr., Missoula, MT 59808, Phone: 406-721-0908

BARNES JR., CECIL C.
141 Barnes Dr., Center Ridge, AR 72027, Phone: 501-893-2267

BARNETT, VAN
Barnett Int'l Inc., 1135 Terminal Way Ste. #209, Reno, NV 89502, Phone: 866 ARTKNIFE or 304-727-5512, Fax: 775-201-0038

BARNGROVER, JERRY
RR. #4, Box 1230, Afton, OK 74331, Phone: 918-257-5076

BARNHART, TODD
350 Jennifer Ln., Driftwood, TX 78619 512-847-9679

BARR, A.T.
153 Madonna Dr., Nicholasville, KY 40356, Phone: 859-887-5400

BARR, JUDSON C.
1905 Pickwick Circle, Irving, TX 75060, Phone: 972-790-7195

BARRETT, CECIL TERRY
2514 Linda Lane, Colorado Springs, CO 80909, Phone: 719-473-8325

BARRETT, RICK L. (TOSHI HISA)
18943 CR .18, Goshen, IN 46528, Phone: 574-533-4297

BARRON, BRIAN
123 12th Ave., San Mateo, CA 94402, Phone: 650-341-2683

BARRY III, JAMES J.
115 Flagler Promenade No., West Palm Beach, FL 33405, Phone: 561-832-4197

BARTH, J.D.
101 4th St., PO Box 186, Alberton, MT 59820, Phone: 406-722-4557

BARTLOW, JOHN
5078 Coffeen Ave., Sheridan, WY 82801, Phone: 307 673-4941

BARTRUG, HUGH E.
2701 34th St. N., #142, St. Petersburg, FL 33713, Phone: 813-323-1136

BASKETT, LEE GENE
427 Sutzer Ck. Rd., Eastview, KY 42732, Phone: 270-862-5019

BATLEY, MARK S.
PO Box 217, Wake, VA 23176, Phone: 804 776-7794

BATSON, RICHARD G.
6591 Waterford Rd., Rixeyville, VA 22737, Phone: 540-937-2318

BATSON, JAMES
176 Brentwood Lane, Madison, AL 35758, Phone: 540-937-2318

BATTS, KEITH
450 Manning Rd., Hooks, TX 75561, Phone: 903-832-1140

BAUCHOP, PETER
c/o Beck's Cutlery Specialties, 107 Edinburgh S #109, Cary, NC 27511, Phone: 919-460-0203, Fax: 919-460-7772

BAUCHOP, ROBERT
PO Box 330, Munster, Kwazulu-Natal 4278, SOUTH AFRICA, Phone: +27 39 3192449

BAUER, MICHAEL R.
1550 Evanston Ave., Muskegon, MI 49442 231-773-3244

BAUM, RICK
435 North Center St., Lehi, UT 84043, Phone: 801-431-7290

BAUMGARDNER, ED
128 E. Main St., Glendale, KY 42740, Phone: 502-435-2675

BAXTER, DALE
291 County Rd. 547, Trinity, AL 35673, Phone: 256-355-3626

BEAM, JOHN R.
1310 Foothills Rd., Kalispell, MT 59901, Phone: 406-755-2593

BEASLEY, GENEO
PO Box 339, Wadsworth, NV 89442, Phone: 775-575-2584

BEATTY, GORDON H.
121 Petty Rd., Seneca, SC 29672, Phone: 864-882-6278

BEATY, ROBERT B.
CUTLER, 1995 Big Flat Rd., Missoula, MT 59804, Phone: 406-549-1818

BEATY, JIM
518 Sutton Spring Rd., York, SC 29745 803-684-0088

BEAUCHAMP, GAETAN
125, de la Rivire, Stoneham, PQ, CANADA G0A 4P0, Phone: 418-848-1914, Fax: 418-848-6859

BECKER, STEVE
201 1st Ave. N.W., Conrad, MT 59425, Phone: 406-278-7753

BECKER, FRANZ
AM Kreuzberg 2, 84533, Marktl/ Inn, GERMANY 08678-8020

BECKETT, NORMAN L.
102 Tobago Ave., Satsuma, FL 32189, Phone: 386-325-3539

BEERS, RAY
2501 Lakefront Dr., Lake Wales, FL 33898, Phone: Winter 863-696-3036, Fax: 863-696-9421

BEETS, MARTY
390 N. 5th Ave., Williams Lake, BC, CANADA V2G 2G4, Phone: 250-392-7199

BEGG, TODD M.
420 169 St. S, Spanaway, WA 98387, Phone: 253-531-2113

BEHNKE, WILLIAM
8478 Dell Rd., Kingsley, MI 49649, Phone: 231-263-7447

BELL, MICHAEL
88321 N. Bank Lane, Coquille, OR 97423, Phone: 541-396-3605

BELL, DONALD
2 Division St., Bedford, Nova Scotia, CANADA B4A 1Y8, Phone: 902-835-2623

BENDIK, JOHN
7076 Fitch Rd., Olmsted Falls, OH 44138

BENFIELD JR., ROBERT O.
532 Bowie, Forney, TX 75126

BENJAMIN JR., GEORGE
3001 Foxy Ln., Kissimmee, FL 34746, Phone: 407-846-7259

BENNETT, PETER
PO Box 143, Engadine N.S.W. 2233, AUSTRALIA, Phone: 02-520-4975 (home), Fax: 02-528-821 (work)

BENNETT, BRETT C.
1922 Morrie Ave., Cheyenne, WY 82001, Phone: 307-220-3919

BENNETT, GLEN C.
5821 S. Stewart Blvd., Tucson, AZ 85706

BENNICA, CHARLES
Chemin du Salet, 34190 Moules et Baucels, FRANCE, Phone: +33 4 67 73 42 40

BENSON, DON
2505 Jackson St., #112, Escalon, C 95320, Phone: 209-838-7921

BENTLEY, C.L.
2405 Hilltop Dr., Albany, GA 31707, Phone: 912-432-6656

BER, DAVE
656 Miller Rd., San Juan Island, WA 98250, Phone: 206-378-7230

BERG, LOTHAR
37 Hillcrest Ln., Kitchener ON, CANADA NZK 1S9, Phone: 519-745-3260, 519-745-3260

BERGER, MAX A.
5716 John Richard Ct., Carmichae CA 95608, Phone: 916-972-9229

BERGH, ROGER
Eklangsvagen 40, 12051 Arsta, SWEDEN, Phone: 070 5941570

BERGLIN, BRUCE D.
17441 Lake Terrace Place, Mount Vernon, WA 98274, Phone: 360-422-8603

BERTHOLUS, BERNARD
Atelier Du Brute, De Forge 21, Rue Fersen 06600, Antibes, FRANCE, Phone: 04 93 34 95 90

BERTOLAMI, JUAN CARLOS
Av San Juan 575, Neuquen, ARGENTINA 8300

BERTUZZI, ETTORE
Via Partigiani 3, 24068 Seriate (Bergamo), ITALY, Phone: 035-294262, Fax: 035-294262

BESEDICK, FRANK E.
R.R. 2, Box 802, Ruffsdale, PA 15679, Phone: 724-696-3312

BESHARA, BRENT
207 Cedar St., PO Box 1046, Stayner, ON, CANADA L0M 1S0

BETHKE, LORA SUE
13420 Lincoln St., Grand Haven, MI 49417, Phone: 616-842-8268, Fax: 616-844-2696

BEUKES, TINUS
83 Henry St., Risiville, Vereeniging 1939, SOUTH AFRICA, Phone: 27 16 423 2053

BEVERLY II, LARRY H.
PO Box 741, Spotsylvania, VA
22553, Phone: 540-898-3951

BEZUIDENHOUT, BUZZ
10 Surlingham Ave., Malvern,
Queensburgh, Natal 4093, SOUTH
AFRICA, Phone: 031-4632827, Fax:
031-3631259

BIGGERS, GARY
Ventura Knives, 1278 Colina Vista,
Ventura, CA 93003, Phone: 805-
658-6610, Fax: 805-658-6610

BILLGREN, PER
TALLGATAN 9, S815 76
Soderfors, SWEDEN, Phone: +46
293 17480, Fax: +46 293 30124

BIRDWELL, IRA LEE
PO Box 1135, Bagdad, AZ 86321,
Phone: 520-633-2516

BIRNBAUM, EDWIN
9715 Hamocks Blvd. I 206, Miami,
FL 33196

BISH, HAL
1347 Sweetbriar Trace, Jonesboro,
GA 30236, Phone: 770-477-2422

BISHER, WILLIAM M.
2015 Back Rd., Denton, NC 27239
336-859-5486

BIZZELL, ROBERT
145 Missoula Ave., Butte, MT
59701, Phone: 406-782-4403

BLACK, EARL
3466 South, 700 East, Salt Lake
City, UT 84106, Phone: 801-466-
8395

BLACK, HARRY B.
10703 Hiawatha Dr., Boise, ID
83709 208-362-2049

BLACK, TOM
921 Grecian N.W., Albuquerque,
NM 87107, Phone: 505-344-2549

BLACK, SCOTT
570 Malcom Rd., Covington, GA
30209

BLACKTON, ANDREW E.
12521 Fifth Isle, Bayonet Point, FL
34667, Phone: 727-869-1406

BLACKWOOD, NEIL
7032 Willow Run, Lakeland, FL
33813, Phone: 863-701-0126

BLANCHARD, G.R. (Gary)
8900 Condotti Ct., Las Vegas, NV
89117, Phone: 702-645-9774

BLASINGAME, ROBERT
281 Swanson, Kilgore, TX 75662,
Phone: 903-984-8144

BLAUM, ROY
319 N. Columbia St., Covington,
LA 70433, Phone: 985-893-1060

BLOOMER, ALAN T.
116 E. 6th St., Maquon, IL 61458,
Phone: 309-875-3583

BLOOMQUIST, R. GORDON
6206 Tiger Trail Dr., Olympia, WA
98512, Phone: 360-352-7162

BLUM, KENNETH
1729 Burleson, Brenham, TX
77833, Phone: 979-836-9577

BLUM, CHUCK
743 S. Brea Blvd., #10, Brea, CA
92621, Phone: 714-529-0484

BLUNTZNER, OTTO
95 Mariposa Dr., Rochester, NY
14624-2521 716-247-4976

BOARDMAN, GUY
39 Mountain Ridge R., New
Germany 3619, SOUTH AFRICA,
Phone: 031-726-921

BOATRIGHT, BASEL
11 Timber Point, New Braunfels,
TX 78132, Phone: 210-609-0807

BOCHMAN, BRUCE
183 Howard Place, Grants Pass, OR
97526, Phone: 503-471-1985

BODEN, HARRY
Via Gellia Mill, Bonsall Matlock,
Derbyshire DE4 2AJ, ENGLAND,
Phone: 0629-825176

BODNER, GERALD "JERRY"
4102 Spyglass Ct., Louisville, KY
40229, Phone: 502-968-5946

BODOLAY, ANTAL
Rua Wilson Soares Fernandes #31,
Planalto, Belo Horizonte MG-
31730-700 BRAZIL, Phone: 031-
494-1885

BOEHLKE, GUENTER
Parkstrasse 2, 56412 Grossholbach,
GERMANY 2602-5440

BOGUSZEWSKI, PHIL
PO Box 99329, Lakewood, WA
98499, Phone: 253-581-7096

BOJTOS, ARPA D.
Dobsinskeho 10, 98403 Lucenec,
Slovakia, Phone: 00421-47 4333512

BOLD, STU
63 D'Andrea Tr., Sarnia, Ont.,
CANADA N7S 6H3, Phone: 519-
383-7610

BOLEWARE, DAVID
PO Box 96, Carson, MS 39427,
Phone: 601-943-5372

BOLTON, CHARLES B.
PO Box 6, Jonesburg, MO 63351,
Phone: 636-488-5785

BONASSI, FRANCO
Via Nicoletta 4, Pordenone 33170,
ITALY, Phone: 0434-550821

BOOCO, GORDON
175 Ash St., PO Box 174, Hayden,
CO 81639, Phone: 970-276-3195

BOOS, RALPH
5107 40 Ave., Edmonton, Alberta,
CANADA T6L 1B3, Phone: 780-
463-7094

BOOTH, PHILIP W.
301 S. Jeffery Ave., Ithaca, MI
48847, Phone: 989-875-2844

BORGER, WOLF
Benzstrasse 8, 76676 Graben-
Neudorf, GERMANY, Phone:
07255-72303, Fax: 07255-72304

BOSE, TONY
7252 N. County Rd., 300 E.,
Shelburn, IN 47879-9778, Phone:
812-397-5114

BOSE, REESE
PO Box 61, Shelburn, IN 47879,
Phone: 812-397-5114

BOSSAERTS, CARL
Rua Albert Einstein 906, 14051-
110, Ribeirao Preto, S.P. BRAZIL,
Phone: 016 633 7063

BOST, ROGER E.
30511 Cartier Dr, Palos Verdes, CA
90275-5629, Phone: 310- 541-6833

BOSTWICK, CHRIS t.
341 Robins Run, Burlington, WI
53105

BOSWORTH, DEAN
329 Mahogany Dr., Key Largo, FL
33037, Phone: 305-451-1564

BOURBEAU, JEAN YVES
15 Rue Remillard, Notre Dame,
Ile Perrot, Quebec, CANADA J7V
8M9, Phone: 514-453-1069

BOUSE, D. MICHAEL
1010 Victoria Pl., Waldorf, MD
20602, Phone: 301-843-0449

BOWEN, TILTON
189 Mt Olive Rd., Baker, WV
26801, Phone: 304-897-6159

BOWLES, CHRIS
PO Box 985, Reform, AL 35481,
Phone: 205-375-6162

BOXER, BO
LEGEND FORGE, 6477 Hwy.
93 S #134, Whitefish, MT 59937,
Phone: 505-799-0173

BOYD, FRANCIS
1811 Prince St., Berkeley, CA
94703, Phone: 510-841-7210

BOYE, DAVID
PO Box 1238, Dolan Springs, AZ
86441, Phone: 800-853-1617

BOYER, MARK
10515 Woodinville Dr., #17,
Bothell, WA 98011, Phone: 206-
487-9370

BOYSEN, RAYMOND A.
125 E. St. Patrick, Rapid Ciy, SD
57701, Phone: 605-341-7752

BRACK, DOUGLAS D.
119 Camino Ruiz, #71, Camirillo,
CA 93012, Phone: 805-987-0490

BRADBURN, GARY
BRADBURN CUSTOM
CUTLERY, 1714 Park Place,
Wichita, KS 67203, Phone 316-
269-4273

BRADFORD, GARRICK
582 Guelph St., Kitchener ON,
CANADA N2H-5Y4, Phone: 519-
576-9863

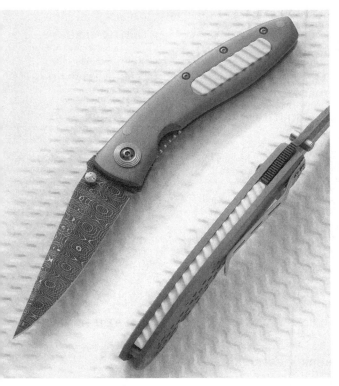

TOM ANDERSON

Tom Anderson's "Warrior Framelock" boasts a 4-inch
blade of Devin Thomas high-carbon damascus, a titanium
handle and ivory insets. Anderson's list price for a similar
piece: **$950**. (Point Seven photo)

BRADLEY, JOHN
PO Box 37, Pomona Park, FL 32181, Phone: 904-649-4739

BRADLEY, DENNIS
2410 Bradley Acres Rd., Blairsville, GA 30512, Phone: 706-745-4364

BRADLEY, GAYLE
1383 Old Garner Rd., Weatherford, TX 76088-8720 817-596-2894

BRADSHAW, BAILEY
PO Box 564, Diana, TX 75640, Phone: 903-968-2029

BRANDON, MATTHEW
4435 Meade St., Denver, CO 80211, Phone: 303-458-0786

BRANDSEY, EDWARD P.
335 Forest Lake Dr., Milton, WI 53563, Phone: 608-868-9010

BRANDT, MARTIN W.
833 Kelly Blvd., Springfield, OR 97477, Phone: 541-747-5422

BRANTON, ROBERT
4976 Seewee Rd., Awendaw, SC 29429, Phone: 843-928-3624

BRATCHER, BRETT
11816 County Rd. 302, Plantersville, TX 77363, Phone: 936-894-3788, Fax: (936) 894-3790

BRAY JR., W. LOWELL
6931 Manor Beach Rd., New Port Richey, FL 34652, Phone: 727-846-0830

BREED, KIM
733 Jace Dr., Clarksville, TN 37040, Phone: 931-645-9171

BREND, WALTER
353 Co. Rd. 1373, Vinemont, AL 35179, Phone: 256-739-1987

BRENNAN, JUDSON
PO Box 1165, Delta Junction, AK 99737, Phone: 907-895-5153, Fax: 907-895-5404

BRESHEARS, CLINT
1261 Keats, Manhattan Beach, CA 90266, Phone: 310-372-0739, Fax: 310-372-0739

BREUER, LONNIE
PO Box 877384, Wasilla, AK 99687-7384

BRIGHTWELL, MARK
21104 Creekside Dr., Leander, TX 78641, Phone: 512-267-4110

BRITTON, ARTHUR
505 N. Lake Shore Dr., Apt. 5702, Chicago, IL 60611 312-836-0176

BRITTON, TIM
5645 Murray Rd., Winston-Salem, NC 27106, Phone: 336-922-9582 336-922-9582, Fax: 336-923-2062

BROADWELL, DAVID
PO Box 4314, Wichita Falls, TX 76308, Phone: 940-692-1727, Fax: 940-692-4003

BROCK, KENNETH L.
PO Box 375, 207 N Skinner Rd., Allenspark, CO 80510, Phone: 303-747-2547

BROMLEY, PETER
Bromley Knives, 1408 S Bettman, Spokane, WA 99212, Phone: 509-534-4235

BROOKER, DENNIS
Rt. 1, Box 12A, Derby, IA 50068, Phone: 515-533-2103

BROOKS, CHARLES E.
1037 Pops Dr., Catawba, NC 28609 828-478-9284

BROOKS, BUZZ
2345 Yosemite Dr., Los Angles, CA 90041, Phone: 323-256-2892

BROOKS, MICHAEL
4645 52nd St .Apt. F4, Lubbock, TX 79414-3802

BROOKS, STEVE R.
1610 Dunn Ave., Walkerville, MT 59701, Phone: 406-782-5114

BROOME, THOMAS A.
1212 E. Aliak Ave., Kenai, AK 99611-8205, Phone: 907-283-9128

BROTHERS, ROBERT L.
989 Philpott Rd., Colville, WA 99114, Phone: 509-684-8922

BROWER, MAX
2016 Story St., Boone, IA 50036, Phone: 515-432-2938

BROWN, TROY L.
22945 W. 867 Rd., Park Hill, OK 74451, Phone: 918-457-4128

BROWN, ROB E.
PO Box 15107, Emerald Hill 6011, Port Elizabeth, SOUTH AFRICA, Phone: 27-41-3661086, Fax: 27-41-4511731

BROWN, DAVID
500 E. Main St., Steel City, NE 68440 402-442-2308

BROWN, DENNIS G.
1633 N. 197TH Pl., Shoreline, WA 98133, Phone: 206-542-3997

BROWN, HAROLD E.
3654 N.W. Hwy. 72, Arcadia, FL 34266, Phone: 863-494-7514

BROWN, JIM
1097 Fernleigh Cove, Little Rock, AR 72210

BROWNE, RICK
980 West 13th St., Upland, CA 91786, Phone: 909-985-1728

BROWNING, STEVEN W.
3400 Harrison Rd., Benton, AR 72015, Phone: 501-316-2450

BRUNCKHORST, LYLE
Country Village, 23706 7th Ave. SE, Ste. B, Bothell, WA 98021, Phone: 425-402-3484

BRUNER, RICK (sheathmaker)
7756 Aster Lane, Jenison, MI 49428, Phone: 616-457-0403

BRUNER JR., FRED, BRUNER BLADES
E10910W Hilldale Dr., Fall Creek, WI 54742, Phone: 715-877-2496

BRUNETTA, DAVID
PO Box 4972, Laguna Beach, CA 92652, Phone: 714-497-9611

BRYAN, TOM
14822 S Gilbert Rd., Gilbert, AZ 85296, Phone: 480-812-8529

BUCHMAN, BILL
63312 South Rd., Bend, OR 97701, Phone: 503-382-8851

BUCHNER, BILL
PO Box 73, Idleyld Park, OR 97447, Phone: 541-498-2247

BUCHOLZ, MARK A.
PO Box 82, Holualoa, HI 96725, Phone: 808-322-4045

BUCKBEE, DONALD M.
243 South Jackson Trail, Grayling, MI 49738, Phone: 517-348-1386

BUCKNER, JIMMIE H.
PO Box 162, Putney, GA 31782, Phone: 912-436-4182

BUEBENDORF, ROBERT E.
108 Lazybrooke Rd., Monroe, CT 06468, Phone: 203-452-1769

BULLARD, BILL
Rt. 5, Box 35, Andalusia, AL 36420, Phone: 334-222-9003

BULLARD, RANDALL
7 Mesa Dr., Canyon, TX 79015, Phone: 806-655-0590

BULLARD, TOM
117 MC 8068, Flippin, AR 72634, Phone: 870-453-3421

BUMP, BRUCE D.
1103 Rex Ln., Walla Walla, WA 99362, Phone: 509 522-2219

BURDEN, JAMES
405 Kelly St., Burkburnett, TX 76354

BURGER, FRED
Box 436, Munster 4278, Kwa-Zulu Natal, SOUTH AFRICA, Phone: 27 393216

BURGER, JAY
RR2, Box 76B, Ft. Branch, IN 47648-9619 812-753-4940

BURGER, PON
12 Glenwood Ave., Woodlands, Bulawayo, Zimbabwe 75514

BURKE, BILL
12 Chapman Ln., Boise, ID 83716. Phone: 208-756-3797

BURKE, DAN
22001 Ole Barn Rd., Edmond, OK 73034, Phone: 405-341-3406, Fax: 405-340-3333

BURNETT, MAX
537 Old Dug Mtn. Rd., Paris, AR 72855, Phone: 501-963-2767

BURRIS, PATRICK R.
11078 Crystal Lynn C.t, Jacksonville, FL 32226, Phone: 904-757-3938

BURROWS, CHUCK
Wild Rose Trading Co, PO Box 5174, Durango, CO 81301, Phone: 970-259-8396

BURROWS, STEPHEN R.
3532 Michigan, Kansas City, MO 64109, Phone: 816-921-1573

BUSFIELD, JOHN
153 Devonshire Circle, Roanoke Rapids, NC 27870, Phone: 252-537-3949, Fax: 252-537-8704

BUSSE, JERRY
11651 Co. Rd. 12, Wauseon, OH 43567, Phone: 419-923-6471

BUTLER, JOHN R.
20162 6TH Ave. N.E., Shoreline, WA 98155, Phone: 206-362-3847

BUTLER, JOHN
777 Tyre Rd., Havana, FL 32333, Phone: 850-539-5742

BUTLER, BART
822 Seventh St., Ramona, CA 92065, Phone: 760-789-6431

BUTTON-INMAN, DEE
3705 Arctic Blvd. 111, Anchorage, AK 99503 907-562-2597

BYBEE, BARRY J.
795 Lock Rd. E., Cadiz, KY 42211-8615

BYRD, WESLEY L.
189 Countryside Dr., Evensville, TN 37332, Phone: 423-775-3826

C

CABE, JERRY (BUDDY)
62 McClaren Ln., Hattieville, AR 72063, Phone: 501-354-3581

CABRERA, SERGIO B.
25711 Frampton Ave. Apt. 113, Harbor City, CA 90710

CAFFREY, EDWARD J.
2608 Central Ave. West, Great Falls, MT 59404, Phone: 406-727-9102

CAIN, LARRY
4867 Fallon Pl., Dallas, TX 75227 214-388-0747

CAIRNES JR., CARROLL B.
RT. 1 Box 324, Palacios, TX 77465, Phone: 369-588-6815

CALDWELL, BILL
255 Rebecca, West Monroe, LA 71292, Phone: 318-323-3025

CALLAHAN, F. TERRY
PO Box 880, Boerne, TX 78006, Phone: 830-981-8274, Fax: 830-981-8279

CALLAHAN, ERRETT
2 Fredonia, Lynchburg, VA 24503

CALVERT JR., ROBERT W. (BOB)
911 Julia, PO Box 858, Rayville, LA 71269, Phone: 318-728-4113, Fax: (318) 728-0000

CAMERER, CRAIG
287 E. Main, Hettick, IL 62649, Phone: 618-778-5704

CAMERON, RON G.
PO Box 183, Logandale, NV 89021, Phone: 702-398-3356

CAMERON HOUSE
001 Delaney Rd. Se., Salem, OR
7306, Phone: 503-585-3286

CAMPBELL, DICK
0000 Silver Ranch Rd., Conifer,
CO 80433, Phone: 303-697-0150

CAMPBELL, COURTNAY M.
PO Box 23009, Columbia, SC
9224, Phone: 803-787-0151

CAMPOS, IVAN
R.XI de Agosto, 107, Tatui, SP,
BRAZIL 18270-000, Phone: 00-55-
5-2518092, Fax: 00-55-15-2594368

CANDRELLA, JOE
219 Barness Dr., Warminster, PA
8974, Phone: 215-675-0143

CANNADY, DANIEL L.
Box 301, Allendale, SC 29810,
Phone: 803-584-2813

CANNON, RAYMOND W.
PO Box 1412, Homer, AK 99603,
Phone: 907-235-7779

CANNON, DAN
0500 Leon, Dallas, TX 75217,
Phone: 972-557-0268

CANNON, RAYMOND W.
PO Box 1412, Homer, AK 99603
907-235-7779

CANOY, ANDREW B.
3420 Fruchey Ranch Rd., Hubbard
Lake, MI 49747, Phone: 810-266-
5039

CANTER, RONALD E.
96 Bon Air Circle, Jackson, TN
38305, Phone: 731-668-1780

CANTRELL, KITTY D.
19720 Hwy. 78, Ramona, CA
92076, Phone: 760-788-8304

CAPDEPON, ROBERT
829 Vatican Rd., Carencro, LA
70520, Phone: 337-896-8753, Fax:
318-896-8753

CAPDEPON, RANDY
553 Joli Rd., Carencro, LA 70520,
Phone: 318-896-4113, Fax: 318-896-
8753

CAREY JR., CHARLES W.
1003 Minter Rd., Griffin, GA
30223, Phone: 770-228-8994

CARLISLE, JEFF
PO Box 282 12753 Hwy. 200,
Simms, MT 59477, Phone: 406-
264-5693

CARLISLE, FRANK
5930 Hereford, Detroit, MI 48224,
Phone: 313-882-8349

CARLSON, KELLY
54 S. Holt Hill, Antrim, NH 03440,
Phone: 603-588-2765, Fax: 603-588-
4223

CARLSSON, MARC BJORN
Hansgade 31, 4000 Roskilde,
DENMARK, Phone: +45 46 35 97
24, Fax: +45 33 91 17 99

CARNAHAN, CHARLES A.
27 George Arnold Lane, Green
Spring, WV 26722, Phone: 304-
492-5891

CARNAHAN, WILLIAM N.
POB 7027, Natchitoches, LA 71457
318-354-0445

CARPENTER, RONALD W.
RT. 4 Box 323, Jasper, TX 75951,
Phone: 409-384-4087

CARR, TIM
3660 Pillon Rd., Muskegon, MI
49445, Phone: 231-766-3582

CARRIGER, JAMES V.
2460 Stone Rd., Wylie, TX 75098

CARROLL, CHAD
12182 McClelland, Grant, MI
49327, Phone: 231-834-9183

CARSON, HAROLD J. "KIT"
1076 Brizendine Lane, Vine Grove,
KY 40175, Phone: 270 877-6300,
Fax: 270 877 6338

CARTER, FRED
5219 Deer Creek Rd., Wichita
Falls, TX 76302, Phone: 904-723-
4020

CARTER, GEORGE
350 Emily Park Rd., RR2, Omemee,
Ontario, CANADA K0L 2W 705-
799-5608

CARTER, MURRAY M.
2506 Toyo Oka, Ueki Kamoto,
Kumamoto, JAPAN 861-0163,
Phone: 81-96-272-6759

CASH, TERRY
113 Sequoyah Cir., Canton, GA
30115, Phone: 770-345-2031

CASHEN, KEVIN R.
5615 Tyler St., Hubbardston, MI
48845, Phone: 989-981-6780

CASTEEL, DOUGLAS
PO Box 63, Monteagle, TN 37356,
Phone: 931-723-0851, Fax: 931-723-
1856

CASTEEL, DIANNA
P.O .Box 63, Monteagle, TN 37356,
Phone: 931-723-0851, Fax: 931-723-
1856

CASTON, DARRIEL
3725 Duran Circle, Sacramento,
CA 95821, Phone: 916-359-0613

CATOE, DAVID R.
4024 Heutte Dr., Norfolk, VA
23518, Phone: 757-480-3191

**CAWTHORNE,
CHRISTOPHER A.**
PO Box 604, Wrangell, AK 99929

CENTOFANTE, FRANK
PO Box 928, Madisonville, TN
37354-0928, Phone: 423-442-5767

CHAFFEE, JEFF L.
14314 N. Washington St., PO Box
1, Morris, IN 47033, Phone: 812-
934-6350

CHAMBERLAIN, JOHN B.
1621 Angela St., Wenatchee, WA
98801, Phone: 509-663-6720

**CHAMBERLAIN, CHARLES
R.**
PO Box 156, Barren Springs, VA
24313-0156, Phone: 703-381-5137

CHAMBERLAIN, JON A.
15 S. Lombard, E. Wenatchee, WA
98802, Phone: 509-884-6591

CHAMBERLIN, JOHN A.
11535 Our Rd., Anchorage, AK
99516, Phone: 907-346-1524, Fax:
907-562-4583

CHAMBLIN, JOEL
960 New Hebron Church Rd.,
Concord, GA 30206, Phone: 770-
884-9055

CHAMPAGNE, PAUL
48 Brightman Rd., Mechanicville,
NY 12118, Phone: 518-664-4179

CHAMPION, ROBERT
1806 Plateau Ln, Amarillo, TX
79106, Phone: 806-359-0446

CHAPO, WILLIAM G.
45 Wildridge Rd., Wilton, CT
06897, Phone: 203-544-9424

CHARD, GORDON R.
104 S. Holiday Lane, Iola, KS
66749, Phone: 620-365-2311

CHASE, ALEX
208 E. Pennsylvania Ave., DeLand,
FL 32724, Phone: 386-734-9918

CHASE, JOHN E.
217 Walnut, Aledo, TX 76008,
Phone: 817-441-8331

CHASTAIN, WADE
Rt. 2, Box 137-A, Horse Shoe, NC
28742, Phone: 704-891-4803

CHAUVIN, JOHN
200 Anna St., Scott, LA 70583,
Phone: 337-237-6138, Fax: 337-230-
7980

CHAUZY, ALAIN
1 Rue de Paris, 21140 Seur-en-
Auxios, FRANCE, Phone: 03-80-97-
03-30, Fax: 03-80-97-34-14

CHAVAR, EDWARD V.
1830 Richmond Ave., Bethlehem,
PA 18018, Phone: 610-865-1806

CHEATHAM, BILL
PO Box 636, Laveen, AZ 85339,
Phone: 602-237-2786

CHELQUIST, CLIFF
PO Box 91, Arroyo Grande, CA
93421, Phone: 805-489-8095

CHERRY, FRANK J.
3412 Tiley N.E., Albuquerque, NM
87110, Phone: 505-883-8643

CHEW, Larry
515 Cleveland Rd., Unit A-9,
Granbury, TX 76049, Phone: 817-
326-0165

CHOATE, MILTON
1665 W. County 17-1/2, Somerton,
AZ 85350, Phone: 928-627-7251

CHRISTENSEN, JON P.
7814 Spear Dr., Shepherd, MT
59079, Phone: 406-373-0253

CHURCHMAN, T.W.
7402 Tall Cedar, San Antonio, TX
78249, Phone: 210-690-8641

CLAIBORNE, RON
2918 Ellistown Rd., Knox, TN
37924, Phone: 615-524-2054

CLAIBORNE, JEFF
1470 Roberts Rd., Franklin, IN
46131, Phone: 317-736-7443

CLARK, NATE
484 Baird Dr., Yoncalla, OR 97499,
Phone: 541-680-6077

CLARK, D.E. (LUCKY)
126 Woodland St., Mineral Point,
PA 15942, Phone: 814-322-4725

CLARK, R.W.
R.W. CLARK CUSTOM KNIVES,
1069 Golden Meadow, Corona, CA
92882, Phone: 909-279-3494, Fax:
909-279-4394

CLARK, HOWARD F.
115 35th Pl., Runnells, IA 50237,
Phone: 515-966-2126

CLARK, MARK
1612 Williams Rd., Plant City, FL
33565 813-752-9326

CLAY, J.D.
5050 Hall Rd., Greenup, KY 41144,
Phone: 606-473-6769

CLAY, WAYNE
Box 125B, Pelham, TN 37366,
Phone: 931-467-3472, Fax: 931-467-
3076

CLICK, JOE
305 Dodge St.#3, Swanton, OH
43558, Phone: 419-825-1220

COCKERHAM, LLOYD
1717 Carolyn Ave., Denham
Springs, IA 70726, Phone: 225-665-
1565

COFER, RON
188 Ozora Rd., Loganville, GA
30052

COFFMAN, DANNY
541 Angel Dr. S., Jacksonville, AL
36265-5787, Phone: 256-435-1619

COHEN, N.J. (NORM)
2408 Sugarcone Rd., Baltimore,
MD 21209, Phone: 410-484-3841

COHEN, TERRY A.
PO Box 406, Laytonville, CA 95454

COIL, JIMMIE J.
2936 Asbury Pl., Owensboro, KY
42303, Phone: 270-684-7827

COLE, DAVE
620 Poinsetta Dr., Satellite Beach,
FL 32937, Phone: 321-773-1687

COLE, JAMES M.
505 Stonewood Blvd., Bartonville,
TX 76226, Phone: 817-430-0302

COLE, WELBORN I.
3284 Inman Dr. N.E., Atlanta, GA
30319, Phone: 404-261-3977

COLEMAN, KEITH E.
5001 Starfire Pl. N.W.,
Albuquerque, NM 87120-2010,
Phone: 505-899-3783

COLEMAN, VERNON
141 Lakeside Park Dr.,
Hendersonville, TN 37075 615-
824-7002

COLLINS, BLACKIE
POB 100, North, SC 29112 803-
568-2444 Fax 803-568-2481

COLLINS, HAROLD
503 First St., West Union, OH
45693, Phone: 513-544-2982

COLLINS, LYNN M.
138 Berkley Dr., Elyria, OH 44035,
Phone: 440-366-7101

COLTER, WADE
PO Box 2340, Colstrip, MT 59323,
Phone: 406-748-4573

COLTRAIN, LARRY D.
PO Box 1331, Buxton, NC 27920

COMAR, ROGER N.
RT. 1 Box 485, Marion, NC 28752,
Phone: 828-652-2448

COMPTON, WILLIAM E.
106 N. Sequoia Ct., Sterling, VA
20164, Phone: 703-430-2129

COMUS, STEVE
PO Box 68040, Anaheim, CA
92817-9800

CONKEY, TOM
9122 Keyser Rd., Nokesville, VA
22123, Phone: 703-791-3867

CONKLIN, GEORGE L.
Box 902, Ft. Benton, MT 59442,
Phone: 406-622-3268, Fax: 406-622-
3410

CONLEY, BOB
1013 Creasy Rd., Jonesboro, TN
37659, Phone: 423-753-3302

CONN JR., C.T.
206 Highland Ave., Attalla, AL
35954, Phone: 205-538-7688

CONNELL, STEVE
217 Valley St., Adamsville, AL
35005-1852, Phone: 205-674-0440

CONNER, ALLEN L.
6399 County Rd. 305, Fulton, MO
65251, Phone: 573-642-9200

CONNOLLY, JAMES
2486 Oro-Quincy Hwy., Oroville,
CA 95966, Phone: 916-534-5363

CONNOR, MICHAEL
Box 502, Winters, TX 79567,
Phone: 915-754-5602

CONNOR, JOHN W.
PO Box 12981, Odessa, TX 79768-
2981, Phone: 915-362-6901

CONTI, JEFFREY D.
4640 Feigley Rd. W., Port Orchard,
WA 98367, Phone: 360-405-0075

COOGAN, ROBERT
1560 Craft Center Dr., Smithville,
TN 37166, Phone: 615-597-6801

COOK, JAMES R.
3611 Hwy. 26 W., Nashville, AR
71852, Phone: 870 845 5173

COOK, LOUISE
475 Robinson Ln., Ozark, IL 62972,
Phone: 618-777-2932

COOK, MIKE
475 Robinson Ln., Ozark, IL 62972,
Phone: 618-777-2932

COOK, MIKE A.
10927 Shilton Rd., Portland, MI
48875, Phone: 517-647-2518

COOMBS JR., LAMONT
546 State Rt. 46, Bucksport, ME
04416, Phone: 207-469-3057, Fax:
207-469-3057

COON, RAYMOND C.
21135 S.E. Tillstrom Rd., Gresham,
OR 97080, Phone: 503-658-2252

COOPER JR., JAMES ROSCOE
501 Broadway St., Marble Hill, MO
63764 573-238-3860

COOPER, TED
322 Sapphire Ave., Balboa Island,
CA 92662 949-675-6214

COOPER, TODD
8208 N. Pine Haven Pt., Crystal
River, FL 34428 352-795-6219

COPELAND, THOM
171 Country Line Rd. S., Nashville,
AR 71852

COPELAND, GEORGE STEVE
220 Pat Carr Lane, Alpine, TN
38543, Phone: 931-823-5214

COPLEY, TONY
Lincoln, MT 59639 406-362-4535

COPPINS, DANIEL
7303 Sherrard Rd., Cambridge, OH
43725, Phone: 740-439-4199

CORBALEY, RICHARD E.
53383 Timberview Rd., North Fork,
CA 93643 209-877-7020

CORBIT, GERALD
1701 St. John Rd., Elizabethtown,
KY 42701 270-765-7728

CORBY, HAROLD
218 Brandonwood Dr., Johnson
City, TN 37604, Phone: 615-926-
9781

CORDOVA, JOSEPH G.
PO Box 977, Peralta, NM 87042,
Phone: 505-869-3912

CORKUM, STEVE
34 Basehoar School Rd.,
Littlestown, PA 17340, Phone: 717-
359-9563

CORRIGAN, DAVID P.
HCR 65 Box 67, Bingham, ME
04920, Phone: 207-672-4879

COSGROVE, CHARLES G.
2314 W. Arbook Blvd., Arlington,
TX 76015, Phone: 817-472-6505

COSTA, SCOTT
409 Coventry Rd., Spicewood, TX
78669, Phone: 830-693-3431

COSTELLO, DR. TIMOTHY L.
30883 Crest Forest, Farmington
Hills, MI 48331, Phone: 248-592-
9746

COTTRILL, JAMES I.
1776 Ransburg Ave., Columbus,
OH 43223, Phone: 614-274-0020

COUGHLIN, MICHAEL M.
414 Northridge Lane, Winder, GA
30680, Phone: 770-307-9509

COURTNEY, ELDON
2718 Bullinger, Wichita, KS 67204,
Phone: 316-838-4053

COURTOIS, BRYAN
3 Lawn Avenue, Saco, ME 04072,
Phone: 207-282-3977

COUSINO, GEORGE
7818 Norfolk, Onsted, MI 49265,
Phone: 517-467-4911, Fax: 517-467-
4911

COVER, RAYMOND A.
Rt. 1, Box 194, Mineral Point, MO
63660, Phone: 573-749-3783

COWLES, DON
1026 Lawndale Dr., Royal Oak, MI
48067, Phone: 248-541-4619

COX, SAM
1756 Love Springs Rd., Gaffney, SC
29341, Phone: 864-489-1892, Fax:
864-489-0403

COX, COLIN J.
107 N. Oxford Dr., Raymore, MO
64083, Phone: 816-322-1977

CRAIG, ROGER L.
2815 Fairlawn Rd., Topeka, KS
66614, Phone: 785-233-9499

CRAIN, JACK W.
PO Box 212, Granbury, TX 76048,
Phone: 817-599-6414

CRAIN, FRANK
1127 W. Dalke, Spokane, WA
99205, Phone: 509-325-1596

CRAWFORD, PAT and WES
205 N. Center, West Memphis, AR
72301, Phone: 870-732-2452

CRAWFORD, DAWNAVAN M.
1727 Bellevue Loop, Anchorage,
AK 99575 907-336-6667

CRAWLEY, BRUCE R.
16 Binbrook Dr., Croydon 3136
Victoria, AUSTRALIA

CRENSHAW, AL
Rt. 1, Box 717, Eufaula, OK 74432,
Phone: 918-452-2128

CROCKFORD, JACK
1859 Harts Mill Rd., Chamblee, GA
30341, Phone: 770-457-4680

CROSS, ROBERT
RMB 200B, Manilla Rd., Tamworth
2340, NSW AUSTRALIA, Phone:
067-618385

CROSSMAN, DANIEL C.
Box 5236, Blakely Island, WA
98222, Phone: 360-375-6542

CROWDER, ROBERT
Box 1374, Thompson Falls, MT
59873, Phone: 406-827-4754

NEIL BLACKWOOD

A pair of small hunters by Neil Blackwood sport mirror-polished, recurve blades of RWL-34 stainless steel and amboyna burl handles. Overall lengths: 7 3/4 inches. Though based on the materials used, Blackwood's list price for a similar set is in the **$1,200** range.
(Point Seven photo)

CROWELL, JAMES L.
O Box 822, Mtn. View, AR 72560,
hone: 870-746-4215

CROWTHERS, MARK F.
O Box 4641, Rolling Bay, WA
8061-0641, Phone: 206-842-7501

CRUZE, DAN
4406 Winterset Dr., Orlando, FL
2832 407-277-8848

CULPEPPER, JOHN
102 Spencer Ave., Monroe, LA
1201, Phone: 318-323-3636

CULVER, STEVE
682 94th St., Meriden, KS 66512,
hone: 785-484-0146

CUMMING, R.J.
CUMMING KNIVES, 35 Manana
Dr., Cedar Crest, NM 87008,
hone: 505-286-0509

CUPPLES, KELLY C.
807 Butterfield Rd., Yakima, WA
8901 509-728-0057

CUTCHIN, ROY D.
960 Hwy. 169 S., Seale, AL 36875,
hone: 334-855-3080

CUTE, THOMAS
State Rt. 90-7071, Cortland, NY
3045, Phone: 607-749-4055

DAILEY, G.E.
577 Lincoln St., Seekonk, MA
02771, Phone: 508-336-5088

DAKE, MARY H.
RT. 5 Box 287A, New Orleans, LA
70129, Phone: 504-254-0357

DAKE, C.M.
19759 Chef Menteur Hwy., New
Orleans, LA 70129-9602, Phone:
504-254-0357, Fax: 504-254-9501

DALAND, B. MACGREGOR
RT. 5 Box 196, Harbeson, DE
19951, Phone: 302-945-2609

DALLYN, KELLY
14695 Deerridge Dr. S.E., Calgary
AB, CANADA T2J 6A8, Phone:
403-278-3056

DAMLOVAC, SAVA
10292 Bradbury Dr., Indianapolis,
IN 46231, Phone: 317-839-4952

D'ANDREA, JOHN
501 Penn Estates, East Stroudsberg,
PA 18301, Phone: 570-420-6050

D'ANGELO, LAURENCE
14703 N.E. 17th Ave., Vancouver,
WA 98686, Phone: 360-573-0546

DANIEL, TRAVIS E.
1655 Carrow Rd., Chocowinity, NC
27817, Phone: 252-940-0807

DANIELS, ALEX
1416 County Rd. 415, Town Creek,
AL 35672, Phone: 256-685-0943

DARBY, JED
7878 E. Co. Rd. 50 N., Greensburg,
IN 47240, Phone: 812-663-2696

DARBY, RICK
71 Nestingrock Ln., Levittown, PA
19054

DARBY, DAVID T.
30652 S 533 Rd., Cookson, OK
74427, Phone: 918-457-4868

DARCEY, CHESTER L.
1608 Dominik Dr., College Station,
TX 77840, Phone: 979-696-1656

DARPINIAN, DAVE
15219 W. 125th, Olathe, KS 66062,
Phone: 913-397-8914

DAVENPORT, JACK
36842 W. Center Ave., Dade City,
FL 33525, Phone: 352-521-4088

DAVIDSON, EDMUND
3345 Virginia Ave., Goshen, VA
24439, Phone: 540-997-5651

DAVIDSON, JIM
1030 South 8th St., Coos Bay, OR
97420

DAVIDSON, LARRY
921 Bennett St., Cedar Hill, TX
75104, Phone: 972-291-3904

DAVIS, JOHN
235 Lampe Rd., Selah, WA 98942,
Phone: 509-697-3845, Fax: 509-697-
8087

DAVIS, BARRY L.
4262 U.S. 20, Castleton, NY 12033,
Phone: 518-477-5036

DAVIS, CHARLIE
ANZA Knives, PO Box 710806,
Santee, CA 92072, Phone: 619-561-
9445, Fax: 619-390-6283

DAVIS, JOEL
74538 165th, Albert Lea, MN
56007, Phone: 507-377-0808

DAVIS, W.C.
19300 S. School Rd., Raymore, MO
64083, Phone: 816-331-4491

DAVIS, JESSE W.
7398A Hwy. 3, Sarah, MS 38665,
Phone: 662-382-7332

DAVIS, JIM JR.
5129 Ridge St., Zephyrhills, FL
33541, Phone: 813-779-9213

DAVIS, JOHN
235 Lampe Rd., Selah, WA 98942

DAVIS, KEN
POB 922, Riverview, FL 33568
813-677-7888

DAVIS, STEVE
3370 Chatsworth Way, Powder
Springs, GA 30127, Phone: 770-
427-5740

DAVIS, TERRY
Box 111, Sumpter, OR 97877,
Phone: 541-894-2307

DAVIS, VERNON M.
2020 Behrens Circle, Waco, TX
76705, Phone: 254-799-7671

DAVIS, DON
8415 Coyote Run, Loveland, CO
80537-9665, Phone: 970-669-9016,
Fax: 970-669-8072

DAVISSON, COLE
25939 Casa Loma Ct., Hemet, CA
92544, Phone: 909-652-8588

DAWKINS, DUDLEY L.
221 NW Broadmoor Ave., Topeka,
KS 66606-1254

DAWSON, LYNN
10A Town Plaza, Suite 303,
Durango, CO 81301, Fax: 928-772-
1729

DAWSON, BARRY
10A Town Plaza, Suite 303,
Durango, CO 81301

DELAGE, JOSSE
1719 2nd Ave. North #3, Seattle,
WA 98109 206-691-0163

DE MARIA JR., ANGELO
12 Boronda Rd., Carmel Valley, CA
93924, Phone: 831-659-3381, Fax:
831-659-1315

**DE VILLIERS, ANDRE and
KIRSTEN**
Postnet Suite 263, Private Bag X6,
Cascades 3202, SOUTH AFRICA,
Phone: 27 33 4133312

DEAN, HARVEY J.
3266 CR 232, Rockdale, TX 76567,
Phone: 512-446-3111, Fax: 512-446-
5060

DeBRAGA, JOSE C.
76 Rue de La Pointe, Aux Lievres
Quebec, CANADA G1K 5Y3,
Phone: 418-948-0105, Fax: 418-
948- 0105

DEFEO, ROBERT A.
403 Lost Trail Dr., Henderson, NV
89014, Phone: 702-434-3717

DEFREEST, WILLIAM G.
PO Box 573, Barnwell, SC 29812,
Phone: 803-259-7883

DEL RASO, PETER
28 Mayfield Dr., Mt. Waverly,
Victoria, 3149, AUSTRALIA,
Phone: 613-9807 6771

DELAROSA, JIM
202 Maccarthur Dr., Mukwonago,
WI 53149, Phone: 262-363-9605

DELL, WOLFGANG
Am Alten Berg 9, D-73277 Owen-
Teck, GERMANY, Phone: 49-7021-
81802

DELLANA
Starlani Int'l. Inc., 1135 Terminal
Way Ste. #209, Reno, NV 89502,
Phone: 775-352-4247, Fax: 775-201-
0038

D'ELIA, RALPH JR.
8021 Liriope Loop, Lehigh Acres,
FL 33936 239-368-6977

DeLONG, DICK
17561 E. Ohio Circle, Aurora, CO
80017, Phone: 303-745-2652

DEMENT, LARRY
PO Box 1807, Prince Fredrick, MD
20678, Phone: 410-586-9011

DEMPSEY, DAVID
103 Chadwick Dr., Macon, GA
31210, Phone: 478-474-4948

DEMPSEY, GORDON S.
PO Box 7497, N. Kenai, AK 99635,
Phone: 907-776-8425

DENNEHY, DAN
PO Box 2F, Del Norte, CO 81132,
Phone: 719-657-2545

DENNING, GENO
Caveman Engineering, 135
Allenvalley Rd., Gaston, SC 29053,
Phone: 803-794-6067

DENT, DOUGLAS M.
1208 Chestnut St., S. Charleston,
WV 25309, Phone: 304-768-3308

DERINGER, CHRISTOPH
625 Chemin Lower, Cookshire
Quebec, CANADA J0B 1M0,
Phone: 819-345-4260

DERR, HERBERT
413 Woodland Dr., St. Albans, WV
25177, Phone: 304-727-3866

DETMER, PHILLIP
14140 Bluff Rd., Breese, IL 62230,
Phone: 618-526-4834

DEWITT, JOSEPH R.
13200 NE 39 Terrace, Anthony, FL
32617 352-620-0619

DI MARZO, RICHARD
2357 Center Pl., Birmingham, AL
35205, Phone: 205-252-3331

DICKERSON, GORDON S.
152 Laurel Ln., Hohenwald, TN
38462, Phone: 931-796-1187

DICKERSON, GAVIN
PO Box 7672, Petit 1512, SOUTH
AFRICA, Phone: +27 011-965-
0988, Fax: +27 011-965-0988

DICKISON, SCOTT S.
Fisher Circle, Portsmouth, RI
02871, Phone: 401-419-4175

**DICRISTOFANO, ANTHONY
P.**
PO Box 2369, Northlake, IL 60164,
Phone: 847-845-9598

DIEBEL, CHUCK
PO Box 13, Broussard, LA 70516-
0013

DIETZ, HOWARD
421 Range Rd., New Braunfels, TX
78132, Phone: 830-885-4662

DIETZEL, BILL
PO Box 1613, Middleburg, FL
32068, Phone: 904-282-1091

DIGANGI, JOSEPH M.
Box 950, Santa Cruz, NM 87567,
Phone: 505-753-6414, Fax: 505-753-
8144

DILL, DAVE
7404 NW 30th St., Bethany, OK
73008, Phone: 405-789-0750

DILL, ROBERT
1812 Van Buren, Loveland, CO
80538, Phone: 970-667-5144, Fax:
970-667-5144

DILLUVIO, FRANK J.
13611 Joyce Dr., Warren, MI
48093, Phone: 810-775-1216

DILLUVIO, MIKE
7544 Ravenswood, Wales, MI 48027
810-531-7760

DION, GREG
3032 S. Jackson St., Oxnard, CA
93033, Phone: 805-483-1781

DIOTTE, JEFF
Diotte Knives, 159 Laurier Dr.,
LaSalle Ontario, CANADA N9J
1L4, Phone: 519-978-2764

DIPPOLD, AL
90 Damascus Ln., Perryville, MO
63775, Phone: 573-547-1119

DISKIN, MATT
PO Box 653, Freeland, WA 98249,
Phone: 360-730-0451

DIXON JR., IRA E.
PO Box 2581, Ventura, CA 93002-
2581, Phone: 805-659-5867

DODD, ROBERT F.
4340 E Canyon Dr., Camp Verde,
AZ 86322, Phone: 928-567-3333

DODDS, DAVID
Rt. 1, Box 157, Belington, WV
26250 304-823-3503

DOGGETT, BOB
1310 Vinetree Rd., Brandon, FL
33510, Phone: 813-786-9057

DOIRON, DONALD
6 Chemin Petit Lac Des Ced,
Messines PQ, CANADA JOX-2JO,
Phone: 819-465-2489

DOLAN, ROBERT L.
220, ÄiB Naalae Rd., Kula, HI
96790, Phone: 808-878-6406

DOLE, ROGER
DOLE CUSTOM KNIFE
WORKS, PO Box 323, Buckley, WA
98321, Phone: 253-862-6770

DOMINY, CHUCK
PO Box 593, Colleyville, TX 76034,
Phone: 817-498-4527

DOOLITTLE, MIKE
13 Denise Ct., Novato, CA 94947,
Phone: 415-897-3246

**DORNELES, LUCIANO
OLIVERIRA**
Rua 15 De Novembro 2222, Nova
Petropolis, RS, BRAZIL 95150-000,
Phone: 011-55- 54-303-303-90

DOTSON, TRACY
1280 Hwy. C-4A, Baker, FL 32531,
Phone: 850-537-2407

DOUGLAS, JOHN J.
506 Powell Rd., Lynch Station, VA
24571, Phone: 804-369-7196

DOUGLAS, ROBERT
29 Castor Ave., Ottawa, Ontario,
Canada K1K 2H5 613-845-4237

DOURSIN, GERARD
Chemin des Croutoules, F 84210,
Pernes les Fontaines, FRANCE

DOUSSOT, LAURENT
6262 De La Roche, Montreal,
Quebec, CANADA H2H 1W9,
Phone: 516-270-6992 Fax: 516-722-
1641

DOWELL, T.M.
139 NW St. Helen's Pl., Bend, OR
97701, Phone: 541-382-8924

DOWNEY, PATRICK J.
2326 Chelteham, Toledo, OH
43606

DOWNIE, JAMES T.
10076 Estate Dr., Port Franks, Ont.,
CANADA NOM 2LO, Phone: 519-
243-1488, Fax: 519-243-1487

DOWNING, PATRICK, T.
4951 Clairemont Suire 281, San
Diego, CA 92117 760-497-5532

DOWNING, TOM
2675 12th St., Cuyahoga Falls, OH
44223, Phone: 330-923-7464

DOWNING, LARRY
12268 Hwy. 181N, Bremen, KY
42325, Phone: 270-525-3523, Fax:
270-525-3372

DOWNS, JAMES F.
35 Sunset Rd., Londonderry, OH
45647, Phone: 740-887-2099

DOX, JAN
Zwanebloemlaan 27, B 2900
Schoten, BELGIUM, Phone: 32 3
658 77 43

DOZIER, BOB
PO Box 1941, Springdale, AR
72765, Phone: 888-823-0023/479-
756-0023, Fax: 479-756-9139

DRAPER, MIKE
#10 Creek Dr., Riverton, WY
82501, Phone: 307-856-6807

DRAPER, AUDRA
#10 Creek Dr., Riverton, WY
82501, Phone: 307-856-6807 or 307-
851-0426 cell

DRESCHER, ADAM
520 Washington Blvd. #122, Marina
Del Rey, CA 90292 310-574-3689

DREW, GERALD
2 Glenn Cable, Asheville, NC
28805, Phone: 828-299-7821

DRISCOLL, MARK
4115 Avoyer Pl., La Mesa, CA
91941, Phone: 619-670-0695

DRISKILL, BERYL
PO Box 187, Braggadocio, MO
63826, Phone: 573-757-6262

DROST, MICHAEL B.
Rt. 2, Box 49, French Creek, WV
26218, Phone: 304-472-7901

DROST, JASON D.
Rt. 2, Box 49, French Creek, WV
26218, Phone: 304-472-7901

DUBLIN, DENNIS
728 Stanley St., Box 986, Enderby,
BC, CANADA V0E 1V0, Phone:
604-838-6753

DUBRO, PAUL
3535 Hanger Louie Rd., Mansfield,
TX 76036

DUFF, BILL
14380 Ghost Rider Dr., Reno, NV
89511, Phone: 775-851-9331

DUFOUR, ARTHUR J.
8120 De Armoun Rd., Anchorage,
AK 99516, Phone: 907-345-1701

DUGAN, BRAD M.
422 A Cribbage Ln., San Marcos,
CA 92069, Phone: 760-752-4417

DUGGER, DAVE
2504 West 51, Westwood, KS 66205,
Phone: 913-831-2382

DUNCAN, BRAD
469.247.1275 www.duncanknives.
com

DUNCAN, RON
Rt. 1, Box 21A, Cairo, MO 65239
660-263-8949

DUNKERLEY, RICK
PO Box 582, Seeley Lake, MT
59868, Phone: 406-677-5496

DUNN, STEVE
376 Biggerstaff Rd., Smiths Grove,
KY 42171, Phone: 270-563-9830

DUNN, CHARLES K.
17740 GA Hwy. 116, Shiloh, GA
31826, Phone: 706-846-2666

DURAN, JERRY T.
PO Box 80692, Albuquerque, NM
87198-0692, Phone: 505-873-4676

DURBIN, ERIC
2868 Grosvenor Dr., Cincinnati,
OH 45251

DURHAM, KENNETH
BUZZARD ROOST FORGE,
10495 White Pike, Cherokee, AL
35616, Phone: 256-359-4287

DURIO, FRED
144 Gulino St., Opelousas, LA
70570, Phone: 337-948-4831

DUVALL, LARRY E.
Rt. 3, Gallatin, MO 64640, Phone:
816-663-2742

DUVALL, FRED
10715 Hwy. 190, Benton, AR 72015,
Phone: 501-778-9360

DYER, DAVID
4531 Hunters Glen, Granbury, TX
76048, Phone: 817-573-1198

DYESS, EDDIE
1005 Hamilton, Roswell, NM
88201, Phone: 505-623-5599

DYRNOE, PER
Sydskraenten 10, Tulstrup, DK 3400
Hilleroed, DENMARK, Phone: +45
42287041

E

EAKER, ALLEN L.
416 Clinton Ave., Dept KI, Paris, IL
61944, Phone: 217-466-5160

EALY, DELBERT
PO Box 121, Indian River, MI
49749, Phone: 231-238-4705

EASLER JR., RUSSELL O.
PO Box 301, Woodruff, SC 29388,
Phone: 864-476-7830

EATON, AL
PO Box 43, Clayton, CA 94517,
Phone: 925-672-5351

EATON, RICK
9944 McCranie St., Shepherd, MT
59079 3126

EBISU, HIDESAKU
3-39-7 KOI OSAKO NISHI KU,
Hiroshima City, JAPAN 733 0816

ECHOLS, ROGER
46 Channing Rd., Nashville, AR
71852-8588, Phone: 870-451-9089

EDDY, HUGH E.
211 E Oak St., Caldwell, ID 83605,
Phone: 208-459-0536

EDEN, THOMAS
PO Box 57, Cranbury, NJ 08512,
Phone: 609-371-0774

EDGE, TOMMY
PO Box 156, Cash, AR 72421,
Phone: 501-477-5210

EDMONSON, GREGORY K.
8605 Koch Field Rd., Flagstaff, AZ
86004-1451 520-522-0776

EDMONSON, RANDEL
POB 399, Oakville, WA 98568 360-
273-6211

EDWARDS, LYNN
778 CR B91, W. Columbia, TX
77486, Phone: 979-345-4080, Fax:
979-345-3472

EDWARDS, FAIN E.
PO Box 280, Topton, NC 28781,
Phone: 828-321-3127

EDWARDS, MITCH
303 New Salem Rd., Glasgow, KY
42141, Phone: 270-651-9257

**EHRENBERGER, DANIEL
ROBERT**
6192 Hwy 168, Shelbyville, MO
63469, Phone: 573-633-2010

EKLUND, MAIHKEL
Föne 1111, S-820 41 Farila,
SWEDEN

ELDER JR., PERRY B.
1321 Garretsburg Rd., Clarksville,
TN 37042-2516, Phone: 931-647-
9416

ELDRIDGE, ALLAN
7731 Four Winds Dr., Ft Worth, TX
76133, Phone: 817-370-7778

ELISHEWITZ, ALLEN
PO Box 3059, Canyon Lake, TX
78133, Phone: 830-899-5356

ELKINS, R. VAN
PO Box 156, Bonita, LA 71223,
Phone: 318-823-2124, Fax: 318-283-
6802

ELLEFSON, JOEL
PO Box 1016, 310 S. 1st St.,
Manhattan, MT 59741, Phone:
406-284-3111

ELLERBE, W.B.
3871 Osceola Rd., Geneva, FL
32732, Phone: 407-349-5818

ELLIOTT, GORDON
1133 East Butler, Phoenix, AZ
85020 602-943-3566

ELLIOTT, JERRY
507 Kanawha Ave., Charleston, WV 25304, Phone: 304-925-5045

ELLIOTT, JIM
8175 Hwy. 98 N., Okeechobee, FL 34972-3904 863-763-3265

ELLIOTT, MARCUS
Pen Dinas, Wyddfydd Rd., Great Orme, Llandudno Gwynedd, GREAT BRITAIN LL30 2QL, Phone: 01492-872747

ELLIS, CARROLL
205 Spring Rd., Flora, MS 39071 601-879-3737

ELLIS, WILLY B.
WILLY B CUSTOM STICKS and PICKS, 10 Cutler Rd., Litchfield, NH 03052, Phone: 603-880-9722, Fax: SAME

ELLIS, DAVE/ABS Mastersmith
380 South Melrose Dr. #407, Vista, CA 92083, Phone: 760-643-4032 Eves: 760-945- 7177

ELLIS, WILLIAM DEAN
3875 N. Barton, Fresno, CA 93720, Phone: 209-299-0303

ELROD, ROGER R.
58 Dale Ave., Enterprise, AL 36330, Phone: 334-347-1863

EMBRETSEN, KAJ
FALUVAGEN 67, S-82821 Edsbyn, SWEDEN, Phone: 46-271-21057, Fax: 46-271-22961

EMERSON, ERNEST R.
PO Box 4180, Torrance, CA 90510-4180, Phone: 310-212-7455

ENCE, JIM
145 S 200 East, Richfield, UT 84701, Phone: 435-896-6206

ENGARTO, EDWARD
406 Shepard Rd., Sayre, PA 18840 607-751-6172

ENGLAND, VIRGIL
1340 Birchwood St., Anchorage, AK 99508, Phone: 907-274-9494

ENGLE, WILLIAM
16608 Oak Ridge Rd., Boonville, MO 65233, Phone: 816-882-6277

ENGLEBRETSON, GEORGE
1209 NW 49th St., Oklahoma City, OK 73118, Phone: 405-840-4784

ENGLISH, JIM
14586 Olive Vista Dr., Jamul, CA 91935, Phone: 619-669-0833

ENNIS, RAY
1220S 775E, Ogden, UT 84404, Phone: 800-410-7603, Fax: 501-621-2683

ENOS III, THOMAS M.
12302 State Rd. 535, Orlando, FL 32836, Phone: 407-239-6205

ENTIN, ROBERT
127 Pembroke St. 1, Boston, MA 02118

EPTING, RICHARD
4021 Cody Dr., College Station, TX 77845, Phone: 979-690-6496

ERICKSON, L.M.
PO Box 132, Liberty, UT 84310, Phone: 801-745-2026

ERICKSON, WALTER E.
22280 Shelton Tr., Atlanta, MI 49709, Phone: 989-785-5262

ERIKSEN, JAMES THORLIEF
dba VIKING KNIVES, 3830 Dividend Dr., Garland, TX 75042, Phone: 972-494-3667, Fax: 972-235-4932

ESSEGIAN, RICHARD
7387 E. Tulare St., Fresno, CA 93727, Phone: 309-255-5950

ESSMAN, JUSTUS P.
502 Appian Way NE, St. Petersburg, FL 33704 727-894-5327

ETCHIESON, DAVID
60 Wendy Cove, Conway, AR 72032 501-513-1019

ETZLER, JOHN
11200 N. Island, Grafton, OH 44044, Phone: 440-748-2460

EVANS, CARLTON
PO Box 815, Aledo, TX 76008, Phone: 817-441-1363

EVANS, BRUCE A.
409 CR 1371, Booneville, MS 38829, Phone: 662-720-0193

EVANS, VINCENT K. and GRACE
6301 Apache Trail, Show Low, AZ 85901, Phone: 928-537-9123

EVANS, RONALD B.
209 Hoffer St., Middleton, PA 17057-2723, Phone: 717-944-5464

EWING, JOHN H.
3276 Dutch Valley Rd., Clinton, TN 37716, Phone: 615-457-5757

F

FAGAN, JAMES A.
109 S 17 Ave., Lake Worth, FL 33460, Phone: 561-585-9349

FALTAY, JOHN
13606 W. Lake Rd., Vermillion, OH 44089

CRAIG CAMERER

A 6 1/2-inch blade forged from 1084 carbon steel, an afzelia-lay-wood handle, and nickel-silver guard and fittings top off Craig Camerer's San Francisco spear-point bowie. His list price for a similar piece: **$375**. (Hoffman photo)

FANT JR., GEORGE
1983 CR 3214, Atlanta, TX 75551-6515, Phone: (903) 846-2938

FARID R., MEHR
8 Sidney Close, Tunbridge Wells, Kent, ENGLAND TN2 5QQ, Phone: 011-44-1892 520345

FARR, DAN
285 Glen Ellyn Way, Rochester, NY 14618, Phone: 585-721-1388

FASSIO, MELVIN G.
420 Tyler Way, Lolo, MT 59847, Phone: 406-273-9143

FAUCHEAUX, HOWARD J.
PO Box 206, Loreauville, LA 70552, Phone: 318-229-6467

FAUST, DICK
624 Kings Hwy. N, Rochester, NY 14617, Phone: 585-544-1948

FAUST, JOACHIM
Kirchgasse 10, 95497 Goldkronach, GERMANY

FECAS, STEPHEN J.
1312 Shadow Lane, Anderson, SC 29625, Phone: 864-287-4834, Fax: 864-287-4834

FEIGIN, B.
Liir Corp, 3037 Holly Mill Run, Marietta, GA 30062, Phone: 770-579-1631, Fax: 770-579-1199

FELIX, ALEXANDER
PO Box 4036, Torrance, CA 90510, Phone: 310-320-1836

FELLOWS, MIKE
PO Box 166, Velddrie 7365, SOUTH AFRICA, Phone: 27 82 960 3868

FERDINAND, DON
PO Box 1564, Shady Cove, OR 97539-1564, Phone: 503-560-3355

FERGUSON, JIM
32131 Via Bande, Temecula, CA 92592, Phone: 909-719-1552

FERGUSON, JIM
PO Box 764, San Angelo, TX 76902, Phone: 915-651-6656

FERGUSON, LEE
1993 Madison 7580, Hindsville, AR 72738, Phone: 479-443-0084

FERGUSON, LINDA
1993 Madison 7580, Hindsville, AR 72738 479-443-0084

FERRARA, THOMAS
122 Madison Dr., Naples, FL 33942, Phone: 813-597-3363, Fax: 813-597-3363

FERRIER, GREGORY K.
3119 Simpson Dr., Rapid City, SD 57702, Phone: 605-342-9280

FERRIS, BILL
186 Thornton Dr., Palm Beach Garden, FL 33418

FERRIER, ROBERT THOMAS III
16005 SE 322nd St., Auburn, WA 98092 253-939-4468

FERRY, TOM
16005 SE 322nd St., Auburn, WA 98092, Phone: 253-939-4468

FIKES, JIMMY L.
PO Box 3457, Jasper, AL 35502, Phone: 205-387-9302, Fax: 205-221-1980

FILIPPOU, IOANNIS-MINAS
7 KRINIS STR NEA SMYRNI, ATHENS 17122, GREECE, Phone: (1) 935-2093

FINCH, RICKY D.
2446 HWY 191, West Liberty, KY 41472, Phone: 606-743-7151

FINLAYSON, SEAN W.
4 Garden Dr., Gales Ferry, CT 06335 860-464-8993

FIORINI, BILL
E2371 Axlen Rd., DeSoto, WI 54624, Phone: 608-780-5898

FISHER, THEO (TED)
8115 Modoc Lane, Montague, CA 96064, Phone: 916-459-3804

FISHER, JAY
1405 Edwards, Clouis, NM 88101, Phone: 505-763-2268, Fax: 505-463-2346

FISK, JERRY
10095 Hwy. 278 W, Nashville, AR 71852, Phone: 870-845-4456

FISTER, JIM
PO Box 307, Simpsonville, KY 40067

FITCH, JOHN S.
45 Halbrook Rd., Clinton, AR 72031-8910, Phone: 501-893-2020

FITZGERALD, DENNIS M.
4219 Alverado Dr., Fort Wayne, IN 46816-2847, Phone: 219-447-1081

FLINT, ROBERT
2902 Aspen, Anchorage, AK 99517, Phone: 907-243-6706

FLORES, HENRY
1000 Kiely Blvd #115, Santa Clara, CA 95051-4819, Phone: 408-246-0491

FLOURNOY, JOE
5750 Lisbon Rd., El Dorado, AR 71730, Phone: 870-863-7208

FOGARIZZU, ANTONIO
Via Enrico Fermi N7, Pattada 07016 ITALY 0039 (0) 79 755003

FOGARIZZU, BOITEDDU
via Crispi, 6, 07016 Pattada, ITALY

FOGARIZZU, TORE
Piazza Vitt Veneto 11, Pattada (SS) 07016, ITALY Phone/Fax 39-079-755066

FOGG, DON
40 Alma Rd., Jasper, AL 35501-8813, Phone: 205-483-0822

FONTENOT, GERALD J.
901 Maple Ave., Mamou, LA 70554, Phone: 318-468-3180

FORREST, BRIAN
FORREST KNIVES, PO Box 203, Descanso, CA 91916, Phone: 619-445-6343

FORSTALL, AL
38379 Aunt Massey Rd., Pearl River, LA 70452, Phone: 504-863-2930

FORTENBERRY JR., STANLEY THOMAS
103 Country Rd. E, Lexington, TX 78947 512-273-1160

FORTHOFER, PETE
5535 Hwy. 93S, Whitefish, MT 59937, Phone: 406-862-2674

FOSTER, BURT
23697 Archery Range Rd., Bristol, VA 24202, Phone: 276-669-0121

FOSTER, R.L. (BOB)
745 Glendale Blvd., Mansfield, OH 44907, Phone: 419-756-6294

FOSTER, NORVELL C.
619 Holmgreen Rd., San Antonio, TX 78220, Phone: 210-333-1675

FOSTER, RONNIE E.
95 Riverview Rd., Morrilton, AR 72110, Phone: 501-354-5389

FOSTER, TIMOTHY L.
723 Sweet Gum Acres Rd., El Dorado, AR 71730, Phone: 870-863-6188

FOSTER, AL
118 Woodway Dr., Magnolia, TX 77355, Phone: 936-372-9297

FOWLER, RICKY and SUSAN
FOWLER CUSTOM KNIVES, 18535-B Co. Rd. 45, Robertsdale, AL 36567, Phone: 251-550-6169

FOWLER, JERRY
610 FM 1660 N., Hutto, TX 78634, Phone: 512-846-2860

FOWLER, ED A.
Willow Bow Ranch, PO Box 1519, Riverton, WY 82501, Phone: 307-856-9815

FOWLER, CHARLES R.
226 National Forest Rd. 48, Ft McCoy, FL 32134-9624, Phone: 904-467-3215

FOWLER, RONNIE C.
226 National Forest Rd. 48, Ft. McCoy, FL 32134-9624 904-467-3215

FOX, JACK L.
7085 Canelo Hills Dr., Citrus Heights, CA 95610, Phone: 916-723-8647

FOX, PAUL
4721 Rock Barn Rd., Claremont, NC 28610, Phone: 828-459-2000, Fax: 828-459-9200

FOX, WENDELL
1480 S 39th St., Springfield, OR 97478, Phone: 541-747-2126

FRALEY, D.B.
1355 Fairbanks Ct., Dixon, CA 95620, Phone: 707-678-0393

FRAMSKI, WALTER P.
24 Rek Ln., Prospect, CT 06712, Phone: 203-758-5634

FRANCE, DAN
Box 218, Cawood, KY 40815, Phone: 606-573-6104

FRANCIS, VANCE
2612 Alpine Blvd., Alpine, CA 91901, Phone: 619-445-0979

FRANCIS, JOHN D.
FRANCIS KNIVES, 18 Miami St., Ft. Loramie, OH 45845, Phone: 937-295-3941

FRANK, HEINRICH H.
13868 NW Keleka Pl., Seal Rock, OR 97376, Phone: 541-563-3041, Fax: 541-563-3041

FRANKL, JOHN M.
12 Holden St., Cambridge, MA 02138, Phone: 617-547-0359

FRANKLIN, MIKE
9878 Big Run Rd., Aberdeen, OH 45101, Phone: 937-549-2598

FRAPS, JOHN R.
3810 Wyandotte Tr., Indianapolis, IN 46240-3422, Phone: 317-849-9419, Fax: 317-842-2224

FRAZIER, RON
2107 Urbine Rd., Powhatan, VA 23139, Phone: 804-794-8561

FRED, REED WYLE
3149 X S., Sacramento, CA 95817, Phone: 916-739-0237

FREDERICK, AARON
1213 Liberty Rd., West Liberty, KY 41472, Phone: 606-743-3399

FREEMAN, JOHN
160 Concession St., Cambridge, Ont., CANADA N1R 2H7, Phone: 519-740-2767, Fax: 519-740-2785

FREER, RALPH
114 12th St., Seal Beach, CA 90740, Phone: 562-493-4925, Fax: same

FREILING, ALBERT J.
3700 Niner Rd., Finksburg, MD 21048, Phone: 301-795-2880

FREY, STEVE
19103 131st Drive SE, Snohomish, WA 98296, Phone: 360-668-7351

FREY JR., W. FREDERICK
305 Walnut St., Milton, PA 17847, Phone: 570-742-9576

FRIEDLY, DENNIS E.
12 Cottontail Ln. - E, Cody, WY 82414, Phone: 307-527-6811

FRIGAULT, RICK
3584 Rapidsview Dr., Niagara Falls ON, CANADA L2G 6C4, Phone: 905-295-6695

FRITZ, JESSE
900 S. 13th St., Slaton, TX 79364, Phone: 806-828-5083, Fax: 915-530-0508

FRIZZELL, TED
14056 Low Gap Rd., West Fork, AR 72774, Phone: 501-839-2516

FRONEFIELD, DANIEL
137 Catherine Dr., Hampton Cove, AL 35763-9732, Phone: 256-536-7827

FROST, DEWAYNE
1016 Van Buren Rd., Barnesville, GA 30204, Phone: 770-358-1426

FRUHMANN, LUDWIG
Stegerwaldstr 8, 84489 Burghausen, GERMANY

FUEGEN, LARRY
517 N. Coulter Circle, Prescott, AZ 86303, Phone: 928-776-8777

FUJIKAWA, SHUN
Sawa 1157 Kaizuka, Osaka 597 0062, JAPAN, Phone: 81-724-23-4032, Fax: 81-726-23-9229

FUJISAKA, STANLEY
45-004 Holowai St., Kaneohe, HI 96744, Phone: 808-247-0017

FUKUTA, TAK
38-Umeagae-cho, Seki-City, Gifu-Pref, JAPAN, Phone: 0575-22-0264

FULLER, JACK A.
7103 Stretch Ct., New Market, MD 21774, Phone: 301-798-0119

FULLER, BRUCE A.
1305 Airhart Dr., Baytown, TX 77520, Phone: 713-427-1848

FULLER, PATRICK N.
17750 Sharon Valley Rd., Manchester, MI 48158 734-428-9143

FULLER, E. NELSON
17750 Sharon Valley Rd., Manchester, MI 48158 734-428-9143

FULTON, MICKEY
406 S Shasta St., Willows, CA 95988, Phone: 530-934-5780

FURRER, RICHARD
720 W. Walnut Dr., Sturgeon Bay, WI 54235 920-746-0313

FURUKAWA, SHIRO
1416-5 Yoshino Fujino, Tsukui, Kanagawa, Japan 199-0203 0426-87-4006 Fax 0426-87-4007

G

GADBERRY, EMMET
82 Purple Plum Dr., Hattieville, AR 72063, Phone: 501-354-4842

GADDY, GARY LEE
205 Ridgewood Lane, Washington, NC 27889, Phone: 252-946-4359

GAETA, ROBERTO
Rua Shikazu Myai 80, 05351 Sao Paulo, BRAZIL, Phone: 11-37684626

GAETA, ANGELO
R. Saldanha Marinho, 1295 Centro Jau, SP-17201-310, BRAZIL, Phone: 0146-224543, Fax: 0146-224543

GAGSTAETTER, PETER
Nibelungenschmiede, Bergstrasse 2, 9306 Freidorf Tg, SWITZERLAND

GAINES, BUDDY
GAINES KNIVES, 155 Red Hill Rd., Commerce, GA 30530

GAINEY, HAL
904 Bucklevel Rd., Greenwood, SC 29649, Phone: 864-223-0225

GALLAGHER, BARRY
135 Park St., Lewistown, MT 59457, Phone: 406-538-7056

GALLAGHER, SEAN
24828 114th PL SE, Monroe, WA 98272-7685

GALLANT, JACQUES
58 Sunset Ln., RR#3, Antigonish, Nova Scotia, Canada B2G 2L1 902-863-6219

GAMBEE, JESSE
115 Shoalford Dr., Huntsville, AL 35806 256-837-2093

GAMBLE, ROGER
2801 65 Way N., St. Petersburg, FL 33710, Phone: 727-384-1470

GAMBLE, FRANK
3872 Dunbar Pl., Fremont, CA 94536, Phone: 510-797-7970

GANSTER, JEAN-PIERRE
18, Rue du Vieil Hopital, F-67000 Strasbourg, FRANCE, Phone: (0033) 388 32 65 61, Fax: (0033) 388 32 52 79

GARCIA, MARIO EIRAS
R. Edmundo Scanapieco, 300 Caxingui, Sao Paulo SP-05516-070, BRAZIL, Fax: 011-37214528

GARDNER, ROB
3381 E Rd., Loxahatchee, FL 33470, Phone: 561-784-4994

GARNER, LARRY W.
13069 FM 14, Tyler, TX 75706, Phone: 903-597-6045

GARNER JR., WILLIAM O.
2803 East DeSoto St., Pensacola, FL 32503, Phone: 850-438-2009

GARRITY, TIMOTHY P.
217 S Grandview Blvd., Waukesha, WI 53188, Phone: 414-785-1803

GARVOCK, MARK W.
RR 1, Balderson, Ontario, CANADA K1G 1A0, Phone: 613-833-2545, Fax: 613-833-2208

GASTON, BERT
7501 Fluid Dr., Little Rock, AR 72206 501-372-4747

GASTON, RON
330 Gaston Dr., Woodruff, SC 29388, Phone: 803-433-0807, Fax: 803-433-9958

GATHERWOOD
Rob Sprokholt and Denise, Werkendelslaan 108, 1851VE Heiloo, Nederland Europe, Phone: 0031-72-5336097

GAUDETTE, LINDEN L.
5 Hitchcock Rd., Wilbraham, MA 01095, Phone: 413-596-4896

GAULT, CLAY
#1225 PR 7022, Lexington, TX 78947, Phone: 979-773-3305

GEDRAITIS, CHARLES J.
GEDRAITIS HAND CRAFTED KNIVES, 82 Campbell St., Rutland, MA 01543, Phone: 508-886-0221

GEISLER, GARY R.
PO Box 294, Clarksville, OH 45113, Phone: 937-383-4055

GENSKE, JAY
283 Doty St., Fond du Lac, WI 54935, Phone: 920-921-8019/Cell Phone: 920-579-0144

GEORGE, HARRY
3137 Old Camp Long Rd., Aiken, SC 29805, Phone: 803-649-1963

GEORGE, LES
1703 Payne, Wichita, KS 67203, Phone: 316-267-0736

GEORGE, TOM
550 Aldbury Dr., Henderson, NV 89014

GEPNER, DON
2615 E. Tecumseh, Norman, OK 73071, Phone: 405-364-2750

GERNER, THOMAS
939 German Rd., Glentui RD, Oxford, NEW ZEALAND 8253

GERUS, GERRY
PO Box 2295, G.P.O. Cairns, Qld. 4870, AUSTRALIA 070-341451, Phone: 019 617935

GEVEDON, HANNERS (HANK)
1410 John Cash Rd., Crab Orchard, KY 40419-9770

GIAGU, SALVATORE AND DEROMA MARIA ROSARIA
Via V. Emanuele 64, 07016 Pattada (SS), ITALY, Phone: 079-755918, Fax: 079-755918

GIBERT, PEDRO
Gutierrez 5189, 5603 Rama Caida, San Rafael Mendoza, ARGENTINA, Phone: 02627 441138

GIBO, GEORGE
PO Box 4304, Hilo, HI 96720, Phone: 808-987-7002

GIBSON SR., JAMES "HOOT,"
90 Park Place Ave., Bunnell, FL 32110, Phone: 904-437-4383

GILBERT, CHANTAL
291 Rue Christophe-Colomb est. #105, Quebec City Quebec, CANADA G1K 3T1, Phone: 418-525-6961, Fax: 418-525-4666

GILBREATH, RANDALL
55 Crauswell Rd., Dora, AL 35062, Phone: 205-648-3902

GILJEVIC, BRANKO
35 Hayley Crescent, Queanbeyan 2620, N.S.W., AUSTRALIA 0262977613

GIST, JOEL
Rt. 1, Box 7, Chinook, MT 59523 406-357-4183

GITTINGER, RAYMOND
6940 S Rt. 100, Tiffin, OH 44883, Phone: 419-397-2517

GLENDENNING, ANDREW
1720 E. 8th, Greeley, CO 80631 970-356-1330

GLOVER, WARREN D.
dba BUBBA KNIVES, PO Box 475, Cleveland, GA 30528, Phone: 706-865-3998, Fax: 706-348-7176

GLOVER, RON
7702 Misty Springs Ct., Mason, OH 45040, Phone: 513-398-7857

GOBEC, STEFAN
Weinserstr. 42, A-3680 Persenbeug, Austria Phone/Fax 43-7414-7675

GODDARD, WAYNE
473 Durham Ave., Eugene, OR 97404, Phone: 541-689-8098

GOERS, BRUCE
3423 Royal Ct. S., Lakeland, FL 33813, Phone: 941-646-0984

GOERTZ, PAUL S.
201 Union Ave. SE, #207, Renton, WA 98059, Phone: 425-228-9501

GOFOURTH, JIM
3776 Aliso Cyn Rd., Santa Paula, CA 93060, Phone: 805-659-3814

GOGUEN, SCOTT
166 Goguen Rd., Newport, NC 28570, Phone: 252-393-6013

GOLDBERG, DAVID
1120 Blyth Ct., Blue Bell, PA 19422, Phone: 215-654-7117

GOLDING, ROBIN
PO Box 267, Lathrop, CA 95330, Phone: 209-982-0839

GOLTZ, WARREN L.
802 4th Ave. E., Ada, MN 56510, Phone: 218-784-7721

GONZALEZ, LEONARDO WILLIAMS
Ituzaingo 473, Maldonado, CP 20000, URUGUAY, Phone: 598 4222 1617, Fax: 598 4222 1617

GOO, TAI
5920 W Windy Lou Ln., Tucson, AZ 85742, Phone: 520-744-9777

GOODE, BRIAN
104 Cider Dr., Shelby, NC 28152, Phone: 704-484-9020

GOODE, BEAR
PO Box 6474, Navajo Dam, NM 87419, Phone: 505-632-8184

GOODLING, RODNEY W.
6640 Old Harrisburg Rd., York Springs, PA 17372

GORDON, LARRY B.
23555 Newell Cir. W, Farmington Hills, MI 48336, Phone: 248-477-5483

GORDON, TIM
6761 N. Paddock Pl., Tucson, AZ 85743 520-579-7521

GORENFLO, GABE
9145 Sullivan Rd, Baton Rouge, LA 70818, Phone: 504-261-5868

GORENFLO, JAMES T. (JT)
9145 Sullivan Rd., Baton Rouge, LA 70818, Phone: 225-261-5868

GORRELL-KNIEPS, CHRISTINA
1302 33rd Ave. S., Seatle, WA 98144-3933

GOTTAGE, JUDY
43227 Brooks Dr., Clinton Twp., MI 48038-5323, Phone: 810-286-7275

GOTTAGE, DANTE
43227 Brooks Dr., Clinton Twp., MI 48038-5323, Phone: 810-286-7275

GOTTSCHALK, GREGORY J.
12 First St. (Ft. Pitt), Carnegie, PA 15106, Phone: 412-279-6692

GOUGH, RAYNE
3089-C Clairemont Dr. Pmb #316, San Diego, CA 92177 858-273-8586

GOUKER, GARY B.
PO Box 955, Sitka, AK 99835, Phone: 907-747-3476

GOYTIA, ENRIQUE
2120 E Paisano Ste. 276, El Paso, TX 79905

GRAFFEO, ANTHONY I.
100 Riess Place, Chalmette, LA 70043, Phone: 504-277-1428

GRAHAM, GORDON
Rt. 3 Box 207, New Boston, TX 75570, Phone: 903-628-6337

GRANGER, PAUL J.
2820 St. Charles Ln., Kennesaw, GA 30144, Phone: 770-426-6298

GRAVELINE, PASCAL and ISABELLE
38, Rue de Kerbrezillic, 29350 Moelan-sur-Mer, FRANCE, Phone: 33 2 98 39 73 33, Fax: 33 2 98 39 73 33

GRAY, DANIEL
GRAY KNIVES, 686 Main Rd., Brownville, ME 04414, Phone: 207-965-2191

GRAY, BOB
8206 N. Lucia Court, Spokane, WA 99208, Phone: 509-468-3924

GREBE, GORDON S.
PO Box 296, Anchor Point, AK 99556-0296, Phone: 907-235-8242

GRECO, JOHN
100 Mattie Jones Rd., Greensburg, KY 42743, Phone: 270-932-3335, Fax: 270-932-2225

GREEN, RUSS
6013 Briercrest Ave., Lakewood, CA 90713, Phone: 562-867-2305

GREEN, MARK
1523 S Main St. PO Box 20, Graysville, AL 35073, Phone: 205-647-9353

GREEN, BILL
706 Bradfield, Garland, TX 75042, Phone: 972-272-4748

GREEN, WILLIAM (BILL)
46 Warren Rd., View Bank Vic., AUSTRALIA 3084, Fax: 03-9459-1529

GREENAWAY, DON
3325 Dinsmore Tr., Fayetteville, AR 72704, Phone: 501-521-0323

GREENE, DAVID
570 Malcom Rd., Covington, GA 30209, Phone: 770-784-0657

GREENE, CHRIS
707 Cherry Lane, Shelby, NC 28150, Phone: 704-434-5620

GREENE, STEVE
DUNN KNIVES INC., PO Box 204, Rossville, KS 66533, Phone: 785-584-6856, Fax: 785-584-6856

GREENFIELD, G.O.
2605 15th St. #522, Everett, WA 98201, Phone: 425-258-1551

GREGORY, MICHAEL
211 Calhoun Rd., Belton, SC 29627, Phone: 864-338-8898

GREINER, RICHARD
1073 E. County Rd. 32, Green Springs, OH 44836

GREISS, JOCKL
Herrenwald 15, D 77773 Schenkenzell, GERMANY, Phone: +49 7836 95 71 69 or +49 7836 95 55 76

GREY, PIET
PO Box 363, Naboomspruit 0560, SOUTH AFRICA, Phone: 014-743-3613

GRIFFIN, RENDON and MARK
9706 Cedardale, Houston, TX 77055, Phone: 713-468-0436

GRIFFIN, THOMAS J.
591 Quevli Ave., Windom, MN 56101, Phone: 507-831-1089

GRIFFIN JR., HOWARD A.
14299 SW 31st Ct., Davie, FL 33330, Phone: 305-474-5406

GRIFFITH, LYNN
5103 S Sheridan Rd. #402, Tulsa, OK 74145-7627, Phone: 918-366-8303

GROSPITCH, ERNIE
18440 Amityville Dr., Orlando, FL 32820, Phone: 407-568-5438

GROSS, W.W.
109 Dylan Scott Dr., Archdale, NC 27263-3858

GROSSMAN, STEWART
24 Water St., #419, Clinton, MA 01510, Phone: 508-365-2291, 800-mysword

GROSSMAN, SCOTT
RAZORBACK KNIVES, PO Box 815, Forest Hill, MD 21050, Phone: 410-452-8456

GRUSSENMEYER, PAUL G.
310 Kresson Rd., Cherry Hill, NJ 08034, Phone: 856-428-1088

GUARNERA, ANTHONY R.
42034 Quail Creek Dr., Quartzhill, CA 93536, Phone: 661-722-4032

GUESS, RAYMOND L.
7214 Salineville Rd. NE., Mechanicstown, OH 44651, Phone: 330-738-2793

GUIDRY, BRUCE
24550 Adams Ave., Murrieta, CA 92562, Phone: 909-677-2384

GUIGNARD, GIB
Box 3413, Quartzsite, AZ 85359, Phone: 928-927-4831

GUNDERSEN, D.F. "DOC"
5811 S Siesta Lane, Tempe, AZ 85283

GUNN, NELSON L.
77 Blake Rd., Epping, NH 03042, Phone: 603-679-5119

GUNNELL, DAVID
4004 Vinson Rd., Little Rock, AR 72206 501-565-6677

GUNTER, BRAD
13 Imnaha Rd., Tijeras, NM 87059, Phone: 505-281-8080

GURGANUS, MELVIN H.
2553 N.C. 45 South, Colerain, NC 27924, Phone: 252-356-4831, Fax: 252-356-4650

GURGANUS, CAROL
2553 N.C. 45 South, Colerain, NC 27924, Phone: 252-356-4831, Fax: 252-356-4650

GUTH, KENNETH
35 E. Wacker Dr., Ste. 1840, Chicago, IL 60601 312-346-1760 Fax 312-282-6890

GUTHRIE, GEORGE B.
1912 Puett Chapel Rd., Bassemer City, NC 28016, Phone: 704-629-3031

H

HAGEN, PHILIP L. "DOC,"
PO Box 58, Pelican Rapids, MN 56572, Phone: 218-863-8503

HAGGERTY, GEORGE S.
PO Box 88, Jacksonville, VT 05342, Phone: 802-368-7437

HAGHJOO, CYRUS
Pleistalstr, 98A, 53757 Sankt Augustin, Germany 49 2241 341562

HAGUE, GEOFF
The Malt House, Hollow Ln., Wilton Marlborough, Wiltshire, ENGLAND SN8 3SR,Phone: (+44) 01672- 870212, Fax: (+44) 01672 870212

HAINES, JEFF, HAINES CUSTOM KNIVES
302 N. Mill St., Wauzeka, WI 53826, Phone: 608-875-5002

HALL, JEFF
PO Box 435, Los Alamitos, CA 90720, Phone: 562-594-4740

HALLIGAN, ED
14 Meadow Way, Sharpsburg, GA 30277, Phone: 770-251-7720, Fax: 770-251-7720

HAMADA, TOMONORI
5-12-83 Kaminagaya Kohonan-ku, Yokohama Kanagawa Pref., 233-0012 Japan Phone/Fax 045-844-2567

HAMLET JR., JOHNNY
300 Billington, Clute, TX 77531, Phone: 409-265-6929

HAMMOND, JIM
PO Box 486, Arab, AL 35016, Phone: 256-586-4151, Fax: 256-586-0170

HANCOCK, TIM
10805 N. 83rd St., Scottsdale, AZ 85260, Phone: 480-998-8849

HAND, BILL
PO Box 773, 1103 W. 7th St., Spearman, TX 79081, Phone: 806-659-2967, Fax: 806-659-5117

HANKINS, R.
9920 S Rural Rd. #10859, Tempe, AZ 85284, Phone: 480-940-0559

HANSEN, LONNIE
PO Box 4956, Spanaway, WA 98387, Phone: 253-847-4632

HANSEN, ROBERT W.
35701 University Ave. N.E., Cambridge, MN 55008, Phone: 612-689-3242

HANSON III, DON L.
PO Box 13, Success, MO 65570-0013, Phone: 573-674-3045

HANSEN, SHAUN
15505 So. Camp Williams Hwy., Bluffdale, UT 84065 801-254-7363

HARA, KOUJI
292-2 Ohsugi, Seki-City, Gifu-Pref. 501-32, JAPAN, Phone: 0575-24-7569, Fax: 0575-24-7569

HARDY, SCOTT
639 Myrtle Ave., Placerville, CA 95667, Phone: 530-622-5780

HARDY, DOUGLAS E.
114 Cypress Rd., Franklin, GA 30217, Phone: 706-675-6305

HARILDSTAD, MATT
18627 68 Ave., Edmonton, AB, T5T 2M8, CANADA, Phone: 780-481-3165

HARKINS, J.A.
PO Box 218, Conner, MT 59827, Phone: 406-821-1060

HARLEY, RICHARD
348 Deerfield Dr., Bristol, TN 37620, Phone: 423-878-5368/423-571-0638

HARLEY, LARRY W.
348 Deerfield Dr., Bristol, TN 37620, Phone: 423-878-5368 (shop)/ Cell: 423-571-0638, Fax: 276-466-6771

HARM, PAUL W.
818 Young Rd., Attica, MI 48412, Phone: 810-724-5582

HARMON, JAY
462 Victoria Rd., Woodstock, GA 30189, Phone: 770-928-2734

HARPER-MURRAY, BRENT
0140 S. Artresian, Chicago, IL
0655 773-779-6888

HARRINGTON, ROGER
Beech Farm Cottages, Bugsell
Ln., East Sussex, ENGLAND TN
2 5 EN, Phone: 44 0 1580 882194

HARRIS, CARL
9942 Upland Terrace, Ashburn,
VA 20147

HARRIS, CASS
9855 Fraiser Hill Ln., Bluemont,
VA 20135, Phone: 540-554-8774

HARRIS, JAY
91 Johnson St., Redwood City, CA
4061, Phone: 415-366-6077

HARRIS, JEFFREY
05 Olive St., Ste. 325, St. Louis,
MO 63101 314-241-2442

HARRIS, JOHN
4131 Calle Vista, Riverside, CA
2508, Phone: 909-653-2755

HARRIS, RALPH DEWEY
607 Bell Shoals Rd., Brandon, FL
3511, Phone: 813-681-5293, Fax:
13-654-8175

HARRIS, TEDD
50 NE Simmental St., Hillsboro,
OR 97124

HARRISON, DAN
492 Van Zandt CR 4812, Edom, TX
75754 903-852-3791

HARRISON, JIM (SEAMUS)
721 Fairington View Dr., St. Louis,
MO 63129, Phone: 314-894-2525

HARSEY, WILLIAM H.
82710 N. Howe Ln., Creswell, OR
97426, Phone: 519-895-4941

HART, BILL
647 Cedar Dr., Pasadena, MD
21122, Phone: 410-255-4981

HARTMAN, ARLAN (LANNY)
340 Ruddiman, N. Muskegon, MI
49445, Phone: 231-744-3635

HARTSFIELD, PHILL
PO Box 1637, Newport Beach, CA
92659-0637, Phone: 949-722-9792
and 714-636-7633

HARVEY, KEVIN
HEAVIN FORGE, PO Box 768,
Belfast 1100, SOUTH AFRICA,
Phone: 27-13-253-0914

HARVEY, MAX
14 Bass Rd., Bull Creek, Perth 6155,
WESTERN AUSTRALIA, Phone:
09-332-7585

HARVEY, HEATHER
HEAVIN FORGE, PO Box 768,
Belfast 1100, SOUTH AFRICA,
Phone: 27-13-253-0914

HASLINGER, THOMAS
164 Fairview Dr. SE, Calgary AB,
CANADA T2H 1B3, Phone: 403-
253-9628

HATCH, KEN
PO Box 203, Dinosaur, CO 81610

HAWES, CHUCK
HAWES FORGE, PO Box 176,
Weldon, IL 61882, Phone: 217-736-
2479

HAWK, GRANT and GAVIN
Box 401, Idaho City, ID 83631,
Phone: 208-392-4911

HAWK, JACK L.
Rt. 1, Box 771, Ceres, VA 24318,
Phone: 703-624-3878

HAWK, JOEY K.
Rt. 1, Box 196, Ceres, VA 24318,
Phone: 703-624-3282

HEADRICK, GARY
Garage Wilson 122, Blvd. Wilson,
06160 Juan Les Pins +E761, France
(33149) 361-2515

HEDGES, DION
90 Hebble Loop, Banjup, Western
Australia AUS 06164 61 89 414
5701

HILLMAN, CHARLES
225 Waldoboro Rd., Friendship,
ME 04547, Phone: 207-832-4634

HINDERER, RICK
5423 Kister Rd., Wooster, OH
44691, Phone: 216-263-0962

HINK III, LES
1599 Aptos Lane, Stockton, CA
95206, Phone: 209-547-1292

HINMAN, TED
183 Highland Ave., Watertown, MA
02472

HINSON and SON, R.
2419 Edgewood Rd., Columbus,
GA 31906, Phone: 706-327-6801

HINTZ, GERALD M.
5402 Sahara Ct., Helena, MT
59602, Phone: 406-458-5412

HIRAYAMA, HARUMI
4-5-13 Kitamachi, Warabi City,
Saitama Pref. 335-0001, JAPAN,
Phone: 048-443-2248, Fax: 048-
443-2248

HIROTO, FUJIHARA
, 2-34-7 Koioosako Nishi-ku
Hiroshima-city, Hiroshima, JAPAN,
Phone: 082-271-8389

HITCHMOUGH, HOWARD
95 Old Street Rd., Peterborough,
NH 03458-1637, Phone: 603-924-
9646, Fax: 603-924-9595

HOBART, GENE
100 Shedd Rd., Windsor, NY
13865, Phone: 607-655-1345

RAYMOND W. ENNIS

The "Sub-hilt Silhouette" by Ray Ennis has a 440C stainless steel blade, a black canvas Micarta® handle and an aluminum guard. Ennis' list price for a similar piece: **$247.50**. (Hoffman photo)

HOCKENBARY, WARREN E.
1806 Vallecito Dr., San Pedro, CA 90732

HOCKENSMITH, DAN
33514 CR 77, Crook, CO 80726, Phone: 970-886-3404

HODGE, J.B.
1100 Woodmont Ave. SE, Huntsville, AL 35801, Phone: 205-536-8388

HODGE III, JOHN
422 S. 15th St., Palatka, FL 32177, Phone: 904-328-3897

HODGSON, RICHARD J.
9081 Tahoe Lane, Boulder, CO 80301, Phone: 303-666-9460

HOEL, STEVE
PO Box 283, Pine, AZ 85544, Phone: 602-476-4278

HOFER, LOUIS
GEN DEL, Rose Prairie BC, CANADA V0C 2H0, Phone: 250-630-2513

HOFFMAN, KEVIN L.
28 Hopeland Dr., Savannah, GA 31419, Phone: 407 207-2643, Fax: 407 207-2643

HOFFMANN, UWE H.
PO Box 60114, Vancouver, BC, CANADA V5W 4B5, Phone: 604-572-7320 (after 5 p.m.)

HOGAN, THOMAS R.
2802 S. Heritage Ave., Boise, ID 83709, Phone: 208-362-7848

HOGSTROM, ANDERS T.
Granvagen 2, 135 52 Tyreso, SWEDEN, Phone: 46 8 798 5802

HOKE, THOMAS M.
3103 Smith Ln., LaGrange, KY 40031, Phone: 502-222-0350

HOLBROOK, H.L.
PO Box 483, Sandy Hook, KY 41171, Phone: 606-738-9922 home/606-738-6842 Shop

HOLDEN, LARRY
PO Box 2017, Ridgecrest, CA 93555, Phone: 760-375-7955

HOLDER, D'ALTON
7148 W. Country Gables Dr., Peoria, AZ 85381, Phone: 623-878-3064, Fax: 623-878-3964

HOLLAND, JOHN H.
1580 Nassau St., Titusville, FL 32780, Phone: 321-267-4378

HOLLAR, BOB
701 2nd Ave. SW, Great Falls, MT 59404, Phone: 406-268-8252

HOLLOWAY, PAUL
714 Burksdale Rd., Norfolk, VA 23518, Phone: 804-588-7071

HOLMES, ROBERT
1431 S Eugene St., Baton Rouge, LA 70808-1043, Phone: 504-291-4864

HONEY, MICHAEL
6733 W. Carol Ann Way, Peoria, AZ 85382 623-334-5092

HORN, DES
5 Wenlock Rd., NEWLANDS, 7700 Cape Town, SOUTH AFRICA, Phone: 27 21 6715795, Fax: 27 21 671 5795

HORN, JESS
2526 Lansdown Rd., Eugene, OR 97404, Phone: 541-463-1510

HORNE, GRACE
182 Crimicar Ln., Sheffield Britian, UNITED KINGDOM S10 4EJ

HORRIGAN, JOHN
433 Twin Creek Dr., Burnet, TX 78611 512-756-7545

HORTON, SCOT
PO Box 451, Buhl, ID 83316, Phone: 208-543-4222

HOSSOM, JERRY
3585 Schilling Ridge, Duluth, GA 30096, Phone: 770-449-7809

HOUSE, LAWRENCE
932 Eastview Dr., Canyon Lake, TX 78133, Phone: 830-899-6932

HOUSE, GARY
2851 Pierce Rd., Ephrata, WA 98823, Phone: 509-754-3272

HOUSTON, MICHAEL
8200 Foxfire Dr., Orangevale, CA 95662 916-723-9032

HOWARD, DURVYN M.
4220 McLain St. S., Hokes Bluff, AL 35903, Phone: 256-492-5720

HOWE, TORI
13000 E Stampede Rd., Athol, ID 83801

HOWELL, TED
1294 Wilson Rd., Wetumpka, AL 36092, Phone: 205-569-2281, Fax: 205-569-1764

HOWELL, JASON G.
213 Buffalo Trl., Lake Jackson, TX 77566, Phone: 979-297-9454

HOWELL, LEN
550 Lee Rd. 169, Opelika, AL 36804, Phone: 334-749-1942

HOWELL, ROBERT L.
Box 1617, Kilgore, TX 75663, Phone: 903-986-4364

HOWSER, JOHN C.
54 Bell Ln., Frankfort, KY 40601, Phone: 502-875-3678

HOY, KEN
54744 Pinchot Dr., North Fork, CA 93643, Phone: 209-877-7805

HRISOULAS, JIM
330 S. Decatur Ave., Suite 109, Las Vegas, NV 89107, Phone: 702-566-8551

HUCKABEE, DALE
254 Hwy 260, Maylene, AL 35114, Phone: 205-664-2544

HUDSON, ANTHONY B.
PO Box 368, Amanda, OH 43102, Phone: 740-969-4200

HUDSON, ROB
340 Roush Rd., Northumberland, PA 17857, Phone: 570-473-9588

HUDSON, C. ROBBIN
22280 Frazier Rd., Rock Hall, MD 21661, Phone: 410-639-7273

HUDSON, ROBERT
3802 Black Cricket Ct., Humble, TX 77396, Phone: 713-454-7207

HUGHES, DAN
13743 Persimmon Blvd., West Palm Beach, FL 33411

HUGHES, ED
280 1/2 Holly Lane, Grand Junction, CO 81503, Phone: 970-243-8547

HUGHES, DARYLE
10979 Leonard, Nunica, MI 49448, Phone: 616-837-6623

HUGHES, GENE
8545 CR 39, Mancos, CA 81328 970-533-1099

HUGHES, LAWRENCE
207 W. Crestway, Plainview, TX 79072, Phone: 806-293-5406

HUGHES, TONY
7536 West Trail N Dr., Littleton, CO 80125 303-346-9548

HULETT, STEVE
115 Yellowstone Ave., West Yellowstone, MT 59758, Phone: 406-646-4116

HULL, MICHAEL J.
1330 Hermits Circle, Cottonwood, AZ 86326, Phone: 928-634-2871

HULSEY, HOYT
379 Shiloh, Attalla, AL 35954, Phone: 256-538-6765

HUME, DON
2731 Tramway Cir. NE, Albuquerque, NM 87122, Phone: 505-796-9451

HUMENICK, ROY
PO Box 55, Rescue, CA 95672

HUMPHREYS, JOEL
3260 Palmer Rd., Bowling Green, FL 33834-9801, Phone: 863-773-0439

HUNT, MAURICE
2492 N. 800 E, Winter: 2925 Argyle Rd. Venice FL 34293, Avon, IN 46123, Phone: 317 272-2669/ Winter: 941-493-4027, Fax: 317 272-2159

HUNTER, HYRUM
285 N. 300 W, PO Box 179, Aurora, UT 84620, Phone: 435-529-7244

HUNTER, RICHARD D.
7230 NW 200th Ter., Alachua, FL 32615, Phone: 386-462-3150

HURST, JEFF
PO Box 247, Rutledge, TN 37861, Phone: 865-828-5729

HURST, COLE
1583 Tedford, E. Wenatchee, WA 98802, Phone: 509-884-9206

HURST, K. SCOTT
68 Spruce St., Abington, MA 02351

HURT, WILLIAM R.
9222 Oak Tree Cir., Frederick, MD 21701, Phone: 301-898-7143

HUSIAK, MYRON
PO Box 238, Altona 3018, Victoria, AUSTRALIA, Phone: 03-315-6752

HUTCHESON, JOHN
SURSUM KNIFE WORKS, 1237 Brown's Ferry Rd., Chattanooga, TN 37419, Phone: 423-667-6193

HYDE, JIMMY
5094 Stagecoach Rd., Ellenwood, GA 30049, Phone: 404-968-1951, Fax: 404-209-1741

HYTOVICK, JOE "HY"
14872 SW 111th St., Dunnellon, FL 34432, Phone: 800-749-5339

I

IKOMA, FLAVIO YUJI, R. Manoel R. Teixeira, 108, Centro Presidente Prudente, SP-19031-220, BRAZIL, Phone: 0182-22-0115

IMBODEN II, HOWARD L.
620 Deauville Dr., Dayton, OH 45429, Phone: 513-439-1536

IMEL, BILLY MACE
1616 Bundy Ave., New Castle, IN 47362, Phone: 765-529-1651

INMAN III, PAUL R.
3120 B Blake Ave #224, Glenwood Springs, CO 81601, Phone: 970-963-5951

IRIE, MICHAEL L.
MIKE IRIE HANDCRAFT, 1606 Auburn Dr., Colorado Springs, CO 80909, Phone: 719-572-5330

ISAO, OHBUCHI
702-1 Nouso Yame-City, Fukuoka, JAPAN, Phone: 0943-23-4439

ISGRO, JEFFERY
1516 First St., West Babylon, NY 11704, Phone: 631-587-7516

ISHIHARA, HANK
86-18 Motomachi, Sakura City, Chiba Pref., JAPAN, Phone: 043-485-3208, Fax: 043-485-3208

J

JACKS, JIM
344 S. Hollenbeck Ave., Covina, CA 91723-2513, Phone: 626-331-5665

JACKSON, DAVID
214 Oleander Ave., Lemoore, CA 93245, Phone: 559-925-8547

JACKSON, CHARLTON R.
6811 Leyland Dr., San Antonio, TX 78239, Phone: 210-601-5112

JACKSON, JIM
7 Donnington Close, Chapel Row Bucklebury RG7 6PU, ENGLAND, Phone: 011-89-712743, Fax: 011-89- 710495

JACKSON, SAMUEL AARON
381 Gladstone St., Idaho Falls, ID 83401 208-542-4540

JAKSIK JR., MICHAEL
427 Marschall Creek Rd., Fredericksburg, TX 78624, Phone: 830-997-1119

JANIGA, MATTHEW A.
2090 Church Rd., Hummelstown, PA 17036-9796, Phone: 717-533-5916

JARVIS, PAUL M.
30 Chalk St., Cambridge, MA 02139, Phone: 617-547-4355 or 617-666-9090

JEAN, GERRY
25B Cliffside Dr., Manchester, CT 06040, Phone: 860-649-6449

JEFFRIES, ROBERT W.
Route 2, Box 227, Red House, WV 25168, Phone: 304-586-9780

JENNINGS JR., MELVIN
POB 6235, Elberton, GA 30635 706-283-8311

JENSEN, JOHN LEWIS
dba MAGNUS DESIGN STUDIO, PO Box 60547, Pasadena, CA 91116, Phone: 626-449-1148, Fax: 626-449-1148

JENSEN JR., CARL A.
1130 Colfax St., Blair, NE 68008, Phone: 402-426-3353

JERNIGAN, STEVE
3082 Tunnel Rd., Milton, FL 32571, Phone: 850-994-0802, Fax: 850-994-0802

JOBIN, JACQUES
46 St. Dominique, Levis Quebec, CANADA G6V 2M7, Phone: 418-833-0283, Fax: 418-833-8378

JOEHNK, BERND
Posadowskystrasse 22, 24148 Kiel, GERMANY, Phone: 0431-7297705, Fax: 0431-7297705

JOHANNING CUSTOM KNIVES, TOM
1735 Apex Rd., Sarasota, FL 34240 9386, Phone: 941-371-2104, Fax: 941-378-9427

JOHANSSON, ANDERS
Konstvartarevagen 9, S-772 40 Grangesberg, SWEDEN, Phone: 46 240 23204, Fax: +46 21 358778

JOHNS, ROB
1423 S. Second, Enid, OK 73701, Phone: 405-242-2707

JOHNSON, BRAD
41046 Rue Chene, Ponchatoula, LA 70454 225-294-0413 Fax 225-294-4518

JOHNSON, RUFFIN
215 LaFonda Dr., Houston, TX 77060, Phone: 281-448-4407

JOHNSON, RANDY
2575 E. Canal Dr., Turlock, CA 95380, Phone: 209-632-5401

JOHNSON, HAROLD "HARRY" C.
98 Penn St., Trion, GA 30753-1520

JOHNSON, GORDEN W.
5426 Sweetbriar, Houston, TX 77017, Phone: 713-645-8990

JOHNSON, DURRELL CARMON
PO Box 594, Sparr, FL 32192, Phone: 352-622-5498

JOHNSON, C.E. GENE
5648 Redwood Ave., Portage, IN 46368, Phone: 219-762-5461

JOHNSON, R.B.
Box 11, Clearwater, MN 55320, Phone: 320-558-6128

JOHNSON, JOHN R.
5535 Bob Smith Ave., Plant City, FL 33565, Phone: 813-986-4478

JOHNSON, STEVEN R.
202 E. 200 N., PO Box 5, Manti, UT 84642, Phone: 435-835-7941

JOHNSON, RICHARD
W165 N10196 Wagon Trail, Germantown, WI 53022, Phone: 262-251-5772

JOHNSON, RYAN M.
7320 Foster Hixson Cemetery Rd., Hixson, TN 37343, Phone: 615-842-9323

JOHNSON, DAVID A.
1791 Defeated Creek Rd., Pleasant Shade, TN 37145, Phone: 615-774-3596

JOHNSON, THOMAS
POB 451, Baldwin, MI 49304 231-745-8336

JOHNSTON, DR. ROBT.
PO Box 9887, 1 Lomb Mem Dr., Rochester, NY 14623

JOHNSON, W.C.
225 Fairfield Pike, Enon, OH 45323 937-864-7802

JOKERST, CHARLES
9312 Spaulding, Omaha, NE 68134, Phone: 402-571-2536

JONES, BARRY M. and PHILLIP G.
221 North Ave., Danville, VA 24540, Phone: 804-793-5282

JONES, FRANKLIN (FRANK) W.
6030 Old Dominion Rd., Columbus, GA 31909, Phone: 706-563-6051

JONES, BOB
6219 Aztec NE, Albuquerque, NM 87110, Phone: 505-881-4472

JONES, CHARLES ANTHONY
36 Broadgate Close, Bellaire Barnstaple, No. Devon E31 4AL, ENGLAND, Phone: 0271- 75328

JONES, ROGER MUDBONE
GREENMAN WORKSHOP, PO Box 367, Waverly, OH 45690, Phone: 740-947-5684

JONES, JOHN A.
779 SW 131 HWY, Holden, MO 64040, Phone: 816-850-4318

JONES, CURTIS J.
39909 176th St. E., Palmdale, CA 93591, Phone: 805-264-2753

JONES, JOHN
12 Schooner Circuit, Manly West, QLD 4179, AUSTRALIA, Phone: 07-339-33390

JONES, ENOCH
7278 Moss Ln., Warrenton, VA 20187, Phone: 540-341-0292

JORGENSEN, GERD
Jernbanegata 8, N-3262 Larvik, NORWAY, Phone: (+47) 33 18 66 06, Fax: (+47) 33 18 66 06

JURGENS, JOHN
3650 Emerald St. Apt. Y-1, Torrence, CA 90503, Phone: 310-542-3985

JUSTICE, SHANE
425 South Brooks St., Sheridan, WY 82801, Phone: 307-673-4432

K

K B S, Knives
RSD 181, North Castlemaine, Vic 3450, AUSTRALIA, Phone: 0011 61 3 54 705864, Fax: 0011 61 3 54 706233

KACZOR, TOM
375 Wharncliffe Rd. N., Upper London, Ont., CANADA N6G 1E4, Phone: 519-645-7640

KADASAH, AHMED BIN
PO Box 1969, Jeddah 21441, SAUDI ARABIA, Phone: (26) 913-0082

KAGAWA, KOICHI
1556 Horiyamashita, Hatano-Shi, Kanagawa, JAPAN

KAHN, DAVID E.
503 N. Las Palmas Ave., Los Angeles, CA 90004 323-476-7922

KAIN, CHARLES
KAIN DESIGNS, 5412 N College Ave., Indianapolis, IN 46220

KAJIN, AL
PO Box 1047, Forsyth, MT 59327, Phone: 406-356-2442

KALFAYAN, EDWARD N.
410 Channing, Ferndale, MI 48220, Phone: 248-548-4882

KALUZA, WERNER
Lochnerstr. 32, 90441 Nurnberg, GERMANY, Phone: 0911 666047

KANDA, MICHIO
7-32-5 Shinzutumi-cho, Shunan-shi, Yamaguchi 7460033, JAPAN, Phone: 0834-62-1910, Fax: 011-81-83462-1910

KANKI, IWAO
14-25 3-CHOME FUKUI MIKI, Hydugo, JAPAN 673-0433, Phone: 07948-3-2555

KANSEI, MATSUNO
109-8 Uenomachi Nishikaiden, Gitu-city, JAPAN 501-1168, Phone: 81-58-234-8643

KANTER, MICHAEL
ADAM MICHAEL KNIVES, 14550 West Honey Ln., New Berlin, WI 53151, Phone: 262-860-1136

KARP, BOB
PO Box 47304, Phoenix, AZ 85068, Phone: 602 870-1234, Fax: 602 331-0283

KATO, SHINICHI
3233-27-5-410 Kikko Taikogane, Moriyama-ku Nagoya, JAPAN 463-0004, Phone: 81-52-736-6032

KATO, KIYOSHI
4-6-4 Himonya Meguro-ku, Tokyo 152, JAPAN

KATSUMARO, SHISHIDO
2-6-11 Kamiseno Aki-ku, Hiroshima, JAPAN, Phone: 090-3634-9054, Fax: 082-227-4438

KAUFFMAN, DAVE
120 Clark Creek Loop, Montana City, MT 59634, Phone: 406-442-9328

KAUFMAN, SCOTT
302 Green Meadows Cr., Anderson, SC 29624, Phone: 864-231-9201

KAWASAKI, AKIHISA
11-8-9 Chome Minamiamachi, Suzurandai Kita-Ku, Kobe, JAPAN, Phone: 078-593-0418, Fax: 078-593-0418

KAY, J. WALLACE
332 Slab Bridge Rd., Liberty, SC 29657

KAZSUK, DAVID
PO Box 39, Perris, CA 92572-0039, Phone: 909-780-2288

KEARNEY, JAROD
7200 Townsend Forest Ct., Brown Summit, NC 27214, Phone: 336-656-4617

KEELER, ROBERT
623 N. Willett St., Memphis, TN 38107 901-278-6538

KEESLAR, STEVEN C.
115 Lane 216, Hamilton, IN 46742, Phone: 260-488-3161

KEESLAR, JOSEPH F.
391 Radio Rd., Almo, KY 42020, Phone: 270-753-7919, Fax: 270-753-7919

KEETON, WILLIAM L.
6095 Rehobeth Rd. SE, Laconia, IN 47135-9550, Phone: 812-969-2836

KEHIAYAN, ALFREDO
Cuzco 1455, Ing. Maschwitz, CP B1623GXU Buenos Aires, ARGENTINA, Phone: 03488-4-42212

KEIDEL, GENE W. AND SCOTT J.
4661 105th Ave. SW, Dickinson, ND 58601

KEISUKE, GOTOH
105 Cosumo-City Otozu 202 Ohita-city, Ohita, JAPAN, Phone: 097-523-0750

KELLER, BILL
12211 Las Nubes, San Antonio, TX 78233 210-653-6609

KELLEY, THOMAS P.
4711 E Ashler Hill Dr., Cave Creek, AZ 85331, Phone: 480-488-3101

KELLEY, GARY
17485 SW Pheasant Lane, Aloha, OR 97006, Phone: 503-649-7867

KELLEY, THOMAS P.
4711 E. Ashler Hills Dr., Cave Creek, AZ 85331 480-488-3101

KELLOGG, BRIAN R.
19048 Smith Creek Rd., New Market, VA 22844, Phone: 540-740-4292

KELLY, LANCE
1723 Willow Oak Dr., Edgewater, FL 32132, Phone: 904-423-4933

KELSO, JIM
577 Collar Hill Rd., Worcester, VT 05682, Phone: 802-229-4254, Fax: 802-229-0595

KENNEDY JR., BILL
PO Box 850431, Yukon, OK 73085, Phone: 405-354-9150

KERBY, MARLIN W.
Rt. 1, Box114D, Brashear, TX 75420, Phone: 903-485-6201

KERN, R. W.
20824 Texas Trail W, San Antonio, TX 78257-1602, Phone: 210-698-2549

KESSLER, RALPH A.
PO Box 61, Fountain Inn, SC 29644-0061

KEYES, DAN
6688 King St., Chino, CA 91710, Phone: 909-628-8329

KEYES, GEOFF
1126 203 Pl. SE, Bothell, WA 98012 425-486-5457

KHALSA, JOT SINGH
368 Village St., Millis, MA 02054, Phone: 508-376-8162, Fax: 508-376-8081

KHARLAMOV, YURI
Oboronnay 46, 2, Tula, 300007, RUSSIA

KI, SHIVA
5222 Ritterman Ave., Baton Rouge, LA 70805, Phone: 225-356-7274

KIEFER, TONY
112 Chateaugay Dr., Pataskala, OH 43062, Phone: 740-927-6910

KILBOURN JR., CHARLES M.
Rt. 2, Box 247, Harlingen, TX 78550 956-440-7684

KILBY, KEITH
1902 29th St., Cody, WY 82414, Phone: 307-587-2732

KIMBERLEY, RICHARD L.
86-B Arroyd Hondo Rd., Santa Fe, NM 87508, Phone: 505-820-2727

KIMSEY, KEVIN
198 Cass White Rd. N.W., Cartersville, GA 30121, Phone: 770-387-0779 and 770-655-8879

KING, DAVID R.
12 Moonbeam St., Hutchins, TX 75141 972-225-8024

KING, FRED
430 Grassdale Rd., Cartersville, GA 30120, Phone: 770-382-8478

KING, BILL
14830 Shaw Rd., Tampa, FL 33625, Phone: 813-961-3455

KING, HERMAN
PO Box 122, Millington, TN 38083, Phone: 901-876-3062

KING, JASON M.
Box 151, Eskridge, KS 66423, Phone: 785-449-2638

KING JR., HARVEY G.
Box 184, Eskridge, KS 66423-0184, Phone: 785-449-2487

KING, KENNETH
1305 Taramore, Dr., Suwanee, GA 30024 770-476-1475

KINGERY, FREDERICK D.
465 Springwood Ct., Longwood, FL 32750-3036 407-830-9871

KINKADE, DONALD E.
9272 Hoffman Rd., Maybee, MI 48159 734-587-3014

KINKADE, JACOB
197 Rd. 154, Carpenter, WY 82054, Phone: 307-649-2446

KINKER, MIKE
8755 E County Rd. 50 N, Greensburg, IN 47240, Phone: 812-663-5277, Fax: 812-662-8131

KINNIKIN, TODD
Eureka Forge, 8356 John McKeever Rd., House Springs, MO 63051, Phone: 314-938-6248

KIOUS, JOE
1015 Ridge Pointe Rd., Kerrville, TX 78028, Phone: 830-367-2277, Fax: 830-367-2286

KIRK, RAY
PO Box 1445, Tahlequah, OK 74465, Phone: 918-456-1519

KITSMILLER, JERRY
67277 Las Vegas Dr., Montrose, CO 81401, Phone: 970-249-4290

KLIENSMID, BRAD
POB 1031, Penn Valley, CA 95946 530-271-4669

KNICKMEYER, HANK
6300 Crosscreek, Cedar Hill, MO 63016, Phone: 314-285-3210

KNICKMEYER, KURT
6344 Crosscreek, Cedar Hill, MO 63016, Phone: 314-274-0481

KNIGHT, JASON
110 Paradie Pond Ln., Harleyville, SC 29448, Phone: 843-452-1163

KNIPSCHIELD, TERRY
808 12th Ave. NE, Rochester, MN 55906, Phone: 507-288-7829

KNIPSTEIN, R.C. (JOE)
731 N. Fielder, Arlington, TX 76012, Phone: 817-265-0573,817-265-2021, Fax: 817-265-3410

KNOTT, STEVE
KNOTT KNIVES, PO Box 963, Rincon, GA 31326, Phone: 912-754-4326

KNUTH, JOSEPH E.
3307 Lookout Dr., Rockford, IL 61109, Phone: 815-874-9597

KOHLS, JERRY
N4725 Oak Rd., Princeton, WI 54968, Phone: 920-295-3648

KOJETIN, W.
20 Bapaume Rd., Delville, Germiston 1401, SOUTH AFRICA, Phone: 27118733305/mobile 27836256208

KOLITZ, ROBERT
W9342 Canary Rd., Beaver Dam, WI 53916, Phone: 920-887-1287

KOMMER, RUSS
9211 Abbott Loop Rd., Anchorage, AK 99507, Phone: 907-346-3339

KOPP, TODD M.
PO Box 3474, Apache Jct., AZ 85217, Phone: 480-983-6143

KOSTER, STEVEN C.
16261 Gentry Ln., Hunting Beach, CA 92647, Phone: 714-840-8621

KOVAR, EUGENE
2626 W. 98th St., Evergreen Park, IL 60642, Phone: 708-636-3724

KOYAMA, CAPTAIN BUNSHICHI
3-23 Shirako-cho, Nakamura-ku, Nagoya City 453-0817, JAPAN, Phone: 052-461-7070

KRAFT, ELMER
1358 Meadowlark Lane, Big Arm, MT 59910, Phone: 406-849-5086, Fax: 406-883-3056

KRAFT, STEVE
315 S.E. 6th, Abilene, KS 67410, Phone: 785-263-1411

KRAMER, BOB
5881 Storr Rd., Ferndale, WA 98248 360-312-8244

KRAPP, DENNY
1826 Windsor Oak Dr., Apopka, FL 32703, Phone: 407-880-7115

KRAUSE, ROY W.
22412 Corteville, St. Clair Shores, MI 48081, Phone: 810-296-3995, Fax: 810-296-2663

KREH, LEFTY
210 Wichersham Way, "Cockeysville", MD 21030

KREIBICH, DONALD L.
1638 Commonwealth Circle, Reno, NV 89503, Phone: 775-746-0533

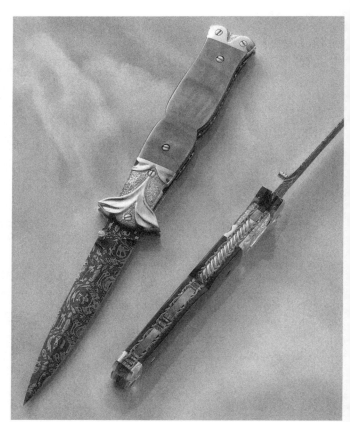

DON HANSON III

A 3-inch blade of mosaic damascus steel, carved bolsters, 18k-red-gold inlays and a black-lip mother-of-pearl handle help complete Don Hanson III's folding dagger. His list price for a similar piece: **$6,500**. (Point Seven photo)

KRESSLER, D.F.
Schloss Odetzhausen, Schlossberg 1-85235, Odetzhausen, GERMANY, Phone: 08134-998 7290, Fax: 08134-998 7290

KRETSINGER JR., PHILIP W.
17536 Bakersville Rd., Boonsboro, MD 21713, Phone: 301-432-6771

KUBAIKO, HANK
10765 Northvale, Beach City, OH 44608, Phone: 330-359-2418

KUBASEK, JOHN A.
74 Northhampton St., Easthampton, MA 01027, Phone: 413-532-3288

KYLE, DANNY L.
570 Brunswick Forge Rd., Troutville, VA 24175 540-992-4707

L

LADD, JIMMIE LEE
1120 Helen, Deer Park, TX 77536, Phone: 713-479-7186

LADD, JIM S.
1120 Helen, Deer Park, TX 77536, Phone: 713-479-7286

LAGRANGE, FANIE
12 Canary Crescent, Table View 7441, South Africa, Phone: 27 21 55 76 805

LAINSON, TONY
114 Park Ave., Council Bluffs, IA 51503, Phone: 712-322-5222

LAIRSON SR., JERRY
H C 68 Box 970, Ringold, OK 74754, Phone: 580-876-3426

LAKE, RON
3360 Bendix Ave., Eugene, OR 97401, Phone: 541-484-2683

LALA, PAULO RICARDO P. AND LALA, ROBERTO P.
R. Daniel Martins, 636, Centro, Presidente Prudente, SP-19031-260, BRAZIL, Phone: 0182-210125

LAMB, CURTIS J.
3336 Louisiana Ter., Ottawa, KS 66067-8996, Phone: 785-242-6657

LAMBERT, JARRELL D.
2321 FM 2982, Granado, TX 77962, Phone: 512-771-3744

LAMEY, ROBERT M.
15800 Lamey Dr., Biloxi, MS 39532, Phone: 228-396-9066, Fax: 228-396-9022

LAMPREY, MIKE
32 Pathfield, Great Torrington, Devon EX38 7BX, ENGLAND, Phone: 01805 601331

LAMPSON, FRANK G.
3215 Saddle Bag Circle, Rimrock, AZ 86335, Phone: 928-567-7395

LANCASTER, C.G.
No 2 Schoonwinkel St., Parys, Free State, SOUTH AFRICA, Phone: 0568112090

LANCE, BILL
PO Box 4427, Eagle River, AK 99577, Phone: 907-694-1487

LANDERS, JOHN
758 Welcome Rd., Newnan, GA 30263, Phone: 404-253-5719

LANDRUM, LEONARD D.
861 Middle Creek Rd., Cosby, TN 37722 423-487-5448

LANE, BEN
4802 Massie St., North Little Rock, AR 72218, Phone: 501-753-8238

LANE, REESE
219 N. Westpoint Rd., Glencoe, OK 74032 405-743-2707

LANER, DEAN
1480 Fourth St., Susanville, CA 96130, Phone: 530-310-1917

LANG, KURT
4908 S. Wildwood Dr., McHenry, IL 60050, Phone: 708-516-4649

LANGLEY, GENE H.
1022 N. Price Rd., Florence, SC 29506, Phone: 843-669-3150

LANKTON, SCOTT
8065 Jackson Rd. R-11, Ann Arbor, MI 48103, Phone: 313-426-3735

LAPEN, CHARLES
Box 529, W. Brookfield, MA 01585

LAPLANTE, BRETT
4545 CR412, McKinney, TX 75071, Phone: 972-838-9191

LARAMIE, MARK
181 Woodland St., Fitchburg, MA 01420, Phone: 978-353-6979

LARGIN
KELGIN KNIVES, PO Box 151, Metamora, IN 47030, Phone: 765-969-5012

LARSEN, MARC
3944 E. Lark Dr., Camp Verde, AZ 86322 520-567-3926

LARSON, RICHARD
549 E. Hawkeye Ave., Turlock, CA 95380, Phone: 209-668-1615

LARY, ED
651 Rangeline Rd., Mosinee, WI 54455, Phone: 715-693-3940

LAURENT, KERMIT
1812 Acadia Dr., LaPlace, LA 70068, Phone: 504-652-5629

LAWRENCE, ALTON
201 W Stillwell, De Queen, AR 71832, Phone: 870-642-7643, Fax: 870-642-4023

LAY, L.J.
602 Mimosa Dr., Burkburnett, TX 76354, Phone: 817-569-1329

LAY, R.J. "BOB,"
Box 122, Falkland BC, CANADA V0E 1W0, Phone: 250-379-2265, Fax: SAME

LEACH, MIKE J.
5377 W. Grand Blanc Rd., Swartz Creek, MI 48473, Phone: 810-655-4850

LEAVITT JR., EARL F.
Pleasant Cove Rd., Box 306, E. Boothbay, ME 04544, Phone: 207-633-3210

LeBATARD, PAUL M.
14700 Old River Rd., Vancleave, MS 39565, Phone: 228-826-4137, Fax: 228-826-2933

LEBER, HEINZ
Box 446, Hudson's Hope, BC, CANADA V0C 1V0, Phone: 250-783-5304

LEBLANC, GARY
7342 145th Ave., Royalton, MN 56373 320-584-5859

LeBLANC, JOHN
Rt. 2, Box 22950, Winnsboro, TX 75494, Phone: 903-629-7745

LECK, DAL
Box 1054, Hayden, CO 81639, Phone: 970-276-3663

LEDBETTER, RANDELL
506 E. 2nd St., Emmett, ID 83617 208-365-5036

LEE, RANDY
PO Box 1873, St. Johns, AZ 85936, Phone: 928-337-2594, Fax: 928-337-5002

LEE, ROBERT M.
3804 Purdue St., Dallas, TX 75225 214-987-2269

LELAND, STEVE
2300 Sir Francis Drake Blvd., Fairfax, CA 94930-1118, Phone: 415-457-0318; Fax: 415-457-0995

LEONARD, RANDY JOE
188 Newton Rd., Sarepta, LA 71071, Phone: 318-994-2712

LEONE, NICK
9 Georgetown, Pontoon Beach, IL 62040, Phone: 618-797-1179

LEPORE, MICHAEL J.
66 Woodcutters Dr., Bethany, CT 06524, Phone: 203-393-3823

LERCH, MATTHEW
N88 W23462 North Lisbon Rd., Sussex, WI 53089, Phone: 262-246-6362

LEVENGOOD, BILL
15011 Otto Rd., Tampa, FL 33624, Phone: 813-961-5688

LEVERETT, KEN
PO Box 696, Lithia, FL 33547, Phone: 813-689-8578

LEVIN, JACK
7216 Bay Pkwy., Brooklyn, NY 11204, Phone: 718-232-8574

LEVINE, BOB
101 Westwood Dr., Tullahoma, TN 37388, Phone: 931-454-9943

LEWIS, MIKE
21 Pleasant Hill Dr., DeBary, FL 32713, Phone: 386-753-0936

LEWIS, TOM R.
1613 Standpipe Rd., Carlsbad, NM 88220, Phone: 505-885-3616

LEWIS, BILL
PO Box 63, Riverside, IA 52327, Phone: 319-629-5574

LEWIS, K.J.
374 Cook Rd., Lugoff, SC 29078, Phone: 803-438-4343

LICATA, Steven
LICATA CUSTOM KNIVES, 142 Orchard St., Garfield, NJ 07026, Phone: 973-341-4288

LIEBENBERG, ANDRE
8 Hilma Rd., Bordeauxrandburg 2196, SOUTH AFRICA, Phone: 011-787-2303

LIEGEY, KENNETH R.
132 Carney Dr., Millwood, WV 25262, Phone: 304-273-9545

LIGHTFOOT, GREG
RR #2, Kitscoty AB, CANADA T0B 2P0, Phone: 780-846-2812

LIKARICH, STEVE
PO Box 961, Colfax, CA 95713, Phone: 530-346-8480

LINDSAY, CHRIS A.
1324 N.E. Locksley Dr., Bend, OR 97701, Phone: 541-389-3875

LINKLATER, STEVE
8 Cossar Dr., Aurora, Ont., CANADA L4G 3N8, Phone: 905-727-8929

LINTON, KEN
2153 Rolling Creek, Spring Branch, TX 78070

LISTER JR., WELDON E.
9140 Sailfish Dr., Boerne, TX 78006, Phone: 210-981-2210

LITTLE, LARRY
1A Cranberry Ln., Spencer, MA 01562, Phone: 508-885-2301

LITTLE, GUY A.
486 W Lincoln Ave., Oakhurst, NJ 07755

LITTLE, GARY M.
HC84 Box 10301, PO Box 156, Broadbent, OR 97414, Phone: 503-572-2656

LITTLE, JIMMY L.
PO Box 871652, Wasilla, AK 99687, Phone: 907-373-7831

LIVELY, TIM AND MARIAN
PO Box 8784 CRB, Tucson, AZ 85738

LIVESAY, NEWT
3306 S. Dogwood St., Siloam Springs, AR 72761, Phone: 479-549-3356, Fax: 479-549-3357

LIVINGSTON, ROBERT C.
PO Box 6, Murphy, NC 28906, Phone: 704-837-4155

LOCKE, KEITH
PMB 141, 7120 Rufe Snow Dr. Ste. 106, Watauga, TX 76148-1867, Phone: 817-514-7272

LOCKETT, LOWELL C.
66653 Gunderson Rd., North Bend, OR 97459-9210, Phone: 541-756-1614

LOCKETT, STERLING
527 E. Amherst Dr., Burbank, CA 91504, Phone: 818-846-5799

LOERCHNER, WOLFGANG
WOLFE FINE KNIVES, PO Box 255, Bayfield, Ont., CANADA N0M 1G0, Phone: 519-565-2196

LONEWOLF, J. AGUIRRE
481 Hwy 105, Demorest, GA 30535, Phone: 706-754-4660, Fax: 706-754-8470

LONG, GLENN A.
10090 SW 186th Ave., Dunnellon, FL 34432, Phone: 352-489-4272

LONG, PHILLIP
2204 Chestnut Ct., Finksburg, MD 21048 410-857-4268

LONGWORTH, DAVE
1811 SR 774, Hamersville, OH 45130, Phone: 513-876-3637

LOOS, HENRY C.
210 Ingraham, New Hyde Park, NY 11040, Phone: 516-354-1943

LORO, GENE
2457 State Route 93 NE, Crooksville, OH 43731, Phone: 740-982-4521, Fax: 740-982-1249

LOTT-SINCLAIR, SHERRY
112 E Main St., Campbellsville, KY 42718, Phone: 270-465-0577

LOVE, ED
19443 Mill Oak, San Antonio, TX 78258, Phone: 210-497-1021

LOVELACE, JIM
1323 NE Drost Dr., Bend, OR 97701 541-388-5476

LOVELESS, R.W., "BOB,"
PO Box 7836, Riverside, CA 92503, Phone: 909-689-7800

LOVESTRAND, SCHUYLER
1136 19th St. SW, Vero Beach, FL 32962, Phone: 561-778-0282, Fax: 561-466-1126

LOZIER, DON
5394 SE 168th Ave., Ocklawaha, FL 32179, Phone: 352-625-3576

LUBECKI, STEVEN
269 Danforth St. #1, Portland, ME 04102 207-775-0211

LUCHAK, BOB
15705 Woodforest Blvd., Channelview, TX 77530, Phone: 281-452-1779

LUCHINI, BOB
1220 Dana Ave., Palo Alto, CA 94301, Phone: 650-321-8095

LUCIE, JAMES R.
4191 E. Fruitport Rd., Fruitport, MI 49415, Phone: 231-865-6390, Fax: 231-865-3170

LUCKETT, BILL
108 Amantes Ln., Weatherford, TX 76088, Phone: 817-613-9412

LUDWIG, RICHARD O.
57-63 65 St., Maspeth, NY 11378, Phone: 718-497-5969

LUI, RONALD M.
4042 Harding Ave., Honolulu, HI 96816, Phone: 808-734-7746

LUM, ROBERT W.
901 Travis Ave., Eugene, OR 97404, Phone: 541-688-2737

LUMAN, JAMES R.
Clear Creek Trail, Anaconda, MT 59711, Phone: 406-560-1461

LUNDSTROM, JAN-AKE
Mastmostigen 8, 66010 Dals-Langed, SWEDEN, Phone: 0531-40270

LUNN, LARRY A.
PO Box 48931, St. Petersburg, FL 33743, Phone: 727-345-7455

LUNN, GAIL
PO Box 48931, St. Petersburg, FL 33743, Phone: 727-345-7455

LUPOLE, JAMIE G.
KUMA KNIVES, 285 Main St., Kirkwood, NY 13795, Phone: 607-775-9368

LUTZ, GREG
127 Crescent Rd., Greenwood, SC 29646, Phone: 864-229-7340

LYLE III, ERNEST L.
LYLE KNIVES, PO Box 1755, Chiefland, FL 32644, Phone: 352-490-6693

LYONS, WILLIAM R.
51245 WCR 17, Wellington, CO 80549 970-897-2956

LYTTLE, BRIAN
Box 5697, High River, AB, CANADA T1V 1M7, Phone: 403-558-3638

M

MacDONALD, JOHN
9 David Dr., Raymond, NH 03077, Phone: 603-895-0918

MACDONALD, DAVID
2824 Hwy 47, Los Lunas, NM 87031, Phone: 505-866-5866

MACKIE, JOHN
13653 Lanning, Whittier, CA 90605, Phone: 562-945-6104

MACKRILL, STEPHEN
PO Box 1580, Pinegowrie 2123, Johannesburg, SOUTH AFRICA, Phone: 27-11-886-2893, Fax: 27-11-334-6230

MADISON II, BILLY D.
2295 Tyler Rd., Remlap, AL 35133, Phone: 205-680-6722

MADRULLI, MME JOELLE
RESIDENCE STE CATHERINE B1, Salon De Provence, FRANCE 13330

MAE, TAKAO
1-119, 1-4 Uenohigashi, Toyonaka, Osaka, JAPAN 560-0013, Phone: 81-6-6852-2758, Fax: 81-6-6481-1649

MAESTRI, PETER A.
S11251 Fairview Rd., Spring Green, WI 53588, Phone: 608-546-4481

MAGEE, JIM
319 N 12th, Salina, KS 67401, Phone: 785-820-8535

MAHOMEDY, A. R.
PO Box 76280, Marble Ray KZN, 4035, SOUTH AFRICA, Phone: +27 31 577 1451

MAIENKNECHT, STANLEY
38648 S.R. 800, Sardis, OH 43946

MAINES, JAY
SUNRISE RIVER CUSTOM KNIVES, 5584 266th St., Wyoming, MN 55092, Phone: 651-462-5301

MAISEY, ALAN
PO Box 197, Vincentia 2540, NSW AUSTRALIA, Phone: 2-4443 7829

MAJER, MIKE
50 Palmetto Bay Rd., Hilton Head, SC 29928, Phone: 843-681-3483

MAKOTO, KUNITOMO
3-3-18 Imazu-cho Fukuyama-city, Hiroshima, JAPAN, Phone: 084-933-5874

MALABY, RAYMOND J.
835 Calhoun Ave., Juneau, AK 99801, Phone: 907-586-6981

MALLOY, JOE
1039 Schwabe St., Freeland, PA 18224, Phone: 570-636-2781

MANABE, MICHAEL K.
3659 Tomahawk Lane, San Diego, CA 92117, Phone: 619-483-2416

MANARO, SAL
10 Peri Ave., Holbrook, NY 11741 631-737-1180

MANCUSO, BOB
769 N. Thorp Ave., Orange City, FL 32763 386-774-2926

MANEKER, KENNETH
RR 2, Galiano Island, B.C., CANADA V0N 1P0, Phone: 604-539-2084

MANKEL, KENNETH
7836 Cannonsburg Rd., Cannonsburg, MI 49317, Phone: 616-874-6955

MANLEY, DAVID W.
3270 Six Mile Hwy., Central, SC 29630, Phone: 864-654-1125

MANN, TIM
BLADEWORKS, PO Box 1196, Honokaa, HI 96727, Phone: 808-775-0949, Fax: 808-775-0949

MANN, MICHAEL L.
IDAHO KNIFE WORKS, PO Box 144, Spirit Lake, ID 83869, Phone: 509 994-9394

MARAGNI, DAN
RD 1, Box 106, Georgetown, NY 13072, Phone: 315-662-7490

MARKLEY, KEN
7651 Cabin Creek Lane, Sparta, IL 62286, Phone: 618-443-5284

MARKS, CHRIS
Rt. 2 Box 527, Ava, MO 65608, Phone: 417-683-1065

MARLOWE, CHARLES
10822 Poppleton Ave., Omaha, NE 68144, Phone: 402-933-5065

MARLOWE, DONALD
2554 Oakland Rd., Dover, PA 17315, Phone: 717-764-6055

MARSHALL, STEPHEN R.
975 Harkreader Rd., Mt. Juliet, TN 37122

MARSHALL, GLENN
PO Box 1099, 1117 Hofmann St., Mason, TX 76856, Phone: 915-347-6207

MARTIN, MICHAEL W.
Box 572, Jefferson St., Beckville, TX 75631, Phone: 903-678-2161

MARTIN, BRUCE E.
Rt. 6, Box 164-B, Prescott, AR 71857, Phone: 501-887-2023

MARTIN, JIM
1120 S. Cadiz Ct., Oxnard, CA 93035, Phone: 805-985-9849

MARTIN, ROBB
7 Victoria St., Elmira, Ontario, CANADA N3B 1R9

MARTIN, RANDALL J.
51 Bramblewood St, Bridgewater, MA 02324, Phone: 508-279-0682

MARTIN, PETER
28220 N. Lake Dr., Waterford, WI 53185, Phone: 262-895-2815

MARTIN, JOHN ALEXANDER
821 N Grand Ave., Okmulgee, OK 74447, Phone: 918-758-1099

MARTIN, GENE
PO Box 396, Williams, OR 97544, Phone: 541-846-6755

MARTIN, TONY
108 S. Main St., PO Box 324, Arcadia, MO 63621, Phone: 573-546-2254

MARTIN, WALTER E.
570 Cedar Flat Rd., Williams, OR 97544, Phone: 541-846-6755

MARTIN, HAL W.
781 Hwy. 95, Morrilton, AR 72110, Phone: 501-354-1682

MARZITELLI, PETER
19929 35A Ave., Langley, BC, CANADA V3A 2R1, Phone: 604-532-8899

MASON, BILL
1114 St. Louis, #33, Excelsior Springs, MO 64024, Phone: 816-637-7335

MASSEY, AL
Box 14, Site 15, RR#2, Mount Uniacke, Nova Scotia, CANADA B0N 1Z0, Phone: 902-866-4754

MASSEY, ROGER
4928 Union Rd., Texarkana, AR 71854, Phone: 870-779-1018

MASSEY, RON
61638 El Reposo St., Joshua Tree, CA 92252, Phone: 760-366-9239 after 5 p.m., Fax: 763-366-4620

MATA, LEONARD
3583 Arruza St., San Diego, CA 92154, Phone: 619-690-6935

MATHEWS, CHARLIE and HARRY
TWIN BLADES, 121 Mt Pisgah Church Rd., Statesboro, GA 30458, Phone: 912-865-9098

MATSUNO, KANSEI
109 Uenomachi Nishikaiden, Gifu City 501-1168 Japan Phone/Fax 81-58-234-8643

MATSUSAKI, TAKESHI
MATSUSAKI KNIVES, 151 Ono-Cho Sasebo-shi, Nagasaki, JAPAN, Phone: 0956-47-2938

MAXEN, MICK
2 Huggins Welham Green, "Hatfield, Herts", UNITED KINGDOM AL.97LR, Phone: 01707 261213

MAXFIELD, LYNN
382 Colonial Ave., Layton, UT 84041, Phone: 801-544-4176

MAXWELL, DON
3164 N. Marks, Suite 122, Fresno, CA 93722, Phone: 559-497-8441

MAYNARD, LARRY JOE
PO Box 493, Crab Orchard, WV 25827

MAYNARD, WILLIAM N.
2677 John Smith Rd., Fayetteville, NC 28306, Phone: 910-425-1615

MAYO JR., TOM
67-420 Alahaka St., Waialua, HI 96791, Phone: 808-637-6560

MAYVILLE, OSCAR L.
2130 E. County Rd. 910S., Marengo, IN 47140, Phone: 812-338-3103

McABEE, WILLIAM
27275 Norton Grade, Colfax, CA 95713, Phone: 530-389-8163

McADAMS, DENNIS
1607 MaAmis Rd., Signal Mountain, TN 37377 423-267-4743

McCALLEN JR., HOWARD H.
110 Anchor Dr., So Seaside Park, NJ 08752

McCARLEY, JOHN
4165 Harney Rd., Taneytown, MD 21787

McCARTY, HARRY
1479 Indian Ridge Rd., Blaine, TN 37709

McCLURE, JOE AND SANDY
3052 Isim Road, Norman, OK 73026, Phone: 405-321-3614

McCLURE, JERRY
3052 Isim Road, Norman, OK 73026, 405-321-3614

McCLURE, MICHAEL
803 17th Ave., Menlo Park, CA 94025, Phone: 650-323-2596

McCONNELL, CHARLES R.
158 Genteel Ridge, Wellsburg, WV 26070, Phone: 304-737-2015

McCONNELL JR., LOYD A.
1710 Rosewood, Odessa, TX 79761, Phone: 915-363-8344

McCONNELL, STERLING E.
726 N. McDonald Rd. #97, Spokane, WA 99216 505-912-9554

McCORNOCK, CRAIG
MCC MTN OUTFITTERS, 4775 Rte. 212, Willow, NY 12495, Phone: 914-679-9758

McCOUN, MARK
14212 Pine Dr., DeWitt, VA 23840, Phone: 804-469-7631

McCOY, FREDRICK L.
200 Farmgate Ln., Silver Springs, MD 20905 301-236-0152

McCRACKIN, KEVIN
3720 Hess Rd., House Spings, MO 63051, Phone: 636-677-6066

McCRACKIN and SON, V.J.
3720 Hess Rd., House Springs, MO 63051, Phone: 636-677-6066

McCULLOUGH, JERRY
274 West Pettibone Rd., Georgiana, AL 36033, Phone: 334-382-7644

McDERMOTT, MICHAEL
151 Hwy F, Defiance, MO 63341, Phone: 314-798-2077

McDONALD, RANDY J.
9237 W. 480 N., Cromwell, IN 46732 219-886-2316

McDONALD, RICH
4590 Kirk Rd., Columbiana, OH 44408, Phone: 330-482-0007, Fax: 330-482-0007

McDONALD, ROBERT J.
14730 61 Court N., Loxahatchee, FL 33470, Phone: 561-790-1470

McDONALD, W.J. "JERRY"
7173 Wickshire Cove E., Germantown, TN 38138, Phone: 901-756-9924

McDONALD, ROBIN J.
6509 E Jeffrey Dr., Fayetteville, NC 28314

McFALL, KEN
PO Box 458, Lakeside, AZ 85929, Phone: 928-537-2026, Fax: 928-537-8066

McFARLIN, ERIC E.
PO Box 2188, Kodiak, AK 99615, Phone: 907-486-4799

McFARLIN, J.W.
3331 Pocohantas Dr., Lake Havasu City, AZ 86404, Phone: 928-855-8095, Fax: 928-855-8095

McGILL, JOHN
PO Box 302, Blairsville, GA 30512, Phone: 404-745-4686

McGOWAN, FRANK E.
12629 Howard Lodge Dr., Sykesville, MD 21784, Phone: 410-489-4323

McGRATH, DONALD
9 Old Mill Terrace, Toronto, Ontario, Canada M8X 1A1 416-233-6636

McGRATH, PATRICK T.
8343 Kenyon Ave., Westchester, CA 90045, Phone: 310-338-8764

McGRODER, PATRICK J.
5725 Chapin Rd., Madison, OH 44057, Phone: 216-298-3405, Fax: 216-298-3405

McGUANE IV, THOMAS F.
410 South 3rd Ave., Bozeman, MT 59715, Phone: 406-586-0248

McHENRY, WILLIAM JAMES
Box 67, Wyoming, RI 02898, Phone: 401-539-8353

McINTOSH, DAVID L.
PO Box 948, Haines, AK 99827, Phone: 907-766-3673

McKENZIE, DAVID BRIAN
2311 B Ida Rd., Campbell River B, CANADA V9W-4V7

McKIERNAN, STAN
205 E. Park St., Vandalia, MO 63382, Phone: 573-594-6135

McLENDON, HUBERT W.
125 Thomas Rd., Waco, GA 30182, Phone: 770-574-9796

McLUIN, TOM
36 Fourth St., Dracut, MA 01826, Phone: 978-957-4899

McLURKIN, ANDREW
2112 Windy Woods Dr., Raleigh, NC 27607, Phone: 919-834-4693

McMANUS, DANNY
413 Fairhaven Drive., Taylors, SC 29687, Phone: 864-268-9849, Fax: 864-268-9699

McNABB, TOMMY
CAROLINA CUSTOM KNIVES, 4015 Brownsboro Rd., Winston-Salem, NC 27106, Phone: 336-924-6053, Fax: 336-924-4854

McNEIL, JIMMY
1175 Mt. Moriah Rd., Memphis, TN 38117, Phone: 901-544-0710 or 901-683-8133

STEVEN R. JOHNSON

Steven R. Johnson reproduced these three dropped hunters in the style of Blade Magazine Cutlery Hall-Of-Famer© Bob Loveless. Blade steel is ATS-34 stainless and overall lengths are 8 inches. Handle materials are, from top: big horn sheep, giraffe bone and mammoth ivory. Johnson's list prices for similar knives: **$1,800** each. (Point Seven photo)

McRAE, J. MICHAEL
6100 Lake Rd, Mint Hill, NC 28227, Phone: 704-545-2929

MEERDINK, KURT
120 Split Rock Dr., Barryville, NY 12719, Phone: 845-557-0783

MEHAFFEY, MAXIE
23155 NE Hwy. 314, Ft. McCoy, FL 32134 352-685-0009

MEIER, DARYL
75 Forge Rd., Carbondale, IL 62901, Phone: 618-549-3234

MELIN, GORDON C.
11259 Gladhill Rd Unit 4, Whittier, CA 90604, Phone: 562-946-5753

MELLARD, J. R.
17006 Highland Canyon Dr., Houston, TX 77095, Phone: 281-550-9464

MELOY, SEAN
7148 Rosemary Lane, Lemon Grove, CA 91945-2105, Phone: 619-465-7173

MENSCH, LARRY C.
578 Madison Ave., Milton, PA 17847, Phone: 570-742-9554

MERCER, MIKE
149 N. Waynesville Rd., Lebanon, OH 45036, Phone: 513-932-2837

MERCHANT, TED
7 Old Garrett Ct., White Hall, MD 21161, Phone: 410-343-0380

MEREDITH, MICKEY
4035 Saddle Club Dr., New Smyrna, FL 32168 386-426-5105

MERRIN, WALTER
4359 Robbins St., San Diego, CA 92122 858-546-0727

MERZ III, ROBERT L.
1447 Winding Canyon, Katy, TX 77493, Phone: 281-391-2897

MESHEJIAN, MARDI
33 Elm Dr., E. Northport, NY 11731, Phone: 631-757-4541

MESSER, DAVID T.
134 S. Torrence St., Dayton, OH 45403-2044, Phone: 513-228-6561

METHENY, H.A. "WHITEY"
7750 Waterford Dr., Spotsylvania, VA 22553, Phone: 703-582-3228

METZ, GREG T.
c/o James Ranch HC 83, Cascade, ID 83611, Phone: 208-382-4336

MICHINAKA, TOSHIAKI
I-679 Koyamacho-nishi, Totton-shi, Tottori 680-0947, JAPAN, Phone: 0857-28-5911

MICHO, KANDA
7-32-5 Shinzutsumi-cho Shinnanyo-city, Yamaguchi, JAPAN, Phone: 0834-62-1910

MICKLEY, TRACY
42112 Kerns Dr., North Mankato, MN 56003, Phone: 507-947-3760

MILFORD, BRIAN A.
RD 2 Box 294, Knox, PA 16232, Phone: 814-797-2595, Fax: 814-226-4351

MILITANO, TOM
CUSTOM KNIVES, 77 Jason Rd., Jacksonville, AL 36265-6655, Phone: 256-435-7132

MILLARD, FRED G.
27627 Kopezyk Ln., Richland Center, WI 53581, Phone: 608-647-5376

MILLER, DON
1604 Harrodsburg Rd., Lexington, KY 40503, Phone: 606-276-3299

MILLER, HANFORD J.
Box 97, Cowdrey, CO 80434, Phone: 970-723-4708

MILLER, JAMES P.
9024 Goeller Rd., RR 2, Box 28, Fairbank, IA 50629, Phone: 319-635-2294

MILLER, M.A.
11625 Community Center Dr., Northglenn, CO 80233, Phone: 303-280-3816

MILLER, MICHAEL E.
1400 Skyview Dr., El Reno, OK 73036, Phone: 405-422-3602

MILLER, MICHAEL K.
28510 Santiam Hwy., Sweet Home, OR 97386, Phone: 541-367-4927

MILLER, R.D.
10526 Estate Lane, Dallas, TX 75238, Phone: 214-348-3496

MILLER, RICK
516 Kanaul Rd., Rockwood, PA 15557, Phone: 814-926-2059

MILLER, RONALD T.
12922 127th Ave. N., Largo, FL 34644, Phone: 813-595-0378 (after 5 p.m.)

MILLER, BOB
7659 Fine Oaks Pl., Oakville, MO 63129, Phone: 314-846-8934

MILLER, STEVE
1376 Pine St., Clearwater, FL 33756 727-461-4180

MILLS, MICHAEL
5604 Lanham Station Rd., Lanham, MD 20706-2531, Phone: 301-459-7226

MILLS, LOUIS G.
9450 Waters Rd., Ann Arbor, MI 48103, Phone: 734-668-1839

MINK, DAN
PO Box 861, 196 Sage Circle, Crystal Beach, FL 34681, Phone: 727-786-5408

MINNICK, JIM (& JOYCE)
144 North 7th St., Middletown, IN 47356, Phone: 765-354-4108

MIRABILE, DAVID
1715 Glacier Ave., Juneau, AK 99801, Phone: 907-463-3404

MISCHKE, STEVE
1378 Friendly Pines, Groom Creek, AZ 86303

MITCHELL, JAMES A.
PO Box 4646, Columbus, GA 31904, Phone: 404-322-8582

MITCHELL, MAX, DEAN AND BEN
3803 V.F.W. Rd., Leesville, LA 71440, Phone: 318-239-6416

MITCHELL, WM. DEAN
PO Box 2, Warren, TX 77664, Phone: 409-547-2213

MITSUYUKI, ROSS
94-1071 Kepakepa St, C-3, Waipahu, HAWAII 96797, Phone: 808-671-3335, Fax: 808-671-3335

MIVILLE-DESCHENES, ALAIN
1952 Charles A, Parent, QC, CANADA G2B 4B2, Phone: 418-845-0950

MIZE, RICHARD
FOX CREEK FORGE, 2038 Fox Creek Rd., Lawrenceburg, KY 40342, Phone: 502-859-0602

MOEN, RICK
408 Camino Vista Verde, San Clemente, CA 92673 949-498-3078

MOMCILOVIC, GUNNAR
Nordlysv, 16, Waipahu, NORWAY, Phone: 0111-47-3287-3586

MONCUS, MICHAEL STEVEN
1803 US 19 N, Smithville, GA 31787, Phone: 912-846-2408

MONK, NATHAN P.
1304 4th Ave. SE, Cullman, AL 35055, Phone: 205-737-0463

MONTANO, GUS A.
11217 Westonhill Dr., San Diego, CA 92126-1447, Phone: 619-273-5357

MONTEIRO, VICTOR
31, Rue D'Opprebais, 1360 Maleves Ste Marie, BELGIUM, Phone: 010 88 0441

MONTJOY, CLAUDE
706 Indian Creek Rd., Clinton, SC 29325, Phone: 864-697-6160

MOON, SIDNEY "PETE"
982 Bellevue Plantation Rd., Lafayette, LA 70503 337-981-7396

MOONEY, MIKE
19432 E. Cloud Rd., Queen Creek, AZ 85242 480-987-3576

MOORE, BILLY R.
806 Community Ave., Albany, GA 31705-9031 912-438-5529

MOORE, TED
340 E Willow St., Elizabethtown, PA 17022, Phone: 717-367-3939

MOORE, MARVE
HC 89 Box 393, Willow, AK 99688, Phone: 907-232-0478

MOORE, MICHAEL ROBERT
61 Beauliew St., Lowell, MA 01850, Phone: 978-459-2163, Fax: 978-441-1819

MOORE, JAMES B.
1707 N. Gillis, Ft. Stockton, TX 79735, Phone: 915-336-2113

MOORE, SHAWN ROBERT
61 Beaulieu St., Lowell, MA 01850 978-459-2163

MORAN JR., WM. F.,, "BILL"
PO Box 68, Braddock Heights, MD 21714, Phone: 301-371-7543

MORETT, DONALD
116 Woodcrest Dr., Lancaster, PA 17602-1300, Phone: 717-746-4888

MORGAN, JEFF
9200 Arnaz Way, Santee, CA 92071, Phone: 619-448-8430

MORGAN, TOM
14689 Ellett Rd., Beloit, OH 44609, Phone: 330-537-2023

MORRIS, DARRELL PRICE
92 Union, St. Plymouth, Devon, ENGLAND PL1 3EZ, Phone: 0752 223546

MORRIS, C.H. and JASON
1590 Old Salem Rd., Frisco City, AL 36445, Phone: 334-575-7425

MORRIS, ERIC
306 Ewart Ave., Beckley, WV 25801, Phone: 304-255-3951

MORTENSON, ED
2742 Hwy. 93 N, Darby, MT 59829, Phone: 406-821-3146, Fax: 406-821-3146

MOSES, STEVEN
1610 W Hemlock Way, Santa Ana, CA 92704

MOSIER, RICHARD
52 Dapplegran Ln., Rollings Hills Est, CA 90274

MOSIER, JOSHUA J.
SPRING CREEK KNIFE WORKS, PO Box 442/802 6th St., Edgar, NE 68935

MOSSER, GARY E.
11827 NE 102nd Place, Kirkland, WA 98033-5170, Phone: 425-827-2279

MOULTON, DUSTY
135 Hillview Lane, Loudon, TN 37774, Phone: 865-408-9779

MOUNT, DON
4574 Little Finch Ln., Las Vegas, NV 89115, Phone: 702-531-2925

MOUNTAIN HOME KNIVES
PO Box 167, Jamul, CA 91935, Phone: 619-669-0833

MOYER, RUSS
HC 36 Box 57C, Havre, MT 59501, Phone: 406-395-4423

MUELLER, JAMES W.
8709 East Mulberry St., Scottsdale, AZ 85251 480-423-8061

MULLER, JODY and PAT
PO Box 35, Pittsburg, MO 65724, Phone: 417-852-4306/417-752-3260

MULLIN, STEVE
500 Snowberry Lane, Sandpoint, ID 83864, Phone: 208-263-7492

MUNROE, DERYK C.
PO Box 3454, Bozeman, MT 59772

MURRAY, BILL
1632 Rio Mayo, Green Valley, AZ 85614

MURSKI, RAY
12129 Captiva Ct., Reston, VA
22091-1204, Phone: 703-264-1102

MYERS, PAUL
644 Maurice St., Wood River, IL
62095, Phone: 618-258-1707

MYERS, RON
6202 Marglenn Ave., Baltimore,
MD 21206 410-866-6914

NATEN, GREG
1804 Shamrock Way, Bakersfield,
CA 93304-3921

NAVAGATO, ANGELO
5 Commercial Apt 2, Camp Hill,
PA 17011

NEALEY, IVAN F. (FRANK)
Anderson Dam Rd., Box 65, HC
#87, Mt. Home, ID 83647, Phone:
208-587-4060

NEALY, BUD
1439 Poplar Valley Rd.,
Stroudsburg, PA 18360, Phone: 570-
402-1018, Fax: 570-402-1019

NEDVED, DAN
206 Park Dr., Kalispell, MT 59901,
Phone: 406-752-5060

NEELY, GREG
5419 Pine St., Bellaire, TX 77401,
Phone: 713-991-2677

NEELY, THOMAS CONOR
5419 Pine St., Bellaire, TX 77401
713-664-4864

NEILSON, J.
RR 2 Box 16, Wyalusing, PA 18853,
Phone: 570-746-4944

NELSON, KEN
11059 Hwy 73, Pittsville, WI 54466,
Phone: 715-884-6448

NELSON, DR. CARL
2500 N Robison Rd., Texarkana,
TX 75501

NELSON, TOM
PO Box 2298, Wilropark 1731,
Gauteng, SOUTH AFRICA

NELSON, BOB
21 Glen Rd., Sparta, NJ 07871

NESBITT, KEN
416 Moore St., San Marcos, TX
78666 512-787-3000

**NETO JR., NELSON AND DE
CARVALHO, HENRIQUE M.**
R. Joao Margarido, No. 20-V,
Guerra, Braganca Paulista, SP-
12900-000, BRAZIL, Phone: 011-
7843-6889, Fax: 011-7843-6889

NEUHAEUSLER, ERWIN
Heiligenangerstrasse 15, 86179
Augsburg, GERMANY, Phone:
0821/81 49 97

NEVLING, MARK
BURR OAK KNIVES, PO Box 9,
Hume, IL 61932, Phone: 217-887-
2522

NEWCOMB, CORBIN
628 Woodland Ave., Moberly, MO
65270, Phone: 660-263-4639

NEWHALL, TOM
3602 E 42nd Stravenue, Tucson, AZ
85713, Phone: 520-721-0562

NEWTON, RON
223 Ridge Ln., London, AR 72847,
Phone: 479-293-3001

NEWTON, LARRY
1758 Pronghorn Ct., Jacksonville,
FL 32225, Phone: 904-221-2340,
Fax: 904-220-4098

NICHOLSON, R. KENT
PO Box 204, Phoenix, MD 21131,
Phone: 410-323-6925

NIELSEN, RANDY LARS
1823 Teton View Dr., Rexburg, ID
83440 208-356-4266

NIELSON, JEFF V.
PO Box 365, Monroe, UT 84754,
Phone: 801-527-4242

NIEMUTH, TROY
3143 North Ave., Sheboygan, WI
53083, Phone: 414-452-2927

NILSSON, JOHNNY WALKER
Tingsstigen 11, SE-133 33
Arvidsjaur, SWEDEN, Phone: 46-
960-130-48

NISHIUCHI, MELVIN S.
6121 Forest Park Dr., Las Vegas, NV
89156, Phone: 702-438-2327

NIX, ROBERT T.
4194 Cadillac, Wayne, MI 48184,
Phone: 734-729-6468

NOLEN, R.D. and STEVE
1110 Lakeshore Dr., Estes Park, CO
80517-7113, Phone: 970-586-5814,
Fax: 970-586-8827

NORDELL, INGEMAR
Skarpå 2103, 82041 Färila,
SWEDEN, Phone: 0651-23347

NOREN, DOUGLAS E.
14676 Boom Rd., Springlake, MI
49456, Phone: 616-842-4247

NORFLEET, ROSS W.
3947 Tanbark Rd., Richmond, VA
23235, Phone: 804-276-4169

NORRIS, DON
8710 N Hollybrook, Tucson, AZ
85742, Phone: 520-744-2494

NORRIS, PAUL T.
POB 1406, Greenwood Lake, NY
10925 845-477-3470

NORTH, WILLIAM
163 Onteora Blvd., Asheville, NC
28803 828-277-0228

NORTON, DON
7517 Mountain Quail Dr., Las
Vegas, NV 89131, Phone: 702-648-
5036

NOTT, RON P.
PO Box 281, Summerdale, PA
17093, Phone: 717-732-2763

NOWLAND, RICK
3677 E Bonnie Rd., Waltonville, IL
62894, Phone: 618-279-3170

NUNN, GREGORY
HC64 Box 2107, Castle Valley, UT
84532, Phone: 435-259-8607

OBENAUF, MIKE
355 Sandy Ln., Vine Grove, KY
40175, Phone: 270-828-4138/270-
877-6300

OBRIEN, GEORGE
22511 Tullis Trails Ct., Katy, TX
77494-8265

OCHS, CHARLES F.
124 Emerald Lane, Largo, FL
33771, Phone: 727-536-3827, Fax:
727-536-3827

O'DELL, CLYDE
176 Ouachita 404, Camden, AR
71701, Phone: 870-574-2754

ODGEN, RANDY W.
10822 Sage Orchard, Houston, TX
77089, Phone: 713-481-3601

ODOM, VIC
PO Box 572, North, SC 29112,
Phone: 803-247-5614

OGDEN, BILL
OGDEN KNIVES, PO Box 52,
Avis, PA 17721, Phone: 570-753-
5568

OGLETREE JR., BEN R.
2815 Israel Rd., Livingston, TX
77351, Phone: 409-327-8315

O'HARE, SEAN
PO Box 374, Fort Simpson, NT,
CANADA X0E 0N0, Phone: 867-
695-2619

**OLDHAM, RAYMOND
FRANK**
2129 Muskingum Ave., Cocoa, FL
32926 321-633-4531

OLIVE, MICHAEL E.
HC 78 Box 442, Leslie, AR 72645,
Phone: 870-363-4452

OLIVER, TODD D.
RR5 Box 659, Spencer, IN 47460,
Phone: 812-829-1762

OLLER, VINCE
dba OMEGA TACTICAL
RESOURCES, LLC, PO Box
835072, Miami, FL 33283-5072

OLOFSON, CHRIS
29 KNIVES, 1 Kendall SQ Bldg.
600, Cambridge, MA 02139, Phone:
617-492-0451

OLSEN, JOE
RR1, Box 4A, Geyser, MT 59447
406-735-4404

OLSON, DARROLD E.
PO Box 1539, Springfield, OR
97477, Phone: 541-726-8300/541-
914-7238

OLSON, WAYNE C.
890 Royal Ridge Dr., Bailey, CO
80421, Phone: 303-816-9486

OLSON, ROD
Box 5973, High River, AB,
CANADA T1V 1P6, Phone: 403-
652-2744, Fax: 403-646-5838

OLSSON, JAN OLAV (JO)
Svardlangsvagen 2-16E, 12060
Arsta, Sweden 46 8 722 4266

OLSZEWSKI, STEPHEN
1820 Harkney Hill Rd., Coventry,
RI 02816, Phone: 401-397-4774

O'MALLEY, DANIEL
4338 Evanston Ave. N, Seattle, WA
98103, Phone: 206-527-0315

ONION, KENNETH J.
47-501 Hui Kelu St., Kaneohe, HI
96744, Phone: 808-239-1300, Fax:
429-4840 (cell)

ORTEGA, BEN M.
165 Dug Rd., Wyoming, PA 18644,
Phone: 717-696-3234

ORTON, RICH
3625 Fleming St., Riverside, CA
92509, Phone: 909-685-3019

OSBORNE, WARREN
215 Edgefield, Waxahachie, TX
75165, Phone: 972-935-0899, Fax:
972-937-9004

OSBORNE, DONALD H.
5840 N McCall, Clovis, CA 93611,
Phone: 559-299-9483, Fax: 559-298-
1751

OTT, FRED
1257 Rancho Durango Rd.,
Durango, CO 81303, Phone: 970-
375-9669

OVEREYNDER, T.R.
1800 S. Davis Dr., Arlington, TX
76013, Phone: 817-277-4812, Fax:
817-277-4812

OWENS, DONALD
2274 Lucille Ln., Melbourne, FL
32935, Phone: 321-254-9765

OWENS, JOHN
14500 CR 270, Nathrop, CO
81236, Phone: 719-395-0870

OWNBY, JOHN C.
3316 Springbridge Ln., Plano, TX
75025

OYSTER, LOWELL R.
543 Grant Rd., Corinth, ME 04427,
Phone: 207-884-8663

PACELT, JEFF
2567 Charter Oak Dr., Aurora, IL
60504-7401

PACHI, FRANCESCO
Via Pometta, 1, 17046 Sassello
(SV), ITALY, Phone: 019 720086,
Fax: 019 720086

PACKARD, BOB
PO Box 311, Elverta, CA 95626,
Phone: 916-991-5218

PADGETT JR., EDWIN L.
340 Vauxhall St., New London, CT
06320-3838, Phone: 860-443-2938

PADILLA, GARY
PO Box 6928, Auburn, CA 95604,
Phone: 530-888-6992

PAGE, REGINALD
6587 Groveland Hill Rd.,
Groveland, NY 14462, Phone: 716-
243-1643

PAGE, LARRY
1200 Mackey Scott Rd., Aiken, SC
29801-7620, Phone: 803-648-0001

PALAZZO, TOM
207-30 Jordon Dr., Bayside, NY
11360, Phone: 718-352-2170

PALERMO, ANTHONY P.
10017 Springdale Dr., Spring
Grove, IL 60081 815-675-0469

PALM, RIK
10901 Scripps Ranch Blvd., San
Diego, CA 92131 858-530-0407

PALMER, TAYLOR
TAYLOR-MADE SCENIC
KNIVES INC., Box 97, Blanding,
UT 84511, Phone: 435-678-2523

PANAK, PAUL S.
9000 Stanhope Kellogsville Rd.,
Kinsman, OH 44428, Phone: 330-
876-8473

PANKIEWICZ, PHILIP R.
RFD #1, Waterman Rd., Lebanon,
CT 06249

PAPP, ROBERT
252 Narseukkles Ave., Elyria, OH
44035 440-336-5868

PARDUE, MELVIN M.
Rt. 1, Box 130, Repton, AL 36475,
Phone: 334-248-2447

PARDUE, JOE
PO Box 693, Spurger, TX 77660,
Phone: 409-429-7074, Fax: 409-429-
5657

PARKER, ROBERT NELSON
5223 Wilhelm Rd. N.W., Rapid
City, MI 49676, Fax: 248-545-8211

PARKER, CLIFF
6350 Tulip Dr., Zephyrhills, FL
33544, Phone: 813-973-1682

PARKER, EARL
POB 2441, Marysville, CA 95901
530-743-7154

PARKER, J.E.
11 Domenica Cir., Clarion, PA
16214, Phone: 814-226-4837

PARKS, BLANE C.
15908 Crest Dr., Woodbridge, VA
22191, Phone: 703-221-4680

PARKS, JOHN
3539 Galilee Church Rd., Jefferson,
GA 30549, Phone: 706-367-4916

PARLER, THOMAS O.
11 Franklin St., Charleston, SC
29401, Phone: 803-723-9433

PARRISH, ROBERT
271 Allman Hill Rd., Weaverville,
NC 28787, Phone: 828-645-2864

PARRISH III, GORDON A.
940 Lakloey Dr., North Pole, AK
99705, Phone: 907-488-0357

PARSONS, MICHAEL R.
MCKEE KNIVES, 7042
McFarland Rd., Indianapolis, IN
46227, Phone: 317-784-7943

PASSMORE, JIMMY D.
316 SE Elm, Hoxie, AR 72433,
Phone: 870-886-1922

PATRICK, BOB
12642 24A Ave., S. Surrey, B.C.,
CANADA V4A 8H9, Phone: 604-
538-6214, Fax: 604-888-2683

PATRICK, PEGGY
PO Box 127, Brasstown, NC 28902,
Phone: 828-837-7627

PATRICK, CHUCK
PO Box 127, Brasstown, NC 28902,
Phone: 828-837-7627

PATRICK, WILLARD C.
PO Box 5716, Helena,, MT 59604,
Phone: 406-458-6552

PATTAY, RUDY
510 E. Harrison St., Long Beach,
NY 11561, Phone: 516-431-0847

PATTERSON, L.D.
6666 Southwest 64th Pl., Miami,
FL 32314-5914 305-663-1106

PATTERSON, PAT
Box 246, Barksdale, TX 78828,
Phone: 830-234-3586

PATTON, DICK and ROB
6803 View Ln., Nampa, ID 83687,
Phone: 208-468-4123

PAULICHECK, GARTH
POB 812, Williston, ND 58802-
0812 701-774-8803

PAULO, FERNANDES R.
Raposo Tavares, No. 213, Lencois
Paulista, 18680, Sao Paulo,
BRAZIL, Phone: 014-263-4281

PAWLOWSKI, JOHN R.
804 Iron Gate Ct., Newport News,
VA 23602, Phone: 757-890-9098

PAYTON, GARY
19426 Lake Hollow Ln., Houston,
TX 77084

PEAGLER, RUSS
PO Box 1314, Moncks Corner, SC
29461, Phone: 803-761-1008

PEASE, W.D.
657 Cassidy Pike, Ewing, KY 41039,
Phone: 606-845-0387

PECK, MICHAEL
1808 Simsbury, Plano, TX 75025

PEELE, BRYAN
219 Ferry St., PO Box 1363,
Thompson Falls, MT 59873,
Phone: 406-827-4633

PENDLETON, LLOYD
24581 Shake Ridge Rd., Volcano,
CA 95689, Phone: 209-296-3353,
Fax: 209-296-3353

PENDRAY, ALFRED H.
13950 NE 20th St., Williston, FL
32696, Phone: 352-528-6124

PENFOLD, MICK
PENFOLD CUSTOM KNIVES, 5
Highview Close, Tremar, Cornwall
PL14 5SJ, ENGLAND Phone:
01579-345783

PENNINGTON, C.A.
163 Kainga Rd., Kainga
Christchurch 8009, NEW
ZEALAND, Phone: 03-3237292

PEPIOT, STEPHAN
73 Cornwall Blvd., Winnipeg,
Man., CANADA R3J-1E9, Phone:
204-888-1499

PERMAR, JOHN W.
630 Dartmouth St., Orlando, FL
32804-5817 407-649-0199

PERRY, JOHN
9 South Harrell Rd., Mayflower, AR
72106, Phone: 501-470-3043

PERRY, CHRIS
1654 W. Birch, Fresno, CA 93711,
Phone: 209-498-2342

PERRY, JOHNNY
PO Box 4666, Spartanburg, SC
29305-4666, Phone: 803-578-3533

PERRY, JIM
Hope Star, PO Box 648, Hope, AR
71801

PERSSON, CONNY
PL 588, 820 50 Loos, SWEDEN,
Phone: +46 657 10305, Fax: +46
657 413 435

**PETEAN, FRANCISCO AND
MAURICIO**
R. Dr.Carlos de Carvalho Rosa,
52, Centro, Birigui, SP-16200-000,
BRAZIL, Phone: 0186-424786

PETERSEN, DAN L.
10610 SW 81st, Auburn, KS 66402,
Phone: 785-256-2640

PETERSON, KAREN
THE PEN AND THE SWORD
LTD., PO Box 290741, Brooklyn,
NY 11229-0741, Phone: 718-382-
4847, Fax: 718-376-5745

PETERSON, ELDON G.
260 Haugen Heights Rd., Whitefish,
MT 59937, Phone: 406-862-2204

PETERSON, CHRIS
Box 143, 2175 W. Rockyford,
Salina, UT 84654, Phone: 801-529-
7194

**PETERSON, LLOYD (PETE)
C.**
64 Halbrook Rd., Clinton, AR
72031, Phone: 501-893-0000

PEYTON III, CLAY C.
4830 Coxey Brown Rd., Frederick,
MD 21702 301-293-2403

PFANENSTIEL, DAN
1824 Lafayetta Ave., Modesto, CA
95355, Phone: 209-575-5937

PFEIFFER, KENNETH
POB 550, Broadalbin, NY 12025
518-883-8283

PHILIPPE, D.A.
PO Box 306, Cornish, NH 03746,
Phone: 603-543-0662

PHILLIPS, JIM
PO Box 168, Williamstown, NJ
08094, Phone: 609-567-0695

PHILLIPS, RANDY
759 E. Francis St., Ontario, CA
91761, Phone: 909-923-4381

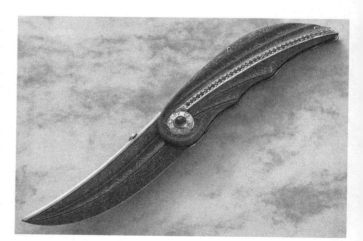

KENNETH KING

Kenneth King's carved damascus steel folder comes in different "trim" levels, starting at King's list price of about **$950**. His list prices for the pictured knife range from around **$3,500** to over **$6,000**, depending on the quality of the gems used. This folder has 9.22 carats of Ceylon sapphires, .88 carat of diamonds inlaid into the spine and pivot disc, and over 2 1/2 ounces of 18k gold.
(Point Seven photo)

PHILLIPS, DENNIS
16411 West Bennet Rd., Independence, LA 70443, Phone: 985-878-8275

PHILLIPS, SCOTT C.
671 California Rd., Gouverneur, NY 13642, Phone: 315-287-1280

PICCOLA, BENJAMIN P.
563 CR 2917, Hughes Springs, TX 75656 903-639-3349

PICKENS, SELBERT
Rt. 1, Box 216, Liberty, WV 25124, Phone: 304-586-2190

PIENAAR, CONRAD
19A Milner Rd., Bloemfontein 9300, SOUTH AFRICA, Phone: 051 436 4180, Fax: 051 436 7400

PIEPER III, RAY
POB 72, Benton, AL 36785

PIERCE, DIANE
POB 99325, Seattle, WA 98199 206-706-4545

PIERCE, HAROLD L.
106 Lyndon Lane, Louisville, KY 40222, Phone: 502-429-5136

PIERCE, RANDALL
903 Wyndam, Arlington, TX 76017, Phone: 817-468-0138

PIERGALLINI, DANIEL E.
4011 N. Forbes Rd., Plant City, FL 33565, Phone: 813-754-3908

PIESNER, DEAN
2633 Herrgott Rd., St. Clements ON, CANADA N0B 2M0, Phone: 519-699-4319, Fax: 519-699-5452

PIOREK, JAMES S.
PO Box 335, Rexford, MT 59930, Phone: 406-889-5510

PITMAN, DAVID
PO Drawer 2566, Williston, ND 58802, Phone: 701-572-3325

PITTMAN, LEON & TRACY
661 Hubert Pittman Rd., Pendergrass, GA 30567 706-654-2597

PITT, DAVID F.
6812 Digger Pine Ln., Anderson, CA 96007, Phone: 530-357-2393

PLUNKETT, RICHARD
29 Kirk Rd., West Cornwall, CT 06796, Phone: 860-672-3419, Toll free: 888-KNIVES-8

POK, OTAKAR
Sokolovska 52, 323 00 Plzen, CZECH REPUBLIC 00420-377-524-176 Tel/Fax 00420-377-225-518

POLK, CLIFTON
4625 Webber Creek Rd, Van Buren, AR 72956, Phone: 479-474-3828

POLK, RUSTY
5900 Wildwood Dr., Van Buren, AR 72956, Phone: 479-410-3661

POLKOWSKI, AL
8 Cathy Ct., Chester, NJ 07930, Phone: 908-879-6030

POLLOCK, WALLACE J.
806 Russet Vly Dr., Cedar Park, TX 78613

POLZIEN, DON
1912 Inler Suite-L, Lubbock, TX 79407, Phone: 806-791-0766

PONZIO, DOUG
3212 93rd St., Pleasant Prairie, WI 53158, Phone: 262-694-3188

POOLE, STEVE L.
200 Flintlock Trail, Stockbridge, GA 30281, Phone: 770-474-9154

POOLE, MARVIN O.
PO Box 552, Commerce, GA 30529, Phone: 803-225-5970

POPLAWSKI, JON R. "POP,"
27957 Helton Dr., Saugus, CA 91350 661-296-5371

POSKOCIL, HELMUT
Oskar Czeijastrasse 2, A-3340 Waidhofen/Ybbs, AUSTRIA, Phone: 0043-7442-54519, Fax: 0043- 7442-54519

POSNER, BARRY E.
12501 Chandler Blvd., Suite 104, N. Hollywood, CA 91607, Phone: 818-752-8005, Fax: 818-752-8006

POTIER, TIMOTHY F.
PO Box 711, Oberlin, LA 70655, Phone: 337-639-2229

POTOCKI, ROGER
Route 1, Box 333A, Goreville, IL 62939, Phone: 618-995-9502

POTTER, FRANK
25 Renfrew Ave., Middletown, RI 02842, Phone: 401-846-5352

POTTER, BILLY
6280 Virginia Rd., Nashport, OH 43830, Phone: 740-454-7412, Fax: 740-319-1751

POWELL, JAMES
2500 North Robinson Rd., Texarkana, TX 75501

POWELL, ROBERT CLARK
PO Box 321, 93 Gose Rd., Smarr, GA 31086, Phone: 478-994-5418

POYTHRESS, JOHN
PO Box 585, 625 Freedom St., Swainsboro, GA 30401, Phone: 478-237-9233 day/478-237-9478 night

PRATER, MIKE
PRATER AND COMPANY, 81 Sanford Ln., Flintstone, GA 30725

PRESSBURGER, RAMON
59 Driftway Rd., Howell, NJ 07731, Phone: 732-363-0816

PRICE, TIMMY
PO Box 906, Blairsville, GA 30514, Phone: 706-745-5111

PRIMOS, TERRY
932 Francis Dr., Shreveport, LA 71118, Phone: 318-686-6625

PRINCE, JOE
190 Bulman Rd., Roebuck, SC 29376 864-576-7479

PRINSLOO, THEUNS
POB 2263, Bethlehem 9700 SOUTH AFRICA 27-58-30337111

PRITCHARD, RON
613 Crawford Ave., Dixon, IL 61021, Phone: 815-284-6005

PROVENZANO, JOSEPH D.
3024 Ivy Place, Chalmette, LA 70043, Phone: 504-279-3154

PRYOR, STEPHEN L.
HC Rt. 1, Box 1445, Boss, MO 65440, Phone: 573-626-4838, Fax: same

PUDDU, SALVATORE
Via Lago Bunnari, 11 Localita Flumini, Quartu s Elena (CA), ITALY 09046

PUGH, VERNON
701-525 3RD Ave. N, Saskatoon SK, CANADA S7K 2J6, Phone: 306-652-9274

PUGH, JIM
PO Box 711, Azle, TX 76020, Phone: 817-444-2679, Fax: 817-444-5455

PULIS, VLADIMIR
Horna Ves 43/B/25, 96 701 Kremnica, SLOVAKIA, Phone: 00427-45-6757274

PULLIAM, MORRIS C.
560 Jeptha Knob Rd., Shelbyville, KY 40065, Phone: 502-633-2261

PURSLEY, AARON
8885 Coal Mine Rd., Big Sandy, MT 59520, Phone: 406-378-3200

PURVIS, BOB and ELLEN
2416 N Loretta Dr., Tucson, AZ 85716, Phone: 520-795-8290

PUTNAM, DONALD S.
590 Wolcott Hill Rd., Wethersfield, CT 06109, Phone: 203-563-9718, Fax: 203-563-9718

Q

QUAKENBUSH, THOMAS C.
2426 Butler Rd., Ft Wayne, IN 46808, Phone: 219-483-0749

QUARTON, BARR
PO Box 4335, McCall, ID 83638, Phone: 208-634-3641

QUATTLEBAUM, CRAIG
2 Ridgewood Ln., Searcy, AR 72143

QUICK, MIKE
23 Locust Ave., Kearny, NJ 07032, Phone: 201-991-6580

R

R. BOYES KNIVES
N81 W16140 Robin Hood Dr., Menomonee Falls, WI 53051, Phone: 262-255-7341

RACHLIN, LESLIE S.
1200 W. Church St., Elmira, NY 14905, Phone: 607-733-6889

RADFORD JR., JOHN R.
7138 Sylar Rd., Ooltewah, TN 37363 423-238-6437

RADOS, JERRY F.
7523 E 5000 N Rd., Grant Park, IL 60940, Phone: 815-405-5061, Fax: 815-472-3944

RADZINSKI, JOSEPH E.
144 Burhans Ave., Yonkers, NY 10701-4917 914-588-3816

RAGSDALE, JAMES D.
3002 Arabian Woods Dr., Lithonia, GA 30038, Phone: 770-482-6739

RAINVILLE, RICHARD
126 Cockle Hill Rd., Salem, CT 06420, Phone: 860-859-2776

RALEY, R. WAYNE
825 Poplar Acres Rd., Collierville, TN 38017, Phone: 901-853-2026

RALPH, DARREL
BRIAR KNIVES, 4185 S St. Rt. 605, Galena, OH 43021, Phone: 740-965-9970

RAMEY, MARSHALL F.
PO Box 2589, West Helena, AR 72390, Phone: 501-572-7436, Fax: 501-572-6245

RAMEY, LARRY
1315 Porter Morris Rd., Chapmansboro, TN 37035-5120, Phone: 615-307-4233

RAMSEY, RICHARD A.
8525 Trout Farm Rd., Neosho, MO 64850, Phone: 417-451-1493

RANDALL JR., JAMES W.
11606 Keith Hall Rd., Keithville, LA 71047, Phone: 318-925-6480, Fax: 318-925-1709

RANDALL MADE KNIVES
PO Box 1988, Orlando, FL 32802, Phone: 407-855-8075, Fax: 407-855-9054

RANDOLPH, DAVID L.
7070 South 40th St., Cimax, MI 49034-8700 616-746-4347

RANDOW, RALPH
4214 Blalock Rd., Pineville, LA 71360, Phone: 318-640-3369

RANKL, CHRISTIAN
Possenhofenerstr. 33, 81476 Munchen, GERMANY, Phone: 0049 01 71 3 66 26 79, Fax: 0049 8975967265

RAPP, STEVEN J.
7273 South 245 East, Midvale, UT 84047, Phone: 801-567-9553

RAPPAZZO, RICHARD
142 Dunsbach Ferry Rd., Cohoes, NY 12047, Phone: 518-783-6843

RARDON, ARCHIE F.
1589 SE Price Dr., Polo, MO 64671, Phone: 660-354-2330

RARDON, A.D.
1589 SE Price Dr., Polo, MO 64671, Phone: 660-354-2330

RAY, ALAN W.
PO Box 479, Lovelady, TX 75851, Phone: 936-636-2350, Fax: 936-636-2931

REAGAN, MIKE
6013 Wakefield Dr., Sylvania, OH 43560 419-885-0170

REBELLO, INDIAN GEORGE
358 Elm St., New Bedford, MA 02740-3837, Phone: 508-999-7090

RED, VERNON
2020 Benton Cove, Conway, AR
72032, Phone: 501-450-7284

REDDIEX, BILL
27 Galway Ave., Palmerston North,
NEW ZEALAND, Phone: 06-357-
0383, Fax: 06-358-2910

REED, DAVE
Box 132, Brimfield, MA 01010,
Phone: 413-245-3661

REED, JOHN M.
257 Navajo Dr., Oak Hill, FL
32759, Phone: 386-345-4763

REEL, JIMMY
c/o Roger Comer, 895 Randolph
Rd., Marion, NC 28752 828-652-
2448

REEVE, CHRIS
11624 W. President Dr., Ste. B,
Boise, ID 83713, Phone: 208-375-
0367, Fax: 208-375-0368

REGGIO JR., SIDNEY J.
PO Box 851, Sun, LA 70463,
Phone: 504-886-5886

REPKE, MIKE
4191 N. Euclid Ave., Bay City, MI
48706, Phone: 517-684-3111

REVERDY, PIERRE
5 Rue de L'egalite', 26100 Romans,
FRANCE, Phone: 334 75 05 10 15,
Fax: 334 75 02 28 40

REVISHVILI, ZAZA
2102 Linden Ave., Madison, WI
53704, Phone: 608-243-7927

REXROAT, KIRK
527 Sweetwater Circle, Box 224,
Wright, WY 82732, Phone: 307-
464-0166

REYNOLDS, DAVE
Rt. 2, Box 36, Harrisville, WV
26362, Phone: 304-643-2889

REYNOLDS, JOHN C.
#2 Andover, HC77, Gillette, WY
82716, Phone: 307-682-6076

RHO, NESTOR LORENZO
Primera Junta 589, (6000) Junin,
Buenos Aires, ARGENTINA,
Phone: (02362) 15670686

RHODES, JAMES D.
205 Woodpoint Ave., Hagerstown,
MD 21740, Phone: 301-739-2657

**RICARDO ROMANO,
BERNARDES**
Ruai Coronel Rennò, 1261, Itajuba
MG, BRAZIL 37500, Phone: 0055-
2135-622-5896

RICE, STEPHEN E.
11043 C Oak Spur Ct., St. Louis,
MO 63146, Phone: 314-432-2025

RICHARD, RON
4875 Calaveras Ave., Fremont, CA
94538, Phone: 510-796-9767

RICH, HOWARD
916 Greeup St., Corington, KY
41011

RICHARDS JR., ALVIN C.
2889 Shields Ln., Fortuna, CA
95540-3241, Phone: 707-725-2526

RICHARDSON JR., PERCY
PO Box 973, Hemphill, TX 75948,
Phone: 409-787-2279

RICHTER, JOHN C.
932 Bowling Green Trail,
Chesapeake, VA 23320

RICHTER, SCOTT
516 E. 2nd St., S. Boston, MA
02127, Phone: 617-269-4855

RICKE, DAVE
1209 Adams, West Bend, WI 53090,
Phone: 262-334-5739

RIDER, DAVID M.
PO Box 5946, Eugene, OR 97405-
0911, Phone: 541-343-8747

RIEPE, RICHARD A.
17604 E 296 St., Harrisonville, MO
64701

RIETVELD, BERTIE
PO Box 53, Magaliesburg 1791,
SOUTH AFRICA, Phone: +2714
577 1294, Fax: 014 577 1294

RIGNEY JR., WILLIE
191 Colson Dr., Bronston, KY
42518, Phone: 606-679-4227

RILEY, DENNIS
POB 72, Cushman, AR 72526 870-
793-3779

RINALDI, T.H.
RINALDI CUSTOM BLADES, PO
Box 718, Winchester, CA 92596,
Phone: 951-926-5422

RINKES, SIEGFRIED
Am Sportpl 2, D 91459,
Markterlbach, GERMANY

RIZZI, RUSSELL J.
37 March Rd., Ashfield, MA 01330,
Phone: 413-625-2842

ROATH, DEAN
3050 Winnipeg Dr., Baton Rouge,
LA 70819, Phone: 225-272-5562

ROBBINS, HOWARD P.
1407 S. 217th Ave., Elkhorn, NE
68022, Phone: 402-289-4121

ROBERTS, E. RAY
191 Nursery Rd., Monticello, FL
32344, Phone: 850-997-4403

ROBERTS, MICHAEL
601 Oakwood Dr., Clinton, MS
39056-4332, Phone: 601-924-3154,
Pager 601-978-8180

ROBERTS, GEORGE A.
PO Box 31228, 211 Main St.,
Whitehorse, YT, CANADA Y1A
5P7, Phone: 867-667-7099, Fax:
867-667-7099

ROBERTS, CHUCK
PO Box 7174, Golden, CO 80403,
Phone: 303-642-0512

ROBERTS, JACK
10811 Sagebluff Dr., Houston, TX
77089, Phone: 218-481-1784

ROBERTSON, LEO D.
3728 Pleasant Lake Dr., Indianpolis,
IN 46227, Phone: 317-882-9899

ROBINSON, ROBERT W.
1569 N. Finley Pt., Polson, MT
59860, Phone: 406-887-2259, Fax:
406-887-2259

ROBINSON, CHUCK
Sea Robin Forge, 1423 Third Ave.,
Picayune, MS 39466, Phone: 601-
798-0060

**ROBINSON, CHARLES
(DICKIE)**
PO Box 221, Vega, TX 79092,
Phone: 806-267-2629

ROBINSON III, REX R.
10531 Poe St., Leesburg, FL 34788,
Phone: 352-787-4587

ROCHFORD, MICHAEL R.
PO Box 577, Dresser, WI 54009,
Phone: 715-755-3520

RODEBAUGH, JAMES L.
9374 Joshua Rd., Oak Hills, CA
92345

RODEWALD, GARY
447 Grouse Ct., Hamilton, MT
59840, Phone: 406-363-2192

RODKEY, DAN
18336 Ozark Dr., Hudson, FL
34667, Phone: 727-863-8264

ROE JR., FRED D.
4005 Granada Dr., Huntsville, AL
35802, Phone: 205-881-6847

ROGERS, RODNEY
602 Osceola St., Wildwood, FL
34785, Phone: 352-748-6114

ROGERS, RICHARD
PO Box 769, Magdalena, NM
87825, Phone: 505-854-2567

ROGERS, CHARLES W.
Rt. 1 Box 1552, Douglas, TX 75943,
Phone: 409-326-4496

ROGERS JR., ROBERT P.
3979 South Main St., Acworth, GA
30101, Phone: 404-974-9982

ROGHMANS, MARK
607 Virginia Ave., LaGrange, GA
30240, Phone: 706-885-1273

ROHN, FRED
7675 W Happy Hill Rd., Coeur
d'Alene, ID 83814, Phone: 208-
667-0774

ROLLERT, STEVE
PO Box 65, Keensburg, CO 80643-
0065, Phone: 303-732-4858

ROLLICK, WALTER D.
2001 Cochran Rd., Maryville, TN
37803, Phone: 423-681-6105

RONZIO, N. JACK
PO Box 248, Fruita, CO 81521,
Phone: 970-858-0921

**ROSA, PEDRO GULLHERME
TELES**
R. das Magnolias, 45 CECAP
Presidente Prudente, SP-19065-410,
BRAZIL, Phone: 0182-271769

ROSE, DEREK W.
14 Willow Wood Rd., Gallipolis,
OH 45631, Phone: 740-446-4627

ROSENFELD, BOB
955 Freeman Johnson Rd.,
Hoschton, GA 30548, Phone: 770-
867-2647

ROSS, TIM
3239 Oliver Rd., RR #17, Thunder
Bay, ONT, CANADA P7B 6C2,
Phone: 807-935-2667

ROSS, GREGG
4556 Wenhart Rd., Lake Worth, FL
33463, Phone: 407-439-4681

ROSS, STEPHEN
534 Remington Dr., Evanston, WY
82930, Phone: 307-789-7104

ROSS, D.L.
27 Kinsman St., Dunedin, NEW
ZEALAND, Phone: 64 3 464 0239,
Fax: 64 3 464 0239

**ROSSDEUTSCHER, ROBERT
N.**
133 S Vail Ave., Arlington Heights,
IL 60005, Phone: 847-577-0404

ROTELLA, RICHARD A.
643-75th St., Niagara Falls, NY
14304

ROTH, GEORGE R.
POB 1211, New Boston, TX 75570
903-628-6698

ROULIN, CHARLES
113 B Rt. de Soral, 1233 Geneva,
SWITZERLAND, Phone: 022-757-
4479, Fax: 022-757-4479

ROWE, STEWART G.
8-18 Coreen Court, Mt. Crosby,
Brisbane 4306, AUSTRALIA,
Phone: Ph: 073-201-0906, Fax: 073-
201-2406

ROWE, FRED
BETHEL RIDGE FORGE, 3199
Roberts Rd., Amesville, OH 45711,
Phone: 866-325-2164

ROZAS, CLARK D.
1436 W "G" St., Wilmington, CA
90744, Phone: 310-518-0488

RUANA KNIFE WORKS
Box 520, Bonner, MT 59823,
Phone: 406-258-5368

RUPERT, BOB
301 Harshaville Rd., Clinton, PA
15026, Phone: 724-573-4569

RUPLE, WILLIAM H.
PO Box 370, Charlotte, TX 78011,
Phone: 830-277-1371

RUSS, RON
5351 NE 160th Ave., Williston, FL
32696, Phone: 352-528-2603

RUSSELL, MICK
4 Rossini Rd., Pari Park, Port
Elizabeth 6070, SOUTH AFRICA

RUSSELL, TOM
6500 New Liberty Rd., Jacksonville,
AL 36265, Phone: 205-492-7866

RUTH, MICHAEL G
3101 New Boston Rd., Texarkana,
TX 75501, Phone: 903-832-7166

RUTHERFORD, BRAD
7932 Calico St., San Diego, CA
92126 858-693-6235

RYAN, C.O.
902-A Old Wormley Creek Rd., Yorktown, VA 23692, Phone: 757-898-7797

RYBAR JR., RAYMOND B.
726 W Lynwood St., Phoenix, AZ 85007, Phone: 605-523-0201

RYBERG, GOTE
Faltgatan 2, S-562 00 Norrahammar, SWEDEN, Phone: 4636-61678

RYDBOM, JEFF
PO Box 548, Annandale, MN 55302, Phone: 320-274-9639

RYDER, BEN M.
PO Box 133, Copperhill, TN 37317, Phone: 615-496-2750

RYUICHI, KUKI
504-7 Tokorozawa-shinmachi Tokorozawa-city, Saitama, JAPAN, Phone: 042-943-3451

RZEWNICKI, GERALD
8833 S Massbach Rd., Elizabeth, IL 61028-9714, Phone: 815-598-3239

SAHLI, WILLIAM
1824 Sycamore Ave., Hanover Park, IL 60103 630-289-3971

SAINDON, R. BILL
233 Rand Pond Rd., Goshen, NH 03752, Phone: 603-863-1874

ST. CLAIR, THOMAS K.
12608 Fingerboard Rd., Monrovia, MD 21770, Phone: 301-482-0264

ST. AMOUR, MURRAY
RR 3, 222 Dicks Rd., Pembroke ON, CANADA K8A 6W4, Phone: 613-735-1061

ST. CYR, H. RED
1218 N Cary Ave., Wilmington, CA 90744, Phone: 310-518-9525

SAKAKIBARA, MASAKI
20-8 Sakuragaoka, 2-Chome Setagaya-ku, Tokyo 156-0054, JAPAN, Phone: 81-3-3420-0375

SAKMAR, MIKE
1451 Clovelly Ave., Rochester, MI 48307, Phone: 248-852-6775, Fax: 248-852-8544

SAKURAI, HIROYUKI
Higashi-Senbo 15, Seki-City, Gifu Pref., Japan 501-3224 011-81-575-22-4185 Fax 011-81-575-24-5306

SALLEY, JOHN D.
3965 Frederick-Ginghamsburg Rd., Tipp City, OH 45371, Phone: 937-698-4588, Fax: 937-698-4131

SAMPSON, LYNN
381 Deakins Rd., Jonesborough, TN 37659, Phone: 423-348-8373

SANDBERG, RONALD B.
24784 Shadowwood Ln., Browntown, MI 48134, Phone: 734-671-6866

SANDERS, A.A.
3850 72 Ave. NE, Norman, OK 73071, Phone: 405-364-8660

SANDERS, BILL
335 Bauer Ave., PO Box 957, Mancos, CO 81328, Phone: 970-533-7223

SANDERS, MICHAEL M.
PO Box 1106, Ponchatoula, LA 70454, Phone: 225-294-3601

SANDERSON, RAY
4403 Uplands Way, Yakima, WA 98908, Phone: 509-965-0128

SANDLIN, LARRY
4580 Sunday Dr., Adamsville, AL 35005, Phone: 205-674-1816

SANDS, SCOTT
2 Lindis Ln., New Brighton, Christchurch 9, NEW ZEALAND

SARGANIS, PAUL
1710 Colombard Rd., Petaluma, CA 94954 707-765-9409

SARVIS, RANDALL J.
110 West Park Ave., Fort Pierre, SD 57532, Phone: 605-223-2772

SASS, GARY N.
23 Baker Ave., Hermitage, PA 16148, Phone: 724-342-7833

SAUER, CHARLES
CUSTOM SAUER KNIVES LLC, 1079 1/2 Hodgson Rd., Columbia Falls, MT 59912-9027, Phone: 406-257-9310, Fax: 775-213-9883

SAVIANO, JAMES P.
124 Wallis Rd., Douglas, MA 01516 508-476-7644

SAWBY, SCOTT
480 Snowberry Ln., Sandpoint, ID 83864, Phone: 208-263-4171

SCARROW, WIL
c/o LandW Mail Service, 919 E Hermosa Dr., San Gabriel, CA 91775, Phone: 626-286-6069

SCHALLER, ANTHONY BRETT
5609 Flint Ct. NW, Albuquerque, NM 87120, Phone: 505-899-0155

SCHANZ, JUERGEN
Rheinstrasse Ost 64, 76297Stutensee-Friedrichstal GERMANY 0049-7249-952-509, Fax 0049-7249-4379

SCHEID, MAGGIE
124 Van Stallen St., Rochester, NY 14621-3557

SCHEMPP, MARTIN
PO Box 1181, 5430 Baird Springs Rd. N.W., Ephrata, WA 98823, Phone: 509-754-2963, Fax: 509-754-3212

SCHEMPP, ED
PO Box 1181, Ephrata, WA 98823, Phone: 509-754-2963, Fax: 509-754-3212

SCHEPERS, GEORGE B.
PO Box 395, Shelton, NE 68876-0395

SCHEURER, ALFREDO E. FAES
Av. Rincon de los Arcos 104, Col. Bosque Res. del Sur, C.P. 16010, MEXICO, Phone: 5676 47 63

SCHILLER, ROY
POB 687, Carrot River, Saskatchewan CANADA S0E 0L0 Phone/Fax 306-768-3821

SCHILLING, ELLEN
95 Line Rd., Hamilton Square, NJ 08690, Phone: 609-448-0483

SCHIPPNICK, JIM
PO Box 326, Sanborn, NY 14132, Phone: 716-731-3715

SCHIRMER, MIKE
312 E 6th St., Rosalia, WA 99170-9506, Phone: 208-523-3249

SCHLOMER, JAMES E.
2543 Wyatt Pl., Kissimmee, FL 34741, Phone: 407-348-8044

SCHLUETER, DAVID
PO Box 463, Syracuse, NY 13209, Phone: 315-485-0829

SCHMIDT, RICK
PO Box 1318, Whitefish, MT 59937, Phone: 406-862-6471, Fax: 406-862-6078

SCHMITZ, RAYMOND E.
PO Box 1787, Valley Center, CA 92082, Phone: 760-749-4318

SCHMOKER, RANDY
SPIRIT OF THE HAMMER, HC 63 Box 1085, Slana, AK 99586, Phone: 907-822-3371

SCHNEIDER, CRAIG M.
5380 N Amity Rd., Claremont, IL 62421, Phone: 217-377-5715

SCHNEIDER, KARL A.
209 N. Brownleaf Rd., Newark, DE 19713, Phone: 302-737-0277

SCHOEMAN, CORRIE
Box 28596, Danhof 9310, SOUTH AFRICA, Phone: 027 51 4363528 Cell: 027 82-3750789

SCHOENFELD, MATTHEW A.
RR #1, Galiano Island, B.C., CANADA V0N 1P0, Phone: 250-539-2806

SCHOENINGH, MIKE
49850 Miller Rd, North Powder, OR 97867, Phone: 541-856-3239

SCHOLL, TIM
1389 Langdon Rd., Angier, NC 27501, Phone: 910-897-2051

SCHRADER, ROBERT
55532 Gross De, Bend, OR 97707, Phone: 541-598-7301

SCHRAP, ROBERT G.
CUSTOM LEATHER KNIFE SHEATH CO., 7024 W. Wells St., Wauwatosa, WI 53213-3717, Phone: 414-771-6472, Fax: 414-479-9765

SCHROCK, MAURICE & ALAN
1712 S. Oak St., Pontiac, IL 61764 815-842-1628 (Maurice) 815-844-7507 (Alan) Fax 815-842-3288

SCHROEN, KARL
4042 Bones Rd., Sebastopol, CA 95472, Phone: 707-823-4057, Fax: 707-823-2914

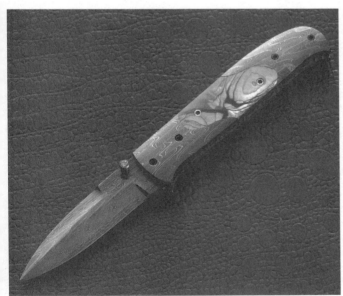

LOYD MCCONNELL

Mosaic damascus steel comprises the handle frame and 2-inch blade of Loyd McConnell's "Little Gem" folder. Green abalone inlay in the handle, filework, and a diamond inset in the thumbstud complete the ensemble. McConnell's list price to make a similar piece: **$1,095**. (Point Seven photo)

SCHULTZ, ROBERT W.
PO Box 70, Cocolalla, ID 83813-0070

SCHWARZER, STEPHEN
PO Box 4, Pomona Park, FL 32181, Phone: 386-649-5026, Fax: 386-649-8585

SCIMIO, BILL
HC 01 Box 24A, Spruce Creek, PA 16683, Phone: 814-632-3751

SCOFIELD, EVERETT
2873 Glass Mill Rd., Chickamauga, GA 30707, Phone: 706-375-2790

SCORDIA, PAOLO
Via Terralba 143, 00050 Torrimpietra, Roma, ITALY, Phone: 06-61697231

SCOTT, AL
2245 Harper Valley Rd., Harper, TX 78631, Phone: 830-864-4182

SCROGGS, JAMES A.
108 Murray Hill Dr., Warrensburg, MO 64093, Phone: 660-747-2568

SCULLEY, PETER E.
340 Sunset Dr., Rising Fawn, GA 30738, Phone: 706-398-0169

SEALE, BERT
POB 16279, Lake Charles, LA 70616 318-587-2440

SEARS, MICK
1697 Peach Orchard Rd. #302, Sumter, SC 29154, Phone: 803-499-5074

SEATON, DAVID D.
2914 Bayshore Dr., Tallahassee, FL 32309 850-668-6838

SEIB, STEVE
7914 Old State Rd., Evansville, IN 47710 812-867-2231

SELENT, CHUCK
PO Box 1207, Bonners Ferry, ID 83805-1207, Phone: 208-267-5807

SELF, ERNIE
950 O'Neill Ranch Rd., Dripping Springs, TX 78620-9760, Phone: 512-858-7133

SELLEVOLD, HARALD
S.Kleivesmau:2, PO Box 4134, N5834 Bergen, NORWAY, Phone: 55-310682

SELZAM, FRANK
Martin Reinhard Str 23, 97631, Bad Koenigshofen, GERMANY, Phone: 09761-5980

SEMONES, DAVID G.
295 Deerfoot Rd., Deland, FL 32720 386-736-5733

SENTZ, MARK C.
4084 Baptist Rd., Taneytown, MD 21787, Phone: 410-756-2018

SERAFEN, STEVEN E.
24 Genesee St., New Berlin, NY 13411, Phone: 607-847-6903

SERVEN, JIM
PO Box 1, Fostoria, MI 48435, Phone: 517-795-2255

SETO, YOSHINORI
1-20 3-Chome, Asahigaoka, Seki-City, Gifu Pref., Japan 501-3829 81575-23-9519 Fax 81575-23-9690

SEVEY CUSTOM KNIFE
94595 Chandler Rd., Gold Beach, OR 97444, Phone: 541-247-2649

SFREDDO, RODRITO MENEZES
Rua 15 De Novembro 2222, Nova Petropolis, RS, BRASIL 95150-000, Phone: 011-55- 54-303-303-90

SHADLEY, EUGENE W.
26315 Norway Dr., Bovey, MN 55709, Phone: 218-245-3820, Fax: 218-245-1639

SHADMOT, BOAZ
MOSHAV PARAN D N, Arava, ISRAEL 86835

SHARRIGAN, MUDD
111 Bradford Rd., Wiscasset, ME 04578-4457, Phone: 207-882-9820, Fax: 207-882-9835

SHAVER II, JAMES R.
1529 Spider Ridge Rd., Parkersburg, WV 26104, Phone: 304-422-2692

SHEEHY, THOMAS J.
4131 NE 24th Ave., Portland, OR 97211-6411, Phone: 503-493-2843

SHEETS, STEVEN WILLIAM
6 Stonehouse Rd, Mendham, NJ 07945, Phone: 201-543-5882

SHEPHERD, BRAD
1554 South Hempel Ave., Windmere, FL 34786 407-295-3200, Fax 407-294-9669

SHIFFER, STEVE
PO Box 582, Leakesville, MS 39451, Phone: 601-394-4425

SHIKAYAMA, TOSHIAKI
259-2 Suka Yoshikawa City, Saitama 342-0057, JAPAN, Phone: 04-89-81-6605, Fax: 04-89-81- 6605

SHINOSKY, ANDY
3117 Meanderwood Dr., Canfield, OH 44406, Phone: 330-702-0299

SHIPLEY, STEVEN A.
800 Campbell Rd. Ste 137, Richardson, TX 75081, Phone: 972-644-7981, Fax: 972-644-7985

SHOEBOTHAM, HEATHER
HEATHER'S BLACKSMITH SHOP, POB 768, Belfast 1100, SOUTH AFRICA, Phone: +27 11 496 1600, Fax: +27 11 835 2932

SHOEMAKER, CARROLL
380 Yellowtown Rd., Northup, OH 45658, Phone: 740-446-6695

SHOEMAKER, SCOTT
316 S. Main St., Miamisburg, OH 45342, Phone: 513-859-1935

SHOGER, MARK O.
14780 SW Osprey Dr., Suite 345, Beaverton, OR 97007, Phone: 503-579-2495

SHORE, JOHN I.
ALASKA KNIFEMAKER, 2901 Sheldon Jackson St., Anchorage, AK 99508, Phone: 907-272-2253

SHOSTLE, BEN
1121 Burlington, Muncie, IN 47302, Phone: 765-282-9073, Fax: 765-282-5270

SIBERT, SHANE
PO Box 241, Gladstone, OR 97027, Phone: 503-650-2082

SIGMAN, CORBET R.
Rt. 1, Box 260, Liberty, WV 25124, Phone: 304-586-9131

SIGMAN, JAMES P.
10391 Church Rd., North Adams, MI 49262, Phone: 517-523-3028

SIMMONS, H.R.
1100 Bay City Rd., Aurora, NC 27806, Phone: 252-322-5969

SIMMONS, KEN
417 Sugarcreek Dr., Grovetown, GA 30813 706-860-0086

SIMONELLA, GIANLUIGI
15, via Rosa Brustolo, 33085 Maniago, ITALY, Phone: 01139-427-730350

SIMONICH KNIVES
PO Box 278, Clancy, MT 59634, Phone: 406-933-8274

SIMONS, BILL
6217 Michael Ln., Lakeland, FL 33811, Phone: 863-646-3783

SIMS, BOB
PO Box 772, Meridian, TX 76665, Phone: 254-435-6240

SINCLAIR, J.E.
520 Francis Rd., Pittsburgh, PA 15239, Phone: 412-793-5778

SINYARD, CLESTON S.
27522 Burkhardt Dr., Elberta, AL 36530, Phone: 334-987-1361

SISEMORE, CHARLES RUSSEL
RR 2 Box 329AL, Mena, AR 71953, Phone: 918-383-1360

SISKA, JIM
6 Highland Ave., Westfield, MA 01085, Phone: 413-568-9787, Fax: 413-568-6341

SJOSTRAND, KEVIN
1541 S. Cain St., Visalia, CA 93292, Phone: 209-625-5254

SKETOS, S. TED
5232 County Rd. 34, Hartford, AL 36344 334-588-3172

SKIFF, STEVEN
SKIFF MADE BLADES, PO Box 537, Broadalbin, NY 12025, Phone: 518-883-4875

SKOW, H. A. "TEX"
TEX CUSTOM KNIVES, 3534 Gravel Springs Rd., Senatobia, MS 38668, Phone: 662-301-1568

SLEE, FRED
9 John St., Morganville, NJ 07751, Phone: 908-591-9047

SLEZAK, JAN
Mendlova 1535, Nove Mesto Na Morave, 592 31 CZECH REPUBLIC

SLOAN, SHANE
4226 FM 61, Newcastle, TX 76372, Phone: 940-846-3290

SLOBODIAN, SCOTT
4101 River Ridge Dr., PO Box 1498, San Andreas, CA 95249, Phone: 209-286-1980, Fax: 209-286- 1982

SMALE, CHARLES J.
509 Grove Ave., Waukegan, IL 60085, Phone: 847-244-8013

SMALL, ED
Rt. 1, Box 178-A, Keyser, WV 26726, Phone: 304-298-4254

SMALLWOOD, WAYNE
146 Poplar Dr., Kalispell, MT 59901

SMART, STEVE
907 Park Row Cir., McKinney, TX 75070-3847, Phone: 214-837-4216, Fax: 214-837-4111

SMART, STEATEN
15815 Acorn Cir., Tavares, FL 32778, Phone: 352-343-8423

SMIT, GLENN
627 Cindy Ct., Aberdeen, MD 21001, Phone: 410-272-2959

SMITH, RICK
BEAR BONE KNIVES, 1843 W Evans Creek Rd., Rogue River, OR 97537, Phone: 541-582-4144

SMITH, J.D.
69 Highland, Roxbury, MA 02119, Phone: 617-989-0723

SMITH, D. NOEL
12018 NE Lonetree Ct., Poulsbo, WA 98370, Phone: 360-697-6992

SMITH, JOHN M.
3450 E Beguelin Rd., Centralia, IL 62801, Phone: 618-249-6444, Fax: 618-249-6444

SMITH, JOHN W.
1322 Cow Branch Rd., West Liberty, KY 41472, Phone: 606-743-3599

SMITH, JOSH
Box 753, Frenchtown, MT 59834, Phone: 406-626-5775

SMITH, MICHAEL J.
1418 Saddle Gold Ct., Brandon, FL 33511, Phone: 813-431-3790

SMITH, NEWMAN L.
676 Glades Rd., Shop #3, Gatlinburg, TN 37738, Phone: 423-436-3322

SMITH, RAYMOND L.
217 Red Chalk Rd., Erin, NY 14838, Phone: 607-795-5257

SMITH, LENARD C.
PO Box D68, Valley Cottage, NY 10989, Phone: 914-268-7359

SMITH, GREGORY H.
8607 Coddington Ct., Louisville, KY 40299, Phone: 502-491-7439

SMITH JR., JAMES B. "RED"
Rt. 2, Box 1525, Morven, GA 31638, Phone: 912-775-2844

SMITH, RALPH
POB 1690, Greer, SC 29652-1690 864-895-3592 Fax 864-281-6027

SMOCK, TIMOTHY E.
1105 N Sherwood Dr., Marion, IN
46952, Phone: 765-664-0123

SMOKER, RAY
113 Church Rd., Searcy, AR 72143,
Phone: 501-796-2712

SNARE, MICHAEL
3352 E. Mescal St., Phoenix, AZ
85028

SNELL, JERRY L.
235 Woodsong Dr., Fayetteville, GA
30214, Phone: 770-461-0586

SNODY, MIKE
7169 Silk Hope Rd., Liberty, NC
27298, Phone: 888-393-9534

SNOW, BILL
4824 18th Ave., Columbus, GA
31904, Phone: 706-576-4390

SNYDER, MICHAEL TOM
PO Box 522, Zionsville, IN 46077-
0522, Phone: 317-873-6807

SOAPER, MAX
2275 Zion Rd., Henderson, KY
42420 270-827-8143

SOARES, JOHN E.
3139 Ozark Ave., Port Arthur, TX
77640

SOLOMON, MARVIN
23750 Cold Springs Rd., Paron, AR
72122, Phone: 501-821-3170, Fax:
501-821-6541

SONNTAG, DOUGLAS W.
906 N 39 ST, Nixa, MO 65714,
Phone: 417-693-1640, Fax: 417-582-
1392

SONTHEIMER, G. DOUGLAS
12604 Bridgeton Dr., Potomac, MD
20854, Phone: 301-948-5227

SOPPERA, ARTHUR
"Pilatusblick", Oberer
Schmidberg, CH-9631 Ulisbach,
SWITZERLAND, Phone: 71-988
47 57, Fax: 71-988 23 27

SORNBERGER, JIM
25126 Overland Dr., Volcano, CA
95689, Phone: 209-295-7819

SOUTHWELL, TYLER JOHN
1800 Fallsburg Park Rd., Lowell, MI
49331 616-897-7262

SOWELL, BILL
100 Loraine Forest Ct., Macon, GA
31210, Phone: 478- 994-9863

SPARKS, BERNARD
PO Box 73, Dingle, ID 83233,
Phone: 208-847-1883

SPARLING, DAVID R.
12814 Selma Ct., Poway, CA 92064

**SPICKLER, GREGORY
NOBLE**
5614 Mose Cir., Sharpsburg, MD
21782, Phone: 301-432-2746

SPINALE, RICHARD
4021 Canterbury Ct., Lorain, OH
44053, Phone: 440-282-1565

SPIVEY, JEFFERSON
9244 W. Wilshire, Yukon, OK
73099, Phone: 405-721-4442

SPRAGG, WAYNE E.
PO Box 508, 1314 3675 East Rd.,
Ashton, ID 83420

SPROUSE, TERRY
1633 Newfound Rd., Asheville, NC
28806, Phone: 704-683-3400

STAFFORD, RICHARD
104 Marcia Ct., Warner Robins, GA
31088, Phone: 912-923-6372

STALCUP, EDDIE
PO Box 2200, Gallup, New Mexico
87305, Phone: 505-863-3107

STANCER, CHUCK
62 Hidden Ranch Rd. NW, Calgary
AB, CANADA T3A 5S5, Phone:
403-295-7370

STANLEY, JOHN
604 Elm St., Crossett, AR 71635,
Phone: 970-304-3005

STAPEL, CHUCK
Box 1617, Glendale, CA 91209,
Phone: 213-66-KNIFE, Fax: 213-
669-1577

STAPLETON, WILLIAM E.
BUFFALO 'B' FORGE, 5425
Country Ln., Merritt Island, FL
32953, Phone: 407-452-8946

STECK, VAN R.
260 W Dogwood Ave., Orange City,
FL 32763, Phone: 386-775-7303

STEFFEN, CHUCK
504 Dogwood Ave. NW, St.
Michael, MN, Phone: 763-497-6315

STEGALL, KEITH
2101 W. 32nd, Anchorage, AK
99517, Phone: 907-276-6002

STEGNER, WILBUR G.
9242 173rd Ave. SW, Rochester, WA
98579, Phone: 360-273-0937

STEIER, DAVID
7722 Zenith Way, Louisville, KY
40219

STEIGER, MONTE L.
Box 186, Genesee, ID 83832,
Phone: 208-285-1769

STEIGERWALT, KEN
PO Box 172, Orangeville, PA 17859,
Phone: 717-683-5156

STEINAU, JURGEN
Julius-Hart Strasse 44, Berlin
0-1162, GERMANY, Phone: 372-
6452512, Fax: 372-645-2512

STEINBERG, AL
5244 Duenas, Laguna Woods, CA
92653, Phone: 949-951-2889

STEINBRECHER, MARK W.
4725 Locust Ave., Glenview, IL
60025, Phone: 847-298-5721

STEKETEE, CRAIG A.
871 N. Hwy. 60, Billings, MO
65610, Phone: 417-744-2770

STEPHAN, DANIEL
2201 S. Miller Rd., Valrico, FL
33594, Phone: 813-684-2781

STERLING, MURRAY
693 Round Peak Church Rd.,
Mount Airy, NC 27030, Phone:
336-352-5110, Fax: 336-352-5105

STEVENS, BARRY B.
901 Amherst, Cridersville, OH
45806, Phone: 419-221-2446

STEWART, EDWARD L.
4297 Audrain Rd. 335, Mexico, MO
65265, Phone: 573-581-3883

STIMPS, JASON M.
374 S Shaffer St., Orange, CA
92866, Phone: 714-744-5866

STIPES, DWIGHT
2651 SW Buena Vista Dr., Palm
City, FL 34990, Phone: 772-597-
0550

STOCKWELL, WALTER
368 San Carlos Ave., Redwood City,
CA 94061, Phone: 650-363-6069

**STODDARD'S, INC.,
COPLEY PLACE**
100 Huntington Ave., Boston, MA
02116, Phone: 617-536-8688, Fax:
617-536-8689

STODDART, W.B. BILL
917 Smiley, Forest Park, OH 45240,
Phone: 513-851-1543

STOKES, ED
22417 Cardinal Dr., Hockley, TX
77447, Phone: 713-351-1319

STONE, GREGORY
14903 Oak Pines, Houston, TX
77040 832-467-2956

STONE, JERRY
PO Box 1027, Lytle, TX 78052,
Phone: 512-772-4502

STORCH, ED
R.R. 4 Mannville, Alberta T0B
2W0, CANADA, Phone: 780-763-
2214

STORM, JAMES D.
105 Richard St., Daleville, AL
36322 334-598-8707

STORMER, BOB
10 Karabair Rd., St. Peters, MO
63376, Phone: 636-441-6807

STOUT, CHARLES
RT3 178 Stout Rd., Gillham, AR
71841, Phone: 870-386-5521

STOUT, JOHNNY
1205 Forest Trail, New Braunfels,
TX 78132, Phone: 830-606-4067

STOUT JR., JOHN K.
211 East 15 St., Irving, TX 75060
972-253-0837

STOVER, HOWARD
100 Palmetto Dr. Apt. 7, Pasadena,
CA 91105, Phone: 765-452-3928

STOVER, JAMES K.
HC 60, Box 1260, Lakeview, OR
97630 541-947-4008

STOVER, TERRY "LEE"
1809 N. 300 E., Kokomo, IN 46901,
Phone: 765-452-3928

STRAIGHT, DON
PO Box 12, Points, WV 25437,
Phone: 304-492-5471

STRAIGHT, KENNETH J.
11311 103 Lane N., Largo, FL
33773, Phone: 813-397-9817

STRANDE, POUL
Soster Svenstrup Byvej 16, Dastrup
4130 Viby Sj., DENMARK, Phone:
46 19 43 05, Fax: 46 19 53 19

STRICKLAND, DALE
1440 E. Thompson View, Monroe,
UT 84754, Phone: 435-896-8362

STRIDER, MICK
STRIDER KNIVES, 120 N Pacific
Unit L-7, San Marcos, CA 92069,
Phone: 760-471-8275, Fax: 503-
218- 7069

STRONG, SCOTT
2138 Oxmoor Dr., Beavercreek, OH
45431, Phone: 937-426-9290

STROYAN, ERIC
Box 218, Dalton, PA 18414, Phone:
717-563-2603

STUART, STEVE
Box 168, Gores Landing, Ont.,
CANADA K0K 2E0, Phone: 905-
342-5617

STUMPHY JR., ROBERT E.
3293 Solstice Ct., Jefferson, MD
21755 301-834-9311

SUEDMEIER, HARLAN
RFD 2, Box 299D, Nebraska City,
NE 68410, Phone: 402-873-4372

SUGIHARA, KEIDOH
4-16-1 Kamori-Cho, Kishiwada City,
Osaka, F596-0042, JAPAN, Fax:
0724-44-2677

SUGIYAMA, EDDY K.
2361 Nagayu Naoirimachi
Naoirigun, Ohita, JAPAN, Phone:
0974-75-2050

SUMMERS, ARTHUR L.
1310 Hess Rd., Concord, NC
28025, Phone: 704-795-2863

SUMMERS, DAN
2675 NY Rt. 11, Whitney Pt., NY
13862, Phone: 607-692-2391

SUMMERS, DENNIS K.
827 E. Cecil St., Springfield, OH
45503, Phone: 513-324-0624

SUNDERLAND, RICHARD
Av Infraganti 23, Col Lazaro
Cardenas, Puerto Escondido
Oaxaca, Mexico 71980, Phone: 011
52 94 582 1451

SUTTON, S. RUSSELL
4900 Cypress Shores Dr., New
Bern, NC 28562, Phone: 252-637-
3963

SWEAZA, DENNIS
4052 Hwy 321 E, Austin, AR 72007,
Phone: 501-941-1886

SWEDER, JORAM
TILARU METALSMITHING, PO
Box 4175, Ocala, FL 34470, Phone:
352-546-4438

SWEENEY, COLTIN D.
1216 S 3 St. W, Missoula, MT
59801, Phone: 406-721-6782

SWITZER, JOHN
6774 Blue Jay Dr., Parker, CO
80138 303-841-4432

SWYHART, ART
509 Main St., PO Box 267, Klickitat, WA 98628, Phone: 509-369-3451

SYMONDS, ALBERTO E.
Rambla M Gandhi 485, Apt 901, Montevideo 11300, URUGUAY, Phone: 011 598 27103201, Fax: 011 598 5608207

SYSLO, CHUCK
3418 South 116 Ave., Omaha, NE 68144, Phone: 402-333-0647

SZAREK, MARK G.
94 Oakwood Ave., Revere, MA 02151, Phone: 781-289-7102

SZILASKI, JOSEPH
29 Carroll Dr., Wappingers Falls, NY 12590, Phone: 845-297-5397

TAKAHASHI, KAORU
2506 TOYO OKA YADO UEKI, Kamoto Kumamoto, JAPAN 861-01, Phone: (8196) 272-6759

TAKAHASHI, MASAO
39-3 Sekine-machi, Maebashi-shi, Gunma 371 0047, JAPAN, Phone: 81 27 234 2223, Fax: 81 27 234 2223

TAKESHI, SAJI
46-1-9 Ikenokami-Cho, Takefu, Fukui, Japan 915-0783

TALLY, GRANT
26961 James Ave., Flat Rock, MI 48134, Phone: 734-789-8961

TAMBOLI, MICHAEL
12447 N. 49 Ave., Glendale, AZ 85304, Phone: 602-978-4308

TASMAN, KERLEY
9 Avignon Retreat, Pt. Kennedy, 6172, Western Australia, AUSTRALIA, Phone: 61 8 9593 0554, Fax: 61 8 9593 0554

TAY, LARRY C-G.
Siglap PO Box 315, Singapore 9145, SINGAPORE, Phone: 65-2419421, Fax: 65-2434879

TAYLOR, SCOTT
18124 B LaSalle Ave., Gardena, CA 90248, Phone: 310-538-8104

TAYLOR, SHANE
18 Broken Bow Ln., Miles City, MT 59301, Phone: 406-232-7175

TAYLOR, C. GRAY
560 Poteat Ln., Fall Branch, TN 37656, Phone: 423-348-8304

TAYLOR, BILLY
10 Temple Rd., Petal, MS 39465, Phone: 601-544-0041

TELESCO, ANTHONY J.
5070 Fischer Store Rd., Wimberly, TX 78676 512-847-0294

TERAUCHI, TOSHIYUKI
7649-13 219-11 Yoshida, Fujita-Cho Gobo-Shi, JAPAN

TERRILL, STEPHEN
21363 Rd. 196, Lindsay, CA 93247, Phone: 559-562-1966

TERZUOLA, ROBERT
3933 Agua Fria St., Santa Fe, NM 87501, Phone: 505-473-1002, Fax:

505-438-8018

TESTER, WILLIAM E.
20618 NE 138th St., Kearney, MO 64060-9098 816-628-5561

THAYER, DANNY O.
8908S 100W, Romney, IN 47981, Phone: 765-538-3105

THEIS, TERRY
21452 FM 2093, Harper, TX 78631, Phone: 830-864-4438

THEUNS PRINSLOO KNIVES
PO Box 2263, Bethlehem, 9700, SOUTH AFRICA, Phone: 27 58 3037111, Fax: same

THEVENOT, JEAN-PAUL
16 Rue De La Prefecture, Dijon, FRANCE 21000

THIBAULT, RAYMOND J.
HC 85 Box 9295, Eagle River, AK 99577 907-694-7800

THIE, BRIAN
11987 Sperry Rd., Sperry, IA 52650, Phone: 319-985-2276

THILL, JIM
10242 Bear Run, Missoula, MT 59803, Phone: 406-251-5475

THOMAS, KIM
PO Box 531, Seville, OH 44273, Phone: 330-769-9906

THOMAS, ROCKY
1716 Waterside Blvd., Moncks Corner, SC 29461, Phone: 843-761-7761

THOMAS, DEVIN
90 N. 5th St., Panaca, NV 89042, Phone: 775-728-4363

THOMAS, DAVID E.
8502 Hwy 91, Lillian, AL 36549, Phone: 251-961-7574

RICHARD ROGERS
Richard Rogers' reproduction of a Joseph Rodgers three-blade wharncliffe whittler features engraving by Simon Lytton, a mother-of-pearl handle and gold filework on the backsprings. Rogers' list price to make a similar piece: **$1,350**. (SharpByCoop.com photo)

THOMAS, BOB G.
RR 1 Box 121, Thebes, IL 62990-9718

THOMAS, JACK
POB 1926, Mountainview, AR 72560 870-269-2716

THOMAS, PHIL
POB 8840, Chico, CA 95927 530-899-3860

THOMPSON, LLOYD
PO Box 1664, Pagosa Springs, CO 81147, Phone: 970-264-5837

THOMPSON, LEON
45723 S.W. Saddleback Dr., Gaston, OR 97119, Phone: 503-357-2573

THOMPSON, TOMMY
4015 NE Hassalo, Portland, OR 97232-2607, Phone: 503-235-5762

THOMPSON, KENNETH
4887 Glenwhite Dr., Duluth, GA 30136, Phone: 770-446-6730

THOMSEN, LOYD W.
HCR-46, Box 19, Oelrichs, SD 57763, Phone: 605-535-6162

THORBURN, ANDRE
POB 74081, Lynnwood Ridge, 0040 South Africa 011 27 12 809 1271

THOUROT, MICHAEL W.
T-814 Co. Rd. 11, Napoleon, OH 43545, Phone: 419-533-6832, Fax: 419-533-3516

THUESEN, ED
21211 Knolle Rd., Damon, TX 77430, Phone: 979-553-1211, Fax: 979-553-1211

TICHBOURNE, GEORGE
7035 Maxwell Rd. #5, Mississauga, Ont., CANADA L5S 1R5, Phone: 905-670-0200

TIENSVOLD, JASON
PO Box 795, Rushville, NE 69360, Phone: 308-327-2046

TIENSVOLD, ALAN L.
PO Box 355, Rushville, NE 69360, Phone: 308-327-2046

TIGHE, BRIAN
RR 1, Ridgeville, Ont, CANADA L0S 1M0, Phone: 905-892-2734, Fax: 905-892-2734

TILL, CALVIN E. AND RUTH
211 Chaping, Chadron, NE 69337

TILTON, JOHN
24041 HWY 383, Iowa, LA 70647, Phone: 337-582-6785

TINDERA, GEORGE
BURNING RIVER FORGE, 751 Hadcock Rd., Brunswick, OH 44212-2648, Phone: 330-220-6212

TINGLE, DENNIS P.
19390 E Clinton Rd., Jackson, CA 95642, Phone: 209-223-4586

TIPPETTS, COLTEN
PO Box 1436, Ketchum, ID 83340, Phone: 208-578-1690

TODD, RICHARD C.
RR 1, Chambersburg, IL 62323, Phone: 217-327-4380

TOICH, NEVIO
Via Pisacane 9, Rettorgole di Caldogna, Vincenza, ITALY 36030, Phone: 0444-985065, Fax: 0444-301254

TOKAR, DANIEL
Box 1776, Shepherdstown, WV 25443

TOLLEFSON,, BARRY A.
177 Blackfoot Trail, Gunnison, CO 81230-9720, Phone: 970-641-0752

TOMBERLIN, BRION R.
ANVIL TOP CUSTOM KNIVES, 825 W Timberdell, Norman, OK 73072, Phone: 405-202-6832

TOMES, P.J.
594 High Peak Ln., Shipman, VA 22971, Phone: 804-263-8662

TOMEY, KATHLEEN
146 Buford Pl., Macon, GA 31204, Phone: 478-746-8454

TOMPKINS, DAN
PO Box 398, Peotone, IL 60468, Phone: 708-258-3620

TONER, ROGER
531 Lightfoot Place, Pickering, Ont., CANADA L1V 5Z8, Phone: 905-420-5555

TOOLE, BOBBY L.
2 Briarwood Pl., Vicksburg, MS 39180 601-636-6267

TOPLISS, M.W. "IKE"
1668 Hermosa Ct., Montrose, CO 81401, Phone: 970-249-4703

TORGESON, SAMUEL L.
25 Alpine Ln., Sedona, AZ 86336-6809

TORVINEN, MARK
POB 2427 Eiko, NV 89803-2427 775-738-6200

TOSHIFUMI, KURAMOTO
3435 Higashioda Asakura-gun, Fukuoka, JAPAN, Phone: 0946-42-4470

TOWELL, DWIGHT L.
2375 Towell Rd., Midvale, ID 83645, Phone: 208-355-2419

TOWNSEND, ALLEN MARK
6 Pine Trail, Texarkana, AR 71854, Phone: 870-772-8945

TRACY, BUD
495 Flanders Rd., Reno, NV 8951-4784

TRAVIESO III, JOE E.
30890 Olympus, Bluverde, TX 78163 830-438-2991

TREIBER, LEON
PO Box 342, Ingram, TX 78025, Phone: 830-367-2246

TREMAIN, JOE
1330 Losey Rd., Rives Junction, MI 49277 517-569-2359

TREML, GLENN
RR #14, Site 11-10, Thunder Bay, Ont., CANADA P7B 5E5, Phone: 807-767-1977

TRINDLE, BARRY
1660 Ironwood Trail, Earlham, IA 50072-8611, Phone: 515-462-1237

TRISLER, KENNETH W.
6256 Federal 80, Rayville, LA 71269, Phone: 318-728-5541

TRITZ, JEAN JOSE
Schopstrasse 23, 20255 Hamburg, GERMANY, Phone: 040-49 78 21

TROUT, GEORGE
POB 13, Cuba, OH 45114 937-382-2331

TRUDEL, PAUL
525 Braydon Ave., Ottawa ON, CANADA K1G 0W7

TRUJILLO, ALBERT M.B.
2035 Wasmer Cir., Bosque Farms, NM 87068, Phone: 505-869-0428

TRUJILLO, THOMAS A.
3001 Tanglewood Dr., Anchorage, AK 99517, Phone: 907-243-6093

TRUJILLO, ADAM
3001 Tanglewood Dr., Anchorage, AK 99517, Phone: 907-243-6093

TRUJILLO, MIRANDA
3001 Tanglewood Dr.., Anchorage, AK 99517, Phone: 907-243-6093

TSCHAGER, REINHARD
Piazza Parrocchia 7, I-39100 Bolzano, ITALY, Phone: 0471-970642, Fax: 0471-970642

TURCOTTE, LARRY
1707 Evergreen, Pampa, TX 79065, Phone: 806-665-9369, 806-669-0435

TURECEK, JIM
12 Elliott Rd., Ansonia, CT 06401, hone: 203-734-8406
TURNBULL, RALPH A.,14464 Linden Dr., Spring Hill, FL 34609, Phone: 352-688-7089

TURNER, KEVIN
17 Hunt Ave., Montrose, NY 10548, Phone: 914-739-0535

TURPIN, JAMES
91766 Marcola Rd., Springfield, OR 97478 541-933-2628

TYCER, ART
23820 N Cold Springs Rd., Paron, AR 72122, Phone: 501-821-487

TYSER, ROSS
1015 Hardee Court, Spartanburg, SC 29303, Phone: 864-585-7616

U

UCHIDA, CHIMATA
977-2 Oaza Naga Shisui Ki, Kumamoto, JAPAN 861-1204

UEKAMA, NOBUYUKI
3-2-8-302 Ochiai, Tama City, Tokyo, JAPAN

VAGNINO, MICHAEL
PO Box 67, Visalia, CA 93279, Phone: 559-528-2800

VAIL, DAVE
554 Sloop Point Rd., Hampstead, NC 28443, Phone: 910-270-4456

VALLET, LOUIS
82 Palm Dr. Bay Point, Key West, FL 33040 305-745-1044 Fax 305-296-4311

VALLOTTON, THOMAS
621 Fawn Ridge Dr., Oakland, OR 97462, Phone: 541-459-2216

VALLOTTON, SHAWN
621 Fawn Ridge Dr., Oakland, OR 97462, Phone: 503-459-2216

VALLOTTON, RAINY D.
1295 Wolf Valley Dr., Umpqua, OR 97486, Phone: 541-459-0465

VALLOTTON, BUTCH AND AREY
621 Fawn Ridge Dr., Oakland, OR 97462, Phone: 541-459-2216, Fax: 541-459-7473

VALOIS, A. DANIEL
3552 W. Lizard Ck. Rd., Lehighton, PA 18235, Phone: 717-386-3636

VAN CLEVE, STEVE
Box 372, Sutton, AK 99674, Phone: 907-745-3038

VAN DE MANAKKER, THIJS
Koolweg 34, 5759 px Helenaveen, HOLLAND, Phone: 0493539369

VAN DEN ELSEN, GERT
Purcelldreef 83, 5012 AJ Tilburg, NETHERLANDS, Phone: 013-4563200

VANDEVENTER, TERRY L.
3274 Davis Rd., Terry, MS 39170-8719 601-371-7414

VAN EIZENGA, JERRY W.
14227 Cleveland, Nunica, MI 49448, Phone: 616-842-2699

VAN ELDIK, FRANS
Ho Flaan 3, 3632BT Loenen, NETHERLANDS, Phone: 0031 294 233 095, Fax: 0031 294 233 095

VAN HEERDEN, ANDRE
POB 905-417, Garsfontein 0042, Pretoria, South Africa 011 27 12 361 7121

VAN RIJSWIJK, AAD
AVR KNIVES, Arij Koplaan 16B, 3132 AA Vlaardingen, THE NETHERLANDS, Phone: +31 10 2343227, Fax: +31 10 2343648

VAN RIPER, JAMES N.
PO Box 7045, Citrus Heights, CA 95621-7045, Phone: 916-721-0892

VANCE, TED
749 S. 2nd Ave., Tucson, AZ 85701 520-623-3796

VANDERFORD, CARL G.
Rt. 9, Box 238B, Columbia, TN 38401, Phone: 615-381-1488

VANDEVENTER, TERRY L.
3274 Davis Rd., Terry, MS 39170-9750, Phone: 601-371-7414

VANHOY, ED and TANYA
24255 N Fork River Rd., Abingdon, VA 24210, Phone: 276-944-4885

VASQUEZ, JOHNNY DAVID
1552 7th St., Wyandotte, MI 48192, Phone: 734-281-2455

VAUGHAN, IAN
351 Doe Run Rd., Manheim, PA 17545-9368, Phone: 717-665-6949

VEATCH, RICHARD
2580 N. 35th Pl., Springfield, OR 97477, Phone: 541-747-3910

VEIT, MICHAEL
3289 E. Fifth Rd., LaSalle, IL 61301, Phone: 815-223-3538

VELARDE, RICARDO
7240 N Greefield Dr., Park City, UT 84098, Phone: 435-940-1378/Cell 801-360-1413/801-361-0204

VENSILD, HENRIK
Gl Estrup, Randersvei 4, DK-8963 Auning, DENMARK, Phone: +45 86 48 44 48

VIALLON, HENRI
Les Belins, 63300 Thiers, FRANCE, Phone: 04-73-80-24-03, Fax: 04 73-51-02-02

VIDITO, C.A.
829 E. Meadow Dr., Bound Brook, NJ 08805 732-627-0453

VIEHMAN, MICHAEL
1031 Lafayette Pl., Lake Saint Louis, MO 63367 636-561-3928

VIELE, H.J.
88 Lexington Ave., Westwood, NJ 07675, Phone: 201-666-2906

VILAR, RICARDO AUGUSTO FERREIRA
Rua Alemada Dos Jasmins, NO 243, Parque Petropolis, Mairipora Sao Paulo BRAZIL 07600-000, Phone: 011-55-11-44-85-43-46

VILLA, LUIZ
R. Com. Miguel Calfat, 398 Itaim Bibi, Sao Paulo, SP-04537-081, BRAZIL, Phone: 011-8290649

VILLAR, RICARDO
Al. dos Jasmins, 243, Mairipora, S.P. 07600-000, BRAZIL, Phone: 011-4851649

VISTE, JAMES
Edgewize Forge, 13401 Mt Elliot, Detroit, MI 48212, Phone: 313-664-7455

VISTNES, TOR
N-6930 Svelgen, NORWAY, Phone: 047-57795572

VITALE, MACE
925 Rt 80, Guilford, CT 06437, Phone: 203-457-5591

VOGT, DONALD J.
9007 Hogans Bend, Tampa, FL 33647, Phone: 813 973-3245

VOGT, PATRIK
KUNGSVAGEN 83, S-30270 Halmstad, SWEDEN, Phone: 46-35-30977

VOORHIES, LES
14511 Lk. Mazaska Tr., Faribault, MN 55021, Phone: 507-332-0736

VOSS, BEN
362 Clark St., Galesburg, IL 61401, Phone: 309-342-6994

VOTAW, DAVID P.
Box 327, Pioneer, OH 43554, Phone: 419-737-2774

VOWELL, DONALD J.
815 Berry Dr., Mayfield, KY 42066, Phone: 270-247-2157

VREYS, LUC
Hoofdstraat 14, 3941 Eksel, Belgium 32 11 734746

VUNK, ROBERT
3166 Breckenridge Dr., Colorado Springs, CO 80906, Phone: 719-576-5505

W

WACHOLZ, STEVE "DOC"
19344 Fishburne, Dr., Springhill, FL 34610 352-544-0179

WADA, YASUTAKA
Fujinokidai 2-6-22, Nara City, Nara prefect 631-0044, JAPAN, Phone: 0742 46-0689

WAGAMAN, JOHN K.
107 E Railroad St., Selma, NC 27576, Phone: 919-965-9659, Fax: 919-965-9901

WAHLSTER, MARK DAVID
1404 N. Second St., Silverton, OR 97381, Phone: 503-873-3775

WALDROP, MARK
14562 SE 1st Ave. Rd., Summerfield, FL 34491, Phone: 352-347-9034

WALKER, JOHN W.
10620 Moss Branch Rd., Bon Aqua, TN 37025, Phone: 931-670-4754

WALKER, BILL
431 Walker Rd., Stevensville, MD 21666, Phone: 410-643-5041

WALKER, DON
3236 Halls Chapel Rd., Burnsville, NC 28714, Phone: 828-675-9716

WALKER, MICHAEL L.
PO Box 1924, Rancho de Taos, NM 87571, Phone: 505-751-3409, Fax: 505-751-0284

WALKER, JIM
22 Walker Lane, Morrilton, AR 72110, Phone: 501-354-3175

WALKER, GEORGE A.
PO Box 3272, 483 Aspen Hills, Alpine, WY 83128-0272, Phone: 307-883-2372, Fax: 307-883-2372

WALKER, JAMES
2334 E. Main, Ottumway, IA 52501

WALKER III, JOHN WADE
2595 HWY 1647, Paintlick, KY 40461, Phone: 606-792-3498

WALLACE, ROGER L.
4902 Collins Lane, Tampa, FL 33603, Phone: 813-239-3261

WALLINGFORD JR., CHARLES W.
9024 US 42, Union, KY 41091, Phone: 859-384-4141

WALTERS, A.F.
PO Box 523, 275 Crawley Rd., TyTy, GA 31795, Phone: 229-528-6207

WARD, J.J.
7501 S.R. 220, Waverly, OH 45690, Phone: 614-947-5328

WARD, RON
1363 Nicholas Dr., Loveland, OH 45140, Phone: 513-722-0602

WARD, W.C.
817 Glenn St., Clinton, TN 37716, Phone: 615-457-3568

WARD, CHUCK
1010 E. North St., Benton, AR 72015, Phone: 501-778-4329

WARD, KEN
5122 Lake Shastina Blvd., Weed, CA 96094, Phone: 530-938-9720

WARDELL, MICK
20, Clovelly Rd., Bideford, N Devon EX39 3BU, ENGLAND, Phone: 01237 475312, Fax: 01237 475312

WARDEN, ROY A.
275 Tanglewood Rd., Union, MO 63084, Phone: 314-583-8813

WARE, GARY D.
3706 Montego Dr., Baytown, TX 77521 281-420-2419

WARE, TOMMY
PO Box 488, Datil, NM 87821, Phone: 505-772-5817

WARENSKI, BUSTER
PO Box 214, Richfield, UT 84701, Phone: 435-896-5319

WARREN, DANIEL
571 Lovejoy Rd., Canton, NC 28716, Phone: 828-648-7351

WARREN, AL
1423 Sante Fe Circle, Roseville, CA 95678, Phone: 916-784-3217/Cell Phone: 916-257-5904

WARTHER, DALE
331 Karl Ave., Dover, OH 44622, Phone: 216-343-7513

WASHBURN, ARTHUR D.
ADW CUSTOM KNIVES, 10 Hinman St/POB 625, Pioche, NV 89043, Phone: 775-962-5463

WASHBURN JR., ROBERT LEE
244 Lovett Scott Rd., Adrian, GA 31002, Phone: 475-275-7926, Fax: 475-272-6849

WATANABE, WAYNE
PO Box 3563, Montebello, CA 90640

WATERS, HERMAN HAROLD
2516 Regency, Magnolia, AR 71753, Phone: 870-234-5409

WATERS, GLENN
11 Shinakawa Machi, Hirosaki City 036-8183, JAPAN, Phone: 172-33-8881

WATSON, PETER
66 Kielblock St., La Hoff 2570, SOUTH AFRICA, Phone: 018-84942

WATSON, TOM
1103 Brenau Terrace, Panama City, FL 32405, Phone: 850-785-9209

WATSON, BERT
PO Box 26, Westminster, CO 80036-0026, Phone: 303-426-7577

WATSON, BILLY
440 Forge Rd., Deatsville, AL 36022, Phone: 334-365-1482

WATSON, DANIEL
350 Jennifer Ln., Driftwood, TX 78619, Phone: 512-847-9679

WATT III, FREDDIE
PO Box 1372, Big Spring, TX 79721, Phone: 915-263-6629

WATTELET, MICHAEL A.
PO Box 649, 125 Front, Minocqua, WI 54548, Phone: 715-356-3069

WATTS, WALLY
9560 S. Hwy. 36, Gatesville, TX 76528, Phone: 254-487-2866

WATTS, JOHNATHAN
9560 S State Hwy 36, Gatesville, TX 76528, Phone: 254-487-2866

WEDDLE JR., DEL
2703 Green Valley Rd., St. Joseph, MO 64505, Phone: 816-364-1981

WEEBER, CHARLES
5285 E. Tu Ave., Vicksburg, MI 49097 269-649-2486

WEEVER, JOHN S.
2400 N FM 199, Cleburne, TX 76033 254-898-9595

WEHNER, RUDY
297 William Warren Rd, Collins, MS 39428, Phone: 601-765-4997

WEILAND JR., J REESE
PO Box 2337, Riverview, FL 33568, Phone: 813-671-0661

WEILER, DONALD E.
PO Box 1576, Yuma, AZ 85366-9576, Phone: 928-782-1159

WEINAND, GEROME M.
14440 Harpers Bridge Rd., Missoula, MT 59808, Phone: 406-543-0845

WEINSTOCK, ROBERT
PO Box 170028, San Francisco, CA 94117-0028, Phone: 415-731-5968

WEISS, CHARLES L.
18847 N. 13th Ave., Phoenix, AZ 85027, Phone: 623-582-6147

WELLS, EDDIE
3958 CR 176, Singleton, TX 77831 936-395-2236

WENDELL, GARY
418 1st Ave., St. Albans, WV 25177
304-727-2021

WERNER JR., WILLIAM A.
336 Lands Mill, Marietta, GA
30067, Phone: 404-988-0074

WERTH, GEORGE W.
5223 Woodstock Rd., Poplar Grove,
IL 61065, Phone: 815-544-4408

WESCOTT, CODY
5330 White Wing Rd., Las Cruces,
NM 88012, Phone: 505-382-5008

WEST, CHARLES A.
1315 S. Pine St., Centralia, IL
62801, Phone: 618-532-2777

WEST, PAT
PO Box 9, Charlotte, TX 78011,
Phone: 830-277-1290

WESTBERG, LARRY
305 S. Western Hills Dr., Algona, IA
50511, Phone: 515-295-9276

WESTLAKE, ELSIE
68 Tipperary Rd., Pavellion, WY
82523 307-856-7510

WHEELER, NICK
1109 NW Mill St., Winlock, WA
98596 360-785-4255

WHEELER, ROBERT
289 S Jefferson, Bradley, IL 60915,
Phone: 815-932-5854

WHETSELL, ALEX
1600 Palmetto Tyrone Rd.,
Sharpsburg, GA 30277, Phone:
770-463-4881

WHIPPLE, WESLEY A.
PO Box 3771, Kodiak, AK 99615,
Phone: 907-486-6737

WHITE, ROBERT J.
RR 1, 641 Knox Rd. 900 N., Gilson,
IL 61436, Phone: 309-289-4487

WHITE, BRYCE
1415 W Col. Glenn Rd., Little
Rock, AR 72210, Phone: 501-821-
2956

WHITE, JOHN
308 Regatta Dr., Niceville, FL
32578 850-729-9174

WHITE, LOU
7385 Red Bud Rd. NE, Ranger, GA
30734, Phone: 706-334-2273

WHITE, RICHARD T.
359 Carver St, Grosse Pointe Farms,
MI 48236, Phone: 313-881-4690

WHITE, GENE E.
6620 Briarleigh Way, Alexandria,
VA 22315, Phone: 703-924-1268

WHITE, DALE
525 CR 212, Sweetwater, TX 79556,
Phone: 325-798-4178

WHITE JR., ROBERT J. BUTCH
RR 1, Gilson, IL 61436, Phone:
309-289-4487

WHITENECT, JODY
Elderbank, Halifax County, Nova
Scotia, CANADA B0N 1K0, Phone:
902-384-2511

WHITLEY, L. WAYNE
1675 Carrow Rd., Chocowinity, NC
27817-9495, Phone: 252-946-5648

WHITLEY, WELDON G.
1308 N Robin Ave., Odessa, TX
79764, Phone: 915-584-2274

WHITMAN, JIM
21044 Salem St., Chugiak, AK
99567, Phone: 907-688-4575, Fax:
907-688-4278

WHITMIRE, EARL T.
725 Colonial Dr., Rock Hill, SC
29730, Phone: 803-324-8384

WHITTAKER, ROBERT E.
PO Box 204, Mill Creek, PA 17060

WHITTAKER, RANDY
8850 Little Mill Rd., Cummings,
GA 30041 770-889-5263

WHITTAKER, WAYNE
2900 Woodland Ct., Metamore, MI
48455, Phone: 810-797-5315

WHITWORTH, KEN J.
41667 Tetley Ave., Sterling Heights,
MI 48078, Phone: 313-739-5720

WICKER, DONNIE R.
2544 E. 40th Ct., Panama City, FL
32405, Phone: 904-785-9158

WIGGENS, TIMOTHY L.
Rt. 3, Box 18, Grapeland, TX 75844
936-687-4741

WIGGINS, HORACE
203 Herndon, Box 152, Mansfield,
LA 71502, Phone: 318-872-4471

WILCHER, WENDELL L.
RR 6 Box 6573, Palestine, TX
75801, Phone: 903-549-2530

WILE, PETER
RR 3, Bridgewater, Nova Scotia,
CANADA B4V 2W2, Phone: 902-
543-1373

WILEY, SCOTT
209 N. 37th St., Corsicana, TX
75110 903-874-5033

WILKES, DAVE
735 McCarthy Blvd., Regina,
Saskatchewan, Canada S4X SY1

WILKINS, MITCHELL
15523 Rabon Chapel Rd.,
Montgomery, TX 77316, Phone:
936-588-2696

WILLEY, W.G.
R.D. 1, Box 235-B, Greenwood, DE
19950, Phone: 302-349-4070

WILLIAMS, JASON L.
PO Box 67, Wyoming, RI 02898,
Phone: 401-539-8353, Fax: 401-539-
0252

WILLIAMS, MICHAEL L.
Rt. 4, PO Box 64-1, Broken Bow,
OK 74728, Phone: 580-494-6326

WILLIAMS JR., RICHARD
1440 Nancy Circle, Morristown,
TN 37814, Phone: 615-581-0059

WILLIAMSON, TONY
Rt. 3, Box 503, Siler City, NC
27344, Phone: 919-663-3551

WILLIS, BILL
RT 7 Box 7549, Ava, MO 65608,
Phone: 417-683-4326

WILSON, DAVE
10617 E. Michigan Ave., Sun
Lakes, AZ 85248 480-895-7456

WILSON, WAYNE O.
11403 Sunflower Ln., Fairfax, VA
22030-6031, Phone: 703-278-8000

WILSON, JAMES G.
PO Box 4024, Estes Park, CO
80517, Phone: 303-586-3944

WILSON, RON
2639 Greenwood Ave., Morro Bay,
CA 93442, Phone: 805-772-3381

WILSON, JON J.
1826 Ruby St., Johnstown, PA
15902, Phone: 814-266-6410

WILSON, PHILIP C.
SEAMOUNT KNIFEWORKS,
PO Box 846, Mountain Ranch, CA
95246, Phone: 209-754-1990

WILSON, R.W.
PO Box 2012, Weirton, WV 26062,
Phone: 304-723-2771

WILSON, MIKE
1416 McDonald Rd., Hayesville,
NC 28904, Phone: 828-389-8145

WILSON, III, GEORGE H.
150-6 Dreiser Loop #6-B, Bronx,
NY 10475

WILSON, STAN
1908 Souvenir Dr., Clearwater, FL
33755 727-461-1992

WIMPFF, CHRISTIAN
PO Box 700526, 70574 Stuttgart 70,
GERMANY, Phone: 711 7260 749,
Fax: 711 7260 749

WINBERG, DOUGLAS R.
19720 Hwy 78, Ramona, CA 92076,
Phone: 760-788-8304

WINGO, PERRY
22 55th St., Gulfport, MS 39507,
Phone: 228-863-3193

WINGO, GARY
240 Ogeechee, Ramona, OK 74061,
Phone: 918-536-1067

WINKLER, DANIEL
PO Box 2166, Blowing Rock, NC
28605, Phone: 828-295-9156

WINN, TRAVIS A.
558 E. 3065 S., Salt Lake City, UT
84106, Phone: 801-467-5957

WINSOR, RANDY
606 Straford Dr., Chandler, AZ
85225 480-839-6698

WINSTON, DAVID
1671 Red Holly St., Starkville, MS
39759, Phone: 601-323-1028

WIRTZ, ACHIM
Mittelstrasse 58, WUERSELEN, D
-52146, GERMANY, Phone: 0049-
2405-2587

WISE, DONALD
304 Bexhill Rd., St. Leonardo-
On-Sea, East Sussex, TN3 8AL,
ENGLAND

WITSAMAN, EARL
3957 Redwing Circle, Stow, OH
44224, Phone: 330-688-4208

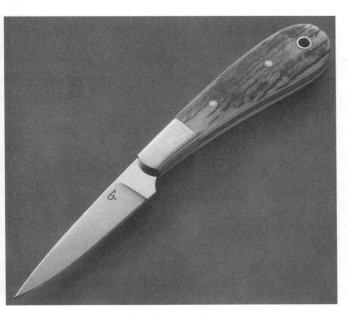

COLTEN TIPPETS

Colten Tippets' Nymph model is a small, slim angler's knife 7.25 inches long overall, with a 3-inch, flat-ground blade of 440C stainless steel. The handle is mammoth ivory and the bolsters are three-color, ladder-pattern mokume. Tippets' list price to make a similar piece: **$350**. (Point Seven photo)

WOJTINOWSKI, FRANK
Bahnhofstrasse 11, 83417
Kirchanschoring, Germany 08685-
1789 Fax 08685-1729

WOLF, BILL
4618 N. 79th Ave., Phoenix, AZ
85033, Phone: 623-846-3585, Fax:
623-846-3585

WOLF JR., WILLIAM LYNN
4006 Frank Rd., Lagrange, TX
78945, Phone: 409-247-4626

WOOD, WILLIAM W.
PO Box 606, Seymour, TX 76380,
Phone: 817-888-5832

WOOD, WEBSTER
22041 Shelton Trail, Atlanta, MI
49709, Phone: 989-785-2996

WOOD, OWEN DALE
6492 Garrison St., Arvada, CO
80004-3157, Phone: 303-466-2748

WOOD, LARRY B.
6945 Fishburg Rd., Huber Heights,
OH 45424, Phone: 513-233-6751

WOOD, ALAN
Greenfield Villa, Greenhead,
Brampton CA8 7HH, ENGLAND,
Phone: 016977-47303

WOODARD, WILEY
4527 Jim Mitchell W, Colleyville,
TX 76034

**WOODCOCK, DENNIS
"WOODY"**
PO Box 416, Nehalem, OR 97131,
Phone: 503-368-7511

WOODIWISS, DORREN
PO Box 396, Thompson Falls, MT
59873-0396, Phone: 406-827-0079

WOODWARD, WILEY
4517 Jim Mitchell W, Colleyville,
TX 76034, Phone: 817-267-3277

WOOTTON, RANDY
83 Lafayett 254, Stamps, AR 71860,
Phone: 870-533-2472

WORRELL, MORRIS
5625 S 25 W. Lebanon, IN 46052-
9766 765-483-0705

WRIGHT, KEVIN
671 Leland Valley Rd. W, Quilcene,
WA 98376-9517, Phone: 360-765-
3589

WRIGHT, TIMOTHY
PO Box 3746, Sedona, AZ 86340,
Phone: 928-282-4180

WRIGHT, RICHARD S.
PO Box 201, 111 Hilltop Dr.,
Carolina, RI 02812, Phone: 401-
364-3579

WRIGHT, L.T.
1523 Pershing Ave., Steubenville,
OH 43952, Phone: 740-282-4947

WRIGHT, TERRY
POB 482, Elaine, AR 72333 870-
827-3257

WUERTZ, TRAVIS
2487 E. Hwy. 287, Casa Grande,
AZ 85222, Phone: 520-723-4432

WYATT, WILLIAM R.
Box 237, Rainelle, WV 25962,
Phone: 304-438-5494

WYMAN, MARC L.
3325 Griffin Rd. Ste. 124, Ft
Lauderdale, FL 33312, Phone: 754-
234-5111, Fax: 954-964-4418

Y

YASHINSKI, JOHN L.
207 N Platt, PO Box 1284, Red
Lodge, MT 59068, Phone: 406-446-
3916

YEATES, JOE A.
730 Saddlewood Circle, Spring, TX
77381, Phone: 281-367-2765

YESKOO, RICHARD C.
76 Beekman Rd., Summit, NJ
07901

YORK, DAVID C.
PO Box 3166, Chino Valley, AZ
86323, Phone: 928-636-1709

YOSHIHARA, YOSHINDO
8-17-11 TAKASAGO, KATSUSHI,
Tokyo, JAPAN

YOSHIKAZU, KAMADA
540-3 Kaisaki Niuta-cho,
Tokushima, JAPAN, Phone: 0886-
44-2319

YOSHIO, MAEDA
3-12-11 Chuo-cho Tamashima
Kurashiki-city, Okayama, JAPAN,
Phone: 086-525-2375

YOUNG, GEORGE
713 Pinoak Dr., Kokomo, IN 46901,
Phone: 765-457-8893

YOUNG, BUD
Box 336, Port Hardy, BC, CANADA
V0N 2P0, Phone: 250-949-6478

YOUNG, CLIFF
Fuente De La Cibeles No. 5,
Atascadero, San Miguel De
Allende, GTO., MEXICO, Phone:
37700, Fax: 011- 52-415-2-57-11

YOUNG, ERROL
4826 Storey Land, Alton, IL 62002,
Phone: 618-466-4707

YOUNG, JOHN
483 E. 400 S., Ephraim, UT 84627
435-283-4555

YOUNG, PAUL A.
168 Elk Ridge Rd., Boone, NC
28607, Phone: 704-264-7048

YOUNG, RAYMOND L.
Cutler/Bladesmith, 2922 Hwy 188E,
Mt. Ida, AR 71957, Phone: 870-
867-3947

YURCO, MIKE
PO Box 712, Canfield, OH 44406,
Phone: 330-533-4928

Z

ZACCAGNINO JR., DON
2256 Bacom Point Rd., Pahokee, FL
33476-2622, Phone: 561-924-7032

ZAHM, KURT
488 Rio Casa, Indialantic, FL
32903, Phone: 407-777-4860

ZAKABI, CARL S.
PO Box 893161, Mililani Town, HI
96789-0161, Phone: 808-626-2181

ZAKHAROV, CARLOS
R. Pernambuco175, Rio Comprido
Jacarei, SP-12305-340, BRAZIL,
Phone: 55 12 3958 4021, Fax: 55 12
3958 4103

ZBORIL, TERRY
5320 CR 130, Caldwell, TX 77836,
Phone: 979-535-4157

ZEMBKO III, JOHN
140 Wilks Pond Rd., Berlin, CT
06037, Phone: 860-828-3503

ZEMITIS, JOE
14 Currawong Rd., Cardiff Hts.,
2285 Newcastle, AUSTRALIA,
Phone: 0249549907

ZIMA, MICHAEL F.
732 State St., Ft. Morgan, CO
80701, Phone: 970-867-6078

ZIMMERMAN, KARL
9822 Ross Lake, Rd., Arbor Vitae,
WI 54368 715-542-2343

ZINKER, BRAD
BZ KNIVES, 1591 NW 17 St.,
Homestead, FL 33030, Phone: 305-
216-0404

ZIRBES, RICHARD
Neustrasse 15, D-54526 Niederkail,
GERMANY, Phone: 0049 6575
1371

ZOWADA, TIM
4509 E. Bear River Rd., Boyne Falls,
MI 49713, Phone: 231-348-5446

ZSCHERNY, MICHAEL
1840 Rock Island Dr., Ely, IA
52227, Phone: 319-848-3629

Harley-Davidson Knives

Information from Bill Claussen

Harley-Davidson motorcycles have a following so dedicated that it verges on the religious. In addition to its splendid vehicles, Harley-Davidson sells a wide array of accessories, clothing and other Harley-brand merchandise, including knives. The contract-made Harley-Davidson knives, both open stock and limited edition, are sold through authorized Harley-Davidson dealers.

The first value chart on this page is of open-stock Harley knives that were sold as regular merchandise in unlimited quantities. Exact numbers were not recorded and most are now discontinued (marked "Obs."). The second chart is of limited-edition Harley knives.

In both charts, the two digits before "V" in each part number indicate the approximate year of first sale (most knives introduced after August bear a part number of the subsequent year). All values are for knives in mint condition with all original packaging. Used open-stock knives generally will be worth substantially less than the indicated values.

I. CURRENT AND OBSOLETE OPEN-STOCK HARLEY-DAVIDSON KNIVES

MANUFACTURER OR DESCRIPTION	ORIGINAL HARLEY PART NUMBER	CURRENT OR OBSOLETE	ORIGINAL CATALOG PRICE	CURRENT RETAIL VALUE
Gerber folder, 3 1/2"	99118-82V	Obs.	$43.95	$175.
Gerber folder, 4"	99119-82V	Obs.	57.95	200.
Buck 110	99116-85V	Obs.	44.95	175.
Buck 112	99115-85V	Obs.	41.95	175.
Swiss Army pocket	99194-87V	Obs.	24.95	40.
Swiss Army folder	99193-87V	Obs.	74.95	175.
Schrade folder 2 3/8"	99114-88V	Current	26.95	34.
Schrade folder 3 3/4"	99115-88V	Current	38.95	47.
Schrade folder 5"	99116-88V	Current	45.95	54.
Schrade 3-blade folder	99113-89VK	Obs.	19.95	25.
Schrade Lite Weight K.R.	99118-89VK	Obs.	17.95	20.
Schrade Lite Weight, sheath	99117-89VK	Obs.	26.95	30.
Schrade skinner, sheath	99112-89VK	Obs.	24.95	50.
Schrade folding pair set	99120-89VK	Obs.	49.95	85.
Zippo knife/scissors	99210-89VK	Obs.	19.95	25.
3 pc. kitchen cutlery set	99189-89VK	Obs.	49.95	50.
6 pc. kitchen cutlery set	99188-89VK	Current	124.95	125.

II. LIMITED-EDITION HARLEY-DAVIDSON KNIVES

MANUFACTURER OR DESCRIPTION	ORIGINAL HARLEY PART NUMBER	ORIGINAL ISSUE QUANTITY	ORIGINAL CATALOG PRICE	CURRENT RETAIL VALUE
Aurum folder (with box)	99117-79V	3,000	$79.95	$500.
Gerber Model 525	99117-81V	3,000	149.95	750.
Buck clip-point bowie	99127-84V	3,000	219.95	700.
Buck Geronimo V-Twin	99158-86V	3,000	199.95	500.
Buck H-D 85th Anniversary	99170-88V	3,000	299.95	300.
Buck Sturgis 50th	99169-90V	3,000	299.95	300.
Buck Superglide 20th	99156-91V	3,000	349.95	300.
Buck "Live to Ride"	99166-92V	3,000	259.95	250.
Gerber H-D 90th Anniversary	99175-93V	3,000	350.00	600.
Buck mastodon H-D 85th	99171-89V	100	995.00	4,000.
Buck Ultra Sturgis	99171-90V	300	995.00	2,500.
Buck Ultra Superglide	99168-92V	300	1,099.95	2,300.
Buck Ultra "Live to Ride"	99154-93V	300	700.00	1,250.
Buck Heritage Folder #1	99158-90V	3,000	99.95	175.
Buck Heritage Folder #2	99157-91V	3,000	109.95	150.
Buck Heritage Folder #3	99155-92V	3,000	134.95	135.
Hog 5th Anniv. set ivory	1091	24?	2,195.00	4,000.
Hog 5th Anniv. bowie, ivory	1092	?	995.00	1,800.
Hog 5th Anniv. dagger, ivory	1093	?	995.00	1,800.
Hog 5th, all four, ivory		1 set	4,435.00	10,000.
Hog 5th Anniv. set, cocobolo	1091-C	75?	2,195.00	2,195.
Hog 5th Anniv. bowie, cocobolo	1092-C	?	995.00	995.
Hog 5th Anniv. dagger, cocobolo	1093-C	?	995.00	995.
Hog 5th, all four, cocobolo	1 set	4	4,435.00	4,000.

Buck Limited-Edition Knives

By Vern Taylor, Larry Oden and Joe Houser

The following list of embellished Buck Knives includes commemorative, animal scene and advertising knives. The list was originally started by Vern Taylor and continued by Joe Houser of Buck Knives. The current list incorporates their work, along with additions by members of the Buck Collector's Club. The list is a work in progress and includes knives produced by Buck, as well as knives that were modified by third-party companies. The market values shown here are only an estimate, at the time of publication, which

assumes that the knives are as new, complete with all original packaging materials. Abbreviations commonly used in the descriptions include:

- DU—Ducks Unlimited;
- NRA—National Rifle Association;
- RMEF—Rocky Mountain Elk Foundation;
- BRK—Blue Ridge Knives;
- H-D—Harley-Davidson;
- NFR—National Finals Rodeo.

For additional information on these and other Buck Knives, please consult the Buck Collector's Club Website at www.buckcollectorsclub.org.

THEME	MODEL	QUANT.	ISSUE	2004
1975				
Shaw-Leibowitz-Deer	501	?	$105.	$200.
1976				
Spirit of '76	Bowie	7600	200.	175.
1977				
"Monroe" Auto Equip.	110	?	?	80.
"Champion" Spark Plugs	110	?	?	81.
N.A. Hunting Club	110	?	?	82.
1978				
Aurum Turkey 8B	501	?	60.	175.
Aurum Mountain Goats 9B	501	?	?	175.
Aurum Mallard Ducklings 10B	501	?	?	175.
Aurum Squirrels 11B	501	?	?	175.
Aurum Goshawk 12B	501	?	?	175.
Aurum Raccoon 13B	501	?	?	175.
Aurum Ruffed Grouse 14B	501	?	?	175.
Aurum Fisherman 15B	110	?	75.	175.
Aurum Bobcat 16B	110	?	?	175.
Aurum Golden Retriever 17B	110	?	?	175.
Aurum Deer 18B	110	?	?	175.
Aurum Caribou 19B	110	?	?	175.
Aurum Grizzlies 20B	110	?	?	175.
Aurum Bighorn Sheep 21B	110	?	?	175.

THEME	MODEL	QUANT.	ISSUE	2004
Aurum Mallards in Flight 01B	112	?	?	175.
Aurum Foxes 02B	112	?	65.	175.
Aurum Mallard 03B	112	?	?	175.
Aurum Raccoon 04B	112	?	?	175.
Aurum Sparrow Hawk 05B	112	?	?	175.
Aurum Pointer 06B	112	?	?	175.
Aurum Cougars 07B	112	?	?	175.
Dillingham Running Rabbit	501	?	?	200.
1979				
Aurum Moose 22B	401	?	125.	250.
Aurum Elk 23B	401	?	125.	250.
Aurum Bobwhite Quails 24B	402	?	115.	250.
Aurum Bobcat and Rabbits 25B	402	?	115.	250.
Aurum Mustang (2 horses)	801/701	5500	68.	75.
Aurum Yearling (horse)	809/709	5500	47.	65.
Aurum Pony	805/705	5500	45.	65.
Arizona Game & Fish	500	?	?	100.
ANCO	501	?	?	45.
Delnau, Miticide for Citrus	501	?	?	?
1980				
Compton Forge	501	?	?	70.
1981				
Mission, San Diego P.D.	110	200+	75.	150.
Ariz. Highway Patrol	500	250	?	150.

THEME	MODEL	QUANT.	VALUES: ISSUE	2004
Bowie w/brass blade back	903	100	?	200.
Tifco Ind.	111	?	?	140.
1982				
Dallas P.D.-black etch	110	290+	**100.**	**150.**
Dallas P.D.-gold etch	110	72+	**125.**	**175.**
Dillingham Grizzlies	110	3	**2,500. set**	**3,000. set**
Dillingham Deer	112	3	**2,500. set**	**3,000. set**
Dillingham Bighorn Sheep	500	3	**2,500. set**	**3,000. set**
Dillingham Elk	501	3	**2,500. set**	**3,000. set**
Dillingham ?	503	3	**2,500. set**	**3,000. set**
Dillingham ?	505	3	**2,500. set**	**3,000. set**
Calif. Highway Patrol	110	1200+	**90.**	**80.**
Stone Sheep (overrun)	501	?	?	**75.**
Desert Bighorn Sheep (overrun)	501	?	?	**75.**
Dall Sheep (overrun)	501	?	?	**75.**
Bighorn Sheep (overrun)	501	?	?	**75.**
Grand Slam set with buckle	501	2500	**450.**	**200.**
1983				
Ducks Unlimited	119	100	?	**175.**
(3) Flying Geese (toward tip)	110	1000	**100.**	**125.**
Calif. Firemans Assoc. 1922/1982	110	590+	**100.**	**125.**
Goodyear Wrangler	432 (112)	10,700	?	**50.**
1984				
Harley-Davidson Bowie	903	3000	**220.**	**350.**
Dr. Pepper	110FG	?	?	**60.**
Apple Blossom Fest.	110	100	**100.**	**200.**
Ducks in Flight I	500	1000	**80.**	**100.**
Ducks in Flight II	500	2000	**90.**	**100.**
Mallards Landing (2)	110	?	?	**150.**
Pewter Handle Eagle Scene	110	2500	**100.**	**200.**
Pewter Handle Deer Scene	110	2500	**100.**	**200.**
Buck Bandit Raccoon	501	250	**70.**	**125.**
Bull Elk Bugling (2)	110	2000	**100.**	**100.**
Coiled Rattler, stag	112	300+	**95.**	**200.**

THEME	MODEL	QUANT.	VALUES: ISSUE	2004
Stone Mtn. Bowie	903	100+	**100.**	**300.**
Turkeys Fighting (W.Va.)	110	250	**125.**	**150.**
White Tail Deer Herd (4)	110	1500	**90.**	**100.**
White Water Canoeing	112	2500	**90.**	**90.**
Sabretooth Tiger, ivory	501	500	**250.**	**400.**
Mastodon, ivory	110	250	**250.**	**500.**
Colt Firearms	500	350	**100.**	**150.**
Tifco Industries	501	?	?	**45.**
1985				
Alaska's 25th (Wine)	110	250	**100.**	**125.**
Alaska's 25th (Black)	110	500	**100.**	**125.**
Alaska's 25th (Orange)	110	?	**100.**	**125.**
S.F. Cablecar	505	250	**65.**	**125.**
D.U. Wetlands, ebony	110	?	?	**100.**
D.U. Wetlands, Medal	110	?	?	**125.**
D.U. Ducks, Red, Medal Set	505/110	4000	?	**175.**
Fighting Bucks (2)	110	750	**100.**	**125.**
Ducks on Pond (2 small)	500	500	?	**125.**
Wood Duck Heads (2)	500	500	?	**150.**
Fighting Tom Turkeys (2)	110	500	?	**125.**
Mallards (2), ivory	501	4	?	**275.**
Kittyhawk	110	4	?	?
Statue of Liberty	501	4	?	**200.**
Mt. Rushmore	704	4	?	?
Prescolite	110	?	?	**60.**
Gary Hawk Cowboy Scene	110	25	?	**175.**
Mr. Peanut	110	?	?	**60.**
Fisherman in boat	110	500	?	**125.**
Grizzly 1-250, stag	500FG	250	?	**150.**
America's Favorite	525AF	?	?	**30.**
Hoffritz, stag	500	?	?	**100.**
Bowman	501	?	?	**30.**
Tamisol/Walco	503	?	?	**30.**
Oxycities Service	506	?	?	**50.**
Buck Logo	525	?	?	**60.**
Running Deer Logo	424	?	?	**40.**
Brown & Root, Inc.	110	?	?	**45.**

THEME	MODEL	QUANT.	VALUES: ISSUE	2004
1986				
Bear & Cubs (in tree)	110	1500.	**100.**	**125.**
Turkeys Feeding (2) (W. Va)	110	100	**80.**	**150.**
Colt Firearms (Reorder)	500	300	**?**	**150.**
Republic Studios- Eagle Logo	110	100+	**?**	**100.**
Fisherman and Bass (Bass Pro)	501	100	**85.**	**125.**
Vietnam Memorial	110	100	**100.**	**250.**
Statue of Liberty II	826	15,000	**55.**	**45.**
Statue of Liberty	826	15,000	**55.**	**40.**
Statue of Liberty (pewter)	825	25,000	**65.**	**50.**
Buck Folding Hunter 25th, N/S	110	2500	**48.**	**75.**
B/K "Legend Lives On"	110	250?	**?**	**175.**
Trophy Buck (Whitetail)	110	500	**125.**	**125.**
Apple Blossom Fest.	402	20	**225.**	**275.**
65 Ford Mustang	501	100	**?**	**200.**
Ford Thunderbird	501	100	**?**	**200.**
Buck Ranger 25th, N/S	112	?	**46.**	**70.**
BSA-Scoutlite	412	?	**?**	**50.**
Harley-Davidson V12 50th	976	3000	**200.**	**350.**
Arkansas 150th	110	?	**?**	**150.**
Colt Firearms	110	?	**?**	**200.**
Colt Firearms Factory, stag	124	40	**?**	**500.**
Colt Firearms, Sam Colt, ivory	124	4	**?**	**1,000.**
Coca-Cola	503	?	**?**	**65.**
Spike	505	?	**?**	**50.**
Ralgro	501	?	**?**	**40.**
Norton	501	?	**?**	**40.**
Running Deer Logo	124	?	**?**	**150.**
1987				
Texas's 150th	110	750	**110.**	**115.**
Quail and Dog	110	250	**125.**	**150.**
Sports Afield 100th, stag	110	100	**144.**	**250.**
Sports Afield 100th, stag	103	100	**156.**	**250.**
Moose Scene	110	200	**100.**	**150.**
Ducks Unlimited 50th	112D1	5000+	**125.**	**125.**
Flying Eagle+Profile	500	1000	**100.**	**125.**
New Mexico 75th	110	200	**100.**	**140.**

THEME	MODEL	QUANT.	VALUES: ISSUE	2004
Liberty (Ellis Is.)	500	5000	**195.**	**175.**
Brown Trout	110	100	**100.**	**150.**
America's Farmers First	110	500	**125.**	**?**
Iditarod Race	110	1000+	**?**	**125.**
Missouri Conserv. 50th	110	250+	**125.**	**100.**
Virginia's 200th	110	250	**125.**	**125.**
Mallards (2 large on pond)	500FG	200	**100.**	**150.**
Arizona's 75th	110	500	**100.**	**115.**
Sportsman's Paradise (La.) N/S	110	250	**100.**	**125.**
Grouse	500	150	**100.**	**150.**
Buck Red Fox	110	150	**125.**	**150.**
Apple Blossom Fest.	501/503	50 sets	**125.**	**250.**
World Record Bass	110	500	**95.**	**110.**
Frontiersman (W. Va.)	110	130	**100.**	**125.**
Buck Black Bear	110	150	**125.**	**150.**
Ford NASCAR Racers	112	250	**?**	**250.**
Ford Street Rods	501	100	**?**	**200.**
Ford Cobra	501	200	**?**	**200.**
S. Carolina Sheriff's Assn.	119	11	**?**	**300.**
Pheasants Standing on Ground	110	1000	**?**	**100.**
Strutting Turkeys	500	250	**?**	**150.**
Arizona Fire Dept. (Aqua)	110	170+	**?**	**125.**
Arizona Fire Dept. (Brown)	110	170+	**?**	**125.**
Arizona Fire Dept. (Ebony)	110	12+	**?**	**100.**
Ducks Unlimited	110FG	?	**?**	**125.**
Geronimo 100th Dagger	976	250	**?**	**300.**
D.U. Wetlands 50th (reorder)	110	?	**?**	**125.**
Cublite-Cub Scouts	414	?	**26.**	**35.**
Yellowhorse Woodsman	102DY	?	**250.**	**100.**
Yellowhorse Maverick	704DY	?	**182.**	**100.**
Yellowhorse Ranger	112DY	?	**250.**	**225.**
Ducks Unlimited	112D2	?	**?**	**125.**
Florida Gators	422 O	?	**?**	**25.**
Georgia Bulldogs	422GE	?	**?**	**25.**
Arkansas Razorbacks	422GE	?	**?**	**25.**
W. Va. Mountaineers	422GE	?	**?**	**25.**
Goodyear	510	?	**?**	**90.**
Deer	426SW	?	**?**	**60.**
Ducks	426SW	?	**?**	**60.**

SECTION V: MODERN, COMMEMORATIVE, CLUB, LIMITED EDITION

THEME	MODEL	QUANT.	ISSUE	VALUES: 2004
Nibco Faucets	505	?	?	40.
Harley-Davidson Logo	110	?	45.	?
Harley-Davidson Logo	112	?	42.	?
Omark	424	?	?	45.

1988

THEME	MODEL	QUANT.	ISSUE	VALUES: 2004
EMS	422	?	?	25.
Clemson Tigers	422GE	?	?	25.
Mallards (2 on pond)	110	750	125.	125.
Flushing Quail	110	750	100.	125.
Pheasants on Ground/Nest	110	1000	95.	100.
Bald Eagle, 4 color	110E5	920	250.	200.
Golden Eagle w/Fish	110	1500	125.	125.
Turkey Standing	110	250	150.	150.
Turkeys Strutting	110	1000	150.	150.
Idaho 100th	110	500	125.	125.
U.S.S. Constitution, Deckwood	500	?	?	175.
U.S.S. Constitution, Birch	500	?	?	125.
Red Tail Hawk	110	750	125.	125.
South Dakota 100th	110	200	100.	125.
North Dakota 100th	110	250	100.	125.
Grazing Deer	110	100	?	150.
Grazing Deer (stag)	500	1000	125.	150.
Old North Church	500	343	225.	175.
Stonewall Jackson	110	250	125.	125.
Canadian Loon & Coin	500	250	175.	150.
Al Buck signature	110	1000	125.	175.
Large Mouth Bass	110	250	125.	125.
Mount Rushmore	110	?	?	250.
Father's Day	500	250	150.	150.
Philmont's Scout Camp 50th	110	500	?	125.
Apple Blossom Fest.	119	25	150.	300.
88 Ford Mustang GT	501	250	?	200.
84-88 Corvette 1-100	501	100	?	200.
H.H. Buck Smithy	903EB	1500	?	200.
U.S. Border Patrol	110	?	?	70.
Ward Bros. Shop, Goose, ivory	110	100	595.	600.
Ward Bros. Blue Bill Duck, stag	110	250	180.	250.

THEME	MODEL	QUANT.	ISSUE	VALUES: 2004
Ward Bros. Barber Pole	526	250	43.	75.
Palmetto Cutlery Club	501	75	?	125.
Cougar at Mtn. Pond	110	250	?	150.
Pitt (Pa. College)	525	?	?	30.
Chemtronics	110FG	?	?	75.
Harley-Davidson Bowie 50th	907	?	300.	?
U. of Ky. Wildcats	424	?	?	75.
Trout-Scrimshaw print	424SW	?	?	45.
Deer-Scrimshaw print	424SW	?	?	45.
Buck-Cowhide	529	?	?	75.

1989

THEME	MODEL	QUANT.	ISSUE	VALUES: 2004
Apple Blossom Fest.	103	25	?	?
H.H. Buck's Smithy	110SP	1500	125.	100.
North Carolina 200th	112	250	195.	200.
Montana's 100th	110	1000	125.	100.
NKCA	103	1700	80.	80.
French Revolution	110	250	165.	125.
Robert E. Lee	110	250	125.	125.
J.E.B. Stuart	110	250	125.	125.
Canvasback Duck, stag	110	500?	300.	225.
Ducks in Flight (4)	110E6	1000	197.	125.
Geese in Flight	110E2	900	197.	125.
Loon on Water/ Nest	110E3	450	197.	125.
Pheasants in Flight	110E1	1000	197.	125.
Turkeys	110E4	960	197.	125.
J.S. Mosby/Gray Ghost	112GG	250	?	100.
Harley-Davidson 50th, ivory	907	?	1,000.	800.
H-D Black Hills 50th	908EB	?	300.	?
Whitetail Deer	525AT4	?	27.	25.
Pheasant	525AT2	?	27.	25.
Rainbow Trout	525AT1	?	27.	25.
Mallard Duck	525AT3	?	27.	25.
Yellowhorse Flag	112Y1	?	380.	350.
Penn State	422GR	?	?	40.
Eagle Print	422SW	?	?	45.
(8) Wild Turkeys print	424WT	?	?	40.
Blackjack Saw	501	?	?	40.
Boeing	503	?	?	40.
Exxon	503	?	?	40.
Container Corp.	501	?	?	45.

THEME	MODEL	QUANT.	ISSUE	2004
1990				
Chuck Buck Signature	103	273	**150.**	**175.**
Buck Collectors Club-Sawby	250	531	**150.**	**225.**
Buck Four Generations	903	363	**295.**	**250.**
USS Arizona	110	250	**150.**	**175.**
Wyoming's 100th	110	1000	**125.**	**150.**
Steam Locomotive-Train	110E7	660	**197.**	**125.**
D-Day, Eisenhower	500	1000	**150.**	**125.**
H-D Founders, Heritage I 3,000	110HD	3000	**175.**	**100.**
H-D Black Hills 50th Gold, Pearl, Ultra	908E1	301	**1,100.**	?
H-D Superglide 20th	909EB	3332	**350.**	?
Christmas Pony	110	1000	**140.**	**125.**
ALCOA	110FG	?	?	**85.**
Dutch Boy Paints	110	200	?	**65.**
Yellowhorse Cuthair Series I	108Y1	?	**840.**	**800.**
Yellowhorse Knight	505Y9	?	**180.**	**125.**
Whitetail Deer 1990	422SW	?	?	**50.**
Huber Flow Control	501	?	?	**45.**
Squadron	501	?	?	**40.**
Raccoons	525A6	?	**28.**	**30.**
Bass	525A5	?	**28.**	**30.**
1991				
Fossil & Hydro Const. Safety	501	?	?	**40.**
West Hazmat	501	?	?	**40.**
Riverboat	110	550	**197.**	**125.**
Steam Locomotive	112	250	**150.**	**125.**
Deer-jumping over log	110E8	1000	**197.**	**125.**
2 Tom Turkeys in Flight	112SP	250	**125.**	**125.**
Buck Collector's Club	531E	500	**119.**	**125.**
Al Buck 1910-91	110	1300	**141.**	**125.**
Sturgis 50th	903E2	?	?	?
Lee & Jackson	110LJ	250	?	**125.**
Superglide 20th Yellowhorse Ultra	909E1	300	**1,100.**	?
Live to Ride, Ride to Live	401EB	3256	**260.**	?
Tulsa Knife Club	531	14	?	?
H-D Humble Beginnings II	110H1	3000	**110.**	**100.**

THEME	MODEL	QUANT.	ISSUE	2004
VA Deer Hunters Assn. 1991	422CM	?	?	**45.**
Yellowhorse Cuthair II	108Y2	?	**900.**	?
Hastin Naat'aani	109Y5	?	**470.**	?
Yellowhorse Deer-Damascus	110Y3	?	**470.**	?
Yellowhorse Mustang-Damascus	110Y2	?	**470.**	?
Collector Set (6)-Damascus	110YW	?	**3,000.**	?
Shriner	503	1500	?	**75.**
Ducks Unlimited (D.U.)	503	?	?	**45.**
Wabash Mine-Safety	503	?	?	**45.**
Buck Knife & Hammer	505	?	?	**75.**
1992				
Al Buck (Kalinga)	401	1000	?	**175.**
Columbus Discover America, gold etch	110	1492	?	**125.**
Buck Collectors Club	535E	500	**71.**	**125.**
LV Maintenance	525	150	?	**30.**
Chevy Truck	110	500	?	**125.**
NRA	525	1500	?	**30.**
H-D Live To Ride, bleached elk	401E1	300	**430.**	**300.**
H-D Early Racers III	110	3000	?	**100.**
Battle: First Manassas	531	100	?	**125.**
Battle: Antietam	531	100	?	**125.**
Battle: Seven Days	531	100	?	**125.**
Battle: New Market	531	100	?	**125.**
Battle: Brandy Station	531	100	?	**125.**
Battle: Chancellorsville	531	100	?	**125.**
Kentucky 200th	531	200	?	**125.**
W. Va. Ch. Wild Turkey	424	1000	?	**45.**
Ellis Island	110	500	?	**150.**
White House 200th	531	500	?	**125.**
Adolphus Busch, Sr.	110	1876	?	**125.**
Fairfield Brewery	525	620	?	**30.**
Eagle, JC Penney	525	600	?	**30.**
Rising Trout, JC Penney	525	600	?	**30.**
Calif. Hwy. Patrol-No Emblem	110	100	?	**125.**
Oshkosh Truck	110	300	?	**115.**

SECTION V: MODERN, COMMEMORATIVE, CLUB, LIMITED EDITION

THEME	MODEL	QUANT.	ISSUE	2004
Roy Clark, Branson	110	1500	?	100.
Roy Clark	525	250	?	30.
Merle Haggard, Branson	110	1500	?	100.
Merle Haggard	525	250	?	30.
River Runs Through It	110	500	?	150.
Ground Hog Day	110	100	?	150.
Ground Hog Day	525	250	?	35.
OwnCo-Georgia Pacific	525	1000	?	30.
Toyota T-100	110FG	110	?	125.
Bass Pro Signature	526	300	?	35.
Buckle Tree-Daytona	110	?	?	75.
Safari Club-Carolina 4/24/92	110	100	?	125.
CIT Group	501	?	?	40.
CCI Speer-Outers Weaver	501	?	?	40.
Wild Turkey	521A7	?	37.	45.
Golfer	521AA	?	37.	45.
Large Mouth Bass	521A5	?	37.	45.
Golden & Black Retrievers	521A9	?	37.	45.
Yellowhorse Confederate Flag	112YA	?	440.	350.
Yellowhorse Thunderbird	112YC	?	310.	300.
Yellowhorse Cactus	112YB	?	310.	300.
Yellowhorse Eagle	112Y5	?	300.	300.
Yellowhorse Ram-Damascus	110Y1	?	480.	500.
Yellowhorse Coyote-Damascus	110Y5	?	480.	500.
Yellowhorse Eagle-Damascus	110Y4	?	480.	500.
Yellowhorse Elk-Damascus	110Y6	?	480.	500.
Yellowhorse Texas	112Y6	?	320.	350.
Yellowhorse California	112Y7	?	310.	350.
Yellowhorse Wolf	112YD	?	310.	350.
Whitetail Deer	521A4	?	37.	45.
Pheasant	521A2	?	37.	45.
Ruffed Grouse	521A8	?	37.	45.
Desert Storm	426	?	?	80.
Snap-On Tools	521	?	?	40.
Buck Collector's Club	525	?	?	40.
Ruffed Grouse	525RG	?	?	30.

THEME	MODEL	QUANT.	ISSUE	2004
Burlington Northern Railroad	531	?	?	75.
Navy	525	?	?	30.
Army	525	?	?	30.
Air Force	525	?	?	30.
Marines	525	?	?	30.

1993

THEME	MODEL	QUANT.	ISSUE	2004
Chris. Columbus 500th	110	?	?	150.
Thomas Jefferson	110	250	?	125.
Battle: Monitor/ Merrimac	531	100	?	125.
Gen. George Pickett	110	250	?	125.
Georgia Flag 1776	110	250	?	125.
Harley-Davidson Combo	426/23ABK	2000	?	?
H-D Country Roads IV	E11073	3002	112.	?
H-D Flathead I 1993	293HD	3000	166.	?
Swiss H-D Club 20th	110	?	?	?
Augustus A. Busch	110	2000	?	100.
Tampa Brewery	525	250	?	50.
Budweiser-King of Beers	549GY	250	?	50.
Dinosaur: Tyrannosaurus	110	525	?	150.
Dinosaur: Tyrannosaurus	525	1656	?	30.
Dinosaur: Pteranadon	110	250	?	125.
Dinosaur: Pteranadon	525	2000	?	25.
Fathers Day	525	1686	?	30.
Father-Son Hunting, stag	110	200	?	200.
Bass Pro Johnny Morris	110	100	?	150.
Calif. Sheriffs Assoc.	525	70	?	50.
Herbertz 10 Yrs. Partner	110	499	?	100.
Weyerhauser	525	1000	?	40.
Buck Continuous Improvement	525	?	?	50.
1st production Zippers	191	50	?	100.
DU Super Raffle Set-USA	?	3000	?	?
DU Super Raffle Set-Canada	?	700	?	?
DU SRS Woodsman pad print Blade, medal in handle	102	?	?	?

THEME	MODEL	QUANT.	VALUES: ISSUE	2004
DU SRS Squire pad print blade, medal in handle	501	?	?	?
DU SRS pad print blade, medal in handle	703	?	?	?
DU SRS Squire pad print blade, medal in handle, overruns	501	?	?	45.
Yellowhorse Dineh	112YG	?	?	?
Yellowhorse Cuthair, Series III	108Y3	?	?	?
Yellowhorse Trapper	314DY	?	?	150.
Marathon '93, Million Manhours	501	?	?	45.
Gabriel	501	?	?	45.
Mare Island Naval Shipyard	501	?	?	45.
West Hazmat Drilling Corp.	501	?	?	45.
Budweiser Beer	426	?	?	40.
Ducks Unlimited	426	?	?	40.
KC 25 Years	424	?	?	35.
VA Bear Hunter	531	75	?	175.
Megasafe	531	?	?	100.
WRCA 1993 Yellowhorse	505Y9	?	?	?
Tiffany's-sterling	507	?	?	100.

1994

THEME	MODEL	QUANT.	VALUES: ISSUE	2004
Buck Collector's Club	192E3	160	110.	100.
NFR-Rodeo, Lakeside, CA	112	100	?	125.
IPRA-Rode, Lakeside, CA	110	116	?	125.
NRA-The Presentation	110	350	?	125.
KC Hilites 1993	110	250	?	125.
Ace Hardware 70th	110	500	?	75.
American Bison	110	75	?	125.
H-D Flathead I Ultra	293H1	500	448.	?
H-D Knucklehead II	293H2	3002	166.	?
H-D Petrali Legend V	11093	3004	112.	100.
Herbertz-Live to Ride	110	300	?	125.
Herbertz-HH Buck	110	60	?	150.
Herbertz-Locomotive	112	80	?	150.
Herbertz-Wild Turkey	112	60	?	150.
Vietnam, JC Penney	692	500	?	100.

THEME	MODEL	QUANT.	VALUES: ISSUE	2004
D-Day 50th Anniv.	192	500	?	125.
WRCA 1994 club knife YH	532	100	?	150.
Yellowhorse Companion	309DY	200	88.	85.
Nevada Gold Mining	916	250	130.	150.
RMEF '95	124	150	?	250.
Buck Founders- Since 1902	110N4	?	60.	60.
Buck Founders- Since 1902	112N4	?	57.	60.
Safari Club International 4/94	110	?	125.	125.
Yellowhorse Eagle Dancer	109Y4	?	490.	?
Yellowhorse Navajo-Land	532Y1	?	278.	300.
Triten	501	?	?	45.
Cadillac	501	?	?	45.
Turkey	525AT	?	31.	30.
Yellowhorse Bull Rider	112DP	?	330.	350.
FG PRCA Folding Hunter	110PR	?	65.	65.
FG PRCA Ranger	112PR	?	63.	65.
PRCA Cocobolo Special	119PR	?	100.	100.
PRCA Black Bucklite II	424PR	?	28.	30.
PRCA Red Bucklite	422PR	?	33.	35.
PRCA Mini-Trapper	312 PR	?	38.	45.
PRCA Blue Knight	505PR	?	41.	45.
PRCA Blue Bucklock	532PR	?	64.	80.
PRCA Gent	525PR	?	32.	30.
PRCA Bronc Rider	525BR	?	33.	30.
PRCA Horse & Rider	525HR	?	33.	30.
PRCA Bull Rider	525BU	?	33.	30.
PRCA Boots	525BO	?	33.	30.
PRCA Companion	309PR	?	25.	30.
PRCA Stockman	301PR	?	38.	40.
PRCA Pony	705PR	?	32.	40.
PRCA Maverick	704PR	?	32.	40.
PRCA Crosslock Horseman	180HP	?	73.	65.
PRCA Crosslock Roper	180PR	?	58.	65.
Ragot D-Day France	110	250	?	125.
Tiffany's-sterling	500	?	?	175.
AMOCO	110	?	?	55.
Sturgis 1990- Road Runner	119RR	50	?	75.

Commemorative and Limited-Edition Knives

Cripple Creek U.S.A. Bench Made Collectible Knives

By Blade Magazine Cutlery Hall-Of-Famer© Houston Price, Publisher of *Knife World*

Brand names such as Remington, Winchester, Case and New York Knife Co. have long held special significance for pocketknife collectors. Finding the high-quality knives made years ago by these famous firms is a constant challenge. Almost all such knives are highly valued, so finding one at a reasonable price means you have a real treasure to keep, or else the makings of a quick profit.

You can add Cripple Creek to that elite list. In a few short years, Bob Cargill's limited-edition brand has earned recognition and respect, as well as a dedicated following of serious collectors.

There are several good reasons for the popularity and collector value of Cripple Creek Knives. First, both the patterns and the quality of workmanship of these American-made knives is reminiscent of knives from the U.S. cutlery industry's "golden years" of the 1920s and '30s.

Second, a very limited number of knives were made following the brand's introduction in 1981. Cripple Creek Knives were bench made one at a time. The company's founder, custom knifemaker Bob Cargill of Ocoee, Tennessee, worked on every knife from the time the design was conceived until production was complete. In fact, until his son, Barry, entered the business in 1984, Cargill performed all the tasks of a one-man factory. From 1993 to 1995, Blackjack Knives owned Cripple Creek, though Cargill remained in charge of production.

Third, Cargill used an effective dating system on his Cripple Creek knives so that it is easy to pinpoint when any knife was made. It is also easy to learn the total production of each pattern. Most Cripple Creeks were made in special limited editions, often for knife clubs, with total quantity marked accordingly.

Identification of a Cripple Creek knife requires noting four features: pattern, handle material, shield and stamping. Cargill's patterns are traditional, so they can be identified from the section, "Pictorial Key to Standard American Folding Knives."

Cripple Creek handle materials are bone, genuine stag and mother-of-pearl. Few pearl Cripple Creeks were made and are much in demand. Most of the knives have bone handles, with the "honey" and the "strawberry" colored being the most popular.

Cripple Creek's standard shield is an oval embossed with a three-legged buffalo, modeled after the one on some 1937-D nickels. Cargill lost a leg in an accident several years ago and this misfortune, combined with his wry good humor, inspired his brand name and trademark. He used the crippled buffalo shield beginning in late 1981. Before then, he sold a few Cripple Creeks without shields. Others had a flat oval shield stamped with the CRIPPLE CREEK brand name. A wise collector would never pass up a knife with the "Cripple Creek" shield.

The small blade of each Cripple Creek knife is tang stamped with the company name in a circle. Cripple Creek knives from 1981 have no date marking, but after that the last two digits of the production year were added to the circle stamping. Cripple Creek devoted most of its 1982 production to making the 2,000 *Knife World* 1st Edition knives. Only about 40 other Cripple Creek knives of different patterns were made that year, any of which would be a rare find.

Several knife collecting clubs have chosen a Cripple Creek as an annual knife. Club knives are made in very limited quantities and are usually sold only to club members. (For more on club knives, see the section, "Knife Club Limited Edition Knives.") Some collectors join local clubs all over the country, by mail, in order to be able to purchase club knives. Also, a few businesses commissioned Cripple Creek limited editions to commemorate special occasions. All these special limited editions are rare and desirable to collectors.

You will not find it difficult to recognize a Cripple Creek. Its distinctive pattern and workmanship will beckon with a whisper of bygone years. A quick check of the handle, shield and stamping will tell you that you have found a pocket-sized treasure.

Early 1981 and 1982 Cripple Creeks. (Weyer photo, courtesy Vanderveen collection)

Fight'n Rooster Limited-Production Knives

by Blade Magazine Cutlery Hall-Of-Famer© Houston Price, Publisher of *Knife World*

In the early 1970s, Blade Magazine Cutlery Hall-Of-Famer© Frank Buster of Lebanon, Tennessee, recognized that finding old knives at reasonable prices was becoming increasingly difficult. Traveling from his middle Tennessee home, he sought out cutlery manufacturers willing to make limited quantities of discontinued traditional patterns of pocketknives that he could sell to his fellow collectors.

Buster learned that most knife factories were geared to producing knives by the tens of thousands. They lacked the flexibility essential for limited-production runs, and they would not consider using old-time methods or old parts and patterns, either.

Finally, Buster located a small factory in Solingen, Germany, which was willing to cooperate with him on a few short-run patterns. In 1976, the factory produced the first knives with Frank Buster's FIGHT'N ROOSTER tang stamping of a pair of fighting cocks.

Since that modest beginning, hundreds of patterns and variations of Fight'n Rooster knives have been offered to the knife-collecting fraternity. Some fans of these knives even carry and use them.

Each of the Fight'n Rooster variations is strictly limited in production. Ordinarily, 300 knives of each style are made, featuring three or four different handle materials. Mother-of-pearl has been a favorite with collectors.

These regular production Fight'n Roosters are offered through dealers at knife shows and by mail. In addition to them, Buster has offered well over 100 different limited-edition club knives. Production of them has varied from 100 pieces for smaller clubs up to 600 for the largest.

Fight'n Rooster knives are made in traditional styles, though Buster has come up with several new variations on old themes. He has offered canoe whittlers, lockback whittlers and multi-bladed stock knives. He has offered many knives with six, eight or even 12 blades. He also has offered a few multi-bladed display knives, including one with 100 blades. A few Fight'n Rooster knives feature genuine old fancy bolsters found in the factory storerooms.

A noteworthy feature of Buster's revival of traditional patterns has been his re-introduction of fancy-patterned celluloid handles. His was the first contemporary knife firm to revive such traditional materials as "butter-and-molasses," "gold flake" and "Christmas tree."

Up until the early 1940s, when the American production of celluloid was halted, celluloid was a popular handle material used by all large knife companies. (For more on celluloid, see the section, "Makers of Picture-Handle Pocketknives.") A few years ago, Buster found the last celluloid factory in Germany. He bought enough of the old-style plastic to last his knife factory several years. In 1984, the celluloid factory went out of business.

Because he also is a knife collector, Buster has been careful to tailor the production of Fight'n Rooster knives to the needs and desires of collectors. He has kept quality high and production strictly limited. He has completely catalogued every pattern produced, including year, quantity and description. He has made Fight'n Rooster a name that will be long remembered.

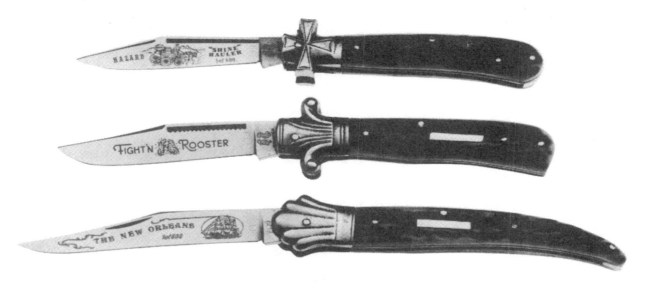

Three Fight'n Rooster knives with genuine stag handles and turn-of-the-century bolsters.
(Weyer photo, courtesy Frank Buster Cutlery Co., Box 936, Lebanon, TN 37087)

Knife Club Limited-Edition Knives

LIMITED-EDITION, annual club knives have remained popular for almost three decades now, enjoying a peak in demand in the late '70s and early '80s. Most are commissioned and sold by local and national knife collecting organizations, both to enhance club treasuries and to allow members to have "something special." Nearly all are very limited in quantity. A few of the clubs, at the end of the list, are commercial undertakings, but this does not diminish the interest or value of their knives.

Newly issued club knives are sold only to club members, but all clubs welcome collectors in distant places to join and to buy knives by mail. An up-to-date list of most knife clubs, with contact names and addresses, is published every month in *Knife World* magazine. For more information contact *Knife World*, Box 3395, Knoxville TN 37927.

All the information in the charts below, including the values, was furnished by the indicated officers or members of the clubs. The original charts and data were collected for *Knife World* by Bill Karsten, beginning in 1981.

If you are interested in older knives from a particular club, your best bet would be to attend a meeting or a show sponsored by the club, or you might write to the club and advertise in its newsletter.

NKCA (National Knife Collectors Association); formerly N.K.C. & D.A. (National Knife Collectors & Dealers Association) Information from Lisa Sebenick. For more information, contact the NKCA, P.O. Box 21070, Dept. BG6, Chattanooga TN 37424-0070 423.892.5007 fax 423.899.9456 nkca@aol.com.

ISSUE	QUANTITY	DESCRIPTION	VALUES ISSUE	VALUES CURRENT
1. 1975	1,200	Kissing Crane	$12.	$862.50
2. 1976	3,000	Case	15.	287.50
3. 1977	5,000	Kissing Crane	17.50	143.75
4. 1978	6,000	Schrade	18.25	115.
5. 1979	12,000	Case	22.	97.75
6. 1980	12,000	Kissing Crane	21.75	86. 25
7. 1981	12,000	Queen	24.50	86.25
8. 1982	10,000	Schrade	24.50	86.25
9. 1983	7,000	Case	45.	172.50
10. 1984	7,000	Hen & Rooster	38.	97.75
11. 1985	7,000	Case	40.	92.
12. 1986	6,200	Gerber	39.	143.75
13. 1987	7,000	Case	42.95	97.75
14. 1988	6,500	Camillus	41.95	172.50
15. 1989A	6,500	Case (folder)	50.	92.
16. 1989B	1,700	Buck (fixed)	80.	115.
17. 1990A	5,000	Kissing Crane (folder)	65.	115.
18. 1990B	1,500	Hen & Rooster (fixed)	85.	115.
19. 1991A	4,000	Case (folder)	69.	86.25
20. 1991B	1,250	Case (fixed)	85.	115.
21. 1992A	3,500	Sarco/Queen (folder)	69.	86.25
22. 1992B	1,000	Bear MGC (fixed)	50.	69.
23. 1993A	2,652	Bear MGC stag (folder)	49.	86.25
24. 1993B	1,370	Bear MGC (fixed)	49.	86.25
25. 1994A	2,058	Case (folder)	69.	115.
26. 1994B	1,131	Bear MGC (fixed)	39.	86.25
27. 1995A	1,850	Case (folder)	65.	86.25
28. 1995B	1,500	German Eye Brand (folder)	64.	103.50
29. 1996A	1,550	German Eye Brand stag whittler	70.	126.50
30. 1996B	1,675	Winchester (folder)	65.	115.
31. 1997	1,720	Smith & Wesson	85.	115.
32. 1998	1,500	Camillus	69.	92.
33. 1999	1,535	Case	69.	92.
34. 2000	1,609	Queen	77.	120.75
35. 2001	1,160	Buck	77.	115.
36. 2002	1,200	Schatt & Morgan (Queen)	77.	110.
37. 2003	1,175	Case	79.	110.
38. 2004	1,075	Schatt & Morgan (Queen)	79.95	100.

GEM CAPITAL KNIFE CLUB, Franklin, North Carolina. Information from Bill Karsten and Dave Culpepper. [Club inactive since 1986.]

ISSUE	QUANTITY	DESCRIPTION	ISSUE	1985	2000
				VALUES	
1. 1980	150	Fight'n Rooster pearl powderhorn with two rubies	$41.	$225.	$300.
2. 1981	250	Fight'n Rooster pearl 5-blade stockman with two sapphires	52.	125.	150.
3. 1982	300	Fight'n Rooster pearl 4-blade canoe with two emeralds	52.	80.	125.
4. 1983	300	Fight'n Rooster pearl muskrat with two garnets	52.	85.	125.
5. 1984	200	Fight'n Rooster black pearl equal-end jack with one diamond	65.	125.	225.
6. 1985	200	Fight'n Rooster pearl 3-blade cattleman with one ruby	65.	80.	125.
7. 1986	150	Fight'n Rooster pearl 3-blade stockman with one sapphire	65.	125.	**Complete set: $1,100-1,175.**

BAY AREA KNIFE COLLECTORS ASSOCIATION, Fremont, California. Information from Ray and Carol Clark. This club's knives are custom knives, mainly by maker members.

ISSUE	QUANTITY	DESCRIPTION	ISSUE	1985	1989	1993	2000
				VALUES			
1. 1980	52	Sornberger rosewood trout/bird, sheath	$70.	$125.	$170.	$190.	$190.
2. 1981	50	Centofante FL2 folder, Micarta®	155.	250.	325.	360.	375.
3. 1982	32	Terrill rosewood semi-skinner, sheath	85.	110.	145.	160.	160.
4. 1983	50	Corrado folder, coin silver	83.	150.	210.	225.	235.
5. 1984	25	Gamble rosewood trailing point, sheath	75.	95.	125.	140.	140.
6. 1985	25	Norton cocobolo drop point, sheath	85.	95.	190.	210.	210.
7. 1986	27	Osborne folder, jigged stag	120.	200.	220.	300.	
8. 1987	30	Ankrom rosewood semi-skinner, sheath	125.	150.	170.	170.	
9. 1988	49	Mendenhall stag drop-point, engraving	125.	200.	225.	225.	
10. 1989	37	Boguszewski cocobolo lockback folder	130.	195.	225.		
11. 1990	37	Crowder ironwood drop point, sheath	145.	175.	175.		
12. 1991	32	Easler stag drop point, sheath, scrim.	135.	150.	165.		
13. 1992	32	Whiskers Allen oosic lockback folder	135.	145.	175.		
14. 1993	28	Maxwell maple fixed blade	175.	225.			
15. 1994	35	Easler stag fixed blade	200.	235.			
16. 1995	30	Tommy Lee ironwood fixed blade	200.	225.			
17. 1996	25	Sawby jigged bone "Self Lock" folder	360.	425.			
18. 1997	—	Berry small hunter					

OREGON KNIFE COLLECTORS ASSOCIATION, Eugene-Springfield, Oregon. Information from Dennis Ellingsen, Jim Kirk, and Jim Chartier.

ISSUE	QUANTITY	DESCRIPTION	ISSUE	1985	1989	1993	2000
				VALUES			
1. 1979	200	Case lockback	$20.	$50.	$50.	$50.	$60.
2. 1980	200	Gerber Knight, stag	27.50	50.	50.	50.	100.
3. 1981	100	Gerber LST	30.	40.	40.	50.	50.
4. 1982	50	Corrado	60.	100.	300.	400.	
5. 1983	50	Gerber/Paul	55.	125.	350.	425.	425.
6. 1984	50	Gerber Touche	30.	75.	75.	85.	85.
7. 1985	50	Gerber FSII	40.	40.	75.	75.	75.
8. 1986	71	Gerber/Loveless	40.	100.	100.	100.	
9. 1987	60	Al Mar tanto	60.	100.	100.	100.	
10. 1988	60	Gerber Benchmark	68.	68.	70.	70.	
11. 1989	50	Cripple Creek	80.	125.	125.		
12. 1990	50	Terry Davis	100.	285.	600.		
13. 1991	50	Mark Wahlster	115.	125.	125.		
14. 1992	50	Gerber FSI	90.	100.	100.		
15. 1993	50	Steve Huey/Terry Davis	80.	100.			
16. 1994	50	Huey/Corrado/Geo. Sherwood	150.	250.			
17. 1995A	50	Corrado/McKenzie	160.	225.			

OREGON KNIFE COLLECTORS ASSOCIATION *(continued)*

ISSUE	QUANTITY	DESCRIPTION	ISSUE	VALUES 1985	1989	1993	2000
18. 1995B	30	Corrado/McKenzie 450.	600.				
19. 1996	50	Gerber/Paul II	140.	140.			
20. 1997	50	Gerber Applegate Combat Folder	120.				
21. 1998	60	Wayne Goddard C16PS Clipit-Special	125.				
22. 1999	50	Gerber Applegate Covert folder	130.				
23. 2000	50	Corrado silver folder-engraving by Phil Grifnee	300.				

GOLDEN CIRCLE KNIFE CLUB, Alamo, Tennessee. Information from Bob Mathes. Club no longer active.

ISSUE	QUANTITY	DESCRIPTION	ISSUE	VALUES 1981	1985	1989
1. 1978	300	Klaas stag serpentine whittler	$18.50	$75.	$100.	$60.
2. 1979	300	Klaas stag 4-blade sleeveboard	30.	50.	90.	60.
3. 1980	500	Klaas white equal-end whittler	30.	50.	60.	
4. 1981	500	Col. Coon stag muskrat	30.		50.	65.
5. 1981A	200	Founders': Col. Coon bone muskrat	35.	50.	60.	
6. 1982	500	Case 6265 SAB red bone fol. hunt.	35.	50.	75.	
7. 1983	300	Case 4254 white comp. trapper	30.	40.	60.	
8. 1983A	150	5th Anniv. Case 2254 trapper	30.	65.	70.	
9. 1984	50	Col. Coon stag trapper	40.	100.	100.	
10. 1985	65	Col. Coon stockman, 3-blade	45.	100.		
11. 1986	60	Col. Coon stockman, 4-blade	45.	100.		
12. 1987	70	Bulldog stag canoe	45.	70.		
13. 1988	44	Case 6199 green bone jack	42.50	50.		

HAWKEYE KNIFE COLLECTORS, Des Moines, Iowa. Information from Jim Reinert.

ISSUE	QUANTITY	DESCRIPTION	ISSUE	VALUES 1989	1993	2000
1. 1986	100	Cripple Creek stag whittler	$60.	$75.	$90.	$90.
2. 1987	100	Cripple Creek stag 3-spring Eureka	65.	75.	85.	85.
3. 1988	100	Boker #280 pearl whittler	48.	55.	60.	60.
4. 1989	50	Boker stag trapper	45.	65.	65.	
5. 1990	40	Larry Duvall cocobolo drop point (fixed)	60.	80.	80.	
6. 1991	45	Larry Duvall maple clip point (fixed)	65.	85.	85.	
7. 1992	50	Sarco/Queen stag swell-center whittler	48.	60.	60.	
8. 1993	64	Sarco stag premium stock	50.	50.	60.	
9. 1994	63	Parker-Case stag wharncliffe whittler	60.	70.		
10. 1995	62	Parker-Case stag sowbelly whittler	60.	70.		
11. 1996	70	Parker-Case stag sowbelly stock, 5-blade	65.	75.		
12. 1997	60	Parker-Case stag swing-guard lockback	75.	75.		

PEACH STATE CUTLERY CLUB, Acworth, Georgia. Club no longer active.

ISSUE	QUANTITY	DESCRIPTION	ISSUE VALUE
1. 1984	60	Ka-Bar stag gunstock, 2-blade	$34.20
2. 1985	60	Case second-cut stag trapper	35.
3. 1986	55	Case ivory mini-trapper	35.
4. 1987	75	Case red bone congress, 3-blade	36.
5. 1988	55	Case stag canoe	40.

MASON-DIXON KNIFE CLUB, Quincy, Pennsylvania. Information from Ralph H. Scruton.

ISSUE	QUANTITY	DESCRIPTION	ISSUE	VALUES 1989	2000
1. 1984A	42	Case 6165 white jigged bone fol. hunter	$42.	$125.	$225.
1984B	33	Case 6165 white bone "Charter Member"	42.	150.	250.

MASON-DIXON KNIFE CLUB (continued)

ISSUE	QUANTITY	DESCRIPTION	ISSUE	VALUES 1989	2000
2. 1985	75	Ka-Bar chestnut jigged bone plowman	39.	50.	45.
3. 1986	75	Queen Winterbottom bone canoe	35.	50.	70.
4. 1987	75	Ka-Bar chestnut jigged bone sunfish	39.	50.	50.
5. 1988	100	Alcas stag large trapper	48.	100.	150.
6. 1989	100	Case R6240 red bone dogleg trapper	40.	50.	
7. 1990	100	Winchester 1924P pearl small toothpick	60.	150.	
8. 1991	110	Winchester 1950 stag	75.	125.	
9. 1992	100	Sargent/ Queen white bone trapper	40.	55.	
10. 1993	62	Blackjack #1-7 sheath knife	75.	75.	
11. 1994	45	Ka-Bar jigged bone large "Coke bottle"	50.	50.	
12. 1995	48	Case 61100 bone saddlehorn	55.	55.	

CENTRAL KENTUCKY KNIFE CLUB, INC. Lexington, Kentucky. Information from George T. Williams.

ISSUE	QUANTITY	DESCRIPTION	ISSUE	VALUES 1989	1993	2000
1. 1983	125	Case 53131 stag canoe, 3-blade	$40.	$125.	$125.	$125.
2. 1984	172	Case 6165L stag lockback folding hunter	50.	75.	75.	75.
3. 1985	201	Case 5254SS stag trapper	40.	50.	50.	50.
4. 1986	108	Bulldog stag equal-end, 3-blade	45.	90.	100.	200.
5. 1987	101	Fight'n Rooster stag lockback whittler	50.	75.	75.	90.
6. 1988	100	Cripple Creek saddlehorn, 1-blade	60.	90.	90.	135.
7. 1989	100	Cripple Creek stag butter-bean, 2-blade	65.	75.	110.	
8. 1990	100	Case 5240 dog-leg trapper	45.	55.	65.	
9. 1991	91	Queen stag gunstock, 2-blade	45.	55.	55.	
10. 1992	50	10th Anniv. Fight'n Rooster pearl canoe	95.	105.	135.	
11. 1992	91	Case 5159LSS stag Hammerhead	45.	60.		
12. 1993	91	Case 53043-1/2 stag whittler	60.	80.		
13. 1994	56	Primble stag congress 4-blade	60.	70.		
14. 1995	70	Bulldog stag Hawbaker muskrat	50.	70.		
15. 1996	62	Case 53052SS stag whittler	42.	50.		

RIVERLAND KNIFE COLLECTORS CLUB, Dunellon, Florida. Information from Charles Piper and Robert Ferring.

ISSUE	QUANTITY	DESCRIPTION	ISSUE	VALUES 1993	2000
1. 1988	55	Fight'n Rooster waterfall cotton sampler	$35.	$50.	$65.
2. 1989	35	Blackton ironwood drop-point hunter	70.	120.	120.
3. 1990	50	Fight'n Rooster stag 2-bl folding hunter	50.	95.	100.
4. 1991	70	Boker stag lockback	55.	55.	55.
5. 1992	50	Boker pearl 2-bl lockback	45.	50.	50.
6. 1993	50	Schatt & Morgan red bone bowtie w/guard	45.	55.	
7. 1994	50	Schatt & Morgan stag scout knife	50.	60.	
8. 1995	50	Case red bone wharncliffe whittler	50.	55.	
9. 1996	50	Fight'n Rooster stag 3-blade barlow	55.	65.	
10. 1997	50	Linder stag drop-point hunter	55.		

PALMETTO CUTLERY CLUB, Greer, South Carolina. Information from Johnny Perry and Hydrick B. Stewart.

ISSUE	QUANTITY	DESCRIPTION	ISSUE	VALUES 1989	1993	2000
1. 1976	50	Queen pearl sleeveboard	$13.	$175.	$175.	$225.
2. 1977	200	Fight'n Rooster pearl canoe, 3-blade	27.	100.	100.	125.
3. 1978	200	Fight'n Rooster pearl muskrat	19.50	75.	75.	90.
4. 1979	200	Fight'n Rooster pearl gunstock	30.	90.	90.	95.
5. 1980	200	Fight'n Rooster pearl physician's 1-blade	29.50	90.	90.	125.
6. 1981	200	Fight'n Rooster pearl teardrop barlow	36.50	90.	90.	125.

PALMETTO CUTLERY CLUB (continued)

ISSUE	QUANTITY	DESCRIPTION	ISSUE	1989	1993	2000
7. 1982	200	Parker pearl baby bullet	20.	40.	40.	45.
8. 1983A	200	Parker pearl sow-belly stockman, 3-blade	27.	30.	30.	55.
9. 1983B	135	Parker pearl congress, 3-blade	16.	25.	35.	65.
10. 1984	135	Case pearl mini-trapper	47.50	90.	100.	150.
11. 1985	140	Queen pearl whittler	40.	75.	75.	125.
12. 1986	105	Queen pearl copperhead	45.	60.	60.	75.
13. 1987	100	Queen pearl half-whittler, 2-blade	38.	38.	45.	45.
14. 1988	75	Buck pearl 501 Squire	42.	42.	75.	150.
15. 1989	75	Hen & Rooster pearl trapper	55.	70.	125.	
16. 1990	90	United/Boker pearl copperhead	45.	55.	65.	
17. 1991	75	Sargent pearl congress 4-blade	45.	55.	75.	
18. 1992	67	Case pearl bow-tie	45.	65.	150.	
19. 1993	75	Case 3-backspring pearl "whittler"	75.	125.		
20. 1994	100	Bulldog pearl toothpick	90.	125.		
21. 1995	48	Russell Easler custom pearl tapered jack	200.	225.		
22. 1996		George Herron pearl skinner (fixed)	275.			

CHESAPEAKE BAY KNIFE CLUB, Baltimore, Maryland. Information from Cathy Berry and Glenn Paul Smit.

ISSUE	QUANTITY	DESCRIPTION	ISSUE	1993	2000
1. 1980	50	R.B. (Ray Beers) custom folder	$100.	$200.	$200.
2. 1980	4	Al Mar folder, standard	50.	100.	150.
3. 1980	18	Al Mar folder, engraved	77.	150.	175.
4. 1981	30	William Antonio skinner	120.	200.	200.
5. 1982	40	R.B. full-tang hunter	150.	250.	250.
6. 1983	100	Case green bone Mako	40.	40.	60.
7. 1983	80	Gary Barnes silver dollar	88.	125.	150.
8. 1984	80	G. & S. Cutlery German drop-point folder	35.	45.	60.
9. 1985	40	KAS Knives (Ken Steigerwalt) folder	125.	175.	200.
10. 1986	40	Victorinox multiblade, black plastic	35.	35.	60.
11. 1987	35	R.B. hunter	95-140.	150-200.	150-250.
12. 1988	19	3-piece Beretta set	85.	100.	125.
13. 1989	75	Goodwin Enterprises red bone trapper	30.	40.	45.
14. 1990A	39	Ray Beers double-edge dagger	100-250.	200-400.	250-400.
15. 1990B	26	Rigid RG101 folder	25.	35.	50.
16. 1991	200	Carvel Hall oyster knives	18.	20-30.	35.
17. 1992	29	Russell Easler scrimshaw hunter (fixed)	100-350.	125-400.	
18. 1993	30	United Cutlery Conquistador	50.	75.	
19. 1994	21	Himalayan Import Kukri	70.	100.	
20. 1995	40	Cripple Creek stag barlow, 1-blade	55.	75.	
21. 1996		Frank McGowan personal model	125-200.		

TENNESSEE VALLEY BLADES KNIFE CLUB, Cleveland, Tennessee. Information from Bob Cargill. Club no longer active.

ISSUE	QUANTITY	DESCRIPTION	ISSUE	1989	1993
1. 1988	25	Parker wood & Frost bone trappers set	$40.	$60.	$65.

NORTH CAROLINA CUTLERY CLUB (disbanded in 1995; club no longer sells the knives). Information from Gene H. Abernethy, 118 Park Ave., Dept. BG6, Fuquay-Varina, NC 27526 919.557.1207 gamewarden007@aol.com.

ISSUE	QUANTITY	DESCRIPTION	ISSUE	CURRENT
1. 1981	150	Parker pearl mini-trapper	$27.50	$100.

NORTH CAROLINA CUTLERY CLUB (continued)

ISSUE	QUANTITY	DESCRIPTION	VALUES ISSUE	CURRENT
2. 1982	150	Parker pearl whittler	20.	40.
3. 1983	200	Boker/Germany gray smooth bone trapper	24.	45.50
4. 1984	200	Boker/Germany gray smooth bone canoe	24.	55.
5. 1985	200	Boker/Germany gray smooth bone copperhead	24.50	40.
6. 1986	166	Case burnt jigged bone whittler	39.	50.
7. 1987	175	United/Boker gray smooth bone folding hunter	29.50	60.
8. 1988	175	United/Boker gray smooth bone stockman	28.75	40.
9. 1989	150	United/Boker gray smooth bone lockback (2006)	32.	55.
10. 1990	175	Boker/Germany gray bone congress	30.	60.
11. 1991	150	Boker/Germany gray bone whittler	29.50	40.
12. 1992	150	United/Boker 2041 jigged gray bone lockback	36.	75.
13. 1993	150	United/Boker jigged gray bone barlow	30.	35.
14. 1994	103	Case mini-trapper appaloosa bone	29.	45.
15. 1995	103	Case B254SS blue Delrin trapper	30.	35.

SOONER KNIFE COLLECTOR CLUB, Oklahoma City, Oklahoma. Information from Mike Ramsey.

ISSUE	QUANTITY	DESCRIPTION	VALUES ISSUE	1989	1993
1. 1984	38	Case stag 5254 trapper	$45.	$80.	$90.
2. 1985	50	Fight'n Rooster lock-back whittler	50.	60.	125.
3. 1986		United Boker bone stockman, 3-blade	20.	40.	
4. 1987		Case red bone muskrat	30.	65.	
5. 1988		United Boker candy-stripe canoe	20.	40.	
6. 1989		United Boker horn congress	20.	40.	
7. 1990		Carl Schlieper trapper	45.	95.	
8. 1991		Schatt & Morgan bone Coke bottle	45.	95.	
9. 1992		Schatt & Morgan bone stockman, 3-blade	45.	95.	
10. 1993		Schatt & Morgan barlow	45.		

BADGER KNIFE CLUB, P.O. Box 511, Elm Grove, WI 53122. Information from Robert G. Schrap.

ISSUE	QUANTITY	DESCRIPTION	VALUES ISSUE	1989	1993	CURRENT
1. 1986	45	Cripple Creek dogleg jack-bone 2 blade	$45.	$85.	$110.	$115.
2. 1987	75	Queen Winterbottom bone whittler 3 blade	30.	30.	30.	40.
1988	None issued...					
3. 1989	50	Mountain Forge - Side Lock I	50.	50.	50.	55.
4. 1990	50	Dave Ricke bird & trout (fixed)	85.	90.	125.	
5. 1991	60	Camillus trapper yellow comp. handle 2 blade	38.	38.	40.	
6. 1992	60	Bill Abbott hunter (fixed)	75.	75.	75.	
7. 1993	50	Fight'n Rooster stag 3-blade trapper	70.	85.		
8. 1994	60	Buck gray bone Duke lockback	55.	60.		
9. 1995	55	Hen & Rooster stag whittler 3 blade	55.	65.		
10. 1996	65	Case "Pocket Worn" canoe bone handle 2 blade	50.	50.		
11. 1997	55	Ron Hembrook mini/fighter bone handle (fixed)	95.	100.		
12. 1998	57	Schatt & Morgan (Queen) stag, "File & Wire Tested" hunter	65.	75.		
13. 1999	60	Fight'n Rooster 4-blade canoe bone handle	59.	75.		
14. 2000	55	Fight'n Rooster 4-blade canoe stag handle	85.	95.		
15. 2001	50	Fight'n Rooster 4-blade canoe	95.	110.		
16. 2002	55	Schatt & Morgan (Queen) 2 blade buffalo-horn-handled baby sunfish	75.	75.		
17. 2003	60	D.H. Russell wood handle lockback	85.	85.		
18. 2004	45	Schatt & Morgan (Queen) 2 blade bone handle wildcat driller	85.	85.		

SOUTHERN CALIFORNIA BLADES, Lomita, California. Information from Lowell Shelhart.

ISSUE	QUANTITY	DESCRIPTION	ISSUE	VALUES 1993	2000
1. 1980	150	Queen stag gunstock	$27.50	$50.	$65.
2. 1981	150	Queen stag trapper	27.50	55.	75.
3. 1982-3	100	Case 051051LSSP lockback	32.50	50.	60.
4. 1984	75	Ka-Bar 0591 bone folding hunter	37.50	50.	65.
5. 1985	75	Ka-Bar DH89 bone Plowman	37.50	50.	70.
6. 1986	70	Cripple Creek buffalo skinner	65.	75.	150.
7. 1987	75	Boker USA 4011 folding hunter	55.	55.	85.
8. 1988	75	Happy Jack trapper	45.	45.	90.
9. 1989	100	Remington Bullet	65.	65.	85.
10. 1990	100	Case ROG 61050	55.	55.	75.
11. 1991	75	Boker 4000	65.	65.	85.
12. 1992	50	Winchester W15 - 1920	60.	60.	80.
13. 1993	50	Schatt & Morgan 06181L Winterbottom bone	50.	85.	
14. 1994	50	Schatt & Morgan 04161C corncob bone	55.	90.	
15. 1995	50	Winchester 1927 bone "toad sticker"	65.		85.
16. 1996	50	Case 625033 elephant toenail red bone	75.	85.	
17. 1997	50	Schatt & Morgan English jack blue bone	55.	65.	
18. 1998	50	Schatt & Morgan 041883 "File & Wire" special stag	70.	85.	
19. 1999	50	Case 80100 stag hobo	65.	75.	
20. 2000	50	Boker 3006 exchange-blade drop point stag	75.	75.	

PERMIAN BASIN KNIFE CLUB, Midland, Texas. Information from Fred Nolley.

ISSUE	QUANTITY	DESCRIPTION	ISSUE	VALUES 1989	1993	2000
1. 1981	151	Case 6254 white smooth bone trapper	$25.	$150.	$150.	$150.
2. 1982	200	Case 6254 blond Pakkawood® trapper	26.	100.	100.	100.
3. 1983	200	Case 9254 dark imitation pearl trapper	28.	135.	135.	135.
4. 1984	200	Case 8254 pearl trapper	70.	175.	225.	225.
5. 1985	200	Case 6254 green jigged bone trapper	36.	85.	85.	85.
6. 1986	200	Case 6254 Rogers-style bone trapper	36.	75.	75.	75.
7. 1987	200	Case IV254 ivory trapper	50.	200.	250.	250.
8. 1988	200	Case B200 black bone trapper	30.	75.	75.	75.
9. 1989	200	Case 6254 mesquite wood trapper	41.	75.	75.	75.
10. 1990	200	Case BH254 buffalo horn trapper	50.	100.	100.	
11. 1991	200	Case DR6254 deep red bone trapper	40.	50.	50.	
12. 1992	160	Case 9254 imitation pearl trapper	45.		75.	75.
13. 1993	120	Case 6254 blue jigged bone trapper	38.			60.
14. 1994	120	Case BW6254 second cut bone stag trapper	40.	75.		
15. 1995	120	Case 5254 India stag trapper	53.	100.		100.

NORTHEAST CUTLERY COLLECTORS ASSOCIATION (New England, New York, New Jersey, Pennsylvania) Mansfield, Massachusetts. Information from Jim and Cindy Taylor. No knives issued after 1989.

ISSUE	QUANTITY	DESCRIPTION	ISSUE	VALUES 1993	2000
1. 1982	150	Case white bone 62131 canoe, scrimshaw	$50.	$125.	$150.
2. 1986	75	Cripple Creek red jigged bone stockman	55.	95.	110.
3. 1987	62	Cripple Creek stag dog-leg whittler	60.	95.	110.
4. 1989	51	Cripple Creek jigged bone "Coke bottle"	68.	68.	75.
5. 1989	45	Jim Turecek red jigged bone drop-point	135.	135.	175.

ONE STAR KNIFE CLUB, Waco, Texas. Information from L. E. Walters.

ISSUE	QUANTITY	DESCRIPTION	ISSUE	1989	1993	2000
1. 1983	50	Case 6275SP moose	$40.	$100.	$100.	$125.
2. 1984	100	Fight'n Rooster pearl toothpick	45.	45.	60.	75.
3. 1984A	?	Founders' knife, Ka-Bar bone fol. hunter	45.	75.	90.	125.
4. 1985	58	Case 5254 stag trapper, engraved	45.	75.	90.	100.
5. 1986	50	Ka-Bar bone Plowman, Lone Star shield	35.	50.	60.	75.
6. 1987	55	Ka-Bar bone toenail, Lone Star shield	45.	100.	100.	125.
7. 1988	55	Case R62131 SS canoe, engraved	45.	60.	60.	70.
8. 1989	35	Ka-Bar smooth bone congress, 4-blade	45.	45.	60.	65.
9. 1990	50	Kissing Crane copperhead, stag	45.	60.	60.	
10. 1991	25	Case muskrat	45.	50.	60.	
11. 1992	25	Queen bone gunstock	45.	45.	50.	
12. 1993	25	Schatt & Morgan bone stockman	50.	60.		
13. 1994	25	Winchester bone sowbelly	55.	75.		
14. 1995	25	Case bone granddaddy barlow	55.	100.		
15. 1996	25	Case peach-bone whittler	45.	45.		

MAHONING VALLEY KNIFE COLLECTORS ASSOCIATION, Canfield, Ohio. Information from Robert W. Brown.

ISSUE	QUANTITY	DESCRIPTION	ISSUE	1989	1993	2000
1. 1986	125	Case 6254 SS brown jigged bone trapper	$25.	$60.	$80.	$100.
2. 1987	125	Case B6254 SS smooth gray bone trapper	37.	60.	80.	90.
3. 1988	125	Case R6294 SS jigged red bone equal-end	40.	60.	80.	90.
4. 1989	150	Case 52131 SS stag canoe	45.	50.	60.	75.
5. 1990	115	Case 51139 SS stag lock-blade	40.	50.	70.	
6. 1990A	40	5th Anniversary Mike Yurco custom	100.	200.		
7. 1991	125	Case 61139 SS red bone lock-blade	35.	45.	60.	
8. 1992	125	Case R61098 red bone toothpick	59.	70.	85.	
9. 1993	125	Case C11098 cracked ice toothpick	59.	59.	85.	
10. 1994	125	Case "Bradford" HB61050 bone	60.	75.		
11. 1995	90	Case "Tested XX" 71050 Zipper	60.	70.		
12. 1996	75	Case 53055 stag wharncliffe whittler	59.	65.		
13. 1996A	44	10th Anniversary Mike Yurco custom	155.	175.		

ROY KNIFE COLLECTORS CLUB, Decatur, Illinois. Information from Jerome F. Greive and Jerry Lutz.

ISSUE	QUANTITY	DESCRIPTION	ISSUE	1989	1993	2000
1. 1982	30	Taylor Cut. "Bob Wong's Phantom" set	$38.	$45.	$45.	$45.
2. 1983	30	Col. Coon stag mini-trapper	29.	75.	80.	100.
3. 1984	30	Case 6154 red bone trapper, 1-blade	24.	34.	34.	34.
4. 1985	23	Cargill stag mini-trapper	46.50	60.	60.	75.
5. 1986	30	Cargill honey bone "butterbean" 3-blade	55.	70.	90.	120.
6. 1987	20	Ka-Bar SF86 brown bone sunfish	34.	45.	50.	65.
7. 1988	30	Hen & Rooster 163DS stag, 3-blade	43.	55.	55.	60.
8. 1989	25	Ka-Bar HMP89 2-blade	38.	38.	45.	
9. 1990	17	Camillus 716 yellow 2-blade	39.	39.	39.	
10. 1991	20	10th Anniv: Sargent/Boker pearl 4-blade	50.	60.	65.	
11. 1992-93	22	Hawes damascus custom hunter	88.	125.		
12. 1994	14	Atkinson custom folder, red Micarta®	125.	125.		
13. 1995	14	Case 62100 gray bone saddlehorn	45.	45.		

OLD DOMINION KNIFE COLLECTORS ASSOCIATION, Troutville, Virginia. Information from John Riddle.

				VALUES		
ISSUE	QUANTITY	DESCRIPTION	ISSUE	1989	1993	2000
1. 1978	75	Case canoe, 2-blade	$16.50	$350.	$400.	$400.
2. 1979	300	Kissing Crane stag whittler	27.50	65.	70.	70.
3. 1980	250	Kissing Crane stag, 4-blade	29.	55.	60.	65.
4. 1981	300	Bulldog stag trapper	27.	65.	90.	100.
5. 1982	300	Bulldog stag gunstock stockman	30.	60.	100.	120.
6. 1983	300	Bulldog stag folding hunter, 2-blade	35.	75.	85.	95.
7. 1984	300	Bulldog stag congress, 4-blade	34.	65.	90.	100.
8. 1985	300	Bulldog stag trapper, 3-blade	37.	75.	100.	120.
9. 1986	225	Boker stag stockman	32.	35.	40.	45.
11. 1988	200	Fight'n Rooster stag folding hunter	47.	50.	50.	52.
12. 1988A	150	10th Anniversary: Boker pearl canoe	39.	50.	60.	65.
13. 1989	200	Fight'n Rooster stag muskrat	38.	38.	38.	50.
14. 1990	125	Fight'n Rooster waterfall sowbelly	38.	50.	75.	75.
15. 1991	200	Fight'n Rooster stag serpentine	40.	45.	50.	
16. 1992	150	Fight'n Rooster gr. bone powderhorn 2-bl.	47.	47.	50.	
17. 1993	100	Bulldog sunfish "purple duck feathers"	82.	85.		
18. 1994	100	Bulldog copperhead "end of day"	45.	50.		
19. 1995	180	Bulldog blue swirl whittler	55.50	55.50		
20. 1996	122	Bulldog red bone physician's jack	60.	85.		

ROCKY MOUNTAIN BLADE COLLECTORS, Louisville, Colorado. Information from Tom Gilroy.

				VALUES			
ISSUE	QUANTITY	DESCRIPTION	ISSUE	1989	1997	2001	CURRENT
1. 1979	72	Case custom pearl whittler	$42.50	$125.	$150.	$150.	$200.
2. 1980	100	Ka-Bar stag folding hunter	30.	100.	135.	140.	150.
3. 1981	100	Ka-Bar stag 2-blade large jack	20.	60.	85.	90.	100.
4. 1982	100	Ka-Bar stag lockback	37.50	75.	100.	115.	125.
5. 1983	55	Ka-Bar bone folding hunter	37.50	125.	155.	165.	175.
6. 1984	100	Ka-Bar stag 2-blade barlow	35.	45.	65.	75.	85.
7. 1986	55	Barminski custom hunter, stag	55.	125.	135.	140.	200.
8. 1987	100	"Rocky Mtn. USA" red-bone lockback, damascus	37.50	60.	65.	65.	70.
9. 1988	55	Barminski custom hunter, Pakkawood®	50.	75.	90.	90.	100.
10. 1989-90	72	Fight'n Rooster 10-blade pearl	85.	?	250.	300.	300.
11. 1991	35	Camillus M-3 Desert Storm commemorative	30.	?	60.	65.	75.
12. 1992	100	Western Valox lockback folding hunter	15.	?	25.	30.	35.
13. 1993	22	Western 628 stag bird and trout	35.	?	45.	60.	95.
14. 1994	50	Case Classic bone moose	45.	?	75.	85.	90.
15. 1995	40	Ken Brock custom "hat band" miniature	55.	?	65.	75.	90.
16. 1996	35	Case Classic bone sunfish	75.	?	105.	125.	130.
17. 1997	45	Barry Wood folder	100.	?	?	225.	295.
18. 1998	50	Colorado Cutlery custom sheath knife	50.	?	?	75.	125.
19. 1999	40	Fight'n Rooster pearl 3-blade trapper	125.	?	?	150.	165.
20. 2000	50	Mark Blevans custom "Grizzly" folding hunter	125.	?	?	200.	275.
21. 2001	75	Owen Wood custom bone locking-liner wharncliffe folder	155.	?	?	?	350.
22. 2002	36	Jim Largent custom burl wood bird and trout	160.	?	?	?	165.
23. 2003	50	Schatt & Morgan pearl 25th anniversary doctor's knife	100.	?	?	?	110.
24. 2004	50	Schatt & Morgan mammoth ivory doctor's knife	110.	?	?	?	110.

PORT CITY KNIFE COLLECTORS CLUB, Cincinnati, Ohio. Information from Bill Powell and Anne Cartwright.

				VALUES		
ISSUE	QUANTITY	DESCRIPTION	ISSUE	1989	1993	2000
1. 1981	150	Fight'n Rooster pearl whittler	$39.50	$115-125.	$150.	$150.
2. 1981	20	ditto, "Founders," gold plated blades	42.50	150-160.	200.	325.
3. 1982	220	Case 5254 SSP stag trapper 8-dot	37.50	40.	50.	75.
4. 1982	15	ditto, etched "Club Officer"	37.50	65.	75.	125.
5. 1983	135	Cripple Creek golden bone barlow	43.	80-90.	80-90.	150.
		(43 were re-etched by Tenn. Knife Works)		95-115.	95-115.	150.
6. 1983	15	ditto, etched "Club Officer"	43.	100-110.	100-110.	200.
7. 1984	100	Swanner honey bone gunstock jack	32.	35.	45.	45.
8. 1984	15	ditto, etched "Club Officer"	32.	40.	75.	65.
9. 1985	65	Hen & Rooster stag congress, 4-blade	41.	60.	75.	85.
10. 1985	10	ditto, etched "Club Officer"	41.	75.	90.	125.
11. 1986	100	Fight'n Rooster pearl lockback whittler	52.50	65.	100.	175.
12. 1986	11	ditto, etched "Club Officer"	61.	80.	125.	250.
13. 1986	35	5th Anniv. Fight'n Rooster pearl 5-blade	72.	100.	150.	325.
14. 1987	75	Fight'n Rooster stag canoe, 4-blade	42.50	45.	65.	125.
15. 1987	10	ditto, but pearl, etched "Club Officer"	68.	100.	150.	350.
16. 1988	50	Kissing Crane red bone copperhead	28.	35.	45.	50.
17. 1988	10	ditto, but pearl, etched "Club Officer"	50.	75.	85.	125.
18. 1989	150	Winchester 1924P pearl toothpick	53.	125.	150.	
19. 1989	10	ditto, etched "Club Officer"	53.	175.	225.	
20. 1990	100	Case R6251 SS red bone	40.	45.	50.	
21. 1990	13	ditto, but wood, etched "Club Officer"	40.	75.	75.	
22. 1991	99	Fight'n Rooster pearl 3-blade	70.	100.	150.	
23. 1991	13	ditto, etched "Club Officer"	70.	135.	225.	
24. 1991	55	10th Anniv. Fight'n Rooster pearl 3-blade	75.	150.	275.	
25. 1992	100	Fight'n Rooster waterfall 4-blade	85.	100.	135.	
26. 1992	14	ditto, gilt blades etched "Club Officer"	85.	140.	200.	
27. 1993	79	Winchester W15 3949 stag 3-blade sowbelly	75.	115.		
28. 1993	15	ditto, etched "Club Officer"	75.	190.		
29. 1994	85	Case Classic 6355 BS stag whittler	65.	115.		
30. 1994	15	ditto, "Club Officer," wharncliffe	65.	170.		
31. 1995	100	Case Classic stag sunfish	80.	125.		
32. 1995	15	ditto, etched "Club Officer"	80.	300.		
33. 1996	120	Fight'n Rooster pearl serpentine whittler	90.			
34. 1996	15	ditto, etched "Club Officer"	90.			
35. 1996	67	15th Anniv. Fight'n Rooster pearl 3-blade	90.			

HEART OF DIXIE CUTLERY CLUB, Trussville, Alabama. Information from Gary G. Nichols, Wade Miller, and Ben Grey.

			VALUES	
ISSUE	QUANTITY	DESCRIPTION	ISSUE	2000
1. 1990	70	Case 5254 SS stag trapper	$50.	$100.
2. 1991	50	Case DR6254 red jigged bone trapper	35.	60.
3. 1992	35	Sargent/Queen smooth brown bone trapper	35.	45.
4. 1993	35	Bear MGC smooth buffalo horn trapper	35.	70.
5. 1993	40	Christmas: Schatt & Morgan slim trapper	50.	75.
6. 1994	50	Hen & Rooster 312DS stag	50.	75.
7. 1994	60	Christmas: Bear MGC trapper, Damascus	45.	75.
8. 1995	40	Schatt & Morgan pearl physician's jack	75.	75.

WHEELER BASIN KNIFE CLUB, Hartselle, Alabama. Information from Earl James.

				VALUES	
ISSUE	QUANTITY	DESCRIPTION	ISSUE	1993	2000
1. 1981	100	Queen stag congress, 4-blade	$25.	$90.	$165.
2. 1982	100	Fight'n Rooster stag stockman, 5-blade	36.	90.	160.

WHEELER BASIN KNIFE CLUB *(continued)*

| | | | | VALUES | |
ISSUE	QUANTITY	DESCRIPTION	ISSUE	1993	2000
3. 1983	150	Fight'n Rooster stag wharncliffe whittler	30.	45.	100.
4. 1984	100	Fight'n Rooster stag stockman, 6-blade	45.	60.	175.
5. 1985	50	"Founders Knife," Fight'n Rooster stag 12-blade	70.	150.	250.
6. 1985	100	Fight'n Rooster stag powderhorn, 1-blade	30.	45.	110.
7. 1986	75	Fight'n Rooster stag trapper	38.	55.	125.
8. 1987	75	Fight'n Rooster stag canoe, 4-blade	45.	60.	115.
9. 1988	100	Fight'n Rooster stag lockback whittler	58.	70.	125.
10. 1989	75	Fight'n Rooster stag sowbelly stockman	45.	55.	100.
11. 1990	40	"Tenth Anniversary" Fight'n Rooster pearl, 10-blade	79.	150.	300.
12. 1991	75	Fight'n Rooster stag copperhead	41.	45.	85.
13. 1992	50	Fight'n Rooster stag 2-side muskrat	100.	125.	275.
14. 1993	50	Fight'n Rooster stag congress, 4-blade	100.		
15. 1994	50	Fight'n Rooster stag sowbelly whittler	110.		
16. 1995	60	Fight'n Rooster stag serpentine whittler	120.		
17. 1996	50	Fight'n Rooster stag congress, 4-blade	100.		

ALLEGHENY MOUNTAIN KNIFE COLLECTORS ASSOCIATION, Hunker, Pennsylvania. Information from Merle Trout.

| | | | | VALUES | | |
ISSUE	QUANTITY	DESCRIPTION	ISSUE	1989	1993	2000
1. 1983	55	Cripple Creek stag "Lil' Trapper"	$54.	$175.	$175.	$200.
2. 1984	94	Fight'n Rooster bone stockman	22.50	45.	45.	45.
3. 1985	61	Cripple Creek stag medium trapper	53.	125.	150.	200.
4. 1986	55	Cripple Creek 2nd-cut stag canoe 3-blade	57.	150.	250.	275.
5. 1987	50	Cripple Creek 2nd-cut stag stock 5-blade	60.	150.	325.	325.
6. 1988	55	Cripple Creek stag saddlehorn 1-blade	63.	125.	150.	160.
7. 1989	50	Cripple Creek bone "Coke bottle"	63.	63.	100.	125.
8. 1990	51	Cripple Creek bone "Hobo," two shields	70.	100.	125.	
9. 1991	35	Cripple Creek stag carpenter's jack	100.	125.	175.	
10. 1992	33	Cripple Creek pearl sowbelly 5-blade	225.	750.		
11. 1993	50	Schatt & Morgan red bone swing-guard	45.	100.		
12. 1994	50	Fight'n Rooster pearl barlow 3-blade	85.	125.		
13. 1995	50	Schatt & Morgan stag swing-guard	55.	125.		
14. 1996	31	Case 61100	50.	75.		

GATOR CUTLERY CLUB, Tampa, Florida. Information from Terry Nicholson and Robert Burtscher.

| | | | | VALUES | |
ISSUE	QUANTITY	DESCRIPTION	ISSUE	1989	1993
1. 1979	300	Fight'n Rooster stag toothpick	$27.	$100.	$100.
2. 1980	350	Parker Cut. Co. pearl toothpick	30.	40.	60.
3. 1981	350	Col. Coon smooth bone toothpick	30.	40.	50.
4. 1982	350	Case smooth green bone toothpick	27.50	45.	65.
5. 1983	200	Ka-Bar stag toothpick	32.	65.	65.
6. 1984	250	R. Klaas #3235 stag whittler	35.	45.	45.
7. 1985	150	R. Klaas pearl whittler	35.	45.	60.
8. 1986	150	Fight'n Rooster red jigged bone whittler	35.	40.	40.
9. 1987	50	Case red jigged bone whittler	30.	40.	45.
10. 1988	75	Fight'n Rooster Xmas tree cell. whittler	45.	50.	50.
11. 1989	50	10th Anniv. Bill Simons ivory physician's	75.	125.	125.
12. 1989	25	Cripple Creek Coke bottle	75.	125.	
13. 1990	25	Ka-Bar smooth white bone slim Coke bottle	60.	70.	
14. 1991	25	Case 61113 red jig bone slim Coke bottle	45.	60.	
15. 1992	25	Queen "S & M" red jig bone Coke bottle	50.	60.	
16. 1993	25	Case 61050 buffalo horn large Coke bottle	?		

·ULF COAST KNIFE CLUB, Pasadena, Texas. Information from Wayne Robertson.

			VALUES	
ISSUE	**QUANTITY**	**DESCRIPTION**	**ISSUE**	**2000**
1. 1986	42	Case Christmas glitter trapper	$37.50	$100.
2. 1987	42	Case B254 smooth gray bone trapper	37.50	75.
3. 1988	42	Case ROG6265 Rogers bone folding hunter	45.	70.
4. 1989	50	Queen smooth white bone gunstock, 2-blade	37.50	60.
5. 1990	55	Case RC61050 SS red bone Coke bottle	45.	60.
6. 1991	35	Schatt & Morgan brown bone Coke bottle	47.50	60.
7. 1992	37	Schatt & Morgan smooth bone swing-guard	47.50	80.
8. 1993A	30	Camillus stag double-lock folding hunter	75.	140.
9. 1993B	8	Tom Lewis stag drop-point hunter	135.	170.
10. 1994A	35	Queen amber jigged bone muskrat	37.50	75.
11. 1994B	8	Marcus McElhannon stag custom hunter	130.	170.
12. 1995A	34	Kinfolks honey jigged bone mini trapper	35.	45.
13. 1995B	9	Henry Heller green jigged bone custom	125.	150.
14. 1996	30	Case 3375 SS yellow composition stockman	35.	35.

WOLVERINE KNIFE COLLECTORS CLUB, P.O. Box 52, Belleville, MI 48112. Information from Patrick Donovan, club president, and Frank Meek, club vice president.

The 2004 club knife for the Wolverine Knife Collectors Club is a Queen two-blade stag canoe in a limited edition of 50. Closed length: 3 3/4 inches. Value: **$80**.

			VALUES	
ISSUE	**QUANTITY**	**DESCRIPTION**	**ISSUE**	**CURRENT**
1. 1980	100	Queen stag gunstock 2 blade, 3 1/2"	$25.	$200.
2. 1981	120	Queen white bone gunstock 2 blade 3 1/2"	20.	75.
3. 1982	150,	Queen pearl gunstock 2 blade 3 1/2"	45.	100.
4. 1983	121	Queen 2nd-cut stag gunstock 2 blade 3 1/2"	32.	50.
5. 1984	106	Case 2nd-cut stag trapper 2 blade 4 1/8"	45.	85.
6. 1985	100	Case 2nd-cut stag mini-trapper 2 blade 3 1/2"	45.	65.
7. 1986	115	Queen 2nd-cut stag/bone trapper 2 blade 4"	32.	40.
8. 1987	100	Queen pearl trapper 2 blade 4"	48.	120.
9. 1988	89	Queen green bone doctor's 2 blades 3 1/8"	36.	75.
10. 1988	30	10th Anniv. Bob Enders bone doctor's 1 blade 3 7/8"	105.	300.
11. 1989	101	Fight'n Rooster pearl doctor's 2 blades 3 5/8"	50.	100.
12. 1990	101	Fight'n Rooster Christmas tree doctor's 2 blades 3 5/8"	35.	70.
13. 1991	101	Case Germany imit. tortoise doctor's 2 blades 3 5/8"	38.	65.
14. 1992	101	Case Classic 6351 green bone split-back whittler 3 blades 4"	55.	85.
15. 1993	101	Case Classic 6351 stag split-back whittler 3 blades 4"	65.	105.
16. 1994	101	Case Classic 6351 red bone split-back whittler 3 blades 4"	55.	75.
17. 1995	80	Case Classic 6355 antique red bone wharncliffe whittler 3 blades 3 5/8"	55.	75.
18. 1996	80	Bulldog stag sunfish/toenail 2 blades 3 1/2"	85.	150.
19. 1997	90	Bulldog grooved brown bone sunfish/toenail 2 blades 3 1/2"	85.	100.
20. 1998	85	Bulldog pearl sunfish/toenail 2 blades 3 1/2"	165.	200.
21. 1998	36	20th anniv. Bill Reh custom fixed blade hunter, 35 diff. Materials, Carlisle sheath	25.	225.
21. 1999	70	Bulldog mastodon bark ivory sunfish/toenail 2 blades 3 1/2"	160.	200.
22. 2000	100	Schatt & Morgan/Queen antique green bone SwingGuard 1 blade 4 1/2"	60.	85.
23. 2001	56	Schatt & Morgan/Queen presentation pearl SwingGuard 1 blade 4 1/2"	162.	250.
24. 2002	55	Schatt & Morgan/Queen dark brown bone SwingGuard 1 blade 4 1/2"	55.	75.
25. 2003	51	Schatt & Morgan/Queen mammoth ivory SwingGuard 1 blade 4 1/2"	160.	195.
26. 2003	21	25th Anniv. Mike Sakmar custom fixed blade stabilized wood, ATS-34, mokume bolsters, leather sheath, padded pouch 1 blade 4"	270.	350.
27. 2004	50	Queen Cutlery Co. stag canoe 2 blades 3 3/4"	65.	80.

ARIZONA KNIFE COLLECTORS ASSOCIATION, Phoenix, Arizona. Information from D'Alton Holder, Mike Mooney and Mike Tamboli.

ISSUE	QUANTITY	DESCRIPTION	ISSUE	VALUES 1993	2000
1. 1982	50	Butch Beaver ironwood hunter (fixed)	$65.	$145.	$300.
2. 1983	50	Ka-Bar stag locking folder	50.	65.	100.
3. 1984	65	Jim Corrado n/s folder, McKenzie engr.	85.	165.	400.
4. 1985	65	Corrado/McKenzie n/s folder, damascus	150.	245.	450.
5. 1986	70	Jim Corrado ivory folder	125.	265.	350.
6. 1987	70	Jim Corrado ironwood folder	100.	145.	300.
7. 1988	70	Corrado/McKenzie mini folder, damascus	125.	165.	300.
8. 1989	55	Case honey bone peanut	35.	40.	90.
9. 1990	50	D'Alton Holder ironwood hunter (fixed)	100.	155.	300.
10. 1991	60	Bill Cheatham stag "flint steel" hunter	100.	145.	300.
11. 1992	60	S. Godfrey stag hunter (fixed), damascus	110.	150.	200.
12. 1993	40	Todd Kopp ebony dagger	110.	200.	
13. 1994	60	Tim Hancock curly maple, wire inlay (fixed)	125.	300.	
14. 1995	60	Greg Sutherland fighter, Micarta® (fixed)	125.	150.	
15. 1996	60	Tim Hancock tanto Micarta (fixed)	125.	300.	
16. 1997	60	Todd Kopp stag hunter (fixed)	110.	110.	
17. 1998	60	Case stag Copperlock	45.	60.	
18. 1998	40	Tom Bryan ironwood locking-liner folder	130.	175.	
19. 1999	60	Lynn Dawson Micarta neck knife (fixed)	90.	90.	
20. 2000	50	Mike Mooney ironwood skinner	120.	120.	

BUCKEYE BLADE KNIFE CLUB, Danville, Ohio. Information from Paul L. Winstead, Jr.

ISSUE	QUANTITY	DESCRIPTION	VALUES ISSUE	1993
1. 1991	21	Red Stag pyrite	$35.	$40.
2. 1992	9	Hen & Rooster pearl	75.	95.
3. 1993	10	Hen & Rooster stag	65.	65.
4. 1994				
5. 1995				
6. 1996				

FORT MYERS KNIFE CLUB, P.O. Box 706, St. James City, FL 33956-0706. Information from Russ Smegal, FMKC secretary/treasurer.

A Queen #20 toothpick with a cocobolo handle is the Fort Myers Knife Club's 2004 club knife. In a limited edition of 35, it has a value of **$50**.

ISSUE	QUANTITY	DESCRIPTION	VALUES ISSUE	CURRENT
1. 1984	100	Case 6264 SSP bone trapper, 7-dot/new grind	$35.	$125.
2. 1985	150	Case 5254 SS stag trapper, 6-dot/new grind	47.	125.
3. 1986	100	Case 7254 SS trapper, 5-dot	32.	50.
4. 1987	50	United red jig bone trapper, gilt blades	36.	45.
5. 1988	40	Cripple Creek stag whittler	55.	120.
6. 1989	40	Cripple Creek stag mini-trapper	52.	110.

FORT MYERS KNIFE CLUB *(continued)*

ISSUE	QUANTITY	DESCRIPTION	VALUES ISSUE	VALUES CURRENT
7. 1990	50	Case B254 small gray bone trapper, 2-dot	34.	45.
8. 1991	40	Case 5254 SS stag trapper, 1-dot	46.	80.
9. 1992	40	Case B254 SS sm. red bone trapper	37.	55.
10. 1993	50	Case 6254 red bone trapper	42.	50.
11. 1994	40	Case 62131 red bone canoe	44.50	50.
12. 1995	30	Case 51050 stag Zipper	76.	90.
13. 1996	30	Case (Classic) 71072 waterfall (12)/candy stripe (18)	74.	100.
14. 1997	35	Bulldog elephant toenail/appaloosa bone	90.	125.
15. 1998	30	Case 51549 stag Copperlock	53.	80.
16. 1999	30	Case 51749 stag Mini-Copperlock	56.	70.
17. 2000	28	Bulldog pearl mini-toenail	144.	175.
18. 2001	35	Case 61953LSS Russlock autumn bone	52.	65.
19. 2002	40	Case 62131SS Pocket Worn red bone canoe	52.	60.
20. 2003	35	Case muskrat black bone	45.	50.
21. 2004	35	Queen #20 cocobolo toothpick	50.	50.
Special 5th Anniversary Issue 1983-88				
1988	12	Charles Anderson stag skinner (fixed)	325.	450.
Special 10th Anniversary Issue 1983-93				
1993	50	Case R510098SS stag Texas toothpick	58.75	135.
Special 20th Anniversary Knife 1983-2003				
2003	10	Bulldog mastodon ivory toenail	175.	175.
2003	15	Bulldog mother-of-pearl toenail	175.	175.

FLORIDA KNIFE COLLECTORS ASSOCIATION, Titusville, Florida. Information from James A. Matthews.

ISSUE	QUANTITY	DESCRIPTION	VALUES ISSUE	VALUES 1993	VALUES 2000
1. 1979	200	Frank Buster stag stockman, 3-blade	$22.	$100.	$100.
2. 1980	300	Frank Buster pearl stockman, 3-blade	28.	65.	65.
3. 1981	300	Frank Buster pearl scroll stockman, 3-blade	28.	68.	68.
4. 1982	300	Frank Buster bone stockman, 3-blade	30.	70.	65.
5. 1983	200	Frank Buster horn stockman, 3-blade	30.	70.	65.
6. 1984	60	Frank Buster stag trapper	35.	65.	65.
8. 1986	30	Ka-Bar stag lockback	30.	60.	50.
9. 1987	25	Ka-Bar bone folder w/hatchet blade	45.	100.	110.
10. 1988	30	F. Buster waterfall gunstock cotton blade	30.	80.	80.
11. 1989	25	Case bone Texas toothpick	25.	35.	35.
12. 1990	25	Case 5150 Classic stag folding hunter	65.	100.	75.
13. 1991	25	Queen bone folder, 1-blade	30.	65.	55.
14. 1992	25	Case Classic saddlehorn	75.	125.	
15. 1993-96	12	Ka-Bar PTP 91 yellow comp. toothpick	32.	50.	

FLINT RIVER KNIFE CLUB, Jonesboro, Georgia. Information from Craig Schneeberger (678.642.6977) and other club members, with appraisals by Jim Sargent.

The Flint River Knife Club's 2003 club knife is a Case muskrat with an antique Pocket Worn bone handle. It comes in a limited edition of 45. Value: **$75**. (photo courtesy Flint River Knife Club)

ISSUE	QUANTITY	DESCRIPTION	VALUES ISSUE	VALUES CURRENT
1. 1982	150	Case 2-blade trapper, red-bone handle	$32.	$85.
2. 1983	150	Case 2-blade trapper, yellow comp. handle	32.	65.
3. 1984	75	Fight'n Rooster 4-blade congress, stag	34.	100.

FLINT RIVER KNIFE CLUB (continued)

ISSUE	QUANTITY	DESCRIPTION	VALUES ISSUE	VALUES CURRENT
4. 1985A	75	Fight'n Rooster 3-blade stag cattleman	32.	75.
5. 1985B	10	Fight'n Rooster 3-blade pearl cattleman	57.	100.
6. 1986	70	Case 2-blade trapper, walnut w/gold filling	35.	75.
7. 1987A	50	Case 2-blade trapper, gray bone	32.	85.
8. 1987B	75	"Show Knife" Case 2-blade trapper, black comp. w/engraved bolster	35.	75.
9. 1988	50	Case 2-blade trapper, yellow comp. w/engraved bolster	30.	75.
10. 1989	50	Case 2-blade copperhead, smooth gray bone	28.	100.
11. 1990	50	Boker lockback, pearl	32.	100.
12. 1991	?	Wayne Hensley custom, 440C, rosewood, sheath	50.	?
13. 1992	50	Case canoe, stag	45.	90.
14. 1993	40	Case whittler, stag	?	125.
15. 1994	40	Case, Texas toothpick, stag	?	100.
16. 1995	40	Case whittler, stag, in memory of John Becker 1928-1994	?	125.
17. 1996	43	Ray Cook custom lockback, 440C, stag	?	125.
18. 1997	43	Case whittler, red stag, collector tin	?	100.
19. 1998	25	Case Copperlock, stag	?	90.
20. 1999	51	Columbia River Knife & Tool Ed Halligan K.I.S.S.	?	?
21. 2000	20/25	Case	?	150.
22. 2001	21/30	Case Russlock, red jigged bone	?	90.
23. 2002	50	Case doctor's knife, 20th anniv. club knife, black and white jigged bone	?	100.
24. 2003	45	Case muskrat, antique Pocket Worn bone	?	75.

OCMULGEE KNIFE COLLECTORS, Macon, Georgia. Information from Joseph P. Wilson.

ISSUE	QUANTITY	DESCRIPTION	VALUES ISSUE	VALUES 1993	VALUES 2000
1. 1983	37	Charter: Col. Coon stag mini-trapper	$30.	$130.	$160.
2. 1983	34	Ka-Bar 1195 stag trapper, dog-head shield	40.	85.	110.
3. 1984	39	Schrade Heritage red bone muskrat	22.	50.	75.
4. 1985	49	Case G6254 SS green bone trapper	33.	65.	85.
5. 1986	60	Case B254 SS blue bone trapper	35.	60.	80.
7. 1988	50	Cripple Creek stag trapper	60.	95.	120.
8. 1989	50	Case 5254 SS stag trapper	35.	60.	80.
9. 1990	50	Case 5165 SS stag folding hunter	45.	60.	80.
10. 1991	50	Zolan McCarty wood drop point (fixed)	65.	110.	145.
11. 1992	50	Zolan McCarty stag folding drop point	125.	150.	200.
12. 1993	50	Case 6251 SPSS brown bone trapper	50.	50.	65.
13. 1994	42	Case 6391 green bone whittler	55.	65.	
14. 1995	32	Bulldog pearl congress, 4-blade	85.	95.	
15. 1996	28	Winchester Model 1950 stag lockback	75.	75.	

JOHNNY APPLESEED KNIFE COLLECTORS, Mansfield, Ohio. Information from Kenneth R. Parker, club secretary, 990 Averill Ave., Dept. BG6, Mansfield, OH 44906 419.747.6939.

ISSUE	QUANTITY	DESCRIPTION	VALUES ISSUE	VALUES 1993	VALUES 2000
1. 1984	40	Case 3254 yellow comp. trapper	$27.50	$65.	$65.
2. 1985	40	Ka-Bar jigged bone congress	35.	50.	50.
3. 1986	50	Fight'n Rooster imit. pearl stockman	29.	29.	100.
4. 1987	50	Case 6275 jigged bone stockman	30.	30.	30.
5. 1988A	55	Case 6265 Rogers bone folding hunter	50.	50.	50.
6. 1988B	54	5th Anniversary Case 6249 green bone	36.	36.	36.
7. 1989	60	Fight'n Rooster pearl canoe	60.	60.	100.
8. 1990	60	Queen stag trapper	35.	35.	35.
9. 1991	70	Case BC61050SS smooth blue bone	45.	45.	45.
10. 1992	50	Case BKC1050SS smooth black bone	45.	45.	45.
11. 1993	50	Schatt & Morgan Winterbottom bone	45.	45.	

JOHNNY APPLESEED KNIFE COLLECTORS *(continued)*

ISSUE	QUANTITY	DESCRIPTION	ISSUE	VALUES 1993	2000
12. 1994	60	Bulldog abalone swirl canoe	55.	55.	
13. 1995	60	Bulldog oystershell muskrat	40.	40.	
14. 1996	50	Bulldog USA stag sowbelly	52.	52.	

WESTERN RESERVE CUTLERY ASSOCIATION, Bolivar, Ohio. Information from Darlene Musgrave.

ISSUE	QUANTITY	DESCRIPTION	ISSUE	VALUES 1996	2000
1. 1977	100	Case 6254 jigged bone trapper	$24.	$85.	$110.
2. 1978A	118	Case 6249 jigged bone	20.	70.	100.
3. 1978B	35	Ka-Bar stag hunter, dog-head shield	50.	150.	200.
4. 1979	100	Case 6383 jigged bone whittler	20.	50.	75.
5. 1980	40	Cargill jigged 2nd-cut stag canoe	40.	75.	125.
6. 1981	150	Fight'n Rooster pearl barlow	40.	80.	100.
7. 1982	150	Case 5254 stag trapper	33.	55.	75.
8. 1983	60	Case 5149 stag copperhead	35.	60.	85.
9. 1984	60	Dale Warther custom bowie, 1/2 scale	75.	300.	400.
10. 1985	65	Hubertus stag side-lever	65.	200.	250.
11. 1986A	35	Hubertus stag side-lever, gold etch	75.	240.	300.
12. 1986B	65	Hubertus stag side-lever, plain etch	65.	150.	200.
13. 1987A	125	Ka-Bar SG865, India stag	42.	75.	100.
14. 1987B	54	Warther ivory, silver dollar bolsters	240.	950.	1200.
15. 1988	100	Ka-Bar DH-92 jigged bone barlow	37.	60.	75.
16. 1989	100	Parker USA ivory stockman, damascus blade	60.	130.	175.
17. 1990A	71	Cargill Cripple Creek stag copperhead	70.	150.	200.
18. 1990B	85	Show Knife: Queen bone toothpick	25.	40.	60.
19. 1991A	80	Sargent/Boker pearl congress	50.	70.	125.
20. 1991B	100	Victorinox Soldier, 100th Anniversary	25.	30.	40.
21. 1992A	70	Tak Fukuta, ceramic blade, magnesium	55.	100.	125.
22. 1992B	150	Expo Knife: Victorinox Tinker	25.	30.	40.
23. 1992C	55	15th Anniversary Warther pearl folder	240.	550.	900.
24. 1993A	100	Buck BU-505-DY David Yellowhorse	55.	175.	200.
25. 1993B	125	Expo Knife: Camillus bone .22 Hornet	25.	40.	45.
26. 1994A	100	Buck 532 rosewood David Yellowhorse	55.	110.	150.
27. 1994B	125	Expo Knife: Sarco white bone Lil Trapper	20.	30.	40.
28. 1995A	100	Hubertus stag knife-fork-corkscrew	65.	75.	90.
29. 1995B	125	Expo Knife: Bear MGC pearl lockback	25.	50.	80.
30. 1996A	85	Schatt & Morgan stag cotton sampler	55.	60.	80.
31. 1996B	150	Expo Knife: Sarco white bone Lil Whittler	20.	20.	30.
32. 1997A	75	Kellam Lappfolder thuya handle	55.	75.	
33. 1997B	35	Rick Hinderer 20th anniv. knife folder, san mai damascus blade	340.	380.	
34. 1997C	85	Expo Knife: Old Cutlery, 2 blades	25.	30.	
35. 1998A	62	Queen Cutlery gunstock folder	75.	90.	
36. 1998B	100	Expo Knife: Swiss Buck Taskmate	25.	30.	
37. 1999-2000	55	Millennium Set of two Schatt & Morgan doctor's knives	133.	133.	
38. 2000	100	Expo Knife: Victorinox Executive	20.	20.	

SUSQUEHANNA KNIFE COLLECTORS ASSOCIATION, Mount Penn, Pennsylvania. Information from Don Howells, Jim Robison, and John Glass.

ISSUE	QUANTITY	DESCRIPTION	ISSUE	VALUES 1993
1. 1990	28	Cripple Creek stag whittler	$85.	$175.
2. 1991	35	Cripple Creek stag Coke bottle, 2-blade	100.	135.
3. 1992	35	Cripple Creek stag buffalo skinner	125.	125.

Commemorative and Limited-Edition Knives

SUSQUEHANNA KNIFE COLLECTORS ASSOCIATION *(continued)*

ISSUE	QUANTITY	DESCRIPTION	VALUES ISSUE	1993
4. 1993				
5. 1994				
6. 1995				
7. 1996				

TEXAS KNIFE COLLECTORS ASSOCIATION, Austin, Texas. Information from Tommy Nolley.

ISSUE	QUANTITY	DESCRIPTION	VALUES ISSUE	1993
1. 1980	310	Schlieper stag & bone toothpicks (2)	$47.25	$125.
2. 1981	340	Case 5165/6165 folding hunters (2)	55.	125.
3. 1982	255	Case 6254 stag & Schlieper bone trappers	75.	125.
4. 1983	248	Ka-Bar stag folding hunter, 2-blade	48.	75.
5. 1984	238	Schlieper red bone giant moose	47.50	125.
6. 1985	217	Alcas stag big trapper, 2-blade	56.	200.
7. 1986	173	Alcas stag big trapper, 1-blade	57.	175.
8. 1987	161	Ka-Bar bone sunfish	55.	95.
9. 1988	124	Mike Allen custom jack, Fischer bone	85.	125.
10. 1989	105	Case 4254/B254 white & black trappers	68.	145.
11. 1990	88	Rob Davidson custom jack, mesquite wood	85.	125.
12. 1991	70	Winchester 1920 stag	85.	120.
13. 1992	62	Case BD347 stockman, bois d'arc wood	55.	100.
14. 1993				
15. 1994				
16. 1995				
17. 1996				

KNIFE CLUB OF THE OZARKS, Ozarks, Missouri. Information from Don Long.

ISSUE	QUANTITY	DESCRIPTION	VALUES ISSUE	2000
1. 1994	40	Case Classic 73091 waterfall	$60.	$90.
2. 1995	45	Winchester 153949 stag	55.	75.
3. 1996	60	Case Classic 5355 stag	55.	75.

SHENANDOAH VALLEY KNIFE COLLECTORS, Singers Glen, Virginia. Information from Wes Shrader and Jim Marshall.

ISSUE	QUANTITY	DESCRIPTION	VALUES ISSUE	1993	2000
1. 1989	25	Ka-Bar USC 88 red jigged bone	$40.	$100.	$175.
2. 1990	34	Remington 1128 cocobolo large trapper	38.	60.	100.
3. 1991	46	Kissing Crane KC-2506 stag	40.	45.	65.
4. 1992	48	Ka-Bar ETN-91 black swirl composition	50.	75.	100.
5. 1993	35	Boker 4525 stag Classic	45.	60.	
6. 1994	40	Kissing Crane KC-2051 stag	52.	52.	
7. 1995	40	Case Classic 62094 green bone	60.	100.	
8. 1996	40	Bulldog USA green bone 3-blade sowbelly	50.	75.	

NORTHERN VIRGINIA KNIFE COLLECTORS, Falls Church, Virginia. Information from Ernie Cook.

ISSUE	QUANTITY	DESCRIPTION	VALUES ISSUE	1993	2000
1. 1981	178	Case 06263 pearl pen knife "CHARTER"	$33.	$50.	$50.
2. 1982	79	Col. Coon stag congress, 4-blade	35.	65.	70.

NORTHERN VIRGINIA KNIFE COLLECTORS *(continued)*

ISSUE	QUANTITY	DESCRIPTION	ISSUE	1993	2000
3. 1983	74	Col. Coon stag barlow, 2-blade	30.	60.	65.
4. 1984	72	Case 21051L SSP smooth black folder	26.	40.	40.
5. 1985	79	Boker stag trapper, 2-blade	20.	45.	50.
6. 1986	71	Don Straight Pakkawood® skinner (fixed)	60.	100.	120.
7. 1987	74	Boker stag canoe, 2-blade	30.	50.	55.
8. 1988	81	Boker smooth white bone muskrat	25.	45.	50.
9. 1989	75	Queen pearl peanut, 2-blade	38.	50.	50.
10. 1990	83	Boker pearl lockback	35.	50.	55.
11. 1991	70	10th Anniv. Gene White maple (fixed)	70.	90.	110.
12. 1992	90	Sarco black handle lockback	25.	30.	30.
13. 1993	63	Gene White cocobolo tanto (fixed)	85.	95.	115.
14. 1994	60	Don Straight black poly pearl caper	65.	85.	
15. 1995	55	Tom Conkey buffalo horn canoe (1/97)	135.	140.	
16. 1996	43	Gene White maroon Micarta® (fixed)	135.	135.	

BECHTLER MINT KNIFE CLUB, Rutherfordton, North Carolina. Information from Hydrick B. Stewart and Neal W. Hunt.

ISSUE	QUANTITY	DESCRIPTION	ISSUE	1993	2000
1. 1983A	93	Charter Knife: Case stag RAZ barlow	$30.	$65.	$75.
2. 1983B	150	Case 5149 SS stag copperhead	38.	50.	60.
3. 1984A	50	Founders' Knife: Col. Coon stag lockback	42.50	60.	65.
4. 1984B	145	Case 5254 stag trapper	45.	60.	65.
5. 1985	129	Case 53032 stag premium stock	50.	62.50	65.
6. 1986	128	Case 54088 stag 4-blade congress	55.	75.	85.
7. 1987	125	Case R62131 red bone canoe	50.	60.	65.
8. 1988	100	Case 52131 stag canoe	50.	60.	70.
9. 1989	100	Case SH2131 sheep horn canoe	55.	70.	80.
10. 1990	113	Case 72131 SS curly maple canoe	50.	62.50	70.
11. 1991	90	Case 5165 stag folding hunter	55.	70.	70.
12. 1992	90	Case 52005 RAZ stag barlow	50.	65.	70.
13. 1993	70	Case 5265 SS stag folding hunter	60.	65.	
14. 1994	70	Case 5347 stag stockman	55.	60.	
15. 1995	61	Case 5240 stag serpentine trapper	55.	65.	
16. 1996	54	Case 5249 stag copperhead	60.	65.	

AMERICAN EDGE COLLECTORS ASSOCIATION, Country Club Hills, Illinois. Information from Charles R. Kelly.

ISSUE	QUANTITY	DESCRIPTION	ISSUE	2000
1. 1979	76	Cripple Creek stag sowbelly	$45.	$125.
2. 1980	76	Cripple Creek stag canoe	50.	50.
3. 1981	70	Cripple Creek pearl gunstock, 2-blade	125.	200.
4. 1982	80	Cripple Creek stag trapper, 2-blade	65.	110.
5. 1983	80	Cripple Creek stag stockman	85.	110.
6. 1984	80	Cripple Creek stag sowbelly, 3-blade	90.	125.
7. 1985	95	Cripple Creek stag jack	85.	95.
8. 1986	85	Cripple Creek stag serpentine jack	85.	85.
9. 1987	48	Happy Jack green jigged bone barlow	55.	75.
10. 1988	39	Happy Jack imitation pearl Norfolk	55.	65.
11. 1989	45	Cripple Creek stag large Coke bottle	70.	90.
12. 1990	42	Cripple Creek stag hobo, 1-blade	70.	90.
13. 1991	40	Cripple Creek stag hobo, 2-blade	90.	95.
14. 1992	43	Cripple Creek stag large clasp	110.	110.
15. 1993	36	Cripple Creek stag sow rat	110.	110.
16. 1994	24	Cripple Creek stag barlow	110.	110.
17. 1995	35	Winchester stag swell-center whittler	65.	65.
18. 1996	45	Winchester stag sow-belly stockman	65.	65.

KANSAS KNIFE COLLECTORS ASSOCIATION, Wichita, Kansas. All knives are made by Queen, all are stamped "KKCA" and all (except 1998) have shields in the shape of the state of Kansas. Information from Bill R. Davis, KKCA knife club chairman, 4456 N. Arkansas, Dept. BG6, Wichita, KS 67204 316.838.0540.

ISSUE	QUANTITY	DESCRIPTION	VALUES	
			ISSUE	CURRENT
1. 1990	165	3 1/2" gunstock, medium brown jigged bone	$35.	$135.
2. 1991	144	4 1/4" trapper, India deer stag	45.	105.
3. 1992	150	4 1/4" stockman whittler, light brown jigged bone	49.	85.
4. 1993	100	3 1/2" barlow, red jigged bone	47.50	95.
5. 1994	100	5 1/4" folding hunter, corn-cob jigged bone	42.50	90.
6. 1995	90	4" premium stockman, dark brown jigged bone	43.	80.
7. 1996	75	4" large congress, deer stag	50.	75.
8. 1997	70	3 3/4" canoe whittler, honey-colored jigged bone	45.	70.
9. 1998	70	3 5/8" doctor's knife, pearl (no shield)	63.	100.
10. 1999	70	4" muskrat, antique green picked jigged bone	42.	60.
11. 2000	65	4 1/2" swedge-ground, burnt red grooved jigged bone	50.	65.
12. 2001	65	4 1/4" toothpick, antique worm-grooved jigged bone	43.	50.
13. 2002	70	3 3/4" baby sunfish, carved stag bone	57.	65.
14. 2003	70	4" moose, amber jigged and worm-grooved bone	50.	60.
15. 2004	65	4 1/2" sleeveboard, crimson Rogers jigged bone	75.	85.
16. Full set	1990-2004: Approx. 1,000			

NORTH STAR BLADE COLLECTORS, Richfield, Minnesota. Information from Sidney Zochert.

ISSUE	QUANTITY	DESCRIPTION	VALUES	
			ISSUE	2000
1. 1982	100	Queen pearl gunstock	$40.	$165.
2. 1983	100	Queen jigged bone gunstock	30.	80.
3. 1984	100	Queen stag gunstock	30.	95.
4. 1985	100	Queen stag 4-blade congress	35.	65.
5. 1986	100	Queen jigged bone 4-blade congress	35.	55.
6. 1987	100	Queen pearl 4-blade congress	45.	120.
7. 1988	100	Queen stag English jack	35.	85.
8. 1989	100	Queen pearl English jack	55.	130.
9. 1990	100	Queen jigged bone English jack	32.	70.
10. 1991	100	Queen jigged bone swell-center hunter	46.	85.
11. 1992	100	Queen jigged bone premium gunstock	45.	65.
12. 1993	100	Queen red jigged bone English jack, lock	44.	60.
13. 1994	100	Queen stag swell-center congress whittler	45.	55.
14. 1995	100	Case stag trapper	45.	45.
15. 1996	100	Queen stag canoe	45.	55.

THREE RIVERS KNIFE CLUB, Rome, Georgia. Information from Jimmy M. Green and B. Dwaine Simmons.

ISSUE	QUANTITY	DESCRIPTION	VALUES	
			ISSUE	2000
1. 1980A	12	Case 278 SS "Merry Christmas" Micarta®	$11.	$30.
2. 1980B	100	Case 6254 SSP jigged bone trapper	30.	150.
3. 1981	164	Case G6207 SSP green bone mini trapper	63.	103.
4. 1982	150	Case Cc5207 SPSSP stag mini trapper	35.	113.
5. 1983	150	Case Cc8207 SPSS pearl mini trapper	50.	150.
6. 1984	100	Case 5207 SPSS 2nd cut stag mini trapper	50.	108.
7. 1985	125	Case 6207 SPSS Rogers bone mini trapper	33.	125.
8. 1986	100	Case IV207 SPSS ivory mini trapper	65.	200.
9. 1987	100	Case 3207 SPSSP yellow mini trapper	33.	78.
10. 1988	100	Case WR6207 SS red/white mini trapper	40.	101.
11. 1989	75	10th Anniv. Case 5207 D stag, damascus	80.	158.

THREE RIVERS KNIFE CLUB (continued)

ISSUE	QUANTITY	DESCRIPTION	VALUES ISSUE	2000
12. 1990	75	Case 8207 SS pink pearl mini trapper	85.	178.
13. 1991	75	Case 7207 SS Santa Fe Stone Medicine Man	69.	112.
14. 1992	75	Case 7207 SS Santa Fe Stone End of Trail	65.	112.
15. 1993	75	Case A8207 SS pearl/abalone mini trapper	120.	225.
16. 1994	75	Case 7207 SS D. Yellowhorse Whitetail	120.	175.
17. 1995	75	Case 7207 SS D. Yellowhorse Thunderbird	120.	166.
18. 1996	75	Case 7207 SS David Yellowhorse Buck	120.	158.

CHATTAHOOCHEE CUTLERY CLUB, Tucker, Georgia. Information from Michael Cowart and Ralph Martin.

ISSUE	QUANTITY	DESCRIPTION	VALUES ISSUE	2000
1. 1977	40	Ka-Bar wood trapper	$16.	$75.
2. 1978	50	Queen green bone mini trapper	16.	40.
3. 1979	50	Queen brown jigged bone stockman	16.	35.
4. 1980	50	stag custom	50.	60.
5. 1981	50	Fight'n Rooster pearl gunstock	40.	65.
6. 1982	50	Fight'n Rooster pearl trapper	40.	65.
7. 1983	50	Fight'n Rooster stag trapper	35.	50.
8. 1984	100	Ka-Bar 1192 stag folding hunter	25.	40.
9. 1985	75	Schrade brown jigged bone stockman	25.	30.
10. 1986	50	August Muller (Solingen) stag trapper	23.	45.
11. 1987	50	Kissing Crane pearl whittler	30.	60.
12. 1988	50	Boker stag 4-blade congress	40.	55.
13. 1989	25	Case WR6207SS red/white bone mini trapper	35.	50.
14. 1990	40	Boker gray smooth bone canoe	35.	50.
15. 1991	40	Case Classic honey bone whittler	35.	50.
16. 1992	50	Schlieper Eye Brand stag copperhead	39.	45.
17. 1993	40	Case 5265SS stag folding hunter	50.	55.
18. 1994	50	Ray Cook custom stag folder	50.	55.
19. 1995	50	Case Classic jigged brown bone toothpick	50.	55.
20. 1996	40	Bulldog stag sunfish	85.	85.

DEEP SOUTH KNIFE COLLECTORS, Pensacola, Florida. Information from Robert T. Lewis.

ISSUE	QUANTITY	DESCRIPTION	VALUES ISSUE	2000
1. 1995A	40	Case Classic 530109 stag	$68.	$75.
2. 1995B	25	Founders Knife: Case Classic 51094 stag	68.	75.
3. 1996	50	Bulldog glitter stripe sunfish	95.	95.

MID-MICHIGAN KNIFE COLLECTORS, Coleman, Michigan. Information from Greg Moe.

ISSUE	QUANTITY	DESCRIPTION	VALUES ISSUE	2000
1. 1994	31	Case 6254 SS Appaloosa bone trapper	$35.	$50.
2. 1995	18	Case 2100R saddlehorn, Winston Cup	48.	55.
3. 1996	22	Case stag mini muskrat	36.	36.

TAR HEEL CUTLERY COLLECTORS, Winston-Salem, North Carolina. Information from George W. Manuel (336.924.6876).

ISSUE	QUANTITY	DESCRIPTION	VALUES ISSUE	CURRENT
1. 1977	200	Fight'n Rooster pearl canoe 2 blade	$25.	$140.

Commemorative and Limited-Edition Knives

TAR HEEL CUTLERY COLLECTORS (continued)

ISSUE	QUANTITY	DESCRIPTION	VALUES ISSUE	CURRENT
2. 1978	350	Fight'n Rooster pearl gunstock whittler 3 blade	29.50	140.
3. 1979	400	Fight'n Rooster pearl copperhead 2 blade	29.50	70.
4. 1980	400	Fight'n Rooster pearl doctor razor 2 blade	33.50	110.
5. 1981	400	Fight'n Rooster pearl lockback whittler 3 blade	49.	150.
6. 1982	350	Fight'n Rooster pearl trapper 2 blade	41.	70.
7. 1983	250	Fight'n Rooster pearl congress, 2-blade	40.	125.
8. 1984	162	Ka-Bar stag barlow 2 blade	22.	60.
9. 1985	120	Case 5207 2nd cut stag mini trapper 2 blade	47.	70.
10. 1986	125	Ka-Bar brown bone congress, 4-blade	39.	90.
11. 1987	125	Case R6215 red bone gunstock 2 blade	30.	50.
12. 1988	60	Case B254 SS blue smooth bone trapper 2 blade	37.	55.
13. 1989	60	Case B254 SS blue smooth bone trapper 2 blade	38.	55.
14. 1990	40	Case HORN C1050 SS horn Coke bottle 1 blade	60.	90.
15. 1991	50	Case 6391 banana bone whittler 3 blade	60.	80.
16. 1992	50	Case 630109 brown bone whittler 3 blade	48.	80.
17. 1993	50	Case bone muskrat 2 blade	39.	75.
18. 1994	45	Sargent stag congress 4-blade	40.	65.
19. 1995	45	Case ROG61050 Rogers bone Coke bottle 1 blade	55.	75.
20. 1996	45	Case 52005 stag "Raz" 2 blade	44.	80.
21. 1997	60	Case 51549L Copperlock stag one blade	46.	100.
22. 1998	45	Case 61549L Copperlock worm groove brown bone 1 blade	46.	100.
23. 1999	60	Case 61549L Copperlock worm groove white bone 1 blade	46.	90.
24. 2000	50	Case muskrat white bone 2 blade	45.	75.
25. 2001	50	Case muskrat antique bone 2 blade	45.	70.
26. 2002	50	Case 6111 1/2 Cheetah natural bone bowtie shield 1 blade	65.	90.
27. 2003	50	Case 61593LSS Russlock jade bone bowtie shield 1 blade	55.	120.
28. 2004	50	Case 6285SPSS doctor's green bone 2 blade w/spatula	50.	?

RANDALL KNIFE SOCIETY OF AMERICA. Information from Rhett Stidham, founder/president.

ISSUE	QUANTITY	DESCRIPTION	VALUES ISSUE	CURRENT
1. 1991A	432	Randall RKSA1 Special 5" fighter, Micarta	$290.	$550.
2. 1991B	568	Randall RKSA1 Special 5" fighter, Stag	290.	595.
3. 1995A	338	Randall RKS2 Special 4 1/2" hunter, Micarta	285.	550.
4.1995B	298	Randall RKS2 Special 4 1/2" hunter, Stag	262.	575.
5. 1997-99	800	Randall RKS3 Special 5 3/4" hunter, Stag	376.	695.
6. 2002A	382	Randall RKS4 Special 8" fighter, Leather	310.	695.
7. 2002B	814	Randall RSK4 Special 8" fighter, Stag	370.	695.
8. 2003C	4	Randall RKS4 Special 8" fighter, Ivory	700.	2,500.
9. 2006	1,500	Randall RKS5 Miniature Drop Point*	478.	n/a

CASE COLLECTORS CLUB, Bradford, Pennsylvania. Information from Jean Cabisca.

[Notes: Li = Life Member knife; Jr = Junior Member knife]

ISSUE	QUANTITY	DESCRIPTION	VALUES ISSUE	2000
1. 1981	5,543	A16151 SSP	$40.	$125.
2. 1982	4,902	6251 SP SS	40.	125.
3. 1983	3,969	6251 FK SS	45.	200.
4. 1984	3,107	G64088 SS	48.50	125.
5. 1985	2,690	C51050	48.50	125.
6. 1986	2,755	6165 SS	48.50	125.
7. 1987	2,100	SB2019 SS	48.50	125.
8. 1988	2,400	5243 SP SS	44.95	125.
9. 1989	2,100	ROG6211 1/2	59.95	125.
10. 1990LiA	279	52019 D	89.	125.

CASE COLLECTORS CLUB (continued)

			VALUES	
ISSUE	QUANTITY	DESCRIPTION	ISSUE	2000
11. 1990LiB	237	52019 SS	89.	125.
12. 1990Jr	373	61009	19.95	75.
13. 1991	611	DR61066 SS	49.99	75.
14. 1991Li	800	DR61066 SS	49.99	75.
15. 1991Jr	318	G61131	19.95	75.
16. 1992	700	GY62005 RAZ SS	49.99	75.
17. 1992Li	500	GY62005 RAZ SS	49.99	75.
18. 1992Jr	400	6207 SS	19.95	75.
19. 1993	731	5299 SS	49.	75.
20. 1993Li	731	5299 SS	49.	75.
21. 1993Jr	347	51052 SS	39.	75.
22. 1994	774	BW10098 SS	61.	75.
23. 1994Li	774	BW10098 SS	61.	75.
24. 1994Jr	331	BW10094 SS	38.	75.
25. 1995	804	61050 SS	49.	75.
26. 1995Li	779	61050 SS	49.	75.
27. 1995Jr	411	6125 1/2	39.	75.
28. 1996Jr	568	Old Red 62109X SS #1638	39.	65.
29. 1996Li	1019	Old Red 6146 SS #1637	49.	70.
30. 1996Reg	970	Old Red 6149 SS #1636	49.	70.
31. 1997Jr	918	Green 61007SS #1670	39.	50.
32. 1997Li	1670	Green 61054 SS #1669	49.	70.
33. 1997Reg	1577	Green 61054 SS #1668	49.	70.
34. 1998Jr	727	Stag Mini-Muskrat #1676	55.	65.
35. 1998Li	1817	Stag Muskrat #1675	65.	75.
36. 1998Reg	1614	Stag Muskrat #1674	65.	75.
37. 1999Jr	713	Gun Metal Black 61749L SS #1597	50.	60.
38. 1999Li	2012	Gun Metal Black 61549L SS #1595	60.	70.
39. 1999Reg	1907	Gun Metal Black 61549L SS #1596	60.	70.
40. 2000Jr	708	Moss Green TH62165 SS #1560	54.50	58.
41. 2000Li	2213	Moss Green 6165 1/2 SS #1558	64.50	68.
42. 2000Reg	2136	Moss Green 6165 SS #1559	64.50	68.
In 2000, the club offered the regular and junior knives to the Life members with their Life number.				
43. 2000Li/Jr	774	Moss Green TH62165 SS #1563	54.60	58.
44. 2000Li/Reg	775	Moss Green 6165 SS #1564	64.50	68.

KA-BAR COLLECTORS CLUB, Olean, New York. Information from Tom Beery.

[Note: ✔ = dog-head shield]

			VALUES	
ISSUE	QUANTITY	DESCRIPTION	ISSUE	2000
1. 1976A	1,500	USMC 200th Anniversary combat knife	$100-300.	250-500.
2. 1976B	3,500	Bicentennial trapper, red-white-blue ✔	30-100.	175.
3. 1977	1,100	1- & 2-blade stag folding hunters ✔	200./pair	325.
4. 1978A	1,200	USMC WWII commemorative combat knife	50-150.	300.
5. 1978B	3,000	1- & 2-blade stag folding hunters ✔	75./pair	375.
6. 1979A	750	CK79 small swell-center lockback, stag	27.50	55.
7. 1979B	500	jack knife, stag ✔	31.50	58.
8. 1979C	940	pearl canoe	33.	95.
9. 1979D	915	stag canoe	29.50	75.
10. 1979E	331	ivory folding hunter	80.	275.
11. 1979F	298	pearl folding hunter	80.	225.
12. 1980A	2,162	CK80 Ka-wood gunstock, 2-blade	27.50	65.
13. 1980B	806	congress pen, pearl	25.	75.
14. 1980C	585	stag lockback hunter, engraved	65.	65.
15. 1980D	150	stag lockback hunter, engraved, initials	67.50	98.
16. 1980E	100	stag lockback hunter	45.	75.
17. 1981A	2,003	CK81 stag Coke bottle hunter	35.	65.

SECTION V: MODERN, COMMEMORATIVE, CLUB, LIMITED EDITION

	KA-BAR COLLECTORS CLUB *(continued)*			VALUES	
ISSUE	QUANTITY	DESCRIPTION		ISSUE	2000
18. 1981B	358	set of stag, pearl, jigged bone gunstocks		125./three	425.
19. 1982A	1,752	CK82 green jigged bone Coke bottle hunter		37.50	85.
20. 1982B	1,308	Large swell-center lockback, stag ✓		35.65	75.
21. 1982C	457	set of stag, pearl, jigged bone trappers		125./three	350.
22. 1983A	1,328	CK83 laminated wood Coke bottle hunter ✓		37.50	65.
23. 1983B	885	jigged bone folding hunter, 1-blade ✓		35.	85.
24. 1983C	352	jigged bone folding hunter, 2-blade ✓		37.50	98.
25. 1983D	2,368	KA-BAR-LO stag barlow ✓		18.75	35.
26. 1984A	1,500	CK84 hickory bone Coke bottle hunter		37.50	95.
27. 1984B	749	jigged bone swell-center whittler		22.50	65.
28. 1984C	251	jigged bone swell-center whittler ✓ gold		50.	175.
29. 1984D	875	jigged bone Texas toothpick ✓		22.50	45.
30. 1984E	333	jigged bone Texas toothpick ✓ gold		50.	175.
31. 1984F	950	jigged bone congress, 4-blades ✓		27.50	55.
32. 1984G	250	jigged bone congress, 4-blades ✓ gold		57.50	225.
33. 1984H	783	jigged bone premium stockman ✓		25.50	48.
34. 1984I	249	jigged bone premium stockman ✓ gold		55.50	200.
35. 1985A	1,474	CK85 pearl Coke bottle hunter, gold shield		45.	325.
36. 1985B	814	jigged bone plowman ✓		29.	47.
37. 1985C	250	jigged bone plowman ✓ gold		52.50	185.
38. 1985D	999	jigged bone swing-guard lockback ✓		28.50	48.
39. 1985E	250	jigged bone swing-guard lockback ✓ gold		52.50	375.
40. 1985F	736	jigged bone sleeveboard pen ✓		20.	45.
41. 1985G	200	jigged bone sleeveboard pen ✓ gold		39.50	150.
42. 1985H	779	jigged bone barlow ✓		24.	45.
43. 1985I	200	jigged bone barlow ✓ gold		47.	125.
44. 1985J	62	Albemarle wood Coke bottle hunter, scrimshaw inlay, engraving, etching		72.50	425.
45. 1986A	1,673	CK86 stag Grizzly		42.	75.
46. 1986B	1,061	multi-color lady leg		32.50	50.
47. 1986C	250	laminated lace lady leg, 2 diamonds		75.	125.
48. 1986D	890	stag swing-guard lockback		35.	85.
49. 1986E	251	pearl swing-guard lockback		45.	125.
50. 1986F	246	set of bone, chestnut bone, black sunfish		110./three	275.
51. 1986G	747	jigged chestnut bone sunfish		32.50	47.
52. 1987A	1,640	CK87 smooth chestnut bone Grizzly		42.	68.
53. 1987B	684	stag physician's jack		25.	65.
54. 1987C	300	pearl physician's jack		39.	95.
55. 1987D	637	jigged bone axe folding hunter		32.50	58.
56. 1987E	400	smooth green bone axe folding hunter		37.50	85.
57. 1987F	600	stag swell-end "bomb" jack		28.	45.
58. 1987G	500	scrimshaw biplane swell-end "bomb" jack		28.	55.
59. 1987H	698	stag sleeveboard whittler		32.	85.
60. 1987I	400	picture handle sleeveboard whittler		35.	95.
61. 1988A	1,165	CK88 bubinga wood Grizzly		42.	57.
62. 1988B	400	scrimshaw Grizzly		55.	150.
63. 1988C	723	stag J.BOWIE knife		55.	100.
64. 1988D	389	bone bowie, laser engraved blade		67.50	125.
65. 1988E	673	red jigged bone curved center-lock hunter		31.	45.
66. 1988F	399	smooth brown bone curved hunter, engraving		37.50	58.
67. 1988G	711	stag "gunfighter" sw-center coffin jack		29.	75.
68. 1988H	406	briar root "banker" sw-center coffin jack		34.	47.
69. 1988I	686	red jigged bone congress, 4-blades		32.50	52.
70. 1988J	401	ivory white congress, 4-blades, engraving		37.50	57.
71. 1989A	1,566	CK89 Prairie jigged brown bone Grizzly		42.	120.
72. 1989B	784	moss green jigged bone dolphin lockback		34.	44.
73. 1989C	488	cinnamon bone dolphin lockback, engraving		37.50	57.
74. 1989D	776	Prairie jigged brown bone humpback jack		33.	40.
75. 1989E	475	smooth green bone humpback jack, engraving		38.	44.

KA-BAR COLLECTORS CLUB (continued)

ISSUE	QUANTITY	DESCRIPTION	VALUES ISSUE	2000
76. 1989F	766	briar root one-hand razor jack	29.50	33.
77. 1989G	431	smooth red bone razor jack, engraving	32.50	37.
78. 1989H	774	smooth white bone whaler	31.	46.
79. 1989I	496	scrimshaw whaler, laser engraved blade	38.50	57.
80. 1990A	1,400	CK90 picture handle Grizzly	45.	125.
81. 1990B	762	smooth white bone Long John swell-center	38.	55.
82. 1990C	501	stag Long John swell-center ✔	43.	48.
83. 1990D	720	strawberry bone "Rancher" stockman	39.	43.
84. 1990E	527	stag "Rancher" stockman ✔	42.	47.
85. 1990F	530	mahogany bone "Boxcar" whittler, engraving	37.	39.
86. 1990G	519	whittler, engraving ✔	42.	48.
87. 1990H	719	blue jigged bone curved barlow	35.	40.
88. 1990I	480	jade green smooth bone curved barlow ✔	40.	53.
89. 1990J	?	USMC 50th Anniversary WWII combat knife	45.	190.
90. 1991A	1,473	CK91 maple curved center-lock hunter	45.	58.
91. 1991B	775	stag balloon pen ✔	35.	53.
92. 1991C	501	alternative ivory balloon pen	39.	44.
93. 1991D	737	maize Delrin "Swashbuckler" toothpick	35.	38.
94. 1991E	426	black Delrin "Swashbuckler," engraving	39.50	44.
95. 1991F	740	black swirl poly jumbo whittler	44.50	65.
96. 1991F	740	alternative ivory jumbo whittler, elephant	49.50	85.
97. 1991G	942	USMC 50th Anniv. Pearl Harbor combat knife	48.	150.
98. 1991H	5,256	USMC Desert Storm commemorative, engraving	48.	150.
99. 1992A	1,293	CK92 stag curved center-lock hunter	47.50	55.
100. 1992B	791	brown jigged bone "Copperhead" jack	37.50	45.
101. 1992C	480	stag "Copperhead" serpentine jack ✔	42.	50.
102. 1992D	802	jigged brown bone muskrat	37.50	45.
103. 1992E	500	stag muskrat ✔	45.	53.
104. 1992F	801	brown jigged bone Coke bottle hunter	47.50	55.
105. 1992G	500	smooth brown bone Coke bottle hunter ✔	52.	58.
106. 1993A	967	CK93 brown jigged bone center-lock hunter	47.50	48.
107. 1993B	802	cherry wood cotton sampler	42.50	120.
108. 1993C	?	USMC Vietnam commemorative, gold etched	60.	200.
109. 1994A	?	CK94 smooth brown bone center-lock hunter	47.50	54.
110. 1994B	730	brown jigged bone swing-guard lockback	49.	55.
111. 1994C	?	Set-jigged bone Texas toothpick	31.	36.
112. 1994D	?	Set-stag Texas toothpick	36.	40.
113. 1994E	?	Set-congress, 4-blades	39.	32.
114. 1994F	?	Set-congress, 4-blades	44.	50.
115. 1994G	?	US Army D-Day 50th Anniv. combat knife	60.	120.

THE KNIFE COLLECTORS CLUB, INC., 1920 N. 26th St., Lowell, AR 72745-8489, 800-255-9034, www.agrussell.com. Information from Goldie Russell.

ISSUE	QUANTITY	DESCRIPTION	VALUES ISSUE	2000
BI-ST	3,000	1976 Hen & Rooster stainless coffin handle Bi-Centennial by Bertram	$29.95	$175.
BI-BR	2,000	1976 Hen & Rooster brass coffin handle Bi-Centennial	34.95	250.
BI-SG	1,000	1976 Hen & Rooster silver coffin handle Bi-Centennial	59.95	495.
BI-AG	28	1976 Hen & Rooster 14k-gold coffin handle Bi-Centennial	495.	1,900.
ENT	400	1976 Hen & Rooster stainless Entebbe	25.	175.
ENT	100	1976 Hen & Rooster sterling silver Entebbe	43.	400.
US-1	1,000	1987 Liberty Bell 2-blade equal-end jack, Cattaraugus	25.	50.
ST-1.	500	Sting I Integral Forged Boot Knife: issue	125.	200.
ST-2.	500	Sting II Integral Forged Boot Knife: issue	125.	200.
ST-3.	1,000	Sting IA Integral Forged Boot Knife: issue	95.	200.
ST-4.	101	1984 Robert W. Loveless Limited Edition Semi-skinner: issue	495.	2,000.

THE KNIFE COLLECTORS CLUB, INC. *(continued)*

ISSUE	QUANTITY	DESCRIPTION	ISSUE	2000
ST-5.	37	1985 A. G. Russell Limited Edition Bowie: issue	295.	1,250.
ST-6.	100	1985 D. F. Kressler Gentleman's Hunter: issue	495.	1,250.
ST-7.	100	1986 Frank Centofante Limited Edition Lockback: issue	205.	600.
ST-8.	200	1987 Mike Franklin Limited Stellite® Hunter: issue	275.	400.
ST-9.	200	1988 Bill Cheatham Limited "Chipped Flint" Hunter: issue	145.	250.
ST-10.	100	1989 S. R. Johnson Gentleman's Hunter: issue	375.	850.
ST-11.	100	1990 D'Holder Amber & Oosic Hunter: issue	495.	600.
CM-1.	12,000	1971 Kentucky Rifle Stock Schrade	12.	150.
CM-2.	12,000	1973 Granddaddy Barlow Camillus	25.	75.
CM-3.	3,700	1974 Luger Wharncliffe Puma	35.	200.
CM-4.	1,800	1975 Hen & Rooster Ivory Barlow	19.	485.
CM-5.	1,200	1977 Hen & Rooster .44 Magnum Whittler	39.	200.
CM-6.	2,500	1978 Hen & Rooster Straight Arrow Coffin Jack	34.	375.
CM-7.	2,800	1978 Hen & Rooster .45 Long Colt Hunter	39.	175.
CM-8.	2,200	1979 Hen & Rooster .219 Zipper Barlow	30.	200.
CM-9.	3,000	1980 Hen & Rooster .300 Savage Canoe	35.	150.
CM-10.	3,600	1985 20th Century Barlow Cattaraugus	25.	150.
CM-11.	3,000	1987 Pocket Barlow Cattaraugus	25.	150.
CM-12.	3,000	1989 Split Bolster Jack Cattaraugus	25.	150.
CM-14.	1,700	1990 Sleeveboard Whittler Cattaraugus	50.	150.
CM-15.	700	1991 2 7/8" Muskrat Cattaraugus	40.	150.
CM-16.	700	1991 3 3/8" Muskrat Cattaraugus	45.	150.
CM-17.	800	1993 Mediterranean Barlow Cattaraugus	40.	150.
FH-1.	3,000	1988 Slim Wharncliffe Jack Cattaraugus	25.	150.
FH-2.	1,600	1990 Clasp Knife A.G. Russell	50.	150.
FH-3.	1,200	1991 European Folding Hunter Cattaraugus	50.	150.
USFH-4.	1,000	1993 American Folding Hunter A.G. Russell	100.	175.
USFH-5.	1,000	? Folding Hunter A.G. Russell	125.	150.

Schrade Limited-Edition Knives

by Debbie L. Chase and Craig R. Henry

Name or Pattern	Issued	Value
Schrade-Walden BB166 Buffalo Bill fixed blade	1969	$45.
Schrade-Walden BB125 Buffalo Bill fixed blade	1969	35.
Set of Two: BB166 and BB125.		
American Revolution Set 1776-1976 (Junior Stock)		
Minute Man (Battle of Concord)	1973	15.
Paul Revere	1973	20.
Liberty Bell	1973	25.
Set of Three on Wooden Display		65.
Grand Dad's Old Timer Series (Schrade 70th Anniversary)		
4" Stockman	1974	35.
Barlow	1974	25.
Junior Stockman	1975	30.
Sharp Finger	1975	20.
1775-1975 U.S. Army, Navy, Marine Corps	1975	45.
Bicentennial Set of Three 4" Stockmen		
Longhorn 4" Stockman	1975	35.
Spirit of St. Louis 4" Stockman	1975	35.
Jim Bowie 4" Stockman	1975	30.
Daniel Boone 4" Stockman	1976	35.
Buffalo Bill 4" Stockman	1976	35.
Covered Wagon 4" Stockman	1976	35.
American Eagle Set/Five 4" Stockmen, Frame	1976	135.
1776-1976 Village of Walden, N.Y., Pen Knife	1976	25.
Mayflower	1977	35.

Name or Pattern	Issued	Value
Schrade-Loveless CH-1 Drop-point, 154-CM/white	1978	175.
Schrade CH-2 Custom Hunter Drop-point (Loveless design) 440-A/burgundy	1978	90.
Schrade 75th Anniversary Large Clasp, Staglon	1979	175.
Schrade 75th Anniversary, Gold Etch, Stag	1979	1,000.
Walden, N.Y., Firefighters 125th Anniv.	1980	30.
Schrade-IX*L, Made in Sheffield		
Schrade-IX*L Stockman, 1787-1980	1980	50.
Schrade-IX*L Set/Five in Box	1980	150.
Schrade-IX*L Set/Five in Box	1981	150.
Schrade-IX*L Set/Two: Canoe, Stockman	1981	50.
Schrade-IX*L Set/Two Lockbacks	1981	75.
The Tradesman		
"The Farmer" Extra Large Stockman	1981	30.
"The Miner"	1981	30.
"The Fisherman"	1981	30.
"The Lumberman"	1981	30.
"The Rancher"	1981	30.
Set of Five		
Schrade Cutlery Classics, Set/Five	1981	125.
Bald Eagle 200th Anniversary	1982	35.
Silver Set/Two, Gold Inlaid Fox, Bear	1982	80.

Name or Pattern	Issued	Value
Schrade "Heritage" Set/Six, Box: Stockman, Junior Stock, Barlow, Muskrat, Whittler, Trapper (brown, red, or green bone)	1983	**200.**
Schrade 80th Anniversary Daddy Barlow, bone	1984	**100.**
Schrade 80th Anniversary Daddy Barlow, plastic	1984	**50.**
Old Timer 25th Anniversary Stockman, bone	1984	**50.**
Los Angeles Olympic Games Cub	1984	**25.**
Schrade Custom Made, Large SCM7, Engraved	1985	**80.**
Schrade Custom Made, Medium SCM5, Engraved	1985	**70.**
Schrade LB-5DM Damascus Steel Blade	1985	**100.**
Boy Scouts 75th Anniversary Utility	1985	**30.**
Boy Scouts 75th Anniversary Lockback	1985	**35.**
Boy Scouts 75th Anniversary Lockback, 10k Gold	1985	**100.**
Boy Scouts 75th Anniversary Lockback, Sterling	1985	**65.**
"Mink" Junior Stockman	1985	**20.**
Old Timer red smooth bone 4" Stockman	1985	**40.**
Old Timer red smooth bone Junior Stockman	1985	**35.**
Old Timer red smooth bone Tiny Stockman	1985	**25.**
Statue of Liberty, Wood Plaque	1986	**75.**
Statue of Liberty Gold Etch, Wood Plaque	1986	**150.**
Mississippi Trapper	1986	**15.**

Indian Series (Scrimshaw Lockbacks, special sheath, box)

Name or Pattern	Issued	Value
Thunderbird	1981	**200.**
Morningstar	1982	**125.**
Kachina	1983	**75.**
Indian Turtle	1984	**70.**
Bear Cult	1985	**65.**
Sundance	1986	**60.**

Pioneers of America Series (each with sheath)

Name or Pattern	Issued	Value
The Cowboy	1987	**50.**
Pony Express	1988	**50.**
Eagle Has Landed (Apollo 11 20th Anniv.)	1989	**45.**
The Gold Rush Story	1990	**45.**

Federal Duck Stamp Series

Name or Pattern	Issued	Value
94OT Gunstock Trapper, Ebony	1987-88	**55.**
94OT Gunstock, Bird Hook, Goncalo Alves	1988-89	**55.**
LB7 Large Lockback, Goncalo Alves	1989-90	**125.**

Name or Pattern	Issued	Value
877UH Double-End Trapper, Goncalo Alves	1990-91	**90.**
160OT Fixed Blade, Winewood	1991-92	**125.**
125OT Large Clasp, Winewood	1992-93	**140.**
8OT 4" Stockman, Winewood	1993-94	**55.**
8OT 4" Stockman, Winewood	1994-95	**55.**
5OT 4" Bruin Lockback	1995-96	**70.**
503SC Scrimshaw	1995-96	**20.**
Gunstock, Bird Hook, 10th Anniv.	1996-97	**80.**

Aviation History Series

Name or Pattern	Issued	Value
Flight of the Flyer (Wright Brothers)	1991	**50.**
Wings of Victory (P51 Mustang)	1992	**50.**
Breaking the Sound Barrier	1993	**50.**
Guide's Choice 158OT Guthook Hunter	1988	**15.**
Schrade Cut. 85th Anniversary Stag Whittler	1989	**125.**
The Whaler Scrimshaw Set of Three, Wood Box	1990	**90.**
Checkered Flag Collection, Set/Three, Box	1991	**100.**
National Park Service 1916-1991, Stag, Box	1991	**250.**
National Park Service 1916-1991, Wood, Box	1991	**124.**
National Park Service 1916-1991, Scrimshaw	1991	**40.**
Pearl Harbor Commemorative Bowie, Box	1991	**900.**
World War II 50th Anniversary, Set/Seven, Box	1991	**2500.**
Discovery of Americas, Set/Six Fixed Blades	1992	**1800.**
Rolling Thunder, Race Cars, Set/Three	1992	**225.**
Rolling Thunder II, Race Cars, Set/Three	1993	**240.**

NASCAR Series

Name or Pattern	Issued	Value
Dale Jarrett	1993	
Harry Gant	1993	
Ernie Irvan	1993	

Sporting Dogs Series

Name or Pattern	Issued	Value
Labrador Retriever	1994	**50.**
English Pointer	1995	**55.**
Golden Retriever	1996	**63.**

Frontier Series

Name or Pattern	Issued	Value
Mountain Man Trapper	1994	**25.**
Daniel Boone Trapper	1995	**25.**
Davy Crockett Trapper	1995	**25.**
Schrade Cut. Co. 90th Anniversary	1994	**100.**
Whitetails Unlimited	1994	**65.**
Compliments of Imperial Schrade	1995	**30.**

Commemorative and Limited-Edition Knives

Selected Private Limited-Edition Knives

Manufactured by Imperial Schrade

Note: These knives were made for the indicated clients as one-time fixed quantity lots. The factory cost was usually not recorded (for ones marked ?, even the client was not recorded). Some issues were then resold, at whatever markup the client deemed appropriate, while others were given away as awards or promotions. We have never seen most of these knives, let alone seen them offered for sale, so we have no idea what they might be worth. A few, such as the Skoal "Event Enhancement" knives, were both fancy and expensive.

Issuer and Name or Pattern	Issued	Value
Adolphus Busch, Stanhope Lens, Enamel	1954	**150.**
Adolphus Busch, Stanhope Lens, Enamel	1959	**140.**
Keen Kutter 100th Anniv. Junior Stockman	1969	**65.**
A. G. Russell Kentucky Rifle	1972	**100.**
Belknap Hdw. Kentucky Rifle	1972	**50.**
J. Russell & Co. Barlow Reproduction, wood box	1974	**85.**
National Knife Collectors [and Dealers] Association		
Eagle Series, Liberty or Death, Set/Five	1974	**100.**
Tennessee-Kentucky Whittlers, Cased Set/Two	1976	**125.**
Rodgers-Wostenholm Cattle, Annual Knife	1978	**100.**
Museum Founders Knife (in Founders' Set)	1981	**125.**
Stag Trapper, Annual Knife	1982	**65.**
Parker-Frost Cutlery		
Thirteen Colonies, Set/Thirteen	1976	**445.**
Trail of Tears, Large Clasp	1977	**150.**
Custer's Last Fight, Large Clasp	1977	**150.**
Otasco Stores		
Teddy Roosevelt, Junior Stockman	1978	**25.**
Will Rogers Junior Stockman	1979	**30.**
Mac Tool		
Mac Tool Trademark of Quality (Imperial)	1979	**30.**
Mac Tool 45th Anniversary	1983	**50.**
Mac Tool 1938-1985 Daddy Barlow	1985	**55.**
Mac Tool	1986	**30.**
Don Prudhomme "Snake's Final Strike"	1994	**30.**
? Dixie Collection, Four Sets of Two Knives	1980	**125.**
Snap-On Tools 60th Anniversary 4" Stockman	1980	**35.**
Orgill Bros. Deluxe Scrimshaw Pearl Canoe	1980	**45.**
? California Gold Rush, Set/Two	1980	**100.**
? Battle of New Orleans	1981	**65.**
? Judge Parker Commemorative	1981	**65.**
? Seminole Indian Commemorative	1981	**65.**
Collegiate Concepts, Bear Bryant	1981	
Warren Tool Co., Warren Whittler Set/Two	1982	**120.**
Warren Tool Co., Warren Whittler HCM Set/Two	1982	**150.**
Hoffritz Cutlery 50th Anniversary	1982	
Moore Handley Hdw. 100th Anniversary	1982	
? Stratton Baldwin Commemorative (1882-1980)	1982	
? Bear Bryant Commemorative	1983	
Montgomery Ward, Indian Lance	1983	**55.**
Matco		
Matco KC-83 Special Edition	1983	
"Quic Shine 99" N.H.R.A. Top Fuel Funny Car	1995	
Cotter True Value Hardware, Scrimshaw Series		
Cotter True Value, Covered Wagon	1983	**45.**
Cotter True Value, Raccoons	1985	**45.**
Cotter True Value, Rainbow Trout	1986	**45.**
Cotter True Value, Appaloosa Stallion	1987	**45.**

Issuer and Name or Pattern	Issued	Value
Cotter True Value, Deer Head (color)	1988	**20.**
Cotter True Value, Pheasants	1989	
Cotter True Value, Bald Eagle	1990	
Cotter True Value, Columbus and Ships	1992	
Sears Roebuck, Currier & Ives Limited Editions		
1st Ed. Folding Hunter, Lightning Express	1984	**50.**
2nd Ed. Sheepfoot Jack, Flying Cloud	1985	**40.**
Ace Hardware		
Ace Hardware 60th Anniversary	1984	
Ace Hardware 70th Anniversary	1994	
Ace Tool		
Armadillo/Cactus Scrimshaw Lockback	1985	
Motorcycle/Indian Head Scrimshaw	1992	
Merchant Marine Maritime Academy	1984	
Walkill Correctional Facility, 50th Anniv.	1984	
Woodbourne Correctional Facility 50th Anniv.	1984	
Westwind Productions, '84 U.S. Shooting Team	1984	
American Express Scrimshaw Presidents Set/Five	1985	**250.**
Big C Sales Set/Three Stockmen, red bone	1985	**60.**
Nat. Wildlife Galleries, Migratory Bird Stamp	1985	
Fleetwood Duck Stamp Commemorative	1985	
American Hdw. Supply 75th Anniversary	1985	
Sports Afield	1987	
? Constitution Commemorative	1987	
A.B. Carter Traveler Co. Office Knife	1987	**25.**
A.B. Carter Mill Devices Co. Office Knife	1987	**25.**
Village of Ellenville, 4th of July		
LB7 Large Lockback	1986	
SC500 Scrimshaw Large Lockback	1987	
SC506 Scrimshaw Barlow	1988	
SC502 Scrimshaw SharpFinger	1989	
LTD Special Limited Edition	1990	
SC500 Scrimshaw Large Lockback	1991	
SC524 Scrimshaw Tradesman	1992	
296Y Yellow Trapper	1993	
LTD Special Limited Edition	1994	
SC507 Ellenville Riverboat Scrimshaw	1995	
L.L. Bean, Freeport, Maine		
167UH Steelhead	1987	
168UH Walleye	1987	
LB7 Large Lockback	1988	
152OT = LLB #6042	1988	
LB1BR = LLB #C637	1989	
225OT = LLB #C832	1989	
SP1BK, Black	1991	
SP1G, Green	1991	
SP1R, Red	1991	
SP2BK, Black	1991	

Issuer and Name or Pattern	Issued	Value
SP2G, Green	1991	
SP2R, Red	1991	
SP3BK, Black	1991	
SP3G, Green	1991	
SP3R, Red	1991	
SP3BK, Black	1991	
SP3G, Green	1991	
SP3R, Red	1991	

Ducks Unlimited (U.S.A.)

Issuer and Name or Pattern	Issued	Value
50DU	1987	
162DU	1988	
502SC Iowa D.U. - 50 Years of Conservation	1988	
165DU, Black	1989	
498DU	1989	
158OTB	1989	
5OTB	1989	
DUGS1 (158OTB/167UHB/5OTB) Set/Three	1989	
13DU	1990	
108DU	1990	
172DU	1990	
225DU	1990	
36DU Greenwing	1990	
AP31DU AP5/AP26 Set/Two	1990	
DU3R (153UH/LB8/885UH) Set/Three	1990	
14 DU (14UH with Staglon handles)	1991	
DU94 Hunting Dog Scene, Oak Box	1991	
PH2DU (Pro Hunter 2, Burgundy)	1991	
DU3OTG (3OT, Greenwing blade etch)	1992	
DU34OT	1992	
DU5OT	1992	
DUCN22	1992	
507DU93, Scrimshaw Mallard Scene	1993	
DU1GS (147OT/CN24) Set/Two	1993	
DU3R94 (147DU/142DU/SP8DU GS) Set/Three	1993	
DU507CO, Colorado D.U. Scrimshaw	1993	
DU507IL, Illinois D.U. Scrimshaw	1993	
DU507OH, Ohio D.U. Scrimshaw	1993	
141DU (141OT)	1994	
143DU (143OT)	1994	
502DU (Flying Mallards)	1994	
707DU95 (707UH)	1994	
CNDU25 (CN21)	1994	
CNDU45 (CN41)	1994	
DU502MO, Flying Mallards, Missouri Map	1994	
DU95R (147DU/143/141DU) Raffle Set/Three	1994	
DUFLYWAY Set/Five Fixed Blades	1994	**770.**
PH1TXDU, Budweiser Salutes Texas D.U.	1994	
SGS3DUDK, Set/Two, North & South Dakota	1994	
SGS9DUDK, Set/Two, North & South Dakota	1994	
SGS9DUNY, Set/Two, New York	1994	
SGS7DU, Set/Two, Waterfowl Blade Etch	1994	
104OT, Green	1995	
154, Ivory Delrin	1995	
96, Green	1995	
LB7DUM, Black	1995	
LB7, Black, Budweiser-D.U. Mississippi	1995	
DDU154SC, North Dakota D.U. Sponsor	1995	
DDULB9SC, North Dakota D.U. Sponsor	1996	
DDU296SC, North Dakota D.U. Sponsor	1997	

Ducks Unlimited (Canada)

Issuer and Name or Pattern	Issued	Value
108DU	1990	
172DU	1990	
225DU	1990	
14DU	1991	

Issuer and Name or Pattern	Issued	Value
30DU, Greenwing	1991	
707DU	1991	
152DU	1993	
513DU	1993	
DUC94R, Set/Three for Raffle	1993	
DUC498, Deer Scene on Blade	1994	

B.A.S.S. Series

Issuer and Name or Pattern	Issued	Value
B.A.S.S. Classic Team Scrimshaw 505SC	1987	
B.A.S.S. Classic Team Scrimshaw 513SC	1988	
B.A.S.S. Classic Team Scrimshaw 515SC	1989	
B.A.S.S. Classic Team Scrimshaw 507SC	1990	
B.A.S.S. Classic Team Scrimshaw 502SC	1991	

Committee to Save Stuyvesant Park

Issuer and Name or Pattern	Issued	Value
Peter Stuyvesant Barlow	1988	
Peter Stuyvesant Daddy Barlow	1988	

Cornwell Tools

Issuer and Name or Pattern	Issued	Value
Cornwell Tools 1919-1989 Scrimshaw	1988	
Cornwell Tools 75 Years of Quality	1993	
Cornwell Tools, Limited Edition, Red	1994	
Cornwell Tools, Limited Edition, Blue	1994	
Eli Lily & Co. for Hubbard Milling, Apralan	1988	
Eli Lily & Co., Elanco	1988	
Culbert Cutlery Co., Sturgis 1988 Ltd. Ed.	1988	
Bass Pro Shops Lockback	1989	
Coast to Coast, 1988 Top Gun Award Commem.	1989	
Walker Valley Fire Dept. 75th Anniversary	1990	
H.K.B. Desert Storm Limited Edition Sets	1991	
U.S. Border Patrol LB7, Engraved	1992	
Anheuser-Busch, Official Beer of NASCAR	1992	
Fishkill Penitentiary, 513SC	1992	
Pennsylvania Bingo, Fire Wagon Scrimshaw	1992	
N.W. Transport Services, Safe Driver 23 Years	1992	
Chromate Co. Race Cars Scrimshaw, Set/Three	1992	

? Classic Car Series

Issuer and Name or Pattern	Issued	Value
'56 Thunderbird	1990	
'53 Corvette	1990	
'57 Chevrolet	1991	
'65 Mustang	1992	

New Jersey Division of Fish Game & Wildlife

Issuer and Name or Pattern	Issued	Value
152OT with Logo on Sheath	1992	
507SC with Deer Scene in Red Scrimshaw	1992	
147OT with Etched Blade	1993	**14.**
CN2545 Set/Two, Green	1993	
96OT, Green	1994	**20.**

Smoky Mountain Knife Works

Issuer and Name or Pattern	Issued	Value
296SC Smoky Mountain Trapper	1992	
Harry Gant, 4" Stockman, green	1994	
Endangered Species Set/Five: Eagle, Elephant, Tiger, Panda, Grizzly	1994	

Town of Wawarsing Fourth of July

Issuer and Name or Pattern	Issued	Value
U.S.S. Constitution	1992	
Fireworks Scrimshaw 4" Stockman	1994	

Town of Wawarsing Happy Holidays

Issuer and Name or Pattern	Issued	Value
Horse-Drawn Sleigh	1993	
Boy with Boot	1994	

I.S.C.-Europe

Issuer and Name or Pattern	Issued	Value
4" Lockback, Genuine Stag	1993	
Pro Hunter 1, Burgundy Micarta	1993	
Pro Hunter 2, Burgundy Micarta	1993	
Pro Hunter 1, Genuine Stag	1993	
Pro Hunter 2, Genuine Stag	1993	
Medco Tools, Vietnam Veterans Memorial	1993	
American Motorcycle Assoc. 5" Lockback	1993	

Issuer and Name or Pattern	Issued	Value
Accessory Wholesalers Small Lockback	1993	
Paul Charles Ltd., Turkey Power	1993	
Milton Sales, Large Lockback, Moose Scene	1993	
Sons of Amvets "Lest We Forget," Blue	1994	
Superior Officers Assoc. Captains' Unit, Blue	1994	
Purina Chow 1894-1994, 505SC Checkered	1994	
National Foundation to Protect America's Eagles: Set/Four 4" Stockmen, Winewood	1994	
Allis Chalmers Tractors 80th Anniv., Set/Five	1994	210.
Promac John Deere LB5	1994	
John Deere 5OT Lockback	1995	
G.M.C. U.S.A. (on tang) Large Lockback	1995	
Hardware Wholesale 50th Anniv. 5OT, Black	1995	
Coors/Integer Holiday, Rocky Mtn. Scene	1995	

National Rifle Association

Hunter Education: Continuing the Heritage	1991	
N.R.A. LB7 Lockback	1992	
N.R.A.-I.L.A 20th Anniv. PH1 Pro Hunter	1995	
N.R.A.-I.L.A 20th Anniv. 34OT Stockman	1995	

? College Football Teams Series

University of Alabama	1993	
Florida State	1994	
University of South Carolina	1994	
University of Georgia	1994	
Clemson University	1994	
Louisiana State University	1994	
University of Tennessee	1994	

Rowland Specialties

U.S. Army LB7	1993	
U.S. Navy LB7	1993	
U.S. Air Force LB7	1993	
U.S. Marine LB7	1993	

Professional Bullriders' Association

Ty Murray Commemorative, 296TYM	1993	40.
Ty Murray, 50TYM	1994	

U.S. Tobacco

167UH Steelhead Filet, Fishermen in Boat	1992	
LB7 "Skoal Bandit Racing" for Gant's crew	1992	

Issuer and Name or Pattern	Issued	Value

U.S. Tobacco / Copenhagen Skoal "Event Enhancement"

P.R.C.A. Stock Contractor (rodeo)	1994	
Black 165OT, Copenhagen shield	1994	
Black 5OT, Copenhagen shield	1994	
Black 877UH, Copenhagen shield	1994	
Black 33OT, Copenhagen shield	1994	
Black LB7, gold Copenhagen shield, blued	1994	70.
Copenhagen Skoal Outdoors Set/Three maple	1994	
Copenhagen Skoal Pro Rodeo Set/Three maple	1994	
Copenhagen Skoal Bandit Racing Set/Three	1994	
Copenhagen Skoal Pulling Circuit Set/Three	1994	

U.S. Tobacco / Skoal Limited Editions

Skoal SK154, Green	1994	
Skoal SK194	1994	
Skoal SK36, 36OT, Green	1994	
Skoal SK5, 5OTG	1994	
Skoal SK72, 72OT	1994	
Skoal SK89, 89, Green	1994	

Rocky Mountain Elk Foundation

Pro Hunter 1, Elk	1994	
LB7, Large Lockback, Elk	1994	
513, Elk	1994	
Pro Hunter 1, Elk	1995	
5OT Medium Lockback, Black, Elk	1995	
Set/Three: 153UH/LB8/885UH, Elk	1995	
Set/Three: 140/141/142, Elk	1995	

Future Farmers of America

Agco-Allis Tractor 4" Stockman	1995	
Massey Ferguson Tractor 4" Stockman	1995	
Farmers Pride 4" Stockman, Blue	1995	20.

Ace Imports, Playing Card Promotion

6OT with Deck of Cards	1995	
8OT with Deck of Cards	1995	
96OT with Deck of Cards	1995	
152OT with Deck of Cards	1995	

Buck Folding Knives

by Vern Taylor, Joe Houser and Larry Oden

Editor's note: Vern Taylor founded the Buck Collectors Club in 1988. After more than a quarter century as a sales representative for Buck Knives, he retired to his ranch in northern California in the early 1990s. Vern passed away in June 2003. Joe Houser and Larry Oden of the Buck Collectors Club have expanded and updated Vern's following original article. For additional values and history of Buck Knives, see "Buck Fixed Blade Knives" in the segment, "Pioneers of Modern Handmade Knives." All values are for knives in excellent, unsharpened condition.

Buck Folding Hunters

The Buck Model 117

In 1946, Hoyt Buck made the first Buck folding knives, the Model 117. Actually, he just made the blades and put them into handles from war surplus lifeboat knives (see sailor's knives in the "Special Purpose Jack Knives" segment of the chapter, "Named Jack Knife Patterns"). In 1963, the 117's curved handle with squared ends, along with its hollow-ground clip blade, would reappear enlarged and redesigned as the Model 110. Buck's circa 1948 catalog says, "No. 117 a handy single-bladed knife of the same steel as in the sheath knives. Blade large enough to use as a pocket hunting knife if desired. 3 1/2" hollow ground blade, 4 3/8" hardwood handle. Price $5.00."

Few 117s were made. An unused example (see accompanying photo) belongs to Tom George, whose father was Buck's first retailer, in San Diego, from 1946-48. An authentic example would be very valuable, but since such a knife would be simple to counterfeit, do not pay a premium for one without having it authenticated. Buck also offered a service whereby a customer could send in a broken pocketknife, regardless of manufacturer, and it would be repaired with a BUCK-stamped blade.

Hoyt Buck made the first Buck folding knives, the Model 117, in 1946. The value of an authentic example is **$450-500**, but since such a knife would be simple to counterfeit, do not pay a premium for one without having it authenticated.

Buck Folding Hunter Model 110

In 1962, Blade Magazine Cutlery Hall-Of-Famer© Al Buck began work on a new style of lockback folding hunting knife. The Model 110 was the design that would make his knife company world famous and the trade name "Buck Knife" just as familiar—and as often misused—as "Kleenex™" or "Xerox™." Though Al Buck popularized the lockback folding hunting knife, he did not invent it. Big lockback knives had been available in the United States in the eighteenth and nineteenth centuries, and they still had been fairly popular up into the 1930s.

The popularity of big lockbacks had declined after the '30s for several reasons. They cost more than sheath knives of the same size, and most of them were more fragile than sheath knives. As pocketknives they were too big for modern pants pockets, so they were more awkward to carry than small sheath knives. By the early 1960s, there were few models of lockback folding knives still available on the American market.

What Al Buck did was rebirth the whole idea of the lockback hunting knife. He gave it sleek, modern lines. He made it stout and sturdy enough to do almost anything a fixed-blade knife could do. He gave it its own belt sheath, like the one with the old Marble's safety folder. This got the knife's bulk out of the user's pocket, while making a much more compact and convenient package than any fixed-blade sheath knife.

When Al Buck designed the original Buck 110, he saw it as a knife that an average hunter might carry for two or three weeks per year, much the way the same hunter carried a sheath knife. However, when the 110 came on the market in 1964, it was quickly adopted by building tradesmen, truckers and many other workmen as an ideal, all-around, heavy-duty work knife.

Because of the 110's heavy everyday use, Al Buck realized that the design had to be beefed up, which led to the first of several major structural modifications. Within the major variations are many minor ones. Today, the variations are of keen interest to collectors of early Buck knives. Here they are in summary form.

First-Version 110: 1964-65

The handle frames of the first 110s were made from die-cast brass with recesses for the Macassar-ebony-wood handle slabs. In the first version, the two sides of the handle were designed initially to be press-fitted together. One side was cast with projecting studs, the other with matching holes. Consequently, the rivets are visible only on the left-hand side bolsters of the first-version knives. The BUCK marking on these earliest knives is stamped along the back of the blade. Etching was briefly used in place of

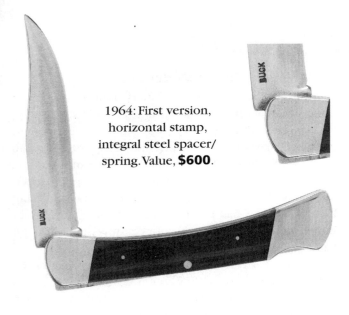

1964: First version, horizontal stamp, integral steel spacer/spring. Value, **$600**.

1965: Second version, horizontal stamp on same side as nail nick, hard fiber spacer. Value, **$400**.

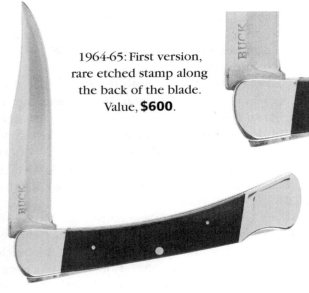

1964-65: First version, rare etched stamp along the back of the blade. Value, **$600**.

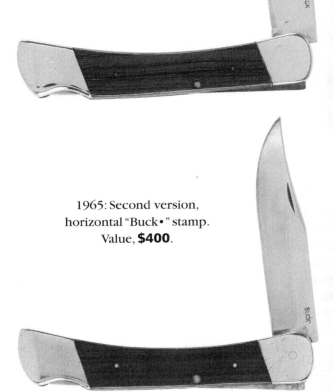

1965: Second version, horizontal "Buck•" stamp. Value, **$400**.

stamping, and vintage 110s so etched are very hard to find today. All the earlier 110s are 1/2-inch thick through the bolsters. The nail mark is struck and very thin. The spacer between the cap bolsters is a separate piece of steel.

Second-Version 110: 1965

In the second version of the 110, the spacer between the cap bolsters is made of a bone-hard reddish fiber. The brass handles on this version are also castings and designed to go together much like the first-version knives. Polished areas of the brass on knives made from castings will consequently show minor porosity. Second-version 110s are about 1/2-inch thick. They have the thin, stamped nail mark. Later-version 110s have a wider, machined nail mark. The BUCK marking on these knives is stamped along the back of the blade. In one variation within this version, the blade rivet is a separate piece and no longer part of the right-hand cast side.

Third-Version 110: 1966-70

The third basic modification of the Buck 110 was to replace the bone-hard fiber spacer used between the cap bolsters. As a result, the spacer was integral to the right-hand side bolster. Third-version 110s will be stamped BUCK and sometimes will have a small dot after the K. The stamp will be located along the tang area as in the 110s of today, only the stamp on the third versions is read with the tip of the blade pointed down. In 1967, Buck added "U.S.A." to the blade stamp, a common marking on knives from this version. There are at least seven major variations within this version, as Buck was constantly perfecting the design of the increasingly popular knife. Knives can be found where the cap-bolster rivets are only visible on the left-hand side, on both sides, and some will even have just one large rivet visible on both sides of the cap bolsters. The inlays will be held in place with two small rivets, though one rare variation has no inlay rivets at all.

1966-67: Third version, spacer integral with right-hand-side bolster, Buck• stamp. Value, **$200**.

Fourth-Version 110: 1970-71

In 1970 Buck went to a separate insert, made of brass, between the cap bolsters. Fourth-version 110s will be stamped BUCK, U.S.A. and the rocker rivet in the first knives from this version will be brass, as in all earlier versions. Later, the rocker rivet was changed to stainless steel, and the rivets are still made that way today. The fourth version marks the first of the "squared-off" bolsters. All previous knives were rounded. Rivets will be visible through both sides of the cap bolsters and the blade-end bolsters.

1970-71: Fourth version w/steel rocker rivet, brass spacer, BUCK/U.S.A. stamp. Value, **$150**.

Fifth-Version 110: 1972-74

After only a couple of years, Buck changed the bolster insert—or "spring holder" as it is known at the Buck factory—from brass to stainless. Fifth-version 110s will be stamped BUCK, U.S.A. and later, BUCK, 110, U.S.A., read with the knife pointed toward the ground. This is often referred to as a *three-line inverted stamping*, and knives with such a stamping are very rare. The more common stamping from this version will have the BUCK, 110, U.S.A. read with the knife pointed up.

Sixth-Version 110: 1974-80

The sixth version marks the beginning of the use of small dots (•), located on either side of the model number, to designate major design changes in the 110. In 1974, Buck redesigned the 110 to make it harder to flick open with one hand. Several internal changes were made and the blade stamping went to BUCK, •110•, U.S.A. This is referred to as a *two-dot 110*. During this timeframe, Buck added an extra inlay rivet to the rear end of the Macassar-ebony inlay.

Seventh-Version 110: 1980-81

In 1980, the rocker material was changed and another dot was added to the blade stamping. The change placed one dot on the left of the 110 model number and two dots on the right side of the model number.

Eighth-Version 110: 1981-85

Until this time, all 110s were made with 440C stainless steel blades. In 1981, Buck started using a steel developed at the mill especially for Buck knives. Buck had made the move to fine-blanked parts, and 440C did not lend itself to that application. The blade stamping was changed to show two small dots on both sides of the 110, called a *four-dot 110*. It is also the last version of the 110 with the squared-off bolsters. In about 1982, Buck began to hand radius the handles to give the knife a more "pocket friendly" use. Apparently, a lot of customers liked to carry the knife in their pockets, and the sharp corners were rough on pants. Later, the radius was incorporated into the handle tooling. You can identify the hand-radiused knives by the thumb depression. If the knife is radiused around the entire handle but has sharp corners inside the thumb depression, it was radiused by hand. Finger-grooved 110s were introduced for the first time during this version.

Date Marks

In 1986, Buck dropped the dots and began to incorporate a code in the stamping of all knives to indicate the year of manufacture. The codes thus far are:

1986	<	1993	/	2000	⊐
1987	>	1994	\	2001	⊓
1988	∧	1995	⊂	2002	✕ ANVIL
1989	∨	1996	⊃	2003	⊤
1990	×	1997	∩	2004	⊥
1991	+	1998	∪	2005	⊢
1992	−	1999	⊏	2006	⊣

*Please note that the following stamp has been used on several special project and limited-edition knives since 2002: BUCK/Anvil/CUSTOM/U.S.A.

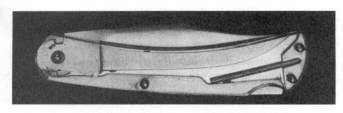

Transparent demonstrator models of 1984 production 110s were used by salesmen to show the internal mechanism.

In 1992, Buck again switched steel and phased in 420HC stainless for blades across the product line. However, no dots or symbols were incorporated to signal the change. Only the tang-stamp year symbol gives any indication. The last major change for the 110 came in 1994 when the inlay material was switched to a more "earth-friendly" laminate made from layers of pressure-treated Obeechee wood. From when the first 296 Model 110s were introduced up until this point, the inlay material had been Macassar ebony from India.

Buck Ranger Model 112

The Buck 112 Ranger was introduced in 1972 and was a smaller version of the 110. As with its larger counterpart, there are quite a few variations to be found and they are listed here with mention of the minor variations found within each category. The dates listed for the versions between 1972-74 are estimates, as no clear records were kept.

First-Version 112: 1972

The first version of the 112 had brass bolsters with a brass spring holder and black Micarta® inlays. The inlays were held in place with two tiny inlay rivets. The 440C blade was stamped BUCK, U.S.A. read with the knife pointed down. The knives do not have the now-popular nail nick in the blade.

1972: First version, Micarta® inlays, BUCK/U.S.A. stamp. Value, **$100**.

Second-Version 112: 1972

Very soon after its introduction, the spring holder on the 112 was changed from brass to stainless. Later in this version, the first three-line 112s can be found and they will be stamped BUCK, 112, U.S.A. read with the knife pointed up.

1973: Third version, Segua wood inlays, BUCK/112/ U.S.A. stamp. Value, **$100**.

Third-Version 112: 1973

There were a lot of changes in the early months of the 112, some of which did not last for very long. The third-version 112 certainly fits into that category. The knife is virtually the same as the second version except that the inlays are of Segua, a heavy-grained wood that tends to be rust brown in color. Third versions in good shape are very hard to find today.

Fourth-Version 112: 1973

The fourth-version 112 marks the beginning of the use of Macassar-ebony inlays. Imported from India, the wood was the same as that used on the model 110 Folding Hunter. Fourth-version 112s are stamped BUCK, 112, U.S.A.

1973: Fourth version, ebony inlays, BUCK/112/U.S.A. stamp. Value, **$75**.

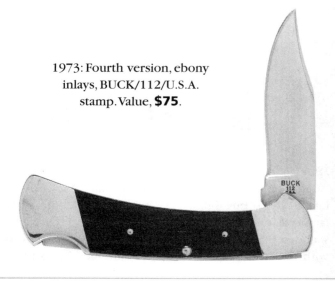

Fifth-Version 112: 1974-80

In 1974, the 112 went through the same changes as the 110 in that it was redesigned to make it more difficult to flick open with one hand. When the adjustments were made, the blade stamping was changed to BUCK, •112•, U.S.A., with a small dot located on either side of the model number. Variations in the number of inlay rivets vary and you can find knives with two, three or even four rivets. Four-inlay-rivet 112s are pretty rare and those found are often in poor condition.

Sixth-Version 112: 1980-81

In 1980, the rocker material was changed and a third dot was added to the stamp. Sixth-version 112s are stamped BUCK. •112••, U.S.A. It was at this time that the marketing department at Buck addressed a suspicion that the 112 was not selling as well as the 110 due to the 112's lack of a nail nick. Though the nail nick was added, 112 sales did not increase. First, radiused handles and, later, finger-grooved handles were introduced during this timeframe.

Seventh-Version 112: 1981-85

In 1981, Buck made the switch from 440C stainless to 425 modified and a fourth dot was added to the blade stamp to designate the change. The knives are stamped BUCK, ••112••, U.S.A.

Other Buck Locking and Slip-Joint Pocketknives

In addition to the 110 Folding Hunter and its downsized, nearly identical twin 112 Ranger, Buck has offered several other series of folding knives. Some of them have been "contract" models made by Schrade or Camillus but that carry the Buck name. However, Buck manufactured the overwhelming majority of these folders.

300 Series Pocketknives

The Buck 300 series of slip-joint pocketknives is very collectible. The knives are readily available, easy on the pocketbook and found in many configurations. Perhaps the most compelling reason to collect this series is because three different companies have produced the knives since 1966.

Schrade Models

Learning to identify the manufacturer is the starting point for any in-depth discussion of the knives in the 300 series. In 1966, Buck contracted with Schrade to build the model 301 Stockman. Later, the model 303 Cadet was added to the contract. Both Schrade-made models have pinned handles of black delrin with simulated saw cuts. The master blade is stamped BUCK/MADE IN/U.S.A. and there is *no* model number on the knife. Each of the knives sports an oval shield with the familiar Buck knife, hammer and bolt logo. Bolsters are steel.

Summary of Schrade Models

The 301 Stockman is a 3 7/8-inch, three-blade premium stock knife. The earliest versions have grooved bolsters.

The second-version 301s have plain bolsters and the two secondary blades are each stamped "BUCK" on the tang. Finally, the third and last Schrade 301 model lacks the "BUCK" stamp on the secondary blades and does not have grooved bolsters. Like all Schrade-made knives in this series, it is identified by the lack of a pivot rivet through the bolsters.

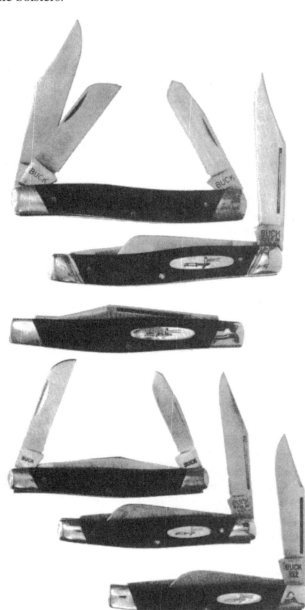

Contract-made Buck 300 series pocketknives are, from top: 1) Reverse side of Schrade-made 301 with plain bolsters and all blades marked. Value, **$90-100**; earliest Schrade-made 301 with grooved bolsters: **$85-90**; Camillus-made 301. Value, **$35-50**; Reverse side of Schrade-made 303 with all blades marked. Value, **$90-100**; early Camillus-made 303 marked BUCK/MADE IN/U.S.A. Value, $50-65; and last Camillus-made 303 marked BUCK/303/U.S.A. (Note lack of handle rivets.) Value, **$35-50**.

The 303 Cadet is a 3 1/4-inch, three-blade junior stockman with two variations: One knife has only the master blade marked and the other variation has "BUCK" stamped on both secondary blades. Again, there will not be a pivot rivet through the bolsters. It is unclear which of these variations came first, but the one with all the blades marked may be the best candidate.

Because of Buck's lifetime guarantee, broken blades needed to be easily replaced. Schrade's method of construction made it impossible to replace the blade of a returned knife in a simple manner. However, Camillus utilized solid bolsters that did allow efficient repairs, and Buck switched the contract for the 301 and 303 models to Camillus sometime around 1972. By the way, the use of solid bolsters explains why the pivot rivets are visible on Camillus-made knives in the 300 series.

Camillus Models

Following is a chronological, model-by-model summary for the Camillus-made 300 series knives. Please remember that during the years that Camillus made the knives, there were assorted commemorative, etched and advertising variations produced. Also, some of the models were offered with stag inlays, and the Buck Custom shop often enhanced the knives in the series at customer request. The following listing focuses only on the standard-production models.

A 2 5/8-inch premium penknife, the 305 Lancer was introduced in 1969 and was apparently the first Buck model contracted to Camillus. The master clip blade and the secondary coping blade each pivoted at opposite bolsters, and the same pinned, black-delrin handle material was used for inlays. Buck must have been pleased with the arrangement, especially since it allowed the easy replacement of blades. In a letter to Buck dealers dated Oct. 31, 1972, Al Buck wrote: "Our line of new pocketknives features an important engineering breakthrough: a tough stainless steel pivot pin and bolster that will not rust, corrode or break." Buck's letter indicated that the Schrade-made 301 and 303 models had finally run their course and that, thenceforth, Camillus would manufacture the knives exclusively.

Outwardly, the earliest 301 and 303 models by Camillus were nearly identical to their Schrade-made predecessors. The master-blade tang stamp, pinned handles of black, sawcut delrin and oval shield with the Buck logo remained consistent. The French (or long) nail pull was continued on the master blade, but none of the secondary blades were stamped with the Buck name. Also, the body of the 301 models was less serpentine than on the Schrade-made knives. As explained earlier, the easiest and best way to differentiate the early Camillus-made knives from their Schrade-made counterparts is by the existence of pivot rivets through the bolsters. If the knife lacks the rivets

while being otherwise identical to the Camillus-made models, it is a Schrade contract knife.

The earliest Camillus 301 models can be found in two configurations. The first models have three brass spacers and the second group has four brass spacers. (The spacers are also known as *center scales* and *side center scales*.)

Soon after the switch to Camillus, Buck began to stamp model numbers on the master blade. The Camillus-made slip joints of the era were unchanged in appearance and construction save for the addition of the model number on the pile-side tang of the master blade.

The next variation of the 300 series involved the removal of the handle pins and coincided with the introduction of two new models: the 307 Wrangler, a jumbo stockman, and the 309 Companion, a two-bladed pen knife that is larger than the model 305.

Buck advertising literature dated 1972 pictures four new 300 series pocketknives: the 311 Trapper (a light or slim model); 313 Muskrat (one blade is a spey); 315 Yachtsman (with locking marline spike); and 317 Trailblazer (a two-bladed, clasp-type folding hunter). The earliest of the knives also featured the familiar BUCK/MADE IN/U.S.A. tang stamp, with the model number stamped on the pile side of the tang. The construction materials were unchanged and all the newer models are visually compatible with the earlier knives. The one exception for the newer models was the use of a crescent nail nick in place of the long pull on the master blade.

Occasionally, one of the newer 300 series models turns up with handle pins. The knives may have been transition models or early sales samples. Whatever the explanation, the models with pinned handle inlays are quite rare.

In about 1973, the tang stamp on all the 300 series knives was changed to incorporate the model number: BUCK/301/U.S.A. Two new models were added to the series later in the 1970s: The 319 Rancher debuted in about 1976, and the 321 Bird Knife was unveiled in about 1978. The master blade on the 319 originally incorporated a long nail pull, while a crescent nail nick was used on the 321. The 319 was a stockman pattern similar to the 301 but substituted an awl or harness punch for the sheepfoot blade. The 321 was modeled after the 313 Muskrat, but incorporated a gutting hook for game birds in place of the spey blade.

Buck 300 Series Production

In about 1984, Buck began to make four of the most popular models in its plant. On these models—the 301, 303, 305 and 309—Buck replaced the long nail pull with the more common crescent nail nick. The logo shield was temporarily replaced with one that spelled out "BUCK" in block letters. The shield lasted only two or three years, as Buck returned to the tried-and-true knife, hammer and bolt logo shield. By the way, at least two of the Camillus-made models also can be found with the block "BUCK" shield.

In 1986, Buck started using year marks on its knives, and all 300 series models actually manufactured by Buck were so stamped. Later offerings of existing models without a year mark were still made on contract by Camillus. Also in 1986, Buck began to reduce the number of 300 series models by discontinuing the 317 Trailblazer. In 1991, the 319 Rancher was removed from the line. By 1992, the 311 Trapper and 321 Bird Knife were dropped. In 1998, the 307 Wrangler, 315 Yachtsman and 313 Muskrat were discontinued.

The 300 series has had a few additions since Buck began to manufacture the knives. In 1990, the 312 Mini-Trapper and the 314 Trapper were introduced. The trappers were designed to be stronger than the slim, contract-made 311. Also for 1990, the 305 Lancer was converted to a Clipper with the substitution of a scissors for the standard coping blade. The Clippers were offered with several delrin colors—black, red, blue, pink and lavender—and jigged brown bone before their run was completed. In 1998, Buck added a three-blade version of the 309 Companion. Dubbed the 310 Whittler, it originally had been made as a limited-edition, special-order knife in 1994.

The 300 series knives have been manufactured with various handle materials and colors. You can find gray, red and yellow delrin, several jigged-bone variations and stag. David Yellowhorse also has handled some of the models in his Navajo Indian motif. The gray delrin knives are Buck Workman series models and often have the Workman logo etched on the master blade. In recent years, Buck has scaled the series back to just the four models it originally began to produce in 1984. The four models—the 301, 303, 305 and 309—were the best-selling models in the series and apparently are still well received by the knife-buying public.

500 Series Lockbacks

The 500 series of slimline lockback folders was launched in 1975 with the introduction of the model 501 Esquire. According to research of Buck archives, the first blueprint for the 501 is dated December 1973 but it was February 1975 before the first knives were shipped to dealers. The earliest 501s had an exposed rocker rivet and burgundy linen Micarta® inlays. Closed length: 3 3/4 inches.

The combination of the rich-looking burgundy linen Micarta, integral stainless steel bolsters/liners—both polished—and a polished rocker bar made for a classy looking knife, especially after Buck began to hide the rocker rivet sometime in 1977. The 440C blade with Buck's superior heat treatment added more value to the package. The tang stamp was the familiar three-line BUCK [script]/501/U.S.A.

The 503 Prince debuted in the March 1977 catalog and was a shorter version—3 3/8 inches—of the Model 501. In 1978 and 1979, the 500 Duke, 505 Knight and 506 Lady Buck were added to the line. The Duke was the largest at

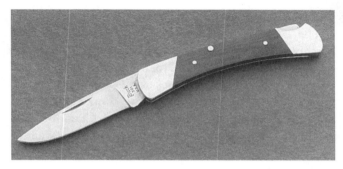

The Model 501, introduced in 1975 as the Esquire (changed to the Squire in 1985), featured an exposed rocker rivet. The blade is 440C stainless and the handle is burgundy linen Micarta®. Its price new: **$18**. Today's value, **$65-75**.

4 1/4 inches, while the 505 and 506 were almost identical with the exception of their closed lengths—2 3/4 inches. The knives shared the same construction characteristics, except for the use of white Micarta inlays on the 506. However, Buck marketing quickly realized that the Lady Buck name needed to be de-feminized so that men would buy the knife, so the name was changed to White Knight sometime in late 1979. In 1980, another version of the model 505 was offered. Called the 507 Ultima I, it was dressed up with mother-of-pearl inlays and a mirror-polished blade.

A major construction change was announced in the 1981 catalog. Each of the four basic models in the series sported handle inlays of impregnated birch. About 1982, Buck switched to 425 modified steel. No other changes were made to the series until about 1984-85, when the tang stamps were switched from script-style lettering to a block-letter font. Examples with a dot after the model number or on each side of the model number may also be found from the time period. The significance of the dots is unknown. Also, in about 1985, the 501 Esquire name was shortened to Squire.

By 1986, when Buck started using year symbols to indicate year of blade manufacture, the perimeter areas of the frame were sanded rather than polished. There could be transition knives that are exceptions but it seems that all the 500 series knives with year marks—excepting the 507 in mother-of-pearl and some stag models—have the sanded finish.

In the late 1980s and continuing through today, various 500 series models have been offered with special inlays or as limited-edition models. Stag, various jigged bones, bonded stone and synthetic plastics, and impregnated woods have all been featured. Around 1992, Buck again replaced the standard steel, this time selecting 420HC. Finally, over time, Buck has switched the integral stainless steel bolsters and liners to sintered (powdered-metal) nickel-silver technology.

700 Series Pocketknives

The 700 series of Buck pocketknives represents perhaps the most distinctive-looking factory-produced slip joints of the era. With their heavier bolsters and beefier backsprings, the knives were designed by Buck to be upgraded replacements for the contract-made 300 series. As it turned out, Buck dealers welcomed the new models but made it known to Buck that they also wanted the less expensive contract pocketknives to be retained in the Buck lineup. As would be expected, Buck acquiesced to the dealers' wishes. Instead of replacing the popular 300 series knives, the 700 series became an upgraded option in the Buck stable.

Stable is an appropriate term as the knives' names suggest, but the planned original names of two of the models characterized a "south-of-the-border" flavor. Originally, Buck planned to name the Model 705 the Amigo, while the 709 was to be known as the Compadre. However, Buck decided to go with an equine/cowboy theme in naming them.

The knives' bolsters and liners originally were made of stainless steel but at some point the bolsters were switched to nickel silver. The knives were heavier and stronger than their 300 series counterparts and remained in the Buck lineup for over 20 years.

Summary of 700 Series Models

Model 703 Colt: Three-bladed stockman pattern, 3 1/4 inches closed, first produced in December 1979;

Model 701 Mustang, renamed Bronco in 1983 catalog: Larger, three-bladed stockman pattern, 3 7/8 inches closed. In March 1981, finished knives were in shipping;

Model 705 Amigo/Pony: Small, two-bladed executive knife, 2 5/8 inches closed. In May 1981, finished knives were in shipping. Earliest boxes had Amigo name printed on them;

Model 709 Compadre/Yearling: Medium, two-bladed executive knife, 3 inches closed. In September 1981, finished knives were in shipping; and;

Four 700 series Buck pocketknives with the script tang stamp and script shield were made circa 1980-85. Model numbers and values are, clockwise from top: 701 and **$65**; 703 and **$65**; 705 and **$45**; and 709 and **$45**.

Model 704 Maverick: Single-bladed jack knife, 3 1/4 inches closed. First mentioned in a 1982 order form but not featured in the '82 catalog. Only knife in the series with a non-equine name.

The earliest 700 series models featured three-line tang stamps of BUCK [script]/model #/U.S.A. Also, the handle escutcheon, or shield, was imprinted BUCK in old English script. Both the tang stamp and the shield maintained the script style until about 1984 or '85, when Buck began to use block letters. Thenceforth, documenting tang stamp and shield fonts gets difficult. Various combinations that are not chronologically logical may be found on the knives manufactured immediately preceding Buck's switch to tang stamps with year marks in 1986.

The perimeter of 700 series knives—the liners, backsprings and bottoms of the bolsters—was polished until the introduction of year marks in 1986. Sometime around then, Buck began to place a sanded finish on the knives' perimeters. In 1986, on the three-bladed Model 703 and later on the Model 701, each blade was given its own backspring instead of the secondary blades sharing a backspring. To accommodate a better fit where the closed blades nested in the well of the knife, Buck also swapped ends for the secondary blades. The sheepfoot blade was placed where the spey blade had been and vice versa. Around the same time, the two-bladed models also were equipped with backsprings for each blade.

Buck also produced each of the knives in the 700 series with brass bolsters and liners in the late 1980s. They could have been a special project because they are not mentioned in any of the catalogs of the era.

The 1987-94 catalogs each featured one to three different 700 series models with stag inlays. Because the Buck Custom shop also was making stag-handled 700 series knives through 1993, it is difficult to know which stag-handled knives from the time period were factory production and which were custom knives. Knives from the Custom shop should have polished perimeters but there probably are exceptions. If a knife has a polished blade, it is most likely from the Custom shop.

The Custom shop also turned out many other enhanced 700 series knives. Various woods, mastodon ivory and mother-of-pearl inlays were offered. The knives may be found with or without handle rivets. Damascus blades as well as other steels were offered, so there is a diverse mix of possibilities to be found in the series.

As noted, in 1992 Buck phased in 420HC for its standard steel across the product line. The blades were not marked and, short of metallurgical testing, there is practically no way to discern the difference. In 1994, Buck produced the 703, 705 and 709 models in jigged bone as a special project for a large hunting and fishing outlet. The handles were pinned and the knives are now very difficult to find because production was limited to 200 of each model.

In 1999, Buck started to wind down the run by removing the 704 from the catalog. The 2000 catalog featured the remaining four models in the series with the shields removed. It was likely a cost-saving measure on a series that was declining in sales. In 2001, the 701 was removed from the catalog and, by 2002, the remaining models were discontinued. However, special orders were possible for at least the model 703 during 2002.

The 700 series now seems to be history. For collectors who appreciate the more traditional knives in Buck's lineup, there is often a twinge of regret when old "friends" are discontinued. On the bright side, discontinued models can boost collector interest by creating a decrease in the supply.

Gerber Folding Knives

For more Gerber history, see "Gerber Fixed Blade Sport Knives" under the section "American Hunting Knives."

Fh and FS

Gerber Legendary Blades was established in 1938 and began its own manufacturing in 1945 in the first of several rented facilities. Two decades later, Gerber began to build its own big factory at 14200 Southwest 72nd Ave. in Portland, Oregon, still its home today. Feb. 1, 1966, was move-in day but, even before then, Francis "Ham" Gerber was at work there designing new products. The most radical of them was Gerber's first folder, the Fh, inspired by Thomas Lamb's 1945 patent handle. Like some eighteenth-century French folders, the Fh had no visible rivets.

Today, a mint Fh with a high-speed-steel blade and a checkered wood handle commands about **$300** (up to **$2,000** in Japan). Delrin, smooth-wood and stainless-blade versions can bring up to **$250**. From 1981 to 1983, Gerber imported "Ebony Folding Hunters" from Japan. Similar in profile to the Fh, they bring about **$100**.

The Fh never competed well with Buck's robust Model 110 folding hunter, introduced in 1963, so Gerber phased out the Fh in favor of brass-framed wood-inlaid lockbacks, the Folding Sportsman series. The first FS was contract made in Solingen in 1972 (**$95**). The mid-sized FS II was made in Portland, beginning in 1973, joined by the larger FS III in 1975, and both the smaller FS I and the FS IId drop-point in 1976. There have been engineering changes over the years in these models, which may someday come to interest collectors, as may the smaller Pk series.

Gerber PAUL

In 1977, Gerber introduced a new folder more radical than the Fh—the Gerber PAUL. The knife was designed by Paul Poehlmann, an engineer and part-time maker of his own sleek, strong, **$500** axial-locking PAUL folders (**$2,500** and up now). Made until 1986, Gerber PAUL knives now bring from **$250** (standard) to about **$450** (factory specials) in mint condition with box. The Gerber PAUL II came out in 1996. Circa 2002, Lone Wolf Knives, also of Portland and in collaboration with Poehlmann, reintroduced the Lone Wolf PAUL folder.

Wada, Sakai and Loveless

In 1977, Blade Magazine Cutlery Hall-Of-Famer® Pete Gerber and his Japanese distributor, Sake Wada of Osaka, signed a contract with Susumo Sakai of Seki, Japan. Sakai and his five sons then built a new factory in Seki called Gerber-Sakai, and made a variety of Gerber knives to be marketed worldwide. Initially called Silver Eagle, the name of the Gerber-Sakai line was soon changed to Silver Knight. The last of 31 Silver Knight patterns was dropped in 1995. Another successful Gerber-Sakai line was the "Gentlemen's" series, pen, money-clip and smoker's knives designed by Blade Magazine Cutlery Hall-Of-Famer Bob Loveless in 1981. Loveless also designed a lockback folder that Gerber made in Portland in 1983, but it did not catch on (about **$125**).

Blackie Collins Designs

In 1981, Gerber pioneered a radical new concept, the plastic-framed folder, which every other major cutlery firm has since been obliged to emulate. Plastic-handled folders with metal liners had been around for over a century then, but prolific knife designer and Blade Magazine Cutlery Hall-Of-Famer Walter "Blackie" Collins saw that the newest engineered plastics were strong enough to obviate the need for liners. Of his first three folder designs for Gerber in the early 1980s, one is still going strong—the LST (Light Smooth Tough). The Touche Belt Buckle knife series eventually totaled 51 variants, but it was dropped in 1989. The Bolt Action was dropped in 1997.

The first LSTs had Micarta® frames. Molded Rynite came next on the LST, as well as on the first Bolt Actions. Then, in 1985, glass-reinforced, molded DuPont Zytel® was adopted for both knives, and the world of pocketknives has never been the same. For the 1990s, Gerber added two new plastic-framed folding knives designed in-house, the Gator and the E-Z-Out. Today, however, Gerber's biggest selling folder by far is the MultiPlier, introduced in 1992 (see the section, "Plier and Wrench Knives").

Chronology of Gerber Folding Knives

Fh [Folding Hunter] (design by Francis "Ham" Gerber)

HS=High speed tool steel 440C=Stainless steel
Delrin handle, HS 4100: 1968-1971 (-1974)
Delrin handle, 440C 4101: 1968-1971 (-1974)
Walnut handle, HS 4102: 1968-1971 (-1974)
Walnut handle, 440C 4103: 1968-1971 (-1974)
Checkered walnut handle, HS 4104: 1968-1973 (-1974)
Checkered walnut handle, 440C 4105: 1968-1973 (-1974)
Checkered ebony handle, HS 4107: 1973-1974 (-1976)
Checkered ebony handle, 440C 4106: 1973-1974 (-1976)
Deluxe sheath: 1968-1969
Deluxe sheath with steel: 1968-1974

Brass Frame Folders

Folding Sportsman wood, Solingen: 1972 (-1974)
Folding Sportsman stag, Solingen: 1972 (-1974)
Folding Sportsman I: 1976-present
Folding Sportsman I Stag: 1977-1985
Folding Sportsman I Red Bone: 1991-1993
Folding Sportsman I Outdoor Scene Train: 1991
Folding Sportsman I Outdoor Scene Elk: 1991
Folding Sportsman I World War II Set/3: 1995
Folding Sportsman II: 1973-present
Folding Sportsman II Stag: c1974-1985
Folding Sportsman II Red Bone: 1991-1993
Folding Sportsman II Outdoor
    Scene Schooner: 1991
Folding Sportsman II Outdoor Scene Eagle: 1991
Folding Sportsman IId (drop point): 1976-1994
Folding Sportsman IId stag: 1976
Folding Sportsman IId polished stag: 1976
Folding Sportsman IIV (Vascowear blade):
    1982-1988
Folding Sportsman II Alaska Statehood: 1984
Folding Sportsman III: 1975-1995
Folding Sportsman III stag: 1975-1976
Folding Sportsman III polished stag: 1975-1976
FS-III Bicentennial: 1976
FS-III Bicentennial, etched blade: 1976
FS-III Jade, plain, walnut chest: 1976-1979
FS-III Jade, engraved, walnut chest: 1976-1979
FS-III Agate, plain, walnut chest: 1976-1979
FS-III Agate, engraved, walnut chest: 1976-1979
Magnum Folding Hunter: 1975-1987
Magnum Folding Hunter stag: 1975-1976
Magnum Folding Hunter polished stag 4216:
    1975-1976
Classic: 1976-1983

Pk series

Pk-1 Skookum (2 blades both ends): 1973-1981
Pk-2 Pete's Knife: 1974-1981
Pk-2d drop point: 1976-1981
Pk-3 Handyman (2 blades same end): 1975-1981
Legacy (Small, Medium, Large): 1989
Vulcan (Small, Medium, Large): 1989

President's Collections in Walnut Chest

FS-I, II, III, Wood inlays: 1979-1983
FS-I, II, III, Engraved, Wood inlays: 1979-1983
FS-I, II, III, Stag inlays: 1979-1983
FS-I, II, III, Engraved, stag inlays: 1979-1983

PAUL Knife (design by Paul Poehlmann)

PAUL 2P stainless: 1977-1986
PAUL 2W hardwood: 1977-1986
PAUL 2PM ivory colored: 1977-1984
PAUL 2PMS, scrimshaw 2 sides: 1983-1986
Anniversary PAUL: 1979
Optional leather scabbard: 1977-1985

PAUL Knife II (design by Paul Poehlmann):

1996-c1998

TOUCHE Belt Buckle Knife

(design by Blackie Collins) Total 51 variants:
1981-1989
First Models:
Ebony Rynite buckle: 1981-1985
Rynite buckle, hardwood inlay: 1981-1989
Ivory Micarta® inlay: 1981
Micarta inlay, duck scrimshaw: late 1981
Micarta inlay, wagon scrimshaw: late 1981
Basic types:
Rynite buckle, wood inlay, imitation ivory onlay
Brass buckle, wood inlay, imitation ivory onlay
Slimline buckle, imitation ivory onlay

Loveless Designed Folding Knives

Loveless Folder: 1983-1985
Loveless Folder, black inlay, eagle scene: 1985
[see also: Escort Gentlemen's Knives]

MultiPlier (option of nylon or leather sheath)

First models in 1992 had scissors; file added 1994
Multi-Plier, Stainless: 1992-present
Multi-Plier, Black: 1992-present
Multi-Plier, Stainless, with tool kit: 1994-present

Applegate-Fairbairn Combat Folder

(Design by Col. Rex Applegate, Bill Harsey, Butch
Vallotton): 1996-present

Bolt Action (design by Blackie Collins)

Bolt Action-Ebony: 1981-1982
Bolt Action-Ivory Rynite: 1981-1984
Bolt Action Utility black checkered: 1983-1997
Bolt Action Fisherman Black: 1983-1994
Bolt Action Fisherman Orange: 1986-1988
Bolt Action Hunter black checkered: 1985-1997
Bolt Action Skinner black (gut hook): 1988-1997
Bolt Action Skinner, Realtree® camo (gut hook):
    1992-1993
Bolt Action Hunter, black blade: 1984
Bolt Action Utility, black blade: 1984
Bolt Action Exchange Blade utility/saw: 1986-1997
Bolt Action Exchange Blade utility/saw/hunter:
    1986-1990
Bolt Action Exchange Blade utility/saw/skinner:
    1987-1988
Bolt Action Rescue: 1987-1988
Bolt Action Parabellum with two-way sheath: 1987-
    1994
(nylon scabbard standard, deluxe leather optional)

LST = Light Smooth Tough (design by Blackie Collins)

LST Classic ivory Micarta: 1981-1985
LST Classic maroon: 1981-1982
LST FSI ivory Micarta: 1981-1982
LST FSI maroon: 1981-1982

LST Classic black Micarta: 1983-1985
LST checkered black DuPont Rynite: 1983-1985
LST Alaska Statehood: 1984
LST checkered black DuPont Zytel: 1985-present
LST checkered black Zytel, black blade: 1992
LST checkered orange Zytel: 1986-1988
LST checkered camouflage Zytel: 1986-1991
LST checkered red Zytel: 1988-present
LST checkered red Zytel, black blade: 1992
LST checkered black Zytel, clip point: 1991-present
LST checkered black Zytel, clip-point black blade:
   1992
LST Realtree camo: 1992-1993
LST Ultralight black: 1986-present
LST Ultralight red: 1986-1993
LST Ultralight blue: 1986-1993
LST Magnum Black: 1989-present
LST Magnum Realtree camo: 1992-1993
LST Magnum Serrated black: 1991-present
LST Magnum Junior black: 1989-present
LST Magnum Junior Realtree camo: 1992-1993
LST Magnum Junior Serrated black: 1991
LST Microlight black: 1989-present
LST Microlight red: 1989-1993
LST Microlight blue: 1989-1993
LST Microlight green: 1989-1992
LST Microlight pink: 1989-1992
LST Microlight yellow: 1990
LST Microlight purple: 1990
LST Sport Saw: 1989-1993

Other Lightweight Models
Fieldlight (SS III): 1986-1989
Stallion, Black 7557 (imported): 1989-present
Premium Stockman 3 7/8": 1987-1990
Junior Stockman 3 1/4": 1987-1991
Baby Stockman 2 5/8" (two blades): 1987-1991

Gator Series
Gator: 1991-present
Gator, Black Blade: 1992
Gator Serrater: 1991-present
Gator Mate: 1992-present
Gator Mate, black blade: 1992-1993
Gator Mate Serrater: 1992-present
Sport Saw (Gator style): 1994-present

E-Z-Out Series
E-Z-Out; E-Z-Out Serrated;
E-Z-Out Junior; E-Z-Out Junior Serrated:
   1994-present

Imported Folding Knives (by Gerber-Sakai, Japan)
Silver Knight Series (called Silver Eagle 1977-78)
   [A=lockback, B=two-blade]
200A wood: 1979-1994
200A pearl: 1979-1982
200A black pearl: 1981-1994
200A abalone shell: 1981-1994
200A eagle scrimshaw: 1985-1992
200A landing eagle scrimshaw: 1991-1992
200A elk scrimshaw: 1991-1992
200A wood, full onlay: 1986-1990
200SS stainless steel handles: 1981-1994
250A wood: 1977-1984
250A pearl: 1977-1982
250A black pearl: 1981-1994
250A checkered ABS: 1981-1992
250A natural stag: 1983-1985
250A landing duck scrimshaw: 1986-1992
250A mallard scrimshaw: 1991-1992
250A bass scrimshaw: 1991-1992
250A wood, full onlay: 1987-1990
250B wood: 1977-1992
250B pearl: 1977-1982
250B black pearl: 1981-1984
250B hunting dog scrimshaw: 1985-1992
250C combo knife: 1979
250C wood combo knife: 1985-1990
250SS stainless steel handles: 1981-1994
300A wood: 1981-1990
300A black pearl: 1981-1984
300A checkered ABS: 1981-1990
300A deer scrimshaw: 1985-1992
300A schooner scrimshaw: 1991-1992
300A bear scrimshaw: 1991-1992
Silver Knight, comet Kohoutek: c1980
Multiblade camping utility: 1985
350ST Folding Knife: 1985

Escort Gentlemen's Knives
   (design by Bob Loveless)
Money Clip Knife: 1981-1990
Gentlemen's Pocket Knife: 1981-1985
Gentlemen's Pocket Knife: 1986-1990
Smokers Knife: 1981-1983

Ebony Folding Hunter Series
Ebony Folding Hunter I, II and III: 1981-1983
Gerber International
Folding Lockback: 1983-1984
Stainless Steel Pocketknife: 1983
Lockbacks - 250ST, 275ST, 375ST: 1987

"They" Are Out There—Are You?

Choice knife collectibles are still available if you prepare properly, know where to look and how to haggle, and out hustle everyone else

By Richard D. White

There is a mistaken belief that the best antique knives are no longer available to the enterprising collector. This misconception centers on the notion that serious collectors have snatched up all the "good stuff" and embedded the beauties in their own private hoards.

In fact, there are numerous outstanding collections of knives in the United States, carefully assembled by devotees who have spent the greater part of their lives acquiring and upgrading their knives in a systematic way. Collections of Boy Scout knives number in the hundreds, even thousands of knives, as do collections of Remingtons, Case knives, Westerns, Keen Kutters, whittlers, multi-blades, heater knives, easy openers, fishing knives, specialty knives and many others. Perusing published photographs of these assembled collections, a beginning collector might assume that there are not any cutlery treasures left to be discovered.

Though there is some truth to the notion that the heyday of cutlery collecting took place decades ago, there is some good news for individuals who pursue America's most perfect tool. With some diligent preparation and proper collecting strategies, even inexperienced collectors can maximize their efforts in searching for rare and valuable cutlery specimens.

Be Prepared

The Boy Scout motto "Be Prepared" is hardly ever more appropriate than when applied to the pursuit of rare knives. Like the Boy Scout preparing for a campout, the seeker on the quest for outstanding knives has to be

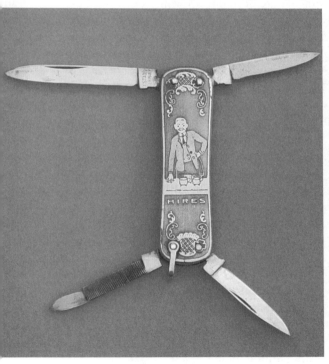

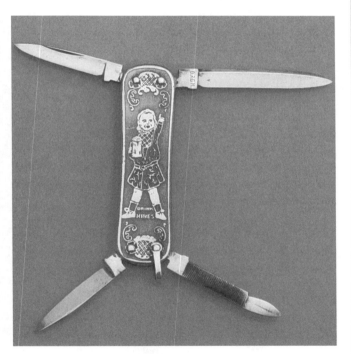

The Hires Root Beer advertising knife made by a German cutlery company is one of a very few known to exist in the United States. Made in a lobster-type pattern, it was probably a watch-fob knife, as indicated by the bail. Well over 100 years old, the knife clearly displays a well-dressed young boy standing behind mugs of Hires Root Beer situated on a counter. Copious metal etchings and polishings provide a 3-D effect. (White photo)

The reverse side of the Hires Root Beer advertising knife is just as intriguing as its opposite.
Using the same repeated metal etchings and polishings, the dramatic 3-D effect shows a girl touting the virtues of Hires by holding a frosty mug in one hand and pointing with the other. The words "Drink Hires" are clearly etched in the metal. Near mint and finely crafted and a wonderful example of early advertising, the knife has a value of **$200-250**. (White photo)

prepared. In fact, a successful collecting foray not only should be preceded by proper preparation but also must take into account location, timing and negotiation.

1) **Preparation**: Proper preparation for a knife show or other collecting opportunity includes gaining as much information about the knife as possible before any purchase is made. Buying well-illustrated knife-collecting books and copies of BLADE® with installments of "Edges" and Knife World is money well spent. Noting knife sizes, numbering systems, handle materials, values, production dates, blade styles and so on will give you a definite edge, and prevent you from buying a knife that is not correct.

Preparation also means wearing a small backpack or belly pack that contains the following:

- An 8x-10x magnifying loupe for reading tang stamps and checking for cracks in the handle material (absolutely necessary);
- A small notebook and pencil for jotting down the location of a potential purchase;
- Photocopied "cheat sheets" of the most important knife information (Case's dating system, for example);
- A blade opener;
- A small, self-contained pocket oiler for making sure that the blades of pocketknives have "snap" or "walk and talk" when opening and/or closing;
- An apple or candy bar for energy and a bottle of water to quench your thirst during your search, and;
- A cell phone for calling collector friends is also becoming standard equipment.

Preparations also include bringing along cash in different denominations. Though most antique malls and shops take credit cards, checks and traveler's checks, most flea-market vendors and some show participants prefer cash as the acceptable form of payment. The old adage "money talks" certainly applies here.

2) **Location**: The location phase must include the inquiry portion of "the quest." Listening to other collectors discuss favorite antique shops, malls, shows and flea markets is necessary to get a sense of where potential knife jackpots are most likely to be found.

Though some collectors are somewhat secretive about their favorite locations, they are generally willing to brag about their latest finds. Ask such questions as, "What time do they open?" "When does that show come back to town?" and "Is the show full of new stuff or antiques?" Visiting local shops and picking up brochures listing antique shop locations is also a wise use of time, especially when visiting new towns or cities.

Do not forget the phone book when searching for possible sites to visit. Most cities publish a monthly collector's newsletter listing times and dates of upcoming shows. Cut the show calendar out of the paper and attach it to your refrigerator, or jot down the dates in your calendar. Subscribing to cutlery publications that regularly list upcoming shows—BLADE, Knives Illustrated and Knife World—is an investment that pays huge dividends. (BLADE also publishes its show calendar on its Website, www.blademag.com.) Many serious antique collectors regularly plan a portion of their vacation to coincide with large tool, toy, cutlery, glassware and antique shows.

Surprisingly, some very valuable cutlery items show up in strange places. One knife collector I know attends automobile swap meets, digging in boxes of small parts in search of knives. Other collectors regularly go to Salvation Army and DAV stores or pawn shops to look for knives that the storeowners often do not know the value of. I have heard of at least one Randall, one Ruana, numerous Marble's knives, and recently a valuable Richtig fighter being purchased in pawnshops and junk shops.

3) **Timing**: Of all the factors listed, timing is by far the most important. Arriving late to any show or flea market is a sure-fire recipe for going home empty handed. A good collector friend of mine looks forward to antique festivals held outdoors in roped-off streets, etc. If the show starts at 8 a.m., he is there by 7:30.

For the novice, arriving early would seem unnecessary and, quite honestly, an intrusion into the dealer's set-up time. There certainly are some dealers who do not want to be interrupted while unloading their merchandise, and get downright testy about people who peer into the backs of their pickup trucks. By the same token, many others seem to enjoy people visiting and looking through their merchandise while they unload and set up their display cases. Buyers must beware, however, that the hour before the official "start time" is for dealers to set up merchandise, not for making deals.

The message, however, is clear: "The early bird gets the worm." Beating out the competition is a technique that often gets results. Nonetheless, for the knife collector, the technique has some pitfalls because of the dealers' concern with theft of valuable objects.

Often, valuable knives that normally are exhibited in display cases are the last to be unloaded, and thus cannot be examined early. However, knife collectors can certainly start asking, "Did you bring any knives today?" as the dealer is unloading. This gives the knife collector valuable information about where to return during a particular show.

In addition, being larger in size, cutlery display cases are generally unloaded along with the larger merchandise. Frequently, small merchandise, such as watches, jewelry and political buttons, are stored in original cutlery display cases. Even though the cases may be used primarily for storage and to prevent theft, when you spot what appears to be an original cutlery display case—which can be a valuable collectible in its own right—you should always ask if it is for sale.

Actually, sellers who specialize in women's jewelry, handkerchiefs, pins and such are prime candidates for having knives, especially knives with mother-of-pearl handles. It is easy to bypass booths that deal primarily with women's items, but two very interesting cutlery purchases took place at different times from booths that looked, on first glance, to be barren of knives. An example occurred recently.

Unexpected Gold Mines

Leaving an antique fair after a fruitless morning of searching, I scanned an aisle to see a display of vintage jewelry and assorted "stuff" sitting before an old white sedan. At first, the open display cases atop the table appeared to be full of cheap custom jewelry and household items, while the area under the table was full of pots, pans and assorted pieces of clothing.

Though I was tempted to avoid the booth, my curiosity got the best of me and I looked into the open display cases. I noticed a small but remarkable jack knife sitting behind some old postcards and political ribbons. The words jumped out at me as I read the engraving on the outside of the knife's metal sides: "JACK KNIFE BEN, CHICAGO."

Quelling my excitement, I asked to look at the knife. Reaching into the case, the unshaven vendor remarked, "You know, that's a special knife." My heart sank. He knew

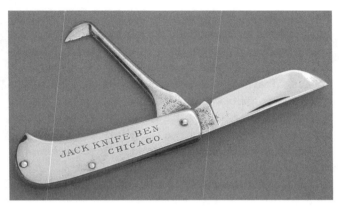

"Rooster-nutters" or any other pocketknives stamped "Jack Knife Ben" are some of the rarest cutlery collectibles extant. Made for Benjamin Choi, who later made a fortune selling knives to cowboys and ranchers in the Chicago stockyards, the pieces are testimonials to the "American-Dream"/wealth-to-riches story. Value: **$250**. (White photo)

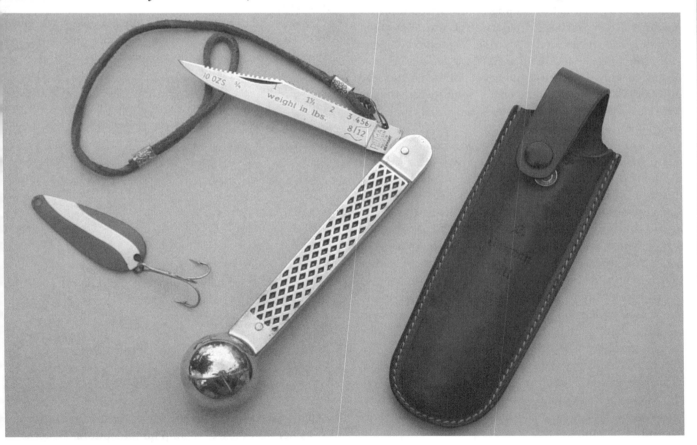

The Puma fisherman's knife is quite rare and a real conversation piece. With its built-in scale for weighing the "catch," etched weights on the blade and notches for hanging fish on a stringer, it is a very unusual design. Add the massive round "priest" for administering the "last rites" to fish and the original leather, owner-inscribed pouch, and the knife is quite rare. It even includes the original leather strap used as part of the knife's counterbalance mechanism. In this condition, with pouch, the knife's value is **$150**. (White photo)

519

"They" Are Out There—Are You?

the story of Jack Knife Ben, I thought, the famous and mysterious 1920s knife entrepreneur from the Chicago stockyards. I waited to hear the story of Jack Knife Ben, aka Benjamin Choi, who went to Chicago with less than $5 in cash and purchased a dozen knives to sell to the cowboys and ranchers who frequented the stockyards, and how this modest endeavor turned into a thriving cutlery business. Instead, the vendor told me another story.

"Yes sir, this knife is very valuable. Did you know that this is the only pocketknife that bears the actual style of the knife engraved on the handle itself? See here, it says Jack Knife [Ben] right here on the sides."

"Very interesting. That's sure unique. How much for the knife?"

"I can't take less than $13, since it's a very unique knife."

"OK, here's $15."

Tucking the $2 change in my pocket, along with the knife, I speed-walked to my car.

Sometimes, knowledge of cutlery history is worth every minute spent reading it. The Jack Knife Ben metal-handled rooster-nutter is worth at least **$125**, and is one of the rarest and most desirable cutlery stampings in existence.

In addition to usually avoiding booths that are mainly jewelry, I also bypass booths filled with glassware, clothing, furniture and newer items. My rule of thumb is "spend your time in those booths that have the greatest chance of having knives." Recently, however, following the lead of other knife collectors, I make it a point to ask, "Do you have any knives?" even in dealer spaces that appear to have no knives on display.

An example took place on the grounds of a major flea market. While walking down a row, I came upon a gentleman lifting a large wooden box out of his truck. It was obvious that he was a knowledgeable antique collector/dealer. Though no knives were evident, I asked if he had any. He walked over to the cab of his truck, reached through the open window and picked up something from the seat. "Only this one," he replied, placing a large leather pouch in my outstretched hand.

With its distinctive bulge I knew instantly what the fine leather pouch contained. I opened the inscribed snap pouch to reveal a mint, Puma fish knife with a distinctive metal "priest," or fish bonker, and engraved scale on the master blade. With the original leather thong used for balancing the knife when weighing a fish, the piece was in pristine, mint condition. Though the knife itself is rare, locating one with an original leather, inscribed pouch was the find of a lifetime.

Actually, opening the blade was merely a formality. Looking at the outside of the pouch, I could see that the knife inside was mint. Quickly arriving at a real "steal" of a price, I slipped the pouch and knife into my pocket and gleefully walked down another show aisle.

4) **Negotiation**: Much of the "art" of acquiring rare knives has to do with negotiating the price. For many potential buyers, one of the greatest frustrations experienced at knife and antique shows is when dealers do not have price tags on the items they have for sale. Minus the displayed prices, buyers sometimes believe that the dealer is sizing them up. I feel that prices on items help the potential buyer decide whether to pursue additional negotiation or to move on to another table.

Negotiating a final price between seller and purchaser is one of the most enjoyable aspects of collecting antique knives. Even knives that you know are already priced significantly below current market value are candidates for negotiation. A dramatic example was the purchase of a lockback folding hunter with the original bone handle made by New York Knife Co. that was negotiated **$5** below the original asking price of **$25**—not bad for a knife worth in the neighborhood of **$500**!

In instances where the asking price is literally a steal and you are tempted to pay it and run, it is sometimes better to seem less anxious and negotiate a bit. That way, the seller will be less likely to back out on the deal thinking that he should do some research before selling the knife.

Remember, a seller will generally not give you a lower price than what is marked on the knife unless you ask questions like, "Can you do anything on that knife?" or "Is that your bottom line?"

It stands to reason that knowing current values for a particular brand or style gives you some basis for comparing prices. Carry copies of recent value guides

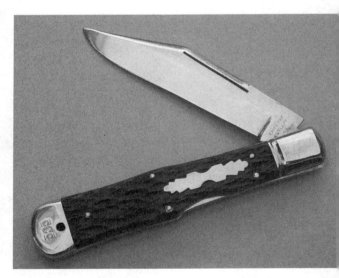

This huge, lockback folding hunter bears the Chipaway Cutlery Co. ("CCC") stamp on the bottom bolster, a pinched and grooved top bolster, and a long pull on the master blade. The knife was contract made by New York Knife Co. before 1931. New York Knife Co. knives are very rare, and one with the CCC stamping is even rarer. Value: **$350-400**. (White photo)

or the knife brands for which you are looking—even if you leave the guides in your car trunk. Buying updated copies of various value guides is cheap insurance against overpayment, and certainly gives you the edge when it comes to negotiations.

After asking for and receiving an offer, you certainly have the right to make a counter offer. If you are dissatisfied with the offer, hand the knife back to the seller and indicate that you want to think about it a little longer. In some cases, dealers will give you a "final" final offer as you walk away in order to make the sale.

It Might As Well Be You

Are rare antique knives still out there, ready to be snatched up by the knowledgeable and prepared

collector? As I sit and examine a turn-of-the-century, Hires Root Beer advertising knife found among a tray of old rings, watches, mechanical pencils and chains, and a KA-BAR fly-fishing knife spotted on the tailgate of a dealer's truck, the answer is a resounding *yes*.

Given the millions of knives produced by scores of different cutlery companies over many decades, it only stands to reason that there are rare collectibles in attics, trunks, barns and myriad other locations, ready to be uncovered by the diligent collector. Even though the competition is usually brisk, rare antique knives are available to the collector who is best prepared—so, be prepared! It might as well be you who find them.

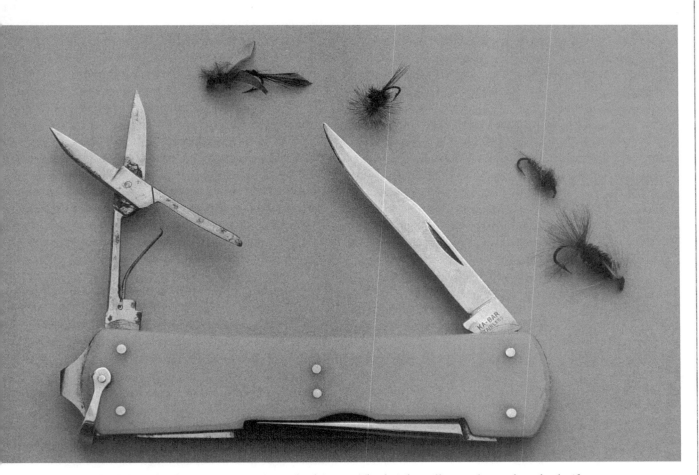

Any antique fly-fishing knife is rare. KA-BAR made this one. The bright yellow color makes the knife easy to spot if it is dropped into the water. This example includes a fish disgorger, fly-line knot awl, master blade, and scissors for trimming fly leaders and hackles. Thanks to the rarity of antique fly-fishing knives and the KA-BAR stamping, the knife has a value of **$300**. (White photo).

The SUVs of Pocketknives

"Bigger is better" reflects not only the vehicles of choice but also the yen for super-sized antique pocketknives

By Richard D. White

In the United States, there is much debate about the size of the cars driven by a significant percentage of the population. The criticism centers on the bigger-is-better mentality that seems to dominate the SUV (sports utility vehicle) crowd. SUVs are the rule, it seems, rather than the exception, and parking lots are literally filled with the oversized, all-wheel-drive vehicles.

"Bigger is better" seems to be the trend in cars, and it has never been more applicable than it is with antique pocketknives. In fact, if trend watching has any value, the fascination with super-sized pocketknives seems to be gaining rapidly in recent years. For the beginning collector or dedicated cutlery aficionado, the move toward larger size means that the value of these knives is climbing, and money spent on oversized pieces will reap loads of collector satisfaction, as well as welcome financial rewards.

The big pocketknives sought most eagerly by collectors are large trappers, folding hunters, coke-bottle folding hunters, folding clasp knives, sunfish and Texas toothpicks (the latter also known as *ticklers*). Each is over 4 inches long closed and was originally designed to fill a specific need.

Except for the Texas toothpick, the knives are heaping handfuls, sporting mammoth blades and huge backsprings Designed to take the punishment of hard, daily use, the best examples snap open and closed—or "walk and talk"—with authority. The nail nick in the master blade is stamped very deep, a necessity in opening the tight-backspringed piece. Some of the knives are so large that they come with their own leather belt pouch.

The heyday of massive pocketknives was circa 1900-1940. The list of companies that produced and/or sold the knives is a who's who of the most famous U.S. cutlery names. They include W.R. Case, Remington, Winchester, New York Knife, Ulster, Challenge, Western States, Camillus, Cattaraugus, Miller Bros., Shapleigh Hardware, Keen Kutter, Boker, Ulster, Imperial, Colonial, Marble's, KA-BAR, Landers Frary and Clark, Maher & Grosh, Valley Forge, John Primble, Schrade and Robeson. The knives also can be found with many other tang stampings from various hardware companies and smaller cutlery companies.

Most of the knives were made specifically for hunters, trappers, ranchers and outdoorsmen. As the names imply, the folding hunter, coke-bottle folding hunter and trapper were specifically designed after input from hunters and outdoorsmen. The oversized blades were used to skin and gut game animals, while the oversized backsprings lessened the likelihood of accidental closure. In fact, some of the knives, like the Marble's safety pocketknife, had a locking mechanism specifically designed to prevent unintentional closings. No respected outdoorsman would dare leave for a hunting trip without his folding hunter weighing heavily in his pants pocket.

Two other pieces qualify for "SUV pocketknife" status and are noteworthy in their own right. Known by a wide variety of nicknames, including *tickler, chaser, powderhorn,*

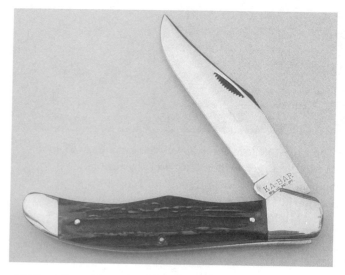

With a closed length of 5 1/4 inches, the early KA-BAR folding hunter in stag has remained one of the old company's most popular collectibles. Value in mint condition: **$200**. (White photo)

An extremely rare Camillus elephant toenail in jigged bone, double pulls on the master blade, and near mint condition has a value of **$400-450**. (White photo)

This Case 6254 trapper was made in the mid-1970s, as indicated by the company's dot-pattern stamping. Value, in mint condition: **$200-225**. (White photo)

tango knife, society knife, dance knife or, as mentioned, the Texas toothpick—in Texas, even the toothpicks are big—they were large, single-blade, serpentine jack knives with a slender, California-clip master blade. In the open position, the knives measure over 9 inches long.

They proved to be the fashion accessory of choice for the 1920s-40s "zoot-suiters" dressed in exaggerated pants, large hats covering "ducktail" hairdos, fingertip chains and double-soled shoes. Moreover, teenagers all over the Southern United States carried them on their "Saturday night" outings. Flicking the knives open and closed—as a result, they were sometimes referred to as switch knives—provided the favorite pastime for youths out on the town. As some of the nicknames imply, the knives were advertised as the special piece to be carried to the Saturday night dance. For partygoers, the slender knives, though seldom used as such, made the perfect self-defense companion. While some can be found in jigged bone, most were handled in colorful celluloid, ranging from candy stripe to Christmas tree.

The knives are very collectible because of their large size, storied history and use of colorful handle material. In addition, they were made and/or sold by a wide variety of companies, including Imperial, Colonial, Remington, Winchester, Wards, Hibbard Spencer Bartlett & Co., Case, Robeson, Western States, Boker, Cattaraugus, Camillus, Maher & Grosh, New York Knife, John Primble and many others.

Pachyderm of a Pocketknife

One of the strangest pocketknives is also one of the largest. Shaped like a huge oval, it has a number of nicknames, including *sunfish, elephant toenail* and *English rope knife*. The sunfish and elephant-toenail nicknames give some clues as to the overall dimensions of the giant piece.

With a closed length of just over 4 inches and a width of almost 2 inches, the knife literally fills the hand. Boasting extra-wide backsprings, it was designed for use by early surveyors to make surveying stakes. Surveyors placed the master blade edge first on a large board and struck the blade on the back with a mallet to cut stakes. Other sources indicate that sailors would place the blade edge first on a hank of rope and whack the blade on the spine with a belaying pin to cut the end of the rope clean and straight. Like the folding hunter, it was designed for the daily rigors of men who lived off the land—or on the sea—and who considered the knife indispensable.

Because many early examples were literally used up, elephant toenails in excellent condition are very rare and remain a conversation piece in any condition. Owners of outstanding examples guard them carefully and use them as centerpieces in their collections. Because of their rarity and odd shape, specimens that reach the marketplace often are significantly overpriced.

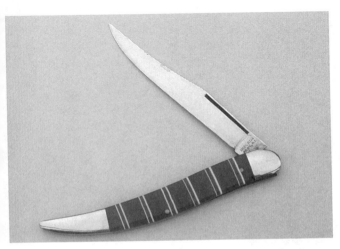

Candy stripe remains perhaps the most popular celluloid handle material. This rare Texas toothpick by Imperial, probably made in the 1930s, has a long pull on the master blade. Value: **$75-100**. (White photo)

This Chipaway lockback folding hunter with jigged-bone handles is perhaps the "find of a lifetime." With its "CCC"-stamped bottom bolster and distinctive shield, this 1930s super-sized pocketknife shouts "New York Knife Co." It is a duplicate of a New York Knife lockback that is extremely popular with collectors. Value: **$300-400**. (White photo)

By the mid-1970s, Case was the last to produce elephant toenails (the 6250 pattern in Case's numbering system). Camillus also made them, as did Marble's, Napanoch, New York Knife and a few others. Elephant toenails generally are handled in celluloid, though jigged bone and, rarely, mother-of-pearl, were used.

Five Value Keys

So what's all the fuss about these fist-filling pocketknives?

- First, they are extremely rare. Most have been used or abused by people who used the knives daily with no regard for their potential future value. The knives were crushed, dropped into streams, broken, used as pry bars, lost in the woods, both hammered and used as hammers, and literally sharpened to death. Others have found their way into collections as showpieces. Finding a folding clasp knife, lockback hunter or elephant toenail in excellent condition is unusual indeed.

- Second, they remain high in demand because they represent what a "real knife" is supposed to look like, with their mammoth blades, beautiful nickel-silver bolsters, jigged bone or striking celluloid handles, inset shields, dark, shiny ebony sides, and finely shaped blades with deep pulls, many of them the "matchstriker-pull" type. (The latter has a series of regularly spaced notches on which a match could be struck.)

- Third, they are examples of prime cutlery from some of America's finest cutlery companies, and are high on the list of those who collect the knives of specific companies. What's more, they are downright impressive, a real "hunk" of a knife.

In addition, several eminently collectible examples of super-sized patterns have been produced over the years.

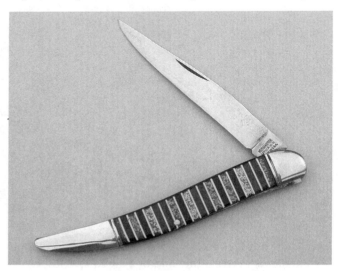

Curiously, glitter-stripe celluloid was used only on Kutmaster knives, a lower-end brand, and Case Tested knives, the latter on the upper end of the value spectrum. In mint condition, this Kutmaster Texas toothpick is valued as **$70-85**. (White photo)

Striking in appearance, linoleum-patterned-celluloid handles make this Colonial folding hunter a special find for collectors. The knife is perhaps Colonial's most desirable pattern and handle material combination. Value: **$75-100**. (White photo)

Most notable are the Remington Bullets, KA-BAR Grizzly, Western States folding clasp knife, Cattaraugus "King of the Woods" lockback, Marble's lockback safety folding hunter, Winchester model 1920 folding hunter, Utica Nessmuk trapper with bull's-head shield, and Case Tested XX stag trapper.

- Fourth, because the knives hearken back to a time in American history when men made a living off the land, they are desirable to those who have and/or admire the same qualities. Like all pocketknives, the larger-than-life pieces are representative of someone who uses tools to build things.

- Fifth, when talking about the potential value of antique pocketknives, "bigger is better." It took more steel, larger blades and a bigger chunk of stag or mother-of-pearl to make a super-sized pocketknife. The knives also

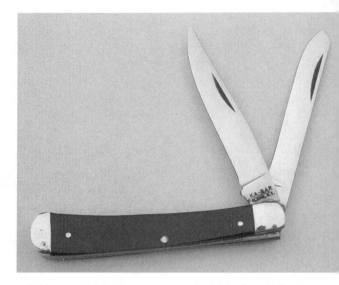

This rare KA-BAR trapper in slick-black celluloid was made in the 1950s. Value in mint, unsharpened condition, **$175-200**. (White photo)

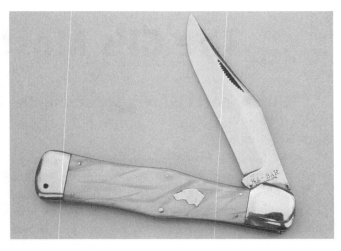

Case was the last company to produce an elephant toenail on a regular basis. This 6250 pattern was made in the 1970s. Some, like this one, had the image of a bull elephant etched on the master blade. In mint condition, with Pakkawood® handles, the knife's value is **$100-125**. (White photo)

KA-BAR "dog's-head" knives are among the most-sought-after large pieces. This early KA-BAR folding hunter, handled in cracked-ice celluloid, has a "matchstriker" pull on the master blade and is valued at **$300**. (White photo)

benefit from being personifications of the cutler's art. Because of the incredible demand for big pocketknives, lesser-known examples have followed the demand and value curve upward.

Editor's note: Though most, if not all, of the knives in the story are at least as big as today's handmade folders, the term folders is eschewed

for pocketknives to help delineate the differences between handmade and antique factory knives. In other words, for the purposes of knife definitions in BLADE's Guide, folders are handmade knives that fold and pocketknives are antique factory knives that fold. Though there are exceptions to every rule, for the most part, these are the definitions BLADE's Guide endorses.

The GI's Most Trusted Tools

Military pocketknives are among the hottest World War II cutlery collectibles

By Richard D. White

On Dec. 8, 1941, President Franklin D. Roosevelt declared war on Japan and the United States was thrust into a conflict that would encompass thousands of miles and cost millions of lives. Within days of FDR's declaration of war, America was changed from a country somewhat isolated from the battles devastating Europe to one that held the destiny of the free world in its grasp.

Aside from the clothing, feeding and transporting of U.S. forces to the various theaters of action, the equipping of the forces was a major hurdle that had to be overcome. The list of necessities needed by individual soldiers and units in the field included not only boots, jackets, food, guns, ammo, tents and communications equipment, but also the specialty items that were necessary for actual combat and to support troop movement, re-supply efforts and evacuation. Binoculars, first-aid supplies, flares, mosquito nets, repair kits, lifeboats, cooking supplies, fuel, landing craft, surgical tents, fuel, jeeps, maps, blankets, shovels and every other imaginable item had to be produced, shipped and supplied to individual soldiers.

One of the most essential pieces of equipment issued to the American soldier was the ever-present combat knife. Most movies and publications point to the bayonet or fixed blade as the indispensable tool for the fighting man, and certainly the straight knives saved countless lives.

For the average soldier, however, whether on the front lines or in the rear supplying the needs of the combatants, the knife that proved most useful in all situations was the military pocketknife. Carried in the pants pocket or hooked to the uniform with a cord, the knives were used to open crates, cut plastic, punch holes in leather and canvas, trim rubber, slash parachute cord, sharpen stakes, pry open containers, and serve as emergency medical instruments.

Classified as a "general utility knife" and sometimes known as the "engineer's pocketknife," most contained a standard four blades. The general configuration included a large master blade, leather punch, can opener, and combination cap lifter-screwdriver. With the four blades, an almost endless variety of tasks could be performed, making the knife the perfect combination tool. The four-blade general utility knives were 3 1/2-3 3/4 inches long closed, almost always handled in jigged bone, and fitted with a bail for attachment to a lanyard to be clipped to a coat, pants or what have you.

Thanks to the soldiers' insatiable demand, military contracts for the knives were awarded to a variety of cutlery companies, including Pal Cutlery, Kutmaster, KA-BAR, Western, Boker, Case, Camillus, Imperial, Ulster, Made in USA, and several others. Within these brand names collectors can find individual differences in can openers, punch styles, bone jigging, and use of steel or brass liners. In fact, as research continues, other cutlery company tang stampings no doubt will be revealed as a result of freshly discovered examples of the knives.

Many general utility knives have "shields" inset into the bone handles. Engraved on the shields are a variety of different letters—such as USA, USN, USMD and MD-USN—which indicate the knives' military branch of origin, or the purpose for which the knives were issued. Collectors of bone-handle specimens look for knives with inscriptions on the shields, with the USN and MD-USN being by far the rarest. Camillus made the majority of the knives, with some estimates putting the company's total production at over 5 million for the Army and Navy.

Boy Scout Connection

Traditionally, those who accumulate the knives have been collectors of Boy Scout knives who add them to their scout knife collections, since the blade configuration, use of bail and size duplicate many Boy Scout patterns. However, because of the recent anniversaries associated with World War II, the dedication of the World War II Memorial, and the upswing in military knives in general, collector demand for the four-blade-utility variety has risen rather quickly. Moreover, the knives are riding the crest of popularity for all military knives, with both values and collector interest on the increase.

Because of the millions of the knives made, it is still possible to buy examples in mint condition that look exactly as they did some 60 or so years ago. Those with shields are particularly prized, with bidders raising the ante in recent internet auctions.

Unlike the extreme scarcity of many military pieces and with some perseverance and a little luck, four-blade utility knives can form the basis of a good military pocketknife collection. Many dealers do not realize that the bone-handle examples without inscribed shields were military issue, and that those marked "USA" probably were made by Imperial or in a joint effort between Ulster and Imperial.

Some dealers also seem to think that the military-issued utility knives always had steel liners, knowing that brass—the standard material for knife liners—was saved for use in brass shell casings. In fact, the earliest of the knives did indeed have brass liners, as brass was still in good supply. The knives with brass, instead of being dated after World War II in the late 1940s or early '50s, may have been made in the early '40s.

The knives are an excellent value, with examples available in the $35-$65 range, or slightly more depending on the tang stamping and inscription on the knife shield.

I believe that, thanks to their bone handles, sturdy construction and a proud military history, the knives are sure to significantly appreciate in the next few years. It would not surprise me if mint examples of rare engineer's pocketknives reach values up to **$100** in the next five years. At that time, collectors will be kicking themselves when they think of all the **$40** knives they passed up.

TL-29

As diverse as the four-blade general utility knives are in terms of shield types and brands, the "TL-29" or "Tool, Lineman" knives issued to military electricians and field wiremen during the Second World War are almost as varied.

Fairly large—3 1/2 inches closed—for a pocketknife, the TL-29 had two blades. The big spear-point master blade was used to open electrical equipment boxes, slice wiring, cut away insulation and for other knife chores. The second blade was specialized and served as a wire stripper and screwdriver. For added strength and multiple uses, the second blade locked. A specialized center liner slid over and locked the screwdriver blade in the open position to help prevent accidental closure.

Generally, TL-29s had wood handles, usually rosewood or walnut, though a few can be found in jigged bone. The knife had a nickel-silver bolster on the blade end only, and could be described as a swell-end, barehead jackknife. Almost all were fitted with a bail for attachment to a lanyard or for clipping to a soldier's pants or belt loop.

Until recently, collectors largely overlooked TL-29s. However, with the increased interest in military knives in general, TL-29s may be the hottest collectible military knives going. One of the reasons for the upsurge is that TL-29s were made by many companies, a fact that endears the knives to both collectors who collect one specific brand and those looking for a varied collection with lots of different brands. Pal, Kutmaster, Camillus, KA-BAR, Ulster, Case, Cattaraugus, Remington, Robeson, Schrade, Utica and several others made TL-29s. In fact, discovering TL-29s with different tang stampings is part of the intrigue of collecting them.

Many TL-29s had blank shields or the TL-29 shield stamped into the side of the wood handle. Some companies painted the stampings to make the "TL-29" stand out.

TL-29s were made in the millions and many still can be found in mint condition. Numerous companies made them after World War II, both with wood sides and newer plastic ones, many of the latter bearing advertisements.

As issued, the TL-29 was contained in a leather pouch along with a large pair of pliers/wire cutters. The challenge for collectors is to find a genuine TL-29 pouch, an original pliers—designated by the military as a "TL-13A"—and an original TL-29.

10th Mountain Division Knife

Another collectible military pocketknife is the 1st Special Service Force knife or the 10th Mountain Division knife, a bone-handled, five-blade utility piece made by one

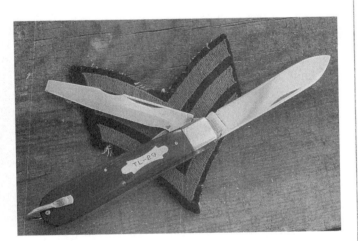

A TL-29 electrician's pocketknife with the very desirable TL-29 inset shield and wood handle is very high on the collector list. Camillus made this one. Value: **$60**. Pal and Kutmaster versions have the same value, while those made by KA-BAR and Cattaraugus are valued at **$110** each, Remington even higher. (White photo)

Two of these TL-29s have the very desirable bone handles. Each has the combination screwdriver-wire stripper blade. Value: **$70-95** each. Only Pal and Camillus made bone-handled TL-29s. (White photo)

company only—Ulster. Unlike the four-blade utility knives, it had a Phillips screwdriver.

What makes the addition of the Phillips screwdriver notable is that it was used by the troops of the 10th Mountain Division to adjust the binding on their snow skis. A specialized combat unit that fought the Germans in the Swiss Alps and other rugged mountain ranges in Europe, the 10th Mountain Division trained at Camp Hale in the Rocky Mountains of Colorado. Because of the knife's many blade styles and because it was used in the Alps, some collectors liken it to the Swiss Army knife.

There are several variations. Some had the Phillips screwdriver attached to the extra wide and sturdy bail, though this configuration was not as efficient as having the screwdriver in the knife body itself. Others have different master blade shapes, including sheepfoot, spear and clip patterns.

Rope & Fish Knives

Another military pocketknife often overlooked by collectors was made by Camillus, Imperial and Kutmaster for the United States Coast Guard. Called the *rope knife*, it was designed to cut ropes on masted ships. The oversized sheepfoot master blade could be laid on a section of heavy rope and struck on the back with a belaying pin or wooden mallet. The knives are sometimes marked "approved USCG," a bonus to collectors. All had a stout bail for attachment to a lanyard or belt hook, a necessary precaution against loss when using the knife in heavy seas.

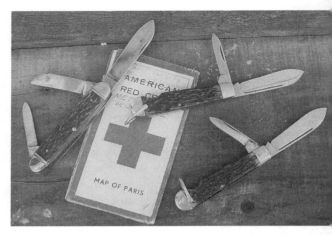

At left is a World War II Army Air Corps-issued pocketknife made by Camillus. Value: **$125-135**. At right are two general utility pocketknives with an easy-open notch near the rear bolster. All have jigged-bone handles. Values: **$60-75** each. (White photo)

The Camillus variety is the most common. Most, i[f] not all, bear the four-line marking "Camillus Cutlery Co[.] Camillus, N.Y. USA" stamped on four separate lines o[n] the tang of the master blade. Most had wood handle[s] frequently jigged to duplicate jigged bone, but also t[o] provide a better grip. Most had steel bolsters on the blade end, with brass liners, though some can be found with[h] steel liners as well. A barehead jack style, the knives had no bottom bolster.

Camillus also made another military pocketknife fo[r] use as an emergency-fishing knife. The rare knives were included in life rafts contained on military planes in case

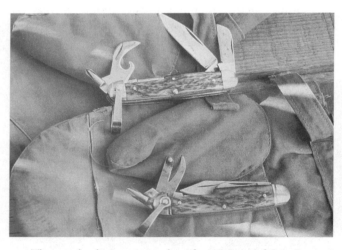

The pocketknives issued to the 1st Special Service Force and the 10th Mountain Division were made by Ulster exclusively. These examples are notable because of the Phillips screwdriver blade, which was used to adjust the ski bindings for the mountain troops. Notice the two different can-opener blades. The bottom one (value: **$400-475**) is the older style with a knob or button-opening mechanism, and the top one (value: **$350-400**) is more of a modern nail-nick, can-opening style. (White photo)

The massive sheepfoot blade of the Camillus "rope knife" was designed to be placed on a rope and then struck on the back with a belaying pin or wooden mallet. According to some, the blades had blunt points to prevent the stab wounds that occurred in knife fights between sailors. Value: **$45-60** (with wood handle). (White photo)

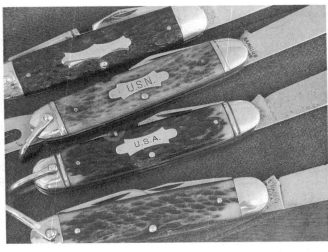

e planes crashed into water. Many dealers are unaware
at the knives were World War II military issue.

Always handled in "jigged-black" celluloid and classified
Texas toothpicks, the knives were thin serpentine jacks.
hey were bolstered on both ends, and the blade end
ontained a bail. Between the two bolsters was a groove
at could be used to remove the hook from a fish. The
rrow lower bolster, common on Texas toothpicks, aided
the hook-removal effort as well. The bottom bolster
as stamped "hook remover." In addition, the blade had a
ries of striations for scaling fish.

asy Open & Big Homely

Often overlooked as a military-issue knife was the
gged-bone, two-blade "easy-open" pocketknife made by
everal companies, including Pal, Camillus, Imperial, Utica
nd "Made in USA" (probably Kingston). With a jigged-
rown-bone handle and an "EZ" open notch, the knives
re very collectible and reasonably priced.

One of the most massive of World War II pocketknives
vas a heavy-duty piece contained in the survival kits of
ircraft pilots. Made by United of Grand Rapids, Michigan,
nd Colonial, the knife was 6 inches long closed and had
large clip master blade with a locking center liner. It
ncluded a saw blade for cutting through the metal sides
f aircraft. The blades were blackened and the checkered
lack handles were affixed with small screws.

Some of the knives came in camouflaged pouches,
vhich are rarely found with the knives. The Navy
contracted the knives for use by its pilots, who carried
hem in their survival vests. Some came with a bail. With
ts massive size, it has been called the largest military

A close-up shows some of the shield possibilities
on the general utility knife. From top: a plain shield,
the very desirable "USN" (United States Navy) shield,
the "USA" shield, and no shield.
(See accompanying chart for values.) (White photo)

pocketknife, and some include it among the rarest. Because
of its unattractive appearance, it has never caught on with
collectors. For the beginning military collector, this may
be its greatest asset.

Paratrooper Switchblades

Perhaps the most intriguing of the military pocketknives
were the switchblades issued to paratroopers. The knives
were designed for one-hand opening to cut parachute
shroud lines in situations where the paratrooper could
use only one hand.

A collection of World War II utility knives,
some with inset shields, some without. All are four
blades with jigged-bone handles and were produced
by such companies as Imperial, Pal, Boker, Valley Forge,
Camillus and Ulster. The newspaper is an edition of
Stars and Stripes published in 1945 reporting
Germany's surrender to the Allies.
(See accompanying chart for values.) (White photo)

Switchblades made by Schrade Walden with jigged-bone
handles were issued to U.S. paratroopers during World
War II. The knives were designed for paratroopers who
might have the use of only one hand to cut ensnared
parachute lines. The example at left has a folding guard.
Values: **$500-550** each. (White photo)

VALUES FOR WORLD WAR II GENERAL UTILITY KNIVES

Knife	Value*
4 blades, utility or camp, jigged bone, w/o shield	**$65-85**
With inset shield, no inscription	**$75-95**
With inset, inscribed shield; USA inscription most common; ITSA, USN, USMC, USMD very rare	**$95-150**

Values based on condition of both the knife and shield inscription. The knife must be in mint or near-mint condition, with full blades that snap ("walk and talk") in both the open and closed positions, and complete bone sides with no cracks or breaks. Brand names have little impact on value.

Schrade Walden made the knives with jigged-bone and, later, jigged-black-composition handles. The knives were extremely well made but the automatic opening mechanism has been worn out on most due to repeated operation. Finding one in mint condition is almost unheard of. Some had folding guards. In addition, the knives had a lock safety that prevented the blade from opening accidentally.

Conclusion

Military pocketknives are commanding what for them are unprecedented prices. Because of the numbers of knives produced and the general lack of knowledge about them, the beginning collector can still buy outstanding examples for reasonable prices. All are sure to appreciate in value in the near future.

Editor's note: According to the third edition of U.S. Military Knives, *the Ulster five-blade utility knife was issued to the 1st Special Service Force and, later, to the 11th Mountain Division. However, according to Richard White, records show that a Congressional Medal of Honor was awarded posthumously to PFC John D. Magrath, a member of the 10th Mountain Division killed near Castel d'Aiano, Italy, during World War II. Also, in a story dealing with the ecological restoration of Camp Hale, the Denver Post reported that Camp Hale was the birthplace of "the storied 10th Mountain Division."*

Values for all knives pictured herein are for knives as described in mint or near-mint condition. Significant wear, breakage or non-working parts decrease values dramatically.

The four-blade utility piece was classified as a "general utility knife." The one at top has a master blade with regular pull, combination cap lifter-screwdriver, can opener and leather punch. The can opener varies depending on the manufacturer. From top, the knives were made by Ulster, Pal and Camillus.
(See accompanying chart for values.) (White photo)

Western's contribution to the war effort included these utility knives in jigged bone. They have the standard configuration of four different blade styles and a bail for attachment to a belt, pack, etc. Also known as "engineer's pocketknives," here they surround an authentic World War II engineer's compass.
(See accompanying chart for values.) (White photo)

Worth Their Weight in Merit Badges

Interest in antique scout pocketknives—both "official" and unofficial—is on the rise

y Richard White

Prior to 1900, the utility knife, generally referred to as a *boy scout knife* or *camp knife*, was almost an unknown commodity in the USA. owever, the bone camp or utility knife with four blades ecame popular in America almost overnight, when, in 910, the Boy Scouts of America (BSA) was formed and lopted the pattern as its "official" camping knife.

The Boy Scout knife is generally described as a four-blade camp" knife, approximately 3 1/2 inches closed, normally icluding a bail and displaying a nickel-silver shield inset ito one side of the jigged-bone handle. The blades are master, leather punch, can-opener, and a combination crewdriver/cap lifter. The bail was used to attach the ocketknife to a lanyard or, with a clip, to the "scouter's" ants bell. The large master blade found hundreds of uses, ncluding whittling, cutting rope, making marshmallow oasting sticks, peeling fruit and cutting meat.

The concern designated to produce the first "official" oy Scout knife was New York Knife Co. in Walden, New York. Though it went out of business in the first year of the Depression in 1931, New York Knife made some of the finest American pocketknives during its "glory days." The company's official Boy Scout pocketknife was no exception.

New York Knife had a monopoly on scout pocketknives after World War I on into the early 1920s, when several other major cutlery companies, noting the rapid expansion of the Boy Scouts, began to produce several varieties of "unofficial" scout knives. To not infringe on the BSA's "official" scout designation, the other companies changed the logos slightly, avoiding the "official scout knife" etching on the master blade and adding several other designations to the nickel-silver shields.

During the early 1920s, several cutlery companies petitioned the BSA to allow them to produce an "official" bone-handle scout knife. The obvious intent was to compete with New York Knife and to be an option for Boy Scouts in the scouting literature and catalogues. At least three well-known cutlery companies—Remington,

Though these three "official" bone-handle Boy Scout camp knives were made by Ulster and carry the official "Be Prepared" shield, they vary greatly in the color and jigging pattern of the bone handles. The knives also bear three different master-blade tang stamps, indicating a difference in production dates. The knives and their stampings are, from left: "Ulster Dwight Devine and Sons" (the earliest example); "Dwight Devine and Sons, USA"; and "Ulster Knife Company." (For values, see the accompanying chart.) (White photo)

Though the most desirable of the "unofficial" scout knives are handled in jigged bone, these examples are proof that interesting scout knives can be found with celluloid handles as well. From left: a black-and-yellow IKCO junior scout pattern; a "snakeskin"-celluloid IDEAL brand scout knife; a gold celluloid Utica scout; a jigged-white-composition Ulster scout; a maroon-and-black Imperial scout; and a jigged-black, imitation-stag Seneca scout. (For values, see the accompanying chart.) (White photo)

Ulster and Landers Frary & Clark (L.F. & C.)—were given the "official" designation and began to produce "official" Boy Scout knives.

In the ensuing years, several other cutlery companies applied for and received the "official" designation and have produced knives for the Boy Scouts. The official knives expanded over the years from pocketknives to sheath knives, and later to knives for the Girl Scouts, Camp Fire Girls, Cub Scouts and Brownies. Today, Camillus is the maker of the official Boy Scout knives.

In addition to pocketknives, some companies made Boy Scout sheath knives, chow knives, lockbacks, Sea Scout knives, and scout knives with less than four blades. In fact, Joseph Richard Kerr, a Boy Scout authority and writer living in Birmingham, Alabama, penned an informative, copiously illustrated book entitled *600 Scout Knives* (copyright 1997, Morris Publishing Co., Kearney, Nebraska). Scout knife aficionados should read Kerr's book. It outlines the extremely varied cutlery types in the Boy Scout knife category.

The list of makers of official scout knives includes not only those mentioned but also Pal, Cattaraugus, Camillus, Imperial, Western Cutlery, Schrade Walden Cutlery,

Marble's, KA-BAR, and even Victorinox. The majority of these companies produced quality knives designed to endure the rigors of scout use. However, like other forms of cutlery, most of the knives manufactured by the earlier companies are literally worn out, with most exhibiting a shortened master blade, broken bone scales, and one or the other blades snapped off. Thousands have been lost over the years.

Skyrocketing Values

For the beginning collector of Boy Scout knives, the availability of many of them, especially those in at least very good condition, is extremely limited, with values skyrocketing. For example, a New York Knife four-blade scout knife in mint condition will set you back about $375. A Remington Boy Scout model #RS3333, bone handle four-blade—the most common Remington scout knife—carries a value of about $300 in mint condition.

An Ulster Boy Scout knife with a bone handle and four blades is worth about $150-$200 in mint condition. A Cattaraugus "Whit-L-Kraft" model fetches about $475—if you can find one. Even an L.F. & C. four-blade, standard

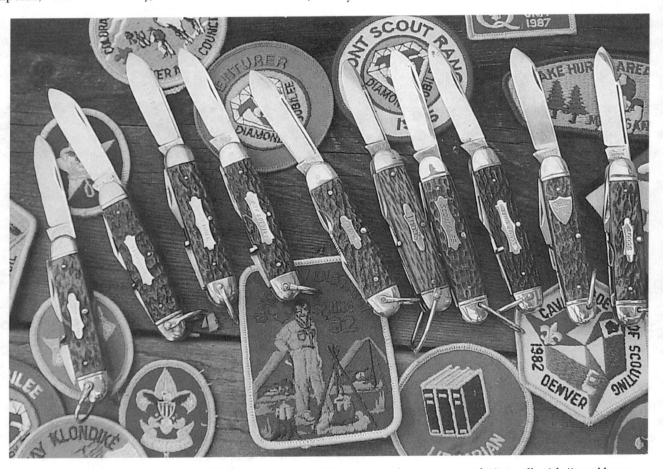

A handsome arrangement of unofficial American- and German-made scout camp knives, all with jigged-bone handles, include: Finedge (Solingen, Germany); Camillus; Richartz (Germany); Specialty Trading Co. (Germany); Premier Lifetime (Germany); Buffalo Cutlery Co; Hibbard Spencer & Bartlett; and a rare Royal Brand. (For values, see the accompanying chart.) (White photo)

ze scout will cost you around **$200**. All have jigged-bone handles except the L.F. & C., which has a jigged-black-composition handle.

Given the escalating price and extreme scarcity of the officially designated "Boy Scout knives, serious collectors have turned to the hundreds of "unofficial" scout knife variations. Contrary to the high price and scarcity of the official scout knives, the unofficial scout/camp knives give both the novice and serious collector an almost endless source of knives handled in bone and a variety of other handle materials.

It is the great diversity of scout-knife-producing companies that has spurred collector interest in scout knives. The list of companies that manufactured "unofficial" scout knives is almost endless and includes not only American concerns but a host of German cutlery producers as well.

Unofficial scout knives were made/offered by Pal; Imperial; Colonial; Remington; Camillus; Ulster; Specialty Trading Co. (Germany); Boker (Germany); Richartz (Germany); Buffalo Cutlery Co.; Premier-Lifetime (Germany); Ulster USA; Simmons Hardware; Utica; Robeson; IKCO (Imperial); Imperial Cutlery; The Ideal;

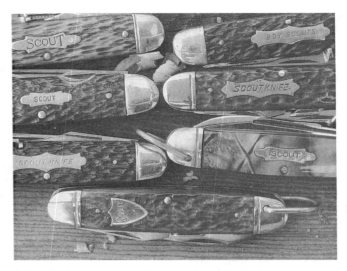

The shields inset into the sides of most Boy Scout camp models often contain an inscription designed to help sell the knives. These pieces were made/offered by the Buffalo Cutlery Co.; Premier Lifetime (Germany); Camillus; Hibbard Spencer & Bartlett; Specialty Trading Co. (Germany); Camillus; and Utica. (For values, see the accompanying chart.) (White photo)

SCOUT KNIFE VALUES

Description	Value*
Cattaraugus, 3 5/8", 4-blade camp knife, bone	**$150-175**
Schrade, 4-blade camp knife, bone	**$100-125**
Miller Bros., 3 5/8", 4-blade camp knife, stag	**$175-200**
Robeson, 3 5/8", 4-blade camp knife, bone	**$125-150**
Keen Kutter, 3 1/2", 4-blade camp knife, bone	**$150-175**
Remington, R3335, 4-blade camp knife, red-white-blue celluloid, 3 3/4"	**$350-400**
Richartz (Germany), 4-blade camp knife, jigged bone	**$50-75**
Buffalo Cutlery Co., peachseed bone, 4-blade camp knife	**$75-100**
Royal Brand, 4-blade camp knife, bone	**$75-100**
Camillus, 4-blade camp knife, bone	**$75-100**
Hibbard Spencer & Bartlett, 4-blade camp knife, bone	**$100-125**
Imperial, 4-blade camp knife, celluloid	**$50-75**
Premier Lifetime (Germany), 4-blade camp knife, bone	**$50-75**
Utica, 4-blade camp knife, bone	**$75-100**

Values are the author's and are for knives in near-mint or mint condition, full blades with few scratches, and no rust or nicks. All blades must snap both open and closed. The backsprings must be level with the spine of the knife in both the open and closed positions. The handle material must be in perfect shape, with no cracks or missing pieces. The bail and inset shield must be present, the inscription on the shield readable, and the knife must exhibit little or no use. All lengths are for knives in the closed position.

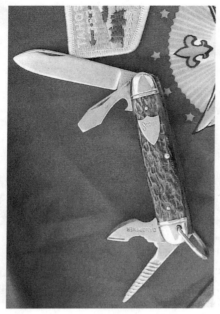

Generally, scout camp knives have a nickel-silver shield inset into one side of the handle. This example, with a rare "federal" shield, was offered by Hibbard Spencer & Bartlett, forerunner of the Tru-Value Hardware chain. (For values, see the accompanying chart.) (White photo)

Royal Brand USA; Hibbard Spencer & Bartlett; Seneca; E. Brueckmann (Germany); Valley Forge; Schrade Cutlery; W.R. Case; Union Cutlery; Dixon Cutlery; John Primble; Keen Kutter; Sword Brand (Camillus); Wards; Challenge Cutlery; Crucible Cutlery; Enderes Cutlery; Empire Cutlery; Napanoch; Kutmaster; Van Camp; Western Cutlery; Frankfurth Hardware; Bingham; and Bieco (Germany).

Other Variables

In addition to the vast diversity of brands mentioned, there are a couple of other variables available to collectors of Boy Scout knives. The first is the variety of words inscribed into the handle shields. In order to convey to the potential purchaser that the knives were to be bought and used by Boy Scouts, the various cutlery companies inscribed words certain to get the point across. Unofficial scout knives carry such inscriptions as *Scout*, *Boy Scout*, *Boy Scouts*, *Camp Knife*, *Scouter*, *Scout Junior*, *Junior Scout*, *Scout Knife*, *Scouts Prepare*, *Be Prepared* and *OVB Scout*. Though mostly engraved on "banner" shields of some sort, the inscriptions also can be found on shields resembling federal insignia, elongated ovals or other shapes.

Handles are another variable. Though dyed and jigged are by far the most popular bone, there are many other varieties. German-produced scout knives have distinctively jigged-bone sides that are quite different from American scout knives. Even among American cutlery producers, the jigging on scout knives varies radically. Boy Scout knives can be found with green, peachseed (made famous by Schrade), Rogers and even the very distinctive New York Knife jigged bone.

Another variable is the assorted colors of celluloid handles. From the jigged black used by Seneca and Kutmaster to the various colored celluloids by Imperial, Simonds and Utica, to the gorgeous red-white-blue celluloids by Schrade, Imperial and Remington, all add to any scout knife collection. Add to this mix a variety of different leather punch styles, blade pulls, and different can-opener and cap-lifter blades, and you have an almost endless spectrum of scout knives.

Because of the significant numbers of early Boy Scout members reaching retirement age, the interest in scout knives has increased significantly. Though scout knives are a very specific and identifiable cutlery pattern, the wide variety of stamps, handle materials, official and unofficial styles, and diversity of shield etchings make the collecting of scout knives interesting and challenging.

Moreover, Boy Scout knives are one of the older cutlery genres, approaching almost 100 years of continuous production in the USA alone, and are one of the few patterns with U.S. origins. Add the number of newer scout models, most handled in the synthetic known as Delrin, and you have yet another source of scout models to collect. Older examples of "unofficial" scout knives can still be found in mint or near mint condition, still reasonably priced, and those by other cutlery companies are appearing on a consistent basis.

With the scout knife being duplicated for use in the U.S. military in World War II, the pattern has a proud history of service. For these reasons, the scout knife has ranked near the top of collector preferences for many years.

Premium Stockmen are Prime-Time Players

Antique examples of the all-purpose multi-blades are plentiful, valuable and high on collectors' want lists

By Richard D. White

The American cowboy certainly can be credited with bringing life to the U.S. cattle industry. The breeding, feeding, branding and transportation of millions of livestock are generally taken for granted, but formed the foundation of the cattle industry Americans rely on so much today.

The tools of the cowboy were simple: a bedroll, poncho, rifle and scabbard, saddle and saddlebags, and a few staples such as coffee, match safe, tobacco and rolling paper, liquor, beans, grease, frying pan, canteen, eating utensils—and the ever-present pocketknife.

The pocketknife was perhaps the most important utensil because it was by far the most versatile. Used for a myriad of tasks—everything from removing splinters to castrating cattle and a host of others—it was always close at hand.

For the cowboy, the knife had to be large enough to be held with a gloved hand and strong enough to perform its many required tasks on a daily basis. That knife most often was the *premium stockman*, named after the person responsible for raising and herding cattle.

Two Case premium stockmen include one (top) in stag—rare among stockmen—and the 6375 pattern in jigged red bone. Measuring 4 1/4 inches closed, the latter is an example of perhaps the largest production premium stockman made. (For values, see the accompanying chart.) (White photo)

The premium stockman is a large pocketknife, usually over 3 1/2 inches long closed, though frequently almost 4. The knife is serpentine in shape, with at least two backsprings. Though most stockmen had three blades, some had four. A few even had five or six blades and three backsprings.

The blade patterns on the three-blade stockman were fairly consistent: clip-point master, spey and sheepfoot. A few models substituted a leather punch for the sheepfoot, and even fewer substituted a pen blade. Many of the master blades had a *match-striker pull*. The match-striker nail pull got its name because it had a jigged surface on which a match could be struck and lighted.

The stockman came into existence around 1890 and was, as you might expect, marketed mainly in the West. By far the most common handle material was jigged bone, with the bone, fittingly enough, coming from the shinbone of cattle. The next favorite handle material was celluloids in various colors, followed by mother-of-pearl. Stag also was used, though infrequently. Mother-of-pearl stockman knives often were saved for special occasions, such as going to church on Sunday.

Premium stockmen had several nicknames, each of which depended on shape variations. Those with an exaggerated swell in the handle were called *humpback* or *sowbelly*. Those with a center swell were called *gunstock* stockmen.

Names associated with the American West frequently were etched on the master blades. One popular etching was *vaquero*, the name given to the Mexican cowboy. Other etchings included *Great Western, Texan, Colorado Stock Knife, Montana Mountaineer, El Dorado, Texas Steer, Kattle King, The Rancher, Stockman's Pride, Big Bronco* and *Rodeo Prize*. The etchings hinted as to the purpose behind the knife's design and capitalized on the Western mystique.

Of special interest to collectors are the models with four or more blades. The four-blade stockman had master, sheepfoot and spey blades, and a leather punch. Each additional blade made production of the knife more difficult because every blade had to be shaped so that it closed easily without hitting the other blades in the process.

Compared to the number of three-blade premium stockmen, the knives having four, five or even six blades—and three backsprings—are significantly rarer and command much higher prices. Obtaining one of these stockmen is a real find.

In addition to the standard blades, a few companies substituted a special blade in place of the regular spey. Henry Boker and Co. and Remington, for example, added an especially long spey blade, the length of which rivaled that of the master clip blade. Almost without exception, the models containing the long spey blade were known as *Great Western* premium stockmen.

Along with the 3 1/2-4-inch premium stockman, most companies also made a junior premium stockman. Made with the same blade configuration, the junior knives measured about 3 3/8 inches or smaller in the closed position. Though highly collected, the smaller knives have lower values than the premium style and few, if any, contain more than three blades—certainly not five or six. As with many other classic antique pocketknives, size and price complement each other, with the larger knives commanding higher values.

Many cutlery companies produced a cattle pattern, which is also a three-blade pocketknife. Unlike the premium stockman, the *cattle pattern* is a straight-sided knife resembling a cigar in shape. As with the premium stockman, the cattle pattern also was used by ranchers and cowboys.

By The Thousands

Almost every major cutlery company made several models of premium stockman by the thousands. Remington, for example, made over 25 models, with the most famous being the 84283, a five-blade sowbelly in jigged-bone valued at a hefty $3,000. As you might expect, you could spend years collecting Remington stockmen without even looking for other brands.

Other brands of stockmen do, however, exist en masse. The antique 6347 pattern by Case is a 3 7/8-inch stockman with a variety of handle materials, including metal, green bone, Rogers bone, stag, red stag and assorted celluloids—Christmas tree, yellow, cracked ice and rough black. In addition, the 6347 was available with a variety of blade configurations and different steels, making the pattern desirable and popular with Case collectors. Case also made a larger stockman with the 6375 stamping. Highly valued by Case collectors, the knife was a whopper at over 4 1/4 inches closed.

Case also made a premium stockman with the "92" designation. Officially known as the 6392, it was 4 inches

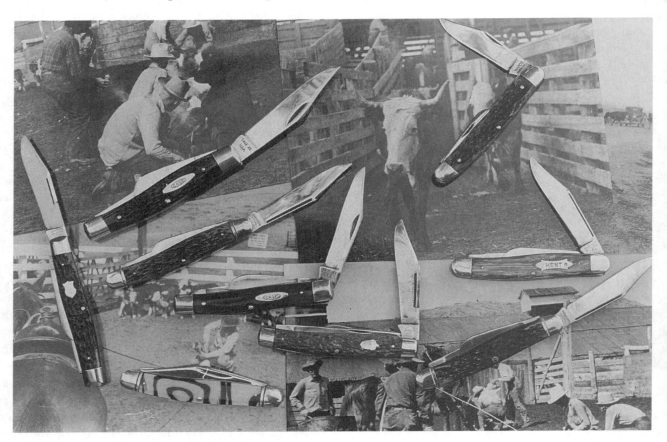

Examples of antique premium stockmen, "The Knife That Won The West," include these marked Remington, Western Boulder, High Carbon Steel (Camillus), Wright and Wilhelmy Hardware Co. (Ulster), Wards, Kent and Case. (For values, see the accompanying chart.) (White photo)

osed and came in a variety of handle materials, including nyx and rough black celluloid, green and red bone, and ag.

Along with Case, Remington and Boker, other valuable ntique premium stockmen bear the marks of Ulster; /inchester; Schrade; Camillus; Miller Bros.; Western States; anders Frary & Clark; Robeson; American Shear & Knife; al; Queen; Cattaraugus; Imperial; Kent; New York Knife Co.; libbard Spencer & Bartlett (OVB); John Primble; Henry

Sears and Sons; Utica; Valley Forge; George Wostenholm; Bridge; W. Bingham and Co.; and Shapleigh Hardware.

In addition to the well-known Shapleigh Hardware (Diamond Edge) edition, other cutlery companies provided premium stockmen for a variety of U.S. hardware companies. For example, a recently acquired model is stamped "Wright & Wilhelmy Co." on the master blade, and "Ulster Knife Co." on the remaining two blades. Wright & Wilhelmy was a hardware store in Omaha, Nebraska.

PREMIUM STOCKMAN VALUES

Knife	Value*
Remington, R3053, bone, 3-blade, 4"	$350-400
Remington, R3054, mother-of-pearl, 3-blade, 4"	$450
Remington, R3055, celluloid, 3-blade, 4"	$350-400
Remington, R3063, bone, 3-blade w/punch, 4"	$300
Remington, R3133, bone, 4-blade w/punch, 4"	$300
Ulster, bone, 3-blade, 3 3/4"	$225-275
Keen Kutter, gunstock, bone, 3 3/4"	$300
Miller Bros., bone, 3-blade, 3 7/8"	$250-275
Western Boulder, bone w/shield, 3-blade, 4"	$200-225
Western Boulder, butter & molasses celluloid, 3-blade	$200-225
Case, 6392, bone, XX stamping, 3-blade, 4"	$250-300
Case, 6392, bone, Tested XX, stag, 4"	$300-350
Case, 6375, rough black, XX 4 1/4"	$300
Case 6375, green bone, XX, 4 1/4"	$300-325
Case, 6375, bone, 1970 10 dot, 4 1/4"	$75-100
Case, 3347SPPU (spey, punch), yellow comp., XX	$225
Case, 6347SPPU (spey, punch), green bone, XX, 3 7/8"	$225-$250
Case, 6347SHSP (sheepfoot, spey), bone, XX	$175-200
Case, 6347SHSP, (sheepfoot, spey), stag, USA, 3 7/8"	$100-125
Case, 6347SHSP, (sheepfoot, spey), flat yellow comp., 3 7/8"	$60-75
H. Boker, bone stag, w/Great Western long spey, 4"	$300
Western States Cutlery, 6347PU (punch), bone, 4"	$350-400
Wards, bone, 4-blade w/punch, 3 7/8"	$200-225

*Values are the author's estimates based on knives in mint or near-mint condition. Mint and near-mint knives may not have any cracks, nicks or deterioration in the bone or celluloid. All blades must be full, free from rust, nicks and observable wear, and must walk and talk" (open and close freely with "snap"). All blades must fit together in the correct position when the knife is closed. In addition, the knife's overall fit and finish must be excellent. Knives that exhibit worn or broken blades or handles, missing parts, etc., will be valued significantly less. All lengths are for knives in the closed position.

Premium Stockmen are Prime-Time Players

Enduring Popularity

Because they were working knives used by ranchers, stockmen and cowboys on a daily basis, premium stockmen in good-to-excellent condition can be a challenge to find. The good news is that literally hundreds of thousands of them were produced over a significantly long period of time. Examples can still be found without an excessive amount of investment in time or money. Though some models—especially sowbelly stockmen with four or more blades or other specialized features—can cost hundreds of dollars, excellent examples can be had for under **$100**.

Since the knives are of an imposing size and represent an important time in American history, they will remain quite popular, as they have for decades. Because of the thousands, perhaps millions, produced, it is still not too late to start a premium stockman collection, with the values of knives in good condition sure to increase.

Rare among stockmen is the four-blade model. The shield-less one stamped "WARDS" (made for Montgomery Ward) contains master, pen and sheepfoot blades, and a punch. The one with the acorn shield—which indicates the knife has a punch blade—is a Remington R3133. It sports a punch and long-pull master and sheepfoot blades, and an extremely rare "Great Western" extra-long spey blade. (For values, see the accompanying chart.) (White photo)

The American West could not have been settled an tamed without the stockman. Because of its size an weight, it easily could be felt in the front pocket, ready t be accessed and opened for the task at hand. Some say tha most cowboys would rather have gone without their boot than without their trusty premium stockman knives.

The size difference between a premium and junior stockman is illustrated here. At left is a premium model by Western Boulder. Closed length: 3 7/8 inches. At right is a junior stockman in winterbottom bone by Queen. Closed length: 3 1/2 inches. (For values, see the accompanying chart.) (White photo)

Advertising Cutlery's Rich Potential

By Richard D. White

Examples of cutlery bearing advertisements have, until very recently, been under-collected, undervalued and unappreciated by most knife collectors. The reason why such pieces have been overlooked may be due to their relatively simple construction—most are senator, two-bladed knives—and their unassuming handle material—many were made with smooth metal sides. In fact, perhaps the specific geographical nature of the advertisements themselves failed to connect with many potential collectors. In recent years, however, advertising knives seem to be coming into their own as collectors and dealers are discovering the proud history and important lineage associated with these early cutlery examples.

Upon closer examination, collectors are finding that advertising knives were made or offered frequently by such major companies as Shapleigh Diamond Edge; George Wostenholm I*XL (Sheffield, England); Schrade Cutlery Co.; A. Kastor and Sons (Germany); H. Keschner and Co. (Germany); W.H. Morley and Sons (Germany); Robeson Shuredge; D. Herder; D. Perez; and a host of others all over the world.

In addition, collectors and dealers are finding that many of the knives often contain intricate and beautiful craftsmanship, with beaded backgrounds, fleur-de-lis patterns, fancy scrollwork, graphic lettering and pictures of various buildings, tools and specific advertised products. Others are being collected because of their unusual shapes and blade configurations. In short, they are being noticed for their artwork in addition to the products they advertise.

Finally, like other forms of collectible advertising pieces, they help us identify with our own past. Examples bearing the advertisements of Goodyear Tires, Metropolitan Life Insurance, Miracle Whip, Disston Saws, Coca-Cola™, Westinghouse, Peter's Leather Shoes, Travelers Insurance, and many others helps us preserve and remember the good times of days gone by. For many, the local nature of the advertising and being able to establish the link between a particular company and its location is becoming more important as people spend more time researching their family history.

With the publication of the first-ever cutlery book devoted entirely to advertising, *Advertising Cutlery*, by this writer for Schiffer Press, 1999, the secret of advertising's special niche in the cutlery scheme is "out of the bag." Advertising cutlery, both metal-handled and celluloid examples, holds rich potential for today's knife collectors

A striking metal knife advertising Metropolitan Life Insurance Co., New York. Given away as a premium, it is one of the most significant advertising knives ever produced. It was made by A. Kastor and Co., New York (Germany). In mint condition, the knife is worth at least **$125**.

The reverse side of the Metropolitan advertising knife shows the company building in New York. In addition to the exquisite graphics, in three dimensions, the knife reads "Tallest Building in the World" (which the edifice was from 1913-1915).

An old Peters Solid Leather Shoes advertising knife, produced by Richartz Bros. and Sons Ltd., Germany, in the 1930s. The reverse side advertises Peters Weatherbird Shoes. Value: **$65**.

A noteworthy Linz Bros. Jewelers (established in 1877) advertiser produced by W.H. Morley and Sons, New York (Germany). The reverse side of this highly decorated advertising knife shows the Linz Bros. shop in Dallas, Texas. Value: **$100**.

This advertising knife is known as a "turn ring," with the blades opened by twisting the small ring attached to each end of the handle. It advertises Western Iron Stores, Co., and was made by Bom Cleff and Co., Germany. Value: **$80**.

A fairly common but still unusual knife made for Simonds, Worden, White, Co., Dayton, Ohio, a concern that produced industrial blades and grinding wheels. Using the "turn-ring" opener, the knife sports brass sides. It was probably made by Camillus Cutlery Co. or W.H. Morley. In mint condition, it has a value of **$90**.

Another Simonds "turn-ring" knife, this is an early model, before Worden and White joined the firm. It features brass, pebbled background and fleur-de-lis at the ends. Value: **$100**.

This very rare "Sunbrite" turn-ring advertiser was made by Camillus. Some researchers think it advertises a carbonated beverage, others a cleaner, perhaps a laundry detergent. Made in the 1940s, in mint condition, its value is **$100**.

This is a 50th anniversary knife for the W.A. Hover & Co., Denver, Colorado, established in 1882. Issued in 1932, the knife was made by Camillus. With brass sides, it is very rare. Anniversary knives tend to be more valuable. It has a value of **$75**.

This smooth, rounded advertiser was made for Goodyear Tire Co. by an old English cutlery company, George Ibberson. Started in the 1700s, Ibberson made knives for over 250 years. This knife is worth **$65**.

This knife advertises the Boyertown Burial Casket Co., Coast to Coast. A simple one-blade knife, it was made by Voos Cutlery Co., New Haven, Connecticut. Rare, it is worth **$50**.

This advertiser for Miracle Whip salad dressing was issued in 1937, four years after the dressing was introduced. The knife was produced by Schrade Cutlery Co. and has a value of **$60**.

The Hallack & Haddock Lumber Co. is the subject of this two-bladed senator-pen advertising knife. Produced by Robeson Cutlery Co., it has the "Shuredge" stamping on the master blade. It has a value of **$80** because of the Robeson name.

Capital Life Insurance, Denver, Colorado, is the name on this metal advertising knife. It was made by Griffon XX Cutlery Co. of Bridgeport, Connecticut. Griffon is known more for its straight razors, so this one is rare. It has a value of **$75**.

The New England Newspaper Supply Co., Worcester, Massachusetts, is advertised on this knife. The knives were made by different companies, this one by Schrade Cutlery. It has a brushed metal finish and strong stamping. It has a value of **$70**.

This watch fob knife contains the traditional bail. It advertises Cook Paint & Varnish. Produced by Landers, Frary and Clark, it is stamped "Universal" on the master blade. The smooth metal sides provide a palette for advertising. It has a value of **$60**.

This knife was made by Camillus for Monroe Hardware of Monroe, North Carolina. Produced in 1978, it is an annual advertising issue. It is a challenge to find several knives with different dates. It has a value of **$60**.

The Midland Bridge Co. knife is an extremely rare advertiser. It was made in 1884 by the Thomaston Knife Co. of Thomaston, Connecticut. The company went out of business in 1934. The knife is valued at **$95** because of its rarity.

This anniversary advertising knife has appeal to both cutlery collectors and tool collectors. It marks the 100th anniversary of the DISSTON Tool Co., a major producer of a multitude of tools, but known for its saws. As an anniversary knife celebrating Disston's history from 1840-1940, it is easy to date. Though the tang of the master blade is stamped only "DISSTON STEEL," the feeling here is that the knife was made by Camillus. Because of its appeal to two different groups of collectors, the knife has a value of **$100-$125**.

This advertiser is perhaps the most noteworthy of all those herein. Promoting the ATLAS ASBESTOS COMPANY, LTD., of both Montreal and Toronto, it advertises an infamous product, asbestos, which has been proved to be a cancer-causing agent. As a Canadian company, Atlas used the George Wostenholm Cutlery Co. of Sheffield, England, to make the knives. The Wostenholm trademark of "I*XL" is stamped deeply into the master blade. It appears likely that the knife was made in the 1920s or '30s. Because of its controversial product, Canadian origin, well-respected maker and mint condition, it is valued at **$125**.

A very simple but elegant advertiser for J.J. Stiller, Tailor, Chicago. A two-blade knife made by H. Keschner, Germany, whose logo reads "Antelope," it sports brass sides, ornate scrollwork and lettering. Because of its design, condition and beauty, it is valued at **$85-100**.

This advertiser was issued by Cardwell Westinghouse. The reverse commemorates the development of the "Friction Draft Gear." Sold by Shapleigh "Diamond Edge" Hardware Co, it is a watch fob knife with a value of **$70**.

This is one of the premier advertising knives ever made. Produced for A.W. Williams & Co., New York, by H. Keschner, one side touts fine clothing, the other offers a 50 cent discount if you presented the knife at the point of purchase at the Williams store. In mint condition, the knife is worth **$150**.

A real show stopper, this advertiser is shaped like an automobile tire. Made for Goodyear by E. Bonnsman Co., Solingen, Germany, it is extremely detailed and finely crafted. It is valued at **$150**.

E.H. Best, a Boston manufacturing company, produced unusual advertising knives with tooled aluminum handles. Depending on the tang stamping—Ulster, Schrade, New York Knife—these knives are valued at **$75-85**.

Another noteworthy clothing advertiser, made for the Boyles Bros. Co. by Albert Lyman & Co., this knife carries the slogans "Money's Worth or Money Back" and "A Knife With Every Suit." It features raised lettering, a pebbled background and fine scrollwork. Value is **$150**.

Pocketknife Blade Openers

Information contributed by Dennis Ellingsen, Janie Stidham and Dee Muehlberger.

A BLADE OPENER is a little slip of tool steel, narrowed and thinned at one end, sometimes with handle scales attached, that is used for opening pocketknife blades. The narrow end is placed in a blade's nail nick, and may be kept from slipping out by a finger or thumb pressed on the back of the blade. Then the blade is levered open.

There are two traditional types of blade opener: those used by cutlers and those used by salesmen. Add the various modern varieties, such as limited-edition, counterfeit and even a few handmade blade openers, and there are three basic types altogether.

The first traditional type, blade openers used by cutlers, may be as old as the folding knife itself. In the old days, a cutler made each knife from start to finish. In modern knife factories, however, a cutler is a skilled man or woman who performs the final inspection and, when necessary, adjustment on pocketknives before they are packed for shipment. A cutler must open and close thousands of blades a day, and no one's thumbnails are that strong. Cutlers usually make their own blade openers, so most such openers are personalized and few are marked. Many come with interesting stories, though the stories are nearly impossible to verify. In our view, the relative ease of fakery limits the potential value of such one-of-a-kind artifacts.

The second traditional type of blade opener seems first to have appeared early in the 20th century. It is the mass-produced advertising blade opener made by or for knife companies, and given both to their traveling salesmen and to the retail dealers and hardware clerks who sold their knives to the public. Such openers were given only to sales people—rarely, perhaps never, to consumers—so their production was limited and they are now very scarce.

The value of such a blade opener is influenced somewhat by the popularity of the brand of knife it advertises, but far more by the age and rarity of the opener itself. For example, Case knives are popular to collect but Case openers are relatively common, so their value is only around **$25**.

The list below includes all the advertising blade openers that we have seen or heard of so far. Each is all steel, unless a handle material is listed. Estimated values are for openers in excellent or better condition.

AMERICAN MANUFACTURERS
ULSTER KNIFE OPENER. **$40**.
ULSTER QUALITY (celluloid). **$45**.
COMPLIMENTS OF CHALLENGE CUTLERY (pearl). **$150**.
NORTHFIELD KNIFE CO., HAND FORGED POCKET KNIVES, UN-X-LD, * CONN. **$250**.

COMPLIMENTS ... EMPIRE KNIFE CO., WINSTED, CONN. **$100**.
NAPANOCH KNIFE CO., NAPANOCH, N.Y. **$100**.
CATTARAUGUS CUTLERY CO., LITTLE VALLEY, N.Y. **$100**.
BARNSLEY BROS. CUTLERY CO., MONETT, MO., PAT. JAN. 27, '03 HAND FORGED CUTLERY (with cap lifter). **$75**.
ALWAYS SHARP, GRIFFON KNIVES (ivory). **$150**.
STELLITE. **$30**.
REMINGTON UMC/REMINGTON CUTLERY (Bullet). **$200**.
REMINGTON UMC/REMINGTON CUTLERY (Bullet) FOR SALE BY SLOSS & BRITTAIN, SAN FRANCISCO, CAL. **$350**.
REMINGTON DUPONT/FINE CUTLERY (Bullet). **$350**.
REMINGTON (bone, with bail). **$375**.
REMINGTON (green celluloid). **$350**.
WINCHESTER TRADEMARK MADE IN U.S.A. **$100**.
WESTERN STATES, BOULDER, COLO., MADE IN U.S.A. **$60**.
ROBESON SHUREDGE, ROCHESTER, N.Y. (bone). **$75**.
ROBESON U.S.A. CUTLERY (jigged bone). **$75**.
UNIVERSAL RESISTAIN STEEL. **$65**.
QUEEN CUTLERY CO., TITUSVILLE, PA. **$20**.
W.R. CASE & SONS, BRADFORD, PA. **$25**.
CASE XX TESTED CENTENNIAL. **$25**.
CAMILLUS HAS THE EDGE! **$25**.
MARBLE'S-GLADSTONE, MICH. U.S.A. (recent) **$25**.

AMERICAN IMPORTERS AND DISTRIBUTORS
JUDSON CUTLERY CO., SOLINGEN, GERMANY; NEW YORK, U.S.A. (pearl, with bail). **$100**.
THE CANTON HARDWARE CO., CANTON, OHIO ADV. NOVELTY CO.-CHICAGO. **$50**.
MAGNETIC CUTLERY CO., 1013 ARCH STREET, PHILADELPHIA PA. BARREL BRAND (white celluloid, with bail). **$100**.
STILETTO CUTLERY CO. **$50**.
[FARWELL] OZMUN KIRK & CO., ST. PAUL. HENRY SEARS & SON CUTLERY. **$50**.
HIBBARD SPENCER BARTLETT, CUTLERY, OUR VERY BEST. **$50**.
KEEN KUTTER, SIMMONS HARDWARE, GERMANY. **$80**.
KEYSTONE (picture) (Simmons Keen Kutter). **$70**.
NORVELL-SHAPLEIGH HDWE. CO. SAINT LOUIS. **$80**.
SHAPLEIGH D-E HDW. CO. **$80**.
TENK'S CLIPPER. **$50**.
HEN & ROOSTER, GERMANY. A.G. RUSSELL... **$20**.
"SHAVIN QUALITY" WORLD KNIFE DISTRIBUTORS, CHATTANOOGA, TENN. **$30**.
PARKER CUT. CO., JAPAN. **$15**.
FROST CUTLERY E-Z OPENER. **$15**.
AMERICAN BLADE, U.S.A., JAPAN. **$15**.
SWANNER CUTLERY, JAPAN. **$15**.

GERMAN MANUFACTURERS
H. BOKER & CO., TREE BRAND, GERMANY. **$50**.
J.A. HENCKELS TWINWORKS, SOLINGEN GERMANY. **$45**.
PUMA IST RICHTIG. **$30**.
CARL SCHLIEPER, SOLINGEN, GERMANY (turquoise, burgundy, black, white or green plastic). **$20**.

MODERN COLLECTOR SPECIALS
Custom openers by TOM BEERY, MEL BREWSTER, BOB RICHARDSON, MARVIN ANDERSON, RICHARD VEATCH, LEON THOMPSON, CARL SONNTAG, GEORGE ROUSSEAU, TERRY DAVIS.
Specials for: NORTH CAROLINA CUTLERY CLUB, OREGON KNIFE COLLECTORS ASSOCIATION.
REMINGTON UMC/REMINGTON CUTLERY (counterfeit). **$5**.
WINCHESTER (Blue Grass Cut. reproduction). **$20**.

Award-Winning Buck Collection

The author's Buck Knife collection has garnered major awards at the BLADE Show and other knife events.

By Larry Oden

For many years I have been interested in knives, Buck knives in particular, so I decided to begin collecting Buck production models. Never did I realize how extensive my collection and the resulting display of all the knives in it would become, but it's been a pleasure all the way.

Once my display grew to a respectable size, I began entering it in the BLADE Show, held in Atlanta, Georgia, each summer, to showcase my knives for others to enjoy. With more than 175 Buck knives and axes, including sheaths and samples of every knife, sharpening device, honing oil and stone from the Buck 1980 catalog, my display is quite complete. In fact, in 1998, 2000, 2003 and 2004, it was judged "Best of Show" of all the displays at the BLADE Show. In 1999 and 2001 it won the show's "Judge's Award."

As an aid to other collectors who may want to show their knives at one or more shows around the country, I'll explain my display. Because there is a limit for most of us as to how many knives we can collect, I set out to concentrate on the factory knives produced by Buck Knives, Inc., between the years 1960-1980. All of my knives are displayed in chronological order with appropriate literature nearby. Framed, matted originals and copies of Buck advertising literature from the period complement the knives, which are all attractively labeled under glass.

Framed explanations of what is displayed give the viewer enough information to learn what is special about the knives. The goal is to provide much more than a plethora of knives to observe. The viewer can actually learn a great deal about the progress of one of the world's leading cutlery manufacturers. Buck employees—and especially people who once sold Buck knives—continually tell me that the display takes them down memory lane.

My display also includes a comprehensive collection of virtually every knife offered by Buck during this period. Many examples of rare, special-order knives are exhibited, too. There is an example of every standard production knife produced by Buck during this time frame.

While the Buck family has made knives for a century now, the company was incorporated in 1961. During the years since then, Buck would introduce new designs or revised models, and this is what makes collecting so exciting—waiting for that all-new knife you just have to have.

This is a section of the author's Buck display at the 1998 BLADE Show, where he won the event's "Best of Show" award for the first time.

The author (right) stands before his display at the 2000 BLADE Show with Chuck Buck, CEO of Buck Knives, Inc., and a Blade Magazine Cutlery Hall Of Famer®. The author's display won "Best of Show" at the 2000 BLADE Show, as well as the 1998, 2003 and 2004 shows.

In 1999, the author's display of Buck knives produced between 1960 and 1980 won the "Judge's Award" at the BLADE Show.

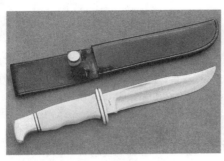

The Buck Special, model 119, was very popular when first introduced in 1961 at a suggested retail price of **$20**. A barrel-nut model, this one features a white melamine handle, aluminum fittings and a 440C stainless blade. The value today for a 119 in exceptional condition: **$400**.

This version of the Buck model 106 Hunter's Axe was made in 1966 and features a black phenolic handle. It sports a stamp on the throat, rather than the face. The sheath is rare in that it has a snap. Cost new: **$20**. The value today for such a 106 in perfect condition: **$200**.

The Buck model 106 Hunter's Axe was introduced in 1965. Featuring a full black Micarta® handle (fairly rare), it sports a 440C stainless blade. This version was made in 1971 and retailed for **$20**. Value in mint condition: **$175**.

The initial period in my collection runs from 1961-67. The six original Buck factory production knife models were: 102 Woodsman, 103 Skinner, 105 Pathfinder, 118 Personal, 119 Special, 120 General, and the model 116 Caper, introduced in 1962.

The earliest Buck factory knives were of fixed-blade design, featuring "barrel-nut" construction. The tang mark was a one-line stamp of 'BUCK'. In 1962, a switch was made to flat-tang and pin construction. Standard handle materials were black phenolic resin. Elk stag, white melamine or desert ironwood were also available.

In 1964, another fixed-blade knife, the model 121 Fisherman, was introduced. This fillet knife features a fish scaler on the blade spine. The scaler was later eliminated when it was found to fatigue the blade. Model 121s with the scaler are now a very rare find.

The famous model 110 Folding Hunter debuted in 1964. At introduction, Buck management was concerned abut public acceptance of a large, folding, lock-blade knife. The concern proved to be needless as a positive, overwhelming response quickly made the 110 one of the most successful and most copied knives in history. Various

design changes were incorporated over the years as Buck improved its best seller.

In 1966, Buck started offering pocketknives made under contract with Schrade. The 301 Stockman and 303 Cadet were introduced during this period, and several of these early models are in my display. The knives were the first models in what became the 300 series.

In the early days of factory production, Buck offered elk-horn-tipped knives on a special-order basis. Very few of the knives were produced and even less are known to be in existence, making them desirable collector pieces. Byron "Mac" McKinney, who headed the Buck Custom Shop some years ago, was known to have reproduced these knives using blades salvaged from knives returned under Buck's lifetime warranty program. A complete set of the knives is also in my display. This is possibly the only complete set of these knives in existence. As a bonus, a Nemo/Frontiersman example is also in my collection. The model was never actually produced by Buck with the elk horn-tip handle.

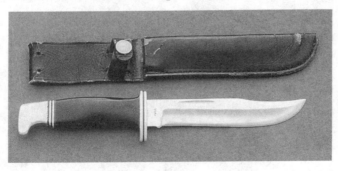

Another Buck Special, made in 1961, this version carries a black phenolic handle. It is a barrel-nut model. Note the extra spacer at the pommel. The value today for such a knife in perfect condition: **$275**.

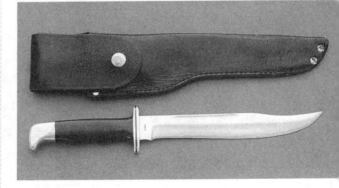

Buck's General, model 120, was introduced in 1961. This version, made between 1962-64, features a custom desert ironwood handle, very rare in production knives. When made, its list price was **$22**. Today's value: **$250**.

Nemo is the name. Buck gave this big blade. The model 122, it was introduced in 1967 at a price of **$30**. Black Micarta scales are on a full-tang 440C blade. It also features a lanyard hole and partial serrations. In like-new condition, the knife is valued at **$225** today.

In 1967-68, Buck Knives began to phase in a new tang stamp of "BUCK/U.S.A." It is believed that the change was the result of Buck's first export order to Canada. Starting with the new model 122 Nemo, the two-line stamp was soon incorporated across the board on all Buck models. The change helps collectors place knives chronologically.

Buck introduced a down-size version of the model 110 folder in 1971. This model, the 112 Ranger, was originally manufactured with black Micarta® handle inserts. The handle material was soon changed to wood and an example of each is in my collection.

In 1968, Buck switched its pocketknife contract to Camillus. The 301, 303 and 305 models were originally produced and featured tang stamps of 'BUCK/MADE IN/ U.S.A.' In about 1970, several other models were added to the series and an example of each is displayed with this tang stamp. The earliest of these knives features handle pins.

Buck also developed a heavy-duty bowie-style knife in the late '60s that ultimately was offered as two distinct models: the model 122 Nemo, which was especially suited to underwater use, and the model 124 Frontiersman,

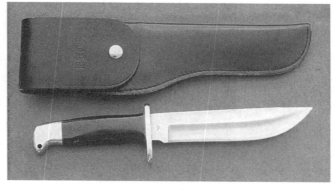

The Buck Frontiersman, model 124, measures 12 inches overall, features a 440C stainless blade, a through tang with black phenolic handle, and comes with a leather sheath. Introduced in 1967 (this one is circa 1968-69), it cost **$30** new. The exact same knife, with a plastic sheath, is the model 122 Nemo. In mint condition the knife is valued today at **$250**.

which Buck marketed to outdoors men. Several variations of the knives exist with differences in serrations, lanyard holes and handle materials. The earliest models were not serrated and were stamped 'BUCK/U.S.A.'

The advertising from this era shows pictures of the same knife and describes both models. It appears that the exact same knife was marketed as two different models, with plastic and leather sheaths provided for the 122 and 124, respectively.

The model 401 Kalinga, a top-of-the-line hunting knife with a Micarta handle and brass guard, was introduced in 1970. This knife was stamped 'BUCK/KALINGA/USA.'

Other models introduced by Buck between 1971 and 1980 include: the 402 Akonua (around 1972); 500 Slimline Series (1975-79); 319 Rancher (around 1976); 107 Scout (around 1976); 200 Empress Trio (kitchen knives, around 1976); 206 Windsor Set (steak knives, around 1977); 321 Bird knife (around 1978); and 703 Colt (around 1980).

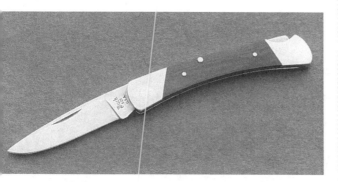

Buck is also famous for its folders. The model 501, introduced in 1975 as the Esquire (changed to Squire in 1985), featured an exposed rocker bar pin. The blade is 440C stainless and the scales are burgundy Micarta. The knife's original suggested retail price was **$18**. Today's value: **$75**.

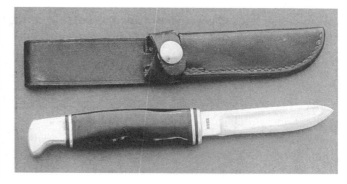

If you're a trophy hunter, you'll want to carry a Buck model 116 Caper afield. Introduced in 1962 at a price of only **$14**, it features a 440C blade and black phenolic handle. This early barrel-nut model has leather spacers and no guard. In mint condition, the knife carries a value of **$225**.

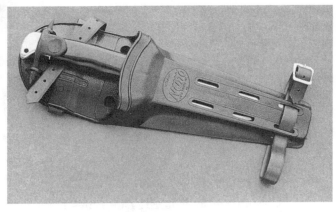
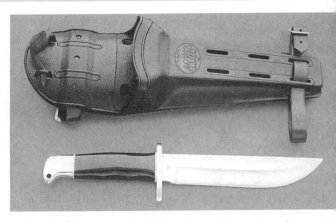

Designed for divers, the Buck Nemo was introduced in 1967 at a **$30** price, including its all-plastic sheath. The handle is black phenolic. This is the first production model to feature white Teflon® spacers (probably less than 500 made), and is rare. Today, the knife is valued at **$300**.

At times during the decade of the 1970s, Buck alternated the use of burgundy and black Micarta handle material. Whether this was due to a lack of availability or an attempt to test market consumer preference may be debated. The result is that both colors of Micarta can now be found on several of the models. My collection includes the 401 Kalinga, 402 Akonua, 124 Frontiersman and 106 Hunter's Ax, displayed with the burgundy Micarta handles, a material not readily found on these models.

Of the new model introductions from the 1970s, only the 500 and 700 series of pocketknives remain in the Buck line. It is interesting to note that the 500 series is based on the same positive-locking action found on the highly successful 110 and 112 models.

The 1980 portion of my display is introduced as follows: "Welcome to Buck Knives—1980! The Pittsburgh Steelers win Super Bowl XIV, American hostages are being held in Iran, and Ronald Reagan is elected President of the United States. Buck Knives, Inc., is moving into its new 200,000 square foot facility in El Cajon, California, and the company has geared up to ride the wave of economic growth in the '80s."

Each knife and related item I displayed at the BLADE Show is featured in the 1980 Buck Dealer Catalog. Listed below are items of interest to collectors.

Sheath Knives: All but two have a tang stamp of BUCK/MODEL #/U.S.A. The Kalinga (model 401) and Akonua (model 402) have each of their names on the tang in place of the model number.

Folding Knives: A close examination of the Folding Hunter (model 110) and Ranger (model 112) proves both have three brass handle pins and a steel rocker pin. Also, each of these models has a tang stamp of BUCK/MODEL #/U.S.A. The Ranger displayed also does not have a nail nick. This model didn't feature a nail nick until 1983.

In 1980, the 300 Series of pocketknives was made by Camillus for Buck Knives, carrying the tang stamp detailed immediately above.

The facts detailed above touch but lightly on the fine cutlery offered by Buck Knives, and the knives and products in my collection, but it gives the reader an idea of where my fascination with knives has taken me. Naturally, I am a member of the Buck Collectors Club (Member #402). Whether you concentrate on collecting Buck knives or another brand matters little. The fact is if you go about it with determination, you, too, can have an enjoyable time collecting.

To demonstrate what goes into making a knife, the author's display shows one type of construction used in making a through-tang knife. Known as "barrel-nut" construction, it is where a round nut goes into the pommel, is tightened, and the excess is ground away and polished.

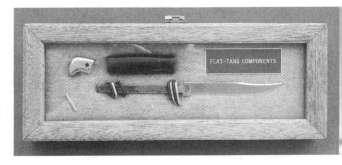

In flat-tang construction, the pommel is pinned in place as the knife goes together.

Cutlery Display Cases

Originally designed for cutlery outlets, these cases are in demand by collectors.

By Richard D. White

Cutlery showcases and display cases full of assorted knives were at one time a standard fixture in almost all hardware, general and sporting goods stores, as well as most lumber yards. Provided by the various cutlery manufacturers as an incentive for handling a particular brand of knives, the cases gave the customer something to admire while browsing through merchandise or picking up supplies for the ranch or farm. In fact, all early cutlery brochures, even as late as the 1960s, pictured various-size display cases available for the merchant to special order.

The showcases came in an almost endless variety of sizes and shapes. They ranged from very simple wooden cases with slanted, glass fronts, to large, ornate models that lighted up, swiveled, or served as large, glass countertops in general stores. Some cases were made of fine hardwoods, such as oak or cherry. They were quite decorative, with regal-looking felt lining and gilded lettering. Knives were generally wired onto flat, cloth-covered boards, then placed upright behind the display case glass. Most cases also included small, round porcelain buttons with the knife style number and price inked on it wired next to each knife.

Regardless of the design, all showcases sported the company name and slogan. The slogan was usually painted either on the sides or near the top or bottom of the case front. On some cases, decals were used to illustrate the name of the cutlery contained therein. Slogans used by the Camillus Cutlery Co. were "Every Inch the World's Finest Knife" and "Custom Made by American Craftsmen." Keen Kutter showcases can be found with the Keen Kutter logo etched into the glass fronts of the large floor models. It is the lucky collector who can find a showcase with the name of the cutlery company etched into the glass front, with the glass free of cracks.

Cutlery display cases are the perfect way to exhibit cutlery collections so that the individual pocketknives or sheath knives can be viewed much as they were in their original setting. For the collector who specializes in a particular brand, cutlery display cases provide the incentive to look for special examples or styles of knives that would complement other pieces produced by the same company.

Unfortunately, many of these cases have been stripped of their original logos and names, and have been transformed into receptacles for other items. Still others have been destined for storage in the backs of old buildings, such as small, rural hardware stores that have closed down permanently. Because of their rarity, these cases are becoming much in demand by cutlery collectors.

Cases with the greatest value are from rare cutlery companies like New York Knife, Holley, American Shear and Knife, The Dollar Knife Co., Western States, Challenge Cutlery, and others. Cases that retain their original decals, have moving/rotating tops or motorized parts, or are unusually constructed are eagerly sought by collectors.

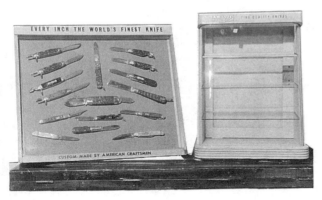

Here are two distinctive Camillus showcases. The left one is a glass, slant-front showcase made with oak sides. It contains all original Camillus knives, including the rare "elephant's toenail" in the center. The showcase on the right is an upright, curved-glass model of painted oak construction and a grooved oak base.

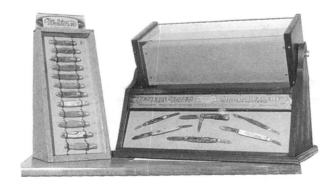

This pair of Western Cutlery showcases demonstrates the evolution of Western's cutlery displays. The small, upright showcase on the left—filled with Western knives—is made of particle board, with the familiar Western rope emblem. The remarkable showcase on the right features a revolving top with four glass sides. It could be rotated by potential customers. The bottom section contains six Western States knives, some with the original "buffalo" etching on the master blade. With decal intact, it is one of the rarest cases in existence.

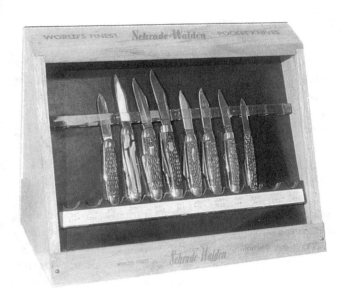

This Schrade Walden showcase contains Schrade Walden knives. It is a slant front, upright showcase with original prices still penciled onto the white board on which the knives stand.

This unusual Remington case features all-glass construction—a curved front, sides and bottom. The back, wooden spring door—held open by an Edworth tin—is painted black. The showcase is very rare, with notable red Remington lettering on both ends.

Collectors who are searching for original display cases, however, might look for reasonably priced models from the "ordinary" cutlery companies, or larger companies who have decades of cutlery production. The latter include Kutmaster, Camillus, Schrade Walden, Queen, Primble, Buck and Case. Cutlery enthusiasts are becoming much more interested in collecting various cutlery "ephemera," which include bill heads, knife-blade openers, razor hones, postcards, original boxes and, of course, original display cases.

A complete collection of showcases, from left: Camillus (with curved glass front); Schrade Walden; Case XX (upper left); Western Cutlery (bottom center); Kutmaster; Camillus (upper right); and Imperial (bottom right).

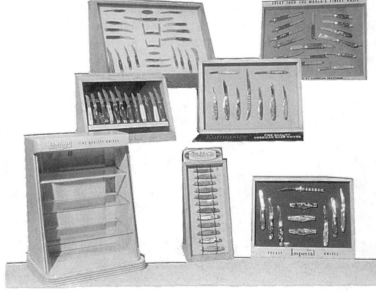

Throwing Knives

Through the years, people have been throwing knives, and others make knives for this particular passion.

By Bobby Branton

Think about it! Like most of us, you and your friends have engaged in throwing knives more than once in your lifetime. It was something that just came natural and you enjoyed it. For some of us, knife throwing became an obsession of sorts, and we really got involved in this exciting sport. Naturally, this means we also either make our own throwing knives or buy them, and in many cases, collect them.

I have samples of throwing knives in my collection that date back to the 1930s, and most were made by or for professional knife throwers. Naturally, these knives were made to perform a specific task, and that is to stick into a target. Some of the knives in my collection were made in other countries—evidence that knife throwing is not a local phenomenon. Some of the throwing knives I've seen and used were made by major cutlery manufacturers, though many are simply too small to be used by serious throwers.

The modern handcrafted throwing knife did not become popular until the early '60s, but it was back in the '40s that a young craftsman named Harry K. McEvoy, a Blade Magazine Cutlery Hall-Of-Famer© from Grand Rapids, Michigan, tried his hand at designing and making a quality throwing knife that would stand up to the rigors of throwing on a daily basis. During the next decade McEvoy produced many designs, but it was 10 years or so before he developed the Bowie Axe and his Number

One professional throwing knife, creations that proved his skills.

Harry's Tru-Balance Knife Co. would set the standard by which all handmade throwing knives would be judged. Cutlery companies such as W.R. Case & Sons, Boker, Cold Steel, United Cutlery and Buck Knives have offered throwing knives at one time or another. On the handmade side of the ledger, John Nelson Cooper, Harvey Draper W.W. Cronk and Cutlery Hall-Of-Famers William Scagel, Bo Randall and Rudy Ruana made throwing knives. Today, among others, Dan Dennehy and Cutlery Hall-Of-Famer Gil Hibben make throwing knives for enthusiasts.

Many of the custom makers either produced their own designs or made knives to customer specs. Ruana made

W.R. Case & Sons produced two different sets of throwers in the early 80s. Two knives were carried in "piggy-back" leather sheaths. Smaller set (#304) cost **$80-90**, valued at **$250** in prime condition today. The larger set (#305) cost **$80-90**, are now valued at **$250** per set in prime shape.

E. Latimer made this knife for the throwing legend, Skeeter Vaughn.

Blade Magazine Cutlery Hall-Of-Famer© Harry McEvoy of Tru-Balance Knife Co. made his Bowie Axe model during the Vietnam War era. Original price was **$19**.

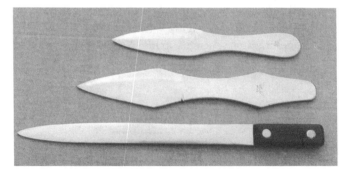

A trio of John Nelson Cooper knives are, from top: a standard model; a larger model that Cooper and friends used at the targets behind his shop; and a set made for Skeeter Vaughn that wasn't picked up and was later given to Dan Dennehy by Cooper.

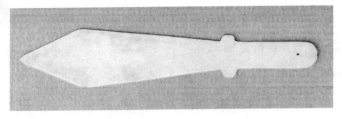

A very early thrower, this knife was made by
Sylvester Braun in the 1930s. It was given to the
author by the maker. Value? Hard to say.

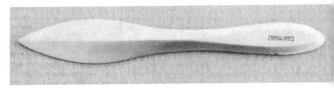

This was one of the first throwing knives
made by Blade Magazine Cutlery Hall-Of-Famer©
Bo Randall. Circa early 1950, it cost **$13.50**.
Today it's valued at **$350-400**.

a few all-metal throwing knives over the years, and was famous for throwing large bowies. One story making the rounds dealt with whether or not bowies could be used as throwing knives. More than once Rudy reportedly would spin around in his shop and throw one of his big bowies across the room, sticking it in a large beam.

Dan Dennehy's interest in throwing knives began at around age 7. He claims to have literally destroyed most of his mom's kitchen knives. Years later, Dennehy bought a small factory throwing knife from a sporting goods store, and achieving no success with it, returned to using screwdrivers and old bayonets. While in the Navy and stationed in Florida, Dan recalls hitchhiking to Orlando to see the knives made by Bo Randall.

As luck would have it, Dan was invited to a shop tour once Bo discovered his deep interest in knives. When the conversation turned to throwing knives, the youngster was invited to throw at a target in the rear of the shop. Dan hefted Bo's throwing knife for a few seconds, then threw it by the blade. As the knife stuck in the target, Dan complimented Bo on the thrower by telling him how well it handled. Bo then asked Dan why he hadn't thrown the knife by the grip. His response was that was the only way he knew how. Bo then walked to the target, retrieved the knife, paced off his distance for a handle throw, and proceeded to amaze the young sailor with his throwing skill. At this, the kid learned a new way to throw—from a pro.

In the '50s Dan began experimenting with throwing-knife designs, and was highly influenced by McEvoy. He found one of Harry's designs to his liking and devised one

that was similar. Thus began Dan's venture into making throwers.

John Nelson Cooper began making throwing knives in the mid-'60s. He also had a target set up to the rear of his shop, where he and his nephew, George Cooper, would throw every chance they got. Some of their throwing buddies included Victor Anselmo, Jody Samson, Alex Collins, and even Sammy Davis, Jr. A regular at Cooper's shop was Skeeter "Grey Otter" Vaughn, of Cherokee heritage, who spent hours at Cooper's throwing knives and tomahawks.

The popularity of knife throwing seems to go in cycles. With the rebirth of the American Knife Throwers Alliance, the sport seems to be growing again. Naturally, you can buy throwers new or used. The choice is yours. For more information, contact yours truly at 4976 Seewee Rd. Awendaw, SC 29429 (843) 928-3624 Email: profly001@aol.com; Tru-Balance Knife Co., PO Box 140555, Grand Rapids, MI 49514-0555; Dan Dennehy, PO Box 2F, Del Norte, CO 81132 (719) 657-2545; Bob Karp, PO Box 47304, Phoenix, AZ 85068 (602) 870-1234; John L. Bailey, 240 E. Bahama Rd., Winter Spring, FL 32708 (407) 696-7255 Email: bahamajohn@sprintmail.com; or Koch Throwing Knives, 1012 Thorndale Ave, Waterloo, IA 50701.

Dan Dennehy made this model in 1996
for a list price of **$45**. Today it's valued at **$100-125**.

Buck Custom Shop Knives

One-of-a-kind knives that were created by the Buck Custom Shop are the focus of the author's collection.

By John Foresman

Ifirst began to seriously collect knives in May 1988. My bride-to-be, Georgia, gave me a Buck custom bowie, model 903, as a wedding gift. I had an accumulation of knives but this knife really impressed me with its quality. From that moment on, I was really sold on Buck knives.

When I first started collecting knives, I bought any knife I could find that was stamped *Buck*. My collection grew for several years with no apparent direction. I slowly came to realize that I couldn't collect every knife that Buck ever made, and it was then that I knew I had to narrow my focus.

Looking over my collection closely, it became apparent that my favorite knives were the ones crafted in the Buck Custom Shop. Buck custom knives appealed to me for several reasons. They were hand-crafted knives but were made by a large knife manufacturer. To my knowledge,

Buck Knives is the only knife company that operated a custom shop in its own plant, where factory-profiled blades were the basis of a custom knife. These custom knives feature custom handles, engraving and other art work. In my opinion, these factors make Buck custom knives more collectible than most factory knives.

The Buck Custom Shop opened in January 1981, having started life as the repair shop. Byron "Mac" McKinney was supervising the repair shop when Blade Magazine Cutlery Hall-Of-Famer© Chuck Buck approached him about setting up a new custom shop. Thus it was an area constructed in the plant and outfitted with mandrels, belt sanders and other tools more often found in one-man handmade knife shops. The shop was stocked with mastodon ivory, Sambar stag, sun-bleached elk horn, mother-of-pearl, and many different exotic hardwoods for handle materials.

When the shop first opened, a couple of the plant's best craftsmen were chosen to help Mac McKinney. Eventually, there would be a total of seven craftsmen making custom Buck knives. Mac ran the shop until he retired, at which time CJ Buck took over the helm. CJ is now president of Buck Knives.

During the 12 years of the Buck Custom Shop's existence, the shop's craftsmen created approximately 8,000 custom Buck knives. The knives fall into three distinct categories:

Category 1) Standard production Buck knives with customized handles and mirror-polished blades. The knives retained their original model numbers;

Category 2) A separate line of handmade Buck custom knives. The knives have model numbers in the 900s; and;

Category 3) True custom knives made to the customer's exact specifications.

The Buck Custom Shop created only four of these dirks in July 1981. They are custom reproductions based on an original design by Blade Magazine Cutlery Hall-Of-Famer® Al Buck in the early '50s for a U.S. serviceman. The handle is lignum vitae. Today's value: **$1,050**.

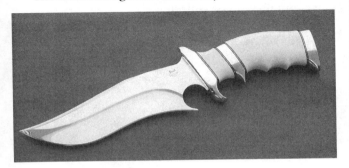

Buck's custom sub-hilt bowie (model 904) measures 13 inches overall and sports brass fittings. It was available in a variety of handle materials. This model features a rare mastodon-ivory grip. Today's value: **$2,200**.

This custom model is the 937, a combination sub-hilt fighter and hunter. It features a random-pattern damascus blade and stainless fittings, and its mother-of-pearl handle sets it apart from the ordinary. Like many of the author's custom Bucks, this one resides in a fine wooden case. Today's value: **$1,425**.

Popular with outdoors men, the Buck model 102 looks totally different in custom dress. This one-of-a-kind version has a damascus blade and sun-bleached elk-horn handle. Today's value: **$600**.

The first 100-200 knives crafted in the Buck Custom Shop were tang stamped BUCK/U.S.A. However, after several months, all custom knives, with the exception of slip-joint pocketknives with customized handles, had a special tang stamp: BUCK/CUSTOM/U.S.A.

Knives from categories 2 and 3 also were serialized, with the exception of prototypes. The knives were serialized in order to keep records of each one. Data such as handle and bolster materials, along with the finish date, were recorded. Three-digit serial numbers represent employee service awards. Four-digit numbers indicate regular custom knives. Many of the custom knives have the initials of the craftsman who made them stamped on the choil.

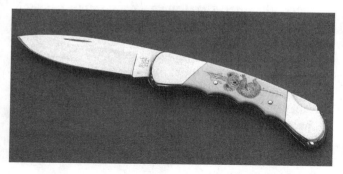

One of the few folders to make its way through the Buck Custom Shop, this model 500FG boasts mastodon ivory scales and scrimshaw. Today's value: **$525**.

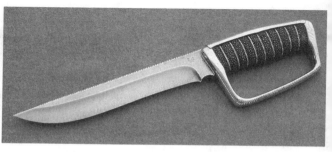

Only one of 10 made, the "Branded Bowie" (model 915) came from Buck's Custom Shop. It includes a stainless damascus blade, mokume gane guard, ray-skin handle wrapped with twisted stainless wire, and a blade spine fileworked in a rope pattern. Retail price in 1993 was **$6,480**. Today's value: **$6,480**.

For approximately the first six months of operation, the knives crafted in the custom shop had satin-finished blades. Later, the blades were mirror polished.

Many Buck custom knives are documented with letters of authenticity. The letters state the type of blade steel, Rockwell hardness, and bolster and handle materials. The letters are signed by Chuck Buck, then president of Buck Knives. Wooden presentation cases were optional with any knife.

The Buck Custom Shop was opened in the hopes that it would turn a nice profit. However, profits were low, and most of the time Buck broke even on the knives. However, the knives were used as a marketing tool. They created a top-level line that helped to pull the rest of the line up with it. The shop was closed in 1993. Buck still has one custom knifemaker, though. His name is Wilde Bill Cody. He makes employee service award knives, prototypes, special projects and knife-display-award knives.

Even though the shop is now closed, there are still so many different variations of Buck custom knives waiting to be found. I have collected over 210 of them, and my collection is nowhere near complete. With all the different handle materials that were used, there are still plenty of knives out there to be collected.

Some Specialists in Collectible Knives

We are acquainted with most but not all of these specialists in collectible knives. They range from hobbyist knife traders to major wholesale and retail merchants. Think about time zones before telephoning. "SASE" means *self-addressed stamped envelope*.

"Guild" means The Knifemakers' Guild annual show of handmade knives made by member makers. "BLADE" means the annual *BLADE* Show, the world's largest all-knife show. "BLADE Show West" is the Western version of the BLADE Show, though much smaller. NKCA shows are put on by the National Knife Collectors Association.

For exact show dates and locations, consult the "Show Calendar" in *BLADE*® (c/o K-P Publications, 700 E. State St., Iola, WI 54990 [715] 445-4612 Email: blademagazine@krause.com), sold on newsstands and in bookstores, or its website, www.blademag.com. In addition, *Knife World* (P.O. Box 3395, Knoxville TN 37927), *Knives Illustrated* (265 S. Anita Dr., Ste. 120, Orange, CA 92868-3310 (714) 939-9991, Ext. 306. website: www. Knivesillustrated.com), and www.knifeshows.com also have knife show calendars.

Federal Switchblade Laws

Title 15 U.S.C.A. 1241(b) [United States Code Annotated], enacted in 1958 as Public Law 85-623, bans the manufacture, transportation, or distribution in interstate commerce of switchblade knives. The only exception is for manufacturers who deal directly with government contracting agencies. Closely related is **Title 18 U.S.C. 1716,** "Injurious Articles as Nonmailable." This law bars the mailing of switchblade knives, even within a state. Section (h) of this title adds, "Any advertising, promotional, or sales matter which solicits or induces the mailing of anything declared nonmailable by this section is likewise nonmailable ..." These are federal laws that apply in all states, regardless of state or local laws. State and local laws concerning switchblades, or automatics, vary.

United States

A&J Enterprises and Hawthorn Galleries (Stephen D'Lack), P.O. Box 313, Turners, MO 65765 (417) 866-6660. Fax (417) 866-6693. Email hg_inc@hotmail. com. Since 1979. Handmade knives. Mail order. SASE for list. Sponsors East Coast Custom Knife Show and New York Custom Knife Show (New York, NY). Displays at BLADE, Guild, Paris, Munich, Swiss, East Coast (NYC), Solvang and other knife shows.

A.G. Russell (A.G. and Goldie Russell), 1920 N. 26th St., Lowell, AR 72745-8489 (800) 255-9034 fax (479) 631-0130.

Website: www.agrussell.com. Since 1964. Handmade and antique knives. Mainly consignments. 25-35% commission on consignments. Also, color catalog of select factory knives, Randalls, premium factory brands, specials. Mr. Russell is a Blade Magazine Cutlery Hall Of Famer© and honorary president of The Knifemakers' Guild. He is also president of the "Knife Collectors Club," which offers limited production knives. Displays at BLADE, East Coast Custom (NYC), New York Custom and other knife shows.

Bill Adams, PO Box 666, Roberta, GA 31078 (478) 836-4195. Mr. Adams is a Blade Magazine Cutlery Hall Of Famer© and an authority on antique knives, especially bowies and nineteenth-century Sheffield pieces.

American Bladesmith Society (Jan DuBois), PO Box 1481, Cypress, TX 77410-1481 (281) 225-9159 fax (281) 225-9163 Email: spqjan1@aol.com. Largest organization of knifemakers; dedicated to the forged blade. Annual meeting held in conjunction with BLADE Show, annual show in Reno.

American Knife & Tool Institute (Jan Billeb), 22 Vista View Ln., Cody, WY 82414 (319) 752-8770. An organization that works for the knife rights of those in the knife industry.

American Military Edged Weaponry Museum (Larry Thomas), 3562 Old Philadelphia Pike, Intercourse, PA 17534

(717) 768-7185 Email: athomas815@aol. com. Antique knives. American military edged weapons museum. Buy and sell U.S. military edged weapons.

Arizona Custom Knives (Julie Hyman), 5099 Medoras Ave., St. Augustine, FL 32082 (904) 460-9579 fax (904) 273-0273. Web site www.arizonacustomknives.com.. Since 1992. Handmade knives, mostly current makers; premium factory brands. Mail order. Catalog (6/year; sample copy $3). Displays at BLADE, Guild and other knife shows.

Atlanta Cutlery Corp. (Pradeep Windlass), 2147 Gees Mill Rd., PO Box 839, Conyers GA 30013. (770) 922-7500 fax (770) 918-2026. Since 1971. Military knives, foreign and exotic knives, factory close-outs from Europe and Asia, knife books, supplies. Mail order catalog. Also Museum Replicas: functional replicas of antique edged weapons. Displays at larger knife shows in the Southeast.

Atlantic Bladesmiths, 50 Mill Rd., Apt. 221, Littleton, MA 01460 (978) 952-6448 Email: j.galt1@verizon.net. Purveyors since 1977. Buys, sells, trades carefully selected, handcrafted, bench-made and factory knives.

The Automatic Knife Resource Guide and Newsletter, 2269 Chestnut St., #212-B, San Francisco, CA 94123 (415) 664-2105. Web site: thenewsletter.com. Automatic knife newsletter.

L. Bainbridge & Co., Inc., (Lyle & Donna Bainbridge), 3480 Salish Trail, Stevensville MT 59870.. Since 1982. Old factory pocket and sheath knives; some new factory brands; handmade knives by Montana makers. Displays at BLADE, Las Vegas, Southern California Blades, Oregon, Montana Knifemakers and other knife shows.

Roger Baker, PO Box 620417, Woodside CA 94062. Since 1966. Antique bowie knives, dirks, and folding dirks. Send want list. Displays at Oregon Knife Show.

Peter Baribault, 58 Stuyvesant Ave., East Haven CT 06512. Since 1976. Resale dealer of factory and handmade knives. Mail order, send want list. Displays at Northeast knife shows, and at eastern New York and most Connecticut gun shows.

Barrett-Smythe Limited (Donald Mendelson), 954 Lexington Ave. #GF291, New York, NY 10021 phone/fax (212) 249-5500 Fine engraved handmade folders by top makers. Hand engraved silver and gold Zippo lighters. Photos on request.

Beck's Cutlery Specialties (Ronnie & Patsy Beck), SHP CENTER #109 MacGregor Village, 107 Edinburgh South Dr., Cary, NC 27511 (919) 460-0203 fax (919) 460-7772 Website: www.beckscutlery.com. Email: beckscutlery@mindspring.com. Since 1985. Premium factory brands; handmade knives, Randalls, agents for Robert and Peter Bauchop of South Africa, Allen Blade of Washington. Monthly list. Displays at Oregon knife show, Soldier of Fortune and other knife shows.

Beckwith's Blades, Web site: www. beckwithsblades.com. Factory knives.

Bestblade, (866) 312-4077. Web site: www.bestblade.com. Factory knives.

Best Knives, (800) 956-5696. Web site: www.bestknives.com. Factory knives.

Barry and Vicky Billings, (903) 965-4490. Web site: www.BVBRanchKnives. com. Buy and sell new and antique knives.

Jim Blackburn, 3008 Lake Park Cir., Birmingham AL 35242. Antique bowie knives. Displays at Birmingham AL, Lake Ozark MO, and Atlanta GA antique shows.

BLADE® (Joe Kertzman), 700 E. State St., Iola, WI 54990 (715) 445-4612 fax (714) 445-4087. Email: blademagazine@krause. com. Web site: www.blademag.com. World's No. 1 Knife Publication.

BladeArt.com (Larry Brahms), 14216 SW 136 St., Maimi, FL 33186 (305) 255-9176 Website: www.bladeart.com. Handmade knives, swords and daggers.

Bladeforums.com (Kevin Sparks), 340 Production Ct., Louisville, KY 40299 (502) 671-5570 Website: www.bladeforums.com. Internet discussion group.

BladeGallery.com (Daniel O'Malley), 107 Central Way, Kirkland, WA 98033 (425) 889-5980 Website: www. bladegallery.com. Online knife community, handmade knives and swords.

Blanchard's Cutlery (Pam Blanchard), POB 709, Pigeon Forge, TN 37868 (865) 908-7466 Website: www. blanchardscutlery.com. Since 1993. Knifemaking and engraving on premises, handmade knives, Randalls, limited edition sets, complete factory knife lines. Retail store. Displays at Guild, Las Vegas Custom and other knife shows.

Blue Ridge Knives (Tom Clark), 166 Adwolfe Rd., Marion, VA 24354-6664 (276) 783-6143 fax (276) 783-9298 Website: www.blueridgeknives.com. Since 1979. Wholesale of most brands (catalog to the trade); buys complete collections: old, new, and custom (occasional lists). Displays at BLADE, Oregon, Cincinnati, Springfield MO, Dalton, Pigeon Forge TN, New York Custom, Northeast Cutlery and other knife shows.

Dick Botbyl, 1800 Claflin Rd. #120, Manhattan KS 66502. Since 1993. Older Gerber folding knives. List quarterly, $2.

David Boye Knives Gallery (Francine Martin, David Larstein), 111-B Marine View Ave., Davenport CA 95017. Since 1972. Art gallery representing David Boye Dendritic knives, other makers, artists. Catalogs. Displays at Oregon, Southern California Blades, Bay Area, San Jose Custom, BLADE Show West and other knife shows.

Harrell Braddock Jr., 1412 Los Colinos, Graham TX 76046. Since 1985. Old and new Case knives, handmade knives. Occasional free list. Sponsors Displays at

Wichita Falls, Abilene, Fort Worth gun and knife shows.

Don Breier, 14044 Ventura Blvd. Suite 100, Sherman Oaks CA 91423. Since 1978. Handmade folding knives. Mail list $1 (revised quarterly). Displays at most California knife shows.

Buck Collectors Club (John Foresman), 110 New Kent Dr., Goode, VA 24556. Email: buckcustom@aol.com.

Carmel Cutlery (Scott Autrey), Dolores & Sixth, PO Box 1346, Carmel CA 93921. Handmade art knives, premium factory brands, reproduction swords. Retail store.

Case Collectors Club, (800) 523-6350. Web site: www.wrcase.com.

Ted Cheldin, PO Box 6694, Woodland Hills CA 91365-6694. Antique pocket, hunting, military knives; buys collections. Mail order (1-2 lists/year). Displays at Southern California Blades knife show.

Deepak Chopra Cutlery & Accessories, Inc., (925) 454-0595 fax (925) 454-0289 (pst). Email: chopra@pacbell.net. Web site: deepakcutlery.com. Wholesaler with a retail knife store location.

Chow's Cutlery (Louis Chow), PO Box 16252, San Francisco, CA 94116 (415) 309-4973 subhilt6@aol.com. Classic and other handmade knives.

Classic Cutlery (Dave Lewis), 576 Francestown Rd., #805, Door 30, Bennington, NH 03442 Website: www. classiccutlery.com. Since 1983. Handmade and factory knives, including many exclusive designs. Catalog. Displays at 49 shows, including Northeast Cutlery, East Coast Custom (NYC), Chicago knife shows.

Tom Clinton/Sharp Stuff, 1475 E Riverside, Belvidere, IL 61008 (815) 885-3396 fax (815) 885-3202. Email: tlclinton@aol.com. Randall knife dealer.

Cohan, Pete – Antique Pocket Cutlery – Also appraisals and evaluations. 118 Newhaven Rd., Oak Ridge, TN 37830 (865) 482-2177 cell (865) 806 3775.

Columbus Cutlery, 358 Columbus Avenue, San Francisco CA 94133. Factory knives, wide range of imported and domestic brands. Retail store only. No list or catalog.

Eiler R. Cook, Historic Edged Weaponry, 1021 Saddlebrook Dr., Hendersonville, NC 28739 (828) 692-0323. E-mail: histwpn@bellsouth.net. Since 1985. High-quality modern reproductions of historical knives and swords; Scandinavian/Lapland/Viking knives and weaponry; antique knives from around the world (brochures). Mail order. Displays at BLADE Show, Asheville, NC, Land-of-Sky gun and knife show.

Larry Cook, PO Box 5777, Aloha OR 97006. Since 1975. Old pocketknives and fixed blades. Mail order (send want list). Displays at most West Coast knife shows.

Corrado Cutlery/Otto Pomper, 26 N. Clark St., Chicago IL 60602. Email info@otto-corrado.com. Branch at Old Orchard Center, Skokie IL (708) 329-9770. Since 1905. Retail stores. Premium factory brands, handmade (Randall, Granton, Wright, Ellefson), antique. Catalog, website.

Country Knives (N. Brian & Catherine R. Huegel), 4134 Old Philadelphia Pike/ mail to: PO Box 70, Intercourse PA 17534. Since 1976. Retail store. 275+ brands of factory knives, some handmade.

Custom Knife Directory (Jonathon Loose), PO Box 674, Moretown, VT 05660 (802) 496-3687 www. customknifedirectory.com. Internet-based sales of folding knives, autos, fixed blades, swords and daggers, art and exotic knives, hunting knives and bowies.

Custom Knife Gallery of Colorado (Bob Glassman), 11898 W. Cooper Dr., Littleton, CO 80127 (303) 904-4471 www. customknifegallery.com. Handmade knives.

Cutlery Shoppe (Jeff Loffer), 3956 E. Vantage Point Ln., Meridian, ID 83642 (208) 884-5250 www.cutleryshoppe.com. High-grade factory knives, special designs, limited editions. Retail store and museum. Mail order. Catalog.

Lawrence Danielkiewicz, c/o Great Lakes Cutlery, 33744 Lighthouse Pt., Lake Baltimore, MI 48047 (248) 258-7378. Handmade and other knives.

J.W. Denton, PO Box 429, Hiawassee GA 30546-0429 (706) 896-2292 fax (706) 896-1212. Email: jwdenton@alltel.com. Since 1980. Buyer and seller of Loveless knives. Displays at BLADE, New York Custom, East Coast Custom (NYC) and Guild, knife shows.

Discount Custom Knife Co. (James Slyman), 411 S. Gay St., Knoxville, TN 37902 (423) 521-7416. Antique and handmade knives.

Michael Donato, 261 Neptune Dr., Manahawkin, NJ 08050. Handmade knives.

Ted Dzialo, 20090 NW Nestucca Dr., Portland OR 97229-2822. Since 1974. Antique and handmade knives. Displays at Oregon and Southern California Blades knife shows, and at West Coast gun shows. No list. Call with wants.

The Edge of the World (Albert & Cyrilla Ernst), 30 Jack London Square, Oakland CA 94607. Since 1976. Retail store. Premium factory brands, knives and swords.

EuroChasse (Hani Hafez), 398 Greenwich Ave., Greenwich CT 06830. Since 1989. Handmade knives by Horn, Lake, Loveless, Randall, Schmidt, Pease, Terzuola. European hunting clothes. Displays at Guild, Paris, and East Coast Custom (NYC) knife shows.

Exquisite Knives (Dave Ellis), 380 S. Melrose Dr., Ste. 407, Vista, CA 92081 (760) 643-4032 www.exquisiteknives. com. Loveless and Moran knives.

Fazalare International Enterprises (Roy Fazalare), PO Box 663, Somis, CA 93066 ourfaz@aol.com. Limited-edition pocketknives, specializing in high-grade and collectible factory cutlery and handmade multi-blade folders by Bose, Davis, Shadley and Rogers.

Fisher Knives (Theo Fisher), 8115 Modoc Ln., Montague CA 96064. Since 1982. Old and new knives, including military. Displays at Oregon, Bay Area, Southern California Blades, and Sacramento knife shows.

Tony Foster/Case Collectibles, 302 Jamesbury Rd. Wando, SC 29492-7813 (843) 971-4777 (after 4 p.m. ET) mcdknif@bellsouth.net. Old and new Case knives. Detailed Case price guide updated monthly. Displays at BLADE, Oregon, Southern California Blades, and all major NKCA knife shows.

Fourth Avenue Knives & Swords (Robert Charles Golden), 203 4th Ave. #216, Olympia WA 98501. Since 1988. Retail Store. Old and new, factory and handmade, exotic. Displays at Oregon knife show.

George & Son Cutlery (Carl L. George), 424 SW Washington, Portland Or 97204. Since 1870. New premium factory brands. Retail store.

Global Outlet (Peter Porada), 3324 N. Harlan Ave., Chicago, IL 60634 (773) 237-2047 www.globaloutlet.com. Swords, sabers and exotic knives.

Gobles Knife Exchange (Tom Goble), 2148 New London Pl., Snellville GA 30278. Since 1982. Resale dealer of custom knives by Guild members. Displays at BLADE, Guild, and Las Vegas knife shows, Atlanta area gun shows.

Grand Prairie Knives, 2230 Liebler Rd., Troy, IL 62294 (866) 667-5965. Web site: www.gpknives.com. Factory knives.

Great Lakes Custom Knives (Bud Angelo), (574) 293-8936 or (574) 596-9906. Email: bud@customknives.info. Web site: www.customknives.info. Handmade and art knives.

The Gun Runner (Robert H. Disbrow), 1426 South 167th St., Omaha NE 68130. Since 1985. Old, new, discontinued folders, fixed, and military. Mail order. Catalog. Displays at gun and knife shows in eastern Nebraska, western Iowa.

Happy Jack Knives (Jack Bromley), 15623 East Scorpion Drive, Fountain Hills AZ 85268-1555. [Summer: PO Box 1202, Pine AZ 85544.] Since 1978. Handmade, new, and antique knives. Mail order, free list. Displays at Arizona, Oregon, Southern California Blades, Texas, and Solvang knife shows.

Ray F. Harris, 1040 Ashwood Place, Knoxville TN 37917-4415. Since 1985. Knife club knives. Free list.

Heritage Antique Knives (Blade Magazine Cutlery Hall-Of-Famer© J. Bruce Voyles), Box 22171, Chattanooga

TN 37422. (423) 894-8319. Email: bruce@jbrucevoyles.com. Since 1972. Handmade, old pocketknives and discontinued commemorative knives. List free. Inquire about auction service (www.knifeauctions.net). Displays at BLADE, Guild, Texas, Spirit of Steel, all NKCA, Bowie Knife Association knife shows.

Hickory Hill Cutlery (Lynn Watkins), 308 Tom Franklin, Jefferson City, TN 37760 (865) 475-4447. Both new and old knives, manufacturing cutlery rolls.

Bill Horn, (931) 537-9662. Email: knifeboy@charter.net. Web site: www.cumberlandknifeworks.com. Case.

House of Blades (B.C. Adams), 6451 N.W. Loop 820, Ft. Worth, TX 76135 (817) 237-7721 fax (817) 237-7041. Since 1964. Retail store. Antique, handmade and factory knives.

House of Cutlery (Bob & Germaine Miller), 8604 On The Mall, Buena Park CA 90620. Since 1980. Handmade knives, Randalls, limited-edition sets, complete factory knife lines. Retail store. Displays at Southern California Blades show.

Hunter Services (Fred Hunter), PO Box 14241, Parkville MO 64152. Since 1991. Old American and English pocketknives, some fixed and handmade. Mail order, catalog. Displays at Springfield MO NKCA knife show, Tulsa and Kansas City gun and knife shows.

Investment Cutlery (Arthur H. Marois), PO Box 544, Auburn MA 01501. Since 1987. Puma knives, current and discontinued. List.

J.T.'s Knife Shop, 264 E. Main St., Port Jervis, NY 12771 (845) 856-6904. Web site: www.jtknives.com. Factory and handmade knives.

J. Bruce Voyles Auctioneers, (Blade Magazine Cutlery Hall-Of-Famer© J. Bruce Voyles), PO Box 22007, Chattanooga, TN 37422 (423) 894-8319 bruce@jbrucevoyles.com. Knife auctions.

Johnson Reference Books (LTC Thomas M. Johnson USA Ret), 312 Butler Rd. #403, Fredericksburg VA 22405. World War I and II German edged weapons. Author of standard reference books. Sales list;

book brochure. Displays at MAX Militaria Antiques Xtravaganza Show.

Doug Kenefick, 29 Leander St., Danielson CT 06239. (860) 774-8929. Since 1977. Randall knives, Ruana knives. Retail store, by appointment. Call for current inventory.

Knife City (Karl and Ofelia Lange), I-40, Exit 294, Sun Valley, AZ 86029 (928) 524-1426 Email: knifecity@frontiernet.net. Knife store carrying all knives.

Knife 4 Auction, www.knife4auction.com. Buys and sells collectible, handmade and other knvies.

Knife Mart, 596 W. 300 S., Heyburn, ID 83336 (800) 331-3213 (orders). Web site: www.knifemart.com. Autos and other factory knives.

Knife World, (Blade Magazine Cutlery Hall-Of-Famer© Houston Price and Mark Zalesky), P.O. Box 3395, Knoxville TN 37927 (865) 397-1955 fax (865) 397-1969. Email: knifepub@knifeworld.com. Web site: www.knifeworld.com.. Knife magazine.

KnifeCenter of the Internet, POB 600, College Park, MD 20740 (800) 338-6799. Web site: www.knifecenter.com. Knives, rescue knives, razors, scissors and much, much more.

Knifeforums.com/KnifeForums.com Magazine (James Nowka), 2387 S. Advance Rd., East Jordan, MI 49727 (231) 536-7913. Web site: www.knifeforums.com. Internet knife discussion group.

The Knifemakers' Guild (Eugene Shadley), 26315 Norway Dr., Bovey, MN 55709-9405 (218) 245-1639 (phone/fax). Email: bses@uslink.net. Oldest organization of knifemakers, annual show in Orlando.

Knifemasters Custom Knives, PO Box 208, Westport, CT 06881 (203) 226-5211 fax (203) 226-5312. Buyer and seller of handmade and other knives. Appraisals.

Knives Illustrated (Viga Hall), 265 S. Anita Dr., Ste. 120, Orange, CA 92868-3310 (714) 939-9991, Ext. 306. Web site: www.Knivesillustrated.com. Knife publication.

Knives Plus (800) 687-6202. Web site: www.knivesplus.com. Factory knives.

Kris Cutlery (Cecil B. Quirino), PO Box 133, Pinole CA 94564. Medieval swords and daggers; Chinese, Japanese, Indonesian, Philippine swords. Mail order. Displays at Great Western gun show.

LDC Custom Knives (Bob Neal), PO Box 20923, Atlanta, GA 30320 (770) 914-7794 fax (770) 914-7796. Email: bob@bobnealcustomknives.com. Exclusive limited-edition handmade knives, sets and singles.

George Leray, PO Box 3002 Church Street Station, New York NY 10008-3002. Since 1989. Antique pocket and hunting knives. Mail order. List. Displays at Northeast Cutlery, eastern Pennsylvania, and Shenandoah VA knife shows.

Bernard Levine, PO Box 2404, Eugene, OR 97402 (541) 484-0294. Web site: www.knife-expert.com. Mr. Levine is a Blade Magazine Cutlery Hall Of Famer©, former editor of the book you hold in your hands and noted knife author. "Knife expertise."

Gary Levine Fine Knives (Gary Levine), PO Box 382, Chappaqua, NY 10514 (914) 238-5748. Web site: www.levineknives.com. Email: gary @levineknives.com. Handmade knife dealer.

Marc & Caroline Levine, PO Box 415, Dracut MA 01826. Antique pocket and hunting knives, some bowie and custom. Mail order. Catalog. Displays at Louisville, Springfield MO, and Dearborn NKCA shows, Northeast Cutlery knife shows.

Ray Lew, PO Box 213, Yorba Linda CA 92885. Since 1989. Handmade folders by Appleton, Boyd, Fox, Lake, Walker, Wright. List. Displays at BLADE, Guild, BLADE Show West, East Coast Custom (NYC), San Jose Custom, Bay Area, and Southern California Blades shows.

Rick London Collectibles (Rick London), 5676 Yorkshire Ct., Lake Oswego, OR 97035 (503) 684-6494. Since 1986. Collector-grade handcrafdted folding knives. Consignments. List on request. Displays at BLADE, Guild, Solvang, and Bay Area knife shows.

Dwight E. Long, Rt. 1 Box 30-B-3, Grandview TX 76050. Since 1992. Buy/sell/trade all types. List. Displays at Dallas, TX and Tulsa, OK knife and gun shows.

Hugh Lowe, 4937 Hine Dr., Shadyside, MD 20764 (410) 867-4418. Knife purveyor.

Dr. Jim Lucie, 4191 E. Fruitport Road, Fruitport, MI 49415; (231) 865-6390 fax (231) 865-3170. Email: scagel@netonecom. net. Dr. Lucie not only makes authentic replicas of knives by the late master and Blade Magazine Cutlery Hall-Of-Famer©, William Scagel, but he deals in Scagel knives and is an authority in their design and value.

Charlie Mattox, PO Box 1565, Gallatin, TN 37066 (877) 520-9192 cell (615) 419-5669. Web site: www.mattoxknife.com. Case pocketknives, especially 10 dot and older.

McGrady Ent., Inc. (Bruce McGrady), 5060 Mark David, Swartz Creek, MI 48473 (810) 635-4282. Email: MEI@TIR.COM. High-end factory retail/purveyor.

Mal Mele, Box 1112, Covington, LA 70434 (985) 892-6711. Email: mal@airmail. com. Handmade knives, including D.E. Henry.

Midwest Gun Exchange (Brad Foster), 2516 Lincolnway West, Mishawaka, IN 46544 (574) 257-0020 fax (574) 257-0021. Web site: www.midwestgunexchange. com. Microtech knives, handmades, limited editions and exclusives.

Perry Miller, c/o Spaceport Supply, 2189 N US 2, Titusville, FL 32796 (321) 383-2355. Knife dealer/purveyor.

Ernie Modlin, Manhattan Beach CA. (310)379-1245. Since 1970. Antique knives, especially military. Displays at Oregon and Southern California Blades knife shows.

Moore Cutlery, Lockport, IL (708) 301-4201. Email: gary@knives.cx. Web site: www.knives.cx. Handmade knives; buys collections.

N. Flayderman & Co., Inc. (Norm Flayderman), PO Box 2397, Ft. Lauderdale, FL 33303 (954) 761-8855. Web site: www. flayderman.com. Web site catalog of many antique knives, including bowies, swords and dirks, antique weapons and militaria. Author of the book, *The Bowie Knife*.

Nagel's Gunshop & Knife Gallery (Robin Nagel, Robert Nagel), 6201 San Pedro, San Antonio TX 78216. Since 1950s. Retail store. Premium factory brands, custom, Randalls.

Nashoba Valley Knife Works (Phil & Elaine Fallon), 19 South Lenox St., Worcester MA 01602-2501. (508) 799-0724. Since 1984. Handmade knives, Randalls, Ruanas, knives by Guild members. List. Displays at Guild show and at most knife shows in the Northeast.

National Knife Collectors Association (Lisa Broyles-Sebenick), PO Box 21070, Chattanooga, TN 37424 (423) 892-5007. National association of antique pocketknife collectors, sponsors several shows nationwide in the USA.

National Knife Distributors, 125 Depot St., Forest City, NC 28043 fax (828) 245-5121. Web site: www.nkdi.com. Email: nkdi@nkdi.com.

New Graham Knives, 566 Virginia Ave., Bluefield, VA 24605 (866) 333-4445. Web site: www.newgraham.com. A wide range of factory knvies.

N.I.C.A., 2636 Bogue Dr., Glendale, CA 91208-2206. Web site: www.nicacutlery. org (site lists store locations). National Independent Cutlery Assocation, an association of retail knife stores, most of which are in the Western USA. Exclusive factory knives.

Nordic Knives (David & Grace Harvey), 1634-C Copenhagen Drive, Solvang CA 93463. (805) 688-3612. Fax (805) 688-1635. Web site: www.nordicknives. com. Since 1975. Retail store. Handmade knives, Randalls. Sponsors Solvang Custom knife show. Displays at Solvang, BLADE, East Coast Custom (NYC) knife shows. Handmade and Randall list.

Norris & Son (formerly Pumphreys), (Knowles), 3613 Park Ridge Dr., Grand Prairie, TX 75052 (972) 264-3307. Web site: www.norrisandsonknives.com. Cutlery distributors.

Northwest Knives & Collectibles (Bill Claussen), 355 Court St. NE, Salem, OR 97301 (503) 362-9045 fax (503) 364-1331. Web site: www.nwknives.com. Retail knife store. Co-author of the book, *Sheffield Exhibition Knives*. Antique pocket, hunting, bowie, military, exotic knives; older handmade knives. Mail order, consignments. Catalog. Displays at BLADE, Oregon, Northeast Cutlery, Southern California Blades, Texas knife shows; Springfield MO, Lakeland FL NKCA knife shows; Tulsa, and Las Vegas Antique gun and knife shows.

Northwest Safari (Erik Remmen), PO Box 7172, Olympia WA 98507. Exclusive handmade and high-grade factory knives. Sponsors Cutlery Rendezvous, Displays at Oregon knife show.

Larry Oden Co., 1112 Veach's Ct., Peru, IN 46970 (765) 472-2323. Buck custom and Yellowhorse.

John Ogden-Bruton, 130 West 26 St., New York NY 10001. Since 1991. Antique pocketknives. Mail order. List.

1 Stop Knife Shop (Kevin Sparks), 340 Production Ct., Louisville, KY 40299 (866) BUY-1SKS or (502) 671-5510 fax (502) 671-5560. Email: info@onestopknifeshop. com. Web site: onestopknifeshop.com. Knives, sharpening supplies, tactical, automatic knives.

Oso Grande Knife & Tool, (760) 742-0385 or (888) 676-6050 (orders). Web site: www.osograndeknives.com. Factory knives.

Ozark Cutlery Supply (Mike Hoag), 5230 Hearnes Blvd., Joplin, MO 64804 (417) 782-4998 (800) 722-4998 fax (417) 782-8100. Email: ozrkcut@joplin.com. Web site: myknifesource.com. A wide range of contemporary factory brand knives.

Ozark Knife & Gun (Daniel L. Honeycutt), 3165 So. Campbell, Springfield MO 65807 (417) 886-2888. Fax (417) 886-2635. Email: danhoneycutt@SBLglobal.net. Since 1977. Handmade knives, Randalls. Retail store. Mail order, SASE for list. Displays at BLADE Show; Kansas City, St. Louis, and Tulsa gun and knife shows.

Paragon Sports (Jerry Blank, Joe Kirdahy), 871 Broadway (at 18th St.), New York NY 10003. Since 1908. Retail store. Handmade knives.

Parkers' Knife Collector Service (Buzz Parker), 6715 Heritage Business Ct., Chattanooga, TN 37422 (423) 892-0448 fax (423) 892-9165. Knife mail-order service that specializes in collectible knives.

Paul Charles Basch, 3091 A Yorkshire Cir., Springdale, AR 72764 (479) 751-2728. Email: paulbasch@hotmail.com. Knife purveyor.

The Pen and the Sword Ltd. (Karen Patterson, Steve Berg), POB 290741, Brooklyn NY 11229-0741 (718) 382-4847. Fax (718) 376-5745. Email: info@pensword.com. Since 1974. Retail store. Handmade knives. Current list on request. Collectible pens and watches. Displays at BLADE, Guild, New York, East Coast (NYC), Chesapeake Bay, Allegheny Mountain, Northeast Cutlery, and Northeast Custom knife shows.

Piranha Knife Co., (Josh Hazen), PO Box 5934, Twin Falls, ID 83303 (208) 732-5525 fax (208) 732-5535. Email: piranha@pmt.org. Folders and autos.

Plaza Cutlery (Dan Delavan, N.I.C.A. member), South Coast Plaza, Costa Mesa CA 92626. (714) 549-3932. Fax (714) 549-1371. Since 1974. Handmade knives, limited editions, older Case knives, most extensive selection of factory knife lines on the West Coast. Retail store. Mail order. No lists. Produces exclusive biennial handmade knife show in Huntington Beach, CA. Displays at BLADE Show West knife show.

Quintessential Cutlery (Grazyna Shaw), 24 Central Ave., Ridgefield Park, NJ 07660 (201) 641-8801 fax (201) 641-0872. Email: gshaw@quintcut.com. Web site: www.quintcut.com. Since 1989. Handmade knives, antique bowies, folders, military. Displays at BLADE, Guild, East Coast Custom (NYC), New York Custom, Meadowlands, Chicago, Detroit, Oregon, Cincinnati NKCA, Northeast Cutlery, BLADE Show West and Las Vegas knife shows.

R. & C. Knives (Ray and Carol Clark), PO Box 1047, Manteca CA 95336-1047. Handmade knives from top makers. Mail order, catalog (4-5/year). Displays at BLADE, Guild, Oregon, Solvang, Sacramento, Las Vegas, New York Custom, East Coast Custom (NYC), Southern California Blades, Bay Area knife shows.

RFG Safe and Knife, 7301 32nd Ave. N, Crystal, MN 55427 (763) 533-9441 fax (763) 533-6290. Email: jesseh@attglobal. net. Huge selection of handmade and current production knives, antique knives.

Randall Knife Society (Rhett and Janie Stidham), PO Box 158, Meadows of Dan, VA 24120 (276) 952-2500 fax (276) 952-6245. Email: rstidham@gate.net. Randall knife club.

Reimold Brothers, (800) 772-7653 fax (724) 646-1776. Knife auctions.

Floyd Ritter, 6017 Sunrise Dr., Collinsville, IL 62234 (618) 345-9814. Antique bowies.

Robertson's Custom Cutlery (Les Robertson), 4960 Sussex Dr., Evans, GA 30809 (706) 650-0252. Since 1986. Handmade knives, presentation and combat. Catalog (5/year). Also LDC Knives (Les Robertson & Bob Neal). Since 1996. Exclusive handmade and limited-edition combat knives. Catalog (2/year). Displays at BLADE, Las Vegas, Southeast Custom, East Coast Custom (NYC), Chesapeake Bay, and Arkansas Custom knife shows.

Hank Rummel, 10 Paradise Ln., Warwick, NY 10990 (845) 469-9172. High-end handmades.

S4 Supply (Patrick Moyes), 194 Center St., Raynham, MA 02768 (508) 822-8269. Email: sales@S4supply.com. Web site: www.s4supply.com. Outdoor, combat, tactical, military semi-production and handmade knives.

S&S & Sons Cutlers (Lowell & Jackie Shelhart), PO Box 501, Lomita CA 90717. (310) 326-3869. Fax (310) 784-1330. Web site: www.snsandsonscutlery.com. Email: snsandsons@earthlink.net. Collector-grade knives, Queen knives, Schatt & Morgan, Robeson, Remington repros. Displays at Southern California Blades and Oregon knife shows; and Ventura gun shows.

Sanders, Steve Antique pocket cutlery + Randalls and Marble's. Route 1 Box 371A, Leavenworth, IN 47137 (812) 739-2700.

San Francisco Gun Exchange (Beth Posner, Bob Posner), 124 Second Street, San Francisco CA 94105. Since 1948. Handmade knives, Randalls; premium factory brands, large selection. Retail store.

SARCO Cutlery LLC (Gina or Jace Sargent), 449 Lane Dr., Florence AL 35630. (256) 766-8099. Fax (205) 766-7246. Web site: www.sarcoknives.com. Email: sarcoknives@earthlink.net. Since 1967. Shows and mail order. Lists (6/year) SASE. Old pocket and hunting knives, emphasis on Case, Remington, Winchester, Schrade and other older knives. Sarco Knives; retail catalog. Displays at most NKCA shows, southeastern gun shows. Jim Sargent, company founder, is author of the knife value guide, *American Premium Guide to Knives & Razors* (one of best for Case knife values).

Schrank's Smoke 'n Gun Inc. (John Schrank, Mike Schrank), 2010 Washington St., Waukegan IL 60085. Since 1976. Antique and used pocket and sheath knives. Retail store. Displays at Chicago and Wisconsin knife shows.

Jerry Schroeder, PO Box 11055, Cincinnati, OH 45211 (513) 262-8037. High-end handmades.

Joe Seale, 11711 Buckingham Rd., Austin, TX 78759 (512) 258-3925. Email: jsealecutlery@aol.com. Rare, collectible cutlery.

Seaside Pocket Knives (Tom & Gloria Baker), 461 South Franklin, Seaside OR 97138. Since 1980. Kershaw and other factory folders, some used. Retail store, also door-to-door sales.

Self Defense Supply, 783 N. Grove Rd. #111, Richardson, TX 75081 (800) 211-4186. Web site: www.selfdefensesupply. com. Automatics and other factory knives.

Sharp Stuff (Sam and Helen Smith), 3655 N. Campbell Ave., Tucson AZ 85719. Since 1977. Retail store. Factory brands, handmade knives, Randall knives, some antique knives. No catalog. Displays at Arizona and California knife shows.

Shepherd Hills Cutlery (Randy Reid), PO Box 909, Lebanon, MO 65536 (800) 727-4643. Web site: www.casexx.com. Specializes in Case knives, including Case exclusives. Holds annual Case Celebration in Lebanon, MO.

Bob Skelton, 313 Peach Valley Dr., Spartanburg SC 29303. Since 1996. Case folding knives, production and limited edition. Mail order, SASE w/2 stamps for list.

Skelton Enterprises (Jerry Skelton), 3795 Hwy. 188, Alamo TN 38001-0733. (731) 656-2443. Since 1978. Old pocketknives, popular brands, automatics. Mail order, list (3/year). Displays at Louisville KY, Cincinnati, Chattanooga NKCA knife shows; BLADE, Lexington KY, Pigeon Forge TN knife shows; area gun and knife shows.

Skylands Cutlery, PO Box 87, Ringwood, NJ 07456-0087 (973) 962-6143. Web site: www.skylandscutlery.com.

Smoky Mountain Knife Works (Clayton Suttles), PO Box 4430, Sevierville TN 37864. (800) 251-9306 (orders). Web site: www.eKnifeWorks.com. Huge selection of current factory brands. Limited editions and some antique and handmade knives. Antique cutlery and knife advertising museum in huge retail store. Mail order, free color catalogs. Was in process of making room for the National Knife Museum at press time.

Robert Soares, 999 North Lincoln St., Stockton CA 95203-2424. Since 1970. Antique cutlery and medical instruments; antique pocketknives. No lists. Displays at Pasadena and Santa Clara antiques shows, and at Oregon knife show.

Angelo Solino, c/o Collectible Kingdom, 201 Toronto Ave., Massapequa, NY 11758 (516) 798-4252. Email: castleh2@ix. netcon.com. Randall, Scagel, Ruana, Richtig, Morseth, Bone, Cooper, Loveless, Moran, Lile, etc. Also military knives and pocketknives.

Sonoma Cutlery (Harry Johnson), 730 Coddingtown Mall, Santa Rosa CA 95401. Since 1979. Retail store. Premium factory brands; handmade knives, limited editions.

Sooner State Knives, PO Box 67, Konawa, OK 74849 (580) 925-3708. Email: ssknives@swbell.net. Web site: www. soonerstateknives.com. Factory knives.

Spartan Cutlery (Cindy Koures), 4750 N. Division St., Ste. 255, Spokane, WA 99207 (509) 482-7554 fax (509) 482-0299. Web site: www.knivescentral.com. Knife dealer.

Spring River Trade Co. (Tye Nance), PO Box 28, Webb City, MO 64870 (417) 623-5400 or (800) 346-3252. Wholesale and retail of knives, Southwest and pre-1840 fur-trade-era items.

David A. Springer, PO Box 1361 Stratford CT 06497-1361. Old factory folding and fixed-blade knives. Mail order, SASE for list. Displays at Northeast Cutlery knife shows.

Steel Addiction Custom Knives (Dave Stark), (909) 731-3903. Email: davestark@s teeladdictionknives.com. Web site: www. CustomKnifeDealer.com. Handmade knives, buys collections.

Stidham's Knives (Rhett and Janie Stidham), 2554 Jeb Stuart Hwy., Meadows Of Dan, VA 24120 (276) 952-2500 fax (276) 952-6245. Web site: www.randallknifesociety.com. Email: rstidham@gate.net. Purveyor of fine handmade and antique knives, military knives. Founder of Randall Knife Collectors Society.

Stoddard's (Steve Weinograd), Copley Place #25, 100 Huntington Ave., Boston MA 02116. Since 1799. Stores at 50 Temple Place and in Chestnut Hill Mall. Retail stores. Selected handmade knives, Randalls, factory knives, French knives. Handmade knife mailer.

Stone Enterprises, Ltd. (Jim Stone), Rt. 609, PO Box 335, Wicomico Church, VA 22579 (804) 580-5114 fax (804) 580-8421. Knives, general, specialty sporting goods merchandise.

Suomi Shop (Lester Ristinen), Box 303, Wolf Lake MN 56593. Since 1980. Factory and handmade Finnish puukko and leuku knives, also factory and handmade Norwegian and Swedish knives, supplies. Mail order, catalog. Displays at Minnesota, Wisconsin, Texas, Detroit, Cincinnati, and Chicago knife shows.

Jim & Cindy Taylor, c/o Celebrated Cutlery, PO Box 741279, Boynton Beach, FL 33473 (561) 742-2337. Since 1978. Illustrated catalogs of antique bowies, pocketknives, fixed blades, razors, and cutlery ephemera. Display at BLADE, Oregon, Northeast Cutlery, Chicago; Detroit, Cincinnati, Springfield MO, and other NKCA knife shows.

Larry P. Thomas, Sr., 2705 Tennyson Avenue, Sinking Springs PA 19608. Since 1954. U.S. military knives. Mail order and some shows. Send want list or write for show schedule. Founder of the American Military Edged Weaponry Museum, 3562 Old Philadelphia Pike, PO Box 6, Intercourse PA 17534 (717) 768-7185.

Tactical Knives, c/o Harris Publications (Steven Dick), 1115 Broadway, New York, NY 10010 (212) 807-7100 fax (212) 807-1479. Web site: www.tacticalknives. com. Email: harrismags@aol.com. Knife magazine.

Tennessee Cutlery (Peter L. McMickle), 770 Chatwood Cove, Memphis, TN 38122 (901) 458-1800. Antique knives, including Michael Price originals.

The Knife Collectors List, tkc-l-request@ellerbach.com. Internet knife discussion group.

Tirdell's Cutlery (Steve Tirdell), 783 Fairmont Ave., Mohnton, PA 19540 (610) 777-3096 fax (610) 796-0858. Bowies, camp knives, hunting/survival, fillet, household cutlery, hunting knives, swords.

TreemanKnives.com, (586) 749-9069. Handmade, factory, modern and vintage knives.

2 The Hilt (Philip DeVries), 560 Fifth St NW Suite 204, Grand Rapids, MI 49504 (616) 456-6569 fax (616) 456-6577. Email: phil@2thehilt.com.

UsefulKnives.com, Email: Answers@UsefulKnives.com. Factory knives and kitchen knives.

The Usual Suspect/usualsuspect.net (Eric Blair), Web site: www.usualsuspect. net. Email: webmaster@usualsuspect.net. Internet knife discussion group.

Vtech Knives (Steven Garsson), 5629 Copley Dr., San Diego, CA 92111 (888) 727-8858 fax (858) 715-0066. Web site: www.balboamfg.com. Bowies, camp knives, tacticals, hunting knives, pocket folders, specialty and throwing knives.

West Creek Cutlery (Jim Markovich), Box 208, Cedar Lake, IN 46303 (219) 696-6842. Current production knives and sharpening products.

We Be Knives (Philip DiCicco), Pier 39, San Francisco CA 94133. Since 1988. Premium factory brands. Some antique and handmade knives. Retail store only. No list or catalog.

Gordon White, PO Box 181, Cuthbert GA 39840 (229) 732-6982. Since 1980. Sheath knives by Marble's, Remington, Ruana, Loveless, Randall, Scagel. Mail order, list. Displays at BLADE, Springfield, MO, NKCA, and Pigeon Forge, TN, knife shows.

World Knives, PO Box 2092, Olympia, WA 98507 (360) 923-1938. Email: chris@worldknives.com. Imported hunting, folding, pocket and collector knives.

World Of Knives (Steve, Jesse, Ward, Glenn), 7301 32nd Ave. N, Crystal, MN 55427 (763) 533-9441 fax (763) 533-6290. Email: jesseh@attglobal.net. Huge selection of handmade and current production knives, and antique knives.

International

Australasian Knife Collectors (Keith Spencer), PO Box 268, Morley 6062, Western Australia. Email: spencer@akc.iinet.net.au. Factory, limited edition, Australian handmade, and a few military knives. Newsletter.

Maurizio Bergomi, Via Zucchi, 46 (ang. Via Mose Bianchi), 20052 Monza, Italy. (39-39) 324194. Fax (39-39) 2300798. Fine handmade knives, Loveless.

Le Briquet, Via Roma 46, 12100 Cuneo, Italy. (39-171)631605. Retail store. Factory and some handmade knives.

Cargasacchi SAS, S. Marco 265, Venice, Italy. (39-41)5234557. Retail store. Factory and handmade knives.

Rolf Freiberg, Bodarna 3, S-75591 Uppsala, Sweden. (46)18-36-01-36. Fax (46)18-36-04-40. Email: rolf.friberg@prisma-marketing.se. Handmade knives.

Frediani Coltelli Finlandesi, Via Lago Maggiore 41, 1-21038 Leggiuno, Italy 0039-332-647362. Purveyors of Finnish knives.

Kindal (Mai Kindal), 33 Avenue de l'Opera, 75002 Paris, France. (33-1)42-61-70-78. Fax (33-1)42-61-75-34. Retail store

and mail order. J. Mongin knives. Fine American and European handmade knives.

Leading Edge Distributors (Kevin Phillips), 3611 Strathcona Ave., Powell River, British Columbia, Canada VBA 2V5 (604) 485-7573. Production knives and Mick Langley damascus and forged knives.

Elvira Lorenzi, Siebensterngasse 41, A-1070 Wien (Vienna), Austria. (43-1)526-2187. Fax (43-1)526-9500. Retail store. Factory and handmade knives.

G. Lorenzi (Aldo and Edda Lorenzi), 9, Via Montenapoleone, 20121 Milan, Italy. (39-2)760-228-48. Fax (39-2)760-033-90. Email: lorenzi.ae@libero.it. Since 1929. Retail store. American and European handmade knives, factory knives.

Matrix-Aida (Mr. Yoshimasa Aida), 26-7 Narimasu 2-Chome; Itabashi-ku; Tokyo 175, Japan. (81) 33939-0052. Fax (81) 33939-0058. Since 1914. Fine handmade knives, Loveless. Displays at Japan Knifemakers Guild Tokyo and East Coast Custom (NYC) knife shows.

Messer Hessel (Wolf & Brigitte Schulz-Tattenpach), Steinweg 14, D-38100 Braunschweig, Germany. (49) 531-41098. Home (49) 531-343528. Fax (49) 531-13114. New and old factory and handmade knives.

Messer Klotzli (H.P. Klotzli), Postfach 104, CH-3400 Burgdorf 2, Switzerland. (41-34) 22-23-78. Fax (41-34) 227-693. Retail stores in Bern and Burgdorf (Hohengasse 3). Handmade and factory knives.

OK-Yess Knife Dealer / Okayasu Steel Co., Ltd., (Mr. Kazuo Okayasu), Taito-Ku Higashi-Ueno 1-12-2, Tokyo 110; Japan. (81) 33834-2323. Fax (81) 33831-3012. Handmade and antique knives. Retail store. Mail order, catalog.

Patrick Custom Knives (Bob Patrick), 12642 - 24A Ave. White Rock BC Canada V4A 8H9. (604) 538-6214. Fax (604) 888-2683. Web site: www.knivesonnet.com. Email: bob@knivesonnet.com. From U.S.: 816 Peace Portal Dr. #18, PO Box 880, Blaine WA 98231-0880. Since 1987. Knifemaker who takes all types of knives in trade. List. Displays at Oregon, Vancouver, Las Vegas knife shows.

David & Jane Petty, 2 The Grange, Green Lane, Burnham, Bucks, SL1 8EN,

England. (44) 1628-605519 phone and fax. Since 1964. Antique knives. Display at BLADE and Louisville NKCA knife shows, Baltimore and European gun shows.

The Razor Man (Neil Wayne), The Cedars, Field Lane, Belper, Derbyshire, England DE56 1DD. (44) 1773-824157. Fax (44) 1773-825573. Email Neil_Wayne@Freedmus.demon.co.uk. Since 1981. Antique European straight razors, related items. Mail order, list.

Salu Trading Co. (Paul Chen), 6 Fl. No. 136, Minchuan West Rd., Taipei, Taiwan. Handmade knives, swords.

Samuel Setian, c/o Alhambra Antiques, Defensa 1030, Buenos Aires, 01065, Argentina phone/fax 5411 4361 8998. Email: setians@ciudad.com.ar. Since 1962. Antique bowie knives, pocketknives, South American knives. Retail store. Author of *Joseph Rodgers & Sons*.

Seki Cut, www.SekiDirect.com. Brand knives from Seki, Japan.

Seto Cutlery Mfg. Co. Ltd. (Mr. Yohichi Seto), 674 Inaguchi-cho, Seki City, Gifu Prefecture 501-32 Japan. (81) 575-22-8892. Fax (81) 575-24-1895. Email: sunny@setocut.co.jp. Web site: http://www.setocut.co.jp/. All types of knives. Catalog. Displays at Seki Outdoor knife show.

True North Knives (Neil Ostroff), PO Box 176, Montreal, Quebec, Canada H3Z 2T2 (514) 748-9985. Web site: www.truenorthknives.com. Email: info@truenorthknives.com. Dealer/purveyor specializing in camp, diving/deck, exotic, combat, hunting, pocket, folders, semi-production, handmade, specialty and utility knives.

Many other knife dealers and purveyors can be found at knife shows, gun shows, and swap meets around the world. Also, check the knife magazines for dealer ads.

If you are a dealer in collectible knives and would like to be listed in the next edition of this book, write, enclosing SASE, to *BLADE's Guide To Knives & Their Values*, K-P Publications, 700 E. State St., Iola, WI 54990

Combined Index and Glossary

Names of companies and individuals mentioned in the text (an index of geographic names and the glossary and index of cutlery terms follow).

A.C. CO., 372, 374-375, 380-381
ABERCROMBIE & FITCH, 46, 324-325, 337, 340, 345, 350, 423
AERIAL CUTLERY CO. (A. C. Co.), 46, 68, 145-146, 273, 332, 375
ALCAS CUTLERY CO. (CUTCO), 46-47, 56-57, 69, 92, 135, 479, 492
ALEXANDER (made in Sheffield), 46, 56, 300
ALLEN CUTLERY CO., 46
ALLEN, JOSEPH, & SONS, 46, 56, 77, 169, 270, 323
ALVORD, CHARLES L., 127
ALVORD, CHARLES L. and JAMES, 31
AMERICAN CUTLERY CO. (A.C. Co.), 46, 372, 381, 417
AMERICAN KNIFE CO., 46, 51, 70, 127, 135, 250
AMERICAN SHEAR & KNIFE CO., 47, 51, 87, 92, 128, 135, 148, 191, 220, 225, 233-234, 249, 268, 537, 547
AMERICAN TAP & DIE CO., 416-417
AMES MFG. CO., 47, 128, 301-302, 308, 369-370
ANDERSON (Glendale CA), 380
ANHEUSER-BUSCH, 15, 47, 52, 241, 503
APPLEGATE, COL. REX, 386, 515
ARBUCKLE, ANGUS, 385
ARDENNLAME, 283
ARNACHELLUM (Salem, India), 401
ASHMORE, JOHN, 47, 132, 301, 308
ASHMORE, JOHN and MARY, 47, 308
ASKHAM, JOHN, 47, 62, 84, 88, 116
AU LION, 374
AUSTIN (Trichinopoly, India), 401
B4-ANY, 91-92, 116
BAEKELAND, LEO H., 30
BAER, ALBERT M., 45, 58, 89, 119, 140-143, 376
BAER, HENRY, 89, 140-142
BAER, ALBERT M. and HENRY ("Uncle Henry"), 84, 89, 140-142
BAKER & HAMILTON, 48, 57, 59, 63, 76, 78, 86
BAKER, LEO F., 379
BAKER, W. JNO., 48, 291, 406-407
BARGE, HENRY, 48, 116
BARKER (Australia), 376
BARLOW (knife and family), 2, 48, 50-51, 62, 74, 77-78, 83, 96, 106, 116, 119, 129, 137, 156, 159-160, 173, 188, 190, 195, 217, 479-481, 483-486, 491, 493-494, 496, 498-503
BARR BROTHERS, 55, 72, 417
BAXTER, SIDNEY R., & CO., 316
BAYONNE KNIFE CO., 132
BEARDSHAW, 38
BEATTY, WILLIAM & SON, 416
BEAVER FALLS CUTLERY CO., 130, 132
BELL, SAMUEL, 299, 306, 309
"BELL BOWIE", 332
BERG, ERIK ANTON, 125
BERNARD, 11, 25, 45, 132, 139, 201, 283, 302, 323, 353, 388, 434, 459, 556
BILLINGS & SPENCER, 128, 294, 331
BIMSON, A. G., 379
BLACK, JAMES, 297-299, 305
BOKER, H., 131, 161-165, 168-170, 173, 177, 183, 186, 215-217, 219, 222, 225-226, 228-229, 235, 237, 242, 248-249, 265, 268, 270-271, 306, 331, 375, 542
BONAPARTE, NAPOLEON, 122, 394
BOOG, (ANDREW?), 393
BOOTH BROS., 131, 133
BOOTH, HENRY C., 116
BOOTH, LUKE, 116
BOWIE, JAMES, 37, 201, 295-299, 305
BOWIE, REZIN, 295-297, 299, 305, 307
BOY SCOUTS, 255, 320, 531-532, 534
BOYT, 372
BRADFORD, MARTIN, 116
BRADLEY, GERSHOM W., 412
BRADLEY, LYMAN, 126-127, 308
BRADLEY, THOMAS and TOM, 130, 235
BREARLEY, HARRY, 30, 118, 331
BRIDDELL, CHARLES, 372
BROOKES & CROOKES, 117
BROOMHEAD & THOMAS, 300
BROWN FAMILY, 51, 130, 135
BROWN, MERRILL E., 379
BROWNIE SCOUTS, 255
BROWNING, 200, 385, 436
BUCK Family, 361, 543
BUD, BRAND, 127
BUNTING, RICHARD, 116
BURKINSHAW, AARON, 128
BURNAND, JAMES, 300
BURRELL CUTLERY CO., 135
BUTCHER, WILLIAM, 107, 116, 300
BUTCHER, SAMUEL, 116, 201, 300
CABAU, JEAN, 299
CALMELS, PIERRE, 283
CAMILLUS CUTLERY CO., 31, 42, 45, 97, 130, 135, 139-143, 148-149, 157-158, 170-171, 180, 187, 191, 195, 197, 221, 226, 230, 240, 243, 246, 250-253, 255, 262-263, 266, 272, 326, 335-336, 369, 373, 375, 377-378, 380, 417, 509-511, 522-524, 526-530, 532-534, 536-537, 540-542, 545-548
CAMP FIRE GIRLS, 255, 321, 532
CANASTOTA KNIFE CO., 130
CANTON CUTLERY CO., 144-145, 148
CAPITOL KNIFE CO., 127
CARGILL, BOB, 474, 480
CARLSON'S SECOND MARINE RAIDERS, 373
CARRIER CUTLERY CO., 130
CASE FAMILY and CASE BRANDS, 13, 17, 33, 35, 38, 114, 118, 130, 133, 135-137, 148-149, 158-161, 164-166, 168, 170-172, 174, 176-180, 185, 189, 192-199, 203, 214-216, 218-219, 221, 227-228, 230-231, 233, 236-238, 248, 250-251, 254, 262-269, 271-272, 277, 325-326, 330-331, 334-335, 351, 353, 369, 373-378, 410, 416-417, 419, 428, 474, 489, 496, 517-519, 522-528, 534-537, 542, 547-549, 551, 554-559
CATTARAUGUS CUTLERY CO., 31, 42, 130, 132-133, 135, 148, 157, 164, 174, 180, 183, 191, 194, 196, 214, 223, 226, 232, 252, 255-256, 267, 270, 272-273, 334-335, 373, 377-378, 522-524, 527, 532, 537, 542
CENTRAL CITY KNIFE CO., 130
CHALLENGE CUTLERY CO., 128, 141, 180
CHAMPION & CO., 118

Geographic Name Index

Glossary and Index of Cutlery Terms

A

ADVERTISING KNIFE (Knives). A give-away knife embellished with advertising, 15, 126, 148, 240-241, 243, 467, 539, 517, 521, 539-541

AIKUCHI, 403.

AIRPLANE KNIFE (Japanese), 382.

AMERICAN INDIAN KNIVES, 116, 310-317

AMES RIFLEMAN'S KNIVES, 369-370

ANACHRONISMS, 37

ANGLO-SAXON. Oval pen knife, 216, 225

ASSORTMENTS. Preselected pocketknives of assorted patterns and handle materials, packed one dozen to a decorated counter display box or card. At first these were assortments of standard patterns, but by the 1930's they were often made up of special low-priced "assortment knives," 139, 566

AXE, 172, 307-308, 318, 325-326, 329, 340, 347, 363-364, 544, 549

B

BACK. 1) Of a knife blade, the edge opposite the cutting edge. 2) Of a jack knife or a pen knife other than a lobster, the side of the handle opposite the opening for the blade(s); the backsprings are visible on the back, except on a "closed-back" knife. 3) The reverse or pile side of a blade, opposite to the front, obverse, or mark side.

BACKSPRING. A spring in the back of folding knife that applies pressure to the end of one or more blades. Most modern factory lockbacks (q.v.) instead have a rocker bar in the back that is tensioned by a "music-wire" spring, 29, 155, 205, 266, 283, 285-286, 288, 294, 513

BADE BADE or RENTJONG (Malayan), 404

BAIL. Shackle. A metal loop attached to one end of a knife that allows the knife to be secured to a cord or chain, 121, 174, 176, 178-179, 232, 252, 255, 262, 272, 517, 526-531, 540, 542

BAIL-OUT KNIFE. An emergency knife used by military airmen, 380

BAKELITE, 30, 150, 326, 329, 338, 340

BALANCE KNIFE. Crutch knife. Berge knife. Springless folding knives with back-to-back blades and split interleaved tangs, 290

BALISONG, see butterfly knife (1)

BALLET KNIFE. Leg knife.

BALLOCK or KIDNEY DAGGER, 392

BALLOON. Said of a pocketknife that has bulbous rounded ends, 38, 137, 145-146, 152, 156, 165, 169, 171, 213, 220, 224, 230-231, 234, 263, 266, 275

BANANA KNIFE, 420

BAR SHIELD, 162

BAREHEAD. A jack knife with no cap bolsters, 137, 155, 158-159, 161-165, 167, 179, 196, 222, 262, 273, 527-528

BARLOW KNIFE. A type of jack knife, 2, 48, 50-51, 62, 74, 77-78, 83, 96, 106, 116, 119, 129, 137, 156, 159-160, 173, 188, 190, 195, 217, 479-481, 483-486, 491, 493-494, 496, 498-503

BARONG, 404

BARREL KNIFE, SWEDISH. A take-apart sloyd knife, 391

BASELARD, 393

BERGE KNIFE, see balance knife, 205, 290

BHUTAN DAGGER, 402

BIRD CARVER. A small slicing knife, 419

BIRD FIGURAL KNIFE (Lebanese), 286

BIRDSEYE RIVET (mouche). A pin with a round burr used without a bolster at the joint of a folding knife. In old Sheffield pins with small burrs were called "birds-eyes," those with large burrs were called "bullseyes," 155, 178

BLACK POLISH, German name for crocus polish (q.v.)

BLADE. The business end of a knife, usually made of steel.

BLADE ETCHING, 31, 301, 505

BLADE OPENER, POCKETKNIFE. Blade pick. A device for opening folding knife blades and saving wear on one's thumb-nail, 518, 542

BLANKED (or FLAT STOCK) BLADE. A blade that was die-stamped or sawn from a flat sheet or strip of steel. Compare forged blade, 37, 316

BOLO. A heavy bladed brush chopping knife, usually with a curved cutting edge, 369, 371-372, 405-406

BOLSTER. 1) A metal end on a folding knife handle that protects the handle cover, and that also usually reinforces the joint. 2) A swelling of, or a metal attachment to, the blade of a fixed blade knife just in front of the handle; it stiffens the blade and protects the front end of the handle, 19, 141, 157, 160, 176, 186, 191-192, 195, 198, 220, 294, 319, 330, 389, 400, 402, 413, 418, 425, 506-507, 510, 520, 523, 527-529, 552

BONE. As used on knife handles, usually cattle shin bone, 15, 33, 36, 38, 40, 132-133, 136, 141, 150, 156-175, 177-180, 182-183, 186-199, 201, 203, 211-213, 215-223, 225-231, 236-238, 245-246, 248-254, 257, 262-270, 280, 282, 288-289, 292, 310, 317, 324, 326, 343, 390-391, 393, 395-396, 399-400, 403-404, 411, 418-420, 451, 458, 474, 489, 511, 513, 515, 520, 522-524, 526-528, 530-538, 542, 559

BONE STAG. Jigged bone, see jigged, 15, 33, 136, 141, 156, 158-173, 175, 178-180, 182-183, 188, 190-198, 203, 213, 215-223, 225-226, 228-231, 237, 245-246, 248-249, 251-254, 257, 262-266, 268-270, 536

BONING KNIFE. Butcher knife with a short narrow blade, used for de-boning meat, 414

BOTTLE OPENER KNIFE, 249

BOUNDARY RIDER'S SHEATH KNIFE, 407

BOWIE KNIFE. A relatively large knife, either folding or fixed blade, intended primarily for use as a weapon, 16, 22, 35, 37-38, 114, 133, 201-203, 295-300, 302-305, 321, 324, 344, 407-408, 417-419, 430, 556-557

BOWIE-STYLE HUNTING KNIVES. Late 19th and 20th century knives similar to earlier bowie knives, 321-323, 331-332

BOXES, CUTLERY DISPLAY, 518, 547

BOY'S KNIFE. A small cheap jack knife, 153, 159, 186-187

BRASS. An alloy of copper and zinc, 31, 34, 37-38, 126-127, 136, 150, 157, 178, 180-181, 183, 185-186, 190-192, 194-196, 198, 203, 212-214, 223, 232, 238-242, 244, 248, 267, 270, 280, 282, 285-286, 288-291, 294, 300-304, 308, 312-313, 319, 332, 344, 347, 349, 355, 357-358, 364, 369-374, 380, 383, 389-392, 394-395, 398-403, 416, 421, 424, 426-429, 505-508, 510, 513, 515, 526-528, 540-541, 545-546, 551

BREAD KNIFE. A kitchen or carving knife, usually with a serrated blade, used for slicing bread, 412, 419

BREAKING KNIFE. A medium sized butcher's knife with a curved sharp-pointed blade, used for disjointing carcasses.

BRONZE. An alloy of copper and tin, 34, 125, 181, 228, 301-302, 304, 308, 358, 392, 397, 399

BRONZE KNIVES, 392, 397, 399

BUCK KNIFE. A knife made by the Buck Knives company, especially their Model 110 folding hunter, 362, 505, 509, 543

BUDDING. A type of grafting (q.v.), 137, 153, 156, 165, 169, 173, 175, 177-178

BUTCHER KNIFE. Any utilitarian fixed blade knife intended for cutting up raw meat, often specifically a clip-point butcher knife, 199, 296, 298, 308, 310-311, 315, 318, 330, 357, 370, 410, 412, 415-416

BUTTER KNIFE. 1) A short-bladed specially shaped table knife for buttering bread. 2) A flatware butter spreader. 3) (also butter spade) A wide spatula with a stiff squared blade for digging butter out of firkins.

BUTTERCUP. Jenny Lind. A small balloon pen knife, 220

BUTTERFLY KNIFE. 1) (also BALISONG) A springless pivot handle folding knife. 2) One of a pair of mirror image Chinese fighting knives with triangular blades and heavy knuckle bows carried together in a single sheath, 128, 294, 402

DAG or DAGUE. A broad-bladed dagger made for the American Indian trade, 310-314

DAGGER. A knife with two or more sharp edges that is designed primarily for stabbing, 32, 37-39, 108, 116, 201, 282, 295, 299, 301-302, 312, 315-316, 338, 349, 375-376, 378, 382-383, 390, 392-393, 396-400, 402-403, 405, 425, 427, 448, 466

DAGGERS, CHINESE DOUBLE. Matched pair of daggers or short swords that are flat on one side, and that are carried together in a single sheath, 402. See butterfly knife (sense 2).

DAMASCUS STEEL. Laminated steel showing "grain" made up of alternating layers of harder and softer alloys, made commercially in India, France, and Germany at least since the 17th century, and in the U.S. since the 1970's, 290, 299, 397, 400, 426, 428, 431, 448, 454, 457. In original non-laminated Wootz or "natural" damascus, the grain results from the method of heat treatment.

DAMASCENING. Inlaying steel with gold and silver wire, 400

DEERFOOT KNIFE. A knife with handle made from a deer's foot, complete with hoof and fur, 395

DHA. Burmese knife or sword, 402

DICE KNIFE. A novelty knife with built-in dice cup, 282

DIRK. 1) A small dagger. 2) A Scottish knife intended as a sidearm, 201-202, 295, 302, 304, 324, 390, 392-393

DISPLAY CASES, 518-519, 547

DIVER'S KNIVES, 380

DOG-LEG. A serpentine folding knife handle shape, 154, 229, 482

DOG-STRIPPING (or DOG-GROOMING) KNIFE, 185

DOLPHIN. A fish candle-end lobster pen knife, 232, 234

DOUBLE-END(ED). Said of folding knives with blades at both ends, 145-147, 152-153, 155-157, 169-171, 175, 178, 181, 185, 194, 204-205, 210, 216, 221, 234, 236-237, 244, 263, 267, 277-279, 281, 290

DOUBLE-END JACK KNIVES, 152, 156, 169-171, 175, 204, 216

DROP POINT. A style of hunting knife blade designed by Robert W. Loveless, based on an old New England pattern, 340, 515

E

EASY-OPEN(ER). Said of a jack knife with large half-round cut-outs in the handles, 189, 211, 240, 255, 272, 528-529

EDGE. The sharp part(s) of a knife blade, 20, 28, 30, 36-37, 40, 106-107, 138, 148, 157, 181, 205, 210, 221, 289, 298, 301-302, 308, 310, 315, 317, 324, 326, 342, 347, 354-355, 358-360, 371, 373, 380, 383, 397, 410, 414, 417, 427, 440, 493, 518, 521, 523, 537, 539, 541-542, 555, 560

EIGHT-TWELVE. A 19th century pocketknife pattern or size name, not identified.

ELECTRICIAN'S KNIFE, 194. Also see Plier and Wrench Knives, 120, 152, 159, 174, 226, 273

ELEPHANT TOENAIL, see sunfish, 137, 234, 522-525

ELLERY HUNTER, 330, 332

ENGINE TURNING. Pattern of circles on metal handles, 212

ENGINEER'S KNIFE. 1) A jumbo whittler. 2) An army engineer's machete, 226, 372

ENGLISH JACK. A large traditional style jack knife, 153, 159, 190

ENGRAVING. Decoration cut into a surface, 20, 35, 116, 206, 212, 288, 389, 397, 425, 460, 519, 551, 554

EQUAL-END. A folding knife handle shape, 120, 137, 144, 146, 152, 154, 156, 158, 164, 166, 169, 171, 173, 177, 182, 185, 194, 211, 215-216, 221, 224-226, 232-234, 238, 240, 244, 252, 263, 266, 271, 291

ERASER. A knife designed for scraping ink from paper or vellum, 211, 238, 420, 422

ETCHING. Marking or decoration applied to a surface by a chemical reaction, 15, 31, 212, 239, 301-302, 375, 505, 531, 535, 547

EUREKA. A swell-center serpentine (q.v.) jack or cattle knife, 135, 137, 146, 152, 156, 167, 169, 171-172, 222, 230, 263, 266, 433, 448

EXPOSITION KNIVES, 116, 155, 236, 244, 277

F

FACA DE PONTA. A Brazilian Indian trade knife, 390

FACTORS and OUTWORKERS. In the cutlery industry, a factor was a merchant in a manufacturing district who contacted with independent artisans, called outworkers, to make cutlery articles to his specifications and bearing his mark, 13-14, 98, 106, 115, 118, 122 147, 149-150, 206, 246, 312, 315, 425, 518, 551

FACTORY. Originally the warehouse of a factor (q.v.) or other merchant then a building or complex of buildings where most or all the operations of a manufacturing process are carried out under a single management, 11, 13-14, 16-19, 21-22, 29, 32, 40-42, 45, 106, 115-117, 119-122, 124-128, 131-132, 136, 140-143, 145, 201, 211, 267 280, 294, 300-301, 303, 305-306, 312-313, 317, 325-326, 331, 337-339 354-355, 365, 395, 415, 417, 430-432, 474-475, 502, 507, 513-514, 525, 543-544, 550-551, 553-560

FAIRBAIRN-SYKES DAGGER, 375, 383

FALSE EDGE. A partially sharpened area on the backs of some knife blades. Some blades have a "sharp false edge" which, though sharp, is not nearly as sharp as the main cutting edge, 298, 301, 324, 355, 359, 383

FASCINE KNIFE. A short handled bill-hook or brush-hook formerly used for cutting fasces, bundles of sticks used to reinforce earthworks and ditches.

FARMER'S CLASP KNIFE. Schlactmesser Zum Zulegen (German: folding butcher knife). A large lightweight folding knife with no bolsters, 199

FARMER'S JACK. A double-end jack with a pruning blade and a spey or grafting blade, 152, 169-170, 172, 175

FARRIER'S (HORSE SHOER'S) KNIFE, 420

FEATHER CURLING KNIFE, 421

FIGURAL KNIFE. A knife, usually a folder, with the handle formed in the shape of an object, animal, or person, 37, 143, 286, 290

FINISH BLADE, 40-41

FIREFIGHTER'S QUICK RELEASE KNIFE, 383

FISH CANDLE END LOBSTER. Dolphin, 232-234

FISH JACK. A jack knife handle shape, 152

FISH KNIFE. 1) Any knife for cleaning or filleting fish. 2) A tickler jack knife with a fish scaler back or blade, 137, 153, 192-193, 198, 329-330, 335, 520

FISH SCALER BLADE, for scraping fish, 188, 192, 198

FISH SLICE. A knife with a silver-plated non-ferrous blade once used in England for serving or eating fish.

FISHTAIL. A jack knife handle shape, 137, 152, 156, 168, 284-285

FIXED BLADE. A knife that does not normally fold, 19-21, 42, 125, 195, 201, 236, 238, 248, 262, 276, 295, 297, 301, 303, 318, 324, 326, 334, 336-337, 340-341, 353-354, 361, 367, 369, 371, 373-375, 377, 379-383 387-388, 390, 392-393, 431, 505, 514, 526

FLEAM. A sharp pointed veterinary instrument used for phlebotomy (blood letting) on livestock (compare lancet), 153, 185, 244-245, 291

FLY FISHING KNIFE, 192

FLYSSA, 398

FLORIST KNIFE. A jack knife pattern, 178

FOLDING BOWIE KNIFE and FOLDING DIRK, 201-202

FOLDING HUNTING KNIFE or FOLDING HUNTER. Any of several types of large jack knife, 35, 137, 147, 195-196, 198-200, 286, 325, 505, 508-510, 514-516, 520, 522-525, 544, 546

FOLDING KNIFE or FOLDER. Any knife with a pivoting or folding blade. Smaller folders are also called pocketknives, 11, 19-20, 28, 38, 42, 119, 128, 147, 149-150, 155-156, 183, 199, 201, 210-211, 214, 224, 232, 262, 279, 283, 292, 294, 300, 305-306, 345, 347, 358, 380, 386, 454, 457, 465-466, 505, 514-516, 542, 545

FORGED BLADE. A blade that was hammered to shape from a red hot bar of steel, 12, 343. Compare blanked blade, 37, 280, 314, 319, 396, 553

FORGED BOLSTER. A bolster (2) (q.v.) integral with a blade, and forged at the same time as the blade and tang, 319, 400, 402

FRAME. A folding knife's liners and bolsters, sometimes including the spring(s). Not originally a cutlery term, 120, 124, 189, 420, 457, 511, 515, 543

FRENCH CHEF'S KNIFE, see chef's knife, 415

FRENCH NAIL MARK. Long pull, see nail mark, 14

FRIEND KNIFE. A French slot knife (q.v.) made up of two nearly identical halves, 293

Cutlery Exhibitors at the 1876 Centennial Exhibition, Philadelphia, Pennsylvania

1) U.S. Cutlery Manufacturers

Ames Manufacturing Co., Chicopee, Mass. Swords.

The Collins Co., New York, N.Y. [Collinsville, Conn.]. Machetes, swords, bayonets; cast steel tools.

Wm. Rose & Bros., Philadelphia, Pa. Saddlers' tools.

Buck Bros., Riverlin Works., Millbury, Mass. Edge tools.

Beaver Falls Cutlery Co., Beaver Falls, Pa. Table, pocket, and miscellaneous cutlery. Special exhibits, large carving knife and fork, nine and a half feet long, cost $1500; revolving knife with 365 blades.

Will & Finck, San Francisco, Cal. California carving sets and cutlery, bar tools.

L. Herder & Sons., Philadelphia, Pa. Shears and scissors.

John Russell Cutlery Co., Green River Works, New York, N.Y. [Turners Falls, Mass.]. Table cutlery, butchers', hunters', painters', and druggists' knives, etc. [The largest exhibit in this class.]

Howard W. Shipley [Coquanoc Works], Philadelphia, Pa. Pocket cutlery.

Henry Seymour & Co., New York, N.Y. [Newark, N.J.]. Tailors', bankers', and sheep shears trimmers, and scissors.

Hotchkiss's Sons, Bridgeport, Conn. Pruning shears.

Meriden Cutlery Co., New York, N.Y. [Meriden, Conn.]. Table cutlery. [The first ivory celluloid handles.]

Holley Manufacturing Co., Lakeville, Conn. Pocket cutlery.

The Lamson & Goodnow Manufacturing Co., Shelburne Falls, Mass. Table and butchers' cutlery.

United States Steel Shear Co., Meriden, Conn. Scissors and shears.

Miller Bros. Cutlery Co., West Meriden, Conn. Pocket cutlery.

R. Heinisch's Sons., Newark, N.J. Tailor shears and scissors.

J. Wiss, Newark, N.J. Cutlery, shears, and scissors.

Friedman & Lauterjung, New York, N.Y. Razors. Leopold Funke, St. Louis, Mo. Knife with 366 blades.

Thos. Hessenbruch & Co., Philadelphia, Pa. Shears and scissors [import].

Robbins, Clark, & Biddle, Phila., Pa. Cutlery.

Northfield Knife Co., Northfield, Conn. Pocket cutlery.

Breeden & Nelke, New York, N.Y. Spring scissors and shears.

Goodell Company, Antrim, N.H. Cutlery and shoe knives.

Star Knife Co., Taunton, Mass. Knives and cutlery.

Marx Bros., New York, N.Y. Folding pocket scissors.

Walden Knife Co., Walden, N.Y. Pocket cutlery.

New York Knife Co. Walden, N.Y. Table, pen, and pocket cutlery, pruning knives.

2) U.S. Surgical and Dental Instrument Makers

Geo. Tiemann & Co., New York.

Geo. P. Pilling, Philadelphia,

J.H. Gemrig, Philadelphia.

Moritz Leiner, New York.

D.W. Kolbe, Philadelphia.

Horatio G. Kern, Philadelphia.

F.G. Otto & Sons, New York.

J.J. Teufel, Philadelphia.

Codman & Shurtleff, Boston.

Samuel S. White, Philadelphia.

3) England Cutlery Manufacturers

George Wostenholm & Son, Sheffield. Razors, pocketknives, scissors, and general cutlery. [The judges rated this the highest quality exhibit in this class.]

John Needham, Sheffield. Cutlery: daggers, table and dessert knives and forks, fish eaters.

Brookes & Crookes, Atlantic Works, Sheffield. Pen, pocket, sportsman's, bowie, and table knives; hunting knives and dirks; scissors, razors, and dressing case instruments.

James Burnand & Co., Sheffield. Fine cutlery, table and pocket knives, hunting knives.

Wilson Hawksworth, Ellison, & Co. Carlisle Works, Sheffield. Pocket and table cutlery, scissors, butchers' knives and steels, and chisels.

J.B. Addis & Sons, Arctic Works, Sheffield. Carving and turning tools.

William Wilkinson & Sons, Sheffield. Pruning shears and farriers' knives.

Thomas Kingsbury, London. Razors, knives, scissors, and dressing case instruments.

John Neal & Co., London. Table, dessert, and fish cutlery.

Mayer & Meltzer, London. Pocketknives, scissors, and razors.

4) Canada

Spilur Bros., St. John, New Brunswick. Tools and cutlery. [Most of St. John burned down in 1877.]

5) France Cutlery Manufacturers

H. Denizet, Langres. Shears and knives.

hinet, Paris. Cutlery.

itry Bros., Paris.

. Perard, Paris. Sheep shears. Group exhibit of cutlers from Haute Marne, displaying hunting and pocket knives, kitchen and mincing knives, daggers, razors, folding and common scissors, corkscrews, and pruning shears.

Renaut Guillemin, Nogent.

Charles Girard, Nogent.

Gommelet, Courcelles. Scissors, shears, and kitchen knives made by reform school inmates.

Felix Thevenot, Nogent.

. Charbonne-Thuillier, Nogent.

Wichard Couvreaux, Nogent.

Thomachot-Thuillier, Nogent.

Dissoire, Nogent.

6) Germany Exporting Cutlery Manufacturers

Heinrich Boker & Co., Solingen. Exhibition pocketknives and scissors.

T. Hessenbruch & Co., Ronsdorf.

J.S. Holler & Co., Solingen. Cutlery.

Fr. Wellmann, Altona. Cutlery.

7) Austria-Hungary (Bohemia)

Wenzel Schneider, Prague. Fine pocket cutlery.

8) Switzerland

C.F. Schneider, Geneva. Complicated pocketknives. Knives both with single and multifarious blades.

Jacques Le Coultre, Sentier, Ct. Vaud. Razors.

9) Sweden

Eskilstuna Iron Manufacturing Stock Co., Eskilstuna. Blades of swords, sabres, foils, and hunters' hangers.

S.O. Morell & Co., Stockholm. Sword ornamented in old Norse style.

Alf Norrstrom, Eskilstuna. Knives and hangers.

Alb. Stille, Stockholm. Surgical instruments.

Sandvikens Iron & Steel Co., Gefle. Razors, knives, and scissors made from Bessemer steel. Collective Exhibit of Manufacturers of Hardware and Metallic Products in Eskilstuna [including] B. & O. Liberg, Rosenfors. Edge tools, cutlery. Job. Engstrom. Razors.

. Gustafson. Knives.

A. Halling. Hunting knives, kitchen knives, and dirks.

Christoffer V. Heljestrand. Razors with engraved ivory handles, knives, and corkscrews.

L.F. Stahlberg, Stahlfors. Cutlery.

E.M. Svalling. Knives.

F.W. Soderen. Knives; shears and scissors.

10) Norway

Jean Mette, Christiania [Oslo]. National daggers.

John B. Michelsen, Bergen. Cutlery, brass goods.

11) Russia

John Kaliakin & Sons, Pavlovo, Nijni Novgorod. Table and pocket cutlery, pruning knives, and shears.

Demetrius Kondratov, Vatcha, Vladimir. Table, pocket, and other cutlery.

Alexis Zavialoff, Vorsma, Nijni Novgorod. Table and pocket cutlery, heavy pruning knives and shears.

12) Italy

B. Giulivo & Co., Turin. Iron and tin knives, forks, and spoons.

"After a general survey of the cutlery exhibition, we are forced to give America the first place for table cutlery.

"For pocket and fine cutlery the pre-eminence of Sheffield was maintained by Wostenholm and Brookes & Crookes. France did scarcely justice to herself in the exhibits sent to Philadelphia.

"The display of Germany in pocket cutlery was no doubt equal to any from the United States, showing great beauty and high excellence of finish.

"The Russian exhibits from Novgorod showed an advance which we were scarcely prepared to see; and Sweden also deserves to be noticed, her products being somewhat of the same quality as those of Russia."

General Report of the Judges of Group XV

Major Watersheds in Modern Cutlery History

1742—Sheffield clockmaker Benjamin Huntsman invented crucible cast steel, the first modern cutlery blade steel. The last commercial crucible was teemed (poured) in 1968.

NAPOLEONIC ERA—Napoleon's rule of Solingen, ended the city's medieval guild system, permitting the rapid development of the German cutlery industry.

WAR OF 1812 AND AFTER—Wartime embargoes showed Sheffield's cutlers that most of their livelihood had been coming from the American trade. Thenceforth, Sheffield actively courted American business, and until the 1890s her cutlery industry grew in step with America's expansion and prosperity.

CALIFORNIA GOLD RUSH AND WESTWARD EXPANSION—These movements fostered the bowie knife trend, and provided a strong home market for the burgeoning American cutlery industry, as well as a growing market for the cutlers of Sheffield.

U.S. CIVIL WAR AND AFTER—Capital-intensive, mechanized, industrial production methods developed during the war were applied afterward in the American cutlery industry, enabling U.S. fixed-blade manufacturers to be strong competitors in the world and domestic markets. The most influential innovators were two former Sheffield men, Matthew Chapman, manager of the Russell Green River Works, and Joseph Gardner, manager of the rival Lamson & Goodnow Shelburne Falls Works.

U.S. "PROTECTIVE" TARIFFS, 1890s-1920s—At the expense of American consumers, the high tariffs fostered rapid growth in the American cutlery industry, especially in pocket cutlery, along with concomitant declines in Sheffield and Solingen. A large pool of immigrant English and German cutlers, thrown out of work and forced to emigrate by the tariffs, enabled American cutlery makers to enjoy a "Golden Age" of quality, variety and high profits. Leaders of the protection movement for cutlery were William Rockwell of Miller Bros., Charles Alvord of Empire, and Tom Bradley of New York Knife Co.

1903—The Hemming brothers of New Haven, Connecticut, introduced the first successful automatic blade-grinding machine. Hemming grinders have been supplanted by computer numerically controlled (CNC) Berger and Siepmann grinders from Germany, and cam-operated Nicholas grinders from Ohio.

1907—French metallurgist Paul Louis Toussaint Heroult (1863-1914), who had invented today's Hall-Heroult aluminum smelting process in 1886, invented the electric furnace for precision steel making. Within a year, the furnace had been adopted in England, Europe and the USA. Today, all tool and many blade steels are made by the method. An electric furnace can make 25 tons of high-grade tool steel in a few hours. A crucible took several days and skilled guesswork to make 60 pounds.

1914—Sheffield metallurgist Harry Brearley and Indiana chemist Elwood Haynes independently invented stainless steel, though its commercial development was delayed by World War I.

WORLD WAR I AND AFTER—The war ended the ascendancy of England and Austro-Hungarian Bohemia in the world cutlery market, while setting the stage for the postwar dominance of German and American cutlery firms. In the 1920s, Remington revolutionized knife marketing, while Imperial revolutionized knife manufacturing. However, the Great Depression, aside from closing a few old firms and forcing most others to reduce their variety and staffing, had little effect on the world's cutlery industry.

WORLD WAR II AND AFTER—During the war, most of the world's cutlery firms devoted all of their efforts to military knives and other hardware, while two of the world's biggest cutlery producers, Remington and Winchester, had quit the cutlery business. Because of the long suspension of the commercial market for cutlery, the immediate postwar years were a period of profound change and painful readjustment in the cutlery industry. Many established channels of distribution, such as hardware wholesalers, had disappeared. A glut of military surplus pocket and sheath knives crippled the key segments of the American cutlery industry. In the postwar years, many American cutlery firms that had grown dependent on war contracts failed or faded away. Surviving American and German cutlery manufacturers were compelled to reorganize, some to accommodate changes in ownership, all to adjust to unprecedented changes in the marketplace.

Most cutlery lines were redesigned, cheapened and radically shortened after the war. The recovery years of the 1950s and '60s witnessed gradual declines in the American and German cutlery industries, counterbalanced by rapid advancement in Japan, Switzerland, Italy, Pakistan, China, Spain, India, Brazil and Taiwan.

1950—Emerson Case of Robeson perfected the freeze treatment of stainless blade steels, allowing knife factories to achieve quality hitherto attainable only in the laboratory.

RECENT YEARS—The boom in all types of collecting since the mid-1960s has included knives, helping in the revival of the American cutlery industry, and in fostering the creation of a custom knifemaking sector that rivals the domestic cutlery manufacturing sector in personnel numbers, if not dollar volume.